A

GAZETTEER

OF THE

STATE OF NEW JERSEY.

COMPREHENDING

A GENERAL VIEW OF ITS PHYSICAL AND MORAL CONDITION,

TOGETHER WITH

A TOPOGRAPHICAL AND STATISTICAL ACCOUNT

OF ITS

COUNTIES, TOWNS, VILLAGES, CANALS,
RAIL ROADS, &c.

ACCOMPANIED BY A MAP.

BY

THOMAS F. GORDON.

Trenton:
PUBLISHED BY DANIEL FENTON.
John C. Clark, Printer, Philadelphia.
1834.

ADVERTISEMENT.

The author of the following work has sought to present to the public, a full and correct portraiture of the State in the year 1833. To this end, he has, personally, visited almost every portion of it; communed with many of its most distinguished and enlightened citizens, and collected, from numerous but scattered sources, a mass of useful and curious information, which must prove alike grateful to the present and succeeding generations. Errors will undoubtedly be discovered in the work; for such a work is peculiarly liable to them; being exposed, not only to the misconceptions of the author, but, to those of his thousand informants. Distance of places from each other, and the area of the townships and counties are, specially, subject to misstatement. The first has been given from the returns of the General Post-Office, measures upon the map, and verbal information of residents; the only and best sources, save actual admeasurement. The area of the townships has been obtained from calculation of their contents, as delineated on Mr. Gordon's map, by means of a reticulated scale of square miles. The result corresponds, so nearly, with the returns of the assessors of such townships, as contain no unimproved lands, as to give considerable confidence in its approximation to the truth. It must be observed, however, that this area comprises roads, lakes, ponds, marshes and, in a word, every thing within the lines.

The abstract which has been given of the laws relating to the administration of the government, generally, and of the counties and townships, specially, will appear, to many, trite and familiar; but to the great mass of the people, particularly, to the rising generation, it will not prove the least acceptable portion of the work. To those about to enter on the duties of the citizen, it will communicate much valuable knowledge; and will be useful to all, for occasional reference; comprising, in a small compass, matter of daily interest, which must, elsewhere, be sought, in many volumes. More of this species of information might have been usefully given; but, the volume collected, exceeds, by one-third, the quantity originally proposed; and to get it within the size of a convenient manual, resort has been had to a small type for the prefatory chapters.

To the many gentlemen to whom the author is indebted for communications, he tenders his unfeigned thanks; and solicits from them, and others, such corrections and additions as may render the next edition of his work, still more valuable.

Philadelphia, January 1, 1834.

GAZETTEER OF NEW JERSEY.

PREFATORY CHAPTER.

PART I.

Containing a Physical View of the State.

I. *General Boundary.*—II. *Principal Divisions.*—III. *Southern and Alluvial Division.—Bounds—Surface—Nevisink Hills—Sandy Hook—Sea Beach—Bays or Lagunes—Soil: Forest—Pine Lands—Oak—Cedar Swamp—Marl—Ferruginous Sand—Proportions of Marl used in Agriculture.—Cultivation of the Alluvial District.—Bog Ore—Streams.*—IV. *Middle and Secondary District: Bounds—Area—Formation—Trap Ridges—Bergen Ridge—First and Second Mountains—Bituminous Coal—Mountains from Springfield to Pluckemin.—Pompton Plain: Abundance of Minerals there—Ridges extending to the Delaware—Character of the surrounding Country—Quarries of Freestone near Princeton—Sandy Hill—Primitive Rocks near Trenton.—Copper Mines: at Belleville, Brunswick, Somerville, Greenbrook.*—V. *Mountainous District: Extent—Blended Geological Formation—Limits—Primitive Ridges, Minerals of—Tongue of Transition Formation, Minerals of—Primitive resumed—Valley of the Wallkill, or of Sparta—Singular Geology and Mineralogy—Valley of Paulin's Kill—Alternation of Slate and Limestone—Blue or Kittatinney Mountains—Transition Limestone on Delaware River—Precious Marbles—Manganese—Rivers and Lakes of the Third Section—Timber of the Middle and Northern Sections.*—VI. *Turnpike Roads.*—VII. *Rail Roads: Camden and Amboy, West Jersey, Patterson and Hudson, Patterson Junction, Patterson and Fort Lee, Elizabethtown and Somerville, New Jersey, New Jersey, Hudson and Delaware, Delaware and Jobstown.*—VIII. *Canals; Morris, Delaware and Raritan, Manasquan, Salem.*—IX. *Population—Increase—Tables—Slavery.*—X. *Statistical Table.* XI. *Agriculture, Manufactures and Commerce.*—XII. *Climate.*

I. The State of New Jersey is bounded on the N. E. by Orange and Rockland counties, of the State of New York; on the E. by Hudson River and Bay, Staten Island Sound, Raritan Bay and the Atlantic Ocean; on S. E. and S. by the Atlantic; on S. W. by the Delaware Bay, dividing it from the State of Delaware; and on the W. and N. W. by the Delaware River, separating it from Pennsylvania. The N. E. line from Carpenter's Point, at the mouth of the Nevisink, or Mackackomack River, in north lat. 41° 21′, to a point on the Hudson River, in 41° north latitude; is in length 45 miles; the E. 60; the S. E. from Sandy Hook to Cape May, 120; and the S. W., W. and N. W. from Cape May to Carpenter's Point, 220 miles—making the extent of its exterior limit 445 miles. The extreme length of the State, by a line almost due north from Cape May, to the northern angle on the Delaware, is 164 miles; its greatest breadth due E. and W. through Salem, Gloucester, Burlington and Monmouth counties, about 75 miles; and through Warren, Sussex, Morris and Bergen counties, to the extreme N. E. point, on the Hudson River, about 60 miles. It may be crossed, however, by a direct line from S. W. to N. E., from Bordentown to South Amboy, in about 30 miles. The nearest approximation we can make to its area, measuring the map by a reticulated scale of square miles, is about 7,276 square miles, or 4,656,330 acres, contained between 38° 58′ and 41° 21′ northern latitude.*

II. This area is distributed into three strongly marked divisions; the alluvial and southern; the secondary, hilly and middle; and the mountainous and northern, comprising primitive and transition formations.

III. The triangular peninsula, or southern division, bordered on the S. and E. by Delaware Bay and the Ocean, on the N. and W. by the Delaware River, about 110 miles in length, and 75 in breadth, is entirely alluvial. South of the Nevisink Hills, the surface seldom rises 60 feet above the sea. Those hills, adjacent to the Ocean, are 310 feet above its level; and stand where the waves formerly rolled, resting in some places on banks of oyster shells and other marine relics, blended with clay and

* Morse gives 8,320 square miles, or 5,324,800 acres; Smith's Hist. N. J. 4,800,000 acres; and Darby 6,851 square miles, or 4,384,000 acres.

A

sea mud. A sandy earth, highly coloured by oxide of iron, and imbedding reddish brown sand and puddingstone, cemented by iron, composes the higher strata; and large rocks and beds of ferruginous sandstone, apparently in place, of a more recent formation than the alluvial below, containing sufficient metal to be called an ore of iron, are of frequent occurrence. Particles of iron are blended with the sands of the beach; and some of the streams which descend from the top of the clay strata, are red with iron oxide. Efflorescences of the sulphates of iron and alumine, are often observed; and flame, proceeding from the spontaneous combustion of gases, generated, probably, in beds of sulphuret of iron, has been noticed here. The strata of the steep eastern declivity are exposed by frequent land slips.

A small portion, only, of these hills is cultivated. They are rough, broken, and covered with wood, in which deer still find covert. From their summit, a view is disclosed of the ocean, unrivalled in grandeur upon the seaboard of this State; and the coast on the N. E. and S. may be seen as far as the eye can reach. The land prospect, though not so extensive, is scarce less interesting. In this hill, on the side of a branch of the Nevisink River, is a remarkable cave, 30 feet long by 15 broad, divided into three apartments. The entrance and roof are low, the latter arched, and of soft rock, through which the water percolates; the bottom is of loose sand.

Sandy Hook, east of, and divided from, the Nevisink Hills by a narrow bay, is six miles in length. It was formerly, and is now, isolated by a channel running from Shrewsbury River, which was first opened in 1778, closed in 1810, but reopened in 1830. The beach running northward several miles from Long Branch, invites to a promenade on the hard sand when the tide is low; but the wrecks of vessels, visible at short intervals, oppress the spectators with recollections of the perils of the sea. From the Hook, this beach extends 125 miles to Cape May, varying in width from half a mile to two miles, but broken in several places by channels communicating with the sea. South of Manasquan it covers a number of bays or salt water lakes, of which Barnegat, Little Egg Harbour, and Great Egg Harbour, are the chief. West of these runs a belt of marsh, in some places from four to five miles wide, intersected by small rivers, with broad and shallow estuaries.

The soil of this alluvial district consists of sand and clay, sometimes one overlaying the other; but frequently intimately blended, forming a tolerably fertile loam, which prevails on its northern and western border with a variable breadth. Above Salem, this breadth is from five to twelve miles, but below that town it is sometimes contracted to a mile. East of this strip of loam, and west of the marsh which girds the sea shore, lies an immense sandy plain, scarce broken by any inequality, and originally covered by a pine and shrub-oak forest—a great portion of which has been once, and some of it twice, cut over. There are many square miles on which there is not a human inhabitant, and where the deer, foxes and rabbits are abundant, and the wolf and the bear find a lair to protect their race from extirpation. But in many places the echo is awakened by the woodman's axe, and the louder din of the forge hammer, and the forest glares with the light of the furnace or glass house. In this sandy desert there are found veins of generous soil, which yield a compensatory crop of corn and rye to the labours of the husbandman.

This immense forest covers probably four-fifths of the alluvial district; and forty years ago a large portion of it was not worth more than from six to ten cents the acre. There was little demand for the timber, oak being preferred for architectural and economical uses, nor was the land worth clearing for agricultural purposes. The establishment of furnaces and glass manufactories first gave additional value to the woodland near their locations; but for a while they made little apparent reduction of the vast wilderness. Then came the steamboats, which for some years traversed our waters, propelled by timber from New Jersey, without sensibly diminishing the density of the forest. In a few years more, however, their number was doubled, trebled, quadrupled. Their huge maws, though fed with thousands of shallop loads of pine wood, were insatiable. The demand for fuel became immense; the almost worthless pine lands rose rapidly in value, and the hitherto almost idle population of the sea-board, found abundant and profitable employment in supplying the growing markets. The introduction of anthracite coal diminished the consumption of oak wood as fuel, but increased that of pine, vast quantities of charcoal being required to ignite the fossil. Yet the invention of the simple portable culinary furnace increased the demand still more, thousands of these convenient utensils being constantly, during the summer months, fed by charcoal. These circumstances have produced an entire revolution in the value of pine lands. They have risen from ten cents, to an average price of six dollars the acre; and, where very well timbered, and convenient to market, bring from fifteen to twenty-five dollars. Indeed, the soil, denuded of the timber, is worth from four to sixteen dollars the acre, the purchaser looking to the growth of wood for profit on his investment. Where the forest has been felled, an extraordinary change takes place in the subsequent product. The oak springs up where the pine has flourished, and pine where the oak has grown. The second growth becomes fit for the axe, in a space varying from 25 to 40 years.

Upon the clay and loam soils, oak grows abundantly; frequently of great size, and of quality much valued in the construction of ships. It is the common timber of the western border, and covers almost exclusively the central portion of the county of Cape May. In the sandy region, are extensive swamps which bear the beautiful and valuable white cedar, much sought for fencing, and which sells readily at from one to three hundred dollars the acre.

Throughout a great portion of the alluvial district, from four to twenty feet beneath the surface, is a species of greenish blue earth, mixed with shells, and generally known as marl. As this substance is of great importance to the agricultural interest of the section, some remarks on its physical properties and use will not be out of place here. The essential ingredient of marl, as a manure, is lime; and its value depends upon the proportion of calcareous matter which it contains. When this abounds in connexion with sand only, it produces indurated marl, classed with the limestones, and frequently forming marble of great variety and beauty. We have discovered none of this precious character; but shell limestone, similar to that of the alluvion of North Carolina, Georgia, and Mississippi Territory, has been discovered in several places, and is burned for lime on the banks of the Rancocus, between Eayrstown and Vincent-town. The Jersey marls, at present, are chiefly known as the shell, clay and stone marls. The first is composed of testaceous matter, in various quantities and degrees of combination; and sometimes imbeds bones of marine and land animals.* The quantity of clay in union with calcareous substances, gives name to the second sort. This absorbs and retains moisture better than other kinds, and varies greatly in colour—being brown, blue, red and yellowish. In the third species, sand is combined with calcareous and argillaceous matter, giving hardness proportionate to its quantity; when of thin and laminar structure, this is termed slate marl. From the clay they contain, all these species are softened by water, and, when exposed to the atmosphere, gradually fall into powder.

By reason of their calcareous principle, all marls effervesce with acids; but as water, alone, frequently produces the same effect when poured on dry clay, it may be necessary, in order to guard against mistake, in making trials upon substances supposed to be marl, to let them remain a short time in mixture with water, previous to the test of acids. The best marls containing the largest proportion of calcareous earth, it is important to know how to ascertain the quantity. Some are so poor as to have only a thirtieth part of their weight of lime. A simple method has been suggested, founded on the fact, that marl commonly contains about forty per cent. of its weight of fixed air or carbonic acid. It is merely by saturating the marl with muriatic or some other acid, and marking correctly the loss of weight which it sustains by the extrication of the fixed air. So, also, if the substance supposed to be marl falls readily to powder when exposed to the air; if the powder, when dry and thrown on hot coals, crackles like salt; and if, when dry, and mixed with water, it have a soapy feel and effervesces much, its quality may be pronounced good.

Some marls in England, and probably here, have eighty-four per cent. of carbonate of lime, which is more than limestone generally possesses; and the refuse being often of peaty substances, is more useful as manure than that of limestone, which is mostly sand or clay. Such marl may be converted into quicklime by burning; and its solution changes vegetable colours to green, possessing all the other properties of caustic lime. Marl is further distinguished by its feeling fat and unctuous, and appearing when dry, after exposure to the weather, as if covered with hoar frost, or sprinkled with fine salt; and even when mixed with the land, giving to the whole surface a whitish appearance.

The farmers in Staffordshire, England, consider the soft blue marl, commonly

---

* Among the latter, it is said, are bones of the rhinoceros and other animals of the eastern continent, some of them of extinct species; elephant's teeth, deer's horns, bones of the whale, shark's teeth, and entire skeletons of fish, together with graphytes, belemnites, cardites, and various shell-fish.

found under clay, or low black ground, at the depth of seven or eight feet, the best for arable land, and the grey sort for pasture. But that which is of a brownish colour, with blue veins, and small lumps of chalk or limestone lying under stiff clays and very hard to dig, is most esteemed in Cheshire. The marl having a light sand in its composition, usually found at the depth of two or three feet, on the sides of hills, and in wet, boggy grounds, is fat and close, and reckoned the strongest and most beneficial on sandy lands. It is usually called peat or delving marl. What is sometimes called paper marl, frequently lies near coals, and flakes like leaves or pieces of brown paper, being of somewhat lighter colour. That which some call clay marl is very fat, and is sometimes mixed with chalk stones. There is another sort of marl, which breaks of itself into square cubical bits. The two last kinds generally lie under sand and clay; sometimes about a yard deep under the former, but often much deeper under the latter. The stone, slate or flag marl, which is a kind of soft stone, or rather slate, of a bluish colour, is generally allowed very good. It easily breaks down, and dissolves with frost or rain; is found near rivers and on the sides of hills, and is very lasting when used as manure.

In many places marl discovers itself to the most negligent eye, particularly on the sides of broken hills or deep hollow roads. Many rivers are bordered with a vast treasure of this sort, which is plundered by every flood. Boggy lands frequently cover it, and in them it seldom lies above three feet deep. It is somewhat lower under stiff clays and marshy levels. The lowest parts of most sandy lands abound with it, at the depth of three, seven, nine or more feet. The depth of the marl itself can seldom be found; for when the upper crust is removed, all that can be seen or dug is marl, to so great a depth that there are few if any instances of a pit having been exhausted. Much of the preceding description of the English marls is applicable to those of New Jersey.

The marl region of this State, is classed by some authors with the ferruginous sand formation of the United States. It may be located, so far as it has yet been explored, between two lines; one drawn from Amboy Bay to Trenton, the other from Deal, on the Atlantic, to the mouth of Stow Creek, in Cumberland county, upon the Delaware River: but there is much reason to believe that this formation occupies a great portion of the triangular peninsula south of the Raritan River. Much of the ferruginous sand region, however, is overlaid by deposites of clay containing lignite. Above these is an almost uniform covering of grey sand; yet in many places the marl, with its peculiar fossil, is found immediately beneath the soil. This formation has been traced southward in many places, and most probably extends nearly the whole length of the Atlantic frontier of the United States.

In all its localities, it has been identified by similar genera and species of organic remains, though all the genera do not exist in every locality. Thus, at the Deep Cut of the Delaware and Chesapeake Canal, the strata are characterized by great numbers of ammonites, baculites, and other multilocular univalves. These remarks apply to various parts of Burlington and Monmouth counties, in New Jersey. Near New Egypt, are ten or twelve beds, one above the other, with the genera terebratula and gryphæa. (*Ostrea*, Say.) Near Horner's Town, the marl is extremely indurated; and contains terebratulæ exclusively. Near Walnford, the fossils are chiefly exogyræ and belemnites; while at Mullica Hill, in Gloucester county, the beds contain bivalves, and quantities of belemnites; and the calcareous beds of this county contain gryphæa, teredo, alcyonium? sparangus, and several species of Linnæan madrepores.

The mineralogical characters vary considerably. Of the species of marl in minute grains, loose and friable, and of an uniform dull bluish or greenish colour, often with a shade of grey, and called gunpowder marl, Mr. Seybert has given the following constituents: silex 49.83, alumine 6.00, magnesia 1.83, potash 10.12, water 9.80, protoxide of iron 51.53, loss 89=100 grains. A less cautious analysis by Mr. J. P. Wetherill and Dr. S. G. Morton, of a specimen, apparently similar, from another locality, gave silex 49.00, protoxide of iron 50.00, alumine 5.50, lime 4.70; the remainder being chiefly water and carbonic acid. Hence the predominant constituents of these marls are silex and iron. They often contain beds of a dark bluish tenacious clay, sometimes mixed with the marl, forming marley clay; at others, the marl and clay alternate.

Again, marl is seen of a yellowish brown colour, friable or compact, and filled with green specks of the silicate of iron. Some of the greenish varieties are also very compact, rendering it extremely difficult to separate the fossils from their matrix. The friable blue marls often contain a large proportion of mica, in minute scales.

Other localities present beds of silicious gravel, the pebbles varying from the size of coarse sand, to one and two inches in diameter, cemented together by oxide and phosphate of iron, and containing fossils, similar to those above described. The most striking instance of this kind is at Mullica Hill. Some of the blue marls, which effervesce strongly with acids, contain but five per cent. of lime. But we find large beds of calcareous marl, containing at least thirty-seven per cent.; the remainder being silex, iron, &c. Also a hard, well characterized, subcrystalline limestone, filled with zeophytes. All these diversified appearances pass, by insensible degrees, into each other, exhibiting an almost endless variety of mineralogical character.

The mineral substances found in these beds, are iron pyrites in profusion; chert in the calcareous beds, amber, retinasphalt, lignite and small spherical masses of a dark green colour, and compact texture, apparently analogous to those found in the green sand of France. Their structure does not appear to be organic, although they have, often, a shark's tooth, or a small shell for a nucleus. Larger spherical bodies also occur, resembling the nodules of clay in ironstone, common in some parts of England.

As the quality of the marl varies greatly, so does the quantity used in manuring lands. In Monmouth county, south of the Shrewsbury River, there is marl so strong, that five cart-loads the acre are as much as the land will bear advantageously: in other places, from twenty to one hundred and forty loads to the acre are profitably used. It is asserted, that a good dressing will last from twelve to twenty years. It would be difficult to calculate the advantages which the state has gained, and will yet derive from the use of marl. It has already saved some districts from depopulation, and increased the inhabitants of others; and may, one day, contribute to convert the sandy and pine deserts into regions of agricultural wealth.

Pine lands, in the counties of Columbia, Albany, and Saratoga, and other parts of the state of New York, of a character similar to those of New Jersey, have been rendered very valuable by gypsum, and rotation of crops, often producing from twenty to twenty-five bushels of wheat to the acre. The sandy soil is in time changed to a rich vegetable mould—and gypsum, therefore, may probably be used with marl to render the pine lands of this State productive.

The occupation of a vast proportion of the inhabitants of this section is agricultural. Upon the loam soils large quantities of grass and grain, particularly rye, corn and oats, are produced; and the sandy lands, treated with marl, also give abundant crops of grain and grass. In convenient situations for supplying the markets of New York and Philadelphia, the farmers give much attention to the more profitable culture of garden vegetables, potatoes, melons, fruit, &c. The peach orchards of E. and W. Jersey, give abundance of that delicious fruit to both cities; so low, at times, as fifty cents the bushel. At a distance from the navigable waters, and from market, the grain is commonly fed to stock, and few portions of the United States, of equal area, produce more, or better, pork, than the counties of Monmouth, Burlington and Gloucester; scarce less famed for the quality of their horses. In the counties of Gloucester, Cumberland and Salem, upon the fresh waters of their streams whose shores are subject to overflow by the tides, many thousand acres have, by embankment, been converted into productive meadows, which maintain large herds of cattle, and furnish adequate means for enriching the upland. Adjacent to the Delaware Bay and sea coast, are wide tracts of salt meadow, some of which have also been reclaimed by embankment; and the rest afford abundance of coarse hay, free in many places to all who seek it, and valuable in the maintenance of stock and making manure. The climate is so mild, near the coast, that herds of cattle subsist, through the winter, upon these meadows, and in the neighbouring thickets, without expense to the proprietors. The sea coast is said also to be favourable to the production of good mutton and wool. The great inducements to enterprise and industry constantly operating in the markets upon the borders of this section, have already produced wonderful effects, and cannot fail to excite the inhabitants to still greater efforts to improve the advantages they possess.

Extensive beds of the variety of argillaceous oxide of iron, called bog ore, are common throughout this district, which when mixed with mountain ore, in the furnace, makes good iron for castings and the forge. From these furnaces, and those of the glass-houses, fed by the wood of the forest, a considerable portion of the annually growing wealth of the district is derived; and if we add to these, the cord wood, and lumber, and vessels built upon its southern waters, we shall have enumerated the chief sources of the prosperity of the peninsula. In this part of the state, 14 furnaces, including cupolas, and 14 forges, one extensive rolling and slitting mill and nail factory, and 11 glass manufactories, engaged in the manufacture of window-glass and hollow ware, provide a valuable and steady market for large portions of the agricultural product.

The whole of this district is tolerably well watered; but the streams are neither large nor rapid, and are remarkable for the depth of their beds, which cause, indeed, almost the only inequalities of its surface. Those of the northern part of the peninsula interlock their sources in various ways; some flow N. and N. E. as the Millstone and the South Rivers, with their many tributaries; some E. to the Atlantic, as the Swimming, Shark, Manasquan, Metetecunk and Tom's Rivers; whilst others seek the Delaware, as the Assunpink, the Crosswicks, the Rancocus, Cooper's, Big Timber, Mantua and Oldman's Creeks. Those on the south either flow S. E. to the ocean, as the Mullica, Great Egg Harbour and Tuckahoe rivers, or run S. W. into the bay, as Salem, Stow and Cohansey creeks and Maurice River. Most of the streams have a crooked course, and flowing through a flat country, are commonly navigable some miles from their mouth. Unlike the rivers of hilly countries, they are steady in their volumes, and uniform supplies of water can be more confidently relied upon.

IV. The second of our divisions of the State is included by a line drawn from Hoboken, running S. of New Brunswick to Trenton, and another from the Ramapo Mountains, on the boundary of New York, curving by the Pompton Mountain or Highlands, Morristown, Baskingridge and Flemington, to the Delaware, between Alexandria and Milford. This section, from N. E. to S. W. has about 70 miles in length, and an average breadth of about twenty miles. It possesses considerable variety of surface and soil, but is strikingly distinguished by its geological formation, which is chiefly secondary or old red sandstone, upon which rest hills of greater or less elevation, crowned with trap or greenstone rock. Its area includes four-fifths of Bergen county, the whole of Essex, a small portion of Morris, nearly all of Somerset, one-half of Middlesex, and one-half of Hunterdon counties. The sandstone base is found in various states of induration and aggregation. Generally, on the eastern portion of the section, from the Palisades, on the North River, westerly to Hunterdon county, it is compact, hard, and well adapted for building, frequently assuming the form of puddingstone and wacke, and occasionally affording considerable organic remains. Between the south branch of the Raritan and Delaware, still underlaying mountain and valley, the red rock assumes a slaty, shaly form, has more clay in its composition, and, taken from whatever depth, readily disintegrates into loam more fertile than that formed from the harder stone. But for the trap hills which have been thrown upon it, the whole of this section would be a vast plain, whose only inequalities would be formed by the excavations made by the streams in their tortuous and generally sluggish passage to the Ocean.

From this general formation, however, we must admit the following exceptions. The alluvial borders the first south-eastern trap ridge, known as the first Newark Mountain, from Boundbrook to Springfield, and westward it approaches the Raritan within two miles, forming the bed of that river a little below Brunswick. Wherever excavations have been made in this alluvial tract, strata of sand, gravel, and clay are disclosed, but no rocks in place. Ochres of good quality have been found in many parts of it, and at Uniontown, near Springfield, compact peat of superior quality, resting on marl, supposed to extend through a morass of five hundred acres. Bones of the mastodon were discovered a few years since in this swamp. Extensive beds of white pipe clay, composed principally of alumine, and infusible, have been observed between Woodbridge and Amboy, and marine shells in various parts of the district.

The alluvial section we have just described, is connected with another five miles in breadth by twenty in length, formed of the deposits of the Hackensack and Passaic Rivers, between the secondary valley and the Bergen ridge. In this tract, the depth of the deposit is from 12 to 20 feet, its basis sand and shells like the shore of the sea. The whole was formerly covered with wood, of which some groves of cedar still remain, and bodies of trees but little decayed are frequently found at various depths. Indeed, so abundant and sound are the logs on these marshes, that they are used for the foundation of the New Jersey Rail-road, now being constructed here. In this bog, N. of the turnpike road, between Newark and Jersey City, rises an island *(Secaucus)* about four miles long by one wide, composed, like the adjacent shores, of red and grey sandstone, and having a promontory at either end. That on the south known as Snake Hill, has a conical form, is of trap rock on sandstone rising into mural precipices, and having cubical masses of the trap piled at its southern base. From its wood clad, rocky and precipitous summit, the spectator may behold the Hackensack and Passaic Rivers almost at his feet, and for several miles dragging their slow length through a sea of verdure; on the west, populous villages and ranges of mountains; on the east the great city of New York, and on the south the wide expanded ocean. Through the grey sandstone of this island, micaceous iron ore is abundantly dispersed; and pectenites and other marine shells are found on its elevated parts.

The trap ridges which traverse this division excite much interest. Trapstone is known in many cases to have an igneous origin. Whether it may be ascribed to the same cause in all, is still a vexed question. That it has been found here subsequently to the sandstone on which it reposes, is most obvious; but when or how it has been poured over its base, throughout such great extent of country, in Connecticut, New York, and Pennsylvania, will probably never be discovered. We observe the first mountainous range of this district, on the eastern border adjacent to the Hudson River. It rises gradually from Bergen Point, bounds the State for about 28 miles, and runs a greater distance into the State of New York. In this State this ridge has an average width of two and a half miles, with a summit of table land. From its western brow there is a gradual descent into the valley of the Hackensack and Passaic. On its eastern side it is uniformly precipitous. At Weehawk, four miles N. of the City of Jersey, the mountain presents a perpendicular wall, elevated 200 feet above the Hudson, commanding a fine view of the surrounding country. From Weehawk to Fort Lee, a distance of about 7 miles, there is an alternation of precipitous ledges and steep declivities, mostly clothed with various verdure. The hills, retiring at intervals from the shore, give room for narrow but fertile and well cultivated strips of ground, adorned with neat dwellings, environed by fruit trees and diversified crops. From Fort Lee to the state line, the mountain has a uniform appearance. The eastern front rises perpendicularly from 200 to 550 feet; numerous vertical fissures cross each other at various angles, forming basaltic columns, from which the name of Palisades has been derived. The face of the ledge is bare, but vegetation is occasionally seen in the crevices. From the base of the precipice to the edge of the water, a distance of 3 or 400 feet, there is a steep declivity covered with angular blocks of stone fallen from the heights, and shaded with trees. The summit of the mountain is slightly undulating table land, gradually rising to the north, with an average width of about two miles, generally covered with wood in all the wildness of nature. The western side of the mountain has a very gradual descent, is cleared and well cultivated, and neat farm houses of freestone line its base, like a village street, for near 20 miles. The prospect is one of the most delightful; numerous farms, rich in luxuriant vegetation, and extensive alluvial meadows through which the Hackensack and its tributaries flow, are bounded by the mountain ranges of the west. The greenstone of this mountain, resting on sandstone, is not so dark as that of New Haven, and is an aggregate of hornblende, feldspar, and epidote, with which prehnite compact and radiated is sometimes associated. At the base of the mountain bordering the river, in many places, secondary argillaceous shist, conglomerate, red, white, yellow and purple sandstone, and indurated clay, alternate, exhibiting a stratification nearly horizontal, the underlaying inclination being from 8 to 10 degrees. These layers are sometimes visible on the mountain's side, at considerable elevations above the river. The sandstone is generally a coarse aggregate of quartz and feldspar, often friable, but sometimes very firmly combined; exhibiting winding vertical fissures. In this base may be observed, in some few places, a compact white sandstone, resembling the Portland stone of England.

A metallic vein was worked, at Fort Lee, at the commencement of the revolutionary war, under the impression that it contained gold; but Dr. Torrey has determined, that the ore is pyritous and green carbonate of copper; and the matrix quartz, dipping under the greenstone.

Two other prominent mountain ranges intersect the country now under view. They rise near the primitive highlands, two miles north of Pompton, and run about sixty miles in an almost semicircular course. The first ridge, at its commencement, is about twenty miles E. from the Palisades; but at, and south of Patterson, it is not more than twelve, from the North River. The most elevated point of these mountains is six miles N. W. from Patterson, where a sugar-loaf peak rises near 1000 feet above the level of the ocean. Its trap rock is generally covered with a thin mould and verdant surface; and a walnut grove, without underwood, occupies, exclusively, about forty acres upon the summit, from which there is a very extensive view, towards the E. N. E. and N. over a tolerably level country. On the N. W. the waving tops of the Preakness ridge are observed, extending for several miles, indented by ponds of considerable magnitude and depth. North of this ridge is another high and detached hill, sweeping in a semicircle, rising and terminating near the Highlands. Many of the summits are under cultivation, and afford fine views of the great secondary valley, bounded by the Highlands, the Hudson and the Preakness ridge. On the east of the last chain is another section of the trap ranges, called the Totoway mountain. It rises near the Preakness mountain, six miles from Patterson, and unites with the Newark chain, at the Great Falls. It is in many places free from rocks, but on the east side are precipices of considerable height and extent, with waving or denticulated mural faces, presenting columns of basaltic regularity. An insulated semicircular wall of greenstone, with projecting columns, bearing some resemblance to a castle or fort in ruins, occupies a summit of the Totoway ridge. Sandstone quarries are opened in several places at the base of the greenstone; and one, three miles from Patterson, on the Preakness mountain, affords the best freestone of New Jersey. Fine red and grey sandstone sprinkled with mica, alternates with argillaceous strata, dipping under the greenstone, with a western inclination of about 12°. Bituminous coal, in layers two inches thick, has frequently been found in this and other parts of the Preakness ridge, in connexion with sandstone and shale, and the neighbourhood is supposed to exhibit indications of more valuable beds of this combustible. Gneiss, granite, pudding and sandstone, in rolled masses, abundantly cover the surface, in many parts of this region. The greenstone of the Preakness range rarely offers interesting imbedded minerals; but prehnite, agate, chalcedony, and a mineral resembling cachelong, have been discovered in it.

At the falls of the Passaic, in Patterson, perpendicular mural precipices of greenstone, with wide vertical fissures and amorphous masses at their base, may be observed. The lower strata of this rock contain much argillaceous matter, which partially takes the place of hornblende. The ledges rest on porous rocks, horizontally posited, resembling the toadstone of Derbyshire. Carbonate of lime and other minerals, subject to decay, are imbedded in it; and by their decomposition give a cellular and volcanic appearance. A friable amygdaloid, with an argillaceous base, enclosing nodules of carbonate of lime of a spheroidal oval or almond shape, from the size of a pea to that of a walnut, may also be noticed. The nodules, easily disengaged from the base, exhibit a smooth dark green surface of chlorite. The layers beneath the amygdaloid, are red and grey conglomerate, connected with red sandstone, too porous for use, absorbing much moisture and breaking by the expansive power of frost. Good freestone in nearly a horizontal position, is the basis layer, and forms the bed of the Passaic. In many places the greenstone occupying the summit appears but a few feet in thickness; and it is not arranged in columns of basaltiform regularity. Prehnite, calcareous spar and carbonate of copper, zeolite, stilbite, analcime and datholite, have been found here.

Mural precipices of dark fine grained fissile greenstone, are observed at the Little Falls of the Passaic, five miles above Patterson. Vertical seams cross each other here, at various angles, in the ledges, giving to detached pieces a regular prismatic form, with three or four sides, often truncated on one or more of the lateral edges—the tabular form is common. Rock of similar character is observable in other parts of the Preakness ridge. Marine organic remains, such as *orthocerites*, *madrepores*, tubipores, pectenites, terebratulas, encrinites, bilabites, serpulites, and other species, generally in an argillaceous base, in mountain and valley, have been observed here, as in other parts of this region.

From Patterson to Springfield, the trap ridges are called first and second Newark mountains, and Caldwell mountain. Their direction is nearly south, with great uniformity of altitude; their eastern declivity steep, their western descent gradual, as is common with mountains of North America. Mural precipices are rarely seen, except at Patterson and Springfield. Wherever ledges appear, the mountain side is covered with small amorphous stones. The red sandstone appears in place, both upon the sides and base. Much of the eastern side is under cultivation; the summit and western declivity are generally covered by coppice of small oak, chesnut, walnut, butternut and cedar. The second Newark mountain runs a parallel course with, and is distant from, the first, about a mile. It is less elevated and rocky, and has a more gradual ascent than the other. The view from the first embraces the thickly settled and highly cultivated valley, whose surface appears like a plain, painted with meadows, grain fields and orchards, and studded with the villages of Bloomfield, North and South Orange, and the large towns of Newark and Elizabeth;—beyond which we have in sight the salt meadows, the city and harbour of New York, parts of Long and Staten Islands and the distant ocean. In this valley, fine red and grey freestone alternates with shale. Bituminous coal, in thin layers, is associated with argillaceous shale, in freestone quarries, adjacent to the Passaic. At the termination of the Newark Mountain, at Springfield, and in many parts of the trap ranges, smoke, and in some instances, flame issuing from the crevices of the rock, have been observed by the inhabitants; proceeding probably from carbonated hydrogen gas indicating coal below. Animal and vegetable organic remains have been observed in this freestone. Near Belleville a tooth, almost two inches in length, was discovered, some years since, fifteen feet below the surface.

The Newark Mountains terminate at Springfield, where the continuity of the trap range is broken. From this place the greenstone ridges take a S. W. direction of seventeen miles to the vicinity of Boundbrook, and thence, N. W. about ten more to Pluckemin: the second mountain following the curvature of the first. Secondary greenstone is, exclusively, the rock, in place, of the summits and sides of both ridges, but it seldom appears in ledges of magnitude. Sandstone is as usual the base, and has been observed under the greenstone, in nearly a horizontal posi tion, with a small dip, sometimes alternating with secondary compact limestone, in layers, from two inches to two feet in thickness. Prehnite is found in considerable quantities, near the foot of the mountain, in amygdaloid with a greenstone base, much of it partly decomposed. It is sometimes imbedded in the rock, in long parallel columns in various directions, its fibres radiating from the centre. Zeolite, stilbite, crystals of quartz, and carbonate of lime, are frequently seen in the valley between the mountains. North of Scotch Plains, sulphat of barytes appears associated with carbonate of lime. A small portion only of these ranges is cleared and cultivated.

The mountain, running a S. W. course from Springfield, has been termed, by some geologists, the Granite Ridge. It is described as passing through the State, bordering the oceanic alluvial, and having its highest point near Hoboken—alluding, doubtless, to the height near Weehawk. The *Greenstone Ridge* would be the more appropriate name. For excepting the serpentine, at Hoboken, there are no primitive rocks in place, between the Hudson and Highland chains; the summit rock of all the ranges being, uniformly, secondary greenstone. The Highland chain runs from S. E. to N. W., the general direction of the primitive strata; but none of the secondary ranges of New Jersey pursues a course parallel with the primitive. The latter, in many places, preserve for miles an even summit of table-land, whilst the Highland ridges display sugar loaf eminences, and a waving profile, characteristic of the primitive. The extensive secondary range commencing near Pompton, within half a mile of the Highlands, and extending in a semi-circular course until it again approaches them, corroborates, by its direction and the character of its summit, the correctness of these positions. The broad valley, encircled by the Greenstone ridge and the Highlands, contains much fresh water alluvial. Many of its small hills have no rock in place. The plain bordering the Passaic is generally extensive—in some places four miles wide. Peat is observed in several places between the source of the river and Little Falls; and a considerable quantity has been cut, adjacent to the Newark and Morristown turnpike, and the bed discovered to be more than six feet deep.

Pompton Plain, near twenty miles in circumference, and environed by mountains, presents a decided fresh water alluvion—strata of gravel, sand, and clay, without rocks in place, have uniformly been found wherever wells have been dug; and it was, probably, at a remote period, the bed of a lake. The waters of the Pequannock Long Pond and Ramapo Rivers pass through it. The southern and much of the western part of the plain is marshy, and embraces about 1500 acres of peat ground, apparently of good quality, judging by a ditch of four miles in length which has been dug through it. In the southern part of the plain, good granular argillaceous oxide of iron, or pea ore, is found over a space of about 200 acres. The Highlands form the west and north-west boundary of the plain, which in other directions is skirted by the Pacganack Mountain, pursuing a serpentine course from North Pompton, to the vicinity of Morristown, separating the wide alluvial plains watered by the Pompton and Passaic Rivers. Upon this range, the summit rock, in place, is, uniformly, a fine grained dark secondary greenstone, often in a state of partial decomposition, exhibiting mural precipices of considerable height and extent, with sandstone at the sides and base. The first contains prehnite, zeolite, analcime, chalcedony, agate, amethyst, jasper, crystals of quartz, and narrow veins of satin spar, in jasper. The part of this range adjacent to Pompton Plains, may, perhaps, from the abundance of these minerals, be useful to the lapidary, as well as to the mineralogist. The agates are from the size of a pin's head to three pounds weight, mostly chalcedony—The eyed and fortification agate has been observed here in a few instances. A mineral specimen was found in this mountain by Judge Kinsey, of near 16 pounds weight, containing agate, amethyst, and white quartz.

Another greenstone range, of minor extent, called Long Hill, is situate in the great valley, under review, rising near Chatham, and running westerly about ten miles. The trap of this ridge is in such state of decay, that rocks seldom appear in place. The Passaic pursues a winding course along the base of the mountain, sometimes concealed in groves, at others glancing sheen in the verdant meadows. About the centre of Long Hill are mural precipices, composed of what the farmers call shell rock, resembling the stone on the banks of the Raritan.

This secondary formation accompanies the Highlands to the Delaware, and is pierced in several places by broken ridges of the same trap character we have described. Such is the Rocky or Nashanic Mountain, the heights near Rocktown, Lambertville, Belmont, Herberttown, and Woodville, and Rocky Hill, immediately north of Princeton. The sandstone, generally, in this portion of the section, differs materially from that of the Passaic. It extends northerly to the first primitive ridge, north of Flemington, and forms the soil of the broad red shale valley, spreading from that ridge to the Rocky Hills, underlays the last, and extends south of Penington. Its colour is of a darker red than the Newark stone—it appears to be without grain, yields a strong argillaceous odour when breathed upon, and is readily decomposed by exposure to air and moisture. It is, probably, composed of iron, alumine, and silex, with a small portion of sulphur, and may be termed ferruginous shist. The rock is stratified, splitting readily into thin brittle laminæ, and is said to rest in some places on good freestone. But on the S. E. near Princeton, are quarries of excellent red and white freestone, similar to that of the Preakness ridge.

Sandy Hill, an elevation of the secondary region, situate between Kingston and Brunswick, is alluvial, like the Nevisink Hills, composed of sand, white and coloured clay, containing beds of ferruginous sand and puddingstone.

Upon the south-western angle of this district, and particularly at and around Trenton, there is a small portion of primitive, rising through the secondary, into abrupt rocks of granitic character, varying from loose micaceous shale to massive granite, but composed chiefly of hard and compact gneiss. This rock forms the Falls of the Delaware at the head of tide, and stretches away in a S. W. direction through Pennsylvania. From a mass in the bed of the river, large and beautiful specimens of zircon have been taken.

The portion of New Jersey which we have now described, is the most populous, and perhaps the most wealthy of the State. Its soil is not so productive as the limestone of the primitive and transition regions; but there is less of it waste, than in those regions, and it is divided into smaller farms, and more assiduously laboured, under the excitement of proximity to the markets of New York and Philadelphia, and that created in the eastern portion by its own manufacturing towns; as Patterson, Little Falls, Godwinsville, New Prospect, Bloomfield, Belleville, North and South Orange, Springfield, Plainfield, Newark, Elizabethtown, Rahway, Woodbridge, New Brunswick, Princeton, Trenton, &c.

Besides the minerals already mentioned, large deposits of copper ore have been discovered in this section, at Belleville, at Griggstown, near Brunswick, Woodbridge, Greenbrook, Somerville, and Pluckemin; and it would seem probable that a vein of this metal extends S. W. across the secondary region from Fort Lee.

The following account of the mine near New Brunswick is extracted from Morse's Gazetteer:—

"About the years 1748, 1749, 1750, several lumps of virgin copper, from 5 to 30 lbs. weight, (in the whole upwards of 200 lbs.) were ploughed up in a field belonging to Philip French, Esq., within a quarter of a mile of the town. This circumstance induced Mr. Elias Boudinot to take a lease of the land of Mr. French, for 99 years, with a view to search for copper ore. A company was formed, and about the year 1751, a shaft was commenced in the low ground 300 yards from the river. The spot selected had been marked by a neighbour, who, passing it in the dark, had observed a flame rising from the ground, nearly as large as the body of a man. At about 15 feet, the miners struck a vein of blue stone, about two feet thick, between loose walls of red sand stone, covered with a sheet of pure copper, somewhat thicker than gold leaf. The stone was filled with grains of virgin copper, much like copper filings, and occasionally lumps of virgin copper of from 5 to 30 pounds were found in it. This vein was followed about thirty feet, when the accumulation of water exceeded the means of the company to remove it. A stamping mill was erected, where, by reducing the ore to powder, and washing it, many tons of pure copper were obtained and exported to England. Sheets of copper of the thickness of two pennies, and three feet square, have been taken from between the rocks, within four feet of the surface, in several parts of the hill. At about fifty or sixty feet deep, a body of fine solid ore was struck in the same vein, but between rocks of white flinty spar, which was soon worked out."

Some efforts were made to renew the mining operations here, at various periods, but never with encouraging success. The excavations have been extensive. A shaft of great depth is yet visible; an adit, it is said, was driven several hundred yards beneath the bed of the river, and hydraulic pumps were worked by Lyell's Brook to free the mine from water. The stones around the vicinage are every where coloured by the oxide of copper, and beautiful copper pyrites are obtained from the neighbouring quarries.

The Schuyler copper mine, near Belleville, on the left bank of the Passaic, seven miles from Jersey City and Hoboken, was discovered about the year 1719, by Arent Schuyler. The ore cropping out on the side of a hill was easily raised; and as the policy of Great Britain prohibited every species of manufacture in the colonies, it was exported in the crude state to England. From the books of the discoverer, it appears that before the year 1731, he had shipped 1,386 tons to the Bristol copper and brass works. His son, Col. John Schuyler, prosecuted the work with more numerous and skilful hands; but the quantity of ore raised by him is unknown, his books having been lost during the war.

In 1761, the mine was leased to a company, who erected a steam engine, of the imperfect construction then in use, and worked the mine profitably for four years. In 1765, however, a workman, who had been dismissed, having set fire to the engine-house, the works were discontinued. Several gentlemen in England, acquainted with the superior quality of the ore of this mine, obtained permission from the crown to erect works for smelting and refining copper in America, and offered to purchase the estate of Mr. Schuyler, containing the mine, at £100,000 sterling. This offer he refused, but agreed to join them in rebuilding the engine and working the mine. But the revolutionary war, and the deranged state of the country subsequent thereto, and other circumstances, caused the mine to be neglected until 1793, when a new company undertook the work with much vigour, but it would seem with little prudence. They collected miners from England and Germany, purchased a freehold estate, convenient for the erection of furnaces and manufactories, with an excellent stream of water, rebuilt the engine, and commenced and partly completed other works. Their labours were interrupted by the death of the principal shareholder in the company, the whole interest of which soon after was vested in Mr. Nicholas I. Roosevelt, whose many engagements debarred him from prosecuting this enterprise.

Another company, organized in 1825, procured some Cornish miners, and cleared out two adit levels, three old shafts, and sunk one new one about 60 feet deep; erected a new steam engine, and prepared most of the necessaries for working the mine in the deep levels. But, when they were ready to break out ore, some inefficient machinery designed to pump the water from the vein to the great shaft, gave way, and the funds or patience of the company were insufficient to prosecute the enterprise further. Their lease, conformable to its terms, was forfeited. We understand that during the present year (1833), a new association has been formed for working this mine.

There are many veins well worth working, particularly those near the surface, containing what is termed stamp ore. The principal vein, which has proved very profitable, is imbedded in a stratum of freestone, from 20 to 30 feet thick, and is called a pipe vein. It dips about 12 degrees from the horizon, rather by steps than a straight line, and increases in richness with its depth. It has been followed 212 feet below the surface, and about 112 feet beneath the adit cut for draining; hence, the water must be pumped to that level. A large shaft has been sunk 140 feet below the adit, 30 feet of which have been filled with mud and rubbish. The engine at the mine has a cylinder 31½ inches in diameter, and eight feet stroke, and has ample power to free the mine from water. Excellent cast iron pumps are fixed from the level of the vein to the adit, and from the adit to the surface, for supplying the engine. The vein has been worked about 150 feet, horizontally, from the shaft, declining from the entrance a few feet: hence, though the leakage is inconsiderable, some method is required to carry it into the shaft, which may be readily done if the shaft be cleared to the bottom.

The ore of the principal vein, it is said, yields from 60 to 70 per cent. of copper; and the vein will produce, it is supposed, from 100 to 120 tons of ore annually, which yields from four to seven ounces of silver to the hundred pounds; and, like most copper ores, a small portion of gold. When pure copper was sold in England at £75 sterling the ton, the ore of this mine was shipped from New York for that market at £70 the ton. The quality of the ore, and condition of the mine, are attested by several respectable persons, who have skill and proper means to judge of them.

If the statement respecting the proportion of silver in this ore be correct, it is more productive than many of the much-worked and highly valued mines of Mexico. The mines of Biscayna, of Royas, of Tehuilotepec, and of Gautla, do not yield more than three ounces of pure silver to one quintal of the ore; whilst the remarkable rich mines of the Count de la Valenciana, at Guanaxuato, gave only 5.1-10 ounces the quintal. The mean product of the whole Mexican mines, when in their best condition, did not exceed 2½ ounces the quintal; and that of the ores of Peru was still less; giving at most at Potosi, 53-100, and at Pasco, 1.3-50 ounces, the quintal. If the ores of the Schuyler mine give from four to seven ounces of silver the quintal, and are abundant, they must be better worth working for the silver alone than most of the silver mines of the world; and the copper product must add enormously to their value.

The copper mine in the trap ridge, two miles north of Somerville, commonly known as Cammam's, has been wrought at intervals for many years, but without profit; more, it is said, because of the want of capital, and public confidence in the operators, than from the poverty of the ores. The following, according to Dr. Torrey, are the principal minerals found here, viz: native copper in irregular masses, weighing from one ounce to eight pounds, and one block has been obtained of 23 pounds; phosphate of copper, massive, and of a verdigris colour, generally accompanying native copper; carbonate of copper, green, in connexion with the phosphate; red oxide of copper; the massive variety of which is the common ore of the mine, found crystallized in octahedra, whose surfaces are extremely brilliant and beautiful; native silver, in small masses, disseminated through the phosphate and crystallized oxide; green quartz, in tabular, partly noded masses, a beautiful mineral, resembling chrysoprase; prehnite, in cavities in the greenstone, very fine; and mountain leather, in thin plates, very tenacious when moistened. Drifts have been made in various directions in this mine, and the ore is said to be abundant, yielding from 25 to 75 per cent. of pure metal.

North of the village of Greenbrook, in the same ridge, a vein of copper, many years since, was wrought to a considerable extent; but it, too, has been long abandoned.

To these locations of copper, we are now to add another, lately discovered, near Flemington, in a vein remarkably, but not yet extensively, explored.

V. The third section, into which we have divided the State, and which we have called the mountainous, is in breadth from 10 to 40 miles, measured at right angles with the direction of the mountains. This district is the most interesting, as it is the most varied, in its geological formation, surface, soil, mineral and vegetable productions.

The geological formations here are much blended and confounded; and the most we can attempt is to designate and describe the strongly marked divisions. The secondary section we have above noticed, is bounded on the N. W. throughout its range by a broad district of primitive; containing, however, a large proportion of transition. The southern limits of this district are marked by the chain of highlands running S. W. from the Ramapo and Pompton Mountains, on the line of New York, by Morristown, Baskingridge and Flemington to, and across, the Delaware, near Saxtonville. The extension, northward, is limited to a line running west of the Wallkill Mountains, and thence crossing the Delaware in the neighbourhood of Belvidere. A belt of transition, having an average breadth of about six miles, including Long Pond, Raffenberg and Greenpond Mountains, continues, we believe, along the eastern foot of Musconetcong and Schooley's Mountains, across the State. The continuity of the eastern ridges of the primitive, with its belt of transition, is interrupted in many places by the streams; yet the hills form few valleys of considerable extent, and are generally less elevated in this State than in the vicinity of the Hudson River, where they rise to 1600 feet. They are usually crowned by sugarloaf eminences, forming a waving profile, characteristic of primitive regions. The summits are commonly covered with masses of rock, which render them unfit for culture.

The primitive ridges contain rocks of pretty uniform character; in general coarse, well crystallized aggregates of quartz and feldspar; often enclosing shorl, garnets, hornblende and epidote, with little mica; and in many places, for a considerable extent, none. These simple materials, variously combined, form granite, gneiss and sienite. Primitive greenstone is observable also in some cases.

In the transition section, grauwacke and grauwacke slate, are the most common rocks. The extensive ranges in Bergen and Morris counties, of Long Pond, Raffenberg, and Green Pond Mountains, for miles present stupendous mural precipices, facing the east, of a reddish brown grauwacke, composed of red and white quartz, red and grey jasper, and indurated clay. The rocks are stratified, inclining to the north-west at an angle of about 40°. They are scattered in abundance on the banks of the Pequannock, from Newfoundland to Pompton. Grauwacke, in place, is sometimes observed, resting on sienite adjacent to the Pequannock. Extensive beds of magnetic iron ore are found on these ranges at Ringwood and Mount Pleasant, and at Suckasunny, at the mines of General Dickenson, being on the strata which extends 300 miles from the White Hills of Newhampshire, to the end of the primitive ridge near Black River. These beds are from 8 to 12 feet thick; and the ore from the mine of General Dickenson produces the best iron manufactured from highland ore. Calcareous spar and asbestos are frequent, and sulphuret of iron abounds in various parts of the Highlands. Probably, the most extensive bed of the last is in Morris county, near the eastern base of Copperas Mountain, and opposite to Green Pond. Copperas was manufactured here extensively during the late war with Great Britain. Many rich beds of iron ore in this region, are rendered useless for the forge by sulphur. Graphite or black lead, in various stages of purity, is common.

At Monro Iron Works, (N. Y.) on the River Ramapo, large plates of black mica, crystallized in hexaedral form, are seen sometimes a foot in diameter. Compact feldspar and epidote, are in the elevated primitive ranges west of the transition district, and compact limestone at various parts of the transition range; and in the vicinity of New Germantown, and on a line running N. E. and S. W. from that point, pudding limestone, not inferior in beauty to that employed in the capitol of Washington, is abundant, and frequently converted into lime. In the primitive range of Morris county, west of Pompton Plains, called Stony Brook Mountains, chlorite slate is common, and granular limestone has recently been found in the same mountain. The latter is in colour clear white, admits of good polish, and is often associated with beautiful amianthus and talc, alternating in narrow veins. In the same vicinity there is a greyish white marble, rendered porphyritic by grains of noble serpentine disseminated through it. It is hard and receives a fine polish. In the talc, metallic crystals supposed to be chromate of iron, have been observed. From the last mentioned mineral an acid is extracted, which, united with lead, forms chromate of lead, a valuable pigment. Galena has been observed in the grauwacke ranges adjacent to Green Pond, and beautiful tremolite is connected with the white granular limestone of Stoneybrook.

North-west of the transition, the primitive resumes its empire, and includes the Wallkill and Hamburg Mountains, which are continued in Schooley's and the Musconetcong Mountains, from the line of New York to the line of Pennsylvania, undivided by any stream. In this ridge and the portion of the primitive sections west of it, the primitive, the transition, and the secondary formations seem combined. This region also includes Marble Mountain, Scott's Mountain, Jenny Jump, Furnace Mountain, Pimple Hill, Pochuck Mountain, and other innominate hills. This, also, is a remarkable mineral district. Schooley's Mountain and the Musconetcong, abound with highly magnetic iron ore, blended however with foreign substances, which render liquefaction difficult. Along the valleys and hill sides of this mountain there is an abundance of excellent flints suitable for guns.

West of the Hamburg Mountain lies the valley of the Wallkill, or, as it is sometimes called, the Valley of Sparta; running east of north twenty miles to the State of New York, much noted for the number and variety of its minerals. A white crystalline limestone and marble occupies the bottom of the valley, and rises on the west into a low subsidiary ridge following the course of the stream eight or nine miles. The metalliferous deposits, however, claim the greatest interest. The first or eastern bed, which at Franklin appears like a black mountain mass, contains an ore of iron commonly little magnetic, and, as a new metalliferous combination, has received the name of Franklinite, and is composed of 66 per cent. of iron, 16 of zinc, and 17 of the red oxide of manganese. On its supposed richness the great furnace of Franklin was built, but it was soon discovered that this ore was not only irreducible to metallic iron, but that it obstructed the fusion of other ores. If employed in quantity exceeding one-tenth of the magnetic oxide of iron with which it was economically mixed, there resulted what the smelters term a *salamander;* an alloy of iron with manganese, which resisted fusion and crystallized even under the blast, so that all the metal was lost, the hearth demolished, and 10 or 12 yoke of oxen required to drag away the useless mass. At Franklin, it is but sparingly intermixed with the red oxide of zinc. About two miles north, the bed ceases to be apparent at the surface, but may be traced seven miles to the south-east. Three miles from the furnace, at Stirling, is another huge mass of this mineral, but so combined with the red oxide of zinc, that the crystals of Franklinite are imbedded in the zinc, forming a metalliferous porphyry. This ore, merely pounded and mixed with copper, was profitably employed during the late war for forming brass. Often, within a few feet west of the Franklinite, appear beds of well characterized magnetic oxide of iron, but always accompanied by hornblende rock. A species of this last ore, found near the furnace, is intimately blended with plumbago. Here, also, are curious beds of yellow garnet, imperfect sienitic granite, in which are beautiful opaque blackish brown masses of garnet of a high resinous lustre, and crystallized on the surface, accompanied with laminated epidote; white and compact massive or minutely laminated augite, in some parts intimately blended with specks of violet, granular feldspar, resembling petrosilex; sphene, brown garnet, dark green granular augite, like the cocolite of Lake Champlain; phosphate of lime; spinelle and black spinelle or fowlerite, from Dr. Fowler, of Franklin, its discoverer; specular iron ore; brucite, bronzite, pargazite and idocras, zircon, tremolite, imbedded in crystals of white augite; actynolite, short crystals of augite almost black, like those of volcanic rocks; apatite, a beautiful apple green feldspar, in crystalline carbonate of lime, accompanied with perfect crystals of mica, and hexagonal plates of plumbago, soft and almost as fusible as hornblende; a very brilliant pale green hornblende, passing into actynolite, which has been denominated maclureite, in honour of him who has done so much for American geology, and natural science in general;—blue and white sapphire, enormous green crystals of augite, at least an inch and a half in diameter, presenting hexaedral or octahedral prisms, with almost equal faces, and terminated by oblique tetrahedral pyramids, accompanied, near the junction of granite and crystallized carbonate of lime, with large crystals of feldspar; scapolite, or wernerite; arsenical pyrites, mixed with others resembling the sulphuret of cobalt, or nickel, with a substance like blende, accompanied by dendrodite, and argillaceous fluate of lime.

The crystalline calcareous rock which here alternates with granitines of feldspar and quartz, or with beds of sienitic granite, at other places, disappears, and a confluent grauwacke, almost porphyritic, and contemporaneous, apparently, with the other formations, is observed, directly overlaid by a bed of leaden, minutely granular, secondary limestone, containing organic remains of the usual shells and corallines, and layers of blackish hornstone or petrosilex. This rock, as well as the grauwacke *beneath* has disseminated crystals of blue fluate of lime. In the limestone the cavities are sometimes very numerous, and lined both with pseudomorphous masses and cubes, and white fluate and quartz crystals. Thus we have here before us, as at Lake Champlain, the rare and interesting spectacle of an union of every class of rocks, but passing decidedly into each other, as if almost contemporaneous. This singular formation, to which slate should be added, extends into Orange county, State of New York. Immense masses, some miles in length, of the red oxide of zinc, lie in the mountains, near Sparta; and as this ore may be easily converted into metal, they will probably one day add greatly to the wealth of this portion of the State. The white crystalline limestone, which is so interesting a feature of this region, has been distinctly traced from Mounts Adam and Eve, in the state of New York, to Byram township of Sussex county, in an uninterrupted line of twenty-five miles, with a width varying from two and a half miles, to that of a few rods, its greatest breadth being at the state line. Its inclination, except at Mounts Adam and Eve, is low, often falling below the adjoining limestone of more recent date. It crops out, only here and there, in large masses; and its continuity is to be observed, solely, by boulders and loose stones, scattered over the surface. It most probably extends, with occasional breaks, to Easton on the Delaware. Silver and gold are asserted to have been found in several places of the primitive region, and attempts have been made at various times, by the ignorant, who have been self-deceived, and by the knavish who have deceived others, to work veins of pyrites, which have a resemblance to those metals.

Among these primitive ridges, we must notice, upon the S. W., Scott's Mountain, and Jenny Jump, in both of which, are extensive deposits of magnetic iron ore, and other interesting minerals. In the first, near Oxford furnace, the mining of iron was many years ago very extensively conducted, and shafts of great depth, and drifts of great length, are still visible. The works, however, had been long abandoned, when Messrs. Henry and Jordan, from Pennsylvania, with praiseworthy enterprise recommenced them in 1832. They are now prosecuting a vein of productive magnetic ore, blended with carbonate of lime, from 10 to 12 feet wide, enclosed by parietes of mica shale. Throughout these mountains, the elements of primitive rock may be found variously and curiously combined; but we are not aware, that they have been subjected to minute examination by the naturalist.

N. W. of the primitive hills we have described, there lies a valley, having an average breadth of about 10 miles, but broadest near the Delaware, extending over the northern parts of Sussex and Warren counties. It is drained for the greatest part by Paulin's Kill, flowing to the Delaware, and may, therefore, properly be termed Paulin's Kill Valley. It is bounded on the N. W. by the Blue Mountain. The valley is covered with knolls and low ridges, at first view apparently in much confusion, but which may be traced on the inclination of the mountains. Transition limestone alternates here with slate. A notable ridge of the latter bounds the Paulin's Kill on the S. E. side, from near its mouth to Newton, whilst the N. W. side is as strikingly distinguished by its range of limestone, which may be traced to Orange county, New York. North of the limestone, there is another ridge of slate, of a character well adapted for roofing and ciphering slate, quarries of which are extensively worked on the Delaware. Between this slate and the Blue Mountain lies a bed of grauwacke. The mountain contains the usual species of transition rocks, grauwacke, in every variety of aggregation, slate, mountain limestone, and greenstone, and rising from 1400 to 1600 feet high, is covered with wood, in which the deer, bear, wolf, and most wild animals, indigenous, still roam. N. W. of the mountain, bounded by the Delaware River, lies a fertile tract of transition limestone land, watered by the Flat Kill, and varying in width from one to seven miles.

The mountains of this third section are, generally, in a state of nature. There are, however, some cultivated spots, which reward the husbandman. But the valleys form the most fertile portions of the State. They are generally based on limestone; and since lime has been extensively adopted as manure, they have rapidly improved. This is especially the case among the Highlands, at Clinton, New Germantown, in the valleys of the north and south branches of the Raritan and of Lamington rivers, in the valleys of the Musconetcong, the Pohatcong, the Pequest and its tributaries, and valleys of Paulin's Kill and Flat Kill. All these produce wheat in abundance, and where wheat abounds and finds a ready way to market, no other good thing is absent. Wheat and iron are the staples of the country, which in the lower part of the section, seek the market by the Morris canal. There were, in 1832, by the report of the assessors, fifteen furnaces and eighty-seven forge fires in operation in the counties of Sussex, Warren, Morris and Bergen. By the completion of the Morris canal, the iron mines are growing into vast importance; great demand for the ores having been created in West Jersey, Pennsylvania and New York. From the valley of the Musconetcong immense quantities of wheat are exported, individual farmers raising from one thousand to three thousand bushels per annum.

Marble for ornamental architecture is abundant in this district. At Mendham,

Morris county, it occurs with dendritic impressions in which it resembles the beautiful marble of Florence. White marble and noble serpentine, we are told, are found in large masses on the Pompton Mountain, and also near Phillipsburg. Manganese, too, is said to be abundant in various parts of the section, and a water lime, similar to that of New York, has been discovered at Mendham and other places.

South-east of the Musconetcong Mountain, this district is drained by the Ramapo River, which divides the primitive formation from the secondary, in Bergen county; by Longpond or Ringwood River, which rises in Longpond or Greenwood Lake; by the Pequannock, which has its source in the Wallkill Mountains: these streams uniting in Pompton and Saddle River townships, Bergen county, form the Pompton River, which joins the Passaic, about four miles N. W. of the Little Falls. The Passaic receives also the Rockaway, Whippany and Dead Rivers. The remainder of this part of the section is tributary to the Raritan River, which receives from it, three of its main branches; the North, the Lamington and the South; each of which has a tortuous course, and waters a great extent of surface, but all having their source S. W. of the Musconetcong and Hamburg Mountains, which separate entirely the whole of the section.

There are several lakes, of from four to six miles in compass, and others larger. The principal is Greenwood Lake, upon the confines of New York, about 16 miles in circumference; lying in a narrow valley of the Highlands, scarce a mile wide. Mackepin, in the southern part of Pompton township, covers less surface, and is supposed to be 600 feet above the waters of an adjacent mountain valley. Greenpond, on the south of the Hamburg turnpike and near the valley of Newfoundland, is a beautiful sheet of water, about eight miles in circumference, bounded E. by the woodclad Copperas Mountain, and W. by a high and savage hill, which bears its name. Two or three farm houses, pleasantly situated, on a sandy beach, on its northern bank, serve as an hostelrie, for the sportsmen of Morris and Bergen counties, when resorting to this their favourite spot. Some of the lakes in the transition region have their borders girded by lofty walls of grauwacke, and rival in their romantic scenery the celebrated sheets of Cumberland and Westmoreland. Budd's Pond upon Schooley's Mountain is also remarkable for its fish, as were Hurds and Hopatcong Lakes; but the last is now celebrated as the perennial source of the supply of water for the Morris Canal, being on the summit level, and the principal feeder. In its natural state the Hopatcong poured forth its waters to the Delaware, only, by the Musconetcong Creek, which courses the north-western base of the Musconetcong Mountain.

The streams that drain the interval, between the Musconetcong and the Blue Mountain, westwardly, are, the Musconetcong, Pohatcong, Lapatcong, Pequest, and Paulinskill; and eastwardly, the Wallkill. In this valley there are also several small lakes, the most curious of which are the White Ponds, near Marksboro', and Pimple Hill, both noted for the quantity of the shells of the small white fresh water snail, which covers the bottom and banks. At the first, the mass of these shells is enormous, covering the sides and bottom of the pond many feet thick. North of the Blue Mountain the only stream worth special notice is the Flatkill.

Oak, walnut, beach, birch, ash, elm and sugar maple, are the predominant timber of the third section. Pine, hemlock, and cedar, are scattered through the forest, adjacent to the lakes and streams. On the high points of ground, walnut and oak are the most common trees. Shrub oak is the most frequent in the transition highland district which passes through Morris county. It occupies almost exclusively an extensive level interval on the north of Suckasunny Plain, attaining the height of six or eight feet, and forming an entangled thicket, beneath which the ground is covered with loose stones.

We have already mentioned the number of peach orchards in the alluvial of the State, and we may observe here, that the apple orchards of the secondary, primitive, and transition sections, are not less worthy of notice. The cider of New Jersey is justly preferred to any other of the United States, and the quantity of ardent spirit distilled from it, may be conjectured by a glance at the list of distilleries in the general statistical table.

For a more particular notice of the rivers of the State, and of the bridges which cross them, we refer the reader to the names of the streams, respectively, in the subsequent part of the work. But we will conclude this physical sketch by a view of the turnpike roads, rail roads, and canals, which traverse the State.

VI. Turnpikes. Since March, 1801, authority has been given for making 54 turnpike roads. The object of these improvements seems threefold. 1. The facilitating the communication between the great cities of New York and Philadelphia. 2. The more ready approach from the interior to the markets of New York and Easton, for the products of agriculture and the mines; and 3. The drawing the produce of the Delaware river, to the waters of East Jersey and New York, all which has been much aided by the capital of that great city. The following list gives the titles of these acts, the dates of their enactment, with their respective supplements. Those marked with an asterisk, (*) have been wholly, or partially, carried into effect.

1801, March 9. *1. Morris Turnpike, from Elizabethtown, through Morristown and Newton, over the Minisink Mountain, at Culver's Gap, to the Delaware, opposite Milford. Supplement, Nov. 10, 1803.
1802, Nov. 30. *2. Hackensack and Hoboken. Supplement, Nov. 16, 1807.
1804, Feb. 23. *3. Union, from Morristown to Sparta.
1806, Nov. 11. *4. Union continued from Sparta, through Culver's Gap, to the Delaware. Supplement, Feb. 4, 1815.
1804, Nov. 14. *5. Trenton and New Brunswick. Supplement, Nov. 28, 1806. Feb. 1, 1814.
1804, Dec. 1. *6. City of Jersey and Hackensack. To which the state subscribed $12,500. Supplement, Nov. 4, 1808.
1806, Feb. 24. *7. Newark and Pompton. Supplement, Nov. 28, 1806. Jan. 28, 1830.
„ 27. *8. Newark and Mount Pleasant. Supplement, May 9, 1820.
„ *9. Jersey, from New Brunswick to Easton Bridge, on the Delaware. Supplement, Nov. 28, 1806. Feb. 22, 1811. Feb. 14, 1815. Feb. 15, 1816. Feb. 16, 1831.
„ March 3. *10. Essex and Middlesex, from New Brunswick to Newark. Supplement, Nov. 17, 1821.
„ „ *11. Washington, from Morristown to the Delaware, opposite to Easton. Supplement, Nov. 15, 1809.
„ „ *12. Patterson and Hamburg, from Acquackanonck landing to Deckertown. Supplement, Nov. 26, 1806. Nov. 23, 1822.
1806, March 3. 14. Springfield and Newark.
„ *15. Franklin, from New Prospect to the New York line.
„ March 12. 16. Hunterdon and Sussex.
1807, Dec. 3. *17. Princeton and Kingston—branch of Trenton and New Brunswick turnpike.
„ „ 18. Jefferson, through Berkshire valley to the Patterson and Hamburg road.
„ Nov. 16. 19. Belleville, from Belleville bridge to the Newark and Pompton road, between Bloomfield and Cranetown.
1808, Nov. 22. *20. Perth Amboy, to Boundbrook. Supplement, Feb. 18, 1820.
„ „ *21. Woodbridge, from New Brunswick, through Piscataway and Woodbridge, to Rahway.
„ Nov. 24. 22. Burlington, through Bordentown, to intersect the Trenton and New Brunswick turnpike. Supplement, November, 1809. Feb. 6, 1811.
„ Nov. 28. 23. Jersey and Acquackanonck, from Acquackanonck to Belleville turnpike.
„ 28. *25. Deckertown and Milford. Supplement, Feb. 10, 1813. Dec. 7, 1825. Dec. 16, 1826.
1809, Nov. 28. *13. Patterson and Hamburg, continued from Deckertown over the Blue Mountain, to the Delaware opposite to Milford. Supplement, Feb. 11, 1815. Feb. 15, 1816. January 23, 1818.
„ 29. *24. Parsippany and Rockaway, from Vanduyns, through Rockaway, to the Union turnpike.
1811, Feb. 8. 26. Water Gap, from the Morris and Sussex turnpike, near the 34 mile post, through Milton and Hope, to the Delaware, near the Water Gap. Supplement, Feb. 3, 1813.
„ 9. *27. Ringwood and Longpond, and division line between the 29th and 30th mile stones. Supplement, Feb. 10, 1813. Feb. 6, 1819.

1811, Feb. 9. 28. Farmers, from Springfield, through New Providence, Long Hill, Pluckemin, to the Jersey turnpike near Potterstown.
„ 11. *29. Newark and Morris, from Newark, through S. Orange to Bottle Hill or Morristown. Supplement, Feb. 12, 1817. Jan. 15, 1818. Feb. 7, 1820. Dec. 5, 1823.
„ 14. 30. Vernon, from the division line, near Decay's, to the Patterson and Hamburg turnpike.
„ 31. New Milford, from the division line between the 29th and 30th mile stones.
1813, Jan. 12. 32. Dover, to Suckasunny.
„ *33. Spruce Run, from Clinton, in Hunterdon county, to the Washington turnpike road, near Sherard's mill, in Sussex county. Supplement, Jan. 26, 1814. Jan. 27, 1818.
„ Feb. 11. 34. Hope and Hackettstown.
„ *35. New Germantown, from Bayle's Mill and White House to New Germantown.
1814, Jan. 27. *36. Deckertown and Newton. Supplement, Feb. 4, 1817. Feb. 4, 1831.
„ 37. Vernon and Newton, from Decay's, in the division line, by Hamburg, to Sussex Court House.
„ Feb. 11. 38. New Brunswick and Middleburg.
1815, Jan. 18. *39. Hackensack and Hoboken. Supplement, Jan. 21, 1818.
„ Feb. 6. *40. Patterson and Hackensack. Supplement, Feb. 27, 1824. Nov. 6, 1827.
„ Feb. 11. 41. Mount Hope and Longwood. Feb. 7, 1820.
„ 42. New Providence, from Morristown to Scotch Plains.
1816, Feb. 15. 43. Georgetown and Franklin. Supplement, Jan. 20, 1819. Dec. 12, 1823. Feb. 25, 1828.
„ Feb. 16. *44. Bordentown and South Amboy. Supplement, January 20, 1817. Nov. 6, 1819. Dec. 8, 1826.
„ 45. Belleville, to the Newark and Pompton road, at the Little Falls.
„ 46. Woodbridge, to the New Blazing Star.
„ 47. Patterson and Hamburg, to the Hudson, from Acquackanonck Bridge, to the Hackensack and Hoboken roads near the Three Pigeons. Supplement, Dec. 7, 1824.
1817, Feb. 12. *48. Pochuck, from Hamburg to Goshen, N. Y.
1819, Jan. 21. 49. Columbia and Walpack, to intersect the Sussex and Morris turnpike.
„ Feb. 6. 50. Newton, from near Andover furnace, through Newton, to the third district of the Morris and Essex turnpike, near the Blue Mountain.
1825, Nov. 23. 51. Patterson and New Prospect.
„ 52. Patterson and New Antrim, from Patterson through Saddle River and Franklin townships.
1828, Jan. 23. 53. Hackensack and Fort Lee.
„ 54. Passaic, from Patterson to Little Falls.

Not more than half the projects for roads, which have received legislative sanction, have been executed; but in some instances the new laws were wholly, or partly, substituted for others, of which the designated routes had been abandoned. There have been made, however, about 550 miles of turnpike road, principally of earth and gravel. We do not recollect to have seen, in any direction, five continuous miles of road paved with stone. The main highways of the State are preserved in pretty good condition, and generally during the summer and fall seasons may be travelled with pleasure, in every direction. Some of them are preferable to the turnpikes, particularly such as pass over the slate and sandstone regions, where the hard rock approaches the surface.

VII. Up to the year 1833, nine companies have been chartered for making rail-roads, with authority to employ the sum of $7,140,000 towards these objects. The Camden and Amboy Rail-road Company was incorporated under the act of February 4th, 1830, authorizing a capital stock of $1,000,000, with privilege to increase it $500,000, divided into shares of $100 each, to be employed in the construction of rail-road or roads, with all necessary appendages, from the Delaware River, at some point between Cooper's and Newton Creeks, in the county of Gloucester, to some point on the Raritan Bay; the road to be one hundred feet wide, with as many set of tracks as may be necessary, with a lateral road to Bordentown; reserving to the legislature the right to subscribe one-fourth, or less, of the capital stock, within a limited time—which right was not exercised—with condition, also, that the road should be commenced within two, and be completed within nine, years; and that the company should make quarterly returns of the number of passengers, and tons of merchandise, transported upon the road, to the state treasurer; and pay a transit duty of ten cents for each passenger, and fifteen cents for each ton of merchandise, in lieu of all other taxes. The company was empowered to decide upon the description of carriages to be used on the road, the weight to be transported on each, the times of starting and rates of travelling, and to regulate the tolls; and was required to provide suitable steam or other vessels, at either extremity of the road, for the transportation of passengers. The State, also, reserved to itself the right to purchase the road at and after the expiration of thirty years, at a valuation to be made according to law; stipulating, that if the legislature shall authorize the construction of any other rail-road for the transportation of passengers across the State from New York to Philadelphia, which road shall be constructed and used, and which shall commence and terminate within three miles of the commencement and termination of the road authorized by the act, then the transit duties shall cease; and that such other rail-road shall be liable to a tax not less than the amount payable to the State by this company.

By an act passed 4th February, 1831, it was further stipulated between the State and the company, that the latter should transfer to the former 1000 shares of the capital stock, the instalments thereon to be paid by the company; the State to appoint one director, on condition, that it should not be lawful to construct any rail-road for the transportation of passengers across the State, within three miles of the road of the company, until after the expiration of the term of nine years from the date of the act of incorporation, (Feb. 4th, 1830.) And that when any other rail-road for the transportation of passengers and property between New York and Philadelphia shall be constructed and used, by virtue of any law of this State or of the United States, authorizing or recognising such road, that the dividends on the stock should cease, and the stock be retransferred to the company.

By the act of 15th February, 1831, the Camden and Amboy Rail-road and the Delaware and Raritan Canal Companies were consolidated, for the purposes of completing the canal and road, subject to the provisions, reservations and conditions of their respective charters; the directors appointed under which are empowered to manage the affairs of the companies in joint meeting; and the companies are jointly liable on the contracts made by either; and are prohibited from charging more than three dollars for the transportation of passengers from and to the cities of New York and Philadelphia. This act further provides that the canal and rail-road shall be completed within the time specified in the respective charters; and that if one of the works at the expiration of such time be completed without the other, that the work completed shall be forfeited to the State.

By the act of 2d March, 1832, 1000 shares of the joint capital stock are transferred to the State; and the companies contract that, if within one year from the time that the rail-road shall be completed, the transit duty received by the acts incorporating such companies, and the dividends on the stock so transferred, shall not amount to $30,000, the companies shall pay the deficiency to the State; and so, annually, out of the joint funds, and before any dividend be made to the stockholders, so as to secure to the State the sum of $30,000 at least, annually, during the charter; and that the State may appoint one director to represent the stock, but shall not vote thereon at any election of the stockholders. The state directors are appointable by the governor. The companies further covenant to construct a lateral rail-road from the village of Spottswood to the city of New Brunswick, to be completed so soon as any rail-road shall be made from that city to the Hudson River; and that they will not charge more than $2.50 for every passenger carried to and from the cities of New Brunswick and Philadelphia. The condition of these grants, however, is, that it shall not be lawful at any time during the rail-road charter, to construct any other rail-road in the State, without the consent of the companies, which shall be intended or used for the transportation of passengers or merchandise between the cities of New York and Philadelphia, or to compete in business, with the Camden and Amboy Rail-road.

The united companies have completed one track of rail-road from a point below Bordentown, on the Delaware River, to South Amboy, passing through, or rather over, Hight's Town and by Spottswood, a distance of 35 miles, at an expense, it is said, of more than $18,000 the mile. Upon this road passengers and merchandise have been carried since February, 1833. It is constructed in a very substantial manner of cast iron rails, supported upon blocks of stone, or wooden sleepers, placed three feet distant from each other in the line. Until September, 1833, the carriages were commonly drawn by horses; at that time steam locomotives were applied to one of the three daily lines which traverse it.

The remainder of the road from Bordentown to Camden is in progress, and is being constructed of wood, faced with iron bars; it being supposed that it will not be employed more than two or three months in the year, and will therefore not require the strength of the portion between Bordentown and New York.

By the power which this company has to regulate the tolls on the road, they are enabled to exclude all other persons from its use, and to secure to themselves a monopoly thereof; and this they have effected.

The West Jersey Rail-road was designed to be connected with the Camden and Amboy Rail-roads, at Camden; and to run, thence, to any point upon the Delaware River, in the township of Penn's Neck, in the county of Salem. The company was authorized to have a capital of half a million, and to increase it to one million of dollars; and the road was to be commenced within two years from the passage of the act, (12th February, 1831,) and to be completed within five years. The road not having been commenced, the charter may be deemed void.

The Patterson and Hudson River Rail-road Company, was incorporated under the act of 21st January, 1831, with a capital of $250,000, and the privilege to extend it to half a million; and was authorized to make a rail-road or lateral roads from one or more suitable places in the town of Patterson, one at least of which to commence at or pass in its course within 50 feet of the corner of the present lower race-way in the town of Patterson, at the intersection of Congress and Mill streets, near the Catholic Chapel, to Weehawkin; and from thence to any other suitable place or places on the Hudson River opposite to the city of New York, within 50 feet of high-water mark, not exceeding 66 feet wide, with as many tracks as they may deem necessary, crossing the Hackensack River upon or near the bridge of the New Barbadoes Company. By act 18th November, 1831, the company was empowered to locate the road from the east side of Berry's Hill, in the county of Bergen, to the Hudson River, and on making a tunnel through Bergen Hill, to charge additional toll.

The company are empowered also to purchase and employ all means necessary in the transportation of merchandise, passengers, &c. upon the road, but the road is declared a public highway, free to all persons paying the prescribed toll, and may be purchased by the State after the expiration of fifty years from its completion. The treasurer of the company is required to make to the State treasurer annual returns of the number of passengers, and tons of merchandise, &c. transported on the road, and after the expiration of five years from the passing of the act, to pay to the State, annually, one-quarter of one per cent., and after the expiration of ten years, one-half per cent. on the capital stock paid in, in lieu of all taxation.

By an act of 3d February, 1831, the Patterson Junction Rail-road Company was incorporated with a capital of $20,000, which may be increased to $40,000, and a power to construct a rail-road or lateral roads from the Morris Canal, distant not more than one and a half miles from the corner of Congress and Mill streets, in the town of Patterson, to intersect the Patterson and Hudson River Rail-road, within the town of Patterson. This is also declared a public highway, and the company are required, when the road shall be completed, to file a statement of its cost in the office of the secretary of state, and annually thereafter to report to the legislature the proceeds of the road, until they shall amount to seven per cent. upon its cost, and afterwards annually to pay to the State a tax of one-half per cent. on such cost in lieu of all taxes. And the legislature have reserved the right to purchase such road upon terms similar to those annexed to the charter of the Patterson and Hudson River Rail-road Company; and the charter of this, as of that company, is declared void, if the road be not commenced in one year, and finished in five years from the 4th July, 1831.

The Patterson and Fort Lee Rail-road Company, incorporated by the act of 8th March, 1832, has authority to employ a capital of $200,000 in making a road from the town of Patterson to Fort Lee, on the Hudson River, not further than 50 feet from high-water mark; to be commenced within one year from the 4th July, 1832, and completed within six years from that time, under penalty of forfeiture of the charter; and subject to be purchased by the State at the expiration of thirty years from the completion of the road, and to a transit duty of the one-quarter of one per cent. yearly, after the expiration of six years from the passage of the act, and the half of one per cent. after the expiration of ten years, upon the capital stock, in lieu of all other taxes.

The Elizabethtown and Somerville Rail-road Company, by the act of 9th February, 1831, was empowered to construct a road from the village of Somerville to Elizabethtown, passing as near as practicable by Boundbrook, Plainfield, Scotch Plains and Westfield, subject to a tax of one-half of one per cent. upon the cost, annually, after the proceeds of the road shall yield seven per cent. thereon, and to the avoidance of the charter in case the road be not completed within seven years from the 4th July, 1831. This road is to be a public highway, and may be purchased by the State on the terms established in the case of the Patterson and Hudson road, and the State may subscribe $25,000 to the stock of the company, at any time before, or within, twelve months after the road shall be completed.

The capital stock originally permitted to the company, was $200,000, with the privilege of increase to $400,000; but, by the act of 8th February, 1833, authority was given to add $500,000 immediately to the stock, and, eventually, should it be found necessary, $500,000 more; and to extend the road from the village of Somerville, by the village of Clinton, in the county of Hunterdon, to the Delaware River, opposite to the village of Belvidere, in the county of Warren, with a branch, if the company deem it expedient, to the Delaware River, between the mouth of the Musconetcong Creek and the Easton Delaware Bridge; subject to all the restrictions and reservations made by the original act. The great object of this extension of the road, is to unite it with the North-western Rail-road, which it is proposed to commence at the Delaware, opposite Belvidere, and to run through the Blue Mountain at the Water Gap, and by Stroudsburg, through a densely wooded country to Pittston, on the Susquehanna; being located for about 18 miles upon an inexhaustible coal bed. From this coal region, the road may be connected with several *authorized* roads into western New York. If this road be executed, it will open a convenient way to the New York market, not only from one of the most fertile and interesting portions of the State of New Jersey, but will give a direction to the produce of a portion of New York territory, otherwise destined to reach the city of Philadelphia. A portion of the stock for this route has, we understand, been subscribed.

The New Jersey Rail-road and Transportation Company was incorporated by the act of 7th March, 1832, with a capital of $750,000, and the privilege to double it, divided into shares of $50 each; with power to make a rail-road not more than 66 feet wide, with as many tracks as they may deem proper, from such point in the city of New Brunswick, as shall be agreed upon by them and the corporation of that city, through or near the villages of Rahway and Woodbridge, within half a mile of the market house, in Elizabethtown, and through Newark, by the most practicable route, and thence contiguous to, or south of the bridges, over the Hackensack and Passaic River; crossing Bergen Ridge, south of the turnpike road to some convenient point not less than 50 feet from high-water mark, on the Hudson river, opposite to the city of New York: and to make a branch road to any ferry on the Hudson opposite to New York, which shall join the main road within 100 yards of the Hackensack River, if the main road cross that river within 100 yards of the present bridge: but if more than 100 yards from that bridge, then the branch to join it, at such point, west of the river, as shall best give to the ferries equal facilities of communication with Newark. And if the company do not construct such branch, as soon as the main road from Newark to the Hudson shall be made, then the law authorizes the owner of the ferry so to do, with the same power and liabilities as the company. The act, also, empowers the company to regulate the time and manner of transporting goods and passengers, the description and formation of carriages; and the rates and modes of collecting toll within the following limits; viz. for empty carriages, weighing less than a ton, two cents; more than one, and less than two tons, four cents; above three tons, eight cents per mile; and in addition thereto, six cents per ton for goods, and three cents for each passenger, per mile. Provided, that no farmer of the State shall pay toll for carrying the produce of his farm, in his own wagon, not weighing more than a ton, when such produce does not weigh more than 1000 lbs.: but shall pay, only, for carriages, as if empty. It also authorizes the company to construct branches to any landing, on or near the Passaic, not north of Belleville, and to any place in the township of Newark; and requires them to commence the road at Jersey City and New Brunswick, within one year, and to complete the whole route in five years, under penalty of forfeiture of their charter. The company are further empowered to purchase any turnpike road and bridges on the route; but the act reserves to the State and individual stockholders of the Newark Turnpike Company, the right, at any time, within two years from the opening of the books, to take stock of the company in exchange, or to sell to the company, at market value; but the Newark turnpike and the bridges over the Raritan, Passaic and Hackensack, are to be kept as public roads, without obstruction: to build or purchase carriages for the transportation of persons or property; but not to charge more than six cents a mile for transporting passengers and each ton of goods, nor more than $1.25 for carrying passengers from New York to New Brunswick: to hold real estate, at the commencement and termination of their roads, not exceeding three acres at each place; and to build thereon, warehouses, stables, machine shops, &c. and over the Hackensack and Passaic Rivers, such bridges, piers, &c. as may be necessary. The State has reserved the right to purchase the road after the expiration of the charter, (30 years) and of subscribing one-fourth of the stock, and has imposed an annual tax of 1-4 per cent. upon the capital paid in; and should the road be continued across the State, a transit duty of 8 cents for each passenger and 12 cents for every ton of goods transported over the whole road. By a supplement to the act relative to the Delaware and Raritan Canal, and Amboy Rail-road, the companies are required to construct a lateral rail-road from the village of Spottswood to the city of New Brunswick, as soon as a rail-road shall be made from New Brunswick to the Hudson River; consequently, when the Camden and Amboy Rail-road and the New Jersey Rail-road shall be completed, there must be a rail-road through the state, from Jersey City to Philadelphia.

The New Jersey Rail-road Company commenced operations in the summer of 1832, and have confident expectations of completing the road from Hackensack River, through Newark to Elizabethtown, by the fall of 1833; and from the Hudson to Elizabethtown in the summer of 1834; and the whole line, from the Hudson to New Brunswick, within two years. The estimated cost of the whole road for one track, with suitable passing places, including the purchase from the Bridge and Newark Turnpike Companies, the bridges over the Hackensack, Passaic and Raritan, and the moving power, cars, &c. as per report of N. Beach, the engineer, is - - - - - - - - - - $718,912

Cost of superstructure for a second track on the whole line, 30 miles, at $4,710 80 per mile, - - - - - - - 141,324

Total, - - - - $860,236

Upon this capital, the company, after paying for annual repairs, cost of moving power, cars, &c. the sum of $35,640 per annum, anticipate to receive a profit of $134,775, equal to 15½ per cent.

By an arrangement with the Patterson Rail-road Company, the road for both companies, from the west side of Bergen Ridge, through the Deep Cut, and across the heavy embankments, on the east of the Ridge, and to the Hudson River, is to be constructed under the charter of this company, as joint property of the two companies; the Patterson company paying two-fifths, and this company three-fifths of the expense of construction, each company using the road without accounting to the other. This arrangement reduces the expense of the New Jersey Company $55,171.

The company, in order to avoid litigation, has purchased of the United Passaic and Hackensack Bridge Companies their stock, at $150,000, equal to $150 per share, upon which amount it had, for some years, paid seven per cent. and created a surplus fund of $30,000. With this stock, they obtained also all the right which the bridge company possessed, to pass the Passaic and Hackensack Rivers, by bridges, for sixty years to come. A very large majority of the stockholders of the bridge companies used the right of election stipulated for, to take rail-road stock, and have thus become identified in interest with the company.

The New Jersey, Hudson and Delaware Rail-road Company was incorporated by an act of 8th March, 1832, with a capital stock of $1,000,000, and authority to increase it to $2,000,000, to be employed in making a rail-road and public highway, commencing at any point on the Delaware River, between the New York state line and the mouth of Paulin's Kill, (and constructing a bridge over said river,) and to run thence to Snufftown, in the county of Sussex, and thence to the Hudson River, opposite the city of New York; or to join any rail-road chartered or to be chartered, leading to or terminating at the Hudson River, opposite the city of New York: but if extended to the Hudson, not to cross the Passaic south of the village of Belleville, nor to approach any point within three miles of the present bridge over the Passaic, at Newark, nor to run south of the turnpike road, a causeway leading from Newark to Jersey City; such road to be commenced within two and finished within twenty years; and when the dividends upon its stock shall amount to seven per cent. to be subject to a tax of one-half of one per cent. per annum on the cost of the road and appendages, in lieu of all taxes; reserving to the State the right, at any time within three years after the expiration of ninety-nine years, of taking the road and appendages at cost.

The Delaware and Jobstown Rail or Macadamized Road Company, was incorporated under the act of 11th February, 1833, with a capital of $60,000, and liberty to increase it to $200,000, for the purpose of making a public road from the mouth of Craft's Creek, upon the Delaware River, by the villages of Columbus, Jobstown and Juliustown, to New Lisbon, a distance of 13 miles; the road to be commenced within three and completed within ten years from the passage of the act, on penalty of forfeiture of the charter: and when the annual net proceeds shall amount to more than seven per cent. to pay half per cent. tax annually to the State; reserving the right to the State to purchase the road upon appraisement after the expiration of fifty years. The stock of this road, we are told, is subscribed.

VIII. There are four canals in the State completed or about to be completed, viz. the Morris Canal, the Delaware and Raritan Canal, the Salem Creek Canal, and the Manasquan Canal.

The Morris Canal is among the most original and boldest efforts of the spirit of internal improvement. The idea of making it was first conceived by George P. M'Culloch, Esq. of Morristown, whilst on a fishing party at the Hopatcong Lake, near the summit of the Musconetcong Mountain, more than 900 feet above the level of the sea, and the enterprise was commenced through his zealous and active exertions. This lake, the source of the Musconetcong River, in its original state covered an area of about five square miles. To dam up its outlet, husband the spring freshets, to double its capacity, and by leading its accumulated waters to the eastern declivity and valley of the Rockaway, to pursue the western descent until a practical route could be obtained across the country to Easton, were the means he proposed to open the way to market for the rich mineral products and the iron manufactured at the many furnaces and forges of this mountainous district. At one period, 81 forges and 12 furnaces flourished in the district, but when the canal was proposed, 30 of the former and 9 of the latter had fallen into ruins; whilst the remainder were greatly limited in their operations by the growing scarcity of fuel and increasing cost of transportation. A ton of iron might have been brought to New York from Archangel on the White Sea, at nearly the same price it could have been transported from Berkshire valley; and thus, this great branch of manufacture, alike interesting to the State and the Union, was in imminent danger of perishing.

But how might a canal penetrate from the Delaware to the Hudson, 100 miles, through the mountainous chain repeatedly crossing its path? How might the elevation, rapid and unavoidable, be surmounted, and how should the pecuniary sources be provided for an enterprise vast, novel, hazardous and expensive? The lake at the summit level would supply water to be sure; but to raise boats 900 feet high, and again to lower them to their first level of lockage, would have required an amount of money for the construction, and of time in the passage, alike fatal to the enterprise. Mr. M'Culloch, therefore, adopted the expedient of inclined planes for the greater lifts, and locks for the less. Such planes had never before been applied to boats of much magnitude, nor to an operation so extensive.

Mr. M'Culloch endeavoured to induce the State to adopt the enterprise; and at the instance of him and others, the legislature, by act 15th November, 1822, appointed G. M'Culloch, Charles Kinsey, of Essex, and Thomas Capner, Esqrs. commissioners, with authority to employ a scientific engineer and surveyor to explore, survey and level the most practicable route for this canal; and to report an estimate of the expense thereof, with such information relative to the minerals along its lines as they could obtain, and to deposit specimens thereof in the state library. The commissioners reported, in 1823, and received the thanks of the legislature for the intelligence, industry and zeal displayed in the execution of their commission. But that cautious and prudential policy which has hitherto prevented the State from yielding her treasury and resources to the blandishment of projectors, charm they ever so wisely, deterred her from making the Morris Canal a state enterprise. A private company was therefore formed, and incorporated under the act of 31st December, 1824, with a capital of $1,000,000, and the right to increase it to $1,500,000, for canal purposes; and, likewise, to employ in banking operations, additionally, the sum of $200,000, for every $200,000 actually expended on the canal, so that the banking capital did not exceed a million of dollars.

The route of the canal was selected, and the estimate of cost made, by Major Ephraim Beach, under whose direction the work was executed. This route, and the estimate of cost, were approved by General Bernard and Major Totten, of the engineer corps of the United States, and by Judge Wright; and the plan of inclined planes, suggested by professor James Renwick, of Columbia College, New York, also received the sanction of the like authority; but much modification was afterwards found necessary in this particular.

In 1825, the excavations were prosecuted with alacrity, while the planes were deferred; an arrangement which experience proves should have been reversed, since the latter could be perfected only by many and tedious experiments. The erection of the planes, too, was entrusted to ordinary mechanics, who, deficient in scientific knowledge and manual skill, caused much disappointment, which was aggravated by great and useless expenditure; but, finally, proper engineers were employed, and the planes have become effectual to establish a regular intercourse along the line of the canal with the Delaware and Lehigh Rivers, and with the Hudson. The machinery of the inclined plane, so far as we have examined it, consists of a double railway connecting the upper and lower portions of the canal, up which a carriage supporting a boat is drawn by means of iron chains, wound round a cylinder, set in motion by a water wheel turned by a stream from the upper level; whilst another chain regulates the descent of another boat to the lower level, if there be one to pass, or if none, of the empty cradle.

The cost of the canal, originally estimated at $817,000, has been about $2,000,000. The length completed is about 90 miles from the Passaic River, at Newark, to the Delaware, at Philipsburg, opposite to Easton; 11¾ miles between Jersey City and Newark remain to be executed, and are estimated to cost $100,000; but the cost will, as usual, probably exceed the estimate. This excess of cost over the estimate is not peculiar to the Morris Canal, but is common, perhaps unavoidable, in all the public works of the country. The engineer can judge only from an imperfect knowledge of the surface of the ground through which he is to make his way: an unexpected bed of stone, a limestone sink, a quicksand, a sudden freshet or frost, may mock his calculations. Adventurers, therefore, in canals and rail-roads, should be content when their agents display reasonable intelligence and full fidelity. The canal was completed to Newark in August, 1831. It is deeply in debt, and pays no dividend to the stockholders; but its use has been most beneficial upon the business of the country through which it passes, and its portage will increase with population and business; and should the anthracite coal be successfully applied to the extraction of iron from ore, the consumption of that article alone will add greatly to the tolls. The transportation of the Lehigh coal to the New York market, originally counted on by the projectors of this canal, will be effected by the Delaware and Raritan Canal. The Morris Canal was adapted to boats of 25 tons only, which in many cases have proved too heavy for the chains of the inclined planes. The passage from Easton to Newark has been performed in less than five days.

The width of the canal is 32 feet at top, and 20 feet at bottom, four feet deep. The locks are 75 feet long between the mitre sills, and nine feet wide. The line is naturally divided into two divisions, the Eastern and Western. The first has 12 planes, whose united elevations make 748 feet, and 18 locks rising, together, 166 feet, making the whole rise, 914 feet. The highest lift by planes is 80 feet. There are two of that height, one at Boontoon Falls, and another at Drakeville; and the highest lift of the locks is 10 feet. This division now ends at the Passaic River, near Newark—the section designed to connect it with the Hudson, 11¾ miles, has not yet been commenced. The length of the division is 51 miles 32-100ths. The western division has 11 planes rising 691 feet, and 7 locks, whose aggregate lifts are 69 feet—total, 760 feet. Its length from the summit level to the Delaware, is

38 miles, 91-100ths, making the length of the whole line 90 miles 23-100ths. The annexed table shows at one view the number of the planes and locks, their location, elevation, grade of the planes, and lift of the locks; and is, perhaps, the best exposition that can be given of the work short of an engraved profile.

EASTERN DIVISION.

Plane.	Lock.	No. of the plane or lock.	LOCATION.	No. of the section.	Elevation of plane in feet.	Inclination of the plane.	Lift of the Lock in feet.
1		1	Summit.	2	50	1-12	
1		2	Drakeville.	4	80	1-10	
1		3	Near do.	5	38	1-12	
	2	1 and 2	do. do.	6			20
1		4	Baker's Mills.	12	52	1-8	
	1	3	Near do.	13			8
1		5	Above Dover.	15	66	1-9	
	1	4	do.	16			9
	1	5	do.	17			9
	2	6 and 7	At do.	19			18
1		6	Rockaway.	25	52	1-12	
	1	8	Near do.	29			7
	2	9 and 10	Powerville.	34			15
	1	11	Booneton.	36			10
		7	Booneton Falls.	37	80	1-10	
	1	12	Near do.	38			12
1		8	Montville.	40	76	1-11	
1		9	do.	41	74	1-11	
1		10	Near Pompton.	48	56	1-12	
	1	13	do.	42			8
		11	Bloomfield.	84	54	1-12	
	1	14	Near do.	86			10
	1	15	Above Newark.	95			10
1		12	Newark.	96	70	1-12	
	3	16, 17, 18	do.	97			30
					748		
12	17				166		166
			Planes and Locks.		914		

WESTERN DIVISION.

Plane.	Lock.	No. of the plane or lock.	LOCATION.	No. of the section.	Elevation of plane in feet.	Inclination of the plane.	Lift of the Lock in feet.
1		1	Great Meadow.	3	58	1-10	
1		2	Stanhope.	5	70	1-11	
	1	1	Near Sayers.	6			12
		3	do. do.	6	55	1-12	
1		4	Old Andover.	10	80	1-8	
	1	2	Guinea Hollow.	16			10
1		5	Near Anderson.	38	64	1-12	
1		6	Monté Rose.	41	50	1-10	
	1	3	Near do.	43			10

Western Division, continued.

Plane.	Lock.	No. of the plane or lock.	LOCATION.	No. of the section.	Elevation of plane in feet.	Inclination of the plane.	Lift of the Lock in feet.
1		7	Pohatcong.	47	75	1-10	
	1	4	Near N. Village.	61			10
1		8	Hulzesers.	63	62	1-11	
1		9	Near Bridleman's Brook.	67	100	1-10	
1		10	Nr. Green's mills.	70	44	1-12	
	1	5	do. do.	71			9
	1 and 2	6 and 7	do. do.	72			18
1		11	Delaware River.	74	33	1-12	
11					691		69
					69		
			Planes and Locks.		760		

RECAPITULATION.

Planes.	Eastern Division,	12	748	
	Western Division,	11	691	
		22		1439 feet.
Locks.	Eastern Division,	17	166	
	Western Division,	7	69	
		24 locks.		235
				1674 feet.

Of the interesting works on the line of the canal, our limits permit us only to notice, the aqueduct of stone of a single arch, 80 feet span, 50 feet above the river, over the Passaic at the Little Falls, built of beautiful dressed freestone, in the most substantial and durable manner—and the wooden aqueduct 236 feet long, supported by nine stone piers, over the Pompton River.

The State is indebted, as we have already observed, for the inception of this great work, to the genius and zeal of George M'Culloch, Esq., and she is not less indebted to the skill and perseverance of Cadwallader D. Colden, Esq., the actual president of the company, for its completion.

The Delaware and Raritan Canal, one of the great links of the chain of internal navigation, which is to give to the domestic trade of the country the greatest facility and security, has for years been a subject of deep interest to all who have reflected on the means of increasing our prosperity. The construction of this canal has been a favourite project,—with speculators desirous to deal in a marketable commodity; with capitalists seeking for safe and profitable investments; and with many statesmen of New Jersey, who believed they saw, in it, the means of creating a permanent and large revenue for the State, which would forever relieve her citizens from taxation, for the ordinary support of government.

So early as the year 1804, the project of a canal to connect the waters of the Delaware and Raritan Rivers, was earnestly considered. A route was then examined by a company of experienced and intelligent gentlemen, and a law passed authorizing its construction by a private company; but the state of our trade, and our inexperience in works of this character, prevented its execution. In 1816 and in 1823, commissioners, appointed by the legislature, explored the route, and by accurate examination demonstrated its practicability. At a subsequent period, a second joint-stock company was authorized to make this canal, and paid to the State treasury, for the privilege so to do, the sum of $100,000; but failing to obtain the sanction of the State of Pennsylvania to the use of the waters of the Delaware, they were compelled to abandon the enterprise, receiving back from New Jersey the premium they had paid. Many citizens of the State rejoiced in this failure, by which the power of making the canal reverted to her; anticipating that she would immediately use it. To this end, many petitions were presented to the legislature, at their session of 1828–9; and a committee appointed thereon, made an able and elaborate report, accompanied by a bill, authorizing the canal to be constructed by the State. But the settled policy of the State, safe at least, if not eminently prosperous or sagacious, which carefully eschews all prospective advantages to be purchased by loans, or by the taxation of her citizens, marred this measure. Finally, by the act of 4th February, 1830, the enterprise was again committed to a joint-stock company, with certain beneficial reservations to the State. The act provides, that a capital stock be created of $1,000,000, which may be enlarged to $1,500,000, divided into shares of $100 each, and that the company have all the powers necessary to perfect an expeditious and complete line of communication from Philadelphia to New York: That, if the capital were not subscribed within one year, or the canal and feeder not commenced within two, and completed within eight, years, the charter should become void: That, the company might make the canal between, and improve the rivers below, where the canal shall empty into them; the canal to be at least 50 feet wide at the water line, and at least five feet deep, and the feeder not less than 30 feet wide and four feet deep: That they may charge tolls for the transport of persons and merchandise, not exceeding five cents per mile for the first, nor four cents per ton per mile for the second, nor more than half those rates respectively on the feeder: That they may alter the route of the canal; that it shall be a public highway; and that, no other canal shall be constructed within five miles of any point of the canal or feeder, without the assent of the company: That at the expiration of thirty years from the completion of the canal and feeder, a valuation of them shall be made by six appraisers, appointed by the company and State; who, in case of difference, may choose an umpire; that such appraisement shall not exceed the first cost, with the lands and appendages, and that the State shall have the privilege for ten years of taking the canal and feeder at the appraisement, upon payment of the amount thereof: That the treasurer of the company shall, on oath, make quarterly returns of the number of passengers and tons of merchandise transported on the canal across the State, and pay to the treasurer of the State, eight cents for each passenger, and eight cents for each ton of merchandise so transported thereon, except for coal, lumber, lime, wood, ashes, and similar low priced articles, for which two cents only per ton shall be paid; and that no other impost shall be levied upon the company.

By the act of 3d February, 1831, in consideration, that the company would make the canal 75 feet wide on the water line, seven feet deep throughout, and the locks at least 100 feet in length, by 24 feet in width in the clear, the State extended the time after which the appraisement should be made, to 50 instead of 30 years, and engaged that neither the company, nor any other person, should construct any rail-road across the State, between the Delaware and Raritan Rivers, within five miles of any point of the canal, until after the expiration of the period allowed for the construction of the canal, reserving existing rights.

As we have already mentioned, when speaking of the Camden and Amboy Rail-road, the Canal and Rail-road Company were consolidated pursuant to the act of 15th February, 1831. By act 2d March, 1832, the united company, in consideration, that no other rail-road should be constructed which might compete with that road, covenanted to convey to the State one thousand shares of the joint stock, and guaranteed to the State an annual income of $30,000 at least, should not the dividends on stock and the transit duties amount to that sum; and engaged that they would annually divide the whole of the net profits, except such surplus fund as might be necessary, not exceeding $100,000.

Under these provisions the canal was commenced, and has progressed nearly to its completion. (Oct. 1833.) It begins at the confluence of the Crosswicks Creek and the Delaware, at Bordentown, and runs thence, through the city of Trenton and the valley of the Assunpink, crossing the creek by a noble stone culvert, to Lawrence's Meadows, whence it passes into the valley of Stony Brook; thence down the right side thereof, one mile S. of Princeton, to the junction of Stony Brook with the Millstone River; thence across the river by an aqueduct of eight arches, and by the right bank of the river to the Raritan River; thence along the right bank of the Raritan to New Brunswick, where it unites with the tide. It passes through or near Bordentown, Lamberton, Trenton, Princeton, Kingston, Griggstown, Millstone, Somerville, and Boundbrook. Its whole length is 42 miles, within which there are 116 feet lockage, viz: 58 between Trenton and the Delaware River, overcome by seven locks; one at Trenton of seven feet; one at the State Penitentiary of seven feet; three at Lamberton of nine feet each; one below Lamberton of seven feet, and one at Bordentown of 10 feet, lift. The last, by reason of the badness of the foundation, has cost an extraordinary portion of time, labour and money, in its construction. The lockage between Trenton and New Brunswick is also 58 feet, and is overcome by seven locks; one at Kingston, one at Griggstown, and one at the mouth of the Millstone, each of eight feet; two opposite to Boundbrook, seven feet each; one two miles below Boundbrook, of eight feet, where a dam has been constructed across the river to use it as a feeder, and one at New Brunswick, of twelve feet, lift. At this city, there is also a tide lock sufficiently capacious to admit a steamboat, and a basin extending the whole front of the town, formed by an embankment in the river. By turning the river into the canal, a water power will have been gained at Brunswick, equal, it is supposed, to 400 horse power. Upon the line of the main canal, there are 17 culverts, some of them very large; one aqueduct, and 29 pivot bridges. The canal is 75 feet wide on the water line, and seven feet deep, and the depth may be increased to eight feet should it be found necessary. To avoid bridging, the company have purchased a large quantity of land, in many cases whole farms, at great expense.

The feeder commences at Bull's Island, in the Delaware River, and runs thence along the left bank of the river to Trenton, where it intersects the canal, a distance of 23 miles, with an inclination of two inches in the mile. The works, beside the excavation, consist of a lift lock of 10 feet at Lambertsville; two guard locks, one at Bull's Island, and the other at Prallsville; 15 culverts, and 37 pivot bridges. The width of the excavation is throughout 50 feet; at the water line, its depth six feet; but, where it could be effected without great expenditure, the width has been increased to 60 feet, and thus three-fourths of the distance will afford good sloop navigation. A large basin has been constructed by the company, upon the feeder near the centre of Trenton, for the accommodation of the city.

The canal is adapted to vessels exceeding 150 tons burden, and has been executed in the most substantial manner. Its cost is now estimated at two millions of dollars. The estimate, when the proposition was made to the State to undertake the enterprise, was stated at $1,142,741; but the present canal is every way larger than that originally proposed.

The Manasquan River and Barnegat Bay Canal Company, was authorized under the act of 21st February, 1833, with a capital of $5,000, to make a canal 40 feet wide and five feet deep, from the mouth of the Manasquan River to the head waters of Barnegat Bay, at Layton's pond or ditch, in the county of Monmouth; to erect tide gates, and to take toll for passing through the canal for every scow, eight cents per ton; sail boat or small craft 10 cents per ton; and for every fish boat or skiff, 25 cents per ton; provided that the canal be commenced within two, and finished within five years.

A short canal of about four miles in length, in Upper and Lower Penn's Neck Township, Salem County, connects the Salem Creek with the Delaware River, about four miles above Kinseyville, and saves to sloops that ply in the creek, from 15 to 20 miles of the distance to Philadelphia.

IX. The population of New Jersey, derived from European ancestry, is composed chiefly of the descendants of the Dutch, Swede, English, and New England settlers. For nearly half a century, the country was in the undisturbed possession of the Dutch, who, in that period, spread themselves extensively over East Jersey; not, however, without an intermixture of their New England neighbours, who very early displayed a disposition to abandon their sterile soil for more fertile lands and milder skies; and who had also found their way to the shores of the Delaware, and made one attempt, at least, to colonize them. After the year 1664, the English authority was established over the province, and the settlement of West Jersey was then zealously commenced by English emigrants, chiefly of the sect called Quakers. The liberality of the provincial government must necessarily have drawn population from other European sources; but such acquisitions were not great, inasmuch as her aspiring and successful neighbours, New York and Pennsylvania, possessed greater attractions.

These attractions, too, have operated to prevent that increase of population in the State, which must otherwise have taken place from natural causes. Abounding in all that is necessary to the comfortable enjoyment of life, and stimulated to industry by the growth of the neighbouring cities, whose wants she in no inconsiderable degree supplied, New Jersey, had not her sons and daughters gone forth to people other lands, would have been covered with inhabitants, who, by natural increase, doubling their numbers in about 23 years, would, at this period, have exceeded 700,000 souls. But the State has been an *officina gentium*, a hive of nations, constantly sending out swarms, whose labours have contributed largely to build up the two greatest marts of the Union, and to subdue and fertilize the western wilds. Instead, therefore, of being distinguished for the growth of numbers within her borders, she is remarkable for the paucity of their increase. By adverting to the periodical census, a copy of which we have annexed, it will be perceived that the ratio of increase from 1790, to 1820, has been about 13½ per cent. for each decennial term, and 15½ per cent. for that ending in 1830. The augmentation in the last period may be ascribed to the growth of manufactures, the improvement of agriculture in the northern, and the accession of labour in clearing the forest of the southern, portion of the State.

In the first half of the eighteenth century, the ratio of her increase was about 30 per cent. in about eight years; at which she would have doubled her population in 26 8-12ths years. This is apparent from the census in the annexed tables of the years 1737, and 1745.

COUNTIES.		CENSUS OF 1737.											CENSUS OF 1745.								
		WHITES.					SLAVES AND OTHER NEGROES.						WHITES.					SLAVES.			
		Males above 16.	Females above 16.	Males under 16.	Females under 16.	Total whites.	Males above 16.	Females above 16.	Males under 16.	Females under 16.	Total slaves.	Total of both.	Males above 16.	Females above 16.	Males under 16.	Females under 16.	Quakers	Males	Females.	Whole number	Increase since 1737.
Morris,	West Jersey.												1,109	1,190	957	1,087	22	57	36	4,436	} 8,080
Hunterdon,		1,618	1,230	1,270	1,170	5,288	75	53	49	42	219	5,570	2,302	2,182	2,117	2,090	240	244	216	9,151	
Burlington,		1,487	1,222	1,190	996	4,895	134	87	58	64	343	5,238	1,786	1,528	1,605	1,454	3,237	233	197	6,803	1,565
Gloucester,		930	757	782	676	3,145	42	24	32	24	122	3,267	913	786	797	808	1,436	121	81	3,506	239
Salem,		1,669	1,391	1,313	1,327	5,700	57	56	40	31	184	5,884	1,716	1,746	1,603	1,595	1,090	90	97	6,847	963
Cape May,		261	219	271	211	962	12	10	9	11	42	1,004	306	284	272	274	54	30	22	1,188	184
													8,132	7,716	7,331	7,308	6,079	775	649	31,911	11,031
Bergen,	East Jersey.	939	822	820	708	3,289	256	203	187	160	806	4,095	721	494	590	585	0	379	237	3,006	
Essex,		1,118	1,720	1,619	1,494	6,644	114	114	84	63	375	7,019	1,694	1,652	1,649	1,548	35	244	201	6,988	
Middlesex,		1,134	1,085	1,086	956	4,261	181	124	91	107	503	4,764	1,728	1,651	1,659	1,695	400	483	396	7,612	2,848
Monmouth,		1,508	1,339	1,289	1,295	5,431	233	152	129	141	655	6,086	2,071	1,975	1,783	1,899	3,131	513	386	8,627	2,541
Somerset,		967	940	999	867	3,773	255	175	170	132	732	4,505	740	765	672	719	91	194	149	3,239	
		11,631	10,725	10,639	9,700	63,388	1,359	998	849	775	3981	47,402	6,954	6,537	6,353	6,446	3,557	1,813	1,369	29,472	
													15,086	14,253	13,684	13,754	9,636	2,588	2,018	61,383	

COUNTIES.	Census of 1790. Free White Males of 16 years and upwards.	Census of 1790. Free White Males under 16 years.	Census of 1790. Free White Females, including Heads of Families.	Census of 1790. All other Free Persons.	Census of 1790. Slaves.	Census of 1790. Total Number.	Census of 1800. Free White Males. Under 10 years.	Census of 1800. Free White Males. Of 10 and under 16.	Census of 1800. Free White Males. Of 16 and under 26.	Census of 1800. Free White Males. Of 26 and under 45.	Census of 1800. Free White Males. Of 45 and upwards.	Census of 1800. Free White Females. Under 10 years.	Census of 1800. Free White Females. Of 10 and under 16.	Census of 1800. Free White Females. Of 16 and under 26.	Census of 1800. Free White Females. Of 26 and under 45.	Census of 1800. Free White Females. Of 45 and upwards.	Census of 1800. All other Free Persons, except Indians not taxed.	Census of 1800. Slaves.	Census of 1800. Total number.
Hunterdon,	4,966	4,379	9,316	191	1,301	20,153	3,363	1,558	1,698	1,872	1,366	3,031	1,509	1,929	1,965	1,230	520	1,220	21,261
Sussex,	4,963	4,939	9,094	65	439	19,500	4,080	1,981	1,926	2,061	1,381	3,779	1,717	2,013	1,853	1,127	102	514	22,534
Burlington,	4,625	4,164	8,481	598	227	18,095	3,569	1,637	1,742	2,229	1,289	3,459	1,418	1,933	2,166	1,121	770	188	21,524
Essex,	4,339	3,972	8,143	160	1,171	17,785	3,343	1,663	1,928	2,084	1,285	3,344	1,718	1,857	2,088	1,240	198	1,521	22,269
Monmouth,	3,843	3,678	7,448	353	1,596	16,918	3,144	1,353	1,375	1,864	1,190	3,106	1,309	1,412	1,736	1,282	468	1,633	19,872
Morris,	4,092	3,938	7,502	48	636	16,216	2,998	1,318	1,405	1,563	1,197	2,905	1,277	1,564	1,616	1,032	100	775	17,750
Middlesex,	3,995	3,375	7,128	140	1,318	15,956	2,819	1,307	1,419	1,564	1,088	2,619	1,278	1,397	1,577	995	263	1,564	17,890
Gloucester,	3,287	3,311	6,232	342	191	13,363	2,861	1,332	1,230	1,578	936	2,661	1,169	1,285	1,511	845	646	61	16,115
Bergen,	2,865	2,299	4,944	192	2,301	12,601	2,887	920	665	1,560	925	2,048	1,008	649	1,410	857	202	2,825	15,956
Somerset,	2,819	2,390	5,130	147	1,810	12,296	1,798	819	879	1,027	822	1,804	767	968	1,115	778	175	1,863	12,815
Salem,	2,679	2,396	4,816	374	172	10,437	1,759	946	856	1,329	500	1,876	745	895	1,276	497	607	85	11,371
Cumberland,	2,147	1,966	3,877	138	120	8,248	1,672	783	844	961	453	1,541	685	844	941	459	271	75	9,529
Cape May,	631	609	1,176	14	141	2,571	487	242	334	264	197	449	227	272	279	137	80	98	3,066
	45,251	41,416	83,287	2762	11,423	184,139	34,780	15,859	16,301	19,956	12,629	32,622	14,827	17,018	19,533	11,600	4402	12,422	211,949

CENSUS OF 1810.

COUNTIES.	FREE WHITE MALES.					FREE WHITE FEMALES.							
	Under 10 years.	Of 10 and under 16.	Of 16 and under 26.	Of 26 and under 45.	Of 45 and upwards.	Under 10 years.	Of 10 and under 16.	Of 16 and under 26.	Of 26 and under 45.	Of 45 and upwards.	All other free persons except Indians not taxed.	Slaves.	Total number.
Hunterdon,	3664	1827	2114	2074	1769	3572	1608	2240	2188	1694	687	1119	24,556
Sussex,	4472	1927	2510	2188	1627	4301	1851	2339	2120	1413	269	478	25,549
Burlington,	4108	1789	2060	2221	1716	3868	1853	2310	2428	1590	946	93	24,972
Essex,	3795	1867	2535	2375	1640	3519	1967	2448	2335	1616	758	1129	25,984
Monmouth,	3356	1698	1655	1876	1557	3286	1452	1808	1851	1475	632	1504	22,150
Morris,	3625	1983	1813	1969	1315	3374	1750	1820	1882	1237	204	856	21,828
Middlesex,	2878	1697	1675	1751	1402	2860	1642	1286	1778	1449	665	1298	20,381
Gloucester,	3249	1531	1821	1714	1290	3154	1411	1722	1738	1154	886	74	19,744
Bergen,	2122	1037	1180	1338	1202	2130	1040	1232	1276	1081	785	2180	16,602
Somerset,	2003	1022	1226	1128	951	1762	1016	1228	1224	881	316	1968	14,725
Salem,	2014	1050	1141	1146	674	1865	835	1175	1114	681	1037	29	12,761
Cumberland,	1911	1157	1183	1230	662	1811	1128	1244	1108	647	547	42	12,670
Cape May,	617	285	318	384	199	563	234	332	317	191	111	81	3632
	37,814	18,914	21,231	21,394	16,004	36,065	17,787	21,184	21,359	15,109	7843	10,851	245,555

CENSUS OF 1820.

COUNTIES.	FREE WHITE MALES.						FREE WHITE FEMALES.					MALE SLAVES.				FEMALE SLAVES.				FREE COLOURED PERSONS—MALES.				FREE COLOURED PERSONS—FEMALES.					
	Under 10 years.	Of 10 and under 16.	Between 16 and 18.	Of 16 and under 26.	Of 26 and under 45.	Of 45 and upwards.	Under 10 years.	Of 10 and under 16.	Of 16 and under 26.	Of 26 and under 45.	Of 45 and upwards.	Under 14 years.	Of 14 and under 26.	Of 26 and under 45.	Of 45 and upwards.	Under 14 years.	Of 14 and under 26.	Of 26 and under 45.	Of 45 and upwards.	Under 14 years.	Of 14 and under 26.	Of 26 and under 45.	Of 45 and upwards.	Under 14 years.	Of 14 and under 26.	Of 26 and under 45.	Of 45 and upwards.	All other free persons except Indians not taxed.	Total number.
Hunterdon,	4194	1940	586	2539	2515	1967	4175	1907	2547	2646	2024	24	135	81	55	21	148	92	60	351	134	117	109	356	155	131	90	91	28604
Sussex, -	5901	2435	723	3053	3034	1931	5458	2371	3174	2776	1768	37	75	40	20	42	77	60	27	139	55	35	30	119	39	30	26		32752
Burlington,	4334	2176	661	2542	2459	2022	4082	2201	2854	2759	2050	14	12	10	4	10	24	2	6	241	173	146	100	252	139	128	82		28882
Essex, - -	4337	2185	720	3100	2802	1999	4162	2244	2930	2934	2051		181	99	64		126	117	72	391	90	118	68	397	115	131	80		30793
Monmouth,	3777	1758	543	2189	2030	1770	3645	1747	2150	2076	1666	328	233	109	65	129	179	134	71	295	68	82	78	223	86	77	73		25038
Morris, -	3218	1639	536	1855	1857	1522	3110	1556	2096	1917	1484	126	122	46	50	81	103	85	44	139	38	37	32	113	40	34	24		21368
Middlesex,	2999	1430	431	1791	1938	1517	2877	1491	1882	1941	1559	134	168	111	80	111	178	130	100	257	86	77	85	273	108	80	67		21470
Gloucester,	3779	1829	451	2161	2051	1531	3384	1704	2194	1979	1356	11	4		3	6	6	6	3	203	107	138	104	187	120	119	86	18	23089
Bergen, -	2416	1154	302	1330	1489	1435	2306	1148	1406	1465	1247	152	376	218	167	157	241	217	155	389	59	44	56	346	73	50	42	40	18178
Somerset,	2140	1091	308	1342	1319	1096	2044	985	1403	1395	1083	23	269	200	112	27	192	190	109	511	92	99	57	502	99	61	66		16506
Salem, -	2193	1047	350	1340	1289	738	2025	963	1368	1289	754	2	3		2	3	5			222	133	107	91	166	129	74	79		14022
Cumberland,	2065	960	266	1026	1201	747	1999	880	1231	1156	780	5	1	3	1	2	1	1	4	138	64	65	48	125	80	48	37		12668
Cape May,	702	326	79	371	434	262	654	308	402	360	213	4	4		5	3	5	2	5	52	17	25	24	34	15	24	14		4265
	42055	19970	5956	24639	24418	18537	39921	19504	25637	24693	18035	860	1583	917	628	592	1285	1036	656	3328	1116	1090	382	3093	1198	987	766	149	277575

CENSUS, 1830.

Showing the Aggregate Amount of each description of Persons within the District of New Jersey, by Counties.

Names of Counties.	FREE WHITES.																									
	MALES.													FEMALES.												
	Under 5 years.	Above 5 under 10.	Above 10 under 15.	Above 15 under 20.	Of 20 under 30.	Of 30 under 40.	Of 40 under 50.	Of 50 under 60.	Of 60 under 70.	Of 70 under 80.	Of 80 under 90.	Of 90 under 100.	Of 100 and upwards.	Under 5 years.	Of 5 under 10.	Of 10 under 15.	Of 15 under 20.	Of 20 under 30.	Of 30 under 40.	Of 40 under 50.	Of 50 under 60.	Of 60 under 70.	Of 70 under 80.	Of 80 under 90.	Of 90 under 100.	Of 100 and upwards.
Bergen	1558	1401	1268	1082	1778	1270	779	509	415	173	61	5	1	1519	1374	1154	983	1656	1102	750	494	402	140	49	11	
Essex	3024	2572	2482	2571	4062	2522	1449	818	477	211	48	6		2867	2506	2316	2367	3735	2331	1503	923	606	289	63	5	1
Morris	1900	1603	1459	1200	2025	1387	906	565	347	170	53	4		1837	1525	1332	1187	1856	1304	827	609	370	170	58	5	
Sussex	1898	1590	1342	1140	1752	1045	665	445	228	103	28	4		1840	1502	1218	1146	1624	977	626	375	232	79	31	4	
Warren	1614	1363	1205	1090	1773	1062	670	341	234	95	14	2		1507	1268	1128	1042	1467	959	566	387	246	100	23	2	
Somerset	1140	1074	1000	921	1255	809	585	434	269	129	46	3		1152	1029	938	854	1259	887	619	438	319	164	56	2	
Middlesex	1561	1411	1378	1227	1886	1190	813	487	371	183	35	1		1507	1398	1285	1239	1831	1203	812	569	401	186	51	5	
Hunterdon	2345	2079	1899	1592	2376	1550	1121	685	500	232	78	8		2191	1931	1797	1736	2509	1612	1216	821	473	274	81	11	1
Burlington	2389	2053	1926	1580	2638	1660	1041	733	441	196	50	3		2283	2037	1848	1665	2780	1683	1105	789	520	235	66	8	
Monmouth	2491	1893	1776	1419	2290	1528	950	731	435	221	64	2		2296	1904	1603	1363	2212	1454	951	640	437	208	58	8	
Gloucester	2513	1928	1856	1551	2546	1452	907	629	354	151	26	3		2331	1844	1618	1513	2324	1374	871	592	315	148	30	2	
Cape May	411	359	341	227	418	284	178	93	63	22	4			405	353	321	264	373	260	175	85	43	25	4		
Salem	1067	874	892	785	1090	761	500	253	143	66	11	1		1065	822	836	707	1100	765	498	277	156	67	7		
Cumberland	1160	1004	921	738	1112	711	479	330	181	69	16	2		1137	986	873	718	1091	712	488	308	185	75	9		
	25071	21204	19745	17123	27001	17231	11043	7053	4458	2021	534	44	1	23937	20479	18267	16784	25817	16623	11007	7307	4705	2160	586	63	2

CENSUS, 1830 (continued).

Names of Counties.	SLAVES. Males. Under 10 years.	Of 10 under 24.	Of 24 under 36.	Of 36 under 55.	Of 55 under 100.	Of 100 and upwards.	SLAVES. Females. Under 10 years.	Of 10 under 24.	Of 24 under 36.	Of 36 under 55.	Of 55 under 100.	Of 100 and upwards.	FREE COLOURED PERSONS. Males. Under 10 years.	Of 10 under 24.	Of 24 under 36.	Of 36 under 55.	Of 55 under 100.	Of 100 and upwards.	FREE COLOURED PERSONS. Females. Under 10 years.	Of 10 under 24.	Of 24 under 36.	Of 36 under 55.	Of 55 under 100.	Of 100 and upwards.	Total.
Bergen		3	102	120	79		3	2	79	110	86		413	409	136	64	38		341	302	97	58	36		22,412
Essex		2	36	40	29				36	41	34		291	297	162	134	36	1	272	360	174	159	53		41,911
Morris	1	2	30	28	15	1		4	44	26	14		132	182	55	50	17	2	117	134	48	44	21		23,666
Sussex			11	5	5			1	9	14	6		65	86	27	19	9		69	69	26	20	11	1	20,346
Warren	4	3	7	5	2		3	5	9	4	5		83	63	34	24	9		58	72	38	26	14	1	18,627
Somerset		1	71	81	60	1		1	78	98	57		312	408	107	73	45		325	366	115	70	37	2	17,689
Middlesex			53	45	32			1	70	67	38	3	297	319	119	112	55	2	258	333	136	113	72		23,157
Hunterdon			33	25	18	1		3	39	36	17		266	314	138	104	47		279	299	165	113	45		31,060
Burlington			4	2	1		1	2	7	5	1		190	203	139	108	54		199	195	105	103	58	1	31,107
Monmouth			45	32	20		1	1	53	45	29	1	385	382	119	129	79		336	306	137	130	69	1	29,233
Gloucester										3	1		228	172	174	179	81	1	203	175	161	118	56		28,431
Cape May		1	2										32	35	21	18	12		23	33	16	19	16		4,936
Salem			1										216	243	146	101	67		209	158	140	83	48		14,155
Cumberland										2			123	121	81	81	24	1	122	88	70	57	18		14,093
	5	12	395	383	261	3	8	20	424	451	288	4	3033	3234	1458	1196	573	7	2811	2890	1428	1113	554	6	320,823

CENSUS, 1830 (continued).

Names of Counties.	WHITE PERSONS INCLUDED IN THE FOREGOING.					SLAVES & COLOURED Included in the foregoing.			
	Deaf and Dumb under 14 years.	Deaf and Dumb above 14 and under 25 years.	Deaf and Dumb above 25 years.	Blind.	Aliens.	Deaf and Dumb under 14 years.	Deaf and Dumb above 14 and under 25 years.	Deaf and Dumb above 25 years.	Blind.
Bergen	6	2	2	12	213	3			5
Essex	7	11	9	22	1176				1
Morris	2	6	12	11	497	2	1	1	1
Sussex	1	2	3	14	89				
Warren	2	2	1	12	286			5	2
Somerset	4	4	6	17	118				3
Middlesex	5	4	3	7	174				3
Hunterdon	11	11	12	19	210				2
Burlington	5	7	8	41	129		1	1	2
Monmouth	8	5	6	14	81			1	1
Gloucester	11	13	5	22	357				2
Cape May		1							
Salem	2	2	2	7	8				
Cumberland		1	3	7	27				
	64	71	72	205	3365	5	2	8	22

The vice of slavery was early introduced into the State, and took deep root, particularly, in the eastern portion. In the county of Bergen, in 1790, the slaves amounted to near one-fifth of the population; and in Essex, Middlesex, and Monmouth, they were very numerous, the counties having most Dutch population being most infected. In the counties settled by "Friends," Burlington, Gloucester, Salem, Cumberland, and Cape May, there were, comparatively, few slaves: the first, at that period, had only 227: the second, 191: the third, 120; and the last, 141. The whole number in the State was then, 11,423. At the subsequent census, the number had increased to 12,422. The small increase of 999, in ten years, proves that the inhabitants, generally, had discovered the moral and physical evils of slavery, and had applied themselves to diminish them. This became more apparent by the act of 15 Feb. 1804, entitled "An Act for the gradual Abolition of Slavery," under which the number of slaves was reduced, in 1810, to 10,851; and in 1820, to 7,557. This act is supplied by the act of 24th February, 1820, which embraces and extends its principles, and provides, that every child, born of a slave, within the State, since the 4th of July, 1804, or which shall be thereafter born, shall be free; but shall remain the servant of the owner of the mother, as if it had been bound to service by the overseers of the poor; if a male, until the age of 25; if a female, to the age of 21 years: that the owner shall, within 9 months after the birth of such child, deliver to the clerk of the county, a certificate, subscribed by him, containing the name and addition of the owner; the name, age and sex of the child, and the name of the mother; which certificate, whether delivered before or after the nine months, must be recorded by the clerk. The owner neglecting to file such certificate, within the nine months, is liable to a fine of five dollars, and the sum of one dollar per month afterward; but not exceeding in the whole $100, to any one suing therefor, one half to the prosecutor, and the other half to the poor of the township; and for delivering a certificate containing a false relation of the time of the birth of such child, $100, recoverable in the same manner: one-half in favour of the child, and the other, of the township. The time of birth may be inquired into, notwithstanding the certificate.

The traffic in slaves, between this and other states, was prohibited by the act of 14th March, 1798, and by act of 1820, last recited, under the forfeiture of vessels, and severe penalties on persons concerned therein. But slaves may still be brought into the State, by persons removing thereto, with a view to settled, or temporary residence; during the stay of the master only, in the latter case. By these acts, also, the manumission of slaves was permitted under certain formalities therein prescribed. And such has been the beneficial operation of these provisions, that in 1830, the State contained 2,254 slaves only; the counties of Gloucester and Cumberland, none; the county of Cape May, 2; and Salem, 1. So that it is probable, that in another 20 years, this pest will be entirely eradicated from the State.

We may remark, as a curious fact, and one that may prove most encouraging to the southern states, in an attempt at the abolition of slavery, that the coloured population, under the system of manumission adopted by this State, has increased in 40 years only, about 44 per cent. including the free and the slaves; whilst the whites have increased in the ratio of nearly 75 per. cent. In considering this subject, it must be observed, on one hand, that the coloured population has uniformly been treated with humanity and indulgence; and upon the other, that the great cities have absorbed a portion of their increase. But yet, the white population of the State has been kept down in a much greater degree by emigration. Indeed, New Jersey has received a large and unwelcome increase of coloured population from the fugitive slaves of Delaware, Maryland, and the southern states.

To complete our view of the physical condition of the State, we annex a table, framed from abstracts returned by the assessors of the several counties, showing the species and the amount of taxable property, and the amount of tax raised for state, county and township purposes. The returns from several counties have not been as full as they should have been, for our purpose; particularly, in respect to township charges; and we have been compelled, in some cases, to estimate the amount of road and poor tax, in some townships, by the ratio of population compared with that of others.

STATISTICAL TABLE OF THE STATE.

Names of Counties.	Total Number of Acres.	Acres of unimproved Land.	Lots of and under 10 acres.	Householders.	Single Men.	Taxables.	Merchants and Traders.	Grist Mills—run of Stones.	Saw Mills.	Fulling Mills.	Paper Mills.	Rolling and Slitting Mills.
Bergen . .	267,500	108,766	660	1,262	533	5,796	75	84	93	8	3	
Burlington .	553,002	123,524	1,867	3,256	1095	6,549	86	91	48	7	2	
Cape May .	161,500	59,528	188	669	188	1,000	29	8	16			
Cumberland	335,460	209,380	475	774	333	2,742	54	44	21	1		1
Essex . .	154,680		3,316	3,370	1412	8,100	306	42	41	1	19	3
Gloucester .	713,320	205,913	1,113	3,075	978	5,600	102	75	63	4		
Hunterdon .	324,572		1,167		673	6,000	86	80	71	10		
Middlesex .	217,000	6,272	1,143	841	477	6,000	99	42	20			
Monmouth .	665,000	127,505	786	1,385	603	6,000	103	67	52	6		
Morris . .	292,900		437	1,083	528	4,836	83	56	71	12	5	9
Salem . .	204,936	58,989	254	1,103	490	3,092	47	33	19	6		
Somerset .	189,800			668	391	3,500	68	64	44	8		
Sussex . .	352,300	135,555	196	1,075	449	3,611	58	87	55	7		
Warren . .	224,360	89,356	132	1,062	411	3,489	56	84	41	2		
	4,656,330	1,125,788	11,734	19,623	8541	66,315	1252	857	655	72	29	13

Names of Counties.	Furnaces.	Forge Fires.	Cotton Factories.	Woollen Factories.	Carding Machines.	Cider Distilleries.	Tan Vats.	Male Slaves.	Neat Cattle over 3 years.	Horses & Mules over 3 ys.	Stud Horses.	Chairs, Sulkies, and Dear-borns.	Coaches, Phætons, and Chaises.
Bergen . .	4	16	10	5	10	12	127	158	1,287	446	14	320	17
Burlington .	4	3	4		11	40	350		14,210	6,055	19	579	34
Cape May .					2			2	2,093	679		72	
Cumberland	1	1		1	3	4	6	1	5,713	2,053	9	75	
Essex . .	5		22	13	5	5	223	40	9,783	3,849	7	715	4
Gloucester .	4	10	2	2	4	29	158		9,478	4,640	4	235	30
Hunterdon .			1		17	58	524		12,492	7,538	50	894	4
Middlesex .				2	7	39	243	51	7,075	3,684	13	522	59
Monmouth .	5		1		17	46	238	22	12,068	4,942	19	122	81
Morris . .	2	43	5		11	53	215	31	11,820	4,056	23	309	6
Salem . .					2	15	119		7,300	3,103	18	278	6
Somerset .					11	27	211	78	8,634	4,621	25	218	32
Sussex . .	3	28			18	35	227	5	13,070	3,875	17	61	2
Warren . .		7		2	16	25	235	6	7,772	4,324	28		
	28	108	45	25	135	388	2876	394	122,805	53,865	236	4400	275

Names of Counties.	Covered Wagons.	Two and Four Horse Stages. 4	Two and Four Horse Stages. 2	Ferries and Toll Bridges.	Fisheries.	Township Taxes. Poor. Dolls.	Township Taxes. Road. Dolls.	Township Taxes. School. Dolls.	County Tax. Dolls.	State Tax. Dolls.	Population, 1830.	Represent. in Assembly.†
Bergen . .				8	7	2,500	600	100	5,000	2,631.43	22,412	3
Burlington .	977	11	22	2	16	13,450	*		15,000	4,607.12	31,107	5
Cape May .	148		1			1,125	1,650		2,000	646.01	4,936	1
Cumberland		1	4	2	2	3,150	4,000		4,115	1,586.18	14,093	3
Essex . .		14	9			9,261	13,860		10,000	3,822.04	41,911	5
Gloucester .	967	2	4	8	21	4,993	15,100		9,993	3,379.26	28,431	4
Hunterdon .		3	7	9	17	6,850	8,300		10,000	4,535 84	31,060	5
Middlesex .	56	22	8	2		5,850	3,600		4,000	3,253.26	23,157	4
Monmouth .	380					6,650	9,646		11,769	3,723.68	29,233	4
Morris . .		5				5,650	10,900		7,100	3,171.23	23,666	4
Salem . .	663			1	6	5,076	4,620		7,000	2,156.60	14,155	3
Somerset .		12	3			4,476	5,837		6,000	2,642.86	17,689	3
Sussex . .	16	1	1			3,400	8,600	766	5,475	2,025.70	20,346	3
Warren . .				3	2	5,700	6,146	500	6,714	2,185.50	18,627	3
	3207	71	59	35	71	78,131	92,859	1366	104,166	40,366.71	320,823	50

* Township generally. † Each county sends one member to Council.

There are in the State—17 Oil Mills—6 Calico Printing Works—4 Plaster Mills—13 Glass and 1 Delf Work—11 Grain Distilleries.

The number of acres in each county in the above table, is given from the measurement of the area of the county upon Gordon's map, with a reticulated scale of square miles. The result corresponds sufficiently well with the returns of the assessor from the counties in which there are no unimproved lands. But in the others, the returns of the assessors fall much short of the estimate in the table. We do not know, exactly, what is meant by "unimproved lands," in the returns of the assessors. We have copied from them.

XI. It will be seen by reference to the preceding table, that the State is, in the aggregate, agricultural; and such is the character of all the counties, except Essex, part of Bergen, and part of Morris. The glass and iron manufactures of the counties of Burlington, Gloucester, and Cumberland, are not sufficient to exempt them from this classification. Of the agricultural products of the several portions, we have already spoken, and will observe, only, generally, here, that the valleys of the two northern sections are well adapted to wheat, and that under the improved mode of culture they may become equally productive with any lands east of the mountains. The southern district, composed of the alluvial country, is productive, chiefly of corn, rye, fruits, grass, and vegetables; and sends to market large quantities of pork, cured in a manner that can scarcely be surpassed. New Jersey hams, bacon, and barrelled pork, bear the highest prices in all markets. Nor is the reputation of the farmers of this district, much less for their beef, and especially for their veal. Its gardens and orchards supply the Philadelphia markets with the best fruits. Indeed the whole state is remarkable for the abundance and quality of its peaches and apples, and the quantity of cider, and brandy made from the latter. Notwithstanding the influence of Temperance Societies upon distilling, and it has been confessedly great, there are yet in the State 388 cider distilleries. The counties of Burlington, Gloucester, Monmouth, Hunterdon, Warren, and Sussex, are renowned for the number and quality of the horses which they breed.

Yet, notwithstanding this agricultural character of the State, she claims no mean rank in manufactures. By the preceding table, 28 furnaces are given; but 12 of these, only, we believe, are blast furnaces, employed in making iron from the ore; the remainder are cupola furnaces, used in the reduction of pig and other metal to castings. The furnaces of New Jersey, by the report of the committee of the tariff convention, holden in New York, October, 1831, produced in 1830, 1,671 tons of pig iron, and 5,615 tons of castings; and her 108 forges, 3000 tons of bar iron.

The first valued at $30 the ton, yields - - - - - -	$50,130
The second, at $60, - - - - - - - - - - -	336,900
The third, at $90 the ton, - - . - - - - - -	270,000
Making - - - - -	$657,030

for her manufacture of iron in pigs, castings and bars. This iron, however, is further improved in value by the aid of 10 rolling and slitting mills, 16 cupola furnaces, and the extensive machine shops of Patterson. And we shall not, we presume, underrate the annual value of the iron manufacture of the State, when we state it at one million of dollars; all of which is obtained from her mines, her forests, and her labour, not one cent of foreign matter entering into the composition.

There are in the State,

1 flint glass manufactory, producing annually, - - - - -	$80,000
12 glass houses, employed on hollow ware and window glass, estimated each to produce annually $30,000, - - - - - - -	360,000
	440,000
And 1 delf ware establishment, whose product may exceed $ -	50,000
	$490,000

Beside several extensive clay potteries.

We may set down, therefore, the annual product of glass and pottery ware at full half a million.

Of the 25 woollen manufactories most are small; and having no data for determining their respective products, we conjecturally average them at $10,000 per annum.

From the Abstracts of the Assessors, we obtain but 45 cotton manufactories in the State; but the Committee of the New York Convention, of 1831, return 51—of which they give the following interesting results:

Capital employed	$2,027,644	Pounds of cloth	1,877,418
Number of spindles	62,979	Males employed	2,151
Number of power-looms	815	Wages per week, each	$6 00
Pounds of yarn sold	3,212,184	Females employed	3,070
Yards of cloth	5,133,776	Wages per week, each	$1 90

Children under 12 years of age	217	Bushels of charcoal	820
Wages per week, each	$1 40	Gallons of oil	13,348
Pounds of cotton used	5,832,204	Value of other articles	18,208
Bbls. of flour, for sizing	975	Spindles building	11,000
Cords of wood	671	Hand weavers	1,060
Tons of coal	1,007	Total dependants	12,750

The price of the raw material, viz. 5,832,204 lbs. at 11 cts. was		$641,542
Price of yarn sold, 3,212,184 lbs. at 30 cts. the lb. average, was	$963,655	
Price of cloth, 5,133,776 yards, at 15 cts.	770,066	
Gross return of cotton manufacture	$1,733,721	

The six calico bleaching and printing establishments, belong to the cotton manufacture. Some of these, as at Patterson, Belleville, and Rahway, are very extensive, but we have not the means to give their results.

The four machine factories at Patterson alone, employ above 400 hands; and the Phœnix Manufacturing Company, in addition to their cotton establishment, have 1,616 spindles employed in spinning flax, consuming 493,000 lbs., and employing 196 hands. The flax is manufactured into duck and bagging. In the cotton establishment of Mr. John Colt, there were manufactured in 1831–2, 460,000 yards of cotton duck.

The 29 paper mills produce large returns. Some of these mills, as at Patterson, Springfield, Mount Holly, &c. are built on the best models, and employ the most improved machinery.

The manufacture of leather from the hide into the various articles of its use, is very extensively conducted. There are 2,876 tan vats; and the fabric of shoes, boots and harness, gives employment and wealth to many individuals in Newark, Bloomfield, Rahway, Burlington, &c. &c.; and its product forms a large item in the exports of the commonwealth. Hats and clothing for the southern market, are also made in the first three towns last mentioned; and, also, in large quantities in the thriving village of Plainfield.

Coaches, cabinetware and chairs, form also large articles of export both from East and West Jersey, from Camden, and from Newark and Rahway.

Unfortunately, we do not possess the means of giving in detail, or in gross, the results of many of these valuable branches of business; for we want, in relation to this state, the usual data for determining the quantum of surplus production, which an account of her exports would afford. Her whole foreign trade, and the far greater proportion of her domestic business, centers in New York and Philadelphia, to swell the business tables of these two great marts. But we are assured that, from Rahway alone, the amount furnished to the general coasting trade is not less than a million of dollars annually; whilst the products of the manufactures of Belleville and its vicinity, are valued at 2,000,000, and those of Patterson at more than double that amount. By the treasury report of 1832, the whole tonnage was 573 90.100, registered, and 32,499 24.100, enrolled and licensed. And the whole amount of exports, foreign and domestic, $11,430; but of the tonnage of the State, 5,000 are said to be enregistered in the New York districts.

We confess, that the view we have thus given of the condition of the State is very imperfect; but it suffices to show, that, in agriculture, in manufactures, in the great improvements by canals and rail-roads, she nobly maintains a course of emulation with her great adjacent sister states. By the Morris and Raritan Canals, and by the rail-way of the Trenton Falls Company, new and great acquisitions of water power for machiney have been attained, with increased facilities of communication with the best markets; and there remain unemployed upon the mountain streams, now cheaply accessible, a vast number of mill sites, among which we may mention those at Belvidere and Clinton as entitled to great attention. The Musconetcong river throughout its course may also be profitably employed, since ready communication may be had with the Morris Canal from all points. The upper falls of the Passaic, the waste waters of the Rockaway, the Pequannock and Ramapo Rivers, will all, probably, be brought into use by the improvements already made and projected. Her mines, her limestones, her marbles, her marls, nay her very sands and clay, will be shortly all better known and more highly valued, and will greatly increase her wealth; her copper profusely scattered over a large area, accessible as any in the world; her inexhaustible and unsurpassed beds of iron; her stupendous veins of zinc will, at no distant day, give employment to additional thousands of intelligent and contented labourers, and instead of pouring forth her population to fertilize, enrich, and bless other lands, she will give to her sons full employment, and the means of wealth, within her own limits. Already has the reflux of population commenced. Newark, Patterson, Bloomfield, Trenton, Boonton and Rahway, will, in ten years, have doubled their population; and New Jersey will, we believe, at the census of 1840, have increased her inhabitants in a ratio equal to that of any of the original states; and among the stars which form the bright constellation of the Union, though small, she will not be the least brilliant.

Climate.—It is supposed that the climate of our country has undergone, and is still undergoing, a material change; that thunder and lightning are less frequent; the cold of our winters, and heat of our summers, less, and more variable; the springs colder, and the autumns more temperate. It is possible, but we think doubtful, that the variability of the climate has increased; but the average severity of heat and cold has not been diminished. The following description of the weather, by a settler of East Jersey, in 1683, will be recognised as true at the present day. "As for the temperature of the air, it is wonderfully suited to the humours of mankind; the wind and weather rarely holding in one point, or one kind, for ten days together. It is a rare thing for a vessel to be windbound for a week together, the wind seldom holding in a point more than 48 hours; and in a short time we have wet and dry, warm and cold weather, which changes we often desire in England, and look for before they come."* Alternations of cold and mild winters, of hot and cool summers, of early and late commencements of frosts, of drought and superabundant rain, have been continued, from the earliest period to which our knowledge of the country extends. A review of the seasons from 1681, shows no less than 39 years in which the navigation was obstructed by ice, in the month of December. On the 10th of that month, 1678, the good ship *The Shield*, moored to a tree before the town of Burlington; and, on the following morning, her passengers walked to the shore upon the ice, so hard had the river suddenly frozen. In 1681, December 10th, the Bristol Factor arrived at Chester; and, on the next day, her passengers, also, went on shore on the ice. On the 19th December, 1740, the navigation was stopped, and the river remained closed until the 13th March. In 1790, it closed on the 8th, and in 1797, on the 1st of that month. In 1831, rigorous cold weather began in November; and the Delaware was frozen fast on the 7th December. In 1780, in the month of January, the mercury stood, for several hours, at 5° below 0, F.; and, during the month, except on one night, never rose in the city of Philadelphia to the freezing point. In 1817, February 7, the water froze in most of the hydrant plugs, and some of the street mains, in that city. The earliest notice we have seen of the weather, on the shores of the Delaware, is in the Journal of De Vries. He left the Texel on the 12th December, 1630, and arrived in the Delaware at the close of January, or commencement of February, the period of our coldest weather; when, unimpeded by the season, which he reports as so mild that his men could work in the open air, in their shirt sleeves, he erected, on Lewis's Creek, the fortress of *Oplandt*. The winter of 1788–9, was also uncommonly mild; but there was ice sufficient to obstruct the navigation. On the 22d March, the orchards were in full bloom, and the meadows as green as ordinarily in the month of June; but, on the 23d, snow fell two feet deep, destroying nearly all the fruits of the year. In 1827–8, the navigation of the Delaware was altogether unobstructed. The atmosphere was filled with dense fog, in the months of December, January and February; during which, including days when the sun was apparent for some hours, there were not more than 17 days of clear weather. By a table for January, during 20 years, from 1807 to 1827, the mean temperature of the month varied from 42° to 27°; and the mean of the whole period was 39° of Fahrenheit.

There are seldom more than from 20 to 30 days, in summer, in which the mercury rises above 80°, or, in winter, falls below 30°. The warmest part of the day is from 2 to 3 o'clock; from which time the heat gradually diminishes until the ensuing morning. The coldest part of the four-and-twenty hours is at the break of day. There are seldom more than three or four nights of the summer, in which the heat of the air is nearly the same, as in the preceding day. After the hottest days, the evenings are generally agreeable, and often delightful. The higher the mercury

* Smith's N. J. 169.

rises in the day, the lower it falls the succeeding night. From 80°, it commonly falls to 66°; but from 60° only to 50°. This disproportion between the temperature of the day and night, in summer, is always greatest in the month of August, when the dews are heavy in proportion to the coolness of the evening. They are sometimes so considerable as to wet the clothes; and marsh meadows and creeks, drained by the heat, have been supplied with their usual water from this source, in this month and the first weeks of September. The violent heats of summer seldom continue more than two or three days, without intermission. They are generally broken by showers of rain, sometimes accompanied by thunder and lightning, and succeeded by a north-west wind, which produces an agreeable and invigorating coolness in the air.

The warmest weather is generally in July; but intensely hot days are often felt in May, June, August and September, and the mean heat of August has been greater than that of July. The transitions from heat to cold are often sudden, and sometimes to very distant degrees. After a day in which the mercury has been at 86° and even at 90°, it has fallen in the course of a single night to 60°, and fires have been found necessary the ensuing morning, especially if the change in the temperature of the air has been accompanied by rain and a S. E. wind. In a summer month, the mercury has been known to fall 20° in an hour and a half. There are few summer months in which fires are not agreeable in some part of them. Mr. Rittenhouse informed Dr. Rush, that there was not a summer during his residence in the country, in which he did not discover frost in every month.

The weather is equally variable during the winter. The mercury has fallen from 37 to 4½° below 0 in 24 hours. In this season, nature seems frequently to play at cross-purposes. Heavy falls of snow are often succeeded by a thaw, which, in a short time, wholly dissolves them. The rivers are frozen sufficiently hard to bear horses and carriages, and thawed so as to be navigable, several times in the course of the winter. Ice is commonly formed gradually, and seldom until the rivers have been chilled with snow. Yet, sometimes its production is sudden, and the Delaware has frequently been frozen over in a night, so as to bear the weight of a man.

In the alluvial district of New Jersey, frost and ice appear in the latter end of October, or beginning of November. But intense cold is rarely felt, until about Christmas. Hence the vulgar saying, "as the day lengthens, the cold strengthens."

The coldest weather is from the middle of January, to the middle of February. As in summer there are often days in which fires are agreeable, so in winter they sometimes are incommodious. Vegetation has been observed in all the winter months. Garlic was tasted in butter in January, 1781; the leaves of the willow, the blossom of the peach, and the flowers of the dandelion, were all seen in February, 1779, and Dr. Rush says, that 60 years since, he saw an apple orchard in full bloom, and small apples on many of the trees in the month of December. In February, 1828, we gathered flowers from the unprotected garden, and saw cattle cropping good pasturage in the fields. A cold day is often the precursor of a moderate evening. The greatest degree of cold recorded in Philadelphia, is 5° below zero, and of heat 95° F. The standard temperature of Southern Jersey may be 52°, which is that of our deepest wells and the mean heat of common spring water.

The spring is generally unpleasant. In March, the weather is stormy, variable and cold; in April, and sometimes far in May, moist and raw. From the variableness of the spring, vegetation advances with unequal pace in different seasons. The colder the spring, the more favourable the prospect of fruit. The hopes of the farmer from his fruit-trees, are, in a warm spring, often blasted by frost in April or May, and sometimes even by snow, at a later period. The colder the winter, the greater is the delay of the return of spring. Sometimes the weather, during the spring months is cloudy and damp, attended occasionally with gentle rain resembling the spray from a cataract.

June is the only month of the year which resembles the spring in the southern countries of Europe. Then, generally, the weather is temperate, the sky serene, and the verdure of the country universal and delightful.

The autumn is the most agreeable season of the year. The cool evenings and mornings, which begin about the middle of September, are attended with a moderate temperature of the air during the day. This kind of weather continues, with an increase of cold scarcely perceptible, till the middle of October, when it is closed by rain, which sometimes falls in such quantities as to produce destructive freshets; at others, in gentle showers, which continue, with occasional interruption by a few fair days, for two or three weeks. These rains are the harbingers of winter, and the Indians long since taught us, that, the cold of that season is proportionate to the quantity of rain which falls during the autumn. From this account, it is apparent, that there are seldom more than four months of the year in which the weather is agreeable without fire.

In winter the winds generally come from the N. W. in fair, and from the N. E. in foul weather. The N. W. winds are dry and cold. The winds, in fair weather in the spring, and in warm weather in the summer, blow from the S. W. and W. N.W. The S. W. winds usually bring with them refreshing showers of rain in spring and summer, which moderate the heat when succeeded by a N. W. wind. Sometimes showers come from the W. and N. W.

The moisture of the air is said to be greater than formerly; occasioned, probably, by the exhalations which fell in the form of snow, now descending in rain. The depth of the snow is sometimes between two and three feet; in 1828-9, it was near four, but in general it is from six to nine inches. Hail frequently falls with snow in the winter. At intervals of years, heavy showers of hail fall in the spring and summer, running commonly in veins from 40 to 50 miles long, and from half a mile to two miles in breadth. On such occasions, destruction of grain, grass and windows, to great value, is not unfrequent. From sudden changes of the air, rain and snow often fall together, forming what is commonly called sleet. In the northern parts of the State, in protected spots, snow sometimes lies until the first of April. The backwardness of the spring has been ascribed to the passage of the air over the ice and snow which remain, after the winter months, on the plains and waters of the north-west country.

The dissolution of the ice and snow is sometimes so sudden, in the spring, as to swell the creeks and rivers to such a degree as to lay waste the hopes of the husbandman, and in some instances to sweep his barns, stables, and even his dwelling into their currents. Of this power of the flood, the years 1784 and 1832, afford memorable examples. The wind, during a general thaw, comes from the S. W. or S. E.

The air, when dry, has a peculiar elasticity, which renders the heat and cold less insupportable than the same degrees of both in moister countries. It is only when summer showers are not succeeded by N. W. winds, that the air becomes oppressive by combination with moisture. With the removal of the forest the waters have decreased considerably.

The average quantity of water which falls yearly, is from 24 to 26 inches, according to the statement of Dr. Rush: but this would seem much too small, since a table of 20 years, from 1810 to 1829, inclusive, 14 of which were kept by P. Legeaux, Esq. at Springmills, and 6 at the Pennsylvania Hospital, give 35.16 inches; and a table for 10 years, ending 1827, kept by Dr. Darlington, of West Chester, gives 49.92. In the first table, the highest was 43.135 inches, in 1814; and the lowest, 23.354, in 1819. In the last table the highest was 54.1 inches in 1824, and the lowest 39.3 inches in 1822.

From the foregoing remarks we may justly conclude that, in New Jersey no two successive years are alike; that even the successive seasons and months differ from each other every year. Perhaps there is but one steady trait in the character of our climate, and that is, that it is never steady, but uniformly variable. The foregoing remarks apply generally to the whole State, yet with some variation. Thus, in the low flat country in the alluvial district, the climate is warmer in winter and hotter in summer, than in the more northern and elevated lands of the other sections. The heat of the summer and the cold of the winter are, however, tempered by the waters which bound it on three sides. In summer, upon the ocean and bay, the sea breeze prevails, and with the prostration of the forest, it finds its way yearly further interior. As the country north of Trenton rises in aerial height, as well as in latitude, its temperature necessarily decreases from both causes. The change, however, is not very considerable until we reach the mountains, where the diminution of heat is apparent in the difference of the seasons. Vegetation in the spring is from one to two weeks later than in the lower country, and the approach of winter is so much earlier. It is to their altitude more than latitude, that the mountains owe their cool and invigorating breezes which render them attractive in the summer season.

PREFATORY CHAPTER.

PART II.

Containing a Moral View of the State.

Division of the Political Power into Three Great Branches.—I. Legislative Council and Assembly—by whom Elected—Nominations—Form of Elections—Legislative Council—how Composed—Powers—Assembly—how Constituted—Powers.—II. Executive Branch—What—Governor—his Powers and Duties—Secretary of State—Powers and Duties—Treasurer—Powers and Duties—Revenue and Expenditures of the State—Burden on the Citizens—Attorney General—Sheriff—Coroner—Officers of State Prison—Political Division of Counties and Townships—of Township Officers—Services in Taxation—Relief of the Poor—Making and Repairing Roads—Executive Duties of County Clerk—Militia System.—III. Judiciary—Courts for Trials of Small Causes—Court of Quarter Sessions—Common Pleas—Orphans' Court—Supreme and Circuit Courts—Court of Chancery—Court of Appeals—Compensation of Officers.—IV. Provisions for Religious, Moral, and Intellectual Improvement—Religious Societies—Literary Institutions established by Individual Largess—Common Schools established by the State—Publication of the Laws—Newspapers in the State.

In the organization of the Commonwealth, the political power here, as elsewhere in well constituted States, has been divided into three great branches; the Legislative, Executive, and Judicial. But, in the existing constitution, these divisions have not been well preserved, the first having received the greater proportion of the province of the second, and having the third wholly dependent upon it.

I. The legislative power is vested in a council and assembly, chosen by qualified electors, on the second Tuesday of October, and the day succeeding, annually. The election is then holden for State officers, and on the first Tuesday of November, when occasion requires, for members of congress and electors of president and vice president. Such electors must be free white citizens, of full age, who have resided within the county in which they claim to vote, for twelve months immediately preceding the election, and who have paid a tax or been enrolled on any duplicate list of the last State or county tax, and possess fifty pounds, clear estate. But, from the requisite of taxation or enrolment, as the case may be, are exempted persons who may have arrived at the age of twenty-one years since the date of the last duplicate; persons removing from the township where they have paid tax, to another in the same county; and persons who have been inadvertently overlooked by the assessor; the names of the last being immediately entered upon the tax list. The property qualification, though demanded by the constitution, has been virtually annulled by the act of 1st June, 1820, providing that every person paying a State or county tax, whose name shall be enrolled on such duplicate list, shall be taken to be worth fifty pounds clear estate; and thus by the omnipotence of the legislature, things essentially different are made the same.

The electors vote only in the township in which they reside. An attempt to vote a second time, is punishable by a fine of fifty dollars to the use of the poor, recoverable by the overseer of the township. The assessor or collector enrolling one under age, or non-resident in the township, with intent to admit him to vote, is subject to the penalty of $100 to the like use, and recoverable in like manner.

Such elections are conducted after the following mode. The clerks of the respective courts of Common Pleas, attend at the court house, on the first Mondays of September, annually, to receive from voters, lists of candidates for public suffrage, signed by the nominator, and transmitted by letter or delivered in person. From these, the clerk makes a general list of the nominees for the several offices, a copy whereof he sends, within a week from the nomination, to the clerks of the several precincts of the county; and, in case of nominations for congress or electors of president, a copy to the governor, who transmits a copy of all the nominations to the clerk of every county, who sends these also to the township clerks. At the election, no vote can be given unless for such nominee.

The precinct clerks, by public advertisement fourteen days before that of the election, make known the time and place of holding it, and the names of the candidates, when and where the election officers, viz. the judge, assessor, collector, and town clerk, attend. The clerk posts on the door of the house where the election is holden, the list of the nominees, and the other officers open the polls at 10 o'clock of the day. If any one of such officers be in nomination, he is disqualified from assisting at the election, unless before its commencement he publicly decline; and should he assist, and be elected, his election is void. The town clerk, with the approbation of his fellow officers, may appoint a substitute; or, if he be absent, dead, or otherwise disqualified, and no substitute have been appointed, such officers may nominate a clerk for the occasion. And if the judge, assessor, or collector be absent or disqualified, his place may be filled by the voters present, and the absentee is subject to punishment by fine, unless he satisfactorily excuse himself to the court of common pleas. Malfeasance by an officer of the election, is punishable by a fine of $100 for the use of the poor. Each officer swears or affirms to the faithful performance of his duty, and may administer like oath or affirmation to his fellows. For the preservation of order, the judge and inspectors may commit riotous or disorderly persons either to the charge of the constable, or to the common gaol for any time not exceeding twenty-four hours.

The poll is open for two days; but may be adjourned for short periods, as occasion may require, in case no voters appear. On the evening of the first day, it is closed at 9 o'clock; and opened on the morning of the 2d at 8; and is finally closed at 7 o'clock of the evening of the second day.

All elections, for representatives in Congress, electors of President and Vice-President of the United States, members of council and assembly, sheriffs and coroners, are by ballot, which may be written or printed, or partly both, and must be delivered by the voter to the judge or either of the inspectors; and the name of such voter, being pronounced, by the officer, in an audible voice, and being unobjected to, is entered upon the poll-list, and the ballot deposited in the ballot-box.

When the poll is closed, the poll-list is signed by the officers, the ballots read, registered, and filed. If there be a greater number of ballots than names on the list, no more ballots are enumerated than names: if two or more ballots be folded, or rolled together, or a ballot contain more names than it ought, or otherwise appear to be fraudulent, it is rejected, and as many numbers, deducted from the poll-list as there are ballots, cast away. The number of votes being ascertained, the election officers, or any two of them, certify the number for each candidate, after a prescribed form; a duplicate of which, duly attested, is filed in the office of the town clerk, with the poll-list; and the original is transmitted to the clerk of the pleas, on or before the Saturday, next after the day of election; who makes a list of the votes for each candidate, from the several certificates, and ascertains who are duly elected, by a plurality of votes; files the certificates and list in his office, and makes a certificate of the election of each officer, a copy of which, with a copy of the list filed, he transmits to the governor.

In case the election be for members of Congress, or electors of President, the governor, within five days of the receipt of the list, before a privy council, determines the persons elected, whom the governor commissions under the seal of the State.

In case two or more candidates, nominated for council, assembly, sheriff, or coroner, have an equal number of votes, there not being a sufficient number having a plurality, the county clerk proclaims, by advertisement, that he will attend at the county court-house, at a day certain, to receive nominations of persons to supply the vacancy; and the nomination and the election, holden thereon, are conducted in the manner already described; except that, the nominations are made ten days, only, previous to the election.

In case of vacancy in the council, or assembly, the vice-president of council, or speaker of the house, as the case may be; or in case there be no vice-president or speaker, the governor, causes the vacancy to be filled; unless it be probable that the services of the member will not be required during the remainder of the unexpired legislative year. But if the board of freeholders, of the county in which the vacancy happens, desire that the vacancy be filled, it is done without delay. Thus, if a member refuse to take his seat pursuant to his election, or to send a satisfactory excuse within twenty days after the meeting of the legislature, die, remove from the state, or be expelled, the vice-president, or speaker, as the case may be, issues his warrant, to the clerk of the county, who takes measures similar to those above described, for filling the vacancy.

The legislative council consists of the governor, who is its perpetual president, having a casting voice; of a vice-president elected by the members, who presides in the absence of the president; and a member from each county, elected annually. It has powers co-ordinate with the assembly, except in the preparation or alteration of money bills, which is reserved to the latter. It is convened, from time to time, by the governor, or vice-president, and must be convened at all times, when the assembly sits; its members must be, and have been, for one whole year, next before election, inhabitants and freeholders in the county for which they are respectively chosen, and worth at least one thousand pounds of real and personal estate, within such county. Seven members form a quorum for business. This property qualification, in practice, is scarce more respected than that of the voters.

The assembly is composed of such number of delegates, from each county, as the legislature may, from time to time, direct; making together, not less than thirty-nine. The delegate must be, and have been, for one whole year next before his election, an inhabitant of the county he represents, and worth five hundred pounds, in real and personal estate, therein. The assembly have power to choose a speaker, and other their officers; to judge of the qualifications and election of their own members; sit on their own adjournments; prepare bills to be passed into laws; and to empower their speaker to convene the members when necessary.

No judge of the Supreme, or other court, sheriff, or person holding any post of profit under the government, other than justices of the peace, may sit in the assembly. On the election of such person his office becomes vacant.

On the second Tuesday next after the day of election, the council and assembly meet, separately, and the consent of a majority of all the representatives in each body, is requisite to the enactment of a law. At their first meeting, after each annual election, the council and assembly, jointly, by a majority of votes, elect the governor; they appoint the field, and general officers of the militia; the judges of the Supreme Court for seven years, the judges of the inferior courts of Common Pleas, justices of the peace, clerks of the Supreme Court, and of the Common Pleas and Sessions, the attorney general and secretary of state, for five years; and the state treasurer, for one year; all of whom are commissioned by the governor; are capable of reappointment, and are liable to be dismissed, when convicted by the council on the impeachment of the assembly. Each member of council and assembly makes oath, that he will not assent to any law, vote, or proceeding which shall appear to him injurious to the public welfare, nor that shall annul or repeal that part of the third section of the constitution which makes the election of members of the legislature, annual; nor that part of the twenty-second section, which provides for trial by jury; nor the eighteenth and nineteenth sections which relate to religion. And such oath may be administered to the members by any member of the respective houses. The oath of the legislators being to preserve a part only of the constitution, sound construction warrants the induction, that they have a constitutional authority to change all other parts of that instrument; and thus, their power is unrestrained, as much as that of the British Parliament, which may, by a simple act of legislation, remodel the State, as has been lately done in Great Britain.

II. The executive power is vested in the governor, secretary of state, treasurer, the attorney general, and county prosecutors, and in the officers of the several townships, counties, and other precincts, viz: in the township clerks, assessors, collectors, commissioners of appeals, surveyors and overseers of the highways, pound keepers, overseers of the poor, judges of elections, township committees, and constables: and in the chosen freeholders of the county, the county clerk, collector, sheriff, coroners, and the militia.

By the 8th article of the constitution, the governor is said to have the supreme executive power; but his executive duties are circumscribed by very narrow limits, and in their performance he may be aided, perhaps controlled, by any three or more of the council, whom he is authorized to call as his privy council. Before entering on his office he swears faithfully and diligently to execute his office, and to promote the peace and prosperity, and to maintain the lawful rights of the State to the best of his ability. He is captain-general, and commander-in-chief of all the militia, and other military force of the State, and is by special act of assembly, trustee of the school fund. He is empowered, when the post of vice president of council, or speaker of assembly is vacant, to cause vacancies in the respective chambers to be filled. He may proclaim rewards of not more than $300 for one offender, for the apprehension of any person charged with murder, burglary, robbery, or other dangerous outrage upon the person or property of the citizen, for the apprehension of their accessories, and for the arrest of any unknown perpetrator of such offences;

may demand fugitives from justice from this State, and draw his warrant for the expenses of their reclamation; may remit costs of prosecution and debts due to the State, from any criminal, on the recommendation of the inspectors of the State prison; may suspend the execution of the sentence of death against any criminal until the rising of the next meeting, thereafter, of the governor and council; and in conjunction with the legislative council, may grant pardon for any offence after condemnation; he may authorize the owner of a slave condemned for certain offences, to send him from the State; distribute copies of the laws to the United States and other States; license pedlars; appoint notaries, who hold their offices during good behaviour; appoint inspectors of flour in certain cities, removable at his pleasure; order out the militia in case of invasion or other emergency, when and so long as he may deem necessary, not exceeding two months; and perform other duties specially imposed upon him by the legislature.

The secretary of state, as we have seen, is elected by the assembly in joint meeting, for five years. Before entering on the duties of his office, he makes oath that he will faithfully perform them, and gives bond conditioned to like effect. He must reside at Trenton. He must file in his office the laws of the State as they are enacted, so that those of each session be kept in separate bundles, and give copies of them when required, under his hand and seal of office; and, within four weeks from the end of every session, deliver a copy of the laws therein passed, to the printer thereof, assist him in comparing the proof sheets with the laws, and make marginal notes thereto. He must record all papers which come to his hands pertaining to his office; and tri-monthly report to the governor, an account of the business done in his office, relating to the record of wills, letters of administration and guardianship, and of the unfinished business therein; and must lay a general statement of the business in his office before the legislature at their first session, annually; must keep the books and papers of the late auditor's office, and settle the accounts, if any be unsettled, of any of the agents of forfeited estates; must record all deeds delivered to him for record, duly acknowledged and proved, and must index such deeds; must in all cases, where money is paid into the public treasury, and the receipt of the treasurer therefor is brought to him, enter the same in the public books in his office, in an account with the treasurer, and indorse such entry upon the receipt, without which it is not available against the State. He must prosecute clerks of courts, on the report of the treasurer, who fail to return the abstracts of fines, amercements and judgments on forfeited recognizances for use of the State. He is register of the prerogative office and court, and is required to record the names of testators of all wills, and of intestates, the inventories of whose estates he may receive, and to file such wills and inventories. He must record bonds given by the keeper of State prison; and the partition lines of townships and counties, as returned by the commissioners of survey. He is also clerk of the court of appeals, and trustee of the school fund; and he must keep suspended for public view a list of the fees payable in his several offices.

The treasurer, before entering on his office, is required to take and subscribe an oath of office, and give bond with sufficient sureties approved by the legislature, in the sum of fifty thousand dollars, conditioned for the faithful performance of his duties and for the fidelity of those employed by him; which oath and bond are to be made before the vice president or justice of the Supreme Court, and to be deposited in the office of the secretary of state. His duty is to receive and keep the monies of the State, and to disburse them agreeably to law; to take receipts for all payments; to keep accounts of receipts and expenditures, and of all debts due to, and from the State; to make reports and give information to either branch of the legislature in person or in writing, as he may be required, respecting matters referred to him by the council or assembly, or appertaining to his office; and generally to perform all services relative to the finances which he may be directed to perform; to state, in books, the account of monies which he shall receive for taxes, or other account in behalf of the State, or which he shall pay, in pursuance of the acts and resolutions of the legislature, so that, the net produce of the whole revenue, as well as of each branch thereof, and the amount of disbursements, may distinctly appear; and to lay such accounts, from time to time, before the legislature; to receive reports of clerks of courts, of fines, amercements and judgments on forfeited recognizances, and within two days after the first day of November, annually, to return the name of every delinquent clerk, to the secretary for prosecution; to cause to be set up in his office, that clause of the act of 19th Nov. 1799, which requires the treasurer's receipt for monies paid him, to be entered in the office of the secretary, and endorsed by him; to receive taxes collected for the State from the county collector, and to prosecute for the same when wrongfully withheld; to prosecute for the recovery of the tax upon bank stock, when not paid according to law; to sue for all sums of money which may become due to the State, and receivable in his office, and to make distribution, annually, of the laws of the State according to law; he is also a trustee of the school fund.

The following abstract from the report of the State Treasurer made to the Legislature, Oct. 1832, exhibits the condition of the Treasury, and the sources of its revenue, with the exception, that $30,000 at least is to be added to receipts of the current and future years, for the annual bonus of the Camden and Amboy Rail-road, and the Delaware and Raritan Canal. It will also be observed, that besides the $40,000 tax levied directly upon the State, there is a further sum of about $11,000 annually, but indirectly, levied upon the holders of Bank stock, and appropriated to the school fund. We append, also, the treasurer's report on the banks, exhibiting in detail the income derived from that source, and the actual condition of this branch of business in the State. We may also remark, here, that the only property possessed by the State, save a small tract of land at Patterson, and some lots and buildings at Trenton, and the oyster beds in her rivers and on her coasts, and the stocks mentioned in the treasurer's report, consists of 2000 shares of Camden and Amboy Rail-road stock and Delaware and Raritan Canal stock, valued at par at $200,000.

Dr. 1832.				Dolls. Cts.
Surplus monies loaned			$20,000 00	
Commissioners for negotiating loan			50 00	
Deaf and Dumb, amount of account			2,089 04	
State Library,	do.		117 48	
Jurisdiction, amount of account for defence of suit against New York in relation to boundary			1,401 36	
Legislature,	amount of account		18,728 98	
Printing account,	do.		2,253 00	
State Prison,	do.		5,800 20	
Salaries,	do.		6,636 00	
				57,076 06
Incidentals,	do.		1,716 91	
Transportation of Criminals,	do.		1,758 43	
Pensions,	do.		856 86	
Inquisitions,	do.		1,637 36	
Militia,	do.*		398 78	
State account, including salaries of Governor, Judges, &c.			4,019 00	
Constable's account			15 00	
Bills receivable—				
Due from T. G.		$1000		
Due from Presbyterian Church at Patterson		150		
			1,150 00	
				10,552 34
Trenton Bank,				
Due from Bank			9,779 91	
Due from State Bank at Morris			195 47	
Due from State Bank at Newark			87 45	
Due from George Sherman			300 00	
				10,362 83
				$77,991 23

Trenton, October 23d, 1832.

* The annual charge for militia expenses is $620—viz: $30 to the brigade inspector of each county, and $200 to the quartermaster and inspector generals.

CONTRA.			CR.
1832.			Dolls. Cts.
Bills receivable—			
Received for surplus money loaned		$20,000 00	
Received for commissions paid, being part of interest		50 00	
Balance on hand, October 25th, 1831		14,819 66	
Taxes—			
Received from the several counties		40,000 00	
Debts outstanding—			
Amount received on this account	$ 509 34½		
Amount due this account	1,150 80		
		1,659 34½	
Fines and forfeitures—			
Received on this account		760 00	
			77,289 00½
Premiums—			
Received on this account		306 22½	
Revised laws—			
Received for one copy sold		3 00	
Pedlar's license—			
Received for this account		585 00	
Interest account—			
Received balance of interest for use of surplus money loaned		808 00	
			1,702 22½
			78,991 23
Balance due as above per contra—			
Deposited in Trenton Bank			9,779 91
Do. State Bank at Morris			195 47
Do. State Bank at Newark			87 45
Due from George Sherman, for advance made for printing law reports now in progress			300 00
Balance on settlement			10,362 23

When chartered.	INSTITUTIONS.	Amount of capital.	Amt. stock paid in, now subject to tax.	Amt. of tax of one-half of one per cent.	Amount of Bonus.	Amt. of Bonus paid to State Treasurer.
1804,	Newark Banking and Insurance Company	$ 800,000	$ 350,000 00	$ 1,750 00	$ 1,482 00	$ 1,482 00
"	Trenton Banking Company	600,000	214,740 00	1,073 70	(*A*)	
1807,	New Brunswick Bank	200,000	90,000 00	450 00	6,000 00	6,000 00
1812,	State Bank at Camden	800,000	300,000 00	1,500 00	25,000 00	25,000 00
"	State Bank at New Brunswick	400,000	88,000 00	440 00	7,000 00	7,000 00
"	State Bank at Elizabeth	200,000	132,924 00	664 62	2,625 50	2,625 50
"	State Bank at Newark	400,000	280,000 00	1,400 00	4,025 00	4,025 00
"	State Bank at Morris	200,000	78,440 23	392 20	1,000 00	1,000 00
1815,	Patterson Bank	(*B*)			6,000 00	6,000 00
"	Cumberland Bank at Bridgeton	200,000	52,025 00	260 12	(*C*)	
1816,	Farmers Bank at Mount Holly	200,000	100,000 00	500 00	3,500 00	3,500 00
1818,	Sussex Bank	100,000	27,500 00	137 50	(*D*)	
1822,	Commercial Bank at Amboy	100,000	30,000 00	150 00	No Bonus.	
"	Salem Banking Company	75,000	30,000 00	150 00	do.	
1824,	People's Bank at Patterson	250,000	75,000 00	375 00	7,000 00	4,000 00
"	Morris Canal and Banking Company*	1,000,000	40,000 00		No Bonus.	
1825,	Washington Bank, Hackensack	200,000	93,460 00	467 30	8,000 00	(*E*) 5,000 00
1828,	Farmers and Mechanics Bank at Rahway	100,000	60,000 00	300 00	No Bonus.	
"	Orange Bank,	100,000	80,000 00	400 00	do.	
1830,	Farmers and Mechanics Bank at Middletown Point	50,000	10,000 00	50 00	do.	
"	Belvidere Bank	50,000	25,000 00	125 00	do.	
1831,	Mechanics Bank at Newark	250,000	200,000 00	1000 00	do.	
1832,	Union Bank at Dover	100,000	50,000 00	(*G*)		
		$6,525,000	$2,317,089 23	$11,585 44	$71,632 50	$65,632 50

* Eleven years after the charter, to pay one-half of one per cent. per annum, on the stock paid in for banking purposes.

(*A*) Trenton Banking Company—no bonus given—the State reserving the right of subscribing for 1200 shares; which shares were subscribed, and, on the 2d of February, 1828, sold to the Trenton Banking Company.

(*B*) Patterson Bank. This bank was chartered in 1815, with a capital of $200,000. It has recently closed its concerns.

(*C*) Cumberland Bank—40 shares of $50 each, given as a bonus.

(*D*) Sussex Bank—20 shares, of $50 each, given as a bonus.

(*E*) Formerly the Weehawk Bank at Weehawk. A supplement was passed 30th of November, 1825, changing its name to Washington Bank, and locating it at Hackensack.

(*G*) Union Bank at Dover. This institution has lately commenced operations.

STATEMENT RELATIVE TO INSOLVENT BANKS.

When chartered.	INSTITUTIONS.	Amount of capital.	Amount of capital paid in.	Amount of Bonus.	Amt. of Bonus paid to Treasurer.
1812,	State Bank at Trenton	$ 300,000	$ 92,400	$ 1,601	$ 1,601
1818,	Jersey Bank at Jersey City	200,000			
1822,	Salem and Philadelphia Manufacturing and Banking Company	75,000	The amount of notes circulated not known.		
1823,	New Jersey Manufacturing and Banking Company at Hoboken	150,000	150,000	4,000	4,000
1824,	Franklin Bank of New Jersey at Jersey City	500,000	300,000	25,000	15,000
"	Monmouth Bank at Freehold	200,000	40,000	4,000	800
"	New Jersey Protection and Lombard Bank	400,000	50,150	25,000	
"	Hoboken Banking and Grazing Company	300,000			
		$2,125,000	$832,550	$59,601	$21,401

Perhaps no country of equal territorial extent and population, in the world, is governed at less cost than the State of New Jersey; and if the happiness of the people be the object and evidence of good government, we do not hesitate to say, that none is better governed. The sum actually levied on the people directly and indirectly, for the maintenance of the State government, exclusive of the township and county polity, will not exceed $ 55,000, and is more likely to be diminished than increased. The whole population, at the present period, 1833, is not less than 330,000, which gives to each individual 16 2-3 cents tax; or dividing the number of individuals by six, for the number of families, gives one dollar for every head of a family in the State. This, it will be observed, is only the tax levied by the State, as contradistinguished from township and county taxes. To ascertain the burden actually supported by the people, we must include not only the latter, but also the sums paid for the maintenance of the militia, and of religious instruction. An opportunity is thus afforded, we trust, of settling, satisfactorily, the question which has lately been agitated, relative to the proportions paid by the inhabitants of the North American republics, and the subjects of European kingdoms, for the maintenance of the social relations.

By the singular character of our political association, each citizen contributes to the maintenance of two governments. The sum paid to the general government, by the whole community of the United States, is the net amount of duties after the deduction of drawbacks.

Taking that amount at twenty-five millions,* and dividing it by fourteen millions, the probable population of the United States, in January, 1834, we have a charge of $ 1 78½ nearly. But a more favorable view may be taken of this subject. The extent of revenue, required for a liberal administration of the government, is estimated at fifteen millions of dollars, and it is highly probable, that the nation will not, for many years, consent to pay a larger sum than is requisite, and which, from accumulation, may become dangerous to her welfare. This sum would impose a tax, supposing it be collected from commerce alone, and the proceeds of lands to be divided among the states, of $ 1 06 and a fraction upon each individual.

From the general statistical table of the State, it appears, that for the year 1832,

there were levied, for State purposes, exclusive of the tax on banks,			$ 40,366 71
Tax on banks, per treasurer's report,			11,585 44
County tax, as per return of assessors,			104,166 00
Township taxes, viz:	Poor,	78,131 00	
	Road,	192,859 00	
	School,	1,366 00	
			271,386 00
			427,504 15

The militia expenses, actually paid by the treasury of the State, are included in the foregoing amount; but the time devoted, we had like to have said, wasted, in militia duties, together with the money uselessly expended, cannot be estimated at less than one dollar for every prescribed day of service, for each person enrolled, or placed on the exempt list. There are three training days in the year. The fine for non-attendance is two dollars per day, and the sum paid by the exempt is five dollars per annum, in form of tax. Every officer and private expends, on the day of service, more than would support him at home. The military force of the State, by the adjutant general's report for 1832, amounted to $ 35,360; that number multiplied by four dollars, which we take as the mesne expense of each officer, private, and

exempt, gives a total annual amount of	141,440 00
The annual cost of religious instruction, according to the statement hereinafter given,	120,000 00
General government for duties at 179 per head,	590,700 00
State charges, including township and county rates, at one dollar twenty-nine cents and five mills per head, nearly,	427,504 15
	$ 1,279,644 15

* The receipts of the treasury, for the three first quarters of 1832, were $ 21,730,717 19; and the treasurer's estimate, for 1833, was twenty-one millions; but it is generally supposed that the receipt will much exceed the estimate.

This sum divided by the number of inhabitants, (330,000,) gives a charge of $3 86,* nearly, upon each inhabitant,—for the payment of principal and interest of the public debt—the pension list—for the support of the General and State governments—for the maintenance of schools in part—for the support of the clergy, and the founding and preservation of churches—for the support of the poor—for making and repairing all other than turnpike roads, and the erection of bridges by the townships and counties—and in a word, for all kinds of public expenditure.

The attorney general is the representative of the State in all the courts of the commonwealth, and prosecutes in her name all offenders against her peace and dignity, and sues and defends all suits in which she has an interest. Deputy attornies are appointed by the legislature for the counties respectively, whose term of office is five years; they are vested in their respective districts with the same powers, entitled to the same fees, and subject to the same penalties as the attorney general. Yet, notwithstanding such appointment, he may act in such counties when present; and any court is empowered to appoint a special substitute, for the term, in case neither the attorney general nor the general deputy shall attend. For neglect of duty, in prosecuting forfeited recognisances, fines, debts, &c. due to the State, he may, on conviction before council, on impeachment by the assembly, be disabled to act as attorney or solicitor in any court of the State, for one year. The attorney general is one of the trustees of the school fund.

A sheriff is annually elected by each county, who is eligible three times consecutively, but who, after the third year, cannot be again re-elected, until after the lapse of three years. He must be, and have been, an inhabitant and freeholder of his county for at least three years next preceding his election; must give bond to the State with five sureties in the sum of $20,000, approved by the judges of the Common Pleas, conditioned for the faithful performance of his duty, and make oath or affirmation to like effect; both of which are filed in the office of the county clerk. If he fail to give such bond and take such oath, a new election may be had; but this done, he may act before receipt of commission from the governor. When occasion requires, suits may be instituted on his bond, by order of that officer. He is *par excellence* the executive officer of his county, is the chief conservator of its peace, and has authority to call forth and direct its physical force to maintain the laws. He has charge of the jails of the county, and is responsible for the conduct of their keepers. He summons all juries, and executes all process civil and criminal issuing from the courts, and carries their judgments into effect. He may appoint deputies, who give bond and make oath for faithful performance of their duties, and have their appointment filed with the county clerk. At the request of the United States, and by the statute of this State, he has charge of prisoners committed by authority of the general government. He may not, during the continuance of his office, act as justice of the peace or keep tavern; nor become bail in any suit. In case of his death, removal or disability, a new election is had upon certificate thereof by a justice of the peace, to the county clerk; and during the vacancy, the duties of his office may be performed by the coroner.

Three coroners are annually elected in each county, must be inhabitants and freeholders, and be commissioned by the governor; but may act before commission; and must take oath, faithfully to execute their duties. The coroner, as we have seen above, is the substitute for the sheriff where the office of the latter is vacant, or where under particular circumstances, as when the sheriff is interested or

---

* The *Revue Britanique*, No 12, for 1831, avers, that notwithstanding the asserted economy of the American republic, its expenses exceeded, proportionably to its population, those of the French monarchy. The charge upon each individual in France is admitted, by the reviewer, to be 31 francs, and that in the United States is asserted, to be 35 francs. The French estimate does not include ecclesiastical expenses, the sums paid for the extinction of the public debt, the maintenance of the poor, the charges for education and other expenses, whilst our estimate contains all these. Valuing the dollar at 5 francs 33 centimes, the charge on each individual in the State of New Jersey would be 20 francs 69 cts. But if we include, in the American impost, no other charges than those of the French estimate, the American citizen, by the rate paid in this State, does not pay for every species of taxation, more than one-third of the amount of the French subject, whose burden is less than that of the subject of any other of the principal monarchies in Europe. The burden on the people of New Jersey is, perhaps, something less than that upon the citizens of some of the other States, which may have contracted considerable debts; but it is larger than is imposed in most of the Western States, and, we think, may be taken as a fair average of charges throughout the Union.

has not given bond, he is disqualified. Where any writ from any court is directed to the coroner, the return made and signed by one of them is sufficient, but such return does not prejudice or affect the rest. The most ordinary duty of the coroner, however, is to take inquests relative to deaths in prison, and of all violent, sudden or casual deaths within his county; which he performs through a jury summoned on his writ, by the constable, and over which he presides.

The constable is the next in grade, but is not the least important of the executive officers. He is annually elected by the qualified voters of the township, of which he may be considered the sheriff. He makes oath or affirmation, and gives bond to the township, for the faithful performance of his duty. He executes all process from the justices' courts, and that issued by coroner on inquest of death; and he is charged with various executive duties, the performance of which moves from himself. Thus, he is a conservator of the peace, and may arrest and confine persons found in breach of it, or contravening the act for the suppression of vice and immorality; may call out the inhabitants to extinguish fires in forests, &c.; may make proclamation in case of riots, and seize rioters; may arrest and disperse slaves meeting together in an unlawful manner, and the like.

All officers of the State appointed by the legislature in joint meeting, must reside within the State, and execute in person such office; except, that, the surrogate general may appoint deputies; officers of counties must reside within their respective counties, and are prohibited from farming out their offices to others, under penalty of five hundred pounds. Such officers desirous of resigning, must make their resignation during the sitting of the legislature, and to the members thereof in joint meeting, attending in person for that purpose, or by letter. And every officer issuing or executing a warrant for removing a prisoner out of the State, an inhabitant thereof, as prohibited by the habeas corpus act, is disqualified to hold office, and is punishable by fine and imprisonment at hard labour. The civil office of any person held under the State, is vacated by election and acceptance by the incumbent of a seat in congress; the office of governor is also vacated, if incumbent accept of any office or appointment under the United States, except such as may be for defence of the State or adjoining posts; and the seat of a member of council or assembly is also vacated by such election and acceptance, and by the acceptance of any appointment under the government of the United States. All officers elected in joint meeting neglecting or refusing to qualify themselves for the space of two months after information of their election, make void their posts. No alien can hold, or elect to any office.

The officers of the state prison are essential arms of the executive power, since they aid in executing the judgments of the law. They consist of three inspectors, two of whom make a quorum, appointed annually, in joint meeting by the assembly; the keeper nominated and removable by the inspectors, and his deputies and assistants appointed by him and approved by the inspectors. The inspectors are empowered to examine the accounts of the keeper, and any witness in relation thereto, including the keeper, upon oath; to appoint annually or oftener, one of their number acting inspector; to meet as often as shall be necessary, and at least quarterly; and the acting inspector is required to attend the prison, at least once a week to inspect the management thereof, and the conduct of the keeper and his deputies; to make regulations to give effect to the law, for the punishment of crimes and the good government of the prison; to punish prisoners in case of refractory, disorderly behaviour, or disobedience to the rules of the prison, by confinement in the cells and dungeons on bread and water for any time not exceeding twenty days for one offence, and for prevention or escapes, to put prisoners in irons; to appoint an agent where they may deem proper, for the sale of articles manufactured in the prison. If any vacancy happen in the board during the recess of the legislature, it may be filled by the governor. The inspectors are allowed one dollar and fifty cents per day, for every day necessarily employed in the duties of their office.

The keeper, before entering on the duties of his office, is required to give bond to the State treasurer, with two sureties in the sum of $1,000, conditioned that he, his deputy and assistants, shall faithfully perform their trusts, to be filed in the office of the secretary of state. He receives a salary of $1,000, and his six assistants each $475, per annum. The keeper is required to receive all prisoners duly committed to his custody, to treat them as directed by law and the rules of the prison; to provide, with the approbation of the inspectors, stock, materials and tools for prisoners; to contract for their clothing and diet, and for the sale of the produce of their labour; to keep accounts of the maintenance of offenders, of the materials furnished, and manufactures produced, subject to the inspection of inspectors, and to furnish an abstract thereof to the legislature. He may punish offenders guilty of assaults, where no dangerous wound or bruise is given, of profane cursing or swearing, indecent behaviour, idleness, negligence or wilful mismanagement in work, or disobedience to regulations, by confining offenders in the cells or dungeons on bread and water, for a time not exceeding two days; and in case of offences which he is not authorized to punish, he is required to make report to the inspectors. The keeper, his deputy or assistant, who shall obstruct the inspectors in the exercise of their powers, is subject to a fine of $30, and removal from office.

It is not within the scope of this work to detail the system of criminal jurisprudence in the State. But we may, with propriety, observe, that so early as 1789, she adopted the humane principles which now characterize the criminal laws of the Union; abolishing the punishment of death in all cases, save treason and murder, and applying imprisonment and hard labour to the correction of other offences in proportion to their enormity, and seeking to reclaim the offender from the evil of his ways. With these views she has constructed and regulated her penitentiary, and advancing with the improvements of the age, has, in the year 1833, directed the building of a new State prison upon the latest and most approved models.

The first steps in the science of reforming criminals in this, as in other States, have been unsteady, uncertain, and tending to thwart, rather than to effect, the proposed object. The prisons have every where been too small, and have not been constructed upon plans which would admit of the indispensable separation of the prisoners; and have, from the free intercommunion of the criminals, been converted into schools of vice, instead of asylums for repentance, where the convict might securely and unimpeded by ridicule or seduction, pursue the work of his own regeneration. The effects of this system are but too truly stated by the late governor De Vroom, in his message to the legislature of 1832. "The situation of our prison," he says, "is such as to invite to the commission of crime within our State. Its condition is well known to that class of offenders who are familiar with punishments. It offers to them all the allurements of that kind of society which they have long been accustomed to, freed from the restraints to which they would be obliged to submit in other places of confinement, and at the same time holds out a prospect of speedy escape. To this may be attributed the great number of our convicts, and as long as it continues, we may expect our prisons to be filled. Within the last three years, the number has increased from eighty-seven to one hundred and thirty, being an increase of fifty per cent. The remedy for these evils, now obvious, was the adoption of a system of penitentiary discipline, combining solitary confinement at labour, with instruction in labour, in morals, and religion." This system has been partially adopted by the act of 13th February, 1833, authorizing the construction of a penitentiary on the plan of the Eastern Penitentiary of Pennsylvania, with such alterations and improvements as the commissioners may approve, adhering to the principle of separate confinement of the prisoners, with hard labour. The estimate of the cost of this building is $150,000, and it is to be of sufficient capacity for the confinement of one hundred and fifty persons. The system will be further perfected by modelling the criminal law to the new species of punishment, when the prison shall have been completed. That the reader may have some idea of the plan of the penitentiary now being erected on the lot belonging to the State, near the old state prison, we give the following description of its model.

"The Eastern State Penitentiary is situated on one of the most elevated, airy, and healthy sites in the city of Philadelphia. The ground occupied by it, contains about 10 acres. The material with which the edifices are built is gneiss, in large masses; every room is vaulted, and fire proof. The design and execution, impart a grave, severe and awful character to the external aspect. The effect on the imagination of the spectator is peculiarly impressive, solemn and instructive. The architecture is in keeping with the design. The broad masses, the small and well proportioned apertures, the continuity of lines, and the bold simplicity which characterize the façade, are happily and judiciously combined. This is the only edifice in this country, which conveys an idea of the external appearance of those magnificent and picturesque castles of the middle ages, which contribute so eminently to embellish the scenery of Europe. The front is composed of large blocks of hewn stone; the walls are 12 feet thick at the base, and diminish to the top, where they are 2 3-4 feet in thickness. A wall of forty feet in height, above the interior platform, incloses an area 640 feet square; at each angle of the wall is a tower, for the purpose of overlooking the establishment; three other towers are situated near the gate of entrance. The façade or principal front is 670 feet in length, and reposes on a terrace, which, from the inequalities of the ground, varies from three to nine feet in height; the basement or belting course, which is 10 feet high, is scarped, and extends uniformly the whole length. The central building is 200 feet in length, consists of two projecting massive square towers, 50 feet high, crowned by projecting embattled parapets, supported by pointed arches, resting on corbets or brackets. The pointed, munnioned windows in these towers, contribute in a high degree to their picturesque effect. The curtain between the towers is 41 feet high, and is finished with a parapet and embrasures. The pointed windows in it are very lofty and narrow. The great gateway in the centre is a very conspicuous feature; it is 27 feet high, and 15 wide, and is filled by a massive wrought iron portcullis, and double oaken gates, studded with projecting iron rivets, the whole weighing several tons; nevertheless, they can be opened with the greatest facility. On each side of this entrance, (which is the most imposing in the United States,) are enormous solid buttresses, diminishing in offsets, and terminating in pinnacles. A lofty octangular tower, 80 feet high, containing an alarm bell and clock, surmounts this entrance, and forms a picturesque proportional centre. On each side of this main building, (which contains the apartments of the warden, keepers, domestics, &c.) are screen wing walls, which appear to constitute portions of the main edifice; they are pierced with small blank pointed windows, and are surmounted by a parapet; at their extremities are high octangular towers, terminating in parapets, pierced by embrasures. In the centre of the great court is an observatory, whence long corridors, eight in number, radiate. On each side of these corridors, the cells are situated, each at right angles to them, and communicating with them only by small openings, for the purpose of supplying the prisoner with food, &c., and for the purpose of inspecting his movements without attracting his attention; other apertures, for the admission of cool or heated air, and for the purpose of ventilation, are provided. A novel and ingenious contrivance in each cell, prevents the possibility of conversation, preserves the purity of the atmosphere of the cells, and dispenses with the otherwise unavoidable necessity of leaving the apartment, except when the regulations permit—flues conduct heated air from large cockle stoves to the cells. Light is admitted by a large circular glass in the crown of the arch, which is raking, and the highest part 16 feet six inches above the floor, (which is of wood, overlaying a solid foundation of stone.) The walls are plaistered, and neatly whitewashed; the cells are 11 feet nine inches long, and seven feet six inches wide; at the extremity of the cell, opposite to the apertures for inspection, &c., previously mentioned, is the door-way, containing two doors; one of lattice work or grating, to admit the air and secure the prisoner; the other, composed of planks, to exclude the air, if required; this door leads to a yard (18 feet by eight, the walls of which are 11½ feet in height,) attached to each cell. The number of the latter, erected on the original plan, was only 266, but it may be increased to 818 without resorting to the addition of second stories."

For the better administration of the government, the State has been divided into counties, townships, cities and boroughs. The object of these divisions is to allocate and circumscribe the duties of the various administrative officers, in the enforcement of the laws, civil and criminal, the collection of the revenues required by the commonwealth and its subdivisions, and, more especially, the better to enable the citizens to promote their own happiness by the improvement of the roads, bridges, &c., the education of their offspring, and the maintenance of the indigent. The division into counties is the most general, and embraces the others, all of which were readily adopted by the first English settlers, upon their coming hither, from models to which they had been accustomed in Europe. Several of the counties were organized before the year 1709; but many inconveniences having arisen from the imperfect definition of their boundaries, the limits of Bergen, Essex, Somerset, Monmouth, Middlesex, Burlington, Gloucester, Salem, and Cape May, were accurately designated by an act of assembly, passed 21st January, of that year. These limits have been since modified, in the erection of Hunterdon, Morris, Salem, Sussex, Warren, and Cumberland counties (for which see the titles respectively of these counties). By an act of 9th March, 1798, provision has been made for ascertaining the bounds of each county and township, in case of any dispute in relation to them.

The State contains at present 14 counties and 125 townships. The use of these divisions will be better understood by examining first the constitution of the townships. These are made bodies corporate by the act of 21st February, 1798; and new ones are created, and so constituted, by special laws, as the public convenience requires. They are thus empowered to sue, and be sued, by process left with the county clerks. And the qualified inhabitants are authorized to hold town meetings in their respective townships, upon specified days, and, also, on special convocation, at such places as the electors may from time to time appoint. At such meetings, every white male citizen of the State, of the age of twenty-one years, having resided within the township six calendar months, and paid taxes therein; or being seized of a freehold, or having rented a tenement, of the yearly value of five dollars, for the term of one year therein, is entitled to vote. A presiding officer, appointed by a plurality of voices, directs the business of the meeting, and determines who have or have not the right to participate therein; and to preserve order he may expel, and fine not exceeding one dollar, the unruly, and even imprison an offender during the session of the meeting. The voters of the township may make regulations and by-laws, from time to time, as they may deem proper, for improving their common lands in tillage or otherwise, and for the making and maintaining pounds; and may enforce such regulations by fine, not exceeding twelve dollars, for each offence; the regulations to be recorded by the clerk of the township, in a book kept for the purpose. Such meeting may, also, provide and allow rewards for the destruction of noxious animals; may raise money for the support of the indigent, and education of poor children; the building and rearing of pounds, the making and repairing of roads, the ascertaining the lines of the township, defending its rights, and for other necessary charges and legal objects and purposes as the major part may deem proper; being such as are expressly vested in the inhabitants of the several townships, by some act of the legislature. The meeting may elect annually, and whenever there shall be a vacancy, one clerk, one or more assessors, one or more collectors, who must give bond, with surety, for the faithful performance of their duties; three or more freeholders, to determine appeals relative to assessments in taxation; three school committee men; two freeholders, commonly called chosen freeholders; two surveyors of the highways; one or more overseers of the poor; one or more constables; so many overseers of the highways, and pound-keepers, as they shall judge necessary; one reputable freeholder as judge of elections; and five freeholders, denominated the township committee—whose duty is to examine and report to the town meeting the accounts and vouchers of the township officers, to superintend the expenditure of monies of the township, and in case of neglect of the township meeting to supply vacancies, to fill such vacancies, among the township officers as may occur. Service in a township office for one year, or payment of a fine for refusal to serve, excuses the party from services in such office for five years thereafter.

The townships being thus empowered to select their officers, and to provide for their wants, are made responsible for the proper performance of duty by their agents; and may be fined for the bad condition of the roads, and compelled to make good any loss sustained in the collection of state and county taxes, by the unfaithfulness of the collectors.

The chosen freeholders of the several townships of each county, form the administrative council, or board of the county. They are, also, incorporated, by the act of 13th February, 1798, with power, to sue and liability to be sued; to hold lands and chattels, &c. in trust for their respective counties, and for such uses as may be designated by law, and to sell and dispose of the same; to make and enforce such regulations as may be necessary for the government of their respective corporations, not contrary to the laws of the State; to raise, at their annual or other meeting held for the purpose, monies for the building, purchase or repairs of poor-houses, gaols, court-houses and bridges; the surveying and ascertaining the lines, the prosecuting and defending the rights, defraying the public and other necessary charges, and executing the legal purposes and objects of the county, as the major part of them shall deem proper; which monies are expended under the direction of the corporation: to elect, annually, and pro tempore in case of absence or refusal to act, a director to preside at the meeting of the board; to meet, annually, upon the second Wednesday in May, at the county town; to elect a clerk annually, who shall record the proceedings of the board; and a county collector, a freeholder and resident of the county, who shall give bond, with sureties, for the faithful performance of his duty;

to raise monies voted by the board, by precepts to the assessors of the respective townships, commanding them to assess such amount on the inhabitants and their estates, agreeably to the law for the time being, for raising money by taxation for the use of the State.

When the lines of the county have not been surveyed and distinctly marked, the freeholders, by prescribed form, may apply to the Supreme Court for commissioners to survey them. They may, also, at their discretion, build or purchase a workhouse within their county, and provide for its government, and the employment of its inhabitants; and may establish a market, once or oftener in every year, within the county, for the sale of live stock, to continue not more than four days, and establish laws for its regulation.

From all assessments, an appeal lies to the commissioners of appeal, who hold stated and special meetings at the usual place of the respective town meetings, attended by the proper assessor, and have power to summon and qualify witnesses, and whose decision upon the case is final.

The township collector is charged, with the collection, within his precinct, of all taxes, whether levied by the township, county or state; to make return of defaulters in payment, on oath, to a justice of the peace, who is required to issue his warrant, to the constable of the township, for levying the tax by distress and sale of the goods, or imprisonment of the delinquent; and the constable must account with the township collector. And such collector and constable are respectively required to render to the people, in township meeting, an account of monies by them received, and to pay, according to their direction, any overplus which may be in their hands.

All monies levied for county use are to be paid by the respective township collectors, on or before the 22d day of December, annually, to the proper county collector, who, in case of default, may proceed summarily against them. Monies levied for State use, are to be paid to the state treasurer by the county collector on or before the 30th December, annually; and such tax money, as he may receive from sheriffs, within ten days after the same shall have been paid; and in case of the default of any county collector, the state treasurer may recover from him, for the use of the State, the penalty of fifty dollars, before a justice of the Supreme Court, who has exclusive cognizance thereof; and when such collectors shall not have paid over monies received by them, the same may be recovered by the state treasurer by proper action at law. The counties are responsible for all monies belonging to the State, received by the county treasurer, and not paid over by him to the state treasurer. And it is the duty of the latter to add the annual deficiency of each county, to the quota of the county for the subsequent year; and of the county collector to charge such deficiency, and also deficiency of county tax, to the delinquent township.

The county collector disburses the monies of the county upon the orders of the board of chosen freeholders, and for neglect or refusal so to do, or to perform any of the duties connected with the levy of taxes imposed by such board, he is subjected to a penalty of 300 dollars.

Thus, in these subdivisions of the State, we have examples of a pure democracy and simple representative government. The people in their township meetings, (and the word township comprehends precincts and wards,) discuss their common wants, propose the remedies, and appoint the agents to give them effect. In the larger districts, where legislation in their proper persons would prove inconvenient, as well by the distance of the people from each other, as from their number when collected, the citizens have devolved the necessary legislative power upon agents, endowed also with an adequate executive capacity. This system works well, and might, possibly, be beneficially extended, by enlarging the sphere of action of the chosen freeholders, particularly, in giving effect to a general and uniform system of education.

Having thus incidentally noticed the taxation of the townships and counties, we may give here the provisions for raising revenues for the State, to which those in other cases are analagous. [See Note A.]

1. The legislature annually ascertains what sum of money will be requisite for State expenses during the succeeding year, and passes an act apportioning such sum among the several counties, in a ratio of their wealth and population, and fixes a day for the payment of the respective quotas.

2. On certain subjects of taxation, they direct specific sums to be levied, viz: on stud horses above three years old, any sum not exceeding 10 dollars; on other horses and mules of like age, any sum not exceeding six cents; and on neat cattle three years old and upwards, any sum not exceeding four cents.

3. The following subjects of taxation are valued and rated at the discretion of the assessor, viz: tracts of land at any sum not exceeding 100 dollars the hundred acres. But houses and lots of ten acres and under, are rated with regard to their yearly rent and value.*

Householders, (under which description all married men are included, the estimated value of whose rateable estate does not exceed 30 dollars,) three dollars over and above their certainties and other rateable estate; merchants, shopkeepers and traders, not exceeding ten dollars; fisheries, ten dollars; grist mills, six dollars the run of stones; cotton manufactories thirty dollars; sail duck manufactories, ten dollars; woollen manufactories, ten dollars; carding machines, unconnected with cotton or woollen manufactories, and propelled by water or steam, three dollars; all furnaces, (other than blast) ten dollars; blast furnaces, thirty dollars; saw mills, for each saw, eight dollars; forges that work pig iron, and forges and bloomeries that work bar iron immediately from ore or cinders, for each fire, six dollars; rolling and slitting mills, ten dollars; paper mills, eight dollars; snuff and oil mills, nine dollars; powder mills, fifteen dollars; fulling mills, unconnected with woollen manufactory, four dollars; every ferry or toll bridge, twenty dollars; tan yards, each vat, thirty cents; every single man, two dollars; but if he possess rateable estate, the tax whereof amounts to that sum, then for such estate only; no person taxed as a single man may be taxed as a householder; every male slave, able to labour, under the age of sixty years, one dollar; distillery for grain, molasses or other foreign material, thirty-five dollars; other distillery, nine dollars; coach or chariot, five dollars; phæton, coachee or four-wheeled chaise, with steel or iron springs, four dollars; four horse stage wagon, five dollars; two horse stage wagon, two dollars and fifty cents; covered wagon, with frame or fixed top, one dollar; two horse chair, curricle, and every two horse riding chair, with steel or iron springs, one dollar and fifty cents; riding chair, gig, sulkey or pleasure wagon, dearborn wagon, with steel, iron or wooden springs, seventy-five cents; printing, bleaching and dying company, five dollars; glass factory, five dollars.

The assessor is required to enter in his tax book and duplicate, a valuation of the real estate, having regard to the yearly rent and value thereof, and the amount of tax assessed in each township, above that raised from the certainties, is to be levied by a per centage upon such valution.

He is required between the 20th of June and 20th August, annually, to make an exact list of the persons, lands, chattels and estates, including certainties, made rateable by law in that year, by which all assessments during the year is regulated; and persons refusing to render an account, or rendering a false one, are liable to be doubly taxed.

The assessors of the several townships of the county meet at the seat of justice, on the first Monday of September, annually, to ascertain the amount of the certainties, and to estimate the estates, real and personal, taken by the assessors of each township, at such valuation as a majority present shall think just, according to law, and thereby to adjust and fix the quota of tax to be levied in each township; and it is their duty at such meeting to make out two abstracts of the rateables in each township, signed by the assessors present, and to deliver the same to the county treasurer, who is required to lay one of such abstracts before the legislature during the first week of their stated annual session; and within fifteen days after their meeting, a duplicate of such assessment shall be delivered by the assessors to the township and county collectors; the last of whom is required also to lay such duplicate, at the time abovementioned, before the legislature.

The amount of the certainties being deducted from the quota of each township,

---

* The rationale of this arbitrary limitation to the value of the lands, is not very apparent. It is not possible in any case, due regard to relative value being preserved, that the valuation can approximate to the true marketable value of lands, which is in many cases more than fifty times the maximum of the statutory limitation. The assessor must make his valuation by adopting a maximum or minimum, always arbitrary, from which to commence his gradation, and determine the value of the several classes of property by the best comparison in his power. If the rule for valuation be uniform in all the counties, the taxation will be equal? But how is this uniformity to be obtained—to what standard shall an appeal be made. It is certain that this mode of valuation affords no means of judging of the wealth of the several counties, nor of comparing the value of lands in this state with that of lands in other states. If the standard of valuation were the marketable value of lands, though a variable one, it would be one of easy attainment; and inequality, designed or accidental, could be detected by a standard that was notorious.

the remainder, with the fees of assessment, collection and paying over to the treasurer, is assessed on the other taxable property within the township, at such rate per dollar as will produce the sum required. Any party aggrieved by such assessment, may seek redress from the commissioners of appeal, who, for that purpose, meet on the second Tuesday of November, annually.

The township collector is required, within thirty days after receipt of the duplicate, to demand payment of the tax from each individual of his township, in person or by notice left at his place of residence, and also to give notice of the time and place of the meeting of the commissioners of appeal; and to pay the taxes, fines and forfeitures by him received, by virtue of any law of the State, to the collector of the county, by the 22d December, annually; and such sums as may be recovered by prosecution, thereafter, as soon as received. If the taxes be not paid at the time appointed, the collector is to make return to a justice of the peace, on the 22d December, annually, of delinquents, with the sums due from them, declaring on oath that he had in relation to them, respectively performed his duty according to law; and to take a receipt for such list from the justice.

Within five days after receipt of such list, it is the duty of the justice to deliver warrants to the constables, requiring them to levy the tax in arrears, with costs, &c. by distress and sale of chattels of delinquent—or, in default of chattels, to imprison the body until payment be made; giving four days notice, at least, by advertisement, of the time and place of such sale. And it is the duty of the constable to pay such tax to the township collector, within forty-five days from the date of the warrant; to return the warrant to the justice, with an account of the manner of his executing the same; a copy of which warrant and return, the justice shall, if demanded, give to the collector, and return the original warrant, if not fully executed, to the constable.

The constable is liable for so much of the taxes, which by such warrant he was required to collect, as shall not be paid over to the collector, unless the deficiency happen without neglect, fraud or default, on his part, in suit, by township collector, before a judge of the Common Pleas; and like suit may be brought against township collector, by the county collector, for monies collected by him, or received from constable, and not paid over, according to law; and in case the constable be prosecuted, such warrant, on cause shown, may be taken from him, and transferred to another.

Tenants or persons having charge of lands, and tenements and their chattels, are liable for taxes imposed on such lands; and on payment, may deduct the amount from their rent, or recover it by suit, where no contract prevents; and when the tax is on unimproved or untenanted land, or the tenant is unable to pay, the tax may be levied by the constable on the warrant of a justice, at the instance of the collector, by sale of timber, wood, herbage, or other vendible property of the owner, on the premises.

The justices, constables and township collectors, render to the township committee, when required, an account of the monies they or any of them may have received on any assessment, and not paid to the county collector, and must pay to such committee, on demand, such monies; and in default, are liable to suit by the clerk of the township, in the name of the inhabitants thereof.

Due provision is made for the compensation of the respective township and county officers, for enforcing performance of their duties by proper sanctions, and for levying monies becoming due from them by virtue of their official stations.

Another prominent use made of the township and county division, is in the system for the maintenance of the poor.

The provisions for this purpose, like the political subdivisions themselves, have, in their principal features, been copied from Great Britain. The wisdom of this system is less than equivocal, but the genius of legislation has not yet been able to substitute a better. Each township, or precinct, is required to maintain the poor *settled* within it. A settlement is gained by the acquisition of a freehold estate of fifty pounds value, and residence of a year; apprenticeship, or servitude by indenture, for a year; residence of one year by a mariner, or a person arriving directly from Europe; and such residence and notice to the overseer, recorded by the town clerk, in case of other persons. From these provisions are excepted servants procured from gaols and hospitals in other states. Bastard children have the settlement of the mothers. Penalties are inflicted upon such inhabitants as receive into their houses, vagabonds, vagrants, sturdy beggars, and idle strolling aad disorderly persons; and they are liable to maintain such wanderers, and to pay the expenses of their funerals in case of death. A person may remove from one precinct to another, bearing the certificate of the overseers of the poor of the precinct in which he has a settlement, attested and allowed by two justices of the peace, declaring such settlement, and delivering such certificate to the overseers of the district into which he shall remove. But such person, becoming chargeable, may be returned to his place of settlement; residence under the certificate not giving settlement; and expenses incurred by the township for maintenance, relief or burial of such resident, must be paid by the precinct in which he has a legal settlement.

Relief is granted to paupers, on the order of a justice, at the application of the overseers; the order fixing the amount, and serving as the voucher for expenditure. And, as a check upon the overseers, they are required to register the name and description of the pauper, and such order, in the township book, together with the account of monies received or disbursed for the use of the poor, and registry of transactions of their office, and to lay such book before the inhabitants in town meeting.

Before relief granted, the goods of the applicant are to be inventoried, and in case of death, sold; and the proceeds applied to reimburse the expenditure for the pauper.

Poor children, who have no parents, or whose parents are applicants for relief, and children of paupers brought up in sloth and ignorance, may, by the overseers, with the assistance and application of two justices, be bound apprentices for such number of years as they may think proper, males until 21, and females until 18 years; inserting in the indenture, a clause binding the master to cause such apprentice to be instructed to read and write. And the overseers and justices continue the guardians of the apprentice.

Where the father deserts his family, or a widow her children, leaving them a public charge, and leaving estate, real or personal, such estate may be taken by the overseers, upon the warrant of two justices, and the rents of the land, and the proceeds of the sale of the chattels, applied to the maintenance of the deserted family.

The overseers, with the assent of the town meeting, may purchase or rent a workhouse, in which to employ and maintain the poor of the precinct, applying the proceeds of their labour to the poor fund; and such house may be erected by two or more townships conjointly. Or the overseers of the township may contract with the overseers of any other place, for the maintenance and employment of the poor of such other place; or the chosen freeholders of the county may purchase or build a poorhouse for the whole county. Persons claiming relief and refusing to be lodged, kept to work, and maintained in such house, are rejected.

When the overseers have reason to believe, that any person not having a settlement in their precinct is, or is likely to become, chargeable, they may bring him, by warrant from two justices, directed to and served by the constable, before such magistrates, who shall examine such person on oath touching his last place of settlement, and direct him to remove thither by a stated time; and on his neglect or refusal to comply with such order, may issue their warrant to the constable, commanding him to convey such person to the constable of the next precinct; and so, from precinct to precinct, until he reach the place of his legal settlement. And in case such person return to the place from which he was removed, and does not depart therefrom, within 24 hours after notice given, such person, if male, is liable, on the order of a magistrate, to receive fifteen lashes; if female, in the discretion of the magistrate, to be sent away again, or committed to close confinement, and fed, at the expense of the township, on bread and water only; and both to be sent back to the place to which they may have been first ordered. But if any person complained of, as a pauper, give bond with two sufficient sureties, conditioned to indemnify the precinct against the charge of his maintenance, he shall not be removed.

The overseers of the township, to which such pauper shall be legally removed, are required to receive him, under penalty of five pounds, on conviction of refusal, before a justice, to the use of the place from which the removal was made. An appeal from the order of removal lies by the pauper, or other person aggrieved, to the sessions.

An idle vagrant, vagabond, or beggar, strolling and begging through the country, may be apprehended by the constable, or any inhabitant, and carried before a justice, who is required to examine him on oath; and if it appear that he have a settlement, to grant a warrant for removal as abovementioned, but if he have no settlement in the State, then to direct by such warrant that he be conveyed back by every precinct through which he had wandered, until he be transported out of the State: and such vagrant returning into the State, is liable to punishment by whipping. These provisions respecting the removal of indigent persons, though in force, are not often executed.

The fund for maintenance of the poor is augmented by fines imposed for breach of the laws, and by the personal estates of such persons as may die intestate, without any representative. The pauper may sue without costs, and have counsel appointed him by the court, who shall conduct his cause without fee or reward. Authority is given to the respective townships to raise, as for other township purposes, such sum of money as may be deemed proper for the education of pauper children and children of paupers.

The father and grandfather, mother and grandmother, child and grandchild, when competent, are liable to maintain the pauper.

A third essential benefit, promoted by the territorial subdivision of townships and counties, is the formation and preservation of roads. The common roads of the country are either public or private. When ten or more freeholders deem a new public road necessary, or one existing, unnecessary or proper to be altered, they may by petition, after giving ten days public notice in the townships through which the road is intended to pass, obtain from the court of Common Pleas the appointment of six surveyors of the highways, having regard to those of the township in which the road lies or is to be made. When the road is to be on the county line, the application must be made to, and the surveyors appointed by, the Supreme Court, three being taken from each county. The surveyors, after a prescribed notice has been given, meet and view the road or ground proposed for the road, and lay out, vacate or alter it, as the case may require; and return a map thereof, with the time when the same may be opened, to the clerk of the Common Pleas, or to the clerk of the Supreme Court, as the case may be, who records the return, and the road so laid out and opened becomes, or if vacated ceases to be, a public highway; unless a caveat be entered thereto within fifteen days, which operates as a supersedeas of proceedings until the succeeding court.

Upon the complaint of any one alleging himself aggrieved, the court will appoint six of the chosen freeholders of the county, who, after due notice as prescribed by law, also view the road proposed to be made, vacated or altered, and concurring in report with the surveyors, it is definitively confirmed, so that no further proceedings may be had thereon for one year. But, if their report differ from that of the surveyors, the latter becomes void, and the road or alteration may be again applied for under a year. If no caveat have been entered, or the person entering it do not prosecute it according to law, or the freeholders make no unfavourable report, or be equally divided in their opinions, the proceedings of the surveyers become valid. If the application for review be in Cape May county, and the proposed or actual road run through lands of any of the chosen freeholders, one or more justices of the peace may be appointed on the review. And where the application relative to the road is in the Supreme Court, three such freeholders from each county are appointed to review, and like proceedings are had in regard to their report, as in the former case. Any neglect of the officers in regard to these proceedings, is punishable by a fine of sixteen dollars, to the use of the prosecutor. Four of the surveyors or freeholders, where the road proposed to be made or altered is in one county, and two from each of the counties, where there are more than one, are necessary to, and sufficient for, the return.

The proceedings for making, vacating, or altering private roads, are similar in most respects, to those in the case of public ones. Such roads, however, are made and preserved at the expense of those interested in them, who may hang gates thereon, which are protected by a penalty against those injuring them. By-roads, if shut up, may be laid out by three of the chosen freeholders, and remain as private roads until vacated, or altered in the manner abovementioned.

For the purpose of making or repairing roads, the township committee assign, in writing to the overseers of the roads respectively, their several limits of the highways within the township. And it is the duty of such overseers to provide labourers, animals, implements and materials for the work, and to erect such bridges as can be built by common labourers; the monies for which are raised by order of the town meeting, as in other cases of township expense, and the overseer accounts with the town meeting.

If the township be fined upon the presentment of the grand jury, or information of attorney general, for the bad condition of the roads, the overseer within whose limits the cause arose, is responsible therefor with costs, or he may be proceeded against in the first instance. The road tax payable by any individual, may be paid in labour on the road by himself or substitute; and the roads over mill-dams are to be kept in good and safe condition by the owners of the mills respectively, so long as they shall be upheld.

The town meeting may determine whether the highways shall be maintained by hire or by labour. But if the resolution be to maintain the roads by labour, the township committee divide the highways, in their township, into convenient districts, and assign the inhabitants to them, in equitable proportions. And whatever mode be thus adopted, must be continued for three years. Inhabitants who neglect to perform their quota of work, are each finable one dollar per day, for absence themselves; one dollar and a half for a horse and cart, and two dollars for wagon or cart with two horses or oxen, which have been warned out and shall be absent. If the township vote to maintain the roads by hire, but do not supply the money therefor, the overseers must resort to the labour system. If the overseer neglect his duty, he is liable to an action, and the magistrate on complaint of three freeholders, may issue his precept against overseer, and on conviction, fine him any sum not over twenty, nor under five dollars. The board of freeholders is authorized, at the county's expense, to erect guide posts and mile stones, where they may deem expedient.

When bridges are required in a township, or between two townships, they are built at the county expense, and if between two counties, at their joint expense. Where the cost does not exceed thirty dollars, the overseer and chosen freeholders of the township, are competent to order its execution; where the cost does not exceed one hundred and fifty dollars, the approbation of the overseers of the township, and of the chosen freeholders of that, and of the two adjacent townships, are necessary; and where the expense will exceed one hundred and fifty dollars, the assent of the overseers of the highway, and of the board of chosen freeholders of the county, is required.

In addition to his services as register of the proceedings of the Circuit Courts, the Court of Sessions and Common Pleas, the county clerk performs many other executive duties. We have already noticed his ministry in general elections. He is the recorder of deeds, mortgages, and other conveyances of lands in his county, and register of marriages returned to him by justices of the peace and ministersof the gospel; the receiver of monies for tavern licenses, which he pays over to the county freeholders; and is the depository of the dockets of the justices of his county, after their deaths. He is forbidden to act as surrogate, or practice as an attorney, within his county.

The township clerk records the proceedings of the town meetings, registers estrays, and receives for the use of the township its share of money produced by the sale of unclaimed beasts impounded for damage feasance; and registers all births and deaths in his township duly communicated to him.

The present militia system of the State, is founded on the act of 18th February, 1815, and the supplements of 1818, 1819, and 1830; which require, that every free able bodied white male inhabitant, of the age of 18, and under 45, years, shall be enrolled by the commanding officer of the company within whose bounds he may reside. From this requisition are exempted, ministers of the gospel; the vice president of the United States; the officers, judicial and executive, of the government of the United States; the judges of the Supreme Court of this State; the members of both houses of congress, and their respective officers; all custom house officers, with their clerks; all post officers and stage drivers employed in the transit of the mail; ferrymen; inspectors of exports; pilots; mariners actually employed in the sea service of any merchant within the United States; all students of divinity and students of the two colleges in this State, except in cases of actual invasion; and persons who shall have served ten years in any uniform corps of the State; and, at the discretion of the brigade board, an officer who has held a commission for one year in the army of the United States, or under the authority of any one of the States, and any soldier who may have faithfully served 18 months in the late war.

A brigade is formed in each county, except Cape May; in that, there is an independent regiment, under the command of a lieutenant colonel, whose field officers form a regimental board, with the power of a brigade board, in many particulars. The brigades are formed into four divisions, of which those of Burlington, Gloucester, Salem and Cumberland, with the Cape May regiment, make the first; those of

Bergen, Essex, and Morris, the second; those of Somerset, Middlesex, and Monmouth, the third; and those of Hunterdon and Sussex, the fourth.

The governor is commander in chief. There is a general staff, of which he appoints his four aids-de-camp, with the rank of lieutenant colonel; one quartermaster and one adjutant general, with the rank of brigadier; and, when the service may require it, one deputy adjutant, and one deputy quartermaster general, to each brigade or division, with rank of lieutenant colonel. To each division there is one major general, and two aids-de-camp appointed by him, with the rank of major; to each brigade, one brigadier general, with a brigade inspector, acting also as brigade major, one aid-de-camp taken from the line, appointed by the general, judge advocate, paymaster and quartermaster; to each regiment, one colonel; to each battalion or squadron, one major; to each company of infantry, light infantry and grenadiers, one captain, one lieutenant, one ensign, four sergeants, four corporals, one drummer, and one fifer; to each troop of horse, one captain, two lieutenants, one cornet, four sergeants, four corporals, one saddler, one farrier, one trumpeter, and the foot and cavalry companies contain not more than 64, nor less than 40, privates. Companies of horse can be raised only by permission of the commander in chief. To each company of artillery there are a captain, two lieutenants, four sergeants, four corporals, one drummer, one fifer, not more than six, nor less than three, gunners and bombardiers, nor more than 62, nor less than 15, matrosses. The regimental staff consists of one adjutant and quartermaster, ranking as lieutenants, taken from the subalterns of the regiment, a paymaster to each battalion; a surgeon, surgeon's mate, chaplain, sergeant major, drum major, fife major, and quartermaster sergeant; all of whom, except the paymasters, are appointed by the field officers. To each company of riflemen there belong a captain, three lieutenants, four sergeants, four corporals, and drummer, fifer, or bugler. Such companies are attached to the battalion in whose bounds a majority of the members reside. To each troop of horse artillery, there are a captain, four lieutenants, one quartermaster sergeant, four sergeants, four corporals, one saddler, one farrier, one bugler, one trumpeter, and not more than 100, nor less than 40, privates.

All officers take rank from the date of their commissions, except when they are of the same date, and then by lot. The captains, and all other inferior officers of the militia, are chosen by the companies; but field and general officers by the council and assembly, and all are commissioned by the governor. The brigade and regimental staff officers, are commissioned by him on certificates of their appointment by the officers making them; non-commissioned officers and musicians, are appointed by the captains and subalterns. The uniform is that worn by officers of the United States.

The commanding officers of each regiment, independent battalion, and squadron, are required to convene their respective officers twice a year; and at one of such meetings, the orderly sergeants; and at the meeting not attended by the non-commissioned officers, may direct the attendance of one of the companies under their command, for the purpose of military improvement. The attendance of such company is in lieu of company training, and absence is punishable as in other cases of neglect of military service. And the non-commissioned officers attending such drill, is entitled to fifty cents per day.

The militia meet three times, annually, for improvement in discipline and martial exercise; once by companies or troops, on the 3d Monday in April; once by battalion or squadron, and once by regiment or independent battalion. The fine for non-attendance on days of exercise, absence from roll call, or leaving parade without permission, is, on a field officer, eight dollars; every other commissioned officer, four dollars; on every non-commissioned officer and private, two dollars per day; and for appearance on parade without appropriate arms, fifty cents, where the soldier is able to provide them. When called into active service, every militiaman must appear fully equipped, with every article required by act of congress, under penalty, if an officer, of ten dollars; and if a private, two dollars. No militiaman having a substitute in actual service, is thereby excused from duty on parade days. But no militiaman is finable more than two dollars in one year, for neglect of duty, if he have attained thirty-five years; provided, that when he shall attend at any one of the days required by law, and perform military duty, he shall be fined one dollar for every other day's absence therefrom. And when the brigade board shall disband any company, its officers may be exempted from military duty.

Delinquents are marked at roll call by the orderly sergeant, and reported to the company court, composed of the officers of the company or troop, of which the officer first in rank is president. Such court is empowered, to hear and decide on, the excuse of delinquents reported, and the president is required to make return within ten days, to the commanding officer of the battalion, of all delinquents, and the sum imposed on each. The battalion court of appeal, consists of the commanding officer of the battalion, the surgeon, or surgeon's mate, and the senior captain, or, in his default, of the captain next in rank; and is empowered to hear excuses on appeal, and to remit fines; and in case of permanent inability, by certificate, to discharge from military duty. The president of this court, makes returns of delinquents and the fines imposed, to the battalion and brigade paymasters. Failure to attend such court by its members, or the president to make return, is punishable, in the first case, by a fine of ten, and in the second, by a fine not exceeding thirty, nor less than fifteen, dollars.

The battalion paymaster, on receipt of the return, and such fines as may have been collected by the battalion commandant, after efforts to collect, and after the first Monday in September, delivers the list of delinquents to a justice of the peace, who issues execution against them, as in case of taxation; the constable being required to levy the same on the goods of the delinquent, or in default of goods, to commit him to prison, until payment, &c. But the brigade board, or any three of them, may discharge delinquent unable to pay. If, upon levy and sale, there be a balance in the hands of the constable which the delinquent will not receive, he pays it to the paymaster of the battalion, to be accounted for in his settlement with the brigade board, and certifies the same to the judge advocate, or brigade board. The fines and penalties imposed on minors, are payable by the parent, guardian, or master.

The battalion paymaster returns to the brigade board the list of delinquent commissioned officers certified by the orderly; keeps a journal of their proceedings; an account of fines and the modes of their payment, whether voluntary or involuntary, and of such as may not be recovered, with the reason thereof; all which is submitted to the brigade board. The battalion and brigade paymasters are appointed by such board, and give bond with sureties, the first in five hundred, and the second in two thousand dollars, conditioned for the faithful performance of their duties; to which effect, they, also, make oath before the county clerk. The brigade paymaster receives all vouchers and returns, and keeps distinct accounts of the monies arising from fines and forfeitures in the several regiments and battalions in the brigade, and of monies received and paid by him, subject to the examination of the brigade board; collects the fines imposed by the board on delinquent officers, and, in case of non-payment for sixty days, puts the list into the hands of a justice of the peace, which is then proceeded upon as above stated.

The brigade board is composed of the brigadier general, brigade major and commandants of regiments, independent battalions, and squadrons of the respective brigades; a majority of whom form a quorum, meeting annually on the third Monday in December, at a place of their own appointment, within the brigade. The officer of first grade and seniority presides, and the board has power: To compel the attendance of its members by fine, not exceeding twenty dollars—to arrange the regiments, battalions, squadrons, troops, and companies, as they may deem expedient—to authorize the formation of new uniform companies, and to attach them to such battalion or regiment as they may deem proper—to draw orders on the brigade paymaster for lawful expenses—to make a reasonable compensation to the brigade and battalion paymasters for their services; adjust their accounts, remove them in case of malfeasance, and to appoint a successor who in case of brigade paymaster shall prosecute his predecessor for monies of the brigade in his hands—and also the battalion paymasters who may be in arrears—to allow adjutants for extra services—to compensate brigade judge advocates—to assess fines on delinquent officers, returned by the brigade major or battalion paymaster—to preserve order at their meetings by imposition of fines not exceeding ten dollars, upon transgressors, and to erect a covering for the protection of field artillery—to keep an account of all sums by them received from their several battalion paymasters, and disbursements, with an account of the expenses of the militia system, and the appropriations made for arms, &c.—and make reports thereof, annually, to the legislature.

The judge advocate is appointed by the brigade board, of which he is *ex officio* clerk, and is required to attend its meetings and record its proceedings.

The adjutant general distributes all orders of the commander in chief, to the several corps, attends public reviews, if required, when the commander in chief reviews the troops,—obeys all orders from him, executing or perfecting the military system established by law,—furnishes blank forms of the different returns directed by the commander in chief,—receives from the several officers returns of all militia under their command, together with reports of the state of the arms, ammunition, &c. from which he reports proper abstracts to the commander in chief, who lays them before the legislature. He annually reports all the militia of the State to the president of the United States—Keeps a record of all orders, returns names of commissioned officers, and proceedings relative to the details of the military force ordered out by the commander in chief upon requisitions of the president or Congress of the United States, in cases of invasion, or other emergency—Records all certificates of election of officers before commissioned by the commander in chief—and lays his accounts, annually, before the legislature, who appropriate, annually, one hundred dollars for his services.

The brigade inspectors attend the brigade, regimental and independent battalion meetings of the militia composing their several brigades, during the time of their being under arms, to inspect their arms, &c.—makes returns, annually, to the adjutant general of the militia of his brigade, reporting particularly the name of the reviewing officer, the state of the arms, &c. and every thing which, in his judgment, may advance good order and military discipline. He receives for ordinary duty, thirty dollars per annum, and for extra duty, such allowance as the brigade board may direct; and is subject to a fine of fifty dollars for malfeasance, and the forfeiture of his annual salary, unless he produce the acknowledgment of the adjutant general for his returns. In the absence of the brigade inspector, the commanding officer appoints some one to perform his duties.

Company officers report their acceptance of office to the commanding officer of the battalion, within ten days after notice of their election, otherwise the election is deemed void. Resignations are made to the brigade commander; and where vacancy happens in the company, by death, removal or resignation, such commander directs his warrant to the battalion commandant, to hold an election to supply the vacancy.

Persons enrolled in a uniform company are, upon the certificate of the commanding officer, excused from service in the militia: but such certificate may not be given until such persons have appeared in uniform, under penalty of ten dollars upon the officer.

The majors are charged with organizing the several companies under their respective commands. Where the militiamen of any company or district, fail to choose officers, the major may appoint a sergeant, to take command of the company until proper officers are duly qualified; and to constitute his company court, such sergeant may appoint persons from the list of the company, who may elect one of their number president.

No officer or private, on his way to, or return from, militia service, may be charged toll or ferriage, and refusal to permit his passage is punishable by fine of eight dollars; nor can he be arrested on civil process on any legal day for training, nor can his arms, &c. be levied on and sold under execution.

The commander in chief may, in case of invasion or other emergency, order out any proportion of the militia of the State, to march to any part thereof, and continue so long as he may think necessary, not exceeding two months. In such case, substitutes may be received for any person called on to do a tour of duty, but no substitute is admissible at ordinary training, under penalty on the officer, of ten dollars. Horses of militiamen, taken into service, are registered and appraised, and their value paid to the owner, in case the horse be killed or taken by the enemy. The accounts of the quartermaster, for rations or ammunition, must be approved by the commanding officer of the regiment or independent battalion, and by the governor, before payment at the treasury.

Courts martial are appointed, for the trial of officers above the rank of field officers, by the commander in chief,—for field officers, by the major generals, in their respective divisions,—for captains and subaltern commissioned officers, by the brigadier generals, each in his own brigade. And the commandant of regiments and independent battalions may institute a regimental court martial whenever they shall find it necessary. Officers appointing such court must, in all cases, approve or disapprove its sentence, and may mitigate or remit the punishment, except where the offence is of a personal nature, when the sentence is conclusive. And such officer may, in case of emergency, appoint a judge advocate, *pro tempore*.

The regimental court martial is composed of five members, the president of whom shall not be under the rank of captain. The general court martial consists of thirteen commissioned officers, not under the rank of captain, the senior of whom is president. The concurrence of two-thirds of the court is necessary, in every sentence for inflicting punishment; and each member, with the judge advocate, swears to determine the case according to the evidence, that he will not divulge the sentence until it have been approved or disapproved; and will at no time, discover the vote or opinion of any member, unless required to give evidence thereof in a court of justice.

The expense of a court martial, trying an officer of the general staff, is payable from militia fines in the State treasury; trying an officer above the grade of major, by the paymaster of the brigade; trying a major, or inferior officer, by the battalion paymaster. Members of courts martial receive $1 50 per day, and witnesses fifty cents—payable on certificates of the judge advocate.

Commissioned officers guilty of unofficer-like conduct, may be cashiered by the court, or punished by fine, not exceeding fifty dollars. The commanding officer of a regiment, battalion, or squadron, failing to give orders for assembling his command, as directed by his brigadier, or in case of invasion, may be cashiered, and punished by a fine not exceeding one hundred dollars: and a commissioned officer of a company, guilty of like offence, under the orders of the commandant of the regiment, &c., is subject to like punishment; and a non-commissioned officer, to a fine not exceeding thirty dollars. The commanding officer of a company, &c., failing to return a list of persons, notified to perform a tour of duty, to the colonel, &c., may be cashiered, or fined in a sum not exceeding one hundred dollars.

Non-commissioned officers, or privates, appearing drunk upon parade, disobeying orders, using reproachful or abusive language to officers, quarrelling or promoting quarrels among fellow-soldiers, may be disarmed and put under arrest, until the company be dismissed, and be fined by court martial, not exceeding eight dollars. A militiaman deserting whilst on a tour of duty, may be fined not exceeding one hundred dollars, and imprisoned not more than two months; and if a non-commissioned officer, shall be degraded to the ranks. Non-commissioned officer, or private, bringing on parade, or discharging, within a mile thereof, any loaded fire arms, on the day assigned for improvement or inspection, without permission from a commissioned officer, is subject to a fine of one dollar.

When ordered out for improvement or inspection, the militia are under military discipline, from the rising to the setting of the sun, and none, during such time, may be arrested on civil process: on days of exercise they may be detained under arms, on duty, in the field, six hours; but not more than three hours without time being allowed to refresh themselves. The retailing of spirituous liquors, on, or within a mile of the parade, is prohibited under a penalty of forfeiture of such liquors. The rules of discipline are such as may be established by Congress for disciplining the regular troops of the United States.

By-standers at any muster, molesting or insulting, by abusive words or behaviour, any officer or soldier, while on duty, may be put under guard, and kept at the discretion of the commanding officer, until sundown; and if guilty of like misconduct, before a court martial, may be fined not exceeding twenty dollars, and costs of prosecution.

Fines imposed by courts martial, are certified by the judge advocate to the brigade board, and are collected by the brigade paymaster, in the manner above directed. The surplus money in the hands of the brigade paymaster, is appropriated to the purchase of arms, accoutrements, colours, instruments of music, and the preservation of arms (the arms being subject to the order of the commander in chief, in case of invasion, insurrection, or war). And the judge advocate is required, after the annual meeting of the brigade board, to transmit to the adjutant general, a statement of the disbursements, and arms, &c., to be laid by him before the legislature. The commandants of regiments, independent battalions, and squadrons, account to the brigade board for the monies received by them for teaching music, and other purposes.

The commander in chief, or of brigade, when the militia may be called into actual service, may receive uniform companies from any brigade in the State as volunteers, who having served their tour, are exempted from draft, until their battalions, regiment, or brigade shall have performed like service; and their brigade is accredited for the number so volunteering. Due authority is given to the commander in chief for organizing companies on the sea-board when necessary for its protection: and he may furnish any uniform company with arms, the property of the State; the officers giving bond for keeping them in repair, and returning them when required. Uniform companies are attached to the battalion within the bounds of which a majority of the company resides.

Any person desirous to be exempt from militia duty, is required, on or before the first of April, annually, to report himself to the commanding officer of the company, in the bounds of which he may reside. Such officer returns the list of exempts to the township collector, on or before the twentieth of June, annually, who taxes each, the sum of five dollars, in addition to his other taxes; designating it in his duplicate, delivered to the township collector; and he, also, furnishes the collector of the county, on or before the first of December, annually, two certified abstracts of the names of such exempts. The township collector pays to the county collector, such taxes, and his certificate of the death, insolvency, or absconding of the exempt, is a sufficient voucher against the tax; and the county collector pays to the State treasurer, the exempt taxes, with other State taxes, and the treasurer carries them to the credit of the school fund.

The commanders of the respective companies enrol all persons within their bounds liable to perform militia duty, not returned as exempts, and fine them for non-attendance on days of parade, according to law, under the penalty of thirty dollars for omission. But exempts may be classed as enrolled militia when called into actual service. And due provision is made by law for classifyng the militia for actual service when required.

The following is the state of the militia, apparent from the last return of the adjutant general, viz: Commander in chief, 4 aids-de-camp; 1 quartermaster general, 4 deputies; 1 adjutant general, 4 deputies; 4 major generals, each having two aids; 13 brigades and brigadiers, and the independent battalion of Cape May county.

Brigade Staff, consisting of 13 brigade majors and one adjutant, 13 paymasters, 11 quartermasters, 6 surgeons, 13 judges advocate.

Cavalry:—1 brigadier general, 4 colonels, 9 majors, 31 captains, 63 lieutenants, 25 cornets, 86 sergeants, 73 corporals, 11 saddlers, 10 farriers, 36 trumpeters, and 1673 privates, making an aggregate of 1810. Cavalry arms: sabres 734, pairs of pistols 609, holsters 733, cartridges 376, cartridge-boxes 359, horses, saddles, and bridles, each, 963.

Artillery:—30 captains, 54 lieutenants, 93 sergeants, 75 corporals, 40 bombardiers, 68 gunners, 36 drummers, 25 fifers, 1802 privates,—total 1886. *Ordnance apparatus and equipments:* 18 six pounders, 8 four pounders, 1 two pounder, 1 swivel, 18 tumbrels and wagons, 25 ramrods and screws, 16 port-fire stocks, 33 dragropes, 14 handspikes, 159 muskets, 19 bayonets, 829 swords, 39 cartouche boxes, 23 powder horns and wires, and 43 knapsacks.

Rifle Corps:—17 captains, 44 lieutenants, 48 sergeants, 16 corporals, 22 drummers, 16 fifers, 12 buglers, 1052 privates,—total 1115. *Arms and equipments:* 54 swords, 336 rifles, 132 fusees, 117 muskets, 17 powder horns and pouches.

Infantry:—Colonels 47, majors 96, adjutants 58, paymasters 98, quartermasters 48, surgeons 47, surgeon's mates 37, drum majors 20, fife majors 21, sergeant-majors 33, captains 406, lieutenants 397, ensigns 327, sergeants 1065, corporals 664, drummers 329, fifers 263, privates 28,882,—aggregate 30,456. *Arms and equipments:* swords 796, espontoons 57, muskets 8268, bayonets 3565, iron ram rods 5084, firelocks, other than muskets, 3373, cartridge boxes 1293.

RECAPITULATION.

COUNTIES.	Commander in chief, Suite, and General Staff.	Division and Brigade General and staff officers.	Cavalry.	Artillery.	Rifle.	Infantry.	Total in each Brigade.	Total in each Division.
Burlington, -			46	44		3288	3378	
Gloucester, -			37	81		1948	2066	
Salem, - -			88	152	120	1508	1868	
Cumberland, -			45	187		1746	1978	
Cape May, -				124		424	548—	9838
Bergen, - -			93	153	21	2074	2341	
Essex, - -			250	422	51	4283	5006	
Morris, - -			155	123	227	2369	2874—	10,221
Middlesex, -			238	93	37	1443	1811	
Monmouth, -			124	50	213	3292	3679	
Somerset, - -			158	107	93	1304	1662—	7152
Hunterdon, -			327			2584	2911	
Warren, - -			77	198	142	1883	2300	
Sussex, - -			172	152	211	2310	2845—	8056
Grand total	15	78	1810	1886	1115	30,456	35,267	35,267

III. The judiciary, as established under the colonial government, was recognised by the constitution, in the general clause continuing the laws existing at the time of its adoption, and in that, limiting the tenure of office of the judges. Some modifications and enlargement of jurisdiction have, however, since been made; and the judiciary power is now vested in a Court of Appeals, Court of Chancery, Supreme and Circuit Courts, Courts of Oyer and Terminer, and General Jail Delivery: Courts of Common Pleas, Quarter Sessions and Orphan's Court, and Courts for the trial of small causes, holden by Justices of the Peace. These institutions will be best viewed, passing from those of the lowest to those of the highest order; and attempting an outline of the constitution of each.

The courts for the trial of small causes or Justices' Courts, now depend upon the act of 12th of February, 1818, and its supplements. By these, every suit of a civil nature, at law, including suits for penalties, where the matter in dispute does not exceed the value of one hundred dollars, is cognizable before a justice of the peace of any county, who holds a court of record, endowed with the usual powers of such courts. From this jurisdiction, however, are excepted, actions of replevin, slander, trespass for assault, battery, or imprisonment, and actions wherein the title to real estate may come in question. The territorial jurisdiction of the justice is coextensive with his county, and his process is confined to it, except in the case of the *subpœna ad testificandum*, which may run into other counties. The constables of the several townships of the county are the ministerial officers of the court, who execute its process, tested on the day it is issued, and signed and sealed, by the justice.

The initiatory process is summons or warrant. The first is required when the defendant is a freeholder, and resident of the county where issued, and in cases where defendant cannot be held to bail; and may be used on all occasions, at the election of plaintiff; the warrant may issue against persons not freeholders, or against freeholders about to abscond from the county. The summons is returnable in not less than five, nor more than fifteen days from its date; and must be served at least five days before the day given therein for appearance, personally, upon the defendant, or by a copy left at his dwelling. The warrant is returnable forthwith. Upon arrest the defendant either gives bond, with freehold surety, to the constable for his appearance at a stated day, not more than eight from the service, or is carried before the justice, where he enters into recognisance with like security, conditioned for his appearance, or is committed to prison to await the time of hearing, which must not be more than three days from the return of the warrant; or he is held by the constable, until the plaintiff be notified and have time to proceed to trial.

The amount of the sum demanded is endorsed upon the writ, with the costs, and may be paid to the constable in full discharge of the debt and arrest.

On the appearance of the parties, the trial is had, or the hearing is adjourned, by the justice himself, or on cause shown by either party, not longer than fifteen days: but if the defendant do not appear, judgment may be rendered by default; and by consent of parties may be entered, without process, for any sum within the jurisdiction of the justice.

After appearance of defendant, and plea entered, and before inquiry into the merits of the cause by the justice, either party may demand a trial by jury; upon which, where the sum claimed does not exceed sixteen dollars, six jurymen, and where over sixteen dollars, twelve jurymen may be summoned. The costs of the jury of twelve, when finding for the applicant, above five, and not exceeding twenty-five dollars, are paid, in part by him; but if finding for him, five dollars, or under, then the whole costs are paid by the applicant; the costs of the jury of six, finding in favour of the applicant, under five dollars, are wholly payable by him.

By consent, and at request of the parties, the justice may enter rules of reference of the matters in difference to such persons as shall be nominated by the parties.

Upon judgment rendered before the justice, no execution can issue against a female, when the debt is under two dollars. Where the debtor is a freeholder, and when sued by summons, he is to be taken as such, unless the presumption be disproved, or when a sufficient freeholder of the county shall join with him in confession of judgment to the adverse party, stay of execution may be had, where the judgment is over five, and under fifteen dollars, for one month; when over fifteen and under sixty dollars, for three months, and when over sixty dollars, for six months.

The execution continues in force for one year from the time it is issued; but may be renewed upon *scire facias*, and judgment thereon, and takes priority from the time of levy made, and the surplus proceeds of sale under the first execution are applicable to the satisfaction of others, in successive order. The levy is made on the goods and chattels of defendant; and if another claim property in the goods levied upon, the constable stays the sale for ten days, unless indemnified by plaintiff; during which, the claimant, on application to a justice, may have his rights tried by a jury of six men, and if the application be not made within that time, the claim is deemed abandoned. The verdict, if against the claimant, protects the constable in making sale of the goods. For want of goods whereon to levy, the body of the defendant is liable to imprisonment until the debt and costs be paid, or until delivered by due course of law: and where there are no personal effects an action may be brought in the Common Pleas, on the judgment before the justice, in order to reach the real estate.

From the judgment of the justice, on default, on absence or confession of defendant, or when the matter in dispute does not exceed three dollars in value, there is no appeal. In other cases, an appeal lies by either party to the Common Pleas to be holden next after rendition of judgment; the appellant giving bond, with surety, to the other party conditioned for the prosecution of his appeal. The justice determining the cause is excluded from sitting upon it in the appellate court.

The judgment of the justice may, also, be revised by the Supreme Court, by certiorari (but not by writ of error) issued within eighteen months from the rendition. Any justice is authorized, in cases in a Justice's Court, to take the deposition of infirm, sick, or going witnesses, and to issue commission for the examination of witnesses.

The justices (among whom are to be esteemed the mayor, recorder, and aldermen of any city, borough, or town corporate, within their respective territorial jurisdictions) are chosen by the legislature in joint meeting, for the term of five years, and may be reappointed for such terms, indefinitely, and dismissed upon impeachment by the assembly, and conviction by the council. Such justices are, by the act of 1794, conservators of the peace, and as such, are charged and empowered to cause the laws to be observed, and to apprehend and punish offenders as the laws may direct. They exercise also many ministerial duties, as notaries in certain cases; and act as substitutes for the coroner, &c. &c. As the Justices' Court is that which disposes of the major part of the disputes among the citizens, we have occupied more space in relation to it than we shall give to the courts of higher order.

The Court of Quarter Sessions, in each county, is composed of the justices of the county, or any three of them; and is a court of record, having cognisance of all indictable offences perpetrated in the county: and authority by its precepts to the sheriff, to summon grand and special juries, and to do all necessary things relative thereto, as directed by law; sending, however, all indictments found for treason, murder, manslaughter, sodomy, rape, polygamy, arson, burglary, robbery, forgery, perjury, and subornation of perjury, to be tried in the Supreme Court, or Court of Oyer and Terminer. To this court the several justices of the county send their recognisances for keeping the peace or good behaviour, and the examination of offenders, taken before them; and generally return to it the recognisances of witnesses and of bail in criminal cases. It has cognisance of cases of bastardy; may grant tavern licenses, the sums payable for which, not less than $10 nor more than $70, pertain to the county treasury; may recommend to the governor persons for license as pedlars; may hear appeals from the order of justices, between master and servant, and in pauper cases, and from conviction, by justices, under the acts for suppressing vice and immorality, &c.; and has, generally, the powers of a court of record, relative to the subjects of its jurisdiction.

The Common Pleas consist of judges appointed by the legislature, in joint meeting, who hold their offices for five years. The number in each county is unlimited, and varies from time to time. Any one of the judges may hold the court. They choose their own president for a year, and receive no salary or compensation, but certain bench fees, divided among them, rarely amounting to their expenses at the court. Their territorial jurisdiction is only coextensive with the county, but they may issue subpœnas for witnesses throughout the State. The court has unlimited original jurisdiction, at common law, in all personal actions where the freehold does not come in question, with some restriction as to costs, in cases cognisable before a justice. Its proceedings may be revised on writ of error to the Supreme Court.

The judges of the Court of Common Pleas, in the several counties, or any three of them, constitute the Orphans' Court; which is a court of record, and is holden four times a year, in the same week with the Courts of Quarter Sessions, and at such other times as the judges may deem proper. This court is empowered: to determine all controversies respecting the existence of wills, the fairness of inventories, the right of administration and guardianship, the allowance of the accounts of executors, administrators, guardians, or trustees, audited and stated by the surrogate; to award process to bring before them all persons interested, or witnesses, in any pending cause; or who, as executors, administrators, guardians, trustees, or otherwise, are accountable for any property belonging to an orphan, or person under age. And the ordinary, his register, and surrogates, are required to transmit into this court, upon application, copies of all bonds, inventories, accounts, &c., relating to estates of orphans, &c. Where insufficient surety has been taken on granting letters of administration, or guardianship, this court has power to require administrators or guardians to give further security; and upon refusal, or malfeasance in their trust, to dismiss them and substitute others: and where an executrix having minors of her own, or is concerned for other minors, or is like to marry without securing the minors' estates; or where an executor, guardian, or other trustee of minors' estates is like to prove insolvent, refuses or neglects to account for such estates, to order that he give security to those for whom he is concerned, by mortgage or bond, in such sum as the court may deem proper; conditioned for the performance of their respective trusts: and, where the surety in bond given by an administrator or guardian, alleges that such officer is wasting or mismanaging the estate, whereby the complainant is liable to damage, the court may compel such officer to render an account, and if the malfeasance be apparent, may, on pain of dismissal, compel him to give separate security to his surety for the faithful performance of duty: and where there are two or more acting executors, guardians, or administrators, the court may, from time to time, on the application of any one of them, and sufficient reason shown, order the executor, &c., to account with his coexecutor, &c., and compel him to give separate security to such executor, &c., and on refusal, to authorize such coexecutor, &c., to sue for the assets in the hands of the executors, &c., refusing.

The court has also authority, to make partition of the lands of an intestate, among his heirs, when any of them are under the age of twenty-one years; and also of the lands devised to two or more devisees, under such age, where the bounds of each devisee's share is unascertained; and to appoint commissioners for the admeasurement of dower. But where the lands of such intestate or devisor lie in two or more counties, the duty of partition devolves upon the surrogate general. The court may order sale of lands for the payment of debts when the personalty is exhausted, either upon application of the executor, administrator, or creditor; or the sale of lands of orphans, when necessary for their maintenance and education; and direct the fulfilment of contracts for the conveyance of real estate, made by the testator or intestate, in his life time: and may also compel creditors of the estates of decedents, to render their accounts, within a stated time, under penalty of being barred of their actions. And in case the estate prove insolvent, may direct distribution of proceeds among creditors; and where the debts are paid, may divide the balance among the representatives of decedent.

This court has jurisdiction, also, in the settlement of the accounts of assignees, under the assignment of a debtor for the benefit of creditors.

By the 8th article of the constitution the governor is *ex officio* ordinary, or surrogate general. One deputy or surrogate, in each county, is appointed by the legislature, for five years, whose power is confined within the same, and whose duty is—to take the depositions to wills, (ten days after death of testator) administrations, inventories, and administration bonds, in cases of intestacy, and issue thereon letters testamentary and of administration; but where doubts arise on the face of the will, or a caveat be put in against proving it, or disputes happen respecting the existence of a will, the fairness of an inventory, or the right of administration, he is to issue citations to all persons concerned, to appear at the next Orphans' Court, of the county, where the cause is determined in a summary way, subject to an appeal to the Prerogative Court, to which all other proceedings of the surrogate may, also, be carried directly by appeal: To record all wills and inventories proven before him, or the Orphans' Court, with the proofs; all letters of guardianship and letters testamentary by him granted, a copy of which, under his hand and seal, is evidence in any court of the State. He transmits to the register of the Prerogative Court, on the first Mondays of February, May, August, and November, annually, all wills and inventories proved by him, and a return of all letters of administration granted during the preceding three months, to be filed in the register's office. Files all administration and guardianship bonds, and other writings, required by law, in conducting the business of his office: Gives bond for the faithful performance of his duties, with sureties in the sum of two thousand dollars: Audits and states the accounts of executors and administrators, exhibited to him, and report the same to the Orphans' Court, giving at least two months' notice of his intention, in at least five of the most public places of the county, as near as may be, to the place of residence of the parties concerned. He is required to keep up in his office, at all times, in some conspicuous place, a true list of all fees lawfully demandable by him as surrogate, or as clerk of the Orphans' Court; and he is punishable for extortion by fine.

The jurisdiction of the ordinary or surrogate general extends only to the granting of probate of wills, letters of administration, letters of guardianship and the hearing and finally determining all disputes that may arise thereon. For the last purpose, he holds, at stated periods, a Prerogative Court, at the times and places for holding the Court of Chancery, where he hears, and finally determines, all causes that come before him, either directly or by appeal from any of the surrogates or from the Orphans' Court. Of this court the secretary of state is register, and is required to record the names of the testators of all wills he may receive, in alphabetical order, with the year in which they were proved, and to file such wills in his office, the wills of each year and county to be put by themselves; and in like manner to record the names of all intestates, and all inventories in manner aforesaid; and transcripts of any will or testament registered by him are receivable in evidence in all courts of the commonwealth.

Supreme and Circuit Courts.—The first consists of a chief justice and two associates, and holds, annually, at Trenton, four terms, commencing on the last Tuesday of February, the second of May, the first of September, and the second of November, by the chief justice or any one of the justices. Issues in this court, determinable by jury, are tried in the county where the lands in question lie, or the cause of action arises; unless upon motion upon behalf of the State, when the State is party, or where the amount in dispute is three thousand dollars, and either party order the trial at bar, which he may do, receiving only the costs of a Circuit Court if he do not recover that sum. Transitory actions, at the discretion of the court, are tried in the county in which the cause of action arose; and trials by foreign juries may be had where the court deem it proper. The court has original jurisdiction in all cases without regard to amount, but the party recovering not more than two hundred dollars, exclusive of costs, is not entitled to costs, unless the freehold, inheritance or title to real estate may come in question, or the suit be removed into this court by the defendant. But no suit may be removed from an inferior court by *habeas corpus* unless the value of the matter in controversy exceed two hundred dollars. It has power to appoint commissioners of bail, and to make rules for justifying such bail; to try treason committed out of the State; to review proceedings of justices in cases of landlords and tenants; to authorize the filing of an information in the nature of a *quo warranto;* to make partition of land and tenements between jointtenants and tenants in common; to appoint commissioners to ascertain county lines; to entertain prosecutions against vessels seized for engaging in the slave trade; to issue writs of dower, and admeasurement of dower, &c.; and writs of error in all cases to the Common Pleas, and to determine thereon, and also to determine causes removed hither by certiorari from the Orphans' Court: to appoint viewers of roads in certain cases, and to receive and determine on their report.

The chief justice, or one of his associates, twice in a year, holds a Circuit Court in every county except in that of Cape May, for the trial of issues which have been joined in, or brought into the Supreme Court, and which may be triable in the county: but the same judge does not hold the court twice in succession in the same county, unless on special occasions; and the clerks of the Common Pleas, in the several counties, are clerks of the Circuit Courts, and of the Courts of Oyer and Terminer and General Jail Delivery.

The Court of Oyer and Terminer is holden semi-annually, in each county, except that of Cape May, where it is holden annually only, by one of the justices of the Supreme Court, and the judges of the Courts of Common Pleas, or any three of them. It has cognisance of all crimes and offences within the county; and authority to deliver the jails of the prisoners therein. Its process runs into all the counties of the State, and it may direct that indictments found in it for offences indictable in the Quarter Sessions be sent to the sessions for trial.

The Supreme Court has original jurisdiction in criminal cases, and appellate jurisdiction from the Court of Oyer and Terminer, &c.

The governor is, by the constitution, chancellor of the State, and holds at Trenton, annually, four stated terms on the third Tuesday of January, the first in April, the second in July, and the second in October, and such stated terms as he may from time to time appoint. If the court be not opened at any of the said terms, the process returnable, and the suits pending therein, are continued, of course, until the court shall sit. This court is considered as always open for the granting of injunctions, writs of *ne exeat* to prevent the departure of defendants from the State, and other writs and process in vacation. The chancellor may call to his assistance the chief justice or other justice of the Supreme Court, or one or more masters of chancery, to advise with on the hearing of a cause, argument, or motion; or he may send any matter of law to the Supreme Court for its opinion; or if a matter of fact render the intervention of a jury necessary, he may send an issue for trial to such court. The masters in chancery are appointed by the chancellor, and the clerk of the court formerly named by him, is now, by virtue of the act of 14th February, 1831, appointed by the legislature in joint meeting, and continues in office five years.

In addition to the subjects of jurisdiction abovementioned, we may add here, that of foreclosure of mortgages as a prominent one. But the jurisdiction of this court is extensive and complex, embracing those many subjects on which the law cannot justly operate, by reason of its generality, and is not defined by the statutory law. A knowledge of it can be obtained, therefore, only from the thousand volumes of English and American law, and it must remain a mystery to all but the erudite student.

To the Supreme and Chancery Courts a reporter is attached, whose duty is, to report and publish their decisions.

The governor and council, seven of whom make a quorum, constitute the court of appeals in the last resort, in causes of law or equity removed from the Supreme

Court, or from Chancery, after final judgment; and possess the power of granting pardons to criminals after condemnation, in all cases of offence. This court holds annually at Trenton, two terms; one commencing on the third Tuesday in May, and the other on the first Tuesday of November; but, if the legislature be elsewhere in session at either of the said terms, the court is holden where the legislature may be; and the governor, with the advice of the council, or three of them, may hold another term, at Trenton, annually. The secretary of state is the clerk of the court. The members of council, sitting as judges, receive the same pay and mileage, as when sitting in council; and the clerk, as when acting as clerk of council. If a sufficient number of members do not attend the court, on the first day of term, it may adjourn from day to day, or until the next term, and all proceedings therein are continued, of course.

Compensation of Officers. The compensation of the chancellor, judges of the Common Pleas, Orphans' Courts, Quarter Sessions, and justices, and of the clerks, sheriffs, coroners and constables, engaged therein, secretary of state, attorney general and deputies, is by fees, respectively, allotted to them by law.

The chief, and other justices of the Supreme Court, are allowed a per diem compensation for attending the Circuit Courts, in addition to their annual salaries, and certain fees on law proceedings, and an allowance for travelling expenses, which may increase their compensation on the whole to $1,300 or $1,400 per annum. The statutes regulating fees are perpetual; but those which fix salaries are annual; and thus the chief officers of State are kept dependent upon the legislature. The act of 2d Nov. 1832, allotted for the then next succeeding year, to the governor, at the rate of $2,000; chief justice, $1,200; associate justice of Supreme Court, $1,100; treasurer, $1,000; law reporter and chancery reporter, each $200; attorney general, $80; quartermaster general, $100; adjutant general, $100. All of which are payable, on warrants signed by the governor or vice president. The salary ceases on the removal of the officer by death or otherwise.

The same act, allotted to the vice president of council and speaker of assembly, $3 50; and to every member of council and assembly, $3 per day; and $3 for every twenty miles of travel to and from the seat of government; to the secretary of council and clerk of assembly, each $3 50 per diem; and eight cents per sheet of 100 words, for recording minutes, and the like for copy for the printer, and per sheet to engrossing clerk. To the sergeant at arms and door keepers, $2 per day.

IV. Having, as fully as our limits will permit, pourtrayed the physical and political condition of the State, it remains, to complete our view, that we trace an outline of the provisions which exist for religious, moral, and intellectual improvement. The principal religious associations are the Presbyterian, Baptist, Methodist, Dutch Reformed, Quaker, and Catholic. Beside these, there are several other Christian denominations, such as Universalists, *Chris-ti-ans*, &c. &c., but the number of members pertaining to them, are inconsiderable. We have sought to give the condition of each from their records, and where such documents were not accessible, from other authentic sources.

The Synod of the Presbyterian Church of New Jersey, comprises the Presbyteries of Newark, Elizabethtown, New Brunswick, Newton, and Susquehanna. But we do not note the latter. The reader will observe, that in the following table, P. attached to a minister's name, denotes that he is pastor of some church, and P. attached to a church, that it has a pastor. W. C. stands for, *without charge;* S. S. for stated supply; O. S. for occasional supply; V. for vacant; *Presb.* for Presbytery; *Prest.* for president of some college; *Prof.* for professor in some college or theological seminary; *Miss.* for missionary; *Chap.* for chaplain to the navy or some public station; *Ch.* for church; *Cong.* for congregational. The expense of each church will not exceed $600.

MINISTERS AND LICENTIATES.	NAMES OF CHURCHES.	Com. added on examina.	Com. added on certific.	Total of Communicants.	Total of Baptisms.	Missionary Funds raised.	Funds for Commissioners.	Education Funds raised.	Contingent Fund of the Assembly.	POST-OFFICE ADDRESS.
Presbytery of Newark.										
Stephen Grover, P.	Caldwell, P.	34		291	19		$ 2 12	$ 5 28	2 12	Caldwell, N. J.
Asa Hillyer, D. D. P.	1st Church, Orange, P.			439	46		2 53	5 54	2 53	Orange, N. J.
Cyrus Gildersleeve, S. S.	South Orange, S. S.	13		41	13		1 13		1 13	Bloomfield, N. J.
Aaron Condit, W. C.										Hanover, N. J.
Noah Crane, W. C.										
Samuel Fisher, D. D. P.	Patterson, P.	28	7	294	28		5 50	12 00	5 50	Paterson, N. J.
Barnabas King, P.	Rockaway, P.	18	4	233	38		3 25		3 25	Rockaway, N. J.
Humphrey M. Perrine, W. C.										
John Ford, P.	Parsippany, P.	15		223	9			5 00		Parsippany, N. J.
Gideon N. Judd, P.	Bloomfield, P.	76	7	404	36		3 38	10 52	3 38	Bloomfield, N. J.
Edward Allen, Teacher.										Harmony Vale, N. J.
Enos A. Osborn, P.	Succasunna, P.	20	8	87	19			1 75		Succasunna, N. J.
Philip C. Hay, P.	2d Church, Newark, P.	21	17	370	23		4 60		4 60	
Jacob Tuttle, P.	New Milford, P.	2		114	6			4 56		
Peter Kanouse, P.	Wantage, P.			400			3 00	7 25	3 00	Deckertown, N. J.
Nathaniel Conkling, S. S.	Frankford, S. S.									Augusta, N. J.
Baxter Dickinson, P.	3d Church, Newark, P.	37	17	417	31		7 17	12 75	7 17	Newark, N. J.
William T. Hamilton, P.	1st Church, Newark, P.		22	414	18		9 78	30 01	9 78	Do.
George Pierson, P.	2d Church, Orange, P.	34	33	164	20		2 27	6 03	2 27	Orange, N. J.
Elias R. Fairchild, S. S.	North Hardiston, S. S.	4	3	78	7		1 02		1 02	Harmony Vale, N. J.
Sylvester Graham, W. C.										
Baker Johnson, P.	Caldwell, P.									
William Toby, S. S.	Hanover, S. S.	5	2	274	10		2 17	5 12	2 17	Hanover, N. J.
Thomas Smith, Miss.	Hardiston, V.	36	2	97						
Moses Jewell, W. C.	Newfoundland, S. S.			150	14					
Licentiates.	Stony Brook, V.			12						
Albert Pierson.	Berkshire Valley, V.			35			1 62		1 62	
Festus Hanks.	4th Church, Newark, S. S.			25						
Abraham De Witte.	Camptown, S. S.			9						
	Jersey City, V.									

	African Church, Newark, V.				12						
Totals, 28		24	350	122	4582	337		$49 55	$ 105 81	$49 52	
Presbytery of Elizabethtown.											
Stephen Thompson, P.	Connecticut Farms, P.		6	2	122	4		$ 1 50	$ 50 00	$ 1 50	Union, N. J.
John M'Dowell, D. D. P.	1st Ch. Elizabethtown, P.		38	4	576	51	$ 236 00	10 25	500 00	10 25	Elizabethtown, N. J.
Jacob Briant, W. C.	Mount Freedom, V.				70						Mount Freedom, N. J.
Alexander G. Fraser, P.	Chatham, P.		1	2	175	6		1 22	5 00	1 22	Bottle Hill, N. J.
David Magie, P.	2d Ch. Elizabethtown, P.		34	6	184	24	150 00	6 00	110 00	6 00	Elizabethtown, N. J.
Abraham Williamson, P.	Chester, P.				105			1 65	9 06	1 65	Chester, N. J.
William B. Barton, P.	Woodbridge, P.		24	3	166	14		2 50	12 00	2 50	Woodbridge, N. J.
James B. Hyndshaw, P.	New Providence, P.		13	3	127	12	12 00	2 00	3 50	2 00	New Providence, N. J.
Holloway W. Hunt, P.	2d Church, Woodbridge, P.		41	9	205	28	8 15	4 50	8 56	4 50	Metuchin, N. J.
Lewis Bond, P.	Plainfield, P.		34	10	98	33	19 13	1 25	2 25	1 25	Plainfield, N. J.
Daniel H. Johnson, P.	Mendham, P.				257			3 25	39 00	3 25	Mendham, N. J.
Alfred Chester, W. C.											Morristown, N. J.
Joseph M. Ogden, P.	Chatham Village, P.		20	6	103	27		2 31	4 00	2 31	Chatham Village, N. J.
Charles Hoover, P.	Morristown, P.				659						Morristown, N. J.
James M. Huntting, P.	Westfield, P.		7	1	268	21	150 00	3 91		3 91	Westfield, N. J.
Thomas L. Janeway, P.	Rahway, P.		46	14	199	36			10 00		Rahway, N. J.
Horace Doolittle, P.	Springfield, P.		1	2	204	10	47 00	1 42	2 20	1 42	Springfield, N. J.
Licentiates.	Perth Amboy, S. S.		7	2	37	1		1 50		1 50	
John T. Halsey.											
Arthur Granger.											
Isaac Todd.											
Augustus O. B. Ogden.											
Totals, 21		17	272	64	3555	267	$ 622 28	$43 26	$ 755 57	$43 26	
Presbytery of New Brunswick.											
Samuel Miller, D. D. Prof.											Princeton, N. J.
Arch. Alexander, D. D. Prof.											Do.
George S. Woodhull, P.	Princeton, P.		36	6	250	38		$ 7 50		$ 7 50	Do.
David Comfort, P.	Kingston, P.		51	1	189	48	$ 114 25	9 75		5 50	Kingston, N. J.
James Carnahan, D. D. Prest.											Princeton, N. J.
Isaac V. Brown, W. C.	Freehold, V.							4 50	$ 4 50		Lawrenceville, N. J
Eli F. Cooley, P.	1st Church, Trenton, P.		6	2	143	7	52 32	2 43		2 05	Trenton, N. J.

MINISTERS AND LICENTIATES.	NAMES OF CHURCHES.	Com. added on examina.	Com. added on certific.	Total of Communicants.	Total of Baptisms.	Missionary Funds raised.	Funds for Commissioners.	Education Funds raised.	Contingent Fund of the Assembly.	POST-OFFICE ADDRESS.
Presbytery of New Brunswick.										
Symmes C. Henry, P.	Cranbury, P.	8	1	403	23	$ 27 56	$ 5 00	$ 15 00	$ 5 00	Cranbury, N. J.
Ravaud K. Rodgers, P.	Boundbrook, P.	42	7	272	27	100 00	5 00	50 00	5 40	Boundbrook, N. J.
Henry Perkins, P.	Allentown & Nottingham, P.	12	3	175	11	40 75	5 00	18 00		Allentown, N. J.
Peter O. Studdiford, P.	Solebury, P.	1		81	3	5 00	2 00		2 00	Lambertsville, N. J.
	Lambertsville, P.	5	2	53	2	5 00	2 00	37 00	2 00	
Charles Hodge, Prof.										Princeton, N. J.
Charles S. Stewart, Chap.										
Joseph H. Jones, P.	New Brunswick, P.	34	10	260	30	308 40	12 31	40 00	12 31	New Brunswick, N. J.
Jared D. Fyler, W. C.										
Benjamin Ogden, P.	Pennington, P.			202		20 63		3 00		Pennington, N. J.
William H. Woodhull, P.	2d Ch. Upper Freehold, P.									Hightstown, N. J.
James W. Alexander, P.	Trenton City, P.	19	6	298	17	175 00	5 00	30 00		Trenton, N. J.
Clifford S. Armes, S. S.	Middletown Point, S. S.	10		50	14	10 00				Middletown Point, N. J.
Peter J. Gulick, Miss.										
John Maclean, Vice-President.										Princeton, N. J.
Robert Baird, Agent.										Philadelphia, Pa.
	Dutch Neck, V.									
Henry Axtell, P.	Lawrence, P.	29	4	140	19	8 00	4 00	11 86		Lawrenceville, N. J.
James W. Woodward, S. S.	Shrewsbury, S. S.	6	2	44	7	45 79		18 85		Shrewsbury, N. J.
Albert B. Dod, Prof.										Princeton, N. J.
Licentiates.										
	1st Church, Howell, V.									
Theodore Gallaudette.										
Alexander N. Cunningham.										
James W. Blythe.										
John S. Rice.										
Sidney S. M'Roberts.										
Thomas Martin.										
Rezeau Brown.										
John B. Pinney.										
Sloan M'Intire.										
William A. Holiday.										

George B. Bishop.												
James Bucknall.												
Totals, 37		19	259	44	2560	246	$ 912 70	$64 49	$ 228 21	$42 21		
Presbytery of Newton.												
Holloway W. Hunt, Sr. P.	Bethlehem, P. and		6	2	133	14						Perryville, N. J.
	Alexandria, P.		2		79	12	$ 2 50	$ 1 50				
William B. Sloan, P.	Greenwich, P.		53	1	192	33	34 10					Bloomsbury, N. J.
Joseph Campbell, P.	Hacketstown, P.				311							Hacketstown, N. J.
Jacob Kirkpatrick, P.	Amwell United 1st, P.		52	1	132	30						Ringoes, N. J.
	Amwell 2d, P.		5		112	8						
Joseph L. Shafer, P.	Newton, P.		75	4	289	49	23 11	5 50	$ 17 50			Newton, N. J.
Jacob R. Castner, P.	Mansfield, P.		19	1	166	24		3 00		$ 3 67		Asbury, N. J.
John F. Clark, P.	Flemington, P.		2		117	6	25 00	2 00	5 00	5 00		Flemington, N. J.
	Amwell 1st, P.		9		68		25 00	3 00	5 00	4 00		
Jehiel Talmage, P.	Knowlton, P.		11	2	109	13	1 75					Centreville, N. J.
John C. Vandervoort, P.	Baskingridge, P.				432							Baskingridge, N. J.
Benjamin I. Lowe, P.	Hardwick, P.				120			2 00	1 58			Johnsonborough, N. J.
	Marksborough, P.				65							
William W. Blauvelt, P.	Lamington, P.		33	2	209	7		2 00	2 00	1 50		Germantown, N. J.
Mantius S. Hutton, P.	German Valley, P.		9	1	74	8	17 75	1 52				Washington, N. J.
	Fox Hill, P.		1		30	17						
Isaac N. Candee, S. S.	Oxford, W. S.		36	10	150	27	96.25	5 00	5 00	11 00		Belvidere, N. J.
James G. Force, Miss.	Pleasant Grove, V.											Schooley's Mount. N. J.
	Harmony.											
Licentiates.	Lower Mount Bethel, V.											
James Wyckoff, Miss.	Scott's Mountain, V.		11	1	30	12						Clinton, N. J.
George M'Lin, S. S.	Clinton, S. S.											
	Kingwood.											
	Stillwater.											
Totals, 16		25	322	25	2818	260	$ 225 46	$25 02	$ 36 08	$25 17		

The Baptists in New Jersey have sixty-one churches, whose location and condition, in some measure, appears from the following table. Their general affairs are directed by a state convention, which assembles, annually, on the first Wednesday of November, at such place as may be fixed at the prior meeting. It maintains six missionaries, and its funds, in 1832, amounted to $1143 74. The cost of maintaining each church, including the funds raised for all kinds of ecclesiastical purposes, is estimated at $300, making in the whole, $18,300.

STATISTICAL TABLES OF ASSOCIATIONS AND CHURCHES.

NEW JERSEY ASSOCIATION.—"There is a healthful action in this body. Sabbath schools, tracts, temperance and missionary operations, are encouraged to a very laudible extent by the churches; and in many of them seasons of refreshing have been enjoyed during the year past. There is an efficient body of ministers belonging to the association, most of them in the prime of manhood."

CHURCHES.	MINISTERS.	POST OFFICES.	Bap.	Total	Consti.
Cohansey, -	H. Smalley, *W. Sheppard*, -	Roadstown, -	55	188	1900
Cape May, -	Samuel Smith, - - -	Cape May, -	7	80	1712
Salem, - -	Charles J. Hopkins, - -	Salem, - -	5	141	1755
Dividing Creek,	Thomas Brooks, - - -	Dividing Creek,	5	55	1762
Tuckahoe, -	William Clark, - - -	Tuckahoe, -		20	
Pemberton, -	Clarence W. Mulford, - -	Pemberton, -	28	170	1764
Pittsgrove, -	William Bacon, - - -	Pittsgrove, -	4	34	1771
Upper Freehold,	James M. Challiss, - -	Imlaytown, -	16	196	1766
Manahawkin, -	C. C. Park, - - - -	Manahawkin,	5	25	1770
Jacobstown, -	—*Ezekiel Sexton*, - -	New Egypt, -	6	62	1785
West Creek,	— - - - - - -	- -	4	33	1792
Burlington, -	—G. Allen, P. Powell, J. Boozer,	Burlington, -	1	77	1801
Mount Holly, -	J. Sheppard, J. Maylin, - J. E. Welsh, *E. W. Dickerson*,	Mount Holly,	7	92	1801
Evesham, -	— - - - - - -	Evesham, -	12	58	1803
Trenton and Lamberton, -	Morgan J. Rhees, - -	Trenton, - -	20	159	1805
Williamsburg,	— - - - - - -	Princeton, -	2	38	1805
Port Elizabeth,	— - - - - - -	Millville, - -	2	11	1805
Haddonfield, -	John Sisty, *S. Hervey*, -	Haddonfield,	2	54	1818
Canton, - -	E. M. Barker; J. P. Thompson,	Canton, - -	12	64	1811
Bordentown, -	— - - - - - -	Bordentown,		36	1821
Woodstown, -	— - - - - - -	- - -	11	43	1821
2d Cohansey,	J. C. Harrison, - - -	Bridgetown,	5	74	
Allowaystown,	— - - - - - -	Allowaystown,	3	50	1830
2d Cape May, -	Ambrose Garrett, - -	Cape May, -		42	1828
Churches 24.	Ministers 24.	Totals	213	1802	

NEW YORK ASSOCIATION.

CHURCHES.	MINISTERS.	CLERKS.	POST OFFICES.	Bapt.	Total	Consti.
Middletown, -	— - - -	- -	Middletown, -	14	132	1688
Piscataway, -	— - - -	- -	New Brunswick,	18	129	1689
Scotch Plains,	John Rogers, *E. Frost*, - -	- -	Scotch Plains,	18	126	1747
Morristown, -	P. C. Broome,	- -	Morristown, -	1	39	1752
Mount Bethel,	M. R. Cox, -	- -	- -	22	83	1767
Lyon's Farms,	P. Sparks, - J. Wilcox, -	- -	- -	14	58	1769
Northfield, -	A. Elliott, -	- -	- -	2	72	1785
Samptown, -	L. Lathrop, -	- -	- -	30	133	1792
Newark, - -	Daniel Dodge,	- -	Newark, -	8	120	1801
Randolph, -	—M. Quin, sup.	- -	- -		20	1802
New Brunswick,	G. S. Webb, -	P. P. Runyon,	New Brunswick,	29	111	1816
Perth Amboy,	Jacob Sloper,	- -	- -	1	35	1818
Plainfield, -	D. T. Hill, -	D. Dunn, -	Plainfield, -	24	113	1818
Paterson, -	D. D. Lewis, -	- -	Paterson, -	1	48	1825
Churches 15.	Ministers 14.		Totals	190	1319	

WARWICK ASSOCIATION.

CHURCHES.	MINISTERS.	CLERKS.	POST OFFICES.	Bap.	Total	Consti.
1st Wantage,	Tim. Jackson,	H. Martin, -	Deckertown,		245	1756
2d Wantage,	A. Harding, -	Israel Dillison,	- -		39	1797
Newfoundland,	— - -	I. Dean, - -	Newfoundland,	1	27	
Hardiston, -	Henry Ball, -	T. Beardsley,	- -	4	63	
1st Newton, -	T. Teasdale, -	J. B. Maxwell,	Newton, - -	23	50	
Hamburg, -	John Teasdale,	I. H. Wood,	Hamburg, -	11	88	
Churches 6.	Ministers 4.		Totals	39	512	

CENTRAL ASSOCIATION.

CHURCHES.	MINISTERS.	POST OFFICES.	Bap.	Total	Consti.
1st Hopewell, -	John Boggs, - -	Hopewell, -	7	172	1715
Hightstown, -	John Seger, - -	Hightstown, -	5	220	1745
Amwell, - -	C. Bartolett, Thos. Burrass, Wm. Pollard, *E. Burrass*,	- -	23	164	1798
2d Hopewell, -	C. Suydam, - -	- -	1	48	1803
Squan, - -	— - - - -	Manasquam, -		40	
Nottingham Square,	— - - - -	Trenton, - -		115	
Sandy Ridge, -	Joseph Wright, -	- -	7	79	
Lambertsville, -	D. B. Stout, - -	Lambertsville, -	4	27	
Oxford, - -	— - - - -	- -	18	30	1831
Washington, -	J. C. Goble, - -	South River, -	27	129	
Churches 10.	Ministers 10.	Totals	92	1024	

HUDSON RIVER ASSOCIATION.

2d Newark, -	P. L. Platt, - -	Newark, - -	15	33	1831

PHILADELPHIA ASSOCIATION.

Kingwood, -	Wm. Curtis, *A. Williamson*, *W. R. Robinson*, -	Kingwood, -	7	198	1742

CENTRAL UNION ASSOCIATION.

Camden, - -	—A. Smith, C. Sexton,	Camden, -		33	1818

UNASSOCIATED CHURCHES.

Schooly's Mountain,	—Michael Quin, -	Schooly's Mountain,	4	14	1832
Hackensack, -	Henry Tonkin, - -	Hackensack, -		8	1832

SUMMARY VIEW.

ASSOCIATIONS.	Chs.	Va. Ch.	Or. Min.	Lic's.	Bapt'd.	Total.	Consti.	MEETINGS IN 1833.
New Jersey, -	24	9	21	3	213	1802	1811	Upper Freehold, Sept. 24.
Central, - -	10	3	9	1	92	1024		Washington, Oct. 16.
New York, -	15	3	13	1	190	1319	1791	1st. Ch. N. Y. city, May 28.
Warwick, - -	6	1	4		39	512	1791	Orange, N. Y. June 11.
Hudson River,	1		1		15	33	1815	Oliver Street Church, June 19.
Philadelphia, -	1		1	2	7	198	1707	Spruce Street Church, Oct. 1.
Central Union,	1		2			33	1832	Second Street Church, May 28.
Unassociated chs.	3	1	2		4	60		
Totals	61	17	53	7	560	3981		

The clergymen report, that during the years 1831 and 1832, 1000 persons have been baptized in the State, and that a spirit of enlightened liberality is diffusing itself among the churches.

In addition to what is done for the objects of the convention, from two to three hundred dollars are annually raised for foreign missions.

The Methodist Episcopal Church, in New Jersey, is divided into three districts, each under the charge of a presiding elder, always a minister, appointed by the bishop, and changed at least once in four years. Each district is divided into circuits and stations; thus, the district of West Jersey, comprehending Burlington county, and the country south thereof, contains eight circuits and three stations, and supernumeraries included, twenty-three ministers; the district of East Jersey, including the country as far north as Flemington and Belleville, four circuits and ten stations, and twenty-three ministers; and Asbury district, comprehending the remainder of the State, eight circuits, three stations, and eighteen ministers.

Circuits are formed of territories of greater or less dimensions, including several churches, under the charge of one pastor, aided, commonly, by one or more assistants, who serve the churches in rotation. Stations consist, generally, of one church, but occasionally, of more, confided to the care of one pastor, who, sometimes, where there are more churches than one, has an assistant. The circuits and stations depend, in their government, upon the annual conference of Philadelphia, and upon the quarterly conferences held in them respectively. Disputes among the members of any church, may be considered, in the first instance, by a committee of their church, from whose decision an appeal lies to the quarterly conference, composed of the pastor, local preachers, exhorters, stewards, and class leaders, at whose head is the presiding elder of the district; and its determination is conclusive, unless one of the parties be a minister; in such case, he may appeal to the annual conference; and if he be a travelling minister, from the annual, to the general, conference.

The whole number of clergymen of this denomination, in the State, is sixty-four; the cost of whose maintenance, including donations of every character, together with the expenses of maintaining the churches, is estimated at about $412 each, per annum; which, distributed among the whole number of members, (15,467,) gives an average charge of $1 77, annually, upon each member. And the annual cost of establishing and repairing churches, is stated at twenty-five cents, each member; so that the whole average annual charge, for religious instruction, upon each member of the Methodist Church, may be set down at about two dollars.

The following table shows the circuits and stations of the several districts, with the number of communicants and clergymen, in each, for the year 1832.

WEST JERSEY DISTRICT.	Mem's.	Min's.
Burlington, - -	424	2
Pemberton, - -	878	4
Tuckerton, - -	848	2
Bargaintown, -	989	2
Cumberland, -	894	2
Bridgeton, - -	357	1
Gloucester, - -	955	2
Salem, - - -	1160	5
Camden, - -	713	2
Presiding Elder, -	-	1
	7218	23

EAST JERSEY DISTRICT.	Mem's.	Min's.
New Brunswick and Somerville,	268	2
Freehold, - -	678	4
Trenton, - -	360	1
Crosswicks, - -	539	2
Pennington, - -	156	1
Plainfield, - -	32	1
Rahway, - -	152	1
Elizabethtown, -	136	1
Woodbridge, -	75	1
Bloomfield and Orange,	450	2
Belleville, - -	160	1
Newark, - -	779	2
Somerset Mission, -	106	4
Bergen Neck, do. -	33	1
Presiding Elder, -	-	1
	3924	23

ASBURY DISTRICT.	Mem's.	Min's.
Kingswood, - -	170	1
Asbury, - -	698	2
Belvidere and Warrent.	167	4
Newton and Hamburg,	937	4
Milford, - -	50	
Haverstraw, - -	210	1
Paterson, - -	420	1
Essex, - -	445	2
Morristown, - -	178	1
New Providence, -	150	1
	4425	18
	3924	23
	7218	23
	15,567	64

The condition of the Episcopalian Church is drawn from the report of the general convention of the Protestant Episcopal Church, in the United States of America, held in the city of New York, October 1832, and from the report of the 50th annual convention of the church in the diocese of New Jersey, held at Camden in May 1833. From these it appears that during the year, ending October 1832, there were three persons admitted to the order of the priesthood, and one to that of deacon: That there have been eleven institutions within the last three years; that eight clergymen have been received in the diocese, and there were therein eighteen resident, all presbyters: That the number of Episcopal families is 340; of communicants, 900; baptisms reported, 517; persons confirmed,168; candidates for the ministry, 2; and congregations, 33; located and supplied, as mentioned in the following list.

NAME.	PLACE.	INCUMBENTS.
Christ,	New Brunswick,	J. Croes.
St. Matthew's,	Jersey City,	E. D. Barry, D. D.
St. Paul's,	Paterson,	R. Williston, Minister.
Trinity,	Newark,	M. H. Henderson.
Christ Chapel,	Belleville,	(Vacant.)
St. John's,	Elizabethtown,	B. G. Noble.
St. Mark's,	Orange,	B. Holmes.
St. Peter's,	Morristown,	H. R. Peters.
Christ,	Newton,	C. Dunn.
St. Luke's,	Hope,	P. L. Jaques, dea. M'y.
St. James's,	Knowlton,	P. L. Jaques, dea. M's.
St John's,	Johnsonsburgh,	P. L. Jaques, dea. M'y.
St. Peter's,	Spotswood,	J. M. Ward.
St. Peter's,	Freehold,	J. M. Ward, Minister.
Christ,	Shrewsbury,	H. Finch.
Christ,	Middletown,	H. Finch.
St. Peter's,	Perth Amboy,	J. Chapman
St. James's,	Piscataway,	W. Douglass, Minister.
Trinity,	Woodbridge,	W. Douglass, Missionary.
St. Thomas's,	Alexandria,	W. Douglass, Missionary.
St. Michael's,	Trenton,	F. Beasley, D. D.
Trinity,	Princeton,	(Just organized.)
St. Mary's,	Burlington,	C. H. Wharton, D. D.
St. Andrew's,	Mount Holly,	G. Y. Morehouse.
St. Mary's,	Colestown,	(Vacant.)
St. Paul's,	Camden,	(Vacant.)
St. Peter's,	Berkeley,	(Vacant.)
Trinity,	Swedesborough,	N. Nash, Rector Elect.
St. Thomas's,	Glassborough,	(Vacant.)
St. John's,	Chew's Landing,	(Vacant.)
St. Stephen's,	Mullica Hill,	(Vacant.)
St. John's,	Salem,	H. M. Mason.
St. George's,	Penn's Neck,	H. M. Mason.

It also appears, that the Sunday schools flourish, and are gradually connecting themselves with the diocesan Sunday school society; that the missionary fund amounts to $4,500, which contributes to aid, most materially, in reviving and supporting old and decayed, as well as new congregations; the episcopal fund, to $2,049.33; that the fund for the relief of widows and children of deceased clergymen, has of late years rapidly increased, and now amounts to almost $15,000; and that the Episcopal Society for the promotion of Christian Knowledge and Piety pursues the even and noiseless tenor of its way, doing good by the distribution of Bibles, prayer books, tracts, and aiding the missionary fund, and candidates for orders. Its permanent fund exceeds $1,500. Six hundred dollars per annum is estimated as the annual expense of each church.

The want of full parochial reports renders it impracticable to give an accurate statement of the actual condition of the respective churches.

The Reformed Dutch Church of New Jersey consists of three classes, attached to the particular synod of New York, the condition of which is apparent from the annexed tables. We are unable to furnish a detailed account of the cost to the members of maintaining this church, but we are instructed, from good authority, that $650 will amply cover all the expenses of each church. There are 36 churches, and consequently the whole charge, about $23,400, annually, including theological and missionary contributions.

CLASSIS OF NEW BRUNSWICK.

CHURCHES.	PASTORS.	Census.		Communicants.							Bapt.	
		Number of Families.	Total of the Congregation.	In communion per last Report.	Rc'd. On Certificate.	Rc'd. On Confession.	Dismissed.	Suspended.	Died.	Total in Communion.	Infants.	Adults.
New Brunswick,	Samuel B. Howe,				20	24	5		2	345	25	3
Six Mile Run,	Vacant,											
Hillsborough,	J. L. Zabriskie,	130		279	8	14	9		8	284	26	4
Raritan,	A. Messler,	310	1700		7	12	8		11	355	16	
Bedminster,	Isaac M. Fisher,											
North Branch,	A. D. Wilson,											
Rockaway,	Jacob I. Shultz,	78	508	101		9	1		1	108	17	2
Lebanon,	Do.	110	600	100	1	3	3		1	100	12	1
Spotswood,	Henry L. Rice,	208	1160			15	1			115	21	5
Freehold,	S. A. Van Vranken,											
Middletown,	J. T. Beekman,	110	600	125		17				142	8	12
Minisink,	C. C. Eltinge,					90	2	2	2	190	11	25
Mahakkamak,	Do.				1	29	2	3		130	4	5
Walpack,	Vacant,											

CLASSIS OF BERGEN.

Bergen,	B. C. Taylor,	185	1050	195	2	12	1		10	198	24	2
Hackensack,	J. V. C. Romeyn,	90		98								
E. Neighbourhood,*	Philip Duryea,	100			12	16	1	1	8	71	32	
Belville,	Gustavus Abeel,	120		118	9	21	1		2	145	30	
Fairfield,	Henry A. Raymond,	170	1000	133		2	1		2	132	18	
Pompton Plains,	James R. Talmage,	170	1060	108		6				114	25	
Pompton,	Isaac S. Demund,	130		100	2	11	1	1		111	8	1
Montville,	Frederic F. Cornell,	100	500	50	3	17			1	70	10	1
Ponds,	Z. H. Kuypers,	65	353	46		16	1			65	19	
Preakness,	Do.	55	251	48						53	10	
Wyckoff,	Do.	78	457	62						67	15	
Bergen Neck,	Ira C. Boice,	64	384	35	1	5			2	39	7	
Jersey City,	Vacant,	56	254	63	2	1	2		3	61	9	
Schraalenberg,	Vacant,	166		157								
Stonehouse Plains,	Vacant,											

Minister without charge—Rev. John Duryea.

* N. B. The Report from the Church at English Neighbourhood is for four years.

CLASSIS OF PARAMUS.

Tappan,	N. Lansing,	161	617	150	1	13	4		5	155	34	3
Clarkstown,	Alex. H. Warner,	159	714		3	3			5	160	11	
Saddle river and Pasgack	Stephen Goetchius,	147	611	248	1	5	3	2	3	250	16	
	Do.	72	225	51						51	8	
Paramus & 1st Ref. D. C. of Totowa,	W. Eltinge,	170	1065	286		10		3	2	291	25	
	Do.	130	765	112		9				121	23	2
Warwick,	J. I. Christie,				2	5	7		1		3	1
2d Ref. D.C. Totowa,	Isaac D. Cole,	100	450	11	5	4				90	23	
Aquackinunck,	Wm. R. Bogardus,	200	1068	119	3	42			2	160	29	2
West New-Hampstead & Ramapo,	J. Wynkoop,											
	Do.											

The Quakers, or Society of Friends, as is well known, have been divided into two great parts, each claiming to hold the ancient doctrines of the church. As these parts do not concur in the account of their former or present condition, we have deemed it proper to publish the statement of each. Both parties claim the venerated name of "Friends," but we are compelled to distinguish them by the titles they give to each other. The first of the following statements is given by the *Hicksite*, and the second by the *Orthodox* party.

1st. "Friends' meetings in New Jersey, and members.—Burlington quarterly meeting, before the division, was composed of five monthly meetings, eighteen meetings for worship, and 1849 members.

Burlington quarterly meeting of Friends, since the division, is composed of four monthly meetings, fourteen meetings for worship, and 1049 members.

And that of the Orthodox Friends, four monthly meetings, thirteen meetings for worship, and 800 members.

Haddonfield quarterly meeting, before the division, was composed of five monthly meetings, ten meetings for worship, 1686 members.—Haddonfield quarterly meetings of Friends, since the division, is composed of four monthly meetings, six meetings for worship, 859 members. That of the Orthodox Friends consists of five monthly meetings, nine meetings for worship, and 827 members.

Salem quarterly meeting, before the division, was composed of five monthly meetings, ten meetings for worship, 1536 members.—Salem quarterly meeting of Friends, since the division, is composed of five monthly meetings, ten meetings for worship, and 1238 members. And that of the Orthodox Friends, three monthly meetings, four meetings for worship, and 298 members.

Shrewsbury quarterly meeting, before the division, was composed of four monthly meetings, eight meetings for worship, and 925 members.—Shrewsbury quarterly meeting of Friends, since the division, is composed of four monthly meetings, eight meetings for worship, and 750 members. And that of the Orthodox Friends, of two monthly meetings, three meetings for worship, and 175 members. About 6000 members, in New Jersey, in all."

2d. "The following statement of the number of members in the Society of Friends previous to the late division, and also of the two portions into which it has been separated, is made out from authentic sources, and a careful examination of the state of the respective meetings.

At the time of the separation, there were in the state of New Jersey four quarterly meetings, nineteen monthly meetings, and forty-six meetings for divine worship. Friends now hold five quarterly meetings, fourteen monthly meetings, and twenty-nine meetings for divine worship.

The quarterly meetings are as follow:—Burlington quarterly consisted, before the separation, of five monthly meetings, and eighteen meetings for worship, comprising two thousand one hundred and twenty-five members. Since the separation, it has four monthly meetings, twelve meetings for worship, and one thousand one hundred and eighty-eight members. The Hicksites, in this quarter, are nine hundred and thirty-seven in number, and hold four monthly meetings.

Haddonfield quarterly meeting, both before and since the separation, consisted of five monthly meetings, and ten meetings for worship, embracing one thousand seven hundred and eighty-eight members, of whom six hundred and forty-four went with the Hicksites, and forty-seven remained undivided, leaving one thousand and ninety-seven Friends. The Hicksites, in this quarter, hold four monthly meetings.

Salem quarterly meeting, before the division, had five monthly meetings, and ten meetings for worship, including one thousand six hundred and three members. Since the separation, Friends hold four meetings for worship, and three monthly meetings, embracing four hundred and fifty-four members. The Hicksites have one thousand one hundred and forty-five members, and hold five monthly meetings.

Shrewsbury and Rahway quarterly meeting, at the time of the separation, was composed of four monthly meetings, eight meetings for worship, and eight hundred and eighty-eight members. Friends now hold two monthly meetings, and three meetings for worship, including two hundred and thirty-three members. The Hicksites, in this quarter, are six hundred and fourteen in number, and hold four monthly meetings. There were forty-one members who did not side with either party."

The whole number of Friends in New Jersey is, - - - - - - - - -	2,972
Hicksites, - - - - - - - - - - - - - -	3,344
Neutrals, - - - - - - - - - - - - - -	81
Total, -	6,404

See Foster's Report, vol. II. p. p. 388 and 395.

Of the forty-five meeting houses in which meetings of Friends were held previous to the separation, there are now *five* in the exclusive possession of Friends—*fifteen* which are occupied by Friends and Hicksites, jointly,—and *twenty-five* in the exclusive possession of the Hicksites."

RECAPITULATION.

Thus it appears that the Presbyterians have	85	churches.
Baptists, - - -	61	do.
Methodists, - -	64	ministers.
Episcopalians, -	33	churches.
Dutch Reformed,	36	do.
Quakers, - - -	67	meetings.
Other denominations, conjectural,	10	
Total number, - - - - - - - -	356	

In this summary, we have given, we believe correctly, the number of churches of each denomination, save that of the Methodist, which has many more churches than ministers; but we have not been able to ascertain the number of churches, although we have taken much pains for that purpose. In the circuits, there are commonly not less than two churches or congregations to a minister; but in such cases the congregations consist of few members. Many of the churches have no pastors. The Quakers, it is well known, have none; and of the 289 churches which remain in the list after deducting their meeting houses, we consider that 39 may continue constantly vacant. We have then 250 churches whose maintenance may be deemed a steady charge upon the people.

In the maintenance of the churches, we include all the expenditures for religious purposes, comprehending the sums conventionally paid to the pastors, the donations of every kind, made directly to them or for their use, the amount expended in the erection and repair of churches, and in aids to bible missionary and tract societies; and we, upon consultation with distinguished clergymen of various denominations, set down as an average expenditure for each church, the sum of $480 per annum, which, multiplied by 250 churches, make the actual charge of $120,000, upon the state for all the expenses of religion, and which we consider sufficiently liberal to cover the expenses of the Society of Friends for the like purpose. The Quakers, have no salaried clergy; and the expenses of their association consist of the very small sums requisite to keep their meeting houses and grave yards inrepair, and the contributions for the support and education of their poor members. Demands of this kind are rare and occasional, only; and the interest of funds vested for schools, by Friends, has been employed in the education of the poor children of other denominations.

In addition to the 356 churches of all denominations, which the State contains, the inhabitants have exemplified their disposition to sustain and improve their moral condition, by the establishment of bible societies, missionary societies, Sunday school unions, and temperance societies. In every county there are bible societies, in most, considerable sums are collected for the missionary cause, and almost every thickly settled neighbourhood has its Sunday school. Temperance societies, in many districts, have effectually bruised the head of the *worm of the still.*

The cultivation of literature and science has, until of late years, been too little regarded; but not less, than in the adjacent and more wealthy states. Yet in the higher departments the "College of New Jersey," at Princeton, has for more than eighty years maintained a reputation unsurpassed in the Union; Rutger's College, at New Brunswick, has, for several years, been in successful operation; academies have been established in most of the county towns and large villages; and common schools are every where seen in populous districts. The "School Fund," which has lately been established, will rapidly increase, and will, at no distant day, furnish means to teach the rudiments of science to the whole population. We proceed to give a more particular notice of the colleges and the school fund.

The "College of New Jersey" was first incorporated in the year 1746, and in 1748 obtained, through the aid of Governor Belcher, an ample and liberal charter from George II., which, after the revolution, was confirmed by the legislature of this State. The institution was located, first, at Elizabethtown, under the direction of the Rev. Jonathan Dickenson. Upon his death, in 1748, it was removed to Newark, and the Rev. Aaron Burr became its president. In the year 1756, it was permanently established at Princeton, whither president Burr removed with his pupils, and where for nearly eighty years it has maintained a high and unvarying reputation, as a seat of literature and science; and, with occasional diminution of numbers, has continued to command a large share of public confidence and patronage.

The present number of under graduates (1833) is one hundred and forty-four. The faculty consists of a president, seven professors, and three tutors.

Provision is made for imparting instruction in the Greek, Latin, French, Spanish, German, Italian, and English languages; in mathematics, (the study of which is pursued to an extent, not excelled by any college in the country,) in natural philosophy, in chemistry, and the various branches of natural history; in belles lettres, in mental and moral philosophy, in logic, political economy, natural theology, the evidences of christianity, and the exposition of the holy scriptures; in anatomy and physiology, in architecture, and civil engineering. The libraries of the college, and two literary societies connected with it, contain about twelve thousand volumes. The college has a very valuable philosophical and chemical apparatus, a museum of natural history, a small anatomical museum, and a mineralogical cabinet.

The principal edifice, called Nassau Hall, is one hundred and seventy-six feet long, fifty wide, and four stories high, and is used chiefly for the lodging of students: another building, erected for the same purpose in 1833, is one hundred and twelve feet in length, and four stories high. There are two other buildings, each sixty-six feet in length, by thirty-six in breadth, and three stories high. One of them contains the library and recitation rooms; the other the refectory, museum, and chemical laboratory.

There are also, at Princeton, several other literary institutions, (see Princeton,) among which, the theological seminary claims the first place.

This school was founded by the General Assembly of the Presbyterian Church of the United States, and is under its control and patronage. The plan of the institution was formed in 1811, and carried into effect in May, 1812, by the appointment of trustees, and a professor of didactic and polemical theology. The latter was inaugurated, and entered upon his duties, with three students only, on the 12th August following. In May, of 1813, a professor of ecclesiastical history was named, and ten years afterwards, the plan was completed by the nomination of a professor of oriental and biblical literature.

The edifice for the use of the seminary, commenced in 1813 and rendered habitable in the autumn of 1817, is of stone, one hundred and fifty feet long, fifty wide, and four stories high, including the basement; and is regarded as a model of economical, neat, and tasteful architecture. Besides the apartments for the library, recitations, refectory, and the steward, there are accommodations for eighty students.

This institution is conducted on very liberal principles; for, though founded and supported by the Presbyterian church, and primarily intended to promote the training of a pious and learned ministry for that church, students of all Christian denominations are admitted into a full participation of its benefits, upon equal terms. It is wholly unconnected with the college, but enjoys, by contract, the free use of the college library.

The funds of the institution, though considerable, are yet inadequate to the full support of its officers. The endowment of four professorships has been commenced, but none is fully completed. Twenty-three scholarships have been founded, by as many benevolent individuals, and maintain that number of poor and pious youth, in a course of theological study. There are, here, two public libraries; one called after the Rev. Ashbel Green, D. D. L. L. D., one of the most ardent and liberal of its contributors; and the other presented by the synod of the Associate Reformed Church, and named the "Mason Library," in honour of the Rev. John M. Mason, D. D. by whose exertions, chiefly, it was collected. The former contains six, and the latter four thousand volumes.

The course of study is extended through three years. The first is devoted to the Hebrew language, exegetical study of the scriptures, biblical criticism, biblical antiquities, introduction to the study of the scriptures, mental and moral science, evidences of natural and revealed religion, sacred chronology, and biblical history. The *second* to the continued exegetical study of the Hebrew and Greek scriptures, and to didactic theology and ecclesiastical history. The *third* to polemic theology, church government, pastoral theology, composition and delivery of sermons. The classes are distinguished, numerically, into *First, Second and Third.* The members of the first, or highest class, are required to exhibit original compositions, once in two weeks; those of the second class, once in three weeks; and those of the third class, once in four weeks.

There are three vacations in each year. The first of six weeks, from the first Thursday of May; the second of six weeks, from the last Wednesday of September; and the third of two weeks, in the month of Feb., at the discretion of the professors.

Board may be obtained at various prices, from $1 25 to $1 75 per week; firewood from $4 to $6 per annum; washing, $7; each student pays to the seminary $10 per annum, towards the general expense fund; but there is no charge for tuition, use of library, &c. The number of students on the catalogue of the institution for the current year (1833) is 132.

Rutgers' College, located at New Brunswick, was chartered by George III. in 1770, and was called Queen's College, in honour of his consort. The present name was substituted by the legislature of the State, in 1825, at request of the trustees, in honour of Col. Henry Rutgers, of New York, to whom the institution is indebted for liberal pecuniary benefactions. The charter was originally granted to such Protestants as had adopted the constitution of the reformed churches in the Netherlands, as revised by the national synod of Dordrecht, in the years 1618 and 1619. That synod, composed of distinguished delegates from almost all denominations of Protestant Europe, formed one of the most august ecclesiastical assemblies of modern times. Their doctrines as embodied in the confession of faith and catechisms of the Reformed Dutch Church in America, substantially comports with the 39 articles of the church of England, and entirely with the doctrines of the Presbyterian church in the United States; and the government of the church is strictly Presbyterian. This denomination of Christians is established chiefly in New York, New Jersey, and Pennsylvania. In the city of New York, alone, it has twelve churches, in which divine worship has long been exclusively conducted in the English language.

Dr. Jacob R. Hardenburg, an American, was appointed first president of the college, in 1789; he was distinguished by a powerful mind, great piety and industry, and success in the ministry. He died in 1792.

The Theological College of the Reformed Dutch Church is established here, and intimately blended with the literary institution. At a meeting in New York, Oct. 1771, of *Coetus* and *Conferentie*, until then, contending parties in the church, peace was restored, and a plan laid for the organization of this, the first theological school in America. Its completion, however, was delayed by the revolutionary war, until 1784, when the Rev. Dr. John H. Livingston, was chosen professor of didactic and polemical theology, who performed the duties of this office, in New York, in connexion with his pastoral services. In 1807, by a covenant between the trustees and the synod, the professorate was united with the college; of which, in 1810, Dr. Livingston was chosen president, on the death of Dr. Ira Condict. The duties of the literary institution were at this time suspended, for want of funds. Dr. Livingston died, 20th January, 1825, in the 79th year of his age, the 55th of his ministry, and the 41st of his professorial labours.

At a general synod, convened at Albany, in February, 1825, the Rev. Philip Milledoler, D. D., was chosen professor of didactic and polemical theology; and in the September following, was elected, by the trustees, president of the college, and professor of the evidences of christianity and moral philosophy. At the same time a plan was matured for reviving the literary institution; by which, one of the theological professors must always be chosen president of the college, and each of such professors must hold a professorship therein, and be a member of its faculty.

The effect of this amalgamation of theology and literature, is said to have been highly favourable to the moral character of the institution, and not to have imparted to it a sectarian influence.

The college edifice, of dark red freestone, is a handsome spacious building, surmounted by a cupola. It is reared on an eminence near the town, a site of great beauty, presented to the institution by the honourable James Parker, of Amboy. The views from thence, embracing great variety of scenery, of mountain and valley, forest and river, are delightfully picturesque, and the country is as healthy as it is lovely. The institution may be considered in a flourishing condition. The number of students in September, 1833, was eighty, with the prospect of much increase during the session. The charge for board and tuition is about $125 per annum. The students board in respectable private families, under the supervision of the faculty, where their habits, morals, and manners are duly regarded. The number of students in theology has varied from sixteen to thirty. There are three libraries; that of the college is large and valuable, and those pertaining to the Peithesopian and Philoclean Societies, are respectable. The cabinet of minerals is considerable, and increasing; and the philosophical and chemical apparatus extensive.

The faculty (in 1833) consists of the Rev. *Philip Milledoler*, D. D., president, professor of moral philosophy and didactic and polemical theology; the Rev. *Jacob J. Janeway*, D. D. vice president and professor of rhetoric, evidences of christianity, political economy, &c.; the Rev. *James S. Cannon*, D. D., professor of metaphysics and philosophy of the human mind, of ecclesiastical history, church government, and pastoral theology; *Theodore Strong*, A. A. S., C. A. S., professor of mathematics and natural philosophy; the Rev. *Alexander M'Clelland*, D. D., professor of oriental and biblical literature; *Lewis Black*, M. D., professor of chemistry and natural history; *John D. Ogilby*, A. M., professor of languages; and *Frederic Ogilby*, A. B., assistant instructer of languages.

The grammar school attached to the college, and under the immediate inspection of the trustees and faculty, is committed to the rectorship of the Rev. *Cornelius D. Westbrook*, D. D., assisted by *Isaac A. Blauvelt*, A. M., an alumnus of the college.

The location of this college equidistant from Philadelphia and New York, the healthfulness and beauty of the adjacent country, the excellent morals which prevail in the city as in the college, the high character and capability of the professors, and the cheapness of tuition and subsistence, give this institution strong claims to the attention of the public.

The first step towards the establishment of the school fund of this State, commenced with the act of 9th February, 1816, which directed the treasurerto invest in the public six per cent. stocks of the United States, the sum of $15,000, arising from the payment of the funded debt, and from the dividends on the stock held by the State in the Trenton Bank; and at the end of every year, to invest the interest on the capital, in the same manner.

On the 12th February of the succeeding year, the "Act to create a fund for free schools" was passed, setting apart the stock and its accumulations vested under the act of 1816; the dividends on the stock held by the State, in the Cumberland Bank, and in the Newark Turnpike Company, the proceeds of the sale of a house and lot, in New Brunswick, the property of the State, and one-tenth part of all monies, thereafter raised by tax for State use; and the treasurer was instructed to vest these as they came to his hands, in the public stocks of the United States. By the act of 12th February, 1818, the governor, vice-president of council, speaker of assembly, the attorney general, and secretary of state, for the time being, were appointed "Trustees for the support of Free Schools;" and the treasurer was directed to transfer to them the school funds, to be by them applied in the mode to be prescribed by the State, reserving to the legislature the authority to change the existing fund, and to dissolve the trust at pleasure; and requiring an account of the fund to be annually laid before the legislature. This act made the following additions to the fund.—The balance of the old six per cent. stock, due 12th February, 1817, with the interest and reimbursement thereof since 9th Feb., 1816; the three per cent. stock of the U. States, belonging to the State on the 12th February, 1817; the shares of the State in the Trenton and Cumberland Banks, with the dividends since 9th February, 1816; all monies receivable from the foregoing items, future appropriations, and such gifts and grants, bequests and devises, as should be made for the purposes contemplated by the act; and one-tenth part of the State tax for the year 1817. The last appropriation, being, specifically, one-tenth of the tax, has been construed as repealing the general appropriation on the tax under the act of 1817.

The fund thus augmented and transferred to the trustees amounted to $113,238 78, and consisted of the following sums:—

1st. Six per cent. stock U. States, purchased under the law of 1816,	$15,000 00
2d. Six per cent. stock United States, purchased under act 1817,	16,224 15
3d. Stock in Newark Turnpike Company, - - - - -	12,500 00
4th. Three per cent. stock of United States, - - - - -	7,009 12

5th.	Interest, and reimbursement, of the principal of the deferred six per cent. stock of United States, - - - - - -	7,810 73
6th.	Twelve hundred shares Trenton Bank stock, - - - -	36,000 00
7th.	Forty shares in the Cumberland Bank, - - - - -	2,000 00
8th.	Interest and dividends from the several stocks since 9th Feb. 1816,	10,429 66
9th.	Cash and one-tenth of State tax for 1817, - - - -	6,265 12

Since 1818, there have been added to the principal of the fund the following items by legislative appropriation:—

1st.	Proceeds of sale of the State House in Jersey City, - -	$4,907 64
2d.	Twenty-two shares in Sussex Bank, - - - - - -	1000 00
3d.	Donation from William J. Bell & Co. - - - - -	23 15
4th.	Bonus of People's Bank at Paterson, recd. 26th Sept. 1825,	4,000 00
5th.	Bonus from Monmouth Bank, 9th June, 1825, - - -	800 00
6th.	Sale of part of a lot in Trenton, - - - - - -	1,061 00
7th.	Under the act 28th December, 1824, one-tenth of State tax, and tax on Monmouth bank for the year 1826, - - -	2,200 00
	Same, 1827, - - - - - - - - - - -	2,200 00
	Same, 1828, - - - - - - - - - - -	3,200 00
8th.	Under the act 5th March, 1828, repealing act of 28th December, 1824, and in lieu of one-tenth of the State tax, giving all the tax from banking, insurance and other incorporated companies, which, in the year 1829, amounted to - - - - - -	11,709 58
	And estimated to produce, annually, $10,000.	
		$31,101 37
	Making whole amount of appropriations by legislature, in 1830,	$144,240 15

In the management of the fund, great advantage has arisen from the act of 18th Feb. 1829, directing the investment of the annual income in advance, by which the trustees were empowered, to invest on or before the first of March, annually, an amount equal to the estimated receipts of the fund during the year, to be advanced by the State treasurer, and to be replaced by him as the monies accruing from the fund shall be received; thus enabling the trustees to invest at one time all the income of the year.

The sources of income of the school fund, are now, the dividends on the various stock which the trustees hold, and which, in October 1832, amounted to $228,611 75. And the annual tax of half per cent. upon the dividends of the several bank and insurance companies of the State, which amounts annually to near $11,000.

The first expenditure which has been directed out of the fund, was by the "act establishing common schools," passed 21st February, 1829, appropriating annually $20,000 from the income of the fund, for the establishment and maintenance of schools. This act was altered and amended by the act of 1st March, 1830. But both acts were repealed by that of 16th February, 1831, by which the system of common schools is now regulated. That act appropriates $20,000 annually, from the income of the school fund, to the establishment and maintenance of such schools; and directs, in case such annual income shall not have been received in full on the first Monday of April, or shall be insufficient to cover the appropriation, the trustees to draw from the State treasury for the deficiency; such amount to be replaced from the annual receipts of the school fund. The act further provides, that the trustees shall apportion the sum, so appropriated, among the several counties, in the ratio of their taxes paid for the support of government, and shall file a list of such apportionment with the treasurer, that he may notify the collectors of the several counties, to draw for the same; that the boards of chosen freeholders, of the respective counties, shall at their annual meetings, apportion among the several townships, the monies received by the collectors, in the ratio of the county tax paid by the several townships, a list of which apportionments, the clerk of the freeholders is required, to file, to deliver a copy thereof, to the county collector, and to notify the collectors of the several townships of the amounts so apportioned, suce collectors report such amounts to the inhabitants, at their next annual town meeting; that may, (and they are recommended so to do,) at such meetings, raise, by tax or otherwise, such additional sum for the same object, as they may deem proper; and may authorize the township collector, to draw on the county collector, for the amount apportioned, and may apply the sum received from the State, to schooling the indigent poor of the township, if they so elect; that the inhabitants at their town meetings, annually, shall choose, as other town officers are chosen, three or more persons, who shall constitute the school committee, and whose duty is to recognise and ascertain the number of common schools within their respective townships; that the patrons, supporters, or proprietors of the several common schools in the respective townships, be authorized to organize such schools, by the appointment of a board of trustees, in such form, and consisting of such number, as they may deem proper; and any board of trustees so organized shall transmit to the school committee, of the proper township, a certificate of its organization, and shall thereon be recognised by the committee as entitled to an apportionment of the monies assigned to such township from the school fund. And such trustees are required to render to the school committees, on or before the first Monday of April, annually, a statement of the average number of scholars resident in the township, taught in such school during each quarter of the preceding year, and where from convenience, scholars from an adjoining township attend such school, to report their number &c. to the school committee of such adjoining township; to visit and inspect the affairs of their respective schools, to apply the monies received, at discretion, for their benefit, and at the end of every year, to exhibit to the school committee, a correct account of the expenditure of such monies; that the school committees, at or before the end of their term of service, shall apportion the whole of the monies assigned to their respective townships, and raised therein, among such common schools, in the ratio of the number of scholars reported to them, respectively, during the preceding year; or where any township may elect to appropriate such funds exclusively to the education of the poor, to apportion the same among the several schools, in proportion to the number of poor children taught; and shall draw in favour of the boards of trustees respectively, for the amount of their several dividends, on the town collector; and shall on or before the first Wednesday of May, yearly, transmit to the clerk of the board of chosen freeholders of their respective counties, a written statement, embracing the number of common schools duly organized within their respective townships, the number of scholars taught therein, the amount of the monies received by them from the township collector, and raised by the township, and the manner in which the same has been applied; that such clerk shall condense such statements into a report, in writing, and transmit the same to the trustees of the school fund, to be laid before the legislature, in a condensed form. No compensation is allowed under this act.

It will be observed, that in framing this system, no attempt has been made to coerce the respective townships into raising monies, in addition to their allotted share of the sum appropriated from the school fund; but, in accordance with the spirit of the government of the State, which considers the townships as integral corporations, whose inhabitants are competent to judge of their wants, and possess the means to supply them, the legislature has, we think, wisely left with each township, the liberty to tax itself for the purposes of education, as to it may seem meet; whilst it has promptly offered all the aid which it has to bestow. It is possible, that learning may advance less rapidly, than if urged by a forced culture; but we are not sure, that the happiness of the people will be less promoted. We would not be understood to mean that literature is not a source of happiness; but it is not the only one. He who is compelled to a diet which is unacceptable to his appetite, will not boast of his enjoyment; and we have no difficulty in determining, which is the most hospitable host, he who forces manna upon the revolting stomach of his guest, or he, who, placing the dish before him, permits him to eat at pleasure, whilst he expatiates upon its agreeable and nourishing properties. None, properly instructed, would reject the joys of paradise; but, were paradise a prison, we should long to leap its crystal walls. Emulation, we think, will soon be awakened among the townships of each county, and among the counties, upon this all-important subject; and although the sum of $20,000 is a small one to distribute among a population of 330,000 souls, it will have one excellent effect; it will turn, periodically, the attention of the people to the means of mental improvement, will set them to compare their condition with that of their neighbours, and when inferior, to improve it. For it may be taken as a truism, that when the people are at liberty to consider and improve their condition, they will, when dissatisfied, amend it.

Among the provisions for enlightening the public mind, we may justly include those for publishing the laws, not only of the State, but also of the general government. The act of 7th June, 1820, directs: 1st, That the secretary of state shall cause the laws of the State to be published immediately after the passing thereof, in one of the public newspapers, of the city of Trenton; and that they shall also be published in a pamphlet form, together with the votes and proceedings of assembly, the journals of council, and minutes of joint meetings, and delivered by the printer within sixty days from the rising of the legislature, to the State treasurer, who shall distribute them in the following manner, at the expense of the State, viz:—to himself, two copies; to the governor, for himself, three copies, and also to be forwarded by him, and presented to the secretary of state of the United States, four copies; to the executive of each state, and territory of the United States, for the use of the executives and legislatures, three copies; to each of the senators, and representatives of this State, in congress, one copy; to the president of the American Antiquarian Society, one copy; to the justices of the Supreme Court, the attorney general, secretary of state, clerk of council, assembly, Courts of Chancery and Supreme Court, each one copy; to the clerk of the council, for the use of council and assembly, sixty copies; and the remainder among the several counties in the ratio they contribute to the support of the government, directed to the county collector. The county collector, retaining a copy for himself, transmits, at the expense of the county, one set of the laws and proceedings, to each of the following officers:—the judges and clerk of the Common Pleas, the justices of the peace, the magistrates of corporate towns, the sheriff, surrogate, clerk of the board of chosen freeholders, and the representatives of the county in the legislature, and each incorporated library company; and divides the remainder among the several townships of the county, transmitting equal proportions to the clerk of each township, who, retaining one copy for the use of the township, causes the residue to be distributed among the officers of the township, giving preference in the following order:—to the assessor, collector, chosen freeholders, and overseers of the poor, each one set.

The laws of the United States, apportioned to this State by Congress, are distributed by the treasurer, at the expense of the State; to himself, to the governor, attorney general, justices of Supreme Court, secretary of state, members of the legislature, each one set; to the clerk of council, and the clerk of the assembly, four sets; to the librarians of Princeton college, and to the two library societies in the college, each one set; and the remainder, among the counties in proportion to their quota of State taxes, to be transmitted to the collectors, and by them distributed to the clerk and judges of the court of Common Pleas, each one set, and to every public library one set; and the residue, as may be directed by the board of chosen freeholders.

Reports of the decisions of the Supreme and Chancery Courts are annually prepared by officers appointed by the legislature for a term of five years, who receive a compensation of $200 per annum. Such reports are printed, and distributed, annually, with the pamphlet laws.

Lastly, and certainly not least, among the agents of moral improvement, we must rank the periodical journals of the State. The commonwealth partakes largely in the benefits flowing from the press, in the cities of Philadelphia and New York, and we therefore might suppose would not extensively encourage newspapers within her own boundaries; yet she has not less than thirty-one weekly papers, engaged in sowing broadcast the germs of literature and science. Of these useful auxiliaries we annex the following table.

NEWSPAPERS.	EDITORS.	WHERE PUBLISHED.
Bergen County Courier,		Jersey City, Bergen Co.
Sussex Register,	Hall,	Newton, Sussex Co.
N. J. Herald,	Grant Fitch,	Do. do.
Belvidere Apollo,	Franklin Ferguson,	Belvidere, Warren Co.
Warren Journal,	Fitch & Co.	Do. do.
Palladium of Liberty,	John R. Eyres,	Morristown, Morris Co.
Jerseyman,	Robbins,	Do. do.
Rahway Advocate,	Thomas Green,	Rahway, Middlesex.
Fredonian,	Randolph and Carman,	New Brunswick, do.
Times,		Do. do.
Sentinel of Freedom,	George Bush & Co.	Newark, Essex.
Daily Advertiser,		Do. do.
Newark Monitor,	S. L. B. Baldwin,	Do. do.
Do. Eagle,	Bartlett and Crowell,	Do. do.

Princeton Courier,	Baker and Connolly,	Princeton, Somerset.
American System,	J. Robinson & Co.	Do. do.
Somerset Messenger,	Gore and Allison,	Somerville, do.
State Gazette,	George Sherman,	Trenton, Hunterdon.
National Union,	E. B. Adams,	Do. do.
Emporium,	Joseph Justice,	Do. do.
Hunterdon Gazette,	Chas. George,	Flemington, do.
Monmouth Enquirer,	John J. Bartleson,	Freehold, Monmouth,
Burlington Herald,	Joseph Pugh,	Mount Holly, Burlington.
Mount Holly Mirror,	Nathan Palmer,	Do. do.
Camden Mail,	Sickler and Ham,	Camden, Gloucester.
National Republican,	Josiah Harrison,	Do. do.
Village Herald,	Joseph Sailor,	Woodbury, do.
Salem Statesman,	H. H. Elwell,	Salem, Salem.
Do. Messenger,	Elijah Brooks,	Do. do.
Washington Whig,	Nelson and Powers,	Bridgeton, Cumberland.
Bridgeton Observer,	F. Pierson,	Do. do.

GAZETTEER OF NEW JERSEY.

Absecum, post town of Galloway t-ship, Gloucester co., 50 miles S. E. from Woodbury, 95 from Trenton, and 105 from W. C., upon Absecum creek, about two miles above Absecum bay, contains a tavern, store, and 8 or 10 dwellings, surrounded by sand, and pine forest.

Absecum Creek rises by several branches, on the line between Galloway and Egg Harbour t-ship, Gloucester co., and flows S. E., by a course of 8 or 9 miles, into Absecum bay. It gives motion to several saw mills.

Absecum Bay, a salt marsh lake, Gloucester co., on the line of Egg Harbour and Galloway t-ship, circular in form, and about 2 miles in diameter, communicating with Reed's bay, and by a broad channel, called Absecum Inlet, 4 miles in length, with the ocean.

Absecum Beach, on the Atlantic Ocean; extends, eastwardly, from Great Egg Harbour Inlet, about 9 miles to Absecum Inlet; broken, however, by a narrow inlet, near midway between its extremities.

Ackerman's Run, small stream, 2 miles long, flowing to the Passaic River, about 3 miles below Paterson, from Saddle River t-ship, Bergen co.

Acquackanonck, t-ship, Essex co., bounded on the N. W., N. E. and E. by the Passaic river, which forms a semi-ellipsis, N. by Paterson t-ship, and S. by Bloomfield and Caldwell t-ships; centrally distant, N. from Newark, 10 miles; greatest length, E. and W. 7, breadth N. and S. 6½ miles; area about 14,000 acres. Mountainous on the W., rolling on the E.; soil red shale, and where well cultivated, productive. Acquackanonck, Little Falls, and Weasel are villages, of the t-ship; the two first, post towns. Acquackanonck, on the Passaic river, distant 5 miles S. E. of Paterson, is at the head of tide water, and consequently the outport of Paterson. Pop. in 1830, about 1,300. In 1832, the t-ship contained 300 taxables, 125 householders, 47 single men, 7 merchants, 6 grist mills, 2 cotton factories, 5 saw mills, 1 paper mill, 13 tan vats, one printing and bleaching establishment, 1 woollen factory, 345 horses and mules, and 766 neat cattle above 3 years of age; and it paid state tax, $230 62 cents; county, $607 37 c.; poor, $500; and road, $700. Aquackanonck town is a p-t, 8 miles N. E. of Newark, 224 from W. C., 58 from Trenton, 10 from New York, to which there is a turnpike and rail road. It contains 3 taverns, 6 stores, about 80 dwellings, and a Dutch Reformed church; has six sloops trading with New York. A small stream, which may be termed the Fourth river, runs near the town, and gives motion to several mills. Blatchley's mineral spring lies about 1½ miles W. of the town. This is the depot of lumber for the neighbourhood.

Alamuche, p-t. of Independence t-ship, Warren co., on the eastern part of the t-ship; by the post route 228 miles N. E. of W. C., and 65 from Trenton, and 17 from Belvidere the C. T.; seated on a small tributary of Pequest creek, and near a lake of the same name, contains a grist and saw mill, a grain distillery, a store, tavern, and 12 or 15 dwellings. It is surrounded by a limestone soil of excellent quality, well cultivated.

Alamuche Lake is one of the many mountain ponds which characterize this country, and which are, in many cases, reservoirs formed in limestone rock. This is about a mile in diameter, and sends forth a tributary to the Pequest creek.

Alamuche Mountain is one of the chain of hills which bounds the valley of the Musconetcong creek in Warren county.

Alberson's Brook, a tributary of Spruce Run, a fork of the south branch of the Raritan river, rises at the south foot of the Musconetcong mountain, and flows easterly by a course of 7 or 8 miles to its recipient.

Alexandria, p-t. of Alexandria t-ship, Hunterdon co., on the bank of the Delaware river, at the junction of Nischisakawick creek with that stream, 11 miles W. of Flemington, 35 N. of Trenton, 189 from W. C.; contains a tavern, store, grist mill, and 8 or 10 dwellings, a Presbyterian and an Episcopalian church.

Alexandria t-ship, Hunterdon co., bounded on the N. E. by Bethlehem t-ship, N. W. by the Musconetcong creek, which separates it from Warren co., and S. W. by the river Delaware; centrally distant, N. E. from Flemington, 12 miles; greatest length, E. and W., 12 miles; breadth, N. and S., 9 miles; area 33,000 acres. Surface on the N., mountainous, the Musconetcong mountain running N. W. across the t-ship. Soil, on the S. E., red shale; at the foot of the mountain, grey limestone; and on the mountain, clay, sand and loam. It is drained, S. W. by the Nischisakawick, the Hakehokake, and other small mill streams. Alexandria, Milford, Mount Pleasant, and Pittstown are p-towns of the t-ship. Pop., in 1830, 3,042. In 1832, the t-ship contained 10 saw mills, 7 grist mills, 4 oil mills, 4 ferries and toll bridges, 6 distilleries, 8 stores, 861 horses, 1287 neat cattle above the age of 3 years; and it paid poor tax, $1000; road tax, $800; and state and county tax, $1413 48 cents.

Allentown, p-t. of Upper Freehold t-ship, Monmouth co., near the western line of the county, between Doctor creek and Indian run, on the road from Bordentown to Freehold, 8 miles from the former and 18 from the latter, 177 from W. C., and 11 from Trenton; contains from 75 to 80 dwellings; 1 Presbyterian church, with cupola and bell, handsomely situated on the hill on the west; an academy, 2 schools, 1 Methodist Church, grist mill, saw mill, and tilt mill, on Doctor creek, and saw mill on Indian run; below which, at a short distance west of the town, is a cotton manufactory. This is a compact pleasant village, with some very good frame and brick houses; but the lands around are sandy, and not of the best quality. A considerable business is done in the town.

Alexsocken Creek, a small mill stream of Amwell t-ship, Hunterdon co., which flows westerly into the Delaware river, by a course of 5 or 6 miles, about a mile above Lambertville.

Alloways Creek, Salem co., rises in the N. W. angle of Pittsgrove t-ship, and flows by a S. W. course of more than 20 miles, through Upper and Lower Alloways, and Elsinborough t-ships, to the Delaware river, below Reedy island. It is navigable above Allowaystown, in Upper Alloways t-ship, a distance of about twelve miles from the mouth, for wood shallops; along its margin for about 10 miles, are some excellent banked meadows.

Allowaystown, p-t. of Upper Alloways t-ship, Salem co., about 7 miles E. of Salem, 177 N. E. from W. C., and 71 S. from Trenton; contains from 70 to 80 dwellings, 2 taverns, 4 or 5 stores, 1 Methodist, and 1 Baptist church. The Messrs. Reeves, have here 2 very powerful saw mills, engaged principally in cutting ship timber, and a valuable grist mill, on the Alloways creek. They employ from 75 to 100 horses in drawing timber &c., to their works.

Alloways Creek, Upper, t-ship, Salem co., bounded N. E. by Pittsgrove t-ship, S. E. by Deerfield, Hopewell, and Stow creek t-ships, Cumberland co.; S. W. by Lower

Alloways creek t-ship, and N. W. by Elsinborough and Mannington t-ships; centrally distant, S. E. from Salem 7 miles. Greatest length E. and W. 10½, breadth N. and S. 9 miles. Area, about 34,000 acres; of which more than 10,000 are unimproved. Soil upon the N. E., stiff clay and loam; on the S. E. sand and gravelly loam, with rolling surface. The forest known as the "Barrens," runs here, producing much white oak and pine wood for market, which finds its way to Philadelphia, by Alloways creek. By the census of 1830, the township contained 2136 inhabitants, and by the assessor's abstract of 1832, 415 taxables, 5 grist mills, 10 saw mills, 2 carding machines, 1 fulling mill, 2 distilleries, 416 horses and mules, and 854 neat cattle, upwards of 3 years old; and it paid t-ship tax, $400; county tax, $834 10; State tax, $218 74. The t-ship is drained by Alloways creek, which runs centrally through it, by a S. W. course, and by Stow creek, which forms part of the southern boundary. Allowaystown and Quinton's Bridge, are villages and post-towns of the t-ship. Guineatown is a name given to a few negro huts, on the northern boundary. Friesburg, lies near the south line.

Alloways Creek, Lower, t-ship, Salem co., bounded N. by Elsinborough, Salem and Upper Alloways creek t-ships; on the E. by Upper Alloways creek t-ship; on the S. by Stow creek, which divides it from Stow creek and Greenwich t-ships, of Cumberland co., on the W. by the river Delaware; centrally distant, S. from Salem, 9 miles; greatest length N. and S. 12 miles; breadth E. and W. 9 miles; area, about 30,000 acres; surface level; soil on the W. for more than half the t-ship, marsh meadow, much of which is embanked; and on the E. a deep clay and loam well cultivated. It is drained by Alloways creek on the N., and Stow creek on the S., and by Hope creek, Deep creek, and Muddy creek, small streams which flow into the Delaware, from the marsh between them. Pop. of the t-ship by census of 1830, 1222. By the assessor's abstract of 1832, it contained 260 taxables, 3 stores, 2 grist mills, 2 distilleries, 255 horses and mules, and 881 neat cattle above 3 years old. It has 3 schools, 1 Methodist, and 1 Friend's meeting house.

Amboy. See *South Amboy, Perth Amboy*.

Amwell t-ship, Hunterdon co., bounded N. by Lebanon t-ship, N. E. by Readington t-ship, E. by Hillsborough t-ship, of Somerset co., S. E. by Hopewell t-ship, and S. W. by the river Delaware, and N. W. by Ringwood t-ship. Greatest length N. and S. 16; breadth E. and W. 15 miles; area, 77,000 acres; surface hilly on the N. W. and S. E.; on the first, there being a clay ridge well timbered and productive, and on the latter, a chain of trap hills, rough, broken, and barren. The intervening space is undulating valley, of red shale, which, where covered with sufficient soil, is grateful for the care bestowed upon it, producing particularly fine crops of grass. The t-ship is drained on the N. E. by the south branch of the Raritan, on the N. W. by the Laokatong and Wickhechecoke creeks; S. W. by the Alexsocken and Smith's creeks, on the S. by Stony brook, flowing easterly to the Raritan river. Pop. in 1830, 7385; in 1832, the t-ship contained 2 Presbyterian churches, 4 stores, 8 fisheries, 15 saw mills, 21 grist mills, 3 oil mills, 2 ferries and toll bridges, 88 tan vats, 12 distilleries, 4 carding machines, 2 fulling mills; and it paid poor tax, $1200; road tax, $2500; State and county tax, $3722 62. Flemington, Sergeantsville, Ringoes, Prallsville, Lambertsville, are p-ts. of the t-ship.

Anderson, p-t. of Mansfield t-ship, Warren co., on the turnpike road leading from Philipsburg to Schooley's mountain, and between the Morris canal and Musconetcong creek, within a mile of either; distant by the post route from W. C. 205, from Trenton 49, and from Belvidere, the co. town, E. 11 miles; 16 miles from Easton, and 25 from Morristown; contains 2 stores and 15 dwellings; situate in a fertile limestone valley. Lands valued at $50 the acre.

Andover p-t., Newton t-ship, Sussex co., on the south angle of the t-ship on the Newton turnpike road, distant by the post-route from W. C. 228, from Trenton 65, and from Newton 5 miles.

Andover Forge, Byram t-ship, Sussex co., on the N. bank of the Musconetcong river, at the junction of Lubber run with that stream, and within 2 miles of the Morris canal, is situate in a very narrow valley, and has around it a store, saw mill, and some 6 or 8 dwellings.

Anthony, hamlet on Schooley's mountain, Lebanon t-ship, Hunterdon co., 18 miles N. E. of Flemington, on Spruce run; contains a saw mill, and some half dozen dwellings.

Arneystown, p-t. of Hanover t-ship, Burlington co., near the eastern line; 13 miles N. E. of Mount Holly, 175 from W. C., 11 from Trenton S. E., and 8 E. from Bordentown; contains a store, tavern, 15 dwellings, and a large meeting house pertaining to "Friends," surrounded by a country of fertile loam.

Arthur's Kill. See *Staten Island Sound.*

Artles' Brook, tributary of the north branch of the Raritan river, Bedminster t-ship, Somerset co., unites with its recipient after a S. course of five miles.

Asbury, p-t. of Mansfield t-ship, Warren co., in the S. W. angle of the t-ship near the Musconetcong creek, by post-route 199 miles from W. C., and 40 from Trenton, 11 miles S. E. from Belvidere; lying in a deep and narrow valley on a soil of rich limestone, contains a Methodist church, 2 grist mills, 1 saw mill, an oil mill, a woollen factory, 1 tavern, 3 stores, and about thirty dwellings.

Assiscunk Creek, Burlington co., rises on the line between Mansfield and Springfield t-ships, and flows westward about 14 miles, forming, for the greater part of that distance, the boundary between the t-ships, uniting with the Delaware river, between the city of Burlington and the point of Burlington island. It has one or two mills upon it.

Atquatqua Creek, branch of the Atsion river, rising on, and forming part of the S. W. boundary of Burlington co. It may be deemed the main stem of the river under another name.

Atsion, p-t. and furnace, on the Atsion river, partly in Galloway t-ship, Gloucester co., and partly in Washington t-ship, Burlington, co., 9 miles above the head of navigation, 12 miles from Medford, 17 from Mount Holly, on the road leading to Tuckerton, and 57 from Trenton. Besides the furnace, there are here, a forge, grist mill, and three saw mills. The furnace makes from 800 to 900 tons of castings, and the forge from 150 to 200 tons of bar iron annually. This estate, belonging to Samuel Richards, Esq., embraces what was formerly called Hampton furnace and forge, and West's mill, and contains about 60,000 acres of land. There are about 100 men employed here, and between 6 and 700 persons depending for subsistence upon the works.

Atsion River, main stem of Little Egg Harbour river, forming in part, the boundary between Gloucester and Burlington cos. It bears this name for about 14 miles above Pleasant Mills, and is formed by the union of the Atquatqua and Tuscomusco creeks. Atsion furnace is on the north side of the river, in Burlington co.

Augusta, p-t. of Frankford t-ship, Sussex co., distant by post-route from W. C. 233, from Trenton 75, and from Newton 7 miles, contains 7 or 8 dwellings and a Presbyterian church.

Babcock's Creek, Hamilton t-ship, Gloucester co., rises by 4 branches, viz: North, East, Main, and Jack Pudding, which, uniting near May's landing, flow westerly into the Great Egg Harbour river at that village.

Back Creek, Fairfield t-ship, Cumberland co., flows about 6 miles into Nautuxet cove, Delaware bay.

Back Water, branch of Maurice river, Millville t-ship, Cumberland co., has a westerly course to its recipient, of about 7 miles.

Bacon Creek, a tributary of Pequest creek, Independence t-ship, Warren co., having a westerly course of 2 or 3 miles.

Bacon's Neck, a strip of rich land, in Greenwich t-ship, Cumberland co., between Cohansey and Store creeks.

Back Neck, a strip of land of Fairfield t-ship, Cumberland co., comprehended by the bend of Cohansey creek and Cohansey cove.

Bambo Creek, small tributary of the Lamington river, rising in Chester t-ship, Morris co., and flowing by a southerly course of about 4 miles, to its recipient in Bedminster t-ship, Somerset co.

Baptisttown, Middletown t-ship, Hunterdon co. See ***Holmdel.***

Baptisttown, p-t. Ringwood t-ship, Hunterdon co., 9 miles W. of Flemington, 33 N. of Trenton, and 187 from W. C., contains a tavern, a store, 8 or 10 dwellings, and a Baptist church. There is a Presbyterian church within a mile of the town. The surrounding country is level, with soil of red shale, of good quality, and carefully cultivated.

Bargaintown, Egg Harbour t-ship, Gloucester co., p-t., on Cedar Swamp creek, 4 miles from Great Egg Harbour bay, 45 S. E. from Woodbury, 90 from Trenton, and 200 by post-route from W. C., contains 2 taverns, 1 store, a grist mill, Methodist church, and about 30 dwellings.

Barnegat Bay, Monmouth co., extends N. from Barnegat Inlet to Metetecunk river, the distance of 20 miles, varying in breadth from 1 to 4 miles. It is separated from the ocean by Island Beach and Squam Beach, narrow strips of land no where exceeding a mile in width. It receives the waters of Metetecunk river, Kettle creek, Toms' river, Cedar creek, and Forked river. The inlet from the ocean is over a mile wide. By act of assembly, 21 Feb. 1833, authority was given to a company, by a canal, to connect the head of this bay with Manasquan Inlet, by which much time and space will be saved to vessels bound thence to New York. The capital proposed for this undertaking is $5000.

Barnegat, p-t. of Stafford t-ship, Monmouth co., near Barnegat Inlet, 36 miles S. from Freehold, 78 S. E. from Trenton, and 202 N. E. from W. C., contains about 50 dwellings, 3 taverns, 4 stores, on a sandy soil, surrounded by pine forest.

Barnesborough, village, of Greenwich t-ship, Gloucester co., 6 miles S. W. from Woodbury, contains a store, tavern, and 12 or 15 dwellings. It lies on the edge of the pines.

Barrentown, Freehold t-ship, Monmouth co., on the road from Freehold to Middletown, 4 miles from the one, and 10 from the other, contains some 6 or 7 dwellings, in a poor sandy country.

Baskingridge, p-t. of Bernard t-ship, Somerset co., 11 miles N. E. of Somerville, 213 from W. C., and 47 from Trenton, beautifully situated in a high, rich, well cultivated, and healthy country; contains a Presbyterian church, an academy for young gentlemen, in much repute, formerly under the care of Drs. Brownlee and Findlay. The residence and estate of General Lord Sterling were near this town.

Bass River Hotel, p-o., Little Egg Harbour t-ship, Burlington co., 183 miles N. E. from W. C., and 71 S. E. from Trenton.

Batsto River, Washington t-ship, Burlington co., a large branch of Little Egg Harbour river, which rises in Northampton t-ship, and flows by a southerly course of 16 miles, to the Atsion river, below Pleasant Mills; the united streams form the Little Egg Harbour river. Batsto Furnace is on the former within 2 miles of their junction, and near the head of the stream, are Hampton Furnace and Forge, now in ruins.

Batsto Furnace is about 8 miles above Gloucester Furnace, about 30 miles S. E. from Woodbury, and one from Pleasant Mills. There are made here 850 tons of iron, chiefly castings, giving employment to 60 or 70 men, and maintaining altogether near 400 persons. There are here also, a grist and saw mill, and from 50 to 60,000 acres of land appurtenant to the works.

Bear Fort Mountain, near the W. boundary of Pompton t-ship, Bergen co. It is broken through by Wood-ruff's Gap, from which runs a branch of Belcher's creek, and by which passes the Ringwood and Long Pond turnpike road. The whole length of the range of hills in this t-ship is about 11 miles.

Bear Brook, western branch of Pequest creek, rises in Hunt's Pond, Green t-ship, Sussex co., and flows S. W., through the S. E. angle of Hardwick t-ship, Warren co., and joins the main stream, in the Great Meadows, Independence t-ship, having a course of about 10 miles.

Bear Swamp, a noted swamp of Downe t-ship, Cumberland co., near Nantuxet or Newport, through which flows the Oronoken creek. The timber upon it is chiefly oak and poplar.

Bear Swamp, Burlington co., near the west boundary of Northampton t-ship, about 2 miles in length by 1 in breadth.

Beasley's Point, Upper t-ship, Cape May co., on Great Egg Harbour Bay. There are here, upon a neck of land, between the salt marshes, of about 1 mile wide, 2 taverns, and several farm houses, where visiters to the shore may find agreeable accommodations.

Beatty's Town, on the N. E. angle of Mansfield t-ship, Warren co., on the bank of the Musconetcong creek, and at the west foot of Schooley's Mountain, within 2 miles of the mineral spring, and 16 E. of Belvidere. The Morris Canal is distant 2 miles from it on the north. The village contains 1 store, 1 tavern, a grist and saw mill, a school, and from 15 to 20 dwellings. The land around it is limestone, of excellent quality, and valued, in large farms, at 50 dollars the acre.

Beaver Brook, tributary of the Rockaway river, Pequannock t-ship, Morris county, flows by a S. W. course of 8 miles through a hilly country, giving motion to several forges.

Beaver Brook, Warren co., rises by two branches, one in Hardwick t-ship, from Glover's Pond, the other in Knowlton t-ship, from Rice's Pond, which unite in Oxford t-ship, near to, and south, from the village of Hope, and thence join the Pequest creek, about 3 miles from its mouth, having a course of about 14 miles.

Beaver Run, Galloway t-ship, Gloucester co., a tributary of Nacote creek, flowing to its recipient below Gravelly Landing.

Beaver Dam Run, a tributary of the south branch of Rancocus creek, which flows to its recipient, by a north course of about 4 miles, at Vincent-town.

Beaver Branch, of Wading river, rises in Little Egg Harbour t-ship, and flows westerly by a course of about 6 miles, to its recipient, about a mile below Bodine's bridge and mill.

Beden's Brook, a mill stream, rises in the Nashanic mountain, Hopewell t-ship, Hunterdon co., and flows E. about 8 miles, through Montgomery t-ship, Somerset co., to the Millstone river, receiving several tributaries by the way.

Bedminster Township, Somerset co., bounded N. by Washington, Chester, and Mendham t-ships, Morris co.; E. by the north branch of the Raritan, dividing it from Bernard t-ship; S. by Bridgewater t-ship, from which it is divided by Chamber's brook and Lamington river; and W. by Lamington river, forming the boundary between it and Tewksbury and Readington t-ships, Hunterdon co.; Centrally distant, N. W. from Somerville, 8 miles; greatest length, N. and S., 8 miles; breadth, E. and W., 4½ miles; area, 19,300 acres; surface, hilly; soil, lime, clay, and red shale; generally well cultivated and fertile. Pepack, Little Cross Roads, Pluckemin, Lamington, and Cross Roads, are villages; the three first, p-ts. of the t-ship. Pepack and Artle's brooks are tributaries of the N. branch, flowing through the t-ship. Pop. in 1830, 1453. In 1832, the t-ship contained about 300 taxables, 60 householders, whose ratables did not exceed $30, 40 single men, 8 merchants, 6 saw mills, 6 grist mills, 19 tan vats, 3 distilleries, 499 horses and mules, and 818 neat cattle, 3 years old and upwards; and paid state tax, $242 48; county tax, 626 30. There is a Dutch Reformed church in the t-ship.

Belcher Creek rises near the centre of Pompton t-ship, Bergen co., and flows northerly about 7 miles, to mingle its waters with those of Long Pond, or Greenwood lake.

Belle Mount, a circular hill in the N. W. angle of Hopewell t-ship, Hunterdon co., on the shore of the Delaware river, between which and an oval hill on the south, flows Smith's creek.

Belvidere, p-t., and seat of justice of Warren co., situate on the river Delaware, in Oxford t-ship, at the junction of the Pequest creek, with that stream; by the post road, 210 miles from W. C., and 54 from Trenton, 69 from Philadelphia, 13 from Easton, 70 from New York, and 19 from Schooley's mountain springs. The town is built on an alluvial flat, based on limestone, and extends for about half a mile, on both sides of the creek, over which there are 2 bridges for carriages, and 1 for foot passengers. The town, which rapidly increases, contains a spacious court house, of brick, with offices attached, and a prison in the basement story; the doors of which, to the honour of the county, are commonly unclosed, and its chambers tenantless, save by the idle warder; a very large and neat Presbyterian church, a Methodist church, an academy, in which the classics are taught; a common school, 2 grist mills, 2 saw mills, a clover mill, 6 stores, 3 taverns, a turning lathe, driven by water, and an extensive tannery; a bank, chartered in 1829, with a capital of $50,000, but which may be extended; a county bible society, a county Sunday school union, auxiliary to the great charity established at Philadelphia; tract and temperance societies; 2 resident clergymen, 3 lawyers, and 2 physicians; 2 weekly journals, viz: The Apollo, edited by Franklin Ferguson; and the Warren Journal, by James J. Browne; and above 80 dwellings, most of which are neat and commodious, and many of brick and stone; among which, the residence of Dr. Green deserves particular notice, as well from its size and finish as from its beautiful and commanding situation. A very extensive business is done here, in general merchandise, in flour and lumber, the saw mills being abundantly supplied with timber from the Delaware. The Pequest creek having a large volume of water, and a rapid fall, affords very advantageous mill sites. Within 144 chains from the mouth of the creek the available fall is 49 feet 64-100, equal to 768 horse power, the whole of which is the property of Garret D. Wall, Esq., who offers mill seats for sale here on advantageous terms. But in addition to this great power derived from the creek, the Delaware river, within 2 miles of the town, offers a still greater, where the whole volume of that stream may be employed. A company has been incorporated, with a capital of $20,000, for erecting a bridge across the river at or near this place, for which three sites have been proposed. 1st. At the Foul Rift, where the channel is 170 yards wide. 2d. The mouth of the Pequest, where it is 205 yards. 3d. At the Deep Eddy, above the creek, where the channel is divided by Butz's island, and the stream, on the Jersey side, is 127 yards, the island 86 yards, and the remaining water 23 yards. The proposed rail road through New Jersey, from Elizabethtown, is designed to cross the Delaware here, and to connect with the Delaware and Susquehanna rail road.

Belleville, p-t. of Bloomfield t-ship, Essex co., beautifully situated on the right bank of the Raritan river, 3½ miles N. E. from Newark, 218 from W. C., 52 from Trenton, and 9 from New York. The margin of the river, here, has width sufficient for a road or street, and for dwellings with spacious lots on both its sides, from which the gently sloping hill, clad in rich verdure, has a very pleasant appearance. Including North Belleville the town is considered as extending 3 miles along the river, and in that distance contains a handsome Dutch Reformed church, having a very large congregation, 1 Methodist and 1 Episcopalian church, 2 large schools for boys, a school for girls, under the superintendence of a lady, a boarding school for males and females, under the care of the Rev. Mr. Lathrop; 2 public houses, one a very large and well finished hotel, kept by Mr. Chandler, where many summer boarders may be accommodated, in this delightful retreat, from the bustle and noise of the great neighbouring city; 6 stores, and about 200 dwellings. Two streams, which flow into the Passaic, at about 3 miles distance from each other, and which, within 2 miles of their course have, respectively, a fall much over an hundred feet, render this place as interesting for its manufactures as for its beauty. There are here 1 brass rolling mill and button manufactory, belonging to Messrs. Stevens, Thomas, and Fuller, occasionally engaged in copper coinage for Brazil; the copper founderies and rolling mills of Messrs. Isaacs, and of Hendricks and brothers; the calico print works of Mr. Andrew Gray, the silk printing establishment of Messrs. Duncan and Cunningham; the Brittania metal factory of the Messrs. Lee; the lamp factory of Stephens and Dougherty, and the grist mill of Mr. Kindsland. These works are estimated to produce, annually, manufactured articles worth two millions of dollars. Two thousand tons of merchandise are supposed to be transported to and from the wharves of Belleville annually.

Belleville, p-o., Sussex co., 241 miles N. E. from W. C., and 75 from Trenton.

Ben Davis' Point, W. Cape of Nantuxet cove, in the Delaware bay, and in Fairfield t-ship, Cumberland co.

Bergen County, was established with its present boundaries, by the act of 21 January, 1709-10, which directed "That on the eastern division, the county shall begin at Constable's Hook, and so run up along the bay and Hudson river, to the partition point between N. Jersey and the province of N. York, and along that line between the provinces, and the division line of the eastern and western division of this province, to Pequanock river; thence by such river and the Passaic river, to the Sound; thence by the Sound to Constable's Hook, where it began." Bounded N. E. by Orange and Rockland co., N. Y.; E. by N. Y. bay and North river; S. by the strait, which connects N. Y. bay with Newark bay, S. W. by Essex and Morris co., and N. W. by Sussex co. It is shaped like an T. Greatest width N. W. and S. E. 32 miles; greatest breadth N. E. and S. W. 28 miles. Area 267,500 acres, or about 418 square miles.

S. E. of the Ramapo mountain, the county consists of the old red sandstone formation, which appears under the form of red shale, and of massive stone, well adapted to buildings; large quarries of which, have been worked on the Passaic near Belleville, and at other places. This formation is in places, covered with trap rock, which in the Closter mountain, assumes a columnar form, in the palisades, 400 feet high, on the North river; and the same form is visible in the continuation of the First and Second mountains across the Passaic at Paterson and

Little Falls. In the Ramapo mountain, and upon the N. W. of it, the primitive formation prevails, and the large township of Pompton is broken into ridges and knolls, of considerable elevation. Limestone is found in the valleys, here, and magnetic iron ore in the hills. The great vein of such ore, which is first discoverable in the White Hills of New Hampshire, may be traced through this county.

The surface of the country W. of the Saddle river, is hilly, with broad and fertile valleys. The left bank of that river, is also high ground, and a very fine valley lies between it and the Closter mountain, which is drained by the Hackensack river. The southern part of the valley is low, and admits the tide to the town of Hackensack, 20 miles from the sound. In this distance, there is a body of salt marsh and valuable cedar swamp. The northern part of the valley and its banks, on the Saddle river, the Passaic and the Hudson, are divided into small well cultivated farms, whose neat, cleanly, and cheerful appearance, declare the thrift and content of their owners. There are few spots in New Jersey presenting more pleasing attractions than this country above the Hackensack, and on the highlands on each side of the river. The houses, generally, built in the ancient Dutch cottage form, of one full story, with its projecting pent houses, and dormitories within the slopes of the roof, are sometimes large, always painted white, and surrounded with verdant lawns, shrubbery, and well cultivated gardens. And we may here remark, that the taste for horticulture and ornamental shrubberies, appears more general in the central and northern parts of New Jersey, than in the southern parts, or in the state of Pennsylvania.

Extensive deposits of copper are found on the banks of the Passaic, in Lodi t-ship, about 1 mile S. E. of Belleville.

The county is well watered, having, beside the rivers on its boundaries, Ringwood, Ramapo, and Saddle rivers; all of which, rising in New York, flow S. to the Passaic; each having considerable tributaries, which though short, are by their rapid falls made available for hydraulic purposes. Ringwood river receives a considerable accesion to its waters, from Long pond or Greenwood lake, in a high and narrow valley between a ridge of the Wawayanda mountains and Sterling mountain. The lake is nearly 5 miles long, but only about a mile of its length is within the state of New Jersey. It pours forth its tribute through Long Pond river.

Hohokus Brook is a rapid stream of Franklin t-ship, which, after having, in a course of 9 miles, given motion to many mills, unites with the Saddle river. The Hackensack, also rising in New York, has an independent course to Newark bay, and receives several tributaries from either hand.

In this county, the first settlements of the state by Europeans were made. The Hollanders were here the pioneers of civilization, aided probably by some Danes or Norwegians, who adopted the name of Bergen from the capitol of Norway. Their descendants occupy the lands of their ancestors, and retain much of their primitive habits and virtues, their industry, cleanliness, and love of flowers; for the latter is a taste so pure and delightful, that we dare to rank it among the virtues. New York is much indebted to the Dutch gardeners for her supplies of flowers and vegetables.

After the country was reduced under the English rule, in 1764, English settlers came in considerable numbers from Long Island and Barbadoes. They were not so numerous, however, as immediately to lose their character of strangers, and they resided chiefly in the "*English Neighbourhood*," and at New Barbadoes.

In 1830, the population of the county was 22,412, divided as follows: white males 10,299, white females 9634, free coloured males 1061, females 834, male slaves 306, female slaves 280. Of these, there were aliens 213; deaf and dumb whites 10, blacks 3; blind, whites 12, blacks 5.

The provisions for moral instruction are the religious societies, consisting of the German Reformed, Episcopalian, Presbyterian, Baptist, and Methodist; a county bible society, Sunday schools, and temperance societies; academies in the larger villages, and common schools in every populous vicinity.

The chief towns are Jersey City, Hoboken, Bergen, Hackensack, the seat of justice, Closter, New Milford, New Prospect, Godwinsville, New Manchester, Ryerson's, Ramapo, Boardville, Ringwood, Stralenberg, Old Bridge, New Bridge, New Durham, English Neighbourhood, Communipaw, and Pamrepaw.

In 1832, the county contained 5796 taxables, 1262 householders, whose rateables did not exceed 30 dollars, 533 single men, 75 merchants, 7 fisheries, 84 run of stones for grinding grain, 16 cotton factories, 5 woollen factories, 10 carding machines, 4 furnaces and 16 forges, 93 saw mills, 3 paper mills, 4 fulling mills, 127 tan vats, 13 distilleries, 1 flint glass, and 1 china manufactory, both extensive; 1 printing, dyeing and bleaching establishment, and 4025 horses and mules, and 10,188 neat cattle above 3 years of age; and it paid state tax $2631 43, county tax $5000, poor tax $2500, school tax $100, road tax $6000.

The county is extensively agricultural, raising a large surplus of grain and esculent vegetables for its manufacturing population, and for the New York market.

The improved means for transporting its produce to market, are beside the ordinary country roads, nine turnpikes and two rail-roads, exclusive of that made by Mr. Stephens along the North river. The turnpikes are, two from Jersey City to Newark, one from Hoboken to Paterson, one from Hoboken to Hackensack, one from Hackensack to Paterson, one from New Prospect to the Ramapo works, in the State of New York, the Ringwood and Long Pond road, the Newark and Pompton, and the Paterson and Hamburg. These have been made, and others have been authorized by law. A rail-road has been completed from Jersey City to Paterson, and another is now being made from the Hudson river through Newark, Elizabethtown, Rahway and Woodbridge, to New Brunswick.

The courts of the county are holden at Hackensack; the common pleas, orphans' and general quarter sessions, on the following Tuesdays, viz. 4th January, 4th March, 2d August, 4th October; and the circuit courts, on the Tuesdays of 4th March and 4th October.

Bergen sends 1 member to the legislative council, and 3 to the assembly.

The following notice of the country embraced by this county, taken from Smith's History of New Jersey, will be interesting to its present inhabitants. "Near the mouth of the bay, upon the side of Overprook creek, adjacent to Hackensack river, several of the rich valleys were then, (1680,) settled by the Dutch; and near Snake hill was a fine plantation, owned by Pinhorne and Eickbe, for half of which, Pinhorne is said to have paid £500. There were other settlements upon Hackensack river, and on a creek near it, Sarah Kiersted, of New York, had a tract given her by an old Indian sachem, for services in interpreting between the Indians and Dutch, and on which several families were settled; John Berrie had a large plantation, 2 or 3 miles above, where he then lived, and had considerable improvements; as had also near him, his son-in-law, *Smith*, and one Baker, from Barbadoes. On the west side of the creek, opposite to Berrie, were other plantations; but none more northerly. There was a considerable settlement upon Bergen point, then called Constable Hook, and first improved by Edsall, in Nicoll's time. Other small plantations were improved along Bergen neck, to the east, between the point and a large village of 20 families (*Communipaw*). Further along lived 16 or 18 families, and opposite New York about 40 families were seated. Southward from this, a few families settled together, at a place called Duke's farm; and further up the country was a place called Hobuck, formerly owned by a Dutch merchant, who, in the Indian wars with the Dutch, had his wife, children and servants murdered by the Indians, and his house and stock destroyed by them; but it was now settled again, and a mill erected there. Along the river side to the N. were lands settled by William Lawrence, Samuel Edsall, and Capt. Beinfield; and at Haversham, near the Highlands, governor Carteret had taken up two large tracts; one for himself, the other for Andrew Campyne, and Co., which were now but little improved. The plantations on both sides of the neck, to its utmost extent, as also those at Hackensack, were under the jurisdiction of Bergentown, situate about the middle of the neck; where was a court held by selectmen or overseers, consisting of 4 or more in number, as the people thought best, chose annually to try small causes, as had been the practice in all the rest of the towns at first; 2 courts of sessions were held here yearly, from which, if the cause exceeded £20, the party might appeal to the governor, council, and court of deputies or assembly."

"*Bergen*, a compact town which had been fortified against the Indians, contained about 70 families; its inhabitants were chiefly Dutch, some of whom had been settled there upwards of 40 years."

STATISTICAL TABLE OF BERGEN COUNTY.

Townships, &c.	Length.	Breadth.	Area.	Surface.	Population.		
					1810	1820	1830
Barbadoes, New,	7	4	11,500	level,	2835	2592	1693
Bergen,	13	4	20,000	part hilly,	2690	3137	4651
Franklin,	10	9	45,000	hilly, rolling,	2839	2968	3449
Hackensack,	9	2½	24,000	hill and valley,	1918	2076	2200
Harrington,	9½	7	34,000	do. do.	2087	2296	2581
Lodi,	10	5	22,000	flat,			1356
Pompton,	14	12	70,000	mountainous,	2060	2818	3085
Saddle River,	10	8	41,000	do.	2174	2291	3397
			267,500		16,603	18,178	22,412

Bergen, village, of Bergen t-ship, Bergen co., about 16 miles S. of Hackensack, and 3 west of Jersey city, upon the summit of Bergen ridge, and equidistant between the turnpike roads leading to Newark, contains a Dutch Reformed church, and some twenty or thirty houses. This town was settled about 1616, probably by Danes, who accompanied the Hollanders.

Bergen t-ship, Bergen co., is bounded N. by Hackensack t-ship, E. by Hudson river and New York bay, S. by the strait called Kill Van Kuhl, W. by the Hackensack river and Newark bay; greatest length N. and S. 13, breadth 4 miles; area, 20,000 acres. Surface hilly on the N. E., on the W. and S. level. Soil, red shale and marsh. A large body of the latter, with Cedar swamp, lies on the Hackensack river, extending from the head of Newark bay, through the t-ship. The t-ship is intersected by several turnpike roads running in various directions. New Durham, Weehawk, Hoboken, Jersey City, Bergen, Communipaw, and Pamrepaw, are towns of the t-ship. There are post-offices at Jersey City and Hoboken. Population in 1830, 4651.

In 1832, there were in the t-ship 1167 taxables, 366 householders, whose ratable estate does not exceed 30 dollars, 191 single men, 22 merchants, 2 grist mills, 1 saw mill, 3 ferries, 1 toll bridge, 10 tan vats, 1 grain distillery, 1 glass and 1 china manufactory, and 1 woollen manufactory, 446 horses and mules, and 1287 neat cattle above the age of three years. The t-ship paid state tax, $422 74; county, $613 36; poor, $800; road, $1500.

Berkely. (See *Sandtown.*)

Berkshire Valley, the S. W. part of Longwood valley, Jefferson t-ship, Morris co., W. of Greenpond mountain, 12 miles N. W. from Morristown, 237 from W. C., and 71 from Trenton. A wild and rocky spot, through which runs a branch of the Rockaway river, giving motion to several forges, &c. There is also a post-office and a Presbyterian church here.

Bernard t-ship, Somerset co., bounded N. by Mendham t-ship, Morris co.; E. by the Passaic river, dividing it from Morris t-ship, of the said county; S. E. by Warren t-ship, S. W. by Bridgewater t-ship, and W. by Bedminster t-ship. Centrally, distant N. E. from Somerville, 7 miles; greatest length, N. and S. 9; breadth, E. and W. 7 miles; area, 25,000 acres; surface hilly, and in great part mountainous; soil on hills, clay and loom; in the valleys, limestone; well cultivated by wealthy farmers. The north branch of the Raritan flows on the western boundary, and receives from the t-ship Mine brook and smaller tributaries. Dead run flows to the Passaic, on the S. E. line. Baskingridge, Liberty Corner, Logtown and Vealtown, are villages of the t-ship; the two first post-towns. Population in 1830, 2062. In 1832, the t-ship contained about 400 taxables, 68 householders, whose ratable estate did not exceed 30 dollars, 34 single men, 5 stores, 8 saw mills, 3 grist mills, 1 fulling mill, 5 distilleries, 461 horses and mules, and 1105 neat cattle 3 years old and upwards, and paid state tax, $306 70; county tax, $695 50.

Berry's Creek, a marsh creek of Lodi t-ship, Bergen co., has a southerly course of about 4 miles.

Bethany Hole Run, small tributary of Hains' creek, Evesham t-ship, Burlington co., flows by a course of about 3 miles into the dam of Taunton furnace.

Bethel, mount and church, Mansfield t-ship, Warren co., 12 miles E. of the town of Belvidere.

Bethlehem t-ship, Hunterdon co., bounded N. W. by the Musconetcong river, which divides it from Warren co., N. E. by Lebanon t-ship, S. E. by Ringwood, and S. W. by Alexandria. Centrally distant N. W. from Flemington, 13 miles; greatest length E. and W. 9 miles, breadth N. and S. 9 miles; area 25,000 acres; surface mountainous on the north, elsewhere hilly; soil, clay, red shale, and loam, with a vein of limestone on the east foot of the Musconetcong mountain; drained chiefly by Alberson's brook, a tributary of Spruce run, and some small tributaries of Musconetcong creek. Charleston, Bloomsbury, Hickory, Pattenburg, are villages of the t-ship—Vansyckles and Perryville, post-towns. Population in 1830, 2032. In 1832, the t-ship contained a Presbyterian church, 3 stores, 3 saw mills, 5 grist mills, 1 oil mill, 25 tan vats, 5 distilleries, 480 horses and mules, and 820 neat cattle above the age of 3 years; and paid poor tax, $900; road tax, $700; county and state tax, $791 68.

Bevens, p-o., of Sussex co., named after the postmaster, James C. Bevens, 241 miles N. E. from W. C., and 83 from Trenton.

Billingsport, more properly written Byllingsport, named after Edward Bylling, a merchant of England, the purchaser of Lord Berkeley's undivided moiety of the province. It lies upon the river Delaware below the mouth of Mantua creek, and 12 miles below Camden, and was rendered famous by the fort erected here during the revolutionary war, for defence of the channel of the river, remains of which are still visible. It contains a tavern and ferry, and some half dozen dwellings.

Birmingham, small hamlet of Trenton t-ship, Hunterdon co. 5 miles N. W. from the city of Trenton, contains a tavern and some half dozen dwellings.

Birmingham, formerly called New Mills, village, on the north branch of the Rancocus creek, Northampton t-ship, Burlington co., 4 miles S. E. of Mount Holly, contains a cotton manufactory, a grist mill, saw mill, fulling mill, a cupola furnace, and from 15 to 20 dwellings. Shreve's calico printing works are within two miles of the village, upon the same stream.

Black Creek, Vernon t-ship, Sussex co., rises on the S. E. foot of the Pochuck mountain, flows northwardly, about 5 miles to the Warwick creek.

Blackwoodtown, village of Gloucester co., upon the main branch of Big Timber creek, near the head of navigation; 8 or 9 miles from its mouth, 5 miles S. E. of Woodbury, and 11 miles from Camden; contains 1 Presbyterian and large Methodist church, an extensive woollen manufactory chiefly employed on kerseynette, belonging to Newkirk and Co., 3 stores, 1 tavern, and about 50 dwellings; a 2 horse stage plies daily between this town and Camden.

Black's Creek, S. W. boundary of Chesterfield t-ship, rising by several branches in Hanover t-ship, flowing W. and N. W. about 8 miles to the river Delaware, below Bordentown. The Amboy rail-road crosses its mouth over a wooden bridge. Bacon's run is a branch of the stream, and part of the aforesaid boundary; the creek drives several mills.

Black Horse. (See *Columbus*.)

Black Run, tributary of the S. branch of Toms' river, Dover t-ship, Monmouth co.

Black Brook, tributary of the Passaic river, rises at the N. E. base of Long hill, Chatham t-ship, Morris co., flows westerly along the hill, by a course of 7 or 8 miles to its recipient in Morris t-ship.

Blackley's Mineral Spring, Acquackanonk t-ship, Essex co., 10 miles N. W. from New York, 4 S. E. from Paterson; formerly much frequented as a useful chalybeate.

Blackwood Meadow Brook, a small tributary of the Passaic river, flowing W. to its recipient in the N. W. angle of Livingston t-ship, Essex co.

Black River, is the name given to the Lamington river, above Potter's Falls. It rises by 2 small branches, on the borders of Roxbury and Randolph t-ships, flows under this name a S. W. course of about 16 miles, to the falls at the point of junction, between Hunterdon, Somerset and Morris co., draining a valley of considerable extent, and in parts very fertile.

Black River, or *Cooper's Mills*, is also the name of a small village on the above stream, situate in Chester t-ship, Morris co., on the turnpike road leading from Morristown to Easton, 14 miles N. W. from the former; contains 1 grist mill, 2 saw mills, a store, and 6 or 8 dwellings; it is a place of considerable business; the country around it is hilly, and not very fertile.

Blackwells, hamlet of Hillsborough t-ship, Somerset co., on the left bank of the Millstone river, 6½ miles S. of Somerville, pleasantly situated, in a fertile country; contains a large grist mill, fulling mill, store, and several dwellings; a bridge crosses the Millstone river here.

Black Point, at the confluence of the Shrewsbury and Nevisink rivers, Shrewsbury t-ship, Monmouth co.

Blazing Star Ferry, over Staten Island Sound, on the road from Woodbury to Staten Island, about 7 miles N. E. from Amboy; the post-route to New York, formerly lay by this ferry.

Bloomfield t-ship, Essex county, bounded N. by Acquackanonck t-sp, E. by the Passaic river, which divides it from Bergen co., E. by Newark t-ship, S. and S. W. by Orange, and W. by Caldwell. Centrally distant N. from Newark, 6 miles; greatest length 5, breadth 4½ miles; area, 14,000 acres; surface hilly; mountainous on the west; on the eastern boundary, the ground rises gradually from the river, and offers beautiful sites for country seats, many of which are thus occupied. It is drained by two streams which rise near the foot of the mountain, and flow by tortuous courses to the river, known as the Second and Third rivers. The first has a length scarce exceeding 6 miles, and the last, which forms a semi-ellipsis, and rises in the notch in Acquackanonck t-ship, may be double that length. These streams are the source of the wealth of the t-ship, and have converted it almost wholly into a manufacturing village. The soil is based on red sandstone, in which are exhaustless quarries of fine building stone, vast quantities of which have been sent to New York, and other places. The villages of the t-ship are Belleville, Bloomfield, Spring Garden, and Speertown. At the two first are post-offices. Pop. in 1830, 4309; in 1832, the t-ship contained 500 taxables, 206 householders, whose ratable estate did not exceed $30; 82 single men, 17 merchants, 6 grist mills, 2 cotton manufactories, 5 saw mills, 4 rolling mills for copper, 3 paper mills, 1 paint factory, 2 calico printing and bleaching works, 1 very extensive; 40 tan vats, 3 woollen factories, and several very extensive shoe factories; 387 horses and mules, and 862 neat cattle above three years old. And the t-ship paid state tax $754 50; county $238 37; poor $1200; and road $1200. The annual value of manufactured products, probably exceed 2½ millions of dollars.

Bloomfield, p-t. of the above t-ship, 3½ miles N. of Newark, extending for near 3 miles in a N. W. direction, and including what was formerly known as West Bloomfield. The chief part of the town lies upon the old road, but part of it on the turnpike; it contains about 1600 inhabitants, above 250 dwellings, 2 hotels, an academy, boarding school, 4 large common schools, 12 stores, 1 Presbyterian church, 2 Methodist churches; a very extensive trade is carried on here in tanning, currying, and shoemaking, and the following manufactories are considered as annexed to the town: 2 woollen factories, 1 mahogany saw mill, 1 cotton mill, 1 rolling mill, 1 calico printing work, 2 saw mills for ordinary work, 1 paper mill, and 1 grist mill.

Bloomingdale, village on the Pequannock creek, Pompton t-ship, Bergen co., 20 miles N. W. from Hackensack, upon the Paterson and Hamburg turnpike road; contains 1 forge, a saw mill, grist mill, machine factory, bark mill, 1 tavern, 2 stores, and some 8 or 10 dwellings; the country around it is mountainous and barren.

Bloomsbury, p-t. of Greenwich t-ship, Warren co., on the turnpike road from Somerville to Philipsburg, and on both sides of the Musconetcong creek, part of the town being in Hunterdon co.; by the post-route 198 miles from W. C., 49 from Trenton, and 14 S. from Belvidere, 18 miles N. W. from Flemington; contains 1 grist mill, 1 oil mill, a cotton manufactory, 2 taverns, 1 store, and from 30 to 40 dwellings; the soil of the valley around it is rich limestone.

Bloomsbury, village of Nottingham t-ship, Burlington co., a suburb of the city of Trenton, below the Assunpink creek, and at the head of the sloop navigation of the river. The bridge across the Delaware runs from the centre of the village; there are here a Presbyterian meeting, several taverns and stores, steam-boat landings and wharves, with about 150 dwellings and 900 inhabitants. The race-way of the Trenton water power company, will pass through the village. (See *Trenton.*)

Blue Ball, village of Howell t-ship, Monmouth co., 4 miles S. from Freehold; contains a tavern and store, 10 or 12 dwellings, 1 Presbyterian and

1 Methodist church. The soil here has been so greatly improved by marl, that lands which 15 years since would not bring $20 the acre, now command $50.

Blue Anchor, tavern and hamlet of Gloucester t-ship, Gloucester co., in the heart of the pine forest, about 25 miles S. E. from Camden.

Boonton, manufacturing village of Hanover t-ship, Morris co., on the N. side of Rockaway river, 9 miles N. of Morristown, situate on the side of a high hill, at the entrance of a dark, narrow, rocky valley; contains the works of the East Jersey Iron Manufacturing Company, consisting of an extensive rolling mill, a blast furnace and foundery, 3 stores, and about 40 dwellings, a school house and a handsome church. In forcing the Trowbridge mountain here, the stream has formed a rapid and a picturesque cascade of about 30 feet fall, and this circumstance has made the site a very advantageous one for hydraulic works. The Morris canal ascends from the valley by an inclined plane 800 feet long, having a lift of 80 feet, which is passed over in from 12 to 15 minutes. Pop. between 300 and 400, principally English; the village was founded in 1828, and is one of the most romantic spots in the state.

Bonhamtown, Woodbridge t-ship, Middlesex co., 5 miles N. E. from New Brunswick, on the turnpike road leading thence to Woodbridge, from which it is distant 6 miles; contains 10 or 12 dwellings, 2 taverns, 1 store and school house; surrounded by a gravelly and poor soil.

Boardville, on Ringwood river, and on the Ringwood and Longwood turnpike road in Pompton t-ship, Bergen co., 21 miles N. W. from Hackensack; contains a Dutch Reformed church, a forge, distillery, a school house, and several farm houses. The narrow valley in which it lies is rich and well cultivated.

Bordentown, borough and p-t., of Chesterfield t-ship, Burlington co., situate on the bank of the Delaware river, at the junction of the Crosswick's creek with that stream, 11 miles N. W. from Mount Holly, 170 N. E. from W. C., 30 from Philadelphia, 10 from Burlington, and 7 S. E. from Trenton; contains about 1000 inhabitants, 200 dwellings, a Quaker meeting house, a Baptist and a Methodist church, 5 stores and 5 taverns, and is surrounded by a fertile and well cultivated country of sandy loam. The Camden and Amboy rail-road passes through the town, by a viaduct beneath its principal streets; and stages run from the town, daily, to Trenton, Princeton, New Brunswick, Long Branch, New Egypt, Mount Holly, &c. &c., and 4 steam-boats, to Bristol, Burlington, and Philadelphia.

This town was founded by Mr. Joseph Borden, an early settler here, and a distinguished citizen of the state, and has borne his name for nearly a century. It was incorporated 9th December, 1825. Its site is perhaps the most beautiful on the Delaware, and the village is alike remarkable for its healthiness and cleanliness, and the neatness of its dwellings. Built upon a plain 65 feet above the surface of the river, and from which there is a descent upon three sides, its streets, speedily drained after the rain, are dry; and lined by umbrageous trees, furnish always an agreeable promenade during the summer season. From the brow of the hill, there is a delightful view of the majestic Delaware, pursuing for miles its tranquil course through the rich country which it laves. The beauty of this scene is greatest in the autumn, when the thousand varied and brilliant tints of the forest trees are contrasted with the deep azure of the sky, and the limpid blue of the mirror like waters. The attractions of the scene determined Joseph Buonaparte, Count de Surveilliers, in his choice of a residence in this country; and this distinguished exile, who has filled two thrones, and has pretensions based on popular suffrage to a third, has dwelt here many years in philosophic retirement. He has in the vicinity about 1500 acres of land, part of which possessed natural beauty, which his taste and wealth have been employed to embellish. At the expense of some hundred thousand dollars, he has converted a wild and impoverished tract, into a park of surpassing beauty, blending the charms of woodland and plantation scenery, with a delightful water prospect. The present buildings, plain but commodious, are on the site of the offices of his original and more splendid mansion, which was destroyed by fire, together with some rare pictures from the pencils of the first masters, whose merit made them invaluable. With characteristic liberality, the Count has opened his grounds to the public, but we regret to perceive, that he has been ungratefully repaid, by the defacement of his ornamental structures, and mutilation of his statues.

Bordentown is much resorted to by the citizens of Philadelphia during the hot months, who find excellent entertainment in the large commodious public houses, and in private and more retired mansions. Few places near the city are more desirable as a summer residence, which is now rendered uncommonly convenient to citizens by the almost hourly means of communicating with Philadelphia and New York. The benefit of these advantageous circumstances to the town, becomes apparent in its increase, many new houses having been built in 1832 and 1833. The outlet lock of the Delaware and Raritan canal is in front of the town, which will in all probability become a depot, for much produce of the surrounding country destined for the New York or Philadelphia market. Under these prospects the value of property here, we are told, has risen 50 per cent. within two years.

Borden's Run, an arm of the S. branch of Toms' river, Upper Freehold t-ship, Monmouth co., flows E. about 7 miles through the S. E. angle of the t-ship.

Bottle Hill, p-t., Chatham t-ship, Morris co., on the turnpike road from Elizabethtown to Morristown, 13 miles from the one, and 4½ from the other; 223 N. E. from W. C. and 57 from Trenton; contains a tavern, three stores, a Presbyterian church, an academy, and above 40 dwellings, generally very neat; the surrounding country gently undulating, and well cultivated.

Bound Brook, p-t., of Bridgewater t-ship, Somerset co., on the S. W. boundary of the county, at the confluence of the Green Brook with the Raritan river. A part of the village is in Piscataway t-ship, of the adjoining county of Middlesex, on the turnpike road from New Brunswick to Somerville, 7 miles from the one, and 4 from the other. The town, including Middle Brook, extends a mile from Green Brook to Middle Brook, and contains a large and neat Presbyterian church, an academy, 3 taverns, 4 stores, a large grist mill, &c., and about 50 dwellings. There is a bridge over the river here. The surrounding country is fertile. The Delaware and Raritan canal runs near the town.

Bound Brook, small stream rising in Newark t-ship, and running S. E. through the marsh, into Newark bay, forming the boundary between Elizabeth and Newark t-ships.

Bound Brook. (See ***Green Brook***.)

Bowentown, Hopewell t-ship, Cumberland co., a small hamlet, of some half dozen houses, midway on the road from Bridgetown to Road's town, about 2½ miles from each.

Branchville, p-t., of Frankford t-ship, Sussex co., on the Morris turnpike road, by the mail route, 235 miles from Washington city, 77 from Trenton, 7 from Newton, and 2 from Augusta. There are several mills here upon a branch of the Paulinskill, within the space of two miles.

Bread and Cheese Run, tributary of the south branch of Rancocus creek, Northampton t-ship, Burlington co., unites with that stream 8 or 10 miles below its source.

Brigantine Inlet, Old, formerly

through Brigantine Beach, on the Atlantic, now closed.

Brigantine Beach, on the Atlantic ocean, Galloway t-ship, Gloucester co., extends from Quarter's Inlet, eastwardly, to Old Brigantine Inlet, about 6 miles, by about a half a mile in width. Several salt works have been established here.

Bricksborough, village, of Maurice t-ship, Cumberland co., upon the left bank of Maurice river, 12 miles from its mouth, within 2 of Port Elizabeth, and 14 of Bridgeton, contains from 12 to 15 dwellings. It lies at the confluence of Muskee run, with the river.

Bridgeport, small hamlet of Washington t-ship, Burlington co., upon the left bank of Wading river, 29 miles S. E. from Mount Holly, and 5 from the confluence of Wading with the Little Egg Harbour river, contains a tavern, store, and some 4 or 5 dwellings, in sandy, pine country. The river is navigable above the town.

Bridgeton, p-t. and seat of justice of Cumberland co., upon the Cohansey creek, 20 miles from its mouth, 175 N. E. from W. C., and sixty S. of Trenton. The town is built on both sides of the creek, over which is a wooden drawbridge, from whence it has its name. It formerly bore that of Cohansey. It contains a court-house of brick, in the centre of a street, upon the W. bank of the creek, a prison of stone, and public offices, on the E., a Presbyterian, a Baptist, and a Methodist church; a bank with an authorized capital of $200,000, of which $50,000 have been paid in; a public library, a Masonic lodge, an academy, a woollen manufactory, a grist mill, an extensive rolling mill, foundery, and nail factory. It exports lumber, flour, grain, nails, and iron castings. Thirty schooners and sloops, of from 50 to 80 tons burthen, sail from the port, which is one of entry and delivery. The collection district of Bridgeton comprehends the counties of Gloucester, Salem, Cumberland, and Cape May; excepting such parts of Gloucester and Cape May, as are included in the district of Egg Harbour. The collector resides at Bridgeton.—250 licenses issued from his office in the year 1832. The country around is a sandy loam, rich and productive in wheat, corn, and rye. The most remarkable object, here, is the iron works of Messrs. Reeves and Whitaker, which occupy a number of stone buildings on the W. side of the creek, above the bridge, and are driven by a water power of 15 feet head and fall. They were originally built in 1815, but were consumed by fire in 1822, and rebuilt and enlarged in the same year. The rolling mill is capable of manufacturing into hoop and round iron, from blooms, 25,000 tons per annum. The nail factory contains 29 nail machines, competent to make 1500 tons of nails annually; and the foundery will make 250 tons of castings, from a cupola furnace, with anthracite coal. These works give employment to 125 men and boys, who receive their wages, monthly, in cash, to the amount of $30,000 per annum; and yield the means of support to nearly 500 persons. Two vessels are constantly employed in bringing coal to the works from Richmond, and one in the intercourse with the city of Philadelphia. There are some very good houses in the town, which has quite an air of business.

Bridgeville, small hamlet of Oxford t-ship, Warren co., 4 miles E. of Belvidere, the county town.

Bridgewater t-ship, Somerset co., bounded N. by Bedminster and Bernard t-ships, N. E. by Warren t-ship, S. E. by Greenbrook, dividing it from Piscataway t-ship, Middlesex co., S. by the Raritan river, separating it from Franklin and Hillsborough t-ships, and S. W. by Readington t-ship, Hunterdon co. Greatest length N. E. and S. W. 13 miles; breadth E. and W. 11 miles; area, about 35,000 acres; surface, on the N. E., mountainous, elsewhere level, or gently undulating; soil, generally, red shale, and well cultivated in grain and grass. The N. branch of the Raritan unites with the Lamington river, on the N.

boundary, and flows thence, S. to meet the S. branch, about 4 miles W. from Somerville; the latter river receives from the W., Holland and Campbell's Brooks; Middle Brook crosses the E. part of the t-ship to the main branch of the Raritan, about 5 miles E. of Somerville. Somerville, the county town, North Branch, Bound Brook, and Middle Brook, are villages, the three first named, post-towns. Popu- in 1830, 3549. In 1832 the t-ship contained about 700 taxables, 152 householders, whose ratable estate did not exceed 30 dollars, 93 single men, 17 stores, 5 saw mills, and 3 grist mills, 3 fulling mills, 29 tan vats, 4 distilleries for cider, 6 carding machines, 858 horses and mules, and 1570 neat cattle, 3 years old and upwards; and paid state tax, $464 96; county, $1145 32.

Broadway, village, of Mansfield t-ship, near the S. W. boundary line, Warren co., on the turnpike road from Philipsburg to Schooley's mountain, about 10 miles from the former, and 14 from the latter, contains a store and tavern, 2 grist mills, 1 saw mill, and 10 or 12 dwellings. It lies in the valley of the Pohatcong creek, upon a soil of fertile limestone.

Broad Oyster Creek, Downe t-ship, Cumberland co., flows from Oranoken creek, through the salt marsh, into the Delaware bay.

Brooklyn, hamlet, of Piscataway t-ship, Middlesex co., on Dismal Brook, 6 miles N. E. from New Brunswick, contains a grist mill, saw mill, and some 8 or 10 dwellings.

Brown's Point, on the Raritan bay, at the mouth of Middletown creek, Middletown t-ship, Monmouth co., 5 miles S. E. from Perth Amboy, 14 miles N. E. from Freehold. There are here, a good landing, 2 taverns, 3 stores, and 12 or 15 dwellings; surrounding country, flat and sandy, but made productive by marl.

Brunswick, North, t-ship, of Middlesex co., bounded N. by the river Raritan, E. by South Amboy t-ship, S. by South Brunswick, and W. by Franklin t-ship, Somerset co. Greatest length E. and W. 9 miles; breadth N. and S. 7 miles; area, 23,000 acres, of which 5000 are unimproved; surface level; soil red shale and sandy loam, drained on the N. by the Raritan, N. E. by South river, centrally by Lawrence's Brook, and N. W. by Six Mile run and its branches. The Princeton and Brunswick, and the Trenton and Brunswick turnpike roads run along and through the t-ship; the first on the W. boundary of the t-ship and county. New Brunswick, the seat of justice of the county, Washington, Six Mile Run, and Old Bridge, are villages, and the three first, post-towns of the t-ship. Population in 1830, 5274. In 1832 the t-ship contained about 1050 taxables, whose ratable estates did not exceed 30 dollars, 111 single men, 47 stores, 1 saw mill, 4 run of stones for grain, 1 plaster mill, 3 carding machines and fulling mills, 90 tan vats, 4 distilleries for cider, 593 horses and mules, and 831 neat cattle, above the age of 3 years; and it paid state tax, $456 84; county, $561 76; road, $200; poor, $1250.

Brunswick, South, t-ship, of Middlesex co., bounded on the N. E. by North Brunswick, E. by South Amboy, S. by East and West Windsor, and W. and N. W. by Franklin t-ship, Somerset co. Centrally distant from New Brunswick S. W. 12 miles; greatest length N. and S. 10; breadth E. and W. 7 miles; area, about 36,000 acres; surface, generally, level, with some hills on the west; soil sandy loam and red shale; in places extremely well cultivated and productive; drained N. E. by Lawrence's Brook, S. W. by Millstone river and its tributaries, Cranberry Brook, Devil's Brook, Heathcoat's Brook. Kingston, and Cranberry, are post-towns, lying partly in the t-ship; and Plainsborough Cross Roads and Maplestown are hamlets of the t-ship. Population 2557, in 1830. In 1832 the t-ship contained 527 taxables, whose ratables did not exceed 30 dollars; 32 single men, 10 merchants, 7 saw mills, 8 run of stones for grist, 5 tan vats, 10 distilleries for cider, 755 horses and mules, and 1275 neat cattle; and it paid state tax, $438 79; county, $539 49; poor, $700.

Buck Pond, Pompton t-ship, Bergen co., near Bear Fort mountain, covers about 150 acres, and sends a small tributary to the Pequannock creek.

Buckshutem, hamlet, near the confluence of Buckshutem creek with Maurice river, Milleville t-ship, Cumberland co., 3 miles from Port Elizabeth; contains 8 or 10 dwellings, a grist and saw mill, and store.

Buckshutem Creek, tributary of Maurice river, Cumberland co., rises by 2 branches, one on the line between Milleville and Fairfield t-ships; the other on the line between Fairfield and Downe t-ships, and the main stream divides Milleville from Downe. It is a fine mill stream.

Buddstown, hamlet, Northampton t-ship, Burlington co., on Stop the Jade creek, a tributary of the south branch of the Rancocus; contains a tavern, store, and saw mill, on the edge of the pines.

Budd's Pond, small lake of Roxbury t-ship, Morris co., on the summit of Schooley's mountain, 17 miles N. W. of Morristown, and 7 from the mineral spring, from which the visiters resort hither, for amusement, in boating and fishing.

Bull's Creek, small tributary of Little Egg Harbour river. Spoy's mill is near its mouth.

Bull's Island, in the Delaware river, 23 miles above Trenton, near Saxtonville. The feeder of the Delaware and Raritan canal communicates with the Delaware here.

Burlington County: the first recognition we find of the bounds of this co. is in the act of Assembly, 1694, but its limits were more definitely settled by the act 21st Jan. 1710, declaring, that the line of partition between Burlington and Gloucester counties begins at the mouth of Pensauken, otherwise, Cropwell creek; thence up the same to the fork; thence along the southernmost branch thereof, sometimes called Cole Branch, until it comes to the head thereof; thence by a straight line to the southernmost branch of Little Egg Harbour river; thence down the said branch and river, to the mouth thereof; thence to the next inlet, on the S. side of Little Egg Harbour's most southerly inlet; thence along the sea coast, to the line of partition between East and West Jersey; thence on such line, by Maidenhead and Hopewell, to the northernmost bounds of Amwell t-ship; thence to the river Delaware, and by the river, to the first mentioned station. This surface has been reduced by the act which established Hunterdon county, March, 1714, making the Assunpink creek the N. boundary of the county. It is now bounded N. by Hunterdon co., E. by Monmouth co., S. E. by the Atlantic ocean, S. W. by Gloucester co., and N. W. by the Delaware river. Central latitude, 39° 50′; longitude E. from W. C., 2° 18′; greatest length, N. W. and S. E. 54; breadth, E. and W., 31 miles; area, 553,000 acres, or near 833 square miles.

Except immediately on the border of the Assunpink creek, where some primitive rock appears, the whole of this county is alluvial, composed of sand, gravel, loam and clay, variously blended. It would seem that the diluvian of the mountainous country above has been spread by the Delaware river, over the northwestern border of the county, for some 12 or 14 miles from the present bank, forming with the aggregations from the sea a very fertile loam, which, manured with stable dung, ashes, or marl, produces abundant crops of rye, corn, oats, beans, peas, grass, and potatoes. Strips of sand occur in this loamy belt, and sometimes masses of stiff clay, which were probably once washed by the tides of the ocean. East of the belt of loam, is a mass of sand overlaying clay, and extending, for near 40 miles, to the marshes, which border the sea shore. In this sandy district, there are occasionally spots where the clay, approaching the surface, mingles with the sand, and forms tolerable soil, producing oak; and in low grounds, where marl is near the surface, some natural meadow, easily brought to produce the reclaimed grasses. But the great wealth of this portion of the county is the pine timber, with which it is covered, and which is cut into valuable lumber, or fed to the furnace of the iron foundery or steamboat. Bog ore is found in many places; marl generally through the western part of the county, and possibly may be turned up every where, by digging sufficiently deep. In the marl pits, animal reliques, such as shells, bones, and also petrified vegetables, are frequent. But the most extraordinary relic, yet discovered in these deposits, is a piece of wrought copper bolt, about an inch square, and two inches long, bearing the marks of tools, taken about 10 years since, from a marl pit, 10 feet below the surface, and within a short distance of Mount Holly, on the farm of Mr. Thomas Howell. Of the time when, and the means by which such a deposit was made, it is scarce possible to form a plausible conjecture.

The waters of the county flow, either N. W. to the Delaware river, or S. W. to the Atlantic ocean. The former consist of the Assunpink, Crosswick's, Black's, Craft's, Assiscunk, Rancocus, and Pensauken creeks, and their tributaries; the latter of the Wading and Mullica rivers, and their branches. The dividing ridge between these streams runs nearly parallel with the Delaware, and at about 20 miles distant from it. The streams are generally crooked, and sluggish; and the larger are navigable for 10 or 15 miles from their mouths. In Springfield t-ship, on the farm of Mr. James Shreve, is a well, whose water petrifies wood. Blocks of hickory, cut into the form of hones, have been converted into stone, in 5 years, by immersion therein.

The chief villages, and post-towns of the county are, Arneytown, Atsion, Bass River Hotel, Bordentown, Burlington, Columbus, Crosswicks, Evesham, Jacksonville, Jobstown, Juliustown, Medford, Moorestown, Mount Holly, the seat of justice, Pemberton, Recklesstown, Tuckerton, Vincenton, Wrightstown, &c. &c.

The county contained, by the report of the assessors of 1832, 123,524 acres of unimproved land, which might, with propriety, be nearly doubled; 14,210 neat cattle, 6055 horses over the age of three years, 19 stud horses, 3256 householders, with taxable property not exceeding $30 in value; 1095 single men, 86 merchants, 16 fisheries, 48 saw mills, 91 grist mills, 4 furnaces, 3 forges, 2 paper mills, one extensive, and of the most approved construction; 1 calico printing factory, 7 fulling mills, 4 cotton factories, 1 plaster mill, 350 tan vats, 11 carding machines, 35 distilleries for cider, 29 coaches and chariots, 6 phaetons and chaises, 8 four horse and 19 two horse stages, 392 dearborns, 977 covered wagons, 206 chairs and curricles, and paid state tax, $4607 12; county tax, $15,000; and township tax, $13,450.

The population of the county, in 1830, was 31,705; of whom 14,710 were white males; 15,033 white females; free coloured males, 869; free coloured females, 901; male slaves, 77; female slaves, 115; 174 aliens; 12 white, deaf and dumb; 7 white, and 3 blacks, blind. The county sends 5 members to the Assembly, and one to the Council.

STATISTICAL TABLE OF BURLINGTON COUNTY.

Townships, &c.	Length.	Breadth.	Area.	Surface generally level.	Population.		
					1810	1820	1830
Burlington,	7	7	9,702		2419	2758	2670
Chester,	7	6	22,000		1839	2253	2333
Chesterfield,	8	6	16,000		1839	2087	2386
Egg Harbour, Little,	20	10	76,800		913	1102	1490
Hanover,	16	13	44,000		2536	2642	2859
Mansfield,	10	6½	21,000		1810	1957	2083
Evesham,	15	10	67,000		3445	3977	4239
Northampton,	33	18	135,000		4171	4833	5516
Nottingham,	10	7	25,000		2615	3633	3900
Springfield,	10	6	18,000		1500	1568	1534
Washington,	20	19	112,000		1273	1225	1315
Willingboro',	6	4	7,500			787	782
			553,002		24,360	28,822	31,107

Burlington t-ship, Burlington co., bounded N. E. by Mansfield and Springfield t-ships, S. E. by Northampton, S. W. by Willingboro', and N. W. by the River Delaware. Centrally distant N. W. from Mount Holly, 6 miles; length N. and S. 7; breadth E. and W. 7 miles; area, 9702 acres; surface, level; soil, sandy loam, very well cultivated, and abundantly productive, in grass, corn, wheat, and garden vegetables, and fruits; drained by the Assiscunk creek on the north, and a branch of the Rancocus on the south. Burlington city is in the t-ship. Population in 1830, 2670. In 1832 the t-ship contained, including the city, 575 taxables, 145 single men, 6 stores, 2 fisheries, 2 grist mills, 1 ferry, 34 tan vats, 1 distillery for cider, 14 coaches and chariots, 2 two horse stages, 27 dearborns, 57 covered wagons, 9 chairs and curricles, and 30 gigs and sulkies; and it paid state tax, $373 45; county tax, $1292 16; and t-ship tax, $1000.

Burlington Island, in the river Delaware, above the city of Burlington, and opposite the town of Bristol, originally termed Matenicunk, and also Chygoes island. (See *Burlington City*.)

Burlington Collection District comprehends that part of West Jersey lying on the eastward and northward of Gloucester, and all the waters thereof within the jurisdiction of the state. Burlington city is the port of entry, and Lamberton a port of delivery only; the collector resides at the latter.

Burlington City, of Burlington t-ship, Burlington co., 20 miles N. E. from Philadelphia, 158 from W. C., and 12 S. W. from Trenton, upon the river Delaware, and opposite to the town of Bristol; contains about 300 dwellings, and 1800 inhabitants; one Episcopal, 1 Baptist, and 2 Methodist churches, one of which are for coloured people, and 1 Friend's meeting house; 1 large and commodious boarding school for girls, beautifully situate on the river bank, and 1 large boarding school for boys; the former under the direction of S. R. Gummere, and the latter of John Gummere; a free school maintained chiefly from the rents of Matenicunk or Chygoes island, lying near the town, and which was given to it for that purpose by the proprietaries, by act of Assembly, 28th September, 1682. This island contains about 300 acres, and yields a rent of about $1000 annually. There are here also a boarding school endowed by the "Society of Friends;" five common schools for white, and one for coloured children.

The town is laid out upon 9 streets running N. and S., and 4 E. and W. The lots are generally deep, admitting of spacious gardens, in which much and excellent fruit is produced, among which grapes of various kinds are common. Upon the main street, the houses are closely built, but in other parts of the town they are wide asunder, and surrounded by gardens, orchards, and grass lots. Many of the buildings are very neat and commodious, and occupied as country seats by citizens of Philadelphia—those on the river bank, below the town, are beautifully situated, with a fine verdant velvet sward to the water's edge, giving them a perpetual air of freshness and coolness, most desirable in the summer months. There are here, also, a public library, several fire companies, a beneficial society, a distinguished nursery of fruit trees, 7 considerable stores, 5 taverns, 3 practising attorneys, 3 physicians, and extensive manufactories of shoes, employing near 300 hands. Burlington was laid out as a town in the year 1677, by the first purchasers from Lord Berkeley, and was incorporated by the proprietary government, including the island only, in 1693, and subsequently by Governor Cosby. The present incorporation is by act of the state legislature, 21st December, 1784, constituting the town and port of Burlington, of the length of 3 miles on the Delaware, and such part of the river and islands opposite thereto, within the jurisdiction of the state, and extending from the river at right angles one mile into the county, "*the city of Burlington;*" and authorizing its government, by a mayor, recorder, and 3 aldermen, annually elective, with power to hold a commercial court monthly. Prior to May, 1676, the site of this town was holden by 4 Dutch families, one of whom kept a public house for the entertainment of travellers passing to and from the settlements on the west shores of the Delaware, and New York. The river here is about a mile wide, the harbour pretty good, but the town has no commerce. A great portion of the city is isolated by a creek, over which there are several bridges; the tide has been stopped out, and the marshes, which it formerly covered, are good meadows. The town is deemed healthy. Four steam-boats pass this town, to and from Philadelphia, daily.

Burnt Cabin Brook, principal branch of the Rockaway river, rises in Greenpond, in the valley between Greenpond mountain and Copperas mountain. It has a S. W. course of about 8 miles, before it unites with the main stream.

Burnt Meadow Brook, small tributary of Ringwood river, Pompton t-ship, Bergen co., into which it flows eastwardly by a course of about 6 miles.

Bustleton, hamlet, of Mansfield t-ship, Burlington co., 7 miles N. W. from Mount Holly, and 4 from Burlington city; contains a Friends' meeting house, and some half dozen farm houses, surrounded by a well cultivated country of fertile sandy loam.

Butcher's Forge, on Metetecunk river, on the line between Howell and Dover t-ships, Monmouth co., at the head of navigation, 18 miles S. E. from Freehold. There are here a forge, a grist mill, a tavern, 2 stores, and 15 or 20 dwellings. The mill pond is the largest in the state, having a length of nearly 3 miles, by nearly half a mile in breadth. Wood from the surrounding forest is boated on it to the furnace.

Byram t-ship, Sussex co., bounded N. W. by Newton t-ship; E. by Hardiston t-ship, and by Jefferson t-ship, Morris co.; S. by Roxbury t-ship, of the same co., and W. by Green t-ship, of Sussex co. Centrally distant S. E. from Newton 8 miles; greatest length N. and S. 10 miles, breadth E. and W. 8 miles; area, 21,760; surface mountainous, the t-ship being wholly covered by the South mountain. The t-ship is drained chiefly by Lubber run, which receives the waters of Lion pond, Hopatcong lake upon the E., and by Musconetcong river, which courses the whole of the southern boundary. It is crossed N. W. by the Morris and Newton turnpike road. By the census of 1830 it contained 958 inhabitants; and in 1832 187 taxables, 5 stores, 5 saw mills, 10 forge fires, 6 tan vats, 1 distillery, 123 horses and mules, and 497 neat cattle, over the age of 3 years. Andover, Lockwood, Columbia, and Stanhope, are the names of the forges within the t-ship; Brooklyn forge lies on the S. E. boundary. The Morris canal touches the south boundary of the t-ship at Stanhope. The t-ship is noted for its iron and other minerals.

Cabbagetown, hamlet, of Upper Freehold t-ship, Monmouth co., on the line between that county and Middlesex, 17 miles from Freehold, and 12 from Trenton, contains some half dozen dwellings, a wheelwright, smith and joiner's shop.

Calais, Randolph t-ship, Morris co., on the road from Morristown to Stanhope forge, 6 miles N. W. from the former; contains a Presbyterian church, store, tavern, and 12 or 15 dwellings.

Caldwell t-ship, Essex co., bounded on the W. and N. by the Passaic river, which separates it from Hanover t-ship, Morris co., E. by Acquackanonck and Bloomfield t-ships, S. by Orange and Livingston t-ships. Centrally distant N. E. from Newark 10 miles; greatest length E. and W. 7; breadth N. and S. 6; area, 16,500 acres; surface mountainous on the E., elsewhere rolling, except in the valley of the river; drained, or rather watered, by Deep and Green brooks; soil red shale and alluvion; towns, Caldwell, Fairfield, and Franklin; the first a post-town; population in 1830, 2001. In 1832 the t-ship contained 325 taxables, 36 single men, 8 merchants, 3 grist mills, 1 cotton manufactory, 3 saw mills, 12 tan vats, 1 woollen factory, 325 horses and mules, and 1001 neat cattle, over the age of 3 years: and it paid state tax, $201 06; county, $526 06; poor, $600; road, $1327.

Caldwell, p-t. of preceding t-ship, Essex co., 10 miles N. E. from Newark, 225 from W. C., and 59 from Trenton, contains a tavern, 3 stores, a grist and saw mill on Pine Brook, about 30 dwellings, and 2 Presbyterian churches. The country around it is deep clay loam.

Camden, city and t-ship, of Gloucester co., on the river Delaware, opposite to the city of Philadelphia, and port of entry and delivery of Bridgeton collection district, 8 miles N. W. from Woodbury, 137 N. E. from W. C., and 31 S. from Trenton. The site upon which it stands, was taken up between the years 1681 and 1685, in several parcels, by Messrs. Cooper, Runyon and Morris. The city was incorporated by acts 13 Feb. and 1 March, 1828, and 9 Feb. 1831; and as a t-ship by act Nov. 28, 1831. Its bounds by these acts are as follow: Beginning at the Pennsylvania line in the Delaware, opposite the mouth of a small run of water below Kaighnton, and running E. to the mouth of said run; thence by the same, crossing the public road to Woodbury, from the Camden academy; thence N. by the E. side of said road, to the road from Kaighnton to Cooper's creek bridge; thence by the E. side of the last mentioned road, and the S. side of the causey and bridge, to the middle of Cooper's creek; thence by the middle of the creek to the Delaware; thence due N. to the middle of the channel, between Petty's island and the Jersey shore; thence down the channel to the nearest point on the line between the states of Pennsylvania and New Jersey; thence by said line to the place of beginning. The district has a length of 2¼ miles on the river, by about 1¼ in breadth to the bridge over Cooper's creek. But a small portion only, of this area, is built upon: the greatest portion is employed in tillage, chiefly of fruit and early vegetables, for the Philadelphia market, to which the soil is admirably adapted; and a considerable part is still in woods, yielding shade and recreation to the inhabitants of the great city, in the hot season. The district is divided into 3 distinct villages, separated by vacant grounds from half a mile to nearly a mile in extent. That, opposite to the Northern Liberties, is known as Cooper's Point, at which there is an extensive ferry establishment, tavern, store, livery stable, and a dozen dwellings. The lower village, nearly opposite to the Navy Yard, is called Kaighnton or Kaighn's Point, from the family of that name, which settled on it in 1696, and whose descendants, still residents on, and owners of the greater part of the adjoining property, laid out town lots here, and established the ferry to Philadelphia in 1809. It contains 35 dwellings, a store, school house, 2 taverns, a tannery, an extensive smithery and manufactory of steel springs for carriages. The central and largest part of the city was originally called Camden, about the year 1772, when first divided into town lots, by the then proprietor, Jacob Cooper, and is nearly equidistant between the two Points, and opposite to the central part of Philadelphia. The land at Cooper's Point, and extensive adjacent tracts, were taken up in 1687, by William Cooper, one of the first and distinguished emigrants to the province, after the sale by Lord Berkeley to Byllinge; the whole of which is, at this time, not only possessed by his descendants, but actually, by descendants bearing the name of Cooper; no portion of it, at any time, having, in the space of 146 years, been aliened by the family.

At the period of incorporation, 1828, the population of the district was 1143; in 1830 it had increased to 1987, and now, Sept. 1833, by a census made for this work, amounts to 2341; of whom 417 are heads of families, or housekeepers, 1237 males, 1104 females, 78 widows, and 105 people of colour. It contains 364 dwelling houses, and 60 other buildings used for manufactories, stores, and schools, a Baptist, a Methodist, and a Quaker meeting house, a court-house, or town hall, where the city sessions are holden, quarterly, by the mayor, recorder, and aldermen, for the trial of minor offences, and a prison connected therewith; an academy, at which are taught the rudiments of a common English education; "the State Bank at Camden," with a capital of $300,000 dollars; a turpentine, a patent leather, and a tinware manufactory; 2 tanneries, a steam saw mill and steam grist mill, 2 saddlers and harnessmakers, other than those connected with the coachmakers; 6 coachmakers, whose business exceeds in value $60,000, annually, and whose work, much of which is exported, is remarkable at once, for cheapness, lightness, strength, and beauty of finish; 8 smitheries, connected with 2 of which are manufactories of steel springs; a white or silver smith, a clock and watchmaker's shop, a comb manufactory, a trunk manufactory, 2 bakeries, 2 cooper's shops, 2 druggist's shops, 12 stores, 5 lumber yards, 5 livery stables, 9 taverns, including the ferry houses, 2 cabinetmaker's shops, 2 tailor's shops, 11 master carpenters, 4 master stone and brick masons, 2 painters and glaziers, a gold and silver plater, 2 printing offices, from each of which a weekly newspaper is issued, and 3 physicians and 6 lawyers.

There are here also several handsome public gardens, much frequented by the Philadelphians, who have ready access to them by the steam ferry boats constantly passing the river. Of these useful vessels, there are at present eight belonging to the five ferry establishments, including those at Cooper's and Kaighn's Points; employing a capital of $60,000, exclusive of the real estate, such as wharves, ferry houses, &c. valued at $100,000. The gross income from which, is estimated at not less than $80,000 per annum. The boats adapted for carriages and passengers cross, in from 5 to 15 minutes, according to the state of the tide; and are impelled by steam engines of from 15 to 20 horse power.

The ship channel is on the Philadelphia side of the river. The water on the New Jersey side is too shoal for vessels of the largest size to ascend higher than Kaighn's Point, where it is sufficiently deep for those of any tonnage. Brigs and schooners of 150 tons come to the central parts of Camden at high tide, and unload at the wharves. Efforts are making to convert this into a port of entry, and to annex it to the Philadelphia collection district.

Campbell's Brook rises at the foot of the mountain in Readington t-ship, Hunterdon co., and flows by a S. E. course of about 7 miles to the south branch of the Raritan river, in Bridgewater t-ship, Somerset co.

Camptown, Orange t-ship, Essex co., 3½ miles S. W. from Newark, contains within a circle of a mile and a half in diameter, 75 dwellings, a free church of stone, of three stories, the first used as an academy, the second as a church, open to all denominations of Christians, and the third a masonic lodge; a Presbyterian church, 1 tavern, 3 stores, 1 saw mill, and 1 grist mill, upon Elizabeth river. The lands here vary in value, according to quality, from 50 to $100 the acre. The name is derived from the circumstance that the American army had a camp in the vicinity during the revolution.

Canoe Brook, small tributary of the Passaic river, Livingston and Springfield t-ships, Essex co., has a westerly course of three miles.

Cape May County, by the act of Assembly, 21st of January, 1710, begins at the mouth of a small creek, on the west side of Stipson's island, called Jecak's creek, and continues thence by the said creek, as high as the tide floweth; thence, along the bounds (of what was then Salem county, now Cumberland,) to the southernmost main branch of Great Egg Harbour river; thence down the said river to the sea; thence along the sea coast to Delaware bay, and so up the said bay to the place of beginning. It is, therefore, bounded on the north by Cumberland county, E. and S. by the Atlantic ocean, and W. by Delaware bay. Its greatest length, N. E. and S. W. is 30 miles; greatest breadth E. and W., 15 miles; form semi-oval: area 252 square miles, or about 161,000 acres. Central lat. 39° 10′; long. 2° 7′ E. from W. C.

This county is wholly of alluvial formation. Upon the coast, from the mouth of Great Egg Harbour bay, and for some miles on the Delaware bay, above the capes, is a sand beach: on the east, this beach, from a half mile to two miles in width, is covered with grass which affords pasture for neat cattle and sheep. It is broken by several inlets, by which the sea penetrates the marshes, and forms lagunes or salt water lakes, in several places, two miles in diameter, connected by various channels. The marsh has an average width of about four miles; a similar marsh extends along the N. W. part of the county, on the bay, widening as it advances northward. The Tuckahoe river, on the north, divides this from Gloucester co., receiving from Cape May co. Cedar Swamp creek, which interlocks with Dennis' creek, the latter emptying into the Delaware bay. Both streams flow through an extensive cedar swamp, stretching for 17 miles across the county. Several other, but inconsiderable streams, flow westerly into the Delaware bay. The *fast land* of the county is composed of clay based on sand, generally covered with oak forest, from which large quantities of timber and cord wood are annually sent to the Philadelphia and New York markets. The greater portion of the inhabitants are settled on the east and west margins of this fast land, along which run the main roads of the county. The forest land, when cleared, becomes arable, and, with due cultivation, produces good crops of corn and rye. The farms are generally large, running from the roads landward. Some cleared and cultivated tracts are interspersed with the forest. The wealth of the county is in its timber.

The name of this county is derived from Cornelius Jacobse Mey, a navigator in the service of the Dutch West India Company, who visited the Delaware bay in 1623, for the purpose of colonization, but the settlements, if any were made here by him, were soon abandoned. In 1630 a purchase of land, extending along the bay for sixteen miles, and sixteen inward, was made of the Indians, by the Dutch governor of New Amsterdam, Van Twiller, for the Sieurs Goodyn and Blomaert, directors of the West India Company; but we do not learn that these lands were immediately peopled by Europeans. From the records of the court of this county, it appears probable that some English settlers were established here at an early period, from New England, and we may conjecture that they were colonists from New Haven, some of whose descendants may yet remain in the county.

The county is divided into 4 t-ships; its pop. in 1830, was 4396 souls; being about 20 to the square mile; of whom 2400 were white males, 2308 white females, 118 free coloured males, 107 free coloured females, 3 slaves; among these were 1 deaf and dumb, but there were none blind nor alien.

The seat of justice is centrally situated at Middletown, where there are a frame court house, brick fire proof offices, and a stone prison; the other public buildings of the county, consist of an Episcopalian church, 2 Baptist do., 2 Methodist do.

At an early period of its history the inhabitants were engaged in the whale fishery; at present, their chief support is derived from the timber and cord wood trade, raising of cattle, and supplying the market with oysters, clams, fish, &c. At Cape Island, a considerable revenue is derived from the company who visit the sea shore during the hot weather. By the assessor's report for 1832, the county contained but 20,244 acres of improved land, a little more than one-eighth part of its area; 669 householders, 8 grist mills, the chief part of which are moved by wind, 16 saw mills, 29 stores, 679 horses, and 2093 neat cattle over 3 years of age; and paid for t-ship purposes $324 60; for state purposes $646 01, and $2000 for county uses.

By the act of 8th March, 1797, it sends 1 member to the assembly, and by the constitution, 1 member to council.

The court of common pleas and quarter sessions for Cape May co., sit on the 1st Tuesdays of February, the last of May, the 1st of August, and the 4th of October; and the circuit courts on the last Tuesday of May, annually, at Middletown.

This portion of the state has not generally been holden in due estimation. If its inhabitants be not numerous, they are generally as independent as any others in the state, and enjoy as abundantly the comforts of life. They are hospitable, and respectable for the propriety of their manners, and are blessed, usually, with excellent health. Until lately they have known little, practically, of those necessary evils of social life, the physician and the lawyer. Morse assures us, that their women possessed the power not only of sweetening life, but of defending and prolonging it, being competent to cure most of the diseases which attack it. We learn, however, that their practice in the latter particular, has lately been contested; that one or more physicians have crept in, but we rejoice to hear that they find little employment. We learn also, that the county, like Ireland, refusing nourishment to noxious animals, no lawyer can subsist in it.

STATISTICAL TABLE OF CAPE MAY COUNTY.

Townships.	Length.	Breadth.	Area.	Surface.	Population.		
					1810	1820	1830
Upper,	12½	11½	37,000		1664	2107	1067
Dennis,	14	8½	43,500				1508
Middle,	12	10	60,000		1106	1157	1366
Lower,	8	8	21,000		862	1001	995
			161,500			4265	4936

Cape May Court House, p-t. and seat of justice of Cape May co., centrally situate in Middle t-ship, 104 miles N. E. from W. C., and 102 S. from Trenton, 34 S. E. from Bridgeton; and 74 from Philadelphia; contains a court house of wood, a jail of stone, fire-proof offices of brick, 2 taverns, 8 or 10 dwellings, and a Baptist church of brick. Lat. 39° N. long. 2° 8′ E. from W. C.; it is called Middletown, in the post-office lists.

Cape May, the most southern point of N. J., and the eastern cape of the Delaware bay, formed by the bay and the Atlantic ocean; lat. 38° 56′, long. 2° 18′ E. from W. C.; a light house stands upon the point. The name of this cape should have been written Mey, since it has its name from Cornelius Jacobse Mey, a distinguished navigator, who visited the Delaware in 1623, in the employ of the Dutch West India Company. He gave his Christian name, Cornelius, to the west cape of the bay.

Cape May Island, beach of the Atlantic ocean, near the southern point of the state, in Lower t-ship, Cape May co., 104 miles by post-route from Philadelphia, 115 from Trenton, and 117 from W. C.; it is a noted and much frequented watering place, the season at which commences about the first of July, and continues until the middle of August, or 1st September. There are here six boarding houses, three of which are very large; the sea bathing is convenient and excellent, the beach affords pleasant drives, and there is excellent fishing in the adjacent waters. There is a post-office here.

Carllsburg, hamlet of Deerfield t-ship, Cumberland co., between 3 and 4 miles N. E. of Bridgeton.

Carpenter's Landing, post-town of Greenwich t-ship, Gloucester co., upon Mantua creek, at the head of sloop navigation, 3 miles S. W. from Woodbury; 7 miles by the creek from the Delaware; 42 miles from Trenton, and 148 from W. C. It is a place of considerable trade, in lumber, cord wood, &c., and contains 1 tavern, 2 stores, 30 dwellings, and 1 Methodist church.

Cat-tail, hamlet, of Upper Freehold t-ship, Monmouth co., on Cat-tail creek, on the line between Middlesex and Monmouth cos., 16 miles S. W. from Freehold, and 28 S. E. from Trenton.

Cedar Bridge, hamlet, Stafford t-ship, Monmouth co., upon the Oswego, or E. branch of Wading river, 33 miles S. of Freehold, contains a saw mill, 2 taverns, and several dwellings, surrounded by pine forest.

Cedar Creek, Stafford t-ship, Monmouth co., flows S. W. about 6 miles, into Little Egg Harbour bay, 2 miles below the mouth of Manahocking creek.

Cedar Creek, Dover t-ship, Monmouth co., rises by several branches, and flows eastwardly about 16 miles to the Atlantic ocean. The village of Williamsburg is seated upon it, near the head of tide water, and contains 10 or 12 dwellings, 2 taverns, 2 stores. Goodluck is a thickly settled neighbourhood, a short distance on the S. W. The country on the E. is salt marsh; elsewhere, sandy, and covered with pine forest.

Cedar Creek, Fairfield t-ship, Cumberland co., rises in the t-ship, and flows westerly through it for about 10 miles, giving motion to several mills, and emptying into Nantuxet cove, Delaware bay. It is navigable about 4 miles to Cedarville.

Cedar Pond, small lake of about 100 acres, Pompton t-ship, Bergen co., sends forth a portion of its waters to supply the stream of Clinton forges.

Cedar Swamp Creek, Upper t-ship, Cape May co., rises in the t-ship by 2 branches, and flows N. E. 8 miles, into Tuckahoe river. Its course is through an extensive cedar swamp.

Cedar Swamp Creek, of Egg Harbour t-ship, Gloucester co., a mill stream, which flows S. W., by Bargaintown, about 7 or 8 miles, into Great Egg Harbour bay.

Cedarville, p-t. of Fairfield t-ship, Cumberland co., pleasantly situated, on Cedar creek, at the head of navigation, about 4 miles from the mouth of the creek, 7 S. from Bridgeton, 183, by post route, N. E. from W. C., and 77 S. from Trenton; contains about 60 dwellings, a store, and tavern, grist and saw mill, and an extensive button manufactory. The country about it is sandy and poor; but the lots in the village are carefully cultivated and productive. Trade, wood and lumber. Inhabitants, 375.

Cedarville, of Caldwell t-ship, Essex co., upon Peekman's run, about 2 miles above its confluence with the Passaic river. There are here several small mills, such as grist mill, saw mill, and cotton factory.

Centreville, p-t. of Pittsgrove t-ship, Salem co., upon Muddy run, and upon the line dividing Salem from Cumberland co., 17 miles S. E. from Salem town, and 75 S. from Trenton; contains some 12 or 15 dwellings, tavern, store, and school house.

Centreville, East Windsor t-ship, Middlesex co., upon the turnpike road from Bordentown to Cranberry, 9 miles from the former, and 18 miles S. W. from New Brunswick, contains a tavern and several dwellings.

Centreville, small village, of Knowlton t-ship, Warren co., on the road leading from Hope to Knowlton mills and Columbia; about 4 miles from the first and last, and 10 N. E. from Belvidere; contains a tavern, store, smith shop, Presbyterian church, and several dwellings.

Centreville Post-Office, Hunterdon co.; by post route, 189 miles from W. C., and 30 from Trenton.

Chambers' Brook, tributary of the north branch of the Raritan, and S. E. boundary of Bedminster t-ship, Somerset co., rises in the mountain on the E., and flows S. W., about 4 miles to its recipient.

Chambers' Mill Branch, a small stream, rising in the centre of Montague t-ship, Sussex co., and flowing westerly, about 5 miles, into the river Delaware. It gives motion to several mills near its mouth.

Change Water, furnace, on the Musconetcong creek, in Mansfield t-ship, Warren co., 3 miles from the village of Mansfield, and 10 S. E. from Belvidere, the county town.

Charlottesburg, the name of a furnace, formerly on the Pequannock creek, Pompton t-ship, Bergen co., now in ruins.

Charleston, small village, in the N. E. part of Bethlehem t-ship, Hunterdon co., on the Musconetcong mountain, 13 miles N. of Flemington.

Charleston, hamlet, of Kingwood t-ship, Hunterdon co., 10 miles W. of Flemington; contains a tavern, store, and several dwellings.

Chatham t-ship, Morris co., bounded north by Hanover t-ship; E. and S. E. by the Passaic river, which separates it from Livingston, Springfield and New Providence t-ships, Sussex co.; W. and S. by Morris t-ship. Centrally distant, S. E. from Morristown, 6 miles; greatest length, N. and S. 9 miles, breadth, E. and W. 5 miles; area, 14,400; surface undulating, except on the south, which is covered by Long Hill. Black Brook rises in the t-ship and flows W. to the Passaic river, through Morris t-ship. Bottle Hill, Chatham, and Columbia are villages of the t-ship, the first two post-towns; population in 1830, 1865. In 1832 there were in the t-ship 340 taxables, 40 single men, 9 stores, 3 saw mills, and 5 grist mills, 5 distilleries, 1 fulling mill, 1 carding engine, 254 horses and mules, and 1015 neat cattle, under 3 years old; and the t-ship paid state tax, $248 35; county tax, $556 04; poor tax, $600; road tax, $600. The turnpike roads from Elizabethtown and Newark cross this t-ship to Morristown.

Chatham, p-t. of Chatham t-ship, Morris co., on the road from Elizabethtown to Morristown, 10 miles from the one, and 7½ from the other; 220 N. E. from W. C., and 54 from Trenton; contains 1 Presbyterian and 1 Methodist church, an academy, 3 stores, 2 taverns, a grist mill and saw mill, and between 40 and 50 dwellings. A thriving village, with neat dwellings, surrounded by a pleasant, well cultivated country, watered by the Passaic river, which flows through the town.

Cheapside, agricultural village, of Livingston t-ship, Essex co., on the turnpike road from Newark to Morristown, 10 miles W. of the former.

Cheesequake's Creek, with several branches flowing into the Raritan bay, about 3 miles below Amboy, Middlesex co., drains a swamp of considerable extent.

Chesnut Neck, strip of fast land, lying between Little Egg Harbour river and Nacote creek, Galloway t-ship, Gloucester co.

Chesnut Run, small branch of the Assunpink creek, Upper Freehold t-ship, Monmouth co.

Chester t-ship, Morris co., bounded N. by Roxbury t-ship, N. E. by Randolph t-ship, E. by Mendham t-ship, S. by Bedminster t-ship, Somerset co., and W. by Washington t-ship. Centrally distant W. from Morristown 12 miles; greatest length N. and S. 9, breadth E. and W. 6 miles; area, 18000 acres; surface rolling; soil on the N. loam, on the S. grey limestone, under good cultivation; drained on the W. by the Black river, and on the E. by tributaries of the N. branch of the Raritan river; population in 1830, 1338. In 1832 the t-ship contained 324 taxables, whose ratables did not exceed $30; 23 single men, 3 stores, 5 saw mills, and 2 grist mills, 4 distilleries, 1 forge, 2 fulling mills, and 311 horses and mules, and 669 neat cattle, above 3 years of age; and paid the following taxes: state, $193 14; county, $432 43; poor $400; road, $400.

Chester t-ship, Burlington co., bounded N. E. by the Rancocus creek, S. E. by Evesham t-ship, S. W. by Pensauken creek, which divides it from Gloucester co., Waterford t-ship, and N. W. by the river Delaware. Centrally distant S. W. from Mount Holly 9 miles; greatest length 7, breadth 6 miles; area, 22,000 acres; surface level; soil sand and sandy loam, of good quality, generally, well cultivated, and productive of grass, grain, vegetables, and fruits. Beside the streams already mentioned, the t-ship is drained by the N. branch of Pensauken creek, by Pompeston creek, and Swede's branch, the last two emptying immediately into the Delaware. All are mill streams. The Rancocus Drawbridge, Westfield, and Moorestown, are villages of the t-ship, the last a post-town; population in 1830, 2333. In 1832 the t-ship contained taxables 524, householders 205, whose ratables did not exceed $30; single men 96, stores 8, fisheries 5, grist mills 3, saw mills 6, tan vats 27, carding machines 2, distilleries for cider 3, coaches and chariots 7, two horse stages 2, dearborns 52, covered wagons 90, chairs and curricles 30, gigs and sulkies 22, neat cattle 1060, and horses and mules 570, over 3 years of age; and it paid state tax, $336 38; county, $1173 91; and road tax, $1100.

Chester, p-t. of Chester t-ship, Morris co., on the turnpike road leading from Morristown to Easton, 13 miles N. W. from the former, 50 N. E. from Trenton, and 216 from W. C.; at the foot of a low isolated mountain, which covers it on the north; it extends along the road for more than a mile, and contains 1 Presbyterian, and 1 Congregational church, 2 taverns, 3 stores, and about 30 dwellings, and lies upon, or near, a vein of grey limestone.

Chesterfield t-ship, Burlington co., bounded N. W. and N. by Crosswick's creek, which divides it from Nottingham t-ship, S. E. by Hanover t-ship, S. W. by Bacon's run and Black's creek, and W. by the river Delaware. Centrally distant N. E. from Mount Holly 12 miles; greatest length N. and S. 8 miles; greatest breadth E. and W. 6 miles; surface level; soil, generally, sandy, mixed with clay and loam; drained by the creeks mentioned, which flow to the Delaware river, the bank of which is here considerably elevated, giving a picturesque appearance to the country, especially at and near Bordentown. Bordentown and Recklesstown are the post-towns, and only villages of the t-ship; population in 1830, 2386. In 1832 the t-ship contained 554 taxables, whose ratables did not exceed $30; 75 single men, 1030 neat cattle, and 510 horses, above 3 years old; 10 stores, 1 saw mill, 2 grist mills, 40 tan vats, 6 distilleries for cider, 2 coaches and chariots, 3 phaetons and chaises, 7 four horse stages, 10 two horse stages, 41 dearborns, 58 covered wagons, 8 chairs and curricles, 17 gigs and sulkies; and it paid state tax, $346 49; county tax, $1216 32 and t-ship tax, $1000.

Chew's Landing, p-t. of Gloucester t-ship, Gloucester co., upon the N. branch of Big Timber creek, at the head of navigation, 9 miles S. E. from Camden, and 6 N. E. from Woodbury, 41 S. E. from Trenton, and 149 N. E. from W. C. It is a place of considerable business in lumber and cord wood, and contains 2 stores, 2 taverns, 2 grist mills, and between 30 and 40 dwellings, 1 Episcopal and 1 Methodist church.

Clarkesburg, hamlet, of Upper Freehold t-ship, Monmouth co., on the road from Wrightsville to Freehold court-house, 12 miles from the latter, and 20 from Trenton; contains some half dozen dwellings, store and tavern.

Clarkesborough, p-t. of Greenwich t-ship, Gloucester co., 5 miles S. W. from Woodbury, 44 from Trenton, and 150 from W. C.; contains a store, tavern, and from 25 to 30 dwellings; and within 2 miles S. W. there is a Friend's meeting house.

Clarkesville, (formerly called Sodom) p-t. of Lebanon t-ship, Hunterdon co., on Spruce run, and on the Musconetcong mountain, on the western line of the t-ship, 14 miles N. of Flemington, 37 from Trenton; contains 1 tavern and store, 2 saw mills, 2 grist mills, and 6 or 8 dwellings; the surface is very rough and stony, but parts are productive; iron abounds in the mountain, and plumbago is also found in several places upon it, near the village.

Clarkesville, small hamlet, of West Windsor t-ship, Middlesex co., on the straight turnpike road from Trenton to Brunswick, 7 miles N. E. from the one, and 18 S. W. from the other; contains 2 taverns, and 6 or 8 dwellings; soil good, and country pleasant around it.

Clementon, village, of Gloucester t-ship, Gloucester co., on a branch of Big Timber creek, 5 miles above Chew's landing, 10 miles S. E. of Woodbury, and 13 from Camden; contained formerly some glass works, at present 1 tavern, store, grist and saw mills, and some 12 or 15 dwellings; marl abounds in the vicinity, and is advantageously used upon the soil.

Clinton, formerly called Hunt's Mills, p-t., of Hunterdon co., on the south branch of Raritan river, at the point of junction of Lebanon, Bethlehem, and Kingwood t-ships, lying partly in each, and on the turnpike road leading from Somerville to Easton; about 20 miles from the former, and 17 from the latter; 10 miles N. E. from Flemington, 33 from Trenton, and 210 from W. C. The town is built in a valley surrounded on all sides by hills, which on the N. N. E. and N. W., approach closely to it, but are more distant on the south. It contains 1 Presbyterian church, 1 common English, and a Sunday school, 2 large grist mills, 2 runs of stones each, an oil mill, at which from 8000 to 10,000 bushels of flaxseed are annually manufactured, a woollen manufactory, with fulling mill and cards for country work, 3 stores, 3 taverns, and 35 dwellings. The fall used at the water-works here, is 8½ feet only, but a very great power may be obtained, the stream having a very rapid descent, and large volume. The surrounding country is very fertile, and carefully tilled, being enriched by lime made from a grey stone, which in a broad vein skirts the Musconetcong mountain, and which rises in cliffs at the village, nearly 100 feet high. The average product in wheat here, is rated at 18 bushels the acre, and from the best farms 25 bushels the acre are obtained. Iron ore, and plumbago, abound in the neighbouring mountain, and the inhabitants look for increased prosperity from a rail-road contemplated to be made through their town, leading from Elizabethtown to Belvidere. The town lies 177 feet above tide water. By act of 19th February, 1833, authority was given to incorporate a company for any species of manufacture here, with a capital of $120,000.

Clinton Forge, Pompton t-ship, Bergen co., on a small stream flowing from Hanks, Cedar, and Buck ponds, and emptying into Pequannock creek, 28 miles N. W. from Hackensack.

Clonmell Creek, small stream of Greenwich t-ship, Gloucester co., flowing by a course of 2 or 3 miles into the Delaware river, opposite to Little Tinicum island.

Closter, village, of Hackensack t-ship, Bergen co., 4½ miles N. E. of Hackensack town, near the W. foot of the Palisade Hills, surrounded by a soil of rich loam, contains a tavern, a store, and from 12 to 15 dwellings.

Closter Mountain, part of the Bergen ridge, Bergen co., Hackensack and Harrington t-ships, forming the right bank of the North river, and the Palisades. Its formation is trap, resting upon red and grey sandstone. Height about 400 feet; the eastern side precipitous, the west gently declining; thickly settled and well cultivated; the top generally covered with wood.

Clove River. (See ***Deep Clove River***.)

Clove Church, on the bank of Clove river, Wantage t-ship, Sussex co.

Cohansey River, rises in Upper Alloways creek t-ship, Salem co., its head waters interlocking with those of Alloways creek. It flows, thence, by a due S. course of 15 miles, by Bridgeton, forming the division line between Deerfield and Hopewell t-ships, Cumberland co., into Fairfield t-ship; turning, thence, westerly, it runs about 8 miles to the town of Greenwich, and thence by a meandering course S. W. of 7 or 8 miles, it unites with the Delaware bay. The river is banked in, above Greenwich, to which place it is navigable for large brigs and schooners; vessels of 80 tons burthen ascend to Bridgeton, 20 miles from the mouth. Above Bridgeton the stream is not navigable, but affords a very valuable water power, which is used at the town for driving a rolling and slitting mill, nail factory, and gristmill, &c. &c. (See ***Bridgeton.***)

Cohansey Cove, bay of the Cohansey creek, Fairfield t-ship, Cumberland co., an inlet from the Delaware bay.

Cold Spring Inlet, Lower t-ship, Cape May co., between Two Mile Beach, and Poverty Beach, upon the Atlantic sea-board. It is less than half a mile in width. It has its name from a spring about 3 or 4 miles inland, which sends its tribute to the ocean by this passage.

Cold Spring, p-t., of Lower t-ship, Cape May co. Centrally situated on the road to Cape May Island, 9 miles S. from Cape May court-house, 112 from Trenton, and 117 N. E. from W. C.; contains 1 tavern, 2 stores, from 15 to 20 dwellings, and an Episcopal church. It derives its name from a remarkble spring near it, which rises in the marsh, and is overflowed at every tide.

Cold Brook, small tributary of Lamington river, flowing into it S. W. from Tewkesbury t-ship, Hunterdon co., by a course of about 4 miles, giving motion to a mill near its mouth.

Cold Branch, tributary of Hospitality creek, an arm of the Great Egg Harbour river, Hamilton t-ship, Gloucester co.

Colestown, hamlet, of Evesham t-ship, Burlington co., 12 miles S. W. of Mount Holly, and 3 from Moorestown; contains an Episcopal church and several dwellings.

Collard Branch, of the west arm of Wading river, rises in Northampton t-ship, Burlington co., and flows S. W. about 8 miles, to its recipient, in Washington t-ship, at the head of the mill pond of Martha furnace.

Colt's Neck, p-t., Shrewsbury t-ship, Monmouth co., 6 miles N. E. of Freehold, 206 from W. C., and 41 from Trenton; contains from 15 to 20 dwellings, 1 tavern, 2 stores, 3 grist mills, 2 saw mills, a place of considerable business, on a soil of red and fertile sand.

Columbia, village, of Chatham t-ship, Morris co., on the turnpike road from Newark to Morristown, 13 miles from the one, and 4 from the other; contains 1 store, 1 tavern, and 5 or 6 dwellings, in a level pleasant country.

Columbia Forge, on Lubber run, centrally situate in Byram t-ship, Sussex co.

Columbia, p-t. and village, of Knowlton t-ship, on the Delaware river, near the mouth of Paulinskill, distant 253 miles from W. C., 94 from Trenton, and 10 from Belvidere; contains 2 taverns, a store, a Presbyterian church, a glass house, a saw mill, and 20 dwellings. The town is prettily situated on a high bank of the river, and surrounded by a limestone soil, tolerably well cultivated. A company was incorporated by act of 12th February, 1833, with authority to employ $100,000 in the conduct of the glass works here.

Columbia, p-t., of Hopewell t-ship, Hunterdon co., on the turnpike road from New Brunswick to Lambertville, 10 miles S. E. from Flemington, 17 N. from Trenton, formerly called Hopewell Meeting House; contains 1 Baptist meeting, 2 taverns, 1 store, and 10 or 12 dwellings.

Columbus, or Black Horse, p-t., of Mansfield t-ship, Burlington co., 7 miles N. E. of Mount Holly, 5 S. E. from Bordentown, 13 from Trenton, and 163 from W. C.; contains a tavern, store, and about 30 dwellings, surrounded by a fertile country.

Communipaw, village, on New York bay, 2 miles S. of Jersey city, Bergen t-ship, Bergen co., one of the earliest settlements of the Dutch, and remarkable for the tenacious adherence of its inhabitants to their primitive costume and manners; some 15 or 20 dwellings, whose inhabitants are chiefly agriculturists.

Congassa Run, tributary of the S. branch of Toms' river, Dover t-ship, Monmouth co.

Cooper's Creek, Gloucester co., rises by two branches, the N. near the E. boundary of the county, and the S. on, and forming, the line between Waterford and Newton and Gloucester t-ships, uniting N. of Haddonfield, above which the stream is not navigable. There are mills on both branches near their sources.

Cooperstown, Willingboro' t-ship, Burlington co., 7 miles N. W. from Mount Holly, and 3 S. W. from Burlington; contains a Friends' meeting house, tavern, store, and 8 or 10 dwellings.

Copperas Mountain, Pequannock t-ship, Morris co., on the S. W. side of Greenpond valley, thus named on account of the large quantity of the sulphate of iron found here, and which was formerly made into the copperas of commerce.

Corson's Inlet, a passage of the sea, through the beach, to the lagunes and marshes of Upper t-ship, Cape May co., about half a mile in width.

Coursenville, p-t. of Stillwater t-ship, Sussex co., distant by post-route from W. C. 239 miles, from Trenton 81 miles, and from Newton, S. W., five miles; contains a store and some half dozen dwellings; adjacent country, slate.

Cove, small village of Upper Penn's-neck t-ship, Salem co., about 12 or 13 miles N. of Salem, and 2 S. of Penn's Grove, on the river Delaware; contains 8 dwellings, a tavern and store.

Cox Hall Creek, small stream of Lower t-ship, Cape May co., flowing into the Delaware bay.

Crabtown, Howell t-ship, Monmouth co.; contains 10 or 12 dwellings, 2 taverns, and a store.

Craft's Creek, Mansfield t-ship, Burlington co.; rises near the eastern border of the t-ship, and flows W. and N. W. about 9 miles to the river Delaware, opposite the lower point of Newbold's island. By act of assembly passed 11th February, 1833, authority was given to make a rail or Macadamized road from the mouth of this creek to the neighbourhood of New Lisbon, a distance of 13 miles 39 chains.

Cranberry p-t., lying partly in South Brunswick t-ship, and partly in South Amboy t-ship, Middlesex co., on the turnpike road leading from Bordentown to South Amboy, 16 miles from the former, 185 from W. C., and 15 from Trenton; pleasantly situated in a level country, and light sandy soil; contains a Presbyterian church with cupola and bell, an academy, a grist mill, 2 tanneries, 3 taverns, 2 stores, and from 60 to 80 dwellings. Cranberry brook, tributary of the Millstone river, flows through the town.

Cranberry Inlet, formerly from the ocean to Barnegat Bay, between Island beach and Squam beach.

Crane's Gap, in the first mountain, Bloomfield t-ship, Essex co., through which passes the turnpike road from Newark to Rockaway.

Craven's Ferry, p-o., Salem co.

Cropwell, village of Evesham t-sp, Burlington co., near the western boundary, 11 miles S. W. of Mount Holly; contains a tavern, store, 12 or 15 dwellings, and a Quaker meeting house; soil, sandy loam.

Cross Keys, hamlet of Trenton t-ship, Hunterdon co., on the road from Trenton to Pennington; contains 4 or 5 dwellings.

Cross Creeks, name given to small tributaries of Back creek, Fairfield t-ship, Cumberland co., near the Delaware bay, which intersect each other.

Cross Roads, Bedminster t-ship, Somerset co., between 7 and 8 miles N. W. of Somerville, on Artle's brook, in a level, fertile, limestone country; contains a store, tavern, and 5 or 6 dwellings.

Cross Roads, hamlet of South Brunswick t-ship, Middlesex co., 9 miles S. W. from New Brunswick; contains 2 taverns, a store, and several dwellings; soil, light and sandy.

Cross Roads, hamlet of Evesham t-ship, Burlington co., 8 miles S. from Mount Holly; contains a tavern, a store, a Methodist church, and 8 or 10 dwellings; soil, sandy loam.

Crosswick's Creek, the Indian name of which is said to be *Closweeksunk, a separation*, rises by two branches, the north in Hanover t-ship, Burlington co., near Wrightstown; and the south in Upper Freehold, Monmouth co., uniting in the latter t-ship and county near New Egypt, thence running northerly and north westerly across Chesterfield t-ship, Burlington co., to the River Delaware, at Bordentown. It is a steady and serviceable mill-stream, whose course is semicircular, and in length about 25 miles; it is navigable to Grove Mill, about 6 miles from the mouth; marl is frequently found on its banks.

Crosswicks, p-t. of Chesterfield t-ship, Burlington co., on the high southern bank of Crosswick's creek, 4 miles E. from Bordentown, 14 N. E. from Mount Holly, 174 from W. C., and 8 S. E. from Trenton; contains from 40 to 50 dwellings, a very large Quaker meeting house and school, 4 taverns, 5 or 6 stores, a saw mill and grist mill; the village is pleasantly situated in a fertile country, whose soil is sandy loam; near the town is a bed of iron ore, from which considerable quantities are taken to the furnaces in the lower part of the county.

Culver's Pond, Frankford t-ship, Sussex co., at the foot of the Blue mountain; one of the western sources of the Paulinskill.

Culver's Gap, in the Blue mountain, between Sandistone and Frankford t-ships, Sussex co., through which the turnpike road from Milford passes; distant from Newton N. W. 10 miles.

Cumberland County, was taken altogether from Salem, by the act of 19th January, 1748, with the following boundaries. Beginning at the mouth of Stow creek, thence up the creek to John Buck's mills, leaving the mills in this county; thence up Stow creek branch to the house of Hugh Dunn, leaving such house within the new county; thence by a straight line to Nathan Shaw's house, also within the new county; thence by a N. E. course, intersecting the Pilesgrove line; thence leaving Pilesgrove, in Salem co., along such line till it intersects the line dividing the counties of Gloucester and Salem; thence S. E. down the Gloucester line to the boundaries of Cape May co.; thence by such county to the Delaware bay, and up the bay to the place of beginning. By the same act, the county was divided into six precincts or townships, viz. Greenwich, Hopewell, Stow creek, Fairfield, Deerfield, and Maurice river; to which Milleville, taken from Maurice river and Fairfield t-ships, in 1801, and Downe t-ship, have been since added. The county is bounded by the Delaware bay on the S. S. W., Salem co. N. W., Gloucester N. E., and Cape May co. on the S. E. Its greatest length is about 30 miles N. and S., and breadth 30 miles E. and W.; area, 524 square miles, or 33,500 acres; central lat. 39° 20′ N.; Long. 2° E. from W. C.

Geologically considered, Cumberland co. belongs to the belt of diluvial and alluvial formation, which extends along the continent of North America, from Long Island to the Gulf of Mexico, and contains in place, the deposits of greenish blue marl, intermixed with shells, similar to those found in the limestone and grauwacke of the transition, and abundantly in the secondary horizontal limestone and sandstone, with beds of bog iron ore, and ochre. The elevated ridges between the streams, are crowned in places with sandstone and puddingstone cemented with iron ore. The marl beds yet developed, lie chiefly on Stow creek, and the iron ore in Greenwich t-ship. The marl is used for manure with much advantage upon the lighter soils, and its use is daily extending. The surface of the country is generally flat; the soil south of Cohansey creek is generally sandy. A salt marsh extends along the Delaware bay, in breadth from half a mile to two miles, adjoining which, eastwardly, is a strip of clay and loam, having an average width of about a mile, tolerably fertile and covered with farms. A prolific marsh borders the creeks, which are embanked, at various distances from their mouths, and employed for grazing cattle. The northern part of the county, particularly, that portion of it lying north and west of the Cohansey creek, is composed of clay and sandy loam, on which considerable quantities of wheat, oats and corn, are grown. The timber above Cohansey, consists of white oak, black and red oak, and hickory, which also characterize the clay and loam of the western belt. Below Cohansey, it is generally pine; forests of which cover the greater portion of the eastern part of the county, which, having been generally once, at least, cut over, are now in various stages of growth.

The principal streams are Stow creek on the N. W. boundary; Cohansey creek in the N. W. section, Maurice river running centrally through the co., and Tuckahoe river upon the east.

The chief towns are Bridgeton, the seat of justice, Greenwich, Deerfield, Roadstown, Millville, Port Elizabeth, Nantuxet, or Newport, Dividing Creek, Mauricetown, Bricksboro', Dorchester, Leesburg, and Marshallville, or Cumberland Works, Cedarville, and Fairton.

There are in the county 2 furnaces, one at Millville, and the other above Port Elizabeth, on the Manamuskin creek; and three extensive glass manufactories, one at Millville, one at Port Elizabeth, and the third at Marshallville. At the last place, and on Maurice river, there is considerable ship building, in vessels of from 50 to 100 tons burthen. Large quantities of grain are exported from Bridgeton, and timber and cordwood from every creek of the county.

The religious sects are Episcopalians, Presbyterians, Baptists, Methodists, and Quakers.

A county Bible society holds its meetings at Bridgeton, and temperance societies have been established with great success in the townships. The provisions for education consist of an academy at Bridgeton, another at Port Elizabeth, and common schools in the several towns and townships.

The inhabitants of the county are derived chiefly from English, Swiss, and German settlers; and it is probable, from several circumstances, that a colony of Puritans, from Newhaven, was settled near the margin of the Delaware so early as 1640, some of whose descendants may yet remain.

By the census of 1830, the population amounted to 14,093, of whom 6723 were white males; 6582 white females; 2 female slaves; 431 free coloured males; 355 free coloured females; of which 27 were aliens, 4 deaf and dumb, and 7 blind.

By the abstract of the assessors, there were, in 1832, in the county, 2742 taxables, 774 householders, whose ratables did not exceed $30; 33 single men; 54 storekeepers, or merchants; two fisheries, 1 woollen manufactory, 1 cupola furnace, 2 blast furnaces, 44 runs of stones for grinding grain, 21 saw mills, 1 forge, 1 rolling and slitting mill, 1 fulling mill, 6 tanneries, 4 glass manufactories, 4 distilleries for cider, 2053 horses, 5713 neat cattle, above the age of 3 years, and 9 stud horses.

By the act of 3d November, 1814, the county sends 3 members to the Assembly, 1 member to Council.

The courts of common pleas and general quarter sessions, are holden annually at Bridgeton, on the third Tuesday of February, the fourth Tuesday of September, the first Tuesday of June, and the last Tuesday of Nov. The circuit court is holden at the same place on the first Tuesday of June, and last Tuesday of November, annually.

STATISTICAL TABLE OF CUMBERLAND COUNTY.

Townships.	Length.	Breadth.	Area.	Surface generally level.	Population.		
					1810	1820	1830
Deerfield,	11	9	34,000		1889	1903	2417
Downe,	14	11½	58,240		1501	1749	1923
Fairfield,	15	8	46,720		2279	1869	1812
Greenwich,	7	6	13,440		858	890	912
Hopewell,	10	6	20,000		1987	1952	1953
Maurice River,	19	11	79,360		2085	2411	2724
Milleville,	16	16	73,500		1032	1010	1561
Stow Creek,	7	6	10,240		1039	884	791
			335,460		12,670	12,668	14,093

Cumberland Furnace, on Manamuskin creek, Maurice river t-ship, about 5 miles above Port Elizabeth, and 17 east of Bridgeton.

Cumberland Works, (See ***Marshallville.***)

Daretown, Pittsgrove t-ship, Salem co., near the N. W. boundary, on the head waters of Salem river, 13 miles, a little N. of E. from Salemtown; contains 12 or 14 dwellings, 2 stores, one Presbyterian, and one Methodist church.

Dead River, a tributary of the Passaic river, rising by several branches in the Mine mountain of Bernard t-ship, Somerset co., and flowing E. to its recipient, along the N. base of Stony Hill; including Harrison's brook, its longest branch, its length may be about 9 miles.

Dayton's Bridge, post-office, Salem county.

Danville, post-office, Warren co.

Deal, small hamlet, and watering place, 220 miles N. E. from W. C., and 64 from Trenton, on Poplar Swamp creek, about a mile from the sea, in Shrewsbury t-ship, Monmouth co., 16 miles E. from Freehold, and 3 S. of Long Branch boarding houses. There are several boarding houses at this place, where from 50 to 100 persons may be comfortably accommodated.

Deckertown, p-t., of Wantage t-ship, Sussex co., at the intersection of the Newton and Bolton, with the Paterson and Hamburg turnpike road; 244 miles from W. C., 86 from Trenton, and 14 from Newton. The town contains a grist mill, a Presbyterian church, 4 stores, 2 taverns, and from 15 to 20 dwellings, and lies in a rich limestone country.

Deep Brook, Caldwell t-ship, Essex co., rises in the Second mountain, and flows N. to the Passaic river, having a semicircular course of 3 or 4 miles, and receiving a small tributary, called Green Brook.

Deep Creek, Lower Alloways creek t-ship, Salem co., rises in that t-ship, and flows S. W., a meandering course, through the meadows and marshes for 7 or 8 miles, to the Delaware. It is not navigable.

Deep Creek, Shrewsbury t-ship, Monmouth co., makes in from the ocean, between 1 and 2 miles; less than a mile above Shark inlet.

Deep Clove River, a tributary of Wallkill river; rises at the east foot of the mountain, in Wantage t-ship, and flows S. E. by a course of 12 miles, to its recipient; receiving from the S. W. the Papakating creek, a short distance below Deckertown. There are several mills on both these streams.

Deep, or ***Great Run***, a tributary of the Great Egg Harbour river, Hamilton t-ship, Gloucester co., into which it flows from the west, about a mile below Weymouth furnace.

Deep Run, tributary of South river, rises in Upper Freehold t-ship, Monmouth co., and flows by a N. W.

course of between 8 and 9 miles, to its recipient, in South Amboy t-ship, Middlesex co., a mill stream.

Deerfield Township, Cumberland co., bounded N. E. by Pittsgrove t-ship, N. W. by Upper Alloways creek t-ship, Salem co.; S. by Fairfield and Millville t-ships, and W. by Hopewell t-ship, Cumberland co. Greatest length, N. and S. 11 miles, breadth, E. and W. 9 miles; area, 34,000 acres. Surface, level; soil, clay, gravel and sand, and not remarkable for fertility, but improving under the application of marl. It is drained by the Cohansey creek, which runs southward along its western boundary, and by Muddy run, a branch of Maurice river, which flows on the S. E. line. Population in 1830, 2,417: In 1832, there were in the t-ship, taxables, 305; 2 Presbyterian, 1 Baptist and 1 Methodist church; 1 academy and several schools; 118 householders, whose ratables did not exceed $30; 11 stores; 9 pairs of stones for grinding grain; one woollen manufactory; 2 saw mills; 1 fulling mill; 316 horses, and 560 neat cattle, above the age of 3 years; and the township paid for township purposes, $500, and for county and state tax, $835 25. Bridgeton, Deerfield and Carllsburg are towns of this t-ship.

Deerfield Street, post town of Deerfield t-ship, Cumberland co., 7 miles N. of Bridgeton; 165 miles N. E. of Washington city, and 63 S. from Trenton; contains from 20 to 25 dwellings, occupied chiefly by agriculturists, 1 tavern, 1 store, and a Presbyterian church.

Dell's Brook, small branch of the Rockaway river, flowing eastwardly about 5 miles through Pleasant valley, Randolph t-ship, Morris co.

Delaware River and *Bay*, called by the Indians, *Poutaxat, Marisqueton, Makeriskitton, Makeriskkiskon, Lenape-Wihittuck* (stream of the Lenape,) by the Dutch, *Zuydt* or South river, Charles river, and Nassau river, and by the Swedes, *New Swedeland stream*, one of the most considerable in N. America, rises by two principal branches, in the state of New York. The northernmost, the *Mohawk* or *Cooquago*, issues from Lake Utsaemthe lat. 42° 45′, takes a S. W. course, and turning S. E. crosses the Pennsylvania line in lat. 42°. Seven miles below this point it receives the *Popachton* branch, which rises in the Katskill mountain, from the S. E. It touches the N. W. corner of N. Jersey, in lat. 41° 24′, at Carpenter's Point, at the mouth of the Nevisink or Mackackomack river. The course of the current, above and below the Blue mountain, is crooked; and is through a mountainous country, until it leaves the Water Gap. The Delaware Water Gap is one of the greatest natural curiosities of the state. It would seem, from the quantity of alluvial lands, above the mountain, that at some remote period, a dam of great height, here, impeded the progress of the river. Had the dam been half as high as the mountain, it would have turned the water into the North river. It may have had an elevation of 150 or 200 feet, forming a lake of more than 50 miles in length; extending over the Minisink settlements. It has been conjectured that this dam was engulphed by some great convulsion of the earth; and the opinion is supposed to be sustained by the extraordinary depth of the channel in several places of its passage through the mountain. An hundred years ago the boatmen reported, that they could not reach the bottom with their longest lines; and even now we are informed that the bottom in these places cannot be attained with two plough lines attached to each other. But we see nothing in these appearances that renders it necessary to resort to the conjecture, that an earthquake was employed to open an adequate passage for the river, and that it performed its office with such accuracy, and economy of power, as to do no more than was indispensable, and to leave the rugged and lofty wall, 1600 feet high, rising almost precipitously from the water's edge, unbroken. The distance through the mountain is about two miles. The rock presents a great variety of strata, in which granitic rock, slate, grauwacke and the old sandstone alternate. The sandstone is, at one place, at least, and probably at others, so soft as to disintegrate rapidly. At the place referred to, the water has scooped out a basin from the hill of many acres in extent, which are now under cultivation. Before the bed of the river was broken down, there must have been a cataract here, higher than that of Niagara. Supposing the waters to have been poured over the precipice upon a bed of soft or disjointed stones, very deep excavations must have been made, which the great mass of waters, in seasons of freshet, would continue to preserve. It is probable that so much of the mountain as forms the present bed of the river was, throughout, of soft or very friable material. The stream has obviously sought the most practicable passage; and to attain it, has formed an almost right-angled course through the mountain. Whatever may have been the resistance, the conquest has been complete, and it now flows through the deep ravine in calm and silent majesty, without a ripple to tell of its whereabout; and occasionally resting in motionless pools, of from two to three hundred yards wide, as if to reflect the picturesque scenery which surrounds and hangs over it.

The lovers of diversified nature cannot visit this spot without high gratification. The "Gap," the break, in the almost unvarying line of the Kittatinny mountain is visible at nearly as great a distance as the mountain itself. As we approach it from the S. E., the ground rises rapidly, almost precipitously, differing in this particular, as do all the mountain ranges of our country, from the N. W. declivity, whose descent is long and gradual. At the entrance, the sides of the mountain, close to the water's edge, leave scarce room for a road, overhung by immense masses of rock, threatening destruction to the traveller beneath. The passage, however, widens as we proceed, and the scenery assumes a less imposing character. Verdant isles stud the bosom of the stream, and contrast beautifully with the rocky and wood-clad eminences, which now have a more rounded form. These islands are rich, and bear the most luxurious harvests. About two-thirds of the way through the mountain from the Jersey shore, may be seen, most advantageously, near Dutotsburg, on the Pennsylvania bank, the pretty cascade formed by Cherry creek, which precipitates its waters in foam and spray, over a declivity of more than 50 feet.

> "The sunbow's rays still arch
> The torrent with the many hues of heav'n,
> And roll the sheeted silver's waving column
> O'er the crags headlong perpendicular,
> And fling its lines of foaming light along,
> And to and fro, like the pale courser's tail,
> The giant steed, to be bestrode by Death,
> As told in the Apocalypse."—Byron.

On the top of the mountain, 2 miles from the "Gap," is a large chalybeate spring, which deposits much ferruginous ochre, similar to that of the Paint spring of Freehold t-ship, Monmouth co.; and, also, a deep lake, near a mile in circumference, well stored with fish. The margin of the river, above the mountain, is narrow, but very fertile; and, on the Pennsylvania side, abounds in lime. A road follows each bank through the mountain. That on the Jersey shore, rough, but safe, was made in the year 1830, by the aid of a donation of $2000 from the state. Before its completion, we are told, that the inhabitants, north of the mountain, made their way over the precipices by means of ladders of ropes.

We know no more admirable spot for a summer retreat than at the foot of the mountain, on the north side of the Gap. Here might be enjoyed the charms of diversified and always delightful scenery; a revivifying breeze, which follows the river through the sinuosities of its valley—fine rides on its banks, into the rich limestone country of the Wallpack; renovated vigour from the bracing mineral fountain; fine fishing upon the lake, the river and mountain brooks, of which the richest spoil is the gilded perch and speckled trout; and the more manly exercise of shooting, the country abounding in game. A good house established at Brotzmanville, upon the prattling stream, which there makes the air musical, and which might be used with great convenience for baths, and other purposes, we think would be much encouraged, provided the road through the mountain be kept in good order.

From New Jersey, the principal tributaries to the Delaware, above tide water, are Flatkill, Paulinskill, Pequest, Musconetcong, Laokatong, the Wickhechecoke, and the Assunpink; below tide, the Crosswicks, Rancocus, Cooper's, Oldman's, Salem, Stow, and Cohansey creeks, and Maurice river. At Easton, the Delaware receives, from Pennsylvania, the Lehigh river. From the South mountain, below Easton, to the tide water at Trenton, the river has a S. W. course of about 60 miles, in which there are 25 noted rapids, with an aggregate fall of 165 feet. But the navigation has been improved, and is safe at the ordinary height of the water. From Easton to Bristol, the Delaware division of the Pennsylvania canal has been completed, and in connexion with the Lehigh canal, affords advantageous communication with the coal mines, and the valley of the Lehigh river. Two surveys have been made for a canal along the valley of the Delaware from Easton to Carpenter's Point.

The Delaware and Raritan canal receives its water by a feeder, which taps the river on the left bank, about 23 miles above Trenton. The Morris canal enters the river below Phillipsburg, and opposite to Easton.

At Camden, opposite Philadelphia, the river is divided into two channels, by Petty's and Smith's islands. The western, near the centre of Philadelphia, is 900 feet wide, with a mean depth of 30 feet; the eastern is 2100 feet wide, with a mean depth of 9 feet; the whole area equal to 46,350 feet, affording a commodious and safe harbour, to which ships of the line may ascend.

At the head of the bay, at Delaware City, and opposite to Fort Delaware, which commands the passage of the river; the Delaware and Chesapeake canal, 14 miles in length, connects this with the Chesapeake bay, and its many tributary rivers. This point is distant from Camden 45 miles, and the bay extends, thence, 75 miles to the ocean, with a width varying from 3 to 30 miles, occupying an area of 630,000 acres. Its navigation is difficult and dangerous, being infested with shoals, which often prove destructive. It opens into the Atlantic, between Cape Henlopen, on the S. E., and Cape May, on the N. E., which are about 20 miles apart. The length of the bay and river, to the head of tide, at Trenton, is 155 miles. A 74 gun ship may ascend to Philadelphia, 120 miles; sloops, to Trenton falls; boats, of 8 or 10 tons, 100 miles above them; and canoes 150 miles higher.

Below Port Penn, 70 miles from the sea, the bay affords no safe harbourage; nor is there S. of New York, for several hundred miles, any place, where a vessel, during the rudest season of the year, when approach to the coast is most dangerous, may seek protection against the elements. The losses from this cause have induced the national government to form an artificial port, or breakwater, at the entrance of the bay. The law for this purpose was enacted, in 1828-9, and the work is in steady progression, and will be speedily completed. The anchorage ground, or roadstead, is formed by a cove in the southern shore, directly west of Cape Henlopen; and the seaward end rests on an extensive shoal, called the Shears; the tail of which makes out from the shore about 5 miles up the bay, near Broadkill creek; whence it extends eastward, and terminates at a point, about 2 miles to the N. of the shore, at the cape. The breakwater consists of an isolated dyke, or wall of stone; the transversal section of which is a trapezium, the base resting on the bottom, and the summit line forming the top of the work. The other sides represent the inner and outer slopes of the work; that to the seaward being the greater. The inward slope is 45°, the top horizontal, 22 feet in breadth, and raised 5½ feet above the highest spring tides; the outward, or sea slope, is 39 feet in altitude, on a base of 105¾ feet; both these dimensions being measured, in relation to a horizontal plane, passing by a point 27 feet below the lowest spring tides. The base bears to the altitude nearly the same ratio as similar lines in the profiles of the Cherbourg and Plymouth breakwaters. The opening or entrance from the ocean is 650 yards wide, between the north part of the cape and east end of the breakwater, and will be accessible by all winds from the sea. The *Breakwater*, proper, is a dyke in a straight line from E. S. E. to W. N. W., 1200 yards in length. At the distance of 350 yards from the upper or western end, that space forming the upper entrance, a similar dyke, 500 yards long, is projected in a direct line W. by S. ½ S., forming an angle of 146° 15′ with the breakwater. This part of the work is designed as an icebreaker.

The whole length of the two dykes will be 1700 yards, and they will contain, when finished, 900,000 cubic yards of basalt and granite rock, weighing from a quarter of a ton to three tons, and upwards. The depth of water, at low tide, is from 4 to six fathoms, over a surface of 7 tenths of a square mile. Although unfinished, this magnificent work has already proved its utility, saving many vessels and many valuable lives.

There are five bridges erected over the Delaware river, viz. at Trenton, at Lambertville, at Prallsville, at Philipsburg, and at Columbia. Authority has also been given to erect a bridge over the river at Philadelphia, and another opposite Taylorsville. The Delaware and Hudson canal crosses the river by means of a dam, constructed below the mouth of the Lackawaxan.

Den Brook, mill stream and tributary of the Rockaway river, rises in Randolph t-ship, Morris co., and flows by a course N. E., about 8 miles along the N. W. base of Trowbridge mountain, to its recipient near Danville.

Dennis's Creek t-ship, Cape May co., bounded N. E. by Upper t-ship, S. E. by the Atlantic ocean, S. by Middle t-ship, S. W. by Delaware Bay, W. and N. W. by Maurice River t-ship, Cumberland co. Centrally distant from Cape May court-house N. 9 miles; greatest length E. and W. 14 miles; breadth N. and S. 8½ miles; area, 43,500 acres. Dennis's creek runs on the S. W. border, through a very extensive cedar swamp, and the northern part of the t-ship consists of sandy plains; the population in 1830 was 1508. In 1832 the t-ship contained about 300 taxables, 198 householders, whose ratables did not exceed $30; 3 grist mills, 7 saw mills, 2 carding machines, 8 stores, and 185 horses, 503 head of neat cattle, over 3 years of age; it paid t-ship tax, $94 27; state tax, 162 75; and county tax, $503 54. Part of Ludlam's beach fronts the ocean, between which and Leaming's beach, the tide rushes in over the marshes and lagunes which border the eastern boundary for a breadth of about 2 miles. Dennis's Creek is the post-town. There are 2 churches in the t-ship.

Dennis's Creek, p-t. of Dennis's Creek t-ship, Cape May co., at the head of the navigation of Dennis's creek, 6 or 7 miles from the Delaware bay, 7 miles N. from Cape May court-house, 194 from W. C., and 97 from Trenton; contains from 30 to 40 dwellings, 2 taverns, 5 stores, and a tide grist mill. The town is built on both sides of the creek, extending each way, about half a mile. Ship building and trade in lumber are carried on extensively here. The country around it, above the marsh, is of sandy loam.

Denn's Branch, of Stow creek, a small tributary of Stow creek, Salem co., flowing westerly into its recipient by a course of 3 or 4 miles.

Denville, p-t. of Hanover t-ship, Morris co., on the right bank of the Rockaway river, 7 miles N. of Morristown, 231 N. E. from W. C., and 65 from Trenton; contains a store, tavern, cider distillery, and 6 or 8 dwellings.

Devil's Brook, small tributary of the Millstone river, in South Brunswick t-ship, Middlesex co., flowing S. W. about 5 miles to the river.

Deptford t-ship, Gloucester co., bounded N. E. by Gloucester t-ship, S. E. by Hamilton t-ship, S. W. by Greenwich t-ship, and N. W. by the river Delaware. Greatest length N. W. and S. E. 25, and breadth 7 miles; area, 57,600 acres; surface level; soil sandy: in the northern part, grass, vegetables, and fruit are successfully cultivated; the southern is chiefly pine forest, valuable for timber and cord wood. It is drained northward by Big Timber creek; Mantua creek on the west boundary; and southward by Innskeeps, Squankum, and Faraway, branches of the Great Egg Harbour river. Iron ore, and some chalybeate waters are found within 2 miles of Woodbury. Woodbury, the seat of justice for the county, Malaga, and Glassborough, are post-towns of the t-ship; population in 1830, 3599. In 1832 the township contained 449 householders, whose ratables did not exceed $30 in value, 19 stores, 8 fisheries, 6 grist mills, 1 cotton and 1 woollen manufactory, 1 carding machine, 9 saw mills, 1 ferry, 1 distillery, 1 glass factory, 1389 neat cattle, and 672 horses and mules above the age of 3 years.

Dickerson, the seat of the Hon. Mahlon Dickerson, former Governor of New Jersey, and representative of that state in the United States Senate, and the site of one of the most extensive and valuable iron mines in the state; ten miles N. W. from Morristown, Randolph t-ship, Morris county, upon the northern part, or continuation of Schooley's mountain.

Dillon's Landing, Dover t-ship, Monmouth co., on the north side of Toms' river bay, about 2 miles from its confluence with Barnegat bay.

Dividing Creek, Downe t-ship, Cumberland co., rises centrally in the t-ship, and flows southerly by a very crooked course of 10 or 12 miles, into Maurice creek cove, in Delaware bay. It is navigable to the village of Dividing Creek.

Dividing Creek, p-t. of Downe t-ship, Cumberland co., about 17 miles S. of Bridgeton, 86 from Trenton, and 192 N. E. from W. C.; contains from 25 to 30 dwellings, a store, tavern, and grist mill.

Dogtown, a mountain hamlet, on the line separating Amwell from Kingwood t-ship, Hunterdon co., 5 miles N. W. from Flemington; contains a tavern, a wheelwright shop, and two or three cottages.

Doctor's Creek, branch of the Crosswicks, rises near Clarkeville, in the eastern part of Upper Freehold t-ship, Monmouth co., and flows by a west course of about 14 miles, by Imlaystown and Allentown, to its recipient near the Sand Hills in Nottingham t-ship, Burlington co., turning several mills by the way.

Dorchester, village, of Maurice river t-ship, Cumberland co., on the left bank of the river, about 10 miles from the Delaware bay, and 20 S. E. from Bridgeton; contains between 30 and 40 dwellings, 1 tavern, and 2 stores. The soil about it is sandy.

Dorson's Brook, tributary of the north branch of Raritan river, Mendham t-ship, Morris co., having a course on and near the west t-ship line of about 4 or 5 miles.

Dover t-ship, Monmouth co., bounded N. by Howell and Freehold t-ships, E. by the Atlantic Ocean, S. by Stafford t-ship, S. W. by Northampton and Hanover t-ships, Burlington co., and N. W. by Upper Freehold. Centrally distant S. from Freehold, 24 miles; greatest length E. and W. 22; breadth N. and S. 17 miles; area, including Barnegat bay, and the Atlantic beach, 200,000 acres. It extends from the Atlantic Ocean to the western line of the county. Surface generally level, but there are some hills in the south, at the head of Forked river, called Forked River mountains; soil, generally sand or light gravel, covered with pine forest, whence enormous quantities of timber and cord wood are taken for the New York market, and for the supply of iron works in the t-ship. It is drained E. by Toms' river and its several branches, Cedar creek, and Forked river; on the W. by some branches of the Rancocus. Toms' river, Cedar creek, and Goodluck, are villages; the two first post-towns of the t-ship. Population in 1830, 2898. In 1832, the t-ship contained about 550 taxables, 201 householders, whose ratables did not exceed 30 dollars, 72 single men, 9 stores, 7 saw mills, 2 grist mills, 3 blast furnaces, 350 horses and mules, and 925 neat cattle, 3 years old and upwards; and paid in state and county taxes, $1265 06.

Dover, p-t. of Randolph t-ship, Morris co., on the Rockaway river, 8 miles N. W. from Morristown, 233 N. E. from W. C., and 67 from Trenton; the mountains recede here, and form a small plain, on which the town is built, on several streets and on both sides of the river, which is passed by one, perhaps more bridges. It contains 3 large rolling and slitting mills, boring and turning engines, a cupola furnace or foundery, and saw mill, the property of the heirs of the late Mr. M'Farlane, of New York, a factory of machinery, owned by W. Ford, a bank with an actual capital of $50,000 and the right to extend it to $150,000, an academy, used also as a church, and about 30 dwellings; much business has formerly been done here; the Morris canal descends into the valley by an inclined plane and 4 locks; a valuable iron mine, known as "Jackson's," near the town, is extensively worked, and governor Dickerson's mine is about 3 miles distant.

Downe, t-ship, Cumberland co., bounded N. by Fairfield and Milleville t-ship, E. by Maurice river, S. and W. by the Delaware. Centrally distant, S. E. from Bridgeton, 14 miles; greatest length E. and W. 14, breadth N. and S. 12 miles; area, 58,240 acres; surface, level; soil, marsh upon the bay and Maurice river; loam for a narrow strip of about a mile in width, adjoining the marsh, the remainder sandy. Maurice river follows the whole of the east boundary; Nantuxet creek the north-west, between which flows Dividing, Oranoken, Fishing, Broad, Oyster, and Fortescue creeks. Population in 1830, 1923; in 1832, there were in the t-ship, taxables, 310, householders 93, whose ratables did not exceed $30; stores 6, grist mills 5, saw mills 2, carding machine 1; 120 horses, 901 cattle above the age of 3 years; Mauricetown, Newport, Dividing Creek, Port Norris, and Buckshutem, are villages of the t-ship, of which the three first are post-towns.

Double Pond, a sheet of water in the Wawayanda mountain, Sussex co., which sends forth northwardly a small stream called Double Pond creek, which unites with Warwick creek, in the state of New York.

Drakestown, Morris co., on the line dividing Washington from Roxbury t-ship, on the road from Morristown to Hackettstown, 15 miles from the former and three from the latter, and upon Schooley's mountain; contains a store, and from 12 to 15 dwellings.

Drakesville, Roxbury t-ship, Morris co., on the turnpike road leading from Morristown by Stanhope furnace, 12 miles N. E. from the former, and upon the Morris canal; contains a tavern, a store, and from 12 to 15 dwellings. The country on the S. and S. E. is level, sandy, and poor; on the N. hilly and rough, but improving by the use of lime.

Drowned Lands, on the line separating Wantage from Vernon t-ships, Sussex co., and extending thence into Orange co., of New York. This is a morass of unusual extent for the northern states, and celebrated for the yearly inundation to which it is subject, and the malaria which it occasions during the autumn. It is twenty miles long, and varies in breadth from 1 to 5 miles. Through it flows the Wallkill, with a current scarce perceptible, to whose waters, when swelled by the spring freshets, it owes its annual submergence. It is composed of an accumulation of vegetable matter, whose surface is imperfectly converted into soil, abounding with carbonaceous substance, empyreumatic oil, and gallic acid, and covered in midsummer with rank and luxuriant vegetation. The ditches, made in several places, in forming roads across it, disclose peat of excellent quality. This equivocal lake encircles several islands, the largest of which contains 200 acres of excellent land, well cultivated; the smaller ones are uninhabited, and generally covered with wood, among which the beautiful flowering shrub, *Rhododendron Maximum*, laurelled leaved rose tree, grows abundantly. The rocks on the island, and upon the borders of the morass, indicate that it reposes on blue cherty limestone; but in one place, at least the island near Woodville, primitive limestone, the rock of the neighbouring country appears. No successful effort has yet been made to drain this vast swamp, which is abandoned as pasturing ground to cattle on the subsidence of the spring inundation, for a few weeks only, and is for the rest of the year a desolate waste.

Dry Branch, tributary of Paulin's creek, Knowlton t-p. Warren co.

Duck Island, in the Delaware river, above Bordentown, in Nottingham township, Burlington county. It is somewhat more than a mile in length.

Dunker Pond, south of Bear Fort mountain, Pompton t-ship, Bergen co., sends forth a small tributary to the Pequannock creek.

Dunks's Ferry, a noted and long established ferry on the Delaware river, Willingboro' t-ship, Burlington co., 4 miles below the city of Burlington.

Dyer's Creek, a small marsh stream of Middle t-ship, Cape May co., which flows into the Delaware, after a course of 3 or 4 miles.

Dutch Neck, village of W. Windsor t-ship, Middlesex co., 18 miles S. W. from Trenton; contains a tavern and 3 or 4 stores; soil, gravelly and poor.

East Creek, mill stream of Dennis t-ship, Cape May co., flowing about 7 miles S. W. into the Delaware bay.

East Windsor. (See *Windsor, East*.)

Eayrstown, village of Northampton t-ship, Burlington co., on the S. branch of Rancocus creek, near the junction of Haines' creek with that stream, and at the head of tide, between 3 and 4 miles S. W. from Mount Holly; contains a cotton factory, a grist mill, saw mill, fulling mill, 1 tavern, 1 store, and 12 or 15 dwellings; soil, sandy loam, fertile and well cultivated.

Edinburgh, W. Windsor t-ship, Middlesex co., on the Assunpink creek, 18 miles S. W. from N. B., and 8 miles E. of Trenton; contains a Presbyterian church of wood, 1 store, 1 tavern, a grist mill, and 12 or 14 dwellings; soil, sandy and light.

Eaton, p-t. of Shrewsbury t-ship, Monmouth co., 2 miles S. from Shrewsburytown, upon Shrewsbury river, 11 miles from Freehold, 48 from Trenton, and 213 from W. C., on a branch of Swimming river, 1½ miles above navigable water; contains about 30 dwellings, 5 or 6 stores, 2 taverns, a grist mill, and an academy, in a pleasant and fertile country.

Edgepeling, a tributary of Atsion river, rising in Evesham t-ship, Burlington co., and flowing by a southerly course of 8 or 9 miles, to its recipient in Washington t-ship.

Egg Harbour, Little, t-ship, Burlington co., bounded N. by Oswego, or east branch of Wading river, which separates it from Northampton t-ship, S. E. by Stafford t-ship, Monmouth co., S. by Little Egg Harbour river and bay, and W. by Washington t-ship. Centrally distant from Mount Holly, S. E. 35 miles; greatest length N. and S. 20 miles; breadth E. and W. 10 miles; area, 76,800 acres, including bays and inlets; surface, level; soil, gravel and sand. The northern part of the township, called the Plains, is of the former, covered with low pines and scrub oaks, forming an excellent covert for deer and grouse, which find abundant food in the mast produced by the latter. The southern part of the t-ship is sandy, covered with forest. It is drained chiefly by branches of Little Egg Harbour river, of which Bass river is here the chief. Tuckerton, upon Shorl's mill branch, is the post-town. Population in 1830, 1490. In 1832, the t-ship contained 150 householders, whose ratables did not exceed $30; 347 taxables, 51 single men, 6 stores, 4 saw mills, 3 grist mills, 1 two horse stage, 7 dearborns, 36 covered wagons, 10 gigs and sulkies, 640 neat cattle, 170 horses and mules; and it paid state tax, $127 48; county tax, $444; road tax, $300.

Egg Harbour Bay, Little, partly in Little Egg Harbour t-ship, Burlington co., and partly in Stafford t-ship, Monmouth co.; extends about 14 miles in length, and from 2 to 4 in breadth, from Little Egg Harbour inlet to Barnegat inlet, and contains many islands, the haunts of ducks, geese, and sea-fowl.

Egg Harbour, Little, or *Mullica's River*, rises by several branches in Burlington and Gloucester cos.; the chief of which are Batsto river, near Burlington, Atsion river, on the boundary between the two counties, Mechescalaxin and Nesochcaque, which unite near Pleasant Mills, 25 miles from the sea. Half way below this point, Wading and Bass rivers blend with the main stream, which is navigable, for sloops, to Batsto furnace, 25 miles. The Little Egg Harbour bay and inlet, and Great bay, form a sheet of salt water, separated from the ocean by Brigantine, Tucker's and Long beaches, the communication with which, from the sea, is chiefly by the New inlet, which admits vessels of from 15 to 18 feet draught, many of which, during the late war, entered and discharged valuable cargoes. The Old inlet, to the north from Tucker's island, is now little used, except for vessels of very light burden. The collection district of Little Egg Harbour, comprehends the shores, waters, bays, rivers and creeks, from Barnegat inlet to Brigantine inlet, both inclusively. Tuckerton is the sole port of entry, at which the collector resides.

Egg Harbour River, Great, rises in Gloucester t-ship, Gloucester co., by Inskeep's branch, and flows a S. E. course through Deptford, Hamilton, Weymouth, and Egg Harbour t-ships, to the ocean, about 45 miles; receiving in its way several, but not very considerable tributaries, on either hand, and draining a wide extent of sandy soil and pine forest. It is navigable for sloops of considerable burden, above May's Landing, more than 25 miles; and from this point flows through a continued marsh. Large quantities of wood, coal, and lumber, are annually exported from this river.

Great Egg Harbour bay is entered by Great Egg Harbour inlet, between Absecum and Peck's beaches. The bay is about five miles long, and has a very irregular breadth, varying from half a mile to 4 miles. The inlet, at its mouth, is more than a mile in width, and communicates with the bay by several channels.

Egg Harbour t-ship, Gloucester co., bounded N. E. by Absecum creek, bay, and inlet, which separate it from Galloway t-ship; S. E. by the Atlantic ocean; S. W. by Great Egg Harbour inlet, bay, and river, and N.

W. by Hamilton t-ship. Centrally distant from Woodbury S. E. 48 miles; greatest length E. and W. 12; breadth N. and S. 12 miles; area, 85,000 acres, including beaches, bays, and rivers; surface level; marsh several miles in width, within the beach; sandy elsewhere, and, generally, covered with pine forest. Bargaintown and Somers' Point are post-towns of the t-ship; population in 1830, 2510. In 1832 the t-ship contained 122 householders, whose ratables did not exceed $30; 5 stores, 2 grist mills, 1 carding machine, 6 saw mills, 510 neat cattle, and 260 horses and mules; and paid county taxes, $307 59½; poor tax, $153 90; road tax, $800.

Great Egg Harbour, collection district, comprehends the river of Great Egg Harbour, together with all the inlets, bays, sounds, rivers, and creeks, along the sea coast, from Brigantine inlet to Cape May.

Egg Island, Downe t-ship, Cumberland co., Delaware bay, off the western point of Maurice Cove, of a triangular form, extending about half a mile upon each side.

Egg Island, false, a point of Downe t-ship, about 4 miles higher up the bay, than the foregoing, and which, from similarity of configuration, is often mistaken for it.

Egg Islands, Barnegat bay, Dover t-ship, Monmouth co., about 3 miles below the mouth of Toms' bay, each near a mile in length.

Eight Mile Branch, of Cedar creek, Dover t-ship, Monmouth co., rises west of the Forked mountains, and flows eastwardly to its recipient.

Elizabethtown, and t-ship, Essex co., thus named after Lady Elizabeth Carteret, the wife and executrix of Sir George Carteret. The town lies upon Elizabeth creek, 1½ miles W. from a point of fast land, running through the marsh to Staten Island Sound, and on the turnpike road and rail-road, from New Brunswick to New York, 17 miles by the post road from the former, and 15 from the latter; 42 from Trenton, and 210 from W. C.; pleasantly situated, in a level and fertile country, of clay loam; contains 400 dwellings, 3 handsome churches of brick, one belonging to the Episcopalians, and two to the Presbyterians, the first congregation of whom, is, probably, as old as the town itself; and 1 Methodist church, of wood. There were two churches in this town, in 1748, which the Swedish traveller, Kalm, preferred to any in Philadelphia: 2 temperance societies, having together 450 members, whose beneficial influence is said to be extensively felt, there not being a distillery in the t-ship, and all the respectable farmers conducting their labours without the stimulus of ardent spirit; a bank called the "*State Bank at Elizabeth*," with an authorized capital of $200,000, of which $132,924, have been paid in, conducted reputably and profitably; 5 taverns in the town and two at the Point; 9 stores, at none of which is ardent spirit sold; 1 book store, 2 boarding schools for girls, at which there are about 100 pupils from various parts of the country; 1 classical boarding school for boys, containing 40 boarders, under the care of the Reverend Mr. Halsey, all of which are in high repute; 2 public libraries, one religious, the other miscellaneous, called the Elizabethtown Apprentices' Library, much and advantageously used; 1 printing office, from which is issued the newspaper called the New Jersey Journal, originally founded by the venerable judge Hallock, at Chatham, in 1779, removed to this town in 1786, and conducted by him for nearly half a century; an oil mill, large grist and saw mill, 2 large saw mills for cutting mahogany, with circular saws for veneers; 2 large oil cloth manufactories, belonging to the same company; 2 earthenware, and 1 earthen and stoneware potteries; flax works, which break and dress 2 tons per day, driven by steam; a rope, twine, and cotton bagging factory, also driven by steam, and employing 20 hands; 2 tin, sheet iron, and stove factories, 1 clock manufactory, and 1 shears manufactory, moved by steam; 2 carriage makers, 2 tanneries, one of which dresses oil, morocco, and alum, leather; 1 iron foundery for making malleable castings, connected with which is a steam engine factory, and machine shop, worked by steam; and a book bindery.

The town or t-ship is bounded N. by Newark t-ship, E. by Newark bay and Staten Island Sound, S. by Rahway, and W. by Union t-ships; greatest length N. E. and S. W. 5 miles; breadth, 3½ miles; area, 10,000 acres; soil, red shale, clay, loam, and marsh; from the last of which, large quantities of grass are cut, chiefly for manure. The soil is of excellent quality, and repays the labour of the husbandman abundantly. Bound Brook runs on the north, and Morss Brook on the south boundary. There are 470 dwellings in the t-ship, and the population was, in 1830, 3455. In 1832, the t-ship contained 550 taxables, 235 householders, whose ratable estate did not exceed 30 dollars, 83 single men, 22 merchants, 289 horses and mules, 579 neat cattle over 3 years of age; and it paid in 1833, state tax, $313 13; county, $819 17; road, $800; poor, $900. The t-ship has a house and farm of 50 acres, upon which its poor are kept.

This town was the first English settlement made in the state. The land was purchased for a company called the Elizabethtown Associates, from the Indians in 1664. These Associates, 74 in number, were originally from Jamaica, Long Island. They held adversely to Berkeley and Carteret, the grantees of the Duke of York; and their pertinacious adherence to the right, real, or supposed, obtained under the Indian grant, was cause of disturbance and commotion, not only during the government of the proprietaries, but for many years of the royal administration. During the revolution, the town suffered much from its contiguity to New York. On the 21st January, 1780, the first Presbyterian church was burned by the British, and in the following November, its minister, the Rev. James Caldwell, was shot.

Elizabethtown is a desirable residence, whether health, business, or pleasure, be in view. The excellent order and morals which prevail here, the advantages derived from its schools, the short distance from New York, to which the inhabitants, three times a day, have access, by steam-boats from the Point, and at other times by stages; the rail-road now being constructed through the town, and that to be made by Somerville to Belvidere, cannot fail to increase its population, and the price of its lands. The town is built upon streets uncommonly wide, and has many very handsome buildings, surrounded by large well improved lots. The t-ship was originally incorporated by Governor Philip Carteret, about the same time as its neighbour Woodbridge, by a most liberal charter; and subsequently, 28th November, 1789, by act of Assembly, with bounds including parts of the present adjacent townships. Its area has been greatly diminished by various acts. The corporate officers of the "*Borough of Elizabeth*" are a mayor, deputy mayor, recorder, seven aldermen or assistants, a sheriff, coroner, treasurer, clerk, high constable, and seven constables. It has power to regulate general police, markets, roads, &c., and has a court of common pleas and general sessions, holden 4 times annually, with a jurisdiction like to, and exclusive of, that of the county courts. At Elizabethtown Point there was formerly a ferry by which passengers, from and to New York, crossed to Staten Island.

Ellisburg, small hamlet, of Waterford t-ship, Gloucester co., 6 miles S. E. from Camden, 9 miles N. E. from Woodbury, and 2 from Haddonfield; contains a tavern, store, smith shop, and several dwellings.

Elsinborough, t-ship, Salem co., bounded N. by Salem creek, and Salem t-ship, E. by Lower Alloways t-ship, S. by Alloways creek; and W. by the Delaware river. Centrally distant from the town of Salem, 3 miles; greatest length N. and S. 6 miles; breadth E. and W. 4 miles; area, about 8000 acres; surface, level; soil, rich loam and marsh meadow, highly cultivated. The t-ship is drained by Alloways creek on the south, and Salem creek on the north. Population in 1830, 503. In 1832, the t-ship contained 56 householders, whose ratables did not exceed 30 dollars, 117 taxables, 118 horses and mules, and 547 neat cattle, above the age of 3 years.

Empty Box Run, Upper Freehold t-ship, Monmouth co., a small branch of the Assunpink creek.

Englishtown, p-t., of Freehold t-ship, Monmouth co., upon Matchaponix creek, near the N. W. boundary of the t-ship and county; contains a grist mill, 2 taverns, 2 stores, and about 30 dwellings, surrounded by a light sandy soil.

English Neighbourhood, pleasant village, of Hackensack t-ship, Bergen co., 5 miles S. E. from Hackensack-town, and 5½ from Hoboken, on the turnpike road to Hackensack; contains a post-office, a Dutch Reformed church, and a church of Chris-ti-ans, 3 taverns, 2 stores, and from 15 to 20 dwellings. This village is at a convenient distance from New York, by a good road, which, through a pleasant country, affords a very agreeable drive on a summer's afternoon, to the business-worn citizens.

English Creek, a smart mill stream, of Egg Harbour t-ship, Gloucester co., which flows by a S. W. course of 4 or 5 miles, into the Great Egg Harbour river, about 5 miles from the bay.

English Creek, a tributary of the Hackensack river, which rises, and has its course, in Hackensack t-ship, Bergen co.; and almost the whole of its length of 7 miles is through a cedar swamp. This creek formed the defence of the garrison of 3000, who retreated from Fort Lee, attacked by Lord Cornwallis, 18th November, 1776.

Essex County, had its boundaries fixed by act 21st January, 1709-10, commencing at the mouth of Rahway river, where it falls into the Staten Island Sound; thence up the river to Robeson's branch; thence west to the line between the former eastern and western divisions of the colony; thence by the same line, to Pequannock river, where it meets the Passaic river; thence down the Passaic to the Bay and Sound; thence down the Sound to the place of beginning. These limits were modified by the act of 4th November, 1741, annexing part of the county to Somerset. Essex is now bounded W. N. and E. by the Passaic river, which separates it, W. and N. W. from Morris co., N. and E. from Bergen co., S. E. by Newark bay and Long Island Sound, S. by Middlesex co., and S. W. by Somerset co. Greatest length N. and S. 28 miles, breadth E. and W. 19 miles; area in acres, 154,680, or 241¼ square miles. Central lat. 40° 45′ N.; long. 2° 45′ E. from W. C.

Geologically considered, this county will be classed with the secondary or transition formation, as the old red sandstone shall be determined to belong to either. The whole seems based upon this substratum. It is crossed, however, diagonally from S. W. to N. E., by 2 mountain ridges, entering New Providence and Westfield t-ships from Somerset county, which extend for 25 miles, unbroken by any stream of water, to the Passaic, at Paterson. These are known by the local names of First and Second Mountains, and the latter by that of Short Hills. These ridges, from 1 to 2 miles asunder, are of trap formation, and in some points assume, particularly at the Great and Little Falls, on the Passaic, a columnar character and appearances of the action of fire in their cellular form, which support the igneous origin of that rock. These hills, generally covered with wood, send forth tributaries to the cardinal points of the compass, and their rocky basis have caused the beautiful cataracts of the Passaic Falls.

The great river of the county is the Passaic, whose main stream encompasses it on all sides, save the south, and receives, with few exceptions, all the other streams. On the west of the mountains, these tributaries are Deep, Pine, Black Rock, Meadow, and River Canoe, brooks; on the east, Second and Third rivers, and several inconsiderable streams. Peckman's river runs northward, in the valley between the mountains, emptying into the Passaic, about 2 miles below the Little Falls. The Rahway river, which rises in the same valley, and whose source is not a mile south of the former, runs by an opposite course into Staten Island Sound. Green brook, which rises in the Short Hills, has a south-west course to the Raritan, on the line below Somerset and Middlesex counties. On the east side of the mountains, there are 2 noted chalybeate springs; one in Acquackanonck, and the other in Orange township.

The soil of the county is generally of red shale, except where formed of the *debris* of the mountains. The first is almost every where well cultivated, and in many places highly productive in grain and grass; and, as a large proportion of the population is employed in manufactures, an advantageous market is produced at the door of the farmer for all his productions; consequently, the whole country, almost without exception, has the air of growing wealth and present enjoyment. A large portion of the surface of the county, on each side of the mountains is level, but some of it, hilly.

The principal towns are on the east of the mountain; Newark, the seat of justice; Paterson, Weasel, Acquackanonck, Bloomfield, Belleville, Orange, South Orange, Camptown, Springfield, Elizabethtown, Rahway, Westfield, Scotch Plains, Plainfield, &c.

Four turnpike roads cross the county, north-westerly, leading from Elizabethtown, Newark, and Jersey City, respectively.

In the north part of the county, a considerable portion of the agricultural population is of Dutch descent, whilst the south has been peopled from English sources, and principally from Long Island and New England. The inhabitants have the love of order, decorum, industry, and thrift of their ancestors.

In 1830, the census gave an aggregate of 41,911 souls, of whom 20,242 were white males; 19,502 white females; 921 free coloured males; 1018 free coloured females; 107 male slaves; 111 female slaves. There were 1176 aliens; whites, deaf and dumb 27, and 22 blind; and 1 coloured person blind.

In 1832, the county contained 7710 taxables, 3370 householders, whose ratable estates did not exceed $30; 1412 single men, 306 merchants, 42 grist mills, 22 cotton, and 13 woollen manufactories, 41 saw mills, 5 furnaces, 5 carding machines, 19 paper mills, 1 fulling mill, 223 tan vats, 3 bleaching and printing establishments for cotton, &c., and 5 distilleries. Besides these sources of trade, a very large business is done in the manufacture of shoes and hats for foreign markets.

In the same year, the county paid state tax, $3822 04, county tax, $10,000, poor tax, $10,570, road tax, $10,204.

The means for moral improvement consist of many religious institutions, such as churches pertaining to Episcopalians, Presbyterians, Methodists, Baptists, and Dutch Reformed—bible, missionary, and temperance societies; academies in the principal towns, at which the languages and the higher branches of an English education are taught, and common and Sunday schools, in every vicinity.

STATISTICAL TABLE OF ESSEX COUNTY.

Townships, &c.	Length.	Breadth.	Area.	Surface.	Population.		
					1810.	1820.	1830.
Acquackanonck,	7	6½	14,000	hilly,	2023	3338	7710
Bloomfield,	5	4½	14,000	do.		3085	4309
Caldwell,	7	6	16,500	do.	2235	2020	2004
Elizabeth,	5	3½	10,000	do.	2977	3515	3455
Livingston,	5	4½	13,000	do.		1056	1150
Newark,	7	6	12,000	level,	8008	6507	10,953
New Providence,	6	2½	7680	pt. hill, pt. valley,	756	766	910
Orange,	7	5	14,000	hilly, rolling,	2266	2830	3887
Rahway,	8	4½	10,000	level,	1779	1945	1983
Springfield,	6	5	13,500	hilly,	2360	1804	1653
Union,	5½	5	12,000	level,	1428	1567	1405
Westfield,	7	6	18,000	pt. hilly pt. level,	2152	2358	2492
			154,680		25,984	30,793	41,911

Etna, furnace and forge, and grist and saw mills, on Tuckahoe creek, Weymouth t-ship, Gloucester co., about 15 miles from the sea.

Everittstown, Alexandria t-ship, Hunterdon co., 11 miles N. W. of Flemington, upon the Nischisakawick creek, contains 1 tavern, a grist mill, a Methodist church, and several dwellings.

Evesham t-ship, Burlington co., bounded on the N. E. and E. by Northampton t-ship, S. E. by Washington t-ship, S. W. by Waterford t-ship, Gloucester co., and on the N. W. by Chester t-ship. Centrally distant S. W. from Mount Holly 8 miles; greatest length N. and S. 15 miles; breadth 10 miles; area, 67,000 acres; surface, generally level; soil, sand and sandy loam; the north-western portion pretty well cultivated and productive. The south branch of the Rancocus forms, in part, the N. E. boundary; Haines' creek, and several other tributaries, are on the E.; and on the S. the t-ship is drained by the head waters of the Little Egg Harbour river. Evesham, Medford, Colestown, Lumberton, Fostertown, Evesham Cross Roads, Bodine, Cropwell, &c. are the villages of the t-ship, the two first are post-towns; population in 1830, 4239. In 1832 the t-ship contained taxables 850, householders 366, whose ratables did not exceed $30, single men 90, stores 9, saw mills 12, grist mills 7, fulling mills 2, distilleries for cider 4, phaetons and chaises 3, two horse stages 1, dearborns 40, covered wagons 221, chairs and curricles 39, gigs and sulkies 11, 2303 neat cattle, and 1016 horses and mules, above 3 years old; and it paid state tax, $607 21; county tax, $2119 15; and t-ship tax, $1500.

Evesham, p-t., Evesham t-ship, Burlington co., 8 miles S. W. from Mount Holly, and 4 miles S. E. from Moorestown, 34 from Trenton, and 147 from W. C.; contains a Quaker meeting house and several dwellings.

Evesham Cross Roads, Evesham t-ship, Burlington co., 6 miles S. W. from Mount Holly.

Ewing's Neck, on the Delaware bay, between Tarkiln creek and Maurice river t-ship, Cumberland co.

Factory Branch, of Cedar creek, small stream of Dover t-ship, Monmouth co.

Fairfield t-ship, Cumberland co., is bounded on the N. by Deerfield, Hopewell, and Greenwich t-ships, from the two last of which, it is separated by the Cohansey creek; E. by Milleville t-ship, and S. by Downe t-ship and the Delaware bay. Centrally distant S. from Bridgeton 7 miles; greatest length E. and W. 15 miles; breadth 8 miles; area, 46,720 acres; surface, level; soil, with the exception of a strip of marsh and upland on the bay, the latter of which is clay and loam, is of sand. The t-ship is drained on the north line by the Cohansey creek, on the south line by Nantuxet creek, and intermediately, by several small streams, of which Cedar creek is the most considerable; all of which flow westward; eastward it sends forth some small tributaries to Maurice river; population in 1830, 1812. In 1832 there were in the t-ship 410 taxables, 105 householders, whose ratables did not exceed in value $30; 9 stores, 6 run of stones for grinding grain; 2 saw mills, 1 tannery, 310 horses, and 1188 neat cattle, above 3 years old; and it paid road tax, $100; county and state tax, $868 55. Cedarville and Fairton are post-towns of the t-ship. There are in the t-ship a Presbyterian and Methodist church.

Fairfield, small village, in the northern part of Caldwell t-ship, Essex co.; contains a Dutch Reformed church, and some 8 or 10 dwellings, distant 11 miles north west from Newark.

Fairton, p-t. of Fairfield t-ship, Cumberland co., in the fork formed by Mill creek and Rattle Snake run, which unite and flow into Cohansey creek; distant about 4 miles S. of Bridgeton, 179 N. E. from W. C., and 73 S. from Trenton; contains from 30 to 40 dwellings, 2 stores, a Methodist church, and about 200 inhabitants. There is also a Presbyterian church near the town. Marl has been lately discovered here on the estate of Michael Swing, the use of which adds much to the fertility of the lands.

Fairview, or *Quakertown*, p-t. of Kingwood t-ship, Hunterdon co., 7 miles N. W. of Flemington, 29 from Trenton, and 188 from W. C.; contains a Quaker meeting house, 2 stores, a tavern, and some 12 or 15 dwellings, and several mechanics' shops. The soil here is a stiff clay, which is becoming fertile by the use of lime.

Faraway Branch, small tributary of Hospitality creek, an arm of the Great Egg Harbour river, in Franklin and Deptford t-ships, Gloucester co.

Fenwicke Creek, Mannington t-sp. Salem co., named after John Fenwicke, the first Quaker settler in this country, rises by two branches, one of which, and the main stem, form the eastern and northen boundary of Salem t-ship, separating it from Mannington. The greatest length of the stream may be 6 miles. It empties into Salem creek, at the town of Salem, where it is crossed by a neat covered bridge, to which it is navigable.

Finesville, small village on the Musconetcong creek, a mile above its mouth, and 19 miles S. W. from Belvidere, the county town, and 8 from Easton; lies in a very narrow but fertile valley; contains a grist mill, saw mill, and oil mill, a woollen manufactory, 1 tavern, 1 store, and from 15 to 20 dwellings.

Finn's Point, a noted point on the Delaware, of Lower Penn's Neck t-ship, Salem co., about 4 miles above Salem creek, and 1 above Fort Delaware. It has its name from the first landing or residence of the Finn's here.

Fishing Creek, a small stream of Downe t-ship, which flows from Oranoken creek, through the salt marsh, into the Delaware bay.

Fishing Creek, S. W. boundary of Middle t-ship, Cape May co., flows westerly 4 or 5 miles to the Delaware bay. It gives name to a post-office; distant 109 miles from W. C., and 112 from Trenton.

Five Mile Beach, between Hereford and Turtle Gut inlets, partly in Middle and partly in Lower t-ship, Cape May co., of a wedge-like form, having in its greatest width about a mile.

Flaggtown, p-t., of Hillsborough t-ship, Somerset co., 6 miles S. W. from Somerville; contains 1 tavern, and about a dozen houses. It is 191 miles N. E. from W. C., and 25 from Trenton.

Flanders, p-t., of Roxbury t-ship, Morris co., in the valley of the south branch of the Raritan river, and in a fertile country, at the east foot of Schooley's mountain; 13 miles N. W. of Morristown, 54 N. E. from Trenton, and 220 from W. C.; contains a grist and saw mill, a Methodist church, a school, 2 taverns, 2 stores, and from 20 to 25 dwellings.

Flatkill, Big and Little, creeks, of Sussex co., both of which rise in Montague t-ship, and unite near the southern boundary of Sandistone t-ship; thence the stream flows S. W. into the river Delaware, at the Walpack Bend. The course of the main stream is parallel with the Blue mountain from its source, and for the length of 25 miles, in which it receives some inconsiderable and innominate tributaries from the mountain.

Flat Brookville, post-office, Sandystone t-ship, Sussex co., 247 miles N. E. from W. C., and 89 from Trenton.

Flemington, p-t., of Hunterdon co., situate at the northern extremity of the valley, lying between Rock mountain and Mount Carmel, and near the S. E. foot of the latter, and 2 miles E. of the south branch of the Raritan river, 23 miles N. from Trenton, 45 from Philadelphia, and 182 from W. C., 25 N. W. from Brunswick, and 25 S. E. from Easton; the two last are the principal markets for this portion of the country. The surface for many miles south and east is gently undulating; the valley between the mountains extending about 8 miles; the soil is of red shale, underlaid by the old red sandstone formation, and if not generous in spontaneous production, is grateful for the careful cultivation it receives, yielding abundance of grass, wheat, rye, oats, Indian corn, and flax; of the last, many farmers sow from 12 to 15 acres, for the product of which they find a ready market at Philadelphia. The town is also famed for excellent cheese, made at the extensive dairy of Mr. Capner. Much attention is also given here to raising horses, of which the breeds are greatly admired, and eagerly sought for. The town contains 50 dwellings, and about 300 inhabitants; a very neat Presbyterian church, of stone, built about 35 years since; a Methodist church, of brick, a neat building; and a Baptist church, of wood; two schools, one of which is an incorporated academy, and 3 sunday schools; a public library, under the care of a company also incorporated; a court-house, of stone, rough-cast, having a Grecian front, with columns of the Ionic order. The basement story of this building is used as the county prison: the second, contains an uncommonly large and well disposed room for the court: the third, a grand jury room; and other apartments. From the cupola, which surmounts the structure, there is a delightful prospect of the valley, bounded by mountains on the S. and S. W., but almost unlimited on the S. E., and of the hill, which rises by a graceful and gentle slope on the N. and N. W., ornamented with well cultivated farms to its very summit. The houses, built upon one street, are neat and comfortable, with small court yards in front, redolent with flowers, aromatic shrubs and creeping vines. The county offices, detached from the court-house, are of brick and fire-proof. There are here, 5 lawyers, 2 physicians; a journal, published weekly, called the Hunterdon Gazette, edited by Mr. Charles George; a fire engine, with an incorporated fire association. The name of the place is from its founder, Mr. Fleming, who resided here before the revolution. A valuable deposit of copper is said to have been lately found here.

Fork Bridge, over Maurice river, about 2 miles below the village of Malaga, on the line between Gloucester, Salem and Cumberland counties. It takes its name from the fork of the river above it. There are here two mills and several dwellings.

Forked River, Dover t-ship, Monmouth co., rises at the foot of the Forked river mountains, and flows E., about 10 miles, to the Atlantic ocean.

Forked River Mountains, two considerable sand hills in the southern part of Dover t-ship, Monmouth county.

Forstertown, Evesham t-ship, Burlington co., 6 miles S. of Mount Holly, is a cluster of some 8 or 10 farm houses, upon an excellent soil of sandy loam, highly cultivated.

Fortescue Creek, Downe t-ship, Cumberland co., flows from the Oranoken creek, through the salt marsh into the Delaware bay.

Fort Lee, on the North river, and in Hackensack t-ship, Bergen co., about 5 miles E. of Hackensack town. This was a noted post during the revolutionary war, commanding in common with Fort Washington, on the New York side, the navigation of the river. Both forts were strongly garrisoned by the American troops, and bridled the English forces in New York, after the battle of Long Island. Possession of them was unfortunately holden after their insufficiency to prevent the passage up the river by the British vessels had been experimentally proven. The capture of Fort Washington lost the Americans 3000 men, and the like number in Fort Lee were saved from the same fate only by the timely abandonment of the works, by order of Gen. Greene, on the 18th November, 1776. A metallic vein was worked near this fort, at the commencement of the American war, under the impression that it contained gold. But it has been determined by Dr. Torrey, that the ore is pyritous and green carbonate of copper, in a matrix of quartz and siliceous and calcareous breccia, dipping under green sandstone.

Frankford t-ship, Sussex co., bounded N. by Wantage; E. by Hardiston; S. by Newton, and W. by Sandiston t-ship. Centrally distant, N. from Newton, 8 miles; greatest length, 11; breadth, 8 miles; area, 28,800 acres. The surface of the t-ship is hilly towards the west; the boundary on that side running on the Blue mountain. The remainder consists of valley lands. At the foot of the mountain, Long pond and Culver's pond, are the principal sources of Paulinskill creek, which flows S. W. towards the Delaware. On the N. the t-ship is drained by the Papakating creek, a tributary of the Wallkill river. Two turnpike roads, that from Morristown to the Delaware, opposite Milford, running north-west, and the Newton and Bolton, running north-east, cross the township. Augusta and Branchville are post towns, lying on the former. Population in 1830, 1996. Taxables in 1832, 370. There were in the t-ship, in 1832, 110 householders, whose ratables did exceed $30; 6 stores, 14 run of stones for grinding grain, 2 carding machines; 1 fulling mill, 460 horses and mules, and 1540 neat cattle, above three years old; 48 tan vats, 5 distilleries. The t-ship paid state and county tax, $812 70; poor tax, $900; road tax, $800. Lime and slate alternate in several veins or beds, in the township. Their soils are fertile.

Franklin t-ship, Somerset co., bounded N. by Bridgewater t-ship and river; N. E. by Raritan river, separating it from Piscataway t-ship, Middlesex co.; S. E. by North and South Brunswick t-ships, of that county; and S. W. and W. by Millstone river, dividing it from Montgomery and Hillsborough t-ships, Somerset co. Centrally distant, S. E., from Somerville, 7 miles. Greatest length, N. E. and S. W., 13; breadth, E. and W., 8 miles; area, about 30,000 acres. Surface on the S. W., hilly, elsewhere gently undulating. Drained by the Millstone and Raritan rivers, and by several tributaries, of which Six Mile Run is the chief. Griggstown is a village of the t-ship; near it, at the foot of Rocky hill, is a deposit of copper ore, not wrought. Part of Kingston and Six Mile Run villages are within the east boundary, on the Princeton and New Brunswick turnpike. Population in 1830, 3352. In 1832, there were 716 taxables; 67 householders, whose ratables did not exceed $30, and 58 single men, 10 stores, 4 saw mills, 4 grist mills, 13 tan-vats, 2 distilleries, 862 horses and mules, and 1335 neat cattle above the age of three years; and it paid, state tax, $709 30; county, $996 11.

Franklin t-ship, Bergen co., bounded N. by Rockland co., state of New York; E. by Saddle river, which divides it from Harrington t-ship; S. by Saddle river t-ship, and W. by Pompton. Centrally distant, N. W. from Hackensack, 13 miles; greatest length, N. and S. 10 miles; breadth, E. and W. 9 miles; area, above 45,000 acres. There are elevated grounds on the E. and W.; on the W. lies the Ramapo mountain. The greater part of the township is valley, with undulating surface and diluvial soil, of gravel, loam and sand, poured over a sandstone base; generally well cultivated and productive; and a large portion of the produce is consumed at the numerous manufactories of the township. It is drained by the Ramapo river, coursing the base of the Ramapo mountain, in the N. W. angle, and by Saddle river on the east boundary, with their tributaries. Population in 1830, 3449. In 1832, the t-ship contained 862 taxables, 83 householders, whose ratables did not exceed $30; 7 merchants, 18 grist mills, 13 cotton mills, 25 saw mills, 3 paper mills, 1 woollen factory, 1 furnace, 2 fulling mills, 22 tan vats, 4 distilleries, 803 horses, and 1780 mules, above 3 years old; and it paid state tax, $370 51, county tax, $753 25, poor, $500, roads, $2000. In Franklin there are 4 Dutch Reformed, 2 Seceders, and 2 Methodist churches.

Franklin, t-ship, Gloucester co., bounded N. E. by Deptford t-ship, S. E. by Hamilton, S. W. by Millville t-ship, Cumberland co., and Pittsgrove t-ship, Salem co., and N. W. by Greenwich and Woolwich t-ships. Centrally distant, S. E. from Woodbury, 15 miles, greatest length 16 miles; breadth, 7 miles; area, 72,000 acres; surface, level; soil, sandy, and generally covered with pine forest. It is drained northward by the head waters of Raccoon creek, S. W. by the sources of Maurice river, and S. E. by branches of the Great Egg Harbour river. Glassboro', Malaga, Little Ease, and Union, are villages of the t-ship; at the two first are post-offices. There are iron works at Union. Population in 1830, 1574. In 1832, the t-ship contained 276 householders, whose ratables did not exceed $30; 4 stores, 2 grist mills, 9 saw mills, 1 distillery, 3 glass factories; and paid county tax, $392 72, poor tax, $196 33, and road tax, $1000.

Franklin Furnace, and village, Hardiston t-ship, Sussex co., in the valley of the Wallkill river, 11 miles N. E. of Newton, contains 2 forges of 2 fires each, a cupola furnace, a blast furnace not now in operation, a woollen manufactory for the manufacture of broad cloth, a grist and saw mill, a school house, and a new stone Baptist church, and 24 dwellings. Dr. Samuel Fowler is the chief proprietor here, and is alike distinguished for his hospitality and his pursuit of mineralogy. He has a cabinet of minerals richly meriting notice, and the country around him is considered as one of the most interesting mineral localities of the United States. The manufactures of this place seek a market at New York, or at Dover and Rockaway.

Franklin, small village of Caldwell t-ship, Essex co., 11 miles N. W. of Newark.

Freehold, Upper, t-ship of, Monmouth co., bounded N. and N. W. by East Windsor t-ship, Middlesex co., E. by Lower Freehold, S. and S. E. by Dover t-ship, and W. and S. W. by Northampton t-ship, Burlington co. Centrally distant S. W. from Freehold, the county town, 15 miles. Greatest length N. W. and S. E. 16;

breadth 10 miles; area, about 90,000 acres; surface, level; soil, clay, sandy loam, and sand. The western part of the t-ship contains some excellent lands, abundantly productive in rye, corn, oats, and grass; wheat is not a certain crop, and is not extensively cultivated. The south-eastern part of the t-ship is covered with pine forest. Population in 1830, 4862. In 1832, the t-ship contained about 900 taxables, 253 householders, whose ratables did not exceed $30; 80 single men, 20 stores, 12 saw mills, 15 run of stones for grain, 1 fulling mill, 3 carding machines, 50 tan vats, 16 distilleries for cider, 1036 horses and mules, 2438 neat cattle, 3 years old and upward; and paid state and county taxes to the amount of $3669 33. The t-ship is remarkable for the large quantities of pork which it annually sends to market. It is drained on the N. E. by the Millstone river, on the S. E. by the head waters of Toms' river, N. W. by Crosswick's creek and its tributaries, Lakaway and Doctor's creeks, and by branches of the Assunpink; and S. W. by the tributaries of the Rancocus. Wrightsville, Imlaystown, Allentown, Varminton, Prospertown, and Hernestown, are villages of the t-ship.

Freehold, Lower, t-ship, Monmouth co., bounded N. E. by Middletown t-ship, E. by Shrewsbury and Howell, S. by Dover, S. W. by Upper Freehold, and N. W. by South Amboy t-ships, Middlesex co. Greatest length N. E. and S. W. 23 miles; greatest breadth 11 miles; area, 104,000 acres; surface, level; soil, sand and sandy loam, not more than half of which is in cultivation, being barren, or covered with pine forest. There are, however, some very good farms, which produce abundance of rye, corn, &c. Pork is also a staple product. Englishtown and Freehold are villages and post-towns. The t-ship is drained by the Millstone river on the N. W.; Matchaponix brook, a tributary of the South river, on the north; by branches of the Swimming river on the N. E., and by arms of the Manasquan and the Metetecunk on the S. E., and by Toms' river on the south. Population in 1830, 5481. In 1832, the t-ship contained about 1100 taxables, 203 householders, whose ratables did not exceed $30, 71 single men, 11 stores, 11 saw mills, 16 run of grist mill stones, 2 fulling mills, 4 carding machines, 16 tan vats, 14 distilleries for cider, 1245 horses and mules, and 2569 neat cattle, 3 years old and upwards; and it paid state and county tax, $3563 86.

Freehold, or *Monmouth*, post-town of Freehold t-ship, and seat of justice of Monmouth co., about 4 miles W. of the east boundary of the t-ship, 201 miles N. E. from W. C., and 36 S. E. from Trenton, situate upon a level soil of sandy loam, which is fast improving under the present mode of culture. The town, though long stationary, is now thriving, and contains from 35 to 40 dwellings, a court house, prison, and public offices, an Episcopal, a Methodist, a Presbyterian, Dutch Reformed, and a Baptist church, 3 taverns, 5 or 6 stores, 4 practising attornies, 2 physicians, an academy and printing office. This place is noted in the revolutionary history, on account of the battle of Monmouth, which was fought near it.

Friesburg, a small German settlement of Upper Alloways Creek t-ship, near the south-east boundary, 12 miles S. E. from Salem, and 5 from Allowaystown; contains 1 tavern, a Dutch Reformed church, and a school.

Fredon, post-office, Sussex co., 232 miles N. E. from W. C., and 74 from Trenton.

Galloway t-ship, Gloucester co., bounded on the N. E. by Atsion river, and Mullica or Little Egg Harbour river, and Great Bay, which separate it from Burlington co., S. E. by the Atlantic ocean, S. W. by Hamilton and Egg Harbour t-ships, and N. W. by Gloucester and Hereford t-ships. Centrally distant S. W. from Woodbury, 35 miles; greatest length, 38; breadth, 10 miles; area, 147,000 acres; surface level, and soil sandy. The sea coast is girded by Brigantine beach, within which, for a depth of seven miles, is a space covered with lagunes and salt meadows. Among the small lakes, Absecum, Reed's and Grass bays, are the most considerable. The remainder of the township is chiefly covered with pine forest, through which flow many streams of water, tributary to Little Egg Harbour river. Pleasant Mills, Leed's Point, Gloucester Furnace, Absecum and Smith's Landing, are villages of the township. Population, in 1830, 2960; and in 1820, only 1895, presenting an instance of the greatest increase in the state. In 1832, there were in the township, as reported by the assessor, 165 householders, whose ratables did not exceed $30, 7 stores, 3 grist mills, 1 cotton manufactory, 1 blast furnace, 5 saw mills, 375 neat cattle, and 205 horses and mules over three years of age.

Georgetown, hamlet of Mansfield t-ship, Burlington co., near the N. E. boundary line, 6 miles S. E. from Bordentown, and 9 N. E. from Mount Holly.

Georgia, a small hamlet of Freehold t-ship, Monmouth co., 5 miles S. from Freehold town.

German Valley, Washington t-sp, Morris county, and in Schooley's mountain. It is about 10 miles long, varying, in width, from one to two miles. The soil is grey limestone throughout, and is well cultivated, and highly productive. The inhabitants are of German descent, and retain the industrious and thrifty habits of their ancestors. The valley is drained by the south branch of the Raritan river, and is crossed by the turnpike road from Morristown to Easton, which passes through the post town of Washington, lying in the vale. There is a Presbyterian church here.

Gibson's Creek, small tributary flowing eastwardly into the Great Egg Harbour river, Weymouth t-ship, Gloucester co.

Glassboro', p-t. of Franklin t-ship, Gloucester co., 14 miles S. E. from Woodbury, 22 from Camden, 49 from Trenton, and 155 from W. C.; contains an Episcopal and Methodist church, 2 glass houses or factories which make hollow ware, belonging to Messrs. Stangeer & Co., 1 tavern, 2 stores, and about 30 dwellings.

Gloucester County, was first laid off in 1677, forming one of the only two counties of West Jersey; and its boundaries were fixed by the act of 21st of January, 1709–10: beginning at the mouth of Pensaukin creek; thence, running up the same to the fork thereof; thence along the bounds of Burlington co., to the sea; thence along the sea coast to Great Egg Harbour river; thence up said river to the fork thereof; thence up the southernmost and greatest branch of the same to the head thereof; thence upon a direct line to the head of Old Man's creek; thence down the same to the Delaware river; thence up Delaware river to the place of beginning. It is, therefore, bounded N. W. by the Delaware river, N. E. by Burlington co., S. E. by the Atlantic ocean, and S. W. by the counties of Cumberland and Salem. Greatest length, from Absecum inlet, on the S. E. to Red Bank, on the N. W. 55 miles: greatest breadth, from the head of the Great Egg Harbour bay, to Tuckahoe river, 30 miles; area, 1114 square miles, or 713,000 acres. Central lat. 39° 40′, N. long. from W. C. 2° 10′, E.

The whole county pertains to the alluvial formation. Along the shores of the Delaware, and for several miles inward, a black or dark green mud is raised even from a depth of forty feet, in which reeds and other vegetables, the evidences of river alluvion, are distinctly visible. The remaining part of the county seems to have been gained from the sea; and beds of shells, whole and in a state of disintegration, are found, at various depths, in many places. The green earth, or marl, in which these are imbedded together with the shells, are used with great advantage upon the soil, especially in the cultivation of grass, clover particularly. Bog iron ore is found near Woodbury, and exported for manufacture.

The surface is uniformly level, except where worn down by the streams, and the soil sandy; having, on the N. W. an admixture of loam or clay, in many places. S. E. of a line drawn about 7 miles from the Delaware river, N. E. across the county, the country is universally sandy and covered by a pine forest, generally, (but with occasional cleared patches of greater or less extent,) from which large quantities of timber and cord wood are taken for market. Along the coast, within the beach, is a strip of marsh of an average width of four miles, in which are lagunes, the chief of which are Grass, Reed's, Absecum, and Lake's bays.

The county is drained southwardly by Maurice river, which flows from it, through Cumberland county, into the Delaware bay; by Tuckahoe river, forming the line between it and Cumberland; by Great and Little Egg Harbour rivers, which rise far north in the county, and empty into the Atlantic; the latter, throughout its whole course, forming the boundary between Gloucester and Burlington counties. All these streams are navigable some miles from the sea, and afford great facilities in transporting the lumber and cord wood, the most valuable products of this region, to market. Their inlets, and the small bays on the coast, abound with oysters and clams, the fishing for which gives subsistence to many of the inhabitants. These rivers have also many tributaries, which intersect the forest in almost every direction. The streams on the N. W. are Oldman's, Raccoon, Little Timber, Repaupo, Clonmell, Mantua, Big Timber, Newton, Cooper's and Pensauken creeks, most of which are navigable for a short distance, and furnish outlets for an amazing quantity of fruit and garden truck and firewood, for the supply of the Philadelphia market, and other towns on the western side of the river.

The post towns of the township are, Absecum, Bargaintown, Camden, an incorporated city, Carpenter's Landing, Chew's Landing, Clarkesboro', Glassboro', Gloucester Furnace, Gravelly Landing, Haddonfield, Hammonton, Jackson Glassworks, Leeds' Point, Longacoming, Malaga, May's Landing, Mullica Hill, Pleasant Mills, Smith's Landing, Somers' Point, Stephens' Creek, Sweedsboro, Tuckahoe, and Woodbury, the seat of justice of the county.

There are several academies for teaching the higher branches of education; and primary schools in most of the agricultural neighbourhoods. There are also established, Sunday schools, in most, if not all, of the populous villages; a county bible society, various tract societies, and many temperance associations; which have almost rendered the immoderate use of ardent spirits infamous.

In 1832, by the report of the assessors, the county contained 3075 householders, whose ratables did not exceed $30 in value; 978 single men, 102 stores, 21 fisheries, 45 grist mills, 2 cotton and 2 woollen manufactories, 4 carding machines, 4 blast furnaces, 3 forges, 63 saw mills, 4 fulling mills, 8 ferries, 9 tan yards, 29 distilleries, 7 glass factories, 2 four horse stage wagons, 967 covered wagons with fixed tops, 204 riding chairs, gigs, sulkies, and pleasure carriages, 4 two horse stage wagons, 31 dearborns with steel, iron, or wooden springs; and it paid county tax, $10,000; poor tax, $5000; and road tax, $15,000; state tax, ——

By the census of 1830 Gloucester co. contained 28,431 inhabitants, of whom 13,916 were white males; 12,962 white females; 14 female slaves; 835 free coloured males; 714 free coloured females. Of these there were deaf and dumb, under 14 years, 64; above 14 and under 30, 73; above 25 years, 80; blind, 205 white, 22 black; aliens 3365.

There is a county poor house established upon a farm near Blackwoodstown, but in Deptford t-ship, containing more than 200 acres of land.

The following extract from the records of this county, presents singular features of the polity of the early settlers. It would seem that the inhabitants of the county deemed themselves a body politic, a democratic commonwealth, with full power of legislation, in which the courts participated, prescribing the punishment for each offence, as it was proven before them.

Gloucester, the 28th May, 1686.

By the proprietors, freeholders, and inhabitants of the third and fourth tenths, (alias county of Gloucester) then agreed as follows:

Inprimus. That a court be held for the jurisdiction and limits of the aforesaid tenths, or county, one time at Axwamus, alias Gloucester, and at another time at Red Bank.

Item. That there be four courts, for the jurisdiction aforesaid, held in one year, at the days and times hereafter mentioned, viz: upon the first day of the first month, upon the first day of the fourth month, and the first day of the seventh month, and upon the first day of the tenth month.

Item. That the first court shall be held at Gloucester aforesaid, upon the first day of September next.

Item. That all warrants and summons shall be drawn by the clerk of the court, and signed by the justice, and so delivered to the sheriff or his deputy to execute.

Item. That the body of each warrant, &c., shall contain or intimate the nature of the action.

Item. That a copy of the declaration be given along with the warrant, by the clerk of the court, that so the deft. may have the longer time to consider the same, and prepare his answer.

Item. That all summons and warrants, &c., shall be served, and declarations given, at least ten days before the court.

Item. That the sheriff shall give the jury summons six days before the court be held, in which they are to appear.

Item. That all persons within the jurisdiction aforesaid, bring into the next court the marks of their hogs, and other cattle, in order to be approved and recorded.

Rex vs. *Wilkes.* } Indict. at Gloucester Ct. N. J. 10 Sept. 1686, for stealing goods of Dennis Lins, from a house in Philadelphia. Dft. pleads guilty, but was tried by jury. Verdict guilty, and that prisoner ought to make pay't. to the prosecutor of the sum of sixteen pounds. Sentence. The bench appoints that said Wilkes shall pay the aforesaid Lins, £16 by way of servitude, viz: if he will be bound by indentures to the prosecutor, then to serve him the term of four years, but if he condescended not thereto, then the court awarded that he should be a servant, and so abide for the term of five years. And so be accommodated in the time of his servitude, by his master, with meat, drink, clothes, washing, and lodging, according to the customs of the country, and fit for such a servant.

In 1832 the county was divided into 12 t-ships as in the following table, to which Camden is now to be added.

STATISTICAL TABLE OF GLOUCESTER COUNTY.

Townships, &c.	Length.	Breadth.	Area.	Population.		
				1810.	1820.	1830.
Deptford,	25	7	57,600	2978	3281	3599
Egg Harbour,	12	12	85,000	1830	1635	2510
Galloway,	32	10	147,000	1648	1895	2960
Gloucester,	20	8	60,000	1726	2059	2332
Greenwich,	15	7	35,840	2859	2699	2657
Newton,	6	4	9,000	1951	2497	3298
Franklin,	16	7	72,000		1137	1574
Hamilton,	18	11	106,880		877	1424
Waterford,	25	8	50,000	2105	2447	3088
Weymouth,	12	10	50,000	1029	781	1270
Woolwich,	16	7	40,000	3063	3113	3033
Gloucestertown, (area included in Gloucester township.)					662	686
			713,320	19,189	23,089	28,431

Gloucester, t-ship, Gloucester co., bounded N. by Gloucestertown, N. E. by Hereford t-ship, S. E. by Hamilton, and S. W. and W. by Deptford t-ship. Centrally distant S. E. from Woodbury, 10 miles; greatest length N. W. and S. E. 20; breadth 8 miles E. and W.; area, about 60,000 acres; surface, level; soil, sand more or less mixed with loam, and in the northern part cultivated in vegetables and fruit, the southern being chiefly pine forest, valuable for timber and fuel. It is drained northward by Cooper's creek on the eastern, and Big Timber creek on the western boundary, southward by Inskeep's branch of the Great Egg Harbour river. Chew's Landing, Longacoming, Clementon, Blackwoodtown, Tansborough, and New Freedom, are villages of the t-ship; the two first post-towns. Population in 1830, 2232. In 1832, there were in the t-ship, including Gloucestertown, 781 householders, whose ratables did not exceed $30 in value; 11 stores, 5 grist mills, 9 saw mills, 2 tanneries, and 1 glass factory; and it paid county tax, $799 78; poor tax, $400 73; road tax, $1000.

Gloucestertown, small t-ship of Gloucester co., bounded N. by Newton, E. and S. E. by Gloucester t-ship, S. W. by Big Timber creek, which separates it from Deptford t-ship, and W. by the river Delaware. Centrally distant N. E. from Woodbury 4 miles; greatest length E. and W. 4; breadth N. and S. 3 miles.

Gloucester, small town of Gloucester t-ship, Gloucester co., on the Delaware river opposite Gloucester point; contains a fishery, a ferry from which a team-boat plies, about 20 dwellings, 1 store, and 1 tavern.

Gloucester, post-town and furnace of Galloway t-ship, Gloucester co., upon Landing creek, a branch of the Mullica or Little Egg Harbour river, 36 miles S. E. from Woodbury, 71 from Trenton, and 179 from W. C.; contains a furnace, grist and saw mill, a store, tavern, and a number of dwellings, chiefly for the accommodation of the workmen, of whom there are about 60, constantly employed, whose families may amount to 300 persons. The furnace makes annually about 800 tons of iron, chiefly castings, and has annexed to it about 25,000 acres of land.

Glover's Pond, Hardwick t-ship, Warren co., the extreme source of Beaver brook.

Godwinsville, Franklin t-ship, Bergen co., upon Goffle brook, 8 miles N. W. from Hackensack; contains 1 tavern, 2 stores, 7 cotton mills, having together 5000 spindles, and from

45 to 50 dwellings; soil around it red shale, fertile and well cultivated.

Goffle Brook, rises in Franklin t-ship, Bergen co., about a mile and a half E. of Hohokus, and flows by a southerly course of 5 miles through Saddle river t-ship, to the Passaic. It is a rapid, steady stream, and gives motion to several cotton mills at Godwinsville. About 1½ miles above its mouth, is the small hamlet called Goffle, containing 5 or 6 farm dwellings.

Goodwater Run, small tributary of Batsto river, Washington t-ship, Burlington co., uniting with the river at the head of Batsto furnace pond.

Good Luck, town, or more properly neighbourhood, of Dover t-ship, Monmouth co., a little S. W. of Cedar creek or Williamsburgh, separated from Barnegat bay by a strip of salt marsh, and surrounded by a pine forest and sandy soil.

Good Luck Point, Dover t-ship, Monmouth co., on the S. side of Toms' bay, at its junction with Barnegat bay.

Goose Creek, Dover t-ship, Monmouth co., puts in from Barnegat bay, 2 miles N. of Toms' bay.

Goose Pond, on the sea shore of Shrewsbury t-ship, Monmouth co., about 2 miles above the south boundary of the t-ship.

Goshen, village of Upper Freehold t-ship, Monmouth co., and near the head of Toms' river, 13 miles S. of Monmouth Court House, 23 S. E. from Trenton; contains 1 tavern, 2 stores, 10 or 12 dwellings, a grist and saw mill, and Methodist meeting; country around, sandy and flat; timber, pine.

Goshen Creek, mill-stream of Middle t-ship, Cape May co., rises in the northern part of the t-ship, and flows westerly into the Delaware bay, by a course of 5 or 6 miles; it is navigable for about 3 miles to the landing, for the small village of Goshen. A channel through the marshes, communicates between this stream and Dennis creek.

Goshen, post-town of Cape May co., in Middle t-ship, near the head of navigation of Goshen creek, about 5 miles N. W. from Cape May court-house, 198 N. E. from W. C., and 101 S. from Trenton; contains a tavern, 2 stores, a steam saw mill, and 12 or 15 dwellings, and a school house, in which religious meetings are held.

Grant Pond, on the Pochuck mountain, Vernon t-ship, Sussex co., a source of a tributary to Warwick creek.

Grass Bay, a salt marsh lake, about 5 miles long, and one wide, in Galloway t-ship, Gloucester co., communicating by several channels with Reed's bay and with the ocean.

Grass Pond, Green t-ship, Sussex co., one of the sources of the Bear branch of Pequest creek.

Gratitude, p-t., Sussex co., 221 miles N. E. from W. C., and 68 from Trenton.

Gravel Hill, village and p-t. of Knowlton t-ship, Warren co., in the valley of the Paulinskill, near the east line of the t-ship, distant by post road from W. C. 243 miles, from Trenton 85, and from Belvidere N. E. 15 miles; contains a large grist mill, tavern, store, tannery, and 6 or 8 dwellings; soil limestone.

Gravelly Landing, p-t. of Galloway t-ship, Gloucester co., 40 miles S. E. from Woodbury, 79 from Trenton, and 187 N. E. from W. C., on Nacote creek; contains a tavern, store, and 10 or 12 dwellings.

Gravelly Run, small tributary of Great Egg Harbour river, flowing westerly from Egg Harbour t-ship to its recipient, 2 miles below May's Landing.

Great Meadows, a large body of 6 or 8000 acres of meadow land, in Independence t-ship, Warren co., watered by the Pequest creek.

Great Brook, Morris t-ship, Morris co., rises at the head of Spring valley, and flows by a semicircular course of 8 or 9 miles, partly through the t-ship of Chatham, to the Passaic river, on the S. W. part of Morris t-ship.

Green Brook, or *Bound Brook*, a

considerable tributary of the Raritan river, rising in a narrow valley between New Providence and Westfield t-ships, Essex co., and thence flowing by a S. W. course of about 16 miles, skirting the semicircular mountain of Somerset co., to its recipient at Bound Brook. It is a mill stream of considerable power.

Green Brook, village, on Green brook above described, in Piscataway t-ship, Middlesex co., 8 miles from New Brunswick, 6½ from Somerville; contains a mill, a school house, 2 stores, and 15 dwellings. The country on the south and east, level and fertile, valued at $50 the acre; on the north mountainous.

Green Creek, small stream of Middle t-ship, Cape May co., which by a course of 2 or 3 miles, flows into the Delaware bay. It gives name to a post-office near it, distant 106 miles from W. C., and 109 from Trenton.

Green Pond, *Valley*, and *Mountain*; the first a beautiful sheet of water, 3 miles in length and 1 in breadth, embosomed in the valley to which it gives name, between the Copperas and Green Pond mountains, Pequannock t-ship, Morris co. The pond is much resorted to for its fish, and its beautiful scenery, where nature is yet unsubdued, and the red deer still roam at will. The valley is drained by the Burnt Cabin brook, a principal branch of the Rockaway river. Green Pond mountain, which has its name also from the same source, extends about 13 miles from the Rockaway to the Pequannock creek; it is a high, narrow, and stony granitic ridge, and lies on the boundary between Pequannock and Jefferson t-ships.

Greene t-ship, Sussex co., bounded N. E. and E. by Newton and Byram t-ships, S. by Roxbury t-ship, Morris co., W. by Independence and Hardwicke t-ships, of the same county, and N. W. by Stillwater t-ship, of Sussex co. Centrally distant S. W. from Newton 7 miles; greatest length N. and S. 9 miles; breadth E. and W. 4 miles; area, 14,080 acres; surface on the south mountainous, elsewhere hilly. It is drained by tributaries of the Pequest creek, which flow through it to the southwest. Hunt's and Grass ponds are noted sheets of water in the t-ship; Greenville near the centre is the post-town. By the census of 1830 the t-ship contained 801 inhabitants, and in 1832 150 taxables, 23 householders, whose ratables did not exceed $30, 1 store, 2 grist mills, 1 saw mill, 150 horses and mules, and 400 neat cattle 3 years old and upwards, 12 tan vats; and paid a state and county tax of $279 60; poor tax, 200; and road tax, $400. The mountain on the S. E. is composed of grey rock; the basis of the soil, in the remainder of the t-ship, is limestone and slate, the former prevailing.

Green Bank, settlement on the left bank of Mullica river, Washington t-ship, Burlington co., about 10 miles by the river from its union with Great bay. There are here, 2 taverns, 2 stores, and 12 or 15 dwellings, within a space of 2 miles. The shore is clean and high; the soil sandy loam, of tolerable quality and well cultivated.

Greenville, p-t. and village, of Greene t-ship, Sussex co., by the post route, 222 miles N. E. of W. C., 69 from Trenton, and 8 S. W. from Newton; contains a store, tannery, and 10 or 12 dwellings, and is surrounded by a rich limestone country.

Green Village, Chatham t-ship, Morris co., 3½ miles S. E. from Morristown; contains some 5 or 6 dwellings, situated in a pleasant fertile country.

Greenwich t-ship, Gloucester co., bounded on the N. E. by Deptford t-ship, S. E. by Franklin, S. W. by Woolwich t-ships, and N. W. by the river Delaware. Centrally distant S. W. from Woodbury 7 miles; greatest length 15 miles; greatest breadth 7 miles; area, 35,840 acres; surface level; soil sandy. It is drained N. W. by Mantua on the N. E., and by Repaupo creek on the S. W. boundary; Clonmell and Crab creeks are small intermediate streams; and on the S. W. by Raccoon creek. Byllingsport, Paulsboro', Sandtown, Clarkesboro', Carpenter's Landing, Barnsboro', and Mullica Hill, are villages of the t-ship; population in 1830, 2557. In 1832 the t-ship contained 306 householders, whose ratables did not exceed $30 in value; 9 stores, 3 fisheries, 5 grist mills, 1 woollen manufactory, 5 saw mills, 1 ferry, 2 tan yards, 1054 neat cattle, and 549 horses and mules, under 3 years of age; and paid county tax, $1491 85; poor tax, $745 92; road tax, $1100.

Greenwich, t-ship of Cumberland co., bounded N. by Newport creek, which divides it from Stow Creek t-ship, E. by Hopewell t-ship, S. by Cohansey creek, which divides it from Fairfield t-ship and the river Delaware, and W. by Stow creek, which separates it from Lower Alloway's Creek t-ship. Centrally distant W. from Bridgeton, 8 miles; greatest length N. and S. 7 miles; breadth E. and W. 6 miles; area, 13,440 acres; surface, level; soil, generally of clay and deep rich loam, and well cultivated. Beside the streams named, the t-ship is drained by Mill creek on its south-east boundary, and by Pine Mount creek; Greenwich is the village and post-town. Population of the t-ship in 1830, 912. In 1832, it contained 205 taxables, 72 householders, whose ratables did not exceed in value $30; 5 stores, none of which sell ardent spirits, 3 grist mills, 1 carding machine, 1 tannery, 1 distillery for cider, and 148 horses and 484 neat cattle 3 years old and upwards.

Greenwich, post-town of the above t-ship, on the Cohansey creek, 6 miles from the mouth, and 6 S. W. from Bridgeton, by post-route 195 N. E. from W. C., and 81 from Trenton; contains between 40 and 50 dwellings of stone, frame, and brick; 1 tavern, 3 stores, and a large grist and merchant mill, 2 Quaker meeting houses, 1 Methodist church, a temperance society, counting more than 200 members; the soil clay and rich loam, well cultivated, and very productive in wheat, oats, rye, and corn.

Greenwich, t-ship, Warren co., bounded N. by Oxford t-ship, N. E. by Mansfield, S. E. by the Musconetcong creek, which separates it from Hunterdon co., and W. by the river Delaware. Centrally distant S. from Belvidere, the county town, 10 miles; greatest length N. and S. 13 miles; breadth E. and W. 11 miles; area, 38,000 acres; surface hilly, the South Mountain covering the t-ship. Drained by Lopatcong, Pohatcong, and Musconetcong creeks, all which flow S. W. through the t-ship to the Delaware river. The turnpike road from Somerville runs N. W. and that from Schooley's mountain W. through the t-ship to Philipsburg, on the Delaware, opposite to Easton. Below that town the Morris canal commences, and runs across the t-ship. The population in 1830, was 4486. Taxables in 1832, 830; at that time the t-ship contained 266 householders, whose ratables did not exceed $30 in value; 9 stores, 17 run of stones for grinding grain, 1 fishery, 2 carding machines, 1 cotton factory, 3 oil mills, 1 fulling mill, 3 distilleries, 930 horses and mules, and 1265 neat cattle over 3 years of age. Although this t-ship be very mountainous, it is one of the most productive, not only of the county, but of the state. Whilst the mountains assume a granitic character, the valleys are every where underlaid with limestone, and their soils fertile. The valleys of the Musconetcong, the Pohatcong, and Lopatcong, and even the small vales through which their tributaries wander, are highly cultivated and improved, and there are farmers who send to market from one thousand to three thousand bushels of wheat, annually, beside other agricultural productions. The most interesting minerals yet discovered in the t-ship, are marble, steatite or soapstone, and iron.

Greenwood, forest, east of the Wawayanda mountain, and west of Bear

Fort Mountain, on the borders of Vernon and Pompton t-ships, and Sussex and Bergen counties; extending N. and S. 14 miles into the state of New York.

Griggstown, Franklin t-ship, Somerset co., on the right bank of the Millstone river, and on the Delaware and Raritan canal, 5 miles below Kingston, and 9 south of Somerville; contains a tavern, store, and some half dozen dwellings. A grist mill formerly here has been torn down, being in the route of the canal, which follows the bank of the river. A copper mine near this place has been wrought, but not with success.

Groveville, village of Nottingham t-ship, Burlington co., in a bend of the Crosswick's creek, about 6 miles S. E. of Trenton, and 4 N. E. from Bordentown; contains a large woollen manufactory, grist and saw mill, and 10 or 12 houses. The creek is navigable from the Delaware to the village, a distance of more than six miles.

Guineatown, a small hamlet of Upper Alloways Creek t-ship, near its northern boundary; contains 8 or 10 dwellings, chiefly inhabited by negroes.

Gum Branch, an arm of the south branch of Toms' river, flows easterly about 4 miles through the S. E. part of Upper Freehold t-ship, Monmouth county.

Hackensack t-ship, Bergen co., bounded N. by Harrington, E. and S. E. by Hudson's river, S. by Bergen t-ship, S. W. by Lodi, and N. W. by New Barbadoes. Centrally distant from Hackensacktown, 2½ miles E.; greatest length N. and S. 9 miles; breadth E. and W. 5 miles; area, 24,000 acres; surface on the E. hilly, on the W. level; soil red shale, with some marsh on the Hackensack river and English creek, generally well cultivated and productive. It is drained S. by the Hackensack and by English creek, and N. by other tributaries of the river. There are four bridges over the Hackensack, connecting this with New Barbadoes t-ship, viz. one at New Milford, at Old Bridge, at New Bridge, and one at Hackensacktown; these, with Strahlenburg, Closter, Fort Lee, Mount Clinton, and English Neighbourhood, are the most noted places of the t-ship. The frontier on the North river, is marked by the perpendicular trap rocks, known as the Palisades. Population in 1830, 2200. In 1832 the t-ship contained 535 taxables, 94 householders, whose ratables did not exceed $30 in value, 56 single men, 7 merchants, 11 grist mills, 4 fisheries, 11 saw mills, 2 fulling mills, 1 ferry, over the Hudson, 8 tan vats, 460 horses, and 1170 neat cattle, above 3 years old; and the t-ship paid the following taxes: state, $303 61; county, $615 38; poor, $300; road, $1000.

Hackensack River, rises by two branches in Rockland co., state of New York; one in the Hightorn mountain, a spur of the Ramapo; and the other from a pond, in the high bank of the Hudson river, opposite to Sing Sing. These unite below Clarkestown, and thence pursue their way southwardly, through that county into Bergen co., and thence to Newark bay. Its whole length by meanders of the stream, may be from 35 to 40 miles. Until it meets the tide at Hackensacktown, it is a fine mill stream. Below that town it flows through a marsh to the bay. Sloops ascend to the town.

Hackensack, post and county town of Bergen co., on the right bank of the Hackensack river, 15 miles from its mouth, 12 from New York, 63 from Trenton, and 229 from W. C. It is a pleasant and neat town, stretching through the meadows, on the river, for about a mile in length; containing about 150 dwellings and 1000 inhabitants, principally of Dutch extraction; three churches, viz. one Dutch Reformed, and two formed of seceders from that church: two academies, one boarding school for females, ten stores, three taverns, two paint factories, one coach maker, two tanneries, several hatters, three smiths, and four or five cordwainers. The county court house is a neat and spacious brick edifice; the offices of the surrogate and county clerk are of the same material, and fire proof. Considerable business is done here with the adjacent country, and several sloops ply between the town and New York, carrying from it wood, lumber and agricultural products. The Weehawk Bank, originally established at Weehawk, on the North river, was removed here in 1825, and then received the name of the Washington Bank. Its authorized capital is $200,000, of which $93,460 have been paid in. A good turnpike road runs from Hoboken to Hackensack, and thence to Paterson. Hackensack was the scene of considerable military operations during the revolutionary war.

Hacketstown, p-t., Independent t-ship, Warren co., lying between the Morris canal and Musconetcong river, which are here about one mile distant from each other. The village is by the post road, 215 miles N. E. from W. C., 59 from Trenton, and 15 E. from Belvidere, the county town, and 6 from Belmont Spring, Schooley's mountain; contains 5 large stores, 2 taverns, and from 30 to 40 dwellings of wood and brick, 1 Presbyterian and 1 Methodist church, an academy, in which the classics are taught, 2 common schools, 1 resident Presbyterian clergyman, and 3 physicians, 2 large flour mills, a woollen manufactory and a clover mill. The town is built upon cross streets; is surrounded by a fertile limestone country, where farms sell at from 50 to 75 dollars the acre. This vicinity is rapidly improving by means of the Morris canal.

Haddonfield, p-t., of Newton t-ship, Gloucester co., near the west bank of Cooper's creek, 6 miles S. E. from Camden, 9 N. E. from Woodbury, 144 from W. C., and 36 S. from Trenton; contains 100 dwellings, a Quaker meeting and Baptist church, 2 schools, a public library, 2 fire companies, and 2 fire engines, 7 stores, 2 taverns, 2 grist mills, a woollen manufactory and 2 tanneries. This is a very pleasant town, built upon both sides of a wide road, along which it extends for more than a half mile. The houses are of brick and wood, many of them neat and commodious, and surrounded by gardens, orchards, and grass lots. This was a place of some note, bearing its present name, prior to 1713. The house erected by Elizabeth Haddon, of brick and boards, brought from England, in style which must then have been deemed magnificent, has upon it "1713, Haddonfield," formed of the arch brick. For many years the town has undergone little change, but a disposition to build has lately been awakened. The soil of the surrounding country is of excellent quality, being fertile sandy loam, and is highly productive of corn, vegetables, fruits and grass, which, with its vicinity to market, occasions it to be much sought after, and at high prices; whole farms selling at from 60 to 100 dolls. the acre.

Hagerstown, a small hamlet, of Elsinborough t-ship, Salem co., on the road leading from Salem to Hancock's bridge, about 4 miles S. of the former, contains 10 or 12 cottages, inhabited chiefly by negroes.

Haines' Creek, a considerable tributary of the Rancocus creek, rising by several branches in Evesham t-ship, Burlington co., on all of which there are mills. It flows N. E. by a course of about 14 miles to its recipient, near Eayrstown.

Hakehokake Creek, rises in Alexandria t-ship, Hunterdon co., and flows S. W. by a course of 6 or 7 miles, to the Delaware river, three miles above the town of Alexandria, passing by Mount Pleasant, and giving motion to several mills.

Hall's Pond, small basin of water, in Newton t-ship, Sussex co., 3 miles S. E. of the town of Newton.

Hamburg, p-t., of Vernon t-ship, Sussex co., in the S. W. angle of the t-ship, within 1½ miles of the west foot of the Wallkill mountains, near the E. bank of the Wallkill river, and near the Pochuck turnpike road.

Distant, by post route from W. C., 248, from Trenton, 90, and from Newton, 14 miles; contains a church common to Baptists and Presbyterians, 2 taverns, 4 stores, 2 grist mills, and two saw mills, and 15 or 20 dwellings. This is a thriving village, and the water power on the river offers strong inducements to settlers.

Hamburg, or *Wallkill Mountains*, a local name given to the chain of hills on the South mountain, extending N. E. across the townships of Byram and Hardiston, and interlocking with Wawayanda and Pochuck mountain, in Vernon t-ship; about 25 miles in length.

Hamilton t-ship, Gloucester co., bounded N. E. by Galloway t-ship, S. E. by Egg Harbour and Weymouth t-ships, S. W. by Maurice river and Milleville t-ships, of Cumberland co., and N. W. by Franklin, Deptford and Gloucester t-ships. Centrally distant, S. E. from Woodbury, 30 miles; greatest length, N. and S., 18 miles; breadth, E. and W., 11 miles; area, 106,880 acres. Surface level, and soil sandy, covered generally with pine forest, and drained, southwardly, by Great Egg Harbour river, which runs centrally through it, receiving several small tributaries on either hand. Hamilton and May's Landing are villages of the township; the latter a post town. Population in 1830, 1424. In 1832, the township contained 115 householders, whose ratables did not exceed $30; 7 stores, 2 grist mills, 1 blast furnace, 6 saw mills, 1 forge with 4 fires, 135 neat cattle, and 171 horses and mules, above the age of three years; and paid county tax, $209 62; poor tax, $104 74¼; road tax, $800. The assessor returns but 670 acres of improved land.

Hamilton Village. (See *May's Landing*.)

Hammonton Post Office, Gloucester co., by post-route, 167 miles from W. C., and 59 from Trenton.

Hancock's Bridge, Lower Alloways Creek t-ship, Salem co., over the Alloways creek. There is a post-town here, which contains between 30 and 40 dwellings, a Friend's meeting house, a tavern, and 2 stores. Distant 5 miles S. of Salem, 174 N. E. from W. C., 54 S. from Trenton: the soil immediately about the town is of rich clay, and marsh meadow, banked and productive.

Hank's Pond, covers about 300 acres, in Pompton t-ship, Bergen co., near Clinton forges, to which it pays a tribute of its waters.

Hanover t-ship, Burlington co., bounded N. E. by Upper Freehold and Dover t-ships, Monmouth co., S. by the North and Pole Bridge branches of the Rancocus creek, which separate it from Northampton t-ship, W. and N. W. by Springfield, Mansfield, and Chesterfield t-ships. Centrally distant N. E. from Mount Holly, 12 miles; greatest length N. W. and S. E. 16 miles; greatest breadth, 13 miles; area, 44,000 acres; surface, generally level; soil, sandy loam and sand, and in the S. E. part covered with pine forest. Drained N. E. by tributaries of the Crosswick's creek, on the N. W. by Black's creek, and on the S. by the north branch of the Rancocus, upon which, near the S. W. angle of the t-ship, is the County Poor House. Arney'stown, Shelltown, Jacobstown, Wrightstown, and Scrabbletown, are villages of the t-ship; at the first of which there is a post-office. Population in 1830, 2859. In 1832, the t-ship contained 530 taxables, 298 householders, whose ratables did not exceed $30 in value; 77 single men, 10 merchants, 5 saw mills, 5 grist mills; 1 furnace, called Hanover; 20 tan vats, 1 carding machine, 7 distilleries for cider, 1 two horse stage, 36 dearborns, 85 covered wagons, 5 chairs and curricles, 13 gigs and sulkies, and paid state tax, $392 14; county tax, $1369 19; and township tax, $500.

Hanover t-ship, Morris co., bounded N. by Pequannock t-ship, E. by Livingston t-ship, Essex co., S. E. by Chatham t-ship, S. by Morris, and W. by Randolph t-ships. Centrally distant N. from Morristown, 5 miles; greatest length E. and W. 12; breadth N. and S. 9 miles; area, 35,000 acres; surface on the N. W. hilly, Trowbridge mountain there crossing the t-ship; on the E. and S. E. level; soil, clay, loam and gravel. The Rockaway river forms its northern boundary, running into the Passaic, which on the east divides the t-ship from Essex county. The Whippany and Parsipany rivers also flow through it, uniting about a mile before they commingle with the Rockaway. Population in 1830, 3718. In 1832, the t-ship contained 700 taxables, 173 householders, whose ratables did not exceed $30 in value; 79 single men, 14 stores, 7 saw mills, 7 grist mills, 29 tan vats, 9 distilleries, 3 paper mills, 5 forges, 2 rolling and slitting mills, 2 fulling mills, 2 carding machines, 4 cotton manufactories, 621 horses and mules, and 2080 cattle above 3 years old; and paid state tax, $548 98; county, $1229 08; poor, $1000; road tax, 1000. This t-ship is not remarkable for the extent of its agricultural produce, the soil not being of the best quality, yet it is generally well cultivated. It contains, however, many and various manufactories, and abundant water power for others.

Hanover, post-town of preceding t-ship, on the turnpike road from Newark to Milford, 7 miles E. from Morristown, 225 from W. C., and 59 from Trenton; contains a Presbyterian church and half a dozen dwellings, situate on the plain near the bank of the Passaic.

Hanover Neck post-office, Morris co., 227 miles N. E. from W. C., and 61 from Trenton, by post-route.

Hardinsville p-o., Gloucester co.

Hardiston t-sp, Sussex co., bounded N. by Wantage t-ship, N. E. by Vernon, S. E. by Bergen and Morris counties, and W. by Newton and Frankford t-ships. Greatest length 13½ miles; breadth 9 miles; area, 41,960 acres; surface mountainous, covered principally by the Hamburg or Wallkill mountains. Pimple Hill is also a distinguished eminence. The t-ship is drained chiefly by the Wallkill river, which flows northward, centrally through it, and Pequannock creek, which flows through the eastern angle. Norman's Pond, and White Ponds, are basins which send forth tributaries to the river. Population in 1830, 2588. Taxables in 1832, 450. There were in the t-ship in 1832, 2 Presbyterian churches, 171 householders, whose ratables did not exceed $30 in value; 8 storekeepers, 13 pairs of stones for grinding grain, 2 carding machines, 7 mill saws, 1 furnace, 13 forge fires, 1 fulling mill, 407 horses and mules, and 1437 neat cattle above the age of 3 years; 37 tan vats, 9 distilleries. The t-ship paid state and county tax, $915; poor tax, $500; and road tax, $1200. Sparta and Monroe are post-towns of the t-ship; there is a third post-office at Harmony Vale, in the N. W. angle of the t-ship. The Hamburg or Wallkill mountain, which has an unbroken course through the t-ship, contains an inexhaustible mass of zinc and iron ores, and the t-ship generally is considered as one of the most interesting mineral localities in the United States.

Hardwick t-ship, Warren co., bounded E. by Stillwater and Green t-ships, of Sussex co., S. by Independence t-ship, W. by Knowlton, and N. by Pahaquarry t-ships. Centrally distant N. E. from Belvidere, 15 miles; greatest length N. and S. 11; breadth E. and W. 8 miles; area, 24,320 acres. Population in 1830, 1962. There were in the t-ship in 1832, 82 householders, whose ratable estates did not exceed $30 in value; 5 stores, 13 pairs of stones for grain, 2 carding machines, 1 wool factory, 5 saw mills, 56 tan vats, 4 distilleries; and it paid a state and county tax of $967 59. The surface of the t-ship is generally hilly, and is drained south-westerly by Paulinskill, Beaver brook, and Bear branch of the Pequest creek, and also by some limestone sinks; Marksboro', Lawrenceville, Johnsonburg, and Shiloh, are post-towns of the t-ship. Lime and slate alternate in the t-ship, as in Knowlton; the ridges being of the latter, and the valleys of the former; both are productive, except where the slate rock approaches too near the surface. White Pond in this t-ship, about a mile north of Marksboro', is a great natural curiosity. (See *Marksboro'*.)

Harlingen, p-t., Montgomery t-sp. Somerset co., 9 miles S. W. from Somerville, 185 from W. C., and 19 from Trenton; contains a Dutch Reformed church, a store, tavern, and 4 or 5 dwellings, in a fertile country of red shale.

Harmony, post-office and Presbyterian church, of Greenwich t-ship, Warren co., by the post route, distant from W. C. 200, from Trenton 60, and from Belvidere, 8 miles.

Harmony Vale, p-t., in the N. W. angle of Hardistone t-ship, Sussex co., 240 miles from W. C., 82 from Trenton, and 10 from Newton; contains some 10 or 12 dwellings, and a Presbyterian church.

Harrington t-ship, Bergen co., bounded N. by Rockland co., New York, E. by the Hudson river, S. by New Barbadoes and Hackensack t-ships, and W. by Franklin t-ship. Centrally distant from the town of Hackensack N. 7 miles; greatest length 9½; breadth 7 miles; area, 34,000 acres; surface level, except near the bank of the North river, along which runs the Closter mountains, 400 feet high, forming the Palisades; soil loam, well cultivated and fertile. It is watered by the Hackensack river, flowing southerly and centrally through it, receiving the Paskack brook, which, rising in New York, seeks its recipient near the centre of the t-ship; and by Saddle river, which, rising also in New York, flows along the western boundary; population in 1830, 2581. In 1832 there were 776 taxables, 152 householders, whose ratables did not exceed $30 in value, 46 single men, 10 stores, 20 grist mills, 3 cotton manufactories, 2 furnaces, 23 saw mills, and 685 horses, and 1332 neat cattle, over 3 years of age, 1 fulling mill, 26 tan vats, 2 woollen factories; and it paid state tax, $432 57; county, $910 92.

Harrison's Brook, branch of the Dead river, a tributary of the Passaic, rises in the Mine mountain near Vealtown, and flows S. 5 miles to its recipient, about a mile below Liberty Corner.

Heathcote's Brook, tributary of Millstone river, rising near the Sand Hills, and flowing westerly about 5 miles, to its recipient, near Kingston.

Herberton, town of Hopewell t-sp. Hunterdon co., 11 miles S. of Flemington, 11 N. from Trenton; contains some half dozen dwellings, a Baptist church, store, and tavern; the country around it is hilly, with soil of red shale, well cultivated. The t-ship poor-house, on a farm of 140 acres, is near it, where the average number of 30 paupers are annually maintained by their own labour.

Hereford Inlet, Middle t-ship, Cape May co., a passage of between one and two miles wide, between Leaming's and Five Mile beach, through which the sea enters the lagunes and marshes upon the Atlantic coast.

Hickory, small hamlet of Bethlehem t-ship, Hunterdon co., 12 miles N. W. of Flemington, at the south foot of the Musconetcong mountain, and on the line dividing Bethlehem from Alexandria t-ship.

Hightstown, p-t. of East Windsor t-ship, Middlesex co., on the turnpike road from Bordentown to Cranberry, and on Rocky brook, 13 miles from Bordentown, 183 from W. C., and 18 from Trenton; contains a Baptist and Presbyterian church, 3 taverns, 2 stores, a grist and saw mill, and from 30 to 40 dwellings. The rail-road from Bordentown to Amboy passes through the town, and a line of stages runs thence to Princeton, &c.

Hillsborough t-ship, Somerset co., bounded N. by the main stem, and south branch of Raritan river, which separates it from Bridgewater, E. by Millstone river, dividing it from Franklin, S. by Montgomery, and W. by

Amwell t-ship, Hunterdon co. Centrally distant S. W. from Somerville 5 miles; greatest length E. and W. 10; breadth N. and S. 7 miles; area, about 36,000 acres; surface on the west hilly, the Neshanie or Rock mountain extending over it; the soil clay and loam: on the east level and gently undulating; soil red shale. The whole t-ship is well cultivated. Besides the streams on the boundaries, the only considerable one is Roy's brook, flowing into the Millstone. Flaggtown, Millstone, Neshanie, Koughstown, and Blackwells, are the villages of the t-ship; the two first post-towns. Population in 1830, 2878. In 1832 the t-ship contained about 560 taxables, 95 householders, whose ratables did not exceed $30 in value, 58 single men, 9 stores, 8 saw mills, 8 grist mills, 1 fulling mill, 10 tan vats, 4 distilleries, 2 carding machines, 939 horses and mules, and 1638 neat cattle, of 3 years old and upwards; and paid state tax, $382 92; county, $1182 53. There is a Dutch Reformed church in the t-ship.

Hoboken, village of Bergen t-ship, Bergen co., on the North river, opposite to the city of New York, built chiefly on one street, and contains about 1 hundred dwellings, 3 licensed taverns, many unlicensed houses of entertainment, 4 or 5 stores, and several livery stables and gardens, and between 6 and 7 hundred inhabitants. It is remarkable, however, chiefly as a place of resort, for the citizens of New York, during the hot days of the summer; the bank of the river is high, and the invigorating sea breeze may be enjoyed at almost all hours when the sun is above the horizon. The liberality of Mr. Stevens, who is an extensive landholder here, has opened many attractions to visiters, in the walks along the river bank, over his grounds; and in the beautiful fields studded with clumps of trees, and variegated by shady woods, the business-worn Yorker finds a momentary relaxation and enjoyment in the "Elysian fields;" and the gastronomes, whether of the corporation of New Amstel, or invited guests, find a less rural, though not a more sensual pleasure, in the feast of Turtle grove. The value of the groves of Hoboken to the inhabitants of N. York, is inappreciated and inappreciable. They are the source of health to thousands.—Several steam-boats ply constantly between this town and New York.

Holland's Brook, tributary of the south branch of the Raritan river, rises in Readington t-ship, Hunterdon co., and flows by a S. E. course of about 7 miles, to its recipient in Bridgewater t-ship, Somerset co.

Holmdel or *Baptistown*, p-t. of Middletown t-ship, Monmouth co., 7 miles N. E. from Freehold, 219 from W. C., and 53 E. from Trenton; contains an academy, a Baptist church, 2 stores, 8 dwellings, lying in a highly improved country, producing rye, corn, grass, &c.

Hog Island, in Little Egg Harbour river, Galloway t-ship, Gloucester co.

Hohokus Brook, rises and has its course S. E. 9 miles in Franklin t-ship, Bergen co. It is a rapid wild stream, studded with mills, and gives name to the village of

Hohokus, village, situate on the turnpike road leading thence to the Sterling mountain, N. Y., 9 miles from Hackensack; contains a tavern, store, cotton mill, and several dwellings.

Hope Creek, a small stream of 4 or 5 miles in length, which rises in, and flows through, the meadows and marshes of Lower Alloway's Creek t-ship, Salem co. It is not navigable.

Hope, p-t., on the line dividing Knowlton from Oxford t-ship, on a branch of Beaver brook, 212 miles from W. C., and 59 from Trenton, and 10 N. E. from Belvidere; contains a grist mill and saw mill, 6 stores, 2 taverns, and about 30 dwellings, an Episcopal and Methodist church. The soil around it is limestone, and well cultivated. This was originally a Moravian settlement.

Hopewell t-ship, of Cumberland co., bounded E. by Deerfield, S. E. and S. by Fairfield, W. by Greenwich and

Stow Creek t-ships, and N. by Hopewell t-ship, of Salem co. Greatest length 10, breadth 6 miles; area, 20,000 acres; surface rolling; soil clay loam. Cohansey creek bounds the t-ship on the east and south, and Mount's creek and Mill creek, its tributaries, are on and near the S. W. boundary. Population in 1830, 1953. In 1832 there were in the t-ship 468 taxables, 1 Seventh-day Baptist, and 1 Methodist church, 112 householders, whose ratables did not exceed $30 in value, 4 stores, 5 run stones for grinding grain, 1 cupola furnace, 1 rolling and slitting mill, 3 tanneries, 2 distilleries for cider; and the t-ship paid for road tax, $500; and for county and state tax, $1052 87. Part of the town of Bridgeton is on the eastern boundary, and Shiloh and Roadstown are on the west. Bowentown lies midway on the road between the first and the last.

Hopewell t-ship, Hunterdon co., bounded N. by Amwell t-ship, E. by Montgomery t-ship, of Somerset co., S. E. by Lawrence t-ship, S. by Trenton t-ship, and W. by the river Delaware. Centrally distant S. from Flemington 12 miles; greatest length E. and W. 12; breadth N. and S. 10 miles; area, 36,000 acres; surface on the north hilly, a chain of low, trap mountains extending across it; and on the south level, and abundantly productive; soil red shale, loam, and gravel. It is drained on the west by Smith's and Jacob's creeks, and east by Stony brook. Population in 1830, 3151. In 1832 the t-ship contained 70 houses and lots, 11 stores, 5 fisheries, 6 saw mills, 8 grist mills, 2 oil mills, 17 tan vats, 1 distillery, 1 carding machine, 1 fulling mill, 863 horses and mules, and 1078 neat cattle, over 3 years of age; and paid poor tax, $300; road tax, $1200; state, $1722 84. Pennington and Woodsville are post-towns, and Hebertown and Columbia, villages of the t-ship.

Hopper's or *Ramapotown*, on the Ramapo river, east foot of the Ramapo mountain, 16 miles N. W. from Hackensack; contains a tavern, and some 6 or 8 dwellings.

Hornerstown, hamlet, on Marl Ridge, Upper Freehold t-ship, Monmouth co., 20 miles S. W. of Freehold court-house, and 15 S. E. from Trenton; contains several dwellings, a grist mill, and saw mill, and fulling mill, upon the Lahaway creek, a branch of the Crosswicks. The soil on the north side of the creek is deep, rich loam; and on the south, barren sand. There is here a great deposit of valuable marl.

Hospitality, branch of the Great Egg Harbour river, rises in Deptford t-ship, Gloucester co., and flows S. E. to the river at Pennypot Mill, in Hamilton t-ship, about 14 miles from its source, receiving from the west, Faraway, Lake, and Cold branches.

Howell township, Monmouth co., bounded N. by Shrewsbury, E. by the Atlantic ocean, S. by Dover t-ship, and W. by Freehold t-ship. Centrally distant S. E. from Freehold 11 miles; greatest length E. and W. 13; breadth N. and S. 11 miles; area, 70,000 acres; surface level; soil sand, sandy loam, and clay; drained by Shark, Manasquan, and Metetecunk rivers, which flow east to the ocean; the first on the north, and the last on the south boundary. Manasquan, Squankum, and Howell's Furnace, are post-towns of the t-ship. Population in 1830, 4141. In 1832 there were in the t-ship about 800 taxables, 122 householders, whose ratables did not exceed $30, and 42 single men, 11 stores, 10 saw mills, 5 grist mills, 2 fulling mills, 4 carding machines, 26 tan vats, 2 distilleries, 1 furnace in operation, 365 horses and mules, and 1400 neat cattle, 3 years old and upwards.

Howell Furnace, p-t., Howell t-ship, Monmouth co., 12 miles S. E. of Freehold, 47 from Trenton, and 212 N. E. from W. C., on the left bank of the Manasquan river. The manufacture of iron is extensively carried on here, and for the accommodation of the workmen, there are from 40 to 50 dwellings, and a store.

A company was incorporated for conducting the works, the stock of which, we understand, is now in great part, if not wholly, the property of Mr. James P. Sairs of New York.

Hughesville, village, on the Musconetcong creek, about 5 miles from its mouth, 15 miles S. of Belvidere, and 6 S. E. from Philipsville, in Greenwich t-ship, Warren co., and in a narrow and deep valley; it contains a tavern, a store, a school and from 15 to 20 dwellings. Lead or zinc ore is said to be found in the mountain north of the town; but most probably the latter, as the hill is part of the range of the Hamburg or Wallkill mountains, in which that mineral abounds.

Hunterdon County, was taken from Burlington, by act of Assembly 13th March, 1714, and received its name from governor Hunter. It has been since modified by the erection of Somerset, Morris and Warren cos., and is now bounded N. E. by Morris, E. by Somerset, S. E. by Middlesex, S. by Burlington, S. W. and W. by the river Delaware, and N. W. by the Musconetcong river, which separates it from Warren co. Greatest length N. and S. 43 miles; breadth 26 miles; area, 324,572 acres, or about 507 square miles. Central lat. 40° 3′ N.; long. 2° 5′ E. from W. C.

This county borders S. on the great eastern alluvial formation. The primitive rock is first found in it at the falls of the Delaware river, near Trenton, and may be traced from the respective banks N. E. and S. W. It has in Jersey, however, a narrow breadth, being overlaid by a belt of the old red sandstone which stretches across the country for about 20 miles to the low mountain ridge north of Flemington. About 12 miles north of Trenton, this formation is broken by a chain of trap hills which cross the Delaware below New Hope, and are known in this county by the name of Rocky mountain, &c.; but this chain has the sandstone for its base. Between it and the chain north of Flemington, lies a fertile valley of red sandstone. With the hills north of Flemington, the primitive formation is again visible, but the valleys which intersect them discover secondary limestone, particularly at New Germantown, Clinton, &c., in the German valley, and in the valley of the Musconetcong.

The surface of the county S. and S. E. of Flemington, with the exception of the Rocky hills of which we have spoken, may be deemed level; on the north of Flemington it is mountainous; the ridges, however, are low and well cultivated to the summits. Many of them, particularly those N. and W. of Flemington, produce abundance of excellent ship timber. The red shale of the sandstone formation, is generally susceptible of beneficial cultivation, and is grateful to the careful husbandman. The limestone valleys may be made whatever the cultivator pleases, provided he bounds his wishes by the latitude and climate. And by the use of lime, the cold clay of the primitive hills may be converted into most productive soil. On the whole, this county may be considered one of the finest and most opulent of the state. It is tolerably well watered by streams, part of which seek the Raritan, whilst others flow to the Delaware river: of the first, proceeding from the north, are Spruce run, the main south branch of the Raritan, Lamington river, Rockaway creek, Neshanie creek, and Stony brook: of the second are the Musconetcong river, Hakehokake, Nischisakawick Lackatong, Wickechecoke, Alexsocken, Smith, Jacob's, and Assunpink creeks. The towns of the county are Alexandria, Baptistown, Centreville, Clarksville, Clinton, Flemington, Hepborn's, Hopewell Meeting, Fairview, Lambertsville, Lawrenceville, Lebanon, Mattison's Corner, Milford, Mount Pleasant, New Germantown, New Hampton, Pennington, Pennyville, Pittstown, Potterstown, Prallsville, Quakertown, Ringoes, Sergeantsville, TRENTON, Vansyckle's, White

House, Woodsville, &c., all of which are post-towns. There are beside these, some small hamlets of little note. The county contained in 1832, by the assessor's abstract, 86 merchants, 17 fisheries, 71 saw mills, 80 grist mills, 13 oil mills, 9 ferries and toll bridges, 524 tan vats, 5 distilleries for grain, 58 for cider; 1 cotton manufactory, 17 carding machines, 10 fulling mills, 50 stud horses, 7538 horses and mules, and 12,492 neat cattle, over 3 years of age; and it paid poor tax, $6850; road tax, $8300; county tax, $14,535 84; and state tax, $4146 76.

For the dissemination of moral and religious instruction, there are in the county Bible and tract societies, Sunday schools and temperance societies, in almost all thickly settled neighbourhoods; and the people generally, are remarkable for their sober and orderly deportment.

The population of the county, derived principally from English and German sources, by the census of 1830, amounted to 31,060, of whom 14,465 were white males; 14,653 white females; 869 free coloured males, and 901 free coloured females; 77 male, and 95 female slaves; 34 deaf and dumb, all white; 19 white, and 2 blacks, blind; 210 aliens.

STATISTICAL TABLE OF HUNTERDON COUNTY.

Townships.	Length.	Breadth.	Area.	Surface.	Population.		
					1810.	1820.	1830.
Alexandria,	12	9	33,000	mount's. hilly.	2271	2619	3042
Amwell,	16	15	77,000	p't hilly, p't level.	5777	6749	7385
Bethlehem,	9	9	25,000	mountainous.	1738	2002	2032
Kingwood,	17	7	35,312	hilly.	2605	2786	2898
Hopewell,	12	10	36,000	p't level, p't hilly.	2565	2881	3151
Lawrence,	8	6	13,093	level.		1354	1430
Lebanon,	15	7	42,000	mountainous.	2409	2817	3436
Readington,	12	7½	29,558	generally level.	1797	1964	2102
Tewkesbury,	8	6½	23,000	mountainous.	1308	1499	1659
Trenton,	7	5	10,609	level.	3002	3942	3925
			324,572		23,472	28,604	31,060

Hunt's Pond, a small basin on the N. W. line of Greene t-ship, Sussex co., supplies the Bear branch of Pequest creek.

Hunt's Mills. (See *Clinton.*)

Hurricane Brook, a tributary of the south branch of Toms' river, Dover t-ship, Monmouth co., which unites with Black run, in the mill pond of Dover furnace.

Imlaytown, post-town of Upper Freehold t-ship, Monmouth co., 3 miles E. of Allentown, 180 N. E. from W. C., and 14 miles S. E. from Trenton; contains 12 or 15 dwellings, a grist and saw mill, tannery, 1 tavern, 1 store, wheelwright and smith shop. The surrounding country is gently undulating; soil, clay, and sandy loam, generally well cultivated and productive.

Imlaydale, pleasant hamlet on the Musconetcong creek, Mansfield t-ship, Warren co., 4 miles S. of the village of Mansfield, and within 1 of New Hampton, in the adjacent county of Hunterdon, and 12 miles S. E. of Belvidere; contains a mill, a store, and 3 dwellings.

Independence t-ship, Warren co., bounded N. by Hardwick t-ship, E. by Green t-ship, Sussex co., S E. by Roxbury t-ship, Morris co., S. W. by Mansfield, and W. by Oxford t-ship. Centrally distant N. E. from Belvidere, the county town, 14 miles; greatest length 9 miles N. and S.; breadth E. and W. 8½; area, 29,440 acres; surface hilly on the E. and W., but a valley runs centrally N. E. and S. W. through the t-ship which is drained by the Pequest creek, and on which there is a large body of meadow land. Bacon creek is a small tributary of the Pequest, which unites with it above the village of Vienna. The Musconetcong river forms the S. E. boundary, and in its valley, parallel therewith, runs the Morris canal. Alamuche, Hackets-town, and Vienna, are post-towns of the t-ship; there is a Quaker meeting house in the N. E. part of the t-ship. There were in the t-ship in 1830, 2126 inhabitants; in 1832, 429 taxables, 10,000 acres of improved land, 414 horses and mules, and 1066 neat cattle, over 3 years of age; 146 householders, whose ratables did not exceed $30; 8 stores, 11 pairs of stones for grinding grain, 6 saw mills, 21 tan vats, 4 distilleries; and it paid in t-ship taxes for the poor and roads, $900; and in county and state tax, $880 95. This ranks among the most valuable precincts of the state. The valleys are of fertile limestone, and the hill sides have been subjected to cultivation to a very great extent. The ridges which cross the t-ship from the S. W. to the N. E. are metalliferous, and upon the "*Jenny Jump*," in the N. W., a gold mine is said to exist. Preparations have ostensibly been made for smelting the ore, but the "wise ones" have little confidence in the undertaking, and consider the mineral discovered, if any, to be pyrites or fool's gold.

Inskeep's Mill, at the junction of the N. E. branch of Great Egg Harbour river, called Inskeep's branch, with the Squankum branch of said river, near the south border of Deptford t-ship, Gloucester county, about 33 miles from Camden.

Island Beach, Delaware t-ship, Monmouth co., extends N. 12 miles on the Atlantic ocean and Barnegat bay, from Barnegat inlet to what was formerly Cranberry inlet; it no where exceeds half a mile in breadth.

Indian Branch, a principal tributary of the north branch of the Raritan river, rising in Randolph t-ship, Morris co., on the N. W. foot of Trowbridge mountain, and flowing S. W. through Mendham t-ship, giving motion to several mills in its course.

Indian Run, branch of Doctor's creek, on the N. W. boundary of Upper Freehold t-ship, Monmouth co., flows S. W. by a course of about 2 miles, to its recipient, west of Allentown, giving motion to a saw mill.

Inskeep's Branch, or rather the main stem of the Great Egg Harbour river, above Inskeep's Mill, about 30 miles from the mouth of the river, rises in Gloucester t-ship, Gloucester co., and flows a S. E. course of 12 or 14 miles, to the mill, receiving Four Mile Branch and Squankum Branch.

Jacksonville, on the line between Lebanon and Tewkesbury t-ships, Hunterdon co., about 11 miles N. of Flemington, and on the turnpike road from Somerville to Easton; contains a tavern, store, grist mill, and 2 or 3 dwellings.

Jacksonville, formerly called Imlay's Mills, on Rocky brook, a branch of the Millstone, in Upper Freehold t-ship, Monmouth co., 10 miles E. from Freehold; contains a grist and saw mill, 2 stores, 7 dwellings, and a Presbyterian church. There is a large body of good bog ore at a short distance north of the town, and some indications of extensive mining operations, said to have been carried on near it, many years since, in pursuit of copper.

Jacksonville, post-office, Burlington co., 160 miles N. E. of W. C., and 17 S. of Trenton.

Jackson Glass Works, post-office, Gloucester co., by post route 156 miles from W. C., and 48 from Trenton.

Jacobstown, Hanover t-ship, Burlington co., near the Great Monmouth Road, 12 miles N. E. from Mount Holly, and 9 miles S. E. of Bordentown; contains 2 taverns, a store, and some 12 or 15 dwellings.

Jake's Brook, small tributary of

Toms' river, or rather of Toms' bay, with which it unites, below the village of Toms' River.

Jefferson, village, Orange t-ship, Sussex co., 6 miles W. from Newark, at the foot of the First mountain; contains about 30 dwellings, a Baptist church, and school house.

Jefferson t-ship, Morris co., bounded N. W. by Hardistone t-ship, Sussex co., N. E. by Pompton t-ship, Essex co., S. E. by Pequannock t-ship, and S. W. by Roxbury t-ship, Morris co., and by Byram t-ship, Sussex co. Centrally distant N. W. from Morristown 15 miles; greatest length 14, breadth 3½ miles; area 25,000 acres. The whole surface is covered with mountains, save a deep and narrow valley, the lower part of which is called Berkshire, and the upper Longwood, valley, bounded on the N. W. by the Hamburg mountain, and on the S. E. by Green Pond mountain. Through this valley flows the main branch of the Rockaway river, which has its source in the Hamburg mountain near the county line; and which, in its course through the vale, gives activity to a dozen forges and other mill works. On the top of the Hamburg mountain, near the S. W. line of the t-ship, lies Hurd's pond and Hopatcong lake. The first receives a small stream which has a S. W. course of 4 or 5 miles, and pours its waters into the second. Hurd's pond is about 1½ mile in length, by 1 mile in breadth; and the lake is between 3 and 4 miles long, and about a mile broad, covering about 3000 acres. These waters are remarkable, as well for their place, as their use; being at the summit level of the Morris canal, and employed as its feeders. They are the source also of that fine stream, the Musconetcong creek, and are much celebrated for their fish. The mountain is rough and broken, and the descent into Berkshire valley is wildly picturesque: of which character Longwood also partakes. The base of the whole t-ship is granitic rock, which breaks through the surface in every direction, in rude and heavy masses. From a soil thus constituted, little fertility is expected; but the product of the mountain, in wood and iron, is very valuable. The population in 1830, was 1551. In 1832 the t-ship contained 250 taxables, 127 householders, whose ratables did not exceed $30 in value, 6 stores, 2 grist, 9 saw mills, 3 distilleries, and 18 forges, 206 horses and mules, and 598 neat cattle, over 3 years of age; and paid state tax, $139 79; county, $312 97; poor, $600; and road, $1000.

Jenny Jump, a noted eminence in the northern part of Oxford t-ship, Warren co., extending N. E. and S. W. for about 10 miles, and into Independence t-ship.

Jersey City, lies on a point of land projecting into the Hudson river, opposite to the city of New York, distant therefrom, 1 mile, 1 chain, 47 links, in Bergen t-ship, Bergen co., 13 miles S. of Hackensack, 224 miles N. E. from W. C., 58 from Trenton, and 8 from Newark. It was first incorporated Jan. 28, 1820, comprising "All that portion of the t-ship of Bergen, owned by the Jersey Associates, formerly called Powles Hook, constituted and surrounded by a certain ditch, as the boundary line between the Jersey Associates and the lands of Cornelius Van Vorst, dec'd, on the W. and N. W., and by the middle of the Hudson river, and the bay surrounding all the other parts of the same." By the act of Assembly the municipal government is vested in seven selectmen, who are *ex officio*, conservators of the peace, a president chosen by the board, a treasurer, secretary, city marshal, &c. The town is commodiously laid out into lots, 25 feet by 100, distributed into 45 blocks, each 2 acres, with broad streets, and contains many good buildings. The whole number of dwellings may be 200, and the inhabitants about 1500. There are here, an Episcopalian church of wood, and a new church of stone being erected, and a Dutch Reformed church, 2 select schools, and an academy, owned by the public; the Morris Canal Banking Company, authorized to have a capital not exceeding one million of dollars, of which, $40,000 only, have been paid in; 20 licensed stores, 5 taverns, a public garden on the bay, called the Thatched Cottage Garden; a wind mill, an extensive pottery, at which large quantities of delfware are made, in form and finish scare inferior to the best Liverpool ware; a flint glass manufactory, employing from 80 to 100 hands, at $750 the week wages, yielding an annual product of near $100,000, of the best plain and cut glass ware. Both these large manufactories are conducted by incorporated companies. There are 2 turnpike roads running from this city to Newark, a rail-road to Paterson, and another through Newark to Brunswick; and a basin in this town is proposed to be the eastern termination of the Morris canal, now completed to Newark. Three lines of stages run from Jersey City, to Newark, twice each day. Two steam-boats, belonging to the Associates of the Jersey Company, cross to New York every 15 minutes. This company was chartered in 1804, for the sole purpose of purchasing the place from Cornelius Van Vorst, the former proprietor.

The city is a port of entry, annexed to the collection district of New York, together with all that part of the state of New Jersey, which lies north and east of Elizabethtown and Staten Island. An assistant collector resides at Jersey, who may enter and clear vessels as the collector of New York may do, acting in conformity, however, with such instructions as he may receive from the collector of New York. There is a surveyor also at this port.

Jobsville, or ***Wilkinsville***, named after the proprietor, Deptford t-ship, Gloucester co., near the mouth of Woodbury creek, between 3 and 4 miles W. from Woodbury; contains some half dozen dwellings.

Jobstown, p-t. of Springfield t-ship, on the Great Monmouth road, 6 miles N. E. from Mount Holly, 169 from W. C., and 23 S. E. from Trenton; contains a tavern, a store, and 8 or 10 dwellings, surrounded by excellent farms. The proposed rail-road or Macadamized road from the mouth of Craft's creek to Lisbon, is designed to pass by this village.

Johnsonburg, p-t. and village of Hardwick t-ship, Warren co.; centrally situate in the t-ship, by post route, 218 miles N. E. of W. C., 65 from Trenton, and 16 from Belvidere; contains an Episcopal and a Presbyterian church, a church belonging to the sect of ***Christ-i-ans***, 2 taverns, 2 stores, many mechanic shops, a grist mill, and from 25 to 30 dwellings. The surrounding soil is of fertile limestone, and well cultivated. A small tributary of the Bear branch of Pequest creek, flows through it, and gives motion to the mill of the town.

Jones' Island, Fairfield t-ship, Cumberland co., formed by Cedar creek, Nantuxet creek, and their tributaries, and by Nantuxet Cove.

Jugtown, small village, in a valley of the Musconetcong mountain, and on the road from Somerville to Philipsburg, about 12 miles N. W. from Flemington; contains a tavern, mill, and some half dozen dwellings.

Juliustown, p-t. of Springfield t-sp, Burlington co., 6 miles N. E. of Mount Holly, 163 from W. C., and 25 S. E. from Trenton; contains 1 tavern, 2 stores, and from 20 to 30 dwellings. A rail, or Macadamized road, from the mouth of Craft's creek to Lisbon, is designed to pass by this village.

Jumping Brook, one of the sources of Crosswick's creek, Freehold t-ship, Monmouth co., which, after a west course of about 4 miles, unites with South Run, and forms the creek. It is a mill stream.

Kettle Run, small tributary of Haines' creek, Evesham t-ship, Burlington co., unites with the main stream at Taunton furnace.

Kettle Creek, Dover t-ship, Monmouth co., rises by two branches, north and south, which flow east, the first about 6, and the second about 4 miles. Their union forms an arm of Barnegat bay. There is a post-office in the neighbourhood, named after the creek, about 65 miles from Trenton.

Kill Van Kuhl, the narrow strait between Staten island and the south shore of Bergen co., connecting New York bay with Newark bay, and in length about 5 miles.

Kingston, p-t., on the turnpike road from Princeton to Brunswick, 13 miles from the latter, 180 from W. C., and 13 from Trenton, and on the line separating South Brunswick t-ship, Middlesex co., from Franklin t-ship, Somerset co., so that part of the town lies in each county, and half way between Philadelphia and New York. There are here a Presbyterian church, an academy, 3 taverns, 4 stores, a large grist mill, saw mill, and woollen factory, driven by the Millstone river, which runs through the town. The Delaware and Raritan canal also passes through it, with a lock at this place. There are here also, about 40 dwellings. The soil around the town is of sandy loam, upon red sandstone, fertile, and in a high state of cultivation, and valued, in farms, at $60 the acre. This place was once remarkable for the number of stages which passed through it, for New York and Philadelphia, the passengers in which, commonly dined at the hotel of Mr. P. Withington. Before the completion of the Bordentown and Amboy rail road, 49 stages, loaded with passengers, between the two cities, have halted here at the same time; when more than 400 harnessed horses were seen standing in front of the inn. Mr. Withington has lately made a very large fish pond on his lands, well stocked with trout, and other fish of the country, with which he can, at any time, supply his table in a few minutes.

Kingwood t-ship, Hunterdon co., bounded N. E. by Lebanon, S. E. by Amwell, W. by the Delaware river, and N. W. by Bethlehem t-ship. Centrally distant W. from Flemington 7 miles; greatest length N. E. and S. W. 17, breadth E. and W. 7 miles; area, 35,312 acres; surface, hilly and rolling; soil, red shale, clay, and loam; in many places fertile and well cultivated. The tract known as the Great Swamp, extends on the top of the mountain into this t-ship, and is alike remarkable for its fine timber and extraordinary fertility. The t-p. is drained southwardly by the Laokatong creek. Baptisttown, Fairview, Dogtown, Charleston, and Milltown, are villages and hamlets of the t-ship; at the first there is a post-office, and there is another office bearing the name of the t-ship. Population in 1830, 2898. In 1832 there were in the t-ship 4 stores, 7 saw mills, 7 grist mills, and 1 oil mill, 7 distilleries, 2 carding machines, 733 horses and mules, and 1347 neat cattle, above the age of 3 years; and the t-ship paid state and county tax, $1323 75.

Kinseyville, p-t. of Lower Penn's Neck t-ship, Salem co., on the Delaware river, opposite to the town of Newcastle, 170 miles from W. C., 58 from Trenton, and 7 from Salem. It is named after James Kinsey, the proprietor, and contains 4 or 5 dwellings, 2 taverns, store, and ferry to Newcastle.

Kirkland's Creek, through the salt marsh of Lodi t-ship, Bergen co.; near its head is a saw mill. The length of the creek is about 3 miles.

Kline's Mills, post-office, Somerset co., by post route 206 miles N. E. from W. C., and 40 from Trenton.

Knowlton, t-ship, Warren co., bounded N. by Pahaquarry t-ship, E. by Hardwick t-ship, S. by Oxford t-ship, and W. by the Delaware river. Centrally distant N. E. from Belvidere, 10 miles; greatest length 10 miles, breadth 10 miles; area 44,800 acres. The Blue mountain lies upon the northern boundary, and the Delaware makes its way through it at the celebrated Water Gap, at the N. W. point of the t-ship. The t-ship is every where hilly, and is said to derive its name from its knolls. It is centrally drained by Paulinskill, and its branches; on the south-east by

Beaver brook, and north-east by the Shawpocussing creek. Gravel Hill, Sodom, Columbia, Centreville, Hope, and Ramsaysburg, are villages and post towns of the t-ship. Population in 1830, 2827; taxables in 1832, 630. There were in the t-ship, in 1832, 132 householders, whose ratables did not exceed $30, 13 pairs of stones for grinding grain, 7 saw mills, 10 tan vats, 4 distilleries, 1 glass manufactory, 744 horses and mules, and 1390 neat cattle over three years of age; and the t-ship paid $1300 for t-ship use, and $1550 for state and county purposes. Slate and lime alternate throughout the t-ship; the hills are commonly of the one, and the valleys of the other.

A slate quarry above Columbia is extensively wrought, from whence excellent roof and writing slates are taken. There is 1 Presbyterian and 1 Episcopalian church in the t-ship.

Knowlton, post town and village of the above t-ship, on Paulinskill, 2 miles from its mouth, and by the post route 217 from W. C., 64 from Trenton, and 10 from Belvidere; contains 1 tavern, 1 store, a large grist and saw mill, a clover mill, and 6 or 7 dwellings. The country around is hilly, soil limestone.

Koughstown, village, on the line between the t-ship of Hillsborough, in Somerset co., and the t-ship of Amwell, in Hunterdon co. 5 miles S. E. of Flemington, contains a tavern and some 4 or 5 dwellings.

Koughstown, small village on the line dividing Hillsborough t-ship, Somerset co; from Amwell t-ship, Hunterdon co., 11 miles S. W. from Somerville, and 4 miles S. E. from Flemington; contains a tavern, store, Dutch Reformed church, and several dwellings, pleasantly situated upon soil of red shale, in the valley of the Neshanie creek.

Krokaevall, small mill stream of Saddle river t-ship, Bergen co., rising on the N. border, and flowing by a course of about 5 miles, to the Passaic river, a mile above the great Falls.

Lafayette, post town of Newton t-ship, near the north line of the t-ship, on the Union Turnpike Road, distant by the post route 233 miles from W. C., 75 from Trenton, and 5 miles from Newton; contains 1 tavern, 1 store, a cupola furnace, a grist mill, with 4 run of stones, driven by the Paulinskill, a Baptist church, and some 10 or 12 dwellings. The prevailing soil around it is limestone, in excellent cultivation.

Lahaway Creek, Upper Freehold, t-ship, Monmouth co., rises near the E. boundary, and flows S. W. about 9 miles, to the Crosswicks creek, below Hornerstown, giving motion to some mills at that place and at Prospertown.

Lake Branch, of Hospitality creek, an arm of the Great Egg Harbour river, Franklin and Hamilton t-ships, Gloucester co.

Lake's Bay, in the salt marsh, on the Atlantic ocean, Egg Harbour t-ship, Gloucester co., communicates by several inlets with the ocean; is about 3 miles long and a mile and a half wide.

Lambertsville, post town of Amwell t-ship, Hunterdon co., 11 miles S. W. from Flemington, 16 N. from Trenton, and 170 from W. C.; a thriving, pleasant village, on the bank of the Delaware river, opposite to the town of New Hope, containing 1 Baptist and 1 Presbyterian church, 2 schools, one of which is a boarding school, under the care of the Rev. Mr. Studdiford, and more than 30 dwellings, many of which are neat and commodious. A turnpike road runs from the town to New Brunswick, and a fine bridge is thrown over the river by a joint stock company, with a capital of $160,000, incorporated in 1812, by the Legislatures of Pennsylvania and New Jersey; built in 1814. It is supported on 9 stone piers; length between the abutments 1050 feet, width 33 feet, elevation above the water 21 feet; roofed. The company for some time employed a portion of its capital in banking operations.

Lamington River, tributary of the north branch of the Raritan, rises in Duck pond, Roxbury t-ship, Morris co., and flows thence by a S. W. and S. course of 34 miles, uniting with its recipient in Bedminster t-ship, Somerset co. It is a large and rapid mill stream, on which there are many mills, particularly at Potter's Falls; in the north part of its course it bears the name of Black river.

Lamington, village of Bedminster t-ship, Somerset co., on the road from Somerville to Philipsburg, 10 miles N. W. of the former; contains a Presbyterian church, a tavern, and 3 or 4 dwellings, situate in a pleasant fertile country.

Landing Creek, Galloway t-ship, Gloucester co., rises on the S. W. line of the t-ship, and flows about 9 miles eastwardly, to the Little Egg Harbour river; Gloucester furnace lies upon it. It has two branches, Indian Cabin branch, and Elisha's creek.

Laokatong Creek, a fine mill stream of Kingwood t-ship, Hunterdon co., rises in the t-ship and flows S. W. 10 or 12 miles into the river Delaware; it gives motion in its course to several mills.

Lawrenceville, Knowlton t-ship, Warren co., on both banks of the Paulinskill, 15 miles N. E. of Belvidere, and 3 miles W. of Marksboro'; contains a store and tavern, and 10 or 12 scattering dwellings. The country around it is hilly; the soil slate on the left, and limestone on the right side of the creek.

Lawrence t-ship, Hunterdon co., bounded N. W. by Hopewell, N. E. by Montgomery t-ship, Somerset co., and West Windsor t-ship, Monmouth co., S. E. by Nottingham t-ship, of Burlington co., and S. W. by Trenton t-ship. Centrally distant from Trenton N. E. 6 miles; greatest length 8, breadth 6 miles; area, by assessor's return, 13,093 acres; surface, rolling; soil, loam and clay, generally well cultivated; drained southward by some branches of the Assunpink creek, and northward by Stony brook: Lawrenceville is the post-town, and only village of the t-ship. Population in 1330, 1430. In 1832, there were in the t-ship 1 store, 2 saw mills, 3 grist mills, 8 tan vats, 339 horses and mules, and 710 neat cattle, above the age of 3 years; and it paid poor tax, $500; road tax, $400; state and county tax, $726 80. Two turnpike roads from Trenton to Brunswick run north-easterly through the t-ship, one of which leads by Princeton.

Lawrenceville, post-town of Lawrence t-ship, Hunterdon co., 6 miles N. E. from Trenton, 18 S. E. from Flemington, 172 from W. C., situate on a level and fertile plain, well cultivated in grain and grass, and contains 1 Presbyterian church, 1 tavern, 1 store, a flourishing boarding school and academy, under the care of Mr. Philips.

Lawrenceville, town of Hardwick t-ship, Warren co., near the western t-ship line, 82 miles N. E. from Trenton, and 15 from Belvidere.

Lawrence's Brook, rises in South Brunswick t-ship, Middlesex co., and flows N. E. through New Brunswick t-ship, by a course of about 12 miles to the Raritan river, near 3 miles below New Brunswick.

Leaming's, or ***Seven Mile Beach***, Middle t-ship, Cape May co., extending from Townsend's inlet to Hereford inlet, having an average width of half a mile.

Lebanon Branch, of Maurice river, rises in Deerfield t-ship, Cumberland co., and flows eastwardly to the river, about 2 miles above the town of Milleville; it is a mill stream, and has a tributary called Chatfield run.

Lebanon t-ship, Hunterdon co., bounded N. E. by Washington t-ship, Morris co., E. by Readington and Tewkesbury t-ships, S. by Kingwood t-ship, W. by Bethlehem, N. W. by Musconetcong creek, which divides it from Mansfield t-ship, Warren co. Greatest length N. and S. 15 miles; breadth E. and W. 7 miles; area, 42,000 acres; surface mountainous, and generally hilly; soil, clay and loam on the hills, with grey limestone in the valleys; in parts rich and well cultivated. The Musconetcong mountain and its spurs cover the greater part of the northern part, and there are some high hills on the S. E., encircling Round Valley. It is drained by Spruce run and the south branch of Raritan river, the latter forming part of the eastern and the southeastern boundary, and crossing the t-ship from Morris county. The turnpike road from Somerville to Philipsburg, runs westerly through the township, by the towns of Lebanon and Clinton. New Hampton and Sodom, or Clarkesville, are post-towns of the t-ship. Population in 1830, 3436. The t-ship contained in 1832, 13 saw mills, 16 grist mills, 2 oil mills, 87 tan vats, 1 distillery for grain, 11 distilleries for cider, 2 carding machines, 2 fulling mills, 886 horses, and 1540 neat cattle, above the age of 3 years; and it paid poor tax, $1100; road tax, 800; and county and state tax, $1585 36.

Lebanon, post-town of Lebanon t-ship, Hunterdon co., centrally situated, upon the turnpike road leading from Somerville to Philipsburg; 11 miles N. of Flemington, 47 from Trenton, and 211 from W. C.; contains 1 tavern, 1 store, and several dwellings. There is a Dutch Reformed church in the neighbourhood.

Leed's Point, post-town, Galloway t-ship, Gloucester co., 44 miles S. E. from Woodbury, 83 from Trenton, and 191 N. E. from W. C.; contains a store, tavern, and some 4 or 5 houses.

Leesburg, village of Maurice River t-ship, Cumberland co., on the left bank of Maurice river, about 5 miles from its mouth, and 20 S. E. of Bridgetown; contains 15 or 20 houses, 1 store, 1 tavern, and a Methodist church. There is a considerable quantity of ship building here, such as sloops, schooners, &c., and much trade in lumber and wood. The soil in the village and country immediately around, is very productive; it is one of the oldest settlements upon the river.

Libertyville, p-t., of Wantage t-sp, Sussex co., on the turnpike road leading to Milford, Pennsylvania, about 3 miles E. of the Blue mountain.

Liberty Corner, p-t., Bernard t-sp, Somerset co., 7 miles N. E. of Somerville, 209 from W. C., and 43 from Trenton, near Harrison's brook; contains a tavern, store, and about 20 dwellings, inhabited by intelligent, respectable families, in a fertile and well cultivated valley.

Lion Pond, a source of Lubber run, Byram t-ship, Sussex co., lying near the centre of the t-ship.

Lisbon, small village of Hanover t-ship, Burlington co., in the forks of the Slab Bridge branch, and the north branch of the Rancocus creek; contains a grist mill, saw mill, store, tavern, and 10 or 12 dwellings. A railroad or Macadamized road, is about to be made from this village to the mouth of Craft's creek, upon the Delaware, about 15 miles, in order to bring to market a quantity of excellent pine wood, which grows in the vicinity.

Little Beach, Burlington co., Little Egg Harbour t-ship, between Little Egg Harbour, New Inlet, and Old Brigantine Inlet.

Little Ease, village of Franklin t-ship, Gloucester co., 20 miles S. E. of Woodbury, upon the head waters of Maurice river; contains a tavern, store, saw mill, and some half dozen dwellings; soil, sandy.

Little Egg Harbour River. (See *Egg Harbour River, Little*.)

Little Falls, of the Passaic, name of the manufacturing village and post-town which has grown up here; (See article *Passaic*) and which contains, on the right bank of the creek, 2 saw, and 1 grist mill, 2 cotton mills, one of a thousand, and another of fourteen hundred spindles, a turning mill, a woollen carpet manufactory, 4 stores, 3 taverns, a school house, used also as a church, and 47 dwellings. On the left bank there is a saw mill and turning mill. This is an admirable position for mill works of all kinds. The whole river may be used under a head of 33 feet, 10 of which only are now employed to drive the few works above named, and which would give motion to a much larger quantity. The proprietors of this desirable site, Messrs. Ezekiel and Isaac Miller, and the heirs of Samuel Bridges, offer mill seats for sale on very advantageous terms, and the rights of the former gentlemen to the right bank, with half the water power, have been holden at $50,000 only. The place from its elevation is very healthy; land in the neighbourhood sells at from 30 to 60 dollars the acre, and town lots, 100 feet deep, at 2 dollars the foot, front, in fee simple. The town is 226 miles N. E. from W. C., 60 from Trenton, 10 from Newark, 4 from Paterson, and 5½ from Acquackanonck Landing. It has also the advantage of the Morris canal, which crosses the river by an aqueduct below the falls.

Lamberton. See *Trenton*.

Little Pond, a small basin of water in Newton t-ship, Sussex co., distant about 4 miles west of the town of Newton, which supplies, in part, a small tributary of Paulinskill.

Little Pond, on the sea shore, Shrewsbury t-ship, Monmouth co., about 3 miles north of the south boundary of the t-ship.

Little ⋈ Roads, p-t., Bedminster t-ship, Somerset co., 9 miles N. W. from Somerville, 209 from W. C., and 43 from Trenton; contains a tavern, store, and 5 or 6 dwellings, in the valley of the north branch of the Raritan.

Littletown, p-t., Hanover t-ship, Morris co., on the turnpike road from Newark to Milford, 5 miles north of Morristown, 224 from W. C., and 59 from Trenton; contains 1 tavern, 1 store, and 4 or 5 dwellings.

Livingston, t-ship, Essex co., bounded N. by Caldwell, E. by Orange, S. by Springfield, and W. by the Passaic river, which divides it from Morris co. Centrally distant, N. W. from Newark, 9 miles; greatest length, N. and S. 5 miles; breadth E. and W. 4½ miles, area 13,000 acres; surface on the east, mountainous, elsewhere rolling, except near the river, where it is level. It is drained on the N. by the Black Rock Meadow brook, and on the S. by Canoe creek, which flow to the Passaic by short courses, not exceeding three miles. Towns, Centreville, Livingston, post-town, Northfield, Squiretown, and Cheapside. Population in 1830, 1150. In 1832, the t-ship contained 200 taxables, 65 householders, whose ratables did not exceed $30; 52 single men, 5 merchants, 1 saw mill, 1 woollen factory, 166 horses and mules, and 637 neat cattle under three years of age; and it paid state tax, $120 03; county tax, $314 04; poor tax, $350; and road tax, $525.

Livingston, small village, and post town of preceding t-ship, on the turnpike road from Newark to Dover, 10 miles N. W. from the former, 225 N. E. from W. C., and 59 from Trenton; contains a tavern, store, and some 8 or 10 dwellings.

Lockwood, forge and post-office; on Lubber run, Byram t-ship, Sussex co.; distant by post route 224 miles from W. C., 61 from Trenton, and 9 south from Newton.

Lodi, t-ship, Bergen co., bounded N. by New Barbadoes t-ship, E. and S. E. by Hackensack river, which separates it from Bergen t-ship, and W. and S. W. by the Passaic river, dividing it from Essex co. Centrally distant, S. W. from Hackensacktown, 5 miles. Greatest length 10, greatest breadth E. and W. 5 miles; area 22,000 acres; surface level. More than half the t-ship consists of salt marsh and cedar swamp. On the N. E. there are about 4000 acres of arable land, and on the west a strip running the whole length of the t-ship, and varying from 1 to 2 miles in width. These are of red shale, with a margin of alluvial, on the Passaic, well cultivated, and productive. Along the latter river are strewed many handsome country seats, and about a mile S. E. of Belleville lies the well known Schuyler copper mine. Population of t-ship, in 1830, 1356. In 1832 it contained 527 taxables, 57 householders, whose ratables did not exceed $30; 21 single men, 1 store, 5 grist mills, 4 saw mills, 2 toll bridges, and 291 horses and mules, and 931 neat cattle, above the age of 3 years. And it paid state tax, $208 87; county $427 69; poor, $400; road, $500. There are several creeks through the marsh, such as Berry's, Kirkland's, and Saw-mill creeks.

Logtown, small hamlet of Lower Alloway's creek t-ship, Salem co., 7 miles S. of Salem-town, and 2 from Hancock's bridge.

Logansville, 6 miles S. W. of Morristown, Morris t-ship, Morris co., a fine settlement on Primrose creek, called after the owner, who has a large estate here.

Logtown, on Mine mountain, Bernard t-ship, Somerset co., at the head of Mine brook, 12 miles N. of Somerville, contains a mill and 3 or 4 dwellings.

Longacoming, p-t. of Gloucester co., on the line dividing the t-ship of Gloucester and Waterford, 14 miles S. E. from Woodbury, 45 from Trenton, and 153 N. E. from Washington; surrounded by pine forest, soil sandy, and naturally barren, but improving by the application of marl. The village contains from 20 to 30 dwellings, 2 taverns, 2 stores, and a Methodist church.

Long Beach, upon the Atlantic ocean, Stafford t-ship, Monmouth co., extending about 11 miles from the inlet to Little Egg Harbour bay, to Barnegat inlet. There are several houses on this beach, one of which was erected by a Philadelphia company, for the accommodation of themselves and friends in sea-bathing.

Long Branch, mill stream and tributary of Shrewsbury river, Shrewsbury t-ship, Monmouth co.; has a course of about 4 miles N. W. There is a small village of 12 or 15 houses, 1 tavern, and 2 stores, east of this stream, and between it and the Atlantic, to which the name of Long Branch is given.

Long Branch, well known and much frequented sea-bathing place, on the Atlantic ocean, 75 miles from Philadelphia, and 45 from New York, in Shrewsbury t-ship, and Monmouth co., which has its name from the stream and hamlet above. The inducements to the invalid, the idle, and the hunters of pleasure, to spend a portion of the hot season here, are many. Good accommodations, obliging hosts, a clean and high shore, with a gently shelving beach, a fine prospect seaward, enlivened by the countless vessels passing to and from New York, excellent fishing on the banks, 3 or 4 miles at sea, good gunning, and the great attraction of all watering places, much, and changing and fashionable company. During the season, a regular line of stages runs from Philadelphia, and a steamboat from New York, to the boarding houses here, of which there are several; Wardell's, Renshaw's, and Sear's are the most frequented. Many respectable farmers also receive boarders, who, in the quiet of rural life, enjoy in comfort and ease, their season of relaxation, perhaps more fully than those at the public hotels. Along the beach at Long Branch is a strip of fertile black sand, several miles in length, and exceeding more than a mile in width. The land adjacent to the ocean rises perpendicularly from the beach, near 20 feet. The boarding houses are 20 rods from the water, with lawns in the intermediate space. The high banks are formed by strata of sand, clay, and sea mud.

Long Bridge, over Pequest creek, Independence t-ship, Union co., at the head of the Great Meadows, 16 miles N. E. from Belvidere. There is a hamlet here of 6 or 8 dwellings, and the neighbourhood is settled by members of the society of Friends, who have a meeting house within 2 miles of the Bridge. The soil of the vicinity is limestone, naturally fertile, and susceptible of improvement, as may be supposed from the character of its cultivators; for "Friends" of all vanities, dislike most, vain labour.

Long Pond, a small sheet of water in the Blue mountains, in Walpack t-ship, Sussex co., whence Vancamp creek has its source.

Long Pond, Frankford t-ship, Sussex co., at the east foot of the Blue mountain, the extreme S. W. source of the W. branch of Paulinskill.

Long Pond, Newton t-ship, Sussex co., five miles S. E. of Newton.

Long Pond, or *Greenwood Lake*, crosses the state boundary from Orange co., New York, into Pompton t-ship, Bergen co.; it is about 4½ miles long by near a mile wide, but only a mile of its length is within this state. It sends forth a stream called Long Pond river, which empties into Ringwood river, near Boardville.

Long Pond, Shrewsbury t-ship, Monmouth co., upon the sea-shore, 6 miles S. of Long Branch Boarding Houses, communicates with the sea by a narrow inlet.

Longwood Valley, Jefferson t-ship, Morris co., lying between the Hamburg and Greenpond mountains, extending longitudinally N. E. and S. W. about 10 miles; narrow, deep, and stony, with soil not very fertile; it is drained S. W. by a principal branch of the Rockaway river, on which are several forges for making iron, the ore and fuel for which are supplied abundantly by the adjacent hills; Berkshire Valley is the name given to the S. W. portion of this vale. The scenery here is wild, rude, and picturesque. Newfoundland is the post-office of Longwood Valley.

Lopatcong Creek, rises in the southern part of Oxford t-ship, Warren co., and flows thence by a S. W. course of 9 or 10 miles through Greenwich t-ship, to the river Delaware, 3 or 4 miles below Philipsburg, giving motion to several mills in its course, and draining a fertile valley of primitive limestone.

Lower t-ship, Cape May co., bounded N. by Middle t-ship, E. and S. by the Atlantic ocean, and W. by the Delaware bay. It is the most southern t-ship of the state, nearly one-half consists of sea beach and salt marsh, and the remainder of clay, covered with oak forest. Centrally distant from Cape May Court House, S. 9 miles; length N. and S. 8, breadth 8 miles; area, 21,000 acres, Pond creek, New England creek, and Cox Hall creek, are short streams, which flow westerly into the Delaware bay. Cape May, Cape May island, and the Cape May light-house, are in the t-ship. Population in 1830, 995. In 1832, there were in the t-ship about 200 taxables, 91 householders, whose ratables did not exceed $30; 3 grist mills, 7 stores, 136 horses, 380 neat cattle, over 3 years of age; it paid t-ship tax, $51 92; state tax, $129; county tax, $399 38.

Ludlam's Beach, extends upon the ocean about 6 miles from Carson's to Townsend's inlet, partly in Middle, and partly in Dennis t-ship, Cape May co.

Lumberton, town of Northampton t-ship, Burlington co., on the south branch of Rancocus creek, 3 miles S. W. from Mount Holly; contains 2 stores, 2 taverns, a steel furnace, and from 25 to 30 dwellings, surrounded by very good farms.

Mackepin Pond, Pompton t-ship, Bergen co., about 2 miles in length, by half a mile in breadth; lies among the mountains, and sends forth a small tributary to the Pequannock creek.

Malaga, p-t. of Franklin t-ship, Gloucester co., 23 miles S. E. from Woodbury, at the angle of junction of Salem, Cumberland and Gloucester counties; on the head waters of Maurice river, 58 miles S. from Trenton, and N. E. 164 from W. C.; contains 1 tavern, 2 stores, a glass manufactory, employed on window glass, 30 dwellings and a grist mill.

Mamapaque Brook, an arm of the south branch of Toms' river, Dover t-ship, Monmouth co.

Manahocking River, Stafford

t-ship, Monmouth co., flows S. E. about 9 miles into Little Egg Harbour bay, giving motion to a mill, at the town of Manahocking.

Manahocking, p-t. of Stafford t-ship, Monmouth co., 38 miles S. E. of Freehold, 73 from Trenton, and 197 N. E. from W. C., upon the creek of the same name, about 4 miles from Little Egg Harbour bay, contains a saw and grist mill, 2 taverns, several stores, and from 20 to 30 dwellings, a Friends' meeting house, a Baptist and a Methodist church. There is a considerable trade carried on here in wood and lumber, and cedar rails, supplied by the swamps of the neighbourhood.

Manalapan Brook, or ***South River***, rises in Upper Freehold t-ship, Monmouth co., near Paint Island spring, and flows by a devious, but generally, N. E. course, through South Amboy t-ship, (forming in part the line between it and South Brunswick) a distance of about 28 or 30 miles, to the Raritan river, about 4 miles below New Brunswick, receiving from the south, several considerable tributaries. When the passage to New York was made by the town of Washington on this river, a canal, of about a mile in length, was cut through the marshes, that by turning the river into it the steam-boat might avoid some detours of the Raritan, and shorten her course. The project, we believe, was not successfully executed.

Manaway Creek, Milleville t-ship, Cumberland co., a tributary of Maurice river.

Manantico Creek, a considerable branch of Maurice river, rising near the S. W. border of Gloucester co., and flowing S. W. about 14 miles, uniting with the river about two miles above Port Elizabeth; it turns several mills; it receives two tributaries, Berryman's and Panther branches.

Manasquan River, mill stream of Monmouth co., rises by several small branches in Freehold t-ship, which unite on the boundary line between Freehold and Howell townships; thence the river flows by a S. E. direction 18 miles through the latter township to the ocean, by Manasquan inlet. The tide water of the river, about 3 miles above the mouth, is crossed by Squan bridge.

Mannington t-ship, Salem co., bounded N. by Salem river, which divides it from Upper Penn's Neck creek, and Pilesgrove township, E. by Pilesgrove, S. by Upper Alloways township, and Salem township, and W. by Salem river, which here separates it from Lower Penn's Neck township. Centrally distant N. E. from Salem, 6 miles; length N. and S. 9; breadth E. and W. 8 miles; area, about 90,000 acres, of which more than 18,000 are improved; surface, level; soil, heavy rich loam, well cultivated in wheat and grass. The township is drained by Salem river, bounding it on the N. and W. and by Mannington creek, which has its whole course within it, and is a tributary of the former. Near the village of Mannington Hill, which is the post-town of the township, is a noted nursery of fruit and ornamental trees, planted by Mr. Samuel Reeves, who sold from it during the year 1832, 15,000 peach trees alone. The poor-house of the county lies near the eastern line of the township, in which from 80 to 120 paupers are annually relieved. Population, in 1830, 1726. In 1832, there were in the township 1 Methodist and 1 Baptist church, 102 householders, whose ratables did not exceed $30; 1 store, 2 distilleries, 353 taxable inhabitants; and the township paid for township purposes, $1000; for county purposes, $1085 34; and state tax, $339 64.

Mannington Hill, p-t., and small village of Mannington t-ship, Salem co. Centrally situate in the township, upon Mannington creek. It contains 6 or 8 houses and a store. It is about 175 miles from W. C., 60 from Trenton, and 5 N. E. of Salem.

Mannington Creek, a small tributary of Salem river, which rising on the S. W. border of Mannington township, Salem county, flows westerly by a meandering course of 8 miles to its recipient. It is not a mill stream, but along its banks are some valuable meadows.

Mansfield t-ship, Warren co., bounded N. E. by Independence, S. E. by the Musconetcong river, which separates it from Morris and Hunterdon cos., S. W. by Greenwich t-ship, and N. W. by Oxford t-ship. Centrally distant from Belvidere, the county town, 9 miles; greatest length on the river 15 miles; breadth 6½ miles; area, 33,000 acres; surface, mountainous; drained by the Musconetcong and Pohatcong creeks, which, divided by a chain of lofty hills, run parallel to each other, but at a distance of nearly 4 miles apart. There is a mineral spring, a chalybeate, in the S. W. part of the t-ship, much frequented. Population in 1830, 3303. In 1832 there were 800 taxables, 169 householders, whose ratable estates did not exeeed $30; 11 stores, 12 pairs of stones for grinding grain, 8 carding machines, 5 saw mills, 1 furnace, 1 fulling mill, 36 tan vats, 7 distilleries, 862 horses and mules, and 1407 neat cattle in the t-ship; and the t-ship paid $1200 road and poor tax; and $1659 42 state and county tax. The Morris canal winds through the hills the whole length of the t-ship. This is one of the richest t-ships of the state, having a large proportion of valley land underlaid with limestone. Large quantities of wheat are raised, and some farmers sell as many as 3000 bushels annually. Iron ore abounds in the hills, and silver *is said* to have been discovered near the spring, but most probably this is iron pyrites.

Mansfield, small village of Mansfield t-ship, Burlington co.; centrally situated in the t-ship 8 miles N. of Mount Holly, and 4 miles S. of Bordentown; contains a Friends' meeting house and 4 or 5 dwellings.

Mansfield or *Washington*, p-t. of Mansfield t-ship, Warren co., founded in 1811, on the turnpike road leading from Philipsburg to Schooley's mountain; by the post route 202 miles from W. C., and 46 from Trenton, and 8½ miles S. E. of Belvidere, the county town, 30 from Morristown, 12 from Easton, and 3 miles from Musconetcong creek; contains 1 tavern, 2 stores, from 35 to 40 dwellings, 1 Methodist and 1 Presbyterian church, and 1 school. Iron ore abounds in Scott's mountain north of the village. Around the town the soil is limestone, fertile and well cultivated, and valued at from 20 to 50 dollars the acre. The town is supplied with excellent water from a spring on the south, which is distributed by 4 public fountains.

Mansfield t-ship, Burlington co., bounded N. E. by Chesterfield t-ship, S. by Springfield, W. by Burlington t-ship, and N. W. by the river Delaware. Centrally distant from Mount Holly N. 7 miles; greatest length E. and W. 10 miles; breadth N. and S. 6½ miles; area, about 21,000 acres; surface, level; soil, various, sand, loam, and clay; generally well cultivated, and productive. It is drained north-westerly by Black's, Craft's, and Assiscunk creeks, all of which flow to the Delaware river. Along the river are some noted clay banks, from which clay is taken for the manufacture of fire bricks, and for other purposes requiring great resistance to heat. The towns are White Hill, Georgetown, Mansfield, Bustletown, Columbus or Black Horse, the last of which is a post-town. Population in 1830, 2083. In 1832 the t-ship contained 432 taxables, 216 householders, whose ratables did not exceed $30; 65 single men, 1390 neat cattle, and 548 horses and mules, above 3 years old, 4 stores, 2 saw mills, 3 grist mills, 1 fishery, 1 furnace, 1 fulling mill, 31 tan vats, 1 carding machine, 5 distilleries of cider, 4 coaches and chariots, 3 phaetons and chaises, 49 dearborns, and 84 covered wagons, 3 chairs and curricles, and 18 gigs and sulkies; and it paid state tax, $345 88; county tax, $1212 38; and t-ship tax, $1100.

Mantua Creek, Gloucester co.,

rises on, and forms the line between Deptford and Greenwich t-ships, and flows N. W. by a course of 15 miles to the Delaware river, above Maiden island. It is navigable for sloops 7 or 8 miles to Carpenter's Landing, above which it gives motion to several mills.

Maple Island Creek, sets in from Newark bay about 1½ or 2 miles into the salt marsh, on the S. E. of Newarktown.

Mapletown, hamlet on Millstone river, a short distance above the mouth of Stony Brook, 2 miles S. E. of Princeton, 15 from New Brunswick; contains a fine grist and saw mill, and fulling mill, and 4 or 5 dwellings. North of the hamlet on the river, are some excellent quarries of freestone; a fine grey, with portions of red, standstone, streaked with small veins of quartz. It works well under the hammer, and has been used in the erection of the locks of the Delaware and Raritan canal.

Mare Run, small tributary of the Great Egg Harbour river, flowing from the west to its recipient, in Hamilton t-ship, Gloucester co., about 3 miles above May's Landing.

Marksboro', p-t. and village of Hardwick t-ship, Warren co.; centrally situate in the t-ship, and by post route distant from W. C. 240, from Trenton 82, from Belvidere 15 miles, 10 from Newton, and 12 from Columbia, and on the south bank of the Paulinskill; contains a Presbyterian church, a grist mill, a cotton manufactory making 1500 lbs. of yarn per week, a clover mill, 1 lawyer, 1 physician, and about 20 dwellings. The town itself lies on a slate ridge, which is fertile and well cultivated, but the soil on the north side of the creek is secondary limestone; the most valuable slate lands rate, at about $30, and the lime, at about $40 the acre. The celebrated White Pond lies about 1 mile north of the town. Its shores and bottom are covered with vast quantities of snail shells, and its waters afford abundance of white perch and other fish.

Marshs'bog, town of Howell t-ship, Monmouth co., 9 miles S. E. of Freehold; contains 2 taverns, 2 stores, and 10 or 12 dwellings; the surrounding country is sterile, but there is considerable business done in the village.

Marshallville, or *Cumberland Works*, on Tuckahoe creek, Maurice Creek t-ship, Cumberland co., at the eastern extremity of the co., 28 miles S. E. of Bridgeton; contains from 30 to 40 houses, some extensive glass works belonging to Randall Marshall, Esq., at which much window glass is manufactured, 1 tavern, and 2 stores. There is much ship building carried on here in vessels of from 50 to 100 tons; soil, sandy.

Martha Furnace, Washington t-ship, Burlington co., on the Oswego branch of Wading river, about 4 miles above the head of navigation; there are here also a grist and saw mill. The furnace makes about 750 tons of iron castings annually, and employs about 60 hands, who, with their families, make a population of near 400 souls, requiring from 40 to 50 dwellings; there are about 30,000 acres of land appurtenant to these works.

Martinsville post-office, Somerset co., 203 miles N. E. from W. C., and 37 from Trenton.

Matchaponix Brook, fine mill stream, which has its source in Upper Freehold t-ship, Monmouth co., and flows about 10 miles N. W. by Englishtown, through South Amboy t-ship, to its recipient, the South river, near Spotswood.

Matouchin, p-t. of Woodbridge t-ship, Middlesex co., at the intersection of the turnpike roads leading, one from New Brunswick to Elizabethtown, and the other from Perth Amboy towards Bound Brook, 5 miles from New Brunswick, 6 miles from Perth Amboy, 31 from Trenton, and 198 from W. C.; contains a Presbyterian church, store, 2 taverns, and 10 or 12 dwellings, surrounded by a fertile country of red shale.

Mattison's Corner, post-office Hunterdon co., by post-route 185 miles from W. C., and 26 from Trenton.

Mauricetown, p-t. on Maurice river, 10 or 12 miles from its mouth, 87 miles S. of Trenton, 18 from Bridgeton, and 184 from W. C.; contains some 20 dwellings, store, tavern, an academy, and Methodist church. The town is handsomely situated upon a high belt of rich land, and some of the dwellings are of brick, very neat and pleasant, and surrounded by valuable meadows.

Maurice River t-ship, Cumberland co., bounded N. by Hamilton t-ship, Gloucester co., E. by Weymouth t-ship, of same co., S. by Upper and Dennis t-ships, of Cape May co., and by the Delaware bay, and W. by Maurice river, from its source to its mouth, separating it from Downe and Milleville t-ships, Cumberland co. Centrally distant S. E. from Bridgeton, 20 miles; greatest length 19, breadth 11 miles; area, 79,360 acres; surface, level; soil, generally sandy except along the margin of the creeks, where loam and clay prevail. It is drained E. by Tuckahoe creek and its tributaries, and S. by Tarkill creek. Population in 1830, 2724. In 1832, there were in the t-ship 525 taxables, 117 householders, whose ratables did not exceed $30 ; 11 stores, 6 pairs of stones for grinding grain, 1 blast furnace and forge, 6 saw mills, 2 glass manufactories, 1 at Port Elizabeth, and the other at Marshallville, or Cumberland Works, 295 horses, and 1810 neat cattle, above 3 years old; there are some very valuable meadows on Maurice river, commencing 5 miles from the mouth, and extending nearly to Milleville, 15 miles. Port Elizabeth, Bricksboro', Dorchester, Leesburg, and Marshallville, are villages of the t-ship; all, except the last, upon or near the east bank of Maurice river, and the last upon Tuckahoe creek.

Maurice River, Prince, rises by several small branches in Deptford and Franklin t-ships, Gloucester co., which uniting above Fork Bridge on the line between the S. E. boundary of Salem co. and Cumberland co., form a considerable stream, which there gives motion to several mills. About 8 miles below this point, the river receives from Salem co. a large tributary, called Muddy run, above the head of the dam of the Milleville works. From this dam, which checks the whole river, a canal of near 3 miles in length, supplies the works at Milleville. From this town the river is navigable for 20 miles to the bay, for vessels of 80 or 100 tons, and to within 5 miles of its mouth, its shores are lined with valuable embanked meadows. It receives in its course a number of considerable tributaries, on either hand. The oysters taken at the mouth of this river, are famed for their excellent quality.

Maul's Bridge, over the Maurice river, between Salem and Cumberland counties.

May's Landing, p-t. of Hamilton t-ship, Gloucester co., upon the Great Egg Harbour river, at the head of sloop navigation, 16 miles from the sea, 35 miles S. E. from Woodbury, 73 from Trenton, and 181 N. E. from W. C.; built on both sides of the river, including the village of Hamilton, and contains 3 taverns, 4 stores, a Methodist church, and 25 or 30 dwellings; a considerable trade in cord-wood, lumber, and ship building, is carried on at this place.

Mead's Basin, post-office, Bergen co., 240 miles from W. C., and 74 from Trenton, N. E.

Meekendam Creek, small tributary of Little Egg Harbour river, uniting with it about 4 miles below Pleasant Mills.

Mechescalaxin Creek, tributary of Atsion river, rises in Hereford t-ship, Gloucester co., and by a course of 13 miles S. E., unites with Atsion river, near Pleasant Mills, in Galloway t-ship.

Medford, p-t. Eveham t-ship, Burlington co., on Haines' creek, 7 miles S. W. from Mount Holly, 16 miles E. from Camden, 29 S. E. from Trenton, and 154 N. E. from W. C.;

contains a large Quaker meeting house, 2 taverns, 4 stores, and from 30 to 40 dwellings, surrounded by a pleasant fertile country.

Mendham t-ship, Morris co., bounded N. by Randolph, E. by Morris, S. by Bernard, and Bedminster t-ships, of Somerset co., and W. by Chester co. Centrally distant, W. from Morristown, 7 miles; greatest length, E. and W. 6; breadth, N. and S. 4½ miles; area, 14,000 acres; surface generally hilly, and on the N. mountainous; soil clay, loam and grey limestone; the last fertile and well cultivated; drained southwardly, by arms of the north branch of the Raritan, and E. by Whippany river. Mendham is the post-town. Population in 1830, 1314. In 1832, the township contained 270 taxables, 48 householders, whose ratables did not exceed $30; 30 single men, 5 stores, 4 saw mills, 3 grist mills, 1 cotton manufactory, 2 fulling mills, 2 wool carding machines, 26 tan vats, 7 distilleries and 1 forge, 273 horses and 686 neat cattle, above the age of three years; and paid state tax, $176 03; county tax, 394 12; poor tax, $250; road tax, $800. Sulphur was reported to be found, in this township, in large quantities, during the revolutionary war.

Mendham, p-t. of the preceding township, on the Morris and Easton turnpike-road, 6 miles W. of the former, 221 N. E. from W. C., and 55 from Trenton; contains a Presbyterian church, a boarding school for boys, in much repute, under the care of Mr. Fairchild, 1 grist mill, 1 tavern, three stores, and between 40 and 50 dwellings. Circumjacent country rolling, soil limestone, well cultivated and fertile.

Merritt's Branch of Pohatcong Creek, rises in Oxford t-ship, Warren co. and flows S. through Greenwich township, to its recipient, having a course of about 7 miles.

Metetecunk River, Monmouth co., rises by two branches, the N. and S. in Freehold township, and flowing S. E. about 16 miles, uniting in the pond of Butcher's works, on the line of Dover and Howell townships, about 4 miles above the north end of Barnegat bay, into which the river empties. Each branch gives motion to several mills. The main river is navigable to Butcher's works.

Middle t-ship, Cape May co., bounded N. by Dennis' creek t-ship, E. by the Atlantic ocean, S. by Lower t-ship, and W. by the Delaware bay; greatest length, N. and S. 12, breadth, 10 miles; area, 60,000 acres; surface, level; soil, sand and marsh; Dennis' creek runs on the N. W. border of the township; Leaming's and Seven Mile beaches lie on the Atlantic, between which, is Hereford's inlet, admitting the sea to the marshes and lagunes, which extend westerly, for about four miles. On the bay there is also, a strip of marsh from half a mile to two miles in width, through which flow Goshen, Dyer's, Green and Fishing creeks. The interval land between the marshes, is a stiff clay, covered with oak forest, through which are interspersed some arable lands. The population is chiefly seated along the edge of the marshes, and consisted, in 1830, of 1366 souls. In 1832, the township contained about 320 taxables, 207 householders, whose ratables did not exceed $30; 1 grist mill, 3 saw mills, 218 horses, 650 neat cattle over 3 years of age, 8 stores, and paid township taxes, $101 3; county do. $630 47; and state tax, $203 53. There are two villages in the township; one at Cape May Court House, and the other called Goshen.

Middle Run, Weymouth t-ship, Gloucester co., a marsh creek, which empties into Great Egg Harbour bay.

Middlebrook, Warren and Bridgewater t-ships, Somerset co., rises in and flows through a mountain valley by a S. W. and S. course of about 9 miles, and emptying into the Raritan near the village of Middlebrook in the latter township.

Middlebrook, village. See ***Bound Brook***.

Middlesex co., was first erected by an act of Assembly under the proprietary government in 1682. Its boundaries have been settled by the acts of 1709, 1713 and 1790. It is now bounded N. by Essex county; N. E. by Arthur's Kill or Staten Island Sound; E. by Raritan bay; S. E. by Monmouth county; S. W. by Burlington, and Huntingdon counties; and W. and N. W. by Somerset county; greatest length, N. E. and S. W. 35 miles; greatest breadth, 17 miles; area, in acres, 21,700, or about 339 square miles. Central lat. 40° 25′ N.; long. from W. C. 2° 34′ east.

Geologically considered, the county is based upon the primitive and old red sandstone formations. The former is, in many places, covered by the latter, and appears most conspicuously in the S. W. portion of the county. The red and grey freestone from the quarries of West Windsor township, S. E. of Princeton, and the redstone near New Brunswick, and in many other parts of the county, are admirably adapted for, and have been extensively used in building; the former especially in the locks of the Delaware and Raritan canal. The sand of this stone is mingled in various portions with other constituents of the soil, forming in some places, deep sand, in others, loam, of diverse consistence, from the light sandy, to the heavy clay. Generally, however, the soil is of improvable quality, and is in many places highly cultivated. The surface is as various as the soil; on the S. E. it is generally level, and on the N. and N. E. is undulating, but cannot any where be deemed hilly; except at the sand hills, a few miles E. of Kingston.

Copper ore is found in the red sandstone near New Brunswick. Mines were opened and worked many years ago, but all operations therein have long been suspended.

The river Raritan divides the county into two unequal parts, flowing by a general but serpentine easterly course of 12 or 14 miles through it, into the Raritan bay; receiving from the south, Lawrence's brook and the South river, whose many branches water the country on the S. E.; and from the N. some inconsiderable tributaries. The Millstone river crosses the S. W. portion of the county in a N. W. direction, and is divided from the Assunpink creek, by a neck of land from four to five miles wide. The one, bending to the north, seeks the Raritan river, in Somerset county; and the other turning to the S. W. runs to the Delaware, on the line between Burlington and Hunterdon counties. The Rahway river courses the N. E. line, and Greenbrook the N. W. boundary, both of which receive tribute from the county. The bay of the Raritan affords an excellent harbour, communicating at all times by a single tide, with the ocean; and by Staten Island Sound, with the bay of New York.

Perth Amboy was originally the seat of justice of the county, which has long since been removed to the city of New Brunswick.

Besides these cities, the county contains the following towns, viz. Bridgetown, Samptown, Brooklyn, New Market, New Durham, Woodbridge, Matouchin, Bonhamtown, Piscataway, Washington, Old Bridge, Spotswood, Kingston, Princeton, Williamsburg, Cranberry, Hightstown, Millford, Edinburg, Centreville, &c.

A turnpike road from Trenton runs by Princeton, along the western boundary of the county, to New Brunswick; and thence a like road passes to New York; a second runs from Trenton, by a straight line, N. W., to New Brunswick; and a third from Bordentown to Amboy, which last two places are also connected by the Bordentown and Amboy rail-road. The New Jersey rail-road, now in progress, will unite the cities of Jersey and New Brunswick. The Delaware and Raritan canal runs a very considerable distance through the county, and communicates with the Raritan at New Brunswick.

The population, by the census of 1830, was 23,157: of whom 10,523 were white males; 10,487 white females; 904 free coloured males; 914 free coloured females; 130 male slaves; 179 female slaves; 174 aliens; 12 whites, deaf and dumb, 7 blind, and 3 blacks blind.

The business of the county is chiefly agricultural, but considerable trade is carried on from New Brunswick. In 1832 the county contained about 4500 taxables, 841 householders, whose ratables did not exceed $30; 477 single men, 99 stores, 20 saw mills, 42 run of stones for grinding grain, 2 plaster mills, 2 woollen factories, 7 carding machines, 39 distilleries, and 3684 horses and mules, and 7675 neat cattle over 3 years of age; and it paid state tax, $3253 26; county, $4000; poor, $5850; road, 3600.

The provisions for moral improvement, in the county, consist of the following religious associations: viz. Presbyterian, Episcopalian, Baptist, Seventh-day Baptist, Dutch Reformed, and Methodist; one college, and one theological institution belonging to Presbyterians, several academies and boarding schools, at Princeton; a college and theological seminary pertaining to the Dutch Reformed, a grammar school, and other schools, at New Brunswick; two academies at Rahway, and common schools, at which the rudiments of an English education are given in every populous vicinity; a county bible society, Sunday schools, in almost every village, and temperance societies which are spreading over the county.

The public buildings in addition to the churches and seats of literature, consist of the court-house, public offices, and prison, at New Brunswick.

The following are post-towns of the county: Amboy, Cranberry, Hightstown, Kingston, New Brunswick, New Market, Rahway, Six Mile Run, South or Washington, Spotswood, and Woodbridge.

STATISTICAL TABLE OF MIDDLESEX COUNTY.

Townships, &c.	Length.	Breadth.	Area.	Surface.	Population.		
					1810.	1820.	1830.
Perth Amboy,			2,577	rolling.	815	798	879
South Amboy,	18	6	64,000	partly rolling.	3071	3406	3782
North Brunswick,	9	7	23,000	level.	3980	4275	5274
South Brunswick,	10	7	36,000	do.	2332	2489	2557
East Windsor,	12	6	24,000	do.	1747	1710	1903
West Windsor,	7	5	19,000	do.	1714	1918	2129
Piscataway,	9	7½	27,000	do.	2475	2648	2664
Woodbridge,	9	9	24,000	do.	4247	4226	3969
			219,577		20,381	21,470	23,157

Middletown t-ship, Monmouth co., bounded N. by Raritan bay and Sandy Hook, E. by the Atlantic ocean, S. by Shrewsbury t-ship, and W. by South Amboy t-ship, Middlesex co. Centrally distant N. E. from Freehold 10 miles; greatest length E. and W. 16, breadth N. and S. 10 miles; area, 50,000 acres; surface, on the east and centre, hilly, elsewhere, level; soil, loam, sand, and clay, not naturally of the first quality, but highly improved, in places, by the use of marl, which has become common. Sandy Hook bay runs south into the t-ship from the Raritan, and is bounded on the S. W. by the promontory of the highlands of Nevisink, and on the E. by the sand beach, forming Sandy Hook, running 6 miles north from Shrewsbury Inlet; upon the north point of which stands Sandy Hook Light-house. The t-ship is drained on the S. E., S. and S. W. by Swimming and Nevisink rivers; on the N. W. by Middletown creek; N. by Waycake, and N. E. by Watson's and Shoal Harbour creeks. Middletown, Middletown Point, Baptisttown, or Holmdel and Mount Pleasant are villages, the two first post-towns, of the t-ship. Population in 1830, 5128. In 1832 the t-ship contained about 1000 taxables, 277 householders, whose ratables did not exceed $30; 169 single men, 27 stores, 5 saw mills, 13 run of stones for grinding grain, 1 fulling mill, 36 tan vats, 11 distilleries, 956 horses and mules, and 2286 neat cattle, above 3 years of age; and paid state and county taxes, $2620 20. Good lands will bring in this t-ship an average price of $60 the acre.

In 1682 Middletown contained about 100 families; several thousand acres had been collected for the town, and many thousand for out-plantations. John Browne, Richard Hartshorne, and Nicholas Davis, had well improved settlements here; and a court of sessions was holden twice or thrice a year, for Middletown, Piscataway and their jurisdictions.

Middletown, post-town of Middletown t-ship, Monmouth co., 13 miles N. E. from Freehold, 56 from Trenton, and 221 from W. C., situate in a rolling and fertile country, based on marl; contains an Episcopal, a Dutch Reformed, and a Baptist church, 2 stores, 2 taverns, and from 20 to 25 dwellings, among which, there are several very neat and commodious.

Middletown Point, port of delivery of Perth Amboy district, and post-town of Middletown t-ship, Monmouth co., upon Middletown creek, about 3 miles from the Raritan bay, 11 miles N. of Freehold, 47 N. E. from Trenton, and 213 from W. C.; lies on a bank elevated about 50 feet above the stream, fronting a marsh on the opposite side; contains a Presbyterian church, from 75 to 100 dwellings, many of which are very good buildings, 8 or 10 stores, 4 taverns, and a grist mill. This is the market of an extensive country, and large quantities of pork, rye, corn, cord wood, and garden truck, are thence sent to New York. The soil immediately around the town is sandy. There is a bank here, incorporated in 1830, with a capital of $50,000, of which $10,000 only were paid in, in 1833.

Middleville, Orange t-ship, Essex co., 5 miles S. W. of Newark, contains a tavern, a store, a grist mill, saw mill, and Universalist church.

Mill Brook, a small stream of Montague t-ship, Sussex co., flowing N. E., a course of about 6 miles, to the Nevisink river, in the state of New York, about 1 mile north of the boundary, giving motion to several grist, and other mills.

Mill Creek, a tributary of Cohansey creek, flowing southward into it, and forming the S. W. boundary of Greenwich t-ship, Salem co.; length between 3 and 4 miles.

Mill Creek, another tributary of Cohansey creek, rising in Fairfield t-ship, Cumberland co., and flowing S. W. about 4 miles, by the village of Fairton, to its recipient, giving motion to two mills.

Millford, E. Windsor t-ship, Middlesex co., on Rocky Brook, 17 miles S. W. from New Brunswick, on Rocky Brook; contains a Presbyterian church, a grist mill, and some 10 or 12 farm houses, and dwellings of mechanics. Soil light, and not productive.

Millford, village of Alexandria t-ship, Hunterdon co., on the river Delaware, at the confluence of a small creek with that stream, 13 miles N. W. from Flemington, and 40 from Trenton; contains a tavern, store, grist mill, 2 saw mills, and from 15 to 20 dwellings, a Presbyterian church, and a church of Unitarians, which styles itself ***Christian***, and which admits females to participate in the ministry. This is a place of considerable business, particularly in the lumber trade.

Millhill, village of Nottingham t-ship, Burlington co., on the S. side of the Assunpink creek; contains 2 cotton manufactories, several taverns and stores, a market house, and about 80 dwellings. (See *Trenton*, of which it is a suburb.)

Millington, post-office, Somerset co., 219 miles N. E. from W. C., and 48 from Trenton.

Millstone River, rises near Paint Island spring, Upper Freehold t-ship, Monmouth co., and flows thence by a N. course of about 5 miles, to the line between Monmouth and Middlesex cos.; thence N. W. 13 or 14 miles, through Middlesex to the mouth of Stony Brook, thence N. E. by Kingston, into Somerset co., 16 miles to the river Raritan. It is a strong and rapid stream, receiving the waters of an extensive country, including that drained by Stony Brook; and runs, in many places, through very narrow valleys, and consequently is subject to sudden and great overflows. The Delaware and Raritan canal enters the valley of this river, with Stony Brook, and follows it to the Raritan. The whole length of the Millstone may be about 35 miles, by comparative courses.

Millstone, post-town of Hillsborough t-ship, Somerset co., on the left bank of the Millstone river, 194 miles N. E. of W. C., 28 from Trenton, 5 S. of Somerville; contains 2 taverns, 3 stores, a Dutch Reformed church, and between 30 and 40 dwellings, in a level, fertile, red shale country. Some of the dwellings are very neat and commodious.

Milltown, a small village in the southern part of Kingwood t-ship, Hunterdon co., on the Laokatong creek, 10 miles S. W. from Flemington; contains a mill, store, and 8 or 10 dwellings.

Millville t-ship Cumberland co., bounded N. by Gloucester and Salem cos., and by Deptford t-ship, S. E. by Maurice River t-ship, S. by Downe, and W. by Fairfield t-ships. Centrally distant E. from Bridgeton, 12 miles; length N. and S. 16 miles; breadth E. and W. 15; area, 73,000 acres; surface, level; soil sandy, and generally not very productive. It is drained by Maurice river and its tributaries, of which Manantico creek is here the chief. Millville and Buckshutem, are towns of the t-ship; the first a post-town. Population in 1830, 1561. In 1832, there were in the t-ship 349 taxables, 136 householders, whose ratables did not exceed $30; 7 stores, 6 run of stones for grinding grain, 1 carding machine, 1 blast furnace, 8 saw mills, 2 glass manufactories; and it paid road tax, $800, and county and state tax, $553 58.

Millville, p-t. of Millville t-ship, Cumberland co., on the left bank of Maurice river, 20 miles from its mouth, 11 miles S. E. of Bridgeton, 79 from Trenton, and 176 N. E. from W. C.; contains about 60 dwellings, 2 taverns, 4 or 5 stores, a furnace belonging to Mr. D. C. Wood, and extensive glass works belonging to Messrs. Burgin and Pearsall; consisting of 2 factories, 1 containing an 8, and the other a 7 pot furnace, employed chiefly in the manufacture of bottles, demijohns, carboys, and the various kinds of vials used by druggists and apothecaries, giving employment to from 75 to 100 workmen. The town lies near the head of sloop navigation.

Milton, post-town of Morris co., 242 miles N. E. from W. C., and 79 from Trenton, and 15 N. of Somerville.

Minisink Island, formed by the Delaware river, and making the extreme S. W. part of Montague t-ship, Sussex co.

Mine Mountain, composed of trap rock, Bernard t-ship, Somerset co., extends from the north branch of the Raritan, 6 miles to the Passaic river, and is intersected by tributaries of the respective rivers; the chief of which is

Mine Brook, rising near Logtown, on the summit of the mountain, and running 6 miles S. W. to the north branch of the Raritan. It is a mill stream of great fall, and studded with mills.

Miry Run, tributary of the Assunpink creek, rises in East Windsor t-ship, Middlesex co., and flows N. W. through Nottingham t-ship, Burlington co., by a course of 8 miles, giving motion to several mills.

Miry Run, small stream of Egg Harbour t-ship, Gloucester co., flowing westerly about 3 miles to the Great Egg Harbour river, having a mill at its mouth.

Monroe, p-t. Hardiston t-ship, Sussex co., at the cross-roads N. W. of Pimple Hill, 236 miles from W. C., 78 from Trenton, and 9 from Newton; contains a mill, store, and several dwellings. It is surrounded by soil of primitive limestone.

Monroe, village of Hanover t-ship, Morris co., near the Whippany river, 3 miles N. E. of Morristown; contains a store, 5 or 6 dwellings, and an extensive paper mill. It is surrounded by soil of loam and gravel, well cultivated.

Monmouth County; the bounds of this county were established by the Acts of 21st January, 1709-10, and 15th march, 1713-14; and it is now limited on the N. by Raritan bay; E. and S. E. by the Atlantic ocean; S. W. and W. by Burlington co.; and N. W. by Middlesex; greatest length 65, breadth 33 miles; area, 665,000 acres, or about 1030 square miles. Central lat. 40° 5′ N., long. from W. C. 2° 42′ E. The whole country belongs to the alluvial formation, and consists of clay mingled with sand, gravel, and in low places vegetable mould. In many parts there are large beds of marl, varying in quality from that composed almost altogether of shells, already highly indurated, to that of blue clay and sand, in which the shells are finely broken and sparsely strewed. In the N. part of the county, marl is generally used as manure, and with the greatest advantage. It has restored many tracts of worn-out land to fertility, and preserved much more from exhaustion and abandonment.

The surface of the county, except in Middletown t-ship, is generally level, and a large portion of it covered with pine forest; N. of Manasquan inlet the sea-coast is high, bold, and clean; S. of that channel commences a series of sand beaches, formed into islands, by Barnegat and Little Egg Harbour inlets, having a width, varying from half a mile to a mile, and which extend in this county to Little Egg Harbour inlet, a distance, southwardly of full 40 miles. Behind the beach, a bayou, continues, nominally divided into two, under the names of Little Egg Harbour, and Barnegat bays, which also varies much in width, being from ½ a mile to 4 miles broad; with a broad border of salt marsh, on the west.

The county is well watered, by many small streams, most of which flow E., to the ocean. The principal of these are Manasquan, Metetecunk, Kettle, Cedar, Oyster, Manahocking, and Westecunk creeks, Nevisink, Shrewsbury, Toms', and Forked rivers. From the N. the Millstone and South rivers flow to the Raritan, and the W. sends forth the Assunpink, the Crosswick's, and the Rancocus, tributaries of the Delaware.

The post-towns of the county are, Allentown, Barnegat, Cedar Creek, Colts' Neck, Eatontown, Englishtown, Freehold, the seat of justice, Holmdel, Howel Furnace, Manohocking, Manasquan, Middletown, Middletown Point, New Egypt, Shrewsbury, Squankum, and Toms' River. There are several other less considerable villages.

The business of the county is chiefly agricultural, but many persons are employed in cutting and sawing timber, and in preparing and carying cord wood to market, large quantities of which are sent from Toms' river, and large quantities of the finest pork are annually raised for exportation. Iron is also made in the central parts of the county, at Phœnix, Dover, and other furnaces.

The population, originally composed of a few Dutch, and some New England men, who removed from Long Island, prior to, and about, the year 1664, amounted in 1830, to 29,233: of whom there were, white free males, 13,900; free white females, 13,304; male slaves 97; female slaves, 130; free coloured males, 1794; free coloured females, 978. There were also, 19 deaf and dumb, and 14 blind, of the whites; 1 deaf and dumb, and 1 blind, of the coloured population.

By returns of the assessors of 1832, there were in the county, about 6000 taxables, 1385 householders, whose ratables did not exceed $30; 603 single men, 103 stores, 52 saw mills, 67 run of stones for grinding grain, 6 fulling mills, 17 carding machines, 5 furnaces, 238 tan vats, 46 distilleries for cider, 4942 horses and mules, and 12,068 neat cattle, over the age of 3 years; and it paid county and state taxes, $15,492 80.

STATISTICAL TABLE OF MONMOUTH COUNTY.

Townships, &c.	Length.	Breadth.	Area.	Surface.	Population.		
					1810.	1820.	1830.
Dover,	24	22	200,000	level.	1882	1916	2898
Upper Freehold,	16	10	90,000	do.	3843	4541	4826
Lower Freehold,	23	11	104,000	do.	4784	5146	5481
Howell,	13	11	70,000	do.	2780	3354	4141
Middletown,	16	10	50,000	part hilly.	3849	4369	5128
Shrewsbury,	13	13	64,000	do.	3773	4284	4700
Stafford,	18	12	87,000	do.	1239	1428	2059
			665,000		22,150	25,038	29,233

Montague, N. W. t-ship of Sussex co., bounded on the N. E. by the state of New York, S. E. by the Blue mountains, S. W. by Sandistone t-ship, and on the N. W. by the river Delaware. Centrally distant from Newton, 16 miles; greatest length 8½, breadth 7½ miles; area, 21,620 acres; surface on the S. E. mountainous, on the N. W. line, river alluvion. Population in 1830, 990. There were in the t-ship in 1832, 85 householders, whose ratables did not exceed $30; 6 store keepers, 3 pair of mill stones, 3 saw mills, 208 horses and mules above 3 years old, 843 neat cattle, above that age; 11 tan vats, 1 distillery. The t-ship paid a school tax of $150; state and county tax, $364 89; poor tax, 100; and road tax, $500. It is drained N. E. by Mill brook, W. by Chamber's Mill brook, and S. W. by Big and Little Flat Kills. There is a post-office here, bearing the name of the t-ship; distant 245 miles from W. C., 87 from Trenton, and 17 from Newton. Two turnpike roads run through the t-ship, and unite at the Delaware, opposite Milford bridge; this bridge, completed in 1826, cost $20,000. Between the Blue mountain and Delaware river, the space is six miles, through which runs a vein of transition limestone, bordered by an extensive river flat. The soil is fertile and well cultivated, producing much wheat. The t-ship was originally settled by the Dutch, some years prior to 1680.

Montgomery t-ship, Somerset co., bounded N. by Hillsborough, E. and S. E. by Millstone river, which separates it from Franklin t-ship, W. by Lawrence and Hopewell t-ships, Hunterdon co. Centrally distant S. W. from Somerville 12 miles; greatest length N. and S. 8, breadth E. and W. 8 miles; area, 36,500 acres; surface, hilly; soil, clay, sandy loam, and red shale. Beden's Brook and its tributaries, Rock, Pike, and Nopipe Brooks flow eastwardly through the t-ship to the Millstone river, and Stony Brook crosses the S. W. angle. Rock mountain or the Nashanic, forms the N. W. angle, and Rocky hill spreads itself over the south. Princeton, the northern side of the main street, Rocky Hill, Stoutsville, Harlingen, and Plainville, are towns of the t-ship. Population in 1830, 2834. In 1832 the t-ship contained about 600 taxables, 170 householders, whose ratables did not exceed $30; and 66 single men, 15 stores, 5 saw mills, 5 grist mills, 1 fulling mill, 54 tan vats, 5 distilleries, 743 horses and mules, 1295 neat cattle, 3 years old and upwards; and paid state tax, $352 72; county tax, $900 94.

Montville, village of Pequannock t-ship, Morris co., lying in a deep valley, through which passes the Morris canal, by two inclined planes; the town lies between 10 and 11 miles N. E. from Morristown, and contains a grist mill, saw mill, 2 stores, 1 tavern, and from 10 to 15 dwellings, and a Dutch Reformed church.

Moorestown, p-t., Chester t-ship, Burlington co., on the great road from Camden to Monmouth, 10 miles from the former, and 8 S. W. of Mount Holly, 30 miles from Trenton, and 147 from W. C. This is a very pleasant town, situated on a fertile plain of sandy loam, extremely well cultivated, near the north branch of Pensauken creek; contains a large Quaker meeting house, a Methodist church, a school, 3 taverns, 4 or 5 stores, and between 50 and 60 dwellings, most of which are neat and commodious, some large and elegant. The town has communication by stages, daily, with Camden and Mount Holly.

Morris County, was taken from Hunterdon, by act of Assembly of 15th March, 1738-9, directing that the portion of "said county lying to the northward and eastward of a well known place, being a fall of water, in part of the north branch of the Raritan, called in the Indian language Allamatonck, to the north-eastward of the north-east end of the lands called the New Jersey Society Lands, along the line thereof, crossing the south branch of the said river, and extending westerly to a certain tree marked with the letters L M, standing on the north side of a brook emptying itself into the said south branch, by an old Indian path to the northward of a line to be run northwest from the said tree to a branch of Delaware river called Musconetcong, and so down the said branch to Delaware river." It was named from Lewis Morris, then Governor of the province. These ample limits were contracted by the erection of Sussex county, 8th June, 1753, from which Warren was subsequently taken. Morris county is now bounded on the N. W. by Sussex, N. E. by Bergen, E. and S. E. by Essex, S. by Somerset, S. W. by Hunterdon, and W. by Warren. Greatest length N. E. and S. W. about 30 miles; breadth 27 miles; area, 292,900 acres; central latitude 40° 53′ N.; longitude 2° 28″ E. from W. C.

The county is divided between the transition and primitive formations, two-thirds of it on the south being of the latter, but even in it, the primitive appears in the hills as in the Trowbridge mountain, and the ridge on the north-west of Morristown. The transition also appears in the range most generally primitive, as in the grauwacke of the Copperas mountain, and the grey limestone at its southern base; a bed of which, probably, underlays the country from Potter's Falls on the S. W., to Charlottesburg on the N. E., upon Pequannock creek. Trap rocks are scattered over the county in various places, as in the Pompton Hills, Long Hill, and elsewhere.

The northern portion of the county is mountainous and divided into several ridges, whose continuity is broken as they extend south and east. Schooley's, or the Hamburg mountain, which is a continuation of the Musconetcong, continues in an unbroken mass across the county, varying from three to six miles in width. On the north-east, longitudinal divisions are formed by the branches of Rockaway river, in the Green Pond and Copperas mountains; whilst Pequannock t-ship is covered with short ridges and rounded knolls. The Trowbridge mountain is a considerable eminence near the centre of the county, varying in breadth from one to three miles, and having a length of fifteen miles. South and east of this ridge the county is level, or at most, undulating with a soil in which red shale predominates; it may be deemed the valley of the Passaic. On the south-east border of the county, however, rises another hill, around whose western extremity the Passaic turns, to follow its base north-eastwardly.

The county is rich in iron ore, and we believe that the great bed of red oxide of zinc, found in the Hamburg mountain near Sparta, in the adjacent county, extends into this. Iron ore is indeed here very abundant. and is chiefly of the magnetic character. The great bed first worked in Franconia, near the White Hills in New Hampshire, extends in the direction of the stratification, into this county, and which is said by Mr. M'Clure, to lose itself near Blackwater; but which most probably extends indefinitely S. W.; since iron of the same character is abundant near the spring at Schooley's mountain. The mine of the Hon. Mr. Dickerson, on the head waters of the Black river, is one of the best and most extensively wrought of the district. (See Randolph t-ship.)

The county is abundantly watered; a line drawn almost due south and north from the village of Mendham, to Drakesville, determines the course of the streams east and west. Thus the Rockaway with its tributaries, the Parcippany and Whippany rivers, seek the first; whilst the tributaries of the north and south branches of the Raritan river, have a westerly inclination. The Passaic river has its source in a swamp near the village of Mendham, and forms a natural boundary between this and the county of Somerset on the south, and the county of Essex on the S. E., receiving the Rockaway west of the village of Franklin, and the Pequannock, or Pompton river, north of the village of Fairfield. The last stream forms the N. E. boundary of the county, separating it from Bergen.

The chief villages and post-towns of the county are Berkshire Valley, Bottle Hill, Chatham, Chester, Denville, Dover, Flanders, Hanover, Hanover Neck, Littleton, Mendham, Milton, Montville, Morristown, the seat of justice, Mount Freedom, Newfoundland, New Vernon, Parsippany, Pompton, Powerville, Rockaway, Schooley's Mountain, Stockholm, Suckasunny, Washington, &c.

The provisions for moral improvement in the county, consist in churches of the Presbyterians, the Dutch Reformed, the Methodists, and the Episcopalians; a county Bible Society, a county Sunday school union, and several Sunday schools and temperance societies in various parts of the county; several academies in the larger villages, where the rudiments of the classics and mathematics are taught, and common English schools in almost every vicinity.

By the census of 1830, the population consisted of 23,666 souls, of whom 10,719 were white males; 1108 white females; 77 male slaves; 88 female slaves; 438 free coloured males; 364 coloured free females: and of whom there were 20 whites, and 4 blacks, deaf and dumb; 11 whites, and 1 black, blind; and 497 aliens.

In 1832, the county contained 4836 taxables, 1083 householders, whose ratables did not exceed $30 in value; 528 single men, 83 stores, 71 saw mills, 56 grist mills, 215 tan vats, 53 distilleries, 5 paper mills, 5 four horse stages, 43 forges and 2 furnaces, 9 rolling and slitting mills,

12 fulling mills, 11 carding machines, 1 plaster mill and 6 cotton mills, 4056 horses and mules, and 11,821 neat cattle, above 3 years old; and it paid state tax, $3171 23; county tax, $7100; poor tax, $10,900.

The courts of common pleas, orphans' court, and quarter sessions, are holden at Morristown, on the following Tuesdays; 3d December, 3d March, 1st July, and 4th September; and the circuit courts, on the 3d Tuesdays in March, and 4th of September.

This county abounds with copper, iron, zinc, plumbago, copperas, manganese, ochres of various colours, excellent brick clay, freestone, limestone, precious marbles, oil stone, &c. &c. With such metallic resources, the pioneers in the settlement of this portion of New Jersey, were rather manufacturers than agriculturists; and the narrow valleys of the mountain region, which contain many and excellent mill seats, were only partially tilled for the subsistence of wood cutters and bloomers. The forge was uniformly the precursor of the farm. The iron master occupied large tracts of land, which, when stripped of timber, were subdivided among agricultural successors, operating on the smallest scale. As the country was cleared, the makers of iron gradually retired to the remote, rough, and almost inaccessible regions, where the cost of transportation of the ores, and of the metal to market, rendered their operations very unprofitable. Relief in this respect will be obtained from the completion of the Morris canal, which has been created in a great measure with that view.

A region abounding so much in metallic ores, necessarily produces mineral springs; but that of Schooley's mountain, is the only one which has yet attained celebrity. A few years since, the county was famed for its apple orchards, its cider, and apple whiskey; of the last, large quantities were annually made for market. The annual average product of the Morris orchards was estimated at 800,000 bushels. But a succession of bad crops, for some years, has discouraged the cultivation. Few new orchards are planted, and the old ones are frequently neglected. Attempts have been made to cultivate the foreign grape upon the hill sides, but without success, the frosts proving too severe. It is possible that some indigenous qualities might be planted with profit.

STATISTICAL TABLE OF MORRIS COUNTY.

Townships.	Length.	Breadth.	Area.	Surface.	Population.		
					1810.	1820.	1830.
Chatham,	9	5	13,400	various.	2019	1832	1865
Chester,	9	6½	18,000	rolling.	1175	1212	1338
Jefferson,	14	3	25,000	mountainous.	1281	1231	1551
Hanover,	12	9½	35,000	various.	3843	3503	3718
Mendham,	6	4½	14,000	do.	1277	1326	1314
Morris,	13	6	33,000	hilly.	3753	3524	3536
Pequannock,	16	11	74,000	mountainous.	3853	3820	4451
Roxbury,	12	10	35,000	do.	1563	1792	2262
Randolph,	7	5	18,000	do.	1271	1252	1443
Washington,	8	7½	27,500	do.	1793	1876	2188
			292,900		21,828	21,368	23,666

Morris t-ship, Morris co., bounded N. and N. E. by Hanover t-ship; E. by Chatham; S. E. by New Providence t-ship, of Bergen co.; S. and S. W. by Somerset co.; and W. by Mendham and Randolph t-ships, Morris co. Greatest length N. and S. 13 miles; breadth E. and W. 6 miles; surface, on the north, centre, and south, hilly; elsewhere, generally rolling, with occasional plains; soil, clay and sandy loam; drained on the W. and S. by the Passaic river (and its tributaries) which courses its boundary; and on the N. E. by the Whippany river. The Elizabethtown and Morris, Newark and Morris, Morris and Easton, Morris and Milford turnpike roads cross the t-ship. Morristown, Logansville, New Vernon, Morris's Plains, are villages of the t-ship. Morristown is the seat of justice for the county. Population in 1830, 3536. In 1832 there were in the t-ship 780 taxables, 21 stores, 6 saw mills, 4 grist mills, 11 distilleries, 1 paper mill, 1 fulling mill, 1 carding machine, and 546 horses, and 1674 neat cattle, above the age of 3 years. The t-ship paid state tax, 558 85; county tax, 1251 19; poor tax, $600; and road tax, $2000.

Morristown, Morris t-ship, post-town and seat of justice of Morris co., on the Whippany river, by post-route 221 miles N. E. of W. C., 71 from Trenton, 17 from Newark and Elizabethtown, and 26 from New York; pleasantly seated on a high plain, built upon several streets, with a large area or public ground in the centre of the town; on which, front the Presbyterian church, many of the best houses, and most of the places of business. The town contains 1 Presbyterian, 1 Episcopalian, 1 Baptist, and 1 Methodist church; an academy in which the classics and mathematics are taught; a very large and handsome court-house, newly built of brick, with the prison in the basement story; a grist mill, saw mill, and 2 paper mills; a bank with a capital of $50,000, which may be extended to $100,000, incorporated by act of 28th January, 1812, and continued by act 19th February, 1820; 5 taverns, 18 stores, 4 practising attorneys, and 3 physicians, 2 printing offices, from each of which a weekly newspaper is issued, viz. The Jerseyman and The Palladium of Liberty; a county bible society, Sunday school union, and temperance societies. This is a beautiful town. The houses are generally well built, neatly painted, surrounded with garden plots, and impress upon the visiter the conviction, that comfort at least, reigns here. The town is supplied by water from a fine spring a mile and a half distant, and distributed by subterraneous pipes. A stage runs to Elizabethtown daily; one every other day to Easton and Jersey City, and one to Oswego in New York, three times a week. It was a noted station of the American army during the revolutionary war, and the ruins of a small fort, overgrown by stately trees, still crown the hill which commands the town.

Morris Plains, hamlet and level land, lying S. E. of Trowbridge mountain, with a tolerable soil of sandy loam, watered by a branch of Whippany river. The hamlet is on the line between Morris and Hanover t-ships, 2 miles north of Morristown, and contains a half dozen dwellings.

Moses' Pond, small sheet of water on the Pochuck mountain, Vernon t-ship, Sussex co., which sends forth westerly, an inconsiderable tributary to the Wallkill river.

Mount Bethel, hamlet, on Stony Hill, Warren t-ship, Somerset co., 7 miles N. E. of Somerville; contains a Baptist church, tavern, store, and 4 or 5 dwellings.

Mount Carmel, a mountain hamlet of Amwell t-ship, Hunterdon co., 3 miles N. W. from Flemington; contains a tavern and some 4 or 5 dwellings, and a store. The soil around it is clay, cold, and at present not very productive, but it is improvable by the use of lime.

Mount Clinton,• a village laid out on the Palisade rocks on the North river, in Hackensack t-ship, Bergen co., 5 miles N. E. of Hackensack-town.

Mount's Creek, a small tributary of the Cohansey river, near the S. W. border of Hopewell t-ship, Salem county.

Mount Ephraim, village, of Gloucester t-ship, Gloucester co., 5 miles S. E. from Camden, and the same distance N. E. of Woodbury; contains a store, tavern, and some 20 or 30 dwellings. The hill from which it has its name is, for this country, elevated, and affords an extensive view of the vicinity, even to the Delaware.

Mount Freedom, p-t., Morris co., 227 miles N. E. from W. C., and 61 from Trenton; contains a Presbyterian church, and some 10 or 12 dwellings.

Mount Holly, p-t., Northampton t-ship, and seat of justice of Burlington co., on the road from Camden to Freehold, and at the head of tide and navigation, on the north branch of Rancocus creek, 20 miles N. E. from the city of Camden, 6 S. E. from Burlington, 21 from Trenton, 156 from W. C., and 18 from Philadelphia, has its present name from a mount of sand and sandstone near it, and some holly trees about its base. It was formerly called Bridgetown; and this name was recognised in a charter for a library company here, so early as 1765. At the period of the revolutionary war, the town contained 200 dwellings, and at present, 1833, has not more than 230; many of which are good brick buildings, erected on 7 streets. It contains a court-house of brick, about 40 by 60 ft., two stories high, with cupola and bell; a stone prison, 1 Episcopal, 1 Methodist, 1 Baptist churches, and 2 Quaker meeting houses; 1 boarding school for young ladies, 4 day schools, 5 taverns, 8 stores, 1 grist mill, 1 saw mill, 1 fulling mill, woollen factory, plaster mill, and a paper mill, of the latest and most improved construction, where paper of fine quality is made by machinery, and from 40 to 50 hands are employed.—10,000 reams of paper may be manufactured in this mill yearly. The country around is flat; soil, sandy loam, generally of good quality, well cultivated, and worth from 40 to 120 dollars the acre, in extensive farms; corn, rye, and oats, are the chief products. A bank was established here in 1816, with authority to possess capital to the amount of $200,000; of which $100,000 only have been paid in. There run from the village, 2 stages twice a day to Burlington, 1 to Camden, 1 to Trenton, 1 to Pemberton, 1 to Vincenttown, 1 to New Egypt; and 2 to Manahocking, tri-weekly. There are 2 newspapers printed here, weekly; viz. the Herald, and New Jersey Mail.

Mount Misery, hamlet of Northampton t-ship, Burlington co., 15 miles S. E. from Mount Holly, in the pine forest; contains a tavern, saw mill, and 4 or 5 dwellings.

Mount Pleasant, p-t., Alexandria t-ship, Hunterdon co., 9 miles N. W. from Flemington, 43 from Trenton, and 196 from W. C., on the Hakehokake creek; contains a church, grist mill, store, and some half dozen dwellings.

Mount Pleasant, small village and forge, Pequannock t-ship, Morris co., on the t-ship road leading from Morristown, N. W. 10 miles; there are here a grist mill, and some half dozen houses, and very valuable iron mines, extensively wrought.

Mount Pleasant, village of Middletown t-ship, Monmouth co., on Middletown creek, 10 miles N. of Freehold; contains from 12 to 15 dwellings, a grist mill, a tavern and store. The ground around it is sandy, but high; elevated at least 50 feet above the waters.

Muddy Creek, a small marsh stream of Lower Alloways Creek t-ship, Salem co., which has a course of a mile or two; and empties into the Delaware, between Stow and Deep creeks.

Muddy Run, a branch of the Morris river, running near to, and forming in part, the S. W. boundary of

Pittsgrove t-ship, and the line between Salem and Cumberland cos.

Mud Pond, a small basin in the Wallkill mountains, Vernon t-ship, Sussex co., which sends forth a tributary to the Wallkill river.

Mullica Hill, p-t. and village of Gloucester co., on the line separating Greenwich from Woolwich t-ships, and on Raccoon creek, 7 miles S. E. from Woodbury, and 5 E. from Swedesboro'; 47 S. from Trenton, and 153 N. E. from W. C.; contains a Friends' meeting house, an Episcopal church, 2 taverns, 2 stores, and between 50 and 60 dwellings. The country around the village is much improved by the use of marl which abounds here, and in some places is found in an indurated state, assuming the character of limestone.

Musconetcong Creek, or *River*, issues from the Hopatcong pond, or lake, in Jefferson t-ship, Morris co.; and flows by a course S. W. and nearly straight, through a longitudinal valley of the South mountains, for nearly forty miles. This valley is bounded S. E. by the Musconetcong and Schooley's mountains, and on the N. W. by a southern continuation of the Hamburg hills; it is narrow and deep, and has throughout its whole length a limestone base. The stream has a large volume, and gives motion to a very great number of mills for various purposes.

Musketoe Cove, an arm of Barnegat bay, Dover t-ship, Monmouth co., which makes about two miles inward through the marsh, between Toms' bay and Kettle creek.

Nacote Creek, a tributary of Little Egg Harbour river, rises by two branches, Clark's mill, and Moss branch, which unite at Wrangleboro', in Galloway t-ship, Gloucester co.; the whole length of the stream is about 9 miles.

Nantuxet Creek, said to be more properly called *Antuxet*, Cumberland co., rises on the boundary line between Fairfield and Downe t-ships, and flows along the boundary, about 9 miles to Nantuxet cove, in the Delaware; it is navigable near four miles to Nantuxet, or Newport Landing.

Nantuxet Village. (See *Newport*.)

Nantuxet Cove, inlet to Nantuxet creek, from the Delaware bay.

Nashanic Creek, a tributary of the south branch of the Raritan river, rises by several branches at the foot of a range of hills on the N. W. line of Amwell t-ship, Hunterdon co., and flows by an easterly course to its recipient in Hillsborough t-ship, Somerset co., giving motion to several mills. It is a large stream, and with its several tributaries drains the easterly part of the wide valley between the Nashanic or Rock mountain, and Mount Carmel.

Nashanic Mountain, or *Rock Mountain*, part of the chain of trap hills which extends from below Lambertsville, on the Delaware, to the Raritan river, near Somerville: it is the largest and most prominent of the chain; is about 11 miles long and about 3 miles over at its widest part. Rock brook, a tributary of Beden's brook, almost passes through it.

Nashanic, small stream on the N. W. foot of the Nashanic mountain, 7 miles S. W. from Somerville; contains a Dutch Reformed church, a store and tavern, and 10 or 12 dwellings; soil, clay, sandy loam, and red shale.

Nesochcaque Creek, tributary of Atsion river, rises by several branches in Gloucester, Hereford, and Galloway t-ships, Gloucester co., and unites with the river, at Pleasant Mills, in the last named t-ship.

Nevisink Hills, on the Atlantic coast, and extending across the northern part of the county of Monmouth. Adjacent to the ocean these hills are between 300 and 400 feet high. They consist in the higher strata of sandy earth, coloured by oxide of iron, and imbedding reddish brown sand and pudding stone, cemented by iron, resting on banks of oyster shells and other marine relics, blended with clay and sea mud. A small portion of these hills only, is cultivated, being rough, broken and generally covered with wood. (See *Introductory Chapter*, fol. 1 and 2.)

Nevisink or *Carpenter's Point*, a small neck of land formed by the Delaware and Nevisink rivers, at the extreme northern point of the state.

Nevisink River, called above tide water Swimming river, rises by several branches in Freehold, Shrewsbury, and Middletown t-ships, Monmouth co. The main stream flows about 13 miles to the salt water estuary or arm of Sandy Hook bay; which is about 5 miles long, to the S. E. base of the Nevisink hills, varying in breadth from ¾ to 1½. Swimming river and its north and south branches are mill streams, on which are several mills. The Nevisink is separated from the Shrewsbury river, by a neck of land about 2 miles in breadth.

Newark, p-t., and seat of justice, Newark t-ship, Essex co., on the right bank of the Passaic river, between 4 and 5 miles by the course of the stream from Newark bay, 9 miles a little N. of W. from New York, 215 N. E. from W. C., and 49 from Trenton; stands upon a plain of fertile loam, resting on old red sandstone, bounded westward by rising ground which was probably the primitive bank of the river. Lat. 40° 44′ N., long. 2° 44′ E. from W. C. This is, perhaps, the most flourishing town of the state. In 1830 its population, t-ship included, amounted to 10,953, and in November, 1833, it is ascertained to be nearly 15,000; the increase having been greater during the last three years than in the ten preceding. There are 1712 dwellings, of which 1518 are wooden, and 194 stone and brick. 109 dwellings were built in 1832, and as many in 1833; many of them large and elegant. The town is remarkable for its manufactures, with which it supplies the market throughout the United States; and in which the great proportion of the inhabitants are engaged. The principal of these are saddlery and harness, carriages, shoes, and hats. Sixteen extensive manufactories of saddlery and harness, employ 272 hands, and a capital of $217,300, yielding an annual product of $346,280, and paying wages $70,000 annually. These are independent of the coachmakers who make their own saddlery and harness. Ten carriage manufactories have 779 workmen, an aggregate capital of $202,500, and produce $593,000 annually. These establishments, generally, do all their work, including plating, lamp making, &c. Eighteen shoe manufactories engage 1075 hands, to whom they pay $175,000 yearly wages; have a capital of $300,000, whose annual product is estimated at $607,450: they cut up annually, $400,000 worth of leather. The amount of sales of boots and shoes, in 1832, was $900,000; the balance, over the product of the town, having been procured abroad, in order to supply the orders. This large amount is exclusive of the manufacture for home consumption, which, it is supposed, employs 225 additional hands. Nine hat manufactories employ 487 hands, a capital of $106,000; pay $142,000 in yearly wages, and make an annual return of $551,700. Thirteen tanneries employ 103 hands, a capital of $78,000, and return annually, $503,000. Beside these prominent manufactories, there are others of less, though great consideration.—Thus, there are two soap and candle manufactories, with a capital of $21,000, whose gross product is $165,000; 7 iron and brass founderies, employing 125 men; 2 extensive founderies of malleable iron, employing 60 men; 2 coach spring factories, employing 50 hands; besides 2 others connected with the carriage-making establishments; 5 tin, sheet iron, and stove factories; 1 hardware manufactory, employing 50 workmen; and 2 patent leather manufactories. There are, also, more than 350 tailors engaged in making garments for the home and southern markets; 140 carpenters, 26 sash and blind makers, 100 masons, 60 cabinetmakers, 51 coach lace weavers, 25 chairmakers, 42 trunkmakers, 9 looking glass manufacturers, 12 stone and marble cutters, 10 iron turners, 50 jewellers, and many other species of handicrafts, of which we are unable to give particular details, such as smitheries, wagon-making, manufactories of saddle trees, watches and clocks, segars, silver plating; planes, locks, guns, whips, brushes, coopering, ploughs, pumps, &c.; with the usual number of butchers, bakers, confectioners, painters, glaziers, book binders, &c. &c.

There are here also, 2 breweries, 2 grist mills, 1 extensive steam saw mill, 5 saw mills driven by horses, 1 distillery, 2 rope walks, 1 pottery, and 2 dyeing establishments.

Four printing offices employing 22 hands, from which 3 weekly and 1 daily newspapers are issued; 40 schools with 1669 scholars; and about 1500 scholars receive instruction in the Sunday schools; 4 Presbyterian churches with large congregations, beside a small Presbyterian congregation of coloured persons. The first Presbyterian church was founded in 1787, by the Rev. Alexander M'Whorter, D. D., who presided over the congregation from 1759 until his death in 1807, nearly a half a century; public worship was first offered in it 1st Jan. 1794: The second Presbyterian church in 1808; the third, in 1824; and the fourth, in 1831, 1832. One Episcopal church, with a large and increasing congregation, which was commenced about 1734, by Col. Isaiah Ogden and others, who left the Congregationalists in consequence of the rigour with which his conduct, in saving his grain in a wet harvest, by labouring on the Sabbath, was condemned. The present house for worship was erected in 1808, on a site occupied by a first and older building: Two Baptist churches; the congregation of the first was constituted in 1801, and the church built in 1804, was rebuilt in 1810; the second church was constructed in 1833: 1 Dutch Reformed congregration, recently organized, with a settled minister: 2 large Methodist Episcopal churches; the first congregation was organized in 1806, and the first chapel built in 1810; the second chapel was built in 1832: 1 Primitive Methodist church, and 1 African Episcopal Methodist chapel, built in 1810: a Roman Catholic church, built in 1824. Of these churches the first and second Presbyterian, the Episcopal and the Catholic, are of stone; the third Presbyterian, of brick; the others of wood: the fourth Presbyterian, second Baptist, and second Methodist Episcopal churches are remarkably large, and some of them have great architectural beauty.

Beside the churches, the only public building of the town, of much importance, is the court-house and prison, of brick, under the same roof—in which the keepers' apartments and cells of the prisoners are on the ground floor; the court room, jury rooms, and sheriff's office, on the second; and the apartment for insolvents on the third. The offices of the clerk and surrogate are also in the same building. An election in 1807 for determining the location of the court-house, is still remembered by the inhabitants, as the most exciting recorded in their annals. The contest was between Newark and Day's Hill. By a construction given to the state constitution, the women were then suffered to vote, and they seem to have been so delighted with this privilege of exercising their wills, that they were unwilling to circumscribe it within the legal limit; many ladies voting, we are told, 7 or 8 times, under various disguises.

Of literary institutions in addition to the schools, we may name an apprentices' library, a circulating library, and the mechanics' association for literary and scientific improvement, which possesses a valuable library and philosophical apparatus. It is to the credit of the town, that the New Jersey college was located here for several years subsequent to 1747, under the charge of its second president, the Rev. Aaron Burr, father of the ex-vice President of the United States; who was in 1736, called to the pastoral charge of the first Presbyterian church, and was highly distinguished for his learning, energy, and public spirit, which contributed much to the growth and prosperity of the town.

The commerce of Newark, already considerable, rapidly increases. It is a port of delivery, and efforts are used to make it a port of entry. It employs 65 vessels, averaging 100 tons, in the coasting trade; 8 or 9 of which are constantly engaged in transporting hither various building materials. The Morris canal, which runs through the town, gives it many advantages for internal trade, for which purpose 25 canal boats are supplied by the inhabitants. The facilities for communication with New York, render the town a suburb of that great city. A steam-boat plies twice a day between the two places, carrying an average of 75 passengers each trip, each way; two lines of stages communicate between them almost hourly, conveying at least 800 passengers a week; and this communication will be still more frequent and facile, when the New Jersey Rail-road, now rapidly progressing, shall have been completed. The Directors of the Rail-road Company have not only run the road through part of the town, but have opened a splendid avenue of 120 feet wide, by its side, and propose to cross the Passaic river, about the centre of the town, upon a wooden bridge on stone abutments, which will give an additional trait of beauty to the place.

There are three banks here, viz. "*The Newark Banking and Insurance Company*," incorporated in 1804, with an authorized capital of $800,000, of which $350,000 have been paid in; "*The State Bank at Newark*," incorporated in 1812, with an authorized capital of $400,000, of which $280,000 have been paid in; and "*The Mechanics Bank at Newark*," incorporated in 1831, with an authorized capital of $250,000, of which $200,000 have been paid in. During the year 1833, the business of the town, manufacturing and commercial, has greatly increased, and consequently the demand for banking capital; to meet which, one of the banks has called in a further instalment, and another has availed itself of the privilege given by charter, to double its capital. The rise in the value of real estate, the sure indication of prosperity, has been astonishingly great—a remarkable instance of which is given us in November, 1833; where a property was sold at public auction for $10,000, which but five years, previously, was purchased by the late vendor for $60! A whaling and sealing company has been incorporated, (October, 1833) which is vigorously prosecuting its object.

The town is laid out upon broad streets, and has a great and salubrious ornament, in the greens or commons, which are shaded by noble trees, and bounded by the principal avenues. It is abundantly supplied with wholesome water, by a joint stock company, from a fine and steady spring, about a mile distant; and seven miles of iron pipes have already been laid for the accommodation of the inhabitants. The present style of building, copied from that of the great cities, is costly, elegant, and commodious. Granite basement stories, in the places of business, admit of convenient stores, whilst lofty edifices give accommodation to families. Houses designed for private residence are now generally of brick, neat, and frequently splendid.

We close this interesting account of this thriving town, for which we are indebted to a committee* of the Young Men's Society, &c., with a brief historical notice, much of which has been abstracted from the town records.

* Consisting of Messrs. A. Armstrong, C. H. Halsey, S. H. Pennington, D. A. Hays, and J. B. Congar.

Soon after the arrival of Governor Carteret, in 1665, he published in New England, and elsewhere, the "Concessions" of the proprietaries, and invited settlers to the new colony. The first fruit of this measure was the settlement of Elizabethtown. In the succeeding year, agents were despatched from Guilford, Brandford, and Milford, in Connecticut, to survey the country, and to ascertain the state of the Indians who inhabited it. Upon their favourable report, particularly, of that district "beyond the marshes lying to the north of Elizabethtown," they were empowered to contract for a township, to select a proper site for a town, and to make arrangements for an immediate settlement. Thirty families from the above named towns and New Haven, embarked in the same year, and after a passage, as long and tedious as a voyage in the present time across the Atlantic, arrived in the Passaic river. Their landing was opposed by the Hackensack tribe of Indians, who claimed the soil which the governor had granted to the emigrants, and insisted on a full compensation therefor, previous to its settlement. The governor not being able to remove this obstacle, the discouraged voyagers prepared to return; but were at length, by the solicitation of the governor and others, induced to hold a council with the Indians, from whom they eventually purchased a tract of country on the west side of the Passaic river, extending from ***Woquakick*** (or Bound) creek, on the south, to its fountain head; and thence westerly about seven miles to the ridge of the Great mountain, called by the Indians (***Wacchung***); thence by the said ridge north to the line of Acquackanonck t-ship; thence east by that line to the mouth of (***Yantokah***) Third river; thence down the Passaic river and bay to the place of beginning. These limits formed the original t-ship of Newark, comprehending the present t-ship of that name, and the t-ships of Springfield, Livingston, Orange, Bloomfield, and Caldwell. The price of this purchase was £130 New England currency, 12 Indian blankets, and 12 Indian guns. The title thus derived from the aborigines, was subsequently set up against that of the proprietaries, and was the source of much litigation and forcible contention, which for many years disturbed the peace of East Jersey.

The settlers at first segregated themselves according to the towns whence they came; but the sense of mutual danger soon induced a change in this respect. On the 21st May, 1666, delegates from the several towns resolved to form one t-ship, to provide rules for its government, and "to be of one heart and hand, in endeavouring to carry on their spiritual concernments, as well as their civil and town affairs, according to God and godly government." And for the more speedy accomplishment of their desires, "a committee of eleven were appointed to order and settle the concernments of the people of the place." These rules had a full proportion of the puritanical spirit of the people who made them, and of that religious intolerance which was the distinguishing trait of the inhabitants of Massachusetts, whence they were originally derived; contrasting strongly with the liberality of the "Concessions" of Berkeley and Carteret, to which these emigrants were indebted for the very soil on which they had alighted. "No person could become a freeman or burgess of their town, or vote in its elections, but such as was a member of some one of the Congregational churches:—nor be chosen to the magistracy, nor to any other military or civil office. "But all others admitted to be planters, were allowed to inherit and to enjoy all other privileges, save those above excepted." With a singular disregard of the rights of the proprietaries of New Jersey, and apparently with a resolution of disclaiming all fealty towards them, and of depending on their Indian grants, they, also, resolved "to be ruled by such officers as the town should annually choose from among themselves, and to be governed by the same laws as they had, in the places from whence they came." At this period, (1667,) there were 65 efficient men in the settlement, beside women and children.

At the first distribution of land, each man took by lot six acres as a *homestead;* and as the families from each of the several original towns, had established themselves at short distances from those of other towns, the allotments were made to them in their respective quarters of the new settlement. Seven individuals, selected for the purpose, assessed on each settler his portion of the general purchase money. The lands were eventually divided into three ranges; each range into lots, and parcelled by lottery; first setting apart certain portions, called tradesmen's lots; one of which was to be given to the first of every trade, who should settle permanently in the place; reserving also, the present *Upper Green* of the town for a market place, and the *Lower Green* for a military parade; and that part of the town in and adjacent to Market street, where the tanneries now are, then a swamp, for a public watering place for cattle. This last portion having been sold by the town, is altogether in possession of individual owners.

In 1767, the Rev. Abraham Pierson, the first minister, commenced his official duties here. He is said to have been "episcopally ordained" at Newark, in South Britain, and to have named this town after that of his ordination; by which name it was sometimes called abroad, but was known at others by that of Milford. In the next year, the first "meeting house," 26 feet wide, 34 long, and 13 between the joists, was erected; the town voting £30, and directing that every individual should perform such labour as a committee of five might require, towards its completion.

Robert Treat, and Jasper Crane, were chosen the first magistrates, in 1668; and representatives to the first assembly of New Jersey, convened at Elizabethtown, 26th May, of the same year; by which the first state tax, £12 sterling, of which the proportion of Newark was 40*s.*, was laid. Mr. Treat was also chosen first recorder or town clerk; and after a residence here of many years, returned to Connecticut, where he became governor, and died. The town also established a court of judicature, holding annually one session, on the last Wednesday of February, and another on the 2d Wednesday of September; having cognizance of all causes within its limits. On the 24th May, 1669, the first selectmen, five in number, were chosen. The number was subsequently increased to seven, who continued to administer affairs until 1736, when the present township officers were created by law. And in this year Indian hostility appears to have displayed itself in petty robberies and depredations, the increase of which, in 1675, induced the townsmen to fortify their church as a place of refuge, in case of general attack, and to take proper measures of watch and ward.

On the 23d October, 1676, a warrant was granted by the Governor, for 200 acres of land and meadow, for parsonage ground, and also, for so much as was necessary for landing places, school house, town house, market place, &c.; and in 1696, a patent from the proprietaries to the town, covered all the lots, in various parts of the township, called "Parsonage Lands;" which have been since divided, with some difficulty and contention, among five churches; viz. the three Presbyterian, and the Episcopal, at Newark, and the First Presbyterian church, at Orange.

In 1721, the first freestone was quarried for market; and this article, celebrated for its excellent quality, has long been exported in great quantities.

At the commencement of the revolutionary war, the town was much divided upon the questions agitating the country; and on the Declaration of Independence, by the State, several families, among whom was Mr. Brown, pastor of the Episcopal church, who had ministered from its foundation, joined the royalists in New York. From its vicinage to that strong hold of the enemy, the town suffered greatly, by his visitations, made by regular troops and marauders. On the night of the 25th of January, 1780, a regiment of 500 men, commanded by Colonel Lumm, came from New York, *following the river on the ice*, and burned the academy, then standing on the upper green. This was a stone building, two stories high, with apartments for the teacher. On the same night another British party, unknown to the first, fired the Presbyterian church, at Elizabethtown, the light from which affrighted the incendiaries at Newark, and caused their hasty retreat. They carried away with them Joseph Heddens, Esq., an active whig, who had zealously opposed their previous depredations; dragging him from a sick bed, and compelling him to follow, with no other than his night clothing. The party returned by the route by which they came; and a soldier, more humane than his fellows, gave Mr. H. a blanket, a short time before they reached Paules Hook. At this place Mr. H. was confined in a sugar house, where he perished in a few days, in consequence of the sufferings from that dreadful night.

The prosperity of this enterprising and industrious town, is deservedly great; and being founded on the indispensable manufactures of the country, will necessarily progress with the general population, and with such increased momentum as the highly stimulated spirit of its inhabitants will not fail to give it.

Newark, t-ship, Essex co., bound- on the N. by Bloomfield t-ship; N. E. by the Passaic river, which separates it from Bergen co.; E. by Newark bay; S. by Elizabeth and Union t-ships; and W. by Orange t-ship. Greatest length, E. and W. 7 miles; breadth, N. and S. 6 miles; area, about 12,000 acres; surface level; soil marsh and red shale; a large proportion of this t-ship lying N. of Boundbrook, and E. of the turnpike road from Elizabethtown to Newark, is salt marsh; the remainder consists of well improved land. Population, in 1830, including the town of Newark, 10,953. In 1832, there were 2500 taxables, 1114 householders, wbose ratables did not exceed $30; 527 single men, 95 merchants, 4 grist mills, 3 saw mills, 3 furnaces, 1 fulling-mill, 26 tan vats, 1 wool factory, and 1 distillery. The t-ship paid in state tax, $933 72; county, $2443 92; poor tax, $2500; road tax, $500.

Newark Bay, a large sheet of water, of 7 miles in length, and 2 in breadth, between Bergen and Essex cos., and separated from the New York, by a strip of land one mile wide, but communicating therewith, by the Kill-van-Kuhl. The Passaic and Hackensack rivers debouch in this bay. Its easterly shore is bold and clean, but its westerly, has a broad margin of salt marsh.

New Barbadoes, t-ship, Bergen co., bounded N. by Harrington; E. and S. E. by Hackensack; S. W. by Lodi, and W. by Saddle river t-ships. Greatest length, N. and S. 7; breadth, E. and W. 4 miles; area, 11,500 acres; surface generally level, but towards the N. there is some undulating ground; soil, sandy loam, and red shale, extremely well cultivated, and productive in grass and vegetables for the New York market. The farms are generally small, and remarkable for their neatness. Most of the dwellings are built in the simple Dutch cottage style, with a single story, high gable ends, and projecting pent-houses. The t-ship is drained on the E. boundary, by the Hackensack river, on which are the post-towns of New Milford, and the hamlets of Old and New Bridge; and on the W. line, by Saddle river. The town of Hackensack, the county seat of justice, lies in the S. E. angle. Population in 1830, 1693. In 1832, there were in the t-ship, 440 taxables, 85 householders, whose ratables did not exceed $30; 40 single men, 15 merchants, 5 grist mills, 5 saw mills, 2 carding machines, 1 fulling mill, 1 wool factory, 28 tan vats, 315 horses, and 548 neat cattle, under 3 years old; and paid taxes, state, $188 90; county, $339 97; poor, $500; school, $100; road, $1000.

New Bargaintown, Howell t-ship, Monmouth co., upon Manasquan river, 9 miles S. E. of Freehold; contains a grist mill, and some half dozen dwellings, surrounded by a sandy soil, and pine forest.

Newbold's Island, in the Delaware river, about 2 miles below Bordentown, and ½ a mile from White Hill, in Mansfield t-ship, Burlington co.; has a fertile alluvial soil, and a fine fishery.

New Bridge, hamlet, of Hackensack t-ship, Bergen co., on the Hackensack river, 2 miles above Hackensack town; contains a grist and saw mill, a store, tavern, and 10 or 12 dwellings. Surrounding country, level; soil, fertile loam.

New Brunswick, p-t. and city, and seat of justice for Middlesex co., lying on the right bank of the river Raritan, 15 miles from the head of the bay at Amboy, 40 miles by water and 25 by land S. W. from New York, 26 N. E. from Trenton. The city is partly in North Brunswick t-ship, Middlesex co., and partly in Franklin t-ship, Somerset co., the post-road or Albany street forming the line between the t-ships and counties.

At the close of the seventeenth century, the place where the city now stands, was covered with woods, and called after the name of its proprietor, "*Prigmore's Swamp*." The first inhabitant, of whom any account is preserved, was one Daniel Cooper, who resided where the post-road crossed the river, and kept the ferry which afterwards, in 1713, when the county line was drawn, was called Inian's Ferry. This ferry was granted by the proprietors, 2d Nov. 1697, for the lives of Inian and wife, and the survivor, at a rent of 5 shillings sterling per annum. One of the first houses is said to be still standing, at the foot of Town lane; and some other buildings, erected at an early period, may be distinguished by their antique structure, in Burnet and Albany streets. The first inhabitants of European origin, were from Long Island. About 1730 several Dutch families emigrated from Albany, bringing with them their building materials, in imitation of their ancestors, who imported their bricks, tiles, &c. from Holland. Some of them built their houses upon the present post-road, which thence acquired the name of Albany street; though originally it was called French street, in honour of Philip French, Esq. who held a large tract of land on the north side of it. About this time the name of New Brunswick was given to the place, which had, hitherto, been distinguished as "The River."

The city was incorporated in 1784, and is now divided into five wards. The old market, called Coenties' market, was of ancient date, and stood in Commerce Square; the present was built in 1811. The court-house was erected in 1793; the bridge, originally, in 1796, and was rebuilt by a joint stock company in 1811, at the cost of $86,687. It is a wooden structure about 1000 feet in length, divided into two carriage ways by a wood partition, and rests on eleven stone piers and abutments.

A portion of the town lying immediately on the river, is low, and the streets are narrow, crooked, and lined principally with small frame houses, extending for near half a mile from the bridge to the landings for steamboats. Albany street is a broad, well paved thoroughfare, ornamented with some excellent buildings, and the streets upon the upper shelving bank, are generally wide, and the houses neat and commodious; many of them expensively built, and surrounded by gardens. The streets generally, are paved with boulders. Those unpaved are, in the rainy season, scarcely passable, the red sandy loam of the soil, being easily wrought into deep paste. From the top of the hill or bank, especially from the site of Rutgers' college, there is a wide prospect of miles, terminating on the north by the Green Brook mountains, and on the east by the Raritan bay.

The tide in the river extends to Raritan Landing, about two miles above the town; but immediately above the bridge, at the town, the river is fordable. At this point the ice, when broken up in the spring, sometimes lodging, forms a dam, which raising the water many feet above its usual level, causes it to overflow the lower streets. The Delaware and Raritan canal has its outlet here, by a lock of 12 feet lift, into a basin 200 feet wide, made in the bed of the river, and extending a mile and a quarter in front of the town, where vessels of 200 tons burden may lie. From the canal a very important hydraulic power will be obtained, under a fall of 14 feet, with all the water of the Raritan river, and all the surplus water of the canal. Consequently, New Brunswick may, at no distant period, claim consideration among the manufacturing towns of the United States.

The city contains between 5 and 6000 inhabitants, about 750 dwellings, 120 large stores, among which are 12 extensive grain stores; 20 taverns, 12 practising attorneys, and 8 physicians; 1 Methodist church, built in 1811, and another belonging to blacks of the same denomination: A Dutch Reformed church, the present house being the third pertaining to that profession; the first was built on the corner of Schuremem and Burnet streets, before the year 1717; the second, on the site of the present, between the years 1750 and 1783, during the ministry of the Rev. Johannes Leydt; and the present, commenced in 1812, was completed in 1828, by the construction of a brick stuccoed steeple—a Presbyterian congregation occupying their second house for worship; their first was built before, or during the ministry of the Rev. Gilbert Tennent, who became their pastor in 1726, in Burnet street, below Lyell's Brook; and was wantonly destroyed by the British soldiers in 1776 or 1777; the present edifice was erected in 1784;—The Episcopal church, called Christ church, was built in 1743, the steeple in 1773; but the latter was burned to the stone basement in 1802, and rebuilt in the same year: the Baptist church was erected in 1810, and a small Catholic chapel in 1832. There are in the town a college called Rutgers' college, and grammar school connected with it; 2 academies; an extensive boarding and day school for young ladies; a Lancasterian school, incorporated and endowed with about $4000, and several common schools.

The town has an extensive trade. The enterprising inhabitants have opened a ready communication with Easton and the valley of the Delaware, by the Jersey turnpike road; and have made it the depot of the produce from a large tract of fertile country; its business will be greatly increased by the trade of the Delaware and Raritan canal. There are now 12 sloops employed in its commerce, and 300,000 bushels of Indian corn, and 50,000 bushels of rye are annually exported. Two lines of stages connected with steam-boats here and at Lamberton, on the Delaware, run daily from the town, and stages depart hence daily to various parts of the country; and communication is had four times, daily, by steam-boats, with New York. There are now two banks established here: the State Bank incorporated in 1812, with an authorized capital of $400,000 of which 88,000 have been called in; and the New Brunswick Bank, incorporated in 1807, with a capital of $200,000, 90,000 of which have been paid.

There is a vein of copper ore adjacent to the town, which was formerly very extensively wrought, but which has been for many years abandoned. For an account of this mine, see prefatory chapter, page 10.

New Durham, village on the turnpike-road leading from Hoboken to Hackensack, Bergen t-ship, Bergen co., 3 miles from the one and seven from the other; contains 2 taverns, a store, and some 10 or 12 dwellings.

New Durham, small village of Piscataway t-ship, Middlesex co., 5 miles east of north from New Brunswick, and on the turnpike road leading from Perth Amboy toward Bound Brook; contains a tavern, store, and some half dozen dwellings.

New Egypt, p-t. of Upper Freehold t-ship, Monmouth co., on the Crosswicks creek, 23 miles S. W. from Monmouth Court House, 170 N. E. from W. C., and 16 miles S. E. from Trenton; contains about 20 dwellings, 2 taverns, 2 or 3 stores, valuable grist and saw mills, and a Methodist church within a mile of the town. The country around it is level; soil, of clay and sand. The name is derived from the excellent market the mills formerly afforded for corn.

New England, village of Fairfield t-ship, Cumberland co., near Cohansey creek, 5 miles S. of Bridgeton; contains some 12 or 15 dwellings, scattered along the road within the space of a mile; near it is a Methodist church.

New England Creek, a small stream of Lower t-ship, Cape May co., flowing into the Delaware bay.

New Freedom, small village of Gloucester t-ship, Gloucester co., on the road from Camden to Great Egg Harbour river, 18 miles S. E. from the former, and 14 from the latter; contains a Methodist meeting, a glass manufactory, a tavern and store, and some 12 or 15 dwellings. It is in the midst of the pines, on Inskeep's branch of Great Egg Harbour river.

Newfoundland, is the post-office of Longwood Valley, 17 miles N. W. from Morristown, 245 N. E. from W. C., and 79 from Trenton; there is a Presbyterian church here.

New Germantown, p-t. of Tewkesbury t-ship, Hunterdon co., on the turnpike-road leading from Lamington to Schooley's mountain, 14 miles N. E. from Flemington, 45 from Trenton, and 211 from W. C.; contains about 30 dwellings, 1 tavern, 3 stores, 1 Lutheran, 1 Methodist, and a Presbyterian, church and an academy. The town lies near the foot of a spur of the Musconetcong mountain, and is surrounded by a rich and highly cultivated limestone soil, in which there are masses of brescia or pudding limestone, which are perhaps equal in beauty, to that in the capitol at Washington.

New Hampton, p-t. of Lebanon t-ship, Hunterdon co., in the N. W. angle on the S. side of Musconetcong creek, and on the turnpike leading to Oxford Furnace, 18 miles N. W. from Flemington, 41 from Trenton, and 200 from W. C.; contains 1 grist mill, 1 saw mill, 2 stores, 3 taverns, and from 20 to 25 dwellings.

New Hamburg, post-office, Bergen co.

New Market, village of Amwell t-ship, Hunterdon co., 8 miles S. of Flemington; contains a tavern and store, 6 or 8 dwellings. Snydertown, a small hamlet, divided from it by a branch of Stony creek, contains a grist mill, and 2 or 3 dwellings; the surrounding country is hilly, stony, and poor.

New Market, formerly called ***Quibbletown***, village of Piscataway t-ship, Middlesex co., 7 miles N. of New Brunswick, on the left bank of Cedar creek; contains a grist mill, a tavern, a store, and some 20 dwellings, in a fertile country of red shale.

New Milford, village of Hackensack t-ship, Bergen co., in the extreme N. W. angle of the t-ship, 4 miles N. of Hackensacktown, upon the Hackensack river; contains 2 mills, some half dozen dwellings, a store and tavern; surrounding country, level; soil, sandy loam, with red shale, well cultivated and fertile.

New Mills. (See *Pemberton.*)

Newport Creek, rises on the confines of Stow creek and Greenwich t-ships, Cumberland co., and flows westerly about 6 miles into Stow creek, forming the south boundary of the first, and north boundary of the second t-ship.

Newport, or *Nantuxet*, said to be more properly called "*Antuxet*," p-t. of Dover t-ship, Cumberland co., on the Nantuxet creek, 5 miles above its mouth, 10 miles S. from Bridgeton, 187 N. E. from W. C., and 81 S. of Trenton; contains from 20 to 30 houses, 1 tavern and store. This place is noted as having been the resort of refugees and tories during the revolution.

New Prospect, p-t. of Franklin t-ship, on the Hohokus creek, 241 miles N. E. from W. C., 74 from Trenton, and 11 N. W. from Hackensack; very pleasantly situated upon high ground, on a fertile soil, and in the centre of a thriving manufacturing settlement; what may appropriately be called the town, contains 2 taverns, 1 store, 2 paper mills, 2 grist mills, and chair manufactory, with lathes running by water, and several dwellings.

New Providence t-ship, Essex co., bounded N. E. by Springfield t-ship; E. by Westfield; S. by Warren t-ships, Somerset co.; and W. and N. W. by the Passaic river; which separates it from Morris co. Centrally distant S. W. from Newark, 13 miles; greatest length 6, breadth 2½ miles; area, 7680 acres; surface hilly, on the west mountainous; soil, clay loam, and red shale; carbonate of lime is found on the east, near Green Brook, in which are metallic appearances supposed to be gold and silver, but are perhaps only the deceptive pyrites of iron or copper. Population in 1830, 910. In 1832, the t-ship contained 195 taxables, 45 householders, whose ratables did not exceed $30; 29 single men, 3 merchants, 3 grist mills, 5 saw mills, 1 paper mill, 13 tan vats, 147 horses, and 503 neat cattle, above 3 years old; and it paid state tax, $97 43; county, $254 92; poor, 300; road, $702.

New Providence, p-t. of preceding t-ship, 13 miles S. W. of Newark, 218 N. E. from W. C., and 52 from Trenton; contains a Presbyterian and Methodist church, a tavern, store, and several dwellings.

Newton t-ship, Gloucester county, bounded N. by the city of Camden; N. E. by Cooper's creek, which separates it from Waterford t-ship; S. E. by Gloucester t-ship; S. W. by Gloucestertown t-ship; and W. by the river Delaware. Centrally distant N. E. from Woodbury 6 miles; greatest length E. and W. 6, breadth N. and S. less than 4 miles; area, 9000 acres; surface, level; soil, sandy; timber, chiefly yellow pine; the cultivated land employed principally in raising vegetables and fruit for market. Besides Cooper's creek on the N. W., it has Newton creek on the S. W., which being stopped out, makes some valuable meadows.—Haddonfield and Rowantown are villages of the t-ship, the first a post-town. Population in 1830, including, we presume, the city of Camden, 3298. In 1832 the t-ship contained 199 householders, whose ratables did not exceed $30; 6 stores, 2 fisheries, 3 grist mills, 1 saw mill, 1 fulling mill, 1 tan yard, 2 distilleries, 643 neat cattle, and 287 horses and mules above 3 years of age. The t-ship paid county tax, $532 44; poor tax, $266 47; road tax, $700.

Newton Creek, Newton t-ship, Gloucester co., rises on the south border of the t-ship, and flows N. W. about 5 miles, to the river Delaware. The influx of the tide to the creek is stopped by dam and sluice, by which some valuable meadows are gained along its banks.

Newton or *Pine Creek*, Galloway t-ship, Gloucester co., a tributary of Little Egg Harbour river.

Newton t-ship, Sussex co., bounded N. by Frankford t-ship; E. by Hardiston t-ship; S. E. by Byram t-ship; S. W. by Green t-ship; W. by Stillwater, and N. W. by Sandistone t-ships. Greatest length N. and S. 12, breadth E. and W. 10 miles; area, 65,920 acres; surface, hilly on the N. W. and S. E.; centrally, level. It is watered chiefly by the Paulinskill, which flows S. W. through it, towards the Delaware. (See ***Paulinskill.***) The Newton and Bolton turnpike road runs centrally through the t-ship, and through the town of Newton; and the turnpike road by Sparta to Milford, through the N. E. angle, on which lies the post-town of Lafayette. Population of the t-ship in 1830, 3464; taxables in 1832, 530. There were in the t-ship in 1832, 140 householders, whose ratables did not exceed $30; 14 stores, 14 run of stones for grinding grain, 6 carding machines, 3 fulling mills, 650 horses and mules, and 1330 neat cattle, above the age of 3 years; 4 tan vats, 8 distilleries. The t-ship paid in 1832, state and county tax, $1156 05; poor tax, $400; road tax, $1200.

Newton, borough, county, and post-town, Newton t-ship, Sussex co., on the Newton and Bolton turnpike road, distant by the post-route 228 miles from W. C., and 75 from Trenton, 60 from New York, 40 from Easton, and 100 from Philadelphia. The town lies upon the slope of a gentle hill, of mingled slate and limestone, at whose foot a spring sends forth the first waters of the Paulinskill, the chief river of the county, whose volume is swelled by the tribute from Moore's Pond, covering 8 or 10 acres, distant about 1 mile S. E. from Newton. There are several streets, and a large common or public lot, fronts the court-house and prison, and on which the public offices are erected. It contains about 130 dwellings, and 900 inhabitants, 4 taverns, 8 extensive stores, 2 printing offices, at each of which a weekly journal is published, viz. the New Jersey Herald, by Mr. Fitch, and the Sussex Register, by Mr. Hall; a very large and commodious Presbyterian church, an Episcopal church, with a valuable glebe farm of 200 acres, near the town; and a Methodist church; 2 seminaries, in which the classics are taught—one of which is incorporated as an academy; 6 common schools, 3 Sunday schools, a public library, a lyceum for the promotion of the study of letters and science; a bank with a capital of $100,000, established in a handsome building, specially erected for it. The court-house is a low and ancient looking stone building, finished in 1765, having the prison in the basement story. There are in the town 4 practising attorneys, 4 physicians, and 2 resident clergymen. Some of the dwellings are very neat: the place has an air of business, and there is in fact a very considerable trade carried on with the surrounding country. In healthiness of situation, by the report of the inhabitants, it cannot be excelled.

New Village, p-t., of Greenwich t-ship, Warren co., on the turnpike road from Schooley's mountain to Philipsburg, and on the Morris canal, by the post-route 196 miles from W. C., 52 from Trenton, and 10 miles from Belvidere, the county town; contains 1 store, 1 tavern, and 10 or 12 dwellings. It is surrounded by a fertile limestone country.

New Vernon, p-t., of Morris t-ship, Morris co., 4 miles S. W. from Morristown, 217 N. E. from W. C., and 51 from Trenton; contains a store, an academy, and 4 dwellings.

Nischisakawick Creek, rises in Alexandria t-ship, Hunterdon co., and flows S. W. into the Delaware river, by a course of 7 or 8 miles, at the town of Alexandria.

Norman's Pond, small lake of Hardistone t-ship, Sussex co., on the Hamburg or Wallkill mountain, near the town of Sparta, a principal source of the Wallkill river. The stream from the pond gives motion to a forge immediately on issuing from the lake.

Northampton t-ship, Burlington co., bounded N. E. by Springfield and Hanover t-ships; E. by Monmouth co.; S. by Little Egg Harbour and Washington t-ships; W. by Evesham and Chester t-ships; and

N. W. by Willingboro' and Burlington t-ships. Greatest length N. W. and S. E. 33 miles; breadth E. and W. 18 miles; area, 135,000 acres; surface, generally level; soil, sand and sandy loam; the portion on the north-west of the t-ship well cultivated and productive; southern and easterly parts chiefly pine and oak forests. It is drained north-west by the north and south branches of the Rancocus creek, and southerly by tributaries of the Little Egg Harbour river. Mount Holly, the county town, New Mills, or Pemberton, Vincenttown, Eayrstown, Buddstown, Tabernacle, &c., are villages of the t-ship. Population in 1830, 5516. In 1832, the t-ship contained 1000 taxables, 654 householders, whose ratables did not exceed $30; 183 single men, 2371 cattle, and 1005 horses and mules; 13 stores, 7 saw mills, and 9 grist mills, 2 forges, 1 paper mill, 2 fulling mills, 1 cotton factory, 1 plaster mill, 50 tan vats, 3 carding machines, 6 distilleries for cider, 1 four horse stage, 2 two horse stages, 60 dearborns, 154 covered wagons, 4 chairs and curricles, 43 gigs and sulkies; and paid state tax, $675 87; county tax, $2359 50; t-ship tax, $3900.

North Branch, or *Bailes'*, p-t., of Bridgewater t-ship, Somerset co., on the turnpike road from Somerville to Easton, 4 miles from the former and 29 from the latter, 203 N. E. from W. C., and 29 from Trenton, upon the north branch of the Raritan river, in a level, fertile country; contains a large grist mill and fulling mill, a tavern, 2 stores, and about 20 dwellings. There is a Dutch Reformed church in the neighbourhood.

North Brunswick. (See *Brunswick, North.*)

Northfield, small village of Livingston t-ship, Essex co., 8 miles W. of Newark; contains a Baptist church, store, and 3 or 4 dwellings.

No Pipe Brook, tributary of Beden's brook, rises by two branches in the Nashanic mountain, on the confines of Montgomery and Hillsborough t-ships, Somerset co., which flow S. E. about 5 or 6 miles to their recipient.

Notch, The, a pass over the First, or Newark mountain, Acquackanonck t-ship, Essex co., through which the road leads from Acquackanoncktown to the Little Falls of the Passaic, distant 7 miles from the former.

Nottingham t-ship, Burlington co., bounded N. W. by the Assunpink creek, which divides it from Trenton and Lawrence t-ships, Hunterdon co.; N. E. by East and West Windsor t-ships, of Middlesex co.; S. by the Crosswicks creek, and S. W. by the river Delaware. Centrally distant N. E. from Mount Holly, 17 miles; greatest length N. and S. 10 miles; greatest breadth, 7 miles; area, 25,000 acres; surface generally level, varied only by the abrasion of the streams, which have worn their courses through deep and narrow valleys; soil, various; along the banks of the river and creeks, there is some stiff clay; sandy loam and sand characterize the remainder. Much of the t-ship, with due care, is susceptible of beneficial cultivation, and is productive in wheat, rye, corn, oats, and grass; the latter being much aided by the use of marl, which is abundant. The streams are the Assunpink, on the north, with its tributaries, Miry and Pond runs, and the Crosswicks, on the south, which receives a small stream from the t-ship. The villages are Sandtown, Nottingham Square, Mill Hill, Bloomsbury, Lamberton, and the Sand Hills. Population in 1830, 3900. In 1832, there were in the t-ship 960 taxables, 430 householders, whose ratables did not exceed $30; 165 single men, 11 merchants, 5 fisheries, 4 saw mills, 19 pair of grist mill stones, 1 paper mill, 1 fulling mill, 3 cotton manufactories, 75 tan vats, 2 carding machines, 5 distilleries for cider, 3 four horse stages, 3 two horse stages, 37 dearborns, 37 covered wagons, 50 chairs and curricles, and 2 gigs and sulkies; 1032 cattle, and 604 horses and mules over 3 years of age; the t-ship paid state tax, $486 87; county tax, $1702 05; township tax, $1900.

Nottingham Square, village of Nottingham t-ship, Burlington co., on the road from Trenton to Allentown, 6 miles E. of the former, on a sandy plain; contains 1 Presbyterian, and 1 Baptist church, a store, a tavern, and from 8 to 12 dwellings.

Obhonon, an arm of the south branch of Toms' river, Dover t-ship, Monmouth co.

Ogdensburg, village of Hardiston t-ship, Sussex co., about 75 miles N. E. from Trenton, and about 9 miles from Newton, in the valley of the Wallkill river; contains 21 dwellings, a small store, and saw mill, scattered along the road within the distance of a mile. There are some good lands in the narrow valley here, but the sides of the mountain are broken and stony.

Old Bridge, hamlet of Hackensack t-ship, Bergen co., on the Hackensack river, 4 miles N. of Hackensack town; contains a store, tavern, and 10 or 12 dwellings; country level; soil, fertile loam, well cultivated.

Old Bridge, hamlet of North Brunswick t-ship, Middlesex co., on South river, and on the turnpike-road from Bordentown to South Amboy, 6 miles S. E. from New Brunswick; contains a tavern, and some half dozen dwelling houses; surrounded by a sandy and light soil.

Old Man's Creek, rises in Gloucester co., Franklin t-ship, about 3 miles E. of a point on the Salem co. line; from which line it runs N. W., forming the boundary between Gloucester and Salem cos. for about 25 miles, following the meanderings of the creek to the river Delaware. It is a crooked stream flowing through a flat country, and has considerable tracts of banked meadow on its margin, as high as Pedricktown, to which place wood shallops ascend.

Ong's Hat, hamlet of Northampton t-ship, Burlington co., 10 miles S. E. of Mount Holly.

Orange t-ship, Essex co., bounded N. W. by Caldwell; N. E. by Bloomfield; E. and S. E. by Newark; S. by Union; S. W. by Springfield; and W. by Livingston. Centrally distant, N. W., from Newark, 4½ miles; greatest length, N. and S., 7; breadth, E. and W., 5 miles; surface, on the west, hilly; the First and Second mountains crossing it here; elsewhere rolling; soil, red shale, generally well cultivated; area, about 14,000 acres. Orange, the post town, South Orange, Camptown, Middleville and Jefferson village, are towns of the township. It is drained N. E. by Second river, and S. W. by branches of the Rahway. Population in 1830, 3887; in 1832, there were in the township, 625 taxables, 172 householders, whose ratables did not exceed $30 in value, 76 single men, 15 merchants, 3 grist mills, 2 saw mills, 40 tan vats, 362 horses and mules, and 1099 neat cattle, above the age of three years; and it paid state tax, $298 19; county, 780 20; poor, $600; road, $1050.

Orange, is a straggling village of the preceding township, and a post-town, extending about 3 miles along the turnpike road, from Newark to Dover; and distant about 3 miles N. W. from the former; 219 N. E. from W. C., and 53 from Trenton; contains 1 Episcopal, 2 Presbyterian, and 1 Methodist churches, 2 taverns, 10 stores, 2 saw mills and a bark mill, from 200 to 230 dwellings, many of them very neat and commodious. A large trade is carried on here in the manufacture of leather, shoes and hats. The country about it is level, red shale, and carefully cultivated. A chalybeate spring near the town is much resorted to.

Orange, South, a village of the same township, lies on the turnpike-road from Newark to Morristown, 5 miles W. of the first; it contains about 30 dwellings, a tavern and store, a paper mill and a Presbyterian church; the lands around it are also rich and well farmed.

Oranoken Creek, Downe t-ship, Cumberland co., rises in the township, and flows S. W. 12 or 14 miles, into Maurice River Cove, sending forth several small streams, laterally to the west, which have their mouths higher up in the bay.

Oswego, east branch of Wading river. (See ***Wading River***.)

Oxford t-ship, Warren co., bounded N. W. by Knowlton; E. by Hardwick and Independence; S. E. by Mansfield; S. by Greenwich t-ships, and W. by the Delaware river. Greatest length, N. E. and S. W., 16 miles; breadth, N. W. and S. E., 5½ miles; area, 42,000 acres. Drained chiefly by the Pequest creek and its tributary, Beaver Brook. Population in 1830, 3665; taxables, in 1832, 800. In 1832, the township contained 254 householders, whose ratables did not exceed $30 in value, 17 stores, 18 pair of stones for grinding grain, 1 carding machine, 7 saw mills, 3 furnaces, 10 tan vats, 4 distilleries, and 862 horses and mules, and 1407 neat cattle; and it paid tax for township use, $1200, and for state and county purposes, $2229 02. Belvidere, the county town, lies on the Delaware river, in this township, and Bridgeville, Oxford and Concord are small villages from 3 to 4 miles distant from it. The surface of the township is much broken, and it possesses a great variety of soil and cultivation. The mountains, which are composed of granitic rock and crowned with wood, cover a considerable portion of it, and are cultivated wherever the hopes of reward will justify the labour. The valleys of limestone are very productive; and large quantities of wheat are grown for market. Greenpond is a small lake 1½ mile long by ¾ of a mile wide, on the S. E. declivity of Jenny Jump mountain; mountain and bog ore abound, and manganese on the Delaware below Foul Rift. The towns are Belvidere, the seat of justice of the county, Bridgeville, Oxford, Concord, and Roxburg.

Oxford, small hamlet of Oxford t-ship, Warren co., three miles S. E. of Belvidere, the county town; contains a Presbyterian church, a tavern, 1 grist and 1 clover mill, and 10 or 12 dwellings.

Oxford Furnace, and village, on a branch of the Pequest creek, near the E. line of Oxford township, and five miles E. of Belvidere, the seat of justice, at the N. W. foot of Scott's mountain. This mountain vale is a very ancient site for the manufacture of iron, a furnace having been erected here more than seventy years since by the ancestor of the present owners, Messrs. Robison; but it had been out of blast for more than 20 years, when Messrs. Henry and Jordon, of Pennsylvania, undertook to renew operations. These gentlemen have obtained a lease of the furnace, with 2000 acres of woodland, and have rebuilt the works. Abundance of excellent iron ore is found in the mountain a few hundred yards from the furnace; and the lessees have sunk several shafts, and are now working a vein of magnetic ore about 13 feet thick, enclosed by walls of rotten mica. This ore is very rich and easily smelted. Old excavations are visible in many places, and shafts have recently been discovered more than 100 feet deep, and drifts exceeding 120 yards in length. The rock of Scott's mountain is primitive, and its constituents are found separately in masses, and also variously combined with each other, with hornblende and with iron of various species, forming granite, sienite, &c. The whole range of hills, of which Scott's mountain is part, forms a very interesting study for the mineralogist and geologist.

Oyster Creek, Stafford t-ship, Monmouth co., flows N. E. about 10 miles, and empties into Barnegat bay, on the line separating Stafford from Dover township.

Pacak Creek rises in the Wawayanda mountains, Vernon t-ship, Sussex co., and by a southerly course, of about seven miles, unites with the Pequannock creek, in Hardistone township.

Pahaquarry, N. W. t-ship of Warren co., bounded N. E. by Walpack t-ship; S. E., by Hardwick and Knowlton t-ships; S. W. and W. by the river Delaware. It lies wholly between the Blue mountain and the river; is centrally distant, N. from Belvidere, 15 miles. Greatest length, N. E. and S. W., 13 miles; breadth, 2½ miles; area, 12,800 acres; surface, mountain and river bottom. Population by census of 1830, 258. In 1832, it contained 13 householders, whose ratables did not exceed $30 in value; but no store, and but one grist mill, 4 mill saws, 59 horses and mules, and 121 neat cattle above the age of three years, and paid a state and county tax of $109 61. Vancamp brook flows southerly through the N. W. part of the township. Pahaquarry is the name given to a small cluster of houses, situate in the northern part of the township. The Water Gap, by which the Delaware flows through the Blue mountain, is on the southwestern boundary of the township. Brotzmanville is the post-office. A road has lately been made through the Gap, and partly cut out of the mountain at the expense of the state. Before it was made, even foot passengers were unable to follow the river through the Gap on the Jersey side without the aid of rope ladders to assist them over the precipitous rocks. The narrow margin above the river, which nowhere exceeds the breadth of the fourth of a mile, is fertile. Upon the Pennsylvania side this margin is wider and underlaid with limestone.

Paint Island Spring, on the boundary between Upper and Lower Freehold t-ships, Monmouth co., 5 miles E. of Wrightsville, and near the source of Toms' river. This is a large chalybeate spring whose waters hold so great a quantity of the super carbonate of iron, blended with the black oxyde of iron in solution, that they leave a very extensive deposit of this mineral. By exposure to the air an atom of carbonic acid escapes, the oxyde takes another atom of oxygen from the atmosphere, and is precipitated in the form of oxy-carbonat, an insoluble powder of a yellow colour. The colour may be converted into a beautiful brown by heating the yellow ochre sufficiently to expel its carbonic acid, leaving behind the second oxide of iron. The heat of boiling water is sufficient for this purpose; and the ore so changed has most of the properties of umber. A manufacture of this paint has given name to the spring. It is esteemed by the neighbours for medicinal qualities, and *pic nic* parties are made here frequently in the summer. It was also formerly known as Lawrence's spring, but is now, we believe, the property of Samuel G. Wright, Esq.

Pamrepau, small scattering settlement, in Bergen t-ship, Bergen co., on New York bay, about 5 miles below Jersey City, occupied by descendants of the original Dutch settlers.

Panther Pond, on the N. W. of Byram t-ship, Sussex co., one of the eastern sources of the Pequest creek.

Papaking Creek, rises in Frankford t-ship, Sussex co., and flows, N. E. by a course of about 10 miles, to Deep Clove creek, below Deckertown, Wantage t-ship; giving motion to several mills.

Paramus, small hamlet, on the Saddle River, and on the boundary of Harrington and Franklin t-ships, Bergen co.; contains a church, a tavern, a mill and several dwellings, about 7 miles N. W. from Hackensack.

Parcipany, p-t. of Hanover t-ship, on the turnpike road from Franklin to Mount Pleasant, 7 miles N. of Morristown, 229 N. E. from W. C., and 63 from Trenton, on the Parcipany river; contains 2 grist mills, 2 stores, 2 taverns, a Presbyterian, and a Methodist church, an academy, and from 15 to 20 dwellings. The soil around it, is sandy loam, well cultivated.

Parcipany Creek, rises by two branches, in the Trowbridge mountain, Hanover t-ship, Morris co.; and flows by a S. E. course of about 8 or 9 miles, into the Whippany river, about a mile above its junction, with the Rockaway, giving motion to several mills.

Parvin's Run, Fairfield t-ship, Cumberland co., a tributary of the Cohansey creek, which joins its recipient, 2 miles S. of Bridgeton; notable as part of the boundary between Deerfield and Fairfield t-ships.

Parvin's Branch, of Maurice river, rises in Millville t-ship, Cumberland co., and flows eastwardly to the head of the Pond, of Millville works.

Paskack Brook, tributary of Hackensack river, rises in Rockland co., New York, and flows by a course, S. and S. E., of about 12 miles, to its recipient, in Harrington t-ship, Bergen co., giving motion to many mills.

Passaic River. This stream is endowed with a very singular character. Rising in, and flowing through a mountainous country, it is the most crooked, sluggish, and longest of the state; and yet presents the two most profound cataracts, and the greatest hydraulic force. Its extreme source is near Mendham, Morris co., where its head waters interlock with those of the north branch of the Raritan: thence it flows a little E. of S. about 10 miles; in which distance, it has considerable fall—turns several mills, and forms the boundary between Somerset and Morris cos.; thence turned by Stony Hill, of the former co., at the N. base of which it receives Dead river, it assumes a N. E. course, by the foot of Long Hill, dividing Morris from Essex county. On this line, for 20 miles, it steals its way, partly through a narrow vale, and partly through a broad valley, with scarce a ripple or a murmur to indicate its course; and consequently, with few mill-works of any kind. At the S. W. point of the Horse-Shoe mountain, it receives the Rockaway river, which having had for many miles, a rapid, spirited, and useful course, assumes the torpor of its recipient; and spreads itself as if seeking rest, after its hurried flow and mighty labours. Collecting its waters, the united stream meanders along the curve of the Horse-Shoe, about 8 miles, when deflected by the north-eastern point, it inclines to the Second mountain, still preserving its monotonous and sluggish character. But, in its way through this mountain, that character is suddenly changed for high and admirable energy. By two perpendicular leaps, and a rocky rapid, it descends, at the Little Fall, 51 feet in the distance of a half mile, into the valley N. of the First mountain. The first fall has comparatively a gentle, and certainly, a very beautiful appearance. It is 10 feet deep, and more than an hundred yards broad, and has been artificially formed into a broad angle opening down the stream, over which the whole river, but now still and lifeless, as a sea of glass, is precipitated, in two broad and dense sheets, which are shaken by the shock into clouds of foam, and scarce recover their liquid form, until they encounter the second precipice. This has a depth of 16 feet, over which the flood, confined, in ordinary seasons, to a very limited bed, pours in a deep mass, with tremendous force, covering itself with a perpetual halo of spray, and then hastening rapidly away, beneath the bold and lofty arch of the aqueduct of the Morris canal, as if regretting, and gladly seeking, its broken quiet. The aqueduct, a beautiful piece of architecture, formed of cut stone, with a span of 80 feet, and height of 50 feet, adds an admirable feature to the scene; the whole of which, including the basaltic columnar walls of the ravine, erected upon their broad bases of red sandstone, is best seen from the rocky brink of the river, which may be descended to, from either bank, but more commodiously from the left.

Between the Little and the Great Falls, a distance of 5½ miles, the river is broken by some inconsiderable ripples, which afford sufficient fall for mills, but do not much disturb the placidity of its course; but before the great leap, it is again composed into a steady calm, as if concentrated for a new and more vigorous effort. Ere it reaches the perpendicular pitch, it rolls over the artificial dam, erected by the Passaic Manufacturing Company, and a low ledge of rocks; and then pours itself in one unbroken column, 50 feet in altitude, into a deep and narrow chasm, of about 60 feet in width; through which it dashes, foams and roars, into a broad and still basin, which it has excavated for itself. From this it rushes impetuously, by a rapid descent of 20 feet, beneath the level of Paterson plain, curbed by walls of trap-rock and sandstone, whose loose and disjointed character, has enabled the stream to excavate its passage through the deep chasm.

From Paterson to the port of Acquackanonck, 10 miles, where the river meets the tide, its course is again sweetly still; and the tide waters of no river can present a more charming scene. The shore spreading like an amphitheatre upon either side, is covered with verdure, and studded with dwellings, and other monuments of successful industry, which give it the appearance of a highway, through a thrifty village; whilst the clear and quiet waters tempt the spectator to venture upon their bosom. Few rivers possess more attraction than the Passaic, between Paterson and Newark, above the marshes; nor are the charms of its beautiful scenery diminished, by the sport which the stream offers, to the patient follower of Isaac Walton, in the finny tribe, with which it is stored. From Acquackanonck to the head of Newark bay, the distance may be 15 miles, and thus the whole course of the river is about 70 miles, in passing through which, it has looked to every quarter of the compass, save the west.

Paterson. This thriving manufacturing town is one of the creations of the genius of Alexander Hamilton, the true father of the system of domestic industry, now cherished as the American system. In the early part of the year 1791, on the recommendation, and by the active and influential exertions of this distinguished and patriotic statesman, a number of public spirited individuals of New York, New Jersey, and Pennsylvania, associated themselves for establishing useful manufactures, by the subscription of a capital of more than $200,000. The number of shares originally subscribed was 5000, at $100 the share; but 2267 shares only, were fully paid up. The general object of the company was to lay the foundation of a great emporium of manufactures for all articles not prohibited by law. Their immediate object was the manufacture of cotton cloths; and the attempt is highly characteristic of the enterprising spirit of our countrymen. At this period, the improvements of Arkwright in cotton machinery, though perfected, were not very extensively used, even in England, and were absolutely unknown in all other countries. In America no cotton had been spun by machinery. Having resolved to establish themselves in New Jersey, the "contributors" were incorporated by the legislature on 22d Nov. 1791, by an act authorizing a capital stock of one million of dollars, with the right to acquire and hold property to the amount of four millions, and the power to improve the navigation of the rivers, make canals for the trade with the principal site of their works, and to raise by way of lottery, the sum of one hundred thousand dollars. The act of incorporation, which was drawn, or revised by Mr. Hamilton, also gave a city charter, with jurisdiction over a tract of six square miles.

The society was organized at New Brunswick, on the last Monday of November, 1791, by the choice of its first board of directors, composed of William Duer, John Dewhurst, Benjamin Walker, Nicholas Low, Royal Flint, Elisha Boudinot, John Bayard, John Neilson, Archibald Mercer, Thomas Lowring, George Lewis, More Furman, and Alex. M'Comb. William Duer was chosen the first governor of the company. We give these names, because they are illustrated by the present flourishing condition of the society, the result of their labours.

Mr. Hamilton, who was not a stockholder of the company, and whose disinterested exertions in its behalf, were prompted by higher motives than pecuniary gratification, had, previously to the act of incorporation, at the request of the company, engaged English and Scotch artizans and manufacturers of cotton machinery and cotton goods, to establish their business here. After its organization, the society advertised their desire to purchase a suitable site for their city, with the requisite water power, in any part of New Jersey. They received proposals from the West Jersey Associates, from South River, Perth Amboy, Millstone, Bull's Falls, the Little Falls of the Passaic, and from the inhabitants of the Great Falls of that river; and in May, 1792, they selected, with admirable judgment, the last place, as the principal site of their proposed operations; giving to their town the name of Paterson, after governor William Paterson, who had signed their charter. At this period there were not more than ten houses here.

At a meeting of the directors, at the Godwin hotel, on the 4th July, 1792, appropriations were made for building factories, machine shops, and shops for calico printing and weaving; and a race-way was directed to be made, for bringing the water from above the falls to the proposed mills. Unfortunately, the direction of these works was given to Major L'Enfan, a French engineer, not more celebrated for the grandeur of his conceptions, than his recklessness of expense; and whose magnificent projects commonly perished in the waste of means provided for their attainment. He immediately commenced the race-way and canal, designing to unite the Upper Passaic with the Lower, at the head of tide, near the present village of Acquackanonck, by a plan better adapted to the resources of a great empire than to those of a private company.

In January, 1793, Peter Colt, Esq. of Hartford, then comptroller of the state of Connecticut, was appointed "general superintendent of the affairs of the company, with full powers to manage the concerns of the society, as if they were his own individual property," Major L'Enfan being retained, however, as engineer; but he, after having spent, uselessly, a large sum of money, resigned his office in the following September. Mr. Colt, thus in sole charge of the works, completed the race-way, conducting the water to the first factory erected by the society. The canal to tide water, had been abandoned before the departure of the engineer.

The factory, 90 feet long by 40 wide, and 4 stories high, was finished in 1794, when cotton yarn was spun in the mill; but yarn had been spun in the preceding year, by machinery moved by oxen. In 1794, also, calico shawls and other cotton goods were printed; the bleached and unbleached muslins being purchased in New York. In the same year the society gave their attention to the culture of the silk worm, and directed the superintendent to plant the mulberry tree for this purpose. In April of this year, also, the society, at the instance of Mr. Colt, employed a teacher to instruct, gratuitously, on the Sabbath, the children employed in the factory, and others. This was probably the first Sunday school established in New Jersey.

Notwithstanding their untoward commencement, and the many discouragements attending their progress, the directors persevered in their enterprise; and during the years

1795, and 1796, much yarn of various sizes was spun, and several species of cotton fabrics were made. But, at length satisfied that it was hopeless to contend, successfully, longer with an adverse current, they resolved, July, 1796, to abandon the manufacture, and discharged their workmen. This result was produced by a combination of causes. Nearly $50,000 had been lost, by the failure of the parties to certain bills of exchange purchased by the company, to buy in England plain cloths for printing; large sums had been wasted by the engineer; and the machinists and manufacturers imported, were presumptuous, and ignorant of many branches of the business they engaged to conduct; and more than all, the whole attempt was premature. No pioneer had led the way, and no experience existed in the country, relative to any subject of the enterprise. Beside, had the country been in a measure prepared for manufactures, the acquisition of the carrying trade, which our merchants were then making, was turning public enterprise into other channels. The ruin of the company under these circumstances, cannot now be cause of astonishment. But to this catastrophe the children of Mr. Colt, now deeply interested in the operations of the company, have the just and proud satisfaction to know, that their parent was in no way auxiliary. On closing their concerns, the directors unanimously returned him their thanks "for his industry, care and prudence, in the management of their affairs, since he had been employed in their service; fully sensible that the failure of the objects of the society was from causes not in his power, or that of any other man, to prevent."

The cotton mill of the company was subsequently leased to individuals, who continued to spin candle wick and coarse yarn until 1807, when it was accidentally burned down, and was never rebuilt. The admirable water-power of the company, was not however wholly unemployed. In 1801, a mill seat was leased to Mr. Charles Kinsey, and Israel Crane; in 1807, a second, and 1811, a third, to other persons; and between 1812, and 1814, several others were sold or leased. In 1814, Mr. Roswell L. Colt, the present enterprising governor of the society, purchased, at a depreciated price, a large proportion of the shares, and reanimated the association. From this period, the growth of Paterson has been steady, except during the 3 or 4 years which followed the peace of 1815.

The advantages derivable from the great fall in the river here, have been improved with much judgment. A dam of 4½ feet high, strongly framed and bolted to the rock in the bed of the river above the falls, turns the stream through a canal excavated in the trap rock of the bank, into a basin; whence, through strong guard-gates, it supplies in succession three canals on separate planes, each below the other; giving to the mills on each, a head and fall of about 22 feet. By means of the guard-gate, the volume of water is regulated at pleasure, and a uniform height preserved; avoiding the inconvenience of back-water. The expense of maintaining the dam, canals, and main sluice-gates, and of regulating the water, is borne by the company; who have expended, in raising the main embankment, and constructing the feeder from the river and new upper canal, and for works to supply water to the third tier of mills, the sum of $40,000.

The advantages which Paterson possesses for a manufacturing town, are obvious. An abundant and steady supply of water; a healthy, pleasant, and fruitful country, supplying its markets fully with excellent meats and vegetables—Its proximity to New York, where it obtains the raw material, and sale for manufactured goods; and with which it is connected by the sloop navigation of the Passaic, by the Morris canal, by a turnpike-road, and by a rail-road, render it one of the most desirable sites in the

Union. The transportation of merchandise to and from New York, has heretofore cost from two, to two and a half dollars the ton; but will be reduced on the rail-road to one dollar.

A water-power, consisting of as much water as may be drawn through an aperture one foot square, or of 144 square inches, with a lot for buildings, having 100 feet on the front and rear, was let in the first instance at a rent of $75 per annum; in the second, at $100; in the third, at $160; and the price has been advanced from time to time, to $200, $250, $300, $400, and $500 rent, per annum. At present, the terms of the company for such power and lot, are—rent of $500 per annum, on a lease of 21 years; renewable every 21 years at the same rent, on the payment of a fine of $500, or an absolute right in fee simple for the sum of $10,000. Lots for dwellings, &c., may be obtained at from $150, to $1000 each. In good situations, the ordinary price is about 5 or 6 hundred dollars for 25 feet in front, by 100 in depth.

The city of Paterson is incorporated pursuant to 26th and 27th sections of the act of 22d November, 1791, and the plot, lies partly in the county of Bergen, and partly in the county of Essex, on both sides of the river, and covers 36 square miles, and is governed by a mayor, recorder, common council, &c. It is 15 miles N. from Newark, and 18 N. W. from New York, 61 N. E. from Trenton, 91 from Philadelphia, and 227 from W. C. The following statistics of the town are derived from a very valuable memoir prepared by the Rev. Dr. Fisher, pastor of the First Presbyterian church there, in 1832. The number of dwellings are 765, stores, &c. 76, families 1586, consisting of 4515 males, and 4570 females, of whom 3949 were under 16 years of age, and 250 were coloured persons. During the year ending 4th July, 1832, the number of births was 321, and of deaths 170; excess of births 151. This population is divided into 14 religious denominations, strongly illustrating the diversity of religious opinion in thickly settled districts of the United States, and the harmony which may prevail among the worshippers of the Deity, where lust of temporal dominion cannot be gratified. There were here of heads of families, Presbyterians 384, Reformed Dutch 323, Roman Catholics 288, Methodists 269, Episcopalians 149, Baptists 86, Reformed Presbyterians 35, Dutch Seceders 6, Lutherans 6, Friends 2, Christian Baptist 1, Universalists 2, Unitarians 2, Deists 4; and there were 11 persons who either professed no religion, or whose sentiments were unknown. There are 9 houses for religious worship, viz: Presbyterian 1, Reformed Dutch 2, Roman Catholic 1, Methodist 1, Episcopal 1, Reformed Presbyterian 1, Baptist 1, True Reformed Dutch 1; the eight first of which had, each, its settled minister. The provision for education in the town, consisted of 20 pay schools, 13 for males and 7 for females, having scholars 384; a free school supported by the town for poor children, having 188 pupils; an infant school under the direction and patronage of a society of ladies, selected from the different religious denominations, in which poor children between the ages of 3 and 8 years, are gratuitously instructed, without regard to the religious professions of their parents. At this school, there was 173 pupils, making the whole number of children thus instructed, weekly, 1195. Seven Sabbath schools taught 1531 scholars, a large proportion of whom attended no other schools.

There is here also, a philosophical society composed of young gentlemen, who have associated for literary improvement, and have collected a respectable library; and a mechanics' society, incorporated by the legislature, for advancement in science and the mechanic arts, which has laid the foundation of a library and a collection of philosophical apparatus.

In 1832 the town contained 163 widows, in whose families there were 834 souls, the greater portion of whom, now maintained by the manufacturing establishments, would, otherwise, have been dependant upon public or private charity, for support.

There were, at this time, 12 blacksmiths, besides those immediately connected with the machine shops—in these 22 fires, and 37 hands are employed; 34 shoemakers, employing 183 hands; 13 tailors and tailoresses, employing 70 hands; 9 milliners, employing 34 hands; 3 bookstores; 1 bindery; 1 circulating library, of 1300 volumes; 1 incorporated library company, with a library of 250 volumes; 1 bank, viz. "The People's Bank of Paterson"—Alex. Carrick, president, and James Nazro, cashier; 10 physicians; 6 licensed attorneys; 2 commissioners; 3 masters in chancery, and 5 notaries; 3 judges of the county courts, and 10 justices of the peace; 2 printing offices, from which are issued 2 weekly papers, viz. the "Paterson Intelligencer," printed by David Burnett, the proprietor, and published on Wednesday; and the "Paterson Courier," printed by A. S. Gould, the proprietor, and published on Tuesday: 1 post-office, Moses E. De Witt, post-master; 10 licensed taverns; 40 grocery and provision stores; and 51 grogshops, where little else but ardent spirits is sold; 1 dry good, hardware, crockery, and grocery store; 2 dry good and crockery stores; 14 fancy dry good stores; 2 hardware stores; 1 fancy chair store; 1 fancy chair and looking-glass store; 1 apothecary and paint store, and 4 medicine stores; 5 shoe stores; 1 corset, millinery, and fancy store; 2 hat stores, and 1 hatter, employing 4 hands; 1 poor-house, 21 paupers; 2 breweries; 1 file cutter; 1 girth manufacturer, and 4 looms; 1 reed maker; 4 bakeries; 2 carpet weavers; 1 manufactory of fine ingrained carpets, employing 7 looms and 12 hands; 1 gun and locksmith, &c.; 2 coopers, employing 11 hands; 1 sizing establishment; 3 dyeing establishments, separate from the factories, and 8 hands; 1 umbrellamaker; 1 chair bottomer; several heddlemakers; 2 tobacconists, 9 hands; 2 watchmakers, jewellers and silversmiths; 4 cabinetmakers, 35 hands; 1 candle and 2 soap factories; 2 barbers; 3 lottery offices; 1 tanner and currier, 33 vats and 9 hands; 3 hay scales, Bull's patent; 4 painters and glaziers, 22 hands; 1 Masonic hall; 1 auction mart; 1 counterpane weaver; 1 marble yard, 6 hands; 1 freestone yard, 5 hands; 7 slaughter-houses, and 9 butchers; 4 livery stables; 7 wheelwrights and 19 hands; 2 saddle and harnessmakers, and trimmers, 10 hands; 8 confectionery and toy shops; 2 copper, tin, and sheet iron manufactories, and 24 hands; 2 large and commodious market-houses, and the market is well supplied with meat, fish, and vegetables of the various kinds; 1 museum, fitted up with taste; 1 hoe factory, 4 hands; 1 sashmaker, 2 hands; 4 public engines for extinguishing fires, and 7 private ones—2 moveable and 5 attached to the factories; 15 master carpenters, employing 122 hands; 8 master masons, employing 174 hands; 1 public dispensary, incorporated by act of the legislature.

Paterson contains 1 saw mill, with 2 saw carriages and 2 saws; 1 grist mill, with 2 run of stones; 4 turning and bobbin factories, employing 43 hands; 2 bleaching establishments, employing 18 hands; 5 millwright establishments, employing 59 hands; 1 manufactory of cotton wadding, where wadding of a superior quality is manufactured; 4 machine factories, employing 404 hands. In the last the manufacture of cotton and other machinery is brought to a high state of perfection. In that of Messrs. Plunket and Thompson, are employed between 60 and 70 hands, and being recently established, it contains the latest improvements in their art, and produces machinery of superior quality.

Attached to the works of Godwin, Clark, and Co., and of Rogers, Ketchum, and Grosvenor, are two extensive brass and iron founderies, where mill shafts, wheels, and the various parts of cotton machinery, &c. are cast: 20 manufactories of cotton; in these are 40,501 spindles in operation; they employ 1646 hands, and use annually 3,360,272 lbs. of raw cotton.

The Phenix Manufacturing Company, in addition to their cotton establishment, have 1616 spindles, employed in spinning flax; the flax annually consumed is 493,000 lbs., giving employment to 196 hands. This flax is manufactured into duck and bagging.

In the cotton establishment of John Colt, Esq. were manufactured in 1831, 460,000 yards of cotton duck: A sattinet factory, with a dyeing establishment annexed, employs 1322 spindles, 75 hands, 23 power looms, and 13 hand looms; consuming, annually, 105,000 lbs. of wool.

The power looms in operation in all the factories were 311, hand looms 14. In the village and out of the factories, there were only 50 hand looms.

Total number of power and hand looms 374. Total spindles 43,439. Total cotton, wool, and flax annually consumed is 3,958,272 lbs. Total hands employed in all the establishments 2543: a large proportion of whom are children.

A button factory, employing 28 hands. In this factory are made steel buttons, clasps, ornaments, and a variety of other articles of iron and steel: A gilt button manufactory, employing 20 hands, and manufacturing at the rate 9000 groce of buttons a year. The average price of these buttons is about $4 50 a groce. Annual produce $40,000. The buttons manufactured at this establishment, as it respects perfection of workmanship and elegance of finish, in the opinion of competent judges, are not surpassed by any gilt buttons imported from Europe.

The large four story brick factory of Rogers, Ketchum, and Grosvenor, besides the room occupied by the machinists, is capable of containing 5000 cotton spindles, with the machines for preparation.

One large three storied paper mill.

In the establishment of Messrs. Collet and Smith, were manufactured in 1831, 900 pieces of nankeen, of a superior quality, from nankeen cotton, raised by Governor Forsyth of Georgia.

That part of the village of Paterson, situated on the north side of the Passaic river, usually called New Manchester, had

	dwellings,	families.	souls.
In 1824,	31	48	289
1827,	66	115	625
1829,	89	154	852
1832,	114	217	1214

In the whole village of Paterson, in 1824, there were,

	814	families, &	4787	souls.
In 1825,	849	do.	5084	do.
1827,	1046	do.	6236	do.
1829,	1220	do.	7033	do.
1832,	1568	do.	9085	do.

The spindles in operation in 1825, were 19,036; in 1827, 25,998; in 1829, 30,295; and in 1832, 43,439.

The raw material consumed in 1827, was,

	Cotton,	1,843,100 lbs.
	Flax,	620,000
	Total,	2,463,100 lbs.
In 1829,	Cotton,	2,179,600 lbs.
	Flax,	600,000
	Total,	2,779,600 lbs.
In 1832,	Cotton,	3,360,272 lbs.
	Flax,	493,000
	Wool,	105,000
	Total,	3,958,272 lbs.

In consequence of the great improvement in cotton machinery, yarn of a much finer thread is spun; consequently, the consumption of the raw material has not increased in proportion to the increased number of spindles.

In 1827, there were employed in all the manufacturing establishments, 1453 hands, and the annual amount of wages paid to them, as ascertained from the pay lists of the manufacturers, was $221,123. In 1829, there were employed, 1879 hands; annual wages, $285,453; in 1832, there were employed, 2543 hands; annual amount of wages, $367,003.

The salutary influence of this thriving town, is sensibly felt throughout the whole of the N. E. section of the state. The agriculturist has participated, in no small degree, in its prosperity. His lands have greatly increased in marketable value, and his physical and moral condition has been in all respects improved. If wise, he will maintain this source of present enjoyment to himself, and of future happiness to his posterity, with a zeal becoming its value.

Pattenbury, small village of Bethlehem t-ship, at the S. foot of Musconetcong mountain, on Alberson's brook, 12 miles N. W. of Flemington, Hunterdon county, contains a grist mill, a store, 6 dwellings. Soil, red shale, through or near which a vein of limestone probably passes.

Paulinskill, creek of Sussex and Warren counties, which rises by two branches; the easterly one from a pond on the south of Pimple hill, in Hardiston t-ship, and flowing thence N. W., through Newton township, into Frankford township; the westerly one, from Long and Culver's ponds, at the foot of the Blue mountain, in Frankford, in which township the branches unite near the town of Augusta, and flow thence by a south-west course of 22 or 23 miles, to the Delaware river: the whole length of the stream, by its eastern branch, may be 35 miles. It gives motion to many mills, and flows through a very fertile country of lime and slate formations, separating them for a considerable part of its course.

Paulsboro', town of Greenwich t-ship, Gloucester co., near Mantua creek, 4 miles W. of Woodbury; contains a tavern, store, 10 or 12 dwellings, and a Methodist church.

Paxton's Island, in the Delaware river, Amwell t-ship, Hunterdon co.

Peck's Beach, on the coast of the Atlantic ocean, in Upper t-ship, Cape May co., extends about 10 miles, from Corson's to Egg Harbour inlet.

Pedricktown, p-t. of Upper Penn's Creek t-ship, Salem co., lying on Oldman's creek, about 8 or 9 miles from its mouth; contains between 20 and 30 dwellings, 1 Friends' meeting house, 1 tavern, 2 stores, 1 school; and is inhabited by agriculturists and mechanics. The soil around it is a sandy loam and well cultivated, by means of the marl found in the neighbourhood. The *Palma Christi*, or castor bean, is extensively produced here, and about 1500 galls. of oil manufactured annually. The town is distant, 16 miles N. E. from W. C.; 54 S. from Trenton, and 14 or 15 N. from Salem.

Pemberton, or *New Mills*, p-t. of Northampton t-ship, Burlington co., on the north branch of the Rancocus creek, 6 miles above Mount Holly, 13 from Burlington, 27 from Trenton, and 162 from W. C.; contains a grist mill, saw mill, fulling mill, a cotton manufactory, a cupola furnace, 1 Methodist and 1 Baptist church, a school house, 2 taverns, 5 stores, and about 100 dwellings. This is a thriving town, growing rapidly by reason of its manufactures.

Pennington, p-t. of Hopewell t-ship, Hunterdon co. Centrally situated, 8 miles N. of Trenton; 174 from W. C., and 15 S. from Flemington; in a level country of red shale, fertile and well cultivated; contains 1 Methodist and 1 Presbyterian church, both good buildings of brick, the latter having a cupola and bell, 3 taverns, as many stores, and about 30 dwellings, a public library and an academy. This is a very neat and pleasant village, surrounded by wealthy and liberal farmers.

Penn's Grove, small hamlet and ferry, on the Delaware river, in Upper Penn's Neck t-ship, Salem co., distant about 15 miles N. of Salem; there are here 6 or 8 dwellings, a tavern and store. The Wilmington and Philadelphia steam boat touches here daily, to receive and land passengers, and a 4 horse stage runs daily between the ferry and the town of Salem.

Penn's Neck, (see ***Williamsburg***,) lies in the angle formed by the Stony Brook and Millstone river, West Windsor township, Middlesex county, about a mile S. E. of Princeton.

Penn's Neck, Lower, t-ship, of Salem co, bounded N. by Upper Penn's Neck; E. and S. E. by Salem river, which divides it from Mannington; and S. W. and W. by the river Delaware. Centrally distant, N. W. of Salem, 5 miles; greatest length, 9; breadth, 6 miles; area, 12,645 acres; surface, level; soil, partly rich clay loam, partly sandy loam, and partly excellent marsh meadow. Products, wheat, rye, corn and vegetables for market. Population in 1830, 994. In 1832, the township contained 228 taxables; 73 householders, whose ratables did not exceed $30 in value; 4 school houses, an Episcopal, a Presbyterian and a Methodist church, 2 taverns, 2 stores, 2 fisheries; and it paid township tax, $300; county tax, $722 76; state tax, $226 50.

A canal, of two miles in length, near the northern boundary, cut through a dead level, unites the Salem river with the Delaware at about 12 miles above the mouth of the former, saving to vessels from this point, a circular navigation of 25 miles. Kinseyville is a small village on the Delaware, at which there is a ferry.

Penn's Neck, Upper, t-ship, Salem co., bounded N. and E. by Woolwich t-ship, Gloucester co.; S. E. by Piles Grove t-ship, Salem co.; S. by Mannington t-ship; S. W. by Lower Penn's Neck; and W. by the river Delaware. Centrally distant from Salem, 10; greatest length, 9; breadth, 7½ miles; surface level; soil light sandy loam; generally cultivated with rye and Indian corn; area, 21,053 acres. There are, in the township, 1 Friends' and 1 Methodist meeting, 5 schools, 5 taverns, 6 stores, 1 grist and 1 saw mill, 1 ferry, 1 distillery. In 1832, there were 340 horses and mules, and 900 neat cattle, over three years of age; 117 householders, whose ratables did not exceed $30; 330 taxable inhabitants. In 1830, the population by census, was 1638. In 1832, the township paid township tax, $400; county tax, $738 20; state tax, $230 75.

A valuable bed of shell marl lies in the township, near Pedricktown; the extent of which has not yet been explored. Large quantities have been dug and used with great advantage in this and the neighbouring townships. It is found most useful on the light and sandy soils, in the culture of grass and grain, when applied in quantities of 10 or 12 two horse wagon loads to the acre. In opening the pits a bed of oyster and other shells, at irregular distances from the surface, from three to twenty feet, presents itself. This bed is about three feet thick. Beneath it is a mass of undiscovered depth, composed of black earth and shells, known as gunpowder marl, but it is not in as much repute as the stratum of shells. These shells, when exposed to the air, disintegrate rapidly. The marl is sold at about 50 cts. the wagon load. More than an acre of this bed has been already excavated.

Pennypot, name of a small tributary of the Great Egg Harbour river, and also of a tavern and mill, near the junction of Hospitality branch, with the main stream, in Hamilton t-ship, Gloucester co.

Pensaukin Creek, rises by two branches, one in the N. part of Evesham t-ship, and the other on the line between that t-ship, in Burlington co., and Waterford t-ship, of Gloucester co., uniting about four miles above the mouth, and flowing into the Delaware, three miles above Petty's island. It is a mill stream, navigable for 5 or 6 miles, and forms part of the boundary line between Burlington and Gloucester counties.

Pepack Creek, mill stream, and tributary of the N. branch of the Raritan; rises in Chester t-ship, Morris co., and flows to its recipient, by a southerly course of about 7 miles, in Bedminster t-ship, Somerset co.

Pepack, p-t., of Bedminster t-ship, Somerset co., 11 miles N. W. from Somerville, 212 from W. C., and 46 from Trenton; contains a tavern, store, grist mill, and some 10 or 12 dwellings, in a fertile limestone country.

Pequannock, t-ship, Morris co., bounded N. E. by the Pequannock creek, which separates it from Pompton t-ship, Bergen co.; E. by Pompton river, dividing it from Saddle river t-ship, of the same co.; S. E. by Caldwell t-ship, Essex co.; S. by Hanover and Randolph t-ships, and W. by Jefferson t-ship. Centrally distant, N. from Morristown, 10 miles. Greatest length, E. and W. 16, breadth, 11 miles; area, 74,000 acres. The surface of the t-ship is hilly, being covered with mountain ridges and knolls. On the northern boundary, is Green Pond mountain, girding a narrow valley, through which flows the Burnt Meadow branch of the Rockaway river, and bounded southward, by Mount Hope, and Copperas mountain. Between these and the next ridge, is a wider valley, drained by the Beaver Branch of the same river, and south of this, innominate knolls and ridges make valleys, through which run minor tributaries of the river. The soil of the t-ship is generally loam and clay, but grey limestone is found in the valley, S. of Copperas mountain, and probably in other places. Iron abounds in the hills in the N. W., and is of excellent quality, from which many iron works in the neighbourhood are supplied. From the sulphate of iron in the Copperas mountain, much copperas was formerly made. Green Pond is a large sheet of water, nearly 3 miles long, by a half-mile in width; in the vale between Green Pond and Copperas mountain, much resorted to for boating and fishing; and the wild scenery around it is much admired. The valley is inhabited sparsely, by persons dependant upon the iron works. Pompton plains, on the east border of the t-ship, are level and sandy, but densely inhabited, and tolerably cultivated. Pompton, Montville, Powerville, &c., are post-towns of the t-ship. Population in 1830, 4451. In 1832, the t-ship contained 129 householders, whose ratables did not exceed $30 in value, 132 single men, 1050 taxables, 8 stores, 9 saw mills, 5 grist mills, 37 tan vats, 2 distilleries, 30 chairs and sulkies, 14 forges for making iron, 1 furnace, 1 four horse stage, 4 rolling and slitting mills, 1 fulling mill, 690 horses and mules, and 2265 neat cattle, above the age of 3 years; and it paid state tax, $574; county tax, $1285 10; poor tax, $800; road tax, $3000. The Newark and Milford turnpike road crosses the western, and the Newark and Hamburg, and Paterson and Hamburg, turnpike roads, cross the eastern end of the t-ship, and the Morris canal runs through the southern part, and for some distance along the valley of the Rockaway river.

Pequannock Creek, rises in the Wallkill and Wawayanda mountains, in Sussex co., and flows by a southeast and south course, of about 27 miles, to the Passaic river; forming the boundary between Morris and Bergen cos. Below Pompton village it takes the name of Pompton river. It has a rapid current, through a narrow valley, and considerable volume; and is, therefore, an excellent mill stream.

Pequest Creek, rises by two branches, in the eastern part of Sussex co., which unite in Independence t-ship, Warren co., and flow thence by a S. W. course, through Oxford t-ship, to the Delaware river, at the town of Belvidere. Its whole length is about

30 miles. This is a large and rapid stream, affording abundant water-power, and draining, by the main stem and branches, an extensive valley of primitive limestone. (See *Belvidere.*)

Perryville, small p-town of Bethlem t-ship, Hunterdon co., on the turnpike road from Somerville to Philipsburg, about 10 miles N. of Flemington, 35 from Trenton, and 194 from W. C.

Perth Amboy City, p-t., t-ship, and port of entry of Middlesex co., at the head of the Raritan bay, and at the confluence of the Raritan river with the Arthur Kill, or Staten Island Sound. It lies 14 miles from the sea, at Sandy Hook, 25 miles by the Sound from New York, 15 by the river, and 10 by land, from New Brunswick; 36 by post-route from Trenton, 65 by rail-road from Philadelphia, and 212 from W. C. The port, large and safe, and one of the best on the continent, is easily approached from the sea by a broad estuary, having generally 12 feet water, and in the main channel from 24 to 26 feet.

This advantageous site for a town, was early noticed by the agents of the East Jersey proprietors; in the language of deputy governor Lawrie, in 1684, "there being no such place in all England, for conveniency and pleasant situation." The place was known to the aborigines as *Ambo*, the Point; and was greatly resorted to by them on account of its fish and oysters, the latter of which are yet abundant here. The relics of Indian festivities, are still visible in the large quantities of oyster shells which mingle with, and enrich portions of the soil. The name of Perth was given to it in honour of James, Earl of Perth, one of the 24 proprietaries; and it was called by that name only in the instructions of the proprietaries, until 1698, when we, for the first time, in the instructions to the deputy governor, Basse, find the name of "Perth Amboy."

The town was laid out into 150 lots, by Samuel Groome, one of the proprietaries, and surveyor general, as early as 1683. In the following year, Gawn Lawrie, a proprietary and deputy governor, added large tracts for out-lots. The town plot was designed to contain 1500 acres; and lots were sold at 20 pounds, with condition that the purchasers should each build a house 30 feet long, by 18 feet wide. Lawrie contracted at this time for the erection of several houses for the proprietaries, and one 60 feet long and 18 wide, for the governor. He was directed to make the town the seat of government and the chief mart of the province, and to incorporate the inhabitants by charter, with the necessary privileges and jurisdiction of a city.

This was a favourite spot with the East Jersey proprietaries, who used many efforts to render it the site of a large city, but it was overshadowed by New York, and their exertions were in vain. After the surrender of the proprietary governments to the crown, the general assembly and the supreme court of the province, assembled at this place and Burlington, alternately.

The city was incorporated under the proprietary and royal governments, but its present charter embracing the provisions of the prior ones, is under the act of 21st December, 1784, and gives the following boundaries. "Beginning at the meeting of the waters of the Raritan river with those of the Sound, at that part of Staten Island from the main to the southward of the flat or shoal that runs off from Cole Point; thence up the Sound, on the eastern bank of the channel as the same runs to Woodbridge creek; thence up the creek to the mouth of the stream on which Cutler's mill stands; thence up said creek to a lane leading to a line between George Herriott and Grace Innsley; thence by said lane to the road leading from Amboy to New Brunswick; thence by said road south to a lane leading to Florida Landing; thence by said lane to the north corner of the farm late of Samuel Neville; thence by the line of the same to Raritan river, and across the same to the south bank of the channel thereof; and thence to the place of beginning." The government of the city is under a mayor, recorder, three aldermen, who are justices of the peace, ex-officio, and appointed by the legislature for seven years; and six common councilmen, sheriff, coroner, and sergeant-at-mace, and township officers, elected annually by the people. The mayor, recorder, and aldermen, have power to grant tavern licenses, and to hold a court of record, having jurisdiction of all causes of a commercial nature, wherein the matter in dispute shall have arisen within the corporation, and subsists between foreigner and foreigner, or between foreigner and citizen of the United States. And to induce the settlement of merchants here the port was declared *free*, and they exempt from taxation for 25 years. The township contains 2577 acres of land, of alluvial formation, consisting of clay, sand loam, and gravel, in which, at various depths, are found organic remains. It is elevated above the tide some 40 or 50 feet, and is undulating in its surface. The population, which is principally gathered near the point, there not being more than 20 dwellings separated from the town, amounted in 1830, to 879. The township in 1832, contained about 140 dwellings, 78 householders, whose ratable estates did not exceed $30 in value; 39 single men, 10 storekeepers or traders, 5 taverns, an Episcopal, Presbyterian, and a Baptist church, 1 school for boys, another for girls, and a third established under the school fund of the state. St. Peter's the Episcopal church, was founded probably about the year 1685. In July 30th, 1718, it was incorporated by George I; and William Eier, and John Barclay, were appointed the first church wardens, and Thomas Gordon Esq., John Rudyard, Robert King, and John Stevens, the first vestrymen. The church is indebted to Thomas Gordon, George Willocks, and Margaretta Willocks, his wife, and major John Harrison, for considerable endowments, upon which its prosperity is based. There is an extensive pottery of excellent stone-ware in the town in which the clay from South Amboy is chiefly, if not solely used. But the chief business of the city is the oyster fishery. The shell-fish are abundant in the bay, and the bottom is so favourable to their growth, that large numbers are transplanted thither, not only from the river above, but also from Virginia. A capital of more than $40,000 is said to be thus employed, yielding an annual profit of more than $20,000. The state of New Jersey has leased about 250 acres of land, covered with water, here, in small lots, of a few acres each, whose tenants rear oysters upon them. But the state of New York, claiming exclusive right of property, in the soil under water, to the line of low-water mark, on the shore of the state; conflicting claims have induced vexatious disputes, and even alarming riots, which have prevented the quiet enjoyment of the tenants, and the collection of rents. In 1832, the city paid poor tax, $350; county tax, $135 87; and state tax, $110 56.

From its agreeable position, vicinity to the ocean, and sea-water baths, Perth Amboy is a pleasant residence during the hot months, and is much visited for recreation, by the citizens of New York. Some years since, a very large and commodious hotel, called Brighton, was erected for their accommodation; but, at that period, there was not sufficient support to sustain it, and Brighton-house is now a handsome country-seat.

The destiny of this town, long obscured, notwithstanding its fine port, and pleasant and healthy position, is probably about to receive a favourable change, through the agency of the Delaware and Raritan canal, and the rail-roads to Philadelphia. The ready transportation of merchandise, by these means, may convert this into an out-port of Philadelphia.

The collection district of Perth Amboy, comprehends all that part of East New Jersey, (that part excepted which is included in the district of Little Egg Harbour) south of Elizabethtown, together with all the waters thereof, within the jurisdiction of the state. The towns of New Brunswick, and Middletown Point, are ports of delivery only. The collector resides at Amboy, and a surveyor at New Brunswick.

Peter's Beach, on the Altantic ocean, Galloway t-ship, Gloucester co., at the mouth of Absecum inlet, and between it and Quarter inlet.

Philipsburg, town of Greenwich t-ship, Warren co., on the left bank of the Delaware river, opposite the borough of Easton, in Pennsylvania, 14 miles below the town of Belvidere, and about 60 above Trenton. Contains about 20 dwellings, 4 stores, and 2 taverns. The Morris canal communicates with the Delaware here, opposite to, and a short distance below, the basin of the Lehigh canal. A bridge of wood of three arches, covered, 600 feet long, and 24 feet wide, over the Delaware, which cost $80,000, connects Philipsburg with Easton.

Pike Brook, tributary of No-Pipe Brook, rises in the Nashanic mountain, Montgomery t-ship, Somerset co., and flows S. E. about 5 miles to its recipient.

Pilesgrove, t-ship, Salem co., bounded, N. E. by Woolwich t-ship, Gloucester co., from which it is divided by Oldman's creek; S. E. by Pittsgrove t-ship; S. W. by Upper Alloways, and Mannington t-ships, and N. W. by Upper Penn's Neck t-ship. Centrally distant, N. E. from Salem, 10 miles. Greatest length 9, breadth 6½ miles; area, about 24,000 acres; of which, little more than 1000 may be unimproved. Surface, level; soil, stiff clay and deep loam, well cultivated in wheat, rye, oats, and corn. The Salem creek flows N. W. through the t-ship, and gives motion to a woollen factory, and several mills. Population in 1830, 2150. In the year 1832, there were in the t-ship, 128 householders, whose ratables did not exceed $30; 3 grist mills, 3 saw mills, 4 tan yards, 2 distilleries for cider, 553 horses and mules, and 966 head of neat cattle, above the age of 3 years. Sharptown and Woodstown are villages and post-towns of the t-ship. Near the latter are some valuable marl beds. There are 1 Quaker, 1 Baptist, and 1 African Methodist church in the t-ship.

Pimple Hill, a noted eminence of Hardiston t-ship, Sussex co., near the eastern line of the t-ship.

Pine Brook, Caldwell t-ship, Essex co., rises in the Second mountain, and flows W. to the Passaic river, by a course of about 3 miles. It is a mill stream.

Pine Mount Creek, Greenwich t-ship, Salem co., rises on the E. line of the t-ship, and flows southward, some 3 or 4 miles, when dividing into two branches, in opposite directions, it isolates an eminence covered with pines, and bounded southward by the Cohansey river, of which the creek is a tributary.

Piscataway, t-ship, Middlesex co., bounded N. by Westfield t-ship; E. by Woodbridge; S. and S. W. by the Raritan river, and N. W. by Green Brook, separating it from Warren t-ship, Somerset co. Centrally distant, N. from New Brunswick, 5 miles. Greatest length, N. and S. 9 miles; breadth, E. and W. 7½ miles; area, 27,000 acres. Green Brook receives from the t-ship two tributaries, Amherst and Cedar Brooks. New Market, post-town; Samptown, Green Brook, Brooklyn, New Durham, Piscataway, and Raritan Landing, are villages of the t-ship. Population in 1830, 3969. In 1832, the t-ship contained an Episcopalian church, 695 taxables, 85 householders, whose ratables did not exceed $30 in value; 91 single men, 10 stores, 2 saw mills, 6 grist mills, 1 plaster mill, 4 distilleries, 709 horses and mules, and 1501 neat cattle, above the age of 3 years; and it paid state tax, $495 91; county tax, $609 72; poor tax, $1400; road tax, $1000. The surface of the t-ship is level, soil of loam, clay, and red shale, generally very well cultivated.

Piscataway, village of the above t-ship, 3 miles E. from New Brunswick, and 1 N. from the Raritan river, on the turnpike road from New Brunswick to Woodbridge; contains an Episcopal church, a store, tavern, and some 10 or 12 dwellings, in a tolerably fertile country. This was an old Indian village, and is remarkable for having been the seat of justice for Middlesex and Somerset cos., so early as the year 1683. At that period, the courts were holden sometimes at this place, and sometimes at Woodbridge.

Piscot Brook, a small tributary of the south branch of the Raritan river, rises in Round valley, in the S. E. angle of Lebanon t-ship, Hunterdon co.

Pittsgrove, t-ship, Salem co., bounded N. E. by Franklin and Woolwich t-ships, of Gloucester co.; S. E. by Millville t-ship, of Cumberland co.; S. W. by Upper Deerfield t-ship, of Cumberland, and by Upper Alloway's Creek t-ships, of Salem co. Centrally distant, E. from Salem, 16 miles. Greatest length, 15, breadth, 7 miles; area, about 44,000 acres, of which 26,000 acres are unimproved. Population in 1830, 2216. Surface, partly undulating, and partly level; the soil is chiefly sandy and gravelly loam. A proportion on the N. W. part, is forest, of pine and white oak timber, which has been much cut over, and is known as the *Barrens*. It is drained on the S. E. and S. W. by branches of Maurice run, and on the N. W. by the head waters of Salem and Oldman's creeks. Daretown, Centreville, and Pittstown, are villages of the t-ship; the last two of which are post-towns. There were in 1832, in the t-ship, 1 Presbyterian, 1 Baptist, and 3 Methodist churches; 161 householders, whose ratables did not exceed $30 in value; 510 taxables, 6 stores, 2 grist mills, 5 saw mills, 2 fulling mills, 1 large tan yard, 5 cider distilleries, 525 horses and mules, and 933 neat cattle, above 3 years of age. The t-ship paid tax for t-ship purposes, $300; county, $921 92; state tax, $294 42. By the act of 19th Nov., 1821, and its supplement, 19th Nov., 1823, a township called Centreville, was taken from this, but was returned to it, by act 18th Feb., 1829.

Pittstown, p-t., of Salem co.; centrally situate in Pittsgrove t-ship, 16 miles E. of Salem; 180 N. E. of W. C., and 74 S. from Trenton; contains 15 dwellings, 2 taverns, and 2 stores, a grist mill, saw mill, school house, and masonic hall. The soil around it, light and sandy.

Pittstown, Alexandria t-ship, Hunterdon co., on the line of Kingwood t-ship, and on a tributary of the S. branch of the Raritan river, 8 miles N. W. of Flemington, 31 from Trenton, and 190 from W. C.; contains 1 tavern, 1 store, a grist mill, and between 15 and 20 dwellings. The soil around it is clay, cold and poor; surface hilly.

Plainfield, a large and thriving village of Westfield t-ship, Essex co., on Green Brook, the line between that and Somerset co. 211 miles N. E. from W. C., 65 from Philadelphia, 45 from Trenton, 20 S. W. from Newark, 16 from Elizabethtown, 25 from New York, and 11 N. E. from New Brunswick;—on a plain of very level land, between 2 and 3 miles wide, and about 11 long; contains 1 Presbyterian, 1 Baptist, and 1 Methodist church, 2 Friends' meeting houses, (Hicksite and Orthodox) 2 grist mills, 1 saw mill, 4 stores, 3 schools, 2 clergymen, 1 lawyer, 2 physicians, 2 taverns, 4 stores, 13 master hatters, who manufacture about $75,000 worth of hats annually; 5 master tailors, employing 70 hands, who work for the southern market; a fire engine, and company, a mutual insurance company, established in 1832, which in a few months, executed policies to the amount of more than $150,000; and 120 dwellings; a ladies' library, an apprentices' library. A four-horse mail stage, to New York, three times a week, and as often to Philadelphia, on alternate days, runs through the village. The country around the town is rich, well cultivated, and healthy; the water good, and the society moral and religious, and ambitious of improvement. The neighbouring mountain, about a mile N. of the town, affords an abundant supply of cheap fuel, and screens the valley from the violence of the N. and N. W. winds; and gives a very pleasing prospect to the S. and E., over a space of 30 miles.

Plainsborough, hamlet of South Brunswick t-ship, Middlesex co., 14 miles S. W. of New Brunswick, 14 S. E. from Trenton; contains a tavern, store, and 8 or 10 dwellings. Soil, light, gravelly and sterile.

Plainville, Montgomery t-ship, Somerset co., 8 miles S. W. from Somerville; contains a tavern, store, and 4 or 5 dwellings.

Pleasant Grove, on Schooley's mountain, Washington t-ship, Morris co., on the turnpike road from Morristown to Easton, 21 miles from the former, and 20 from the latter; contains a tavern, store, and several dwellings, and a very neat stone church, belonging to Presbyterians. The surrounding country is pleasant, and is improving much by the use of lime; the soil is a stiff clay.

Pleasant Mills, p-t. of Galloway t-ship, Gloucester co., on the Atsion river, 30 miles S. E. from Woodbury, 65 from Trenton, and 173 from W. C.; contains a tavern, 2 stores, a glass factory, belonging to Messrs. Coffan & Co., a cotton factory, with 3000 spindles, and from 20 to 30 dwellings.

Pleasant Valley, of the South mountain, Mansfield t-ship, Warren co., through which runs a small tributary of the Pohatcong creek. The soil here, as in other valleys of the t-ship, is of primitive limestone. There is a small hamlet in the valley, at which there is a grist mill, and several dwellings, upon the turnpike road to Easton.

Pleasant Valley, Randolph t-ship, Morris co., through which flows Dell's brook. The sides of the vale are of gentle ascent; part of the land good, and well cultivated.

Pluckemin, p-t. of Bedminster t-ship, Somerset co., 6 miles N. W. from Somerville, at the foot of Basking Ridge, 205 miles N. E. from W. C., and 39 from Trenton; contains 1 tavern, 2 stores, and from 25 to 30 dwellings.

Pochuck Mountain, on the W. side of Vernon t-ship, Sussex co., extends about 8 miles northwardly. Along its eastern foot runs the Pochuck turnpike road, leading from Hamburg towards the state of New York. The mountain is composed of primitive rock, of which hornblende is a principal constituent. Its base is surrounded with primitive limestone.

Pohatcong Creek, Warren co., rises near the N. E. boundary of Mansfield t-ship, and flows S. W. through that and Greenwich t-ships, by a course of three or four and twenty miles to the Delaware river, 8 or 9 miles below Philipsburg. This fine stream flows through and drains a wide and fertile valley of primitive limestone, which is very well cultivated, and produces large quantities of wheat. There is a fine view of the valley from the south-eastern acclivity of Scott's Mountain, on the road to Oxford furnace; the creek runs somewhat parallel with the Musconetcong, both following the range of the mountains, and at their mouths are scarce two miles asunder.

Point Comfort, west cape of Sandy Hook bay, Middleton t-ship, Monmouth co., projecting into the Raritan bay, 8 miles S. E. of Perth Amboy, and about an equal distance from Sandy Hook light-house.

Pole Tavern, a noted tavern and cluster of houses in Pitsgrove t-ship, about 4 miles N. W. of Pittstown, and 14 E. of Salem.

Pompeston Creek, mill stream of Chester t-ship, Burlington co., flowing by a N. W. course of about 5 miles, and emptying into the Delaware river, nearly opposite to the mouth of the Pennepack creek.

Pompton t-ship, Bergen co., bounded N. by Orange co., New York; E. by Franklin t-ship; S. by Pequannock and Jefferson t-ships, Morris co.; and W. by Hardiston and Vernon t-ships, Sussex co. Centrally distant N. W. from Hackensack, 23 miles; greatest length E. and W. 14 miles; breadth N. and S. 12 miles; area, about 70,000 acres, of which about 55,000 are unimproved, and much of it covered with forest; surface, very hilly; the Ramapo mountain, extending over the eastern boundary, and Bear Foot mountain along the western; the intervening space is broken into knolls of various sizes and shapes. The soil is generally clay and loam, but some primitive limestone appears near Mackepin lake. In these hills is found an extensive deposit of iron, in the same vein which runs through Schooley's mountain. Ringwood river bathes the western base of the Ramapo mountain; Long Pond or Greenwood lake, which crosses the northern boundary from New York, sends a tributary to it called Long Pond river. Dunker, Buck, Cedar, Hanks, and Mackepin ponds, in the south-west part of the t-ship, give their surplus waters to the Pequannock, which, under the name of Pompton river, flows along the southern boundary; Long House creek flows northerly through the north-west angle. Population in 1830, 3085. In 1832, the t-ship contained 750 taxables, 229 householders, whose ratables did not exceed $30; 79 single men, 6 stores, 15 grist mills 14 saw mills, 16 forge fires, 2 fulling mills, 20 tan vats, 2 distilleries, 519 horses and mules, and 1816 neat cattle over 3 years of age; and paid state tax, $340 13; county, $649 17. The Morris canal crosses the Pompton river about 2 miles above its mouth in this t-ship, by a wooden aqueduct 236 feet long, supported by 9 stone piers.

Pompton Plain, lies between the Pompton mountain and the Preakness hills, and is nearly 20 miles in circumference, with a variable breadth seldom exceeding four miles. It is a fresh water alluvion, and strata of gravel, sand, and clay, without rocks in place, are uniformly found here wherever wells have been dug. It was, probably, at some remote period, the bed of a lake. The Pequannock, Ringwood, and Ramapo rivers, uniting at the head of the Plain, form the Pompton river, which flows along its eastern side to the Passaic, about 8 miles. The southern, and much of the western part of the plain is marshy, and embraces about 1500 acres of peat ground, the fuel from which, so far as can be determined by a ditch running four miles through it, appears to be good. In the southern part of the plain, good granular argillaceous oxide of iron, or pea ore is raised from a space of about 200 acres. There is a straggling village upon the plain, comprising a Dutch Reformed church, a tavern, 3 stores, an academy, and about 30 dwellings: and at the head of the plain is

Pompton, p-t., 18 miles N. E. of Morristown, 236 from W. C., and 70 from Trenton; containing a tavern, store, grist mill, and 12 or 15 dwellings, and a Dutch Reformed church. (See *Ryersons.*)

Pompton Mountain, an angular hill, of Pequannock t-ship, Morris co., bounding the Pompton plains, W. and N. W. The sides of the angle are respectively about 4 miles long.

Pond Creek, Downe t-ship, Cumberland co., a short inlet to the marsh on the W. side of Maurice river cove.

Pond Creek, a small stream flowing from Lower t-ship, Cape May co., into the Delaware bay, near 2 miles N. of the Light-house.

Pond Run, small tributary of the

Assunpink creek, Nottingham t-ship, Burlington co., unites with its recipient, after a N. W. course of about 5 miles.

Ponds; name given to a neighbourhood of the S. W. part of Franklin t-ship, Bergen co.; so called, possibly, from a small lake. There is a German Reformed church here, also called Ponds.

Port Elizabeth, p-t. of Maurice river t-ship, Cumberland co., upon the Manamuskin creek, near its confluence with the Maurice river, about 14 miles from the Delaware bay, 16 S. E. from Bridgeton, 85 from Trenton, and 182 from W. C.; contains from 80 to 100 dwellings, 1 tavern, 4 stores, a Baptist church, an academy—a commodious building; some large glass works, managed by a company of Germans, under the firm of Getz, Zinger, and Co., at which large quantities of window glass and hollow ware are made. The hands of this establishment speak the German language altogether, and are remarkable for their cultivation of music. A considerable lumber trade is carried on from the town, and some ship building is done there. The town is 16 miles from the Delaware bay, by the sinuosities of Maurice river, and 8 by land. The river is navigable for vessels of 120 tons. There are 4 grist, and 3 saw mills within 3 miles of the town. Much business is done here in wood, lumber, and rails. The town is built on good land, and is surrounded by very valuable meadows, worth $100 the acre.

Port Norris, landing and storehouse, with a tavern, store, and 6 or 8 dwellings, on the west side of Maurice river, about 10 miles from the mouth, 5 miles from Dividing Creek village, and 22 from Bridgeton.

Pottersville, p-t. of Hunterdon co., on the line separating Readington from Tewkesbury t-ship, and on the turnpike road leading from Somerville to Philipsburg, 10 miles N. E. from Flemington, 43 miles from Trenton, and 211 from W. C.; contains a tavern, store, and a few dwellings.

Potter's Falls, on the Lamington river, at the angle of junction of Hunterdon, Morris, and Somerset cos.

Poverty Beach, on the Atlantic ocean, immediately north of Cape May Island, Lower t-ship, Cape May co., extends about three miles in length by half a mile in breadth.

Povershon, small village of Bloomfield t-ship, Essex co., 5 miles north of Newark; contains a school house and several dwellings. The poorhouse of the t-ship is in the valley near it.

Powerville, p-t. of Pequannock t-ship, Morris co., in the valley of the Rockaway river, 10 miles N. E. from Morristown, 234 from W. C., and 68 from Trenton; contains a tavern, 2 stores, a forge, a grist and saw mill, and from 10 to 15 dwellings. Country around rough and sterile.

Prallsville, p-t. of Amwell t-ship, Hunterdon co., on the river Delaware, 10 miles S. W. from Flemington, 20 N. from Trenton, and 174 from W. C.; contains 1 store, 1 tavern, some 6 or 8 dwellings, and a grist mill, at the mouth of the Wickhechecoke creek. There is a fine bridge here over the Delaware, erected on stone piers, by an incorporated company. The surrounding country is hilly.

Preakness Mountain, a distinguished hill of Saddle River t-ship, Bergen co., commencing about three miles N. W. from Paterson, and running in a semicircular direction several miles. It is formed by sandstone surmounted by trap rock, and embosoms an extensive valley.

Preakness Brook, Saddle River t-ship, Bergen co., which, after a south course of about 6 miles, flows into the Passaic river, about 2 miles above the Little Falls. Preakness Dutch Reformed church, is in the valley of this stream, near its source.

Primrose Creek, tributary of the Passaic river, Morris t-ship, Morris co., has a course of about six miles from its source to its recipient.

Prospect Plains, level tract of country extending between Cranberry Brook and Manalapan Brook, with a light sandy soil, in South Amboy t-ship, Middlesex co.

Princeton, p-t. and borough, partly in Montgomery t-ship, Somerset co., and partly in Windsor t-ship, Middlesex co., on the main road between New York and Philadelphia, 50 miles from the one, and 40 from the other, 11 from Trenton, 25 from New Brunswick, and 177 from W. C.; situated in a very pleasant country of red shale and alluvion, and remarkable for the salubrity of its climate, the beauty of its villas, and the neatness, generally, of its buildings. It was incorporated as a borough in 1813, and contains about 185 dwelling houses, and at least 1100 inhabitants, exclusive of the youth connected with the public institutions, of whom there are, at present, (1833) about 350.

The Delaware and Raritan canal runs within a half mile of the borough, and has already contributed, in no small degree, to its prosperity. The office of the company is established here.

Besides the buildings belonging to the literary institutions, (for these see pages 84, 85,) there are in Princeton, a Presbyterian church, an Episcopal church, and two other houses for public worship, belonging to the Presbyterian society; one of which is for the use of the coloured population. The literary institutions of Princeton are a college, a theological seminary, three classical schools, two schools for the instruction of young ladies, and three or four common schools; all independent of each other.

The name of Princeton is associated, not only with the literary reputation of our country, but also with her struggle for independence; since, in the immediate vicinity of this place, was fought the memorable battle of January 3d, 1777, in which the British army was routed by the Americans, under the command of General Washington, and in which the lamented Mercer was mortally wounded. A large painting commemorative of these events, is suspended in the chapel of the college.

Quarter's Inlet, from the Atlantic ocean to Reed's bay, between Brigantine beach on the east, and Peter's beach on the west, Galloway t-ship, Gloucester co.

Quaker Bridge, over Batsto river, Washington t-ship, Burlington co., 6 miles S. E. of Shamong village, and 4 from Atsion Furnace. There is a tavern here.

Quakertown. (See ***Fairview***.)

Quinton's Bridge, small village and p-t. on Alloways creek, in Upper Alloways t-ship, Salem co., 5 miles S. E. of Salem, 174 N. E. from W. C., and 68 S. from Trenton; contains some 12 or 15 dwellings, 1 tavern, and 2 stores. It is a landing at which much wood is delivered for the Philadelphia market. The bridge is noted in the county for a massacre of some militia, by a party of British troops, while on a foraging party, during the occupancy of Philadelphia by Sir William Howe, in the revolutionary war.

Raccoon Creek, rises in Franklin t-ship, Gloucester co., and flows thence N. W. through Woolwich t-ship, by a course of 17 miles to the River Delaware, opposite to Shiver's island. It is navigable for sloops 7 or 8 miles to Swedesborough, and for boats to Mullica Hill, 5 miles further.

Rahway River, called by the aborigines Rahawack, *anglicé*, Man's River, rises in the valley between the First and Second mountains, Orange t-ship, Essex co., and flows thence S. W. and S. to Springfield, where it receives several considerable tributaries; thence by a south course of about 8 miles it passes by Rahway village, where it meets the tide; and thence by a south-east course of about 5 miles, dividing Middlesex from Essex co., it unites with Staten Island Sound, 9 or 10 miles N. E. of Perth Amboy. It is navigable to Rahway village for vessels of 80 tons burden, and receives at the village the Middle or Robinson's branch, and the South branch. Upon these branches there are severable valuable mill seats, and on the main branch between Springfield and tide-water, there are 20 mills employed in grinding grain, sawing lumber, and manufacturing paper, cotton, and wool. On the river, there is some of the best brick clay of the United States; and the manufacture of bricks was, at one period, so great here, as to employ steadily about 40 sloops in their transport to New York. Owing to the scarcity of fuel, this manufacture has declined.

Rahway, p-t., including what was formerly called Bridgetown, lies upon the Rahway river, at the head of tide, five miles from its mouth, partly in Woodbridge t-ship, Middlesex co., and partly in Rahway t-ship, Essex co.; distant N. E. 205 miles from W. C., 39 from Trenton, 11 from Brunswick S. W., 10 from Newark, 18 from Jersey City, and 8 from Amboy; consists of four detached villages, Rahway Proper, north of Robinson's branch, Union, Bridgetown, and Leesville, on the south. This diversity of names is productive of some irregularity in the transit of letters to the town, and has induced a wish to change the name; and some of the inhabitants propose to substitute that of "*Athens.*" There are here, about 350 dwellings, containing, it is said, 3000 inhabitants, mostly of New England origin; this would give a greater average number of inhabitants to a house, than in any other district of the state; an elegant Presbyterian church erected in 1831, a Methodist, Baptist, and an African Episcopal church, and two Quaker meeting houses pertaining to the Orthodox and Hicksite parties, respectively. The citizens, with enterprise and liberality worthy of high commendation, have established, under the general incorporation law of the state, a library company, and a Sunday school association, which has erected a commodious house, supposed to be the first designed expressly and exclusively for Sunday schools in the world; and a second Sunday school house is about to be built by the Methodists here. A joint stock company have reared the "*Athenian Academy*," a noble building 68 feet long by 36 wide, two stories high; the upper used as a lecture room; costing 5000 dollars, and which was opened for literary exercises 12th August, 1833, by a neat and exciting address from the president of the trustees of the institution, Mr. Robert Lee. The tutors of this seminary have fixed salaries, and are thus relieved from the anxiety and distraction of mind arising from uncertain and precarious compensation. But we may observe also, that the stimulus to exertion and the attainment of excellence, has been in a great measure thereby removed. The professors in the schools of Germany, certainly inferior to none in the world, are supported by their pupils, whose number depends on the reputation of the teachers. Perhaps the best mode of compensation, is that which, providing certain subsistence, leaves merit to find its own reward from popular favour. "The Athenian Academy", had 106 pupils in the first week of its existence. Besides this institution, Rahway has six common public schools, and a very large and commodious literary institution, built and directed by Mr. Samuel Oliver. There are also in the village a bank, called the "Farmers and Mechanics," incorporated in 1828, with an authorized capital of $200,000, of which 60,000 have been paid in; a fire engine, a mutual insurance company, and a printing office; from which issues a weekly paper, called the Rahway Advocate; 25 stores, 4 taverns, (and be it remembered, 10 schools,) a large building called "The Taurino Factory," originally designed for the manufacture of coarse cloth and carpets from cow's hair, but about to be employed in the colouring and printing of silk; the "Mammoth Saw Mill," said to be the largest in the state; belonging to Mr. Joseph O. Lufberry, and for the supply of which, there was in the river, in September, 1833, more than $30,000 worth of pine and oak timber; a steam-boat company, whose operations will probably be superseded by the Jersey rail-road now making; 5 lumber and coal yards, 1 soap and candle manufactory, 3 bakeries, 2 watchmakers, 4 millinery shops, and extensive manufactories of hats, boots, shoes, carriages, cabinet furniture, and clothing for export; clock, earthenware, coach-lace, plated ware for carriages, &c. &c. On the Rahway river, some distance above the town, are extensive cotton bleaching and printing works, employing about 100 hands. The amount of capital vested in manufactures here and in the neighbourhood, is estimated at 356,000 dollars, and the surplus product of the town and its vicinity, at from 1,000,000 to 1,200,000 annually. Thriving as this place certainly is, new stimulus will be given to its activity by the rail-road now being made from "Jersey City" to New Brunswick, which will pass through the village, and thus bring it within an hour's journey of New York. The town has now communication thrice daily with New York, by stages and steam-boats via Elizabethtown Point, and also by other conveyances.

The soil, for many miles around the town, is well adapted to grass and grain, consisting of a fertile loam resting on sand, gravel and red shale, and much hay and grain are annually sent to market. In 1830, the population of Woodbridge township was 3909, and of Rahway township, 1983, making in the two townships in which the village lies, 5952 souls. It is said, the population of these townships, now, 1833, amounts to 10,000; but, though the increase is certainly great, we fear it has been overrated.

We insert *verbatim*, the following remark, which needs no comment, made by a highly respectable inhabitant of the town. "Leesville, at the southern part of the town, takes its name from a family named Lee, who have long resided there, and furnished our most enterprising and public spirited citizens; and as merchants and manufacturers, were the first to lead the way to our extensive trade with the southern states, and who have, by their industry and perseverance, liberality and enlightened views in other respects, greatly added to the prosperity of the town."

Rahway t-ship, Essex co., bounded N. W. by Union, and N. E. by Elizabeth t-ship; E. by Staten Island Sound; S. by Woodbridge t-ship, Middlesex co.; and W. by Westfield t-ship. Centrally distant, S. W. from Newark, 9 miles. Greatest length, E. and W., 8; breadth, N. and S., 4½ miles; area, 10,000 acres; surface, level; soil, red shale and well cultivated. Drained by the Rahway river, which runs S. centrally through the township, and bounds it on the S. E.; by Robinson's brook, a tributary of that stream; and by Moss's creek, which, after a crooked course of about 7 miles, empties into the Sound, on the N. E. boundary. Rahway post-town, is the only village of the township, and one-half of that is in the adjoining county. Population in 1830, 1983. In 1832, there were in the township, 375 taxables, 177 householders, whose ratables did not exceed $30; 117 single men, 5 merchants, 6 grist mills, 4 saw mills, 1 paper mill, 1 printing and bleaching establishment, 254 horses and mules, and 711 neat cattle, over 3 years of age; and it paid state tax, $212 98; county, $557 25; poor, $600; road, $400.

Ramapo River, rises in the recesses of Sterling mountain, Orange co., New York; and flows thence by a S. course, dividing the Ramapo mountain, to the boundary between that state and New Jersey, 14 miles; thence, deflecting S. W. it follows the base of the mountain, 13 miles to Pompton river, about 2 miles below Ryerson's, forming in part, the boundary between Franklin and Pompton townships. It is a fine mill stream, receiving several small tributaries from the east, which also move mills.

Ramapo Mountain, Bergen co., is a high hill of angular form, with its base upon Ramapo river, in the state of New York, and enclosed by that river on the east, and Ringwood river on the west; partly in Pompton and partly in Franklin townships. Its breadth, at the base, is about 5 miles, and its length about 10. Its height under 1000 feet, composed of primitive rock, and covered with wood.

Ramsaysburg, p-t. of Knowlton t-ship, Warren co., on the bank of the Delaware, 215 miles N. E. from W. C., and 59 from Trenton, and 5 miles N. from Belvidere. Contains a tavern, store, an Episcopal church, and some half dozen dwellings.

Rancocus Creek, rises by two branches; the north, on the western border of Monmouth county, flowing a little north of west, about 28 miles, passing by the town of Mount Holly, to which place it is navigable; the south branch, composed of several streams, which have their source in Burlington county, and flow northwestward, uniting at Eayrstown, and thence running by Lumberton, to the junction with the north branch, four miles below that town. This branch is navigable to Eayrstown. The united streams continue a N. W. course for about 7 miles, to the Delaware. The wood, timber, and produce of a large extent of country find their way to market by this stream.

Randolph t-ship, Morris co., bounded N. by Rockaway river, which separates it from Pequannock t-ship; E. by Hanover and Morris t-ships; S. by Mendham; S. E. by Chester, and W. by Roxbury t-ships. Centrally distant, N. W., from Morristown, 7 miles; greatest length, 7; breadth, 5 miles; area, 18,000 acres; surface, mountainous—Schooley's mountain, filling the northern part, and Trowbridge mountain crossing the southern. In the valley, between them, rises and flows Den branch of Rockaway river. Black river has one of its sources in the northern mountain, near the seat of the honourable Mahlon Dickerson, Esq., near which also rises Dell's brook, a tributary of the Rockaway, flowing eastward through Pleasant valley. The great bed of magnetic iron ore which may be traced in the direction of the stratification from the White Hills, in New Hampshire, terminates in this township near the Black river, upon its western boundary. On this bed the mine of Mr. Dickerson is remarkable for the abundance and excellent quality of its product, and the skill with which it is wrought; and the ore is transported in wagons and by the Morris canal, to the furnaces and forges, not only of this county, but of the neighbouring counties and states. This mine has been wrought many years. Shafts have been sunk to the depth of 70 feet, and drifts driven more than 120 feet. There is carbonate of lime mingled with the iron, which renders any other flux unnecessary in smelting. In 1830, the population of the township was 1443 souls; and in 1832, the township contained 324 taxables, 78 householders, whose ratables did not exceed $30; 40 single men, 5 stores, 6 saw and 4 grist mills, 1 furnace, 1 forge, 1 oil mill, 1 fulling mill, 1 carding machine, 35 tan vats, 250 horses, and 770 neat cattle over three years of age, 4 distilleries; and it paid state tax, $156 70; county tax, $350 82; poor tax, $800; road tax, $800.

Raritan River, is formed by three great branches, the North, the South, and the Millstone river. (For a description of the last, see article *Millstone River.*) The North Branch rises in the valley N. of Trowbridge mountain, in Randolph t-ship, Morris co., and flows S. through that and Somerset co., to the main branch in Bridgewater t-ship, of the latter, about 4 miles W. of Somerville, receiving in its course, Black or Lamington river, a stream longer and larger than itself, and several smaller tributaries. Passing through a mountainous country, it is a rapid stream, with a pretty direct course, and gives motion to several mills. The South Branch has its source in Budd's pond or lake, on the summit of Schooley's mountain, and within three miles, becomes an efficient mill stream, turning several water works. It flows by a S. W. course, through the chain of hills of the South mountain to Clinton; thence deflects easterly through the same chain, passing within a mile and a half of Flemington, to the western boundary of Somerset co.; thence turned to the N. W. by the Nashanic mountain, it receives the North Branch, and by an easterly course, traverses that county to the eastern boundary: flowing within two miles of Somerville, and receiving the Millstone river from the south, about three miles from that town. From Bound Brook it reassumes a S. E. course, and forms the boundary between Somerset and Middlesex counties, to New Brunswick; thence through the latter county by a winding course in the salt marsh, it meets the ocean at Perth Amboy. From this point the Raritan bay extends to the light-house on Sandy Hook, 14 miles. The length of the river is from Amboy to New Brunswick, by the windings 15 miles; from New Brunswick to the mouth of the Millstone 10; from the mouth of the Millstone to the mouth of the North Branch 7; and from thence to its source, 42 miles; in all 74 miles. It may be navigated by small boats beyond Bound Brook; but we believe this is never attempted above New Brunswick. To that town, sloops, schooners, and steam-boats of considerable burden ascend. The Delaware and Raritan canal enters the valley of the river at the mouth of the Millstone, and terminates at New Brunswick. Immediately above Brunswick the river may be forded at low water, when below the town a 20 gun ship may securely ride. In high tide, however, sloops may pass a mile above the ford. The bridge opposite the city, near 1000 feet in length, wide enough for two carriages to pass abreast, with a foot way, built of wood, on 11 stone piers beside the abutments, was first completed in 1796; and rebuilt by a joint stock company, in 1811.

Raritan Bay, extends from the mouth of Raritan river, at Perth Amboy eastward, 14 miles to the ocean, at Sandy Hook, and is about 2 miles wide at Amboy Point, but increases in width between Sandy Hook and the Narrows at Fort Richmond on Staten Island. There are two channels through the bay. The northern carries from 24 to 28 feet water to Amboy; the southern about 12 feet. The bay abounds with oysters, and the lands beneath the water, claimed by the state, are in part divided into small lots, and granted on rent (badly paid) to the fishermen. More than 250 acres have been thus leased, on which oysters are planted from time to time, whose increase gives large annual profits to those concerned in the fishery. (See *Perth Amboy*.)

Raritan Landing, on the left bank of the Raritan river, at the head of tide water, and two miles above New Brunswick, in Piscataway township, Middlesex co. This is a place of considerable business; contains some 20 dwellings, 2 stores and a tavern, chiefly on the primitive bank of the river, which is here high, and having between it and the water, a broad bottom of rich alluvial land. There is a wooden bridge here across the river.

Rattle Snake Run, branch of Mill creek, Fairfield t-ship, Cumberland co., uniting with its recipient at the village of Fairton.

Readington t-ship, Hunterdon co., bounded N. by Tewkesbury t-ship; E. by Bridgewater t-ship, Somerset co.; S. and S. W. by Amwell t-ship; W. by Kingwood, and N. W. by Bethlehem t-ship. Centrally distant N. E. from Flemington 8 miles; length N. and S. 12 miles; breadth

E. and W. 7½ miles; surface, hilly, except on the S. E. where it is level; soil, red shale, clay, and loam. The South Branch of the Raritan river, flows on the S. W., S., and S. E. of the t-ship, and receives from it Campbell's and Holland's Brooks. The northern part is drained by Rockaway creek and its branches. Population in 1830, 2102. In 1832 there were in the t-ship 7 merchants, 5 saw mills, 7 grist mills, 6 distilleries, 2 carding machines, and 2 fulling mills, 705 horses and mules, 1200 neat cattle over 3 years of age. The t-ship paid state and county taxes, $1323 75. White House and Potterstown are post-towns of the t-ship.

Recklesstown, p-t. of Chesterfield t-ship, Burlington co., 12 miles N. E. of Mount Holly, 5 S. E. from Bordentown, 11 from Trenton, and 177 from W. C.; contains a tavern, store, and 10 or 12 dwellings, in a very fertile country of sandy loam.

Red Bank, p-t. of Shrewsbury t-ship, Monmouth co., on the south shore of the Nevisink river, 46 miles E. from Trenton, 13 miles N. E. from Freehold, 3 N. from Shrewsbury; contains within a circle of a mile in diameter about 100 dwellings, 3 taverns and 4 stores. The surrounding country is fertile and pleasant; a steam-boat runs between it and New York, and many persons from that city spend the hot weather of summer here; finding very agreeable entertainment in the families of respectable farmers, in visits to the sea shore, in fishing, and other rural sports. A bridge near 300 feet in length, resting on wooden piers, has been thrown across the river here, at the expense of the county.

Red Bank, on the Delaware river, between Big Timber and Woodbury creeks, named from the colour of the earth of which it is composed; remarkable for a fort called Mercer, erected here during the revolutionary war, and its brave and successful defence by Col. Green, against a detachment from the British army, commanded by Count Donop, on the 22d Oct. 1777; in which the Count and many officers were made prisoners, and a lieutenant colonel, 3 captains, 4 lieutenants, and 70 privates were killed. In commemoration of this event, a monument of handsome grey marble has been reared, bearing the following inscription.

THIS MONUMENT
was erected on the 22d October, 1829,
To transmit to posterity, a grateful remembrance of the
Patriotism and Gallantry of
Lieut. Col. Christopher Green, who with
400 men, conquered the Hessian army
of 2000 troops, then in the British
service, at the Red Bank, on
the 22d October, 1777.
Among the wounded was found their
commander,
COUNT DONOP,
who died of his wounds, and whose body
is interred near the spot where he fell.
A number of the
New Jersey and Pennsylvania
volunteers,
Being desirous to perpetuate the memory
of the distinguished officers and soldiers, who fought and bled in
the glorious struggle for
American Independence,
HAVE
Erected this Monument, on the 22d day
of October, Anno Domini, 1829.

Red Lion, hamlet of Northampton t-ship, Burlington co., 9 miles S. W. from Mount Holly.

Reed's Bay, a salt marsh lake of Galloway t-ship, Gloucester co., about 2 miles in length, and 1 in breadth, communicating with Absecum bay, and with the ocean, by a channel flowing through Absecum inlet.

Repaupo Creek, Gloucester co., rises on the line separating Greenwich from Woolwich t-ship, and flows N. W. 7 or 8 miles, to the Delaware river, opposite to Chester Island.

Rice's Pond, Knowlton t-ship, Warren co., source of Beaver Brook, which flows thence to Pequest creek, by a S. W. course of 10 miles, turning several mills in its course.

Ringwood River, rises in Sterling pond, Sterling mountain, state of New York, and runs by a southerly course of 16 miles, through Pompton t-ship, Bergen co., to the Pequannock creek, forming with it Pompton river. It is a rapid mill stream, and receives several tributaries, which also turn mills.

Ringwood, village, on the above stream, and within a mile and a half of the state line; contains a blast furnace, a forge, a store, and three dwellings beside those for the workmen at the iron works. Surrounding country, mountainous and barren; distant 24 miles from Hackensack.

Ringoestown, p-t. of Amwell t-ship, Hunterdon co., 6 miles S. of Flemington, 17 N. of Trenton, and 176 N. E. from W. C.; contains 1 tavern, 3 stores, 1 Presbyterian church, an academy, and 26 dwellings, saddlery, and smith shop, cotton and woollen factory, and grist mill. This is a delightful village, lying in the valley immediately at the foot of the Rock mountain, and upon a soil of loam, composed of red shale and clay, very deep, and highly cultivated in grain and grass. Lands immediately round the village, readily bring $100 the acre, and those more distant in the valley, $50 the acre.

Roadstown, p-t. of Cumberland co., on the line dividing Stow Creek and Hopewell t-ships, 5 miles W. of Bridgeton, 179 N. E. of W. C., and 73 by post-route from Trenton; contains 20 dwellings, 1 tavern, 2 stores, and a large Baptist church of brick. The town is peopled principally by the cultivators of the soil; the soil is good loam, and improving by the use of marl.

Robinhood, branch of Maurice river, a small tributary, flowing from the east into the river, about 2 miles below Maul's bridge.

Robin's, branch of Batsto river, rises in Northampton t-ship, Burlington co., and flows S. W. about 10 miles, to its recipient in Washington t-ship. It is a mill stream.

Robinson's Brook, tributary of Rahway river, rises on the S. W. border of Rahway t-ship, and flows E. by a course of about 6 miles, to its recipient at Bridgetown or Rahway.

Rockaway river, Morris co., rises by two principal branches in the mountains of Pequannock and Jefferson t-ships; the one flowing through Longwood valley, and the other through Green Pond valley, and commingling about a mile S. E. of Mount Pleasant. The united streams, thence, flow through a deep and rapid channel, by a very serpentine course of about 20 miles, to the Passaic river. The volume and fall of this stream adapt it admirably to hydraulic purposes, and there are many mills upon it, principally for working of iron, as at Dover, Rockaway village, Boonton, &c.

Rockaway Valley, of Hanover and Pequannock t-ships, Morris co., north of Trowbridge mountain; a narrow vale crossed by the Rockaway river.

Rockaway, p-t. of Morris co., on both banks of the Rockaway river, 8 miles N. of Morristown, 229 N. E. from W. C., and 63 from Trenton; contains 1 rolling mill, 2 forges, 1 grist and saw mill, 4 stores, 1 tavern, a Presbyterian or Dutch Reformed church, and from 20 to 25 dwellings. The Morris canal passes through the village.

Rocky Hill, one of the chain of trap rock hills, which extend from the Delaware, below Lambertsville, N. E. across the state, in Amwell t-ship, Hunterdon co., and in Montgomery t-ship, Somerset co., about 2 miles N. of Princeton. The surface of this hill is rugged; soil, deep clay, covered with heavy timber. It extends E. and W. about 6 miles, to the Millstone river, which seems to have forced a passage through it.

Rocky Hill, p-t., Montgomery t-ship, Somerset co., at the N. E. base of Rocky hill, on the Millstone river, and turnpike road from New Brunswick to Lambertsville, 12 miles S. W. of Somerville, 185 N. E. from W. C., and 14 from Trenton; contains a grist and saw mill, a woollen manufactory, 2 stores, 2 taverns, and 12 or 15 dwellings.

Rockaway Creek, Hunterdon co., rises by two branches; one from the northern part of Tewkesbury t-ship, and the other from the western border of Readington t-ship, uniting in the latter t-ship, and thence flowing into Lamington river, or the north branch of the Raritan. By its longest arm the stream has a course of 12 miles. It is a fine, rapid mill stream.

Rock Brook, tributary of Beden's Brook, rises in the Nashanic mountain, Amwell t-ship, Hunterdon co., and by a S. E. course of about 6 miles, unites with its recipient near the centre of Montgomery t-ship, Somerset co.

Rock Mountain, fills the S. E. angle of Amwell t-ship, and the N. E. angle of Hopewell t-ship, Hunterdon co., and extends N. E. into Somerset co., having a length of about 10 miles, with a very irregular breadth. On the north it sends forth tributaries to the south branch of the Raritan river, and on the south to the Millstone river. The hill is of trap rock, imposed on old, red sandstone.

Rocksbury, village of Oxford t-sp, Warren co., 5 miles S. of Belvidere, upon the road leading to Philipsburg; contains a tavern, store, 2 grist and 1 oil mill, an air furnace for small castings, and from 15 to 20 dwellings.

Rocktown, small hamlet, of Amwell t-ship, Hunterdon co., 7 miles S. of Flemington; contains 1 tavern, 1 store, and some 2 or 3 dwellings. It lies in the pass through the Rock mountain, and is named from the abundance of large rocks around it.

Rocky Brook, a tributary of Millstone river, rises in Upper Freehold t-ship, Monmouth co., above Imlay's mill, and flows by a N. W. course through East Windsor t-ship, Middlesex co., about 9 miles to its recipient, on the boundary of South Brunswick t-ship, passing through Hightstown, and turning several mills.

Rotten Pond, covering about 150 acres, on the boundary between Franklin and Pompton t-ships, Bergen co., and on the Ramapo mountain.

Round Valley, in the S. E. angle of Lebanon t-ship, Hunterdon co., nearly surrounded by mountains; drained by Piscot Brook, a tributary of the south branch of the Raritan river.

Rowandtown, small village of Newton t-ship, Gloucester co., on the road from Camden to Haddonfield, about 4 miles from the former, and 2 from the latter; contains some 6 or 8 dwellings, and several mechanics; surrounded by a country of sandy loam.

Roxbury t-ship, Morris co., bounded N. and W. by the Hopatcong lake and Musconetcong river, which separates it from Warren and Sussex counties; N. E. by Jefferson t-ship; E. by Randolph; S. E. by Chester; and S. W. by Washington t-ships. Centrally distant from Morristown N. W. 14 miles; greatest length N. and S. 12, breadth E. and W. 10 miles; area, 35,840 acres; surface, generally mountainous; but the Suckasunny Plains extend some miles in length, by two or three in breadth. Schooley's mountain fills the greater portion of its area. On its summit lies Budd's Pond, two miles in length by one in breadth, whence flows a tributary of the south branch of the Raritan river; the main stream of which has its source in a small pond, two miles north of Drakesville, in this t-ship. Black river forms, in part, its eastern boundary. On the mountain the soil is clay and loam, but limestone is even there mixed with the granitic rock, and is found in the valley on the S. W. Flanders, Suckasunny, Drakestown, and Drakesville, are villages of the t-ship; at the two first of which are post-offices. Population in 1830, 2262. In 1832 the t-ship contained 410 taxables, 92 householders, whose ratables did not exceed $30 in value; 44 single men, 4 stores, 9 saw, 10 grist, and 2 fulling mills, 16 tan vats, 8 distilleries, 15 chairs and sulkies; and it paid state tax, $261 07; county tax, $584 51; poor tax, $300; and road tax, $800.

Roxbury. (See ***Rocksbury***.)

Ryersons, a village at and near the junction of Ringwood and Pequannock rivers, in the S. E. angle of Pompton t-ship. There are here

1 tavern, 3 grist mills, a carding machine, a furnace, and store, a Dutch Reformed church, an academy, and from 15 to 20 dwellings; surrounded by a rich and productive country. The post-office is at Pompton, on the right side of the river, in Morris co.

Roy's Brook, a tributary of the Millstone river, rising at the S. E. foot of Nashanic mountain, and flowing by a devious, but generally, N. E. course of about 7 or 8 miles, to its recipient, below Rogers' mill.

Saddle River, rises in the state of New York, 3 or 4 miles beyond the northern boundary of this state, and flows thence, southwardly, about 18 miles, through Bergen co., forming the boundary between Franklin and Harrington t-ships, Saddle River, and New Barbadoes, and Lodi t-ships, to its recipient, the Passaic river, about a mile above Acquackanonck. It has a rapid course, and considerable volume, and mills are strung thickly along its banks. The valley through which it flows is broad, and shows evidence in the gravel, and boulders, and water-worn hills, that at some day, a much larger volume of water ran through it.

Saddle River t-ship. The t-ship and river both have their name from the shape of the former, which receives from the Passaic river the shape of a saddle. It is bounded N. by Franklin t-ship; E. by Saddle river, separating it from Harrington, New Barbadoes, and Lodi t-ships; S. by the Passaic river; and W. by Pompton river, which divides it from Morris co., and by Pompton t-ship. Centrally distant N. W. from Hackensacktown 8 miles: greatest length E. and W. 10 miles; breadth N. and S. 8 miles; area, 41,000 acres, of which, about 17,000 are improved: the surface is generally hilly, the First and Second mountains of Essex co., crossing the Passaic and continuing through it. On the east, however, between the Passaic and Saddle rivers, there is a neck of low and level land; soil, red shale and loam; the valleys fertile and well cultivated, and the hills well wooded. Through the valleys flow several small brooks, such as Singack, Preakness, Krokaevall, Goffle, and Ackerman's Brooks. Goffle, and New Manchester, a part of Paterson City, are the chief villages of the t-ship. Population in 1830, 3397. In 1832 there were 741 taxables, 496 householders, whose ratables did not exceed $30 in value; 80 single men, 7 stores, 8 grist mills, 1 cotton manufactory, 1 furnace, 10 saw mills, 13 tan vats, 2 distilleries, 1 wool factory, 506 horses and mules, and 1324 neat cattle over 3 years of age; and it paid state tax, $364 10; and county tax, $690 26.

Salem County has its name from its chief town and seat of justice, Salem, founded by John Fenwicke, in the year 1675. By the act for ascertaining the bounds of all the counties in the province, passed 21st January, 1710, the following were the boundaries given to it: "Beginning at the mouth of a creek on the west side of Stipson's island, called Jecak's creek, now West creek; thence by said creek as high as the tide floweth; thence by a direct line to the mouth of a small creek at Tuckahoe, where it comes into the southernmost main branch of the fork of the Great Egg Harbour river; thence up the said branch to the head thereof; thence along the bounds of Gloucester county to the river Delaware, and thence by the river and bay to the place of beginning; and thus it included the whole of Cumberland county. The latter county was taken from it by the act of 19th Jan. 1748; and the boundaries then established, confirmed by the act of 7th Dec. 1763, by which the southern boundary of Salem county was then fixed as follows: Commencing at the middle of the mouth of Stow creek; thence by the same, opposite to the mills formerly of John Brick; thence up the middle of Stow creek branch opposite the house of Hugh Dunn; thence by a direct line to said house, leaving it in Cumberland county; and thence by a straight line N. 51° 15′ E. 94 chains, to the house of Aziel Pierson, leaving that also in Cumberland county; thence N. E. by a line intersecting the line of Pilesgrove t-ship, 305 chains; thence by Pilesgrove line S. 47° E. to the middle of Maurice river, below the mouth of Muddy run; thence up the middle of said river to the foot of Scotland branch; thence up the middle of said branch to Gloucester line." The county is, therefore, now bounded by the Delaware bay and river on the S. W., W., and N. W.; by Gloucester co. on the N. E; and Cumberland co, on the S. E. Greatest length N. and S. about 30 miles; breadth E. and W. 26 miles; area, 320 square miles, or 204,936 acres; central lat. 39° 33′; long. from W. C. 1° 50′ E.

The surface of the county is generally flat. Its soil, in the northern and western parts, clay and loam, mixed more or less with sand, and generally productive, in wheat, grass, oats, &c. In the south-eastern parts, the soil is sandy and gravelly, and less fertile, but yielding much timber and cord wood of oak and pine, which succeed alternately when a clearing is made. This is particularly the case with a strip of about 20 miles long, extending across Lower and Upper Alloways Creek and Pittsgrove t-ships, denominated the *Barrens.* The county is well watered, having Oldman's creek on its northern boundary, Salem and Alloways creeks running through it centrally, and Stow creek on the southern limits.

The county consists of alluvial and diluvial formation, the washings of the ocean and the primitive strata, being very irregularly mingled, and beds of stiff clay, loam, and gravel, are interspersed with white sea sand. From two to twenty feet below the surface, in several places, there is found a species of greenish blue marl, as at Pedricktown and Woodstown, which is used as manure. In it there are shells, as the ammonite, belemnite, ovulite, ostrea, terebratula, &c. similar to those found in the limestone and grauwacke of the transition; and in the horizontal limestone and sandstone. We have not heard of any bog iron ore in the county, though it probably exists; but sandstone and puddingstone, cemented with iron ore, are not uncommon.

Salem, Woodstown, Sharptown, Sculltown, Pedricktown, Daretown, Pittstown, Allowaystown, Friesburg, Canton, Hancock's Bridge, and Quinton's Bridge, are villages of the co.

The county was originally settled by Dutch and Swedes; and subsequently by the English, companions of John Fenwicke, who landed here in 1675; and it derived its principal inhabitants from the same source. Some Dutch fixed themselves at, and gave name to, Friesburg, in Upper Alloways Creek t-ship. The population by the census of 1830, amounted to 14,155, of whom, 6443 were white males; 6300 white females; 1 slave; 673 free coloured males, and 638 free coloured females. There were also in the county, 6 whites, deaf and dumb; 7 blind, and 27 aliens; and in 1832, taxables, 3092; 1103 householders, whose ratables did not exceed $30; 47 storekeepers, 6 fisheries, 13 grist mills, 19 saw mills, 2 carding machines with spinning machines for wool, 6 fulling mills, 7 tanneries, 15 distilleries, 19 stud horses, 3103 horses and mules, 7300 neat cattle, over 3 years of age; and the county paid for t-ship purposes, $5076; for county purposes, $7000; and state tax, $2156 60.

There were in the county 7 Friends' meeting houses, 6 Methodist, 5 Baptist, 1 Seven-day Baptist, 2 Episcopalian, 2 Presbyterian, and 2 African Methodist churches; 1 academy at Salemtown, and sufficient other schools there, and in every t-ship, to teach the rudiments of an English education.

The other public buildings of the county consist of a large court-house, with fire proof offices detached, of brick; a stone prison, a large poor-house, with a farm annexed, and two buildings erected for masonic halls.

The trade of the county consists of wheat, rye, Indian corn, oats, and garden vegetables for market, lumber, and cord wood. Considerable quantities of grain are annually exported from Salem to the Eastern states.

The courts of common pleas and general quarter sessions of the peace, for the county, are annually holden at Salem, on the first Tuesdays of March and December, the second Tuesday of June, and the third Tuesday of September; and the circuit court, on the second Tuesday of June and the first Tuesday of September. The county, by virtue of the constitution, elects one member of council, and three members of the Assembly.

STATISTICAL TABLE OF SALEM COUNTY.

Townships.	Length.	Breadth.	Area.	Surface.	Population. 1810.	1820.	1830.
Upper Alloways Creek,	10½	9	34,000	p't level, rolling.	1921	2194	2136
Lower Alloways Creek,	12	9	30,000	level.	1182	1217	1222
Elsinborough,	6	4	8000	do.	517	505	503
Mannington,	9	8	20,000	do.	1664	1732	1726
Upper Penn's Neck,	9	7½	21,053	do.	1638	1861	1638
Lower Penn's Neck,	9	6	12,645	do.	1163	1158	994
Pilesgrove,	9	6½	24,000	do.	1756	2012	2150
Pittsgrove,	15	7	44,000	p't level, p't roll.	1991	2040	2216
Salem,	2	2	1238	level.	929	1303	1570
			204,936		12,761	14,022	14,155

Salem t-ship and post-town, and seat of justice of Salem county, situate 171 miles N. E. of W. C., 65 S. of Trenton, and 34 S. E. from Philadelphia; lat. 39° 32′; long. from W. C. 1° 35′. The t-ship is of circular form, and is nearly surrounded by water, having on the N. W. the Salem creek, on the N. E. and E. Fenwicke's creek, a tributary of that stream, and on the W. another small tributary of the same stream. The town is distant from the Delaware, by the creek, 3½ miles. The t-ship is about 2 miles in diameter, and contains 1238 acres of well improved land, of a rich sandy loam, divided into town lots and 12 farms. The town contains about 250 dwellings; a fine court-house, about 60 by 40 feet, of brick, with brick fire proof offices adjacent; 1 Episcopalian, 1 Methodist, 1 Presbyterian, 1 Baptist, 1 African Methodist, and 2 Quaker (one being orthodox and the other Hicksite) churches; 1 building of brick, of gothic architecture, designed for a masonic hall, but which is now appropriated to other purposes, the lodge being extinct; a bank with capital paid in of $75,000; a stone jail with yard, surrounded by a high stone wall, both of small dimensions; 1 market house, 2 fire engines, 2 public libraries, 1 academy, and 5 daily schools for teaching the rudiments of an English education; 5 Sunday schools, 2 printing offices, at each of which is printed a weekly newspaper, called, respectively, "*The Salem Messenger*," and "*The American Statesman;*" 21 stores, 2 hotels, 7 physicians, 5 lawyers, 3 lumber yards, 1 steam mill which grinds much grain, 1 horse mill, 5 apothecaries' stores, 1 livery stable. A steamboat leaves the town daily, for Delaware City and Newcastle, to meet the morning steam-boat from Philadelphia; 1 four horse stage runs daily to Philadelphia, another to Pennsgrove, on the Delaware, to meet the Wilmington steam-boat for Philadelphia; a two horse daily line to Bridgetown, and a two horse line to Centerville, once a week. The creek at the town, is 152 yards wide, over which is a wooden bridge, resting on wooden piers, with a draw for the passage of vessels. Over Fenwicke creek, a short distance above its junction with Salem creek, is another wooden bridge, a neat structure, roofed. Vessels of 50 tons may approach the town safely, but the bar at the mouth of the creek prevents the entry of vessels drawing more than eight feet water. Large quantities of wheat, rye, oats, and corn, are exported from this place to the eastern states. The streets of the town are wide—footways paved, and bordered with trees; the houses of frame and brick, the former painted white, are surrounded with gardens and grass lots, and adorned with flowers, giving to the place, a cheerful and healthy appearance, surpassed by few villages in the United States. The t-ship contained in 1830, 1570 inhabitants: in 1832, 267 householders, whose ratables did not exceed $30 in value; and 397 taxables, 2 tan yards, 1 distillery; and it paid taxes for t-ship purposes, $426; county use, $738 25; and state use, $233 35.

The site of the town of Salem was the first spot visited, and we believe, the first settled, by the English emigrants to West Jersey. Soon after the sale by Lord Berkeley of one moiety of the province, to Edward Byllinge, John Fenwicke, the agent of the latter set sail, (in 1675) to visit the new purchase in a ship from London, called the Griffith. After a short passage, he landed at this pleasant spot, which, from its aspect of peace, he called Salem. He brought with him two daughters, and several servants, two of which, Samuel Hedge and John Adams, afterwards married his daughters. Other passengers were, Edward Champness, Edward and Samuel Wade, John Smith, Samuel Nichols, Richard Guy, Richard Noble, Richard Hancock, John Pledger, Hypolite Lefever, and John Matlock, and others, who were masters of families.

Salem Creek, Salem co., rises in Pittsgrove t-ship, and flows N. W. through that and Pilesgrove t-ship, by Woodstown and Sharptown, about 17 miles to the S. W. angle of Upper Penn's Neck t-ship; thence turning S. and S. W., it divides Mannington and Lower Penn's Neck t-ships, and passing by Salem, empties into the Delaware river, 3½ miles below that town. There is a bar at the mouth, on which at high tide there are eight feet water. Vessels of 50 tons approach the town safely; but within the bar, there is water, it is said, for vessels of 300 tons burden. The whole length of the creek may be about 30 miles, and it is navigable for shallops nearly half that distance. A short canal of 3 or 4 miles, through Upper and Lower Penn's Neck t-ships, unites the creek with the Delaware, saving a distance to the craft which navigate the creek, of about 20 miles.

Samptown, Piscataway t-ship, Middlesex co., about 8 miles N. from New Brunswick, on the left bank of Cedar creek; contains a Baptist church, 10 or 12 houses, tavern and store, in a tolerably fertile country of red shale.

Sand Hills, small hamlet of Nottingham t-ship, Burlington co. There is a tavern, and 12 or 15 dwellings here; the turnpike road, and the Camden and Amboy rail-road, run near it. The carriages from and for Trenton meet the rail-road cars here. Distance from Trenton, about 5, and from Bordentown, 3 miles.

Sand Hills, noted hills in the N. W. part of South Brunswick t-ship, Middlesex co., covering an area of about 4 miles by 2; about 7 miles W. from Brunswick.

Sandy Hook, Sandy Hook bay: the first is a sandy beach, extending northward, from Old Shrewsbury inlet, and the S. point of the highlands of Nevisink, 6 miles, of an irregular width, varying from half a mile to a mile, forming the eastern boundary of the bay. The bay sets in from the Raritan bay, southwards, and is about 7 miles wide, between Point

Comfort, the western cape, and the point of the Hook. Its depth to the S. point of the Nevisink hills, which form the coast for about 6 miles, is about 6 miles. The western shore encroaches, eastwardly, upon the water until it is narrowed to three-quarters of a mile.

Sand Pond, a small sheet of water, in Wallkill mountains, Vernon t-ship, Sussex co., which sends forth a small tributary to the Wallkill river.

Sand Pond, the source of Stout's brook, on the N. line of Hardwick t-ship.

Sandtown, or *Berkely*, village of Greenwich t-ship, Gloucester co., on Mantua creek, 4 miles S. W. from Woodbury; contains a store, tavern, 12 or 15 dwellings, and an Episcopal church.

Sandtown, Nottingham t-ship, Burlington co., on the road from Trenton to Cranberry, about 5 miles E. of the former, on a sandy plain; contains a tavern, smithery, and some half-dozen dwellings.

Sandistone t-ship, Sussex co., bounded on the N. E. by Montague t-ship; S. E. by the Blue mountain, which divides it from Newton, Frankford, and Wantage t-ships; S. W. by Walpack t-ship; and W. by the Delaware river; centrally distant, N. W. from Newton, 12 miles; greatest length, 8½, breadth, 7 miles; area, 19,320 acres; surface on the E. mountainous, and on the W. river alluvion. Population in 1830, 1097. There were in the t-ship in 1832, 65 householders, whose ratables did not exceed $30; taxable inhabitants, 240; 4 merchants or traders, 5 pair of stones for grinding grain, 1 carding machine, 4 saw mills, 204 horses and mules, and 841 neat cattle over 3 years; 13 tan vats, 1 distillery. The t-ship paid state and county tax, $426 77; poor tax, $100; road tax, $500. It is watered by the Big and Little Flat Kill creeks, and their tributaries, and by the river Delaware. The Morristown and Milford turnpike road crosses it north-westwardly, on which lies the post-office, distant 241 miles from W. C., 83 from Trenton, and 13 from Newton. Between the Blue mountain and the Delaware, there is a rich flat, increasing from two to six miles in width, through which runs a bed of transition limestone, girded by an alluvial belt. This flat produces excellent crops of wheat. The t-ship was originally settled by Dutch, whilst that people held possession of New York.

Sandy New, small hamlet of Middletown t-ship, Monmouth co., 9 miles N. E. of Freehold; contains a tavern, and some 3 or 4 dwellings, in a fine fertile country.

Sargeantsville, p-t. of Amwell t-ship, Hunterdon co., 6 miles S. W. from Flemington, 23 N. from Trenton, and 177 N. E. from W. C.; contains a tavern, store, and some 6 or 8 dwellings. Surrounding country hilly and poor; lands rated at $20 per acre. Near this village, on a farm of 150 acres, Mr. R. Rittenhouse has established the Mantua Manual Labour Institute, with accommodations for about 30 students, and the purpose to increase them as they may be required. At this institute are taught the Greek and Latin languages, and all other branches of learning, taught at similar institutions. About three hours every day, Saturday and Sunday excepted, are employed in manual labour, by the students, for which they receive reasonable compensation. The charge for tuition, board, washing, lodging, candles, and fuel, is $25 per quarter.

Saw Mill Creek, a marsh stream about 2 miles in length, in Lodi t-sp, Bergen co.

Saxtonville, small hamlet of Amwell t-ship, Hunterdon co., on the river Delaware, 12 miles S. W. from Flemington; contains some 3 or 4 dwellings; named from the proprietor.

Schooley's Mountain, *Schugl's Hills*, form part of the central granitic chain, which extends in a N. E. and S. W. direction, across the state of New Jersey, from the Delaware to the Hudson river. The name, Schooley's Mountain, derived from a family formerly owning a considerable portion of its soil, is applied chiefly, to that portion of the chain which crosses the N. W. part of Morris county. The height of the mountain above its base, has been determined by geometrical measurement, to be more than 600 feet; and a calculation, made by approximation, on the falls of water, on the different mill dams along the rapid channel of the Musconetcong river, to its junction with the Delaware, and on the descent, thence to Trenton, gives to that base an elevation of 500 feet above tide; making the height of the mountain, above the level of the ocean, somewhat more than 1100 feet.

From the top of the mountain a turnpike road runs northward to Sussex, another westward to Easton, a third eastward to New York, and a fourth southward towards Trenton. The mineral spring near the top has given much celebrity to this region. It is said to have been known to the aborigines, and to have been employed by them as a remedy, which, with characteristic selfishness, they would have concealed from the whites. The latter, however, have resorted to it, since the settlement of the country. Remarkable cures have been ascribed to it, and some persons have habitually frequented it, season after season, on account of the benefit they have derived from the use of its waters. It is situated in Washington t-ship, Morris co., 19 miles N. W. of Morristown, 50 from New York, 70 N. E. from Philadelphia, 56 from Trenton, and 213 from W. C.

The spring is, in strictness, a rill which issues from a perpendicular rock, having an eastern exposure, between 40 and 50 feet above the level of a brook, which gurgles over the stones, and foams down the rocks in the channels beneath. A small wooden trough is adapted to the fissure, so as to convey the water to a platform where the visiters assemble, and to the structure containing the baths. The temperature of the water is 56° F. being 6° warmer than the spring water nearer the summit. The fountain emits about 30 gallons per hour; which quantity does not vary with any change of season or weather. The water, like other chalybeates, leaves a deposit of oxidized iron, as it flows, which discolours the troughs, baths, and even the drinking vessels. The bare taste and appearance shows that it is a chalybeate; and it is strongly characterized by the peculiar astringency and savour of ferruginous impregnations. Though remarkably clear when first taken, the water becomes turbid upon standing for some time in the open air, and after a long interval, an irridescent pellicle forms on its surface. Ochre and other indications of iron are dispersed extensively through the surrounding rocks and soil. Iron ore is so plentiful in the vicinity that furnaces are worked, both in the eastern and western district of the chain, and much of the ore is magnetic. Grey limestone is found at the base of the hills and along the valleys. The analysis of the water, by Dr. M'Nevin of New York, has given the following result:

Vegetable extract 92, muriate of soda 43, muriate of lime 2.40, muriate of magnesia 50, carbonate of lime 7.99, sulphate of lime 65, carbonate of magnesia 40, silex 80, carbonated oxide of iron 2, loss 41—total 16.50.

The iron from the mineral water is very easily separated. Exposure to the atmosphere induces metallic precipitation; and transportation to a distance, even in corked bottles, produces a like effect; and when thus freed from its iron, the water may be used in making tea. The heat of ebullition, also, seems to separate the ferruginous ingredient, and to prevent any dusky or black tint; for if an infusion of green tea be mixed with water fresh from the spring, a dark and disagreeable hue is instantly produced. The carbonic acid which this water contains, is altogether in a state of combination, and hence it never occasions flatulence or spasm in the weakest stomach, whilst it gradually strengthens the digestive powers.—This chalybeate is considered by medical men, as one of the purest of this, or any other country, and as beneficial, in most cases of chronic disease, and general debility, and especially in cases of calculus in the bladder or kidneys.

To those in pursuit of health or pleasure, this region presents equal attraction. A short journey brings the patient from the level of tide water to a very desirable elevation, which tempers the summer's heat, and braces the relaxed frame. The plain on the top of the mountain, affords very pleasant rides amid ever changing and delightful scenery, in which cheering views of improved and profitable agriculture are blended with the velvet plain, the craggy hill, and shadowy vale. Thus the invalid has every incentive to exercise, by the highest gratification from his exertions. To him who seeks relaxation from the cares of business, or to change sedentary occupation and feebleness for activity and vigour, the excellent society which assembles here during the summer months, the abundant sport in fowling and fishing, and the delightful scenery, hold forth strong inducements; to which, we would be unjust not to add the excellent fare, cheerful attention, and comfortable accommodation given to visiters at the three hotels, and several farm houses in the vicinity of the spring. Belmont Hall, kept by Mr. G. Bowne, situate on the highest part of the mountain, shadowed and embowered by various fruit, forest, and ornamental trees, is a fine building, 50 feet square and three stories high, with very extensive wings; and the Heath House of Mr. E. Marsh, less showy, but not less commodious or pleasant, afford the visiter all the means of enjoyment usual at watering places; whilst their distance from the fountain, (about ¾ of a mile) by adding the benefits of exercise, does not diminish the salubrious effects of the water. There is, however, a third house, immediately at the spring, where such visiters as desire to be near it, can be accommodated. The season commences here on the 1st of June, and continues during the hot weather.

For the man of science, the mineral region, and geological formation of the country, possesses much interest. It abounds with iron and other minerals. The first, in a mine opened within gun-shot of the Heath House, is highly magnetic; so much so, indeed, as to render the use of iron tools about it very inconvenient. The following extraordinary circumstances we give on the authority of Mr. Marsh. The tools, by continued use, become so strongly magnetized, that in boring the rock, the workman is unable, after striking the auger with his hammer, to separate them in the usual mode of wielding the hammer, and is compelled to resort to a lateral or rotatory motion for this purpose; and the crowbar has been known to sustain, in suspension, all the other tools of the mine, in weight equal to a hundred pounds. These facts are supported by the assurance of General Dickenson, that the magnetic attraction of the tools, used in his mine, adds much to the fatigue of the workmen; and that it is of ordinary occurrence for the hammer to lift the auger from the hole during the process of boring.

Besides the houses for public entertainment, at and near the springs, there are several others, which, with a church and school house built by Mr. Marsh, with the aid of the visiters, and a post-office, give the neighbourhood a village-like appearance. And, among the attractions of the mountain, we must not forbear to mention the fishing and boating on Budd's Pond, a beautiful sheet of water, two miles in length by one in breadth, at seven miles distance from the spring. This little mountain lake of great depth and clear as crystal, abounds with perch, sun, pike, and other fish.

Scotch Plains, p-t. of Westfield

t-ship, Essex county, 14 miles from Newark, Somerville, New Brunswick, Morristown, Elizabethtown Point, and Amboy; 214 miles N. E. from W. C., and 48 from Trenton, on the road from Springfield to Somerville; contains, within the diameter of a mile, 1 Baptist church, an academy, 1 tavern, 2 stores, 3 grist mills, 2 saw mills, 1 oil mill, 1 straw paper mill, and about 70 dwellings. The surface of the adjacent country is level, except on the W. and N. W. which is mountainous; soil, clay loam, well cultivated, and productive, and valued, in farms, at $40 the acre. Within 2 miles of the village, a bed of carbonate of lime has been lately discovered, in which are metallic appearances supposed to be gold and silver, but which are, probably, only deceptive pyrites.

Scott's Mountain, lying in Greenwich, Oxford, and Mansfield t-ships, Warren co., forms part of the chain of the South mountain, of which this portion covers much of the area of the three t-ships above named. The height of the mountain here may be from 700 to 800 feet above tide, and it is composed of granitic rock, based on, or breaking through limestone. It abounds with iron of several varieties, which, for near a century, has been extensively worked, near Oxford furnace; where Messrs. Henry and Jordan are, now, extensively engaged in the iron manufacture. The mountain is generally well wooded, and the valleys fruitful.

Scrabbletown, hamlet of Hanover t-ship, Burlington co., 10 miles E. from Mount Holly, and 12 S. E. from Bordentown; contains a tavern, and 6 or 8 cottages, in a poor, sandy, pine country.

Sculltown, a village of Upper Penn's Neck t-ship, Salem co., on Oldman's Creek, at the head of navigation; containing from 20 to 30 dwellings, a tavern, and 2 or 3 stores. It is about 12 miles N. E. of Salem.

Secaucas, island in the Cedar swamp, of the Hackensack river, in Bergen t-ship, Bergen co. It is near 4 miles long by half a mile wide; terminating in a very distinguished elevation, called Snake-hill. The island is crossed by the turnpike and rail-road from Hoboken to Paterson.

Serepta, a post-office, Warren co.

Seven Causeways, noted union of 7 roads, near the junction of 4 mile branch, with Inskeep's branch of the Great Egg Harbour river, 25 miles S. E. from Camden, on the line of Deptford and Gloucester t-sps, Gloucester co.

Shabacung Island, formed by the Delaware river, and part of the t-ship of Montague, Sussex co., near the remote N. end of the state.

Shark River, mill stream, rises in Shrewsbury t-ship, Monmouth co., and flows along the boundary, between that and Howell t-ship, about 6 miles, into a broad estuary, and thence about 3 miles through Shark inlet, into the Atlantic ocean.

Sharptown, p-t. and village of Pilesgrove t-ship, Salem co., on Salem creek, between 3 and 4 miles below Woodstown, and 8 or 9 miles N. E. from Salem, 162 from W. C., and 56 S. from Trenton; contains between 40 and 50 dwellings, 1 tavern, 2 stores, 1 grist mill, and one school house, used occasionally as a church. The surrounding country is level and fertile.

Shawpocussing Creek, small tributary of the Delaware river, which rises in Knowlton t-ship, Warren co., at the foot of the Blue mountain, and flows S. W. to its recipient, having a course of five miles.

Shelltown, on the line between Hanover t-ship, Burlington co., and Upper Freehold t-ship, Monmouth co., on a small branch of the Crosswicks creek; contains some half-dozen dwellings. There is a Friends' meeting house near it, in Monmouth county.

Shiloh, p-t. in the S. W. angle of Hardwick t-ship, Warren co., 12 miles N. E. of Belvidere, and 60 miles from Trenton.

Shiloh, hamlet of Cumberland co., on the line dividing Hopewell from

Stow Creek t-ship, about 5 miles N. W. of Bridgeton; contains 8 or 10 dwellings, and a Seventh-day Baptist church. The country around it is of light loam, but in an improving condition.

Shipetaukin, small branch of the Assunpink creek, rising in Lawrence t-ship, Hunterdon co., and flowing S. by a course of 5 or 6 miles to its recipient, through an extensive body of meadow land.

Shoal Harbour Creek, small stream at the N. W. foot of the Nevisink hills; runs about a mile and a half N. E. into Sandy Hook bay.

Shrewsbury Inlet, Old, was opened in 1778, from the ocean into the estuary formed by the Nevisink and Shrewsbury rivers, Monmouth co.; was closed by the moving of the sands in 1810, but was reopened in 1830. Vessels now pass through it.

Shrewsbury River, so called, is a continuation of Sandy Hook bay, Shrewsbury t-ship, Monmouth co., which receives from the t-ship, Shrewsbury river proper, a small stream of 6 or 7 miles long, Long Branch, and several other tributaries. This arm of the bay, from the mouth of the Nevisink river, is about 5 miles long, with an average breadth of a mile and a half, and has a considerable quantity of salt marsh on its borders. It is separated from the Nevisink by a high neck of land, 2 miles wide.

Shrewsbury, p-t. of Shrewsbury t-sp., Monmouth co., between Shrewsbury and Nevisink rivers, 12 miles E. from Freehold, 50 S. E. from Trenton, and 215 N. E. from W. C.; contains 12 or 15 dwellings, an Episcopalian and Presbyterian church, 1 tavern, and 2 stores. Soil, sandy and light.

Shrewsbury t-ship, Monmouth co., bounded N. by Middletown t-ship; E. by the Atlantic ocean; S. by Howell t-ship, and W. by Freehold. Centrally distant 7 miles E. from Freehold; length N. and S. 13, breadth E. and W. 13 miles; area, 64,000 acres; drained on the N. E. by the Nevisink and Shrewsbury rivers, and their tributaries; E. by White Pond, and Deal creeks, and S. E. by Shark river; surface level; soil, clay and sandy loam, on marl, of good quality on Swimming river, and its tributaries; on the S. of these, sandy, poor, and covered with pine. On the E., along the shore near and below the Long Branch boarding-houses, is a very fertile black sand. The sea shore in this t-ship, is generally high and bold, and without marsh. The celebrated Long Branch boarding houses, so named from their vicinity to a long branch of Shrewsbury river, are in this township. Population in 1830, 4700. In 1832 the t-ship contained about 900 taxables; 265 householders, whose ratables did not exceed $30; and 150 single men; 21 stores, 5 saw mills, 12 run of stones, for grinding grain, 1 carding machine, 60 tan vats, 730 horses and mules, 1650 neat cattle, 3 years old and upwards; and paid state and county tax, $2144 69. Shrewsbury, Eatontown, Colts Neck, Long Branch, and Tinton's Falls, are villages and post-towns of the t-ship.

Several thousand acres in this t-ship were settled in 1682, and the inhabitants were then computed at 400. Lewis Morris of Barbadoes, the brother of Richard Morris, the first settler at Morrisania, New York, and uncle of Lewis Morris, subsequently governor of New Jersey, had iron works and other considerable improvements here.

Singack, small tributary of Preakness brook, Saddle River t-ship, Bergen co.

Six Mile Run, village and stream. The first, a post-town on the Princeton and Brunswick turnpike, (and on the line between New Brunswick t-ship, Middlesex co., and Franklin t-ship, Somerset co.,) 12 miles from the one, and 4 from the other, 189 from W. C., and 23 from Trenton; contains a Dutch Reformed church, 2 taverns, 1 store, and from 10 to 12 dwellings. Soil, red shale, level, and well cultivated.—The stream flows from North Brunswick, through Franklin t-ship, by a W. course of about 6 miles, to the Raritan river.

Slabtown, hamlet of Springfield t-ship, Burlington co., on the road from Mount Holly to Bordentown, 4 miles N. of the former; contains a Friends' meeting house, and 10 or 12 dwellings, 1 store, and 2 taverns.

Slab Cabin Branch, of the Rancocus creek, rises in Monmouth co., and flows a S. W. course of 10 miles, to its recipient, the North Branch of that creek, on the south boundary of Hanover t-ship, Burlington co. Hanover furnace lies upon it, and it turns several mills.

Slab Cabin Brook, Dover t-ship, Monmouth co., a small stream about 3 miles in length, which flows into the south side of Toms' Bay.

Sleepy Creek, a tributary of Atsion river, rises in Hereford t-ship, and flows by a S. E. course of about 6 miles, to its recipient, in Galloway t-ship, Gloucester co.

Smith's Creek, a small mill stream, which rises near Herbertstown, in Hopewell t-ship, Hunterdon co., and flows S. W. by a course of 6 miles, to the river Delaware, at the foot of Belle Mount.

Smithville, village of Galloway t-ship, Gloucester co., 42 miles S. E. of Woodbury, and 2 miles E. from Leed's Point; contains a tavern, store, Methodist meeting house, and 10 or 12 dwellings; surrounded by pines, and near the salt marsh.

Snake Hill, a noted eminence of Secaucas Island, in the marsh on Hackensack river, and a very prominent object from the road, between Jersey City and Newark. Its formation is of trap rock, on sandstone base.

Snover's Brook, rises in Sucker Pond, Stillwater t-ship, Sussex co., and flows by a S. W. course of about 8 or 9 miles through the north part of Hardwicke t-ship, into Paulinskill, on the northern part of Hamilton t-sp, Warren co.

Snuffletown, a small village of Sandistone t-ship, Sussex co., at the east foot of the Wallkill mountain, and in the valley of the Pacake creek, on the Paterson and Hamburg turnpike road, about 15 miles N. E. of Newton; contains a Methodist meeting house, a store, tavern, and tannery, and 6 or 8 dwellings.

Sodom, p-t. of Knowlton t-ship, Warren co., on Paulinskill, 12 miles N. of Belvidere, 4 E. from Columbia; contains a grist and saw mill, tavern, store, and some half-dozen dwellings. Some smelting works have lately been erected here, said to be for precious metals, discovered in the Jenny Jump mountain.

Sodom, Lebanon t-ship, Hunterdon co. (See *Clarkesville.*)

Somerset County, was taken from Middlesex, by an act of the proprietaries in 1688. Its bounds were subsequently modified by the legislative acts of 1709, 1713, and 1741. It is now bounded on the N. and N. E. by Morris co.; on the E. by Essex and Middlesex; on the S. E. by Middlesex; and on the S. W. and N. W. by Hunterdon co.: greatest length N. and S. 28 miles; breadth E. and W. 20 miles; area, 189,800 acres, or about 297 square miles: central lat. 40° 34′; long. 2° 15′ from W. C.

The whole county lies within the transition formation, if the old red sandstone be included within it. Hills of trap rock, upon the sandstone base, are scattered over it, as at Rock Hill, near the southern boundary, Rocky, or Nashanic mountain on the S. W., and Stony Hill N. of Somerville. The ridges N. of the last, contain grauwacke, and the valleys transition limestone, generally of a grey colour. The surface of the county is various: the N. W. section being mountainous; the S. and S. W. hilly, whilst the centre and S. E., the valley of the Raritan, is either level, or gently undulating. The soil varies with the surface: that of the hills is generally of clay and stiff loam, whilst that of the plains is a sandy loam, formed of the red shale; and the mountain vales, as we have already observed, are of limestone. All are, however, fertile under proper culture, and the county may vie with her neighbours of Hunterdon, Essex, and Middlesex, in the variety and quantity of agricultural products.

The county is well watered. It is cut into two, almost equal parts, by the main stem and south branch of the Raritan river, which receives the north branch, flowing southward and centrally through the northern section, and the Millstone river, flowing northward and centrally through the southern section; and it is thus by these three streams, divided into four parts, intersected by smaller brooks and creeks, in almost every direction. The Delaware and Raritan canal enters the county at Kingston, with the Millstone river, and follows that stream to its junction with the Raritan, 3 miles S. E. of Somerville, whence it pursues the valley of the last stream to Brunswick.

Copper ore has been discovered in considerable veins in the first range of hills, N. E. from Somerville; and mines have been opened in at least two places; the first within 2, and the second within 6 miles of the town. Attempts have been made to work both, but every effort has hitherto been unsuccessful: and yet the ore is said to contain not only a very valuable proportion of copper, but to be worth working on account of the gold which it yields. Public opinion attributes these failures more to the want of adequate capital to sustain the expense of the first steps in mining, than to the want of skill, or poverty of ore. It is said, also, that particles of gold and silver have been discovered in a gangue of carbonate of lime, on Green Brook, N. of the Scotch Plains.

A turnpike road from Brunswick, enters the county by a bridge over Bound Brook, and passes through Somerville, to North Branch, and thence to Philipsburg, opposite to Easton. From North Branch a turnpike road runs northward over Schooley's mountain to Hacketstown, in Warren co.; and a rail-road is in contemplation, through Somerville to Belvidere.

The post-towns of the county are Baskingridge, Bound Brook, Flaggtown, Harlingen, Kline's Mills, Lesser Cross-Roads, Liberty Corner, Martinsville, Millington, Millstone, North Branch, Peapack, Pluckemin, Princeton, Rocky Hill, Somerville, the county town, and Warren.

The county was early settled by the Dutch, whose industrious habits soon rendered it remarkable for its fruitfulness, and it became soon one of the most thickly settled of the province. By the census of 1830, the population amounted to 17,689 souls, of whom 7665 were white males, 7717 white females; 945 free coloured males, 914 free coloured females; 214 male slaves, 234 female slaves. Among these there were 118 aliens; deaf and dumb, 14 whites—blind, whites, 17, coloured, 3.

In 1832, there were in the co., 3500 taxables; 668 householders, whose ratables did not exceed $30; 391 single men, 68 merchants; 44 saw mills, 64 grist mills, or run of stones for grinding grain, 8 fulling mills, 211 tan vats, 28 distilleries, 11 carding machines, 4621 horses and mules, and 8634 neat cattle, above the age of 3 years; and it paid in state tax, $2642 86, and in county tax, $6000.

The courts for the county are holden at Somerville; the common pleas, orphan's court, and general quarter sessions, on the following Tuesdays: viz. last in January, 3d in April, 3d in June, and 1st in October; and the circuit courts on the 3d Tuesday in April, and the 1st in October.

STATISTICAL TABLE OF SOMERSET COUNTY.

Townships.	Length.	Breadth.	Area.	Surface.	Population.		
					1810	1820	1830
Bedminster,	8	4½	19,300	hilly,	1312	1393	1453
Bernard,	9	7	25,000	mountainous,	1879	2063	2062
Bridgewater,	13	11	35,000	level,	2906	3147	3549
Franklin,	13	8	30,000	do. [level,	2539	3071	3352
Hillsborough,	10	7	36,000	part hilly, part	2456	2885	2878
Montgomery,	8	8	26,500	hilly,	2282	2495	2834
Warren,	8	4	18,000	mountainous,	1354	1452	1561
			189,800		14,728	16,506	17,689

Somers' Point, p-t. and port of entry for Great Egg Harbour district, upon the Great Egg Harbour bay, about 43 miles S. E. from Woodbury, 88 from Trenton, and by post-route 196 from W. C. There is a tavern and boarding house here, and several farm houses. It is much resorted to for sea bathing in summer, and gunning in the fall season.

Somerville, p-t. and seat of justice, of Somerset co., situate about a mile N. of the Raritan river, on the turnpike road from New Brunswick to Philipsburg, 11 miles N. W. from the former, 33 S. E. from the latter, or from Easton, 28 N. E. from Trenton, and 199 from W. C. It lies upon a high well cultivated plain of red shale, about 2 miles south of a ridge of the South mountains; in which are some noted copper mines. It contains a Dutch Reformed church, a Methodist meeting, an academy where the classics and mathematics are taught, a boarding school for young ladies, 3 taverns well kept, and 7 stores, 1 large grist mill, 5 practising attorneys, 4 physicians, and 1 resident clergyman, 600 inhabitants, and about 100 dwellings. The court-house and other public buildings, are large and commodious, and many of the private dwellings are very neat; and the town is a healthy, pleasant, and desirable place of residence. The proposed rail road from Elizabethtown to the Delaware, at Belvidere, is designed to pass through it.

South Amboy, p-t. of South Amboy t-ship, Middlesex co., at the head of the Raritan bay and mouth of the Raritan river, 15 miles below New Brunswick, and 35 N. E. from Trenton; contains a hotel and some 15 or 20 dwellings, and an extensive manufactory of stone ware, made from clay obtained in the vicinity. This clay is of excellent quality, and much of it is exported to various parts of the country. It is used in the manufacture of delf ware at Jersey City, and in the fabrication of china at Philadelphia. The beds extend in the hills for several miles around the point. The turnpike road from Bordentown, and the Camden and Amboy rail road terminate here. There is a safe harbour here for vessels, and deep water at the landing.

South Amboy t-ship, Middlesex co., bounded N. by the Raritan river; N. E. by the Raritan bay; S. E. by Middletown and Upper Freehold t-ships, of Monmouth co.; S. W. by Millstone river; and N. W. by North Brunswick and South Brunswick t-ships. Centrally distant S. E. from New Brunswick 9 miles: greatest length N. E. and S. W. 18, and breadth 6 miles; area, 64,000 acres; surface, flat; soil, sandy; drained on the S. W. by the Millstone, and on the N. E. by South river and its tributaries, Tenant's run, Deep run, Matchaponix brook, and Manalapan creek. The turnpike and rail road from Bordentown to Amboy run through the t-ship. Upon the former lie the post-towns of Cranberry and Spotswood, and South Amboy. Population in 1830, 3782.

South River. (See *Manalapan Brook.*)

South Brunswick. (See *Brunswick, South.*)

Sparta, p-t. of Hardistone t-ship, Sussex co., at the west foot of the Wallkill mountain, 236 miles N. E. of W. C., 78 from Trenton, and 8 from Newton, on the Union turnpike road, in the valley, and near the source of the Wallkill river. This is a pleasant village, having some very good houses, a neat Presbyterian church with cupola, a school house, 2 grist mills, 2 saw mills, 4 forges for making iron, in which there are, together, 6 fires; 1 tavern, 3 stores, and from 35 to 40 dwellings. Iron and zinc ores are abundant in the neighbourhood; but only a small portion of the first is used in making iron here; the chief part being carted from the mines in Morris co., at the cost of $2 50 the ton. The zinc ore is not worked. The soil in the valley is limestone, and tolerably well cultivated.

Speertown, agricultural village of Bloomfield t-ship, Sussex co., 7 miles N. of Newark, near the foot of the First mountain; contains from 20 to 30 dwellings, 1 tavern, 1 store, a Dutch Reformed church, and school; surrounded by a country of red shale, carefully cultivated.

Spottswood, thriving p-t. of South Amboy t-ship, Middlesex co., on the turnpike road and rail road from Bordentown to South Amboy, about 25 miles from the former, 202 from W. C., and 26 from Trenton, and on the South river; contains a large gristmill, a fine Presbyterian church of wood, a Dutch Reformed church, 1 tavern, 2 stores, 2 tobacco manufactories, and about 30 dwellings.

Spruce Run, Lebanon t-ship, Hunterdon co., flows S. W. through the north part of the t-ship, and along the west boundary, and is a branch of the Raritan river.

Springfield t-ship, Essex county, bounded N. by Livingston t-ship; E. by Orange and Union t-ships; S. by Westfield and New Providence t-ships; and W. by the Passaic river, which divides it from Chatham t-ship, Morris co. Centrally distant W. from Newark 8 miles: greatest length N. and S. 6, breadth E. and W. 5 miles; area, 13,500 acres; surface, generally hilly; soil, clay loam and red shale. It is washed on the eastern boundary by the Rahway river, which receives several tributaries from the t-ship. Springfield the post-town; Vauxhall and part of Chatham are villages of the t-ship. The pretensions of Springfield, as an agricultural t-ship, are not high, but it claims consideration for its paper manufactories. Population in 1830, 1653. In 1832 there were 365 taxables, 97 householders, whose ratables did not exceed $30; 93 single men, 7 merchants, 1 grist mill, 3 carding machines, 12 paper mills, 6 tan vats, 1 woollen manufactory, 1 distillery, 220 horses and mules, and 818 neat cattle, above the age of 3 years. It paid state tax, 198 96; county, $520 56; poor, $500; road, $8.

Springfield p-t. of the preceding t-ship, on the turnpike road from Elizabethtown to Morristown, 7 miles W. from the one, and 10 E. from the other, 216 N. E. from W. C., and 50 from Trenton, and upon the Rahway river, at the foot of the First mountain; contains about 200 dwellings, some of which are neat structures; 1 Presbyterian church, with cupola and bell; 1 Methodist church, 3 taverns, 5 stores, 2 grist mills, 1 saw mill, and 10 paper mills. The surface of the country around it, is rugged, and the soil, a stiff cold clay, unproductive; and farms are not averaged at more than 20 dollars the acre.

Springfield, t-ship, Burlington co., bounded N. by Chesterfield, and Mansfield t-ships; S. E. by Hanover t-ship; S. W. by Northampton t-ship, and W. and N. W. by Burlington t-ship; centrally distant N. E. from Mount Holly, 5 miles; greatest length, E. and W. 10 miles; breadth, N. and S. 6 miles; area, 18,000 acres; surface level; soil, sand and sandy loam, well cultivated, and productive; drained, N. by the Assiscunk creek, which forms the northern boundary, and its branches, and S. by the tributaries of the north branch of the Rancocus creek. Slabtown, Jobstown, and Juliustown, are villages of the t-ship, at the two last of which, are post-offices. The population, a great portion of which are Friends, was, in 1830, 1531. In 1832, the t-ship contained, 3 Friends' meeting houses, 147 householders, whose ratables did not exceed $30, in value; 61 single men, 330 taxables; 3 stores, 14 tan vats, 1 distillery for cider, 31 dearborns, 100 covered wagons, 17 chairs, 11 gigs and curricles, 1975 neat cattle, and 507 horses and mules, over 3 years of age; and paid state tax, $388 85; county tax, $1358 29; and township tax, $500.

Spring Garden, or *North Belleville*, Bloomfield t-ship, Essex co., upon the Third river, and about a mile W. of the Passaic river; contains from 50 to 70 dwellings, a cotton manufactory, a school, and a Methodist church. (See *Belleville.*)

Spring Mills, village of Alexandria t-ship, Hunterdon co., 13 miles N. W. from Flemington, on a small stream, which empties into the Delaware; contains a grist mill, and several dwellings.

Springtown, small village of Schooley's mountain, on the Somerville and Easton turnpike road, 18 miles W. of Morristown, and 3 miles E. of the mineral spring; contains some 6 or 8 dwellings.

Spring Valley, hamlet of Morris t-ship, Morris co., 4 miles S. E. of Morristown; contains a tavern, and some half-dozen dwellings.

Squan Beach, extends from Old Cranberry inlet, N. 10 miles to Manasquan inlet, dividing for part of that distance, Barnegat bay, from the Atlantic ocean. It no where exceeds half a mile in width.

Squan, a vicinage in the S. E. part of Howell t-ship, Monmouth co., between Manasquan and Metetecunk rivers. It is much frequented for sea-bathing; and comfortable accommodations are found at the farm-houses, of which there are several where boarders are received.

Squankum, p-t. of Howell t-ship, Monmouth co., 10 miles S. E. from Freehold, 44 from Trenton, and 209 N. E. from W. C.; contains a Friends' meeting house, a grist mill, and fulling mill, 2 taverns, 1 store, and 12 or 15 dwellings, surrounded by pine forest, and sandy soil.

Squankum, tavern, and creek; the creek is a tributary of Inskeep's branch of the Great Egg Harbour river, Deptford t-ship, Gloucester county.

Stafford t-ship, Monmouth co., bounded on the N. by Dover t-ship; E. and S. E. by the Atlantic ocean; S. W. by Little Egg Harbour t-ship; and W. by Northampton t-ship, Burlington co. Centrally distant S. from Freehold, 38 miles; greatest length, N. and S. 18 miles, breadth 12 miles; area, 87,000 acres; surface level; soil, sand, gravel, and marsh. On the E. front of the t-ship, Long Beach extends upon the ocean, about 11 miles, with an average breadth of about 1 mile, separating Little Egg Harbour bay from the sea. The bay varies from 2 to 3 miles in width, and between it and the fast land, there is a body of salt marsh of like width, through which flow several creeks; the principal are Manahocking, Gunning, Cedar, and Westecunk. Barnegat, Manahocking, Cedar Bridge, and Westecunk, are villages; the two first post-towns of the t-ship. Population in 1830, 2059. In 1832 the county contained about 400 taxables; 64 householders, whose ratables did not exceed $30; 30 single men; 4 stores, 2 saw mills, 1 grist mill, 1 furnace, 210 horses and mules, and 802 neat cattle, above 3 years of age.

Stanhope, forge, and post-town, on the Musconetcong river, and on the Morris canal, on the S. boundary of Byram t-ship, Sussex co., by the post route, 222 miles from W. C., 59 from Trenton, 11 S. of Newton, and 16 N. W. of Morristown; contains a grist mill, 3 forges, 2 taverns, 2 stores, and from 20 to 30 dwellings, and one large school house. The creek has here been led from its bed, by which means a fine waterfall of 30 feet, available for mill purposes, has been obtained; an inclined plane of the canal at this place, surmounts an elevation of 76 feet. This thriving little town was founded by Mr. Silas Dickenson; and is surrounded by an excellent soil of limestone.

Staten Island Sound, or ***Arthur-Kill***, the strait which divides Staten Island from New Jersey. It has a devious, but general N. E. course, from the head of Raritan bay, and including the ***Kill-van-Kuhl***, extends to New York bay, a distance of about 18 miles, having a breadth, commonly much under, and no where exceeding half a mile. It is the ordinary passage of the steamboats which ply between Brunswick, Amboy, and New York. As the tide flows from, and into both bays, from and into this strait, the navigator never has a current with him through its whole length. The channel is skirted on both sides by an agreeable country. That of New Jersey is the more level, and that of Staten Island the more variegated and picturesque. For several miles from New York bay, the shore of the island is so closely covered with houses, as to have the appearance of a continued street.

Steddam's Neck, a strip of land lying in the N. W. angle of Greenwich t-ship, formed by the junction of Newport and Stow creeks.

Steelman's Creek, small tributary, flowing eastwardly into the Great Egg Harbour river, Weymouth t-ship, Gloucester co.

Stephen's Creek, Weymouth t-ship, Gloucester co., tributary of Great Egg Harbour river, having an easterly course of 8 or 9 miles. Two miles from its mouth, is a village and post-town which bears its name; 39 miles S. E. from Woodbury, 78 from Trenton, and 106 N. E. from W. C. It contains a grist and saw mill, tavern, store, and 6 or 8 dwellings.

Stewartsville, p-t. of Greenwich t-ship, Warren co., centrally situate in the t-ship, on Merritt's branch of Pohatcong creek, 10 miles S. E. of Belvidere; contains a tavern, a store, and 10 or 12 dwellings; surrounded by a fertile limestone country, and lying about a mile south of the Morris canal, and about 5 miles east from Easton, Pennsylvania.

Still Valley, of Greenwich t-ship, Warren co., lying between Lopatcong and Pohatcong creeks, and extending N. E. from the river Delaware. This is a rich valley of limestone land, thickly settled, and highly productive in wheat. There is a post-office here named after the valley, on the turnpike road, between 4 and 5 miles from Easton, Pennsylvania.

Stillwater t-ship, Sussex co., bounded N. E. by Newton t-ship; S. E. by Greene t-ship; S. W. by Hardwick t-ship, Warren co.; and N. W. by Walpack t-ship. Centrally distant from Newton, E. 7 miles; greatest length N. and S. 10 miles; breadth E. and W. 7 miles; area, 28,160 acres; surface hilly, on the N. W. mountainous. It is drained by Paulinskill, which crosses it centrally, and receives a tributary from Swartwout's pond in the t-ship. Population in 1830, 1381. Taxables in 1832, 230. Stillwater and Coursenville are post-offices of the t-ship, which contained, in 1832, 40 householders, whose ratables did not exceed $30, 4 run of stones for grinding grain, 4 stores, 6 saw mills, 277 horses and mules, and 692 neat cattle above three years of age, 1 distillery, 64 tan vats. It paid state and county tax, $378 85; poor tax, $200; road tax, $600. S. E. of the Paulinskill, the soil is slate; N. W.

of the creek, lime, slate, and grey rock, and is generally fertile.

Stillwater, p-t. of the above t-ship, by the post-route, 236 miles from W. C., 78 from Trenton, and 7 S. W. from Newton; contains a tavern, store, a grist and oil mill, a Presbyterian church, formerly Dutch Reformed, and 8 or 10 dwellings. The soil around it is limestone, well cultivated.

Stipson's Island, a neck of fast land, near the west boundary of Dennis t-ship, Cape May co., projecting into the marshes, having a length of about 3 miles.

Stockholm, post-office and forge of Jefferson t-ship, Morris co., upon the Pequannock creek, at the N. E. end of the Greenpond mountain, 18 miles N. W. of Morristown, 249 N. E. from W. C., and 83 from Trenton.

Stockingtown, a small hamlet of 6 or 8 dwellings, of Upper Alloways Creek t-ship, Salem co., about 9 miles E. of Salem t-ship, and 3 from Allowaystown.

Stone House Brook, branch of the Pompton river, rising in Pequannock t-ship, and flowing by a course of 6 miles N. W. to its recipient, giving motion to some forges.

Stony Brook, Pequannock t-ship, Morris co., small tributary of the Rockaway river, which flows by several branches, in length from 4 to 5 miles, through Rockaway valley.

Stony Hill, extends from the north branch of the river Raritan, in Bernard and Bridgewater t-ships, through Warren t-ship, in Somerset co., into Essex co., in the form of a crescent; formed of trap rock, on old red sandstone base. Under this name the mountain, following its curve, is about 12 miles long.

Stop-the-Jade Creek, tributary of the S. branch of the Rancocus creek, Northampton t-ship, Burlington co.; unites with the latter at Vincenttown, after a westerly course of 9 miles.—A mill stream.

Stout's Branch, of Paulin's creek, rises in Sand Pond, Hardwick t-ship, Warren co., at the foot of the Blue mountain, and flows by a southerly course of 7 or 8 miles, to its recipient.

Stoutsville, on the line dividing Montgomery t-ship, Somerset co., from Hopewell t-ship, Hunterdon co., and on the turnpike road from Brunswick to Lambertsville, 13 miles S. W. from Somerville; contains a tavern, and 6 or 8 dwellings, in a fertile, pleasant valley.

Stow Creek t-ship, Cumberland co., bounded N. and W. by Stow creek, which divides it from Salem co.; E. by Hopewell t-ship, and S. by Greenwich t-ship. Centrally distant, N. W. from Bridgeton, 7 miles; greatest length, E. and W. 7; breadth, N. and S. 6 miles; area, 10,240 acres; surface, partly level, partly rolling; soil, clay, loam, sand, and gravel. Population in 1830, 791. In 1832, the t-ship contained 170 taxables, 21 householders, whose ratables did not exceed $30; 4 grist mills, 1 saw mill, 198 horses and 557 cattle, above the age of 3 years, 1 store; and paid road tax, $200; state and county, $437 81. Newport creek forms the boundary between this and Greenwich t-ship.

Stow Creek, rises on the confines of Salem and Cumberland cos., and Hopewell and Upper Alloways Creek t-ships, and by a S. W. and S. course, forms the line between these counties, by the meanders of the creek; 25 miles to the Delaware bay. It is navigable for sloops, about 18 miles, and has some good banked meadow on its borders, for the distance of 9 miles, commencing 9 miles from its mouth.

Straw, hamlet of Greenwich t-ship, Warren co., about 5 miles S. E. of Philipsburg, and 12 miles S. of Belvidere; contains 3 or 4 dwellings only.

Stralenberg, hamlet, Hackensack t-ship, Bergen co., about 5 miles N. E. of Hackensacktown; contains 1 Dutch Reformed, and 1 Seceder's church, some 8 or 10 dwellings, a store and tavern; surrounded by a pleasant, level country, of fertile loam, well cultivated.

Stretch's Point, on Stow creek, Lower Alloways Creek t-ship, Salem co., about 7 miles from the mouth of the creek.

Suckasunny, the name of a village and plain; the latter extending in width from 2½ to 3 miles, and in length about 6 miles; is sandy and not very fertile, and is drained by Black, or Lamington river. On the N. E. of this plain, terminates the great vein of iron which has continued a S. W. course from the White Hills in New Hampshire.

The village and post-town is situate on the Morristown and Easton turnpike road, 11 miles N. W. from the former, 63 N. E. from Trenton, and 226 from W. C.; contains a Presbyterian church, a store and tavern, and some 12 or 15 dwellings.

Sucker Pond, a small basin of water, at the east foot of the Blue mountain, in Stillwater t-ship, Sussex co.

Sussex County, was taken from Morris, by act of Assembly, 8th June, 1753, with bounds which included the present county of Warren. Warren was erected by act of 20th Nov. 1824; and Sussex is now bounded S. by the Musconetcong river and Hopatcong pond; thence by a line running N. E. dividing it from Morris and Bergen counties, to the line of the state of New York; thence along that line N. W., to the Delaware river, at the mouth of the Nevisink, or Macacomac river; thence by the river, to the mouth of the Flatkill; and thence by a line S. E., separating it from Warren co., to the Musconetcong river, somewhat more than a mile below Andover furnace. Its form approaches an oblong, with a mean length of 26, and breadth of 22 miles; area, about 572 square miles, or 366,000 acres: central lat. 41° 8′ N.; long. 2° 15′ from W. C.

The county is divided geologically by the primitive and transition formations. The former passing N. E. by Sparta, and including within its limits, the Hamburg or Wallkill, and the Wawayanda mountains. These mountains abound with a variety of minerals, of which iron and zinc are the most considerable. The country between these hills and the Blue mountain is rolling; nay, hilly; in which, ridges of slate, alternate with valleys of limestone; and is highly fertile, and every where well cultivated. The Blue, or Kittatinny mountain, is skirted on the east by grey rock, which bears great resemblance to the primitive, and certainly contains little evidence of recombination. The mountain itself appears to be composed partly of similar rock, of a bluish green and red sandstone, the colours of which are singularly and intimately blended. Upon the N. W. the mountain is bounded by a broad strip of grey limestone.

A dividing ridge running from Blue mountain, in Frankford t-ship, north of Culver's Pond, through the S. E. angle of that t-ship, on towards Sparta, gives a determination to the waters of the county, sending part N. E. towards the Hudson, and part towards the Delaware river. Thus all the waters of the eastern portion pour from the hills north and south, into the valley of the Wallkill, where the flatness of the surface causes them to spread over a considerable space, and occasions an extensive marsh along the borders of that stream, greatly enlarged within the bounds of the state of New York. The western portion of the county is drained chiefly by the Paulinskill, flowing by a deep and rapid course, through this and Warren county, to its recipient near Columbia.

The face of the country is dotted with large ponds, or small lakes, some of which are on the highest hills. Swartwout's and Culver's ponds are the largest—the first being 3 miles in length, by 1 in breadth, and the other 2 miles in length, by the same breadth. But the most remarkable are the White Ponds, which have been so called, from the appearance of their shores and bottoms, covered with shells of the snail, in very extensive masses. Two of these lie on the line between Newton and Hardiston townships.

The agriculture of the county is in a state of progressive improvement, and is now very productive. The limestone lands yield large crops of wheat, and the slate, where the rock does not come too near to the surface, is scarce less fertile. Lime is not yet much employed as manure, but its use is growing, and will doubtlessly be extensive, when its benefits shall be generally known. Wheat, rye, oats, corn, and iron, are staple products.

The principal towns and post offices, are Newton, the county town, Deckertown, Hamburg, Ogdensburg, Sparta, Andover, Greenville, Stillwater, Branchville, Augusta, and Lafayette. Benville, Coursenville, Flatbrookville, Fredon, Gratitude, Harmony, Hamburg, Lafayette, Libertyville, Lockwood, Monroe, Montague, Sandystone, Stanhope, Vernon, Walpack, and Wantage.

By returns of the assessors, for the year 1832, there were 1075 householders, 58 merchants, shopkeepers, and traders, 87 run of stones for grinding grain, 18 carding machines, 3 iron furnaces, 55 saw mills, 28 forge fires, 7 fulling mills, 3875 horses and mules, 13,070 neat cattle 3 years old and upwards, 6 ferries and toll bridges, 227 tan vats, 36 distilleries, and 101,887 acres of improved land. The amount of state and county tax, was $7500 95; poor tax, $3300; road tax, $8600.

By the census of 1830, the population of the county amounted to 20,346 souls, of whom 10,240 were white males; 9654 white females; 206 free coloured males; 195 free coloured females; 21 male, and 30 female slaves. Of these inhabitants, 89 were aliens; 6 deaf and dumb; 14 blind.

The provision for moral improvement in the county, consist of 2 classical seminaries at Newton, 6 common schools in that town, and others in sufficient numbers for the wants of the people throughout the county; a Lyceum for the cultivation of letters and science, and a public library at Newton; a county Bible society, a county Sunday school union, and district Sunday schools and temperance societies.

The county elects 1 member to the legislative council, and 2 to the Assembly. The courts of common pleas, orphans', and quarter sessions, are holden at Newton, on the last Tuesday of January, the 4th Tuesday of May, the 3d of August, and the 4th of November; and the circuit courts, and sessions of oyer and terminer and general jail delivery, are holden on the 4th Tuesdays of May, and November.

STATISTICAL TABLE OF SUSSEX COUNTY.

Townships.	Length.	Breadth.	Area.	Surface.	Population. 1810.	1820.	1830.
Byram,	10	8	21,760	mountainous.	591	672	958
Frankfort,	11	8½	28,800	valley.	1637	2008	1996
Green,	9	4	14,080	p't hilly, p't level.			801
Hardiston,	13	9	41,960	mountainous.	1702	2160	2588
Montague,	8½	7½	21,620	moun. & riv. flat.	661	964	990
Newton,	12	10	65,920	hilly, p't level.	2082	2743	3464
Sandistone,	8½	7	19,320	moun. & riv. flat.	703	1945	1097
Stillwater,	10	7	28,160	moun. level.			1381
Walpack,	10	4	15,360	moun. & riv. flat.	591	822	660
Wantage,	11	8½	42,880	do. do.	2969	3307	4084
Vernon,	11	10	52,480	mountainous.	1708	2096	2377
			352,300		12,644	16,617	20,346

We have already, in our introductory chapter, noted generally the geological and mineralogical character of this county. But the reader will be gratified with the following special notice from Dr. Samuel Fowler, whose intimate knowledge of the subject, renders the account highly valuable.

Perhaps in no quarter of the globe is there so much found to interest the mineralogist, as in the white crystalline calcareous valley, commencing at Mounts Adam and Eve, in the county of Orange, and state of New York, about three miles from the line of the state of New Jersey, and continuing thence, through Vernon, Hamburg, Franklin, Sterling, Sparta and Byram, a distance of about twenty-five miles, in the county of Sussex, and state of New Jersey. This limestone is highly crystalline, containing no organic remains, and is the great imbedding matrix of all the curious and interesting minerals found in this valley. When burned, it produces lime of a superior quality. A considerable quantity of this stone is burned into lime near Hamburg, and when carted to the towns below, as Patterson, Newark, &c. is sold for one dollar per bushel. It is principally used in masonry, for whitewashing, cornice work, and wall of a fine hard finish, and is considered superior to the best Rhode Island lime. Some varieties, particularly the granular, furnish a beautiful marble; it is often white, with a slight tinge of yellow, resembling the Parian marble from the island of Paros; at other times clouded, black, sometimes veined, black, and at other times arborescent.

Franklinite; a new metalliferous combination, containing, according to Berthier, of oxide of zinc 17, of iron 66, and manganese 16, is very abundant; indeed it appears inexhaustible. It commences about half a mile north-east of Franklin furnace, and extends two miles south-west of Sparta, a distance of nine miles. It is accompanied in this whole distance by the red oxide of zinc, mutually enveloping each other. The greatest quantity appears to be at Franklin furnace. The bed here, is about 100 feet high above the adjoining land, on the west side of it, and from ten to forty feet wide. Various attempts have been made to work this ore in a blast furnace, but without success. It frequently congeals in the hearth, before time is allowed to get it out in a liquid state, in consequence of a combination of the iron with manganese. All this difficulty I apprehend might be overcome, if a method could be discovered of smelting iron ore in a blast furnace with anthracite coal; as the Franklinite requires a greater degree of heat to cause it to retain its liquid state, than can be obtained by the use of charcoal. It occurs in grains imbedded in the white carbonate of lime, and detached in concretions of various sizes, from that of a pin's head to a hickory nut; also, in regular octahedral crystals, emarginated on the angles, small at Franklin, but very perfect, with brilliant faces. At Sterling, the crystals are large and perfect. I have one from that place that measures sixteen inches around the common base.

Red Oxide of Zinc.—At Sterling, three miles from Franklin, a mountain mass of this formation presents itself about 200 feet high. Here, as Mr. Nuttall truly observes, the red oxide of zinc forms as it were a paste, in which the crystals of Franklinite are thickly imbedded; in fact a metalliferous porphyry. This appears to be the best adapted for manufacturing purposes. The Franklinite imbedded in the zinc ore here, is highly magnetic, and may be all separated by magnetic cylinders, recently brought into use to separate the earthy portion of magnetic iron ore. It was long since observed, that this ore is well adapted for the manufacture of the best brass, and may be employed without any previous preparation. It is reduced without any difficulty to a metallic state, and may be made to furnish the sulphate of zinc (white vitriol).

It is remarked by Professor Bull, "that this ore, from its abundance, and the many uses to which it may be applied, promises to be a valuable acquisition to the manufacturing interest of the United States." Berthier found it to contain oxide of zinc 88, red oxide of manganese 12.

Magnetic Iron Ore. On the west side of the Franklinite, and often within a few feet of it, appears an abundance of magnetic iron ore, usually accompanied by hornblende rock. In some places it soon runs into the Franklinite, which destroys its usefulness; and the largest beds are combined with plumbago, which renders it unprofitable to work in a blooming forge, but valuable in a blast furnace. On the Franklin or Warwick mountain, about four miles east of the furnace, are numerous beds of iron ore, from which many thousand tons have been taken; and which still contain a large quantity of the best quality of ore, either for a blooming forge or blast furnace. Iron pyrites occur here, both in the valley and on the mountain, of a proper quality to manufacture sulphate of iron—(copperas.) It also occurs crystallized, in cubes, in octahedrons, and dodecahedrons, frequently perfect, and highly splendid.

The other minerals found in this district are numerous, rare, interesting, and several of them new, and not found in any other place, but better calculated to instruct the naturalist and adorn his cabinet, than for any particular uses to which they have as yet been applied. A catalogue of which I have subjoined, designating the minerals as they occur in each township.

In Byram t-ship, considered the south western extremity of the white carbonate of lime.

1. Spinelle, colour reddish brown, green, and black, in octahedral crystals, associated with orange coloured brucite.

2. Brucite of various shades, from that of a straw colour, to a dark orange, and nearly black.

3. Grey hornblende in six-sided prisms, with diedral summits.

In the Township of Hardiston.

At Sparta:

1. Brucite of a beautiful honey colour—the finest we have is found here.

2. Augite in six-sided prisms, colour brownish green.

At Sterling:

1. Spinelle, black, green, and grey, in octahedral crystals.

2. Brucite of various shades.

3. Brutile, colour steel grey; lustre metallic, in acicular prisms, with longitudinal striad.

4. Blende, black and white; the white sometimes in octahedral crystals, the lustre brilliant.

5. Dysluite, in octahedral crystals, colour brown externally, internally yellowish brown; lustre metallic—(a new mineral.)

6. Ferruginous silicate of manganese, in six-sided prisms, colour pale yellow, associated with Franklinite.

7. Tourmaline, imbedded in white feldspar, in six-sided prisms, longitudinally striated; colour reddish brown.

8. Green and blue carbonate of copper. A number of large excavations were made at the Sterling mine for copper, during the revolutionary war, under an erroneous impression, that the red oxide of zinc, was the red copper ore. It was the property of Lord Sterling; hence the name of the Sterling mine. Of copper, we only find there a trace of the green and blue carbonate.

At Franklin:

1. Spinelle, black and red crystallized.

2. Ceylonite, green and bluish green, in perfect octahedrons truncated on the angles; lustre of the brilliance of polished steel.

5. Garnets, black, brown, yellow, red, and green—crystallized in dodecahedrons.

6. Silicate of Manganese, light brownish red.

7. Ferro Silicate of Manganese, of Professor Thomson, and the Fowlerite, of Nuttall, light red or pink, foliated and splendent, has much the appearance of Feldspar, is also in rectangular prisms.

8. Lesqui-Silicate of Manganese, lamellar in scales or small plates; colour, brownish black.

9. Hornblende, crystallized.

10. Actynolite, do.

11. Tremolite, do.

12. Augite, common variety, do.

13. Jeffersonite, do. do.

14. Plumbago, foliated and crystallized in six-sided balls.

15. Brucite of various shades.

16. Scapolite, white, crystallized.

17. Wernerite, yellow, do.

18. Tourmaline, black, do.

19. Fluate of Lime, earthy and do.

20. Galena.

21. Oolite, in small grains about the size of a mustard seed, disseminated in blue secondary carbonate of lime.

22. Asbestos, connected with Hornblende rock.

23. Green Beryl.

24. Feldspar, green and white, crystallized.

25. Epidote and Pink Carbonate of Lime.

26. Arsenical Pyrites.

27. Serpentine.

28. Sahlite.

29. Cocolite, green and black.

30. Sphene, honey colour, crystallized.

31. Quartz.

32. Jasper.

33. Chalcedony.

34. Amethyst, crystallized.

35. Agate.

36. Mica, black and orange coloured, crystallized.

37. Zircon, crystallized.

38. Sulphate of Molybdena.

39. Phosphate of Iron.

40. Carbonate of Iron.

41. Steatite, foliated with yellow Garnet.

42. Phosphate of Lime, crystallized.

43. Pale Yellow-blende, of a foliated structure—lustre, vitreous.

Near Hamburgh.

1. An ore of Manganese, and iron of a light reddish brown, very compact and heavy.

2. Augite and Brucite.

In the Township of Vernon.

1. Green Spinelle and Brucite, in octahedral crystals.

In Newton Township.

1. Sulphate of Barytes in lamellar masses, and tabular crystals, in a vein traversing secondary limestone.

2. Sapphire, blue and white, in rhombs and six-sided prisms.

3. Red Oxide of Titanium.

4. Grey Spinelle in large octahedral crystals.
5. Mica, copper coloured, in hexahedral crystals.
6. Idocrase, crystallized, yellowish brown.
7. Steatite, presenting the pseudomorphous form of quartz, scapolite, and spinelle.
8. Scapolite, in four-sided prisms. For a more particular account of the Newton minerals, see Silliman's Journal, vol. XXI. page 319.

In Frankford Township.

Serpentine, of a light yellowish green, bears a fine polish, has a glistening lustre, and is quite abundant.

Swartwout's Pond, a large sheet of water, of Stillwater t-ship, Sussex co., which sends forth a tributary to Paulinskill.

Swedesboro', p-t. of Woolwich t-ship, Gloucester co., 13 miles S. W. from Woodbury, 49 miles from Trenton, and 155 from W. C., at the head of sloop navigation, on Raccoon creek, about 5 miles from its mouth; contains about 100 dwellings, an Episcopal and a Methodist church, an academy, 2 taverns, 4 stores, a merchant grist mill, and an extensive woollen factory, belonging to C. C. Stratton, Esq. The country around it is level; soil, sandy loam, fertile, and well cultivated. Battentown, a mile distant from it, contains 1 tavern, and a few dwellings.

Swede's Branch, mill stream of Chester t-ship, Burlington co., flows by a N. W. course of more than 3 miles, to the Delaware river.

Swimming River. (See *Shrewsbury river.*)

Tabernacle, village of Northampton t-ship, Burlington co., 12 miles S. W. of Mount Holly; contains a Methodist church, a tavern, and 10 or 12 houses.

Talman's Creek, small tributary of the Rancocus creek, rising in Evesham t-ship, Burlington co., near Evesham village, and flows six miles to its recipient.

Tansboro', village of Gloucester t-ship, of Gloucester co., on the road from Long-a-coming, to Great Egg Harbour river, 15 miles S. E. from Woodbury, 18 from Camden; contains a tavern, and some half dozen dwellings. Surrounded by a sandy soil, and pine forest.

Tarkiln Creek, mill stream of Maurice River t-ship, Cumberland co., rising in the t-ship, and flowing by a southerly course, of 10 miles into the Delaware bay.

Taunton Furnace, on Haines' creek, Evesham t-ship, Burlington co., 11 miles S. W. from Mount Holly, and 14 S. E. from Camden.

Tenants' Run, a tributary of South river, South Amboy t-ship, Middlesex co., flowing N. W., between 3 and 4 miles to its recipient.

Tewkesbury, t-ship, Hunterdon co., bounded N. by Washington t-ship, Morris co.; E. by Bedminster t-ship, Somerset co.; S. by Readington t-ship, and W. and S. W. by Lebanon t-ship; centrally distant N. E. from Flemington, 14 miles; greatest length, N. and S., 8; breadth, E. and W. 6½ miles; area, 23,000 acres; surface hilly; soil, on the mountain, clay and loam, and in the valley, at its foot, grey limestone, rich and well cultivated; drained by Rockaway creek, and its tributaries, flowing S. E. through the township, and by Lamington river, which runs on the eastern boundary. New Germantown, and Pottersville, are post-towns of the t-ship. Population in 1830, 1659. In 1832 the t-ship contained 8 stores, 6 saw mills, 3 grist mills, 28 tanner's vats, 2 carding machines, 2 fulling mills, 9 distilleries, 417 horses and mules, 696 neat cattle, above 3 years of age; and paid poor tax, $350; road tax, $600; state and county tax, $706 68.

Tice's Pond, at the foot of the Ramapo mountain, Pompton t-ship, Bergen co.; covers about 200 acres of ground, and is the source of a tributary of Ringwood river.

Timber Creek, Big, Gloucester co., rises by two branches, the lesser in Gloucester, and the greater in Deptford t-ship, uniting about 6 miles above the mouth. The north branch is navigable for sloops from the Delaware to Chew's landing, a distance of 8 or 9 miles, and the south, nearly to Blackwoodtown, a distance of about 10 miles. The whole length of the stream, by its meanders, may be 13 or 14 miles. It receives several small tributaries in its course, and drives some valuable mills.

Timber Creek, Little, of Woolwich t-ship, Gloucester co., rises in the t-ship, and flows N. W. 7 or 8 miles, to the Delaware river, below Chester Island. There is a mill upon it, near its head.

Tinton Falls, village, and mill site of Shrewsbury t-ship, Monmouth co., upon a branch of the Nevisink river, 9 miles E. from Freehold; contains from 15 to 20 dwellings, a grist and saw mill, 1 tavern, and 2 stores. The water of the S. E. branch of Swimming river, falls over a sand rock, filled with animal remains, and forming a cascade of about 30 feet high. From this rock flows a copious chalybeate spring, which is frequently visited by those who seek health or amusement at the boarding houses near the coast.

Titusville, post-office, Hunterdon county.

Toms' River, p-t., of Dover t-ship, Monmouth co., upon the head of Toms' River bay, and tide water, 25 miles S. E. from Freehold, 221 from W. City, and 69 from Trenton, and 6 from the confluence of the river with Barnegat bay; a flourishing village, lying on both sides of the creek, united by a wooden bridge, of near 200 feet in length; contains from 50 to 60 frame dwellings, some of which are very neat and commodious; 2 taverns, 5 or 6 stores, and a Methodist meeting. Many sloops and schooners are built here, and more than $200,000 worth of timber and cord-wood, annually exported.

Toms' River, mill stream of Monmouth co.; its main branch rises on the line dividing Freehold and Upper Freehold t-ships, and near Paint Island spring; and flows thence by a S. E. and E. course of 30 miles, into Barnegat bay. Above the village of Toms' river, about 4 miles, it receives the south branch, which is formed by many streams from Dover and Upper Freehold t-ships; and about a mile above the village, Wrangle Brook also unites with it. It drains a wide expanse of forest land, and by the main stream and branches turns many mills and iron works.

Townsbury, post-office, Warren county.

Tranquility, small tributary of the west branch of Wading river, rises and flows about 4 miles in the neck of land, between the east and west branches of the river.

Trap, hamlet of Shrewsbury t-ship, Monmouth co., near Shark river, 11 miles S. E. from Freehold; containing 6 or 8 dwellings, surrounded by a sandy soil and pine forest.

Trenton t-ship, Hunterdon co., bounded N. by Hopewell, E. by Lawrence t-ships; S. E. by Nottingham t-ship, of Burlington co.; and S. W. and W. by the river Delaware. Greatest length N. W. and S. E. 8 miles; breadth E. and W. 6 miles; area, 10,609 acres; surface, level; soil, clay and red shale, generally well cultivated, and productive. It is drained by Jacob's creek on the north, and by the Assunpink and its tributaries, on the south. The town of Birmingham, and the city of Trenton, are within its boundary. Population in 1830, 3925. In 1832, there were in the t-ship 11 merchants, 3 fisheries, 2 saw mills, 3 grist mills, 2 ferries and bridges, 220 tan vats, 2 grain distilleries, 469 horses and mules, and 590 neat cattle, above 3 years old; and it paid poor tax, $900; road tax, $400; and county tax, $1264 98. (See *Trenton City.*)

Trenton, city, and seat of government of the state, on the left bank of the Delaware river, three-fourths of a mile above the tide, opposite the lower falls of the river, and on the north side of the Assunpink creek, Trenton t-ship, Hunterdon co., 30 miles from Philadelphia, 58 from New York; lat. 40° 13′ 41″ N.; long. 0° 21′ 15″ E. of Philadelphia, and 2° 8′ 15″ of Washington City. Incorporated by the act of 13th November, 1792, which established its government under a mayor, recorder, 3 aldermen, and 13 assistants, with the usual city privileges, and power to license taverns within the city; and by the act of 3d January, 1817, the mayor, recorder, and aldermen, or any three of them, of whom the mayor and recorder must be one, are empowered to hold a court of general quarter sessions. There are here, a state house, 100 by 60 feet, with bow at either end, cupola, and bell; the building is of stone, stuccoed in imitation of dark granite, and beautifully situated on the bank of the river, commanding a fine view of the stream, the airy bridge which has been thrown over it, and of the undulating shore of Pennsylvania: a house for the residence of the governor of the state; 3 fire-proof offices, a bank incorporated in 1804, with an authorized capital of $600,000, of which $214,740 only have been paid in; an academy in which the languages are taught, 3 boarding and day schools for females, and several common schools. These are, however, in the city proper; but Trenton, as known in common parlance, including the villages of Mill Hill, Bloomsbury, and Lamberton, extending 1¾ miles down the river bank, has an Episcopal, Presbyterian, Friends', Baptist, Reformed Baptist, Roman Catholic, Methodist, and African Methodist churches. Trenton proper contains 425 dwellings, 13 taverns, about 30 stores, among which are 3 bookstores, and 3 silversmith shops; 3 printing offices, each of which issues a weekly paper, viz. the Union, the True American, and the New Jersey Gazetteer; a public library, established about the year 1750, and a lyceum or literary association. Mill Hill has 78 dwellings, 4 stores, and 4 taverns. Bloomsbury, 145 dwellings, 2 stores, and 5 taverns; and Lamberton, 64 dwellings, 2 stores, and 2 taverns. The Philadelphia steam-boats ply daily, and sometimes several times a day, one from Lamberton, and others from Bloomsbury; and stages run 3 times a day by the rail-road to New York and Philadelphia. Stages also run hence by Princeton to Brunswick, and to various other parts of the country The Delaware and Raritan canal receives its feeder here, on which is an extensive basin for vessels and boats, and the main canal crosses the Assunpink east of the town, over a noble stone aqueduct. The state prison is at Lamberton, where a new prison is also being erected, adapted to the confinement of 150 convicts. The famed bridge over the Delaware, is thrown from Bloomsbury to Morrisville, a span of 1100 feet, having a double carriage-way and foot-paths resting on the chords of, and suspended from, a series of five arches, supported on stone piers. This structure has been much admired for its lightness, grace, and strength. There are on the Assunpink, within the town, two cotton mills, having 5400 spindles, and one mill for power looms, and on the Delaware, two mills for looms; the whole number of looms exceed 200.

For some years past Trenton has not been in a very thriving state, but the late improvements have given new life to business and enterprise, and much prosperity is anticipated from the completion of the canal, and particularly from the construction of the mill race, now being made by the Trenton Falls Company.

This company was incorporated by an act of the legislature, 16th Feb. 1831, with power to purchase, lease, or sell lands, mills, and water privileges useful in the creation of water power; to cut a wing dam in the Delaware river, between the mouth of the Assunpink and the head of Wells' Falls, and a race-way along the bank, not extending more than one and a half miles below the Trenton Falls; to make lateral race-ways and other works; to sell lots, sites, and privileges under the charter; and with a general power of taking lands necessary for their purposes, at the appraisement of the commissioners; and with the customary powers granted to other corporations. Their charter is perpetual, protecting the company from any tax exceeding the half of one per cent. on the actual amount of capital expended in the construction of the work, with the privilege of extending its capital to $200,000. Each share, in the election of managers, is entitled to one vote.

The capital subscribed is $90,000; the cost of constructing the work is estimated at $140,000 exclusive of the lands purchased by the company for mill sites and building lots. The canal and race-way commences at the head of Scudder's Falls, directly opposite the upper end of Slack's Island, and continues down the margin of the river, to a point opposite the centre of White's Island, where, leaving the bank, it enters upon the meadows bordering the river, through which it passes to the Assunpink, in Trenton; thence, it is designed to cross this creek by an aqueduct, and to pass through Bloomsbury, to the precincts of Lamberton, where it debouches into the river.

The fall in the river Delaware, between the head and foot of the raceway is 20 feet, of which, one foot and a half descent is given to the raceway, leaving a head and fall at the Assunpink of 14 feet, and below the foot of the Trenton Falls 18½ feet.

The entire column of the water descending the race-way is estimated at 23,868 cubic feet per minute, at the lowest known state of the water.—This at the Assunpink, will afford a power equal to 335 horses; or if all be expended below the Assunpink, equal to 575 horses: or should one-third of the water be used above, and two-thirds below the creek, the power above will be equal to 145 horses, and that below, to 384 horses. This calculation is based on a depth of six feet water only, in the race-way; the minimum supply, after all deductions for leakage and evaporation at the lowest water.

This, however, is the view of the power, in what is deemed its first stage. The work commences at the upper end of Slack's Island, which is of considerable extent, situate near the middle of the river. The main channel of the stream was formerly on the right, or Pennsylvania side of the island, but a loose stone wall having, some years since, been thrown across this channel to improve the navigation of the river, the larger portion of the water was thrown into the Jersey channel. This wall remains, but it is overflowed at the lowest water. By raising this dam and throwing the whole current of the river into this channel, or by entirely removing it, and erecting a dam from the head of the company's works to Slack's Island, and reopening the channel on the other side, the water in the raceway would be raised two feet beyond its present elevation; and in constructing their work, the company have adapted it to the reception of that body of water. A column of eight feet instead of six, would thus be gained in the race; the velocity of its current increased to 122 feet per minute, and the quantity of water to 52,704 cubic feet in the same time. The power of the water would then be equal to 960 horses at the Assunpink, or 1260 below it: or should one-third of the power be employed above, and two-thirds below the creek, it would afford the company a power above, equal to 330 horses, below, 840, in the whole 1170.

The company propose to let their lands for the erection of mills, above the Assunpink, at 30 cents, and below the creek, at from 40 to 50 cents the foot, perpetual rent, according to situation; with the right of the free use of the company's wharf, rail-road, &c.: and their lands for dwellings, in lots 20 by 75 feet, at $6 per annum. The buildings, in all cases, to be fire proof. And they propose to let the water from the main race-way for mill power, at a perpetual rent of three dollars above, and four dollars below the Assunpink creek, for every square inch area of the aperture, through which it shall be drawn off by a flume, the plan of which is in the office of the company. The aperture to be measured and made according to the standard measure, also kept by the company, and similar to that in the office of the Secretary of State, at Washington, and according to other regulations published by the company.

The advantages of this site for manufacturing purposes are perhaps unsurpassed by any in the country. Intermediately situated between the great markets of Philadelphia and New York, 30 miles from the former, and 60 from the latter--surrounded by a rich agricultural country, producing a large surplus quantity of grain of every description, and capable of quadrupling its productions—upon a river, navigable to the ocean, and for near 250 miles above the falls, flowing through a wide and fertile country, whose products may find a ready market here; having also the feeder of the Delaware and Raritan canal, connecting with the main canal in the heart of the city plot, whilst the canal itself unites with the Delaware, below the bar at Bordentown, and passing through Trenton, along the Millstone and Raritan rivers, to New Brunswick, affords a fine sloop navigation, and all the advantages of cheap and rapid water transportation from and to Philadelphia and New York:—the facility of obtaining an abundant and cheap supply of anthracite coal by the river and the Pennsylvania canal, on the opposite bank:—the rail-roads made, and in progress towards New York and Philadelphia, of which, there are two leading to the latter, one on each side of the river; that on the west running directly from the city, and that on the east from Bordentown, combine all that the manufacturer can require:—a healthy country, abundant and cheap provisions, an adequate supply of labourers, convenience in obtaining raw materials, unfailing power for its manipulation, and a chance of, and ready access to, the best markets of the country.

The following is a description of Trenton, in 1748, as given by the Swedish traveller Kalm—which the citizen will delight to compare with its present condition:

"Trenton is a long, narrow town, situate at some distance from the river Delaware, on a sandy plain. It is reckoned 30 miles from Philadelphia. It has two small churches, one for the people belonging to the Church of England, the other for the Presbyterians. The houses are partly built of stone, though most of them are made of wood or planks, commonly two stories high, together with a cellar below the building, and a kitchen under ground, close to the cellar. The houses stand at a moderate distance from one another. They are commonly built so that the street passes along one side of the houses, while gardens of different dimensions bound the other side; in each garden is a draw-well; the place is reckoned very healthy. Our landlord told us that 22 years ago, when he first settled here, (1726) there was hardly more than one house: but from that time, Trenton has increased so much, that there are at present near an hundred houses. The houses were within, divided into several rooms by their partitions of boards. The inhabitants of the place carried on a small trade with the goods which they got from Philadelphia; but their chief gain consisted in the arrival of the numerous travellers between that city and New York; for they are commonly brought by the Trenton yachts from Philadelphia to Trenton, or from thence to Philadelphia. But from Trenton, further to New Brunswick, the travellers go in wagons, which set out every day for that place. Several of the inhabitants also subsist on the carriage of all sorts of goods, which are sent in great quantities, either from Philadelphia to New York, or from thence to the former place—for between Philadelphia and Trenton, all goods go by water; but between Trenton and New Brunswick, they are all carried by land, and both these conveniences belong to people of this town. For the yachts which go between this place and the capital of Pennsylvania, they usually pay a shilling and sixpence, Pennsylvania currency, per person, and every one pays beside for his baggage. Every passenger must provide meat and drink for himself, and pay some settled fare. Between Trenton and New Brunswick, a person pays 2*s*. 6*d*., and the baggage is likewise paid for separately."

The town was founded a few years prior to 1720, by William Trent, an enterprising trader, who was distinguished for public spirit, and private character, in the provinces of Pennsylvania and New Jersey. He was at one time, Speaker of the Assembly of the former, and at another, Speaker of the Assembly of the latter, province. The site of Trenton, before it bore his name, was significantly called Littleworth. Mr. Trent died on the 29th December, 1724.

Trowbridge Mountain, a long and irregularly shaped hill, of Morris co., extending from the N. branch of the Raritan, through Mendham, Randolph, and Hanover t-ships, to the Rockaway river, ranging S. W. and N. E. It is of granitic formation; many parts of it in cultivation, but generally sterile.

Troy, hamlet of Hanover t-ship, Morris co., on the Parcipany river, about 7 miles N. E. of Morristown; contains a forge, 1 grist mill, a saw mill, and 12 or 15 dwellings. Soil, sandy loam.

Tubmill, branch of Wading river, rises in the west plains of Little Egg Harbour t-ship, Burlington co., and flows S. W. 7 miles to its recipient, about a mile below Bridgeport.

Tuckahoe Creek, rises on the line between Weymouth t-ship, Gloucester co., and Maurice river t-ship, Cumberland co., and forms, in part, the western boundary of the former co., and also, its southern boundary, separating it in the latter case, from Cape May co. Its course, for about 11 miles, is S., thence due E. for about 12 miles; emptying into Great Egg Harbour bay. It is a fine mill stream, driving several mills, at Marshallville, Etna, and other higher points, and is navigable for sloops, above the village of Tuckahoe, more than 10 miles from the ocean.

Tuckahoe, p-t. on both sides of the Tuckahoe river, over which there is a bridge, 10 miles above the sea, 46 miles S. E. from Woodbury, and by post-route 192 from Washington; contains some 20 dwellings, 3 taverns, several stores. It is a place of considerable trade in wood, lumber, and ship building. The land immediately on the river is good, but a short distance from it, is swampy and low.

Tuckerton, p-t, and port of entry, for Little Egg Harbour district, about 35 miles S. E. of Mount Holly, 65 from Trenton, and 189 N. E. from W. C.; situate on a narrow tongue of land, projecting into the marsh on Little Egg Harbour bay, Little Egg Harbour t-ship, Burlington co.; contains between 30 and 40 dwellings, 4 taverns, 5 stores, 2 Methodist churches, a Quaker meeting house. It lies upon a navigable stream, called Shord's Mill Branch, 6 miles from the bay, whence wood scows and flats ascend to the town. There is a large business done here in timber and cord-wood; and salt is, or was manufactured in the vicinity. The town is frequented during the summer season, by many persons for the benefits of sea-bathing, &c. A stage plies regularly between it and Philadelphia.

Tulipehaukin Creek, tributary of the west branch of Wading river, rises in, and has its whole course of about 8 miles, through Washington t-ship, Burlington co.

Turpentine, hamlet of Northampton t-ship, Burlington co., on the road from Mount Holly to Freehold, about a mile east from the former; contains a tavern, a store, and some 8 or 10 dwellings.

Turtle Gut Inlet, Lower t-ship, Cape May co., between Five Mile and Two Mile Beach.

Tuscomusco Creek, a small tributary of the Atsion river, Evesham t-ship, Burlington co.

Two Mile Beach, on the Atlantic ocean, Lower t-ship, Cape May co., between Turtle Gut and Cold Spring Inlet.

Union Cross Roads, hamlet of Deptford t-ship, Gloucester co., 4 miles S. E. of Woodbury; contains 3 or 4 dwellings.

Union t-ship, Essex co., bounded N. by Orange and Newark t-ships; E. by Elizabethtown t-ship; S. by Rahway, and W. by Westfield and Springfield t-ships. Centrally distant from Newark S. W. 6 miles: greatest length N. and S. 5½, breadth E. and W. 5 miles; area, 12,000 acres; surface, rolling; soil, red shale, well cultivated; watered by Elizabeth river on the east, and Rahway river on the west. Population in 1830, 1405.—In 1832 the t-ship contained 350 taxables, 56 householders, whose ratables did not exceed $30 in value; 40 single men, 2 stores, 7 saw mills, 1 woollen factory, 21 tan vats; and paid state tax, $179 65; county, 470 04; poor, $300. There is a fine body of turf here, upon the south branch of Elizabeth river.

Union or "*Connecticut Farms*," is the post-town of the preceding t-ship, situated on the road from Elizabethtown to Morristown, 4 miles N. W. of the former, 5 miles S. E. from Newark, 213 N. E. from W. C., and 47 from Trenton; contains a Presbyterian church, and within a half a mile of it, 3 taverns, a store, and about 30 dwellings.

Up-Clearing Creek, a small tributary of Cohansey creek, which flows westerly into it, from Hopewell t-sp, Cumberland co.

Upper t-ship, Cape May co., bounded N. by Tuckahoe creek, which divides it from Weymouth t-ship, Gloucester co.; E. and S. E. by the Atlantic ocean; S. W. by Dennis t-sp; and N. W. by Maurice river t-ship, Cumberland co. Centrally distant from Cape May court-house N. E. 13 miles: greatest length N. E. and S. W. 12 miles; breadth S. E. and N. W. 11½ miles; area, 37,000 acres; surface, flat; soil, sand and clay; timber, generally oak and cedar. Population in 1830, 1067. In 1832 there were in the t-ship about 200 taxables, 173 householders, whose ratables did not exceed $30; 1 grist mill, 6 saw mills, 6 stores, 140 horses, and 560 cattle above the age of three years. There are 1 Baptist and 1 Episcopalian church, here. The t-ship paid for t-ship expenses, $77 38; county, $466 65; state tax, $150 73. It is drained by Tuckahoe river and Cedar Swamp creek. The last flows N. E. from the S. W. boundary of the t-ship, through an extensive cedar swamp into the river. On the Atlantic front is Ludlam's and Peck's Beaches, having a width of near half a mile, between which the tide flows into several marsh canals and small lagunes. The marsh may have an average width of about two miles. Tuckahoe village lies on the Tuckahoe river, partly in this, and partly in Gloucester co., having a post-office in the latter. Marshallville lies on the line between Cumberland and Cape May counties, but in the former.

Vancamp Brook, rises from two ponds at the west foot of the Blue mountain, Walpack t-ship, Sussex co., and by a S. W. course of about 8 miles empties into the Delaware river, in Pahaquarry t-ship.

Vansickles, tavern, store, and post-office, of Bethlehem t-ship, Hunterdon co., on the S. E. foot of the Musconetcong mountain, 10 miles N. W. from Flemington, 36 from Trenton, and 195 from W. C.

Varmintown, hamlet of Upper Freehold t-ship, Monmouth co., 6 miles S. E. of Allentown, and 16 S. W. of Freehold; contains a wheelwright and smith shop, and 2 or 3 cottages, in a fertile country of sandy loam.

Vauxhall, small hamlet of Springfield t-ship, Essex co., 7 miles W. from Newark, and 2½ N. from Springfield.

Vealtown, in a vale of Mine mountain, on Mine Brook, Bernard t-ship, Somerset co., 11 miles N. of Somerville; contains a mill and some half dozen dwellings.

Vernon t-ship, Sussex co., bounded N. by the state of New York; E. by Pompton t-ship, Bergen co.; S. by Hardiston t-ship; and W. by Wantage t-ship, from which it is separated by the Wallkill river. Greatest length 11, breadth 10 miles; area, 52,480 acres. The whole surface of the t-ship is covered by mountains; the Wallkill and Wawayanda mountains being on the south and east, and the Pochuck mountain on the west. It is drained north by Warwick creek and its tributaries, Black creek and Double Pond creek; south by Pacak creek, a tributary of the Pequannock, and by some small tributaries of the Wallkill river. Population in 1830, 2377; taxables in 1832, 382. There were in the t-ship in 1832, 158 householders, whose ratables did not exceed $30; 2 storekeepers, 5 pairs stones for grinding grain, 1 carding machine, 1 furnace, 3 forges, 8 mill saws, 1 fulling mill, 311 horses and mules, and 1650 neat cattle, 3 years old and upwards, and 6 distilleries. The t-ship paid for school tax, $116; state and county tax, $921 10; poor tax, $300; and road tax, $1200. Hamburg and Vernon are villages and post-towns of this t-ship. The mountains, which on the east, rise to the height of 1000 feet, are composed of primitive rock, in which hornblende is a principal constituent; the valleys are uniformly of primitive limestone. The mountains yield iron abundantly.

Vernon, p-t. of the above named t-ship, lying in the valley between the Wawayanda and Pochuck mountains, 246 miles N. E. from W. C., 88 from Trenton, and 18 from Newton. It contains a tavern, store, and from 10 to 12 dwellings.

Vienna, p-t. of Independence t-ship, Warren co., on the Pequest creek, near the S. W. boundary of the t-sp, by the post-road 220 miles from W. C., 54 from Trenton, and 12 from Belvidere, upon the verge of the Great Meadows; contains a Presbyterian church, a store, tavern, and 6 or 8 dwellings.

Vincenttown, p-t. of Northampton t-ship, Burlington co., at the junction of Stop-the-Jade creek with the south branch of the Rancocus creek, 5 miles S. of Mount Holly, 12 miles S. E. from Burlington, 32 from Trenton, and 159 N. E. from W. C.; contains a grist mill, saw mill, 2 taverns, 4 stores, from 30 to 40 dwellings, a Quaker meeting house, and a house of public worship, free to all denominations; surrounded by a fine fertile country.

Wading River, a considerable arm of Little Egg Harbour river, which rises by two branches; the east in Dover t-ship, Monmouth co., and flows S. W. 15 miles, into Washington township; the west in Northampton t-ship, and flows S. W. about 15 miles, to unite with the east, near Bodine's tavern. The main stem flows by a south course, thence of 8 miles to the Little Egg Harbour river, below Swan's Bay.

Waertown, hamlet of Stafford t-sp, Monmouth co., upon Barnegat bay, near the mouth of Waertown creek, a small mill stream, of about 3 miles long, 35 miles S. E. from Freehold, and opposite to Barnegat Inlet; contains 10 or 12 dwellings, a tavern and store; in a sandy soil, covered with pine forest.

Wallkill Mountains. (See *Hamburg.*)

Wallkill River, rises in Byram t-ship, Sussex co., and flows by a N. E. course of 23 or 24 miles, through Hardiston t-ship, dividing Wantage from Vernon t-ship, into the state of New York, and thence by a like course of 35 or 40 miles, through Orange and Ulster counties, falls into the Hudson river, 3 miles S. E. from the village of Esopus or Kingston. This stream is remarkable for being the drain of a large and valuable tract of marsh meadow land, exceeding 50,000 acres, elevated more than 325 feet above tide water. The waters which descend from the surrounding hills, being slowly discharged from the river, cover these vast meadows every winter, and would render them extremely fertile, could they be effectually drained.

Walnut Valley, post-office, Warren co.

Walpack t-ship, of Sussex co., bounded N. E. by Sandistone t-ship; S. E. by the Blue mountain, which separates it from Stillwater t-ship; S. W. by Pahaquarry t-ship; and W. by the river Delaware. Greatest length 10 miles; breadth 4 miles; area, 15,360 acres; surface on the east, mountainous; on the west, river alluvion. Population in 1830, 660; taxables 137. There were in the t-ship in 1832, 24 householders whose ratables did not exceed $30; 1 storekeeper, 2 saw mills, 146 horses and mules, 3 years old and upwards; 354 neat cattle of like age; 14 tan vats. It paid state and county tax, $293 80; and road tax, $350. It is drained by the Flatkill, which runs centrally through the t-ship, and empties into the Delaware at the Walpack Bend; and by Vancamp Brook, which rises in Long Pond, in the Blue mountain. There is a post-office here, called after the t-ship, distant from Washington 240, from Trenton 82, and from Newton 12 miles. The Blue mountain covers nearly half the t-ship; between its base and the river is a margin, of an average width of two miles, of limestone, bordered and partly covered by alluvion, rich and highly productive of wheat, corn, &c. There is a German Reformed church in the t-ship.

Walpack Bend, a remarkable bend of the river Delaware, at the S. W. angle of Walpack t-ship, about 85 miles above the city of Trenton.

Wantage t-ship, of Sussex co., bounded N. by the state of New York; E. by Vernon t-ship; S. by Frankford and Hardiston t-ships; and W. by the Blue mountain, which separates this from Sandistone and Montague t-ships. Greatest length 11 miles; breadth 8½ miles; area, 42,880 acres; surface on the west, mountainous and hilly; on the east, rolling. Population in 1830, 4034; taxables 643. There were in the t-ship in 1832, 208 householders, 11 storekeepers or traders, 18 pairs of stones for grinding grain, 6 saw mills, 1 fulling mill, 5 carding machines, 939 horses and mules, and 3481 neat cattle, over 3 years of age; 18 tan vats, and 3 distilleries. The t-ship paid a school tax of $500; state and county tax, $1706 27; poor tax, $300; and road tax, $1500. It is drained by Deep Clove river and Papakating creek, uniting south of Deckertown, and thence flowing into the Wallkill river, which forms the whole eastern boundary of the t-ship. The Paterson and Hamburg turnpike road runs N. E., and the Newton and Bolton N. W., through the t-ship; and at their intersection, is the small village of Deckertown. There is a post-office at Deckertown, 444 miles from W. C., 86 from Trenton, and 16 from Newton; and another called Libertyville, 241 miles from W. C., 83 from Trenton, and 10 from Newton. Wantage is a rich t-ship, consisting of limestone and slate soils; the one on the east, and the other on its western side, highly cultivated. Along the Wallkill river, there is a margin of swamp, known as the Drowned Lands, caused by the collection of the waters from the high ground, in a deep and flat valley, through which the river moves sluggishly. These lands are, in places, heavily timbered.

Wardle's Beach, on the Atlantic ocean, Shrewsbury t-ship, Monmouth co., extending south from Old Shrewsbury Inlet.

Warren County, was taken from Sussex, by Act, 20th Nov., 1824, which directed, That all the lower part of the latter, southwesterly of a line, beginning on the river Delaware, at the mouth of Flat Brook, in the t-ship of Walpack, and running thence a straight course to the N. E. corner of Hardwicke church, and thence in the same course to the middle of the Musconetcong creek, thence down the middle of the said creek, to the Delaware, should be a new county. Warren is bounded N. E. by Sussex co.; S. E. by the Musconetcong creek, which divides it from Morris and Hunterdon, and W. and N. W. by the river Delaware. Its greatest length, N. E. and S. W. is 35 miles; greatest breadth, E. and W. 17 miles; area, about 350 square miles; central lat. 40° 50′ N.; long. 1° 58′ E., from W. C.

The county is divided between the primitive and transition formations. A strip of the former crosses it, in the neighbourhood of Beattystown, towards Philipsburg, and the other fills the portion N. of a line running N. W. and S. E. by Sparta, towards Belvidere, including the Blue mountain; leaving an intervening strip of primitive, of a wedge-like form, having its broader part resting on New York. From these formations we may expect a great variety of soils; and indeed all the rocks which belong to them, are singularly blended. The valley of the Musconetcong, on the N. W. side, abounds with transition limestone, bordered by a vein of dark slate; and all the valleys, whether of the primitive or transition, are fertilized by the decomposition of the limestone rock, mingling with the sand, loam and clay, washing from the mountains, making a compound, various as the rocks from which it is derived.

The metals found within the county, are magnetic iron, brown hematite, and bog ore, in several places, but principally in Scott's mountain, Jenny Jump, and on the Delaware river, near Foul Rift. A mine of magnetic iron ore is wrought in Scott's mountain, Oxford t-ship, where a furnace was established nearly a century since, and has lately been repaired and put into operation. Zinc, or lead, appears in the hills which bound the Musconetcong valley, on the N. W.; but most probably zinc, inasmuch as these hills are in the range of the Wallkill mountain, where that metal lies in large masses. Gold and silver are said to have been discovered in the Jenny Jump mountain, but which, though possibly true, may in all likelihood, be iron or copper pyrites, which have so often been mistaken for the precious metals. Marble, steatite, or soapstone, roofing slate, and manganese, may also be obtained in the county, sufficiently near to navigation, to render them valuable in commerce. The state quarries, near the Blue mountain, are already extensively worked.

The county is marked by several prominent mountain ridges, which determine its water courses, and the surface is every where uneven. Entering it from the south, we cross the natural boundary, the Musconetcong creek, which is confined to a narrow valley, by hills, forming a continuation of the Wallkill mountain, whose north-western base is washed by the Pohatcong creek, for nearly the whole breadth of the county; and the valley of that stream is divided from that of the Pequest, by Scott's mountain, which breaks into small and diminished knolls, near the eastern extremity of the county. North of the main branch of the Pequest, but embraced by it and its chief tributary, Beaver brook, lies the Jenny Jump mountain, a narrow and isolated ridge. Beaver brook drains a valley of several miles in width, and covered with knolls of slate, and beds of limestone, and circumscribed northward by a long, unbroken, slaty ridge, which bounds the valley of the Paulinskill. Between that stream, and the Blue mountain, the mean distance may be about five miles. The Blue mountain covers the remaining portion of the county, with the exception of a small strip of alluvial, which borders the Delaware river.

As in most parts of the primitive and transition formations, the streams are rapid and precipitous, affording advantageous use of their volumes for hydraulic purposes, but are in no instance navigable. The waters of the county, without exception, seek the Delaware; and whilst that river boldly cuts its way through the mountains, these tributaries are compelled to pursue the course of the ridges whose bases they lave.

The only artificial road of the county, is that from Morristown to Philipsburg, opposite to Easton. A rail-road has been authorized by the Legislature, which is designed to unite with a similar road, opposite to Belvidere, on the Delaware, and to proceed thence to the Susquehanna river.

The business of the county is chiefly agricultural, and its staples are wheat, corn, rye, oats, and flax; and in the northern part buckwheat. Within a few years, husbandry has made great advances, and yet continues to improve. The use of lime as a manure is becoming general; and the rich valley lands yield very large crops of wheat, which find a ready market at Easton. Flax-seed is also grown in great quantities; of which 12,000 bushels are annually purchased in Belvidere, alone.

In 1830, the county contained, 18,627 inhabitants, of whom 9463 were white males, 8695 white females; 214 free coloured males, 208 free coloured females; 21 male, and 26 female slaves. Of this population, 286 were aliens, 10 were deaf and dumb, and 14 were blind. The inhabitants are chiefly of English extraction, and a considerable portion from New England parents.

By the abstract of the assessors, reported to the Legislature, in 1832, there were 102,377 acres of improved land, making nearly one-half the area of the county; 1062 householders, whose ratables did not exceed $30; 411 single men; 3489 taxables; 56 merchants, 45 grist mills, 41 saw mills, 16 carding machines, 7 furnaces for casting iron, 2 cotton and woollen factories, 2 fulling mills, 3 oil mills, and 1 plaster mill, 235 tan vats, 1 glass factory, 3 distilleries of grain, and 25 of cider; 14 carriages, with steel springs; 177 riding chairs, gigs and sulkies; 4324 horses, and 7772 neat cattle, over 3 years of age; and it paid for t-ship purposes, $5700; and for state and county purposes, $8999 20. The t-ship of Greenwich alone honourably distinguished itself, by appropriating money to *school use*, and paid for this object, $500.

The religious sects of the county are Presbyterian, Methodist, Episcopalian, Baptists, and *Chris-ti-ans.* The last has, we believe, two churches, and admits women to officiate in the ministry. These sects rank in number in the order we have placed them.

The towns and post-offices of the county are, Belvidere, the seat of justice; Finesville, Hughesville, Bloomsbury, Asbury, Imlaydale, Pleasant Valley, Mansfield, Anderson, Beattystown, Hackettstown, Alamuche, Long Bridge, Johnsonburg, Lawrenceville, Marksborough, Philipsburg, Stewartsville, New Village, Broadway, Concord, Rocksbury, Oxford, Hope, Shiloh, Columbia, Knowlton Mills, Centreville, Sodom, Gravel Hill, &c.

The courts of common pleas, orphan's courts, and quarter sessions, are holden at Belvidere, on the 2d Tuesday of February, 1st Tuesday of June, 4th Tuesday of August, and the 1st Tuesday after the 4th in November. The circuit court and sessions of oyer and terminer, and general jail delivery, are holden on the 1st Tuesday in June, and the 1st Tuesday after the 4th in November.

The county elects one member to the council, and two to the general Assembly.

STATISTICAL TABLE OF WARREN COUNTY.

Townships.	Length.	Breadth.	Area.	Surface.	Population. 1830.
Greenwich,	13	11	38,000	hilly.	4486
Hardwick,	11	8	24,320	do.	1962
Independence,	9	8½	29,440	hills and vales.	2126
Knowlton,	10	10	44,800	do.	2827
Mansfield,	15	62	33,000	mountainous.	3303
Oxford,	16	5½	42,000	do.	3665
Pahaquarry,	13	2½	12,800	do.	258
			224,360		18,627

Warren t-ship, Somerset co., bounded N. by Bernard t-ship and by Morris t-ship, Morris co., from which it is separated by the Passaic river; N. E. by New Providence; S. E. by Westfield t-ship, of Essex co.; S. by Piscataway t-ship, Middlesex co.; and S. W. by Bridgewater t-ship, Somerset co. Greatest length N. E. and S. W. 8 miles; breadth N. and S. 4 miles: centrally distant N. E. from Somerville 6 miles; area, 18,000 acres; surface, mountainous, the whole t-ship being covered with hills; bent into elliptic form, with a single narrow valley drained by Middle Brook. These hills are low, well wooded, and composed of trap rock, upon old red sandstone, whose disintegration gives a soil of stiff clay and sandy loam. They contain veins of copper ore, apparently, very rich, and said to be valuable not only for the copper they contain, but also for their gold. Several efforts have been made to work them, but none have been successfully prosecuted. Mines have been opened within 2 miles N. E. of Somerville, which were lately wrought by Mr. Cammams and Dr. Stryker, who have suspended their operations; others, within a mile of the village of Green Brook, and six of Somerville, were worked some 40 years ago. The southern base of these mineral hills is washed by Green Brook. Mount Bethel is a small hamlet at which we believe the post-office of the t-ship is kept, called "*Warren.*" Population in 1830, 1501. In 1832 the t-ship contained about 300 taxables, 56 householders, whose ratables did not exceed $30; 42 single men, 4 stores, 8 saw mills, 4 grist mills, 2 fulling mills, 4 tan vats, 5 distilleries, 3 carding machines, 259 horses and mules, and 873 neat cattle, over 3 years of age.

Warwick Creek, rises in Orange co., in the state of New York, from Wickham's Pond, and flows thence by the town of Warwick S. W. into Vernon t-ship, Sussex co., and into the valley between Wawayanda and Pochuck mountains; thence by a N. W. course re-enters the state of New York, and unites with the Wallkill river, in the Great Marsh. This stream gives motion to several mills.

Washington t-ship, Morris co., bounded N. by Roxbury t-ship; E. by that t-ship and Chester; S. by Tewkesbury and Lebanon t-ships, Hunterdon co.; and W. by Mansfield and Independence t-ships, Warren co., from which it is separated by Musconetcong creek. Centrally distant W. from Morristown 18 miles: greatest length E. and W. 8, breadth N. and S. 7½ miles; area, 27,500 acres; surface, mountainous, Schooley's mountain covering the western portion; on the east of which, lies the German valley, drained by the south branch of the Raritan river: the intervening country between that and the Black river, near the south-eastern boundary, is hilly. The soil of the highlands is generally clay and loam, with grey limestone in the valleys. Much of the mountain is cultivated, and with lime, brings abundant crops. The German valley is very rich, and settled by the industrious descendants of Germans. The celebrated mineral spring and houses of public entertainment, are on the mountain. (See *Schooley's Mountain.*) Springtown and Pleasant Grove are villages of the t-ship.—Population in 1830, 2188. In 1832 the t-ship contained 397 taxables, 124 householders, whose ratables did not exceed $30 in value; 8 stores, 11 saw, 6 grist mills, 3 forges, 20 tan vats, 10 distilleries, 532 horses, and 1015 neat cattle, above 3 years of age; and paid the following taxes: state, $314; county, $703 74; poor, $300; road, $500.

Washington, village of North Brunswick t-ship, Middlesex co., on the left bank of the South river, 5 miles S. E. from New Brunswick, and about 3 miles from the confluence of that river with the Raritan. There are here 2 taverns, 3 stores, and from 30 to 40 dwellings. An unsuccessful attempt has been made to cut a canal, a mile long, between the South river and the Raritan, in order to save several miles in the navigation from the town to Perth Amboy.

Washington t-ship, Burlington co., bounded N. and N. E. by Northampton t-ship; S. E. by Little Egg Harbour t-ship; S. W. and W. by Galloway and Waterford t-ships, Gloucester co.; and N. W. by Evesham t-ship. Centrally distant S. from Woodbury, 22 miles. Greatest breadth, N. and S. 19 miles; greatest length, E. and W. 20 miles; area, 112,000 acres. Surface, level; soil, generally sandy, and covered with forest. Drained S. by the Little Egg Harbour river, and its several branches; Atsion, the main branch, being on the W. boundary, and Wading river running centrally through the t-ship. Shamong, Washington, and Greenbank, are villages of the t-ship. Population in 1830, 1315. In 1832 the t-ship contained 141 householders, whose ratables did not exceed $30; 59 single men; 287 taxables; 6 stores, 3 fisheries, 7 saw mills, 4 grist mills, 2 furnaces, 1 forge, 6 dearborns, 19 covered wagons, 4 gigs and sulkies, 333 neat cattle, 265 horses and mules; and paid state tax, $117 12; county tax, $371 10; township tax, $450.

Washington, p-t. of Washington t-ship, Morris co., in the German valley, Schooley's mountain, on the turnpike road from Morristown to Easton, and on the south branch of the Raritan river, 18 miles W. of Morristown, 54 N. E. from Trenton, and 220 by post route from W. C.; contains 1 Presbyterian, and 1 Lutheran church, a school, 1 store, 2 taverns, and about 20 dwellings. It is surrounded by a fertile, well improved, limestone country. (See ***German Valley.***)

Washington, village of Mansfield t-ship, Warren county. (See ***Mansfield.***)

Waterford t-ship, Gloucester co., bounded N. E. by Chester t-ship; E. by Evesham t-ship, Burlington co.; S. E. by Galloway t-ship; W. by Gloucester and Newton t-ships; and N. W. by the river Delaware. Centrally distant W. from Woodbury 12 miles. Greatest length, N. W. and S. E., 25; breadth, 8 miles. Its form is very irregular, being deeply indented by the adjacent county of Burlington, and being near the middle of its length, scarce more than a mile in width. Its surface is level, broken only by the streams which run through it; soil, sandy, mixed in the northern part, more or less with loam, but generally light, producing tolerable grass, when manured with marl, ashes or lime, and is cultivated in fruit and vegetables for market. The southern part of the t-ship, has a sandy soil, covered with a pine forest, and is valuable chiefly on account of its timber. It is drained, N. E. by Pensauken creek; N. W.

by Cooper's creek, which, respectively, are boundaries; and on the S. E. by several branches of the Atsion river, of which Atquatqua creek runs along the S. E. boundary. Shell marl is found in the t-ship, in the neighbourhood of Long-a-coming, and other places. Waterfordville, and Ellisville, are villages of the t-ship, and Long-a-coming is on the western t-ship line. Population in 1830, 3088. In 1832 the t-ship contained an Episcopal church, 404 householders, whose ratables did not exceed $30, in value; 7 stores, 5 fisheries, 5 grist mills, 4 saw mills, 7 distilleries, 2 glass factories; and paid poor tax, $660 52; county tax, $1321 06; township tax, $1200.

Waterfordville, village of Waterford t-ship, Gloucester co., on the road from Camden to Moorestown, about 5 miles from either; contains a tavern, store, and 8 or 10 dwellings.

Water Street, village of Mendham t-ship, Morris co., on the line between that and Morris t-ship, and on the head waters of Whippany river, 3 miles W. of Morristown; contains a grist mill, store, and half a dozen of dwellings.

Watson's Creek, Middletown t-sp., Monmouth co., runs N. E. 2 miles, into Sandy Hook bay.

Wawayanda Mountain, Vernon t-ship, Sussex co., extends northerly, across the eastern part of the t-ship, about 9 miles. It interlocks on the S. with the Wallkill mountain.

Waycake Creek, Middletown t-sp., Monmouth co., flows N. ahout 5 miles, into the Raritan bay, W. of Point Comfort.

Weasel; the name of a dense settlement, of Acquackanonck t-ship, Essex co., extending for near 4 miles, along the right bank of the Passaic, between Acquackanonck village, and Paterson. There may be in the settlement, about 40 dwellings, many of which are very neat. The country is fertile, and extremely well cultivated;—land, in farms, valued at $100 the acre.

West or *Jecak Creek*, forms the S. E. boundary of Cumberland co., between that and Cape May co. It is a mill stream between 6 and 7 miles in length, upon which are Hughes' grist and saw mills.

Westfield, small village of Chester t-ship, Burlington co., on the road from Camden to Burlington, 7 miles N. of the former, and 11 S. W. from Mount Holly; contains a Friends' meeting house, and some half dozen farm houses, in a very fertile well cultivated country. Soil, sandy loam.

Westfield t-ship, Essex co., bounded N. by Springfield; E. by Union; S. E. by Rahway t-ships; S. by Middlesex co.; W. by Warren t-ship, Somerset co., and by New Providence t-ship. Centrally distant S. W. from Newark 13 miles: greatest length 7, breadth 6 miles; area, 18,000 acres; surface on the N. W. hilly, but subsiding to a plain on the south; soil, clay loam northward, and red shale southward: the latter rich and carefully cultivated. Rahway river courses the eastern, and Green Brook the western, boundary. A more abundant and delightful country is scarce any where to be found, than that along from the foot of the mountain, north of Scotch Plains through the t-ship. Westfield, Plainfield, and Scotch Plains are villages and post-towns of the precinct. Population in 1830, 2492. In 1832 the t-ship contained 475 taxables, 124 householders, whose ratables did not exceed $30; 64 single men, 5 merchants, 5 grist mills, 2 saw mills, 1 paper mill, 423 horses and mules, and 1111 neat cattle, above 3 years old; and paid state tax, $264 78; county, $692 77; poor, $420; road, $800.

Westfield, p-t. of the above t-ship, 11 miles S. W. from Newark, 218 N. E. from W. C., 52 from Trenton, and 3½ from Scotch Plains, on the road leading thence to Elizabethtown; contains a Presbyterian church, a tavern, store, and smithery, and 25 dwellings. The vicinage is level, with a stiff clay cold soil. Lands valued at an average of 25 dollars per acre.

Westecunk Creek, rises by several branches in Little Egg Harbour t-sp, Burlington co., and flows S. E. about 8 miles, through Stafford t-ship, Monmouth co., into Little Egg Harbour bay. There was formerly a forge upon the stream. There are now a grist and saw mill, and in the vicinity, some 15 or 20 dwellings. The *Palma Christi*, or castor bean, is extensively cultivated here.

West Milford, post-office of Bergen co., 248 miles from W. C., and 82 N. E. from Trenton.

Weston, p-t., on the Millstone river, and on the Delaware and Raritan canal, formerly called Rogers' Mill, about a mile and a half from its confluence with the Raritan river, and 2 miles below the village of Millstone, 3 miles in a direct line S. E. of Somerville, Somerset co., and about 30 from Trenton; contains a saw mill, grist mill, store, and some 10 or 12 dwellings.

Weymouth, blast furnace, forge, and village, in Hamilton t-ship, Gloucester co., upon the Great Egg Harbour river, about 5 miles above the head of navigation. The furnace makes about 900 tons of castings annually: the forge having four fires and two hammers, makes about 200 tons bar iron, immediately from the ore. There are also a grist and a saw mill, and buildings for the workmen, of whom 100 are constantly employed about the works, and the persons depending upon them for subsistence, average 600 annually. There are 85,000 acres of land pertaining to this establishment, within which May's Landing is included. The works have a superabundant supply of water, during all seasons of the year.

Weymouth t-ship, Gloucester co., bounded N. by Hamilton; E. by Great Egg Harbour river; S. and W. by Tuckahoe river. Centrally distant from Woodbury 41 miles: greatest length N. and S. 12 miles; breadth E. and W. 10 miles; area, 50,000 acres; surface, level; soil, sandy: eastern boundary on the river, and the portion on the S. E. lying between the two rivers is salt marsh. Stephens' Creek and Tuckahoe are villages and post-towns of the t-ship. Population in 1830, 3333. In 1832 the t-ship contained 90 householders, whose ratables did not exceed $30; 4 stores, 2 grist mills, 1 carding machine, 1 blast furnace, and 2 forges called Etna, 4 saw mills, 315 neat cattle, and 90 horses and mules, above 3 years old; and paid county tax, $157 69; poor tax, $78 82; and road tax, $600.

Whale Pond Creek, Shrewsbury t-ship, Monmouth co., flows easterly about 5 miles to the ocean, about a mile below the Long Branch boarding houses. It gives motion to a mill.

Wheat Sheaf, small village on the line separating Rahway from Elizabethtown t-ship, 8 miles S. W. from Newark, and half-way between Bridgetown and Elizabethtown, 3 miles from either; contains a tavern, from whose sign it has its name; a store, and 8 or 10 dwellings.

Whippany, manufacturing village, of Hanover t-ship, Morris co., on the Whippany river, 5 miles N. E. of Morristown; contains a Methodist church, an academy, 3 stores, 1 tavern, 5 cotton manufactories, 2000 spindles, 3 paper mills, and 56 dwellings. Soil, loam, valued at 25 and 30 dollars per acre.

Whippany River, Morris co., a considerable tributary of the Rockaway, rises in Mendham t-ship, at the foot of Trowbridge mountain, and flows by a N. E. course of 17 or 18 miles, by Morristown, to its recipient about 2 miles above the junction of that stream with the Passaic. This is a fine mill stream, drives many mills in its course, and is well employed at the village of Whippany.

White Hall, hamlet on Schooley's mountain, Lebanon t-ship, Hunterdon co., 18 miles N. E. of Flemington; contains a store, tavern, smith shop, and 4 or 5 dwellings.

White Hill, landing and small village, on the Delaware river, Mansfield t-ship, Burlington co.; contains 2 taverns, 10 or 12 dwellings, and an air furnace. There is also a ferry here.

White House, p-t. of Readington t-ship, Hunterdon co., 10 miles N. E. of Flemington, 33 from Trenton, and 196 from W. C., upon Rockaway creek; contains a grist mill, some 12 or 15 dwellings, 3 stores, 3 taverns, and a Presbyterian or Dutch Reformed church. The surface of the country around it is hilly; soil, loam, clay, and red shale.

White Marsh Run, tributary of Maurice river, rises in Fairfield t-ship, Cumberland co., and flows eastwardly to its recipient, about 6 miles.

White Ponds, two small lakes, connected by a brook, lying at the west foot of Pimple Hill, in Hardiston t-ship, Sussex co., on the western line of the t-ship, distant, in a direct line N. E. from Newton, 8 miles.

Wickhechecoke Creek, rises by two branches in the hills, on the N. W. of Amwell t-ship, Hunterdon co., and flows by a southerly course of 10 miles, into the Delaware, giving motion to several mills.

Williamsville, Orange t-ship, Essex co., 5 miles N. W. of Newark, near the foot of the first mountain; contains 8 or 10 houses.

Williamsburg, or ***Penn's Neck***, West Windsor t-ship, Middlesex co., on the straight turnpike, from Trenton to New Brunswick, 10 miles from the first, 15 from the second, 2 miles from Princeton, and half a mile W. from Millstone river, and Stony brook; contains a Baptist church, of wood; an Episcopalian church; 2 taverns, 1 store, and 12 dwellings. Soil, kind, sandy loam, extremely well cultivated, and productive. There are two large quarries of freestone, of excellent building stone upon the river.

Williamsburg. (See *Cedar Creek*.)

Willingboro' t-ship, Burlington co., bounded N. E. by Burlington t-ship; S. E. by Northampton; S. W. by the Rancocus creek, which separates it from Chester t-ship; and N. W. by the river Delaware. Centrally distant N. W. from Mount Holly, 7 miles. Greatest length, 6, breadth, 4 miles; area, 7500 acres. Surface, generally level; soil, sand and sandy loam, well cultivated, and productive in grass, grain, vegetables and fruit. A small branch of the Rancocus creek, crosses the t-ship. Dunks' ferry, over the Delaware, is within it, 4 miles below Burlington. Cooperstown is the only village. Population in 1830, 782. In 1832 the t-ship contained 160 taxables; 50 householders, whose ratables did not exceed $30; 28 single men; 1 grist mill, 2 distilleries, 2 coaches, 6 dearborns, 36 covered wagons, 4 chairs and curricles, 5 gigs and sulkies, 269 neat cattle, and 176 horses and mules, above 3 years old; and paid state tax, $109 38; county tax, $381 93; township tax, $400.

Windsor, West, t-ship, Middlesex co., bounded N. E. by South Brunswick; S. E. by East Windsor; S. W. by Nottingham t-ship, of Burlington co., and by Lawrence t-ship, Hunterdon co.; and on the N. W. by Montgomery t-ship, Hunterdon co. Centrally distant S. W. from Brunswick, 17 miles. Greatest length, 7, breadth, 5 miles; area, 19,000 acres. Surface, level; soil, sandy loam and clay, generally well cultivated, and producing, abundantly, grain and grass. Drained on the E. by Millstone river; on the S. W. by the Assunpink creek; and on the N. W. by Stony Brook. The road through Princeton divides this from Somerset co. Princeton, Williamsburg, Clarksville, Dutch Neck, and Edinburg, are towns of the t-ship. Population in 1830, 2129. In 1832 the t-ship contained 448 taxables; 226 householders, whose ratables did not exceed $30; 64 single men; 6 merchants; 1 large grist mill, with 3 run of stones; 1 woollen factory, 3 distilleries, and 496 horses and mules, and 848 neat cattle, over 3 years of age; and paid state tax,

$320 49; county, $394 04; road, $200; poor, $450. Excellent freestone, for building, is abundant in the t-ship.

Windsor, East, t-ship of Middlesex co., bounded N. by South Brunswick t-ship; N. E. by South Amboy; S. E. by Freehold t-ship, Monmouth co.; S. W. by Nottingham t-ship, Burlington co.; and N. W. by West Windsor t-ship. Centrally distant S. W. from New Brunswick, 20 miles. Greatest length, 12: greatest breadth, 6 miles; area, 24,000 acres. Surface level; soil, sandy and gravelly loam, light, and not generally productive. Drained by Millstone river, and Rocky brook, on the N. E., and by the Assunpink and Miry run, upon the S. W. Hightstown, Millford, Centreville, and Cattail, are villages, the first a post-town, of the t-ship. The turnpike road from Bordentown, to New Brunswick, crosses the t-ship. Population in 1830, 1930. In 1832 the t-ship contained 487 taxables; 52 householders, whose ratables did not exceed $30; and 41 single men, 3 merchants, 3 saw mills, 4 grist mills, 1 woollen factory, 2 carding machines, and fulling mills, 32 tan vats, 13 distilleries for cider, and 484 horses and mules, and 897 neat cattle, above 3 years of age; and paid state tax, $286 77; county, $352 53; road tax, $400; poor tax, $700.

Woodbridge t-ship, Middlesex co., bounded N. by Westfield, and Rahway t-ships, Essex co.; E. by Staten Island Sound; S. E. by Perth Amboy t-ship; S. by Raritan river; and W. by Piscataway t-ship. Centrally distant from New Brunswick, N. E. 8 miles. Length, E. and W. 9, breadth, N. and S. 9 miles; area, 24,000 acres. Surface, level; soil, red shale, universally well cultivated. Drained on the N. E. by a branch of Rahway river, upon which are some mills. Rahway and Woodbridge, are post-towns, Matouchin and Bonhamtown, villages of the t-ship. Two turnpike roads from New Brunswick, run N. E. through the t-ship, which are crossed by another, from Perth Amboy to New Durham. Population in 1830, 3969. In 1832 the t-ship contained 700 taxables; 180 householders, whose ratables did not exceed $30 in value; 99 single men; 13 stores, 5 saw mills, 3 grist mills, 40 tan vats, 1 distillery, 585 horses and mules, 1555 neat cattle, 3 years old and upwards; and paid state tax, $594 53; county, $731 03; road, 1800; poor, $1000. This t-ship contains a portion of the thriving town of Rahway. It was incorporated by Governor Philip Carteret, prior to 1680, by one of the most liberal charters which had ever been given in America. (See *Records of East Jersey Proprietaries, at Amboy.*) In 1682, it was estimated that there were in the t-ship, one hundred and twenty families. They had then erected a court-house and prison, and had many thousand acres surveyed for plantations. Delaplaine, the surveyor-general, was one of the settlers here.

Woodbury Creek, Deptford t-ship, Gloucester co., rises by two branches; the southern called Matthew's branch, each about 3 miles above Woodbury, and unite below the town. The north branch is navigable from the town to the river Delaware, 3 miles.

Woodbury, p-t., and seat of justice of Gloucester co., on Woodbury creek, at the head of navigation, 8 miles S. of Camden, 39 from Trenton, and 145 from W. C.; contains a spacious court-house of brick, and county offices, fire proof, and of the same material, detached, and a prison, in the rear of the court-house, of stone; 1 Friends' meeting house, large, and of brick; 1 Presbyterian church, frame, with cupola and bell, the upper part of which is used as an academy; and 1 brick Methodist church; 2 common schools; 2 public libraries, one of which was founded by the ladies of the town; 2 sunday schools; a county bible society; and temperance society, which has been productive of very beneficial effects; several store-keepers refusing to sell spirituous liquors; 10 stores, 3 taverns, 4 lawyers, 3 physicians, 1 clergyman, 100 dwelling houses, and 735 inhabitants. The town, for a mile in length, and half a mile in breadth, is incorporated, for the maintenance of a fire engine and fire apparatus, for which eight public wells have been sunk; and the provisions for defence, against this devastating element, are very efficient. The creek was, 70 years since, stopped out; but the obstruction was removed in 1830, much to the convenience and health of the inhabitants. Vessels now load at the landing, in the town.

Woodruff's Gap, through Bear Fort mountain, Pompton t-ship, Bergen co. The Ringwood and Long Pond turnpike road passes through it.

Woodstown, p-t., and village, of Pilesgrove t-ship, Salem co., upon the Salem creek, 10 miles E. of the town of Salem, 161 N. E. from W. C., and 55 S. of Trenton. The town contains about 150 dwellings, 2 taverns, and 6 stores, 3 schools, 1 Friends' meeting, 1 Baptist, and 1 African Methodist church. In the neighbourhood of the town, there are some valuable marl beds—and the use of marl has much improved the agriculture of the t-ship.

Woodsville, p-t. of Hopewell t-sp., Hunterdon co., 10 miles S. from Flemington, 13 N. from Trenton, 179 from W. C., on the turnpike road from N. Brunswick, to Lambertsville; contains a store, tavern, and half a dozen dwellings, mostly new. It lies upon the slope of a gently rising ground, from which there is a delightful prospect of the surrounding country; the soil of which is of red shale, and well cultivated.

Woolwich t-ship, Gloucester co., bounded on the N. E. by Greenwich; on the S. E. by Franklin, t-ships; S. W. by Pittsgrove, Pilesgrove, and Upper Penn's Neck, t-ships, Salem co; and N. W. by the river Delaware. Centrally distant S. W. from Woodbury, 11 miles. Greatest length, 16; breadth, 7 miles; area, about 40,000 acres. Surface, level; soil, sandy, and on the S. E. covered with pine forest. Drained, westerly, by Repaupo, Little Timber, Raccoon, and Oldman's, creeks—the last of which forms the S. W. boundary. Swedesboro' and Battentown, are villages—the first a post-town of the t-ship. Population in 1830, 3033. In 1832 the t-ship contained 333 householders, whose ratables did not exceed $30; 8 stores, 9 grist mills, 4 saw mills, 3 fulling mills, 1 tannery, 8 distilleries, 1433 neat cattle, and 699 horses and mules above the age of 3 years.

Wrangleboro' or *Clark's Mill*, village, on Nacote creek, of Galloway t-ship, Gloucester co., about 37 miles S. E. from Woodbury; contains a store, one or more taverns, and one mill, and 15 or 20 dwellings.

Wrangle Brook, considerable tributary of the south branch of Toms' river, Dover t-ship, Monmouth co., uniting with the main branch, about two miles above Toms' River village.

Wrightsville, on the road from Allentown to Freehold, Upper Freehold t-ship, Monmouth co., 5 miles from the former, and 14 from the latter; contains 8 or 10 dwellings and a Quaker meeting house; soil, sandy. In the rear of the village, upon Cattail creek, are some bog meadows, which, in hot weather, are covered, in places, with an efflorescence of sulphate of iron (copperas).

Wrightstown, Hanover t-ship, Burlington co., 10 miles N. E. from Mount Holly, and 10 S. E. of Bordenton; contains 2 taverns, 2 stores, a Methodist church, and some 15 or 20 dwellings; surrounded by a very fertile country.

Yard's Branch, of Paulinskill, rises in the Blue mountains, in Pahaquarry t-ship, and flows S. W. through Knowlton t-ship to its recipient, near the village of Sodom, having a course of about 8 miles.

THE

HISTORY

OF

NEW JERSEY,

FROM ITS

DISCOVERY BY EUROPEANS,

TO

THE ADOPTION

OF THE

FEDERAL CONSTITUTION.

BY

THOMAS F. GORDON.

Trenton:

PUBLISHED BY DANIEL FENTON.

John C. Clark, Printer, Philadelphia.

1834.

PREFACE.

An attempt has been made in the following pages to narrate, succinctly, but fully, the history of New Jersey, from the time of its discovery by Europeans, to that of the adoption of the constitution of the United States. By the latter event, the individuality of the State, as a historical subject, is merged in the history of the nation; and the subsequent period of unvaried political prosperity, within her borders, presents few matters for the historian.

The story we have told, has, for the inhabitants of the State, the interest of their peculiar and proper affairs; but, like such affairs, may not prove attractive to strangers. Like Pennsylvania, this State was founded by deeds of peace; and no community, in any country, can have undergone less vicissitude. Her prudence and justice preserved her from Indian hostility, and her distance from the frontier protected her from the inroads of the French. She has known, therefore, no wars, save those commanded by the king, or undertaken in defence of her own civil liberty. To pourtray the part, which, as a colony, she took in the one, and as an independent State, in the other, it has been necessary to treat of the general colonial and revolutionary history; yet no further than was indispensable to exhibit the action of New Jersey.

In the compilation of the work, resort has been had to all the known histories of the Anglo-American colonies, to the best writers on the American revolution, and to the minutes of the legislature and the statutes, for a period of more than one hundred and twenty years. From these sources, it is believed, that a faithful and ample narrative has been obtained. More particulars of the horrors which attended the revolutionary war, especially of those which were inflicted by furious tory partisans, might, perhaps, have been added, if full reliance were due to the partial newspaper accounts, frequently written under excitement unfavourable to truth. Yet, enough of these scenes has been described to display the nature and extent of the sufferings of the inhabitants; more would have served rather to disgust, than to entertain, the reader.

The author submits the result of his labours to the many subscribers by whom they have been encouraged, with an assurance of his readiness, in another edition, to supply such omissions, and to correct such errors, as may be discovered in the present.

March, 1834.

CONTENTS.

CHAPTER I.

CHAPTER II.

CHAPTER III.

CHAPTER IV.

CHAPTER V.

CHAPTER VI.

CHAPTER VII.

CHAPTER VIII.

CHAPTER IX.

CHAPTER X.

CHAPTER XVI.

CHAPTER XVII.

CHAPTER XVIII.

THE

HISTORY OF NEW JERSEY.

CHAPTER I.

Comprising Events from the Discovery by Europeans, to the Grant from Charles I. to James Duke of York.—I. Ancient and Modern Principles of Colonization.—II. Voyages of the Spaniards and Portuguese upon the East Coast of North America.—III. Voyages of the Italians, Verrazano and the Cabots.—IV. First English Attempts at Discovery.—V. Efforts of Raleigh to establish a Colony.—VI. Gosnold opens a new Road—London and Plymouth Companies created.—VII. Voyages and Discoveries of Hudson.—VIII. Intercourse of the Dutch East India Company with America, and Formation of the Amsterdam Licensed Trading West India Company.—IX. Settlement of the Puritans at Plymouth.—X. Formation of the Great West India Company in Holland.—XI. Voyage and Proceedings of Cornelius Jacobse Mey.—XII. Measures of the Company to promote Emigration; Purchases of large Tracts of Land from the Indians.—XIII. Voyages of De Vries; Colony planted—The Delaware abandoned by the Dutch.—XIV. Minisink Settlements on the Delaware.—XV. Settlements of the Swedes on the Delaware—first Project of a Colony—first Colony—increase of Settlers.—XVI. Colonial Government established—Colonel Printz first Governor.—XVII. English Settlements upon the Delaware—prostrated by a united Force of Dutch and Swedes.—XVIII. Swedish Government under Printz and his Successors.—XIX. Swedish Colony subjected by the Dutch.—XX. Dutch Colonial Government on the Delaware—Possessions on the East of New Jersey.—XXI. Account of the English Settlements upon the Delaware previous to 1664—under Patent from Lord Baltimore—under Grant to Sir Edward Ploeyden—by Traders from New Haven.—XXII. Plans of New England Settlers for Conquest of the Dutch Colonies.—XXIII. Duke of York's Charter from the Crown and Grant to Berkeley and Carteret.—XXIV. Conquest of New Netherlands, by Colonel Nicholls.—XXV. English Government established on the Delaware.—XXVI. Condition of New Netherlandts at the time of the Surrender.

I. A distinction has frequently been taken between ancient and modern colonization; ascribing the former to military, and the latter to commercial principles. But this classification does not embrace the various species of colonies, in present or past time. A more happy division of the subject would seem to be, into colonies founded by individuals, in their search of happiness; and colonies planted by states, with a view to military or commercial purposes. By the first, our race was originally spread over the face of the globe. It has prevailed at all times, as well among the Egyptians, Athenians, and other ancient people, as among the moderns, who instituted the communities of the North American confederacy. The early Greek colonies, generally, sprung from the desire of the citizens to ameliorate their condition; and the immediate impulse was, excess of population, the ambition of chiefs, the love of liberty, or contagious and frequent maladies. The bonds of filiation connected the colony with the parent state; and the endearing names of daughter, sister and mother, sanctioned and preserved the alliances between them. But in the Grecian colonies of latter date, we trace commercial and political views. The Carthaginians, also, seem to have established colonies upon commercial principles; and two treaties, recorded by Polybius,* between them and the Romans, are in the true spirit of modern colonial policy. On the other hand, the Roman colonies were military establishments, designed to maintain or extend their conquests; and their agrarian allotments, to disbanded veterans and discontented and clamorous citizens, partook of the same character. Commercial motives seem rarely to have blended with the policy of these haughty conquerors. Such, also, in more recent days were the colonies of the Normans, in England, France, and the south of Europe; of the English, in Ireland and Indostan; of the Portuguese and Dutch in either India; and of a portion of the Spanish settlements in the New World.

In general, the civil colonies of the ancients were independent of the authority of the parent state; though, necessarily, influenced by the ties of charity which connected them with her. But, modern history, we believe, furnishes no instance of a colony independent in its inception; unless the short-lived religious communities of the Jesuits, in America, and of the Moravians in the northern parts of both continents, be so considered. The colonies of the western hemisphere were, generally, commenced under the sanction of, and in dependence upon, some European state. Even the ascetic Brownists, in their torpid settlement of New Plymouth, began their labours under the auspices of James I. of England: and though for some years, they were unnoticed by the crown, they claimed and enjoyed the protection due to English subjects.

The colonization of America was prompted and directed by various passions. The Spaniards and Portuguese were inspired by visions of sudden wealth, by the love of that fame which chivalric adventure gave, and by an apostolic desire of spreading their religious faith among the heathen. The founders of states in the northern continent, were actuated by more sober, but not dissimilar views. Raleigh and his associates sought wealth and reputation, by extending the power and fame of their mistress and their country; and the provincial proprietaries, holders of large grants from the crown, were excited by ambition and avarice; which in Calvert and Penn, at least, were blended with a noble philanthropy, delighting to assure religious and civil liberty to their associates and their successors. The subgrantees and settlers who subdued the wilderness, came with great diversity of purpose. Many fled from religious, some, from political persecution; but, the larger portion was induced by that well founded hope of ameliorating the condition of themselves and their posterity, which flowed from the unrestricted possession of a rich and virgin soil, in whose fruits they were protected, against lawful and lawless violence. The religious instruction of the savage is a condition of every royal grant; and afforded to the grantor, doubtless, a full extenuation of the injustice of invasion. The extensive grant of Charles II. to his brother, of York, was moved by political causes, and designed, probably, also, to reward the services of others, which he could not, in a different manner, acknowledge. The immediate grantees of the Duke, were wise enough to see, that their interest lay in the adoption of the most liberal principles of political association, which circumstances would permit; and these circumstances were most favorable, to civil and religious liberty.

The period in which the foundations of the Anglo-American colonies were laid, was rife with events, which sowed the indestructible seeds, and reared into strength the scions of human liberty. The integrity and infallibility of clerical power, had been shaken to pieces by Luther and Calvin; and the divinity of kings had expired with the unhappy Charles. The religious contests, and the transition of power from one religious sect to another,

* Lib. iii. c. 22.

had taught to Catholic and Protestant, the advantages, if not the necessity, of religious toleration. Letters, the cause and power of religious freedom, had been equally serviceable to civil liberty; and the great truth which, for ages, had laid buried in the ruins of civilization, beneath sacerdotal palaces and prisons, and the gothic gorgeousness of the feudal system,—the great truth, that political power belonged to, and was made for, the people, had been rediscovered—was proclaimed abroad, and had become generally understood among men—among Englishmen. That truth had wrenched the sceptre from the grasp of an obstinate and bigoted despot, and borne him to the block—had overthrown a monarchy and created a republic; and because of the abuse of republican forms, had again established a throne. Religious and political freedom were in England terms as familiar as household words, and enforced, even from the hate of her princes, the most profound respect.

It was vain, therefore, to think of the formation of new political societies, without adverting to, and securing these great essentials. Kings and proprietaries, who would establish colonies, were compelled to stipulate for religious toleration, and legislative power in the people. Hence, the first Charles, who abominated a parliament, required the proprietary, Calvert, to obtain all subsidies, by the assent of the people—hence, the second Charles introduced the same principle, in the grant of Pennsylvania—hence, they, and the Carterets, and the Berkeleys, and the minor Proprietaries, were compelled to their liberal charters. All were results of improvement in the moral condition of our species, which individuals might promote, but could scarce retard. We are guilty, therefore, of the worst species of idolatry—of man-worship, when we give to individuals the praise of creating measures, of which they could only be the servants. Our plaudits for their concurrence in the good work, are, however, due; and should be frankly and fully paid, as the just incentive to virtuous actions.

In this spirit, we adopt the expressions of a late writer upon colonial history:—"A North American may feel grateful exultation in avowing himself the native of no ignoble land—but of a land which has yielded as great an increase of glory to God, and happiness to man, as any other portion of the world, since the first syllable of recorded time, has had the honour of producing. A nobler model of human character could hardly be proposed to the inhabitants of the North American States, than that which their own early history supplies. It is, at once, their interest and their honour, to preserve with sacred care, a model so richly fraught, with the instructions of wisdom and the incitements of duty."*

No portion of the history of this great country is more filled with cause for this "grateful exultation," than the State of New Jersey—none can boast greater purity in its origin—none more wisdom, more happiness in its growth. To develope her unpretending, but instructive story, is the object of the following pages; in which, however, we must, necessarily, blend a portion of that of the adjacent states, which for half a century were identified with her.

II. Soon after the discovery of America, by Columbus, the Spaniards and Portuguese explored the northern Atlantic coast, as high as Labrador; to which, the latter gave its present name. As they approached by the West Indies, they may have visited the shores of the Delaware and Hudson rivers; but possessed of the fine climates, and richer countries of the south, they had no inducement to make permanent settlements in regions less attractive. Florida was occupied by the Spaniards, in 1512; and its boundaries, as

* Grahame's History of the American Colonies.

given by the charter of Philip II. to Menendez, extended from Newfoundland to the 22d degree of northern latitude.

III. To the genius of the Italian navigators, the world is deeply indebted, as well for the early exploration, as for the discovery, of America. John de Verrazano, and the enterprising and skilful Cabots, were the worthy successors of Columbus and Americus Vespucius. Verrazano, whilst in the service of Francis I. of France, visited, it is supposed, the bay of New York.* It is certain, that, in 1523, he coasted the American continent, from the 30th to the 50th degree of north latitude, landing and communicating with the natives in several places; and that by virtue of discoveries made by him, and some French navigators, Henry IV. gave to Des Monts, the lands lying between the 40th and 46th degrees of north latitude.† The loss of Verrazano, with his vessel and crew, on a subsequent voyage, (1524) procrastinated, for ten years, the efforts of the French to establish colonies in America. The voyages and discoveries of Quartier, in 1535, directed their attention, particularly, to the shores of the bay and river of St. Lawrence.

IV. Under the patronage of Henry VII. of England, Sebastian Cabot discovered the islands of Newfoundland and St. Johns, and explored the coast of the continent, from the 38th to the 67th degree of north latitude.‡ But no fruit was, immediately, derived from his labours. During the reigns of the voluptuary, Henry VIII., of his son, Edward VI., and daughter, the bigoted Mary, no effort was made to prosecute these interesting discoveries. It was reserved for the maritime enterprise of Elizabeth's reign, to give to the English nation a fuller knowledge of the new world, and a proper sense of the advantages which might be drawn from it. Encouraged by the Earl of Warwick, Martin Frobisher, in three successive voyages, visited the shores of Labrador and Greenland.§ Sir Humphrey Gilbert, in 1580, made two unsuccessful attempts to establish a colony in North America, in the last of which, he perished.

V. But the fate of Gilbert did not deter his half-brother, Sir Walter Raleigh, alike distinguished for his genius and courage, from pursuing the same object; which, indeed, had taken strong hold of the affections of the principal men of the kingdom. He formed a company, under a charter, obtained from the queen,|| granting them all the lands they should discover between the 33d and 40th degrees of north latitude. Two vessels despatched by them, under captains Armidas and Barlow,** visited Pamptico Sound, and Roanoke Bay; and on their return, reported so favourably of the beauty and fertility of the country, that the company were excited to new exertions; and Elizabeth gave, to the newly discovered region, the name of Virginia, as a memorial that it was discovered in the reign of a virgin queen. But the subsequent efforts of this company proved abortive. A colony was, indeed, planted at Roanoke, in 1585; but, having been reduced to distress by the delay of supplies, they returned to Europe, in the following year, with Sir Francis Drake; who touched at their island on his way home, from a successful cruise against the Spaniards. Undiscouraged by this ill success, Raleigh despatched another colony to the same place, under the direction of captain John White,†† which perished by famine, or the sword of the natives; having been deprived, by the preparations of the Spaniards, for invading England, of the succour which White had returned to seek.

* Dr. Miller's Discourse, 1 vol.—N. Y. Historical Collection.

† 2 Hackluyt's, 1. N. Y. Historical Collection. Williamson's History of North Carolina, vol. i. 15. Moulton's History of New York, vol. i. 134.

‡ 1498. A Mr. Hare is said to have followed Cabot, and to have brought to Henry VIII, some Indians from North America.

§ In 1576, 1577, 1578. || 26th March, 1584. ** Sailed, 27th April, returned, 15th September, 1584. †† March, 1590.

VI. Between the years 1590 and 1603, the English do not appear to have made any voyage for the purpose of settlement. In the latter year, Bartholomew Gosnold, abandoning the circuitous route hitherto pursued by all navigators, discovered, by steering due west, a more direct course to the northern continent. He visited, and gave names to Cape Cod, and the islands of Elizabeth, and Martha's Vineyard; and taught his countrymen, that there were many attractions, far north of the lands they had attempted to colonize. His favourable reports, at first disbelieved, were confirmed by persons who sailed, thither, in the service of some merchants of Bristol, the Earl of Southampton, and Lord Arundel, of Wardour. By the zeal of Richard Hackluyt, prebendary of Westminster, to whom England was more indebted than to any man of his age, for her American possessions, an association, embracing men of rank and men of business, was formed, with a view to colonization.*

To this company, James I., on the 10th of April, 1606, granted letters patent, dividing that portion of the continent which stretches from the 34th to the 46th degrees of north latitude, into two, nearly equal, districts. The one, called the first, or south colony of Virginia, was allotted to Sir Thomas Gates, Richard Hackluyt, and their associates, mostly residents of London; the other, to sundry knights, gentlemen and merchants, of Bristol, Plymouth, and other parts of the west of England. Each company was empowered to appropriate to itself, fifty miles each way, along the coast, from the point of its settlement, and one hundred miles of interior extent. From the places at which the colonial councils were respectively established, were derived the titles of the London and Plymouth Colonies.†

Under this and another charter, to the Plymouth company, given in 1620, whose provisions were not the most friendly to political freedom, nor the best adapted to promote the objects for which they were designed, the permanent settlement of Virginia and New England was commenced and prosecuted. It forms, however, no part of our present plan, to trace the various fortune which attended their growth, from weak and sickly plants, to deep-rooted and umbrageous trees.

VII. The hope of discovering a north-west passage from Europe to Asia, which no disappointment seems to have power to extinguish, was the motive of several voyages made by Henry Hudson, a distinguished English mariner. In his third voyage, failing to open a northern route, he explored the eastern coast of America, with the view of determining, whether a passage, to the Pacific Ocean, might not be found through the continent.‡ He ran down the coast, from Newfoundland, to 35° 41′, northern latitude; and returning by the same course, entered the Delaware bay, on the 28th of August, 1609,—but finding the water shoal, and the channel impeded by bars of sand, he did not venture to explore it. Following the eastern shore of New Jersey, he anchored his ship, the Half-Moon, on the 3d of September, within Sandy Hook. He spent a week in examining the neighbouring shores, and in communication with the natives; during which, one of his seamen, named John Coleman, was killed. The boat in which he and several others had passed the Kills, between Bergen Neck and Staten Island, being attacked by two canoes, carrying twenty-six Indians, the unfortunate sailor was shot, by an arrow, through the throat. Thus it would seem, that in the intercourse

* 2 Purchas, 5. Belknap's American Biography.—N. A. R., (new series) vol. vi. p. 36.

† Modern Universal History, vol. xxx. Hazard's State Papers, 1. Stith, Beverly, Robertson.

‡ Voyages undertaken by the Dutch East India Company. Hudson's Journal. Purchas, 1—N. Y. Hist. Col. 81, 162.

between the European and Indian, in this part of America, the Indian committed the first homicide. The shores of the Delaware and Raritan bays were, probably, the first lands of the middle States trodden by European feet.

On the 12th of September, Hudson entered New York Bay, through the Narrows. He spent the time between that day and the 19th of the same month, in exploring the North river.* He ascended, with his ship, as high as the spot where the city of Albany now stands; and his boat proceeded to the sites of Waterford and Lansingburg. The decreasing volume of the stream, and the shoals which obstructed his further way, depriving him of all hope of reaching the Pacific Ocean by this route, he prepared to retrace his steps. Commencing his return on the 22d of September, he slowly descended the river, and on the 4th day of October, put to sea. He reached England on the 7th of November, 1609. His vessel, and part of the crew, returned to Holland; but the jealousy of the king, James the First, forbade him, and his English sailors, to revisit that country.†

In the following year, Hudson re-entered the service of the London company, in which he had made his two first northern voyages; designing to seek again, a north-west passage, through Davis' Straits; but his crew mutinied, and abandoned him, his only son, and some half-dozen of his men, who continued faithful, to perish amid the fields of ice, in the vicinity of the bay which bears his name.‡

Whilst in the North river, Hudson had much intercourse with the natives. Near the coast, they were fierce and inimical—at a distance from the sea, mild and hospitable. But the superior power of the Europeans was exercised upon friend and foe without mercy. Of the former, one was shot to death, for a petty theft—and of the latter, nine were more deservedly slain, in an attack which they made upon the vessel. The first visit of the white man, therefore, to the shores of the Hudson, was signalized by the violent death of ten of the aboriginal inhabitants.

VIII. The Dutch East India Company, although disappointed in the main design of Hudson's voyage, found in the fur trade he had opened, sufficient inducement to cherish commercial intercourse with the Americans. A second voyage, under their authority, in 1610, proving successful, was repeated; but the competition of private adventurers reducing their profits, they endeavoured to monopolize the trade, by a decree of the States-General, granting to all persons who had discovered, or might discover, any bays, rivers, harbours, or countries before unknown, the right, beside other advantages, to the exclusive trade therein, for four successive voyages.§ Under this edict the Amsterdam Licensed Trading West India Company was formed; proposing to maintain the acquisitions on the Hudson and to explore the circumjacent country.

In the service of this company, Adrian Blok and Hendrick Christianse sailed in the year 1614. Blok arrived first at Mannahattan, where, his ship having been accidentally burned, he built a small vessel, with which he passed into Long Island Sound. He fell in with Christianse near Cape Cod. Together, they discovered Rhode Island and Connecticut river; and proceeding to Mannahattan Bay, they erected a fort on Castle Island, and four dwellings on the Greater Island. In the preceding year, a small trading house was built upon an island below Albany; and in the following, a redoubt was thrown up on the right bank of the river, probably, at the present Jersey City

* Hudson's Journal. See Note (A.)—Appendix.
† Lambrechsten, Moulton, Ebeling. ‡ June 21, 1611.
§ De Laet, March 27, 1614; or as it is said 1611, 1612. Moulton, 340.

Point.* The most important event of this period, however, was the alliance by formal treaty, between the Dutch and the Five Nation confederacy of Indians; at the execution of which, it is supposed, the Lenape tribes were also present, and by the united instances of the Dutch and Iroquois, consented to the fatal assumption of the character of the *woman*, in the manner we shall narrate hereafter.†

The Hollanders, directing their efforts at colonization, to their Asiatic, African and South American possessions, and restrained, perhaps, by the claim of the English, to the greater part of North America, had hitherto made little effort to people the shores of the Hudson. It has been asserted, however, that between the years 1617 and 1620, settlements were made at Bergen, in New Jersey, in the vicinage of the Esopus Indians, and at Schenectady; and it would seem, that Sir Thomas Dale and Sir Samuel Argal, in the year 1614, returning from an expedition against the French at Acadie, visited Mannahattan, and compelled the Dutch to acknowledge the English title, and to contribute to the payment of the expenses of their voyage. It would further seem, from the authorities cited in the margin, but which should be received with some allowance, that in 1620, the Dutch West Indian Company, upon application to James the First, of England, obtained leave to build some cottages upon the Hudson river, for the convenience of the ships, touching there for fresh water and provisions, in their voyage to Brazil; under colour of which license, the company established a colony; and that, upon complaint to Charles I. of these proceedings, he remonstrated with the States-General, who disowned the acts of the company.‡

IX. But, although the Dutch did not immediately, themselves, colonize the New Netherlands, (the name given to the country from the Delaware Bay to Cape Cod,) they were well disposed to aid others in such design; encouraging the Puritans, who, under the care of the Rev. John Robinson, had fled to the low countries from England, to seek a safe and more commodious asylum in the New World; notwithstanding these sectarians avowed an intention to preserve their national character, and to hold the title for the lands they should inhabit, in dependence on the English government. This germ of the Plymouth colony, planted in 1620, was designed for the country between New York Bay and the western line of Connecticut. But the season at which the adventurers arrived on the coast, adverse winds and currents, with the discovery of a portion of the country, whence the aborigines had been lately swept, providentially, as the pilgrims supposed, by pestilence, induced them to land at a place, they termed Plymouth.§ The allegation, therefore, that Capt. Jones, with whom they sailed, had faithlessly, in consequence of a bribe from the Dutch, landed them at a distance from the Hudson, is not entitled to credence.

X. In 1621 the great West India Company was formed in Holland, and endowed with the wealth and power of the States-General. The Licensed Trading Company which had hitherto conducted commercial operations in the Hudson, confining themselves to one river and a small portion of the coast, was merged in the new company, to whom we may properly ascribe the first efforts of the Dutch to plant colonies in North America.||

They immediately despatched a number of settlers duly provided with the means of subsistence, trade, and defence, under the command of Cornelius

* De Laet, Moulton. † Heckewelder.

‡ Beauchamp Plantagenet's description of New Albion—Moulton—British Empire in America—Ogilby's America—Elizabethtown Bill in Chancery.

§ Robertson. Dudley's letter. Moulton.

|| See charter of this company in Hazard's Col.

Jacobse Mey; who, with more enterprise and industry than his predecessors, visited the coast from Cape Cod to the Delaware river, where he proposed to establish his own residence. He called the bay of New York, Port May; that of the Delaware, New Port May; its northern cape, Cape May; and its southern, Cape Cornelius. He built Fort Nassau at ***Techaacho***, upon ***Sassackon***, now Timber Creek, which empties into the Delaware, a few miles below the city of Camden. During the same year the forts ***New Amsterdam*** and ***Orange***, were also erected upon the sites, of the now great cities, of New York and Albany.

The administration of the affairs of New Netherlands, was committed to Peter Minuit; with whom came a colony of Walloons, who settled, 1624-5, at the Walbocht, a bend of the Long Island shore, opposite to New Amsterdam. In 1626, Minuit opened a friendly and commercial intercourse with the Plymouth pilgrims; and prosecuted the fur trade with great advantage to the company.

XII. In 1629 the West India Company endeavoured to excite individual enterprise, to colonize the country; granting by charter to the ***patroon*** or founder of a settlement, exclusive property, in large tracts of land, with extensive manorial and seignorial rights.* Thus encouraged, several of the directors, for whose use, probably, the charter was designed, among whom Goodyn, Bloemart, Pauuw and Van Renselaer were most distinguished, resolved to make large territorial acquisitions; and they sent out Wooter Van Twiller, of Niewer Kerck, a clerk of the Amsterdam department, of the company, to assume the management of its public affairs, and to select lands for the individual directors.

One of the three ships which came over in 1629, visited an Indian village on the south-west corner of Delaware Bay; and the agents on board, purchased from the three chiefs of the resident tribe, in behalf of the Herr Goodyn, a tract of land, extending from ***Cape Henloop***, in length thirty-two, and breadth two, English miles. In the succeeding year, several other extensive tracts were purchased; for Goodyn and Bloemart, of nine Indian chiefs, sixteen miles square, on the peninsula of Cape May; for the director Pauuw, Staten Island, and a large plat on the western side of the Hudson, in the neighbourhood of Hoboken; and for Van Renselaer, a considerable territory, along the Hudson, in the vicinity of Fort Orange.† The impolicy of these great and exclusive appropriations was, subsequently, discovered and condemned; and their ratification seems to have been obtained, only, by admitting other directors to participate in them.

XIII. In prosecution of their plans, these directors formed an association, to which they admitted, on equal terms, David Pieterson de Vries, an experienced and enterprising navigator. Their immediate object was to colonize the Delaware river, to plant tobacco and grain, and to establish a whale and seal fishery. The command of the vessel appointed to carry out the colonists was given to De Vries; who left the Texel on the 12th Dec. 1630, and arrived in the Delaware bay in the course of the winter. The country was deserted by the Europeans, who had preceded him. Fort Nassau was in possession of the Indians; Captain Mey having left it, bearing with him the affectionate regrets of the natives, who long cherished his memory. De Vries selected a spot for his settlement, on Lewis Creek, called by the Dutch, on account of the prostitution of the Indian women here, Hoornekill; where, unimpeded by the season, which was uncommonly mild, he erected a trading

* See the charter in Moulton's History of New York.

† See Moulton's History of New York. The territory of Goodyn was denominated Swanwendael; that of Pauuw, Pavonia; and that of Van Renselaer, Renselaerwick.

house and fort, giving it the name of Oplandt. The whole plantation, within Goodyn's purchase, extended to the Little Tree Corner or Boompjes' Hoek.*

Returning to Holland, he committed his infant colony to the care of one Giles Osset; who, in evidence of the claim and possession of the Dutch, set up the arms of the States-General, painted on tin, upon a column, in some conspicuous station. An Indian, ignorant of the object of this exhibition, appropriated the honoured symbol to his own use. The folly of the commandant construed the trespass into a grievous national insult, and he became so importunate for redress, that the harassed and perplexed tribe brought him the head of the offender. This was a result which Osset had neither wished nor foreseen, and he should justly have dreaded its consequences. In vain he reprehended the severity of the Indians, and assured them that had they brought the delinquent to him, he would have suffered a reprimand only. Though the death of the culprit had been doomed and executed by his own tribe, they beheld its cause in the exaction of the strangers, and with the vindictiveness of their character, sought a dire retribution. At a season when the greater part of the garrison was engaged in field labour, distant from the fort, the Indians entered it, under the pretence of trade, and murdered the unsuspicious Osset with the single sentinel who attended him. Thence, proceeding to the fields, they massacred every other colonist, whilst tendering to them the usual friendly salutations. This conduct, with its extenuating circumstances, as related by the aborigines themselves to De Vries, is sufficiently atrocious; but it is highly probable, that the desire of the white man's wealth was as powerful a stimulant to violence as the thirst for vengeance.

In December, 1632, De Vries returned from Holland, to mourn over the unburied bodies of his friends, and the ashes of their dwelling. Attracted by the firing of cannon, the savages approached his vessel with guilty hesitation; but at length, summoned courage to venture on board, and to detail the circumstances we have narrated. The object which De Vries had in view, led him to seek reconciliation; and he was compelled to pardon, where he could not safely punish. He formed a new treaty with the Indians; and in order to obtain provisions, ascended the river above Fort Nassau, where he narrowly escaped from the perfidy of the natives. Pretending to comply with his request, they directed him to enter Timmerkill or Cooper's Creek, which furnished a convenient place for attack; but, the interposition of an Indian woman, so often recorded in favour of the whites, saved him from destruction. She warned him of the design of her countrymen, and that a crew of a vessel (supposed from Virginia) had been there murdered. In the mean time, Fort Nassau was filled with savages, and on the return of De Vries, forty boarded his vessel, whom he compelled to retreat; declaring that the Manitou or Great Spirit, had revealed their wickedness. But, subsequently, with the humane and pacific policy which distinguished him, he consented to their wishes of forming a treaty of amity; which they confirmed with customary presents, declining his gifts, however, saying, that they did not now give with the view of a return.† Disappointed in obtaining provisions, De Vries, leaving part of his crew in the bay, proceeded to Virginia; where, as the first visiter from New Netherlands, he was kindly received and his wants supplied. Upon his return to the Delaware, finding the whale fishery unsuccessful, he hastened his departure, and with the other colonists proceeded to Holland, by the way of Fort Amsterdam. Thus, at the expiration of

* Corrupted into Bombay Hook. De Vries, Moulton.
† De Vries' Journal. Moulton.

twenty-five years from the discovery of the Delaware Bay, by Hudson, not a single European remained upon its shores.

XIV. It is possible, however, that the Minisink settlements on the river, above the Blue Mountain, were made at or near this period. They extend forty miles on both sides of the river, and the tradition, as rendered by Nicholas Depuis, a descendant of an original settler is; "That, in some former age, there came a company of miners from Holland, supposed to have "been rich and great people, from the labour they bestowed in opening two "mines—one on the Delaware, where the mountain nearly approaches the "lower point of Pahaquarry Flat, the other, at the north foot of some mountain, half-way between Delaware and Esopus; and in making the mine "road from Delaware to Esopus, a distance of one hundred miles: That "large quantities of ore had been drawn upon this road, but of what metal, "was unknown to the present inhabitants: That, subsequently, settlers "came to the Minisinks from Holland, to seek an asylum from religious persecution, being Arminians: That they followed the mine road to the large "flats, on the Delaware, where the smooth cleared land, and *abundance of* "*large apple trees*, suited their views, and they purchased the improvements "of the Indians, most of whom, then, removed to the Susquehanna: And that "the new settlers maintained peace and friendship with such as remained, "until the year 1755."* These settlements at the Minisinks were unknown to the government of Pennsylvania until 1729.

XV. It has been affirmed that the Swedes established a colony on the Delaware, in the year 1627, or 1631. This is an error, arising from the historian having mistaken the will for the deed; inferring that a colony had been established, immediately after the proposition for forming it, had been published in Sweden. The design had, indeed, been fondly encouraged by Gustavus Adolphus, but was not effected during his life. This prince fell at Lutzen, in 1632; and several years elapsed, before the ministers of his daughter, Christina, gave encouragement to the enterprise. The success of the Dutch West India Company had excited the Swedes to form a similar association, whose operations should extend to Asia, Africa, and America;—and William Usselinx, or Usseling, a Hollander, who had been connected with the Dutch company, obtained the consent of Gustavus, to this measure.† Designing to plant a colony on the Delaware, he prepared and published articles of Association for that purpose, accompanied with a description of the fertility of the soil, and the commercial advantages of the country. The king, by proclamation, exhorted his subjects to unite with the company,‡ and recommended its plan to a diet of the States, by whom it was confirmed.§ Persons of every rank, from the king to the hind, engaged in the scheme. An admiral, vice admiral, merchants, assistants, commissaries, and a military force, were appointed, and the association received the name of the South Company;—but the intervention of a German war, suspended its operations.||

From 1633 to 1637, no effort was made by any European power, to people the banks of the Delaware, unless during this period, Sir Edward Ploeyden, commenced his ephemeral palatinate of New Albion. It is probable, however, that the Dutch visited the river, with a view to trade, and, occasionally, spent some time at Fort Nassau. That, they vigilantly observed the approach of other nations to these shores, is obvious, from the prompti-

* Letters of Samuel Preston, of Stockport, June 6th, and 14th, 1828, published in the Register of Pennsylvania, Vol. i. No. 28.—July 12, 1828.

† 21st December, 1624. ‡ July, 1626. § 1627. || Campanius, Aurelius, Molton.

tude of their remonstrances against the subsequent attempts of the English and Swedes.

The Swedish project, so far as it relates to colonization on the Delaware, was, at length, revived by the Dutch ex-governor, Minuit, (who had been superseded by Vouter van Twiller,) under the immediate authority of the Swedish government. In 1637 or 1638, an expedition, consisting of the Key of Calman, a ship of war, and a transport named the Bird Grip, (Gryphen) carrying a clergyman, an engineer, and many settlers, with necessary provisions, and merchandise for trade with the Indians, sailed under Minuit's command.* The emigrants landed at Inlopen, the inner cape on the western shore of the Delaware bay, to which they gave the name of Paradise Point—more, we must conjecture, from the pleasant emotions caused by the sight of any land, after a long sea-voyage, than from the beauty or fertility of the spot. They opened communications with the natives, on the bay and river, and purchased the soil, on the western shore, from the capes, to the falls at *Sanhikans*, below the present city of Trenton.

Soon after, in 1638, they laid the foundation of the town and fort of Christina, on a site called by the natives ***Hopohaccan***, north of the ***Minquas***, or ***Suspecough*** creek, and a short distance above its mouth.† Not a vestige of this fort or town remains; but a plan of both, drawn by the engineer, Lindstrom, has been preserved by Campanius. In 1747, during the war of England against France and Spain, a redoubt was thrown up at this spot; and at the distance of three feet below the surface, a Swedish coin of Christina was found, among axes, shovels, and other implements.‡

The author of ***Bescryvinge van Netherlands***, asserts, that Minuit entered the Delaware, under pretence of procuring refreshment, on his way to the West Indies, but betrayed the deception, by erecting this fort. The Dutch soon discovered the intrusion; and Kieft, who, about this time had succeeded Van Twiller, as governor of New York, remonstrated with Minuit, by letter, dated, May 6th, 1638; asserting, that the whole South river of New Netherlands, had been in possession of the Dutch, for many years, above and below Christina—had been studded by forts, and sealed with their blood. This remonstrance was unreasonable and unwarrantable, if, as Campanius asserts, the Swedes had, in 1631, purchased the right of the Dutch. The allegation of purchase, may have induced forbearance on the part of the Dutch authorities, but did not deter them from erecting a fort soon after, at the Hoarkills.

During the year 1640, several companies of emigrants departed from Sweden, for the new world. Among the documents obtained from the Swedish records, by Mr. Russel, minister from the United States, at Stockholm, we find, dated, January 24th, 1640, a passport to captain Jacob Powelson, for a vessel under his command, named Fredenburg, laden with men, cattle, and other things, necessary for the cultivation of the country, departing from Holland to America, or the West Indies, and there establishing himself in the country called New Sweden. Two others were issued in blank, for other captains and their vessels. We learn, also, from a letter of the same date, addressed by the Swedish ministers to the commandant, or commissary, and other inhabitants of Fort Christina, in New Sweden, that permission had been granted to Gothbert de Rehden, William de Horst, and Fenland, and those interested with them, to send out and establish a

* Bescryvinge van Virginie, De Laet, Acrelius.
† Swedish MSS. Records, communicated by the Rev. Nicholas Collin.
‡ Kalm's Travels.

colony on the north side of the South river. In a charter, or grant and privilege, as it is termed, of the same date, to this company, the name of Henry Hochhanmer, is substituted for that of Lieutenant Horst. From this instrument we derive the Swedish principles of colonization. An indefinite quantity of land is given to the company—at least four German miles, (about 15 English) from Fort Christina, in allodial and hereditary property; they paying to the crown of Sweden, three florins of the empire, for each family established upon their territory. The company is empowered to exercise, within their district, high and low justice; to found cities and villages, and communities, with a certain police, statutes and ordinances—to appoint magistrates and officers, and to take the title and arms of a province or colony; conforming themselves, in the use of these rights, to the principles directing the ordinary justice of fiefs. Reservation is made of full sovereignty to the crown; and, especially, of appeals to it, and the governors established by it, whose approbation was necessary to all statutes and ordinances. Besides the Augsburg confession of faith, the exercise of the "*pretended reformed*" religion was permitted, in such manner, however, that those who professed either, should live in peace, abstaining from every useless dispute, from all scandal, and from all abuse. But the patrons of the colony were obliged, at all times, to maintain as many *ministers and schoolmasters* as the number of inhabitants should require; and to choose for this purpose, persons who had at heart, the conversion of the pagan inhabitants, to Christianity.

Permission was given to the colonists to engage in every species of manufacture and commerce, in and out of the country; in vessels, however, which should be built in New Sweden. Gottenburg was made the depot for all merchandise transported to Europe; but merchants were not required to pass the Sound, when destined to some other part of Sweden. Entrance to foreign ports, however, was prohibited, unless in case of necessity; and even in such case, merchants were required to repair to Gottenburg, to account for such entry, and to pay duty on merchandise, they might have sold elsewhere; and to equip their vessels anew. The colonists were exempted, for ten successive years, from every species of impost; but, after that period, were required to pay, in New Sweden, a duty of five per cent. on all imports, and exports, and such further charges as the expenses of government, there, might require. The discoverer of minerals, precious stones, coral, crystal, marble, a pearl fishery, means for making salt, or other like things, was permitted the unrestricted use thereof, for ten years, and to enjoy, subsequently, a preferable right to possession, under an annual rent. Protection was promised to the colonies, in consideration whereof, fealty and allegiance were exacted. But the government expressed the desire, that the colonists and their posterity might be always exempt from enrolments and compulsory military service. Confiscation of property was prohibited: and fines, whatever might be the offence, were limited to forty rix-dollars; every other species of punishment, according to the quality of the offence, was reserved to the crown. And as the patrons of the colony designed, in a few years, to transport other and more considerable colonies, liberty was given to ship, directly from Holland, whatever they might require.

Whilst the arrangements for this colony were in progress, due care was had, by the ministry of Sweden, for the scion they had already planted. One Jost de Bogardt was nominated, rather as an agent and superintendent of the colony of Christina, than as governor. He engaged, by an obligation, called the counterpart of his commission, to be faithful and subject to her majesty; "and not only to aid, by his counsel and actions, the persons who are at Fort Christina, and those who may be afterwards sent there from

Sweden, but to employ his exertions to procure, as occasion may present, whatever will be most advantageous to her Majesty and the crown of Sweden; and, moreover, not to suffer an opportunity to pass of sending information to Sweden, which may be useful to her Majesty and the crown." The reward of these services was stipulated to be two hundred rix-dollars per annum.

XVI. The country, which had been settled, appears to have been purchased, chiefly, by an association called the Navigation Company, who, enjoying the soil, submitted to the political direction of the crown. John Printz, a colonel of cavalry in the Swedish service, was appointed governor. His commission bears date August 16, 1646. His instructions charge him to preserve amity, good neighbourhood, and correspondence with foreigners, with those who depend on his government, and with the natives of the country; to render justice without distinction, so that there shall be injury to no one; and if any person behave himself grossly, to punish him in a convenient manner; and as regards the cultivation of the country, in a liberal manner to regulate and continue it, so that the inhabitants may derive from it, their honest support, and even, that, commerce may receive from it a sensible increase. As to himself, he was required so to conduct in his government, as to be willing and able, faithfully, to answer for it before God, before the Queen and every brave Swede, regulating himself by the instructions given to him. These instructions, remarkable for their simplicity, remind us of the patriarchal era, to which the state of New Sweden, had some resemblance. The salary assured to the governor, was 1200 rix-dollars per annum; a portion of which, at least, was imposed on the colony in a tariff of compensations, which gave to the governor 800 rix-dollars; (half from excise and half in silver;) to a lieutenant governor, sixteen dollars per month; a sergeant major ten, a corporal six, a gunner eight, trumpeter six, drummer five; to 24 soldiers, four, each; to a paymaster ten, a secretary eight, a barber ten, and a provost six. We must not infer from comparison of the wages of the secretary and barber, that the latter was the most valued though the most appreciated. The first had, doubtless, the most honour, though the second had a greater compensation in base lucre.

On the 16th February, 1642-3, Printz, accompanied by John Campanius, a clergyman and subsequent historian of New Sweden, with many emigrants, on board the ship Fame and Transport Swan, arrived in the Delaware. The governor established himself on the island of *Tennekong*, corrupted into, *Tinicum;* which, in Nov. 1643, was granted him by the Queen Christina, in fee; where he built a fort called New Gottenburg, a convenient dwelling for himself, denominated Printz Hoff or Printz Hall, and a church, which was consecrated in 1646. Around this nucleus, the principal settlers reared their habitations. Pursuant to his instructions, he recognised the right of the aborigines to the soil, confirmed the contract made with them by Minuit, for land fronting the river, from the Cape to the Falls, and extending inland, so far, as the necessities of the settlers should require. He refrained from every species of injury to the natives, cultivated their favour by a just and reciprocal commerce, supplying them with articles suitable to their wants, and employed all friendly means to win them to the Christian faith.

The result of these measures was such as they should have produced. The savage was disarmed by respect and gratitude; for, when the presents from the Swedes were discontinued, and councils were holden by the discontented, to weigh the fate of the strangers, the old and wise expatiated on their benevolence and justice, and assured the young and violent, that no easy conquest, would be made, of men, who, whilst cherishing the arts of peace, were armed with swords and muskets, and guarded by vigilance and courage.

The ire of the Indians on one occasion, it seems, was particularly directed against the pastor, who speaking alone, during divine service, was supposed to exhort his audience to hostility against them.*

XVII. Before Printz left Sweden, it was known that an English colony had alighted on the eastern shore of the Delaware; sixty persons having settled near *Oijtsessing*, *Assamohocking*, Hog or Salem Creek, at the close of the year 1640, or commencement of 1741, who were, probably, pioneers of Sir Edmund Ploeyden, or squatters from the colony of New Haven. The Swedes purchased all the lands from Cape May to *Narriticon* or Raccoon Creek, for the purpose of bringing the English under their dominion; and Printz was instructed, either to attach them to the Swedish interests, or to procure their removal without violence.† He disregarded his instructions on this occasion, since, we are told, that the Dutch and Swedes united to expel the English; and that the latter, assuming the task of keeping out the intruders, seized their possessions, and erected a fort; which they called Elftsburg or Elsinborg.‡ But, Acrelius assures us, that this fort was reared in 1651, as a counterpoise to the Dutch power, acquired by the erection of Fort Casimer; and that, the guns of Elsinborg, compelling the Hollanders to strike the flag from their vessels' mast, gave mortal offence, and was the cause of their subsequent wrath, so fatal to the dominion of the Swedes. Be this as it may, all authors agree, that the Swedes were driven out by an invincible, and sometimes invisible, foe,—that the moschettoes, in countless hosts, alike incomparable for activity and perseverance, obtained exclusive possession of the fort, and that the discomfited Swedes, bathed even in the ill-gotten blood of their enemies, were compelled to abandon the post, which, in honour of the victors, received the name of *Moschettoesburg*.

The Salem settlers were not the only Englishmen who endeavoured, at this time, to establish themselves in the vicinity of the Delaware. A colony seated under the patent of Lord Baltimore, was discovered on the Schuylkill, whence they were driven by the watchful Kieft, governor of New Netherlands, without difficulty. His instructions, dated 22d May, 1642, to Jan Jansen Alpendam, commandant of the expedition, strongly assert the right of the Dutch to the soil and trade there.

XVIII. The Swedish government anticipated, that, resistance might be made to their plans of colonization, by the Dutch West India Company, of whose pretensions to the shores of the Delaware, they were well instructed. Yet, Printz was authorized to protest against their claims, supported as they were, by the actual possession of Fort Nassau, now garrisoned by twenty men; and in case of hostile efforts on their part, to contend to the uttermost.

Printz conducted the affairs of New Sweden with due discretion, receiving the thanks and commendations of his sovereign, whose permission he solicited, in 1647, to return to Europe. He remained in America, however, until 1654, when he was succeeded in the government by John Papegoya, his son-in-law. Papegoya had come to the Delaware with the earliest Swedish settlers, probably in 1638; but had returned to Sweden about the time of Printz's departure. In 1643 he revisited New Sweden, bearing letters recommendatory, from the Queen, to the governor, whose daughter he subsequently married. He remained in the government two years; when embarking for Europe, he devolved the administration on John Risingh, who came out, a short time before this period, clothed with the authority of commissary

* "The Indians sometimes attended the religious assemblies of the Swedes; but with so little edification, that they expressed their amazement that one man should detain his tribe with such lengthened harangues, without offering to entertain them with brandy."—*Grahame's Col. Hist.* 2 vol. 200.

† Acrelius. ‡ Beschryvinge van Virginie. Smith's New Jersey.

and counsellor, and continued to preside over the Swedes until they were subjected by the Dutch. He renewed the treaties with the Indians; and at a convention held in 1664, both parties engaged to preserve and brighten the friendly chain. The engineer Lindstrom, who accompanied Risingh, minutely explored several portions of the country, constructed plans for some forts, aided in the fortification of others, and framed a map of the bay, river, and adjacent territory, remarkable for its correctnesss, and curious, as giving the Indian names of the streams. A descriptive memoir, highly interesting, accompanied the map.*

The country on the Delaware was, for some years, holden by the Swedes and Dutch, in common. To the forts at Nassau and the Hoarkills, the latter, in 1651, added Fort Casimer, at Sandhocken, the present site of New-castle.† This near approach to the primitive seat of their American domain, became intolerable to the Swedes. Printz remonstrated, and Risingh formally demanded, that Fort Casimer should be surrendered to him. This having been refused, he manfully resolved to seize it by force or fraud. He approached it in seeming amity, and after firing two complimentary salutes, landed thirty men, whom the garrison, unsuspectingly, admitted within their gates. The Swedes suddenly mastered the place, seized the effects of the West India Company, and even compelled some of the conquered soldiers to swear allegiance to Queen Christina. Not even Dutch phlegm would lie quiet under this grievous insult. The redoubted Stuyvesant, then governor of New York, though busily engaged in restraining the encroachments of his restless mercurial neighbours of Connecticut, resolved on instant and direful vengeance.

XIX. On the 9th September, 1654, he appeared in the Delaware, with seven vessels, carrying between six and seven hundred men. He descended first upon Elsinborg, where the patriotism of the Swedes had again led them, in despite of the moschettoes, and where it was their fate to become prisoners to the invaders. Next, he asailed the fort of the Holy Trinity, and having landed and intrenched his force, demanded its surrender, threatening, in case of refusal, the utmost extreme of military severity. Whether the fort were taken by storm, or surrendered upon capitulation, history has, with reprehensive carelessness, omitted to state: but certain it is, that the Dutch, also, became masters of the Holy Trinity, and striking the Swedish colours, gave from the towering flag-staff, those of the States-General, to the breeze. On the 16th, the fleet anchored in front of Fort Casimer, then commanded by Sven Scutz, or Schute, who, in reply to the summons, asked leave to consult his superior, Risingh; which being denied him, he yielded, upon most honourable terms; marching forth in military pomp, and retaining, not only the arms of his troops, but the battery of the fort. The stronger fortress of Christina was held by Risingh, in person; but even he, unable to resist the invincible Stuyvesant, submitted on the 25th of September; and the fall of New Gottenburg, with its fort, *Printzhoff*, and church, soon followed. Thus perished, never to be revived, the provincial power of New Sweden.‡

Stuyvesant issued a proclamation favourable to such of the Swedes as chose to remain under his government. About twenty swore fealty to the "States-General, the Lords, Directors of the West India Company, their subalterns of the province of New Netherlands, and the Director-General, then, and thereafter to be, established." Risingh and one Elfyth, a noted trader, were ordered to Gottenburg.§ Among those who remained, was the wife of Papegoya, to whom *Tennekong* had descended; and who, subse-

* MSS. Lib. of Am. Phil. Soc. † Campanius, Acrelius.
‡ Acrelius; Smith's N. Y.; Smith's N. J.; Dutch Records. § Smith's N. Y.

quently, sold it to Captain Carr, the English governor, from whom the purchase money, 300 guilders was recovered, by execution from the council at New York.* In March, 1656, the Swedish resident at the Hague, remonstrated against the conduct of the West India Company; but the United Provinces never gave redress. These wars of the Dutch and Swedes have been more minutely and worthily chronicled by the facetious and veracious Knickerbocker. We will add, only, that they appear to have been wholly unstained by blood, and admirably adapted to a country where restraint on population was not needed.

During the government of the Swedes, several vessels, other than we have mentioned, arrived from Sweden with adventurers, who devoted themselves to agriculture. The last ship, thus freighted, through the unskilfulness of her officers, entered the Raritan, instead of the Delaware, river, and was seized by Stuyvesant, then preparing for his campaign against Risingh. Many improvements were made by this industrious and temperate people, from Cape Henlopen to the falls of Alumningh, or Sanhikans. Beside the places we have already named, they founded *Upland* the present Chester, at *Mocoponaca; Korsholm* at *Passaiung;* Fort *Manaiung* at the mouth of the river, called by the Indians *Manaiung*, *Manaijunk*, *Manajaske*, *Nitabacong*, or *Matinacong;* by the Dutch, *Schuylkill*, and by the Swedes, *Skiarkillen* and *Landskillen;* marked the sites of *Nya Wasa* and *Gripsholm*, somewhere near the confluence of the Delaware and Schuylkill rivers, *Strawswijk* and *Nieu Causeland* or *Clauseland;* (the present Newcastle) and established forts, also, at *Kinsessing*, *Wicacoa*, (Southwark) *Findlant*, *Meulandael*, and *Lapananel*. On the eastern shore of the Delaware, they had settlements at Swedesborough, at the site of the present city of Burlington, and other places. Most of these stations are marked on the maps of Campanius and Lindstrom, and were, probably, little else than dwellings of farmers, with such slight defences, as might protect them from a sudden incursion of the natives. Gold and silver mines are said to have been discovered by the Swedes; and the latter are mentioned by Master Evelyn, in his description of the country, reported by Plantagenet, in his memoir on New Albion. The ores were probably pyrites, which have so often proven deceptive.†

* New York Records.

† We are assured by Lindstrom, that a silver mine existed on the eastern shore of the Delaware, in the vicinity of the falls; and that gold was found in considerable quantities higher up the river, on the Jersey side. "The shore before the mountain is covered with pyrites. When the roundest are broken, kernels are found as large as small peas, containing virgin silver. I have broken more than a hundred. A savage Unapois beholding a gold ring of the wife of governor Printz, demanded, why she carried such a trifle. The governor replied, 'if you will procure me such trifles, I will reward you with other things suitable for you.' 'I know,' said the Indian, a mountain filled with such metal.' 'Behold,' rejoined the governor, 'what I will give you for a specimen;' presenting to him at the same time, a fathom of red and a fathom of blue frize, some white lead, looking-glasses, bodkins, and needles, declaring that he would cause him to be accompanied by two of his soldiers. But the Indian, refusing this escort, said, that he would first go for a specimen, and, if it gave satisfaction, he might be sent back with some of the governor's people. He promised to give a specimen, kept the presents and went away; and, after some days, returned with a lump of ore as large as his doubled fist, of which the governor made proof, found it of good quality, and extracted from it a considerable quantity of gold, which he manufactured into rings and bracelets. He promised the Indian further presents if he would discover the situation of this mountain. The Indian consented, but demanded a delay of a few days, when he could spare more time. Content with this, Printz gave him more presents. The savage, having returned to his nation, boasted of his gifts, and declared the reason of their presentation. But he was assassinated by the sachem and his companions, lest he should betray the situation of this gold mine; they fearing its ruin if it were discovered by us. It is still unknown."—*Extract from Lindstrom's MS. Journal. Am. Phil. Soc.*

XX. The Dutch governed the newly recovered country on the Delaware, by lieutenants, subject to the Director-General at New Amsterdam. Johannes Paul Jaquet was the first Vice-Director. His successors were Peter Alricks, Hinojossa, and William Beekman. These officers were empowered to grant lands; and their patents make part of the titles of the present possessors. Alrick's commission, of 12th of April, 1657, indicates the extent of the Dutch claim, on the west of the Delaware. It constitutes him "Director-General, of the Colony of South river, of New Netherlands, and the fortress of Casimer, now called Niewer Amstel, with all the lands dependent thereon, according to the first purchase, and deed of release, from the natives, dated, July the 19th, 1651; beginning at the west side of the Minquas, or Christina Kill, in the Indian language named, *Suspecough*, to the mouth of the bay or river called Boompt Hook, in the Indian language, *Cannaress*, and so far inland, as the bounds and limits of the Minquas land, with all the streams, appurtenances and dependencies." Of the country north of the Kill, or south of Boompt Hook, no notice is taken. In 1658, Beekman was directed to purchase Cape Henlopen, which, for want of goods, was not done, until the succeeding year.* From the order and purchase of 1658, it would seem, that no regard was had, either by the Indians or Dutch, to the contracts made for Goodyn, in 1629, or by the Swedish governors.

Upon the eastern side of the present State of New Jersey, the Dutch had, at this period, acquired several tracts of country. Beside the purchase of Staten Island, for the Heer Pauw,† Augustine Herman purchased an extensive plot, stretching from Newark Bay, west of the present site of Elizabethtown;‡ and the Lord Director-General and Council, a large tract, called Bergen.§ And we may, justly, suppose, that, the road between the colonies, on the Hudson and Delaware, was not wholly uninhabited.

XXI. Although, for fifty years, these extensive possessions of the Dutch, were not disputed by the English government, still the claim of the English nation, founded on the discoveries by Cabot, Hudson, and other navigators, was neither abandoned nor unimproved. The Puritans were making continued pretensions and encroachments upon the east, and emigrants from New Haven settled on the left shores of the Delaware, so early as 1640—some of whose descendants may, probably, yet be found, in Salem, Cumberland, and Cape May, counties. The adventurers of Maryland had penetrated to the Schuylkill, and the agents or grantees of Sir Edward Ploeyden, had attempted to people his palatinate. Of these efforts it is proper that we should speak more particularly.

In 1642, as we have seen, the Dutch expelled the English, from the Schuylkill, as intruders, on rights too notorious to be disputed. But in 1654, Colonel Nathaniel Utie, commissioner of Fendal, governor of Maryland, demanded possession of the shores of the Delaware, by virtue of the patent from the English crown, to Lord Baltimore; visited New Castle to protest against the occupation of the Dutch, to threaten the assertion of Baltimore's right by force, and to offer his protection to the inhabitants, upon terms similar to those given to other emigrants. Beekman proposed to refer the controversy to the republics of England and Holland; and Stuyvesant, by commissioners, at Annapolis, repeated the proposition; asserting, however, the title of the India Company, by prior occupancy, and assent of the English nation; and protesting against the conduct of Fendal, as in breach of the

* Smith's New York.

† Deed, dated, 10th August, 1630. Elizabethtown Bill in Chancery.

‡ Deed, 6th December, 1651.

§ Deed, 30th January, 1658.

treaties between the two nations. In the following year, Lord Baltimore applied, through his agent, captain Neale, to the Dutch Company, for orders to the colonists on the Delaware, to submit to his authority. A peremptory refusal was instantly given; and a petty war in the colonies was prevented, by the weakness of Maryland, and the hopes of redress from measures then contemplated by the English government against all the Dutch possessions in America.*

We learn, from a pamphlet, published in 1648, that a grant had been made by James the First, to Sir Edward Ploeyden, of the greater part of the country between Maryland and New England, which was erected into a province and county palatine, with very comprehensive, if not precise boundaries.†

The rights derived from this patent were unexercised during the reigns of James, and the first Charles—but were acted on, during the revolution. Before 1648, a company was formed, under Sir Edward Ploeyden, for planting this province, in aid of which, our author wrote his description of New Albion. This little work compares New Albion with other countries of the new world, giving all preference to the former, and contains a learned exposition and defence of the rights of an earl palatine, who, among other royalties, having power to create barons, baronets, and knights, of his palatinate, had bestowed a baronage upon our author, and others, as well as upon each of his own children. Thus, there were, the son and heir apparent, and Governor, Francis, Lord Ploeyden, Baron of Mount Royal, an extensive manor, on Elk river; and Thomas, Lord Ploeyden, High Admiral, Baron of Roymount, a manor on the Delaware bay, in the vicinity of Lewistown; and the Lady Winifrid, Baroness of Uvedale, in Webb's Neck, deriving its name from its abundance of grapes, producing the Thoulouse, Muscat, and others.

From circumstances, it is probable, that this New Albion Company sent out agents, who visited different parts of the province, some of whom established themselves there; that the Palatine and some friends, of whom was Plantagenet, sought temporary cover from the storms of civil war in England, amid the American wilds;—that a fort named Erewomec was erected at the mouth of Pensaukin Creek, on the Jersey shore; and that, there was a considerable settlement at *Watcessi* or *Oijtsessing*, the present site of Salem, which was probably broken up, or reduced, by the united force of the Dutch and Swedes. No known vestige of these settlements remains; and all our knowledge in relation to their fate is conjectural.‡

XXII. In 1640, as stated by Trumbull, some persons at New Haven, by Captain Nathaniel Turner, their agent, purchased for *thirty pounds sterling*, a large tract of land, for plantations, on both sides of the Delaware river; erected trading houses, and sent out near fifty families to settle them.§ It is probable, that this number is over-rated. But we gather from the complaints of

* New York Records. New York Hist. Col. vol. iii. p. 368. Smith's New York.

† This pamphlet is addressed by Beauchamp Plantagenet, "To the Right Honourable and mighty Lord Edmund, by Divine Providence, Lord Proprietor, Earl Palatine, Governor, and Captain-General of the province of New Albion; and to the Right Honourable, the Lord Viscount Monson, of Castlemain; the Lord Sherard, Baron of Leitrim, and to all other, the Viscounts, Barons, Baronets, Knights, and gentlemen, merchants, adventurers, and planters, of the hopeful company of New Albion, in all forty-four undertakers, and subscribers, bound by indenture, to bring and settle 3000 able, trained men, in our several plantations, to the said province."

‡ New Albion. Smith's N. J. Bescryvinge van Virginie, New Netherlandts. Penn. Register, 1828, vol. iv. See, for a further account of New Albion, Appendix, note B, and Philadelphia Library, No. 1019, Oct.

§ Trumbull's Conn.

the Connecticut traders, that, they visited the Delaware for the purpose of barter, and were driven thence by the Swedes and Dutch, under Kieft, in 1642; that, their trading house was destroyed, their goods confiscated, and their persons imprisoned. The commissioners of the United Colonies of New England, upon an investigation of the facts, directed governor Winthrop to remonstrate with the Swedish governor, and to claim indemnity for the losses sustained, amounting to one thousand pounds. Winthrop addressed letters to Kieft and Printz, but received no satisfactory answer.

At an extraordinary meeting of the commissioners, in 1649, the court of New Haven, proposed the speedy planting of Delaware Bay. But this, as a general measure, was deemed inexpedient, and the New Haven merchants were left to improve or sell their lands as they should see cause. The treatment of these merchants, by the Dutch, formed part of the grievances submitted to the delegates appointed by Stuyvesant, and the United Colonies, in 1650; when the latter claimed a right to the Delaware under their patents, as well as by purchase from the Indians. These delegates, from want of sufficient light to determine the question, concluded to leave both parties at liberty to improve their interests upon that river.

Encouraged by this declaration, the inhabitants of New Haven and its vicinity, in the following year, fitted out a vessel with fifty adventurers, who proposed to establish themselves on the disputed lands. They put into New York; and the object of their voyage being made known, Stuyvesant, who was wanting, neither in ability, nor resolution, immediately seized the vessel, her papers, and crew, and extorted a promise from the last, to return to their homes; which they more readily gave as the Dutch governor threatened, that he would send to Holland, any of them whom he should find on the Delaware, and would resist their encroachments, in that quarter, even unto blood.

But, the colony of New Haven, with its characteristic pertinacity, was not disposed thus to abandon her pretensions. She brought the subject again before the commissioners of the United Colonies, in 1654, who addressed a missive to Stuyvesant, in which, the rights alleged by the Dutch, are very summarily disposed of, as "their own mistake, or at least, the error of them that informed them;" whilst, the claims of the people of New Haven, appeared "so clear, that they could not but assert their just title to their lands, and desire that they might peaceably enjoy the same." No effect was produced by this letter, and the colony of New Haven would have resorted to hostilities, could she have been assured of the protection of her sisters. But, they were deaf to her appeals, and the Plymouth colony shortly replied, "that they did not think it meet, to answer their desire in that behalf, and that they would have no hand in any such controversy." Thus deprived of all hope of effectual assistance, from their neighbours, the traders of New Haven were compelled to remain at peace. The country was soon after granted to the Duke of York, and their claims were too feebly sustained by justice, to brave the Duke's power.

But this, with other causes of dispute, had implanted in the colonists of New England, such animosity against their Dutch neighbours, that, in 1653, they formed the design to drive them from the continent, and applied to Oliver Cromwell for assistance. He, being then engaged in the two years' war with Holland, which the Parliament had commenced, promptly acceded to their request, by despatching a squadron to aid the colonial troops. The design was, however, arrested, by intelligence of the peace that had been concluded between the Protector and the States-General.* And it is remark-

* **Oldmixon i. 119. Chalmers 574. Trumbull i. 168. Hazard's Col. vol. ii. Grahames' Col. Hist. of North America.**

able, that the treaty has no direct reference to the possessions of either party in North America; but, stipulating for the restoration of peace, between the dominions of the two countries in every part of the world, and the English expedition being countermanded thereon, the validity of the Dutch claim to the country, it is supposed, was manifestly implied and practically acknowledged.* Yet, the New England men, succeeded in impressing different views upon Richard Cromwell; who, during his short protectorate, addressed instructions to his commanders, for the invasion of New Netherlands, and directed the concurrence of the forces of the English colonial governments, in the enterprise; but the subversion of his ephemeral power, prevented the execution of his orders.†

Charles II., however, from enmity to the States-General, certainly not from love of his transatlantic subjects, entered into their designs. His sentiments were enforced by the interest of the Duke of York, who had placed himself at the head of a new African company, with the view of extending and appropriating the slave trade, and which found its commerce impeded by the more successful traffic of the Dutch. Like the other courtiers, the Duke had cast his eyes, on the American territorities, which his brother was about to distribute with a liberal hand; and to other reasons, which he employed to promote a rupture with the Dutch, he solicited a grant of their North American possessions, on the prevailing plea, that they had been originally usurped from the territory, properly belonging to Britain.‡ The influence of these motives on the mind of the King, may have been aided by the desire to strike a blow that would enforce the arbitrary commission, he was preparing to send to New England, and to teach the Puritan colonists there, that he had power to subdue his enemies in America.

XXIII. Charles having failed in repeated attempts to provoke the resentment of the States-General, resolved to embrace the suggestion of his right to the province of New Netherlands. In pursuance of this purpose, a royal charter, dated 20th March, 1664, was executed in favour of the Duke of York, containing a grant of the whole region, extending from the western bank of the Connecticut river, to the eastern shore of the Delaware, together with the adjacency of Long Island, and conferring on his royal highness, all the powers of government, civil and military, within these ample boundaries. This grant disregarded alike, the possession of the Dutch and the recent charter of Connecticut, which, from ignorance or carelessness in the definition of boundaries, it wholly, but tacitly superseded.

As soon as the Duke had obtained this grant, and before investiture, he proceeded to exercise his proprietary powers in their fullest extent, by conveying to Lord Berkeley and Sir George Carteret, all that portion of the territory, which forms the present state of New Jersey. A military force, however, had been prepared to compel possession; and with some secrecy too, although this was scarce necessary, since the Dutch, so far from apprehending an attack, had, but a few months before, sent to their colony, a vessel laden with planters and the implements of husbandry.

XXIV. The command of the English troops in the expedition, and the government of the province against which it was directed, were given to Colonel Nicholls, who had studied the art of war under Marshal Turenne, and who, with George Cartwright, Sir Robert Carr, and Samuel Maverick, also, had a commission to visit the colonies of New England, and investigate

* Oldmixon i. 119. Chalmers 574. Trumbull i. 168. Hazard's Col. vol. ii. Grahame's Col. History of North America.

† Ib. ib. Thurloe's Collec. i. 721.

‡ Sir J. Dalrymple's Mem. ii. 4. Hume's England. Chalmers. Grahame, vol. ii. 214.

and determine, according to their discretion, all disputes and controversies within the various colonial jurisdictions. After touching at Boston, where an armed force was ordered to be raised and sent, to join the expedition, the fleet proceeded to the Hudson river, and anchored before the capital of New Netherlands. The requisition from Boston was so tardily obeyed, that the enterprise was over, before the Massachusetts troops were ready to march; but governor Winthrop of Connecticut, with several of the principal inhabitants of that province, immediately joined the King's standard.*

The armament, consisting of three ships, with one hundred and thirty guns and six hundred men, was too formidable to be resisted by a petty town, hastily and poorly fortified, and manned by peaceful burghers, or mere plodding planters. Yet the spirited governor was exceeding loth to surrender without, at least, having attempted its defence; although the favourable terms offered to the inhabitants disposed them to immediate capitulation. After a few days of fruitless negotiation, during which, Stuyvesant pleaded, in vain, the justice of the title of the States-General, and the peace existing between them and the English nation, the province was surrendered upon the most honourable terms to the vanquished, who preserved their arms, ammunition, and public stores, with leave to transport them, within twelve months, to Holland: the inhabitants were free to sell their estates and return to Europe, or retain them and reside in the province; such as remained, were to enjoy their ancient laws relative to the descent of property, liberty of conscience in divine worship, and church order, and perpetual exemption from military service; and what was yet more extraordinary, all Dutchmen continuing in the province, or afterwards resorting to it, were allowed free trade with Holland;† but this privilege being repugnant to the navigation act, was soon afterwards revoked. Notwithstanding these very advantageous conditions, the mortified commandant could not be brought to ratify them, for two days, after they had been signed by the commissioners.‡ Immediately afterwards, Fort Orange also surrendered. In honour of the Duke, the city of New Amsterdam received the name of New York, afterwards extended to the province, and Fort Orange, that of Albany. The greater part of the inhabitants submitted, cheerfully, to the new government; and governor Stuyvesant retained his property and closed his life, in his beloved city.

XXV. Sir Robert Carr, with two frigates, and the troops not required at New York, was sent to compel the submission of the colony on the Delaware; which he effected with the expenditure of two barrels of powder and twenty shot. By articles of agreement, signed Garret Saunders, Vautiell, Hans Block, Lucas Peterson, and Henry Cousturier, it was stipulated, "that the burgesses and planters submitting themselves to his Majesty, should be protected in person and estate; that, the present magistrates should continue in office; that permission should be given to depart the country, within six months, to any one; that all should enjoy liberty of conscience in church discipline, as formerly; and that any person taking the oath of allegiance, should become a free denizen, and enjoy the privilege of trade in his Majesty's dominions, as freely as any Englishman."§ From this separate convention, it would seem, that the capitulation of New York was not deemed conclusive upon the Delaware settlements; whose affairs were henceforth conducted, until 1768, by their ancient magistrates, under the supervision of Captain John Carr, aided by a council consisting of Hans Block, Israel Holme, Peter Rambo, Peter Cock, and Peter Aldrick, from whom an appeal lay to the governor and council of New York.||

* Trumbull i. 266. † Smith's N. J. Grahame's Col. Hist.
‡ August 27, 1664. § 1st October. || New York Records.

XXVI. Thus, by an act of flagrant injustice and tyranical usurpation, was overthrown the Dutch dominion in North America, after it had subsisted for more than half a century. The actual condition of their possessions was depreciated by Col. Nichols, in his letters to the Duke, from the humane view, it is supposed, of deterring his master from burdening or irritating the people, by fiscal impositions. Early travellers and writers unite in describing the Dutch colonial metropolis, so admirably chosen, as a handsome well built town; and Josselyn declares that the meanest house in it, was worth £100.* Indeed, the various provisions introduced into the articles of surrender, to preserve the comforts of the inhabitants, attest the orderly condition and plentiful estate they had acquired, and explain the causes of their unwarlike spirit. If their manners corresponded with those of their countrymen in the parent state, they were probably superior to those of their conquerors. Of the colonists, who had latterly resorted to the province, some had enjoyed affluence and respectability in Holland, and had imported with them, and displayed in their houses, costly services of family plate, and well selected productions of the Dutch school of painting.† No account has been preserved of the total population of the province and its dependencies; but the metropolis, at this time, is said to have contained about 3000 persons, of whom, one half returned to Holland. Their habitations, however, were soon occupied by emigrants, partly from Britain, but chiefly from New England. Upon the North river, throughout the present county of Bergen, Dutch settlers were numerous, and both shores of the Delaware were studded with plantations of Dutch and Swedes. Three Dutch families were settled at Lazy Point, opposite Mattinicunk Island, the site of Burlington, and four years later, one Peter Jegow, in 1668, (such was the intercourse between the two rivers) received license for, and kept a house of entertainment, for accommodation of passengers, travellers, and strangers, on this point of the Delaware.‡

The capture of New York and its dependencies, led to an European war, between Great Britain and Holland, ending in the treaty of Breda, of July, 1667. Happily, for the prosperity of the colony, which Nicholls, with the aid of the other English provinces, would have defended to the last extremity, neither the States-General, nor the Dutch West India Company, made any attempt to possess themselves of New York during this war; and at the peace, it was ceded to England, in exchange for her colony of Surinam, which had been conquered by the Dutch. This exchange was no otherwise expressed, than by a general stipulation in the treaty, that each nation should retain what it had acquired by arms, since the commencement of hostilities. The Dutch had no reason to regret this result, since they could not long have preserved New York against the increasing strength and rivalry of the inhabitants of New England, Maryland, and Virginia.§

Colonel Nicholls governed the province, for nearly three years, with great justice and good sense. He settled the boundaries with Connecticut; which, yielding all claim to Long Island, obtained great advantages on the main, pushing its line to Mamoroneck river, about thirty miles from New York—prescribed the mode of purchasing lands from the Indians, making the consent of the governor, and public registry, requisite to the validity of all contracts with them for the soil—and incorporated the city of New York, under a mayor, five aldermen, and a sheriff; and although he reserved to himself all judicial authority, his administration was so wise and impartial, that it enforced universal praise.

* Josselyn's Second Voyage, p. 154. Oldmixon i. 119.
† Grant's Memoirs of an American Lady, &c. vol. i. p. 11. Grahame's Col. Hist. vol. ii. 225. ‡ Elizabethtown Bill in Chancery. New Jersey Records.
§ Grahame's Col. Hist. vol. ii 231.

CHAPTER II.

Comprising Events from the Grant to the Duke of York, to the Division of the Colony, into East and West Jersey. I. Nature of the Estate acquired by the Duke of York, by the Grant from Charles I.—II. Motives and Nature of the Grant from the Duke of York, to Berkeley and Carteret.—III. Bounds of the Country ceded.—IV. Proceedings of the Proprietaries, to settle their Province of New Jersey, &c.—their " Concessions."—V. Remarks on the Constitution.—VI. Assumption of Government by Colonel Nicholls—Indian Grants.—VII. Philip Carteret appointed Governor—His Efforts for Colonization—Advantages enjoyed by the New Colonists.—VIII. Unhappy Effects of the Demand of Proprietary Quit Rents.—IX. Recapture of New Netherlands by Holland—and Restoration to the English.—X. Re-grant of the Province to the Duke—Re-grant to Berkeley and Carteret.—XI. Return of Philip Carteret to the Government—Modification of the Constitution.—XII. Oppressive Conduct of Andross, Governor of New York.—XIII. Division of the Province into East and West Jersey.

I. We have seen, in the preceding Chapter, that James, Duke of York, even before he had obtained seizin of his newly granted fief, had conveyed a considerable portion of it to Lord Berkeley and Sir George Carteret. The charter to the duke, though less ample in its endowments than those previously granted to the proprietaries of Maryland and Carolina, resembled them by conferring the powers of ***government*** on the grantee and ***his assigns.*** And thus, even with the light which had been stricken forth by the extraordinary political concussions of the passing century, the allegiance and obedience of freemen, were made transferable as if they were serfs attached to the soil. Nor was this proprietary right merely potential.—Instances in the history of the Carolinas, New Jersey, and Pennsylvania, demonstrate, that the proprietaries regarded their functions less as a trust, than as an absolute property; subject to every act of ownership, and in particular, to mortgage and alienation. It was not until after the British revolution of 1688, that the legality of this power was disputed; when the ministers of William III. maintained its repugnance to the laws of England, which recognised (an absurdity not less), a hereditary, but not a commercial transmission of office and power. The point was never determined by any formal adjudication; but, the evil in process of time, produced its own remedy. The succession and multiplication of proprietaries became so inconvenient to themselves, that, they found relief, in surrendering their functions to the crown. In Carolina and New Jersey the exercise of the right of assignation, materially, contributed to shorten the duration of the proprietary government.*

II. Berkeley and Carteret were already proprietaries of Carolina. Not satisfied with this ample investiture, nor yet certified by experience, of the tardy returns from colonial possessions, they had been induced, by the representations of a projector acquainted with the domain assigned to the Duke of York, to believe, that a particular portion of it would form a valuable acquisition to themselves. This person, we are assured by Colonel Nicholls, had been an unsuccessful applicant for the patent which the Duke had obtained, and revenged his disappointment by instigating these courtiers to

* Grahame's Col. Hist. vol. i. 315.

strip him of a most desirable portion of his territory.* But the claims which the grantees of the duke had upon the royal family, together with the political motives of colonization, may have been sufficient reasons for the grant of a newly acquired, and almost unexplored wilderness in America; and we incline to the opinion, which we think is confirmed by the promptitude with which it was made, after the title of the Duke had accrued, that, the transfer to Berkeley and Carteret was an understood consideration of the grant to the Duke. Both were favoured courtiers;—Berkeley was of the Privy Council, and Carteret, Treasurer of the Navy, and Vice Chamberlain of the royal household.†

III. The cession from the Duke was made by deeds of lease and release, dated, respectively, 23d and 24th June, 1664, and conveyed to the grantees, their heirs and assigns, in consideration of a competent sum, "That tract of "land adjacent to New England, lying westward of Long Island, and Man- "hattan Island; and bounded on the east, part by the main sea, and part by "Hudson's river; and hath upon the west, Delaware Bay, or river; and "extendeth southward to the main ocean, as far as Cape May, at the mouth of "Delaware Bay; and to the northward as far as the northernmost branch of "the said bay, or river Delaware, which is in 41° 40′ of latitude; and "crosses over, thence, in a straight line, to Hudson's river, in 41 degrees of "latitude; which said tract of land is hereafter to be called *Nova Cæsaria*, "or New Jersey." The name was given in compliment to Carteret, who had defended the island of Jersey against the long Parliament, in the civil war. But the powers of government, which had been expressly granted to the Duke, were not in terms conveyed, though it would seem, that both parties deemed them to have passed by the grant.

IV. The first care of the proprietaries was to invite inhabitants to their province; and their exertions for this purpose, though pursued with more eagerness than perseverance, were marked by political sagacity, and held forth those assurances of civil and religious rights which had proven so attractive in New England. They prepared a constitution which they published under the title of "The concessions and agreement of the Lords Proprietors of New Jersey, to and with all and every of the adventurers, and all such as shall settle and plant there."‡ We deem it our duty to give much in detail, the provisions of this instrument; since from it, have sprung, many of the existing institutions of the state.

It provided; 1. That the governor of the province should have power, when occasion required, to appoint a substitute, and to nominate a council, in number, not less than six, nor more than twelve, by whose advice he should govern:—2. That the proprietaries or governor should nominate a secretary or register, to record all public affairs, and all grants or leases for more than one year, of land, from the proprietor, or from man to man; the execution of which, should be acknowledged before the governor or a judge; and giving to such recorded grants, preference to other conveyances:—3. That

* The name of this individual was Scot. Whether it was he, or another with the same name, who afterwards published an account of East New Jersey, we are uncertain. Colonel Nichols acquits Berkeley and Carteret of a design to defraud the Duke. But Carteret did not always enjoy an unspotted reputation. In 1669 he was expelled the House of Commons for *confused accounts* as chamberlain.—*Grahame's Col. Hist. Smith's New Jersey.*

† Clarendon.

‡ The date of this instrument, as given in Scot's model of the province of East New Jersey, in Smith's History of New Jersey, and in Leaming and Spicer's Collection of State Papers, is 10th February, 1664. This date precedes not only that of the grant to Berkeley and Carteret, but, also, that of the grant to the Duke of York. The date is, therefore, erroneous, unless we suppose the instrument was prepared before the charter from the king

a surveyor-general, appointed in the same manner as the secretary, should survey the lands granted by the proprietary, and those of individuals when requested; certifying the same for record, to the register:—4. That all officers should swear (and record their oaths) to bear allegiance to the King, to be faithful to the proprietaries, and duly to discharge their respective trusts; persons subscribing a declaration to like effect *without oath*, being subject to the same punishment, as if they had sworn and broken their oaths:—5. That all subjects of the King of England, swearing allegiance to the King and faithfulness to the Lords, might become freemen of the province:—6. That no person so qualified, should, at any time, be in any way molested, punished, disquieted, or called in question for any difference in opinion or practice, in matters of religious concernment, who do not actually disturb the civil peace of the said province; but that all persons may freely and fully have and enjoy his and their judgments and consciences in matters of religion, they behaving themselves peaceably and quietly, and not using this liberty to licentiousness, nor to the civil injury or outward disturbance of others; any law, statute, or clause contained, or to be contained, usage or custom of the realm of England, to the contrary thereof, in anywise notwithstanding:—7. As a restraint upon the right of advowson, claimed by the proprietaries, under their grant, that the Assembly should have power to constitute and appoint such and so many ministers or preachers as they shall think fit, and to establish their maintenance, giving liberty beside, to any person or persons to keep and maintain what preachers or ministers they please.

The concessions further provided—8. That, the inhabitants being freemen, or chief agents to others, should immediately choose twelve representatives, to unite with the governor and council in making laws; but, so soon as the proper territorial divisions should be made, that the inhabitants or freeholders thereof, respectively, should, annually, elect representatives who, with the governor and council, should form the General Assembly of the province; the governor or his deputy being present, unless he refused, when the Assembly might appoint a president. The Assembly was to have power to meet and adjourn at pleasure, and to fix their quorum at not less than one-third of their number: to enact all necessary laws, as near as may be, conveniently agreeable to the laws and customs of England, and not against the interest of the Lords Proprietors, nor against these concessions, and particularly, not repugnant to the article for liberty of conscience; such laws to be in force for one year, unless contradicted by the Lords Proprietors; within which time to be presented to them for ratification, and being confirmed, to remain in force until expired by their own limitation, or be repealed: to constitute courts, and all that shall pertain to them: to levy taxes on goods or lands, except such of the latter as were unsettled, belonging to the Lords Proprietors: to erect manors, with their courts and jurisdictions, and to divide the province into such districts as they might think proper: to create ports, and harbours; build castles, incorporate cities, towns, and boroughs; create a military force; naturalize foreigners; and prescribe the quantity of land to be allotted, from time to time, to every head, free or servant, within the proportions granted by the "concessions:" to provide for the maintenance and support of the governor, the necessary charges of government, and the collection of the Lords' rents; and lastly, to enact all such other laws, as may be necessary for the prosperity and settlement of the province, conforming to the limitations expressed in the "concessions."

The governor and council were empowered—9. To see that all courts and officers performed their duties, and to punish infraction of the laws:

to nominate and commission the judges and other officers, according to the constitution of the General Assembly, appointing none but freeholders, except by assent of Assembly, and their commissions to revoke at pleasure: to have charge of all places of defence, and direction and officering of the military force, appointing none but freeholders without assent of the Assembly: to reprieve criminals until the pleasure of the Lords, who reserved the power to pardon, was known: to issue writs for supplying vacancies in the Assembly; and to grant warrants for land. They were required, *not to impose, nor suffer to be imposed, any tax upon the province or inhabitants, other than that imposed by the General Assembly:* to take care, that lands quietly held, seven years after survey by the surveyor-general, should not be subject to review by the proprietaries, or their agents.

And that the planting of the province might be the more speedily promoted, it was further provided—10. That, there should be granted to all persons who had already adventured, or should transport themselves or servants, before the 1st Jan. 1665, lands in the following proportions, viz. to every freeman, going with the first governor, armed with musket, ten pounds of powder and twenty pounds of bullets, with bandeliers and matches convenient, and with six months' provision, for his own person, arriving there, one hundred and fifty acres; and like quantity, for every able bodied servant, so armed, whether taken by the master, or sent thither, by him; and for every weaker servant, or *slave*, male or female, exceeding fourteen years, which any one should send or carry, arriving there, seventy-five acres; and to every Christian servant, exceeding such age, seventy-five acres, for his own use: to the master or mistress going before 1st January, 1665, one hundred and twenty acres, and like quantity for an able bodied male servant, taken with, or by, them; and for other servants or slaves, as above, sixty acres, with sixty acres for the servant's own use, when able, and forty-five acres when of the weaker class. Where the party emigrating arrived, from January 1666 to January 1667, armed and provided as aforesaid, he became entitled, for self and able servant, to sixty acres of land for each, and such servant to like quantity, and weaker servants or slaves, thirty acres each. All lands were to be taken up by warrant, from the governor, and confirmed, after survey, by the governor and council, under a seal to be provided for that purpose. All lands were to be divided by general lot, none less than two thousand one hundred, nor more than twenty-one thousand, acres, except cities, towns, &c., and the near lots of townships; and of such lots, towns, &c., one seventh, was reserved, by lot, for the proprietaries. Convenient portions of land were to be given, for highways and streets, not exceeding one hundred feet in breadth, in cities, towns and villages; for churches, forts, wharves, keys and harbours, and for public houses; and to each parish for the use of their minister, two hundred acres, in such place as the General Assembly might appoint. A penny, or half penny, per acre, according to the quality of the land, was reserved to the proprietaries, annually, as quit rent.

V. Such was the first constitution of New Jersey, almost as democratic as the one she enjoys; and certainly a greater safeguard of her liberties, since this was, truly, a constitution, an unalterable paramount law, prescribing and regulating the duties and powers, of the agents of the government, whether legislative, executive, or judicial; whilst all the provisions of the instrument of 1776, save three, are placed at the will of the legislature. What more was necessary, save the perpetuity of the laws, to assure to the people, all the blessings of political union? No laws were in force, save for one year, without the assent of the Lords Proprietors. But, laws which did not infringe their interests, would, commonly, receive their assent; and when it was refused, at the worst, the Assembly was compelled to re-enact such laws, annually. It was, indeed, a singular competition, which these proprietary governments produced, in which despotic sovereigns, and speculative legislators, were compelled, by interest, to vie with each other, in the production of models of liberty, and in offering to their subjects, the most effectual securities against arbitrary government. The competition was, the noble, though compulsory sacrifice to the great and divine principle, that man, in the aggregate, is competent to promote his own happiness.

VI. Upon the conquest of New Netherlands, Col. Nicholls assumed the administration of the whole territory, as governor for the Duke of York. While yet unacquainted with the grant to Berkeley and Carteret, he formed the design of colonizing the district which they had acquired; and for this purpose, granted licenses to various persons, to make purchases of lands from the aboriginal inhabitants; a measure, however wise in its conception, fraught, ultimately, with perplexing consequences to the Duke's grantees, by the creation of a pretence for an adverse title. Three small townships were speedily formed, in the eastern part of the territory, by emigrants, chiefly, from Long Island, who laid the foundation of Elizabethtown, Woodbridge, and Piscataway; and Nicholls, who entertained a very favourable opinion of this region, bestowed on it the name of Albania, in commemoration of one of the titles of his master.* It is uncertain, whether Middletown and Shrewsbury had not been previously settled by Dutch and English. About this time, however, many respectable farmers, comprising almost all the inhabitants from the west end of Long Island, removed to the neighbourhood of Middletown; and to Shrewsbury, there came many families from New England.†

* Smith's N. J. Grahame's Col. Hist.

† The petitioners for the Elizabethtown tract, 26th Sept. 1664, were John Bailey, Daniel Denton, Thomas Benydick, Nathaniel Denton, John Foster, and Luke Watson. The parties to the deed, from the Indians, dated 28th Oct. 1664, are *Mattano*, Manawarne, and Conascomon, of Staten Island, and John Bailey, Daniel Denton, and Luke Watson:—the tract conveyed, is described, as "one parcel of land, bounded on the south, by a river, commonly called the Raritan, and on the east, by the river which parts Staten Island and the main, and to run northward up Arthur Cull Bay, till we come to the first river, which sets westward out of the river aforesaid; and to run westward, into the country, twice the length that it is broad, from the north to the south, of the aforementioned bounds." The consideration given for this broad tract, was twenty fathom of trading cloth, two made coats, two guns, two kettles, ten bars of lead, twenty handfuls of powder, and four hundred fathoms of white, or two hundred of black, wampum, payable in one year from the day of entry, by the grantees, upon the lands. The whole valued at thirty-six pounds and fourteen shillings sterling. One of the grantors attests the conveyance, perhaps the first Indian grant made with technical form, by a mark opposite to his name. This, subsequently, became the common mode of signature; and the illiterate sons of the American forest, like the unlettered noble of the European feudal states, adopted as a sign manual, occasionally, the picture of a bird, or other object, that captivated his fancy. Mattano was the only grantor who signed, and his mark was ∿∿∿∿ or waved line; and, unfortunately for his business character, he had executed a deed, for the same lands, to Augustus Herman, already mentioned. The grant, however, is duly confirmed, probably, in entire ignorance of preceding events, by governor Nicholls.‡ The wampum was the current money of the Indian tribes, the precious material of which their ornaments were made, and the sacred sanction of their contracts, public and private. The name is derived from an Indian word, meaning *muscle*. It was called by the Dutch, *sewant*. It was worked from shells into the form of beads, and perforated, to string on leather. Six beads were formerly valued at a stiver, twenty stivers made a guilder, 6d. currency, or 4d. sterling. The white was fabricated from the inside of the great conchs, the black or purple, from the clam or muscle shell. Several strings, increased in number with the importance of the occasion, formed the belt of wampum. Before

‡ See Elizabethtown Bill in Chancery.

But the hope, which Nicholls had conceived, of rendering the district a valuable appendage of the Duke's possessions, was destroyed by intelligence of the grant to its new proprietaries. He remonstrated, with his master, on the impolicy of thus multiplying statistical divisions, and disjointing, from his own province, a portion distinguished for the fertility of its soil, the commodiousness of its rivers, and the richness of its minerals: and while he urged the Duke, to revoke a grant, so prejudicial to his interests, he predicted, truly, that the attempt of his grantees, to colonize the vacant territory, would disappoint their expectations of profit, and involve them in expenses, of which their remote posterity, only, could hope to gather the fruits.*

VII. Whatever effect this remonstrance may have had upon the Duke, it was too late to revoke the grant; and Nicholls was compelled to surrender the government of New Jersey, to Philip Carteret, who arrived with a company of thirty settlers, from England, and established themselves at Elizabethtown,† regarded as the capital of the infant province. At this period, however, there were only four houses here, and the name was given by him in honour of Lady Elizabeth Carteret.‡ Soon after his arrival, he despatched emissaries to New England, and other adjacent colonies, to make known the proprietaries' "concessions," and to invite settlers; whose efforts were attended with extraordinary success. Among those who came on this invitation, were the founders of Newark, who, in consequence of the inability of the governor, to pay the consideration required by the Indians, took, by his license, an Indian title, which was afterwards vexatiously set up against that of the proprietaries.

It was the happy peculiarity in the lot of these colonists, that establishing themselves in the vicinity of countries already cultivated, they escaped the disasters and privations which had afflicted so severely, the first inhabitants of most of the other provinces. Their neighbourhood to the commerce of New York was considered highly advantageous during the infancy of their settlement; though, in process of time, it was less favourably regarded, as preventing the rise of a domestic mart, which might give more effectual encouragement to their trade. Like the other colonists of North America, they enjoyed the advantage of transporting the arts, and habits of industry, from an old country, where they had been carried to high perfection, into a new land, which afforded them more liberal encouragement, and more unrestricted scope. Their exertions for raising cattle and grain were speedily and amply rewarded, by a grateful soil; and their friendly relations with the Indians enabled them to prosecute their labours, in undisturbed tranquillity, and to add to them a beneficial traffic, in peltry, with the roving tribes, by which the adjacent forests were inhabited. Their connexion with New York, also, gave them the advantage of the alliance, which subsisted between that colony, and the powerful confederacy of the Five Nations, whose influence extending to all the tribes of the new settlement, procured its inhabitants entire exemption from Indian war. Recommended by the salubrity of the climate, as by its many other advantages, it is not surprising that New Jersey was soon celebrated by the early writers, with higher commendations

the advent of the Europeans, the Indians made their strings and belts, of small pieces of wood, stained black or white. For want of proper tools, few were made of shells, though highly valued. But the Europeans soon manufactured them of the latter material, neatly and abundantly. The value of this Indian money, was raised by proclamation, in 1673, from the governor and council of New York, commanding that, "instead of eight white and four black, six white and three black, should pass for a stiver, and three times so much, the value in silver.—*New York Records.*

* Grahame's Col. Hist. † August, 1665. ‡ Elizabethtown Bill.

than any other of the colonies. The proprietaries, stimulated by the hope of a rich revenue, industriously proclaimed its advantages in Europe and America, and, from time to time, despatched from England, vessels freighted with settlers, and stores, to reinforce the numbers, and supply the wants of their people.

VIII. But the period to which they had looked, for the fruition of their hopes, demonstrated their fallacy; and the peace of the province was unhappily interrupted by the arrival of the day fixed for the payment of the proprietary quit rents. The first demand of this tribute excited universal disgust among the colonists, who expressed greater unwillingness, than inability, to comply with it. A party among them, including the few settlers who had seated themselves under the authority of Colonel Nicholls, refused to acknowledge the title of the proprietaries, and in opposition to it, set up the Indian title, which we have already noticed, and also, the right of government within the tract, thus conveyed to them. And the better to support this pretence, they prevailed on James Carteret, a weak and dissolute natural son of Sir George, to assume the government, as by their election, and under an alleged proprietary title, which, he asserted, he was not obliged to show.* For two years, the governor, Philip Carteret, maintained an ineffectual struggle, to enforce the claims of his employers; until, at length, the popular discontent broke forth into insurrection—his officers were imprisoned, their estates confiscated—and he was compelled to fly from the province, and to seek redress in England, leaving John Berry, as deputy Governor, and James Bollen, Secretary of the Province.† His return, with strengthened authority, was retarded by the unexpected events of the following year, when New York, being reconquered by Holland, New Jersey was again united to the province of New Netherlands.

IX. The second war with Holland, most wantonly and unjustly provoked by the dissolute Charles, in subserviency to the ambition of Louis XIV., was declared, March 17th, 1672. A small squadron despatched from Holland, under the command of Binkes and Evertzen, to destroy the commerce of the English colonies, having performed that service, with great effect on the Virginia coast, was induced to attempt a more important enterprise, by intelligence of the negligent security of the Governor of New York. The Dutch had the good fortune to arrive before this, their ancient seat, while Lovelace, the Governor, was absent, and the command was exercised by Captain Manning, who, by his own subsequent avowal, and the more credible testimony of his conduct, was a traitor and a coward. Now was reversed the scene, which had been presented on the invasion by Nicholls. The English inhabitants prepared to defend themselves, and offered their assistance to Manning; but he obstructed their preparations, rejected their aid, and on the first intelligence of the enemy's approach, struck his flag, even before their vessels were in sight. As the fleet advanced, the garrison demonstrated their readiness to fight, but in a transport of fear, he forbade a gun to be fired, under pain of death, and surrendered the place, unconditionally, to the invaders. After this extraordinary and unaccountable conduct, Manning had the impudence to repair to England, whence, he returned, in the following year, after the province had been given up, by the Dutch. He was tried, by a court martial, on a charge of treachery and cowardice, expressed in the most revolting terms; which, confessing to be true, he received a sentence almost as extraordinary as his conduct;—"that, though he deserved death, yet, because he had, since the surrender, been in England, and ***seen the King and the Duke***, it was adjudged that his sword should be

* 1670. † 1672.

broken over his head, in public, before the city hall; and himself rendered incapable of wearing a sword, and of serving his majesty for the future, in any public trust."* The old maxim, that, grace was dispensed by the mere look of a king, was respected on this occasion. The Dutch commanders, in their triumph, imitated the moderation and prudence of Nicholls; and assuring the citizens of their rights and possessions, gratified the Dutch colonists, and left the English cause of complaint, only against their pusillanimous commander. Like moderation being tendered to the other districts of the province, on condition of sending deputies, to swear allegiance to the States-General, induced the whole to submit.† The Dutch dominion was restored more suddenly than it had been overthrown, and the name of New Netherlands was once more revived—but was not destined to long endurance.

Great consternation prevailed in the adjoining English colonies. The government of Connecticut, with apparent simplicity, that ludicrously contrasts with the ordinary astutia of her people, sent a deputation to the Dutch admirals, to remonstrate against their usurpation of dominion, over the territory of England, and the property of her subjects; to desire them to explain the meaning of their conduct, and their further intentions, and to warn them, that the united colonies of New England, entrusted with the defence of their sovereign dominions, in America, would be faithful to their trust. The Dutch commanders, as they well might, expressed surprise at the terms of this message, but declared, that commissioned by their country, to assail her enemies, whilst they applauded the fidelity of the English, to their sovereign, they would imitate the good example, and endeavour to prove equally faithful to the States-General. Active preparations for war, were, forthwith, made by Connecticut, and the confederate colonies; but, as each party stood on the defensive, only a few insignificant skirmishes took place, before winter suspended military operations. Early in the following spring, the controversy was terminated, without further bloodshed, by the treaty of peace, concluded at London, and the restoration of New York, to the English.‡

X. Doubts had been raised, as to the validity of the Duke of York's title, because granted whilst the Dutch were in full and peaceful possession of the country; and which, though originally good, seemed to have been impaired by the subsequent conquest. The Duke deemed it prudent to remedy this defect, and to signalize the resumption of his proprietary functions, by a new patent. Another cause, however, may have contributed to this measure.—He probably, supposed, that it would afford him an opportunity of dispensing with his grant, to Berkeley and Carteret. It was pretended, that the Dutch conquest, had extinguished the proprietary rights, and that the country had been acquired, *de novo*, to the crown. A new charter recited the former grant, and confirmed to him the whole which that had covered. The misfortune, and evident incapacity of Lovelace, precluded his re-appointment to the office of governor, which was conferred on Edmund Andross, who disgraced his superior talents, by the unprincipled zeal and activity, with which he devoted them to the arbitrary designs of his master.

In him, and his council, were vested all the functions of government, legislative and executive, and their power was extended over New Jersey. It seems, however, that the Duke wanted either resolution or authority, to effectuate his iniquitous intentions; for, on the application of Sir George Carteret, he promised the renewal of his charter, which, after some delay and hesitation, he performed. Previous to this second grant, it would seem, that

* Smith's New York. † July, 1673. ‡ 28th February, 1674.

Lord Berkeley and Sir George Carteret, had agreed upon a partition of the province, since the country described therein, was bounded, on the south-west, by a line drawn from Barnagat Creek to the Rancocus. But, though he finally consented to restore New Jersey, he endeavoured to evade the full performance of his engagement, pretending to have reserved certain rights of sovereignty over it, which Andross seized every opportunity of asserting.

XI. In the commencement of the year 1675, Philip Carteret returned to New Jersey, and resumed the government of the settlements, in the eastern part of the province. The inhabitants, who had experienced the rigours of conquest, and the arbitrary rule of Andross, readily received him; and as he postponed the payment of their quit rents, to a future day, and published a new set of "*concessions*," by Sir George Carteret, a peaceable subordination was once more established in the colony. These new "concessions," however, restricted the broad grant of political freedom, originally framed, by giving to the governor and council, the power of naturalization, the right to approve such ministers as might be chosen by the several corporations, and to establish their maintenance; granting liberty, however, to all persons, to keep and maintain what preachers they pleased. They authorized the governor, also, to appoint the times and places of meeting of the General Assembly, and to adjourn them at pleasure, and to separate the counsellors and delegates into two chambers.*

XII. Yet, the only disquiet, during several years, arose from the efforts of Andross, from time to time, to enforce the unjust pretensions of the Duke. Governor Carteret, in hope of procuring to his people, a share of the advantages, which the neighbouring colony derived from her commerce, attempted to establish a direct trade between England and New Jersey. But Andross earnestly opposed this proper measure, as one injurious to New York; and by confiscating vessels engaged in such trade, extinguished the New Jersey commercial enterprise in its infancy. In addition to this outrage, he endeavoured, by various exactions, to render the colonists tributary to his government; and even had the insolence, by a force despatched to Elizabethtown, to arrest governor Carteret, and convey him prisoner to New York. When complaints of these proceedings were made to the Duke, he evinced the same indecision and duplicity, that had characterized all his recent conduct. He could not, he said, consent to depart from a prerogative which had always belonged to him; yet, he directed the relaxation of its exercise, as a matter of favour to his friend, Sir George Carteret.† But the province had now been divided into two proprietary jurisdictions; and it was in the western part, where Carteret had ceased to have an interest, that the Duke most exercised his prerogative. The circumstances which attended this partition, are not the least interesting of the provincial history of the state.

* Leaming and Spicer's Col.

† Douglas ii. 272. S. Smith 68, 77. Chalmers, 616, 618. Smith's N. Y. 45. Grahame's Col. Hist.

CHAPTER III.

From the Division of the Province, into East and West Jersey, to the Purchase of East Jersey, by Quakers.

I. Motives of the Quakers for Emigration.—II. Sale of Lord Berkeley, to Byllinge and Fenwicke.—III. Assignment of West Jersey to William Penn, and others in Trust, for the Creditors of Byllinge.—IV. "Concessions," or Constitution of West Jersey.—V. Measures of the Proprietaries to promote Colonization.—VI. Commissioners appointed to Administer the Government of West Jersey—their Proceedings.—VII. Increase of Emigrants—Success of their Efforts.—VIII. Death of Sir George Carteret—Successful Efforts of the Colonists, to procure Relief, from the Jurisdiction of New York.—IX. Extraordinary Pretensions of Byllinge.—X. Resisted by the Proprietaries, in General Assembly—Samuel Jennings elected Governor—Proceeds to England, as Deputy of the Assembly—The Right of Government, purchased by Doctor Daniel Coxe, and subsequently transferred to the West Jersey Society.—XII. Meeting of the First Assembly—Proceedings.—XIII. Modification of the Law, relating to Religious Faith.—XIV. Death of Carteret—his Disposition of East Jersey.—XV. Troubles at the Close of the Administration of Philip Carteret.—XVI. Review of the Policy of the Proprietary Governments.—XVII. Comparison between the Laws of East and West Jersey.

I. Soon after the restoration of Charles II., the Quakers became objects of suspicion and dread, to his government, from a mistaken supposition, that, like the ***Fifth Monarchy men***, or ***Millenarians***, they held themselves entitled to overthrow, even by force, every temporal authority, which obstructed the advent of their cherished spiritual dominion. This suspicion was increased by the insurrection of the Millenarians, in the first year of the restored monarchy; and the refusal of the Quakers to give assurance of fidelity to the king, by taking the oath of allegiance. In consequence of this error, they were assailed with a rigour and reality of persecution, which hitherto they had never experienced, in England. They were, first, included with the Millenarians, in a royal proclamation, forbidding either, to assemble under pretence of worship, elsewhere, than in the parochial churches; but were soon afterwards, distinguished by the provisions of an act of parliament, that applied exclusively to themselves.* This statute enacted, that all Quakers refusing to take the oath of allegiance, and assembling to the number of five persons, above sixteen years of age, should, for the first and second offences, incur the penalty of fine, and imprisonment; and for the third, should either abjure the realm, or be transported beyond it. Nay, so cordial was the dislike entertained by the court, against them, that, instead of using their complaints as cause of quarrel, with the obnoxious province of Massachusetts, the enmity in this province against the Quakers, was sustained: and the authorities there, were invited to a repetition of the severities, which had been, at one time, prohibited. "We cannot be understood," said the king's letter of 1662, after urging general toleration, "hereby, to direct or wish, that any indulgence should be granted to Quakers, whose principles, being inconsistent with any kind of government, we have found it necessary, with the advice of our parliament here, to make a sharp law against them; and are well content, that you do the like, there."

These unfavourable and erroneous sentiments, it is true, were shortly after exchanged by the king, for a more just estimate of Quaker principles. But, the alteration in his sentiments, produced no relaxation of the legal

* Grahame's Col. Hist. vol. ii. p. 332.

severities to which the Quakers were subjected; and was attended with no other consequence, than a familiar and apparently confidential intercourse, between him, and some of their more eminent leaders, together with many expressions of regard and good will, on his part, which he was unwilling or unable to substantiate. In the persecution, now commenced against all classes of dissenters, the Quakers were exposed to a more than equal share of severity, from the unbending zeal, with which they refused to conform, even in appearance, to any one of the obnoxious requisitions, and the eagerness with which they seized every opportunity of manifesting their forbidden practices, and signifying their peculiar gifts of patient suffering, and untiring perseverance. In every part of England, they were harassed with fine and imprisonment, and great numbers were transported to Barbadoes, and to the American settlements;* where, they formed a valuable addition to the English population, and quickly discovered, that their persecutors, in expelling them from their native land, had, unconsciously, contributed to ameliorate their condition. Instead of the wild enthusiasts who had rushed with headlong zeal to New England, in quest of persecution, there was now introduced into America, a numerous body, of wiser and milder, professors of Quakerism, whose views were confined to the enjoyment of that liberty of worship, for the sake of which, they had been driven into exile.

In several of the American provinces, as in the island of Barbadoes, they experienced full toleration, and friendly reception from the governments, and inhabitants; and, even in those provinces, where they were still objects of suspicion and severity, they rendered their principles less unpopular, by demonstrating with what useful industry, and peaceful virtue, they might be combined. Contented with the toleration of their worship, and diligently improving the advantages of their new lot, many of the exiles obtained, in a few years, to plentiful and prosperous estates: and so willing were they to reconcile their tenets, with existing institutions of the countries, in which they were established, that they united in the purchase and employment of negro slaves. Perhaps, the deceitfulness of the human heart, was never more strikingly exhibited, than in this monstrous association of the characters of exiles, for conscience sake, and the principles of universal peace and philanthropy, with the condition of slave owners and the exercise of arbitrary power. Yet, in process of time, much good was educed from this evil; and the inconsistency of one generation of Quakers, enabled their successors, to exhibit to the world, a memorable example of disinterested regard, for the rights of human nature, and a magnanimous sacrifice to the requirements of piety and justice.†

The principles of the sect continued, meanwhile, to propagate themselves, in Britain, to an extent, that more than supplied the losses occasioned by the banishment of their professors. Almost all the other sects had suffered an abatement of piety and reputation, from the furious disputes, and vindictive struggles, that attended the civil wars; and while the Quakers were exempted from this reproach, they were no less advantageously distinguished, by a severity of persecution, which enabled them to display, in an eminent degree, the primitive graces of Christian character. It was, now, that their cause was espoused, and their doctrines defended, by writers, who yielded to none of their contemporaries, in learning, eloquence, or ingenuity, and who have not been equalled, nor even approached, by any succeeding Quaker authors. The doctrines that had floated, loosely, through the

* In one vessel alone, which was despatched from England, in March, 1664, sixty Quaker convicts, were shipped, for America.—*Williamson's North Carolina*, i. 82.

† Grahame's Col. Hist.

Quaker society, were collected and reduced to an orderly system; the discipline necessary to preserve from anarchy, and restrain the fantastic sallies, which the genuine principle of Quakerism, is peculiarly apt to beget, was explained and enforced;* and in the midst of a persecution that drove many of the Presbyterians of Scotland to despair and rebellion, the Quakers began to add to their zeal and resolution, that mildness of address and tranquil propriety of thought, by which they are universally characterized. Yet, it was long before the wild and enthusiastic spirit, which had distinguished the rise of the society, was banished entirely from its bosom; and while it continued, a considerable diversity of sentiment and language, prevailed among the brethren. This diversity was manifest, particularly, in the sentiments entertained relative to the duty of confronting persecution. While all considered it unlawful to forsake their ordinances, on account of the prohibition of their oppressors, many held it, a dereliction of duty, to abandon their country, for the sake of their enjoyment in a foreign land. Considering Quakerism as a revival of primitive Christianity, and themselves as fated to repeat the fortunes of the first Christians, and to gain the victory over the world, by evincing the fortitude of martyrs, they had associated the success of their cause with the infliction and endurance of persecution, and deemed retreat, to be flight from the contest between truth and error. The promulgation, rather than the toleration, of their principles, seemed their great object; and their success was incomplete, without the downfall of the established hierarchy. But others of more moderate temper, though willing to sustain the character of the primitive Christian, believed it not inconsistent with the exercise of that liberty, expressly given to the apostles, when persecuted in one city, to flee to another. Disturbed in their religious assemblies, harassed and impoverished by fines and imprisonments, and withal, continually exposed to violent removal from their native land, they were led to meditate the advantages of voluntary expatriation with their families and substance; and, naturally, to cast their eyes on that country, which, notwithstanding the severities once inflicted on their brethren, in some of its provinces, had always presented an asylum to the victims of persecution. Their regards were further directed to this quarter, by the number of their fellow sectaries, who were now established in several of the North American states, and the freedom, comfort, and tranquillity, which they were there enabled to enjoy.†

II. Such was the situation of the Quakers when Lord Berkeley, alarmed by the insubordination of the planters of New Jersey, and dissatisfied with the pecuniary prospects of his adventure in colonization, offered his share of his province for sale. He soon received the offer of a price, that was satisfactory, from two English Quakers, John Fenwicke and Edward Byllinge; and on the 18th March, 1673, in consideration of one thousand pounds, conveyed his interest in the province, to the first, in trust for the other. A dispute arising between these parties, respecting their proportions of interest; to avoid the scandal of a law suit, it was submitted to William Penn, who now held a conspicuous place in the society of Friends. With some difficulty, he succeeded in making an award satisfactory to both parties. Fenwicke, in 1675, sailed from London, for the new purchase, in the ship Grif-

* See Appendix, C.

† Gough and Sewell's History of the Quakers, vol. i. chap. 2, 4, 6, 7 and 8, vol. ii. chap. 4. Neal's History of the Puritans, vol. iv. Grahame's Col. Hist. From the last work I have drawn, principally, the preceding view of the Quaker motives for emigration. It has, however, suffered such modification, in my hands, as to render me responsible for it.

fith, with his family and several Quaker associates.* This was the first English vessel that came to New Jersey with emigrants. After a prosperous voyage, she landed her freight, at a rich and pleasant spot on a branch of the Delaware, to which Fenwicke, on account, probably, of its peaceable aspect, gave the name of Salem.

III. Further, immediate, efforts, at colonization, were prevented by the commercial embarrassments of Byllinge, who had sustained such losses, in trade, as rendered it necessary for him to assign his property for the indemnification of his creditors, with a resulting trust, in whatever balance there might be, for himself. Penn, unwillingly, at the solicitation of some of the creditors, became joint assignee, with Gawn Lawrie and Nicholas Lucas, (Quakers and creditors) of Byllinge's interest, in New Jersey. These trustees, under the pressure of circumstances, sold a considerable number of shares, of the undivided moiety, to different purchasers, who, thereby, became proprietaries, in common, with them.

IV. As all men, when, now, emigrating to America, sought, not only religious and civil freedom, but, also, the security which these could receive in the form of permanent records or constitutions, the proprietaries of West New Jersey, published their "*concessions*," comprising many of the provisions of the instrument formed by Berkeley and Carteret, together with others, originating with themselves. The management of the estate and affairs of the province, was committed to the commissioners, appointed by the proprietaries, with power to divide and sell the lands, to lay out towns, and, generally, to govern the province according to the "concessions," until March, 1680; at which time, and thence, annually, ten commissioners were to be elected by the people, until a General Assembly should be chosen. The territory was to be divided into one hundred lots, or proprietaries, ten of which, to be assigned to Fenwicke, and the remainder to the assignees of Byllinge; and the hundred proprietaries were to be divided into ten divisions or tribes, and the *inhabitants* of each, were empowered to elect a commissioner; and, for the avoidance of "noise and confusion, all elections were directed to be by ballot. Lands were given to settlers upon principles analogous to those adopted in the concessions of Berkeley and Carteret.

The instrument then sets forth, the charter or fundamental laws, and declares, that, they shall be the foundation of the government, not to be altered by the legislative authority: that every member of the Assembly, who shall, designedly, wilfully, and maliciously move any thing subversive of such constitution, on proof, by *seven* honest and reputable persons, shall be proceeded against, as a traitor to the government: that, such constitution should be recorded, in a fair table, at the Assembly house, and read at the commencement and dissolution of every Assembly, and be, also, written in fair tables in every common hall of justice, and read, in solemn manner, four times every year, in presence of the people, by the magistrates: that, as no men, nor number of men, upon earth, had power to rule over men's consciences, no one should, at any time, be called in question, or hurt in person, privilege, or estate, for the sake of his opinion, judgment, faith, or worship, towards God, in matters of religion: that, no inhabitant should be deprived of life, limb, liberty, privilege, or estate, without due trial and judgment, passed by twelve good and lawful men of his neighbourhood; and in *all trials*, the

* There came passengers, with Fenwicke, Edward Champness, Edward Wade, Samuel Wade, John Smith and wife, Samuel Nicholls, Richard Guy, Richard Noble, Richard Hancock, John Pledger, Hypolite Lefever, and John Matlock. These, and others with them, were masters of families. Among the servants of Fenwicke, were John Adams and Samuel Hedge, who, subsequently, married his daughters.—*Smith's N. J.* 79.

accused might peremptory challenge thirty-five jurors, and for cause shown, the whole array: that, in civil cases, no inhabitant of the province should be arrested, until after summons and default of appearance; and imprisonment for debt, on surrender of the property of the debtor was prohibited: that, every court should consist of three justices or commissioners, who, sitting with the jury, should assist them in matters of law, but should pronounce such judgment, only, as the jury should give; to whom, only, the right of judgment belonged, in all causes civil and criminal; and should the commissioners refuse, then judgment to be pronounced by one of the jury: that, in all causes, civil and criminal, proof should be made by "the solemn and plain averment" of, at least, two honest and reputable persons; and perjury, in civil causes, was punishable by the penalty the one witnessed against might suffer, and in criminal cases, by fine, disqualification from giving evidence, and from holding office: that, in criminal cases, not felonious, the injured party might compound the offence before, or remit the penalty after, judgment: that, theft should be punished, by twofold restitution, and for lack of means, by the labour of the offender, until such restitution should be made, or as twelve men of the neighbourhood should determine, not extending to life or limb; and that breach of the peace, should be punished according to the nature of the offence, at the discretion of twelve men of the neighbourhood, appointed by the commissioners.

Much providence was displayed in the care of the estates of decedents. Wills were to be registered, and inventories filed, and security given, by executors, before administration. In case of intestacy, like provision was made in regard to administrators; and to secure two parts of the estate, for the children, and one-third to the wife; and if there were no child, half to the next of kin, and half to the wife: and guardians were appointed, of the persons and estates, by the commissioners. Where parents died, leaving children and no estates, the commissioners were to "appoint persons to take care for the children, to bring them up at the charge of the public stock of the province, or a tax to be levied by twelve men of the neighbourhood. No forfeiture was incurred, by suicide, or by way of deodand; and in cases of murder and treason, the sentence, and way of execution thereof, was left to the General Assembly to determine, as they, in the wisdom of the Lord, should judge meet.

As soon as the divisions or tribes, or such like distinctions should be made, the inhabitants, on the first of October, yearly, were to elect one proprietor or freeholder, for each proprietary, "to be deputies, trustees, or representatives, for the benefit, service, and behoof of the people; and whose number was a hundred, corresponding to the number of the proprietaries. Provision was made for the purity of elections, which were not to be determined by the common and confused way of cries and voices; but by putting balls in balloting boxes, for the prevention of all partiality, and whereby every man might freely choose, according to his own judgment and honest intention. This supreme legislature was empowered, to meet and adjourn within the year, at pleasure; to fix the quorum for business, at not less than one-half of the whole, and the votes of two-thirds of the quorum were required for determination. The question frequently agitated, relative to the obligation of the representative, to obey the instructions of his constituents, was, here, fully decided. He was holden, justly, to be their deputy or agent; and they were required, at his election, to give him their instructions at large, and he, to enter into indenture, under hand and seal, covenanting and obliging himself, in that capacity, to do nothing, but what should tend to the fit service and behoof of those that sent and employed him; and on failure of trust, or breach of covenant, he might be questioned in that or the next

Assembly, by any of his electors: And further, each member was allowed one shilling, per day, payable by his constituents, not in compensation of his services, but that he might be known, as the servant of the people. The Assembly was, also, authorized, to constitute and appoint, ten commissioners of estate, for managing the affairs of the province, during the adjournments, and dissolution of the General Assembly: To enact all laws for the well-government of the province: To constitute all courts, together with the limits, power and jurisdiction thereof: To appoint the judges for such time as they may deem meet, not more than two years, their salaries, fees, and appellations: To appoint commissioners of the public seals, treasurers, and chief-justices, embassadors, and collectors. But the justices of the peace, and constables, were to be chosen by the people.*

The faults of this system of government are radical and glaring. A many-headed executive, possessing a temporary, and reflected portion only, of political power, necessarily engendered jealousy, division and favouritism; and distracted councils, produced contempt and disobedience. The legislature, composed of one house, was exposed to the evils of precipitation: and choosing from itself the executive, and the greater proportion of the officers of the commonwealth, to intrigue and corruption. Courts, without permanent judges—with juries, determining, in all cases, the law, as well as the fact, would disregard the established rules of jurisprudence, and produce uncertainty in the administration of justice; whilst the limited tenure of office, made incumbents unskilful and rapacious. Yet, this instrument contained many excellencies, and revealed principles of political science, which the enlightened philosophy of the present age, has not yet fully developed. Thus, the most entire liberty of conscience, was established; and the political power was emphatically in the people, who were absolutely free to pursue their own happiness;—the right of suffrage was universal—the personal liberty of the citizen was cherished, and the barbarism of imprisonment for debt, whether upon initiatory or final process, was abolished. The punishment of crimes, had in view, the reparation of injury, rather than the infliction of vengeance; and in no instance, did it extend to the loss of life or limb. The evidences of property were secured by registering offices;—and rules for the treatment of the aborigines, were framed upon principles of justice and humanity. The love of the proprietaries, for civil and religious freedom, and democratic rule so thoroughly established in the Quaker societies, was certainly conspicuous in their concessions, and had they possessed as much experience, as zeal, they would, probably, have framed a finished system.

V. With the publication of this instrument, the proprietaries gave a special recommendation of the province, to the members of their own religious fraternity, which produced an immediate display of that diversity of sentiment, which had begun to prevail in the society. Many, with lively expectations of future happiness, prepared to embark for the New Utopia; whilst others regarded with jealousy, and vehemently opposed, a secession, which they deemed pusillanimous. To moderate the expectations of the one, and appease the jealousy of the other, of these parties, William Penn, and his colleagues, addressed a circular letter, to "Friends," solemnly cautioning them, against leaving their country, from a timid reluctance to bear testimony to their principles, from an impatient, unsettled temper, or from any motive inferior, to a deliberate conviction, that the God of all the earth, opened their way, and sanctioned their removal. And admonishing them, to remember, that, although Quaker principles were established, in the province, only Quaker safeguards could be interposed for their protection; and

* See Appendix, D.

that, religious toleration must depend for its continuance, on the aid of the Being, with whose will they believe it to concur, and could never be defended by force, against the arm of the oppressor. To this admonitory letter, there was annexed, "A Description of West New Jersey," correcting some trivial exaggerations, which had been bruited abroad, of the excellence of the soil, and climate; but conveying, in the main, a most inviting representation of the country. This neither did, nor was intended, to repress the ardour of Quaker emigration. Numerous purchases of colonial land, were made by Quakers, in various parts of England; and in the course of the year 1677, upwards of four hundred persons of this persuasion, transported themselves to West New Jersey; many of whom, were persons of property and respectability, who carried with them, their children and servants.

The first care of the assignees of Byllinge, was to make a partition of the province, between them and Sir George Carteret, which was effected by a deed, quintipartite,* comprehending, Sir George, William Penn, Gawn Lawrie, of London, merchant, Nicholas Lucas, of Hertford, malster, and Edward Byllinge, of Westminster; directing a straight line to be drawn through the province, from north to south, from the most southerly point of the east side of Little Egg Harbour, to the most northerly point, or boundary on the Delaware. To the portions thus separated, were given the names of East and West Jersey, respectively.†

Soon after,‡ letters were addressed by the West Jersey proprietaries, Penn, Lawrie, Lucas, Byllinge, (who had still an equitable interest,) and John Eldridge, and Edmond Warner, who had become the assignees of Fenwicke's portion, to Richard Hartshorne, Richard Guy, and James Wasse. The two first were Quakers, resident in East Jersey, and the last, an agent, sent out specially, from Europe. They were instructed to resist and control some irregular proceedings of Fenwicke, in the disposition of lands, to prepare for the many emigrants about to depart for the colony, to purchase lands from the natives, and to select a site for, and lay out a town of four or five thousand acres.§ Among the purchasers of West New Jersey, were two companies, one, of *Friends* from Yorkshire, and the other of *Friends* from London, who contracted for very considerable shares, for which they received patents.||

VI. In 1677, the promised commissioners were sent out, by the proprietaries, to administer the government, pursuant to the concessions.** They embarked on board the Kent, Gregory Marlow, master, the second ship from London, to West Jersey. Whilst on the Thames, Charles II., in his pleasuring barge, came along side, and observing the number of passengers, and learning whither they were bound, asked if they were all Quakers, and gave them his blessing. After a tedious passage, they arrived at New Castle, on the 16th of August; and soon after, two hundred and thirty, landed at the mouth of Raccoon creek, where the Swedes had some habitations. Notwithstanding their number, the greatest inconvenience which they suffered, was want of room for lodgings; and some terror, from the abundance of

* Dated 1st July, 1676.

† Leaming and Spicer's Collection.

‡ 26th August, 1676.

§ The surveyor proposed for this duty, was a certain Augustin, of Maryland, or William Elliot, of York river, Virginia.

|| See Appendix, E.

** These commissioners were Thomas Olive, Daniel Wills, John Kinsey, John Penford, Joseph Helmsley, Robert Stacy, Benjamin Scott, Richard Guy, and Thomas Foulke. Richard Guy came in the first ship. John Kinsey died at Shackamaxon, Kensington, soon after his landing; his remains were interred at Burlington, in ground appropriated for a burial ground, but now a street.—*Smith's New Jersey.*

snakes, which were occasionally seen in their chambers, or crawling over the low roofs of their dwellings.* The vessel on the passage had dropped anchor at Sandy Hook, whilst the commissioners proceeded to New York, to exhibit their commission to Andross. He treated them civilly, but demanded, if they had any communication from the Duke, his master. This measure, obviously requisite, the commissioners had strangely neglected, and when Andross declined to recognise their authority, instead of extenuating their imprudence, they strenuously insisted upon their rights, under the assignment of Lord Berkeley. Andross cut short the controversy, by pointing to his sword; and as this was an argument, which they could not retort, they submitted to his jurisdiction, until they could obtain redress from England; taking magistrate's commissions from him, and conducting the land affairs according to their instructions. Fenwicke, who neglected to take a like precaution, in relation to his tenth, was twice seized, and detained, some time, prisoner, in New York.

Upon their arrival in the Delaware, the commissioners obtained, from the Swedes, interpreters, by whose agency they conducted their negotiations with the Indians, and purchased the lands from Timber Creek to Rancocus, from Oldman's Creek to Timber Creek, and from Rancocus to the Assunpink, by three several conveyances.† Not having sufficient goods to make payment for the land last purchased, they covenanted not to settle any portion of it, until full payment should have been made. After examination of the country, the Yorkshire commissioners, Helmesly, Emley, and Stacy, on behalf of their constituents, chose the tract between Rancocus, and the Falls, which hence was called the first tenth; whilst the London commissioners, Penford, Clive, Wills and Scott, selected that below Timber creek, which was called the second tenth. Disastisfied, however, with this separation, the Yorkshire men proposed to the Londoners, that, if they would unite in establishing a town, the latter should have the larger proportion, in consideration, that the Yorkshire men had the better land in the woods. These terms were embraced, and one Noble, a surveyor who came in the first ship, was employed to lay out the town plot, running the main street and dividing the land on either side, into lots, giving those on the east, to the Yorkshire, and those on the west, to the London, proprietors. The town thus founded, was first called New Beverly, after Bridlington, but the name was soon changed to Burlington, which it now bears.§

These pioneers having arrived late in the autumn, the winter was much spent, before they could erect permanent dwellings. In the mean time, they lived in wigwams, built after the manner of the Indians, and subsisted chiefly on Indian corn and venison, supplied by the natives. These simple people, less corrupted, than they afterwards became, from the use of ardent spirits, were kind to their guests, notwithstanding some malicious insinuations, that the strangers had sold to them the small pox in their match coats; that distemper having attacked them at this period.

VII. In the same year arrived two other vessels. ***The Willing Mind,*** John Newcomb, commander, with about seventy passengers, dropped anchor, at Elsinburg, in November. She was soon after followed, by the fly boat, ***Martha,*** of Burlington, Yorkshire, with one hundred and fourteen. On the 10th December, 1768, came ***The Shield,*** from Hull, Daniel Townes, commander. When passing Coaquanock, the site of the present city of Philadelphia, she ran so close to the shore, that in tacking, her spars struck the

* Smith's N. J.
† Dated, respectively, 10th September, 27th September, and 10th October, 1677.
‡ Smith's N. J. § See Appendix, F.

trees, and some one on board remarked, how fine a spot this was for a town. A fresh gale brought her to Burlington, being the first vessel that came so far up the Delaware. She moored to a tree, and the next morning the passengers came ashore on the ice. About the same period, another ship arrived from London, freighted with passengers.*

Although compelled to endure the hardships inseparable from the occupation of a desert land, these were quickly surmounted, by the industry and patience of the emigrants. Their town soon assumed a thriving appearance, and was rapidly enlarged by increasing members. In this, as in other, infant settlements of America, the success of the colonist was commonly proportioned to the original humility of his condition; and he, who emigrated as a servant, was frequently more prosperous than his master. Persevering industry, temperance, and self-reliance, always reaped a full reward, whilst self-indulgence, and dependence upon hirelings, terminated in poverty.

VIII. Sir George Carteret, proprietary of East Jersey, died in 1679; having derived so little benefit from his American territory, that he found it necessary to bequeath it to trustees, to be sold for the benefit of his creditors. The exemption, this district enjoyed, from the jurisdiction of the Duke of York, had not contributed to moderate the discontent of the inhabitants of West New Jersey, with his assumed illegal authority. They, incessantly, importuned him for redress, and were, at length, provoked by a tax of five per cent., which Andross imposed, on the importation of European merchandise, to additional vehemence of complaint, and urgency of solicitation. Wearied, at length, with the importunity of these suitors, rather than moved by the justice of their complaint, the Duke referred the subject to commissioners, by whom, it was finally submitted to Sir William Jones.†

The argument, in behalf of the colonists, on this occasion, prepared by William Penn, George Hutchinson, and others, chiefly Quakers, breathes a firm, undaunted spirit of liberty, worthy the founders of a North American commonwealth; and contains traces of those principles, which, subsequently, led the colonies to full emancipation.‡ "Thus then," they say, after a deduction of their title, "we came to buy that moiety, which belonged to Lord Berkeley, for a valuable consideration; and in the conveyance he made us, powers of government are expressly granted; for that, only, could have induced us to buy it: and the reason is plain, because to all prudent men, the government of a place is more inviting than the soil. For what is good land without good laws?—the better the worse. And if we could not assure people, of an easy, and free, and safe government, both with respect to their spiritual and worldly property,—that is, an uninterrupted liberty of conscience, and an inviolable possession of their civil rights and freedoms, by a just and wise government,—a mere wilderness would be no encouragement; for it were madness to leave a free, good, and improved country, to plant in a wilderness, and there adventure many thousands of pounds, to give an absolute title to another person, to tax us at will and pleasure." Stating the tax imposed by Andross, they proceed: "This is one grievance; and for this, we make our application to have speedy redress, not as a burden only, with respect to the quantum or the way of levying it, or any circumstance made hard by the irregularity of the officers, but as a wrong; for

* See Appendix, G. † Grahame's Col. Hist. vol. ii. 344.

‡ This document, found in Smith's History, is unnoticed by Chalmers; and is imperfectly abridged by Winterbotham (vol. ii. p. 287). Grahame (vol. ii. p. 346) admits that Penn concurred in its presentation, and, probably, assisted in its composition; but denies that he was the sole author, as some of his biographers have insisted; supposing this pretension to be refuted, by the style of the document; in which, not the slightest resemblance is discernible, to any of his acknowledged productions.

we complain of a wrong, done us, and ask, yet, with modesty, ***quo jure?*** Tell us the title, by what right or law, are we thus used, that may a little mitigate our pain? Your answer, hitherto, hath been this. That it was a conquered country; and that the King, being the conqueror, has power to make laws, raise money, &c.; and that this power ***jure regale***, the King hath vested in the Duke; and by that right and sovereignty, the Duke demands that custom we complain of. Natural right and humane prudence, oppose such doctrine all the world over; for what is it, but to say, that people, free by law, under their prince at home, are at his mercy in the plantations abroad; and why? because he is a conqueror there, but still at the hazard of the lives of his own people, and at the cost and charge of the public. We would say more, but choose to let it drop. But our case is better yet; for the King's grant, to the Duke of York, is plainly restrictive to the laws and government of England. Now the constitution and government of England, as we humbly conceive, are so far from countenancing such authority, that it is made a fundamental in our constitution, that the King of England cannot, justly, take his subject's goods without their consent. This needs no more to be proved than a principle; 'tis ***jus indigene***, an home-born right, declared to be law by divers statutes."—"To give up the power of making laws, is to change the government, to sell, or rather, to resign, ourselves to the will of another; and that for nothing. For, under favour, we buy nothing of the Duke, if not the right of an undisturbed colonizing, and that, as Englishmen, with no diminution, but expectation of some increase of those freedoms and privileges enjoyed in our own country; for the soil is none of his; 'tis the natives, by the ***jus gentium***, the law of nations; and it would be an ill argument to convert them to Christianity, to expel, instead of purchasing them, out of those countries. If then, the country be theirs, it is not the Duke's: he cannot sell it; then what have we bought?"—"To conclude this point, we humbly say, that we have not lost any part of our liberty, by leaving our country; for we leave not our King, nor our government by quitting our soil; but we transmit to a place given by the same King, with express limitation to erect no polity contrary to the same established government, but as near as may be to it; and this variation is allowed, but for the sake of emergencies, and that latitude, bounded by these words, for the good of the adventurer and planter." After this, as they term it, the "point of law" of the case, they proceed to insist upon the equity of it; protesting that the "tax is not to be found in the Duke's conveyances; that it was an after business, a very surprise to the planter."—"This, in plain English, is under another name, paying for the same thing twice over."—"Custom, in all governments in the world, is laid upon trade; but this, upon planting, is unprecedented. Had we brought commodities to these parts to sell, made profit out of them, and returned to the advantage of traders, there had been some colour or pretence for this exaction; but to require and force a custom, from persons, for coming to their property, their own ***terra firma***, their habitations; in short, for coming home, is without a parallel. This is paying custom, not for trading, but for landing; not for merchandising, but planting."—"Besides there is no end of this power; for since we are, by this precedent, assessed without any law, and thereby excluded our English right of common assent to taxes; what security have we of any thing we possess? We can call nothing our own, but are tenants at will, not only for the soil, but for all our personal estates. We endure penury, and the sweat of our brows, to improve them, at our own hazard, only. This is to transplant, not from good to better, but from good to bad. This sort of conduct has destroyed government, but never raised one to any true greatness; nor ever will, in the Duke's territories, whilst so many countries, equally good, in soil and air, surround, with greater freedom and security. Lastly, the Duke's circumstances, and the people's jealousies, considered, we humbly submit it, if there can be, in their opinion, a greater evidence of a design, to introduce an unlimited government, than both to exact such unterminated tax from English planters, and to continue it, after so many repeated complaints. And on the contrary, if there be any thing so happy to the Duke's present affairs, as the opportunity he has to free that country with his own hands, and to make us all owers of our liberty, to his favour and justice: So will Englishmen, here, know what to hope for, by the justice and kindness he shows to Englishmen there; and all men, to see the just model of his government in New York, to be the scheme and draught in little, of his administration in Old England, at large, if the crown should ever devolve upon his head."

Unpalatable as this argument must have been to the British court, and the counsellors of the Duke, at this period, it was triumphant. The commissioners were constrained to pronounce judgment, in conformity with the opinion of Jones, "that as the grant to Berkeley and Carteret, had reserved no profit or jurisdiction, the legality of the tax could not be defended." The Duke, therefore, without further delay, abandoned all claims on West Jersey, confirming the territory, or soil of the province, in the fullest terms, to William Penn, Gawn Lawry, and Nicholas Lucas, trustees for Byllinge, and to John Eldridge, and Edmund Warner, assignees of Fenwicke, according to their several interests, whilst he conveyed, expressly, the government to Edward Byllinge, his heirs and assigns.* And soon after, he made a like confirmation, in favour of the representatives of his friend, Sir George Carteret.†

The forcible and spirited pleading, we have noticed, derives special interest, from the recollection of the conflict, then waging between the advocates of liberty, and the abettors of arbitrary power. Probably, none of the writings of which that period was, abundantly, prolific, was characterized by a more magnanimous effort, for the preservation of liberty, than this first successful vindication, of the rights of New Jersey. Its most remarkable feature, is the strong and deliberate assertion, that no tax could be justly imposed upon them, without their consent. The report of the commissioners, and the relief that followed, was a virtual concession of this principle, which subsequently triumphed more signally, in the independence of the United States.‡

* Indenture, dated 6th August, 1680.

† 14th March, 1682. Leaming and Spicer's Collection.

‡ The case between the proprietaries and the Duke, relative to the government, is of some complexity; and from inspection of the documents alone, his pretensions have better grounds than his advocates appear to have assumed for him. The charters of Charles II., to him, in addition to a full fee simple estate, in land, contain an express grant of the powers of government; whilst the deeds from the Duke to Berkeley and Carteret, convey a "*tract of land*," specifically bounded, as in the transfer of a private estate. There is not the slightest allusion to the powers of government in them; and the special care taken to give such powers, in the one case, and to omit them in the other, would be a strong argument, that they were not designed to be granted, if such argument were needed, in the total absence of a grant. It certainly never can be maintained, that, a fee simple, in land, carried with it a political power of government. In all cases where this power was intended to be conveyed, apt words were employed, as in the grants to the Duke of York, to Baltimore, and Penn. Berkeley could convey no other right than he possessed, nor did he attempt it, since that is not asserted in the plea of the New Jersey proprietaries.—Nor in the deed, quintipartite of partition, between Carteret, and the grantees of Berkeley, is there any reference to the powers of government. So far, then, the case would seem to be clearly, that the Duke had retained the integrity of his political powers, as granted him by the crown. But against this paper case, there is strong circumstantial evidence. 1. The assumption, and undisputed exercise of political

IX. But, if we condemn, severely, the tenacious hold of power, on the part of the Duke, how shall we characterize the pretensions of Byllinge, subsequent to the exclusive grant of the government to him? His conduct affords an additional instance of the corrupting force of power, and of human inconsistency. He asserts, as grantee of Berkeley, that he became the participant of political power, even by a deed for lands only; but, when that power was expressly and unequivocally conveyed to himself, he denies the grant of similar power, to his assigns, though he is a party to the "concessions," by which it was clearly conveyed; under the pretence, it would seem, that as such power was not then with him, he could not grant it, and though he had himself, taken the office of governor, by the election of the proprietaries. That his exclusive gubernatorial power might be known and felt, he proposed to remove Jennings, whom he had appointed his deputy, under his delegated powers, in 1679.

X. The proprietaries, in General Assembly of the province, in June, 1683, met this pretension with due firmness and spirit; resolving, that they had purchased the land and government together; that, in their deeds, Byllinge, the grantor, had covenanted, within seven years, to make further assurance of title, and was now bound, as they were, to fulfil his contracts; that the "concessions" were adopted by proprietaries and people, as the foundation of the government of West New Jersey, by which they were resolved to stand; and that "an instrument be drawn up and sent to some trusty friends in London, for Edward Byllinge to sign and seal; whereby, to confirm his first bargain and sale, he made to the freeholders of this province, of land and government together." They further resolved, that upon such confirmation, they were willing to testify their gratitude, as their ability would permit; and should Byllinge visit the province, to show their free and unanimous acceptance, and acknowledgments of his care and diligence in the premises. This subject, it would seem, had been some time under discussion, before the Assembly was wrought to these resolutions; and William Penn had recommended that the people should secure themselves, by the *election* of Jennings, to the office of Governor, and his promise to execute the place, with fidelity and diligence, according to the laws, concessions, and constitutions of the province. This expedient, certainly not flattering to Byllinge, the Assembly adopted, and proclaimed Jennings governor, by virtue of the power vested in six parts in seven, of their body, to alter their constitution; and they bestowed the right to six hundred acres of land, to pay the charges of the office. Upon this occasion, the governor, and all the officers, under the government, signed written engagements, faithfully to perform their duty.*

power, by Berkeley and Carteret, openly promulgated in their concessions. 2. The surrender of the government, by Nicholls, the agent of the Duke, to them, after remonstrance, against such a measure, by that agent. 3. The re-grant of the soil, and the sufferance of the resumption of political power, by the Duke, after the conquest, and reconquest, by the Dutch; and 4th, the continued and unquestioned exercise of such power, by Byllinge, and his assigns, and by Carteret, after partition made. These are facts strangely at variance, with the deeds, and no one can suppose their existence, against an adverse claim, on the part of the heir apparent to the crown. And it is not the least singular part of the case, that whilst the Duke claims a partial political right, that of laying taxes, he suffers undisturbed, the exercise of independent governments, in East and West Jersey. We must, therefore, believe, that there was an implied grant of political power, in the conveyance of the soil, which was too strongly confirmed by more than twenty years enjoyment, to be defeated. Yet, under these circumstances, the ready acquiescence of the Duke, in the award of the commissioners, is extraordinary, when his love of power, and his tyrannical measures, against other colonial governments, are considered.

* See Appendix, H.

Subsequently, at an Assembly, convened on the 29th of March, 1684, Governor Jennings, and Thomas Budd, were deputed to negotiate this matter, in England; and two hundred pounds were voted for their expenses, which were advanced by governor Penn, then in Philadelphia; for the repayment of which, three thousand acres of land, were appropriated, above the falls of the Delaware. Upon his departure, Jennings nominated Thomas Clive, his deputy, who was duly elected governor, in May, 1684, and May, 1685. These measures, on the part of the Assembly, seem to have been attended with the desired effect. A new charter, the precise nature of which, we are left to conjecture, was given by Byllinge, and deposited by the Assembly, in the custody of Clive and Gardiner, their treasurer, and directed to be recorded. This instrument, probably, restored the government to the footing of the "concessions;" and John Skeine was received as the deputy governor, of Byllinge, although the Assembly had, before, rejected Welsh, who had been appointed to the office. Skeine died in February, 1688.*

XI. Upon the death of Byllinge, in 1687, Dr. Daniel Coxe, of London, already a large proprietary, at the instance of other proprietaries, purchased the interest of Byllinge's heirs, in the soil and government. Soon after, (September 5, 1687) he addressed a letter to the council of proprietors in New Jersey, communicating this matter, and reviving the repudiated claim of Byllinge; declaring, "that the government of the province was legally in him, as that of Pennsylvania in Penn, or East Jersey in the proprietaries; and that he was resolved, by the assistance of Almighty God, to exercise the jurisdiction to him conveyed, with all integrity, faith, fulness, and diligence, for the benefit and welfare of those, over whom, Divine Providence had constituted him superintendent, or chief overseer. But as he confirmed the "concessions," and thereby, in fact, transferred, as Jennings had done, the full right of government, to the proprietors, jointly, his naked assertion of exclusive right, appears to have excited no uneasiness in the province. Smith informs us, that, Coxe received the appointment of governor from the proprietaries, and continued in that station until the year 1690; that, in the interval, Edward Hunloke was, at one time, his deputy; and that a like commission had been sent to John Tatham, who, being a Jacobite, was rejected by the Assembly. In 1691, Dr. Coxe conveyed the government to a company of proprietaries, called the West Jersey Society, in consideration of nine thousand pounds sterling, who, in 1692, appointed Andrew Hamilton governor. This view of the governmental question, has carried us in advance of other portions of our subject, to which we now return.

XII. West Jersey, now filled apace with inhabitants; the greater portion of whom were Quakers. Jennings convened the first Assembly, on 25th November, 1681. This body enacted certain *fundamental constitutions*, and many laws. Pursuing the spirit of the "concessions," they, in the first, provided, for the annual election and meeting of the Assembly; the obligation of the laws by them enacted; the appointment and removal by them, of all officers of trust; that no tax or custom should continue longer than one year; and that no one should be incapable of office, by reason of his faith and worship. They prohibited the governor and council, from enacting laws, laying any tax, sending ambassadors, or making treaties, and from proroguing or dissolving that house; and declared, that, upon Jennings' acceptance of these conditions, they would recognise him as deputy governor. These "constitutions were duly signed by Samuel Jennings, deputy governor, and Thomas Clive, speaker. It would be difficult to find

* The salary of Clive was thirty pounds; of Skeine, thirty bushels of rye, beside his fees.

any instrument, in representative government, more democratic, or more liberal, in matters of religious faith. Not even belief in the Deity, was necessary to human equality, whilst the constitution of the *state* of New Jersey, excludes from office all who do not profess belief in the faith of some Protestant sect.

Thirty-six acts embraced, and enforced, most of the provisions of the "concessions." Among them, however, was one authorizing the levy of two hundred pounds, "*in coin, or skins, or money*," for defraying public debts and other public charges of the province. For this great sum, "Thomas Budd and Thomas Gardiner, were appointed receivers-general, with power to constitute and appoint all inferior or sub-collectors, or otherwise, for the best and easiest way of raising the amount, throughout the province of West Jersey." Another enacted, that, if any person shall presume to offer affront to the public authority, or any officiating in that capacity, he shall be punished and fined at the discretion of the court—an offence certainly indefinite, and a latitude of punishment, which, in some governments, would have been very alarming. A third, which was, however, soon after repealed, raised the value of the current coin fifty per cent.: a fourth, directed the making of a highway from Burlington to Salem; and two others, appropriated twenty pounds to the governor, and five to the speaker, for their services. But among the most meritorious, was that imposing a heavy penalty upon the sale of strong liquors to the Indians.

At the next session, holden in May, 1682, the Assembly authorized each of the ten proprietaries, to dispose of five hundred acres of land, within their respective tenths, for defraying the public expenses, in such tenth: made the half-pence, coined by one Mark Newbie, a member of council, and called Patrick's half-pence, current coin of the province; with condition, however, that no one should be obliged to receive more than five shillings of it, in one payment: established Burlington and Salem as ports: empowered justices to solemnize marriages on fourteen days notice, and consent of parents: directed ten bushels of corn, necessary apparel, two horses, and one axe, to be given, as freedom dues, to servants: subjected land to the payment of debts; prohibited the imprisonment of debtors, surrendering their estates; and declared the town of Burlington, the chief city of the province.

At the next session, May, 1683, some modification of the fundamental laws was made. The governor and council, were empowered to prepare bills for laws, promulgating them, twenty days, in the most public place of the province, before the meeting of the General Assembly. The governor, council, and Assembly, met together, were declared the General Assembly; who might affirm, or deny, bills so prepared; and of this Assembly, the governor was declared speaker, with a double voice. During the recess of the Assembly, the government of the state, was lodged with the governor and council.

We have already noticed the proceedings of the Assembly, in relation to the claim of Byllinge; beside which, there were no subjects of interest, in the history of the succeeding decade of years. The planters appeared to have pursued, undisturbed, the noiseless tenor of prosperity. Some efforts, however, were made during this period, by the proprietaries of East and West Jersey, for running the line between their provinces. But of this vexed and still unsettled question, we shall treat fully, in our exposition of the land system of the state.

XIII. In 1693, however, the religious toleration, granted by the laws, was somewhat restricted by an act, which, though declaring that conscientious scruples, against taking oaths, should not incapacitate for office, required from the incumbent, a declaration of fidelity to the King, renunciation of popery and the following profession *of the Christian faith: I,* A B, *profess faith in* GOD, *the Father, and* JESUS CHRIST *his eternal Son, the true* GOD, *and in the Holy Spirit, one* GOD *blessed for ever more; and do acknowledge the Holy Scriptures of the Old and New Testament, to be given by divine inspiration.**

* Can this be deemed a confession of faith, by Quakers? The question derives great interest from the wide schism, at this time existing in the society of Friends, in which the two parties, alike, claim to hold the original faith; one professing that in the text—the other, belief in the unity of the Deity, the humanity of Christ, with a modified view of divine inspiration in the Scriptures. Upon the true solution of the original faith of the Quakers, much property, and a greater value, (if I may thus express myself,) in sentiment, at this moment depends. It is said, that no formal declaration of the Quaker faith, is to be found in the records of the society; and courts of justice have been compelled to seek it, in the partial, equivocal, and unsatisfactory declarations of esteemed preachers, and polemical writers. The best evidence which the nature of the subject admits, is the formal declaration of faith, by the yearly meeting. But an attempt of this kind was one of the immediate causes of the present division. The next best evidence, would be a declaration of faith, by a body of Quakers, at a period when no division existed, among the sect, and when an attempt to force a declaration of faith upon them, would have been resisted, as firmly, to say the least, as at any time, since the ministry of Fox. Was the Assembly of West New Jersey, of the year 1696, such a body? If it was, their declaration of "*The Christian Faith*," is entitled to profound respect and unlimited confidence; having been made when the zeal of the church was most lively, during the life of many of its distinguished primitive apostles, such as Barclay and Penn, and within seven years after the death of its founder, George Fox. This Assembly consisted of about fifty members. It is perhaps impossible, at this day, to declare that every member was a Quaker. This, however, is probable, since the Quakers composed vastly the greater proportion of the population. It is certain, however, that the majority of the Assembly were Friends, and might, therefore, have arrested the promulgation of this creed. That they would have done so, cannot be doubted, had it not been their faith; for they came to the province, that they might enjoy that faith, without molestation. They had purchased the soil, and the government, that they might live under laws of their own enactment. But this act, had it declared a faith different from that, which the Quakers professed, would have disqualified them from participating in the government, and would have placed them at the mercy of the very few Swedes and Dutch, who were in the province. We are, therefore, constrained to believe, that this statutory confession of faith, was the faith of the Quaker church.—*See Leaming and Spicer's Collection, p.* 514.—*And see the Act, in the Appendix,* I.

The confession of faith set forth in the New Jersey act of 1693, is copied in words, from the English toleration act, passed in 1689, (1 William and Mary). The following account of which, is given by George Whitehead.—*Works, page* 635. "Yet to prevent any such (Friends) from being stumbled or ensnared, by some expressions in the aforesaid profession or creed, (which appeared unscriptural,) in the said Bill, we, instead thereof, did propose and humbly offer, as our own real belief of the Deity of the Father, Son and Holy Ghost;"—the form we have given in the text. "Which declaration," he continues, "John Vaughton and I, delivered to Sir Thomas Clergis, who, with some others, were desirous we should give in such confession, of our Christian belief, that we might not lie under the unjust imputation of being no Christians, and thereby be deprived of the benefit of the intended law, for our religious liberty. We were, therefore, of necessity, put upon offering the said confession, it being, also, our known professed principle, sincerely to confess Christ, the Son of the living God, his divinity, and that he is the eternal Word, and that the Three which bear record in heaven, the Father, the Word, and the Holy Ghost, are one; one divine Being, one God, blessed forever."

In what sense the words of this confession were accepted, by Friends, it would, perhaps, be difficult to say. They were, probably, understood by the framers of the toleration act, to be equivalent to the belief in the Trinity, as expressed by the Church of England. But this sense, if not denied, is certainly not conceded by the Quaker writers, generally, who, in relation to this mysterious subject, express themselves with great mystery, and allege that they take up the doctrine as expressly laid down in the Scripture, and are not warranted in making deductions, however specious. It has been supposed, too, that in framing this confession of faith, an outward conformity to the requisition of Parliament, only, was designed: and that every Friend was at perfect liberty to construe the words of his confession, in such sense as the spirit within him should direct. If so, we have advanced nothing in determining

XIV. By the deed of partition of July, 1676, Sir George Carteret became seized of East New Jersey, in severalty. By his testament, December 5th, 1678, he named his wife, Elizabeth, his executrix, and guardian of his heir; and devised the province to trustees, to be sold for payment of his debts.* He died in the following year, but his death made no change in the government, which continued to be administered by his brother Philip, until about the end of the year 1681, or beginning of 1682, when he was superseded by the transfer of the province to other proprietaries.

XV. The latter part of his administration, was embittered by the revival of the disputes which had once rendered him a fugitive from his government, and by the unjust and violent assumption of authority, over his province, by the profligate Andross, governor of New York. The pretension of this ready tool of despotism, was sustained by that portion of the inhabitants, who had derived their land titles through governor Nicholls, from the Duke, and who believed that his Grace would render valid their advantageous purchases from the Indians. Andross seems, first, formally, to have disputed the right of Carteret, in March, 1680, when, by proclamation, he claimed the submission of the inhabitants for the Duke of York. Threats of invasion followed; to resist which, Carteret prepared his military force, amounting to one hundred and fifty men. Andross, however, visited Elizabethtown, attended by a civil suite, only, where he ostentatiously displayed the Duke's title, and his own commission; and, utterly disregarding his master's double grant to Sir George Carteret, demanded the recognition of his authority. This being refused, he retired; but soon after, April 31, 1680, despatched a party of soldiers, who rudely dragged Carteret from his bed, and conveyed him, prisoner, to New York, where he was tried, upon the information of the attorney-general, with having riotously and routously, with force of arms, endeavoured to maintain and exercise jurisdiction and government over his Majesty's subjects, within the bounds of his Majesty's letters patent, granted to his Royal Highness. In despite of the efforts of Andross, who presided at the trial, the jury, though several times sent out by him, magnanimously acquitted the prisoner. The court, however, adjudged, that if Carteret returned to New Jersey, he should engage not to assume any authority there.

Andross met an Assembly at Elizabethtown, on the 2d June, 1680, where he again exhibited the documents of his authority, together with a copy of the laws enacted at New York, which he proposed as the rule of action for New Jersey. Although the Assembly were indisposed, or dreaded, to question the authority of the Duke, they were not unregardful of their rights, nor backward in proclaiming them. They replied, "As we are the representatives of the freeholders of this province, we dare not grant his Majesty's letters patent, though under the great seal of England, to be our rule or joint safety; for the great charter of England, alias, *magna charta*, is the only rule, privilege, and joint safety of every free born Englishman. What we have formerly done, we did in obedience to the authority that was then established in this province, and that being done according to law, they needed no confirmation." They declared, also, their expectation, that, the privileges granted them, by virtue of the concessions of Lord Berkeley and Sir George Carteret, would be confirmed to them; and they re-enacted former laws, and demanded their approval.

the faith of Friends, since they have adopted the remainder of the Scriptures, giving to them, in many cases, a meaning widely different from that assigned by Orthodox Christians.

* The trustees were John Earl of Sandwich, John Earl of Bath, Bernard Granville, brother of the latter, Sir Thomas Crew, Sir Thomas Atkins, and his brother, Edward Atkins.

Complaints against the proceedings of Andross were despatched to England with an appeal to the King. The Duke disavowed the acts of his minion, yet no instructions appear to have been given to rescind them. For, after the departure of Andross, for England, Captain Brochholts, his substitute, maintained his assumption, refusing to recognise the authority of Carteret, until he exhibited a new commission, notwithstanding the Assembly of New Jersey had declared the conduct of Andross illegal. No further forcible effort, however, was made to control the province; the Duke having, in truth, agreed to confirm his former grants with the right of government; and, soon after, by release of this contested power, terminated these troubles.

Disgusted by these contentions, and perceiving that they were not likely to derive either emolument or satisfaction, from their province, the trustees and executrix of Sir George Carteret, offered it for sale to the highest bidder.*

XVI. The sessions of the Assembly, during the administration of Carteret, were commonly holden at Elizabethtown, frequently at Woodbridge, and sometimes at Middletown and Piscataway.† Many laws were enacted during this period, but most of them were local or ephemeral in their character. Those of a more general nature, provided; That, contemners of authority should be punished by fine, or corporal infliction, at the discretion of the court: that males above sixteen, and under sixty, years of age, failing to furnish themselves with arms, should be fined, two shillings per week, for neglect: that, one guilty of arson, should repair the injury done, and in case of inability so to do, be, at the mercy of the court, condemned to death or other corporal punishment: that, murder, false witness, with design to take away life, crimes against nature, witchcraft, *stealing away any mankind*, should be punished by death; burglary or highway robbery, the first offence with burning in the hand, the second in the forehead, and in both cases, with restitution; and the third offence with death: larceny, the first offence by treble restitution; and so the second and third, with such increase of punishment, even unto death, as the court might direct, if the offender were incorrigible; otherwise, and if unable to make restitution, to be sold for satisfaction, or to receive corporal punishment: conspiracies or attacks upon towns or forts, smiting or cursing of parents, unless in self defence, upon complaint of the parent, were also subjected to the penalty of death: rape was punishable with death, or otherwise, severely, at the discretion of the court; fornication, with *marriage*, fine, or corporal punishment; adultery, with divorce, corporal punishment, or banishment, either, or all of them, as circumstances should determine the mind of the judge; night walking and revelling, after nine o'clock, with arrest, and punishment, at the discretion of the court:—That, the members of Assembly should be chosen on the first of January, and their sessions be holden on the first Tuesday in November, annually, or oftener, if the governor and council should deem necessary: that, no marriage should be had without the consent of parent, guardian, or master, as the case might require, unless upon notice, thrice published, at some meeting or kirk, near the parties' abode, or set up in writing, at some public house, for fourteen days previous; nor then, unless solemnized by some approved minister, justice, or chief officer, who was forbidden, under penalty of twenty pounds, and dismission from office, to marry any, who had not fulfilled these requisitions.

XVII. In comparing the laws of East and West Jersey, we are much struck with the difference of the spirit which dictated them. The genius of Calvinism, which rules by terror, and the ever suspended sword, in this and

* Grahame's Col. Hist. vol. ii. 350. See Appendix K.

† The first Assembly was holden 26th May, 1668, at Elizabethtown.

in the future world, is strongly impressed upon the one, whilst a prudent reserve in naming crimes, and a humane forbearance in their punishment, characterize the other. The ancient lawgivers prescribed no punishment for parricide, deeming the offence impossible;—the Quaker legislators, had no enactment against arson—no prescribed punishment for murder or treason, and other heinous offences; and yet, during four-and-twenty years, of their administration, no instance of such crimes was known within their territories. In East Jersey, there were thirteen classes of offences, against which, the penalty of death was denounced; and amongst these, were simple larcenies, and the impossible crime of witchcraft; whilst in West Jersey, such punishment was unknown to the law. The sentence, and mode of its execution, in cases of treason and murder, were by the "Concessions," committed to the Assembly; but that body never prescribed a general rule, nor had occasion to apply their powers to a special case. The legislators of West Jersey, in injuries of every kind, sought reparation, and the reclamation of the offender. Thus, the spoiler of property was condemned, in all cases, to make a fourfold restitution, and to suffer imprisonment at labour; and the perpetrator of personal injuries, might be pardoned by the sufferer. In all cases, mercy presided over the justice-seat. But in East Jersey, the great object of the law seems to have been vengeance. Like to Draco, the legislator deemed small crimes worthy of death, and could find no severer punishment for the greatest. But, though from the enactments against witchcraft, the progress of intellectual light seemed less in East, than in West Jersey, there was an earnest care for the instruction of the people. This was particularly evident in an act, of 1693, providing, that, the inhabitants of any town might, by warrant from a justice, elect three men to establish and levy a rate for the maintenance of a schoolmaster, payment of which, might be enforced by distress. Upon the whole, we may remark, that, though the legislators of East and West Jersey, drew their principles from the same volume, they were from different sources; the first were oppressed, enslaved, by the vengeful God, who prescribed the Levitical law; the others sought and found, a well regulated freedom, in the merciful monitions of a Redeemer.

In East Jersey there was no law for the public support of religion; yet, every township maintained its church and its minister. The people, by the testimony of the first deputy of the Quaker sovereigns, "were, generally, a sober, professing people, wise in their generation, courteous in their behaviour, and respectful to those in office." And Gawn Lawrie, the second deputy, assures us, "that there was not, in all the province, a poor body, or that wants."* Relying on this view, we might impute the dissentions which had prevailed, to the injudicious conduct of the government. But there is reason to believe, that, the blame of these dissentions is chargeable, in a considerable degree, upon the people. A headstrong and turbulent disposition appears to have prevailed among some classes, at least, of the inhabitants: various riots and disturbances broke forth, even under the new government, and the utmost patience of the rulers, were necessary to govern them. A law, enacted about four years after this period, reprobates the frequent occurrence of quarrels and challenges, and interdicts the inhabitants from wearing swords, pistols, or daggers.†

* "The servants work not so much," says Lawrie, "by a third, as they do in England, and I think, feed much better; for they have beef, pork, bacon, pudding, milk, butter, and good beer and cider to drink. When they are out of their time, they have land for themselves, and generally turn farmers. Servants' wages are not under two shillings a day, besides victuals." S. Smith, p. 117, 181.

† Smith, pp. 162, 163, 169, 171, 175, &c. Grahame's Col. Hist.

CHAPTER IV.

From the Purchase of East Jersey, by the Quakers, to the Surrender of the two Provinces to the Crown, 1682–1702.—I. Purchase of East Jersey by Penn and his Associates.—They admit others, not Quakers, to participate in the Purchase. —II. Robert Barclay appointed Governor for Life—Scotch Emigrants—Deputy Governors—Foundation of Amboy—Vain Efforts at Commerce.—III. Efforts of James II. to destroy Colonial Charter—Defeated by the Revolution.—IV. Andrew Hamilton, Deputy Governor—Death of Robert Barclay—Interregnum—Andrew Hamilton, Governor-in-Chief—Superseded by Jeremiah Basse—Reappointed—Discontent of the Colonists.—V. Attempt of New York to tax the Colony.—VI. Proposition from the English Ministers for the Surrender of the Proprietary Governments—Negotiations relating thereto.—VII. Final and unconditional Surrender—Lord Cornbury appointed Governor—Outline of the new Government.—VIII. Stationary Condition of New Jersey—Causes thereof.—IX. Condition of the Aborigines—Purchases of their Lands—Traditions of their Origin—Tribes most noted in New Jersey—Treaty at Crosswicks—at Burlington and Easton—Final Extinction of Indian Title to the Soil of New Jersey.—X. Review of the Title under the Proprietaries of East Jersey.—XI. Review of Title of Proprietaries of West Jersey.—XII. Of the Partition Line between East and West Jersey.

I. The success of their experiment in West Jersey, encouraged the Quakers of Great Britain, to avail themselves of the opportunity, that was now afforded, in the proposition for the sale of East Jersey, of enlarging the sphere of their enterprise, by the acquisition of that province. In February, 1682, William Penn, with eleven others of his religious faith,* purchased the colony from the devisees of Sir George Carteret. This territory, then, contained about five thousand inhabitants, the great majority of whom were not Quakers. There were populous settlements at Shrewsbury, Middletown, upon the Raritan and Millstone rivers; at Piscataway, Woodbridge, and Elizabethtown; at Newark, and upon the banks of the Passaic and Hackensack rivers; at Bergen, and along the bay and bank of the Hudson. Whether to allay the jealousy, with which, the inhabitants might have regarded a government, wholly composed of men whose principles differed greatly from their own, or for the purpose of fortifying their interest at court, by associating influential men with their enterprise, the twelve purchasers hastened to assume twelve other partners, among whom were the Earl of Perth, Chancellor of Scotland, and Lord Drummond, of Gilston, Secretary of State for that kingdom.† In favour of the twenty-four, the Duke of York executed his third and last grant of East Jersey, 14th March,

* The associates of Penn were Robert West, Thomas Rudyard, Samuel Groome, Thomas Hart, Richard Mew, Thomas Wilcox, Ambrose Rigg, Hugh Hartshorne, Clement Plumstead, Thomas Cooper, and John Hayward.

† The names of the additional twelve, were James, Earl of Perth, Sir George M'Kenzie, John Drummond, Robert Barclay, David Barclay, Robert Gordon, Robert Burnett, Peter Sonmans, James Braine, Gawen Turner, Thomas Nairne, Thomas Cox, and William Dockwra.

† From the dedication of Scott's model of East Jersey, it appears that Viscount Tarbet and Lord M'Leod, two other powerful Scotch nobles, became, shortly after, proprietaries. Sir George M'Kenzie, Lord Advocate of Scotland, whom his cotemporaries justly denominated, the bloody M'Kenzie, was infamously distinguished as a witness for the crown, on the trial of Lord Russell.—*Grahame's Col. Hist.* vol. ii. p. 351. n.

† Grahame's Col. Hist.

1682, with full powers of government. To facilitate the exercise of their dominion, they, also, obtained from the King, a royal letter, addressed to the governor, council, and inhabitants of the province, stating, the title of the purchasers to the soil and jurisdiction, and requiring due obedience to their government.*

Among the new proprietaries of East Jersey, was the celebrated Robert Barclay, of Urie, a Scottish gentleman, who had been converted to Quakerism, and, in defence of his adopted principles, had published a series of works, which elevated his name, and his cause, in the esteem of all Europe. Admired by scholars and philosophers, for the stretch of his learning, and the strength and subtlety of his understanding, he was endeared to the members of his religious fraternity, by the liveliness of his zeal, the excellence of his character, and the services which his pen had rendered to them. To the King and the Duke of York, he was recommended, not less by his distinguished fame, than by the principles of passive obedience, professed by the sect of which he was leader; and with the royal brothers, as well as with some of the most distinguished of their Scottish favourites and ministers, he maintained a friendly and confidential intercourse. Inexplicable, as to many, such a coalition of uncongenial characters may appear, it seems, at least, as strange a moral phenomenon, to behold Barclay and Penn, the votaries of universal toleration and philanthropy, voluntarily associating, in their labours, for the education and happiness of an infant community, such instruments as Lord Perth, and other abettors of royal tyranny and ecclesiastical persecution, in Scotland.†

II. By the unanimous choice of his colleagues, Robert Barclay was appointed, for life, first governor of East Jersey, under the new proprietary administration, with dispensation from personal residence, and authority to nominate his deputy. The most beneficial event of his presidency, was the emigration of many of his countrymen, the Scotch, to the province; a measure, effected, it is said, with much difficulty and importunity. For, although the great bulk of the nation was suffering the rigours of tyranny, for their resistance to the establishment of prelacy, they were reluctant to seek relief in exile from their native land. The influence of Barclay and other Scotch Quakers, however, co-operated with the severities of Lord Perth, and the other royal ministers, to induce many, particularly, from Aberdeen, the governor's native county, to seek this asylum. In order to instruct the Scotch, more generally, of the condition of the colony, and to invite them to remove thither, an historical and statistical account of it was published, with a preliminary treatise, combatting the prevailing objection to expatriation. This work was, probably, composed, in part, by Barclay; but was ascribed to George Scott, of Pitlochie, and was eminently successful.‡ As a farther recommendation of the province, to the favour of the Scotch, Barclay, subsequently, displaced Lawrie, a Quaker, whom he had appointed deputy, and conferred this office on Lord Neil Campbell, uncle of the Marquis of Argyle, who resided some time in the province as its lieutenant governor.§ The

* Leaming and Spicer's Col. Grahame, vol. ii. p. 351.

† Grahame's Col. Hist. vol. ii. p. 354. See Appendix, L.

‡ It bore the title of The Model of the Government of the Province of East New Jersey, in America, and contains a minute account of the climate, soil, institutions, and settlements of the province. See Appendix, M.

§ Grahame's Col. Hist. vol. ii. p. 358. Oldmixon and Smith concur, in relating that Lord Neil Campbell succeeded Barclay as *governor*. But this seems an error of Oldmixon, which Smith has incautiously copied; for, from a document, preserved by Smith himself, (p. 196) Barclay, in 1688, as governor of East Jersey, subscribed an agreement of partition between it and West Jersey.

more wealthy of the Scotch emigrants, were noted for bringing with them a great number of servants, and in some instances, for transporting whole families of poor labourers, whom they established on their lands, for a term of years, endowing them with competent stock, and receiving in return, one half of the agricultural produce.

The first Deputy Governor, under Barclay, was Thomas Rudyard, an attorney of London, noted for his assistance at the trial of Penn and Mead, who arrived at his government, early in 1683. He was superseded, however, at the close of the year, by Gawn Lawrie, also of London, who had been one of Byllinge's trustees, for West Jersey. The efforts of Rudyard, of Samuel Groome, who was the surveyor of the proprietaries, and of Lawrie, were strenuously directed to create a city, at Amboy Point; a plan for which, the proprietaries had published, with an invitation to adventurers. They laid the ground out in lots, with out-lots, or small farms, appendant to them, put up houses on account of the proprietaries, in order to entice settlers, and proclaimed the advantages of its situation, in England and America. The town at first called ***Ambo***, the Indian name for point, received soon after, the addition of Perth, in honour of the Earl, and was thenceforth known, as Perth Amboy. The endeavours of the proprietaries, in this respect, were crowned with very partial success; nor were their equally earnest efforts to establish foreign trade with their city, more happy. New York possessed, in her more advantageous position, and greater capital, the means of suppressing all rivalry, to which her governors did not hesitate to add force; seizing, in the very port of Amboy, vessels engaged in foreign trade, carrying them to New York, for adjudication, upon alleged breach of commercial regulations.

The new proprietaries do not appear to have deemed any modification of the civil polity of the country necessary. In their description of the province, they commended the concessions of Berkeley and Carteret, and promised to make such additions to them as might be found necessary. Their administration for several years seems to have been satisfactory to the inhabitants; and with some inconsiderable exception, the discord arising from opposing titles, was stilled.

III. But James II., who had now ascended the throne,* had little respect for the engagements of the Duke of York. Nor could his seeming friendship for Barclay, nor the influence of the Earl of Perth, and the other courtier proprietors, deter him from involving New Jersey in the design he had formed of annulling all the charters and constitutions of the American colonies. A real or pretended complaint was preferred to the English court, against the inhabitants of the Jerseys, for evasion of custom-house duties. The ministers, eagerly seizing this pretext, issued writs of *quo warranto*, against both East and West Jersey; and directed the Attorney-General to prosecute them with the greatest possible expedition. The reason assigned for this proceeding, was, the necessity of checking the pretended abuses "in a country, which ought to be more dependent upon his majesty." Aroused by this blow, the proprietaries of East Jersey presented a remonstrance to the King; reminding him, that, they had not received their province as a benevolence, but had purchased it, at the price of many thousand pounds, to which they had been encouraged, by his assurances of protection; that they had already sent thither several hundreds of the people from Scotland; and that, if satisfactory, they would propose to the New Jersey Assembly, to impose the same taxes there, that were paid by the people of New York. They entreated, that if any change should be made in the condition of the

* On the death of Charles II., 6th February, 1685.

provinces, it might be, by the union of East and West Jersey, to be ruled by a governor, selected by the King from the proprietaries. But James was inexorable, and gave to their remonstrances no other answer, than that he had resolved to unite the Jerseys, New York, and the New England colonies, in one government, dependent upon the crown, and to be administered by Andross. Unable to divert him from his arbitrary purpose, the proprietaries of East Jersey, not only abandoned the contest, for the privileges of their people, but consented to facilitate the execution of the King's designs, as the price of respect, for their interest in the soil. They made a formal surrender of their patent, which being accepted by the King, the proceedings on the *quo warranto* were stayed, with regard both to East and West Jersey.* Seeing no resistance to his will, the King was less intent on consummating his acquisition; and while the grant of the soil to the proprietaries, which was necessary for this purpose, still remained unexecuted, the completion of the design was abruptly intercepted by the British revolution.

IV. Upon the departure of Lord Neil Campbell, from Jersey, after a few months residence only,† Andrew Hamilton, Esq., a respectable Scotch gentleman, became Deputy Governor; which office he continued to exercise, until June, 1689, when, by his return to Europe, it was vacated, and so remained, until his second arrival, in August, 1692. During this interval, there appears to have been no regular government in New Jersey. The peace of the country was preserved, and the prosperity of its inhabitants promoted, by their honesty, sobriety, and industry. In the mean time, Robert Barclay died;‡ having retained the government in chief, during his life. At his death, this power reverted to the proprietaries; who having, by sales and subdivisions of their rights, become too numerous, readily to express their will, some delay occurred in filling the vacancy. In March, 1692, Andrew Hamilton, received the commission of Governor-in-chief; which, the proprietaries were, nevertheless, compelled, very reluctantly, to revoke in March, 1697, in consequence of a late act of parliament, disabling all Scotchmen, from serving in places of public trust and profit, and obliging all colonial proprietors to present their respective governors to the King, for his approbation. In his place, they appointed Jeremiah Basse, who arrived in the province, in May, 1698; but, who, though instructed by the ministers of the King, had not the royal approbation in the form prescribed, nor it seems, the voice of a majority of the proprietaries. These circumstances, added to the hostility borne to the proprietary government, by such of the settlers, as held their lands by adverse title, occasioned disobedience to his authority; to enforce which, he imprisoned some of the most turbulent malcontents. This energetic measure served but to increase the public dissatisfaction; to allay which, Colonel Hamilton was reappointed, notwithstanding the statute, which was now construed, not to extend to the provinces, and without the royal sanction. A new pretence for disobedience was thus afforded, which was immediately seized; and a petition and remonstrance was sent, by the disaffected, to the King, complaining of their grievances, and praying redress. This document betrayed the source of these commotions to be the claims of the proprietors to the exclusive possession of the soil under the Duke of York's grants, their demand of quit-rents, and repudiation of the title alleged to have been derived from Indian grants and the approbation of Colonel Nicholls. The petitioners close their remon-

* April, 1688. Smith, App. 558, &c. Grahame's Col. Hist.

† From 10th Oct. 1686, to March, 1687. MSS. Records, Secretary's Office, Amboy. Smith's Hist. App. 558.

‡ 3d October, 1690.

strance, with a prayer, that if the rights of government be in the proprietaries, his Majesty would compel them to commission for governor, some one qualified by law, who, as an indifferent judge, might decide the controversies, between the proprietaries and the inhabitants.*

V. To these causes of uneasiness, another was at this period superadded, affecting alike, the proprietaries and the people, in the renewed assumption by New York, of supremacy over New Jersey, manifested in an attempt to levy taxes by law upon that province. This effort, though encouraged by King William, was as unsuccessful as those which had preceded it. The Crown lawyers, to whom the complaint of the Jersey proprietors was referred, reported, that no customs could be imposed on the Jerseys, otherwise, than by *Act of Parliament*, or their own assemblies.†

VI. At length, the proprietaries of East and West Jersey, embarrassed by their own numbers, and by the searching and critical spirit of their people, finding that their seignoral functions tended only to disturb the peace of their territories, and to obstruct their own emoluments from the soil, hearkened to an overture from the English ministers, for the surrender of their gubernatorial power to the Crown. They were further induced to this measure, by the desire to avoid a tedious and expensive lawsuit, with which they were threatened: the Lords of Trade having resolved to controvert their rights of Government by a trial at law, in which they would probably have taken the broad ground, that the King was not competent to subdivide and alienate the sovereign power. The determination of the Lords on this head had prevented the confirmation of the appointment of Col. Hamilton to the office of Governor of East and West Jersey, respectively, and such was the confusion in the provinces, consequent upon this rejection, that many of the proprietaries, whilst professing their readiness to surrender the government upon such terms and conditions as were requisite for the preservation of their properties and civil interests, earnestly prayed that Col. Hamilton might be approved, until the surrender could be effected.‡ But, whilst they seemed to make this approbation almost a condition of their surrender, other proprietaries refused to join in the petition to that effect, though expressing their readiness to yield the government. Under these circumstances, the Lords of Trade, upon consideration, that, the disorders into which the province had fallen were so great, that, the public peace and administration of justice was interrupted and violated, and that no due provision could be made for the public defence, recommended that his Majesty should appoint a Governor by his immediate commission, with such instructions as might be necessary, for the establishment of a regular constitution of government, by a Governor, Council, and General Assembly, and other officers; for securing to the proprietors and inhabitants, their properties, and civil rights; and for preventing the interference of the Colony with the interests of his Majesty's other plantations, as the proprietary governments in America had generally done.

VII. The proprietaries were desirous to annex special conditions to their surrender, which they inserted in several memorials. It was finally, however, made, absolutely and unrestricted, by all parties interested in both provinces, before the privy council, on the 17th of April, 1702; and Queen Anne proceeded forthwith to reunite East and West Jersey into one province, and to commit its government, as well as that of New York, to her kinsman Edward Hyde, Lord Cornbury, grandson of the chancellor, Earl of Clarendon. The commission and instructions which this nobleman received, formed the con-

* Smith's Hist. App. 560. † Grahame's Col. Hist. vol. ii. p. 361.
‡ Smith's N. J. App. No. 12, 13, 14.

stitution and government of the province, until its declaration of independence. The confidence of the proprietaries in the crown, exemplified by the unconditional surrender, was not misplaced. The greater part of the provisions they were desirous to obtain, were inserted in the instructions, which were submitted to, and approved by, them, before confirmation in council. Indeed, so much regard was paid to their wishes, that they might have nominated the first governor, could they have united on any individual. All the measures preparatory to the surrender, had been completed prior to the death of King William,* but were not perfected until nearly a year after that monarch's death, by his successor Anne.

The new government was composed of the governor, and twelve counsellors, nominated by the crown, and an Assembly, of twenty-four members, to be elected by the people, for an indefinite term, whose sessions were to be holden, alternately, at Perth Amboy, and Burlington.† Five, or in case of necessity, three members of council made a quorum; and they possessed the right to debate and vote on all subjects of public concern brought before them. Their number was neither to be augmented nor diminished, nor any member to be suspended, without sufficient cause, when report was to be made to the commissioners of trade and plantations. The Assembly was constituted of two members from Amboy, two from Burlington, two from Salem, and two from each of the nine counties, into which the whole province was then divided.‡ No person was eligible to the Assembly, who did not possess a freehold in one thousand acres of land, within the division for which he was chosen, or personal estate to the value of five hundred pounds sterling; and the qualification of an elector was a freehold estate in one hundred acres of land, or personal estate to the value of fifty pounds sterling. The house was to be convened by the governor from time to time, as occasion might require, and to be prorogued, or dissolved at his pleasure. The laws enacted by the council and Assembly were subject to the negative of the governor; and when passed by him, were to be immediately transmitted to England, for confirmation or disallowance by the crown. The governor was empowered to suspend members of council from their functions, and to fill vacancies occurring by death; and with consent of this body, to constitute courts of law, but not other than those established, except by royal order; to appoint all civil and military officers, and to employ the forces of the province in hostilities against public enemies: He was commanded to communicate to the Assembly, the royal desire, that, they would provide means, for a competent salary to the governor, to themselves, to the members of councils, and for defraying all other provincial expenses: He was empowered, with advice and consent of council, to regulate salaries and fees of officers, and such as were payable on emergencies: He was directed to have especial care, that God Almighty be devoutly and duly served, the book of common-prayer, as by law established, read each Sunday and holiday, and the sacrament administered, according to the rights of the church of England; that churches already built, should be well and orderly kept; that more should be built, as the colony improved, and that beside, a competent maintenance to be assigned to the minister of each orthodox church, a convenient house should be built at the common charge, for each minister, and a competent proportion of land, granted him for a glebe, and exercise of his industry; and that the parishes be so limited, as should be most convenient for the accomplishment of this good work: He was to permit liberty of conscience to all persons (except papists), so they be contented

* March 8, 1701. † See note N.

‡ Bergen, Essex, Somerset, Middlesex, Monmouth, Burlington, Gloucester, Salem, Cape May.

with a quiet and peaceable enjoyment thereof, not giving offence or scandal to the government: and he was vested with the right of presentation to all ecclesiastical benefices.

If, on the death or absence of the governor, there were no lieutenant governor commissioned, the eldest counsellor, nominated by the crown, exercised his powers.

Quakers were declared to be eligible to every office, and their affirmation accepted in lieu of oaths.

Due encouragement was directed to be given to merchants, and, particularly, to the Royal African Company, in England, lately established for prosecuting the accursed slave trade, and special care to be taken that they were duly paid for the negroes they should import and vend in the province. Laws were also to be enacted, protecting the slave against inhuman severity, promoting his conversion to Christianity, and punishing his wilful murder, by death.

From the courts of the province, where the value in controversy exceeded one hundred pounds, an appeal lay to the governor in council, excluding such members as might have, previously, sat upon the cause; and where the value exceeded two hundred pounds, the cause might be carried before the privy council in England. And,

Predicating, that great inconveniences might arise by the liberty of printing in the province; no printing press was permitted, nor any book or other matter allowed to be printed, without the license of the governor.

The former proprietaries were confirmed in their rights to the soil and quit-rents, as they had enjoyed them before the surrender, with power to appoint their surveyors, and the exclusive right to purchase lands from the Indians.

The constitution thus framed, gave to New Jersey, a polity similar to that of other royal governments in America; but it fell far short of the uncontrolled political freedom enjoyed under the proprietary concessions. The great and essential principle of political happiness, the popular will, was deprived of its energy, and circumscribed in its action, by the subjugation of the Assembly, in the times of its convention and duration of its sessions, to the pleasure of the governor; and by the double veto of him and the crown upon the laws. The means were thus created, not only of marring the most beneficial measures, when conflicting with the partial interests of the prince or his deputy; but when such measures were indifferent to them, of selling their approbation for selfish considerations. When these consequences of the surrender were felt, and they were not long delayed, the proprietaries and people contended by an ingenious, but alas! by a fallacious reasoning, that, they had reserved, and by the nature of things were entitled to, the privileges of their first and palmy state. Among these privileges, they enumerated, absolute religious freedom; exemption from every species of imposition, not levied by their Assemblies; the establishment of the judiciary by the governor, council, and Assembly; exemption from military duty of those conscientiously scrupulous against bearing arms; the solemnization of marriage, as of other contracts, in presence of disinterested witnesses merely; the determination of all causes, civil and criminal, by jury, and in criminal cases, the right of peremptory challenge, to the number of thirty-five; and the right of the Assembly alone, to enact laws, provided, they were agreeable to the fundamental laws of England, and not repugnant to the concessions. Some of these claims were so entirely incompatible with the right of government, as understood by the crown, that we cannot be surprised that they were disregarded.

VIII. The attractions which the neighbouring province of Pennsylvania, presented to the English Quakers, and the cessation, which the British revolution produced, of the severities that had driven so many Protestant dissenters from both England and Scotland, undoubtedly, prevented the population of New Jersey from advancing with the rapidity which its increase, at one period, seemed to promise. Yet, at the close of the seventeenth century, the province is said to have contained twenty thousand inhabitants, of whom, twelve thousand belonged to East, and eight thousand to West, Jersey.* It is more probable, however, that the total population did not exceed fifteen thousand; the great bulk of whom, were Quakers, Presbyterians, and Anabaptists. There were two Church of England ministers in the province, but their followers were not sufficiently numerous and wealthy to provide them with churches. The militia, at this period, amounted to fourteen hundred men. This province, like several others of the continental colonies, witnessed a long subsistence of varieties of national character among its inhabitants. Patriotic attachment and mutual convenience, had, generally, induced the emigrants, from different countries, to settle in distinct bodies, whence their peculiar national manners and customs were preserved. The Swedes appear to have been less tenacious of these, than the Dutch, and to have copied, very early, the manners of the English. The distinction arising too, from the separation of the province into governments and two proprietaryships, was long continued, and is now scarce wholly obliterated. Yet, the inhabitants of the eastern and western territories, were strongly assimilated by the habits of industry and frugality, common to the Dutch, the Scotch, the emigrants from New England, and the Quakers; and the prevalence of these habits, doubtlessly, contributed to maintain tranquillity and harmony among the several races, which were alike distinguished by the steadiness and ardour of their attachment to those liberal principles which had been incorporated with the foundations of political society in the province. Negro slavery was, unhappily, established in New Jersey, though, at what precise period, or by what class of planters it was introduced, cannot now be ascertained. In spite of the royal patronage which this baneful system received, it did not become inextricably rooted. Yet the Quakers, here, as in Pennsylvania, became proprietors of slaves; but they always treated them with humanity; and so early as the year 1696, the Quakers of New Jersey, united with their brethren, in Pennsylvania, in recommending to their own sect, to desist from the employment, or at least from the further importation of slaves.†

The trade of the province was even at this time considerable. Its exports consisted of agricultural produce, among which, mistakenly, we think, *rice* has been enumerated, with which it supplied the West Indian islands; furs, skins, and a little tobacco, for the English market; and oil, fish, and other provisions, which were sent to Spain, Portugal, and the Canary islands.‡ Burlington, at this time, gave promise of becoming a place of considerable trade; and the comfort and neatness of its buildings, are commended by several writers of this era.§ It possessed a thriving manufactory of linen and woollen cloth, which was soon smothered by the jealous policy of the mother country. In 1695, the governor's salary, in East Jersey, was one hundred and fifty pounds; in West Jersey, two hundred pounds; and those of other officers, at proportionate moderate rates.

* Grahame's Col. Hist vol. ii. 366. Holmes' Ann. vol. ii. p. 45, &c.

† Kalm's Travels, vol. i. and ii. Winterbotham, ii. 279. Warden, vol. ii. 38. Clarkson's History of the Abolition of the Slave Trade, vol. i. 131, 136.

‡ Gab. Thomas' Hist. of West N. J. 13, 33. Oldmixon, i. 141. Blome celebrated the excellence of the New Jersey tobacco.

§ Thomas. Blome, who wrote in 1686.

IX. Having thus brought our history to the termination of the proprietary governments, it may be proper, before we proceed to a narration of events, under the royal administration, to consider the condition of the aborigines, the manner in which their interest in the soil was extinguished, and the principles adopted by the proprietaries, in disposal of their acquisitions.

The strong are every where masters of the weak. In all ages, and with all people, the power to subdue has been accompanied with the pretension of right. The European, eminently endowed with this power, mentally and physically, over the untutored savage of America, unhesitatingly, appropriated to himself, all that the latter possessed, comprehending his labour and his life. From the first landing of Columbus, at Guannahané, or San Salvador, to the present era, the right by discovery has been the right of conquest. The ambition of princes, stimulated by the most sordid motives, was dignified by the approval of grave and politic counsellors, and sanctified by the fathers of the church, who in the plenitude of spiritual arrogance assumed, to dispose of all countries:—of those inhabited by Christians, because the inhabitants, as members of the church, were subjects of the supreme Pontiff—of other countries, because the church would be advanced by the estates and services of infidels. So long as colonization was prompted by state policy, and was effected by the sword, the rights of the original possessors of the soil, whatever they may have been, were wholly disregarded. The most sacred, most venerated spots, endeared to their inhabitants by the long occupancy of themselves and their ancestors, were seized with the same ruthless indifference, as the untrodden wild; and the fruits of cultivation, with the same license, as the spontaneous productions of nature. All the principles of property, growing out of occupancy and manipulation, which society in its simplest form must recognise, were utterly prostrated, in the subjugation of the newly discovered countries of the West. When, however, these countries were sought, not with the view of increasing regal power, or of gratifying the insatiate longings of avarice, but as an asylum against princely misrule and clerical tyranny, that justice which the colonist would obtain for himself, was in a measure, extended to the owner of the soil he would possess. The emigrant did not, perhaps could not, and ought not, divest himself of the idea of right, acquired by discovery of sparsely peopled land, to participate in the occupancy of an uncultivated soil, with the indigene, who exercised over it the slightest of all species of appropriation, that of occasional hunting upon it. But he recognised in this occupant also, a right impeding that full and separate property which his convenience required, and which his conscience forbade him to extinguish without a colour of compensation. The requisitions of conscience, however, in these cases, were easily appeased. In some instances, perhaps, their very existence may be attributed to the fears caused by the fierce, warlike, and indomitable character of the North American savage. The veriest trifles which could be imposed on the ignorance and vanity of the native were deemed adequate compensation for scores of miles of fertile lands; and such contracts of sale, whose nature was not comprehended by the vendors, were enforced by the vendees with as much confidence in the legality and equity of their title, as if a court of chancery had passed upon the adequacy of the consideration.

It has been erroneously supposed, that, the first instance of purchase from the aborigines of America, was given by William Penn; and modern historians and essayists, delighted to contrast the humanity and justice of his conduct with the violence and devastation of other European agents, have by the inflation of his deeds, obscured and almost hidden the scarce inferior merit of others. The Dutch, Swedes, and Fins on the Delaware, the English in Massachusetts, in New York, and New Jersey, had given examples of this just and prudent policy, which Penn gladly followed, but which he dared not reject. He has the merit of conforming to this established practice, with a kindness of spirit and humane consideration, which have made an indelible impression on the Indian race.

Compared with the value of the lands acquired, the sums paid for them were generally inconsiderable; and consisted, but too frequently, of articles of destructive luxury, serving to debase and destroy those who received them. This consideration, small and personal and perishable in its nature, was soon consumed; leaving the vendor, only, vain regrets, which frequently hurried him into imprudent and unjustifiable hostilities. Had it been practicable in the early period of the intercourse between the whites and Indians of North America, to have adopted the annuity system, which has been, in part, pursued by the United States, the Indian race might, possibly, have been improved, enlightened, and preserved.

The Indians inhabiting the country between the great lakes and the Roanoke, belonged, it would seem, either to the *Lenni Lenape*, or the *Mengwe* nations. The former, known among their derivative tribes, also, by the name of the *Wapanachki*, corrupted by the Europeans into *Opennaki*, *Openagi*, *Abenaquis* and *Apenakies*, and among the whites by the name of Delawares, held their principal seats upon the Delaware river, and were acknowledged by near forty tribes as their "grandfathers," or parent stock. They relate, that many centuries ago, their ancestors dwelt far in the western wilds: but emigrating eastwardly, they arrived after many years peregrination, on the *Namæsi Sipu* (Mississippi), or river of fish, where they encountered the *Mengwe*, who had also come from a distant country, and had first approached the river, somewhat nearer its source. The spies of the *Lenape* reported, that the country on the east of the river was inhabited by a powerful nation, dwelling in large towns, erected upon their principal rivers.

This people were tall and robust, some of them were said to be even of gigantic mould. They bore the name of *Alligewi*, from which has been derived, that of the Alleghany river and mountains. Their towns were defended by regular fortifications, vestiges of which are yet apparent, in greater or less preservation. The *Lenape*, requesting permission to establish themselves in the vicinity, were refused; but obtained leave, to pass the river, in order to seek a habitation farther to the eastward. But, whilst crossing the stream, the *Alligewi*, alarmed at their number, assailed and destroyed many who had reached the eastern shore, and threatened a like fate to the remainder, should they attempt the passage. Fired by this treachery, the *Lenape* eagerly accepted a proposition from the *Mengwe*, who had hitherto been spectators of their enterprise, to unite with them, for the conquest of the country. A war of great duration was thus commenced, which was prosecuted with great loss on both sides, and eventuated in the expulsion of the *Alligewi*, who fled from their ancient seats, by way of the Mississippi, never to return. The devastated country was apportioned among the conquerors; the *Mengwe* choosing their residence, in the neighbourhood of the great lakes, and the *Lenape* in the lands of the south.

After some years, during which, the conquerors lived together in much harmony, the hunters of the *Lenape*, crossed the Alleghany mountains, and discovered the great rivers, Susquehanna and Delaware. Exploring the *Sheyichbi* country (New Jersey) they reached the Hudson, to which they, subsequently, gave the name of the *Mahicannittuck* river. Upon their return to their nation, they described the country they had visited, as abounding in game, fruits, fish, and fowl, and destitute of inhabitants. Concluding this to be the home destined for them, by the Great Spirit, the tribe established themselves upon the four great rivers, the Hudson, Delaware, Susquehanna, and Potomac, making the Delaware, to which they gave the name of the *Lenape wihittuck*, (the river or stream of the Lenape) the centre of their possessions.

They say, however, that all of their nation who crossed the Mississippi, did not reach this country; and that a part remained west of the *Namæsi Sipu*. They were finally divided into three great bodies; the larger, one-half of the whole, settled on the Atlantic; the other half was separated into two parts; the stronger continued beyond the Mississippi, the other remained on its eastern bank.

Those on the Atlantic were subdivided into three tribes; the Turtle or *Unamis*, the Turkey or *Unalachtgo*, and the Wolf or *Minsi*. The two former inhabited the coast from the Hudson to the Potomac, settling in small bodies, in towns and villages upon the larger streams, under chiefs subordinate to the great council of the nation. The *Minsi*, called by the English, *Muncys*, the most warlike of the three tribes, dwelt in the interior, forming a barrier between their nation and the *Mengwe*. They extended themselves from the Minisink, on the Delaware, where they held their council seat, to the Hudson on the east, to the Susquehanna on the south-west, to the head waters of the Delaware and Susquehanna rivers on the north, and on the south to that range of hills now known, in New Jersey, by the name of the Musconetcong, and by that of Lehigh and Coghnewago, in Pennsylvania.

Many subordinate tribes proceeded from these, who received names either from their places of residence, or from some accidental circumstance, at the time of its occurrence remarkable, but now forgotten.

The *Mengwe* hovered for some time on the borders of the lakes, with their canoes, in readiness to fly should the *Alligewi* return. Having grown bolder, and their numbers increasing, they stretched themselves along the St. Lawrence, and became, on the north, near neighbours to the *Lenape* tribes.

The *Mengwe* and the *Lenape*, in the progress of time, became enemies. The latter represent the former as treacherous and cruel, pursuing, pertinaciously, an insidious and destructive policy towards their more generous neighbours. Dreading the power of the *Lenape*, the *Mengwe* resolved, by involving them in war with their distant tribes, to reduce their strength. They committed murders upon the members of one tribe, and induced the injured party to believe they were perpetrated by another. They stole into the country of the Delawares, surprised them in their hunting parties, slaughtered the hunters, and escaped with the plunder.

Each nation or tribe had a particular mark upon its war clubs, which, placed beside a murdered person, denoted the aggressor. The *Mengwe* perpetrated a murder in the Cherokee country, and left with the dead body, a war club bearing the insignia of the *Lenape*. The Cherokees, in revenge, fell suddenly upon the latter, and commenced a long and bloody war. The treachery of the *Mengwe* was at length discovered, and the Delawares turned upon them with the determination utterly to extirpate them. They were the more strongly induced to take this resolution, as the cannibal propensities of the *Mengwe* had reduced them, in the estimation of the Delawares, below the rank of human beings.*

Hitherto, each tribe of the *Mengwe* had acted under the direction of its particular chiefs; and, although the nation could not control the conduct of its members, it was made responsible for their outrages. Pressed by the *Lenape*, they resolved to form a confederation which might enable them

* The Iroquois or Mengwe sometimes ate the bodies of their prisoners.—*Heckewelder*, ii. N. Y. Hist. Col. 55.

better to concentrate their force in war, and to regulate their affairs in peace. *Thannawage*, an aged Mohawk, was the projector of this alliance. Under his auspices, five nations, the Mohawks, Oneidas, Onondagoes, Cayugas, and Senecas, formed a species of republic, governed by the united counsels of their aged and experienced chiefs. To these a sixth nation, the Tuscaroras, was added in 1712. This last, originally dwelt in the western parts of North Carolina, but having formed a deep and general conspiracy, to exterminate the whites, were driven from their country, and adopted by the Iroquois confederacy.* The beneficial effects of this system, early displayed themselves. The *Lenape* were checked, and the *Mengwe*, whose warlike disposition soon familiarized them with fire arms, procured from the Dutch, were enabled, at the same time, to contend with them, to resist the French, who now attempted the settlement of Canada, and to extend their conquests over a large portion of the country between the Atlantic and the Mississippi.

But, being pressed hard by their new, they became desirous of reconciliation with their old, enemies; and, for this purpose, if the tradition of the Delawares be credited, they effected one of the most extraordinary strokes of policy which history has recorded.

The mediators between the Indian nations at war, are the women. The men, however weary of the contest, hold it cowardly and disgraceful to seek reconciliation. They deem it inconsistent in a warrior, to speak of peace with bloody weapons in his hands. He must maintain a determined courage, and appear, at all times, as ready and willing to fight as at the commencement of hostilities. With such dispositions, Indian wars would be interminable, if the women did not interfere, and persuade the combatants to bury the hatchet, and make peace with each other.

Their prayers seldom failed of the desired effect. The function of the peace maker was honourable and dignified, and its assumption by a courageous and powerful nation could not be inglorious. This station the *Mengwe* urged upon the *Lenape*. "They had reflected," they said, "upon the state of the Indian race, and were convinced that no means remained to preserve it, unless some magnanimous nation would assume the character of the WOMAN. It could not be given to a weak and contemptible tribe; such would not be listened to: but the *Lenape* and their allies, would at once possess influence and command respect."

The facts upon which these arguments were founded, were known to the Delawares, and, in a moment of blind confidence in the sincerity of the Iroquois, they acceded to the proposition, and assumed the petticoat. The ceremony of the metamorphosis was performed with great rejoicings at Albany, in 1617, in the presence of the Dutch, whom the *Lenape* charge with having conspired with the *Mengwe* for their destruction.

Having thus disarmed the Delawares, the Iroquois assumed over them the rights of protection and command. But, still dreading their strength, they artfully involved them again in war with the Cherokees, promised to fight their battles, led them into an ambush of their foes, and deserted them. The Delawares, at length, comprehended the treachery of their arch enemy, and resolved to resume their arms, and, being still superior in numbers, to crush them. But it was too late. The Europeans were now making their way into the country in every direction, and gave ample employment to the astonished *Lenape*.

The *Mengwe* deny these machinations. They aver, that they conquered the Delawares by force of arms, and made them a subject people. And,

* Smith's New York. Dougl. Summ.

though it be said, they are unable to detail the circumstances of this conquest, it is more rational to suppose it true, than that a brave, numerous, and warlike nation should have, voluntarily, suffered themselves to be disarmed and enslaved by a shallow artifice; or that, discovering the fraud practised upon them, they should, unresistingly, have submitted to its consequences. This conquest was not an empty acquisition to the *Mengwe*. They claimed dominion over all the lands occupied by the Delawares, and, in many instances, their claims were distinctly acknowledged. Parties of the Five Nations occasionally occupied the *Lenape* country, and wandered over it, at all times, at their pleasure.

Whatever credit may be due to the traditions of the *Lenape*, relative to their migration from the west, there is strong evidence in support of their pretensions to be considered the source, whence a great portion of the Indians of North America was derived. They are acknowledged as the "grandfathers," or the parent stock, of the tribes that inhabited the extensive regions of Canada, from the coast of Labrador to the mouth of the Albany river, which empties into the southernmost part of Hudson's Bay, and from thence to the Lake of the Woods, the northernmost boundary of the United States; and also by those who dwelt in that immense country, stretching from Nova Scotia to the Roanoke, on the sea-coast, and bounded by the Mississippi on the west. All these nations spoke dialects of the *Lenape* language, affording the strongest presumption of their derivation from that stock. The tribes of the *Mengwe*, interspersed throughout this vast region, are, of course, excepted. They were, however, comparatively, few in number.

We have no data by which to determine the number of Indians in New Jersey, at the advent of the Europeans. It is certain that it was very inconsiderable. The tribes were small, and scattered over the country; and consisted then, or soon after, of portions of the *Mengwe* and *Lenape* nations. These petty hordes were commonly distinguished in their intercourse with the whites, by the names of creeks, or other noted places, near which they dwelt. Thus, there were the *Assunpink*,* the *Rankokas*,† the *Mingo*, the *Andastaka;* about Burlington, the *Mantas;*‡ the *Raritans*, the *Navisinks*, &c. The most noted nations, who occasionally inhabited the province, and claimed lands within it, were the *Naraticongs*, on the north side of the Raritan river; the *Capitinasses*, the *Gacheos*, the *Muncys*, or *Minisinks*, the *Pomptons*, the *Senecas*, the *Maquas*, or *Mohawks*, and perhaps others, of the confederates of the Five Nations. These tribes were frequently at war with each other, and the heads of their arrows and javelins, are even now occasionally discovered in the battle-fields; and near the falls of the Delaware, on the Jersey side, and at Point-no-Point, in Pennsylvania, and at other places, entrenchments were made against hostile incursions. At some seasons of the year, the country, on the sea shore was probably more thickly covered by swarms, who crowded from the adjacent provinces to enjoy the pastimes, and partake the plenty of the fishing and fowling seasons. And we may conceive, that they were *Mengwe* warriors, whom Hudson encountered in the Kill-van-Kuhl, and the New York Bay.

From the petty resident tribes, purchases of the soil of New Jersey, were from time to time, made by the Dutch, the Swedes, and the English proprie-

* *Stony Creek.*

† *Lamikas*, or *Chichequas*, was the proper Indian name. The Indians did not use the *r*.

‡ *Frogs*. A creek or two, in Gloucester county, are called *Manta*, or *Mantua*, from a large tribe that resided there. The tribes were probably of the same stock.

tors of East and West Jersey. Prior to the conquest of New York, by Nicholls, it is probable, that individuals were permitted to purchase from the natives, such tracts of land as they required. Subsequently to that event, a like practice was for a short time permitted, upon the express license and confirmation of the governor. But after the grant to Berkeley and Carteret was proclaimed, no purchase from the Indians, other than by the general proprietors, could be deemed lawful. These proprietors, appear to have conducted themselves, with much equity; and for nearly a century to have maintained, with the remnant of the tribes, great cordiality and friendship.*

When the war of 1756, unbridled the evil passions of the western Indians, some of those who had usually resided in New Jersey, ungratefully, united with the enemy, and probably, in the year 1758, led the way to the massacres of a few families on the Walpack. Upon the first evidences of Indian hostility, the legislature of New Jersey appointed commissioners to examine into the treatment of those who dwelt within their boundaries, with whom a convention was holden, at Crosswicks, in the winter of 1756, and they were invited to unfold whatever grievances they might have. They complained of some impositions, in grants of lands, to individuals, and in their private traffic, particularly, when intoxicated; of the destruction of the deer, by iron traps; and the occupation of some small tracts of land, the title to which, they had not sold. At the session of 1757, the Assembly imposed a penalty on persons selling them strong drink, so as to intoxicate them—prohibited the setting of traps weighing more than three pounds—avoided all sales and leases of land, made in contravention of the laws—and appropriated sixteen hundred pounds, to the purchase of a general release of Indian claims, in New Jersey; one-half to be expended for a settlement, for such Indians as resided south of the Raritan, where they might dwell, and the remainder, to be applied to the purchase of any latent claims of non-residents. At a second convention, holden also at Crosswicks, in February, 1758, the Indians produced a specification of their claims, appointed attorneys, to represent them in future negotiations, and executed a formal release, to all lands in New Jersey, other than those in their schedule, and also to such of those as might have been before conveyed; excepting the claims of the Minisinks and Pomptons, in the northern parts of the province; reserving the right to hunt and fish, on unsettled lands.†

* The last purchase from the Indians, entered in the East Jersey Records, was made by John Willocks, from the Indian Weequehelah, June 16th, 1703, of a tract of land, in Monmouth county.—*Book F.* 221.

† The Indians who retired to the west, had, to one of the messengers, from Pennsylvania, complained of the death of the sachem, Weequehelah; but this was a mere pretence, to colour their attempts with the appearance of justice; as that Indian was known to have been executed for actual murder, and to have had a legal trial. He was an Indian of great note, among Christians and Indians, of the tribe that resided about South river, where he lived, with a taste much above the common rank of Indians, having an extensive farm, cattle, horses and negroes, and raised large crops of wheat; and was so far English in his furniture, as to have a house well provided with feather beds, calico curtains, &c. He frequently dined with governors and great men, and behaved well; but his neighbour, Captain John Leonard, having purchased a cedar swamp of other Indians, to which he laid claim, and Leonard refusing to take it on his right, he resented it highly, and threatened that he would shoot him; which he accordingly took an opportunity of doing, in the spring, 1728, while Leonard was in the day time walking in his garden, or near his own house.—*Smith's New Jersey*, pp. 440–441, n.

The commissioners for treating with the Indians, were Andrew Johnston, and Richard Salter, esquires, of the council; and Charles Read, John Stevens, William Foster, and Jacob Spicer, esquires. The Indians were, Teedyuscung, king of the Delawares; George Hobayock, from the Susquehannah; *Crosswick Indians*, Andrew

Towards the close of the summer of 1758, and after the inroads on the Walpack, Governor Bernard, through the medium of Teedyuscung, king of the Delawares, summoned the Minisink or Muncy, and the Pompton Indians, who had joined the enemy, to meet him at Burlington. Thither, they despatched deputies, who opened a council, on the 7th of August, 1758, at which a Mingo attended, who, exercising the right of a conqueror, declared, the Muncys to be women, and, consequently, unable to treat for themselves; and proposed to adjourn the conference, to the council fire, about to be lighted at Easton—to which, the governor readily acceded.* The great council holden at this place, in October, 1758, had the general pacification of the Indian tribes, for its chief object. A special conference was, however, had, by Governor Bernard, with the chief of the united nations, the Minisinks, Wapings, and other tribes, on the 18th of that month; when he obtained, in consideration of one thousand dollars, a release of the title of all the Indians, to every portion of New Jersey.

The commissioners, subsequently, with the consent of the Indian attorneys, purchased a tract of more than three thousand acres of land, called "Brotherton," in Burlington county, on Edgepeling creek, a branch of the Atsion river, upon which, there were a cedar swamp, and a saw mill; and adjacent, many thousand acres of poor, uninhabited land, suitable for hunting, and convenient for fishing on the sea shore. This property was vested in trustees, for the use of the Indians, resident south of the Raritan, so that they could neither sell nor lease any part thereof; and all persons, other than Indians, were forbidden to settle thereon. Soon after the purchase, they were assisted by the government to remove to this spot, and to erect commodious buildings. In 1765, there were about sixty persons seated here, and twenty more at Weekpink, on a tract secured, by an English right, to the family of King Charles, an Indian sachem. But no measure has yet been devised, to avert the fiat which has gone forth against this devoted race. This feeble remnant having obtained permission to sell their lands, in number between seventy and eighty, removed, in 1802, to a settlement on the Oneida lake, belonging to the Stockbridge Indians, who had invited their "*Grandfathers* to eat of their dish," saying, "it was large enough for both;" and adding, with characteristic earnestness, that, "they had stretched their necks, in looking towards the fire-side of their grandfathers, until they were as long as those of cranes." The united tribes remained here until 1824; when the encroachments of the whites induced them, with the Six Nations, and the Muncys, to quit New Stockbridge, and to purchase from the Menomees, a large tract of land on the Fox river, between Winnebagoe Lake, and Green Bay, and extending to Lake Michigan. In 1832, the New Jersey tribe, reduced to less than forty, applied by memorial, to the Legislature of the State, setting forth, that they had never conveyed their reserved rights of hunting and fishing, on unenclosed lands, and had appointed an agent, to transfer them on receipt of a compensation. This agent, a venerable chief

Wooley, George Wheelwright, Peepey, Joseph Cuish, William Loulax, Gabriel Mitop, Zeb. Conchee, Bill News, John Pembolus; *Mountain Indians*, Moses Totamy, Philip; *Raritan Indian*, Tom Evans; *Ancocus Indians*, Robert Kekott, Jacob Mullis, Samuel Gosling; *Indians from Cranbury*, Thomas Store, Stephen Calvin, John Pompshire, Benjamin Claus, Joseph Wooley, Josiah Store, Isaac Still, James Calvin, Peter Calvin, Dirick Quaquaw, Ebenezar Wooley, Sarah Stores, widow of Quaquahela; *Southern Indians*, Abraham Loques, Isaac Swanelae. John Pompshire, interpreter.

* The degradation of the Delawares, or Lenape, is apparent upon every occasion, on which the Mengwe assemble with them. Benjamin, who on this occasion replied to Governor Bernard, on behalf of the Muncy Indians, held a belt in his hand, but spoke whilst sitting, not being allowed to stand, until the Mingo had spoken.—*Min. of Treaty.—Smith's Hist. N. J.* 450.

of seventy-one years of age, bore the name of Bartholomew S. Calvin. He had been selected by J. Brainerd, brother of the celebrated Indian missionary, and placed at Princeton College, in 1770; where he continued, until the revolutionary war cut off the funds of the Scotch Missionary Society, by whom he was supported. He afterwards taught school, for a number of years, at Edgepeling, where he had as many white as Indian pupils. As all legal claim of the tribe, was even by its own members, considered barred by voluntary abandonment, the Legislature consented to grant remuneration, as an act of voluntary justice; or rather, as a memorial of kindness and compassion, to the remnant of a once powerful and friendly people, occupants and natives of the State, and as a consummation of a proud fact, in the history of New Jersey, that every Indian claim to her soil, and its franchises had been acquired by fair and voluntary transfer. By the act of 12th of March, the treasurer was directed to pay to the agent, two thousand dollars, upon filing in the secretary's office, a full relinquishment of the rights of his tribe.

In all the measures of the state for the extinction of Indian title, it will be observed that she was moved by principles of justice, humanity, and sound policy. No pecuniary benefit resulted directly to the treasury, as she possessed, in her own right, not a single acre of the soil. This, by every title, legal and equitable, was fully vested in the proprietaries, respectively, of East and West Jersey; and we proceed to consider, concisely, the principles which they adopted for its disposal.

X. By the several "Concessions" of Berkeley and Carteret, and their grantees, the twenty-four general proprietors, lands were given to settlers, masters, and servants, males and females, in designated quantities, subject to an annual quit-rent, and the extinction of the Indian title. This was the common tenure until the 13th January, 1685,* and some few instances occur so late as 1701. Lands thus granted were denominated "*head lands.*"

The mode of the grant was devised with due regard to the ease and safety of the grantees. A warrant signed by the governor and major part of the council, was directed to the surveyor-general, commanding him to survey a specific number of acres. Upon this warrant the surveyor endorsed his return; both were recorded by the register, and upon certificate from the governor and council, he issued a patent, which receiving the signature of the governor and council, was, also, duly registered. A reservation, not ordinarily expressed in the patent, was made of all mines of gold and silver.

There was, however, another source of legal title, to lands in the province, in the Swedish and Dutch authorities; under the latter of which, many tracts were holden in East and West Jersey, accompanied with an Indian title, obtained by the holders. Upon the English conquest, the principle was, immediately, established, that no Indian right could be purchased, except by license from the English proprietors. Thus, that license was required for the Elizabethtown tract, and was given by Colonel Nicholls before, and in ignorance of, the transfer to Berkeley and Carteret. Governor Philip Carteret, also, gave such licenses, but, always subject to the "Concessions," which required the purchaser from the Indians, to take a proper and formal title from the general proprietors. In such case, when the Indian grant covered more than the location of the grantee, he was entitled to contribution from all who were benefitted by it. Thus, when under his license, the Newark settlers procured the Indian release for more lands than they had appropriated to imported heads in 1685, they claimed, and in 1692 received,

* Elizabethtown Bill in Chancery. See ante, p. 26.

from the council of proprietors, a full indemnity, in the grant of one hundred acres of land more than they were entitled to by the Concessions, for each of the original settlers, at a quit-rent of six-pence sterling the hundred, instead of four shillings and two-pence, per annum.

In the year 1680, governor Andross, after his usurpation of authority in New Jersey, encouraged purchases from the Indians, in derogation of the proprietary rights. But the Duke of York, on complaint, not only disowned the acts of his deputy, but removed him from office. Many of such purchasers, afterwards, took title from the proprietors, in due form; but the danger of the practice, induced an act of Assembly, in 1683, prohibiting all treaties with the Indians, without license from the governor. During the confusion resulting from the rival claims of Mr. Basse and Mr. Hamilton to the government, from 1698 to 1702, this act was disregarded, and purchases were made from the natives. But, in 1703, as soon as the government was resettled, another act annulled them, and required the possessor to take a proprietary title, within six months from its passage. This act, also, prescribed the method by which the proprietaries, themselves, individually, should obtain license to treat with the natives; and imposed a penalty of forty shillings per acre, upon every one who should purchase without license.

We have elsewhere spoken, particularly, of the Elizabethtown purchase.* Many of the claimants under the Indian title, took patents from the proprietors; but others have steadfastly relied upon it, resisting all efforts of the proprietors to recover quit-rent, or locate warrants, and have repeatedly disturbed the public peace by their violence. This pertinacity has been maintained, notwithstanding the only plausible pretence of title, was in the sanction of Governor Nicholls, as the deputy of the Duke of York, given after the right had passed from the Duke to his grantees, and notwithstanding such sanction was formally disavowed by the Duke, 25th November, 1672. This claim purchased for a few pounds, the very payment of which is uncertain, covered 400,000 acres, between the Raritan and Passaic Rivers. Irregular Indian titles were also set up in Middletown and Shrewsbury townships, but were early abandoned; the claimants taking patents from the proprietors, and receiving an indemnity for their expenditure in the grant of 500 acres of land, each. Some of the inhabitants of Newark, also pertinaciously claimed an exclusive right under the Indian grant, refusing to pay quit rents, and playing a conspicuous part in the riots which were, from time to time, excited by efforts to enforce proprietary rights. The adverse claims of the Newark people, were, probably, settled by arbitration and acquiescence.† But although many suits have been brought at law, and a most ably drawn bill, containing the whole case has been filed in chancery, the proprietaries have been unable to obtain an effectual determination of the question arising out of the Elizabethtown pretension. The quit rents throughout East Jersey, are due and demandable; but the lapse of time, and the division of tracts and interests render it impossible to collect them. In one instance, only, that of the quit-rent on the town of Bergen, of £15 sterling, per annum, a commutation after suit brought, has been made between the tenants and proprietors.

For a short period after the purchase of the province, by the twenty-four proprietaries, the grant of bounty or head lands, was continued. The proprietaries soon after their acquisition, sold many small shares, to persons who transported themselves and families into the Eastern division. And they

* See page 27.

† See Appendix note O, for a copy of a letter from David Ogden, esq., 20th February, 1767, and see Phila. Lib. No. 1588, octavo.

agreed to divide part of the lands remaining in common, among themselves in proportion to their rights. Dividends were thus made from time to time. The first consisted of 10,000 acres to each share, or twenty-fourth part, and to fractions of a share in the same proportion. These dividends were to be located in any place, not before appropriated. And to restrain the locations within proper limits, a number of the proprietaries, resident in New Jersey, convened from time to time with the governor, to examine the rights of the respective claimants, in order to determine what was due to each; and upon a certificate of five of them, the governor issued the proper warrants of survey. This council first met on the 13th November, 1684. In other respects, the mode of location and of obtaining of title, was similar to that pursued by the first proprietaries under their Concessions, except, that in patents to the proprietors, no quit-rents were reserved. This mode continued until after the surrender of the government, and the arrival of the first governor appointed by Queen Anne.

Upon the 2d of December, 1702, two further dividends having been made, a general order was declared, that the surveyor-general should survey to each proprietor his proportion without further particular warrant, by which the duty of inquiry into the rights of each proprietary, and ordering warrants, devolved upon that officer. At the same time, a former regulation was renewed, directing that no survey should be made to any person, whose title was not upon record with the register; who by means of an account opened with each proprietary, could certify the true condition of his share.

The office of register, which was established by the Concessions, and was always in the nomination of the proprietaries, was recognised by Act of Assembly, 21st February, 1692. Upon the surrender of the government to the crown, it was agreed, that the governors to be appointed, should be instructed to procure from the assembly, such acts, whereby the right of the proprietaries to the soil might be confirmed to them, together with such quit-rents as they had reserved, and that the particular estates of all purchasers, claiming under the general proprietaries, should be also confirmed and settled; and he was required not to permit any person, other than such proprietors and their agents, to purchase lands from the Indians. These instructions were regularly continued to the respective governors.

In 1719, the act for running, and ascertaining the division line between East and West Jersey, and other purposes, required, that the surveyor-general of the respective divisions, should keep by themselves, or deputies, a public office in the cities of Perth Amboy and Burlington, respectively, in which should be, carefully, entered and kept, the surveys of all lands, thereafter, made, which should be of record, and pleadable in the courts. Authority was also given to such officers, respectively, to collect, and preserve all muniments of title, which might be of general use for proving the rights of the proprietaries, or persons claiming under them; and the officers were required to give bond to the governor for the use of the proprietors, in the sum of one thousand pounds, conditioned for the faithful performance of their duties.

As the practice which now universally prevailed, of the proprietaries or their vendees laying their warrants wherever they could, or supposed they could, find vacant lands, and as the surveys were not regularly recorded, many persons not only surveyed lands which had been formally appropriated, but even settled and improved them, and were afterwards ousted. For remedy of this grievance, the same act provided, that all surveys theretofore made, the certificates of which were in the hands of any of the inhabitants of this or the neighbouring province, which were not within two years, and such certificates as were in the hands of persons living beyond seas, which were not within three years, after the publication of the act, duly recorded, either in the recorder's office, or in the surveyor-general's record of the division, in which such lands were surveyed, should be void; and any succeeding survey duly made and recorded, should be as good and sufficient, as if no former survey had been made.

After the surrender of the government, by which the governor ceased to be an officer of the proprietaries, no more patents could be made under the seal of the province. The proprietaries of East Jersey, observing that those of West Jersey had never used that method for appropriating their dividends, but had made all their divisions by warrants from their council of proprietaries, after inspection of the right of the claimant and survey thereon made and certified by their surveyor-general and recorded, resolved to adopt the same form of obtaining their dividends in severalty. And this mode, since 1703, has continued to prevail in both East and West Jersey.

The council of proprietaries of East Jersey, having devolved their principal duties on the surveyor-general, they, after the surrender, ceased to meet, unless on special occasions. But finding this inattention prejudicial to their interests, a majority of the general proprietors, their attorneys, and agents, by an instrument, dated the 25th day of March, 1725, agreed, that, a certain number therein mentioned, having, in their own right, or by proxy, eight whole proprietaries, should make a council, with power to appoint the receiver of the quit-rents, the register, and the surveyor-general, declare dividends, examine claims, grant warrants of survey, and, generally, to do all things requisite for the management of proprietary affairs. The council commonly held two stated meetings, annually, at Perth Amboy, and convened, also, when specially required. From 1725, to the present period, it has continued to administer the affairs of the proprietaries of East Jersey, without intermission.*

The whole number of dividends, made by the proprietaries of East Jersey, are eleven of "*good right*," and three of "*pine right;*" the first, amounting to thirty-eight thousand, and the second, four thousand, acres to each share. A very great portion of these rights have been located, but the stock is not yet exhausted. In Monmouth there is much vacant land, but it is not valuable; in the northern counties, Sussex, Bergen, and Morris, there is little unappropriated; but in Middlesex, Somerset, and Essex, there is none unlocated.†

XI. Soon after the purchase by the West Jersey proprietaries, they resolved to divide their territory into ten parts or precincts, and the whole into one hundred shares or actions. To this end, chapter first of the Concessions, provided, that the commissioners, for the time being, "should take care for the setting forth and dividing all the lands of the province, as were already taken up, or by themselves shall be taken up and contracted for, with the natives, and the said lands to divide into one hundred parts, as occasion shall require; that is to say, for every quantity of land that they shall, from time to time, lay out to be planted and settled on, they shall first, for expedition sake, divide the same into ten equal parts or shares; and, for distinction sake, mark in the register, and upon some of the trees, belonging to every tenth part, the letters A B, and so end at the letter K." The

* Mr. John Rutherford is now, or was lately, its president, and James Parker, Esq. the register. To the latter gentleman I express my obligation, for the readiness and kindness, with which he has communicated much information relative to the eastern land office, and other subjects of general interest. Its first president was Lewis Morris, afterwards governor.

† Proprietary rights of East Jersey have sold, since 1797, generally, at about one dollar the acre, wholesale—sometimes higher, if scarce, before a dividend. The retail price has been about one dollar and fifty cents the acre. The value in 1834, is stated at one dollar, or seventy-five cents per the acre, in large quantities.

commissioners were then instructed to give preference to certain individuals of the county of York,* for themselves and friends, who were described, "as a considerable number of people, who might speedily promote the planting of the said province," in the choice of any one of such tenths. Afterwards, any other person or persons, who should go over to inhabit, and have purchased to the number of ten proprietaries, should have liberty to make choice of any of the remaining parts: and all other proprietaries who should go over to settle, and could make up amongst them the number of ten proprietors, might elect to settle in any tenth, not before appropriated. The commissioners were empowered to see such tenth part, so chosen, laid out and divided into ten proprietaries, and to allot the settlers so many proprietaries out of the same, as they had order for. And the commissioners were instructed to follow these rules, until they should receive contrary directions from the major part of the proprietors.

To encourage the settlement of the province, the proprietaries of West Jersey, also, adopted the plan of granting head lands, as in East Jersey, with some modification, of the conditions. Thus—1. To all persons, who, with the consent of one or more of the proprietaries, should transport themselves or servants to the province, before the 1st April, 1677, there were granted, for his own person and for every able man servant, each, seventy acres; and for every weaker servant, male or female, exceeding the age of fourteen years, fifty acres; and to every servant, when free, fifty acres in fee: 2. To masters and able servants, arriving before the 1st of April, 1678, fifty acres, and to such weaker servants, thirty acres; and to servants, after the expiration of their service, thirty acres: 3. To every freeman, arriving in the province between the 1st of April, 1678, and the 1st of April, 1679, with an intention to plant, forty acres; for every able man servant the like quantity, and for such weaker servant, twenty acres; with twenty acres to each servant at the expiration of service: Upon lands of the first class, there was reserved an annual quit-rent to the proprietor, his heirs and assigns, to whom the said lands belonged, of one penny an acre for what should be laid out in towns, and a half-penny an acre, for what should be laid elsewhere; the rent to commence two years after the lands were laid out: upon lands of the second class, one penny farthing, the acre, when in towns, and three farthings the acre, elsewhere: and on lands of the third class, one penny halfpenny the acre, in towns, and one penny the acre, elsewhere.

Lands so granted and settled, were to be holden, on condition, that every hundred acres should contain, at least, two able men servants, or three such weaker servants, and so proportionately, for a lesser or greater quantity, beside what the master or mistress should possess, as granted for his or her own person. On failure of which, on notice to the occupant or his assigns, three years time was given for completing the number of servants, or for the sale of such portion of the lands, as should not be so peopled. And, if, within such three years, the holder should fail to provide such number of persons, (unless the General Assembly, without respect to poverty, should judge it to have been impossible, to keep such number of servants), the commissioners, upon verdict and judgment of a jury of the neighbourhood, were empowered to dispose of so much land, for any term not exceeding twenty years, as should not be planted with the due number of persons, to some other, that would plant the same; reserving to the proprietor his rents. It was further provided, that every proprietor, who should go over in person, and inhabit, should maintain upon every lot he should take up, one person

* Thomas Hutchinson of Beverly, Thomas Pearson of Benwicke, Joseph Holmesly of Great Kelke, George Hutchinson of Sheffield, and Mahlon Stacy of Hemsworth.

for every two hundred acres. "And all other proprietors, that do *but** go over in person and inhabit, should keep upon every lot of land that should fall to them, one person at least, and if the lot exceed one hundred acres, then, upon every hundred acres, one person. And upon neglect, the commissioners were empowered to dispose of the lands, as in the preceding case. This obligation for keeping servants upon lands was to continue in force for ten years, from the date of the Concessions; unless where, in case of default, the commissioners had let the lands for a longer period.

For the regular laying out of lands, the register having recorded a grant from a proprietor, for any quantity of acres, made out a certificate to the surveyor, or his deputy, enjoining him, to survey such quantity, from the share of such proprietor; which done, the surveyor returned the survey to the register, and such return was duly registered in a book kept for that purpose, and an endorsement of the entry was made on the back of the warrant.

The commissioners elected by the Assembly, in 1681, prescribed additional rules for the settlement of lands; by which, the surveyor was required to measure the front of the river Delaware, beginning at Assunpink Creek, and proceeding thence, to Cape May, that the point of the compass might be found, for running the partition line between each tenth. Each tenth was to have its proportion of front, on the river, and to run so far back into the woods, as to give it 64,000 acres for first settlement, and for subdividing the Yorkshire and London two-tenths: Three thousand two hundred acres, were allowed, where the parties concerned pleased to choose it, within their own tenth, to be taken up in the following manner; one-eighth part of a proprietary, and so for smaller parts, to have their full proportion of the said land, in one place (if they pleased); and greater shares, not to exceed five hundred acres, to one settlement. All lands, so taken up and surveyed, were to be seated within six months, after being taken up; upon penalty, that the choice and survey should become void; in which case, they might be taken up by any other purchaser, he seating them, within one month after they should be taken up: No person was permitted to take up lands on both sides of a creek, for one settlement, unless for special cause· Nor to have more than forty perches front, to the river or navigable creek, for every hundred acres, except it fell upon a point, so that it could not be avoided—when the commissioners might exercise their discretion: All lands were to be laid out, on straight lines, that no vacancies should be left between tracts, except in special cases, to be determined by the commissioners: All persons were allowed their just proportion of meadow, at the discretion of the same officers: Persons already settled, were at liberty to make their settlements their choice, following the rules prescribed: Every proprietor was allowed four hundred acres to his proprietary, and proportionably to lesser quantities, for town lot; over the 3200 above mentioned, which might be taken any where within his own tenth, either within or without the town bounds: No person having taken up a town lot, was permitted to leave it, and take a lot elsewhere; nor could any one take up more land within the town bounds, than belonged to his town lot, by virtue of his purchase: No person, not a purchaser, to whom town lot, or lots, were given, was permitted to sell his lot of land, separate from his house, on penalty of the sale being void, and the lot forfeited to the town of Burlington, to be disposed of therein, at the discretion of the commissioners: No person, thenceforth, was permitted, to take up any land without special order, from two or more

* The word *but* here is found in Leaming and Spicer's Collection, and in Smith's History. *Sed quere* whether the word "*not*" ought not to be substituted.

commissioners for the time being: All settlements were to be modified conformably with the preceding rules: The proprietors in England, were to be notified, that it was necessary for the speedy settlement of the province, and all concerned therein, that there should be allowed to each proprietary 3200 acres, for the first choice (*first dividend*); and in case of the arrival of many adventurers, who purchased no land in England, the commissioners reserved the liberty to take up as much more land, as should give to every proprietor, a quantity not exceeding 5200 acres, which had been allowed for the first settlement (dividend). But that no one should take up any such portion of land, but as they should settle it; and after the 3200 should have been settled: All public high-ways were to be laid out at the discretion of the commissioners, through any lands, allowing the owners reasonable satisfaction: All persons having taken up lands within the first and second tenth, were required to present their muniments of title, to certain of the commissioners, for inspection; and persons thereafter taking up lands, within such tenth, were required to declare, before such commissioners, upon the pains of perjury, that the quantity specified in their respective deeds, did really, and in good conscience, belong to them; upon which such commissioners might grant a warrant to the surveyor, enjoining him to return such warrant and survey, at the next court, after survey, that the same might be registered by order of the court: The proprietors and purchasers, within the first and second tenths, had liberty to take their full proportions, as before, within mentioned, of the first and second choice, provided they did not, respectively, take up more than five hundred acres, in one settlement.

By the subdivision of the proprietys, it soon became difficult to ascertain the sense of those interested; and great detriment arising to the business of the province, it was resolved by the proprietors, on the 14th of February, 1687, to constitute a proprietary council, consisting of eleven commissioners, to be annually elected, from among themselves; which number was in the subsequent year reduced to nine. These commissioners were empowered to act and plead in all such affairs, as should concern the body of the proprietors, as fully and effectually as if every proprietor were present; and two shillings per day were allowed them as a compensation. In November, 1688, the commissioners gave the following instructions relative to the examination of deeds, and granting of warrants, for taking up of lands. 1. That no warrants should be granted, but upon the production of good deeds, authentic copies, or an extract of the record of such deed, under the register's hand. 2. That the deeds signed by Edward Byllinge, only, before the year 1682, were insufficient to sustain warrants. 3. That there should be a particular warrant, for every separate deed or particular purchase. 4. That the president of the council should, from time to time, grant warrants for the commissioners for the taking up their own lands. 5. That warrants, for laying out the lands of the surveyor-general, should not be directed to him, but to some other person, at the discretion of the commissioner, issuing the warrant. 6. That every proprietor demanding a warrant, should engage to pay his proportionate share of expense of the management of the proprietary affairs.

Under this council, the land affairs of West Jersey have been administered, to the present day. The right to head lands, as we have seen, ceased after the first of April, 1678. From that period, all titles were derived from individual proprietors. Dividends were declared from time to time, and carried to the credit of each proprietor, who was then at liberty to locate, or to sell unlocated, the quantity appropriated to his share, wherever it could be found unsurveyed.

XII. The boundary between East and West Jersey, though of no political importance, was long a vexed, and still continues an unsettled question. The line of partition was geographically fixed by the quintipartite deed, between the proprietors, of the first of July, 1676, confirmed by Act of Assembly, 27th March, 1719. But some difficulties occurred, subsequently, in making the partition, to the understanding of which, we must take a review of the titles of the respective proprietors.

The patent from Charles I. to the Duke of York, conveyed all the country now within the states of New York and New Jersey. The deed from the Duke to Berkeley and Carteret, extended New Jersey, "northward as far as the northernmost branch of the bay, or river Delaware, which is in 41° 40′ of latitude, and from thence in a straight line to Hudson's river in 41° of latitude." Lord Berkeley conveyed his undivided moiety in fee to Fenwicke, in trust for Byllinge, and Fenwicke conveyed such moiety to Penn, Lawrie and Lucas, reserving a tenth to himself, which tenth he subsequently assigned to Eldridge and Warner, who conveyed it to Penn, Lawrie, and Lucas, the better to enable them, in conjunction with Byllinge, to make partition of the entire province with Sir George Carteret. These parties by the quintipartite deed, after expressly declaring, that, the province extended northward, as far as the northernmost branch of the river Delaware, which is in 41° 40′ latitude, determine that the line of partition shall be a straight line drawn from the most northerly point or boundary on the Delaware, to the most southerly point of the East side of Little Egg Harbour. The confirmation of the Duke of York, (6th August, 1680,) to the West Jersey proprietor, and his confirmation, (14th March, 1682), to the twenty-four East Jersey proprietors, recognise the northern boundary as above described, and referring to the quintipartite deed, give the limits accordingly.

As the country became populous, much uneasiness was excited by sundry fruitless attempts for running the partition line, and the uncertainty relative to the point at which the designated latitude would fall. For remedy whereof, the Act of Assembly of 1719 was passed. This, after recognizing the quintipartite deed, and prescribing that a straight and direct line from the most northerly point of New Jersey, on the northernmost branch of the river Delaware, to the most southerly point of a beach on Egg Harbour, should be the division line, appoints commissioners to run the line and provides, that, which ever board of proprietors had appropriated lands of the other, should give an equivalent of lands, in satisfaction, and that the then settlers should be quieted.

Pursuant to this act, and another for establishing the boundary line with the province of New York, Governor Hunter commissioned John Johnstone, and George Willocks of the eastern division, Joseph Kirkbride, and John Reading of the western division, and James Alexander, surveyor-general of both divisions, in conjunction with commissiouers from New York, to discover and determine which of the streams of Delaware is the northernmost branch thereof, and also the place on such branch that lies in latitude 41° 40′. These commissioners together with Robert Walter and Isaac Hicks commissioners, and Allain Jarrat surveyor on the part of New York, after designating the Fishkill branch, and fixing the point of latitude in the low land, in the Indian town called Cosheghton, on the east side of the river, executed an indenture tripartite, certifying the above result of their labours. After which, the West Jersey commissioners retired, protesting that their business was completed.

The northern station point thus fixed, appears to have been recognised and acquiesced in by both parties; yet the division line was not run for many years. But random lines were made along the whole distance of the extreme points, that the true line might be marked with the greater certainty and ease; and such lines served to regulate future surveys.

The assigns of Carteret and Berkeley were respectively entitled to a moiety of the province, and unacquainted with the true geography of the country, they imagined that the line given in the quintipartite deed, would nearly effect their intentions; and the idea of equality of partition seems to have prevailed, until about the year 1687, when its propriety was questioned by Dr. Daniel Coxe. Under this idea, in the year 1686 an agreement was made between Robert Barclay, and the proprietors of East Jersey, and Edward Byllinge, and the proprietors of West Jersey, for running the partition line, so as to give "as equal a division of the province" as was practicable. Pursuant to which, Lord Neil Campbell, Governor, and captain Andrew Hamilton, and John Campbell of East Jersey, and John Skene, deputy governor, and Samuel Jennings and others of West Jersey, all of whom were proprietors of their respective divisions, entered into bonds, to stand to the award of John Reed and William Emley, who were appointed to determine the line, and who directed that it should run from Little Egg Harbour, N. N. W. and fifty minutes more westerly, which was more than twelve degrees westward of the quintipartite line; and was so altered, because the umpires as well as the parties to the bonds, were better acquainted with the quantity of land in each division, than the parties to the quintipartite deed. The line so awarded, was actually run in the year 1687, by George Keith, surveyor-general of East Jersey, from the south station point, to the south branch of the Raritan; and now forms the straight line, which in part, bounds the counties of Burlington, Monmouth, Middlesex, Somerset, and Hunterdon. This line was deemed by the West Jersey proprietors to be too far west, and was not continued.

On September 5, 1688, Governors Coxe and Barclay, entered into an agreement for terminating all differences concerning the deed of partition; stipulating that the line run by Keith, to the south branch of the Raritan, should be the bounds, so far, between the provinces, and directing the route by which that line should be continued for perfecting the division.* But this agreement was never carried into effect.

Subsequent to the determination of the north station point, in 1719, several ineffectual attempts were made by the parties to ascertain the line. At length, John Hamilton, and Andrew Johnstone, commissioners under the Act of 1719, (the latter named in 1740), at the request of the eastern proprietors, in the year 1743, appointed John Lawrence to run the line, pursuant to the act of Assembly; which was, accordingly, done in September and October of that year. And this line, the East Jersey proprietors allege, has been frequently recognised by the West Jersey proprietors, particularly, by the issue of warrants of relocation from the year 1745, to 1765, for lands which were found to be east of this line; by directions given to survey and return for the use of the proprietors of the fifth dividend, the gore, or angle formed by Keith's and Lawrence's lines; by numerous surveys inspected, approved and ordered to be recorded, which are bounded by Lawrence's line; and by other acts of acquiescence, entered upon their minutes. To this line of Lawrence, the East Jersey proprietors still firmly adhere.

The division line between the provinces of New York and New Jersey, remained long unsettled, by reason that the latitude of forty-one degrees on Hudson's river, was not ascertained. From the zealous and violent pretensions of the border inhabitants in the respective provinces, such disorders arose, as to demand the interposition of their respective Legislatures; and in 1764, acts were passed in both provinces, referring the subject to the King. His Majesty appointed seven commissioners, who, meeting at New York on the 18th July, 1769, determined that, the boundary should be a straight

* See Smith's Hist. N. J. pp. 197, 198.

and direct line, not from the station point in latitude 41° 40′, as fixed by the commission of 1719, *but from the mouth of the Mackhackamack, at its junction with the Delaware*, in latitude 41° 21′ 37″, to the latitude of 41° on Hudson's river. The controversy with New York, then, and subsequently to the year 1719, was deemed, only, to affect the property of the proprietors of East Jersey,—the Legislature rejecting their application to defray any portion of the expense of settling the boundary line; and the West Jersey proprietors refusing to join in their request; alleging that their stations were already fixed, and must remain.

The alteration of the boundary on the Delaware is supposed to have been produced by corrupt influence over the commissioners; who were all crown officers, and by the change, took from the proprietary government of New Jersey, and gave to the royal government of New York, large tracts of land, to be granted at its pleasure. The effect of the change was to take from the East Jersey proprietors, near two hundred thousand acres, and to produce a new discussion relative to the partition between East and West Jersey.

The new station point, at the confluence of the Mackhackamack with the Delaware, now *the most northerly point or boundary of the province, on the northernmost branch of the river Delaware*, with a line thence to the station point, at Little Egg Harbour, would make a gore or angle with Lawrence's line, near ten miles wide in the northern part, narrowing in proportion as it approached the point of contact, and containing about four hundred thousand acres. On the 25th of January, 1775, the West Jersey proprietors assuming, that, the new northern station point, was the true northerly boundary of the province, from which the partition line should commence, and altogether losing sight of the words of the quintipartite deed and its dependencies, which assigned the point on the river, in latitude 41° 40′ as the station point, petitioned the legislature to pass a law for the final settlement of the said line, either in aid of the act of 1719, or by the appointment of commissioners, out of the neighbouring province, for that purpose. This petition was referred to the succeeding Legislature. On the first of December following, Daniel Coxe, president of the board of western proprietors, requested leave, on their behalf, to bring in a bill for the appointment of commissioners for the same purpose, suggesting the acquiescence of the eastern proprietors to the mode proposed, (which acquiescence the eastern proprietors deny). Leave was granted; but the public commotions, which soon after took place, prevented the execution of the measure. In October, 1782, the application to the Legislature was renewed ,stating the object of the western proprietors to be, "a recompense in value of lands, from the general stock of the eastern proprietors: for which purpose," they say, "they understand and believe, it is generally known, that, certain lands, called Ramapoch, belonging to the general stock of the eastern proprietors, and specially excepted in all the warrants of the eastern proprietors, were particularly allotted as an equivalent, in case the event should take place, which hath since happened, of the station point being fixed farther eastward than was formerly expected." This allegation respecting the Ramapoch lands, the eastern proprietors, scouted as too void of truth and foundation to need comment; and resisting the application to the Assembly, contended, that the subject was a private dispute between individuals, which should be decided by the courts of law or equity. The application of the western proprietors was rejected by the Assembly, on a vote of twenty-one to eleven.

Lawrence's line is now acquiesced in, by the greater part of northern Jersey; but is yet disputed in Monmouth county, and in the region of the pines, where, under West Jersey rights, great destruction of timber is committed. These rights are sought; having, hitherto, been sold at a much less price than those of East Jersey. The line run by Lawrence, in Sussex county, forms the boundary between Byram and Greene, Newton and Greene, and Stillwater, and between Walpack and Sandistone townships; crossing the Delaware into Pennsylvania, about fifteen miles below the present northernmost point of the state, it strikes the Delaware again, in the state of New York, near thirty miles north of the mouth of the Mackhackamack.*

* The authorities on which the foregoing statement is made, are—1. The several deeds cited:—2. The Act of Assembly, 1719:—3. The petitions of the respective parties in 1782:—4. The minutes in the land offices of East and West Jersey:—5. Smith's History; and—6. Circular of West Jersey proprietors, in 1795. The following statistical view is appended to the petition of the East Jersey proprietors, 1782.

1. The angle or gore of land which East Jersey lost in the controversy with New York, amounts to about 210,000 acres. The remaining quantity of land in New Jersey, being the whole amount of the state, is about 4,375,970 acres.

2. Therefore supposing a line was drawn, dividing the state into two equal half parts, and which would be the line of partition between East and West Jersey, each division would then contain about 2,187,985 acres.

3. Supposing Keith's line extended to Delaware river, to be the line of partition between East and West Jersey, the quantity of land in East Jersey would, then, be about 2,214,930 acres: the quantity in West Jersey 2,161,040 acres. And East Jersey would, then, contain 53,890 acres more than West Jersey.

4. Supposing Lawrence's line to be the line of partition, the quantity of land in West Jersey would, then, be about 2,689,680 acres: the quantity in East Jersey, 1,686,290 acres. And West Jersey would, then, contain 1,003,390 acres more than East Jersey.

5. Supposing a line to be drawn from the Mackhackamack, to the line of partition, the quantity of land in West Jersey would, then, be about 3,119,260 acres: the quantity in East Jersey, 1,256,710 acres. And West Jersey would, then, contain 1,862,550 acres more than East Jersey.

6. The angle or gore of land, between Keith's and Lawrence's line, contains about 528,640 acres. The angle or gore between Lawrence's line, and a line to be drawn from the Mackhackamack would contain about 429,580 acres.

CHAPTER V.

Comprising the Administration of Lord Cornbury. I. Arrival of Lord Cornbury—Demands a large and permanent Salary—being refused, dissolves the House.—II. A new Assembly chosen—Part of its Members arbitrarily excluded—Measures of the Governor.—III. Third Assembly convened—Determines to Petition the Queen, and to Remonstrate with the Governor—Public Grievances—Delivery of the Remonstrance, by Samuel Jennings.—IV. Reply of the Governor.—V. Dispute on the Treasurer's Accounts.—VI. The Governor refuses the Message of the Assembly, which they enter upon their Minutes.—VII. The West Jersey Proprietors, in England, address a Memorial to the Commissioners of Trade and Plantations, against Cornbury—Address of the Lieutenant-Governor, and Provincial Council, to the Queen.—VIII. The Governor unable to obtain the gratification of his wishes, by the Assembly, first prorogues, and then dissolves them.—IX. Offensive Conduct of Lord Cornbury, in his Government of New York—His Character.—X. Is reluctantly removed by Queen Anne—Imprisoned by his Creditors.

I. Lord Cornbury arrived in New Jersey, in August, 1703, and met the General Assembly, at Amboy, on the 10th of the succeeding November. The House prepared several bills, but passed, at this session, only, the act prohibiting the purchase of land from the Indians, by any person except the proprietaries. At the next session, holden at Burlington, in September, 1704, his lordship recommended to the Legislature, to ascertain by law, the rights of the general proprietors to the soil, and to establish some permanent fund, for the support of the government. A French privateer having committed depredations about Sandy Hook, he, thence, took occasion, also, to require a militia law, and the erection of a watch-tower, on the Nevisink Hills. All these measures were beset with difficulties. The people had been accustomed to pay, as they still are, small salaries to their officers, and were little disposed to gratify the wishes of his lordship, in this respect. Those who claimed lands under Indian grants, and held adversely to the proprietaries, resisted the attempt of the latter to confirm their rights. And every military effort was repugnant to the consciences of a large portion of the inhabitants. After a dilatory discussion of these embarrassing topics, the House proposed a revenue of thirteen hundred pounds, per annum, to endure for three years. But this sum, being far short of the governor's expectation, he requiring two thousand pounds, per annum, for a term of twenty years, was indignantly rejected; and in the hope of procuring an Assembly, more complaisant, he dissolved the present, and hastily commanded the election of another House.

II. The people, who, in the very wantonness of freedom, had involved themselves in contentious strife, discovered that they had exchanged king Log for king Stork. The precipitate and arbitrary measure of the governor was executed in the spirit with which it was conceived. By corrupt efforts, a House was obtained, with a large proportion, but not a majority, of the members devoted to the governor. To obtain the entire control of this body, his lordship resolved, by the advice of his counsellors, to exclude a portion of its members, under the false pretence, that they were not qualified by the requisite quantity of estate. As the representatives appeared before the governor to take the prescribed oaths, without which, they could not exercise their offices, he refused to administer them to Thomas Gardiner, Thomas Lambert, and Joshua Wright, distinguished delegates from West

Jersey, by whose exclusion, he obtained a majority of one, in the House. John Fretwell, of Burlington, was chosen speaker, by the casting vote of the clerk, who, though nominated by the governor, was admitted by the Assembly, to use the faculty of a member.

The House, thus constituted, complimented his excellency, on conducting the affairs of his government, "with great diligence, and exquisite management, to the admiration of his friends, and the envy of his enemies;" and granted him a revenue for the support of government, of two thousand pounds, for two years; six hundred of which, were given to the lieutenant-governor, Colonel Ingoldsby. Several other acts were passed, among which, we find one of amnesty, for offences during the late unsettled state of the province, and another establishing a militia, which, by its unnecessary severity, gave much disquiet to the Quakers; but no effort was made to confirm the proprietary estates. Having obtained all that he immediately required, the governor adjourned the House, in December, to the succeeding year, with many encomiums on its conduct.

At the next session, however, his power over it had ceased. The rejected members, after eleven month's exclusion, were admitted to their seats; the governor having been forced, by very shame, to recognise their qualification; which the title deeds of their estates had long before confirmed, to every dispassionate inquirer. But the most interesting object of his lordship, had been obtained by the settlement of the revenue, and he was content that the existing House should continue, though he could entertain little hope of service from it, either to himself or the province. It convened again in November, 1705, and October, 1706, but did no business at either session.*

III. When the term of the revenue had expired, the convocation of the Assembly was indispensable for its renewal; but it was impracticable, by any means, to procure another House like to the last. Few of the members of that, which met at Burlington on the 5th of April, 1707, were favourably disposed to the governor. Its most active leaders, Samuel Jennings, the speaker, and Lewis Morris, who had been twice expelled the council, for his resistance to the governor's measures, were among the most respectable and influential inhabitants of the province, intimately acquainted with its interests, and altogether adequate to sustain them. The House, therefore, soon after it met, resolved itself into a committee of the whole, with a clerk of its own appointment, to consider of the public grievances; of which it determined to complain, by petition to the Queen, and remonstrance to the governor.*

In the latter, prepared, most probably, by Morris, they express their regret, that, instead of granting to the governor the revenue required from them, it became their duty, to lay before him the unhappy circumstances of the province, which they attributed, in some measure, to his long and frequent absence from his government. They then proceeded to allege—That, he had obstructed the course of justice, by suspending, for years, the execution of the sentence of death, pronounced against some women, convicted of murder; and that this delay "was not only a very great charge, but that the blood of the innocents cried aloud for vengeance—and just heaven would not fail to pour it down upon their already miserable country, if the guilty were not made to suffer according to their demerits: That, in criminal cases, the accused were condemned to the payment of costs, even when no bill was found: That, the sole office for the probate of wills, together with the secretary's office, were holden at Burlington, to the great inconvenience of the inhabitants, who dwelt in the remoter parts of the province: That patents

* Smith's New Jersey, 284. See Appendix, P.

for the exclusive carriage of goods, on the road from Burlington to Amboy, had been granted for a term of years, contrary to the statute of 21 Jac. 1, against monopolies: That fees had been established without the authority of the General Assembly: And that the governor had put the records of the eastern division of the province into the hands of one, the pretended agent of the proprietors,* who did not reside in the province. Some of these grievances were certainly of a character to rouse public indignation, whilst others were, probably, more the result of circumstances, which would have been removed by the Legislative power, as they were offered for consideration.

But there were other grievances, which the Assembly deemed of higher nature, and attended with worse consequences. Such were—the prohibition to the council of proprietors, to issue warrants for land in West Jersey, and other unauthorised interferences with proprietary rights—the exclusion of the three members from the last House—and the corruption of the governor in receiving large sums of money for the dissolution of the first Assembly, in order that no act should be passed to compel the payment of proprietary quit-rents, and to obtain such officers as the contributors should approve. "This House," continues the remonstrance, "has great reason to believe, that the money so gathered, was given to Lord Cornbury, and did induce him to dissolve the then Assembly, and by his own authority to keep three members out of the next Assembly, and put so many mean and mercenary men in office; by which corrupt practice, men of the best estates are severely harassed, her Majesty's good subjects in this province, so impoverished, that they are not able to give that support to her Majesty's government, as is desired, or as they would be otherwise inclined to:—And we cannot but be very uneasy, when we find by these new methods of government, our liberties and properties so much shaken, that no man can say he is master of either, but holds as tenant by courtesy and at will, and may be stripped of them at pleasure. Liberty is too valuable a thing to be easily parted with, and when such mean inducements procure such violent endeavours to tear it from us, we must take leave to say, they have neither heads, hearts, nor souls, that are not moved by the miseries of their country, and are not forward with their utmost power, lawfully to redress them."

"We conclude by advising the governor to consider what it is, that principally engages the affections of a people, and he will find no other artifice needful, than to let them be unmolested in the enjoyment of what belongs to them of right; and a wise man that despiseth not his own happiness, will earnestly labour to regain their love."

This free and unceremonious remonstrance lost nothing of its force, in the delivery by speaker Jennings. In vain did his lordship attempt to awe his constant and spirited temper, by assumed airs of greatness, and by repeated interruption, with the cry of *stop! what's that?* as the most offensive passages were read to him. Jennings, with an affectation of deep humility, whenever interrupted, calmly desired leave to read the passages again; to all of which, he gave additional emphasis, so that the second reading was greatly more offensive than the first.†

IV. The indignation of the governor, at this remonstrance, is strongly pourtrayed, in a long circumstantial, but not very successful, reply; in which he denied the truth of some of its charges, and sought to justify the others. On the dread, expressed by the house, of divine vengeance for punishments delayed,

* Peter Sonmans.

† When the House had retired, Cornbury, with some emotion, says the historian Smith, told those with him, that Jennings had impudence enough to face the devil.

he remarked; "I am of opinion, that nothing has hindered the vengeance of just heaven, from falling upon this province long ago, but the infinite mercy, goodness, long-suffering, and forbearance of Almighty God, who has been abundantly provoked by the repeated crying sins of a perverse generation among us; and more especially, by the dangerous and abominable doctrines, and the wicked lives and practices of a number of people; some of whom, under the pretended name of Christians, have dared to deny the very essence and being of the Saviour of the world." The practice of extorting fees from the accused against whom no bill was found, he defended on the ground of established custom; admitting, however, that if the juries of the country were such as they ought to be, a different rule might be proper.

"But," he continues, "we find from woeful experience, that there are many men, who have been admitted to serve upon grand and special juries, who have convinced the world, that they have no regard for the oaths they take; especially among a sort of people, who, under a pretence of conscience, refuse to take an oath: and yet, who, under the cloak of a very solemn affirmation, dare to commit the greatest enormities, especially, if it be to serve a "friend," as they call him; these are the designing men, and the vindictive tempers of which all the Queen's good subjects ought to beware, and be protected from; and these are the crying sins which will undoubtedly draw down the vengeance of just heaven upon this province and people, if not timely and seriously repented of."

In considering the more heinous charge of corruption, the truth of which he peremptorily denies, his lordship demands; "who would not, after such assertions, expect to see the governor proved guilty, either of treason or betraying the trust reposed in him, by the Queen, by depriving the subjects of their lives, their estates, or their properties; or, at least, denying them justice, and perverting the laws to their oppression? These, or the like crimes, manifestly proved, are the only things that can justify men in the accusing a governor of corrupt practice, and of shaking the liberties and properties of the people. But if none of these things can be proven, but on the contrary, it does appear plainly, that no one act of severity, much less of injustice or oppression, has been done, since the government of this province come under the Queen, but there has been an impartial, just, and equal administration of justice observed throughout the whole course of my government, and that many acts of mercy have been extended to persons who deserved to be severely punished; then what sort of creatures must these bold accusers appear to be, in the eyes of all impartial and judicious men? That these are truths beyond all contradiction, and which all the people of this province know, I do challenge you, and every one of you, to prove to the contrary. And though, I know very well, that there are several unquiet spirits, in the province, who will never be content to live quiet, under any government, but their own; and not long under that neither, as appears by their methods of proceeding, when the government was in the hands of the proprietaries, when many of these very men, who are now the remonstrancers, were in authority, and used the most arbitrary and illegal methods of proceeding, over their fellow subjects, that were ever heard of; yet, I am satisfied, there are very few men in the province, except Samuel Jennings and Lewis Morris, men known, neither to have good principles, nor good morals, who have ventured to accuse a governor of such crimes, without any proof to make out their accusation; but they are capable of any thing but good."

V. New fuel was added to this flame, already unextinguishable, by a dispute relative to the accounts of Peter Fauconier, the provincial treasurer. In the examination of which the House found several objectionable items, paid upon the governor's order, merely, and without vouchers, which the treasurer refused to render without the governor's commands. Upon application for these, his lordship replied, that, he had already ordered them; therein exceeding his powers; inasmuch as the Lord High Treasurer had appointed an auditor-general, for the province, who had deputed one to settle the accounts of the provincial treasurer; he being responsible only to the Lord High Treasurer. His lordship proffered to explain any articles with which the Assembly were dissatisfied; but this, they very properly, declined, as they would have sanctioned the preposterous claim of irresponsibility of the provincial treasurer to a provincial Assembly, for the funds of the province, and would have placed them still more at the mercy of their extortionate rulers.

VI. In the temper which now prevailed among the officers of the state, there was no prospect of joint and beneficial labours; and the governor, probably, dreading a caustic rejoinder to his reply, prorogued the House on the 16th, to meet in the following September, at Amboy. A subsequent order convened them in October, when they resolved to answer the governor's replication, and to raise no money unless their grievances were redressed; in which case, they proposed to grant, for the support of government, fifteen hundred pounds. On the 28th, they informed the governor, that having seen his reply in print, they were disposed to answer it, and requested to know, when they might present their rejoinder. He promised to receive them in due time; but having waited for his message until next day, and then concluding that he purposed to elude their request, they sent a committee with their message, which, he refusing to receive, they caused to be entered on their journal.

In this address the House reiterated and amplified their former complaints, and spared no opportunity to give to his excellency the retort courteous. From the following examples, the reader will, probably, agree with us, that, their shafts were keen, if not polished. "It is," say they, "the General Assembly of the province of New Jersey, that complains, and not the Quakers, with whose persons (considered as Quakers) or meetings we have nothing to do; nor are we concerned in what your excellency says against them; they, perhaps, will think themselves obliged to vindicate their meetings, from the aspersions which your excellency, so liberally, bestows upon them, and evince to the world how void of rashness and inconsideration your excellency's expressions are, and how becoming it is, for the governor of a province, to enter the lists of controversy, with a people who thought themselves entitled to his protection, in the enjoyment of their religious liberties; those of them who are members of this House have begged leave, in behalf of themselves and their friends, to tell the governor they must answer him in the words of Nehemiah to Sanballat, contained in the eighth verse of the sixth chapter of Nehemiah; viz. *There is no such things done as thou sayest, but thou feignest them out of thine own heart.*"

In reply to the governor's boast, of the purity of his administration, they ask, "are not his Majesty's loyal subjects hauled to gaols, and there lie without being admitted to bail? And those that are," they continue, "is not the condition of the recognizances, that, if your excellency approves not of their being bailed, they shall return to their prisons? Are not several of her Majesty's good subjects forced to abscond, and leave their habitations, being threatened with imprisonment, and having no hopes of receiving the benefit of the law, when your excellency's absolute will is the sole measure of it? Has not one minister of the Church of England, been dragged by a sheriff, from Burlington to Amboy, and there kept in custody, without assigning any reason for it, and at last hauled by force into a boat, by your excellency, and transported, like a malefactor, into another government, and there kept in a garrison, a prisoner; and no reason assigned for it, but your excellency's pleasure? Has not another minister of the Church of England been laid under the necessity of leaving the province, from the reasonable apprehension of the same treatment? Is any order of men, either sacred or civil, secure in their lives, their liberties, or estates? Where these procedures will end, God only knows."

"If these, and what we have named before, be acts of mercy, gentleness, and good nature—if this be the administering laws, for the protection and preservation of her majesty's subjects, then have we been the most mistaken men in the world, and have had the falsest notion of things;—calling that cruelty, oppression and injustice, which is their direct opposite, and those things, slavery, imprisonments, and hardships, which are freedom, liberty, and ease; and must henceforth take France, Denmark, the Muscovian, Ottoman, and Eastern empires, to be the best models of gentle and happy government."

VII. Beside these measures of resistance, in the province, to the usurped authority and irregular proceedings of the governor, the West Jersey proprietors, residing in England, addressed a memorial condemnatory of his conduct, to the lords commissioners of trade and plantations; in which, they exposed at length, the evils resulting from his interference with their lands. The governor sought to repel these attacks, by an address, from the lieutenant-governor, and his council, to the Queen. After partially stating the dissentions in the province, they added, "We are now obliged humbly to represent to your majesty, the true cause; which, we conceive, may lead to the remedy of these confusions."

"The first, is owing to the turbulent, factious, uneasy, and disloyal principles of two men in the Assembly, Mr. Lewis Morris, and Samuel Jennings, a Quaker; men notoriously known to be uneasy under all government—men never known to be consistent with themselves—men to whom all the factions and confusions in the government of New Jersey and Pennsylvania, for many years, are wholly owing—men that have had the confidence to declare, in open council, that your majesty's instructions to your governors, in these provinces, shall not oblige or bind them, nor will they be concluded by them, further than they are warranted by the law, of which, also, they will be the judges; and this is done by them, (as we have all the reason in the world to believe,) to encourage, not only this government, but also the rest of your governments in America, to throw off your majesty's royal prerogative, and, consequently, to involve all your dominions, in this part of the world, and the honest, good, and well-meaning people in them, in confusion; hoping, thereby, to obtain their wicked purposes.

"The remedy for all these evils, we most humbly purpose, is—that your majesty will most graciously please to discountenance those wicked, designing men, and show some dislike to this Assembly's proceedings; who are resolved, neither to support this your majesty's government, by a revenue, nor take care to defend it, by settling a militia. The last libel, called 'The Reply, &c.' came out so suddenly, that as yet, we have not had time to answer it in all its particulars; but do assure your majesty, it is for the most part, false in fact; and in that part of it which carries any face of truth, they have been malicious and unjust in not mentioning the whole truth; which would have fully justified my Lord Cornbury's just conduct."*

It might be questionable at the present day, whether the lieutenant-governor, and his council, did not design to betray the cause they seemed to defend, when they charged it as a crime upon the citizens of a government

* See Appendix, Q., for names of Council.

of laws, that they preferred the laws, as they understood them, to the instructions of the Queen, and would obey the latter, so far only, as they were consistent with the former. But we have, here, only, an additional instance of the subserviency, which the love of power and place, every where produces. It is the law of society, if not of nature, that men should strengthen the hand that feeds them. And ordinary men, like the beast of the stall, lick the hand that fattens them, even for the shambles. The dispenser of official favours, whether he be a prince or a president, will always find minions, ever ready to maintain his prerogative above the law, and we are, therefore, not surprised, that such hoped for protection, from a daughter of James the Second.

VIII. Two days after Lord Cornbury had refused to receive the Address of the Assembly, he prorogued that body, to the spring of the ensuing year; and thus avoided the necessity of a defence, which he found difficult to sustain. The house met in Burlington, on the 5th of May, 1708; and in the illness of Jennings, their former speaker, named Thomas Gordon to that office.* The governor addressed them with the customary speech; to which, they replied, by repetition of former grievances, and recounting of new ones. Perceiving that nothing could be obtained, without the abandonment of the ground he had taken, he adjourned them, until September, to meet at Amboy; and in the interval, dissolved them.

IX. In his government of New York, the conduct of Lord Cornbury was, if possible, more offensive to the people, than in New Jersey; and had been productive of like results, universal dissatisfaction of the people, and entire suspension of legislative action. His character is described as a compound of bigotry and intolerance, rapacity and prodigality, voluptuousness, and cruelty, and the loftiest arrogance, with the meanest chicane. Whether from real difference in sentiment, or from a policy, which in those days was not uncommon, whilst his father adhered to James, the son attached himself to king William, and was among the first officers who deserted to him, on his landing at Torbay. Having dissipated his substance in riot and debauchery, and being obliged to fly from his creditors, in England, he obtained from his patron, the government of New York, which was confirmed by his kinswoman, Queen Anne, who added the government of New Jersey. He first excited the odium of the people of the former province, by the intolerance he exercised against the Presbyterians, and every other religious sect, except the protestant Episcopalians. Though the great body of the inhabitants, including the principal families of the province, were of the former persuasion, he prohibited their ministers from preaching without a license from himself; implying, that they officiated not of right, but by his indulgence. He, in one instance, fraudulently seized upon their church property, and delivered it to the Episcopal party; in another, he indicted two ministers from Virginia, who preached without license, for a misdemeanor; but his malice was defeated, by the independence of the jury, who refused to convict. In every part of the province, he tendered his assistance to the Episcopalians, to possess them of the churches, which other sects had built. Happily, his conduct in other departments of his government, by uniting all parties against him, soon deprived him of the power of instigating one portion of society to harass or oppress the rest. Not content with the liberal grants which the Assembly had made him, for his private use, he embezzled large sums appropriated to the erection of public works, and unable to subsist on his lawful emoluments, even with the addition of enormous pillage, he contracted debts, with every tradesman who would trust him, and set his

* See Appendix, R.

creditors at defiance, by means of his official station. The Assembly proposed, in vain, to establish a body of functionaries, to control the public expenditure, and to account to themselves; and, with as little success, did they transmit remonstrances, against him, to the Queen.* The only immediate result of the latter, was some private instructions to the governor. The proposition, to control the public disbursements, was rejected; and, when they insisted on a scrutiny of his accounts, he warned them not to provoke him, to exert "certain powers entrusted to him by the Queen, and to trouble him less about the rights of the House; as the House possessed no rights, other than the grace and good pleasure of her Majesty, suffered it to enjoy." By such declaration, and a line of policy strictly conformable therewith, he alienated all his adherents; and when he dissolved one Assembly, for its attention to the public interest, he was unable to convoke another of different character. At length the Assemblies refused to vote the smallest supply for the public service, until he should account for all his past receipts and applications of public money, and perform the impossible condition of refunding the sums he had embezzled. His dissolute habits and ignoble tastes and manners, completed and embittered the disgust with which he was, now, universally regarded; and when he was seen rambling abroad in the dress of a woman, the people beheld with indignation and shame, the representative of their sovereign and ruler of their country.†

X. At length Queen Anne was compelled, in the year 1709, by the reiterated and unanimous complaints of New York and New Jersey, to supersede his commission. No sooner was he deprived of office than his creditors threw him into prison. And thus degraded from an honourable station, by his public crimes, and deprived of liberty by his private vice and dishonesty, this kinsman of his Queen, remained a prisoner, for debt, in the province he had governed, till the death of his father, elevating him to the peerage, entitled him to liberation. He then returned to Europe, and died in the year 1723.‡

* See Appendix, S., for resolutions of the Assembly of New York.

† Grahame's Col. Hist. vol. ii. 302. Smith's New York.

‡ Smith's New York, 144, 145, 146, 164. Grahame's Col. Hist. 306. Biograph. Brit.

CHAPTER VI.

Comprising Events from the Removal of Lord Cornbury to the Close of the Administration of Governor Hunter—1709-1719.—I. Lord Cornbury succeeded by Lord Lovelace—His conciliatory Address to the Assembly.—II. Ready disposition of the House to provide for the Support of Government—Change in the Constitution of the Assembly—Assembly obtain a Copy of the Address of the Lieutenant Governor and Council, to the Queen, in favour of Lord Cornbury—Demand a hearing for their Defence before the Governor.—III. Death of Lord Lovelace and Accession of Lieutenant Governor Ingoldsby.—IV. Promptitude of the Province to aid in reducing the French Possessions in North America.—V. Failure of the Expedition, and renewed Efforts of the Colonists to revive it—Visit of the Chiefs of the Five Nations to England.—VI. Capture of Port Royal, &c. by Colonel Nicholson and the American Forces.—VII. Governor Ingoldsby removed—Government administered by William Pinhorne as President of Council—succeeded by Governor Hunter.—VIII. Biographical Notice of Governor Hunter.—IX. Meets the Assembly, which prefers Charges against Members of Council.—X. Expulsion of a Member of the House for his Conduct in Council—Address to the Queen.—XI. Bills proposed for the relief of the Quakers defeated by the Council.—XII. New Efforts for the Conquest of the French Provinces—Unfortunate Result.—XIII. Continued quiet of the Province.—XIV. Division of the Assembly.—XV. Governor Hunter returns to Europe—Testimonials in his favour by New Jersey and New York—Exchanges his Commission with William Burnet.

I. Lord Cornbury was succeeded in his governments of New York and New Jersey, by John, Lord Lovelace, Baron of Hurley, who met the council of the latter province, at Bergen, December 20th, 1708, and a new Assembly, at Perth Amboy, in the following spring.

The principles which directed his administration, were the converse of those of his predecessor. He had more confidence in the melting power of kindness and respect, than in that of haughtiness and reserve; in the influence of justice and frankness, than in force and fraud, to bend the people to his wishes. His address to the House was full of conciliation. He assured them, "that he would not give them any just cause of uneasiness under his administration, and hoped they would bear with one another; and that past differences and animosities would be buried in oblivion, and the peace and welfare of the country, only, would be pursued by each individual." On the subject of the support of government and the establishment of a militia, the contrast is striking between his course and that of the infatuated Cornbury. Instead of peremptorily demanding a large and fixed annual sum, payable for a long period; he observed, that "her Majesty would not be burdensome to her people; but there being an absolute necessity, that government be supported, he was directed to recommend that matter to their consideration; that they knew best what the province could conveniently raise for its support, and the easiest methods of raising it; that the making a law for putting the militia on a better footing than it at present stood, with as much ease to the people as possible, required their consideration; that he should always be ready to give his assent to whatever laws they found necessary for promoting religion and virtue, for the encouragement of trade and industry, and discouragement of vice and profaneness, and for any other matter or thing, relating to the good of the province."

II. These liberal and favourable sentiments were reciprocated by the House; they passed a bill, appropriating a sum exceeding seventeen hundred pounds, for the support of government; an act for settling the militia of the province; an act for the encouragement of the post-office; and an act for explaining grants and patents, for land, in the eastern division of the province. They, also, availed themselves of the present opportunity of changing the constitution of the General Assembly, giving to it a more aristocratical essence, than it received from the royal instructions. The latter required, that, the House should consist of two members elected by the *householders and inhabitants* of the towns of Amboy, Burlington, and Salem, respectively, and five members, chosen by the freeholders of the respective counties. The Assembly now directed that the electors, in all cases, should be *freeholders*, and that two members should be chosen for each of the above mentioned towns, and two for each county, and that the members should be freeholders of that division, for which they were, respectively, elected. The freehold required for the elector and representative, was that specified in the instructions, and the House was made the judge of the qualification of its members. This change was induced by the proprietaries; to whom it was a matter of obvious and deep interest, that, every inhabitant should be an owner of land.

The Assembly obtained from the governor, a copy of the address which the lieutenant governor and council had made to the Queen in favour of Lord Cornbury; and engaged him to hear their defence of the charges against them, in presence of the addressors, but the latter contrived, for a season, to elude the inquiry.

III. The prospect which the province now had of a happy administration, in which the interests of the people were duly consulted, and the officers of government, liberally and satisfactorily maintained, were content with the emoluments the law conferred, was unhappily obscured by the sudden death of their popular governor, in a few days after the passage of the above-mentioned laws, and the devolvement of his power upon the lieutenant governor Ingoldsby.

IV. This officer, pursuant to his instruction from the ministers of the Queen, laid before the Assembly their demand for aid, in an attack upon the French provinces in North America. The French had actively prosecuted the war declared against them by England, on the 4th May, 1702, and the northern English provinces of America, had suffered greatly from their incursions. In the preceding year, they had penetrated to Haverhill, on the Merrimack river, and reduced the town to ashes. Upon the entreaty of the inhabitants of New England, the ministry adopted a plan proposed by Col. Vetch, for the conquest of Arcadia, Canada, and Newfoundland. An attack upon Quebec was to be made, by a squadron of ships carrying five regiments of regular troops from England, and twelve hundred provincials, furnished by the zeal of Massachusetts and Rhode Island; whilst an army of fifteen hundred men from Connecticut, New York, New Jersey, and Pennsylvania, conducted by Colonels Nicholson and Vetch, should attempt Montreal, by way of the lakes. The enterprise, however, was never prosecuted; the exigencies of the war in Europe requiring all the forces of the allies. The quota of troops required from New Jersey, was two hundred. The Assembly entered spiritedly into the views of the ministry; passed one act appropriating three thousand pounds to aid the expedition, to be raised by the issue of bills of credit; another, for enforcing their currency, and a third for the encouragement of volunteers. The few Indian chiefs who were in the province, were summoned before the council, and incited to engage in the enterprise; and Col. Schuyler was commissioned by the governors of Connecticut, New York and Pennsylvania, to direct the efforts of these and of the Five Nations.

V. Upon failure of the expedition, Col. Nicholson returned to England to solicit further assistance, taking with him, five of the Indian sachems of the Five Nations, together with Col. Schuyler, whose influence over these warlike savages was almost unbounded. It suited the ministry to make an exhibition of these sons of the forest. The court being then in mourning for the death of the prince of Denmark, the American kings were dressed in black under clothes, and their coarse and filthy blankets were exchanged for rich scarlet cloth mantles, trimmed with gold. A more than ordinary solemnity attended the audience they had of her Majesty; Sir Charles Cotteral conducted them in coaches to St. James's; and the Lord Chamberlain introduced them into the royal presence, where the chief warrior and orator addressed a speech, with the customary belts of wampum, to her Majesty.

VI. To the solicitations of Colonels Nicholson and Schuyler, the ministry returned the most favourable promises; but their execution was so long delayed, that Nicholson resolved to attack Port Royal, with the means at his disposal in the colonies. With twelve ships of war and twenty transports, having on board one regiment of marines, and four of infantry, raised in New England, he assailed and captured the place, and obtained full possession of Nova Scotia, on the 5th of October 1710.

VII. Lieutenant Governor Ingoldsby was, as we have seen, justly obnoxious to the people of New York and New Jersey, and their remonstrances, also, procured his removal soon after the dismission of Cornbury. But before the arrival of another governor appointed by the crown, the executive powers were exercised in New Jersey, by Mr. William Pinhorne, one of the most unpopular of the council. He was, however, very soon superseded by the arrival of Brigadier General Hunter, on the 14th June, 1710, with the commission of governor general of the provinces of New York and New Jersey.

VIII. Governor Hunter was a native of Scotland, and when a boy, was put apprentice to an apothecary. But he deserted his master and entered the army, and being a man of wit and personal beauty, acquired the affections of Lady Hay, whom he afterwards married. He had been nominated in the year 1707, lieutenant governor of Virginia, under George, Earl of Orkney; but having been captured by the French, in his voyage to that colony, was carried into France. Upon his release, he was appointed to succeed Lord Lovelace. He was, unquestionably, a man of merit, since he enjoyed the intimacy of Swift, Addison, and others, distinguished for sense and learning; by whose interest, it is supposed, he obtained this profitable place. He mingled freely with the world, and was somewhat tainted by its follies; had engaging manners, blended perhaps, not unhappily, for his success in the province, with a dash of original vulgarity. His administration of ten years' duration, was one of almost unbroken harmony, and consequently productive of scarcely aught else, worthy of historical notice.

IX. He met the Assembly of New Jersey on the 6th of December, 1710; to whom he delivered a frank, soldierly, and acceptable speech, much in the spirit of his predecessor Lovelace. The session continued more than two months, during which the joint labours of the governor and House of Representatives were unimpeded, save by the occasional refractoriness of the obnoxious council. This led the House, nothing loth, to the consideration of the charges which a majority of the present council had made to the Queen, against a former Assembly, whose vindication the present House assumed not the less eagerly, that it was composed, almost wholly, of other individuals.*

They presented to governor Hunter a long memorial, in which, these members of council were certainly not spared. And if we may judge of their characters, from their sycophancy, no terms of reprobation could have been too strong. It was scarce possible for the minions of the most despotic and profligate court, to flatter a monarch, more than the council

* Smith's N. Y. Smith's N. J. See note T.

of New Jersey did the good Lord Lovelace, in an address, "which," say the Assembly, "for the peculiarity of the language, (and we might add, the unintelligibleness of the terms), ought never to be forgotten." The address commenced thus: "*Your lordship has not one virtue or more, but a complete accomplishment of all perfections*," &c. &c. The address to the Queen, purporting to be an act of the council, it appears had never been formally considered before that body, but had been prepared at the instance of Lord Cornbury, and was signed by the counsellors at different times and places; and many of them, afterwards, becoming ashamed of its contents, alleged that they had signed it without having read it.

In their defence, the Assembly charge upon the council an attempt to defeat their endeavours, to aid the expedition against Canada, by conspiring to negative the acts which they proposed for that purpose. And they allege such misdeeds against most of the counsellors, that we are driven to believe, that party spirit must have aided much in forming the accusation. Thus Mr. Hall is accused of extortion, of imprisoning and selling the queen's subjects, and "of taking up adrift several casks of flour, denying them to the owner, and selling them."—Mr. Sonmans of being indicted for perjury, "from which, by a pack'd jury he was cleared, there being too much reason to believe he was justly accused, and of being a bankrupt," who at this time, and for some years past, has lived in open and avowed adultery in contempt of the laws. They allege also, that the courts of law, in which the gentlemen of the council were judges, instead of being a protection and security to her Majesty's subjects, became their chief invaders and destroyers—That though the courts were holden, alternately, at Amboy and Burlington, "yet the causes of one division were tried in the other, and juries and evidences carried for that end;" that "the writ of *habeas corpus*, the undoubted right, as well as the great privilege of the subject, was by William Pinhorne, Esq. second Judge of the Supreme Court, denied to Thomas Gordon, Esq. then speaker of the Assembly; and, notwithstanding the station he was in, he was kept fifteen hours a prisoner, until he applied by the said Pinhorne's son, an attorney at law; and then, not before, he was admitted to bail: that, many persons prosecuted upon informations, had been, at their excessive charge, forced to attend, court after court, and not brought to trial, when there was no evidence to ground such information on: that, the people called Quakers, who are by her Majesty, admitted to places of the most considerable trust within this province, are sometimes admitted to be evidences, as in a capital case, at a Court of Oyer and Terminer, holden by Chief Justice Mompesson, Colonel Daniel Coxe, Colonel Huddy and others, on which evidence the prisoner was condemned to be executed; and sometimes, they are refused to be jurors or evidences, either in civil or criminal cases; so that their safety or receiving the benefit of her Majesty's favour, seems not to depend upon the laws or her directions, but the humours and caprices of the gentlemen who were judges of the court: all persons not friends to the gentlemen of the council, or some of them, were sure in any trial at law to suffer; every thing was done in favour of those that were: justice was banished, and trick and partiality substituted in its place: no man was secure in his liberty or estate; but, both, subjected to the caprices of an inconsiderate party of men, in power, who seemed to study nothing more than to make them as precarious as possible:"—that "all the original copies of the laws, passed in the time of the just Lord Lovelace, are somehow or other made away with: Basse* offers to purge himself by his oath, that, he

* **Mr. Jeremiah Basse, once deputy governor under the proprietaries of East Jersey, at this time, secretary of state, clerk of council, and prothonotary of the Supreme Court.**

has them not, nor knows any thing of them; and it may be so, for aught we know; but in this province, where he is known, it is also known, that, few men ever believed his common conversation, and several juries have refused to credit his oaths. It is certain, that the secretary's office is the place these laws should have been." "It does appear to have been the interest of the lieutenant governor and his friends, to destroy it, (the law appropriating eight hundred pounds to Lord Lovelace) for they had got an act passed, which took from the Lord Lovelace three hundred and thirty pounds of that money, and gave it to the lieutenant governor; and two hundred and twenty pounds more of it was given to him for the support of the government. Had he sent the act, made in favour of the Lord Lovelace, to the Queen, for her approbation or disallowance, it would not have served him, had her Majesty approved of it, as, in all probability, she would have done; but had the other gone home first, there was an expectation it might pass, the Queen knowing no more about the first act, than that a vote had passed in favour of the Lord Lovelace."

"We are concerned," say the Assembly in conclusion, "we have so much reason to expose a number of persons combined to do New Jersey all the hurt that lies in their power. Her Majesty has been graciously pleased to remove Colonel Richard Ingoldsby, from being lieutenant governor, and we cannot, sufficiently, express our gratitude for so singular a favour, and, especially, for appointing, your excellency, our governor: we have all the reason in the world to be well assured, you will not forget that you are her subject; but will take care, that justice be duly administered to the rest of her subjects here; which can never be done while William Pinhorne, Roger Mompesson, Daniel Coxe, Richard Townley, Peter Sonmans, Hugh Huddy, William Hall, or Jeremiah Basse, Esquires, continue in places of trust, within this province; nor can we think our persons or properties safe, while they do; but if they are continued, must, with our families, desert this province, and seek some safer place of abode."

These representations are, without doubt, highly coloured; but there must have been great cause for them; since sustained by the governor, they were attended with the desired effect; all the obnoxious counsellors being removed by the Queen.

X. Major Sandford, one of the unfortunate counsellors, who had now been elected a member of the Assembly, from Bergen county, was expelled the House; it having resolved, "that any one who had signed the false and scandalous representation of the representative body of the province, was unfit to sit in the House, unless he acknowledged his fault," which the offending member refused to do. An address to the Queen was, also, prepared, and immediately despatched.

XI. Since the surrender of the government, by the proprietaries, the administration of the province had been greatly embarrassed by the obstacles created by the requisition of oaths from the Quaker inhabitants, who were, thereby, precluded from sitting on juries, and from exercising other offices. This grievance had been foreseen, and, in some degree, provided for, by the instruction of the ministers to Lord Cornbury, directing that he should unite with the Assembly in passing an act, to the like effect as that of the seventh and eighth of King William, entitled, "An act, that the solemn affirmation and declaration of the people, called Quakers, shall be accepted, instead of oath, in the usual form." The disregard of this just and prudent provision, enabled the governor, Cornbury, at will, to admit or reject, the services of Quakers, and became one of the means by which he oppressed the people. The House proposed to provide against similar abuses, in future, by two bills; one for ascertaining the qualification of jurors, and the other for substituting affirmations, for oaths, where a party was conscientiously scrupulous in taking them. But though laws, for these purposes, were subsequently enacted, the opposition of the council, at this time, defeated the efforts of the Assembly. And a bill for explaining the militia law, and relieving persons aggrieved thereby, met a like fate.

XII. Animated by his successes in Newfoundland, Colonel Nicholson again urged upon the ministry, the reduction of Canada, which had been strongly recommended by the Indian chiefs, as the only effectual means of securing the northern colonies. The attempt having been resolved upon, circulars were addressed to the governors of the northern and middle colonies, requiring them to meet and confer with Nicholson, and to prepare their respective quotas of men and provisions. Governor Hunter summoned the Assembly of New Jersey in July, 1711; and informing them that the fleet and army destined for this service, had arrived at Boston, demanded that they should provide three hundred and sixty effective men beside officers, together with the means for their subsistence and pay. The service was one which this, together with the northern provinces, looked upon with great favour. The House, therefore, promptly resolved to aid it, by appropriating twelve thousand five hundred ounces of plate (dollars) in bills of credit, to be sunk, together with the three thousand pounds formerly appropriated, by a subsequent tax; and by measures for raising and supporting the requisite troops.

But the expedition proved most disastrous. Colonel Nicholson, under whom served Colonels Schuyler, Whiting, and Ingoldsby, mustered, at Albany, two thousand colonists, one thousand Germans from the Palatinate, and one thousand of the Five Nation Indians, who commenced their march towards Canada, on the 28th of August. The troops from Boston, consisted of several veteran regiments of the Duke of Marlborough's army, one battalion of marines, and two provincial regiments; amounting to six thousand four hundred men, commanded by Brigadier General Hill, the brother of the Queen's favourite, Mrs. Masham. They sailed on board of sixty-eight vessels, under convoy of Sir Hoveden Walker, the 30th of July, and arrived off the St. Lawrence, on the 14th of August. In ascending the river, the fleet, by the unskilfulness of the pilots, or the obstinacy and distrust of the admiral, was entangled amid rocks and islands, on the northern shore, and ran imminent hazard of total destruction. Eight transports, with eight hundred men, perished. Upon this disaster, the squadron bore away for Cape Breton; and the expedition, by the advice of a council of naval and military officers, was abandoned, on the ground of want of provisions, and the impossibility of procuring a seasonable supply. The admiral sailed directly for England, and the colonial forces for New England; whilst Colonel Nicholson, thus deserted, was compelled to retreat from Fort George. The want of skill and fortitude, were eminently conspicuous in the British commanders of this enterprise.*

* The ministry were, generally, censured by the Whigs for the project of this enterprise, and for the measures taken for its execution. It was never laid before Parliament, though then in session; on account, as it was said, of the greater secrecy; and for the same reason the fleet was not victualled at home. They relied on New England for supplies, and this defeated the design; for the ships tarried at Boston, until the season for attack was past. According to Lord Harley's account, the whole was a contrivance of Bolingbroke, Moore, and the Lord Chancellor Harcourt, to cheat the public of £20,000. The latter of these, was pleased to say, "No government was worth serving, that would not admit of such advantageous jobs."—*Smith's New York*, 131. From the manner in which this and other enterprises against the possessions of France, in America, were conducted, we are almost prepared to agree in opinion with

XIII. During five years, nothing worthy of historical notice, occurred in the province. The Assembly was occasionally convened, and passed such laws as were required. These were few and simple, relating solely to the internal policy of the colony; the peace of Utrecht, 31st of March, 1713, having put an end to hostilities between Great Britain and France, and terminated a merciless war upon the American continent. Some leaven of the political spirit, which had been engendered during the administration of Cornbury, still worked, at times, among the people, and in the Assembly. Gersham Mott, and Elisha Lawrence, members from Bergen, who had been of Cornbury's party, having entered on the minutes of council, reasons for voting against aiding the expedition to Canada, were severally expelled the House of which they had become members, "for having arraigned the honour of the representative body of the province." This would seem to have been a party vote, scarce warranted by circumstances. In the interval, we have mentioned, one Assembly had been dissolved, by the demise of Queen Anne, on the 1st of August, 1714; another, by the arrival of a new commission to the governor, from her successor George I.; and a third, by some cause which is not apparent. A new Assembly was convened at Amboy, on the 4th of April, 1716, in which there was a temporary majority, against the late ruling party; and the party which had suffered for adhesion to Cornbury, seemed about to regain its ascendency. Col. Daniel Coxe was chosen Speaker, and several of the most odious members of Cornbury's council, were members of the House. They contrived to delay the business of the session, until the governor, wearied by their procrastination, prorogued them.

XIV. He summoned the House again, on the 14th of May, when nine, only, out of twenty-four members appeared. These adjourned from day to day, for five days, receiving no accession to their numbers. When it became apparent, that the absentees, intended by desertion to prevent the exercise of the legislative authority, now indispensable to renew the supplies for the support of government, and to provide for the re-emission of the bills of credit, the nine applied to the governor to enforce, by some means, the attendance of the absent members. He issued writs to several of them, commanding their presence, as they would answer the contrary at their peril. Four immediately appeared, making a majority of the House, to whom he recommended the choice of a new Speaker, (Col. Coxe being of the absentees), that they might despatch their sergeant-at-arms to enforce the attendance of others. Mr. John Kinsey of Middlesex, was placed in the chair, and the Assembly proceeded with its usual business. They also entered upon an examination of the conduct of the Speaker and his associates, all of whom they expelled, for contempt of authority and neglect of the service of their country; and resolved that they should not sit, if returned on a new election, during the then session. Several of such members, however, were returned; but being rejected, the electors were compelled to choose again.

A subsequent session of the same House, was holden at Crosswicks,* in consequence of the small pox being at Burlington, at which sixteen public and private bills were enacted. The next session commenced on the 8th of April, 1718, but continued a few days only; being adjourned by the governor, at the request of the House, to the following January, a less inconvenient season of the year; when, also, many acts were passed; among which were, one for ascertaining the division line betwixt New Jersey and New York, and

the Swedish traveller, Kalm, that Great Britain "was not earnestly disposed to drive that power from the continent, preferring to retain it as a check upon the colonists, whom, they feared, would otherwise become powerful and independent."

* October 3d, 1716.

another for running the line between East and West Jersey. The commissioners under the first act, fixed the northern station point, on the 25th July, 1719, in latitude 41° 40′, in the manner we have already stated. But nothing was done under the act for determining the line between the East and West Jersey proprietors.

XV. This was the last session of the Assembly during Governor Hunter's administration. He had grown tired of his residence in America, or was called, thence, by his affairs in Europe; expressing his intention, however, with his Majesty's permission, to return. He left New York on the 13th of July, 1719, and on his arrival at London, exchanged his government with William Burnet, Esq., son of the celebrated bishop of that name, for his office of comptroller of the customs. Perhaps none of the colonial governors have earned a more excellent or more merited reputation than Brigadier Hunter. Preserving all the firmness which the dignity of his station required, and maintaining the royal authority in full vigour, he conciliated the people of both provinces, in a very remarkable degree, and obtained from both, in the form of legislative resolves, the most enviable testimonials.

The last New Jersey Assembly declared to him in their Address, "Your administration has been a continued series of justice and moderation, and from your past conduct, we dare assure ourselves of a continuation of it; and we will not be wanting in our endeavours to make suitable returns, both in providing a handsome support of the government, and of such a continuation as may demonstrate to you and the world, the sense we have of our duty and your worth." The Legislature of New York addressed him thus—

"Sir, when we reflect upon your past conduct, your just, mild, and tender administration, it heightens the concern we have for your departure, and makes our grief such as words cannot truly express. You have governed well, and wisely; like a prudent magistrate—like an affectionate parent;—and wherever you go, and whatever station the divine Providence may please to assign you, our sincere desires and prayers for the happiness of you and yours, shall always attend you. We have seen many governors, and may see more; and as none of those who had the honour to serve in your station, were ever so justly fixed in the affections of the governed, so those to come will acquire no mean reputation, when it can be said of them, their conduct has been like yours. We thankfully accept the honour you do us, in calling yourself our countryman; give us leave, then, to desire, that you will not forget this as your country, and if you can, make haste to return to it. But, if the service of our sovereign will not admit of what we so earnestly desire, and his commands deny us that happiness, permit us to address you as our friend, and give us your assistance, when we are oppressed with an administration the reverse of yours."

Like all other men, who have been in any way remarkable for political success, Governor Hunter selected his associates and agents, with much judgment; and instead of forcibly opposing the public will, sought, successfully, by gentle means, to guide it. In New Jersey, Colonel Lewis Morris, a popular favourite, and chief justice, was his principal adviser; and in New York, he was sustained by that gentleman, and by Messrs. Robert Livingston, De Lancy, and others, of high character, and influence. The province of New Jersey gave him a salary of £600, per annum; commonly, by acts limited to two years. The whole expense of the government, about £1000, per annum, was raised by a levy upon real and personal estate, by an excise on wines and spirituous liquors, and a duty on the importation of Negro and Mulatto slaves—the last, laid, probably, as much with design to prohibit the traffic, as for the sake of revenue. The extraordinary expenses, such as those for the military expeditions, were met by bills of credit, or loans, payable from the surplus of the ordinary revenue. The debt of the province at this time, amounted to eight thousand pounds.

CHAPTER VII.

Containing Events from the arrival of Governor Burnet, to the Death of Governor Morris, 1719–1746.—I. Governor Burnet—Notice of his Character.—II. Meets the Assembly—Proceedings.—III. Paper Currency—an Account of its Rise and Progress.—IV. Bill proposed against denying the Trinity, &c.—V. Governor Bernard removed to Massachusetts.—VI. Is succeeded by John Montgomery—His Administration.—VII. Death of Colonel Montgomery, and Presidency of Colonel Lewis Morris—Arrival of Governor Cosby—Harmony of the Province during his Administration—His Death.—VIII. Presidencies of John Anderson, and John Hamilton, Esquires.—IX. Lewis Morris, Governor of the Province of New Jersey, it being separated from New York—Gratification of the Province.—X. He ceases to meet the Council, in Legislation.—XI. Salaries of Officers.—XII. Unpopular Conduct of Governor Morris.—XIII. War with Spain—Aid required by Great Britain, from the Colonies—promptly afforded by New Jersey—Further disputes between the Governor and Assembly.—XIV. Disingenuous Conduct of the Governor, relative to the Fee Bill.—XV. Opposes the views of the House, on the Bill relative to the Paper Currency—on that, circumscribing the Jurisdiction of the Supreme Court.—XVI. Assembly refuse to provide for the Salaries of the Public Officers.—XVII. Efforts at Accommodation—defeated by the discovery of the duplicity of the Governor—Death of Governor Morris—John Hamilton, Esq., President.—XVIII. Biographical Notice of Governor Morris.—XIX. Application made by his Widow, for arrears of Salary—refused.

I. Governor Burnet, as we have already observed, was a son of the celebrated Bishop Burnet, whose piety and erudition, but more especially, whose zeal and activity, for the revolution and protestant succession, in Great Britain, has rendered his name illustrious in English story. The son was a man of sense and breeding, a well read scholar, and possessed a sprightly and social disposition, which his devotion to study restrained from excess. He cherished, successfully, the arts of popularity—had none of the moroseness of the scholar, but was gay and affable, avoiding all affectation of pomp, and mingled freely with the reputable families of his government, paying great attention to the ladies, by whom he was much admired. His fortune was very inconsiderable, and had been impaired by adventuring in the *South Sea* scheme; yet, he was not avaricious, nor importunate, as most colonial governors were, with the people, for a permanent salary.* His intimacy with Mr. Hunter, enabled him, before his arrival, properly to appreciate both persons and things in the province, and thus to obtain many of the advantages of experience. He connected himself closely with Mr. Lewis Morris, and with Dr. Colden, and Mr. Alexander, men of learning, good morals, and sound judgment. Mr. Hunter had recommended to him all his former friends; and few changes, consequently, were made in the colonial offices.

II. Governor Burnet met the Assembly of New Jersey, soon after his arrival. The session was short, little business was done, and the House being soon after dissolved, writs were issued for a new election. In this respect, the governor's policy, in New Jersey, differed from that which he

* "Whether an alteration in sentiment, or instruction, or both, was the cause, must be left to conjecture; but while governor of Massachusetts Bay, his conduct was different; there he insisted for several years with the greatest firmness, for an indefinite support, and pursued it through the plantation board, and privy council, to the Parliament, when his death prevented its coming to a conclusion."—*Smith's New Jersey.*

pursued in New York; where he continued the Assembly, which he found existing at his arrival, until the people, apprehensive that their representatives might be corrupted, by executive favour, clamorously demanded a dissolution.

The new Assembly met early in the spring of 1721, and chose Dr. John Johnson, of Amboy, their Speaker. The House continued in being, during the whole of the administration of Governor Burnet, until December, 1727; changes being made only in the Speakers; first, consequent on the illness of Mr. Johnson, when Mr. William Trent was chosen; and again on the death of Mr. Trent, in 1725, when Mr. Johnson was re-elected.*

III. The most remarkable acts of this Assembly, were, that for the support of government, in which the salary of the governor was fixed for five years, at £500 per annum; and that, authorizing the issue of £40,000, in bills of credit, with the view, principally, of increasing the circulating medium of the colony. The country, as the preamble to this act sets forth, had been wholly drained of a metallic medium of exchange, and was without any means of replenishment; inasmuch, as the neighbouring colonies of New York and Pennsylvania, to which its produce was exported, had no other than paper currency; and as this was not a legal tender, in the payment of debts, in New Jersey, much vexation and embarrassment of trade, was produced. The payment of taxes was occasionally made, in broken plate, ear-rings, and other jewels; and the law authorized their payment in wheat.

The expedient of paper currency had been long since resorted to by Massachusetts, New York, and South Carolina; but in these provinces, its benefits had been decreased by the want of due provision for its redemption, and by over issues. In Pennsylvania, the measure was introduced in 1723, by Governor Keith, with signal success. New Jersey wisely adopted in the same year, the plan of the last, which preserved her currency from much depreciation. Yet, as from the limited nature of her trade, it was less convertible into gold and silver coin, than that of the adjacent colonies, it was, at times, at a discount in Philadelphia and New York. Small amounts had already been issued to meet the expenses of the Canadian expedition, but the bills on these occasions, were in form, treasury notes, based on the faith of the state, and redeemable by taxation only.

Forty thousand pounds in such bills, in value from one shilling, to three pounds, were issued by the government to borrowers, on the pledge of plate, or real estate, at 5 per cent per annum. Loans on plate were made for one year, and on lands, lots, houses or other valuable improvements, for twelve years; the applicant deposing that the estate offered, was held in his own right, and had not been conveyed to him for the purpose of raising money on loan for others; and that it was free from all incumbrance. The amount loaned to any individual was not less than twelve pounds ten shillings, nor more than one hundred pounds, unless there remained bills in the hands of the commissioner, six months after issue; when two hundred pounds might be loaned, to be repaid in twelve annual instalments, with the interest; or the whole, at any time, at the pleasure of the borrower. In default of payment, for thirty days after any instalment became due, the mortgage was to be foreclosed. All bills thus paid in, were to be destroyed, or when prematurely paid in, to be loaned to others. The whole sum was specifically apportioned to the counties, in which, loan-offices were established, under commissioners named in the act, and created a body politic. The bills were made current for twelve years; were a legal tender in payment of all debts and contracts, under penalty of extinction of the debt, or a fine

* See Appendix, U.

for refusal, of not less than thirty shillings, nor more than fifty pounds, as the case might be. Forgery of the bills was made felony, and punishable with death. If, at the expiration of the term, for which they were made current, any portion of the amount, respectively, allotted to the counties remained unpaid, the county became responsible for it.

For the better credit, and sooner sinking of these bills, and for the additional support of the government, a tax of one thousand pounds a year, was imposed for ten years. Four thousand pounds of the product were appropriated to the redemption of the bills of credit formerly issued; and the interest on the money loaned under the act was applied to the sinking of bills, thereby issued; and as the interest and principal of the sums loaned, when paid in, would much more than pay the bills, the balance was devoted to the support of the government, in such manner as the governor, council, and General Assembly might direct.

In 1730, another act added twenty thousand pounds to this medium, which were made current for sixteen years; and in 1733, the act of 1723, for the issue of forty thousand pounds was renewed; the amounts being loaned upon the same principles as under the first act, and kept in circulation by re-issues, and subsequent issues of such sums as were necessary to supply the place of torn bills. All these issues were fully and duly redeemed.

An additional and floating debt was subsequently contracted by the issue of bills, from time to time, to defray the war requisitions of the British ministry, and other exigencies. This debt bore heavily upon the province, as it was payable solely by taxation; and the Legislature frequently sought relief by the issue of new bills, the interest of which would supply the means of ordinary expenditure, and was cheerfully paid by the enterprising and industrious borrower, who received an adequate consideration. But the English ministry, for many years, could not be prevailed upon to assent to this measure. At one period, they reluctantly consented to the framing a bill for the issue of sixty thousand pounds, with condition that it should receive the sanction of the King; but when the bill had passed the colonial Legislature, that sanction was refused. The governors were uniformly instructed to pass no such act, unless with a clause suspending its operation, until confirmed by the crown. In 1758, a second bill for sixty thousand pounds was sent for the royal approbation, which was rejected by the board of trade on three grounds, which obstructed the passage of every other bill of this character. 1st, That the Assembly reserved to itself, not only a participation with the governor and council, in the disposal of the money granted by the bill for his Majesty's service; but, also, the right to judge of the propriety of its application. 2d, That the surplus of interest from loans, after paying a specific grant to the crown, was appropriated to the redemption of bills before omitted, in lieu of taxes; and 3d, That the bills of credit were made a legal tender, in payment of all debts and contracts. Without these conditions, the inhabitants of the province did not deem the currency worth having, and with them, it could not be obtained; so that no other money bills were issued for a long period, unless based on taxes that would redeem them in five years.

Sound policy certainly required that the paper currency should be kept within narrow bounds, lest over issues should embarrass the commerce of the country with the parent state. But this danger could scarce be dreaded from the small amount required by New Jersey, and we must look to other causes for the pertinacious refusals of the crown. These we shall, probably, find in the independence which the colony acquired by a certain and easy revenue, which it as pertinaciously resolved to keep within its own control. Repeated attempts were made, by the colonial Legislature, to bend the will of the

King, but always without success, until the 20th of February, 1775; when an act passed March 11th, 1774, near the close of the administration of Governor Franklin, authorizing the issue on loan of one hundred thousand pounds, and divested of all the objectional features, was confirmed by the King in council.

At one period the bills of New Jersey were at a discount of sixteen per cent., in exchange for the bills of New York, and, consequently, all contracts, especially, in East Jersey, were based upon the New York currency. The Assembly, with too much disregard for justice, directed, that all such contracts should be discharged, by payment of their nominal value in Jersey bills.

IV. Among the acts proposed at the session of the Assembly, in 1721, was one bearing the singular title, "*An act against denying the Divinity of our Saviour Jesus Christ, the doctrine of the blessed Trinity, the truth of the Holy Scriptures, and spreading Atheistical books.*" "Assemblies in the colonies," says Smith, "have rarely troubled themselves with these subjects. It, probably, arose from the governor's motion, who had a turn that way, and had, himself, wrote a book, to unfold some part of the apocalypse." The bill, however, was rejected, on the second reading, in the Assembly.

V. After a harmonious administration, of nearly seven years, Governor Burnet was removed, much against his will, to the government of Massachusetts Bay. His marriage, in New York, had connected him with a numerous family there; and, besides, an universal acquaintance, he had contracted with several gentlemen, a strict intimacy and friendship. The great merit of his administration consisted, in his effectual exertions to diminish the trade of the French with the northern Indians, and to obtain it for his countrymen; and in the erection of forts, and other means, establishing the English influence over the savages. These were benefits, however, not immediately obvious to the public sense; and some contests with the Assembly of New York, caused by private dissatisfaction, deprived him of that popularity, which his general conduct merited.

"Insensible of his services, the undistinguishing multitude were taught to consider his removal as a fortunate event; and until the ambitious designs of the French monarch, with respect to America, awakened attention to the general welfare, Mr. Burnet's administration was as little esteemed as the meanest of his predecessors."*

"The excessive love of money, a disease common to most of his predecessors, and to some who succeeded him, was a vice from which he was entirely free. He sold no offices, nor attempted to raise a fortune by indirect means; for he lived generously, and carried scarce any thing away with him, but his books. These, and the conversation of men of letters, were to him inexhaustible sources of delight. His astronomical observations were useful; but by his comment on the apocalypse, he exposed himself, as other learned men have done, to the criticism of those who have not ability to write half so well."†

VI. John Montgomery, his successor, received from him the seals of the provinces of New York and New Jersey, on the 15th of April, 1728. Colonel Montgomery was a Scotch gentleman, bred a soldier, but who, in the latter years of his life, had been groom of the bed chamber to his Majesty, George the Second, before his accession to the throne. This station, and a seat in Parliament, had paved his way to preferment in America. Good natured, unenterprising, and fond of his ease, his short administration of

* Smith's New York, 172. † Ibid. 173.

three years, is unmarked with any event of historical interest. In 1727, before the departure of Governor Burnet, a new Assembly had been elected. With settled salaries, and the means for support of government provided for years, the governors had few inducements to invite frequent sessions of the House. Nearly three years had elapsed between the rising of the last, and the convocation of the present Assembly; and in dread that their meetings might be even longer dispensed with, they passed an act providing, that, a General Assembly should be holden once in three years, at the least, alternately, at Burlington and Amboy; and lest, by long continuance in office, the members should be improperly influenced by the executive, or cease to remember their responsibility to, and dependence upon, the people, it was further directed, that, a new Assembly should be thenceforth chosen, triennially, and that the term of the present should expire on the 25th of October, 1727. By this act, the province gained a partial security for popular rights. And by another, it was relieved from the monstrous grievance of the practice, under which the courts compelled parties acquitted upon indictment, to pay costs of prosecution.*

VII. Upon the death of Colonel Montgomery, on the 1st of July, 1731, the government devolved on Colonel Lewis Morris, until the 1st of August, 1732; when William Cosby, Esq. arrived, with the commission of governor of New York and New Jersey. He held these offices until his death, in 1736. His administration in New York was signalized by long and obstinate contests with the Assembly. Some differences, appear, also, to have arisen, between him and the Assembly of New Jersey; the latter complaining, that, the council was filled with members from New York; and the former, that, his maintenance had not been provided for, during a long protracted session. With this exception, the harmony, which had long prevailed, between the governors and Assemblies of this province, was uninterrupted during his administration.

VIII. The executive power, on the demise of Governor Cosby, devolved, first, on the president of the council, John Anderson, Esq., and on his death, about two weeks afterwards, upon John Hamilton, Esq., son of Andrew Hamilton, governor in the time of the proprietaries; who exercised it for nearly two years, and until superseded by the appointment of Lewis Morris, by the crown.

IX. The provinces of New York and New Jersey, although wholly independent of each other, had, uniformly, been governed by the same officer, since the surrender of the proprietary governments of the latter; unless for short periods, when the government was administered by the presidents of their respective councils. Yet, New Jersey, the smaller and less important territory, was treated, almost, as a dependency of her greater neighbour. The governor, attracted by the pleasures, and enchained by the business of the city, spent a small portion of his time in New Jersey. The chief officers of state were taken from New York, or upon their appointment, removed thither. Thus, Mr. Alexander, the secretary of New Jersey, was a distinguished practitioner of law of New York, and Mr. Morris held the office of chief justice in both colonies; and hence, the executive and judicial duties, were fulfilled with much difficulty, and frequently, with vexatious delays. At their January session, 1728, the Assembly of New Jersey, petitioned the King, that when he should shink proper to remove the then incumbent governor, Montgomery, he would separate the governments, and appoint a distinct governor for each colony. The application had been in the colonial office, probably, disregarded, for several years, when Mr. Morris obtained

* See Appendix, note V, for the names of the members of council, in 1727.

its consideration. The lords of trade reported favourably upon it to the privy council, and Mr. Morris was so fortunate, as to receive for himself, the commission of governor of New Jersey, in severalty.

This appointment was highly satisfactory to the people, as well, because the duty of the governor would be, exclusively, confined to the colony, as that the officer was greatly esteemed by them. To the Assembly, which he first met, after his elevation, on the 27th of October, 1738, he addressed a long speech, in which he took full credit for the services he had rendered in separating the governments, and did not leave unnoticed nor unpraised, the qualities he possessed for his station. His self-applause was echoed by the House. "We are," said they, "more deeply sensible of our sovereign's care of us, when we consider, how exactly he has adapted the person to preside, to the nature and circumstances of this province:—a person who has been long distinguished and highly preferred for his profound knowledge of the law, and in that station has behaved, for a long tract of years, with great candour and strict impartiality;—a person well known to ourselves, to be eminent for his skill in affairs of government, which we, more than once, have had experience of; and from his knowledge of the nature and constitution of this province, and other advantages of learning, if his inclinations and endeavours to promote our welfare bear any proportion to his abilities, (which we have no reason to doubt) every way qualified to render us a happy and flourishing people."

X. "And we cannot," they continue, "but observe with pleasure and thankfulness, your excellency's candour and justice, in introducing among us, in some measure, that noble economy so happily maintained in the Legislature of our glorious mother country, by fixing the gentlemen of the council as a separate and distinct part of the Legislature; for all former governors have presided in that House, in a legislative capacity, which, not only very much influenced their debates, but often produced very bad effects, and greatly thwarted and obstructed the despatch of public business."

This arrangement was certainly wise on the part of the governor. By it he relinquished no power, since his right of absolute negative upon all bills was not impaired; but he avoided much trouble, and maintained more securely, the dignity of his office, which, in the debates of a legislative council, must often have been in danger.

XI. With such favourable sentiments, and with full reminiscence of their professions of ability, to maintain an exclusive governor, the House proceeded, with cheerfulness, to appropriate five hundred pounds, as a compensation to Mr. Morris, for his expense and labour in procuring a separation of the governments, and one thousand pounds per annum, for three years, for his salary; together with sixty pounds a year for his house rent. They, at the same time, voted one hundred and fifty pounds per annum to the chief justice; forty pounds to the second judge; forty pounds to the treasurers of East and West Jersey, respectively; thirty pounds to the clerk of council; twenty pounds to each of the clerks of the circuits, and eighty pounds to their agent in Great Britain, whom they had a short time before appointed.

Unhappily, this good understanding did not long continue. The governor whose ardent, restless, and persevering temper, when engaged on the part of the people, had gained him great popularity, was now as little disposed to yield his lightest opinions to their wishes, as he formerly had been, to submit to the executive will. And such was the estimate of his own merits, that, although, he had now received double the salary allowed to former governors, and a considerable gratuity, he informed the Assembly that he accepted their grants only as an earnest of what he expected and deserved: and he wantonly forbade the treasurer to pay them their wages, although duly granted, and certified according to law. Flattered by the deference, which had hitherto been paid him, and confident in his political skill and experience, which he held to be, incomparably, greater than that, of any other person in his province, he was surprised and offended, at the presumption of the Assembly, when it proposed measures which he did not approve, and attained ends which he himself sought, by some unimportant variation from the path he indicated. Passionately fond of argumentation, his addresses to the House were, at times, political lectures, delivered with all the airs of superiority, which he supposed his station, and greater intellect warranted; and at other times, revilings, alike unworthy of him and the House. He rejected several important bills, passed by the Assembly, and to their complaints of the inexpediency of this conduct, objected his power, as a constituent portion of the Legislature to exercise his veto, without question; whilst he denied, practically, to the House, a similar right. And thus, although he proposed no tyrannical or unlawful measures, he defeated, by his opinionated obstinacy, several beneficial bills; harassed the Legislature by repeated adjournments, prorogations, and dissolutions; and became, with the exception of Cornbury, the most obnoxious governor who had, in this province, held a commission under the crown. During the early years of his administration, few instances of this captious temper occur. The most memorable one, was in granting aid to a military expedition against the Spanish West Indies.

XII. A misunderstanding had arisen, in the year 1737, between Great Britain and Spain, on account of injuries alleged to have been done, to the English logwood cutters at Campeachy, and salt gatherers at Tortugas. The Spaniards, not only denied them the privileges they exercised, but claimed, and used with insolence and cruelty, the right to search English vessels, for contraband goods; of which, large quantities were introduced into their colonies. Open war was, for a while, delayed, by a convention, extremely unpopular in England, concluded in January, 1738; but which, not having been observed by Spain, letters of marque and reprisal were issued by Great Britain, and general preparations were made for war; which was finally declared, on the 23d of October, 1739. A fleet, under Admiral Vernon, having on board a body of troops, under Charles, Lord Cathcart, was despatched against the Spanish islands, and aid was required from the several British colonies.

The province of New Jersey showed the same alacrity, upon this, as upon other like occasions; promptly passing a bill for raising, transporting, and victualling her quota of troops; but, some of its details were unsatisfactory to Governor Morris, and he delayed his assent to the bill. Having despatched all other business before them, the House begged his excellency, to inform them, when he would permit them to return to their homes. To this reasonable request, he sullenly replied, "When I think fit;" and he kept the representatives of the people, hanging upon his will, from day to day, from the 25th to the 31st of July, before he sanctioned their bills, and prorogued them.

XIII. This treatment, justly, gave offence, which was heightened by his refusal at subsequent sessions, to concur in several bills deemed essential to the welfare of the province, by the House; and by his pertinacious demand for some unwelcome modification of the existing militia law. The fees of the various officers of the colony were not prescribed by law, but regulated by the governor and council; and were, frequently, exorbitant and oppressive. A fee bill was, at length, proposed by the Assembly, but long resisted by the council and governor, and finally passed, on the 21st of October, 1743, with a clause suspending its operation, until his Majesty's pleasure in relation thereto, should be known. When the sense of the several branches of the Legislature, had thus been obtained, the Assembly, very rationally, inferred, that the inchoate law supplied a more satisfactory rule, than the will of the executive; and on the 5th of December, resolved, that, it ought to have due weight with the judges and all others concerned, and, to govern their practice, until the royal pleasure should be declared. This expression of opinion, awakened the indignation of the governor, who sternly demanded, "By what authority the House ordered an act, not in force, to be printed as a rule for the government of the people?—or indeed, any act? And that, if they had, or pretended to have, such authority, they would let him know whence they derived it, and how they came by it, that his Majesty might be informed of it." In reply to these queries, the House resolved, "That as they had only given their opinion of an act, which had passed the three branches of the Legislature here, and had not assumed to themselves, any unwarrantable authority, they think themselves not accountable for that opinion; and that it is not consistent with the honour and dignity of the House, and the trust reposed in them, to give any further answer." And though the governor prohibited them from printing the act, it was published with votes of the Assembly. Notwithstanding the governor had sanctioned the law, and thereby concurred in opinion, with the Assembly, and the people, in the adequacy of the fees which it prescribed, he, with great duplicity, represented to the ministry, that they were so inconsiderable, that no persons of character or reputation, cared to accept of employments, in the several courts of judicature; and the refusal of the royal assent to the bill, was delayed, only, by the exertions of Richard Partridge, Esq., the provincial agent, at court.

XIV. There were three other measures which the people were desirous to effect. 1st. The renewal of the act, making current forty thousand pounds, in bills of credit, which was approaching its term; 2d. An act to oblige the several sheriffs of the colony, to give security for the faithful performance of their duties, which had become highly necessary, from the improvident appointments of the executive; and, 3d. An act to prevent actions for small amounts, in the Supreme Court. All of which, whilst productive of the public weal, would impair the influence, and lessen the power, of the governor.

The interest on the bills of credit, loaned, as we have already observed, supplied the treasury with ample funds, for the support of government, without resort to taxation, unless upon special occasions, and rendered the Assembly in a measure independent of the governor. A clause in the act made a general appropriation of the interest to the support of government, but as special acts were, from time to time, requisite to allot to the several officers, such portions as the Assembly deemed proper, the amount and duration of their salaries, depended on the pleasure of the Assembly. A full treasury, beyond the control of the executive, was reprobated as a mean of strengthening the people, both by the governors in America, and the ministers of the crown; and both desired, that specific and exhausting appropriations, should be made of the revenue, by the act which created it, which would, besides stripping the Assembly of its power, make the executive independent of its pleasure, for the term assigned, to the currency of the bills. In a word, the executive department was indisposed to continue an acknowledged benefit to the people, unless it received, in payment, what it deemed its full value.

Under the pretence, therefore, that the colonial bills of credit had been injurious to English commerce, the royal instructions forbade the respective governors to assent to any act, for issuing such bills, without a clause suspending its effect, until the act had been approved by the King. But, this prohibition having been disregarded, a bill was, about this time, introduced into Parliament, making it unlawful for any governor, to assent to any act, whereby paper bills of credit should be made, or the time limited, for the sinking of them, protracted; and requiring, that all subsisting bills, should be sunk and destroyed, according to the tenor of the acts creating them. The Assembly of New Jersey prepared their bill, with the suspending clause, yet the governor refused to sanction it, or more properly speaking, influenced the council to refuse their concurrence; whilst he remonstrated with the House, on the unseasonableness of their bill, pending that before Parliament. The true cause of his opposition, was, that the Assembly would not fix the salaries of the officers, for a term concurrent with that of the bills.

The refusal of the governor and council to confine the jurisdiction of the Supreme Court, to actions in which the sum demanded exceeded fifteen pounds, had a selfishness so naked, that they should have blushed to observe it. The compensation of the justices was partly dependent upon fees; hence, it became, indeed, the part of a judge to enlarge his jurisdiction,* to protract the pleadings, and to increase litigation. The chief justice, Robert Hunter Morris, son of the governor, was a member of council, and his fees would, obviously, be diminished by the limitation.

XV. Justly irritated by these scarce gauze-covered attempts, to make the commonwealth a productive estate, regardless of the public weal, the Assembly resolved, to apply for defence, to the passion that oppressed them; and by withholding the salaries of the officers, to make them feel, that, even in a pecuniary point of view, concession to the popular will would be more profitable than resistance. Between October, 1743, and April, 1745, three houses had been dissolved by the governor; each of which had given him distinctly to understand, that, they would pass no act for the support of government, unless, concurrently, with the bills above-mentioned. In considering this offer, the governor in his address to the House, sitting at Amboy, in April, 1745, observed—

"The kings of England have, from time to time, immemorial, refused their assent to many bills passed by both Lords and Commons, without assigning any reason for their so doing; and so have the Lords to bills passed by the Commons, though perhaps not so often; and if it may be lawful to compare small things with great, should the House of Commons deny to support the government, and assign these refusals as a reason for their denial, as is done here, and appeal to the populace upon it; or, in an address, propose to the King to pass their bills previous to their granting the support of government, could it bear a milder construction, than an attempt to alter the constitution? And is it less so here?

"I believe, with some reason, that the House was ashamed of that ridiculous proposal of passing their bills, previous to their granting the support of government; and was willing for their sakes to forget it, and let it drop into the oblivion it deserved; but, since the late House have thought fit to mention it, on the particular occasion they have done, I shall say a few words to it. And, first, it is known to all, and themselves, in particular; that the money in the treasury is appointed for the support of government, and appropriated for that purpose; and all that they have to do in it is, to agree with the council and myself, what quantity of it should be applied to that use; and the council could, with equal propriety, have made the same proposal, to pass their bills, that is, the bills of the proposers, previous to their granting their support. I thought, that, what I had said, when that proposal

* "*Bonis est judicis ampliare jurisdictionem.*"—Law maxim.

was made, and the bills I then passed, left no room for a second mention of it; but since they have done it, on the occasion, they did, and thereby seem to insinuate to the populace, that my passing of their bills, is a condition on my part, to be complied with, before they will agree to the support of the government, I take leave to say, that what they call a proposal, I esteem a most unmannerly threat, that, they would not support the government at all, unless I passed all their bills, before they did it; and then would support it, as they thought fit: To which, I say, that I will assent to none of the bills passed by the Assembly, unless first assented to by the council, and I approve them: But not even then—if I think such not very necessary, unless sufficient provision be made for the support of the government, previous to the passing of any bill, by me. And this, gentlemen, I desire you to take notice of, and govern yourselves accordingly."

To this assertion of the governor's determination, the House, among other things, replied. "As we met your excellency at this time, determined, as in duty to his Majesty, we are bound, to support his government, so we entertained hopes that we might at least, have been encouraged to proceed in preparing some bills we think very necessary, and much wanted by the people, whom we represent. But, since your excellency hath been pleased to assure us, that you will assent to none of the bills passed by the Assembly, unless first assented to by the council, and you approve of them; but not even then, if you think such bill not very necessary, unless a sufficient provision be made for the support of government, previous to the passing of any bill by you; and this you have recommended to our particular notice, to govern ourselves accordingly, it gives us some concern to be thus almost, peremptorily, precluded from proposing such bills as we should think very necessary; but we know this is a power, your excellency can make use of, to check our proceedings. We shall, therefore, according to your prescription, defer such bills until some more favourable opportunity, when reason and argument may have greater influence."

Urged by the necessity, so far as it regarded the crown, of preserving, at least, the appearance of providing for the support of government, the House presented to the governor and council, a bill for granting less than half the usual sums, which was of course rejected.

At length, after several adjournments, and more than a year's delay, the Assembly declared, "that notwithstanding all the foregoing treatment, they were still fond of an accommodation, and solicited his excellency for two or three laws which the country have very much at heart; and they informed him, that they would willingly support the government with salaries as large as had been given during his administration, on condition, that they could obtain those acts that would enable them to do it in a manner they could approve of;—but this could not be done. They therefore begged leave to be plain with his excellency, and hoped that he would not take it amiss, that they are so; they are now willing (if his excellency and council think fit,) to pass the bills which they passed at the last meeting over again, but as they are discouraged from giving so large a support, as they would willingly have done, they are determined to assent to no longer applications, than what in the late meeting they assented to, until they can have an assurance of obtaining some acts they think they have a right to, and very necessary to enable the colony so to do." From this determination, the House did not depart, and the governor equally unyielding, though in very bad health, prorogued them from time to time, twice to Trenton, that they might be near his residence of Kingsbury; and, at length, after another year of fruitless altercation, dissolved them.

XVI. But, the appeal to the people, by the convocation of a new Assembly, did not relieve the governor. The constituents of the former House universally approved their conduct, and the same members were re-elected, two only excepted. The governor's infirmities increasing, the Assembly met at Trenton, on the 26th of February, 1746. Both parties had now become heartily weary of the unprofitable contention, and were disposed to unite by sacrificing a part of their respective wishes. This desirable compromise was induced partly by the war, in which the empire was engaged with France and Spain, and the dangers dreaded to the state from the rebellion in England in favour of the Pretender. These circumstances served as a pretext, if they were not the reason, for accommodation. The leaders of the Assembly agreed to pass the militia law, desired by his excellency, and he engaged to concur in their bills for the paper currency, the requiring security from sheriffs, and curtailing the jurisdiction of the Supreme Court—it being well understood, that the support of government should be provided for, as liberally as heretofore. These bills were all duly approved by the Assembly, and council, and awaited only the signature of the governor, to become laws; but that for the support of government, had not yet passed the House. The governor refused his assent to those before him, until the supply bill should also be presented. Neither party had confidence in the other; and it soon became apparent, that the distrust of the House was but too well founded. For at this period, they received a communication from the provincial agent at London, informing that the fee-bill was about to be defeated, by the representations of the governor, notwithstanding he had given it his official sanction; and it was subsequently disapproved by the king. No reliance therefore, could be placed in the success of their money bill, even when approved by all the branches of the Legislature; since the governor might, and probably would use his endeavours, successfully, under the suspending clause to prevent the royal approbation. The House resolved, therefore, whilst adhering to the letter and spirit of the agreement for accommodation, and providing, as usual, for the compensation of the other officers, to make the governor's salary depend upon his good faith, and upon the final passage of their money bill, by the King.

XVII. "With this view, a committee of the House informed him, that they were willing, upon giving his assent to the bills now before him, to vote to the commander-in-chief for the time being, five hundred pounds per annum, for two years, to commence the 23d of September, 1744, and to end 23d of September, 1746; which, with the other salaries, should be paid out of the money then in the treasury. And as a grateful acknowledgment to his Majesty, and his excellency, for the benefits they hoped the colony would receive from such bills, they further assured him, that, provision should be made in the bill, for the support of government, for the payment of one thousand pounds to him or his representatives, out of the first interest money, arising from the act making current the bills of credit, when his Majesty's assent should be had thereto. With these conditions, the governor refused compliance and prorogued the House until the following day. The effect of prorogation was to put an end to all business before the House, and oblige them to recommence their labours. It had been repeatedly tried without any good effect, and was probably resorted to on this occasion, that the governor, whose illness daily increased, and incapacitated him for business, might obtain a short respite from a vexatious dispute. The House convened on the prorogation, and authorized the speaker, and any two members, to meet and adjourn from day to day.

On the 21st of May, 1746, Governor Morris, after a severe illness, of more than two years, died at Kingsbury, near Trenton. By his death, the office of governor devolved upon John Hamilton, Esq., the eldest member of council, All the bills which had been so obnoxious to him, were passed in February, 1748, by Governor Belcher, without hesitation. The champions of the Assembly, in their long contests with the governor appear to have been Mr. Richard Smith, Mr. Lawrence, Mr. Neville, and Mr. Eaton.

XVIII. The family of Mr. Morris, which for more than a century exercised a controlling influence over the political events of New York, and New Jersey, was derived from Richard Morris; who, wearied with the unsettled condition of affairs in England, consequent on the wars of Cromwell, in whose armies he is said to have been a distinguished leader, turned his views to America, and came over first to the West Indies, and shortly after to New York. He purchased an estate near Haerlem, ten miles from the city, containing more than three thousand acres of land, which by the original grant was endowed with manorial privileges, and called Morrisania. Richard died in 1673, leaving an only son, Lewis, the subject of our story, an infant and an orphan, his mother having died a few years before his father. Thus destitute, he became the ward of the colonial government, which appointed a guardian to his person and estate. Soon after, however, his uncle, Lewis Morris, arrived from Barbadoes, and settling at Morrisania, took his nephew in charge, and finally made him heir to his fortune. The early years of the nephew, were wild and erratic. On one occasion, having committed some folly, or extravagance, displeasing to his uncle, he strolled to the southern colonies, and thence to the West Indies, where he maintained himself some time, as a scrivener. He soon tired of his vagaries, and returned to his uncle, by whom he was kindly received. Ambitious, and possessed of much intellectual power, he entered, at an early age, upon a public career; and though, indolent in the management of his private affairs, the love of power, rendered him active in those of a political nature. In New Jersey, he distinguished himself in the service of the proprietaries and the Assembly; and by the latter was employed to draw up their complaint against Lord Cornbury, and made the bearer of it, to the Queen. No man in the colony equalled him in the knowledge of the law, and the arts of intrigue. He was one of the council of the colony, and judge of the Supreme Court, in 1692. Upon the surrender of the government, to Queen Anne, in 1702, he was named as governor, before the appointment was conferred upon Cornbury. He was several years chief justice of New York, and a member of Assembly;—was second counsellor, named in Cornbury's instructions; but was suspended by him, in 1704; restored by the Queen, and suspended a second time, in the same year. He was a member of the Assembly, in 1707, and was reappointed to the council, in 1708, from which he was again removed, by Lieutenant-Governor Ingoldsby, in 1709, but reappointed in 1710, where he continued, until made governor, in 1738. The love of power was his ruling passion. Unable to gratify it, as a partisan of the governor, he became a leader of the people; and as their power was his, contended strenuously, for its preservation and enlargement; but when that power was opposed to his will, he was not less active to control and abridge it. There was nothing in his conduct or character, to separate him from the herd of politicians, who throw themselves into the public arena, like gladiators, to obtain by combat, with each other, their daily bread, and a few shouts of applause, from the spectators; the memory of which, endures, scarce longer than their reverberation. In his early life, he rendered some service to the colony, for which it was grateful; and his name, borne by one of the counties of the State, will attest, that he was, once, a popular favourite. In private life, he was highly respectable, and happy. Inheriting a large estate, and free from avarice, he was not tempted to increase it, by indirect means. Blessed with the affections of an amiable wife, he became the father of a large family of children, many of whom, he lived to see successfully settled.*

XIX. His widow applied, soon after his death, to the Legislature, for the payment of what she termed the arrears of his salary, at the rate of one thousand pounds, per annum, for nearly two years; and the Assembly having rejected her petition, she solicited the interference of the lords commissioners for trade and plantations. That Board instructed Governor Belcher, in November, 1748, to recommend, in the most earnest manner, to the Assembly, to make provision for the speedy payment of such arrears—declaring, that they earnestly interested themselves in behalf of the petitioner, as the salary was represented to them to have been withheld, merely on account of his adherence to his duty, and obedience to the direction of the board. When this subject was thus brought before the Assembly, for consideration, they replied, by a long enumeration of the political sins of the late governor; and for those causes, trusted that Governor Belcher would deem their conduct just and reasonable. "But," they continued, "to put the matter beyond dispute, although Governor Morris, in his life time, did, and his executors, now, do, insist upon payment of what some are pleased to term arrears, yet the House have his own opinion in a similar case, to justify their not allowing them:"—(Alluding to the case of Lord Cornbury, in which, Mr. Morris had taken, as a member of the Legislature, the present ground of the House.) "The subject," the Assembly further urged, "was so universally disliked in the colony, that there is none except those who are immediately concerned, in point of interest, or particularly, influenced by those who are, will say one word in its favour. And it is altogether unlikely, that, any Assembly in the colony, would look upon that to be a just debt, or apply any money for the discharge thereof; and that they could not conceive, that further recommendation of it, would be advantageous to the executors."

* See Appendix, W.

O

CHAPTER VIII.

Comprehending Events from the death of Governor Morris to the death of Governor Belcher—from 1746 to 1757.—I. War with France—Proposal of Governor Shirley to attack the French Settlements, at Cape Breton—New Jersey votes two thousand Pounds for the Service—Favourable result of the Expedition.—II. Proposed attack on Canada—New Jersey Regiment raised and placed under the command of Colonel Philip Schuyler—March for Albany—Threatened Mutiny.—III. Plan of the proposed Campaign.—IV. Treaty of Peace.—V. Death of President Hamilton—Devolvement of the Government on President Reading—Arrival of Governor Belcher—His Character.—VI. Vexations arising from the Elizabethtown Claims under Indian Grants—the Assembly disposed to palliate the Conduct of the Rioters—Representation of the Council of Proprietors—their grievous Charge against the Members of Assembly, in a Petition to the King—the House transmits a counter Petition—Disingenuous conduct of the House.—VII. Disputes relative to the "Quota Bill."—VIII. Hostile proceedings of the French in America.—IX. Difference between the French and English, in their mode of cultivating Indian favour.—X. Efforts of the French to occupy the English Lands.—XI. Expedition of George Washington to Fort Venango.—XII. Measures of the English Government to resist French encroachments.—XIII. Convention of the Colonies—Plan of Union proposed by Dr. Franklin—Condemned by New Jersey—Military Expedition of Lieutenant Colonel Washington—is captured by the French under De Villiers.—XIV. Extensive military Preparations of Great Britain.—XV. Measures of New Jersey.—XVI. Arrival of Major General Braddock.—XVII. Convention of Governors to determine the Plan of the Campaign. XVIII. Acquisitions in Nova Scotia—Cruel treatment of the Neutrals.—XIX. New Jersey raises a Regiment for the Northern Expedition—Mr. Philip Schuyler named Colonel.—XX. March of General Braddock on the Western Expedition—Fastidiousness and Presumption of the General—is attacked and defeated.—XXI. Universal Consternation on this Defeat—Governor Belcher summons the Legislature—Inroads and Cruelties of the Indians—the Inhabitants of New Jersey give aid to those of Pennsylvania.—XXII. Success of the Northern Expedition.—XXIII. Provision against the Attack of the French and Indians.—XXIV. Plans proposed for the Campaign of 1756—Exertions of the Colonies.—XXV. War formally declared between Great Britain and France.—XXVI. General Shirley removed from the supreme command—General Abercrombie, and, subsequently, Lord Loudon appointed.—XXVII. Suspension of Indian Hostilities.—XXVIII. Sluggish military Efforts of the English—Success of the French in the North—Capture of part of the Jersey Regiment, with Colonel Schuyler, at Oswego—Disastrous termination of the Campaign.—XXIX. Renewal of Indian Barbarities.—XXX. Military Requisitions of Lord Loudon—New Jersey refuses to raise more than five hundred Men.—XXXI. Unsuccessful attempt of Lord Loudon on Louisburg.—XXXII. Success of Montcalm—New Jersey prepares to raise four thousand Men—the remainder of the Jersey Regiment captured by the Enemy.—XXXIII. Death of Governor Belcher—Biographical Notice of.—XXXIV. John Reading, President.

I. A masked war had been, for some time, carried on between France and Great Britain; and hostilities were openly declared by the former, on the 20th, and by the latter, on the 24th of March, 1744. In the spring of 1745, Governor Shirley, of Massachusetts, having conceived the design of attacking the French settlements at Cape Breton, and the conquest of Louisburg, the capital, endeavoured to enlist the other colonies in the enterprise. The capture of this place was greatly desirable, inasmuch as it was the largest and most commodious position of the French in America; affording safe harbourage for their largest vessels, and a rendezvous for their numerous privateers, now infesting the western shores of the Atlantic. As the design originated with the people of New England, and had not been sanctioned by the crown, Commodore Warren, the English commandant on the American station, declined to join Shirley in the attack. The Legislature of New Jersey, to whom the plan was not communicated before the expedition had sailed, also, declined to aid it; because there was not a single vessel in the service of the province, nor a ship belonging to private owners, that was fit for sea; and because the expedition not having received the approbation of the King, might disconcert the measures of the ministry. But when the House was, soon afterwards, informed, that the siege of Louisburg was earnestly prosecuted with his Majesty's consent, they unanimously voted two thousand pounds of the interest money, then in the treasury, for his Majesty's service, to be transmitted, in provisions, to General Shirley.

The plan, when communicated to the British government, had been warmly approved. Warren was commanded to repair to Boston, and to render all possible aid to the views of Shirley. He did not arrive, however, until after the provincial fleet had sailed, with six thousand men, under the command of Mr. Pepperel, a trader of Piscataqua. The result of the enterprise was highly honourable to its projectors and executors. The town surrendered after two months' siege, during which, the provincial forces displayed courage, activity, and fortitude, that would have distinguished veteran troops. The English historians have, shamefully, endeavoured to strip the colonies of this early trophy of their spirit and capacity. Smollet makes an equivocal statement of the facts, by which Warren is brought on the scene, before the departure of the provincial troops from Boston; when, in truth, they sailed without any expectation of his assistance, having a knowledge of his refusal to join them. The English ministry, though sufficiently forward to sustain the exclusive pretensions of their officers, was compelled by the merits of the provincials, to distinguish their leader, Pepperel, and to reward him with a baronetcy of Great Britain.

II. The ministry, having resolved to attempt the conquest of Canada, by a combined European and colonial force, communicated their instructions to the provincial governors, at the close of the month of May, 1746. President Hamilton laid them before the Assembly of New Jersey, on the 12th of June. The House resolved to raise and equip five hundred men for this service; for facilitating which, they offered to the recruit, six pounds bounty. So popular was the enterprise, that, in less than two months, six hundred and sixty men offered themselves for enlistment. From these, five companies were formed, and put at the charge of this province, and a sixth was transferred to the quota of New York. These troops, under the command of Colonel Philip Schuyler, reached the appointed rendezvous at Albany, on the 3d of September; where, the proposed invasion of the French provinces having been abandoned, in consequence of the failure of the supply of forces from England, they remained until the autumn of the next year, serving to overawe the Indians, and to protect the frontier. The pay promised by the crown, was tardily remitted, and the troops, at the rendezvous, became impatient of the delay. In April, 1747, the Jersey companies mutinied, and resolved to go off, with their arms and baggage, unless their arrears were paid up. To avert this evil, Colonel Schuyler despatched an express to President Hamilton, with an account of the disposition of the troops. The president recommended, to the Assembly, to provide for the pay, but the House having expended more than twenty thousand pounds in equipping, transporting, and victualling the detachment, declined to make further appropriations; and it was detained in service chiefly by the generous aid of the colonel, who supplied the wants of the soldiers; advancing many thousand pounds from his private funds.

III. The proposed attack on the French possessions, originated with Governor Shirley, whose solicitations, enforced by the brilliant success at Louisburg, prevailed on the ministry to undertake it. A squadron of ships of war, having on board a body of land forces, commanded by Sir John St. Clair, was, as early as the season would admit, to join the troops of New England, at Louisburg; whence they were to proceed by the St. Lawrence, to Quebec. The troops from New York, and from the more southern provinces, were to be collected at Albany, and to march thence against Crown Point and Montreal. This plan, so far as it depended upon the colonies, was executed with promptness and alacrity. The men were raised, and waited, impatiently, for employment; but neither general, troops, nor orders arrived from England; and the provincial forces continued in a state of inactivity, until the ensuing autumn, when they were disbanded. This affair was one of the thousand instances of incapacity and misrule, which the parent state inflicted upon her dependant American progeny.

IV. No further material transactions took place in America during the war. Preliminary articles of peace were signed on the 30th of April; but hostilities continued in Europe and on the ocean, until October, 1748; when the definitive treaty was executed, at Aix-la-Chapelle; in which the great object of the war was wholly disregarded, the right of the British to navigate the American seas, free from search, being unnoticed. The Island of Cape Breton, with Louisburg, its capital, so dearly purchased by provincial blood and treasure, was given up under the stipulation, that all conquests should be restored; and the Americans had great cause to condemn the indifference or ignorance, which exposed them to future vexation and renewed hostilities, by neglecting to ascertain the boundaries of the French and English territories on the American continent.

V. President Hamilton, whose health was in a very precarious state, when the government devolved upon him, died about midsummer, 1747; and was succeeded by John Reading, Esq., the next eldest counsellor, who was soon afterwards displaced by Jonathan Belcher, Esq., appointed governor, by the crown. He met the Assembly for the first time, on the 20th August, 1747. Between this gentleman and the Legislature, for the space of ten years, considerable harmony prevailed. He seems to have adopted as a rule for his administration, the most entire submission to the wishes of the Assembly, where they did not interfere with the instructions from the king. In the latter case, he threw himself behind the royal will, as an impregnable rampart. He was sparing of words, and generally preferred, when required to communicate any matter to the House, to use those of the ministry, petitioner, or agent, as the case might be; rarely adding comments of his own, or embarking his feelings deeply in the subject. He was never obnoxious to the reproach of failing in his duty, and seldom displayed that indiscreet zeal which creates resistance, by the well known law, ruling alike in physics, as in morals; by which the reaction is always equal to the action. His temper was imperturbable, and though sometimes severely tried by the Assembly, by suspension of his salary, a point in which most colonial governors were extremely sensitive, he was unmoved.

VI. Two questions arising out of proprietary interests, vexed the whole term of his administration; and though he earnestly and successfully endeavoured to avoid becoming a party to them, he was made a sufferer in the contests between the council and Assembly. For more than thirty years, there had been no important controversy between the grantees of Carteret, and the Elizabethtown claimants, under the Indian title. But this peace was altogether consequent on the abstinence of the first, from enforcing their title and attempting the recovery of their rents. A large quantity of East Jersey lands, under the Carteret title, had gotten into the hands of Robert Hunter Morris, and James Alexander, Esquires, who held important offices in the province; the one being chief justice, the other secretary; and both, at times, were in the council. These gentlemen, with other extensive proprietors, during the life of Governor Morris, and towards the close of his administration, commenced actions of ejectment, and suits for the recovery of quit-rent, against many of the settlers. These immediately resorted to their Indian title for defence; and formed an association, consisting of a large proportion of the inhabitants of the eastern part of Middlesex, the whole of Essex, part of Somerset, and part of Morris counties; who were enabled, by their union and violence, to bid defiance to the law, to hold possession of the lands which were fairly within the Indian grant, and to add to their party a great many persons who could not, even under that grant, claim exemption from proprietary demands. The prisons were no longer competent to keep those whom the laws condemned to confinement. In the month of September, 1745, the *associators* broke open the gaol of the county of Essex, and liberated a prisoner, committed at the suit of the proprietaries; and during several consecutive years, all persons confined for like cause, or on charge of high treason and rebellion for resisting the laws, were released at the will of the insurgents; so that the arm of government, was in this regard, wholly paralyzed. Persons who had long holden under the proprietaries, were forcibly ejected; others compelled to take leases from landlords, whom they were not disposed to acknowledge; whilst those who had courage to stand out, were threatened with, and in many instances, received, personal violence.

The council and the governor were inclined to view these unlawful proceedings in the darkest colours; to treat the disturbers of the peace, as insurgents, rebels, and traitors, and to inflict upon them the direst severity of the laws. They prepared, and sent to the Assembly, a riot act, modelled after that of Great Britain, making it felony without benefit of clergy, for twelve or more, tumultuously assembled together, to refuse to disperse upon the requisition of the civil authority, by proclamation, in form set forth in the act. The Assembly not only rejected this bill, but sought to give a more favourable colour to the offences of the associators. The council of the proprietors, in a petition to the king, signed December 23d, 1748, by Andrew Johnson, president, represented, "that great numbers of men, taking advantage of a dispute subsisting between the branches of the Legislature of the province, and of a most unnatural rebellion at that time reigning in Great Britain, entered into a combination to subvert the laws and constitution of this province, and to obstruct the course of legal proceedings; to which end they endeavoured to infuse into the minds of the people, that neither your Majesty nor your noble progenitors, Kings and Queens of England, had any right whatever to the soil or government of America, and that their grants were void and fraudulent; and having by those means associated to themselves, great numbers of the poor and ignorant part of the people, they, in the month of September, 1745, began to carry into execution, their wicked schemes; when in a riotous manner, they broke open the jail of the county of Essex, and took from thence a prisoner, there confined by due process of law; and have, since that time, gone on like a torrent, bearing all down before them, dispossessing some people of their estates, and giving them to accomplices; plundering the estates of others, who do not join with them, and dividing the spoil among them; breaking open the prisons as often as any of them are committed, rescuing their accomplices, keeping daily in armed numbers, and travelling often in armed multitudes, to different parts of the province, for those purposes; so that your Majesty's government and laws have, for above three years last past, ceased to be that protection to the lives and properties of the people here, which your Majesty intended they should be."

"These bold and daring people, not in the least regarding their allegiance, have presumed, to establish courts of justice, to appoint captains and officers over your Majesty's subjects, to lay and collect taxes, and to do many other things in contempt of your Majesty's authority, to which they refuse any kind of obedience: That all the endeavours of the government to put the laws in execution, have been hitherto vain; for, notwithstanding many of these common disturbers stand indicted for high treason, in levying war against your Majesty, yet such is the weakness of the government, that it has not been able to bring one of them to trial and punishment: That the petitioners have long waited in expectation of a vigorous interposition of the Legislature, in order to give force to the laws, and enable your Majesty's officers to carry them into execution: But the House of Assembly, after neglecting the thing for a long time, have, at last, refused to afford the government any assistance; for want of which, your petitioners' estates are left a prey to a rebellious mob, and your Majesty's government exposed to the repeated insults of a set of traitors."

This grievous charge was unknown to the Assembly, until a copy of the petition of the proprietaries, was transmitted by the provincial agent. In October, 1749, the House sent a counter petition to the King, with the design of vindicating its conduct, in which it declared, "that the proprietaries of East New Jersey had, from the first settlement, surveyed, patented, and divided their lands, by Concessions, among themselves, in such manner as from thence many irregularities had ensued, which had occasioned multitudes of controversies and law suits, about titles and boundaries of land:—That, these controversies had subsisted between a number of poor people on the one part, and some of the rich, understanding, and powerful on the other part; among whom were James Alexander, Esq. a great proprietor, and an eminent lawyer, one of your Majesty's council, and surveyor-general for this colony, although a dweller in New York; and Robert Hunter Morris, Esq. chief justice, and one of your Majesty's council in the said colony: That the said Alexander and Morris, not yielding to determine the matter in contest, by a few trials at law, as the nature of the thing would admit, but on the contrary, discovering a disposition to harass those people, by a multiplicity of suits, the last mentioned became uneasy (as we conceive) through fear, that those suits might be determined against them, when considered, that the said Chief Justice Morris, was son of the then late Governor Morris, by whose commission the other judges of the Supreme Court acted; and by whom the then sheriffs, throughout the colony, had been appointed; and should a multiplicity of suits have been determined against the people, instead of a few only, which would have answered the purpose, the extraordinary and unnecessary charges occasioned thereby, would have so far weakened their hands, as to have rendered them unable to appeal to your Majesty in council; from whom they might expect impartial justice: That these are, in the opinion of the House, the motives that prevailed on these unthinking people, to obstruct the course of legal proceedings, and not any disaffection to your Majesty's person or government."*

If the council of proprietors, supported by the Legislative council, was disposed to aggravate the offences of the insurgents into high treason, it is apparent, that the Assembly were not less resolved to consider them of a very venial character; and their conduct, upon this occasion, was highly disingenuous. The House could not refuse, from time to time, to condemn,

* Votes of Assembly.

in strong terms, the conduct of the rioters; but, no representation of the governor or council, could induce them, either to pass the riot act, or to arm the executive with military force, to capture the rioters, guard the prisons, or protect the public peace. If, indeed, the insurgents possessed a colourable title to the lands, and had been oppressed by a multiplicity of suits, which they were disposed to render unnecessary by submission to the law, as apparent on the decision of a few; if they had been content, with defending their own possessions, without disturbing those of others; the representations of the Assembly might have been less reprehensible. But the title of the insurgents was, on its merits, wholly unsustainable in an English court of justice, where a mere Indian right could never prevail against the grant of the King. The true solution of the course taken by the Assembly will be found, most probably, in their sympathy for the rioters, and their hostility towards the leading members of the council, who were large proprietaries. The public peace, from this cause, continued unsettled, for several years.

VII. The other subject which perplexed the administration of Governor Belcher, was a difference between the council and Assembly, on a bill for ascertaining the value of taxable property in each county, with the view to a new apportionment of their respective quotas. Among other property directed to be returned by this "Quota Bill," as it was termed, was "*the whole of all profitable tracts of land held by patent, deed, or survey, whereon any improvement is made.*" To this clause the council took objection on two grounds,—first, that it was in contravention of the royal instruction, prohibiting the governor from consenting to any act to tax unprofitable lands, and second, that it would be gross injustice, by taxing lands according to their quantity and not according to their quality, since tracts of land might, and, probably, would, be deemed *profitable*, when the greater number of acres were wholly unproductive. The council, therefore, proposed, to amend the act, by declaring, that nothing therein was intended, to break in upon the royal instruction, or to warrant the assessors to include any unprofitable lands in their lists. The House, roused by this attempt to modify what they deemed a money bill, denied the right of the council, to amend such bill, and refused themselves to alter it, so as to remove the objection.

There is much reason to believe that the Assembly intended, at a season, when taxation was becoming unusually heavy, to reach a portion of the unprofitable lands held by many of the rich proprietaries, but which had hitherto been protected by the royal instruction; and that they designed to make the whole of the lands pertaining to any improvement, whether wild or in culture, liable to taxation. The council, some of whose members were large proprietaries, were interested in firmly supporting the King's instruction; and in the space of a little more than three years, from 1747 to 1751, they impeded the passage of seven bills of like tenor; and as the "Quota Bill" was an indispensable preliminary to an act for the support of government, all the officers of the state were, during this period, deprived of their compensations. It was certainly unjust to require exemption from taxation for lands which, though yielding no annual returns, were daily growing in value, and increasing the wealth of the owner; yet there would not have been less injustice in exacting a tax proportioned on quantity alone, since one fertile acre happily located, might be worth a thousand of pine barren.

We extract from the minutes of the Assembly, parts of messages between the council and the Assembly, in order to show the manner in which these bodies treated each other, and to give somewhat of the form and colour of the times. Thus the cuoncil, in their address to the Assembly of the 19th of February, 1750, say—

"The Assembly, in their message, and in their address to his excellency, accuse us of having taken liberties upon us; as to which we think we have taken none, but what were our just right to take. But the liberties the Assembly have taken with his Majesty, with his excellency, our governor, with the magistrates of this and other counties, and with us, by those papers, and during this and former late sessions, (as will appear by their minutes) and by spreading base, false, scandalous, and injurious libels against us; we believe all sober and reasonable men will think unjustifiable—God only knows the hearts and thoughts of men. They have, it seems to us, even not left that his province uninvaded; for they take upon them to suggest our thoughts to be ***not out of any great regard to his Majesty's instruction, that we have been led to make our amendment; but to exempt our large tracts of land from taxes;*** when they well knew, that a majority of this House, are not owners of large tracts of land; and those who have such, do declare, they never had the least thought of having their lands exempted from taxes, consistent with reason and his Majesty's instructions."

The House, in their democratic pride, did not deign to reply directly to this reproach. But they ordered an entry to be made upon their minutes, declaring, "That it would be taking up too much time, at the public expense, for the House to make any particular answer thereto; nor, indeed, is it necessary, when considered, that the message itself, will discover the council's aim, in having the improved part, only, of tracts of land taken an account of, in future taxation; which, if admitted, would exempt the unimproved part of such tracts, from paying any part of the public tax: So that, should a gentleman be possessed of a tract of ten thousand acres of land, in one tract, worth ten thousand pounds, and only fifty acres of it improved; and a poor freeholder should be possessed of a tract of one hundred acres, only, worth but one hundred pounds, and fifty acres of it improved; the poor freeholder must pay as much as the gentleman; and this we may venture to say, (without invading the province of God, which the council are pleased to charge us with,) would be the obvious consequence of the bill, in question, if passed in the manner the council insist; and why, a poor man, worth only one hundred pounds, should pay as much tax as a gentleman, worth ten thousand pounds, will be difficult for the council to show a reason; but at present, we may set it down as a difficult and surprising expedient, indeed, to favour the poor.

"The council, instead of making it appear, that they have a right to amend the bill, as they have repeatedly resolved they had, have unhappily fell into the railing language of the meanest class of mankind; in such a manner, that had it not been sent to this House, by one of their members, no man could imagine that it was composed by a deliberate determination of a set of men, who pretend to sit as a branch of our Legislature. For, towards the close of the above said message, they charge us with having taken liberties with his Majesty, with his excellency, our governor, with the magistrates of this, and other counties, and with our having spread false, scandalous, and injurious libels against them, the said council; which, they say, they believe, all sober and reasonable men, will think unjustifiable. What liberties we have taken with his Majesty, otherwise, than to assert our loyalty to him, in our address to the governor, we know not: What liberties we have taken with the governor, unless it be, to tell him, the true reason of the government's being so long unsupported, and to represent the public grievances to him, for redress, we know not: What liberties we have taken with the gentlemen of the council, other than to tell them the truth, in modest, plain English, we know not: What liberties we have taken with the magistrates of this and other counties, unless it be to inquire into their conduct, upon complaints, and after a fair and impartial hearing, to represent their arbitrary and illegal proceedings, for redress, we know not;—and wherein we have been guilty of spreading false, scandalous, and injurious libels against the council, we know not. Therefore, it will be incumbent on them, to point out, and duly prove, some undue liberties we have taken, and libels spread, before any sober and reasonable men, will be prevailed on to condemn our proceedings, as unjustifiable; which we think they will not do, upon the slender authority of the council's insulting message to this House; which, in our opinion, is so far from being likely to prevail on any sober and reasonable men, to believe the false, scurrilous, and groundless charges, therein alleged against us; that it will rather discover the council to be men at least under the government of passion, if not void of reason and truth; and, until they recover the right use of their reason again, it will be fruitless for this House to spend time in arguing with them."

As it was now obviously impossible that the public business could proceed, whilst these important branches of the government ceased to treat each other with ordinary respect, the governor prudently dissolved the Assembly. The new House, which met on the 20th of May, 1751, consisted of a majority of new members, and was earnestly disposed to despatch the affairs of the province, as they evinced, by the passage of the quota bill, in a form, which dissipated the objections, that had hitherto prevailed against it; classifying lands, according to their quality, and making all which could in any way be deemed profitable, liable to taxation, at a rate depending on their class. This difficulty was scarce removed, before another, partaking of the same character, arose. In the adaptation of a new act, for the support of the government, to the principles furnished by the quota act, the council assumed the right to amend the bill; though such right had always been peremptorily denied them, by the House, in relation to all money bills, and in the present case, their amendments were unanimously rejected. As this was a point which the Assembly were resolute to maintain, they sought to get over the delay by making the governor a party to the bill, in their favour; and for that purpose, after it had been returned by council, sent it up directly, to him, that he might place it again before that body, accompanied with his influence for its passage. This course would have brought the form of administering the government back to that which it possessed, before the alteration made by Governor Morris, when the governor sat and debated with the council. But Mr. Belcher, declining to receive their bill, the House, unable to progress with it, was prorogued, and the public treasury still continued empty. Nor was it until February, 1752, after a delay of near four years, that a bill for the support of the government, received the approbation of every branch of the Legislature.

VIII. The treaty of Aix-la-Chapelle, which, in Europe, was but a hollow truce, was scarce regarded by the French, in America. Eager to extend their territories, and to connect their northern possessions with Louisiana, they projected a line of forts and military positions, from the one to the other, along the Mississippi and Ohio rivers. They explored, and occupied the land upon the Ohio; buried, in many places, through the country, metal plates, with inscriptions declaratory of their claims;* caressed and threatened the Indians by turns; scattered liberal presents, and prepared to compel by force, what should be refused to their kindness.

* In 1750.

IX. In their Indian relations, the enterprise and industry of the French, were strongly contrasted with the coldness and apathy of the English. After the peace of 1748, the latter discontinued their attentions, even to those Indians they had induced to take up arms. They suffered the captives to remain long unransomed; their families to pine in want, and utterly disregarded the children of the slain; whilst the former, attentive to the vanity and interests of their allies, dressed them in finery, and loaded them with presents. Their influence over these untutored tribes, might have been greater, had they not sought to convert them to the Catholic faith; for the Indians fancied, that the religious ceremonies, were arts, to reduce them to slavery.* The French had, by this policy, succeeded in estranging the Indians on the Ohio, and in dividing the councils of the Six Nations; drawing off the Onondagoes, Cayugas, and Senecas. Their progress with these tribes, was rendered still more dangerous, by the death of several chiefs, who had been in the English interest, and by the advances of the British in the western country, without the consent of the aborigines.

X. In prosecution of their views of territorial acquisition, and seduction of the Indians, the French attacked the Twightees, and slew many, in chastisement of their adherence to the British and protection of English traders. The Ohio Company having surveyed large tracts of land upon the Ohio river, with the design of settlement, the governor of Canada remonstrated with the governors of New York and Pennsylvania, upon this invasion of the French territories; and threatened to resort to force, unless the English traders abandoned their intercourse with the Indians. These threats being disregarded, he captured some traders, and sent them to France, whence they returned, without redress. He also opened a communication from Presqu'isle, by French Creek, and the Alleghany river, to the Ohio; and though the Six Nations forbade him to occupy the Ohio lands, he contemned the present weakness of those tribes.

XI. Governor Dinwiddie, of Virginia, learning that the French designed to proceed southward, from Fort Venango, on French Creek, resolved to despatch an agent, for the double purpose of gaining intelligence, and remonstrating against their designs. For this duty, he selected Mr. George Washington, then a young man, under twenty years of age. He left the frontier, with several attendants, on the 14th of November, 1753, and after a journey of two months, over mountain and torrent, through morass and forest, braving the inclemency of the winter, and the howling wilderness, and many dangers from Indian hostility, he returned, with the answer of Legardeau de St. Pierre, the French commandant upon the Ohio, dated at the fort, upon Le Bœuff river. The Frenchman referred the discussion of the rights of the two countries to the Marquis du Quesne, Governor-in-chief of Canada; by whose orders, he had assumed, and meant to sustain, his present position. From De la Joncaire, a captain in the French service, and Indian interpreter, Washington received full information of the French designs. They founded their claim to the Ohio river, and its appurtenances, on the discovery of La Salle, sixty years before; and their present measures for its defence, had grown out of the attempts of the Ohio Company to occupy its banks.

XII. The British ministry, instructed in the views and operations of the French nation, on the American continent, remonstrated with the Court of Versailles. But, whilst that court publicly instructed the Governor of Canada to refrain from hostilities, to demolish the fortress at Niagara, to deliver up the captured traders, and to punish their captors, it privately informed him, that strict obedience was not expected. Deceived and insulted, the English

* MSS. Journals of Conrad Weiser. *Penes me.*

monarch resolved to oppose force to force; and the American governors were directed to repel the encroachments of any foreign prince or state.

The English force in America, numerically considered, was much greater than that of the French; but divided among many and independent sections, its combined efforts were feeble and sluggish, whilst the French, directed by one will, had the advantages of union and promptitude, and drew the happiest hopes from the boldest enterprises. To resist them, effectually, some confederacy of the colonies was necessary, and common prudence required, that the affections of the Indians, towards the English, should be assured. A conference between the Six Nations, and the representatives of the colonies, was ordered by the ministry under the direction of Governor De Lancy, of New York. Governor Belcher communicated this order to the Assembly of New Jersey, on the 25th of April, 1754. But the House refused on this, as upon every other occasion, theretofore, to take part in the Indian treaties; assigning as a reason, that their province had no participation in the Indian trade; professing, however, their readiness to contribute their assistance to the other colonies, towards preventing the encroachments of the French, on his Majesty's dominions, but declaring their present inability to do aught, on account of the poverty of their treasury. The reluctance which the Assembly displayed upon this subject, together with their rude reply to a remonstrance from the governor, provoked him to dissolve them.

The Six Nations, although large presents were made them, were cold to the instances of the confederate council, which met on the 14th of June. Few attended, and it was evident that the affection of all towards the English had diminished. They refused to enter into a coalition against the French, but consented to assist in driving them from the positions they had assumed in the West, and to renew former treaties.

XIII. In this convention of the colonies, several plans for political union were submitted, and that devised by Mr. Franklin, of which the following is an outline, was adopted on the 4th of July. A general colonial government was to be formed, to be administered by a president-general, appointed and paid by the crown; and a grand council of forty-eight members to be chosen for three years, by the colonial Assemblies, to meet at Philadelphia, for the first time, at the call of the President. After the first three years, the number of members from each colony was to be in the ratio of the revenue, paid by it to the public treasury; the grand council was to meet, statedly, annually, and might be specially convened, in case of emergency, by the president. It was empowered, to choose its speaker, and could not be dissolved, prorogued, nor kept together longer than six weeks at one time, without its consent, or the special command of the crown; with the president-general, to hold or direct all Indian treaties, in which the general interest of the colonies was concerned, and to make peace and declare war with Indian nations:—to purchase for the crown, from the Indians, lands not within particular colonies:—to make new settlements on such purchases, by granting lands in the King's name, reserving quit-rent to the crown, for the use of the general treasury:—to make laws regulating and governing such new settlements until they should be formed into particular governments, to raise soldiers, build forts and equip vessels of war; and for these purposes, to make laws and levy taxes:—To appoint a general treasurer, and a particular treasurer in each government; disbursements to be made only on an appropriation by law, or by joint order of the president and council; the general accounts to be settled yearly, and reported to the several Assemblies:—Twenty-five members to form a quorum of the council, there being present, one or more, from a majority of the colonies:—The assent of the president-general was requisite to all acts of the council, and it was his duty to execute them:—The laws enacted were to be as like as possible to those of England, and to be transmitted to the King in council for approval, as soon as might be after their enactment, and if not disapproved within three years, to remain in force. On the death of the president-general, the speaker was to succeed him, and to hold his office until the King's pleasure should be known. Military and naval officers, acting under this constitution, were to be appointed by the president, and approved by the council, and the civil officers to be nominated by the council, and approved by the president; and in case of vacancy, civil or military, the governor of the province in which it happened, was to appoint, until the pleasure of the president and council should be ascertained.

This plan was submitted to the board of trade in England, and to the Assemblies of the several provinces. Franklin* says, its fate was singular. The Assemblies rejected it, as containing too much prerogative; whilst in England, it was condemned as too democratic. Had it been adopted, the projector might have been famed as the forger of a nation's chains, instead of the destroyer of a tyrant's sceptre.† As a substitute, the British ministry proposed, that the governors of the colonies, with one or more members of the respective councils, should resolve on the measures of defence, and draw on the British treasury for the money required, to be refunded by a general tax, imposed by Parliament, on the colonies. But this proposition was deemed inadmissible by the provinces. The "plan of union," as adopted by the Congress, was laid before the Assembly of New Jersey in October. The House voted that if it should be carried into effect, "it might be prejudicial to the prerogative of the crown, *and* to the liberties of the people." They instructed their agent, at court, to petition the King and Parliament against its ratification.

In the mean time, Virginia had raised three hundred men, under the command of Colonel Fry and Lieutenant Colonel Washington. The latter marched with two companies, in advance, to the Great Meadows, in the Alleghany Mountains; where he learned, that the French had dispersed a party, employed by the Ohio company, to erect a fort on the Monongahela river; were, themselves, raising fortifications at the confluence of that river with the Alleghany, and that a detachment was then approaching his camp. It was impossible to doubt of the hostile intentions of this party, and Washington resolved to anticipate them. Guided by his Indians, under cover of a dark and rainy night, he surprised the French encampment, and captured the whole party, save one who fled, and Jumonville, the commanding officer, who was killed. Soon after, the whole regiment, the command of which had devolved on Mr. Washington, by the death of Mr. Fry, was united at the Great Meadows; and reinforced by two independent companies of regulars, the one from South Carolina, and the other from New York.—It formed an effective force of five hundred men. Having erected a stockade for protecting their provisions and horses, the troops marched to dislodge the enemy from Fort Du Quesne. But their progress was arrested by information of the advance of twelve hundred French and Indians. As the Americans had been six days without bread, had but a small supply of meat remaining, and dreaded the enemy would cut them off from their stores, they resolved to retreat to their stockade, to which they gave the name of Fort Necessity. Colonel Washington began a ditch around this post, but ere he could complete it, he was attacked by the French force under Mon-

* Memoirs.
† *Cœli eripuit fulmen sceptrumque tyrannis.*

sieur de Villiers. The troops made an obstinate defence, fighting partly within the stockade, and partly in the ditch, half filled with mud and water, from ten o'clock in the morning until dark, when De Villiers demanded a parley, and offered terms of capitulation. During the night, articles were signed, allowing the garrison the honours of war, to retain their arms and baggage, and to return home unmolested. The last clause was not strictly kept, the Indians harassing and plundering the Americans during their retreat. The courage and conduct of Washington, on this occasion, were greatly applauded; and the Assembly of Virginia voted their thanks to him and his officers. The French retired to their post on the Ohio.*

The attack, on the part of Jumonville, without summons or expostulation, was deeply reprobated by the French. Whilst peace prevailed between the two nations, hostility, they said, should not have been presumed. They have called the death of that officer, an assassination, even in the capitulation of Fort Necessity; the attack on which, they state to have been made, in consequence of the outrage upon their advance party. These allegations are refuted, by a review of the conduct of the French, since the development of their designs upon the Ohio. The capture of the persons and property of the settlers, at Logtown, and of the Indian traders, wherever found in the western country, afforded conclusive evidence of their intention to try the disputed title by force; and they could not, justly, complain of the reply to their argument.†

With great industry, the French completed Fort Du Quesne, at the confluence of the Monongahela and Alleghany rivers, where the thriving city of Pittsburg now stands; garrisoned it with one thousand regulars, amply supplied with cannon, provisions, and other munitions; and prepared to occupy the country of the Twightees, with numerous settlers. The Six Nation Indians, now more numerous on the western waters, than in their ancient seats, indifferent to the English cause, and divided among themselves, barely maintained their neutrality. Some of them had removed to Canada, preferring the protection of the active and enterprising French commanders. The small body of British troops, collected on the frontiers, was weakened by desertion, and corrupted by insubordination; whilst the Indians who still adhered to their interest, retired to Aughwick, in Pennsylvania, where they proclaimed their admiration of the courage of the enemy, and their contempt of the sloth of their friends; and were scarcely kept in quiet, by the liberality of the Assembly of Pennsylvania to their families, and its forbearance towards the license of their chiefs.

XIV. At length, however, Great Britain prepared to oppose, energetically, the growing power of her restless rival in the Western World. Two regiments of foot from Ireland, under the command of Colonels Dunbar and Halkett, were ordered to Virginia, to be there enforced; and Governor Shirley and Sir William Pepperell were directed to raise two regiments, of a thousand men each, to be officered from New England, and commanded by themselves. The provinces, generally, were required, to collect men for enlistment, to be placed at the disposal of a commander-in-chief of rank and capacity, who would be appointed to command all the King's forces in America; to supply the troops on their arrival with provisions, and to furnish all necessaries for the soldiers landed or raised within the province; to provide

* Marshall's Washington. Bradford's Journal. Review of Military Operations in North America. London, 1757.

† Colonel Washington, who was ignorant of the French language, was unable to read the articles of capitulation, and was, therefore, obliged to rely on an interpreter, who rendered the word "*assassinat*" into the word "*death*" merely.—*Wash. Lett.*

the officers with means for travelling, for impressing carriages and quartering troops. And as these were "local matters, arising entirely within their colonies, his Majesty informed his subjects, that he expected the charges thereof to be borne by them in their respective provinces, whilst articles of more general concern would be charged upon a common fund to be raised from all the colonies of North America; towards which, the governors were severally requested to urge the Assemblies to contribute liberally, until a union of the northern colonies, for general defence, could be effected.

XV. The Assembly of New Jersey, before whom Governor Belcher laid these requisitions in February, and who were incited to prompt and liberal measures by the solicitations of their constituents, praying the House to pass such bills as might be necessary (in proportion with the other colonies) to assist his Majesty in driving the French from their fortifications on the Ohio, and in defence of the frontiers, appropriated five hundred pounds for the subsistence of the royal troops, during their march through the colony, and transportation of their baggage; and also at the instance of Governor Shirley, passed an act to prevent the exportation of provisions, naval or warlike stores to any of the French dominions. The House excused themselves from appropriating a larger sum, under pretence, that by a bill passed at a previous session, and sent to England for the approbation of the King, they had granted for his Majesty's service, ten thousand pounds. This bill provided for issuing in bills of credit, the sum of seventy thousand pounds; and the House had just reason to believe, that it would receive the royal sanction, since they had the assent of the board of trade and plantations, to issue sixty thousand pounds, and the surplus was given to the national use. But the objections to provincial paper currency in England, could not yet be overcome.

XVI. Major-general Braddock, Sir John St. Clair, adjutant-general, and the regiments of Dunbar and Halkett, which sailed from Cork on the 14th of January, 1755, arrived early in March at Alexandria, in Virginia, whence they marched to Fredericktown, in Maryland. The place of debarkation was selected with that ignorance and want of judgment, which then distinguished the British ministry. The country could furnish neither provisions nor carriages for the army, whilst Pennsylvania, rich in grain, and well stocked with wagons, could readily have supplied food and the means of transportation; and from this source the general, with the aid of Mr. Benjamin Franklin, drew finally the means of making the expedition against the French in the West.

XVII. A convention of the Governors of New York, Massachusetts, Maryland, and Virginia, convened at Annapolis, to settle with General Braddock, a plan of military operations. Three expeditions were resolved on. The first, against Fort Du Quesne, under the command of General Braddock, in person, with the British troops, and such aid as he could draw from Maryland and Virginia,—the second, against Forts Niagara and Frontignac, under General Shirley, with his own and Pepperell's regiments—and the third, originally proposed by Massachusetts, against Crown Point, to be executed altogether with colonial troops from New England, New York, and New Jersey, under Major-general William Johnson.

XVIII. Whilst these measures were in embryo, an attack conducted by Lieutenant-colonel Monckton, a British officer, and Lieutenant-colonel Winslow, a major-general of the Massachusetts militia, was made against the French who had possessed themselves of a portion of the country claimed by the English, for the province of Nova Scotia. In little more than a month, with the loss of three men, only, possession was obtained of the whole province according to the British definition of its boundaries. This easy conquest elated the colonies, and produced sanguine anticipations of the results of their future efforts. But their present success was disgraced by scenes of devastation and misery, scarce paralleled in modern history.

The inhabitants of Nova Scotia were chiefly of French descent. By the treaty of Utrecht, (1713,) they were permitted to retain their lands, taking the oath of allegiance to their new sovereign, with the qualification, that they should not be compelled to bear arms against their Indian neighbours, or their countrymen; and this immunity was, at subsequent periods, assured to their children. Such was the notoriety of this compact, that, for half a century, they had borne the name, and with few exceptions, maintained the character of neutrals. But, now, excited by this ancient love of France, by their religious attachments, and their doubts of the English rights, some of these frugal, industrious, and pious people, were seduced to take up arms. Three hundred were found in the fortress of Beau Sejour, at its capture, but it was stipulated, that they should be left in the same situation, as when the army arrived, and should not be punished for any thing they had subsequently done. Yet, a council was convened by Lawrence, Lieutenant Governor of Nova Scotia, at which Admirals Boscawen and Moyston assisted, to determine the fate of these unfortunate people. Their elders were required to take the oath of allegiance to the British monarch, without the exemption, which, during fifty years, had been granted to them and their fathers. Upon their refusal, although, out of a population of seven thousand, three hundred only had borne arms, the council resolved to expel all from their country, to confiscate their property, money and household goods excepted, to lay waste their estates, and burn their dwellings. The public records and muniments of title, were seized, and the elders of the people treacherously made prisoners. Governor Lawrence, with great presumption, and total disregard of the rights of the neighbouring provinces, imposed a heavy and durable burden upon them, in the reception and maintenance of this devoted race. In transporting them to their several destinations, the charities of blood and affinity were wantonly torn asunder. Parents were separated from their children—and husbands from their wives. Among many instances of this barbarity, was that of René Le Blanc, who had been imprisoned four years, by the French, on account of his English attachments. The family of this venerable man, consisting of twenty children, and about one hundred and fifty grand-children, were scattered in different colonies; and himself, with his wife and two children only, were put on shore at New York.

XIX. The province of New Jersey, in a continental war, dreaded most, an attack from Canada, by the way of New York, and scarce felt any apprehension of danger, from the French and Indians on the Ohio. The Assembly cordially approved of the plan of operation adopted at Annapolis, and, particularly of the expedition against Crown Point; and resolved, immediately, to raise a battalion, of five hundred men, for the maintenance of which, they issued bills of credit, for £15,000, redeemable within five years. The governor nominated Mr. Peter Schuyler, with the rank of colonel, to the command of this force; and that gentleman's popularity was such, that the battalion was not only promptly filled, but a much larger number of men, presented themselves for enlistment, than were required. The arms for these troops, of which the colony was almost wholly unprovided, were procured from Virginia, at the cost of the Assembly.

XX. General Braddock having removed his army to Fort Cumberland, on Wills's Creek, on his way to the west, received there, his wagons, and other necessary supplies; and being, at length, after many delays, amply furnished with all the munitions he required, and also reinforced by a considerable body of Americans and Indians, broke up his encampment on the 12th of June, and passed the Alleghany mountain, at the head of two thousand two hundred men. On reaching the Little Meadows, five days' march from Fort du Quesne, he convoked a council of war, to consult on future operations. Colonel Washington, who had entered his family, as a volunteer aid-de-camp, and who possessed a knowledge of the country, and of the nature of the service, had urged the substitution of pack horses for wagons, in the transportation of the baggage, now renewed his advice; and earnestly and successfully recommended, that the heavy artillery and stores should remain with the rear division, and follow by easy marches, whilst a chosen body of troops, with a few pieces of light cannon and stores, of absolute necessity, should press forward to Fort du Quesne. Twelve hundred men, and twelve pieces of cannon, being selected, were commanded by General Braddock, in person. Sir Peter Halkett, acted as brigadier, having under him Lieutenant-colonels Gage and Burton, and Major Spark. Thirty wagons, only, including those with ammunition, followed the march. The residue of the army remained under the care of Colonel Dunbar and Major Chapman.

The benefit of these prudent measures was lost by the fastidiousness and presumption of the commander-in-chief. Instead of pushing on with vigour, regardless of a little rough road, he halted to level every molehill, and to throw bridges over every brook, employing four days to reach the great crossings of the Youghiogany, nineteen miles from the Little Meadows. On his march, he neglected the advantage his Indians afforded him, of reconnoitering the woods and passages on the front and flank, and even rejected the prudent suggestion of Sir Peter Halkett, on this subject, with a sneer at his caution.*

This overweening confidence and reckless temerity were destined to a speedy and fatal reproof.† Having crossed the Monongahela river, within seven miles of Fort du Quesne, wrapt in security, and joyously anticipating the coming victory, his progress was suddenly checked, by a destructive fire, on the front and left flank, from an invisible enemy. The van was thrown into confusion; but the main body, forming three deep, instantly advanced. The commanding officer of the enemy having fallen, it was supposed from the suspension of the attack, that the assailants had dispersed. But the delusion was momentary. The fire was renewed with great spirit, and unerring aim; and the English, beholding their comrades drop around them, unable to see the foe, or tell whence their death arrived, broke and fled in utter dismay. The general, astounded at this sudden and unexpected attack, lost his self-possession, and neither gave orders for a regular retreat, nor for his cannon to advance and scour the woods. He remained on the spot where he first halted, directing the troops to form in regular platoons against a foe dispersed through the forest, behind trees and bushes, whose every shot did execution. The officers behaved admirably; but distinguished by their dresses, and selected by the hidden marksmen, they suffered severely; every one on horseback, except Washington, was killed or wounded; he had two horses killed under him, and four balls through his coat. Sir Peter Halkett was killed on the spot; and the general himself, having been five times dismounted, received a ball through the arm, and lungs, and was carried from the field of battle. He survived only four days. On the first, he was totally silent, and at night, only said, "Who would have thought it?" He was again silent until a few minutes before his death, when he observed, "We shall better know how to deal with them another time."

The defeat was total—the carnage unusually great. Sixty-four, out of

* Marshall, Wash. Lett. ‡ July 9, 1755.

eighty-five officers, and one-half the privates, were killed or wounded. Many fell by the arms of their fellow soldiers. An absolute alienation of mind, seems to have fallen upon the regular troops. In despite of the orders of the officers, many gathered in squads of ten or twelve deep, and in their confusion, shot down the men before them; whilst the troops in line fired on the provincials wherever they saw a smoke, or heard a shot from behind trees. Captain Waggoner, of the Virginia forces, who had taken an advantageous position on the flank, with eighty men, was driven from it by the British fire with the loss of fifty.* Fortunately, the Indians were held from pursuit by the desire of plunder. The artillery and military stores, even the private cabinet of the commander-in-chief, containing his instructions, fell into the hands of the enemy, whose whole force was computed at three hundred men.

The fugitives continuing their flight to Dunbar's division, so infected it with their terror, that, though the enemy did not advance, all the artillery and stores collected for the campaign, except those indispensable for immediate use, were destroyed, and the remnant of the army marched to Fort Cumberland. The loss in this engagement would have been still greater, but for the coolness and courage of the colonial troops. These, whom Braddock had contemptuously placed in his rear, so far from yielding to the panic which disordered the regulars, offered to advance against the enemy, until the others could form and bring up the artillery; but the regulars could not again be brought to the charge, yet the provincials actually formed and covered their retreat. The conduct of the Virginia troops merits the greatest praise. Of three companies brought into the field, it is said, scarce thirty escaped uninjured. Captain Peyroney and all his officers, down to the corporal, were killed. Captain Polson's company shared almost as hard a fate; the captain himself being killed, and one officer only escaping. Of the company of light-horse, commanded by Captain Stewart, twenty-five out of twenty-nine were slain.†

This misfortune is solely to be ascribed to the misconduct of the general. Presumptuous, arrogant, and ignorant, he had no quality save courage to insure success. Unacquainted with the country, and the Indian mode of warfare, he neglected the suggestions of the Duke of Cumberland, whose instructions seem predicated on a prescience of his conduct, and the advice of his American officers, to employ his Indians in guarding against ambush and surprise. He neglected and disobliged the Virginians, and behaved with insupportable haughtiness to all around him. With a lethargy in all his senses, produced by self-sufficiency, he led his troops to be defeated and slaughtered by a handful of men, who intended only to molest their march.‡

Dunbar proposed to return with his army, yet strong enough to meet the enemy, to Philadelphia; but consented, on the remonstrance of the Assembly of Pennsylvania, to keep the frontiers. He requested a conference with Governor Morris, at Shippensburg; but Governor Shirley having succeeded to the chief command of the forces in America, though at first he directed Dunbar to renew the enterprise on Fort Du Quesne, and to draw upon the neighbouring provinces for men and munitions, changed his mind, and determined to employ his troops elsewhere, leaving to the populous provinces of Pennsylvania, Maryland, and Virginia, the care of their own defence.

* Penn. Records.

† Penn. Gaz.

‡ Modern Univ. Hist. Marshall. Franklin. Richard Peters' Report to Council. W. Shirley's letter to Governor Morris. See note Z, Appendix.

XXI. The defeat of General Braddock, wholly unexpected, produced great consternation throughout all the colonies. Upon receipt of intelligence of this extraordinary event, as Governor Belcher properly termed it, he summoned the Assembly of New Jersey, to meet him on the 1st of August; but it was not until the approach of winter, that they became fully aware of its disastrous consequences, and began to prepare against them. The enemy, long restrained, by fear of another attack, could scarce credit his senses, when he discovered the defenceless state of the frontiers; and now roamed, unmolested and fearlessly, along the western lines of Virginia, Maryland, and Pennsylvania; committing the most appalling outrages, and wanton cruelties, which the cupidity and ferocity of the savage could dictate. The first inroads were in Cumberland County, Pennsylvania, whence, they were soon extended to the Susquehanna; and thence through Berks and Northampton Counties, across the Delaware, into New Jersey. New horrors were given to these scenes, by the defection of the Shawanese and Delaware Indians, who had hitherto continued faithful, and had repeatedly solicited employment against the French and their allies, with threats, that unless engaged with the English, they would take part against them. These threats had been humanely, if not wisely, withstood; and now, irritated by the love of blood, and of plunder, and the hopes fed by the French, of recovering the lands they had sold, these savages openly joined the foe. To the perversion of these tribes, the Delaware chiefs, ***Shingas*** and ***Captain Jacobs***, were highly instrumental. They had been loaded with presents and favours, by the provincial authorities of Pennsylvania, and the principal inhabitants of Philadelphia; and their defection and perfidy, justly awakened the anger of the citizens of that province; who, with the approbation of the governor, proclaimed a reward of seven hundred dollars for their heads.

In the month of November, these barbarous wretches laid waste the settlements in Northampton county, not sparing even those of the Moravians, who had ever treated them and their brethren, with the greatest kindness. Gnadenhutten, on the Lehigh, was attacked, and several of its inhabitants slaughtered; and the other Moravian stations soon shared a like fate. A letter from the Union Iron Works, New Jersey, dated 20th December, 1755, says, "the barbarous and bloody scene, which is now open in the upper parts of Northampton County, is the most lamentable, that has perhaps ever appeared. There may be seen horror and desolation; populous settlements deserted—villages laid in ashes—men, women and children, cruelly mangled and massacred—some found in the woods, very nauseous, for want of interment—some just reeking from the hands of their savage slaughterers—and some hacked, and covered all over with wounds." To this letter was annexed, a list of seventy-eight persons killed, and more than forty settlements burned.

A letter from Easton, of the 25th of the same month, states, that "the country, all above this town, for fifty miles, is mostly evacuated and ruined. The people have, chiefly, fled into the Jerseys. Many of them have threshed out their corn, and carried it off, with their cattle, and best household goods; but a vast deal is left to the enemy. Many offered half their personal effects, to save the rest; but could not obtain assistance enough, in time to remove them. The enemy made but few prisoners; murdering almost all that fell into their hands, of all ages, and both sexes. All business is at an end; and the few remaining, starving inhabitants, in this town, are quite dejected and dispirited."

The panic, which foreran the savage monsters, seemed to deprive their prey, of the means of concerting defence and retaliation. And the farmers, intoxicated with hope, or stupefied by fear, suffered the invader to approach their solitary and undefended homesteads, without an effort to stop them on the way. This was the effect of a long period of peace, and the consequent total inexperience of warfare, as well as of the manner by which the assailants conducted their attacks. They wandered over the country, in small parties, concealing themselves, whilst danger was near, and pouncing, suddenly, upon the unprepared, generally during the darkness of the night; they made undistinguished slaughter; and frequently consumed their victims, upon the funeral piles formed of their dwellings. This senseless, and emasculating fear, seems to have spent itself, on the right bank of the Delaware.

The inhabitants of New Jersey, roused by the sufferings of their neighbours, prepared seasonably, not only to resist the foe, but to protect their friends. Among the energetic citizens of Sussex County, Colonel John Anderson was most conspicuous. With four hundred men, whom he collected, he scoured the country, marched to the defence of Easton, and pursued the dastard enemy, unhappily, in vain. The governor promptly despatched troops from all parts of the province, to the defence of its western frontier; and the wealthy inhabitants advanced the funds requisite for their maintenance, until the Assembly, in the middle of December, took such troops, upon the provincial establishment, and recalled their battalion, under Colonel Schuyler, from the northern service, where it was then idle; and placed them, also, on the frontier. To meet the expenses thus incurred, the House, though greatly chagrined, at the rejection, by the King, of their bill, for a paper currency, voted **£10,000**, in such bills, redeemable at the usual period of five years.*

XXII. The troops destined for the northern expeditions, assembled at Albany, on the close of June, but were not equipped for the field, until the last of August. General Johnson proceeded to the southern shore of Lake George, on his way to Ticonderoga, where he received information of the approach of Baron Dieskau, at the head of twelve hundred regulars, and six hundred Canadians and Indians. He detached Colonel Williams, with one thousand men, to reconnoitre, and to skirmish with the enemy. Engaging with the foe, the detachment was overthrown, put to flight, and its commander killed. A second detachment, sent to the aid of the first, experienced a like fate: both were pursued to the camp, where they found shelter, behind a breast-work of fallen trees, which the American army had thrown up, in its front. The artillery, which had lately arrived, was served with effect; and though the Baron advanced firmly to the charge, his militia and Indians deserted him, and he was compelled with his regulars to retreat. In the pursuit, which was close and ardent, Dieskau, mortally wounded and abandoned, was made prisoner. A scouting party, under the command of Captains Folsom and Maginnis, from Fort Edward, fell on the baggage of the enemy, routed the guard, and immediately after engaged with the retreating army; which, surprised by an enemy whose force it did not know, fled precipitately towards the posts on the lake. This repulse of Dieskau, though not followed up by Johnson, was magnified into a splendid victory; served in some measure, to relieve the effect of Braddock's defeat, and procured the fortunate general, a present of five thousand pounds sterling, from the House of Commons, and the title of baronet, from the King. This army was soon after discharged, with the exception of six hundred men, retained to garrison Forts Edward and William Henry. The French seized and fortified Ticonderoga.

General Shirley, at the head of the expedition against Niagara and Fron-

* Votes.

tignac, did not reach Oswego, on Lake Ontario, until late in August. His force consisting of about thirteen hundred regulars, and one hundred and twenty militia and Indians, he divided; embarking between six and seven hundred men, for Niagara, and leaving the remainder at Oswego. But he had scarce embarked, before the rains set in with fury, and his Indians, discouraged, dispersed. It was apparent, that the season was now too far advanced for the accomplishment of his design, which, by the advice of a council of war, was abandoned. A garrison of seven hundred men was left at Oswego, to complete the works, and the general returned to Albany.

XXIII. The marauding parties of French and Indians hung on the western frontiers during the winter. To guard against their devastations, a chain of forts and block-houses, were erected by Pennsylvania, along the Kittatinny or Blue Mountain, from the river Delaware to the Maryland line, commanding the principal passes of the mountains. In New Jersey, forts and block houses were also erected along the mountain, and at favorable points on the east bank of the Delaware river. Although the inroads of the savages across the river were infrequent, yet the fear which every one on the frontier felt, that his midnight slumbers might be broken by the warwhoop, or that his dwelling and out-houses might be consumed before the morning's dawn, was sufficient to disturb the repose of the most courageous. Many left their homes, and all called loudly upon the Assembly for additional means of defence. And in the spring, when the Jersey regiment was again to proceed to the north, the House authorized the enlistment of two hundred and fifty volunteers, to supply their place and that of the militia on the frontier. Two hundred of this force were also destined to unite with any troops that might be organized by other colonies, for pursuing the brutal enemy to his den, and making him, in the sufferings of his wives and his children, feel the horrors which he had delighted to inflict. The provincial force on the frontier was, subsequently, increased, and the whole was commanded by Colonel De Hart.

XXIV. Governor Shirley, having been appointed commander-in-chief, summoned, in the spring of the year 1756, the governors of the northern and middle colonies to settle the plan of the ensuing campaign. The council resolved on raising ten thousand two hundred and fifty men; to attack Niagara, that the communication between Canada and Louisiana might be cut off; to reduce Ticonderoga and Crown Point, that the command of Lake Champlain might be obtained, and New York be freed from the apprehension of invasion; to besiege Fort Du Quesne; and to detach a body of forces, by the river Kennebeck, to alarm the capital of Canada. This plan was too extensive for the means which General Shirley possessed; and served only to dissipate the strength, which more concentrated efforts might have rendered serviceable.

In enlisting troops for the approaching campaign, the recruiting parties in Pennsylvania and New Jersey, gave great offence to the inhabitants, by the reception, if not, the seduction of their indented servants; and the Assembly of the latter province threatened to discontinue the regiment they had furnished, unless this grievance were redressed. Circumstances, however, did not admit the discharge of such recruits to any great extent; of which the House, becoming sensible, it appropriated £15,000, for the maintenance of that regiment for the ensuing campaign. Extraordinary inducements were offered at this time, for enlistment in the royal regiments. The recruits were exempted from service any where but in North America, and were promised a bounty of two hundred acres of land, free from quit-rents, for ten years, either in the province of New York, New Hampshire, or Nova Scotia, at their option; to be assured, in case they should be killed in the service, to their children. And to stimulate the provinces to liberal appropriations, as occasion might require, Parliament voted £115,000 sterling, to be distributed at the King's pleasure, among the northern and middle provinces, of which New Jersey received five thousand pounds.

XXV. Though France and England had been engaged in the warmest hostilities, in America, since 1754, the peace was not openly and avowedly broken in Europe, until May, of the present year. The events in America, in 1754, had determined each to despatch considerable reinforcements to the colonies. The French, understanding that orders had been given to Boscawen, to intercept their squadron, declared they would consider the first gun fired as a declaration of war; and their minister was recalled from London, in consequence of an attack upon their fleet, by that admiral. The British government instantly issued letters of marque, under which a large number of French merchant ships, and seven thousand French sailors, were captured. A blow which had great effect upon the subsequent operations of the war, in Europe and America.

XXVI. Either from want of confidence in the military talents of General Shirley, or that, he might give them information on American affairs, the ministry removed him from his command, and summoned him to England. General Abercrombie succeeded him; with whom came out two additional regiments. But the chief direction of the war was soon after given to the Earl of Loudon, who was appointed governor of Virginia, and colonel of the royal American regiment, which had been lately formed from the German emigrants.

XXVII. In the mean time, Sir William Johnson had succeeded, by the mediation of the Six Nations, in disposing the Shawanese and Delawares to an accommodation. Hostilities against them were suspended, and the treaty of peace was soon after ratified at Easton. This was the withdrawal of one painful thorn from the side of the colonies; and the chastisement inflicted by Colonel Armstrong of Pennsylvania,* by the destruction of the den of the horde, at Kittanning, soon extracted another. The conflagration of that town, and slaughter of the Indian families there, was a severe stroke upon the savages. Hitherto, the English had not assailed them in their towns, and they fancied, would not venture to approach them. But, now, though urged by unquenchable thirst of vengeance to retaliate the blow, they dreaded, that, in their absence on war parties, their wigwams might be reduced to ashes. Such of them as belonged to Kittanning, and had escaped the carnage, refused to settle again on the east of Fort Du Quesne; resolving to place that fortress and the French garrison between themselves and the English.

XXVIII. Of the many enterprises resolved on by General Shirley, several were unattempted; none were successful. Notwithstanding the exertions in the northern provinces, the recruiting service moved heavily. Much time was lost by the change of commanders; and the season for operation was nearly half spent, before the arrival of Lord Loudon. No preparations were made against Fort Du Quesne. The colonies of Virginia, Maryland, and Pennsylvania, far from pursuing offensive measures, were unable to protect themselves. The expedition against Ticonderoga and Crown Point, was confided to General Winslow, who had won golden opinions during his last campaign, in Nova Scotia. Seven thousand provincialists had assembled near Lake George, but their number was reduced by subtractions for the garrisons in their rear. Winslow refused to proceed without reinforcements; and though soon after strengthened by some British troops, under General Abercrombie,

* September 8th, 1756.

he was perplexed and embarrassed by disputes relative to rank, which grew out of this junction. The regulations of the crown, on this subject, had given great offence in America; and such was the reluctance of the provincialists to serve under British officers, that, in the present case, in order to enable the troops to act, separately, the Americans were withdrawn from the garrisons to the army, and their places supplied with British forces. The expedition to Ontario was rendered hopeless by the successes of the French under Montcalm, who had captured the forts of Ontario and Oswego, situate on either side of the Onondago river, at its junction with the lake. These forts in the country of the Six Nations, he, with sound policy, destroyed, in their presence. At the capture of Oswego, Colonel Schuyler, and half the Jersey regiment, which formed part of the garrison, were made prisoners and sent to Canada; from whence they were not released, until the end of the campaign, and then on parole, not to serve for eighteen months. The regiment was, however, recruited to its original state of five hundred men, at the expense of the province, early in the ensuing spring.

Discouraged and disconcerted by these events, Loudon relinquished all offensive operations, and disposed his troops for the defence of the frontier. Renewed efforts to increase his force were rendered abortive by the appearance of the small-pox at Albany. The troops which were on the march from New England, and the army at Lake George, were panic-struck by the irruption of an enemy more dreadful than the French; and it became necessary to garrison all the posts with British troops, and to discharge the provincialists, excepting one regiment raised in New York. Thus terminated, for a second time, in defeat and utter disappointment, the sanguine hopes, formed by the colonists, of a brilliant and successful campaign. Much labour had been employed, and much money expended, in collecting, by land, from a great distance, troops, provisions, and military stores, at Albany, and in transporting them through an almost unsettled country, to Lake George; yet not an effort had been made to drive the invaders even from their outposts at Ticonderoga.

XXIX. The treaty with Teedyuscung, had neutralized the Delaware and Shawanese tribes on the Susquehanna, but the country was still exposed to the inroads of the French and western Indians, who, growing confident from the late disasters of the English, roamed, in small parties, avoiding or attacking the forts and armed provincialists, as they judged most safe. The counties of Cumberland, Lancaster, Berks, and Northampton, in Pennsylvania, and, occasionally, a part of Sussex, in New Jersey, were, during the spring and summer months of 1757, kept in continual alarm, and some of the scalping parties penetrated to within thirty miles of Philadelphia. Many of these wretches paid with their lives, the just penalty of their temerity. But their sufferings were not comparable with those of the unfortunate inhabitants. Incessant anxiety pervaded every family in the districts we have named; their slumber was broken by the yell of demons, or by dread of attack, scarce less horrible than their actual presence. The ground was ploughed, the seed sown, and the harvest gathered, under the fear of the tomahawk and rifle. Women visiting their sick neighbours, were shot or captured; children, driving home cattle from the field, were killed and scalped; whilst the enemy, dastardly as cruel, shrunk from every equality of force. Many of the richest neighbourhoods were deserted, and property of every kind abandoned: extraordinary heroism was frequently displayed by men, women, and children, in defence of themselves and their homes, and in pursuit of, and combat with, the enemy. There was certainly great want of ability and energy in the constituted authorities, British and Provincial. United councils, and well directed efforts, would have driven the bar-

barians to their savage haunts, and repeated the chastisement, administered at Kittanning, until they sued for peace. The Assembly of New Jersey, however, was not regardless of the danger and sufferings of her frontier citizens, and kept on foot, for their protection, a body of rangers, consisting of one hundred and twenty men, under Captain Gardiner; who, though they could not prevent occasional invasions of the foe, gave as much security to the frontier as circumstances would admit.

XXX. Lord Loudon, in the middle of January, summoned the Governors of the New England provinces to New York. In no very good humour he attributed to them, the disasters of the late campaign. "Their enterprise against Crown Point," he said, "had not been timely communicated to the ministry; their troops were inferior to his expectations, disposed to insubordination, and less numerous than had been promised; the true state of the forts and garrisons had not been reported to him, and the provincial Legislatures had given him votes, instead of men and money." He concluded this reprimand with a requisition for additional troops from New England, New York, and New Jersey. The spirit of the colonists, however, was not to be broken by misfortune, caused by the incapacity of the ministry of the parent state, and her delegated satraps, nor to be perverted by unmerited reproaches. His demands were, generally, complied with; and he was placed, in the spring, at the head of a respectable army, to tempt his fortune under his own star. The New England provinces exerted themselves greatly at this time, and authorized a draft, or conscription, should their quotas not be completed by voluntary enlistment. The force required from New Jersey was one thousand men; but the Assembly conceiving five hundred to be their full proportion, refused to do more than complete their regiment; and in an answer to the proposal of Governor Belcher, that they should, also, authorize a draft, they peremptorily declared by a vote of 12, to 7, "that they were determined not to oblige or compel any of the inhabitants by force, to serve as soldiers."

XXXI. The failures of the past year were attributed to the multiplied objects of the campaign, and the consequent division of the forces. Unity of design, and concentration of the troops, it was presumed, would ensure success. It was therefore resolved, that Louisburg should be attacked; and Halifax was fixed as the rendezvous of the fleet and army. Early in July, Admiral Holburn arrived there with a large squadron of ships and five thousand land forces; and after many delays, was joined by Lord Loudon, with six thousand regulars. Much was properly anticipated from this formidable armament, but the procrastination of the commander-in-chief doomed the country to severe disappointment. For before his preparations were completed, the French had occupied Louisburg with a superior force, despatched from Brest, against which his lordship was not disposed to make an effort.

XXXII. The enemy, however, was not slow to avail himself of the advantages which might accrue to him by the withdrawal of the British troops from the northern frontiers of New York. Montcalm, at the head of nine thousand men, drawn principally from Crown Point, Ticonderoga, and the neighbouring forts, witth some Canadians and Indians, invested Castle William on the southern shore of Lake George. The place was garrisoned by three thousand men, including the unfortunate Jersey regiment, was well fortified and supplied with necessaries, but Colonel Monroe was compelled to surrender it within six days after its investment. Montcalm's triumph was stained by the barbarities of his Indian allies, and though he exerted himself to protect his prisoners, the massacre of many of them will ever be coupled with his name. Major-general Webb made strenuous exertions to relieve the fort by arousing the militia of New York and New Jersey. From the latter province, one thousand men were despatched, and three thousand were put in readiness to march, should they be required. By these reinforcements he was enabled to hold Fort Edward, check the progress of the enemy, who retired when he had learned the return of Loudon to New York. The New Jersey regiment with other prisoners were released, and returned to New York under parole, not to serve again during eighteen months, and being thus rendered useless, were, at the instance of the Assembly, disbanded. This regiment, since the capture of Colonel Schuyler, had been commanded by Colonel Parker.

XXXIII. On August 31, 1757, died Governor Jonathan Belcher, in the 76th year of his age. His health had been so infirm, during the preceding two years, that he summoned the Assembly to attend him at Elizabethtown, much to their dissatisfaction. The House seemed apprehensive of being made a mere satellite of the Executive, to revolve around him, in whatever sphere he chose to move, and they therefore attended Governors Morris and Belcher, even when illness prevented these officers from getting to Burlington, or to Amboy with great reluctance; protesting at all times, that their acquiescence should not be drawn into precedent; and they explicitly refused to adjourn from Burlington to Trenton, on the request of his successor Mr. Readington, although his health also required this indulgence.

Governor Belcher was a native of New England, and inherited, in early youth an abundant fortune, which enabled him to visit Europe, and to mingle extensively in good society, until lavish expenditure dissipated his wealth. He joined the popular side in the colony of Massachusetts, in the long contest with Governor Burnet, on the question of fixing his salary, for an indefinite time, and was sent as an agent of the Assembly to represent their views to the King. Upon the death of Governor Burnet he was appointed to succeed him, and then maintained the pretension of his predecessor, which he had been employed to repel, and with the like ill success. His administration at Boston was distinguished by his taste for ostentation, and his imperious deportment, and he finally so disgusted the influential men of that government, by rejecting several respectable persons nominated to the council, that they successfully united to effect his removal. He afterwards remained several years unemployed, until he was named to the government of New Jersey. "He was now advanced in age, yet lively, diligent in his station, and circumspect in his conduct, religious, generous and affable. He affected splendour, at least equal to his rank and fortune: but was a man of worth and honour, and though, in his last years under great debility of body from a stroke of the palsy, he bore up with firmness and resignation, and went through the business of his government, in the most difficult part of the war, with unremitting zeal in the duties of his office."*

XXXIV. By the death of Mr. Belcher, the administration of the government again devolved on Mr. John Reading, the first named of the counsellors; who being aged and infirm, at first refused, and finally assumed, its duties with great reluctance. For the space of more than a month, the government was directed by the whole council, at whose instance, on the application of Lord Loudon, the Assembly voted one hundred rangers, to be employed on the frontiers during the winter season.†

* Smith's Hist. of N. J. 438.

† The captain of this company received six shillings, the lieutenants five, serjeants four, corporals three and six pence, and the private soldier three shillings per day. And each officer and soldier was furnished at colonial expense, with a blanket, a half thick under jacket, a kersey jacket lapelled, buckskin breeches, two check shirts, two pair of shoes, two pair of stockings, a leather cap, and a hatchet; and 20 shillings was allowed to the captain for each private he should enlist.

CHAPTER IX.

Containing Events from the Presidency of Mr. Reading to the repeal of the Stamp Act—from the year 1746 to the year 1766.—I. Influence of Mr. Pitt and his Policy upon Colonial Affairs—New hopes infused into the Colonists.—II. Successful Attack of the English upon the Northern Forts.—III. Capture of Fort Du Quesne by General Forbes.—IV. Cheerful and ready aid of the Colonies.—V. New Jersey supplies one thousand Men, and builds Barracks for the King's Troops.—VI. President Reading superseded by the arrival of Governor Bernard—His treaty with the Indians—Succeeded by Thomas Boone—He, by Josiah Hardy—He, by William Franklin, the last of the Royal Governors.—VII. Efficient Preparations for the Campaign of 1759.—VIII. Conquest of the French Colonies in North America.—IX. Honourable share of the Provincialists in this Result.—X. Treaty of Peace with France and Spain.—XI. New Confederacy and Hostilities of the Indians—Six hundred Troops raised by New Jersey.—XII. Impressions on the English Ministry, by the Wealth and Power displayed in America.—XIII. Proposition of Mr. Grenville to tax the Colonies.—XIV. Consideration of the Principles relating to Colonial Taxation.—XV. Mr. Grenville commmunicates his purpose to the Colonial Agents in London.—XVI. Views taken by Colonies of this Proposition.—XVII. Propositions by several of the Colonies to raise Money, rejected by Mr. Grenville.—XVIII. Act of Parliament for Tax on Colonial Imports and Exports.—XIX. Effect of the Measures in America—Proceedings of Massachusetts and Rhode Island.—XX. Stamp Act passed—Its reception in the Colonies.—XXI. Temporary suspension of legal proceedings and of the publication of Newspapers.—XXII. Anti-Importation Associations.—XXIII. Organization of the "*Sons of Liberty*."—XXIV. Proposition of Massachusetts for assembling a Congress of Deputies from the Colonies—Action of New Jersey on this proposition.—XXV. Proceedings of the Congress—Messrs. Ruggles of Massachusetts, and Ogden of New Jersey, refuse to join in a General Petition.—XXVI. The Assembly of New Jersey approve the Proceedings of Congress—adopts Resolutions condemnatory of the Stamp Act.—XXVII. Efforts in England for Repeal of the Stamp Act.—XXIX. Inquiry before the House of Commons—Repeal of the Stamp Act.

I. With the opening of the year 1758, a new era dawned upon the colonies, which were roused from a state of apathy by the voice of William Pitt. The enterprise, judgment, and firmness, which had raised England from the depths of humility, were now employed for the reduction of the American continent. The plan of the campaign was wisely matured, and committed for execution, to men who had reputations to lose and fortunes to gain. Loudon was recalled. Abercrombie commanded in chief, with Amherst for his second, aided by Brigadiers Wolfe and Forbes. The fleet, consisting altogether of one hundred and fifty sail, was commanded by Boscawen.

II. The designated objects of the campaign were Louisburg, the forts on the lakes, and Fort du Quesne. Major-general Amherst, with twelve thousand men, aided by the fleet, laid siege to the first, early in June; and captured it, after an obstinate defence of seven weeks. General Abercrombie, with seven thousand regulars and ten thousand colonial troops, undertook the expedition against the northern forts. He first attempted that at Ticonderoga, which had been reared by the French in 1756, on the narrow neck of land dividing Lake George from Lake Champlain. Its position, strong by nature, was well secured by art, and by a garrison of five thousand men. Relying on his superior force, the British general made his attack without artillery, which, from the badness of the roads, could not keep pace with the army. He was repulsed with the loss of two thousand men, chiefly killed; among whom were Brigadier-general Lord Howe, and many other officers of distinction. Though still superior to the enemy, he made a hasty retreat;

but compensated for this ill-timed prudence, by the capture of Fort Frontignac, situate on the north side of the river St. Lawrence, at its entrance from Lake Ontario; commanding the river, and serving as a magazine for the more southern castles. The garrison consisted of one hundred and ten men only; but the fort contained a large stock of arms, stores, and provisions for the western posts. Nine armed vessels, some of which carried eighteen guns, were also taken. The enterprise was projected and executed by Lieutenant-colonel Bradstreet.

III. The reduction of Fort Du Quesne was confided to Brigadier-general Forbes, with a detachment from General Abercrombie's army, strengthened by the southern militia; the whole computed at seven thousand eight hundred and fifty men.* He began his march from Carlisle in the middle of July, to join Colonel Bouquet at Raystown; who, with two thousand five hundred men, was advanced to Loyal Hanna, fifty miles further to the westward. The march of the main body was delayed until September, in consequence of the difficulty in procuring carriages and military stores, and of the tardiness with which the orders to the Virginia regulars, under Colonel Washington, had been given. In the mean time, Major Grant was detached by Bouquet, with eight hundred men, to reconnoitre the fort and adjacent country. He was attacked, surrounded by the enemy, and lost above three hundred men, killed and taken, and was himself among the prisoners; the remainder retired in great confusion.† Colonel Bouquet still continuing at Loyal Hanna, the enemy resolved to attack him, in his camp. A force, estimated at twelve hundred French, and two hundred Indians, commanded by De Vetri, assailed him on the eleventh of October with great vivacity, but was compelled to draw off with considerable loss, after a warm combat of four hours. A second attack was made during the night, but some shells thrown from the camp compelled them to retreat. The loss of Colonel Bouquet amounted to sixty-seven rank and file, killed and wounded. Upon the twenty-third or twenty-fourth of October, General Forbes proceeded from Raystown to Loyal Hanna. He continued there until the seventeenth of November. On the twelfth of that month Colonel Washington, being out with a scouting party, fell in with a number of the enemy about three miles from the camp, whom he attacked, killing one, and taking three prisoners: among the latter was one Johnson, an Englishman, who had been captured by the Indians in Lancaster county, from whom was derived full and correct information of the state of the garrison at Du Quesne. A most unfortunate occurrence happened to the provincials upon this occasion. The fire of Washington's party being heard at the camp, Colonel Mercer, with a number of Virginians, were sent to his assistance. The two parties approaching, in the dusk of the evening, reciprocally mistook each other for enemies; a number of shot was exchanged, by which a lieutenant and thirteen or fourteen Virginians were killed. On the thirteenth of November, a force of one thousand men, under Colonel John Armstrong, was pushed forward, and the general followed on the seventeenth, with four thousand three hundred effective men, leaving strong garrisons at Raystown and Loyal Hanna. For want of practicable roads, the whole march was tedious and difficult—the advance of ten miles a-day being deemed extraordinary progress. The

* 350 Royal Americans; four companies.
1200 Highlanders; thirteen companies.
2600 Virginians.
2700 Pennsylvanians.
1000 Wagoners, sutlers, and followers of the army.
Penn. Gazette, 1758, No. 1553.

† 14th September.

army was greatly afflicted by sickness, and weakened by desertion. Neglecting the road formerly cut by Braddock over the mountains, General Forbes opened a new one, by which he approached the fort. The capture of Frontignac, and the defection of the Indians from the French interest, had already prepared the way for his success. The garrison of Fort Du Quesne, unsustained by their savage allies, and hopeless of reinforcements, the Canadian force lately engaged at Loyal Hanna having retired, held the place, only, until the approach of the English army should justify its abandonment. Accordingly, on the twenty-fourth of November, when Forbes was within a day's march of the fort, they burned and abandoned it, and escaped, by the Ohio river, to the French settlements upon the Mississippi. The ruined fortifications were seized by the English, on the next day, and, being hastily repaired, were garrisoned by four hundred and fifty men, chiefly provincial troops, from Pennsylvania, Maryland, and Virginia, under the command of Colonel Mercer. The remainder of the army was marched into the interior, and quartered at Lancaster, Reading, and Philadelphia.

IV. In the preparations of the colonies for this campaign, we have new evidence of the power which an energetic spirit, directed by wisdom, may obtain, over the mass of mankind. The contributions of the provinces, towards carrying on the continental war, had, for the last campaigns, been merely the cold returns of duty; but in this, the people displayed all the zeal with which men pursue their interests, when animated by well founded hopes of success. Their combined forces, they were now assured, would be applied to remove the enemy from the frontiers; and instead of being required to furnish a specific quota of troops, each colony was directed to raise as large a force as was in its power, with the greatest possible despatch. To render such force effective, Mr. Pitt recommended to the respective governors, to commission popular men for officers, and in bestowing military appointments, to have regard, solely, to the public service. Arms, ammunition, tents, and provisions, were to be furnished by the crown; and the expense of levying, clothing, and pay, was to be borne by the provinces. But, even these charges, he promised to recommend the Parliament to pay, as the vigour and efforts of the provinces should merit.

V. Thus inspirited, the Assembly of New Jersey, instead of raising, reluctantly, five hundred men, doubled that number; and to fill the ranks, in season, offered a bounty of twelve pounds, per man; increased the pay of the officers, and voted a sum of fifty thousand pounds, for their maintenance. They, at the same sessions, directed barracks to be built at Burlington, Trenton, New Brunswick, Amboy, and Elizabethtown, competent, each, for the accommodation of three hundred men. *Nor, did the Assembly fail to remark, on the constitutional method they had been called on to give assistance to the common cause; being left at liberty to furnish to the crown, what their own ability and sense of the occasion required.* This complement of one thousand men, New Jersey kept up, during the years 1758, 1759, and 1760; and in the years 1761 and 1762, furnished six hundred men, beside in the latter year, a company of sixty-four men and officers, especially, for garrison duty; for which she incurred an average expense of forty thousand pounds per annum.

VI. On the 13th of June, 1758, President Reading was superseded by the arrival of Francis Bernard, Esq., who continued to govern the province, in unbroken harmony with the Legislature, until the 4th of July, 1760. The principal service rendered by this gentleman, was the aid he gave in the pacification of the Indians, at the treaty of Easton, in October, 1758, of which we have spoken fully elsewhere. Upon his transfer to Massachusetts, he was succeeded by Thomas Boone, who continued little more than a year;

being removed to South Carolina, and his place in New Jersey supplied by Josiah Hardy. Upon his dismissal, and appointment to the consulate at Cadiz, came in, William Franklin, the son of, Dr. Benjamin Franklin, the last of the colonial governors. Thus, in the space of five years, New Jersey had seen five governors appointed by the crown. This frequent change proved very unacceptable to the colony, which was fully content with the three first we have named; and would have been satisfied to have spared the repeated gift of five hundred pounds, usually made to the new governor, on his arrival, in consideration of the expense and trouble of his voyage. To Governor Franklin this present was not made. But as the cost of living had considerably increased by the diminution of the value of money, consequent on the increased amount of the circulating medium, during the war, the Assembly added two hundred pounds to the annual salary, making it twelve hundred pounds.

VII. Great Britain, having resolved to annihilate the French power in North America, made adequate preparations for the campaign of 1759. An army of eight thousand men, under General Wolfe, was destined to attack Quebec; whilst General Amherst, with 12,000 regular and provincial troops, should reduce the forts of Ticonderoga and Crown Point, cross Lake Champlain, and by the rivers Richelieu and St. Lawrence, join Wolfe; and General Prideaux, assisted by Sir William Johnson, at the head of some friendly Indians, should capture the fort at the falls of Niagara, and proceed by Lake Ontario and Montreal, to unite with the other generals. To General Stanwix, was confided the southern department, with orders to watch the western frontier, and to erect proper forts for its defence.

VIII. This stupendous plan was, only, partly carried into execution. Quebec was purchased with the life of the gallant Wolfe. General Amherst obtained possession of Crown Point and Ticonderoga, but too late in the season, to permit him to accomplish the remainder of the plan assigned to him. General Prideaux invested Niagara, but was slain in the trenches by the bursting of a cohort. The fort was, however, captured by Sir William Johnson, who succeeded him in the command. It was not until September of the succeeding year, that the great object was entirely gained; when, by the union of three British armies, before Montreal, the Marquis de Vaudreuil, was compelled to surrender, by capitulation, the whole of the French possessions to his Britannic Majesty.

Thus fell the great power of France in America. Possessed of the northern and southern parts of the continent, her encroachments became formidable to the British American empire, which she sought to confine, to a narrow slip of sea-coast. She thus brought upon her the united power of England and her colonies, which she baffled, when feebly directed; but which was irresistible in the hands of a wise and energetic minister.

IX. The share of the provincials in this result, gives lustre to the colonial history of the American States. They had kept in the field an average force of twenty-five thousand men during the war; had lost thirty thousand of their young men, and contributed three millions five hundred thousand pounds sterling, to the payment of its expenses.* Four hundred privateers, from their ports, ravaged the French West India islands, and distressed the commerce of France, in all parts of the world. Their troops preserved the remains of the army wrecked by the folly of Braddock; and under Monckton, captured Beau Sejour, in Nova Scotia. Commanded by Sir William Johnson, they destroyed the army of Baron Dieskau; and subsequently reduced Fort Niagara, one of the most important posts on the continent. The merit

* Of this sum, Parliament reimbursed at several times, £1,031,666 sterling.

of these actions, is ascribable to them, solely. In all the marches and battles they were principal sufferers; and where honour was to be gained, the provincial was distinguished, by his fortitude in adversity, and his promptitude and courage in the hour of peril.

X. Spain became party to the war, in January, 1772; but the conflict against the united house of Bourbon, was not of long continuance; peace being made with France and Spain, on the 3d of November, of the same year. We are interested in the terms of the treaty, so far only, as they affected the colonies. France surrendered her pretensions to Nova Scotia, and ceded Canada, including Louisiana. Spain yielded Florida. In exchange for this mighty domain, France received the islands of St. Pierre and Miquelon, near Newfoundland, with a restricted privilege of the fishery, and the islands of Martinique, Guadaloupe, Mariegalante, Deseada, and St. Lucia.—Spain obtained the restoration of the Havana—a price, more than adequate for Florida, which would not have been paid, but with the design of preserving the eastern shore of North America, from foreign influence.

XI. In exclusive possession of this immense territory, comprehending nearly one-fifth of the globe, Great Britain and her colonies rationally looked forward, to its peaceful enjoyment, in full confidence, that the aboriginal inhabitants, no longer exposed to dangerous solicitations, nor supported by alien power, would not dare to provoke the resentment of those upon whom they must entirely depend, for the gratifications supplied by the whites. But the cupidity of the savage had been highly excited, during the late conflict, and as deeply indulged. The present unprotected state of the frontier, held forth irresistible temptations to his whetted appetite for plunder. His barbarities had been rather rewarded than chastised. Every treaty brought him rich presents; and his detention of prisoners, whom he had again and again promised to surrender, was overlooked, on slight apologies; though, obviously, done to afford opportunities for new treaties and additional gifts. But, we must, perhaps, look deeper, for the cause of the wide extended confederacy, which now took place among the aborigines, and which may have been dictated by profound policy. They beheld the French driven out of the whole country, and themselves in danger of becoming wholly dependent upon a power, which already commanded by its forts, the great lakes and rivers; and they may have felt, that an immediate and mighty effort was necessary to restrain the tide, which, if unimpeded, would spread itself over the continent, overwhelming all their nations in its course.

A secret coalition was formed among the Shawanese, the tribes upon the Ohio, and its tributary waters, and about Detroit, to attack, simultaneously, the English posts and settlements, upon the frontier. The plan was deliberately and skilfully projected. The settlements were to be invaded during harvest; the inhabitants, with their corn and cattle, to be destroyed; and the outposts to be reduced by famine. The Indians fell, suddenly, upon the traders, whom they had invited among them, murdered many, and plundered the effects of all, to an immense amount. The frontiers of Pennsylvania, Maryland and Virginia, were overrun by scalping parties, committing their usual enormities. The out-forts, even the most remote, were assailed about the same time; and all, immediately, fell into the hands of the enemy, save Niagara, Detroit, and Fort Pitt, which, being larger and better garrisoned, were enabled to stand a longer siege.

As, in the preceding Indian contest, the frontier inhabitants were driven in, and the enemy again penetrated into the thickly settled country; but more skill and courage were generally displayed in resisting them. Niagara and Detroit were protected by detachments sent to their relief by General Amherst, whilst Colonel Bouquet, after much fatigue and a bloody battle, succeeded in succouring Fort Pitt. These distressing hostilities continued until October, 1764, when they were terminated by Col. Bouquet, who, with fifteen hundred men, overran the Indian country in Ohio, compelling the submission of the tribes, and releasing many white prisoners. The Indians, soon after, entered into a final and satisfactory treaty with Sir William Johnson, who was authorized for that purpose, by the crown.

Governor Franklin, on the approach of the savages to the western frontier of New Jersey, ordered out the militia, remanned the fortifications which had been formerly erected, and built several new block-houses. Yet some parties of Indians crossed the Delaware, made their way through the lines, and massacred several families. On the meeting of the House, 15th of November, he recommended them to provide six hundred men, at the request of General Amherst, to unite with other forces to invade the Indian country, and to provide more effectually for defence of their own limits. The latter, the House undertook, directing two hundred men to be raised for this purpose, and appropriating ten thousand pounds for their support; but they declined to furnish troops for general operations, until a general plan should be formed, and a requisition should be made for aid to the other colonies. At their next subsequent session, however, they passed a bill for raising six hundred men, on condition, that a majority of the eastern colonies should come into the requisition; and when this bill was rejected by the council, and the governor prorogued the House, in order to give them an opportunity to bring in another, they authorized the force required, provided New York should contribute her full proportion. In this shape the bill passed, and the troops joined the northern army.

XII. The great pecuniary advances of the colonies, in the late wars, discovered to the ministry of Great Britain, a mine of wealth, whose existence they had not hitherto suspected; and with the knowledge came an inexpressible longing to subject this wealth to the use of the parent state. But no good genius whispered, that, there existed, also, the spirit, as well as the means, to maintain the political freedom which had been, at once, the source of riches and of colonial happiness. It was supposed, that, if in a few years, these long neglected and distant provinces could pay, without apparent inconvenience, millions for defence, they might, also, be compelled to pay millions for tribute.

XIII. On this assumption, Mr. Grenville, first commissioner of the treasury, flattered himself that he might establish a high financial character, in relieving *his* country by the taxation of her provinces. To a superficial observer, few obstacles were apparent in such a course. Parliament had frequently imposed duties upon the colonial trade; which, as a part of a general system, for regulating the commerce of the empire, had been patiently borne. But, no attempt had been, hitherto, made, avowedly, to raise a revenue from the colonies, for the use of the British treasury.

XIV. Upon the principles which have governed modern colonization, the colony is dependent, either upon the parent *state*, or upon its *chief*, as a distinct *apanage* or property. The first case was, that of the colonies of most of the European states. The second, characterized those of Spain; the kingdoms of Mexico, Peru, &c., being long considered as connected with those of Castile and Arragon, through the monarch alone, who was the king of each, respectively. A different view, however, was taken in relation to these, by the Cortes, in framing the constitution of 1820, when, as integral parts of the Spanish *empire*, they were admitted to representation in the *national* councils. The English colonies held their connexion with Great Britain, to be somewhat similar to that which had prevailed between Spain and her provinces; claiming, however, for their governments, the important and characteristic principle, which animated the polity of the parent state, that the people should have a potential voice, in legislation, through their representatives. This theory was universal, but the practice was variously modified; the Legislative power, being more or less exercised by the people, according to the provisions of the several charters from the crown. One right, however, which controlled all others—the right of the purse, was every where held sacred to the people; and though the crown might create an almost inevitable necessity of disbursement, it could not without the form, at least, of popular volition, take money from the pockets of the people.*

The right of the Parliament to legislate, generally, for the colonies had not been questioned since the year 1692, when Massachusetts and New York denied it by acts of their Legislatures.† These laws were annulled in England; and in 1698 Parliament declared, that "all laws, by-laws, usages and customs, which shall be in practice, in any of the plantations, repugnant to any law made, or to be made, in this kingdom, relative to the said plantations, shall be void and of none effect."

By the charter of Charles II, to Penn, the right of Parliament to lay duties on imports and exports, and to impose taxes or customs on the inhabitants of Pennsylvania, their lands, goods and chattels was clearly reserved. In 1739, Sir William Keith, in conjunction with some American merchants, proposed to raise troops for the western frontier, to be supported by a duty laid by Parliament on stamped paper and parchment, in all the colonies. But the subject was then too inconsiderable to claim the attention of the government. When efforts were made to unite the colonies in 1754, a plan for colonial taxation was suggested; but the ministers finding the colonies averse to their views, did not venture to press it on the eve of a war, in which the cordial and undivided exertions of the whole nation were required.‡

A more favourable occasion seemed now to present itself. The war which had grown out of American interests, had been honourably terminated, and it was supposed, that the provinces, grateful for their deliverance, would cheerfully repay the care of a fostering mother. Nor would such anticipations have been disappointed, had the designs of the ministry no other consequences than a single pecuniary burden upon the people.

XV. Towards the end of the year 1763, Mr. Grenville communicated to the colonial agents in London, his purpose of drawing a revenue from America, by means of a stamp duty to be imposed by Act of Parliament, and directed them to transmit this intelligence to their respective Assemblies, that they might suggest any more preferable duty, equally productive.§ The following view, briefly exhibited, was then taken of this subject, by all the provinces.

XVI. The colonies were considered as integral governments, of which the crown was the head, having exclusive political power within their respective territories, except in cases involving the general interests of the empire, in which, from principles of convenience and necessity, they admitted the supremacy of the British Parliament. On these principles, they had submitted to the general regulations of commerce, however restrictive of their exertions at home and abroad; and where the letter of the law pressed heavily on their

* By the *Concessions* of Berkeley and Carteret, and also of the West Jersey proprietors, it was provided, "that the governor and council are not to impose, or suffer to be imposed, any tax, custom, or subsidy, tollage, assessments, or any other duty whatsoever, upon any colour or pretence, how specious soever, upon the said province, and inhabitants thereof, without their own consent, first had, or other than what shall be imposed by the authority and consent of the General Assembly."

† Smith's N. Y. 75, 76.

‡ Marshall's Life of Washington.

§ One hundred thousand pounds sterling, was the sum required by Mr. Grenville.

natural rights, murmurs were seldom heard, as such acts were not rigidly enforced. The mode of drawing aid from the colonists accorded with these principles. The sovereign having well considered the occasion, in his privy council, directed his secretary of state to apply to each colony through its governor, to grant him such sums as were suitable to its ability. And as the colonies had always made liberal grants on such requisitions, the proposition to tax them in Parliament, was unnecessary, cruel, and unjust. Unjust, because it was diametrically opposite to the letter and spirit of their constitutions, which had established as a fundamental axiom, that taxation and representation are inseparable, and that as the colonies were not, and from local and political obstacles could not be, represented in the British Parliament, it would be the very essence of tyranny to attempt to exercise an authority over them, which, from its nature, must inevitably lead to gross abuse. For, when in absolute possession of the power now claimed, could it be imagined, that Parliament would not rather vote away the money of the colonists, than of their constituents? By the constitution, their business in matters of *aid* was with the King alone; they had no connexion with any financier, nor were the provincial agents the proper persons through whom requisitions should be made. For these reasons, it was improper for the provinces to make propositions to Mr. Grenville, in relation to taxes, especially, as the notice he had sent, did not appear to have been by the King's order, "and was perhaps without his knowledge."*

XVII. These views certainly did not proceed from a desire to avoid contribution, in relief of the public wants. Several of the colonial Legislatures declared, "that as they always had thought, so they always should think, it their duty to grant aid to the crown." Copies of these votes were presented to Mr. Grenville, and an opportunity was thus offered to him, to raise by constitutional means, more than a compulsory tax would produce. But he had resolved on measures, which should establish the absolute supremacy of Parliament over the provinces, and open the way for its unrestrained exercise.

XVIII. When forming his plan of American taxation, Mr. Grenville certainly did not apprehend all its consequences. But, aware that it would be opposed, he was desirous of trying an old measure under a new aspect, and proposed, in distinct terms, to *raise a revenue*, by taxes on colonial imports. This measure, sufficiently obnoxious in itself, was accompanied by a resolution of Parliament, "that it may be proper to charge certain stamp duties in the colonies." The act of Parliament, based on the first proposition, was extremely onerous to the American trade; the duties thereby imposed amounting almost to a prohibition of commercial intercourse with the French and Spanish colonies.† It is true, that this trade, previous to the passage of the act of which we now speak, was unlawful; but it was connived at, and was

* Votes of the Assemblies of the several colonies. Franklin's Letters, March 8th, 1770. Provincial Remonstrances. Marshall's Life of Washington, vol. ii. 68, &c.

† This act was entitled, "An act for granting certain duties in the British colonies and plantations, in America, for continuing, amending, and making perpetual, an act passed in the sixth year of the reign of his late Majesty, King George the Second, (entitled, an act for the better securing and encouraging the trade of his Majesty's sugar colonies in America,) for applying the produce of such duties, and of the duties to arise by virtue of the said act, towards defraying the expenses of defending, protecting and securing the said colonies and plantations, for explaining an act, made in the twenty-fifth year of the reign of King Charles the Second, (entitled, an act for the encouragement of the Greenland and Eastland trades, and for the better securing the plantation trade,) and for allowing and disallowing, several drawbacks on exports, from this kingdom, and those effectually preventing the clandestine conveyance of goods, to and from the said colonies and plantations, and improving and securing the trade between the same and Great Britain."

highly profitable; furnishing to the provinces, gold and silver for their remittances to England. The minister, in his care to prevent smuggling, did not pause to consider the difference between an advantageous trade in the western hemisphere, and the illicit commerce on the British coast. Converting naval officers into officers of the customs, he nearly destroyed the whole colonial trade with the Spanish and French islands. The preamble to the new impost law, declaring it to be just and necessary, that a revenue should be raised in America, and the resolution to follow it up, with a stamp act, gave an unequivocal and odious character to the law, and sent it forth to the colonies, the pioneer of a system of boundless oppression.

The revenue act became still more unpopular, by the means used to enforce it. The penalties for breach of its provisions, were made recoverable in the courts of admiralty, without the intervention of a jury, before judges dependent upon the crown, and drawing their salaries from forfeitures, adjudged by themselves. The duties were required to be paid in gold and silver, now scarce attainable, and consequently, the paper currency, more than ever necessary, was rejected and depreciated.

XIX. The impression, caused by these measures on the public mind, was uniform throughout America. The Legislature of Massachusetts, whose population, essentially commercial, felt most severely the late restrictions, was the first to notice them. That body resolved, "That the act of Parliament relating to the sugar trade with foreign colonies, and the resolution of the House of Commons, in regard to stamp duties, and other taxes proposed to be laid on the colonies, had a tendency to deprive the colonists of their most essential rights, as British subjects, and as men—particularly, the right of assessing their own taxes, and of being free from any impositions, but such as they consented to, by themselves or representatives." They directed Mr. Mauduit, their agent in London, to remonstrate against the ministerial measures, to solicit a repeal of the sugar act, and to deprecate the imposition of further duties and taxes on the colonies. They addressed the Assemblies of the other provinces, requesting them to unite in a petition against the designs of the ministry, and to instruct their agents to remonstrate against attempts so destructive to the liberty, the commerce and prosperity, of the colonies. The colony of Rhode Island, proposed to the provincial assemblies, to collect the sense of all the colonies, and to unite in a common petition to the King and Parliament.

XX. All the efforts of the American colonies to stay the mad career of the English ministry, proved unavailing. The stamp act was passed, with slight opposition, by the Commons, and unanimity by the Lords.* Dr. Franklin, who had been despatched to Europe, in November, 1764, as the agent of Pennsylvania, laboured earnestly to avert a measure, which his sagacity and perfect knowledge of the American people, taught him was pregnant with danger, to the British empire. But, even he does not appear to have entertained the idea, that it would be forcibly resisted. He wrote to Mr. Charles Thompson, "The sun of liberty is set, you must light up the candles of industry and economy." To which Mr. Thompson replied, "He was apprehensive that other lights would be the consequence." To Mr. Ingersol, the agent of Connecticut, the doctor said, "Go home, and tell your people to get children as fast as they can." Intimating that the period for successful resistance had not yet arrived.

* The stamp act was passed on the 22d of March, 1765. It was under the consideration of Parliament, in March, of the foregoing year, bu. was postponed, it was said, by the exertions of Mr. Allen, chief-justice of Pennsylvania, at that time on a visit to London.

The ministry, desirous to render the stamp act as little obnoxious as possible, resolved to appoint the officers of distribution and collection, from among the discreet and reputable inhabitants of the provinces. But, there were no means, by which to reconcile the people to a law, every where regarded as the forerunner of political slavery. The stamp officers, either voluntarily or compulsorily resigned their offices; some were hung or buried in effigy, in several of the provinces, and violent outrages were committed on the person and property of the deputy-governor, and other officers, at Boston. William Coxe, Esq., who had been appointed stamp officer, for New Jersey, voluntarily resigned his office in September, 1765. Subsequently, upon the application of the *Sons of Liberty*, of East Jersey, he published a copy of his letter of resignation, which had been made to the commissioners of the treasury; and declared that he had appointed no deputy, and would never act under the law. Towards the end of November, a number of the inhabitants of Salem county, learning that a Mr. John Hatton was desirous to be employed in the distribution of stamps, compelled him to a similar declaration.

On Saturday, the 5th of October, the ship Royal Charlotte, bearing the stamped papers for Jersey, Maryland, and Pennsylvania, convoyed by a stoop of war, arrived at Philadelphia. As these vessels rounded Gloucester Point, all those in the harbour hoisted their colours, at half mast; the bells were muffled, and every countenance assumed the semblance of affliction. At four o'clock, in the afternoon, many thousand citizens assembled at the state house, to consider of the means for preventing the distribution of the stamps. Their deliberations resulted in forcing Mr. Hughes, the stamp officer, most reluctantly, to decline the exercise of his office, and in securing the stamps on board his Majesty's sloop of war, Sardine.

XXI. The universal refusal of the colonists to submit to the stamp act, occasioned the entire suspension of legal proceedings. In some of the provinces, however, business was speedily resumed; and in nearly all, the penalties of the act were braved before its repeal. The members of the bar in New Jersey, met about the middle of February, 1766, at New Brunswick, to consider of the propriety of continuing their practice; and being *waited on* by a deputation of the *Sons of Liberty*, who expressed their dissatisfaction at the suspension of law proceedings, they determined, at all hazards, to recommence business on the first of the ensuing April. At the same time, deputies from the same self-constituted regulators of public affairs, *waited on* Mr. White, prothonotary of the county of Hunterdon, who was induced by their polite and energetic instances, to promise that his office should be reopened at the same period. By law, the stamp duty was to commence on the first of November. On the previous day, the newspapers, generally, were put in mourning for their approaching extinction; the editors having resolved to suspend their publication, until some plan should be devised to protect them from the penalties for publishing without stamps. The term of suspension, however, was short. On the 7th of November, a simisheet issued from the office of the Pennsylvania Gazette, without title or mark of designation, headed, "*No stamped paper to be had;*" and on the 14th, another, entitled "*Remarkable Occurrences.*" Both were in form of the gazette, which, after the 21st, was again regularly published.*

XXII. "To interest the people of England against the measures of administration, associations were formed in every part of the continent, for the encouragement of domestic manufactures, and against the use of those imported from Great Britain. To increase their quantity of wool, they deter-

* Pennsylvania Gazette.

mined to kill no lambs, and to use all the means in their power, to multiply their flocks of sheep.

XXIII. While this determined and systematic opposition was made by the thinking part of the community, there were some riotous and disorderly proceedings, especially in the large towns, which threatened serious consequences. Many houses were destroyed, much property injured, and several persons, highly respectable in character and station, grossly abused. These violences received no countenance from the leading members of society; but it was extremely difficult to stimulate the mass of the people, to that vigorous and persevering opposition, which was deemed essential to the preservation of American liberty, and yet to restrain all those excesses, which disgrace, and often defeat, the wisest measures. In Connecticut and New York, originated an association of persons, styling themselves the "*Sons of Liberty*," which extended into New Jersey, and other colonies; who bound themselves, among other things, to march to any part of the continent, at their own expense, to support the British constitution in America; by which, was expressly stated to be understood, the prevention of any attempt, which might any where be made, to carry the stamp act into operation. A corresponding committee of these sons of liberty was established, who addressed letters to certain conspicuous characters, throughout the colonies, and contributed materially to increase the spirit of opposition, and perhaps the turbulence, with which it was in some places attended.*

XXIV. On receipt of intelligence of the passage of the stamp act, several of the colonial Legislatures, of which Virginia was the first, asserted the *exclusive* right of the Assemblies to lay taxes and impositions on the inhabitants of the colonies, respectively. But the House of Representatives of Massachusetts, contemplating a still more solemn and effectual expression of the general sentiment, and pursuing the suggestion of Rhode Island, recommended a Congress of deputies from all the colonial Assemblies, to meet at New York, on the first Tuesday in October, to consult on the present circumstances of the colonies. Circular letters, signed by the speaker, communicating this recommendation, were addressed, respectively, to the speakers of the Assemblies in the other provinces. Wherever the Legislatures were in session, this communication was immediately acted upon.

It was laid before the Assembly of New Jersey, (20th June, 1765) on the last day of the session, when the House was thin; and the members, as Governor Franklin asserts, determined "*unanimously, after deliberate consideration, against connecting on that occasion;*" and directed a letter to be written at the table, to the speaker of Massachusetts Bay, acquainting him with their determination. The House, at a subsequent session, question,† but

* Marshall's Life of Washington, vol. i.

† June 27th, 1766. The statement of the Assembly is curious, and evidently betrays a design to make the best of a circumstance, with the remembrance of which, they were not very content. They say, "This House acknowledges the letter from the Massachusetts Bay; that it was on the last day of the session, some members gone, others uneasy to be at their homes; and do assert, that, the then speaker agreed to send, nay urged, that members should be sent to the intended Congress; but changed his opinion upon some *advice* that was given to him; that this sudden change of his opinion displeased many of the House, who seeing the matter dropped, were indifferent about it; and as no minute was made, and no further notice taken of it, the House is at a loss to determine whence his excellency could get the information, that the House took the same into '*deliberate consideration,*' *determined* (as his excellency says, from their own words) '*unanimously against connecting on that occasion:*' they have recollected the whole transaction, carefully examined their minutes, and can find nothing like it inserted therein; an answer to the Massachusetts letter was written, and if the expressions his excellency mentions, were made use of, in it, this House is at a loss to know how they are accountable for it, when it does not appear

do not disprove this statement. But, this determination was so highly condemned by their constituents, that the speaker found it necessary, in order to avoid the indignation of the people, and to preserve the public peace, to convene the members by circulars, at Amboy, and with them to proceed to the nomination of delegates to the Convention of New York, consisting of Mr. Robert Ogden, the speaker, Mr. Hendrick Fisher, and Mr. Joseph Borden. This measure was severely reprehended by the governor, and was the cause of an angry contention between him and the Assembly.

XXV. Delegates from the Assemblies of Massachusetts, Rhode Island, Connecticut, New York, New Jersey, Pennsylvania, Delaware, Maryland, and South Carolina, assembled at New York at the time appointed. New Hampshire, Georgia, Virginia, and North Carolina were not represented; but the two former gave assurances of their disposition to unite in petitions to the King and Parliament. The Assemblies of the two latter not having been in session, since the proposition for a Congress had been made, had no opportunity to act upon the subject.

This Congress adopted a declaration of rights and grievances, upon which they founded a petition to the King and a memorial to Parliament. In these, they claimed the full privileges of English subjects, averred the plenary legislative power of the colonial Assemblies, protested against taxation by Parliament, and the dispensation of the trial by jury; and earnestly pressed upon the attention of the parent state, the burdens imposed by the stamp and other acts, with the utter impossibility of continuing the execution of the former, in consequence of the drain of specie it would produce. A difference of opinion prevailed upon the question, whether the petitions and memorials should be signed and transmitted by the Congress, or be sanctioned and forwarded by the provincial Assemblies, as their several acts. Messrs. Ruggles of Massachusetts, the chairman of the Convention, and Ogden of New Jersey, believing in the propriety of the latter mode, refused to sign with the other delegates; but their conduct was censured by their constituents: and Mr. Ogden, thereupon, resigned his seat in the Assembly, which was convened by the governor, at his special instance,* that they might consider and adopt the best mode of expressing their sense of the obnoxious measures.†

XXVI. The House received from Messrs. Fisher and Borden their report of the proceedings of the Congress, and, unanimously, approved thereof; voting their thanks to those gentlemen, for the faithful and judicious discharge of the trust reposed in them. Mr. Courtlandt Skinner, the newly elected speaker, Mr. John Johnson, Mr. John Lawrence, and Mr. David Cooper were appointed to correspond with the agent‡ of the colony in Great Britain.

The House then proceeded to adopt, unanimously, the following preamble and resolutions: "Whereas, the late act of Parliament, called the stamp act, is found to be utterly subversive of privileges inherent to, and originally

to be an act of the House; but reflection on this passage, satisfies the House, that his excellency has more knowledge of the contents of the letter in answer, than the members of the House themselves."—*votes*. It is impossible not to perceive that the members of this Assembly, had not that vivid sense of evil resulting from the stamp act, which was displayed in other colonies, particularly, when we consider that this was the first opportunity for expressing their sentiments, upon the odious pretensions of Parliament. Upon their return to their constituents, however, the members imbibed opinions and zeal more befitting the times; and hence we have additional evidence, that, resistance to British oppression, was not produced by the efforts of a few leading and aspiring men, but was the spontaneous act of a high spirited people, well instructed in their rights, and resolutely determined to maintain them.

* 27th November, 1765. † Note A A. ‡ Joseph Sherwood, Esq.

secured by, grants and confirmations from the crown of Great Britain to the settlers of this colony: in duty, therefore, to ourselves, our constituents, and posterity, this House thinks it absolutely necessary, to leave the following resolves on our minutes: 1. That his Majesty's subjects inhabiting this province, are, from the strongest motives of duty, fidelity, and gratitude, inviolably attached to his royal person and government; and have ever shown, and we doubt not, ever will show, the utmost readiness and alacrity, for acceding to the constitutional requisitions of the crown, as they have been, from time to time, made to this colony: 2. That his Majesty's liege subjects in this colony, are entitled to all the inherent rights and liberties of his natural born subjects, within the kingdom of Great Britain: 3. That it is, inseparably, essential to the freedom of a people, and the undoubted right of Englishmen, that no taxes be imposed upon them, but with their own consent, given personally, or by their representatives: 4. That the people of this colony are not, and from their remote situation cannot, be represented in the Parliament of Great Britain; and if the principle of taxing the colonies without their consent, should be adopted, the people here would be subjected to the taxation of two Legislatures; a grievance unprecedented, and not to be thought of, without the greatest anxiety: 5. That the only representatives of the people of this colony, are persons chosen by themselves; and that no taxes ever have been, or can be, imposed on them, agreeably to the constitution of this province, granted and confirmed by his Majesty's most gracious predecessors, but by their own Legislature: 6. That all supplies being free gifts; for the people of Great Britain to grant, to his Majesty, the property of the people of this colony without their consent and being represented, would be unreasonable, and render useless legislation in this colony, in the most essential point: 7. That the profits of trade arising from this colony, centering in Great Britain, eventually contribute to the supplies granted there to the crown: 8. That the giving unlimited power to any subject or subjects, to impose what taxes they please in the colonies, under the mode of regulating the prices of stamped vellum, parchment, and paper, appears, to us, unconsitutional, contrary to the rights of the subject, and, apparently, dangerous in its consequences: 9. That any incumbrance which, in effect, restrains the liberty of the press in America, is an infringement of the subject's liberty: 10. That the extension of the powers of the court of admiralty, within this province, beyond its ancient limits, is a violent innovation of the right of trial by jury—a right which this House, upon the principles of their British ancestors, hold most dear and invaluable: 11. That, as the tranquillity of this country hath been interrupted through fear of the dreadful consequences of the stamp act; that, therefore, the officers of the government, who go on in their offices, for the good and peace of the province, in the accustomed manner, while things are in their present unsettled situation, will, in the opinion of this House, be entitled to the countenance of the Legislature; and it is recommended to our constituents, to use what endeavours lie in their power, to preserve the peace, quiet, harmony, and good order of the government; that no heats, disorders, and animosities may, in the least, obstruct the united endeavours, that are now strongly engaged for the repealing the act abovementioned, and other acts affecting the trade of the colonies."

XXVII. Whilst these efforts were being made on this side of the Atlantic to obtain redress for American grievances, the colonial agents, the friends of freedom and equal rights, and the merchants interested in the American trade, were not idle in Great Britain. The refusal to import her manufactures touched her in a vital part. The great diminution of orders for goods, so honourable to the self-control of the colonists, compelled a powerful class of traders to advocate liberal principles, who, under other circumstances, would have gladly sustained any policy which might have lessened their burden of taxation. Powerful as this combination certainly was, it had to contend against the most imperious passions, the pride and avarice of the people. The lofty position assumed by the Americans was intolerable. They had long been viewed as men of an inferior race. The arrogant philosophy of Europe had placed them and the animal productions of their country, low in the scale of perfectibility. By the mass of the English vulgar, they were ranked with savages and negroes. The colonies, the dependencies of Great Britain, on which she had, for years, poured forth the scourings of her prisons, had denied her supremacy, and refused to submit to her Parliament, hitherto deemed throughout her vast empire, politically omnipotent. With the sin of a rebellious temper, they were also charged with ingratitude. Under the pressure of accumulated debt and heavy taxation, the English people envied the display of wealth by the provincialists in the late war, and forgot that its exhibition was made in the common cause, with a generosity which had enforced from English justice, the return of more than a million sterling. Thus supported, the ministry which sought relief for the people, by taxing American industry, would scarcely have been driven from their purpose. But other causes transferred the government to other statesmen, whom consistency required, at least, to reverse measures which they had denounced with unqualified reprobation.

XXVIII. Under the new ministers an inquiry was instituted into the effects of the colonial policy of their predecessors. The merchants and manufacturers gave ample testimony of the paralysis in trade, whilst Dr. Franklin, as the representative of America, before a committee of the whole House of Commons, demonstrated the impossibility of levying the new impositions, and the consequent necessity of their repeal. The majority of Parliament was, now, divided into two parties. The larger one affirmed the right to tax the colonies, but denied the expediency of its present exercise; the other, led by Mr. Pitt, repudiated this right, on the ground that all aids are gifts from the people, and can never be legally obtained without their assent; and that this assent could not be had in Parliament, since the colonists were not there represented. A repeal on these principles, however just, according to the English constitution, would not have saved the pride of the nation, and would have destroyed the hopes of future revenue at the will of Parliament. Hence, the repeal of the stamp act, which took place on the eighteenth of March by a vote of two hundred and seventy-five, to one hundred and sixty-seven, was accompanied by a declaration of the right of Parliament to tax America. It was followed by an act indemnifying those who had incurred penalties on account of stamp duties. The tidings of this event were received in America with joy more temperate than might have been expected from the excitement of the public mind. The prudence displayed on this occasion had been earnestly recommended by a committee of merchants in London trading with America, and by others friendly to American interests.

At the meeting of the Assembly of New Jersey in June, 1766, Governor Franklin congratulated the House on the repeal of the odious stamp act; to which, however, he had been little accessory; and whilst he lauded, with the warmth becoming a dependent of the crown, "the tenderness, lenity, and condescension, the wisdom, justice, and equity, which his Majesty and the Parliament had manifested on this signal occasion," he carefully refrained from reminding the members of the obstacles he had endeavoured to raise, to their action on the case, and the severity with which he reprehended them for sending delegates to the New York convention, and their approval of its proceedings. The Assembly did not fail to use so favourable an opportunity for retaliation, rendered more poignant, that the moderation of the province had received the commendation of the ministry; but the House would have enjoyed its triumph with forbearance, had not the governor, by an angry message, drawn forth a severe retort.

CHAPTER X.

Comprising Events from 1766 to 1769.—I. Remaining discontents in the Colonies, after the repeal of the Stamp Act.—II. Dissatisfaction in Great Britain on account of the repeal—American taxation again proposed in Parliament, by Mr. Townsend—Bill imposing Duties on Goods imported into America, passed.—IV. Circular Letter of Massachusetts to the other Colonies.—V. Promptitude and Unanimity of the Colonies produced by the Farmer's Letters.—VI. Resort to Non-importation Agreements.—VII. The Ministry condemn the Circular Letter. VIII. Menacing Resolutions of Parliament against Massachusetts—The other Colonies approve her conduct.—IX. Modified repeal of the Imposts—Consequent modification of the Non-importation Agreements.—X. Numerous Law Suits—The People complain of the Fees of the Courts.—XI. Disputes between the Governor and the Assembly.—XII. Robbery of the Treasury of East Jersey—The Assembly require the removal of the Treasurer—He is protected by the Governor.—XIII. Efforts of Governor Franklin to encourage the culture of Hemp, Flax, and Silk.—XIV. New apportionment of Members in the Province.—XV. Testimonial of the Northern Indians to the Justice of the Colony.

I. Although the joy produced by the repeal of the stamp act, was common to all the colonies, the same temper did not prevail in all. In the commercial cities, the restrictions on trade excited scarce less disgust than had been created by the stamp act itself; and in the north, political parties had been formed, which betrayed excessive bitterness in opposition to each other. The first measures of Massachusetts and New York demonstrated that the reconciliation with the colonies was not cordial.

With the circular of Mr. Secretary Conway, announcing the repeal of the stamp act, came a resolution of Parliament, declaring, that those persons who had suffered injury by assisting to execute that act, ought to be compensated by the colonies, respectively, in which such injury was done. This, specially, affected Massachusetts, where compliance with the resolution was tardy, reluctant, and ungracious. An act of pardon to the offenders, and of indemnity to the sufferers, was, however, passed; but it was rejected by the King; because the colonial Assembly had no power under their charter, to pass an act of general pardon, but at the instance of the crown.

In New York, where General Gage was expected with a considerable body of troops, the governor required from the Legislature, compliance with the act of Parliament, called the "*Mutiny Act*," which directed, the colony, in which any of his Majesty's forces might be stationed, to provide barracks for them, and certain necessaries in their quarters. The Legislature, reluctantly and partially, complied with the requisition; but at a subsequent session, when the matter was again brought before them, they determined, that the act of Parliament could only be construed to require necessaries for troops on a march, and not while permanently stationed in the country; on a contrary construction, they said, the colony might be grievously burdened, by marching into it several regiments. This reason admits the obligation to obey the act. Yet, its requisitions were, unquestionably, a tax; and between the power of Parliament to levy money by its own authority, and, compulsorily, through the colonial Legislatures, no essential distinction can be drawn. A like requisition was made on the Legislature of New Jersey, in April, 1768, by Governor Franklin, which was fulfilled with cheerful alacrity. Such were the inaccurate ideas, which even then prevailed, in parts of the continent, relative to the control which Parliament might justly exercise over the colonies. The contumacy of New York was punished and removed by prohibiting the Legislature from passing any act, until the requisition of the Parliament had been, in every respect, complied with.*

Some troops having been driven, by stress of weather, into the harbour of Boston, their commander applied to Governor Bernard, for the necessary and usual supplies, which were granted by consent of the council, "*in pursuance of the act of Parliament.*" But the general court which met soon afterwards, (1767) disapproved, in pointed terms, the conduct of the governor, declaring, that, "after the repeal of the stamp act, they were surprised to find, that this act, equally odious and unconstitutional, should remain in force. They lamented the entry of the reason for the advice of council, the more, as it was an unwarrantable and unconstitutional step, which totally disabled them from testifying the same cheerfulness they had always shown, in granting to his Majesty, of their free accord, such aids as his service had, from time to time, required."

II. The repeal of the stamp act, however grateful to the friends of liberty, to the colonists, and to the English merchants trading with them, was not popular with the nation at large. The supremacy of the Parliament was maintained by the mass of the people; the hope of revenue from America was too fascinating to be surrendered without further exertion; and the King beheld, with high indignation, the resistance to his authority, and the political principles which his American subjects had displayed. Moved by these considerations, Mr. Charles Townsend, chancellor of the exchequer, in an administration formed by Lord Chatham, a man of splendid and versatile talents, invited the attention of Parliament, again, to the subject of American taxation. He boasted, "that he knew how to draw a revenue from the colonies, without giving them offence, and animated by the challenge of Mr. Grenville, to make his vaunting true, he proposed and carried almost unanimously, a bill imposing certain duties on tea, glass, paper, and painters' colours, imported into the colonies from Great Britain; the proceeds of which were appropriated to the support of government in America, so far as should be necessary, and the balance to be paid into the British treasury.

This measure was founded in the erroneous belief, that the colonists objected rather to the mode than to the right of taxation. But though there had been some inaccuracies in expressing their views on the statutes regulating trade, there should have been no misapprehension of their determination to resist every attempt to tax them without their consent. The bill of Mr. Townsend had the unequivocal character of a revenue law, and as such was avowedly enacted; nor were the provincialists slow to declare their sense of its true character.

III. Petition and remonstrance were again resorted to by the colonial Legislatures. The tone, generally taken, was not so high, as in case of the stamp act; but the conviction that the one was as great a violation of public liberty as the other, soon became universal.

The colony of Massachusetts, in addition to her other measures, addressed a circular letter (11th February, 1768,) to the Assemblies of the respective colonies, stating her own proceedings to obtain redress. This was laid before the House of Representatives of New Jersey by the speaker, Courtland Skinner, Esq., on the 16th of April, and was referred to Messrs. Borden, J. Lawrence, and R. Lawrence, with instructions to draught an answer thereto. The answer, signed by the speaker, remarks, "sensible that the law you complain of is a subject in which every colony is interested, the

* Marshall.

House of Representatives readily perceived the necessity of an immediate application to the King, and that it should correspond with those of the other colonies; but as they have not had an opportunity of knowing the sentiments of any other colony, but that of the Massachusetts Bay, they have endeavoured to conform themselves to the mode adopted by you. They have therefore given instruction to their agent, and enjoined his attention on the subject of their petition." And it concluded, "the House have directed me to assure you, that they are desirous to keep up a correspondence with you, and to unite with the colonies if necessary, in further supplications to his Majesty, to relieve his distressed American subjects. Pursuant to these sentiments, the House, May 7th, 1768, adopted a petition to his Majesty, in which, after recounting the perils and labours of the primitive settlers, they declared, that "the subjects thus emigrating brought with them, as inherent in their persons, all the rights and liberties of natural born subjects within the parent state. In consequence of these, a government was formed under which they have been constantly exercised and enjoyed by the inhabitants, and repeatedly and solemnly recognised and confirmed by your royal predecessors, and the Legislature of Great Britain."

"One of these rights and privileges vested in the people of this colony, is the privilege of being exempt from any taxations, but such as are imposed on them by themselves, or by their representatives; and this they esteem so invaluable, that they are fully persuaded, no other can exist without it."

Then, after recalling to the remembrance of their sovereign, their past promptitude in furnishing all necessary supplies required from them, and their disposition for the future, to evince "their unfeigned affection for his Majesty's person, their distinguished duty to his government, and their inflexible resolution to maintain his authority and defend his dominions," they proceed;

"Penetrated with these sentiments, this, your people, with the utmost concern and anxiety observe, that duties have lately been imposed upon them by Parliament, for the sole and express purposes of raising a revenue. This is a taxation upon them from which they concieve they ought to be protected, by the acknowledged principles of the constitution: that freemen cannot be legally taxed but by themselves or by their representatives; and that they are represented in Parliament they not only cannot allow, but are convinced from their local circumstances they never can be."

"Very far is it from our intention, to deny our subordination to that august body, or our dependence on the kingdom of Great Britain; in these connections, and in the settlement of our liberties under the auspicious influence of your royal House, we know our happiness consists, and therefore, to confirm those connexions and to strengthen this settlement, is at once our interest, duty, and delight. Nor do we apprehend, that it lies within our power by any means more effectually, to promote these great purposes, than by zealously striving to preserve in perfect vigour, those sacred rights and liberties, under the inspiriting sanction of which, inconceivable difficulties and dangers opposing, this colony has been rescued from the rudest state of nature, converted into a populous, flourishing, and valuable territory; and has contributed in a very considerable degree, to the welfare of Great Britain."

"Most gracious sovereign, the incessant exertions of your truly royal cares, to procure your people a prosperity equal to your love of them, encourage us, with all humility, to pray, that, your Majesty's clemency will be graciously pleased to take into consideration our unhappy circumstances, and to afford us such relief, as your Majesty's wisdom shall judge to be most proper."

IV. The Legislature of Massachusetts, which convened early in January, 1768, addressed remonstrances to the King, to Parliament, and to the ministers, and a circular letter to the several colonies. The latter contained an exposition of the subject of their remonstrances, a recapitulation of the arguments urged against the stamp act, and declared the taxes lately imposed, to be inequitable, because exacting a duty upon the importation into America, on British manufactures, in addition to that paid on exportation from England; and that, the proposed disbursements of the revenue, in the payment of the salaries of the governors and judges appointed by the crown, had a tendency to subvert the principles of equity, and to endanger the happiness and security of the subject.

V. The promptitude and unanimity of the colonies, generally, on this occasion, has been, with great justice, ascribed to the judicious and eloquent essays of Mr. John Dickerson, published as "Letters from a Farmer in Pennsylvania, to the Inhabitants of the British colonies." These papers, in which the rights of the colonists were ably maintained, were republished in every colony; and the people of Boston, and other towns, in town meeting, voted a letter of thanks to their "patriotic, enlightened, and noble spirited author."

VI. In their controversy upon the stamp act, the colonists found their most effectual weapon in their non-importation agreements. Recourse was again had to them. But as New Jersey had little direct commerce, of importation, she could not express her sense of injury, adequately, by this mode; but she was not precluded from giving to her commercial neighbours the stimulus of her approbation. Accordingly, in the October session of 1769, her Legislature resolved unanimously, "That the thanks of the House be given to the merchants and traders of this colony, and of the colonies of New York and Pennsylvania, for their disinterested and public spirited conduct, in withholding their importations of British merchandise, until certain acts of Parliament, laying restrictions on American commerce, for the express purpose of raising a revenue in America, be repealed."

Efforts being made in Rhode Island, to break through the non-importation agreement, the freeholders, merchants and traders, of the county of Essex, convened at Elizabethtown, on the 5th of June, 1770, and resolved, that such agreement was founded on the truest policy, and was a legal and constitutional method of discovering their sense of the acts of Parliament, for raising a revenue in the colonies; and therefore should be firmly adhered to, until such acts were repealed: That they would not themselves, or by others, receive, purchase, sell, or otherwise use, any of the manufactures or merchandise, imported from Great Britain, contrary to the agreement; and that, they would not trade, nor have any commercial intercourse, with such persons, who should import goods or cause them to be imported, or with any person, who shall purchase goods so imported; but would use every lawful means, to hinder the sale of such goods, in any way whatever: That they highly approved the spirited behaviour of their Boston, New York, and Philadelphia brethren, in renouncing all commerce and intercourse with the traders and inhabitants of Newport, in Rhode Island, who had perfidiously deserted them in this struggle; and that they would observe the same rules of conduct they had so properly adopted, with respect to the traders and inhabitants of Newport. And at a meeting held at the same place, on the 16th of July, when having learned, that "the merchants and traders of the city of New York, had lately thought proper, contrary to their own agreement, and in violation of their public faith, to break through the only measure that could have obtained redress, they declared that the signers to the late non-importation agreement, at New York, had perfidiously betrayed the common cause, deserted their countrymen, in their united struggles for the removal of ministerial oppression; and that every person who, contrary to the non-importation agreement, shall import, ought, by the friends of their country, to be treated, not only in like manner, as they themselves set the example, in the late case of the merchants and traders of Newport, but be held in the utmost contempt by all the friends of liberty, and treated as enemies to their country: And that they would strictly adhere to their resolutions, adopted at a former meeting. The conduct of the New York importers was condemned by the inhabitants of Woodbridge, and New Brunswick, and other places, in terms still more energetic. Some of these importers, venturing, soon after, to New Brunswick and Woodbridge, with their goods, were severely handled by the populace.

VII. "On the first intimation of the measures taken by Massachusetts, the Earl of Hillsborough, who, about the close of the year 1767, had been appointed to the then newly created office of Secretary of State, for the department of the colonies, addressed a circular letter to the several governors, to be laid before the Assemblies, in which he treated the circular of Massachusetts, as of the most dangerous and factious tendency, calculated to inflame the minds of his Majesty's good subjects in the colonies—to promote an unwarrantable combination, to excite and encourage an open opposition to, and denial of, the authority of Parliament; and to subvert the true principles of the constitution; and he endeavoured to prevail upon them to treat with resentment, "such an unjustifiable attempt to revive those distractions, which had operated so fatally to the prejudice of the colonies, and of the mother country; but in any event, not to take part with Massachusetts, by approving such proceedings." Instructions accompanied this letter, to dissolve such Assemblies as should refuse to comply with its recommendation. It does not appear, that the Assembly of New Jersey took any order upon the circular of Massachusetts. But other colonies declared, that they could not consider as an unwarrantable combination, a concert of measures to give efficacy to their representations, in support of principles essential to the British constitution.*

"This circular of Massachusetts, together with the violent proceedings which were subsequently had in that colony, were the cause of joint resolutions of both Houses of Parliament, condemning in the strongest terms, the measures pursued by the Americans. An address was agreed upon, approving the conduct of the crown, giving assurances of effectual support to such further measures as should be found necessary to maintain the civil magistrates in a due execution of the laws within the province of Massachusetts Bay; and beseeching his Majesty, to direct the governor of that colony, to obtain and transmit to him, information of all treasons committed therein, since the year 1767, with the names of the persons who had been most active in promoting such offences, that prosecutions might be instituted against them, *within the realm*, in pursuance of the statute of the 35th of Henry VIII."†

VIII. The impression made by these menaces, directed specially against Massachusetts Bay, in expectation that the other provinces would be, thereby, deterred from involving themselves in her dangers, was very unfavourable to the views of the mother country. The resolution to resist the exercise of the authority claimed by her, was not only unshaken, but manifested itself in a still more determined form. The Assembly of Virginia, soon after the receipt of these resolutions, asserted, unanimously, the exclusive right of that Assembly to impose taxes on their constituents, and their undoubted privilege to petition for redress of grievances, and to obtain the concurrence of the other colonies in such petitions. Alluding particularly to the joint ad-

* Marshall. † Ibid.

dress of the two Houses of Parliament to the King, they also resolved, that all persons charged with the commission of any offence, within that colony, were entitled to a trial before the tribunals of the country, according to the fixed and known course of proceedings therein; and that to seize such persons, and transport them beyond seas for trial, derogated, in a high degree, from the rights of British subjects; as, thereby, the inestimable privilege of being tried by a jury, from the vicinage, as well as the liberty of summoning and producing witnesses, in such trial, would be taken from the party accused. This last resolution was also adopted, in terms, by the Assembly of New Jersey.*

IX. Notwithstanding these strong measures on the part of Parliament, the mass of the English trading population, feeling, severely, the consequences of the non-importation agreement, strongly urged the abrogation of the new duties. And the ministry, affected by the commercial distress, were desirous to give relief, but were resolute to maintain the parliamentary right to tax the colonies.

With criminal weakness they adopted a middle course, remarkable for the ignorance it displays of the state of the public mind, and the nature of the public character, in America. The earnest remonstrances and prompt and energetic resistance of the colonies, had failed to convince them, that the assertion of the right, and not the amount of duty levied, was the true source of complaint. The ministers persisted in believing that a reduction of the tax would restore tranquillity. Under this delusion, assurances were given, in 1769, that five-sixths of the taxes imposed in 1767, should be repealed: and, in 1770, the whole were abolished.

Adhering strictly to their principles, the colonists modified their non-importation agreements, to operate on tea alone. This they were better enabled to do, as that article could be obtained from continental Europe, by smuggling, in sufficient quantities, and at less price, than if regularly imported from Great Britain. The anticipation of revenue, by continuance of the impost act, was, therefore, vain; and its preservation on the statute book, served but to keep the jealousies and fears of the provinces in constant activity, and to familiarize the people with opposition to a power, which like the sword of Damocles, threatened, momentarily, their destruction.

In some of the colonies the non-importation agreements were partially violated; but, in the greater part, they were religiously observed. By the revenue act, in its modified form, their rights were exposed to violation, yet their preservation depended on themselves; since, whilst no dutiable commodity was purchased, no duty was paid; and whilst this commodity was, otherwise, cheaply procured, no privation was sustained. Hence, a state of political quiet ensued the repealing act of 1770. The ministry seemed disposed to avoid further aggression, and the Americans, generally, ceased to remonstrate and complain; although they continued to watch, with lynx-eyed vigilance, every movement of the British government, and to discuss, publicly and privately, the value of the union between the colonies and the parent state.

X. The period of four years, which succeeded the modification of the revenue act, contains few incidents of historical interest. The late war, by the great expenditure of money, and consumption of agricultural products, had caused an extraordinary appearance of prosperity in New Jersey, as in other colonies. A ready market and advanced price for grain, increased the value of lands, and seduced the enterprising into improvident purchases. The causes of this excited state ceasing with the peace, great depression

* December 6th, 1769.

of prices, and contraction of business, ensued. Debtors were unable to pay; bankruptcies and suits at law were numerous, and the prosecuting creditor and his attorney became odious to the debtor and his sympathizing friends. In popular distress, as amid arms, the laws are silent. In January, 1770, many citizens of Monmouth county, assembled at Freehold, on the stated day for holding the county court, and violently deterred the judges from executing their office; compelling them to return to their respective homes; and a similar riot, in Essex, was suppressed, only, by the spirited conduct of the sheriffs, magistrates, and the better disposed inhabitants. The cause alleged for these unwarrantable proceedings, was oppression by the lawyers, in their exorbitant charges for costs. The governor, by the advice of his council, issued a special commission for the trial of the offenders, adding to the justices of the Supreme Court, some gentlemen of distinguished character. In Essex, the rioters were immediately tried, convicted, and punished; but, in Monmouth, they were screened from chastisement, by the sympathy of their fellow-citizens. The Assembly was specially convened as well to receive and continue legal process, which had abated by the lapse of a term, as to provide additional means for the preservation of the public peace. And whilst effecting these objects, they inquired strictly into the allegations against the lawyers, acquitting them of extortion, but providing by law against excessive costs, in the recovery of debts under fifty pounds. In suppressing these seditions Mr. Richard Stockton was highly instrumental, supporting with dignity the authority of government, and mildly assuaging the temper of the people.

XI. In the intercourse between Governor Franklin and the Assembly, considerable harmony prevailed. But, occasionally, differences of opinion led to intemperate altercation. Thus, a war of words grew out of the application of the officers of the King's troops, for supplies and accommodations greater than the House was disposed to grant. For, although the statesmen of New Jersey did not take the high ground of Massachusetts, upon this subject, they were reluctant to expend any thing more than the strictest construction of the act of Parliament required. A lengthened discussion was finally terminated by mutual concession. But another dispute soon after arose, on the application of the Assembly, for the removal of the treasurer of the eastern division of the province. With singular policy, a treasurer was retained and located in each of the ancient divisions of the colony; and by policy not less singular, they were appointed by the governor, gave no security for the faithful performance of their duties, but were responsible to, and always accounted with, the Assembly.

XII. Mr. Stephen Skinner was treasurer of East Jersey, and resident at Perth Amboy. On the night of the 21st of July, 1768, his house was broken open, and the iron chest in which he kept the provincial funds, was robbed of sixty-six hundred pounds, chiefly in bills of credit. The character of the treasurer was fair, and his statement of circumstances was received without inquiry, during two years; when no clue being discovered to the robbery, the Assembly, October, 1770, directed an investigation, and came to the conclusion, that the loss was occasioned by the want of that care, which was necessary to the safe keeping of the money; and that the treasurer ought not to be allowed therefor in his accounts. But no further steps were taken in this matter, until September, 1772; when, the treasurer remonstrating against this vote, the then House approved the sentiment of its predecessor, and invited the governor to join them in some method to compel the treasurer to account for the sum, *said to be stolen.*

The committee, addressing his excellency, complained, "that though the treasurer did not apprehend himself accountable for that sum to the public, as in the treasury, he was still continued in office, the public money still depended on his care, and nothing had been done to recover the deficiency." Notwithstanding this broad intimation, the governor insisted, that if the House desired the removal of the treasurer, they should tell him so, in plain terms. He reproached them for their insinuation of neglected duty, and retorted the charge, averring, that for several years, they had taken no order on the matter. The Assembly, thus urged, now left the governor no cause to doubt their wishes, and closed a long argumentative reply, with "humbly requesting his excellency, that he would be pleased to remove the treasurer from his office, appoint some other person therein, and unite with them in passing a law, authorizing the treasurer, so appointed, to commence suit for the deficiency against his predecessor. The governor did not object to a suit for determining the liability of the officer; and a committee of the council, in conference with one from the Assembly, proposed to file an information against the treasurer; but the House rejected the mode, alleging, that a criminal prosecution would not attain their object. On the other hand, the governor refused to commit the injustice of removing a public officer, who, though unfortunate, had not been convicted of malfeasance; and whose conduct and character the Assembly, after examination, had declared unimpeached. He pleaded, also, a royal instruction, forbidding him to displace any officer or minister, in the province, without sufficient cause, to be signified to the king; an instruction, he said, wisely calculated to guard against that arbitrary, despotic temper, which sometimes actuated governors, as well as that levelling, democratic disposition, which too often prevails in popular assemblies.*

This was a subject of angry discussion, between the governor and Assembly, for nearly two years longer; in which the former was encouraged, by the discovery of a gang of counterfeiters and forgers, one of whom, it was probable, from the evidence of his accomplices, had perpetrated the robbery of the treasury. At length, the treasurer, who had repeatedly, but in vain, prayed the Assembly to cause a suit to be instituted against him, resigned his commission; and an act was passed by the Legislature, directing

* May we not here properly remark, that a clause in our republican constitutions, prohibiting the removal of public officers, *without good and sufficient cause*, would protect useful public servants against the arbitrary and despotic temper, which sometimes actuates governors and presidents, as well as that capricious disposition, and proscriptive spirit of party, which too often prevails in popular assemblies? Officers of state are created for the service of the people, as the state itself is constituted for their benefit. The individual emolument which arises from the maintenance of the officer, is an accident, not the object, of the creation. Yet, a fatal misconstruction of the maxim, that offices are created for the people, has been so widely spread throughout our republics, as to threaten their safety and duration. Leaders of parties, in high stations, proclaim "*rotation in office*," to be republican; that all citizens are entitled to participate in official emoluments, and are competent to the performance of official duties. Such doctrines have a demoralizing effect, tending to discourage industry, and to create numerous anxious, idle, venal, expectants of office. Their absurdity becomes apparent, by following them out to their proper results. Even, if we limit the position, by saying, that all men duly qualified, are entitled to participate in official emoluments, it will be obvious that an attempt to reduce it to practice, however impossible, would produce a change every hour, in every office of the country. The true principle is, that public officers are agents of the people, to be appointed, directly or indirectly, by the people, as they shall in their wisdom determine; and should be changed, only, when the public interests require. Like other agents they should receive a moderate, but just, compensation for their services, with the assurance of its continuance, whilst those services are, faithfully, rendered. Towards their public servants, the whole people, the state, should pursue the course which each individual possessing common sense, adopts in his own affairs. No prudent man discharges a competent, experienced, and faithful servant, to receive others in quick succession, who enter his service with a view solely to the wages, and whose capacity for service is to be acquired at his expense.

his successor to sue for the balance. One good effect resulting from this contest, was the requisition on future treasurers, to give adequate security to the province for the faithful disbursement of public moneys.*

XIII. Governor Franklin seems to have been truly solicitous to promote the welfare of the colony, by increasing its agricultural and commercial products. At his instances, which in the present season of political quiet, he earnestly renewed, the Assembly established bounties for the growth of hemp, flax and silk; considerable efforts were made to diffuse the culture of the mulberry tree, and had not this simple branch of industry been prostrated by the war, silk would soon have become a staple commodity of the country. At the suggestion of the governor, also, means were taken by the Assembly, to obtain a full census, and statistical account of the province; but these were rendered ineffective by the scenes of political disquiet which soon after arose.

XIV. Previous to the year 1772, the House of Representatives consisted of twenty members. The cities of Perth Amboy and Burlington, and the counties of Middlesex, Essex, Somerset, Bergen, Gloucester, and Cape May, each sending two representatives, whilst Salem and Cumberland jointly, sent only two, and Hunterdon, Morris, and Sussex jointly, the same number. But in that year, an act of Assembly for increasing the number of representatives, had been approved by the King, and seems to have been a cause of gratulation between the governor and Assembly. By this act, each county was entitled to two representatives, and the whole number was increased to thirty. The representation which appears to have been based upon territorial divisions, merely, without regard to the essential principle of population, was, thus, continued upon an erroneous basis, and has not been fully corrected, even at the present day.

XV. Governor Franklin, on the part of the province, contrary to the policy which it had hitherto pursued, attended two conferences with the northern Indians. The first was in 1769, at Fort Stanwix, at which he was accompanied by the chief justice; and where the *Six Nations* having agreed upon a general boundary line, between them and the northern colonies, (the object of the meeting) publicly acknowledged the repeated instances of the justice of the province, in bringing murderers to condign punishment; and declared that they had no claim, whatever, upon the province, and in the most solemn manner conferred upon the government of New Jersey, the distinguishing name of *Sagorighwiyogstha*, or the great arbiter, or doer of Justice.

* See note B B.

CHAPTER XI.

Comprising Events from the year 1773, to 1776.—I. Committees of Correspondence established in the several Colonies.—II. The British Ministry encourage the shipment of Teas to America, by the East India Company.—III. Alarm of the Colonists—Consignees of the India Company compelled to forego their appointments.—IV. Measures pursued in New Jersey.—V. Reception of the Tea in America.—VI. Indignation of the King and Parliament.—VII. Violent measures adopted against Boston.—VIII. Alarming Act of Parliament, relative to the Provincial Government of Canada.—IX. Proceedings of the Inhabitants of Boston—General commiseration of their fate.—X. New Jersey appoints Members to Congress.—XI. Congress assemble at Philadelphia—Their proceedings.—XII. The Assembly of New Jersey approve the Proceedings of Congress, and appoint Delegates to the next Convention—Instructions.—XIII. The Provincial Governors instructed to impede the Union of the Colonies—Efforts of Governor Franklin.—XIV. Reply of the House.—XV. Rejoinder of the Governor—Address of the Council.—XVI. The Assembly petition the King.—XVII. Reception of the Proceedings of Congress in London.—XVIII. Proceedings of Parliament—Conciliatory Propositions of Lord North.—XIX. Sense of New Jersey upon this proposition.—XX. State of the Dispute with England.—XXI. Second New Jersey Convention called—Encourages Political Associations—Organizes the Militia, and provides funds.—XXII. Meeting of Congress at Philadelphia—Its Measures.—XXIII. Appointment of Commander-in-Chief and subordinate Generals.—XXIV. Congress again petition the King—Ungracious reception of the petition.—XXV. Address their fellow-subjects of Ireland, &c.—XXVI. New Jersey Convention re-assembles—Proceedings—Provision for the continuance of a Provincial Congress—Committee of Safety appointed.—XXVII. Meeting of the Assembly—Address of Governor Franklin—He claims assurance of protection for himself and others, the King's officers.—XXVIII. Reply of the Assembly.—XXIX. Act authorizing the issue of Bills of Credit, for £100,000, approved by the King.

I. It is not our purpose to detail all the remote causes and immediate motives that led to the revolution, which dissolved the connexion between Great Britain and her North American colonies; but to keep up such a connected narrative of circumstances pertaining to that great event, as will enable us to exhibit the part which New Jersey bore in the contest. We do not, therefore, enter upon the various causes of dissatisfaction in Massachusetts, and the measures resulting therefrom, which preserved there a spirit of opposition to the crown, whilst a general calm was elsewhere pervading the continent. It may be proper, however, to note, that, from the commencement of the contest, Massachusetts was particularly solicitous of uniting all the colonies in one system of measures. In pursuance of this object, she devised the plan of electing committees in the several towns for the purpose of corresponding with each other, and with the other colonies, which was adopted by the other provinces. The honour of originating the Legislative committees of correspondence in the several colonies, which afterwards became so essentially useful, is claimed, by Mr. Jefferson, for Virginia.

II. The general state of quiet which had been induced by the prudence of the European and American parties, the one forbearing to ship, and the other to order teas, was, after three years' continuance, terminated by the impolitic avarice of the British ministry. The East India company, the most daring, ambitious, and successful of commercial associations, had became embarrassed by lavish expenditure, the peculations of their servants, and the diminution of their trade in consequence of the American quarrel. Applying to the government for assistance, they proposed, that the duty of three pence per pound, payable on teas imported into the colonies, should be abolished, and that six cents per pound should be imposed on the exportation. This favourable and honourable mode of removing the occasion for dispute between the parent and her offspring was, we cannot, now, say, unfortunately, rejected by the administration; who, as if by extraordinary stimulus to accelerate the coming contest, proposed and carried a bill authorizing the company to export their teas altogether free of duty. Lord North, says the English historian, recommended this measure to Parliament with a twofold view; to relieve the India Company and to improve the revenue. The latter was to be accomplished by tempting the Americans to purchase large quantities of teas at a low price. But the Company would not venture to ship, until assured by the ministry, that in no event they should suffer loss.

III. The export of tea to America, under these circumstances, was, in itself, sufficient to arouse opposition. But the occasion was eagerly seized by those whose interests would be promoted by popular resistance. Merchants in England, whose profits were endangered by this operation of the India Company, and cis-atlantic smugglers, whose trade was threatened with extinction, laboured with the patriot, to convince the people of the immutable determination of the parent state to tax the colonies; and for that purpose, to compel the sale of the tea, in despite of the solemn resolutions, and oft declared sense of the inhabitants. The cry of endangered liberty was again heard from New Hampshire to Georgia. Town meetings were held in the capitals of the different provinces, and combinations formed to obstruct the sale of the fatal weed. The consignees of the Company were, generally, compelled to relinquish their appointments, and substitutes could not be procured.

IV. The most determined spirit of resistance displayed itself, in New Jersey, upon the first favourable opportunity. On the eighth of February, 1774, the Assembly, on the proposition of Virginia, appointed from its members, a standing committee of correspondence,* whom they instructed to obtain the most early and authentic intelligence of all the acts and resolutions of the Parliament of Great Britain, or the proceedings of the administration, which might affect the liberties and privileges of his Majesty's subjects, in the British colonies of America; to maintain a correspondence with the sister colonies, respecting these important considerations, and to inform the speakers of the several continental Assemblies of this resolution, requesting, that, they would submit them to their several Houses. They gave thanks, also, to the burgesses of Virginia, for their early attention to the liberties of America.

V. On the approach of the tea ships destined for Philadelphia, the pilots in the Delaware were warned not to conduct them into harbour; and their captains, apprized of the temper of the people, deeming it unsafe to land their cargoes, consented to return without making an entry at the custom house; the owners of goods, on board, cheerfully submitting to the inconvenience of having their merchandise sent back to Great Britain. The captains of vessels addressed to New York, wisely, adopted the same resolution. The tea sent to Charleston was landed and stored, but not offered for sale; and being placed in damp cellars, became rotten, and was entirely lost. The ships designated for Boston entered that port, but before the tea could be landed, a number of colonists, disguised as Indians, pursuant to a concerted plan, entered the vessels, and without doing other damage, broke open three hundred and forty-two chests, and emptied their contents into the sea. Such

* Consisting of James Kinsey, Stephen Crane, Hendrick Fisher, Samuel Tucker, John Wetherill, Robert Friend Price, John Hinchman, John Mehelm, and Edward Taylor.

was the union of sentiment among the people, and so systematic their opposition, that not a single chest of the cargoes, sent out by the East India Company, was sold for their benefit.

VI. The conduct of the colonists, generally, in relation to the tea ships, and, especially, the daring trespass at Boston, gave great umbrage to the King. In his message* to Parliament, he characterized the colonial proceedings as obstructing the commerce of Great Britain, and subversive of her constitution. High and general indignation was excited in that body. His Majesty's measures were almost unanimously approved, and pledges were given to secure the due execution of the laws, and the dependence of the colonies. To maintain that dependence, the whole nation seemed disposed to approve and support the severest measures of the ministry. All consideration for the just rights of the colonists, was lost in the desire to punish their audacity; and, for the moment, the patriot forgot his principles, and the merchant his interest, whilst fired with indignation at the bold resistance to the will of the parent state.

VII. Upon Massachusetts the vials of wrath were first poured out. Before the magnitude of her guilt the offences of other colonies became insignificant. By one act of Parliament the port of Boston was closed, and the custom house and its dependencies transferred to the town of Salem, until compensation should be made to the East India Company, and until the King in council, should be satisfied of the restoration of peace and good order in the town of Boston: By another act, the charter of Massachusetts was subverted; the nomination of counsellors, magistrates, and other officers, being vested in the crown, during the royal pleasure: By a third, persons indicted in that province, for any capital offence, if an allegation were made on oath to the governor, that such offence had been committed, in aid of the magistracy in the suppression of riots, and that a fair trial could not be had in the province, might be sent to any other colony, or to Great Britain, for trial. A bill was also passed for quartering soldiers upon the inhabitants. But these penal bills were not wholly unopposed, in either house of Parliament; in the Lords, the minority entered their protest against each.

VIII. An act passed simultaneously with the foregoing, making more effectual provision for the government of the province of Quebec, excited as much indignation and more dread among the colonies, than the severe measures against Massachusetts. The latter might be palliated as the result of indignation, violent, but not causeless; while the former, vesting the legislative power in a council dependent on the crown, and subjecting the whole revenue to the King's disposal, bore strong indications of the resolution of the ministry to take from the colonies, generally, the right of self-government. Had sympathy failed to unite the other provinces to the fate of Massachusetts, regard to their common safety, so openly threatened, would have rendered their union indissoluble. Both were intensely felt.

IX. The inhabitants of Boston had foreseen the present crisis, and they met it with undaunted spirit. Information of the passage of the port act was received on the tenth of May, and on the thirteenth, the town resolved, "that if the other colonies would unite with them to stop all importations from Great Britain and the West Indies, until that act should be repealed, it would prove the salvation of North America and her liberties; but should they continue their exports and imports, there was reason to fear that fraud, power, and the most odious oppression, would triumph over justice, right, social happiness, and freedom." A copy of this resolution was transmitted to the other colonies, the inhabitants of which expressed deep sympathy in the sufferings

* 7th March, 1774.

of their brethren in Boston, endured in the common cause; and concurring in opinion with them on the propriety of convening a provincial Congress, delegates for that purpose were generally chosen.

Throughout the continent, the first of June, the day on which the Boston port act was to take effect, on the resolution of the Assembly of Virginia, was adopted as a day of fasting, humiliation, and prayer, to implore the divine interposition to avert the heavy calamity which threatened destruction to their civil rights, and the evils of civil war, and to give one heart and one mind to the people, firmly to oppose every invasion of their liberties.

X. Early in the month of July, the inhabitants of the several counties of New Jersey, assembled at their respective county towns, and adopted resolutions strongly disapprobatory of the course of the ministry and of the late acts of Parliament, closing the port of Boston, invading the charter rights of the province of Massachusetts, subjecting supposed offenders to trial in other colonies and in Great Britain, and sending an armed force to carry these injurious measures into effect. They nominated deputies, to meet in convention, for the purpose of electing delegates to the general Congress, about to convene at Philadelphia. The Convention, consisting of seventy-two members, selected from the most intelligent and respectable citizens of the colony, among whom were many members of Assembly, met at New Brunswick on the twenty-first of July, 1774; and choosing Stephen Crane, chairman, and Jonathan D. Sergeant, clerk, proceeded to reiterate the sentiments of their constituents, and to nominate James Kinsey,* William Livingston, John De Hart, Stephen Crane, and Richard Smith to represent them in Congress, and the following gentlemen as a standing committee of correspondence:† William Peartree Smith, John Chetwood, Isaac Ogden, Joseph Borden, Robert

* Kinsey left Congress in November, 1775, refusing to take the republican oath of allegiance.—*Journal of Congress*, 2d *December*, 1775. He was highly esteemed notwithstanding the course he took at this time. "He is a very good man," says Governor Livingston, in a letter to Samuel Allinson, of the 25th of July, 1778, "though not the best hand on deck in a storm." To Kinsey himself the governor wrote, 6th of October, of the same year: "As I find myself engaged in writing to my old friend, I cannot help embracing this opportunity to express my concern at your standing so much in your own light, as to forego your practice rather than submit to a test, which all governments ever have, and ever will, impose upon those who live within the bounds of their authority * * * *. Your voluntary consent to take the test prescribed by law, would soon restore you to the good opinion of your country, (every body allowing you, notwithstanding unaccountable political obliquities, to be an honest man) and your way to the magistracy would, doubtless, be easy and unincumbered." Some years afterwards Mr. Kinsey became chief justice. He died about 1801.—*Sedgwick's Life of Livingston*, p. 169.

We find the following minute in the votes of the Assembly, November 17, 1775. "Mr. Kinsey and Mr. De Hart, two of the delegates appointed by this House, to attend the continental Congress, applied to the House for leave to resign their said appointments, alleging that they are so particularly circumstanced, as to render their attendance, exceedingly, inconvenient to their private affairs." On the 22d November, their resignations were accepted, and the three remaining delegates, or any two of them, were empowered to represent the colony in Congress.

† Mr. De Hart appears to have soon grown weary in the race. On the organization of the state government he was elected a judge of the Supreme Court, but refused the office. Mr. Smith held out much longer, but his course was equivocal. He was a representative from Burlington, in the first legislative council, but did not attend its session. Upon a requisition to perform his duties, by the council, he tendered his resignation, which was rejected, on the ground that the constitution did not warrant its acceptance. Persevering in his refusal, the council, on the seventeenth of May, 1777, resolved, "that he had neglected and refused to perform the duties of his station, as a member of that House, in divers instances, and, particularly, by contumaciously withholding his attendance at that sitting, though duly and repeatedly summoned; and that he be expelled." He was re-elected to council in the succeeding October, but it does not appear that he served. He was elected state-treasurer, in joint meeting, September 5th, 1776, and performed the duties of that station for about six months.

Field, Isaac Pierson, Isaac Smith, Samuel Tucker, Abraham Hunt, and Hendrick Fisher.

XI. The delegates from eleven provinces assembled at Philadelphia, on the fourth of September; those from North Carolina did not appear until the fourteenth.* On the fifth, Peyton Randolph, of Virginia, was unanimously chosen president, and Charles Thompson elected secretary. As the Congress was composed of men who gave tone to the sentiments of the provinces which they respectively represented, it was in course, that the prominent acts of the colonies should be supported and enforced with the ability and dignity pertaining to their joint endeavours. Still there was a chivalrous disregard of self, in the prompt and energetic approbation of the highest measures of Massachusetts, which history rarely discloses among a temperate and calculating people, even amid the excitements of political revolution; and which leads us to believe, that even at this time, independence of Great Britain was a foregone conclusion, in the bosoms of most members of the Congress, which yet, they scarce dared acknowledge to themselves, still less breathe to others.

Whilst expressing "their sympathy in the sufferings of their countrymen of Massachusetts, under the late unjust, cruel, and oppressive acts of the British Parliament," Congress approved of the resolve of the county of Suffolk, in which Boston lies, "that no obedience was due from that province to such acts, but that they should be rejected as the attempts of a wicked administration." They resolved, that contributions from all the colonies, for supplying the necessities, and alleviating the distresses of their brethren at Boston, ought to be continued in such manner, and so long, as their occasions might require. They requested the merchants of the several colonies to refuse new orders for goods from Great Britain, and to suspend the execution of such as had been sent, until the sense of Congress, on the means to be adopted for the preservation of the liberties of America, should be made public. And soon after, they adopted resolutions prohibiting the importation, the purchase, or use, of goods from Great Britain, or Ireland, or their dependencies, after the first day of the succeeding December; and directing that all exports to Great Britain and the West Indies, should cease on the tenth of September, 1775, unless American grievances should be sooner redressed. An association, corresponding with these resolutions, was then framed, and signed by every member present. "Never," says Mr. Marshall, "were laws more faithfully observed, than were the resolves of Congress at this period, and their association was, of consequence, universally adopted."

The better to enforce these resolutions, Congress recommended the appointment of committees in the several counties and towns, who, soon after their appointment, under the names of committees of superintendence and correspondence, assumed no inconsiderable portion of the executive power and duties in the several colonies, and became efficient instruments in aiding the progress of the revolution.

XII. The New Jersey delegates reported the proceedings of Congress to the Assembly of that colony, on the 11th January, 1775, by whom they were unanimously approved; *such members as were Quakers, excepting, only, to such parts as seemed to wear an appearance, or might have a tendency to force, as inconsistent with their religious principles.*

And the House resolved, that the same gentlemen should represent the colony in the future Congress, should report their proceedings therein to the Assembly at its next session; should propose and agree to every *reasonable*

* Congress held their sessions in Carpenter's Hall.

and constitutional measure, for the accommodation of the unhappy differences subsisting between the mother and her colonies. And having been informed that at the preceding Congress, an attempt was made to give some of the colonies a greater number of votes than others, in determining questions before it, the Assembly, instructed their delegates not to agree to a measure of that kind unless upon condition, that no vote so taken, should be obligatory on any colony, whose delegates did not assent thereto. The equality of the colonies in their deliberations was, however, preserved, and all questions were, throughout the contest, resolved by Congress, each colony having a voice alike potential.

XIII. The joint action of the colonies was, specially, obnoxious to the royal government; and the governors of the respective colonies threw every obstacle in their power in the way of its accomplishment. To this end, Governor Franklin refused to summon the Assembly, notwithstanding the petitions of the people; and the first delegates to Congress were consequently elected by a convention, and not by the House. On opening the session of the Assembly, January, 1775, he observed. "It would argue not only a great want of duty to his Majesty, but of regard to the good people of this province, were I, on this occasion, to pass over in silence, the late alarming transactions in this and the neighbouring colonies, or not endeavour to prevail on you to exert yourselves in preventing those mischiefs to this country, which, without your timely interposition, will, in all probability, be the consequence.

"It is not for me to decide on the particular merits of the dispute between Great Britain and her colonies, nor do I mean to censure those who conceive themselves aggrieved, for aiming at a redress of their grievances. It is a duty they owe themselves, their country, and their posterity. All that I would wish to guard you against, is the giving any countenance or encouragement to that destructive mode of proceeding which has been unhappily adopted, in part, by some of the inhabitants of this colony, and has been carried so far in others, as totally to subvert their former constitution. It has already struck at the authority of one of the branches of the Legislature in a particular manner. And if you, gentlemen of the Assembly, should give your approbation to transactions of this nature, you will do as much as lies in your power, to destroy that form of government, of which you are an important part, and which it is your duty by all lawful means to preserve. To you, your constituents have entrusted a peculiar guardianship of their rights and privileges, you are their legal representatives, and you cannot, without a manifest breach of your trust, suffer any body of men in this, or any of the other provinces, to usurp and exercise any of the powers vested in you by the constitution. It behooves you, particularly, who must be constitutionally supposed to speak the sense of the people at large, to be extremely cautious in consenting to any act whereby you may engage them as parties in, and make them answerable for measures which may have a tendency to involve them in difficulties far greater than those they aim to avoid."

"Besides, there is not, gentlemen, the least necessity, consequently, there will not be the least excuse for your running such risks, on the present occasion. If you are really disposed to represent to the King any inconveniences you conceive yourselves to lie under, or to make any propositions on the present state of America, I can assure you, from the best authority, that such representations or propositions will be properly attended to, and certainly have greater weight coming from each colony in its separate capacity, than in a channel, the propriety and legality of which there may be much doubt."

"You have now pointed out to you, gentlemen, two roads—one evidently leading to peace, happiness, and a restoration of the public tranquillity—the other inevitably conducting you to anarchy and misery, and all the horrors of a civil war. Your wisdom, your prudence, your regard for the true interests of the people, will be best known, when you have shown to which road you give the preference. If to the former, you will probably afford satisfaction to the moderate, the sober, and discreet part of your constituents. If to the latter, you will perhaps give pleasure to the warm, the rash, and inconsiderate among them, who, I would willingly hope, violent, as is the temper of the present times, are not even now the majority. But, it may be well for you to remember, should any calamity hereafter befall them from your compliance with their inclinations, instead of pursuing, as you ought, the dictates of your own judgment, that the consequences of their returning to a proper sense of their conduct, may prove deservedly fatal to yourselves."

XIV. These persuasions were powerless, as we have seen, with the Assembly, who, unanimously approved and adopted the very measures which the governor condemned; and it may be proper to give their justification of their conduct, in the reply of the House to his address.

"We should have been glad," they say, "that your excellency's inclinations to have given us early an opportunity of transacting the public business, as was consistent with our 'convenience,' had terminated in a manner more agreeable to your design, and more favourable to us, than it really has done, on the present occasion. If the petitions, which we understand have been presented to you, had been granted, we should have had a meeting more convenient to us than the present; and that meeting, perhaps, would have prevented some of those 'alarming transactions,' which your excellency's apprehensions of your duty leads you to inform us, as having happened in this colony. We thank you for your intention to oblige us; but that it may not be so entirely frustrated in future, permit us to inform you, it will be much the most agreeable to us, that the meeting of the House, to do public business, should not be postponed to a time later than when the bill for the support of government expires."

"We are sorry to hear, that in your excellency's opinion, there has been of late, any 'alarming transactions' in this and the neighbouring colonies; our consent to, or approbation of which, may lead the good people we represent, into 'anarchy, misery, and all the horrors of a civil war.' It is true you are pleased to tell us, that this destructive mode of proceeding has been adopted, but 'in part,' by some of the inhabitants of this colony. We assure you, that we neither have, nor do intend to give our approbation to measures destructive to the welfare of our constituents, and in which we shall be equally involved with them.—Their interests and our own, we look upon as inseparable. No arguments are necessary to prevail on us to endeavour to prevent such impending calamities; and if we should, at any time, mistake our duty so much, we hope your regard to the public will induce you to exert the prerogative, and thereby give them the choice of other representatives, who may act with more prudence. The uncertainty, however, to what 'alarming transactions,' in particular, you refer, renders it sufficient for us to assure you, only, that we profess ourselves to be the loyal subjects of the King, from whose goodness we hope to be relieved from the present unhappy situation; that we will do all in our power to preserve that excellent form of government, under which we at present live; and that we neither intend to usurp the rights of others, nor suffer any vested in us by the constitution, to be wrested out of our hands, by any person or persons whatever.

"We sincerely lament the unhappy differences which at present subsist between Great Britain and her colonies. We shall heartily rejoice to see the time, when they shall subside, on principles consistent with the rights and interests of both, which we ardently hope is not far off; and though we cannot conceive how the separate petition of one colony, is more likely to succeed, than the united petitions of all, yet, in order to show our desire to promote so good a purpose, by every proper means, we shall make use of the mode pointed out by your excellency, in hopes that it will meet that attention, which you are pleased to assure us, will be paid to the representatives of the people."

This was the language of men who had well weighed their measures, and were resolved to abide their consequences. Nor is such resolution rendered less obvious, by the tone of irony and *persiflage*, which pervades their comments on the specious, but hollow assurances of the governor, of the success which might ensue a departure from the union entered into by the colonies.

XV. The rejoinder of the governor, was remarkable for good temper and moderation; evincing that his course was prompted, more by the duties of his station, than by his judgment, which would probably have united him with the people.

"Were I to give such an answer," he said, "to your address, as the peculiar nature of it seems to require, I should be necessarily led into the explanation and discussion of several matters and transactions, which, from the regard I bear to you, and the people of this colony, I would far rather have buried in perpetual oblivion. It is, besides, now vain to argue on the subject, as you have with the most uncommon and unnecessary precipitation, given your entire approbation to that destructive mode of proceeding, which I so earnestly warned you against. Whether, after such a resolution, the petition you mention, can be reasonably expected to produce any good effect; and whether you or I have best consulted the true interests of the people, on this important occasion, I shall leave others to determine."

The language of the council, however, was in a different tone, and as loyal as the governor himself could desire. "We agree with your excellency," say they, "that it would argue not only a great want of duty to his Majesty, but of regard to the good people of this province, were we, on this occasion, to pass over in silence, the present alarming transactions, which are so much the objects of public attention, and, therefore, beg leave to assure you, that feeling ourselves strongly influenced, by a zealous attachment to the interests of Great Britain and her colonies, and deeply impressed with a sense of the important connexion they have with each other, we shall, with all sincere loyalty to our most gracious sovereign, and all due regard to the true welfare of the inhabitants of this province, endeavour to prevent those mischiefs which the present situation of affairs seems to threaten; and by our zeal for the authority of government on the one hand, and for the constitutional rights of the people on the other, aim at restoring that health of the political body, which every good subject must earnestly desire."

"Your excellency may be assured, that we will exert our utmost influence, both in our public and private capacities, to restore that harmony between the parent state, and his Majesty's American dominions, which is so essential to the happiness and prosperity of the whole empire. And earnestly looking for that happy event, we will endeavour to preserve peace and good order, among the people, and a dutiful submission to the laws."

XVI. The committee appointed for the purpose, composed of Messrs. Wetherill, Fisher, Ford, Tucker, and Shepherd, reported a petition to his Majesty, which was adopted by the House. This instrument contained, in a short compass, the black catalogue of the grievances of the colonies, and prayed for that redress, which his Majesty's gracious assurances signified by their governor, that the representations or propositions of the colonies would be attended to, led them to expect.

In England, the proceedings of the Americans were still viewed with great indignation by the King and his ministry. His Majesty, in his opening speech,* to a Parliament newly elected, declared, before intelligence had been received of the course of the Congress, "that a most daring spirit of resistance and disobedience to the laws unhappily prevailed in the province of Massachusetts, and had broken forth in fresh violences of a very criminal nature; and that these proceedings had been countenanced and encouraged in his other colonies; that unwarrantable attempts had been made to obstruct the commerce of his kingdoms by unlawful combinations; and that he had taken such measures, and given such orders, as he judged most proper and effectual for carrying into execution the laws, which were passed in the last session of the late Parliament, relative to the province of Massachusetts; an address, echoing the royal speech, was carried by large majorities in both Houses of Parliament, but not without a spirited protest from some few lords of the minority.†

XVII. The reception, in London, of the proceedings of Congress appeared to have a momentary beneficial effect upon their cause. The administration was staggered, and the opposition triumphed in the truth of their predictions, that the measures pursued by the ministry would unite all the colonies in resistance. The petition of Congress to the King was declared by the Secretary of State, after a day's perusal, to be decent and proper, and was received, graciously, by his Majesty, who promised to lay it before his two Houses of Parliament. But the ministry had resolved to compel the obedience of the Americans. Hence every representation from America, coming through channels other than ministerial partisans, was unwillingly received, and denied all credit. The remonstrances of the representatives of three millions of men, made under the most awful and affecting circumstances, and the most sacred responsibilities, were treated, perhaps believed, as the clamours of an unruly multitude. In vain did the merchants of London, Bristol, Glasgow, Norwich, Liverpool, Manchester, Birmingham, and other places, by petition, pourtray the evils which must result from such determination, and predict the dangers to the commercial interests of the kingdom: In vain did the planters of the sugar colonies, resident in Great Britain, represent, that the profits on British property in the West India islands, amounting to many millions, which ultimately centered in Great Britain, would be deranged and endangered by the continuance of the American troubles: In vain did the venerable Earl of Chatham, roused from a long retirement, by the danger of losing these colonies, which his own measures had protected, and, seemingly, assured to the parent state, apply his comprehensive mind and matchless eloquence to arrest the fatal course of the administration: In vain, from a prophetic view of events, did he demonstrate the impossibility of subjugating the colonies; and urge the immediate removal of the troops collected by General Gage, at Boston, as a measure indispensably necessary to open the way for an adjustment of the differences with the provinces: In vain, when undiscouraged by the rejection of the motion, did he propose a bill for settling the troubles in America. The period of American emancipation had approached, and the power which might have delayed it, was providentially stultified.

XVIII. Both Houses of Parliament joined in an address to the King, declaring "that they find a rebellion actually exists in the province of Massachusetts." This was followed by an act for restraining the trade and com-

* October 30th.

† Richmond, Portland, Rockingham, Stamford, Stanhope, Torrington, Ponsonby, Wycombe, and Camden.

merce of the New England provinces, and prohibiting them from carrying on the fisheries on the banks of Newfoundland, which was subsequently extended to New Jersey, Pennsylvania, Maryland, Virginia, South Carolina, and the counties on the Delaware.

Pending the consideration of this bill, Lord North introduced what he termed a conciliatory proposition. It provided that when any colony should propose to make provision, according to its circumstances, for contributing its proportion to the common defence, (such proportion to be raised under the authority of the General Assembly of such colony, and ***disposable by Parliament,***) and should engage to make provision also, for the support of the civil government, and the administration of justice in such colony; it would be proper, if such proposal were approved by his Majesty and Parliament, and for so long as such provision should be made, to forbear to levy any duty or tax, except such duties as were expedient for the regulation of commerce; the net produce of such duties to be carried to the account of such colony. This proposition was opposed by the friends of the minister, as an admission of the correctness of the American views as to taxation by Parliament, and as a concession to armed rebels; until it was explained, that the resolution was designed to enforce the essential part of taxation, by compelling the Americans to raise, not only what they, but what Parliament, should think reasonable. The minister declared, "that he did not expect the proposition would be acceptable to the Americans; but, that, if it had no beneficial effect in the colonies, it would unite the people of England by holding out to them a distinct object of revenue; that, as it tended to unite England, it would produce disunion in America; for, if one colony accepted it, the confederacy, which made them formidable, would be broken."

This avowal of the character and tendency of the resolution was not requisite to enlighten the colonists. On its transmission to the provinces, it was unanimously rejected.

XIX. For the sole purpose of communicating this resolution, Governor Franklin convened the Assembly of New Jersey, at Burlington, on the 15th of May, 1775; when, by a long and elaborate speech, he sought to set it before them, in a light, different from that in which it had been viewed by the Legislatures of the other colonies. Soon after the opening of the session, a circumstance occurred, illy adapted to prepare the House for any favourable impression from the governor. Mr. Tucker laid before the Assembly, a copy of "The Parliamentary Register, No. 5," containing, among other things, an extract of a letter, from Governor Franklin to the Earl of Dartmouth, dated the 1st February, 1775, received February 28th; in which the governor represents the House as divided in their approbation of the proceedings of the late Congress. The House sent the governor a copy of the extract, with a request, to be informed, whether it contained a true representation of the words or substance of the letter written by him, relative to the proceedings of the last session of Assembly. His excellency complained of the course of the House, in entering the extract upon their minutes, and endeavouring to inculpate him; but denied the correctness of the extract. The House was still dissatisfied, and referred his answer to a committee, to report thereon, at the next session, when the matter was suffered to fall, without further notice. Under the excitement produced by this affair, the House replied to the governor's address, delivered at the opening of the session.

"As the continental Congress," they said, "is now sitting, to consider of the present critical situation of American affairs, and as this House has already appointed delegates for that purpose, we should have been glad that your excellency had postponed the present meeting, until their opinion could be had upon the resolution now offered for our consideration, and to which we have no doubt a proper attention will be paid; more especially, as we cannot suppose you to entertain a suspicion, that the present House has the least design to desert the common cause, in which all America appears both deeply interested, and firmly united, so far as separately and without the advice of a body, in which all are represented, to adopt a measure of so much importance. Until this opinion be known, we can only give your excellency our present sentiments, being fully of the opinion, that we shall pay all proper respect to, and abide by the united voice of the Congress on the present occasion." * * * * * "We confess that your excellency has put a construction on the proposition which appears to us to be new, and if we could be of the opinion that the resolution 'holds no proposition beyond the avowal of the justice, the equity, and the propriety of subjects of the same state, contributing according to their abilities and situation to the public burdens,' and did not convey to us the idea of submitting the disposal of all our property to others, in whom we have no choice, it is more than probable, that we should gladly embrace the opportunity of settling this unhappy dispute."

"Most Assemblies on the continent have, at various times, acknowledged and declared to the world their willingness, not only to defray the charge of the administration of justice and the support of the civil government, but also to contribute, as they have hitherto done, when constitutionally called upon, to every reasonable and necessary expense for the defence, protection, and security of the whole English empire; and this colony in particular, hath always complied with his Majesty's requisitions for these purposes: And we do assure your excellency, that we shall always be ready, according to our abilities and to the utmost of our power, to maintain the interest of his Majesty and of the parent state. If, then, your excellency's construction be right, and if a 'proposal of this nature,' will, as you are pleased to inform us, be received by his Majesty with every possible indulgence, we have hopes, that the declaration we now make, will be looked on by his Majesty and his ministers, not only to be similar to what is required from us, but also to be, "a basis of a negotiation, on which the present differences may be accommodated—an event which we most ardently wish for."

"We have considered the resolution of the House of Commons. We would not wish to come to a determination, that might be justly called precipitate, in the present alarming situation of affairs. But if we mistake not, this resolution contains no new proposal. It appears to us to be the same with one made to the colonies, the year preceding the passage of the stamp act. America then did not comply with it; and though we are sincerely disposed to make use of all proper means to obtain the favour of his Majesty and the Parliament of Great Britain, yet we cannot in our present opinion, comply with a proposition, which we really apprehend to give up the privileges of freemen; nor do we want any time to consider, whether we shall submit to that, which, in our apprehension, will reduce us and our constituents to a state little better than that of slavery."

"By the resolution now offered, if assented to, we think we shall be to all intents and purposes, as fully and effectually taxed by our fellow subjects, in Great Britain, where we have not any representation, as by any of the late acts of the British Parliament, under which we have been aggrieved, of which we have complained, and from which we have prayed to be relieved; and that, too, in a much greater degree perhaps, than by all those acts put together. We cannot consent to subject the property of our constituents to be taken away for services and uses, of the propriety of which we have no right to judge, while to us, are only left the ways and means of raising the money.

We have always thought and contended, that, we had a right to dispose of our property ourselves, and we have always cheerfully yielded our assistance to his Majesty in that way, when the exigencies of affairs required us so to do, and he has condescended to ask it of us. At this period we cannot form any judgment, either of the extent of the proposition, or of the consequences in which the good people of the colony may be involved, by our assent to a provision so indeterminate, for it appears to us to be impossible to judge what proportion or share the people can bear, until we know what situation they will be in, when any sum is intended to be raised."

"Upon the whole, though sincerely desirous to give every mark of duty and attachment to the King, and to show all due reverence to the Parliament, we cannot, consistently, with our real sentiments, and the trust reposed in us, assent to a proposal big with consequences destructive to the public welfare, and hope that the justice of our parent country will not permit us to be driven into a situation, the prospect of which fills us with anxiety and horror."

If the governor really supposed that he could prevail on the colony over which he presided to separate from the union, he had egregiously mistaken his power; but he laboured so earnestly to effect this object, that his defeat should not, and did not lessen his claim upon the favour of his royal master. He observed, however, that his labour was in vain, and had the good sense to retire from further contest by a short and moderate rejoinder.

Congress had fixed on the month of May, for their next meeting, that the disposition of the parent state might be known previously to their deliberations. They entertained hopes, that their re-assembling might be unnecessary; that the union of the colonies, their petition to the King, and address to the people of Great Britain, might lead to the redress of their grievances. But these flattering delusions now gave place to the stern and gloomy truth, that their rights must be defended by the sword, their quarrel be determined by the god of battles. For this appeal, the colonies, generally prepared, as soon as the proceedings of Parliament, and the resolution of the ministry to send out additional troops were known. Means were every where taken to organize and instruct the militia, and to procure arms and munitions of war.

XXI. The New Jersey committee of correspondence appointed by the convention, met at New Brunswick on the second of May, 1775; when taking into consideration the alarming and very extraordinary conduct of the British ministry for executing the acts of Parliament, as also the several acts of hostility which had been actually commenced for this purpose by the regular forces under General Gage, they directed their chairman, immediately, to call a second provincial convention, to meet at Trenton on the 23d of May, to consider and determine on such matters as should then come before them.*

This important body met at the time and place appointed, and elected Hendrick Fisher their president, Samuel Tucker, vice-president, Jonathan D. Sergeant, Secretary, and William Patterson, and Frederick Frelinghausen, his assistants. On the resignation of Mr. Sergeant, soon after, Mr. Patterson was chosen principal, and Mr. Frelinghausen deputy secretary.

Under a deep and religious sense of the responsibility they had assumed, the members of the Convention declared, that, "Inasmuch as the business on which this Congress are now assembled, and is likely to engage their deliberation, appears to be of the highest moment, and may, in the event, affect the lives and properties, the religion and the liberties of their constituents,

* See Appendix, note CC, for the names of the members.

and of their remotest posterity, it unquestionably becomes the representative body of a Christian community, to look up to that all powerful Being, by whose providence all human events are guided, humbly imploring his divine favour, in presiding over, and directing their present councils, towards the re-establishment of order and harmony between Great Britain and her distressed colonies; and that he would be graciously pleased to *succeed* the measures that may be devised as most conducive to these desirable ends: It is, therefore, ordered, that the president do wait on the ministers of the gospel in this town, and in behalf of this Congress, request their alternate attendance and service, every morning at eight o'clock, during the session, in order, that, the business of the day may be opened with prayer for the above purposes."

The president opened to the Congress, the important occasion of their meeting, recommending the utmost deliberation in determining on the measures to be pursued in the defence of their rights and privileges, to which, by their *happy constitution*, the inhabitants of the province were justly entitled, and that due care might be taken to support the established civil authority, (so far as might consist with the preservation of their fundamental liberties) for the maintenance of good order and the undisturbed administration of justice. The restriction, which regard for "the established civil authority," imposed on the power of the Congress, was, indeed, very inconsiderable. For the Convention, reflecting the majesty of the people, assumed as occasion required, the full power of all the branches of government.

They proceeded, to take into consideration the unhappy contest between Great Britain and the colonies, which they determined was of such a nature, and had reached such a crisis, that the Convention had become absolutely necessary, to provide such ways and means for the security of the province as the exigencies of the times require: and at the same time declared, that they had assembled with the profoundest veneration for the person and family of his sacred majesty, George III., firmly professing all due allegiance to his rightful authority and government. And as a majority of the members of the Legislature, convened at Amboy, in the preceding January, had been instructed by their constituents, to appoint deputies to the Congress, and some of the counties had omitted so to instruct their representatives, who, notwithstanding, had cordially joined in such appointment, the Convention approved the nomination, and rendered thanks to the House, for the regard they had shown for the rights and liberties of the province, in timely adopting the continental association, and resolving in favour of the resolutions and proceedings of the continental Congress. But the Convention, also, resolved, that whenever a continental Congress should again be necessary, that it would be most eligible, for the inhabitants of each county, to apoint deputies for the purpose of electing delegates.

On the twenty-fifth of May, a written message was addressed to the continental Congress, then, in session at Philadelphia, declaring that the provincial Congress was convened "with dispositions most heartily to concur, to the utmost of their abilities, in the common cause of America, but that they did not deem it advisable to enter into any measures of consequence, until some general plan had been adopted by the general Congress: That, in this first instance of such an assembly in the colony, without precedent for their direction, and anxiously desirous to make their provincial measures consistent with that plan, they deemed it necessary, by a special deputation, to request such advice and assistance as the Congress might be disposed to give.* This deputation reported on the thirtieth, that the Congress was not,

* This committee consisted of William P. Smith and Elias Boudinot.

then, prepared to give any advice upon the state of the province, but promised due attention to the request.

The Convention adopted the following form of association, which they directed to be sent to the committees of observation or correspondence in the several counties, which had not already associated in a similar manner, in order that it might be signed by the inhabitants.

"*We*, the subscribers, freeholders and inhabitants of the township of in the county of and province of New Jersey, having long viewed with concern, the avowed design of the ministry of Great Britain to raise a revenue in America; being deeply affected with the cruel hostilities, already commenced in the Massachusetts Bay, for carrying that arbitrary design into execution; convinced that the preservation of the rights and privileges of America depends, under God, on the firm union of its inhabitants; do, with hearts abhorring slavery, and ardently wishing for a reconciliation with our parent state, on constitutional principles, solemnly associate and resolve, under the sacred ties of virtue, honour, and love to our country, that we will, personally, and so far as our influence extends, endeavour to support and carry into execution, whatever measures may be recommended by the continental and our provincial Congress, for defending our constitution and preserving the same inviolate. We do, also, further associate and agree, as far as shall be consistent with the measures adopted for the preservation of American freedom, to support the magistrates and other civil officers in the execution of their duty, agreeable to the laws of this colony, and to observe the direction of our committee, acting according to the resolutions of the continental and provincial Congresses; firmly determined, by all means in our power, to guard against those disorders and confusions to which the peculiar circumstances of the times may expose us." Surely, no more effectual mode could have been devised, of subjecting a people to the will of their leaders, than this association and its written pledge. Happily, the leaders and the people had the same interest, which the former steadily pursued.

Mr. Pierpoint Edwards, having been deputed from Connecticut to New Jersey, for the purpose of obtaining intelligence of the true state of the province, and to communicate the actual condition of his own, the Convention gave their state and purposes as we have detailed them; and they, also, opened a correspondence with the provincial Congress of New York.

The organization of the military force was, in every colony, an object of the first importance, and received from the provincial Congress of New Jersey, due attention. One or more companies of eighty men, each, were directed to be formed in each township or corporation, from the male inhabitants between sixteen and fifty years of age, under the supervision of the respective committees, with power to elect their commissioned officers: The officers of the companies determined the number which should form a regiment, and named the officers. And as the inhabitants of Morris, Sussex, and Somerset counties, had made spirited exertions in raising minute men, pledged to march to any point of the country whenever called on, the Congress approved their conduct, and voted their thanks.

In order to raise the necessary funds, the convention imposed a tax of ten thousand pounds, which they apportioned, specifically, among the several counties; and each county quota was apportioned among the townships, by the township committees, according to the act of Assembly, settling the quotas of the several counties, to be collected by agents nominated by the township committees, and to be paid to the treasurer of the county committees. Then, after appointing a committee of their body, any three of whom, together with the president or vice-president, were empowered to convoke them, the Congress adjourned, upon the 3d day of June, after a session of eleven days.

XXII. Before the continental Congress again met,* hostilities between the colonists and the British troops in America, had commenced. The battle of Lexington was fought,†—and Ticonderoga captured;‡—and soon after, the ever memorable engagement at Breed's Hill,§ gave confidence to the colonists; and the British army, under General Gage, was besieged in Boston. Instead of contending against orations of ministers, votes and acts of Parliament, by petition and remonstrance, addresses and resolutions, Congress was now to be employed, in developing the resources and directing the energies of the colonies, to resist the military power of Great Britain.

Peyton Randolph was again chosen president, but being in a few days called to his duties, as speaker of the house of burgesses, of Virginia, Mr. John Hancock, of Boston, was unanimously elected his successor. Mr. Charles Thompson was re-appointed secretary. The leading patriots had long foreseen, that, the controversy must be decided by arms; yet they were anxious, that the odium of the war should fall on their oppressors. Care was, therefore, taken, to show that the royal troops had been the aggressors at Lexington; and the inhabitants of New York were advised to act, defensively, on the arrival of British troops there; to permit the forces to remain in barracks, but to suffer no fortifications to be erected, nor the communication between the town and country to be impeded. To this cause, we must also assign the resolution of Congress ascribing the capture of Ticonderoga, to the imperious necessity of resisting a cruel invasion from Canada, planned and commenced by the ministry.

Congress promptly proceeded to further measures of offence and defence. They prohibited exports to such parts of British America, as had not joined the confederacy—forbade the supply of provisions, or other necessaries, to the English fisheries on the coast, to the army and navy in Massachusetts, and to vessels employed in transporting British troops and munitions of war; and interdicted the negotiation of bills of exchange, drawn by British officers, agents or contractors, and the advance of money to them, on any terms whatever. To secure the colonies against the forcible execution of the late obnoxious acts of Parliament, they resolved, to put them immediately in a state of defence; recommending to them, severally, to provide the munitions of war—to prepare the militia; so classing them, that a fourth of their number might be drawn into action, at a minute's warning; and to form a corps for continual service;—authorizing each colony, apprehensive of attack, to levy one thousand regulars at the expense of the confederacy. They organized the higher departments of the army, framed regulations for its government, and issued three millions of dollars, in bills of credit, for its maintenance. They prepared an address to the army and the people, reviewing the conduct of Great Britain, exposing the enormity of her pretensions, exhibiting the dreadful alternative she had created, of unconditional submission, or resistance by arms, and asserting the justice of their cause, the competency of the means to maintain it, and their fixed determination to employ, at every hazard, the utmost energy of the powers granted them by their Creator, for the preservation of their liberties. This spirit-stirring manifesto closed with the following solemn protestation.—"In our native land, in defence of the freedom which is our birth-right, and which we ever enjoyed, until the late violation of it, for the protection of our property, acquired solely by the honest industry of our forefathers, and ourselves, against violence actually

* 10th May, 1775.
† 19th April.
‡ 9th May.
§ June 17th, 1775.

offered, we have taken up arms; we shall lay them down when hostilities shall cease on the part of the aggressors, and all danger of their being removed, and not before."

XXIII. Under other circumstances, the selection of a commander-in-chief, amid opposing pretensions, would have been exceedingly difficult. The individual best fitted for this important trust was now a delegate in Congress, and had embarked a high character and splendid fortune, with his life, in the perilous contest. Of mature age, and advantageously known to all British America, by his military talents, sound judgment, firm temper, spotless integrity, and dignified person and demeanour, there could not exist a single personal objection to his nomination. The middle and southern districts possessed no man having superior claims to public confidence; and if the northern had a preference for an individual of their own section, policy and gratitude required its sacrifice. The delegates of Massachusetts, therefore, nominated Colonel George Washington, of Virginia, who was unanimously appointed commander-in-chief of the united colonies.* His commission, revocable by Congress, invested him with "full power and authority to act as he should think for the good and welfare of the service;" subject to the rules of war and the orders of Congress. By a resolution, simultaneous with his appointment, Congress declared, "that for the maintenance and preservation of American liberty, they would adhere to him with their lives and fortunes." The reply of Mr. Washington, to the annunciation of his appointment, by the president of Congress, was marked by that modesty, disinterestedness, and devotion to duty, which eminently distinguished him. As no pecuniary motive had excited him to assume the dangerous honour, he declined all compensation for services that were inestimable; declaring that he would accept only the reimbursement of his expenses.

Soon after the nomination of the commander-in-chief, Congress created and filled the offices of subordinate generals. Artemas Ward, Charles Lee, Philip Schuyler, and Israel Putnam, were appointed major-generals, ranking in the order we have named them; Horatio Gates, adjutant-general; and Seth Pomeroy, Richard Montgomery, David Wooster, William Heath, Joseph Spencer, John Thomas, John Sullivan, and Nathaniel Greene, brigadiers.

XXIV. Although determined to resist to the uttermost the tyranny of the parent state, the colonies had given no public indication of their desire to become independent of her government. Many provincialists, certainly, looked to political independence as the possible result of the contest; some, perhaps, wished and sought it, but none avowed such wishes. The American people were proud of their derivation, and exulted in their connexion with Great Britain. Some of their most distinguished patriots could under no circumstances, resolve to break the bonds which bound them to her. It was characteristic, therefore, that, amid warlike preparations, renewed attempts should be made to propitiate the British government and people. Another petition to the King was, however, opposed by several members of the Congress, from a conviction that it would prove nugatory. But the influence of Mr. Dickenson, by whom it was proposed and written, procured its adoption.

This address, replete with professions of duty and attachment, declared, that "the provincialists not only most fervently desired the former harmony between Great Britain and the colonies to be restored, but that a concord might be established between them upon so firm a basis, as to perpetuate its

* June 15th, 1775.

blessings, uninterrupted by any future dissentions, to succeeding generations in both countries. They, therefore, besought his Majesty to direct some mode by which the united applications of his faithful colonists to the throne, in pursuance of their common counsels, might be improved to a happy and permanent reconciliation. These sincere professions of three millions of his subjects, were contemptuously treated by the King. The petition was presented through the secretary for American affairs, on the first of September, by Messrs. Richard Penn and Henry Lee; and on the fourth, Lord Dartmouth informed them, that "to it no answer would be given." And in a speech from the throne, the colonists were accused of designing "to amuse, by vague expressions of attachment to the parent state, and the strongest protestations of loyalty to their King, while they were preparing for a general revolt; and their rebellious war was manifestly carried on for the purpose of establishing an independent empire." Contumely so unwise and undeserved, served but to confirm the scrupulous in America, in the course of resistance—removing the faintest hope of redress by the humble and pacific means of petition and remonstrance.

Whilst resorting to arms, respect for the opinions of their fellow subjects induced Congress to make an exposition of their motives in addresses to the inhabitants of Great Britain, to the people of Ireland, and to the Assembly of Jamaica. They also published a declaration to the world, setting forth the necessity of assuming arms, and recapitulating the injuries they had sustained. "We are," they said, "reduced to the alternative of choosing an unconditional submission to the tyranny of irritated ministers, or resistance by force. The latter is our choice. We have counted the cost of this contest, and find nothing so dreadful as voluntary slavery."

General Washington, immediately after his appointment to the chief command, repaired to the army before Boston. With incredible difficulty he was enabled to maintain a show of force, which confined the British troops to that town from the month of June, 1775, until the month of March following, when the Americans, having seized and fortified Dorchester Heights, which overlooked and commanded the place, General Howe, who had succeeded General Gage,* abandoned it, and sailed with his command for Halifax.

The capture of Ticonderoga had opened the gates of Canada, and the impetuous spirit of Colonel Arnold was eager to enter them. At his instance, Congress resolved to invade that province; and from the unprepared state of its defence, and the friendly disposition of its inhabitants, well founded hopes were entertained of success. This step, which changed the character of the war from defensive to offensive, was justified by the obvious propriety of depriving the enemy, for such the parent state was now considered, of the means of assailing the colonies from that quarter. The command of this enterprise was given to Generals Schuyler and Montgomery. The former, however, soon retired, in consequence of ill health. The latter, with a force of one thousand men, having captured the fort at Chambleé, and the post of St. Johns, proceeded to Montreal in despite of the opposing efforts of General Carlton, governor of the province; and, having obtained at this place many necessary supplies, led his gallant little army to the walls of Quebec.

During the progress of General Montgomery, Colonel Arnold, with boldness and perseverance rarely surpassed, conducted a detachment to the St. Lawrence, by an unexplored course along the Kennebeck and Chaudiere rivers, through a trackless desert of three hundred miles. His force originally consisted of one thousand men, one-third of whom were compelled to

* October 10th.

return by the want of necessaries. The remainder persevered with unabated resolution; surmounting every obstacle of mountain and forest; progressing at times, not more than five miles a day; whilst so destitute of provisions, that some of the men ate their dogs, cartouch boxes, breeches and shoes. When distant a hundred miles from any habitation, their whole store was divided, yielding only four pints of flour per man; and after having baked and eaten their last morsel, they had thirty miles to travel before they could expect relief. After a march of thirty-one days, they reached the inhabited parts of Canada, where they were kindly received, and their wants supplied by the astonished natives.

Before Montgomery attained Montreal, Arnold had reached Point Levy, opposite Quebec; and had it been possible for the latter to cross the St. Lawrence, that important place would, probably, have been, immediately, surrendered by the astonished and affrighted garrison. But the want of boats occasioned an indispensable delay of a few days, and the inhabitants, English and Canadians, alarmed for their property, united for its defence.

The prospects of the Americans, however, were not desperate. The inhabitants of Canada, many of whom were from the colonies of New England and New York, were friendly to the colonial cause, and excited by the wisdom and humanity of General Montgomery, gave the most efficient aid. The united American forces laid siege to Quebec, but the paucity of their number forbade any just expectations of reducing the place, unless by a *coup de main.* General Montgomery was induced, by various considerations, to attempt it by storm. The depth of winter was approaching; dissentions had arisen between Arnold and his officers; the specie of the military chest was exhausted, and the continental bills were uncurrent; the troops, worn by toil, were exposed to the severities of the season; the term for which many had enlisted was near expiring, and their departure for home was apprehended; and the brilliant success that had hitherto attended them had excited hopes, which their high-spirited and enthusiastic commander dreaded to disappoint. He was not unaware of the danger and hazard of such an attempt. Governor Carlton, who commanded in Quebec, was an experienced and able soldier; and the garrison, provided with every thing necessary for defence, daily acquired firmness. But success had often crowned adventures more hopeless than that which he proposed; and the triumph of Wolfe, on this very field, taught him, that to the brave and resolute, difficult things were not impossibilities.

The escalade of the town was made with a force of less than eight hundred men.* Two feints were directed, one by Colonel Livingston, at the head of his regiment of Canadian auxiliaries, the other by Major Brown; the principal attacks were conducted by Montgomery and Arnold, in person. The former advancing against the lower town, had passed the first barrier, and was preparing to storm the second, when he was killed by the discharge of a cannon fired by the last of its retreating defenders. His death so dispirited the assailants, that Colonel Campbell, on whom the command devolved, thought proper to draw them off. Arnold, at the head of about three hundred and fifty men, with irresistible impetuosity, carried a two gun battery; but in the conflict, receiving a wound from a musket ball, which shattered his leg, he was compelled to quit the field. His party continued the assault, and mastered a second barrier. But, after a contest for three hours with the greater part of the garrison, finding themselves hemmed in, without hopes of success, relief, or retreat, they yielded themselves prisoners. This issue, so unfortunate for the colonists, relieved the town from all apprehensions for its

* December 31st, 1775.

safety; the invaders being so much weakened as to be scarce competent to their own defence. Arnold encamped at three miles distance from Quebec, and maintained his position amid many difficulties and great privations, until the spring, when he was joined by reinforcements.

The fall of General Montgomery was deplored by friends and foes. He was an Irishman by birth, and though scarce thirty-eight years of age, a veteran soldier. He had shared in the labours and triumph of Wolfe; was distinguished for talent and military genius, and blessed with a mild and constant temper, and dauntless courage. The highest honours of his profession awaited him in the British service. These he abandoned for the enjoyments of domestic happiness in the country of his adoption. But, devoted to freedom, he engaged enthusiastically in defence of the American cause, and by his early successes in the Canadian campaign, induced the highest anticipations of future greatness. In Parliament, his worth was acknowledged, and his fate lamented; the minister himself joined in his praise, whilst condemning the cause in which he fell, and concluded his involuntary panegyric, in the language of the poet, crying, "Curse on his virtues, they've undone his country." In Congress he was mourned as a martyr to liberty, and by their direction a marble monument, of beautiful simplicity, with emblematical devices, has been erected to his memory, in front of St. Paul's church, New York.

XXVI. The provincial Congress of New Jersey re-assembled on the fifth of August, 1775, and engaged in devising further means for the collection of the tax they had imposed and for the organization of the militia. They directed fifty-four companies, each of sixty-four minute men, to be organized, allotting to each county a specific number, and assigning the duty of appointing their officers to the respective county committees. The minute men entered into the following engagement: "We, the subscribers, do voluntarily enlist ourselves as minute men in the company of in the county of And do promise to hold ourselves in constant readiness, on the shortest notice, to march to any place where our assistance may be required, for the defence of this and any neighbouring colony; as also to pay due obedience to the commands of our officers, agreeable to the rules and orders of the continental Congres, or the provincial Congress of New Jersey, or during its recess, of the committee of safety." These troops were formed into ten battalions; in Bergen, Essex, Middlesex, Monmouth, Somerset, Morris, Sussex, Hunterdon, and Burlington, one each; in Gloucester and Salem one, whilst in the counties of Cumberland and Cape May were independent light infantry and rangers:—They took precedence of the other militia, and were entitled to be relieved at the end of four months, unless in actual service. Congress, also, resolved, that two brigadier-generals should be appointed, but named, at the time, only Mr. Philemon Dickenson to that command. Mr. Livingston soon after received the other commission. And as there were a number of people within the province, whose peculiar religious principles did not allow them, in any case to bear arms—the Congress declared, that they intended no violence to conscience; and, therefore, earnestly recommended it to such persons to contribute the more liberally, in these times of universal calamity, to the relief of their distressed brethren; and to do all other services to their oppressed country, consistent with their religious profession.

But the chief measure of the provincial Congress was the perpetuation of the authority which they had assumed. To this end they resolved, that, "Whereas, it is highly expedient, at a time when this province is likely to be involved in all the horrors of civil war, and when it has become absolutely necessary to increase the burden of taxes, already laid on the good people of this colony, for the just defence of their invaluable rights and privileges, that the inhabitants thereof should have frequent opportunities of renewing their choice and approbation of the representatives in provincial Congress:—Therefore, the inhabitants in each county, qualified to vote for representatives in General Assembly, shall meet together, (at places designated) on the twenty-first day of September next, and elect, not exceeding five substantial *freeholders* as deputies, with full power to represent such county in provincial Congress to be holden at Trenton on the third of October next:—That during the continuance of the present unhappy disputes between Great Britain and America, there be a new choice of deputies in every county, yearly, on the third Thursday of September:—That on the said Thursday in every year, such inhabitants shall choose a sufficient number of freeholders to constitute a county committee of observation and correspondence, with full power as well, to superintend and direct the necessary business of the county, as to carry into execution the resolutions and orders of the continental and provincial Congresses:—That the inhabitants of each township, so qualified, do immediately choose a sufficient number of freeholders to constitute a township committee, and that on the second Tuesday of March, thereafter, they make a like choice, to act as committee of observation and correspondence, in the townships, respectively, with power within their precincts, similar to that conferred upon the county committees.

Having appointed Jonathan D. Sergeant their treasurer, and a committee of safety to exercise their powers during the recess, the Congress adjourned to the twentieth day of the ensuing September,* at which session no important matters seem to have occurred. The Congress, elected in September, convened in October, when they were employed chiefly in modifying the ordinance for regulating the militia, and in collecting and preparing the scanty stock of munitions of war which the country contained. At their rising, this Congress, also, appointed a committee of safety from among themselves, who, in the vacation, continued the measures for the defence of the country. They called before them persons accused of disaffection to the American cause, fined, imprisoned, or held them to bail, as they deemed meet; and where the accused was an officer of the government, they suspended him from the exercise of his functions. But having received several communications from the continental Congress, relative to raising of additional force for the general service, the establishment of a court of admiralty, and regulations for the continental troops, raised in the colonies, they summoned the provincial Congress to meet at New Brunswick, on the thirty-first of January.†

The procurement of arms and munitions was a labour of very great difficulty. The policy of the continent, in its anterior warfare with the ministry, having prohibited importation, the whole country was bare of these indispensable agents of war; and to equip even one battalion, that of Colonel

* Names of committee of safety—Hendrick Fisher, Samuel Tucker, Isaac Pearson, John Hart, Jonathan D. Sergeant, Azariah Dunham, Peter Schenk, Enos Kelsey, Joseph Borden, Frederick Freelinghausen, and John Schurman.—*Min. of Convention.* This committee was changed, by the Congress holden in Trenton, in October. But I have not been able to find the minutes of the sessions of the provincial Congress of September and October, 1775. The proceedings, then had, do not seem to have been considered important, since they were not printed, so far as my researches have enabled me to dicover. The following are the names of the committee of safety appointed in October; at least of such as attended the session of January 10th, 1776; the proceedings of which have been published, viz. Samuel Tucker, president, Hendrick Fisher, vice-president, Abraham Clark, secretary, Azariah Dunham, Ruloffe Vandyke, John Dennis, Augustine Stevenson, John Pope, John Hart, Joseph Holmes.

† See Appendix, note D D, for the names of the members of provincial Congress, elected in September, 1775.

Maxwell, ordered to march to Canada, the provincial Congress was compelled to apply to the county committees, and to appeal to the patriotism of individuals.

On the sixth of February, 1776, the Convention made a new appointment of delegates, to the continental Congress, for the current year, consisting of William Livingston, John de Hart, Richard Smith, John Cooper, and Jonathan Dickenson Sergeant, who, or any three of them, were empowered to agree *to all measures which such Congress might deem necessary*, and in case of the adjournment of the continental Congress, to represent the province in any other such Congress as might assemble during their delegation. The thanks of the Convention were given to their late representatives.

This Congress, like its predecessors, exercised the whole power of the state, assuming control over its funds, and directing its physical energies. A first measure was an endeavour to protect such points as they deemed most exposed to the forces from the British fleet; which, under the supposition, that New York was adequately defended, they believed to be Perth Amboy, and Swedesborough on the Delaware. For this object the continental Congress was solicited to take into pay two battalions and two companies of artillery; but Congress were unable to do more than order the procurement of twelve pieces of small cannon, and to engage for the maintenance of two companies of artillery, which were raised by the province. An ordinance was passed modifying the form of association, and delaring, that, though it was not the design of the Congress to offer violence to conscience, yet it was highly necessary, that all the inhabitants should associate, so far as their religious principles would permit; and, therefore, directing, that all persons, whose religious principles would not suffer them to bear arms, and to sign the general association, might sign it with the following proviso. "I agree to the above association, as far as the same is consistent with my religious principles." All persons refusing to sign this modified form, were to be disarmed, to give security for their peaceable conduct, and pay the expenses attending thereon. The township and county committees were charged with the execution of this ordinance, and appeal by a party aggrieved was permitted from the township, to the county, committee, and from the latter to the Congress. These committees were also empowered to confine any person, notwithstanding his offer of security, whose freedom might prove dangerous to the common cause. It was further declared, that all such persons, between the ages of sixteen and fifty years, who should not attend, properly accoutred, and bear arms, on the times appointed for the general muster of the militia, should pay ten shillings for each default, to be recovered by warrant of distress. And in order to encourage enlistment into the service of the United Colonies, the Congress granted to the soldiers, exemption of person and goods from execution for small debts, and to procure a supply of nitre and common salt, they established a bounty on the manufacture of both articles.

The impending invasion of New York, filled that city with alarm, and many of its inhabitants actuated by various motives, disposed themselves in the neighbouring counties of New Jersey. So numerous was this emigration that the provincial Congress, doubting, whether it was caused by cowardice or cunning, passed an ordinance to repress it.—Providing, that "whereas, large numbers of people are daily removing from the neighbouring colonies into New Jersey, and it being unknown upon what principles such removals are occasioned, whether to seek an asylum from ministerial oppression, or the resentment of their injured country, to whom they may have become obnoxious, by adhering to the present system of tyranny, now endeavouring to be executed in America; and it being inconsistent with the principles of persons, properly attached to the cause of liberty, to desert their town or county at a time their assistance may be absolutely necessary for its defence, unless the support and maintenance of their families may make such removal necessary—This Congress, therefore, think it advisable, that, although the inhabitants of this colony ought most cheerfully, to receive into their protection, and afford all the relief in their power, to all such as are helpless, and unable to defend themselves, yet they ought to prevent the desertion of places in immediate danger of attack from the enemy, by all who are proper to remain for the defence thereof, and also to prevent persons inimical to the liberties for which the United States are contending, from taking refuge in this province—For remedy whereof, they resolved, that all persons proper to bear arms, who had removed, or should remove into the colony from any city or county of another province, in danger of being suddenly attacked, should immediately return to make that defence, becoming every good citizen, unless they should produce permits from the committee of the precinct, from whence they removed, to reside in this colony, or unless such residence appeared necessary for the support of the resident's family, or he had no visible means of support whence he came, and could procure such support by his industry in this colony. And they further resolved, that all suspected persons removing into the colony, should be immediately returned to the place whence they came, unless their detention as delinquents should be proper; or unless they produced certificates from the committee of the precinct, from which they came, that they had signed the association recommended by Congress, and had not subsequently contravened it." The execution of this ordinance was consigned to the several county and township committees.

Some irregularities having taken place in the election of the existing Congress, this body resolved to dissolve itself, and to direct the election of another, on the fourth Monday of May, following, and thence annually; and repealing a former ordinance, they passed one, for that purpose, in which the right to vote was extended to all persons, who having signed the general association, were of full age, had resided immediately preceding the election, for the space of one year, in the colony, and were worth fifty pounds in personal estate.

XXVII. Governor Franklin convened the Legislature on the 16th of November, 1775, that they might have an opportunity of transacting such business as the public exigencies required. In his opening address he observed. "Having lately said so much to you, concerning the present unhappy situation of public affairs, and the destructive measures which have been adopted in the colonies under the pretence of necessity; and as I do not see, that the urging any more arguments on that head has a chance of producing any good effect, I shall not endanger the harmony of the present session by a further discussion of the subject." He proceeded, however, to inform them from his instructions, "That his Majesty laments to find his subjects in America, so lost to their own true interests, as neither to accept the resolution of the House of Commons of the 20th of February, nor make it the basis of a negotiation, when, in all probability, it would have led to some plan of accommodation, and that, as they have preferred engaging in a rebellion, which menaces to overthrow the constitution, it becomes his Majesty's duty, and is his firm resolution, that the most vigorous efforts should be made, both by sea and land to reduce his rebellious subjects to obedience. But it is hoped, that unfavourable as the prospects are at present, the time will come, when men of sense, and friends to peace and good order will see the fatal consequences of the delusions which have led to the measures the people of America are now pursuing, and that we may yet see the public tranquillity re-established on the ground of the terms held out by his Majesty and the Parliament."

"Although," he continued, "the King's officers in this province, have not, as yet, (except in one or two instances,) met with any insults or improper treatment from any of the inhabitants; yet such has been the general infatuation and disorder of the times, that had I followed the judgment and advice of some of my best friends, I should ere this, have sought, (as others of the King's governors have done,) an asylum on board of one of his Majesty's ships. But, as I am conscious that I have the true interest and welfare of the people at heart, (though I am so unhappy as to differ widely in opinion with their representatives with respect to the best means of serving them, in the present crisis,) I shall continue my confidence in that affection and regard which I have on so many occasions experienced from all ranks during my residence in this colony."

"I have, indeed, the stronger inducement to run this risk and to use my influence with the other crown officers to do the same, because our retreat would necessarily be attributed to either the effect, or well grounded apprehension of violence, and of course subject the colony to be more immediately considered as in actual rebellion, and be productive of mischiefs, which it is my earnest inclination and determination to prevent, as far as may be in my power. Let me, therefore, gentlemen, entreat you to exert your influence likewise with the people, that they may not by any action of theirs, give cause for bringing such calamities on the province. No advantage can possibly result from the seizing, confinement, or ill-treatment of officers, adequate to the certain damage such acts of violence must occasion the province to suffer."

"However, gentlemen, if you should be of a different opinion, and will not, or cannot, answer for our safety, all I ask is, that you would tell me so in such plain and open language, as cannot be misunderstood. For as sentiments of independency are, by some men of present consequence, openly avowed, and essays are already appearing in the public papers, to ridicule the people's fear of that horrid measure, and remove their aversion to republican government, it is high time, that every man should know, what he has to expect. If, as I hope, you have an abhorrence of such a design, you will do your country an essential service, by declaring it in so full and explicit terms, as may discourage the attempt. You may always rely on finding me ready to co-operate with you in every proper expedient for promoting peace, order, and good government; and I shall deem it a particular happiness to have an opportunity of being instrumental in saving this province from the present impending danger."

XXVIII. The prominent objects of this address, seem to have been to obtain from the Assembly, an assurance of personal safety, and a disavowal of all intention to proclaim independence. And in these, the governor was successful. For the House replied, "your excellency's safety, or that of any of the officers of government, we apprehend to be in no danger. We place our own safety in that protection which the laws of our country and the executive powers of government afford to all the King's subjects. It is the only asylum which we have to fly to, and we make no doubt that it will be, as it hitherto hath been, found fully equal to the purpose, both of securing your excellency and others. And we hope to find, that the officers of government will conduct themselves so prudently, as not to invite any ill usage; and that they will not make any supposed 'infatuation or disorder' of the times, a pretence to leave the province, and thereby endeavour to subject the inhabitants to any calamities."

"We know of no sentiments of independency, that are, by men of any consequence, openly avowed; nor do we approve of any essays tending to encourage such a measure. We have already expressed our *detestation* of such opinions, and we have so frequently and fully declared our sentiments on this subject, and particularly, in our petition to the King, at the last session of the Assembly, that we should have thought ourselves, as at present we really deserve to be, exempt from all suspicions of this nature."

The dread of independence seems to have seized, at this time, others than the governor. Several petitions were presented from the freeholders of Burlington county, praying the House to enter into such resolves as might discourage an independency on Great Britain. The petitioners were summoned before the House, and stated, that they had been induced to address it, "from reports that some affected independency." Whereupon, it was resolved, that reports of independency, in the apprehension of the House, are groundless:—That it be recommended to the delegates of the colony, to use their utmost endeavours for obtaining a redress of grievances, and for restoring the union between the colonies and Great Britain, upon constitutional principles; and that, the said delegates be directed not to give their assent, but utterly to reject any propositions, if such should be made, that may separate this colony from the mother country, or change the form of government thereof. The spirit of these resolutions differed widely from that which animated the provincial Congress, which, in the succeeding February, instructed the delegates to agree to all measures which the continental Congress might deem necessary.

XXIX. At this session the governor communicated to the Legislature, the royal approbation of an act, for issuing on loan, bills of credit to the amount of one hundred thousand pounds. For more than twelve years this had been a desirable object with the Assembly, who, as we have, elsewhere, observed, frequently passed bills for this purpose, which had hitherto been rejected by the crown; but as if every concession to the wishes of the people, was a grant of property for which some consideration was due, Lord Dartmouth, in remitting the approval, informed the governor, "At the same time I am commanded by the King, to say to you, that it would have been more agreeable to his Majesty, if the Assembly, instead of a general appropriation of the interest of the loan to the support of government in such manner as shall be directed by future acts, had thought fit to make a settlement, during the existence of that loan, upon the civil officers of government, of salaries more suitable to their respective offices than they now receive; and to appropriate a specific proportion of the said interest, to building houses for the residence of the governor and the meeting of the Legislature, of which you say there is a shameful want. Such an appropriation is no more than what they owe to the dignity of their own government, and his Majesty's just expectations; and, therefore, it is his Majesty's pleasure, that you do require the Assembly, in his Majesty's name, to make such provision accordingly, trusting that they will not make such an ill return to his Majesty's grace and favour, in the confirmation of this law, as not to comply with so just and reasonable a requisition." Thus, a measure was conceded by all parties, having power over it, to be just and necessary, and yet, an individual, who, in all matters relating to the public weal, should have been deemed but an individual, inflated by the worship of crowds, dared to talk of *grace and favour* in the performance of a simple and imperious duty. But the age is passing away, when men will make themselves golden calves for worship, and when a feeble mortal shall

"Assume the God,
Affect to nod,
And seem to shake the spheres."

But the name of the King was no longer a spell sufficiently potent to open the purses of the people, for a prescribed series of years, in favour of royal officers. The Assembly declared, "that though they entertained the most grateful sense of the attention shown to the wishes of the colony, in the allowance of the loan act, and of his Majesty's gracious inclinations to give "every indulgence consistent with the true principles of commerce and the constitution," and are sincerely disposed to grant his Majesty's requisitions; yet, at this time, the House cannot consider it prudent, to go into any increase of the salaries of the officers of government, nor do they apprehend that it will be beneficial for his government over us, to settle them longer than the usual time; or expedient to erect buildings at present, better to accommodate the branches of the Legislature."

On December 6th, 1775, the House was prorogued by the governor until the third day of January, 1776, but it never re-assembled; and thus terminated the provincial Legislature of New Jersey.

CHAPTER XII.

Comprising Civil Events of the year 1776.—I. State of the Public Opinion at the commencement of the year 1776—Gradual growth of the desire of Independence.—II. Resolution of Congress for the establishment of Independent Colonial Governments.—III. Provincial Congress re-assembles—Proceeds to the Formation of a Colonial Constitution.—IV. Review of the Constitution.—V. Oath of Abjuration and Allegiance established.—VI. Tories—their motives.—VII. Law relative to Treason.—VIII. Imprisonment and Relegation of Governor Franklin.—IX. Measures adopted against the Disaffected.—X. Adoption of the Declaration of Independence.

I. For more than a year the whole country had been, not, only, in open rebellion against the King, but its inhabitants had actually made war upon their fellow subjects, who, unconscious of oppression, had preserved their loyalty. Yet, during this period, the governments of the United Colonies, respectively, were administered in the King's name, and the people, every where, professed affection for his person, and attachment to the parent state. In the first half of the year 1755, amongst the great mass of the people and many of their leaders, these sentiments were real. But the more daring and ambitious spirits had, not only foreseen that the continuance of political connexion was not much longer possible, but had, successfully, sought to inspire the people with the desire of independence. And, probably, there was not a profoundly reflecting man in revolted America, who did not, in the depths of his heart, believe, that the severance of the ties between the parent and daughters was, at no very distant period, inevitable; though many, from various causes, such as timidity, selfish policy, and influence of family relations, were disposed to postpone the event.*

But this inconsistent state of things could not continue, without the most odious and useless hypocrisy, nor without the greatest injury to the cause of the colonists. Whilst the expectation of a reunion was suffered to delude the minds of men, a reluctance to pursue those energetic measures which the crisis demanded, would paralyze the best efforts of the patriots who had assumed the direction of affairs. In effecting a change and demonstration of public opinion, perhaps, no single agent was more powerful, than a pamphlet styled Common Sense, written by Thomas Paine; which, in a clear, perspicuous, and popular style, boldly pronounced a continued connexion with England unsafe, as well as impracticable; and successfully ridiculed her

* In 1768 the following language was holden in the *American Whig*, a periodical paper, published in New York, edited by Mr. William Livingston, afterwards, governor of New Jersey; and the article is said to have been written by him.—*Sedgwick's Life of Livingston*, p. 145. "The day dawns in which the foundation of this mighty empire is to be laid, by the establishment of *a regular American Constitution.* All that has hitherto been done, seems to be little besides the collection of materials for the construction of this glorious fabric. 'Tis time to put them together. The transfer of the European part of the great family is so swift, and our growth so vast, that before seven years roll over our heads, the first stone must be laid. Peace or war, famine or plenty, poverty or affluence, in a word, no circumstance, whether prosperous or adverse, can happen to our parent, nay, no conduct of hers, whether wise or imprudent; no possible temper on her part, will put a stop to this building * * * What an era is this to America! and how loud the call to vigilance and activity! As we conduct, so will it fare with us and our children." Notwithstanding this prophecy and the spirit which prompted it, and which filled the bosom of every leading man in every colony, Mr. Livingston was of those who believed, that the time for its fulfilment had not arrived, and that the declaration of independence, when made, was premature.

constitution, which had hitherto been deemed the masterpiece of political workmanship. This pamphlet was universally read, and among those who were zealous in the war, obtained, every where, friends to the measure of independence. The belief became general, that a cordial reconciliation with Great Britain was impossible; that, mutual confidence could never be restored; that, reciprocal jealousy, suspicion, and hate, would take place of that affection, indispensably necessary to a beneficial connexion; that, the commercial dependence of America upon Britain, was injurious to the former, which must derive incalculable benefit from full liberty to manufacture her raw material, and to export her products to the markets of the world; that further dependence upon a nation or sovereign, distant three thousand miles, ignorant and regardless of their interests, was intolerable in the present rapidly increasing strength and power of the colonies; that the hazard in prolonging the contest was as great as in the declaration of independence; and that, since the risk of every thing was unavoidable, the greatest good attainable should be made, in common justice and prudence, the reward of success. It was urged, also, with great force, that foreign aid could be more certainly obtained from the rivals of Great Britain, if they felt assured that such aid would tend to the permanent dismemberment of her empire. The bias given by all these forces was confirmed among the people, on finding, that, they were declared to be in a state of rebellion; that foreign mercenaries were employed to forge their chains; that the tomahawk and scalping knife were engaged in the British service; and that their slaves were to be seduced from their masters and armed against them.

II. The measures of Congress during this remarkable contest, took their complexion from the temper of the people. Their proceedings against those disaffected to their cause became more vigorous; their language relative to the British government, less that of subordinate states—general letters of marquè and reprisal were granted, and the ports were opened to all nations not subject to the British crown. At length, the great and important step of independence was in effect, though not in form, taken. On the 15th May, 1776, Congress declared, that his Britannic Majesty, with the lords and commons, had, by act of Parliament, excluded the united colonies from the protection of the crown; that, not only had their humble petition for redress and reconciliation been received with disdain, but the whole force of the kingdom, aided by foreign mercenaries, was about to be exerted for their destruction; that, therefore, it was irreconcilable with reason and good conscience for the colonists to take the oaths for supporting any government under the crown of Great Britain; and it was necessary that the exercise of every kind of authority under the crown should be suppressed, and that all the powers of government should be exercised by the people of the colonies for the preservation of internal peace, virtue, and good order, and the defence of their lives, liberties, and properties, against the hostile invasions and cruel depredations of their enemies. And they resolved, "That it be recommended to the respective Assemblies and conventions of the united colonies, where no government sufficient to the exigencies of their affairs has been hitherto established, to adopt such government as shall, in the opinions of the representatives of the people, best conduce to the happiness and safety of their constituents in particular, and America in general."

This was virtually a declaration of independence. It was such almost in terms. The renunciation of allegiance to the British crown, and the establishment of governments by the authority of the people, were made, certainly, with no hope of reconciliation, nor desire of re-union with the parent state. When Massachusetts asked advice of Congress on the propriety of "taking up and exercising the powers of civil government,"* they recommended such regulations, only, as were indispensable, and those to be conformed as nearly as possible to the spirit of their charter, and to endure no longer than until a governor of his Majesty's appointment should consent to govern the colony according to that instrument. This was in perfect accord with the professions of the colonies of respect and attachment, and dependence on Great Britain. But the resolution now adopted spoke not of limitation to the powers to be assumed by the people, neither as to their nature nor duration.

In seeking redress from British taxation, and denying to Parliament the right for its unlimited exercise, great unanimity had prevailed. The old parties forgot their animosities, and united to oppose a common oppression. Whilst bound with the band of loyalty to the King, this union appeared indissoluble, but when armed resistance became necessary, still more, after it had commenced, strong repulsive qualities discovered themselves in the mass. The Quakers, opposed to every form of war, and strongly attached to the parent state, and to their church, and family connexions therein, shrunk with deep sensibility from the unnatural contest, and with horror from permanent separation and independence. The royal officers, their dependents and connexions, embracing a large proportion of the wealthy and distinguished of the province, beheld in a change of government the loss of official emolument and influence. The great body of the people, however, led by enterprising spirits, who were not only impatient of oppression, but who saw even in the vicissitudes of war the excitement they loved, and in independence successfully maintained, bright visions of glory and wealth, hailed with rapture the recommendation of Congress to take the first irrevocable step towards political emancipation.

For these parties names were borrowed from English politics. The devotees of American freedom and independence assumed the title of ***whigs***, whilst they designated their opponents by that of ***tories***.

III. The provincial Congress of New Jersey, elected on the fourth Monday in May, pursuant to the ordinance of the preceding Congress, convened at Burlington on the 10th of June, 1776, and was organized by choosing Samuel Tucker, Esq. president, and William Patterson, Esq. secretary. Before the 21st of that month, many petitions were received from East Jersey, for and against the formation of a new government; and on the day last mentioned, the convention resolved, that a government be formed for regulating the internal police of the colony, pursuant to the recommendation of the continental Congress, of the 15th of May, by a vote of 54, against three members. Messrs. Green, Cooper, Jonathan D. Sergeant, Lewis Ogden, Jonathan Elmer, Hughes, Covenhoven, Symmes, Condict, and Dick, were appointed a committee to prepare a constitution on the 24th of June, who reported a draught on the 26th, which, after a very short and imperfect consideration, was confirmed on the 2d day of July.

At this time Congress, impelled by the tide of public opinion, had gone far beyond their resolutions of the 15th of May; and had, actually, resolved on declaring the colonies independent states, thereby severing forever, all political ties which had connected them with Great Britain. Yet, the convention of New Jersey was not disposed to abandon all hopes of accommodation; providing in the last clause of their constitution, that if reconciliation between her and the colonies should take place, and the latter be again taken under the protection and government of the crown, the charter should be null and void. This door of retreat was kept open by the fears of the president of the convention, who, in a few months after, claimed the clemency of the

* June, 1775.

enemy, with whom this clause gave him an interest.* Other clauses of the constitution show also, that it was made for the colony. The laws were to be enacted, and all commissions, writs, and indictments, were to be in the name of the *colony*. On the 18th of July, 1776, the provincial Congress assumed the title of the "convention of the *state* of New Jersey." And after the declaration of independence, in practice, the commissions and writs ran in the name of the *state*, the indictments concluded against the peace of the *state*, and an act of Assembly of 20th September, 1777, substituted the word, *state*, in all such cases for the word, colony.

The collision between the views of the continental Congress, and the New Jersey convention did not escape the reprobation of some of the members of the latter, who moved to defer the printing of the constitution for a few days, that the last clause might be considered by a full House. The effort, however, was negatived, when not more than half the members were present. It must not hence be inferred, that New Jersey was timid or backward in engaging in the contest. She had kept pace with the foremost, and her spirited conduct was the more meritorious, that it had less of the excitement of immediate interest, inasmuch, as she had yet felt no burthen, and was not irritated by the vexations of commercial restrictions. She had no ships, no foreign commerce. Her instructions to her delegates in Congress, chosen on the 21st of June, empowered them to join in declaring the united colonies independent of Great Britain. The convention consisted of sixty-five members, five from each of the thirteen counties, and on the 2d of July when the motion for reconsidering the last clause was made, there were present only twenty-five members; of whom, Messrs. Camp, Hardenburg, Joseph Holmes, Mott, Sparks, Cooper, Clark, Elmer, Harris, Bowen, Leaming, Shaver, Shinn, Tallman, Fennimore, Shreve, and Covenhoven, voted in the negative. And Messrs. Frelinghausen, Paterson, Mehelm, Josiah Holmes, Ellis, Sergeant, Symmes, and Dick, in the affirmative. Had the House been full on this vote, the adoption of the constitution would have, probably, been delayed, and the character of an independent state, at once fearlessly assumed.

IV. This instrument is styled in the proceedings of the convention, and within itself, a constitution. But it is not such, in the present political sense of this word, in America. A constitution of government may now be defined, a written expression of the will of the people of a state, establishing and limiting unalterably, except by themselves, the political powers therein created. Or it may be deemed a power of attorney from the people to their agents, specifying, distinctly, the powers assigned to each.† The constitution and the government are frequently confounded, and treated as synonymous; whereas, they are essentially different; the former being the creator and the law of the latter. The difference between them is not less, than that, between the whole power of the people, and that of their special delegates. Every country has a government, but few have a constitution. The government in England, is by king, lords, and commons, but that nation has no constitution; that is, no instrument restraining the political omnipotence of those agents. No act of theirs can be compared with a designation of their powers, and be thereby corrected or annulled. But, whatever they may do, however oppressive and arbitrary, has necessarily the authority of law. A constitution may create any form of government—may give any quantum of power, less than the whole; for if it give the whole, it destroys itself. And such is the defect,

* Votes of Assembly, 1776.

‡ It might be objected, that the convention which framed the constitution, exceeded their powers, or had, in fact, no power to touch the subject—that they mistook in supposing themselves *the people*, and that it is essential to the existence of a constitution, that the people should formally and expressly pass upon it. But acquiescence must be deemed assent.

and such has been, partially, the fate, of the constitution of New Jersey. The only restriction it contains, upon the agents to which it gave being, is found in the twenty-third article, requiring each member of Council and Assembly, to declare, upon oath or affirmation, that he will "not assent to any law, vote or proceeding, which shall appear to him injurious to the public welfare; *nor that shall annul or repeal that part of the third section of the charter, which establishes, that, the elections of members of the legislative Council and Assembly, shall be annual; nor that part of the twenty-second section, respecting the trial by jury; nor that shall annul, repeal or alter the eighteenth and nineteenth sections;*" which relate to the freedom of religious worship. This specification of things, which the Legislature shall not alter, admits its power to change all others, and puts within its control, the whole form of the government, with the partition of its powers.

The powers of government are commonly divided into the legislative, executive and judicial branches; though the third is but a modification of the second, since the making and executing the laws, comprise the whole duty of every government. Most of the constitutions of the States of North America, define the manner in which these branches shall be constituted, the powers they shall, respectively, exercise, and protect each against the other. But, by the constitution of New Jersey, the executive, and judiciary powers, may be remodelled in any way. The office of governor may be vested in an individual for life, or made hereditary—the judges may be appointed for months, for years, or for life—their number be increased or diminished, and their compensation varied, and the courts continued or abolished, at the pleasure of the Assembly—in a word, all the ordinate branches are dependent on, and at the mercy of, the legislative. And, with the very inconsiderable restrictions already noticed, the whole power of the people, for all purposes, is in the hands of their representatives; who are, thus created universal and not special agents, and have no law but their own will.

We have seen with what extraordinary haste this instrument was formed. Less than two days were employed by the committee in framing, and less than six days by the convention, in considering and confirming, the government of the state. This would be deemed extraordinary and unprofitable haste, at the present day, when political science is more generally understood, the several powers more orderly classified, and models of tried constitutions abound. At that period, resort could be had to two models, only, of free government—those of England, and her colonies. In both, the powers of the state were divided between the king, or his representatives, and the representatives of the people. But most of the powers which had been exercised by the royal governors, were held by this convention to have been taken from the people, and were, by it, restored to their representatives; doubtless, in the conviction, that, they were thereby restored to the people. The government of Great Britain was deemed too exceptionable to copy from; and its hereditary executive and hereditary branch of the Legislature, were not congenial with the habits and wishes of the people.

By the constitution of New Jersey, the legislative power is vested in an assembly and council, annually elected by, and from, the people.

The council is composed of one representative from each county. This allotment seems based upon no political principle. It has regard, neither to extent of territory, nor amount of population; but would seem to be, wholly, arbitrary.

The *minimum* number of the Assembly, was fixed at thirty-nine. Three members were given to each county, with a like disregard of territorial extent and population. But the Legislature was empowered to diminish the number or proportion of the representatives in the Assembly for any county.

The qualification for a member of the Legislature is, that he should be for one whole year, before his election, an inhabitant and freeholder of the county in which he is chosen.—If for council, that he should be worth one thousand pounds.—If for the Assembly, five hundred pounds, in real or personal estate. Neither mature age, nor citizenship, nor oath of allegiance, are required from the law-giver of the land. But notwithstanding the constitution has thus defined the qualification of the representative, the Legislature, exercising the power which it unquestionably possesses, but which would not pertain to it, if the constitution were obligatory upon it, have declared, that no alien should hold office; and that every officer shall take a prescribed oath of allegiance. And it has, thus, by the requisition of qualifications not prescribed by the constitution, added to the instrument.

That the Legislature may be preserved as much as possible from all suspicion of corruption, no judge, sheriff, or other person possessed of any post of profit, under the government, other than justices of the peace, may sit in the Assembly. But, on taking his seat, his office is vacated. This restriction does not extend to the council, and was borrowed from the provincial laws.

The electors are required to be of full age, worth fifty pounds, clear estate, and to have resided within the county for twelve months previous to the election. This qualification also, has been found in practice too broad; admitting all inhabitants, bond and free, white or black, male or female, native or foreign, citizen or alien; and the Legislature has again exercised its power, over the constitution, by limiting, more narrowly, the qualification of electors; declaring that no person shall vote in any state or county election, unless he be a free white male citizen of the state.

The property qualification required in the electors and elected, is a striking, because the only aristocratic, feature in the constitution. It is copied from the law of the colony, and was introduced, probably, into the constitution, by proprietary influence, which still prevailed in both sections of the province. But the people having since condemned the restriction, the Legislature has removed it from the electors, by declaring, that, every person who shall, in other respects, be entitled to a vote, and who shall have paid a tax for the use of the county, or state, and whose name shall be enrolled on any duplicate list of the last state or county tax, shall be adjudged by the officers conducting the election, to be worth fifty pounds. In practice, the property qualification of the elected, is almost wholly disregarded. Under the royal government, a freehold estate was required in the voter. In the convention, an effort was made to give this franchise to all who paid taxes, and the qualification required by the constitution was probably a composition between the parties.

The Assembly has power, under the constitution, to choose its officers—to judge of the qualification and election of its members—to sit upon its own adjournments—prepare bills—and to empower the speaker to convene the members when necessary. Like powers are given to the council; except, that, it may not alter any money bill. In this restriction, we have a striking evidence of the haste, and confusion of ideas, under which the constitution was framed. In the British government, the right to grant money is claimed, exclusively, by the commons, because the other branches of the Legislature are presumed to have an interest, and to be subject to an influence, foreign to the mass of the people. The principle was adopted in the colonies, and the right of framing money bills reserved to the Assembly, for the same cause;—the governor and council being creations of the crown. But the reason ceasing, wholly, with the change of government, the rule should have ceased, also. The members of council, in their relation to the people, differ in nothing from the members of the Assembly. They are not like the senators of the United States, the representatives of territorial divisions; removed in a degree from the people by the mode of their creation, and less responsible by the length of the term of office; but are annually elected, by the same electors, at the same time, and in practice, from the same class, as the members from the lower House. By the letter of the constitution a distinction is made. More property is requisite to qualify them for office. But this distinction makes them safer guardians of the public purse, because it gives them a deeper interest in it.

The Assembly and council have power to make the great seal:—They are required to meet, separately, on the second Tuesday next after the day of election; and the consent of both Houses is necessary to every law.—Seven form a quorum of the council; and no law can pass, unless there be a majority of all the representatives of each body, personally present, and agreeing thereto.

The council and Assembly, in joint meeting, are empowered to elect the governor, annually, by a majority of votes, at their first meeting after each annual election; to elect, in the same manner, the judges of the supreme and inferior courts, justices of the peace, clerks of courts, the attorney general, the secretary of state, the treasurer, and all general and field officers of militia.

It is now a settled principle of political science, that, the legislative and executive powers of government ought not to be in the same hands. That government in which they are blended is a *tyranny* in proportion to the extent of the amalgamation; because, responsibility for the execution of the laws is, proportionately, destroyed. Where the whole of the legislative and executive powers are vested in the same person or persons, the government is despotic; and it may be the despotism of the one, or of the many. Every executive act may be a new volition of the legislative power, and the law may, nay, will be, changeable and uncertain; and ofttimes never proclaimed, never known, until its execution. In the classification of powers, that of appointing the expounders and the subordinate executors of the law, is properly assigned to the executive branch of the government, co-ordinate with, and independent of, the Legislature; but the difficulty of producing a prompt and adequate responsibility, of the executive to the people, has, in practice, occasioned various restrictions on the exercise of this power. When the Legislature appoints these officers, it assumes the functions of the executive. But experience would seem to teach us, that the danger of corrupt administration is equal, where the ministrative or judicial officer depends, for the tenure of his office, upon the chief executive, or upon the legislative Assembly. The corruption most common, and most to be dreaded, in popular governments, is subservience to party spirit. Thus, we daily see officers dependent upon the will of a single headed executive, a council of appointment, or a legislative assembly, changing their opinions, modelling their conduct, or losing their offices, with the mutations of party—following all its phases, or buried in the obscurity of forgetfulness. To preserve the Legislature, whose purity is indispensable to the public weal, from every temptation, to act under any other influence, than that of sound reason and discretion, it should have, neither the power to appoint, nor remove, any other, than such officers, as are necessary to the exercise of its functions. It is, wisely, objected, that the power of appointment should not be exercised by a body composed of several individuals; because responsibility for its deeds is diminished or destroyed, by comminution; and because consociated assemblies, every where, take a latitude in morals, from which unprotected, unsupported individuals, would shrink with dismay. If such power be vested in an individual, although he be not elevated above the temptation to abuse it, he is not only legally responsible for its improper exercise, but he stands constantly before the tribunal of public opinion, and may be instantly arraigned for malversation in this, as in every other department of his office; and when the continuance of the appointee in office, is independent of the will of the appointor, it would seem, that, the constitution, in this particular, possesses all practical guarantees for honest administration.

But the constitution of New Jersey vests in the legislative power, to an alarming degree, all the powers of government. Thus, the incumbents of chief executive offices, including the judiciary, are not only dependent upon the Legislature, for their commissions, but for the amount of their salaries, which is subject to enlargement, or diminution, at its pleasure. The placemen, therefore, moved by ambition or avarice, whether governor, judges, secretary, treasurer, clerks, or chief officers of the army, are the creatures of the Assembly, not of the people; receiving from it, life and daily sustenance, and following it, as the sunflower does the sun, whatever be its course. Officers actuated by such motives, are always attainable; and when the Legislature may be corruptly influenced, its power will be despotic in the direct or indirect exercise of all the functions of the government. If the constitution were, indeed, the supreme law of the land, unchangeable by the Legislature, it would present, in the prescribed tenure of office for some of the officers, a check upon legislative influence. Thus, judges of the Supreme Court, hold their offices for seven—judges of the inferior courts, justices of the peace, clerks of courts, the attorney-general, and secretary, for five years. But the Legislature may alter the constitution, in this, as in other particulars, and make the term of office in these cases annual, as in case of the governor and treasurer; or at will, as in the case of the principal militia officers.*

* The following is given, by Judge Griffiths, as the actual result, in the state, of this commingling of powers. We cannot of our own knowledge, vouch for the truth of the picture, but it has sufficient verisimilitude.

"One of the most threatening effects of the connexion of the legislative and executive in the *same* body, is its apparent tendency to corrupt the Legislature.

"*First.* By placing the power of filling the offices of government in the Legislature, and permitting the choice from their own body, a temptation of the most direct kind is offered to their virtue: offices will be erected for no other purpose, but to gratify the expectations or promote the private ends of popular and ambitious leaders in the Assembly.

"*Second.* But the most pernicious effect of this executive power in the Legislature, is seen in the intrigues and party purposes, which it promotes and cherishes in a body, that ought to be free from every local and every interested consideration.

"It is impracticable here to enter into a detail of facts, to prove, that the virtue of the Legislature has been, and will be, constantly assailed and overcome, by committing to it the nomination and appointment of the executive officers. It shows itself in the very formation of the Legislature. No sooner does an election for a legislative assembly and council approach, than the question is not, who are the wisest and most disinterested, and of most integrity; but who will best answer the views of *party*, of private ambition, or personal resentment. In every county, there will be constantly a succession of people aspiring to appointments, civil or military: some desire to be judges, some justices, some majors, and some colonels; some have interests depending in the courts of law, and some perhaps have resentments against existing officers, and would fain oust them from their seats: all these, and a thousand more passions, are set to work, parties are formed, and nominations to the Legislature will be directed and supported, upon principles altogether beside those, which should form the basis for a right election of legislative characters; the result must, of course, be unfavourable to the public good. But this is not all;—not only are elections rendered vicious, and the morals of the people corrupted in these struggles for personal advantages, but unhappily the candidates partake of the contamination They must promise

By the constitution the governor has the supreme executive power; is captain-general of all the militia and other military force; is chancellor, and ordinary and surrogate-general; and as president of council, is judge of the court of appeals, in the last resort; presides in council, and has a casting vote in their proceedings. The council choose a vice-president, who acts as president, and governor, in the absence of the governor; and any three members of the council, are at all times a privy council, to advise the governor, in all cases where he may find it necessary to consult them.

Whilst the proper powers of the executive are given to the Legislature, the governor is oppressed with various heterogeneous duties, which have been conferred upon him; not because he is the proper organ for their exercise, but because the members of the convention were habituated to behold them lodged with the colonial governors; who engrossed them, that they might increase their emoluments. As chancellor, surrogate, and president of the court of appeals, the governor is a high judicial officer, and as such, gives decisions, which as an executive officer, he may be called upon to enforce. As the president of council, he has a potential voice and influence in legislation, and, thus, exercises, in a limited degree, to be sure, all the powers of government. Thus, in another of its branches, the government assumes the essence of tyranny. This combination of powers, might prove very dangerous, were not the governor so ephemeral in his existence, that he has not space, in his official life, to mature and effectuate a plot; and is wholly dependent upon the Legislature for his compensation, which is, not uncommonly, a principal mean of his subsistence. But, he is not deterred from making his powers subservient to the dominant party of the Legislature,

allegiance to their party—you shall be a judge, and you a justice—you a major, and you a colonel—you a clerk, and you a commissioner, I will solicit your cause in the court of errors, and will vote for your friend to fill a seat in the judiciary. Thus the executive authorities confided to an annual legislature, lay the foundation of corruption at the threshold of its election; instead of being elected with a national view, and for the purpose of forming general laws, for the more equal and salutary government of the people, the persons go there to represent the interests and gratify the desires of a few partisans in their different districts, upon the performance of which will depend their reappointment at the ensuing election!

"When the Legislature is formed, and a joint meeting agreed upon, then begins a scene of intrigue, of canvassing and finesse, which baffles all description, and is too notorious to require proof, and too disgusting for exhibition. The members of a county, in which an office is to be disposed of, are beset by friends and partisans of the candidates; their hopes and fears are excited, by all the arts which can be suggested to influence their choice; from these, the attack extends itself, till it reaches every member of the Legislature; and so strong and so general does the contest become, by the different representations, having each particular objects to attain, that one grand scene of canvass and barter ensues; a vote for one, is made the condition of voting for another, without regard to qualifications; even laws which are to affect the public interest, are made the price of these interested concessions; and not unfrequently almost the whole sitting of the Legislature is spent in adjusting the pretensions, and marshalling the strength of the respective candidates for office. To such a pitch has this grown, that even the members of the Legislature complain of it, as an intolerable evil. These contests again, lay the foundation for new parties and new resentments at the next election. To counteract the opposition which may be stirred up, all the appointments will be made, with a view to strengthen the interest of the sitting members. New commissions, civil and military, judges and justices, general officers, general staff and field officers, will be made with a reference to the state of parties in the county, instead of being dictated by quite a contrary spirit.

"The result of all this, is seen and felt in every quarter. From hence proceed the jars and divisions which destroy the pleasures of social life in every neighbourhood and village; and from hence arises the instability of laws, the multiplication of magistrates, the weakness and divisions of the courts of justice, the heats and ill-directed zeal at elections, and that general languor and dereliction of principle in every department, which menaces the total depravation of the body politic."—*Eumenes*, pp. 130—132.

and thus to submit himself to a corrupt influence. There is another point of view in which this commingling of powers is prejudicial to the state. It demands qualities for their execution, which are so rarely found in the same individual, as to seem incompatible. The qualifications for a commander-in-chief, are not those of the legislator, much less those of the judge.

It is not the fault of the constitution of New Jersey, alone, to vest in the chief executive officer, a portion of the legislative power. It is done by the constitution of the United States, and by many of the states, with an expediency, which daily experience renders less than doubtful. The feature is borrowed from the English government, where its chief use is to preserve the prerogative of the King, against the encroachments of the people.

The inferior executive officers, beside those abovenamed, who are created by the constitution, are a sheriff, and one or more coroners, elected, annually, from each county; who are eligible three years, successively, but after which, not again for three years;—and a constable, and commissioners of appeal, in case of taxation, also, annually elected in each township.

But in no particular, is the imperfection of this constitution more visible, than in its provisions relative to the judiciary. Neither the courts nor the number of judges which shall respectively constitute them, are determined by it. The power is given to appoint the judges of the Supreme Court, and of the inferior courts of Common Pleas, of the several counties. These courts, and the chancery, were established by an ordinance of the King, recognised and confirmed by the acts of Assembly, and are continued under the new constitution, by articles twelve and twenty-two; declaring, that all the laws contained in Allinson's edition, and the common law of England, and so much of the statute law, as had been theretofore practised, shall continue in full force, until altered by the Legislature; such parts only excepted, as were incompatible with the charter. If any difference of opinion may exist, relative to the power of the Legislature over the constitution, there can be none, as to their power over the laws;—consequently, they may alter or abolish, all or either of the courts, at their pleasure; and therefore the constitution has made no provision for the permanence of the judiciary. The fixed term of office of the judges, supposing the constitution unalterable by the Legislature, becomes no protection to their independence, since the laws upon which the courts depend, may be repealed, and the commissions of the judges fall with them. Of the manner in which the courts are at present constituted, there are many seemingly well founded complaints, which it is no part of our province to examine or to judge. But we may remark, with regard to the Court of Chancery, that we cannot conceive, of a worse organization, than that, by which the highest law officer of the state, is not only subject to annual change, but is actually and repeatedly changed from year to year. The judge has no inducement to qualify himself for the duties of his place, since his labour will not be rewarded; and the business of the court must be ignorantly, slovenly and sluggishly executed, inasmuch, as more than one chancellor may frequently intervene between the hearings of the same cause.*

* For the manner in which the system of the inferior courts works, we refer the reader to the following remarks of Judge Griffiths—observing that the judges of these courts are without limit as to number, have not a professional education, and receive no compensation, save some inconsiderable bench fees.

"Let any man go into a county court in New Jersey, and one hour's observation will satisfy him, that it is neither a place of common sense, nor of common justice. He will see disputes maintained with great heat and prolixity, on questions which none would hear debated, but those who feel difficulty in every thing, from their total ignorance of every thing, of a legal complexion; he will see the most preposterous decisions, after those preposterous pleadings; he will see cause after cause

The judges and other officers, chosen by the Assembly, are commissioned by the governor, and may be reappointed at the end of their several terms, and dismissed when adjudged guilty of misbehaviour, by the council, on impeachment of the Assembly.

By article ninth, the governor and council, (seven whereof shall be a quorum,) form the Court of Appeals, in the last resort, in all cases at law, as theretofore; and have power to grant pardons to criminals, after condemnation. By statute, this court has also been made the Court of Appeals in equity cases.

This feature is also copied from the colonial government, in which, it was analogous, somewhat, to the judicial power of the House of Lords; with this important and extraordinary difference, that in England, the executive, or the King, is not a member of the court; and the court there, is always aided by the great law officers of the state, and guided by their collected wisdom and learning. Whilst in New Jersey, the executive forms a part of the court, and the court consisting of members annually chosen, and perhaps annually changed, whose education and pursuits do not qualify them to determine legal questions, sits to revise—and perhaps, to reverse decisions given under the best lights of the land.*

The 18th and 19th articles of the constitution, which are exempted from the power of the Legislature, provide, that no person shall be deprived of the privilege of worshipping Almighty God, in a manner agreeable to the dictates of his own conscience, nor under any pretence, compelled to attend any place of worship contrary to his own faith and judgment, nor be obliged to pay tithes, taxes, or any other rates, for the purpose of building or repairing any church, or place of worship, or for the maintenance of any minister or ministry, contrary to what he believes to be right, or has deliberately or voluntarily engaged himself to perform.

"That there shall be no establishment of any one religious sect, in preference to another; and that no *protestant* inhabitant shall be denied the enjoyment of any civil right, merely on account of his religious principles; but, that all persons professing a belief in *the faith of any protestant sect*, who shall demean themselves peaceably under the government, shall be capable of being elected into any office of profit or trust, or being a member of either

torn by piecemeal from their foundations; the judges perplexed or dismayed with every trifling occurrence, upon which a legal doubt arises; he will see the judges divided in opinion, looking round for help; and finally, he will see the business of the session abandoned where it began, and put off upon frivolous pretexts to a more convenient season; and when he has seen this at one court, at one term, he will have a very accurate sample of the dignity and ability, which pervades the judiciary system of his enlightened country. Those who are best acquainted with the subject of this description, will allow that it is not exaggerated; they know that there is little dignity, and less ability in most of the courts, to which their professional pursuits call them; they know, it is sometimes a subject of ridicule, and oftener of serious regret, that the judges, instead of knowing the laws better than those who advocate them, are generally ignorant of first principles, and instead of *directing* business with that manly confidence, which is always the attendant of knowledge, they are *led* away by their deference to professional eminence, perhaps by the fallacious sophistry of a concluding harangue. Far be it from me to apply this indiscriminately; there are exceptions; and still farther it is from me, to place this general defection in the judiciary, to a depravity of personal character; quite the contrary. It would be difficult to find more private integrity in any equal number of men; but no qualities of the heart, can compensate for the want of knowledge in any science; and in that of the law, however paradoxical it may seem, mere goodness of heart is a dangerous propensity."—*Eumenes*, pp. 107, 108.

* Members of the bar are frequently elected to council. To them, of course, the foregoing remark is not applicable. An increase of business in this court, would probably render it as necessary to have the councillors all lawyers, as it is that the governor should be one.

branch of the Legislature, and shall fully and freely enjoy every privilege and immunity enjoyed by others, their fellow subjects."

This last clause, much less liberal than were the Concessions of the proprietaries, stands a monument of British intolerance; for it is modelled on the laws of England, excluding Catholics from office; yet whilst in Great Britain this intolerance has ceased, it is continued here, and the Catholic christian, together with all who do not profess a belief in the faith of a Protestant sect, are excluded from full participation in civil rights. This restriction is far behind the age, and calls loudly for removal; although, to the honour of the state, in no instance, has it been enforced. Yet, it is a foul blot on the polity of the country.

By the 16th article of the constitution, all criminals were admitted to the same privileges of witness and counsel, as the prosecutor; and by the 18th, the estates of persons destroying their own lives, and chattels occasioning, accidentally, the death of any one, are declared not to be subject to forfeiture.

We have thus given all the provisions of the existing constitution, with a running commentary upon its leading features, in which the deficiency of the instrument, as a constitution, has been chiefly considered. Compared with what such an instrument should be, it has many faults of expediency, which have been frequently noticed by eminent citizens of the state; some of which have been, and others may be, amended, by the Legislature. But as a constitution, the instrument is radically defective; first, that it is not obligatory upon the Legislature, but may be, as it has been, altered, by the power which makes the ordinary law; second, that it does not separate and define the powers of the several departments of the government; and third, that it has made every department subject to, and dependent upon, the Legislature. Consequently a despotic power lies in that body, which may be abused to party purposes, and to the subversion of political liberty. That this power has been so abused, is not less certain, than that every cause in action must produce its appropriate effect. That such abuses have not been intolerable, may be ascribed first, to the want of opportunity of working extensive evil; for no great convulsion of the people has yet arisen, in which individuals could advance their interests, by the utter subversion of established principles, and drawing to themselves as members of the Assembly, the actual exercise of all political power; although a continued assumption of such power might, perhaps, be traced in the Legislature, from the establishment of the state government: 2dly, To the restraining power of public opinion, enlightened by that political science, which sends more or less of its rays into every part of our country, and to which the annual election of the members of the Legislature makes them amenable. But, that the state is subject to all the evils which may result from an unlimited and indefinite government, is as unquestionable, as that the man who dwells beneath the impending avalanche, or on the slumbering volcano, is exposed to destruction from the fall of the one, or irruption of the other. That he has not already been overwhelmed, can be no protection against the next convulsion of nature.

The transition from a provincial to an independent state, was made with as little pain and confusion, at the moment, as a modification might now be effected in an American state, where the sense of a majority of the people, forms the unresisted law. A simple resolution of the convention, "that the judges, justices of the peace, sheriffs, coroners, and other inferior officers of the late government, proceed in the execution of the several offices under the authority of the people, until the intended Legislature, and the several officers of the new government should be settled and perfected, having respect to the present constitution, and the orders of the provincial Congresses; and that all suits of law should be continued, altering only the style and form thereof," was sufficient to continue without much embarrassment, the whole machinery of society.

V. After the adoption of the constitution, the provincial Congress, proceeded by an ordinance, to carry it into effect. The second section of the charter appointed the second Tuesday in August, for the election of the members of the Legislature, sheriffs, and coroners. The ordinance ascertained the places and manner of election, and created a new qualification for the members of council and Assembly, and for the electors, which may be considered the second violation of the constitution just established; requiring, from the voter and member, respectively, an oath or affirmation, that he did not hold himself bound to bear allegiance to George the Third, King of Great Britain, and would not by any means, directly or indirectly, oppose the measures adopted by the colony, or the continental Congress, against the tyranny attempted to be established over the colonies by the Court of Great Britain; but would bear true allegiance to the government established in the colony, under the authority of the people. The council and Assembly, when elected, were directed to meet, the first time, at Princeton.

VI. The period of the revolution has been termed the "*time for trying men's souls*;" and this was emphatically true, at the moment of declaring independence. The unanimity with which resistance against the measures of the parent state had been continued, was then broken. The timid, the interested, and the conscientious, were alike unwilling to sever irreparably, the ties which connected them with her. The professions of loyalty and dependence, were sincerely made by a large majority of the provincialists, and they were adhered to by many, with religious tenacity, who truly believed that political happiness and salvation existed, only, in the British empire. The timid, and especially the timid rich, shrunk from the disgrace and pains of treason—the placeman, and the expectant of place, who looked upon the rising sun, struggling amid clouds as a portentous, but evanescent, meteor, could not turn from the rays of meridian splendour, in which they had long lived or hoped to bask; whilst others united with their fellow subjects of the European isles, by the tenderest charities of blood and affinity, of tastes and business, could not summon resolution to break connexions, which were the great pleasures of their existence. The wonder, therefore, is not that a great many valuable men preserved their loyalty and became distinguished as tories; but, that the declaration of independence had not more equally divided the country. But there was, also, a class of men of desperate character, opposed to American independence, who, confident in the strength and success of Great Britain, availed themselves of her protection to prey upon the country, and under pretence of loyalty and readiness to punish treason, to gratify their own malignant passions, their foul revenge, and cupidity. Bands of these marauders soon haunted the forests and shores of the eastern part of the state, particularly of Monmouth, and the mountains of Morris and Sussex counties; breaking out from time to time, and doing far greater evil, than the regular inimical soldiery. New York, one of the largest, richest, and most powerful of the royal colonies, was the most divided on the question of independence. The tories, there protected by the English forces, were numerous, wealthy, and active; they had many friends, relatives, and dependents in East Jersey, over whom they exercised a dangerous influence. During the whole interval from the commencement of hostilities until the treaty of peace, New Jersey was a frontier state, and exposed to all the miseries of border warfare; at one time, the enemy lay upon her northern and southern boundaries, and her losses in proportion to her wealth and population, were probably greater than those of any other state, save South Carolina.

Upon the arrival of the British army in 1776, the disaffected in New York and New Jersey, were embodied under officers selected from among themselves. Mr. Oliver Delancey, an influential officer of the late government, in New York, was appointed brigadier-general, and empowered to raise three battalions, to consist of fifteen hundred men. But, notwithstanding great exertions on his part, his command did not exceed six hundred. Mr. Courtlandt Skinner, late attorney-general, and speaker of the Assembly of New Jersey, his brother, the late treasurer, who had recently been received in the council, and every member of that family, adhered to the enemy. Courtlandt was, also, appointed a brigadier, and directed to raise two thousand five hundred men, but he could rarely bring into the field more than five hundred.

VII. With the assumption of independent sovereignty, came the duty of supporting it, by the denunciation of the pains and penalties of treason, against such as should attempt its overthrow. An ordinance of the 18th of July, 1776, therefore, prescribed, that, all persons abiding within the state, deriving protection from its laws, owed allegiance to its government, and were members of its community; and, that, sojourners receiving like protection, owed like allegiance whilst within its limits; that all persons, so owing allegiance, who should levy war against, and within, the state, or be adherent to the King of Great Britain, or others, the enemies of the state within the same, or to the enemies of the United States of North America, giving them aid or comfort, should be adjudged guilty of high treason, and suffer the pains thereof (death) as by the ancient laws. This act transmitted the cases of disaffected residents, *en masse*, to the ordinary tribunals.

VIII. To those opposed to the rising order of things, the loyalty of Governor Franklin afforded countenance. The torrent of public opinion was too strong, for him to attempt to turn its course, and he was compelled to stand by, an almost idle spectator, whilst it swept away all the powers and services which, lately, pertained to him; but which he was not disposed to abandon without an effort for their maintenance. Before the resolution to establish a new government had been formally adopted, by this state, the whole political power had passed, by the voice of the people, to their delegates in Convention; which became the government *de facto;* and the powers flowing from royal authority, were suspended by the exercise of those derived from the people. This, however, was a conclusion which the governor was very unwilling to attain, and he resolved to determine whether it were indeed true, by attempting to collect and set in action the component parts of his Majesty's government. Could this be effected, a powerful effort might yet be made in the royal cause; and whatever might be the final result, disunion and distraction in the proceedings of the state would be inevitable. Of the thirty members of Assembly, seven, only, were members of the Convention; and the governor may, probably, have supposed, as some of the former body were distinguished royalists, that he might array one popular Assembly against another. He, therefore, by proclamation of the thirtieth of May, summoned the House, in the name of the King, to meet on the twentieth of June. The provincial Congress, instantly, foresaw the mischief of this measure, and prepared to defeat it. On the fourth of the last month, they resolved, by a vote of thirty-eight to eleven, that the proclamation of William Franklin, late governor, ought not to be obeyed; and on the sixteenth, by a vote of thirty-five to ten, that, by such proclamation, he had acted in direct contempt, and violation, of the resolve of the continental Congress of the fifteenth of May; had discovered himself to be an enemy to the liberties of the country; and that, measures should be immediately taken to secure his person:—And by a vote of forty-seven to three, they further resolved, that all payments of money, on account of salary, or otherwise, to him, as governor, should thenceforth cease; and that the treasurers of the *province* should account for the moneys, in their hands, to the *provincial* Congress, or to the future Legislature of the colony.

Immediately upon the adoption of these resolutions, the Congress issued the following order to Colonel Nathaniel Heard, of the first battalion of the Middlesex county militia. "The provincial Congress of New Jersey, reposing great confidence in your zeal and prudence, have thought fit to entrust to your care, the execution of the enclosed resolves. It is the desire of Congress, that this necessary business, be conducted with all the delicacy and tenderness which its nature can possibly admit. For this end you will find, among the papers, the form of a written parole, in which there is left a blank space for you to fill up, at the choice of Mr. Franklin, with the name of Princeton, Bordentown, or his own farm at Rancocus. When he shall have signed the parole, the Congress will rely upon his honour, for the faithful performance of his engagements; but should he refuse to sign it, you are desired to put him under strong guard, and keep him in close custody, until further orders. Whatever expense may be necessary will be cheerfully defrayed by the Congress. We refer to your discretion, what means to use for that purpose, and you have full power and authority to take to your aid, whatever force you may require."

On the seventeenth, Colonel Heard and Major Deare, waited on the governor at Amboy, and desired him to comply with the order of Congress, and sign the parole. Upon his refusal, they surrounded his house with a guard of sixty men, and despatched an express to report their proceedings to, and ask further instructions from, the Congress; who commanded, that Mr. Franklin should be immediately brought to Burlington.

In the mean time, Mr. Tucker addressed a letter to Mr. Hancock, president of the continental Congress, in the following terms: "Sir, our colony has, of late, been alarmed with sundry attempts of disaffected persons, to create disturbances. The proclamation of Mr. Franklin, our late governor, for calling together the Assembly, is one of those we have thought deserving the most serious attention. Enclosed, we have sent a copy of certain resolves which we have thought necessary to pass on the occasion, together with a copy of our instructions to Colonel Heard. We, this minute, received, by express from Colonel Heard, a letter, of which the enclosed is a copy. We have ordered down to this place, Mr. Franklin, under guard; and now beg leave to submit, to the consideration of the Congress, whether it would not be for the general good of the United Colonies, that Mr. Franklin should be removed to some other colony. Congress will easily conceive the reasons of this application, as Mr. Franklin, we presume, would be capable of doing less mischief in Connecticut or Pennsylvania, than in New Jersey. Whatever advice Congress may think proper to give us, we shall be glad to receive; and would further intimate, that the countenance and approbation of the continental Congress, would satisfy some persons who might, otherwise, be disposed to blame us."

President Hancock replied, transmitting the following resolution: "In Congress, June 19th, 1776—Resolved, that it be recommended to the Convention of New Jersey, to proceed on the examination of Mr. Franklin; and if, upon such examination, they should be of opinion, that he should be confined, to report such opinion to this Congress, and then this Congress will direct the place of his confinement; they concurring in sentiment with the Convention of New Jersey, that it would be improper to confine him in that colony."

On the twenty-first of June, Mr. Franklin was, accordingly, called before the provincial council, to be examined, touching such parts of his conduct, as were deemed inimical to the liberties of America. He refused to answer all questions put to him; denying the authority of this body, which he alleged had usurped the King's government in the province. Whereupon, the Congress resolved, that as by this and his former conduct, in many instances, he appeared to be a virulent enemy to this country, and a person who might prove dangerous, he should be confined in such place and manner, as the honourable continental Congress should direct; and that Lieutenant-colonel Bowes Read, should keep him under safe guard, until further order of the continental Congress. That order was received on the twenty-fifth of June, directing that the deposed governor should be sent, under guard, to Governor Trumbull, of Connecticut, who was desired to take his parole, and in case he refused to give it, to treat him agreeably to the resolutions of Congress, respecting prisoners. This request was immediately complied with. On his release, he sailed to England, where he received a pension for his losses.*

IX. Towards the disaffected the conduct of the patriots was, at first, truly lenient. Those taken in arms were treated as prisoners of war; and no other proceeding was had against those not in arms, from whom danger was apprehended, than such as would prevent them from committing the mischief they meditated. Congress had great confidence in the power of reason and gentle treatment, on the presumption, that the disaffected were, generally, the misinformed. Under this impression, resolutions were adopted, second January, 1776, recommending to the several township and county committees, and other friends of American liberty, to explain to the honest and misguided, the nature of the controversy, and the many, but fruitless efforts which had been made to effect an accommodation; but, at the same time, to proceed with vigour, against active partizans from whom danger might be apprehended, disarming them, keeping them in safe custody, or binding them with sufficient sureties to their good behaviour. Strong measures were not, however, immediately taken against them, in those parts of the country where they were the most powerful. In Long and York islands, where General Lee had been stationed, principally, to counteract their machinations, they maintained, even, after the arrival of the commander-in-

* Governor Franklin was born about the year 1731. He was a captain in the French war, and served at Ticonderoga. After the peace of Paris he accompanied his father to England. Going to Scotland he became acquainted with the Earl of Bute, on whose recommendation, to Lord Halifax, he was appointed governor of New Jersey, in 1763; from which time he continued in office, until deposed in the manner above stated. He died in England, November 17th, 1813, aged eighty-two years. By his first wife, a West Indian, he had a son, William Temple Franklin, who edited the works of his grandfather, suppressing, as it is said, at the instance of the British government, some very important memoirs. He died at Paris, May 25th, 1823. Governor Franklin differed, essentially, in temperament from his illustrious father, prefering ease to action, and gained a life of inglorious comfort, by the sacrifice of an eternity of fame. His own conduct and the reputation of his father, had made him respected in New Jersey, and had he joined the popular party, he would, probably, have attained high distinction among American patriots. Governor Franklin, as well as Governors Bernard and Hutchinson, were Americans, and though sons of the soil, their devotion to the parent state, and the royal cause, was right loyal; and such was the effect of the royal favour, on them, as to give us occasion to rejoice, that it had not been more bountifully dispensed among the patriots of 1776. To carry his points in England, Lord North was profusely beneficent. Ten peers, at once, were called up into the English House, and one day, the 22d of July, 1777, saw the Irish peerage reinforced by eighteen new barons, seven barons further secured by being created viscounts, and five viscounts advanced to earldoms. It was, perhaps, happy for America, that, at the dawn of the rebellion, the griefs of the complainants had not been medicated by a patronage like this.

chief, a regular intercourse with Governor Tryon, and devised plans for co-operating with the enemy. When the contest assumed the form of active hostility, disaffection to the American cause took a decided shape, and its enemies united as a party; still numbers followed with the body of their countrymen, and were not distinguishable until the declaration of independence. That measure effectually separated the mass.

Where the previous measures of the continental and local governments had been generally and cordially supported, the public mind was prepared for independence. In New England, Virginia, and South Carolina, there was scarce a dissentient voice. From New York to Maryland, inclusive, the people were more divided. In North Carolina an efficient majority was friendly, but there was a powerful minority, ready to seize the first opportunity to manifest their hostility. Georgia was weak and disunited.

In New York and New Jersey the British were received with open arms, by the disaffected, as their deliverers from oppression. The tories were so numerous, that, as the army advanced into the country, the militia of the islands were embodied for their defence; and these states afforded corps of regulars, equal to their quotas in the American army. Upon taking possession of Long Island, General Howe assured his army, that they were among friends, and prohibited, under the severest penalties, every species of violence.* As he advanced to the White Plains, the state Convention entertained fears of a dangerous insurrection, and seemed apprehensive of an attempt to punish the disaffected, though actually engaged in enlisting men for the British service. Much dread was felt, that they would seize the important passes of the highlands; and it was thought dangerous to march the militia from some of the neighbouring counties for their protection, lest their absence should encourage the loyalists to assemble in arms.

On entering the Jerseys, Lord Cornwallis gave orders similar to those of General Howe, on Long Island. The proclamation, offering protection to those who would come in and take the oaths of allegiance, within sixty days, also, contained assurances, that the obnoxious laws, which had occasioned the war, would be revised. The effect of these measures, with the military success of the enemy, was to extinguish, nearly, the spirit of resistance. A few militia, only, were in arms, under General Williamson; whose indisposition, compelling him to leave the service, they were afterwards commanded by General Dickenson; but the great body of the country was either with the enemy, or had too little zeal for the cause, to hazard their lives and fortunes in its support. When urged to take up arms, they answered, "that General Howe promised them peace, liberty, and safety, and more they could not require."

The articles of association of 1775, may be deemed the entering wedge of division, between the parties in New Jersey, as in other parts of America. Those who refused to sign, or having signed, disobeyed, their requisitions, were held enemies to their country, and as such, were not only denounced by the county and township committees, but were fined and imprisoned, as well by the order of such committees, as by that of the provincial Conventions and committees of safety. Notwithstanding these measures, counter associations were attempted, resolving to pay no tax levied by order of the provincial Congress, nor to purchase any goods distrained for such taxes, or for non-attendance at militia musters. These, and like demonstrations of hostility, induced the committee of safety of the province, on the fifteenth of January, 1776, earnestly to recommend to the several county and town committees, the execution of the resolve of the continental Congress, of the

* For violation of these orders some soldiers were condemned and executed.

second of that month, recommending due moderation and prudence, and requesting all officers of militia to lend their assistance. Under this resolution several persons, from different parts of the state, were brought before the committee of safety, and the provincial Congress, which sat from the thirty-first of January to the second of March, 1776. Most of the prisoners confessed their faults, craved pardon, and were either dismissed unscathed, or subjected to a small pecuniary mulct, and to give security, in various sums, for future good conduct. But with the progress toward independence, the number of the disaffected, increasing rapidly, gave much employment to the provincial Congress, which assembled on the tenth of June; and which framed the state constitution; and their proceedings assumed a greater degree of severity. Memorials, from several counties, complaining of the hostile intentions and proceedings of the disaffected, particularly, in Monmouth, Hunterdon, Bergen, and Sussex, called forth a reiteration of previous instructions to the county committees, and formal summons to the inculpated, to appear before the Convention. On the twenty-sixth of June, that body having intelligence, that there were several insurgents in the county of Monmouth, who took every measure in their power to contravene the regulations of Congress, and to oppose the cause of American freedom, and that it was highly necessary, that an immediate check should be given to so daring a spirit of disaffection, resolved, that Colonel Charles Read should take to his aid, two companies of the militia of the county of Burlington, and proceed, without delay, to the county of Monmouth, to apprehend such insurgents as were designated to him by the president of the Convention. Authentic information was, at the same time, received, that other disaffected persons in the county of Hunterdon had confederated for the purpose of opposing the measures of Congress, and had even proceeded to acts of open and daring violence; having plundered the house of a Captain Jones, beaten, wounded, and otherwise abused the friends of freedom in the county, and publicly declared, that they would take up arms in behalf of the King of Great Britain. In order, effectually, to check a combination so hostile and dangerous, Lieutenant-colonel Abraham Ten Eick and Major Berry were directed, with the militia of the counties of Hunterdon and Somerset, to apprehend these insurgents. On the first of July the provincial Congress resolved, that the several colonels of the counties, should, without delay, proceed to disarm all persons within their district, who, from religious principles, or other causes, refused to bear arms. Two days after the last, an additional order was given to Colonel Charles Read, Lieutenant-colonel Samuel Forman, and Major Joseph Haight, with two hundred militia of Burlington, and two hundred of Monmouth county, to proceed, without delay, to quell an insurrection in Monmouth, and to disarm and take prisoners, whomsoever they should find assembled, with intent to oppose the friends of American freedom; and to take such measures as they should think necessary for this service. On the fourth of July, Congress resolved, that as divers persons, in the county of Monmouth, who had embodied themselves, in opposition to its measures, had expressed their willingness to return to their duty, upon assurances of pardon, alleging, that they have been seduced and misled, by the false and malicious reports of others; such persons as should, without delay, return peaceably to their homes, and conform to the orders of Congress, should be treated with lenity and indulgence, and upon their good behaviour, be restored to the favour of their country; providing, that such as appeared to have been the leaders and principals in these disorders, and who, to their other guilt, had added that of seducing the weak and the unwary, should yet be treated, according to their demerits.

Under these and like resolutions many persons, among whom were several of large property and great respectability, were brought before Congress. Some were imprisoned, some fined, and others suffered to go at large upon their parole; others were compelled to enter into recognizance with security, conditioned for *their good behaviour;* and others were relegated to such places within the province, as the Congress supposed could give them the least opportunity of evil.*

When the state government was organized, under the constitution, the Legislature enacted a law of like tenor, with the ordinance of the convention, against treason;—and further declared, that any one owing allegiance to the state, who should by speech, writing, or open deed, maintain the authority of the King and Parliament of Great Britain, should be subject, by the first offence, to fine, not exceeding three hundred pounds, and imprisonment, not exceeding one year; and for the second, to the pillory, and the like imprisonment;—that reviling, or speaking contemptuously of the government of the state, of the Congress, or United States of America, or of the measures adopted by the Congress, or by the Legislature of the state, or maliciously doing any thing whatever, which would encourage disaffection, or manifestly tend to raise tumults and disorders in the state; or spreading such false rumours, concerning the American forces, or the forces of the enemy, as would tend to alienate the affections of the people from the government, or to terrify or discourage the good subjects of this state, or to dispose them to favour the pretensions of the enemy, should, also, be punishable in the same manner. By the same act, two justices of the peace were empowered to convene by summons or warrant, any person, whom they should suspect to be dangerous or disaffected to the government; and compel him to take the oath of abjuration, and of allegiance, under penalty of being bound with sufficient sureties to his good behaviour, or imprisoned until the meeting of the Quarter Sessions; when, upon refusal, he might be fined or imprisoned, at discretion of the court. This act drew the cords around the discontented much more closely, than they had hitherto been. But it became necessary to strain them still tighter.

An act of June 5th, 1777, declaring, that divers of the subjects of the state, having, by the arts of subtile emissaries from the enemy, been seduced from their allegiance, and prevailed upon by delusive promises, to leave their families and friends, and join the army of the King of Great Britain, and had since become sensible of their error, and desirous of returning to their duty; that many of such fugitives and others, who had been guilty of treasonable practices against the state, secreted themselves to escape the punishment of their crimes—and that, in compassion to their unhappy situation, the Legis-

* We could give a very long list of names of disaffected persons; but we refrain for very obvious reasons. Persons who are curious to revive the remembrance of these scenes, may have recourse to the journals of the convention, and the columns of the newspapers of the period, where they may find many a name which has since been distinguished for good service to the state. We may, however, make the following extract from the minutes of the Congress.—"The petition from sundry ladies, from Perth Amboy, was read the second time, and ordered, that a copy of the following letter, addressed to Mrs. Franklin, one of the subscribers, be signed by the president and secretary—'Madam: I am ordered, by Congress, to acquaint you, and through you, the other ladies of Amboy, that their petition, in favour of Dr. John L——, has been received and considered. Could any application have promised a greater indulgence to Dr. L——, you may be assured yours could not have failed of success. But, unhappily, madam, we are placed in such a situation, that, motives of commiseration to individuals, must give place to the safety of the public. As Dr. L——, therefore, has fallen under the suspicion of our generals, we are under the necessity of abiding by the steps which we have taken;' &c. The doctor was transferred to Morristown, on his parole, not to depart thence, more than six miles, without leave of Congress."

lature was desirous that no means should be left unemployed, to prevent the effusion of blood, and to give those an opportunity of returning to their allegiance, who should testify their desire to be restored to the inestimable rights of freemen. To this end the act provided, That, such offender, on or before the first of August, then next ensuing, might appear before a judge or justice of the peace, and take the oaths to the state; and should, thereupon, be pardoned his offence, and restored to the privileges of a citizen; That, if he were so far lost to every sense of duty to his country, his family, and his posterity, as to decline the clemency so proffered, his personal estate should be forfeited to the state; and all alienations thereof, and of his real estate, subsequent to the act, were declared void; That commissioners should be appointed in the respective counties, to make inventories of such personal estate, to dispose of perishable parts, or where in danger of falling into the hands of the enemy, of the whole; to keep the proceeds for the owner claiming the benefit of the act, but paying the same to the treasurer for the use of the state, in case of the non-claim of the proprietor within the prescribed time.

This act was followed by another of 18th April, 1778, directing the commissioners of the several counties to make return to a justice of the peace, of the name and late place of abode of each person whose personal estate they should seize, and to obtain from the justice a precept for summoning a jury of freeholders, to inquire whether he had, since the date of the act against treason, (4th October, 1776,) and before the 5th June, 1777, joined the army of the King of Great Britain, or otherwise offended against his allegiance to the state. The jury finding against the accused, their inquisition was returned by the justice, to the next court of Common Pleas; where it might be traversed, either at the return, or the succeeding, term, by the party, on entering into recognisance, to prosecute with effect. But in default, judgment of forfeitures was rendered, and the commissioners empowered to sell all the personal estate of the fugitive, and to take possession of all his books of account, bonds, mortgages, &c., in whose hands soever they might be; and to collect all debts due to him. Similar provisions were made, relative to persons committing like offences, subsequent to the act of pardon, of the 5th of June, 1777. The commissioners were, also, empowered to take into their possession and management, all the real estate of the offender, and lease the same for a term not exceeding a year, and to hold possession of such estate, before inquisition found, when it had been abandoned by the owner. Tenants in possession, were required to attorn to the commissioners. All sales of real or personal estate, by any person, against whom inquisition was found, made after the offence committed, were declared void.

This severity was carried still further by the act of December 11th, 1778, directing, that all the real estate of offenders at the time of the offence, or thereafter, acquired, in fee or otherwise, against whom inquisition and judgment had been, or should be, rendered, should be forfeited to the state; and that, every person, whether an inhabitant of this state, or of any other of the United States, seized or possessed of real or personal estate, who had, since the *19th day of April*, 1775, (the day of the battle of Lexington) and before the *4th day of October*, 1776, aided and assisted the enemies of the state, or of the United States, by joining their armies within the state, or elsewhere, or had voluntarily gone to, taken refuge or continued with, or endeavoured to continue with, the enemy, and aid them by council or otherwise, and who had not since returned and become a subject in allegiance to the present government, by taking the prescribed oaths or affirmations when required, to be guilty of high treason, and on inquisition and judgment, his whole estate, real and personal, was forfeited to the state; but such proceedings affected the estate only, not the person of the offender. The real estates so forfeited were sold, and title made therefor, by the commissioners, and no error in the proceedings affected the purchaser, nor did pardon relieve the forfeiture. The forfeited estates were held liable for the debts of the offender, and some efforts, unsuccessful we believe, were made, to render them responsible for such damages as the former owners might commit in their predatory excursions.

The same act declared, every inhabitant of the state who had joined the enemy by taking refuge among them, or affording them aid by counsel or otherwise, and who should be convicted of high treason, or otherwise forfeit his estate, pursuant to the act, or should be duly convicted of treason, felony, or misdemeanour, for going to, taking refuge with, or affording any aid and assistance to the enemy, incapable of holding any office of trust or profit, or of exercising the elective franchise, and deprived all persons within the state who had suffered fine or imprisonment for refusing to testify their allegiance, by taking the oaths, of the capacity to exercise any military office.

Under these acts, a large mass of property was brought into the market and sold for the benefit of the state, and also of many of the commissioners. In 1781, the market was probably glutted, and property was very greatly sacrificed; when the act of June 26th, declaring, that the continuance of the sales might prove injurious to the interests of the state, directed their suspension until further order, and the authority of the commissioners to cease. Another act of 1781, (20th December,) substituted a single agent, in the respective counties, for the commissioners; and the act of December 16th, 1783, directed such agents to proceed in the sale of such estates, and to receive in payment any obligation of the state. Subsequently, various provisions were made for satisfying the claims of the creditors of the offenders.

During the greater part of the war, the tory refugees from New Jersey were embodied on Staten, Long, and York islands; and when the British were in force in the state, they collected on the eastern and south-eastern border, and occasionally appeared in other districts. Their hostility was more malignant than that of the British soldiery, and being commonly directed by revenge, was more brutally practised, and more keenly felt. Intimately acquainted with the country, they could more suddenly enter it, strike a barbarous stroke and retreat. This spirit was encountered by one almost as fierce and ruthless, in which, however, there was the redeeming quality of patriotism. Many a tale of the romantic daring of the invaders, and of the fearless devotion of the defenders, is yet told, along the eastern shores, and amid the cedar swamps, and pine forests of the state.

The enterprise of the refugee royalists was frequently directed against the persons of the distinguished patriots of the state. Among their first successful attempts, was that on Mr. Richard Stockton. On the entrance of the British army into New Jersey, after the capture of Fort Washington, that gentleman withdrew from Congress in order to protect his family and property, at his seat near Princeton. He removed his wife and younger children into the county of Monmouth, about thirty miles from the supposed route of the British army. On the 30th of November, he was, together with his friend and compatriot John Covenhoven, at whose house he resided, dragged from his bed by night, stripped and plundered, and carried by the way of Amboy to New York. At Amboy he was exposed to severe cold weather in the common jail, which, together with subsequent barbarity in New York, laid the foundation of disease, that terminated his existence in 1781. His release was probably procured by the interference of Congress, in January.

We cannot more fully, nor more truly justify the measures of severity adopted against the disaffected, than by the following extract from the speech of Governor Livingston, to the Assembly, on the 29th of May, 1778.

"I have further to lay before you, gentlemen, a resolution of Congress of the 23d of April, recommending it to the Legislatures of the several states, to pass laws, or to the executive authority of each state, if invested with sufficient power, to issue proclamations offering pardon, with such exceptions and under such limitations and restrictions as they shall think expedient, to such of their inhabitants or subjects as have levied war against any of these states, or adhered to, aided or abetted the enemy, and shall surrender themselves to any civil or military officer of any of these states, and shall return to the state to which they may belong, before the tenth day of June, next; and recommending it to the good and faithful citizens of these states, to receive such returning penitents with compassion and mercy, and forgive and bury in oblivion their past failings and transgressions.

"Though I think it my duty to submit this resolution to your serious consideration, because it is recommended by Congress, I do not think it my duty to recommend it to your approbation, because it appears to me both unequal and impolitic. It may, consistently, with the profoundest veneration for that august Assembly, be presumed, that they are less acquainted with the particular circumstances and internal police of some of the states, than those who have had more favourable opportunities for that purpose. There seems, it is true, something so noble and magnanimous in proclaiming an unmerited amnesty to a number of disappointed criminals, submitting themselves to the mercy of their country; and there is in reality something so divine and christian in the forgiveness of injuries, that it may appear rather invidious to offer any thing in obstruction of the intended clemency. But as to the benevolent religion to which we are under the highest obligations to conform our conduct, though it forbids at all times and in all cases the indulgence of personal hatred and malevolence, it prohibits not any treatment of national enemies or municipal offenders, necessary to self preservation, and the general weal of society. And as to humanity, I could never persuade myself that it consisted in such lenity towards our adversaries, either British or domestic, as was evidently productive of tenfold barbarity on their part, when such barbarity would probably have been prevented by our retaliating upon them the first perpetration; and consequently our apparent inhumanity in particular instances, has certainly been humane in the final result. Alas, how many lives had been saved, and what a scene of inexpressible misery prevented, had we from the beginning treated our bosom traitors with proper severity, and inflicted the law of retaliation upon an enemy, too savage to be humanized by any other argument. As both political pardon and punishment ought to be regulated by political considerations, and must derive their expedience or impropriety from their salutary or pernicious influence upon the community, I cannot conceive what advantages are proposed by inviting to the embraces of their country, a set of beings from which any country, I should imagine, would esteem it a capital part of its felicity to remain forever at the remotest distance. It is not probable that those who deserted us to aid the most matchless connoisseurs in the refinements of cruelty, (who have exhausted human ingenuity in their engines of torture,) in introducing arbitrary power, and all the horrors of slavery; and will only return from disappointment, not from remorse, will ever make good subjects to a state founded in liberty, and inflexibly determined against every inroad of lawless dominion. The thirty-one criminals lately convicted of the most flagrant treason, and who, by the gracious interposition of government, were upon very hopeful signs of *penitence*, generously pardoned, and then with hypocritical cheerfulness enlisted in our service, have all to a man deserted to the enemy, and are again in arms against their native country, with the accumulated guilt of its being now not only the country that first gave them life, but which hath, after they had most notoriously forfeited it, mercifully rescued them from death. Whence it is probable, that a real tory is by any human means absolutely inconvertible, having so entirely extinguished all the primitive virtue and patriotism natural to man, as not to leave a single spark to rekindle the original flame. It is indeed, against all probability, that men arrived at the highest possible pitch of degeneracy, the preferring of tyranny to a free government, should, except by a miracle of omnipotence, be ever capable of one single virtuous impression. They have, by a kind of gigantic effort of villany, astonished the whole world, even that of transcending in the enormities of desolation and bloodshed, a race of murderers before unequalled, and without competitor. Were it not for these miscreants, we should have thought, that for cool deliberate cruelty and unavailing undecisive havoc, the sons of Britain were without parallel. But considering the education of the latter, which has familiarised them to the shedding of innocent blood from the mere thirst of lucre, they have been excelled in their own peculiar and distinguished excellence by this monstrous birth and offscouring of America, who, in defiance of nature and of nurture, have not only by a reversed ambition chosen bondage before freedom, but waged an infernal war against their dearest connexions for not making the like abhorred and abominable election. By them, have numbers of our most useful and meritorious citizens been ambushed, hunted down, pillaged, unhoused, stolen, or butchered; by them has the present contest on the part of Britain been encouraged, aided and protracted. They are therefore responsible for all the additional blood that has been spilt by the addition of their weight in the scale of the enemy. Multitudes of them have superadded perjury to treason. At the commencement of our opposition, they appeared more sanguine than others, and like *the crackling of thorns under a pot*, exceeded in blaze and noise, the calm and durable flame of the steady and persevering. They have associated, subscribed, and sworn to assist in repelling the hostile attempts of our bowelless oppressors; they have, with awful solemnity, plighted their faith and honour, to stand with their lives and fortunes by the Congress, and their general, in support of that very liberty, which, upon the first opportunity, they perfidiously armed to oppose, and have since sacrilegiously sworn, utterly to exterminate. This worthy citizen has lost a venerable father; that one a beloved brother; and a third, a darling son, either immediately by their hands or by their betraying him to the enemy, who, from a momentary unintentional relapse into humanity, were sometimes inclined to spare, when these pitiless wretches insisted upon slaughter, or threatened to complain of a relenting officer, merely because he was not diabolically cruel."

X. From the actual assumption of political independence, to that of a formal declaration, the interval could not be long. On the very day that Congress adopted the resolution recommending to the colonies a change in their form of government; the convention in Virginia resolved unanimously, that their delegates in Congress should propose to that body, to declare the United Colonies free and independent states, absolved from all allegiance to, or dependence on the King and Parliament of Great Britain. The public mind was now fully prepared for this measure. The Assemblies of Maryland, Pennsylvania, and New York, which had displayed the greatest reluctance and forborne the longest, at length assented to it. The proposition was made in Congress, on the 7th of June, 1776, by Richard Henry Lee of Virginia, and seconded by Mr. John Adams of Massachusetts, "*that the United Colonies are, and of right ought to be, free and independent states, and that all political connexion between them and the state of Great Britain, is, and ought to be, totally dissolved.*" This resolution was referred to a committee of the whole Congress, where it was daily debated. In favour of the resolution, Messrs. Lee and Adams were the most distinguished speakers. The latter has been characterized as "the ablest advocate" of independence. Its most formidable opponent was Mr. John Dickenson, whose "Farmer's Letters," had signally served to awaken the resistance of the people to British oppression. Mr. Dickenson's views were those of a sincere, but timid patriot. He lived to discover that his fears were groundless, and to give his aid in maturing and perfecting the institutions of independent America. In resisting the declaration of independence, he was actuated by no ignoble personal fears; his apprehension was for his country. For at this period, no man could be more obnoxious to British statesmen, than the author of the Farmer's Letters, who now, bore a colonel's commission, and was, in the month of July, 1776, upon the lines of New Jersey, and New York. The considerations which weighed upon his mind affected the minds of others; among whom were Wilson of Pennsylvania, R. R. Livingston, of New York, E. Rutledge, and R. Laurens, of South Carolina, and William Livingston, of New Jersey; who, if they did not doubt of the absolute inexpediency of the measure, believed it premature.

On the first day of July, the resolution declaratory of independence, was approved in committee of the whole, by all the colonies, except Pennsylvania and Delaware. Seven of the delegates from the former were present, four of whom voted against it. Mr. Rodney, one of the delegates from the latter, was absent, and the other two, Thomas M'Kean and Gorge Read, were divided in opinion; M'Kean voting for, and Read against, the resolution. On the report of the committee to the House, the further consideration of the subject was postponed until the next day, when the resolution was finally adopted, and entered on the journals.* Pending this memorable discussion, a committee, consisting of Messrs. Jefferson, John Adams, Franklin, Sherman, and R. R. Livingston, was appointed to prepare *the delaration of independence.* Messrs. Jefferson and Adams were named a sub-committee, charged especially with that duty; and the original draught of that eloquent manifesto was made by the former. It was adopted by the chief committee without amendment, and reported to Congress on the twenty-eighth of June. On the fourth of July, having received some slight alterations, it was sanctioned by the vote of every colony.†

The delegation in Congress, from New Jersey, during part of the time, employed in the consideration of the question of independence, had been elected by the Convention, on the fourteenth of February, 1776. It consisted of Messrs. Livingston, De Hart, Richard Smith, John Cooper, and Jonathan Dickenson Sergeant. After the proposition of the fifteenth of May for organizing provincial governments, it would seem that nearly all these gentlemen were reluctant to assume the responsibility of measures which led, eventually, to independence. Richard Smith, alleging indisposition, resigned his seat on the twelfth, John De Hart on the thirteenth, and Mr. Sergeant on the twenty-first of June. Mr. Cooper appears to have taken no part in the proceedings of this Congress. His name, with that of Mr. Sergeant, is regularly on the minutes of the State convention, from the 10th of June, to the 4th of July. Mr. Livingston was withdrawn, on the 5th of June, to assume the duty of brigadier-general of the New Jersey militia. Messrs. Richard Stockton, Abraham Clarke, John Hart, Francis Hopkinson, and Dr. John Witherspoon, were substituted for the previous delegation, on the 21st of June; and were, probably, all present at the time of the final votes upon the resolution, and the declaration of independence. It is certain, that

* Journals of Congress. † Ibid.

on the 28th of June, Mr. Hopkinson appeared in the continental Congress, and presented instructions empowering him and his colleagues to join in declaring the united colonies independent of Great Britain, entering into a confederation for union and common defence, making treaties with foreign nations, for commerce and assistance, and to take such other measures as might appear necessary for these great ends."*

On the 17th of July, the provincial Congress resolved, that, "Whereas, the honourable, the continental Congress have declared the United Colonies free and independent States, We, the deputies of New Jersey, in provincial Congress assembled, do *resolve and declare*, That we will support the freedom and independence of the said States, with our lives and fortunes, and with the whole force of New Jersey." And on the succeeding day they changed the style and title of the "provincial Congress of New Jersey," to that of the "Convention of the State of New Jersey."

* Journals of Congress, vol. ii. p. 230.

We are careful in noting these circumstances, as Mr. Samuel Adams, in a letter, dated 15th July, 1776, to Richard Henry Lee, observes, "We were more fortunate than we expected, in having twelve of the thirteen colonies in favour of the all-important question. The delegates of New Jersey were not empowered to give their voice on either side. Their convention has since acceded to the declaration, and published it, even before they received it from Congress."—*Mem. of Richard Henry Lee*, vol. i. p. 183. This error has been further promulged by the following note, in Mr. Sedgwick's *Life of Livingston*, page 194.—"This delegation, consisting of Witherspoon, Stockton, and others, arrived after the declaration had been signed, but were allowed to fix their names to it." We do not find on the Journal of Congress, the name of any other of the delegates, than Mr. Hopkinson, between the 21st of June, and 4th of July. But the following statement given in the life of R. H. Lee, vol. i. 176, upon, we know not what authority, shows, if correct, that another of the Jersey delegates was present, at the adoption of the declaration. "In the clause of the original draught, that upbraids George III., with the hiring and sending foreign mercenary troops to invade America, among those mentioned, the *Scotch* are specified. It was said that Dr. Witherspoon, the learned president of Nassau Hall College, who was a Scotchman by birth, moved to strike out the word, '*Scotch*,' which was accordingly done."

The following extract from the life of Mr. Stockton, in the Biography of the Signers of the Declaration of Independence, proves, that he, also, was present.—"Mr. Stockton immediately took his seat in the continental Congress, and was present at the debates which preceded the promulgation of that memorable charter of national independence, to which his name is affixed. It has been remarked by Dr. Benjamin Rush, who was a member of the same Congress, that Mr. Stockton was silent during the first stages of this momentous discussion, listening with thoughtful and respectful attention to the arguments that were offered by the supporters and opponents of the important measure then under consideration. Although, it is believed, that, in the commencement of the debate, he entertained some doubts as to the policy of an immediate declaration of independence, yet in the progress of the discussion, his objections were entirely removed, particularly by the irresistible and conclusive arguments of the honourable John Adams, and he fully concurred in the final vote, in favour of that bold and decisive measure. This concurrence he expressed in a short and energetic address, which he delivered in Congress, towards the close of the debate." It may be true, but is not probable, that Mr. Stockton doubted, in Congress, upon this measure. It is certain, that he was instructed by the convention, which appointed him, to support it, and in so doing, performed a delegated trust, which he was too honest to betray. This State had decided the question before she sent him to announce her consent.

CHAPTER XIII.

I. Military Proceedings in Canada.—II. Measures adopted in Great Britain.—III. Objects proposed for the Campaign of 1776.—IV. Operations against New York, and the surrounding Country.—V. Proposals for accommodation, by the British Commissioners.—VI. Condition of the American Forces, at New York—Landing of Lord Howe, on Long Island.—VII. Battle of Brooklyn.—VIII. Retreat of the American Army from Long Island.—IX. Unhappy Effect of the Defeat of the American Army.—X. Lord Howe renews his Attempts for accommodation of the Quarrel—Proceedings of Congress.—XI. Military Movement of the Armies, after the Battle of Brooklyn.—XII. American Army, by advice of General Lee, quit York Island.—XIII. Battle of White Plains.—XIV. Capture of Fort Washington.—XV. Abandonment of Fort Lee, and retreat of the American Army—Its condition—Inhabitants join the British.—XVI. Washington crosses the Delaware—The enemy possess themselves of the left bank.—XVII. Capture of General Lee.—XVIII. New efforts of the Commander-in-Chief—The enemy retire into Winter Quarters.—XIX. Battle of Trenton.—XX. The British re-open the Campaign.—XXI. The American Army re-enters Jersey.—XXII. Battle of Princeton.—XXIII. The American Army retreat to Morristown—Beneficial results of the late actions.—XXIV. Firmness of Congress.—XXV. Condition of New Jersey.—XXVI. The American Army innoculated for the Small Pox.—XXVII. Measures for reclaiming the disaffected of New Jersey.—XXVIII. License of American Troops—restrained.

I. The early successes of General Montgomery, had induced Congress to reinforce the army under his command; and on the intelligence transmitted previous to the assault on Quebec, they resolved, that nine battalions should be maintained in Canada.* Nor did the repulse extinguish this ardour. The council of war, of the army before Boston, resolved, that as no troops could be spared from Cambridge, the colonies of Massachusetts, Connecticut, and New Hampshire, should forward their regiments to Canada; and Congress, in addition to the reinforcements previously ordered, directed four battalions from New York. The indispensable articles, blankets, were procured by contributions of householders, from their family stocks, and specie, by the enthusiasm of patriots, who readily exchanged, at par, their Mexican dollars, for the paper bills of Congress. It was resolved, also, to raise a corps of artillery for this service, and to take into pay one thousand Canadians, in addition to Colonel Livingston's regiment, and to place them under the command of Moses Hazen, a native of Massachusetts, who had resided many years in Canada. A stimulating address to the inhabitants, was published by Congress; and a printing press, and a priest, were despatched, that the cause might have the powerful aid of letters and religion. Dr. Franklin, and Mr. Chase, members of Congress, and Mr. Carrol, who was of the Roman Catholic persuasion, proceeded to Canada, with the design of gaining over the people; having authority to promise them admission to the union of the colonies, upon equal terms, with the full enjoyment of their liberty, and ecclesiastical property. Such was the diligence exerted, that, in despite of the season, the first reinforcements reached the American army, before Quebec, on the eleventh of April, one thousand seven hundred and seventy-six.

Notwithstanding these exertions of the United States, their interest in Canada had daily declined, from the fall of Montgomery. The unsuccessful

* January 8th, 1776.

assault on Quebec, had dispirited the friendly Canadians, and Indians. The small pox, which had been communicated to the army by a woman who had been sent, voluntarily or compulsorily, from the city, so disabled the troops, that, of three thousand men, nine hundred only were fit for duty. The affections of the people were aliened by the misconduct of the continental soldiery, which, in many instances, officered by men from obscure life, without education, or morals, abandoned themselves to plunder, and other crimes, not more disgraceful to themselves than injurious to the cause they were sent to support. And, finally, the early opening of the St. Lawrence, and the arrival of the British succours, compelled the Americans to commence their retreat, very early in the month of May,* with so much precipitation, as to leave their artillery, military stores, and some of their sick, behind. To the last, as well as to such stragglers as were apprehended, or came in, the humanity of General Carlton was exemplary; and more adapted to injure the American cause, than the cruelty of other British commanders. He dismissed his prisoners, after liberally supplying their wants, with the recommendation, "to go home, mind their farms, and keep themselves and their neighbours from all participation in the unhappy war."

A disastrous retreat was pursued, during which, General Thomas, the chief in command, fell a victim to the small pox. On his death, the direction of the army devolved, first on General Arnold, and afterwards on General Sullivan. Brigadier-general Thompson made an unsuccessful attempt on the British post at Trois Rivieres, in which he was made prisoner, though little other loss was sustained. On the first of July, the whole army reached Crown Point, where the first stand was made. The retreat was rendered more painful, by the reproaches of those Canadians, who had united with the invaders, and who were about to be abandoned to the penalties of unsuccessful insurrection, and by the plunder of the merchants of Montreal, by the avaricious and profligate Arnold.

II. Notwithstanding the universal resistance, in America, to the measures of the ministry, the Parliament and people of Great Britain, could not be made to believe, that it would be maintained against a determined spirit on the part of the government, and a few thousand troops to aid the established authorities. This erroneous opinion was confirmed by the royal officers, who were, probably, themselves deceived by their wishes. The military operations, therefore, of the year 1775, were adopted, more to strengthen the civil authority, than to support a contest for empire. But the battles of Lexington, Breed's Hill, and the measures subsequently adopted by Congress, awakened the nation from this delusive dream, and produced an earnest resolution, at all hazards, to establish its supremacy over the colonies.

The speech from the throne, on the opening of the Parliament, twenty-fourth October, 1775, declared, that his Majesty's subjects, in America, "meant, only, to amuse, by vague expressions of attachment to the parent state, while they were preparing for a general revolt;" "that the rebellious war, now levied by them, was become more general, and, manifestly, carried on for the purpose of establishing an independent empire; and that it was become the part of wisdom, and in its effects, of clemency, to put a speedy end to these disorders, by the most decisive exertions." The sentiments of the speech were echoed in the addresses of both Houses of Parliament, but not without a spirited protest in the Lords. Nineteen dissenting members declared the approaching war to be "unjust and impolitic in its principles, and fatal in its consequences," and that they could not approve an address "which might deceive his Majesty and the public, into a belief of

* On the 4th.

their confidence in the present ministers, who had disgraced Parliament, deceived the nation, lost the colonies, and involved them in a civil war, against their dearest interests, and on the most unjustifiable grounds, wantonly spilling the blood of thousands of their fellow subjects."

With the sanction of Parliament, estimates for the public service were made on the basis of operations against a foreign armed power. Twenty-eight thousand seamen and fifty-five thousand land forces were immediately voted; authority was soon afterwards given to employ foreign mercenaries; and to give full efficacy to these measures, an act of parliament* interdicted all trade with the Americans; authorized the capture of their property, whether of ships or goods, upon the high seas; and directed, "that the masters, crews, and other persons found on board captured American vessels, should be entered on board his Majesty's vessels of war, and there considered to be in his Majesty's service, to all intents and purposes, as if they had entered of their own accord. And this, worse than Mahommedan slavery, was insolently represented, as a merciful substitution of an act of grace and favour, for the death which was due to rebellion. This bill, also, authorized the crown to appoint commissioners, with power to grant pardon to individuals, to inquire into general and particular grievances, and to determine whether any colony or part of a colony was returned to that state of obedience, which might entitle it to be received within the King's peace and protection; in which case the restrictions of the law were to cease. In the debate on the bill, Lord Mansfield, whose ability and legal knowledge were known and admired in America, declared, "that the questions of original right and wrong were no longer to be considered—that they were engaged in a war, and must use their utmost efforts to obtain the ends proposed by it—that they must either fight or be pursued—and that the justice of the cause must give way to their present situation." This declaration, justified by circumstances, from the mouth of a ministerial partisan, excited the astonishment, and aided to cement the union, of the colonists; and the act was, justly, characterized by a member of the opposition, as "a bill for carrying more effectually, into execution, the resolves of Congress." By treaties, approved by Parliament, with the Landgrave of Hesse Cassel, the Duke of Brunswick and the hereditary prince of Hesse Cassel,† sixteeen thousand of their subjects were engaged to reduce the rebellious colonies to submission.

In the selection of a general for the royal forces, the command, as a matter of right, was offered to General Oglethorpe, the first on the list of general officers. To the surprise of the minister, the gallant veteran readily accepted the proffer, on condition, that he should be properly supported. A numerous and well appointed army and fleet were promised him. "I will assume the charge," replied he, "without a man or vessel of war, provided, I am authorized, to proclaim to the colonists, that you will do them justice." "I know the people of America well," he added, "and am satisfied that his Majesty has not, in any part of his dominions, more obedient and loyal subjects. You may secure their obedience by doing them justice, but you will never subdue them by force of arms." A commander-in-chief, with such opinions, was unacceptable to the ministry, and the command was given to Sir William Howe.

III. It was resolved, to open the campaign with a force that would look down opposition, and produce submission without bloodshed; and to direct it to three objects: 1. The relief of Quebec; the recovery of Canada; and the invasion of the adjacent provinces: 2. The chastisement of the southern colonies; and—3. To seize New York with a force sufficient to keep pos-

* 20th Nov. 1775. † Feb. 29th, 1766.

session of the Hudson river, to maintain the communication with Canada, or to overrun the adjacent country. The partial success of the first we have already noticed. The execution of the second, was committed to General Clinton and Sir Peter Parker, and eventuated in their repulse, from Charleston, by the vigorous efforts of the colonists, at Fort Moultrie; and the exertions of General Lee, who had charge of the southern department. The third, which involves the operations in New Jersey, asks from us particular detail.

IV. The command of the force, consisting of about three thousand men, destined against New York, was given to Admiral Lord Howe, and his brother, Sir William, officers, high in the confidence of the British nation; who were, also, appointed commissioners for restoring peace to the colonies. On evacuating Boston, General Howe, as we have seen, retired to Halifax, designing, there, to await reinforcements from England. But his situation proving uncomfortable, and the arrival of succours being delayed, he at length (June 10th, 1776) resolved to sail for New York. On the fourth of July his whole force was established on Staten Island, where he resolved to await the arrival of the troops from Europe. The inhabitants received him with great demonstrations of joy, took the oath of allegiance to the crown, and embodied themselves under the command of the late Governor Tryon. He received, also, strong assurances from Long Island, and the neighbouring parts of New Jersey, of the favourable disposition of the greater proportion of the people to the royal cause. Admiral Lord Howe, after touching at Halifax, arrived, with the fleet and auxiliary forces, on the twelfth of the same month.

It had early been conceived by General Washington, that the British would endeavour to possess New York. Its central position, contiguity to the ocean, and capacity of defence, made it highly desirable to both parties. While the English were yet in Boston, General Lee had been detached from Cambridge, to put the city and Long Island in a posture of defence. As the departure of General Howe from Boston became certain, the probability of his going to New York, increased the necessity of collecting a force for its defence. By a resolution of a council of war, (March 13th, 1766) five regiments, with a rifle battalion, were marched upon it, and the states of New York and New Jersey, were requested to furnish—the former two thousand, and the latter one thousand men, for its immediate defence. General Washington soon afterwards followed, and early in April, fixed his head quarters in that city.

The experience which the American commander already had of the material that must necessarily compose his army, determined him to pursue the Fabian mode of war, *a war of posts;* to hazard nothing, but to hover round the enemy, watching his motions, cutting off his supplies, and perpetually harassing him with small detachments, until his own army had became accustomed to military fatigue and danger. With this view, works were erected, in and about New York, on Long Island, and the heights of Haerlem. Congress on the opening of the campaign, had a force far inadequate to its objects. And though feeling the inconvenience of the temporary armies formed of the militia, on short tours of service, they, or the country, probably both, were not prepared to enlist men for periods that would render them efficient soldiers, and therefore they adopted middle expedients. They instituted a flying camp, composed of one thousand men from the states of Pennsylvania, Delaware, and Maryland, engaged until the first day of the ensuing December, and at the same time, called out 13,800 of the ordinary militia. The ranks of the first were chiefly filled, but great deficiencies occurred in those of the second. The difficulty of providing the troops with arms which had hitherto been distressingly great, was now much increased. By the returns of April, the garrison at Fort Montgomery in the Highlands, composed of two hundred and eight privates, had only forty-one guns fit for use; and that at Fort Constitution of one hundred and thirty-six men, had only sixty-eight guns. Flints were scarce, and the lead for musket balls was obtained, by stripping the dwellings.

V. Notwithstanding independence had been declared, the British commanders and commissioners resolved before commencing military operations, to try the influence of their powers for pacification. On the 14th of July, Lord Howe sent on shore, by a flag, a circular letter, addressed severally, to the late governors under the crown, enclosing a declaration which he rerequested them to publish, announcing to the people his authority to grant pardon to all, who having departed from their allegiance, would, by speedy return to duty, merit the royal favour; to declare any colony, town, port, or place, in the peace, and under the protection of the crown, and excepted from the penal provisions of the act of Parliament, prohibiting trade and intercourse with the colonies; and to give assurances, that the services of all persons aiding in the restoration of public tranquillity, should be duly considered. These papers were transmitted to Congress, who caused them to "be published in the several gazettes, that the good people of the United States might be informed of what nature were the powers of the commissioners, and what the terms," offered by them. About the same time, his lordship addressed a letter to "George Washington, Esq.," which the general refused to receive, because his public character was not, thereby, recognised, and in no other, could he have intercourse with the writer. This reason, unquestionably sound, was approved by the Congress. The commissioners, earnest in their purpose, sent Colonel Patterson, adjutant-general of their army, to the American commander, with another letter, directed to "George Washington, &c. &c. &c." When introduced to the general, he addressed him by the title of "Excellency;" and presented the regrets of General Howe, for the difficulty which had arisen with respect to the direction of the letter; observing, that the mode adopted was deemed consistent with propriety, and was founded on precedent in cases of diplomates, when disputes had been made about rank; that General Washington had, in the preceding summer, addressed a letter to "the honourable William Howe;" that the commissioners did not mean to derogate from his rank, or the respect due to him, and that they held his person and character in the highest esteem; but that, the direction, with the addition of &c. &c. &c. implied every thing which ought to follow. The colonel, then, produced a letter, which he said was the same that had been before sent, and which he laid upon the table. But the general declined to receive it. He still urged, that, the address of a letter to one in a public character, should indicate such character, and remarked, that though the et ceteras implied every thing, they also implied any thing: That, his letter to General Howe was an answer to one he had received from him under a like address, and that he would decline any letter relating to his official station, directed to him as a private person. During the subsequent conference, which the adjutant-general wished to be considered as a first advance towards conciliation, he remarked, that "the commissioners were clothed with great powers, and would be very happy in effecting an accommodation." But he received for answer, that "from appearances, they had power only to pardon those, who having never transgressed, sought no forgiveness." Soon after this interview, a letter from General Howe respecting prisoners, properly addressed to General Washington, was duly received.

These seductive efforts of the British agents were repaid by Congress in kind. A resolution of the 14th of August, offered to all foreigners who should leave the armies of his Britannic Majesty in America, and become members of any of the states, protection in the free exercise of their religion, the enjoyment of the privileges of natives, together with fifty acres of land.

VI. The amount of the American force rendered the British commanders cautious in commencing their operations by land. Their fleet, however, gave them great advantages, and soon demonstrated the total inefficiency of the American obstructions to the passage of the North river. Frigates and smaller vessels passed the batteries of New York, Paules Hook, Red Bank, and Governor's Island, almost with impunity. The American army in the vicinity of New York, on the 8th of August, consisted of not more than seventeen thousand men, mostly new recruits, distributed in small and unconnected posts, some of which were fifteen miles distant from others. It was soon after increased by Smallwood's regiment from Maryland, two regiments from Pennsylvania, and a body of New England and New York militia, to twenty-seven thousand; of whom, however, one-fourth were unfitted for duty by sickness. A part of this force was stationed on Long Island, where Major-general Greene had originally commanded, but becoming extremely ill, had been succeeded by Major-general Sullivan.

As the defence of Long Island was intimately connected with that of New York, a brigade had been stationed there, whilst the army was assembling; and had taken a strong post at Brooklyn, where an extensive camp had been marked out and fortified. The village is on a small peninsula, formed by the East river, the Bay, and Gowan's Cove, into which a creek empties itself. This encampment fronted the main land of the island, and the works stretched quite across the peninsula, from Waaleboght Bay in the East river, on the left, to a deep marsh on the creek emptying into Gowan's Cove on the right. The rear was covered by the batteries on Red Hook, Governor's Island, and on the East river. In front of the camp was a range of hills, crowned with thick woods, which extended from east to west, near the length of the island; and though steep, they were every where passable by infantry.

The whole of the English force having at length arrived, General Howe indicated his intention to remove to Long Island—a battle for its possession became inevitable. To this selection he was induced by its abundant product of the supplies which his forces required. He landed on the 22d of August, between the small towns, Utrecht and Gravesend, without opposition; Colonel Hand, with a Pennsylvania regiment, retiring before him to the woody heights commanding the pass leading through Flatbush to the works at Brooklyn. Lord Cornwallis immediately marched to seize this pass, but finding it occupied, took post in the village.

VII. On the 25th of August, Major-general Putnam took command at Brooklyn, with a reinforcement of six regiments. On the same day, General de Heister landed with two brigades of Hessians; and on the next, took post at Flatbush. In the evening, Lord Cornwallis drew off to Flatland. General Washington passed the day at Brooklyn, making arrangements for the approaching action, and returned at night to New York.

The Hessians, under de Heister, composed the centre of the British army at Flatbush; Major-general Grant commanded the left wing extending to the coast; and the greater part of the forces, under General Clinton, Earl Percy, and Lord Cornwallis, turning to the right, approached the opposite shore at Flatland.

The armies were now separated by the range of hills already mentioned. The British centre was scarce four miles from the American lines, at Brooklyn. A direct road, from the one to the other, led across the heights. Another, but more circuitous road ran from Flatbush, by the way of Bedford, a small village on the Brooklyn side of the hills. The right and left wings of the British were nearly equidistant, five or six miles from the American works. The road from the Narrows, along the coast, and by Gowan's Cove, was the most direct route to their left; and their right might either return by the way of Flatbush, and unite with the centre, or take a more circuitous course, and enter a road leading from Jamaica to Bedford. These roads united between Bedford and Brooklyn, a small distance in front of the American lines.

In the hills, on the direct road from Flatbush to Brooklyn, near the former, the Americans had reared a fortress, which had a body of troops with several pieces of artillery, for its defence. The coast and Bedford roads were guarded by detachments, posted on the hills, within view of the English camp, which were relieved daily, and were engaged in obstructing the ways by which the enemy might advance. General Woodhull, with the militia of Long Island, was ordered to take post on the high grounds, as near the enemy as possible; but he remained at Jamaica, scarcely recognising the authority of the officer commanding on the island. Light parties of volunteers patrolled the road from Jamaica to Bedford; about two miles from which, near Flatbush, Colonel Miles, of Pennsylvania, was stationed with a regiment of riflemen.

On the 26th, Colonel Lutz, of the Pennsylvania militia, commanded on the coast road; and Colonel Williams, from New England, on the road leading from Flatbush to Bedford. Colonel Miles, with his regiment, remained where he had been, originally, placed. About nine at night, General Clinton, silently drew the van of the army from Flatland, in order to seize a pass in the heights, about three miles east of Bedford, on the Jamaica road. In the morning of the 27th, about two hours before day, within a half mile of the pass, he captured an American party, which had been stationed on the road, to give notice of the approach of the enemy. He possessed himself of the unoccupied pass, and with the morning light, the whole column passed the heights, and advanced into the level country between them and Brooklyn. They were immediately followed by another column, under Lord Percy. Before Clinton had secured the pass, General Grant proceeded along the coast, with the left wing, and ten pieces of cannon. As his first object was to draw the attention of the Americans from their left, he moved slowly, skirmishing with the light parties in his front.

As it had been determined to defend the passes through the hills, General Putnam, apprized of these movements, reinforced his advance parties, and as the enemy gained ground, employed stronger detachments on this service. About three o'clock in the morning, Brigadier-general Lord Stirling, with the two nearest regiments, was directed to meet the enemy, on the road leading from the Narrows. Major-general Sullivan, who commanded all the troops without the lines, proceeded at the head of a considerable body of New Englandmen, on the road leading directly to Flatbush, while another detachment occupied the heights between that place and Bedford.

About break of day, Lord Stirling reached the summit of the hills, where he was joined by the troops which had been already engaged, and were retiring slowly before the enemy, who almost immediately appeared in sight. Having posted his men advantageously, a warm cannonade commenced on both sides, which continued several hours; and some sharp, but not very close skirmishing took place between the infantry. Lord Stirling being anxious, only, to defend the pass, could not descend in force from the heights; and General Grant did not wish to drive him thence, until the part of the plan intrusted to Sir Henry Clinton, should be executed.

In the centre, De Heister, soon after daylight, began to cannonade the troops under Sullivan; but did not remove from Flatbush, until the British right had approached the left and rear of the American line. In the mean time, the more effectually to draw attention from the point where the grand attack was intended, the fleet was put in motion, and a heavy cannonade commenced on the battery at Red Hook.

About half past eight o'clock, the British right having then reached Bedford, in the rear of Sullivan's left, De Heister ordered Colonel Donop's corps to advance to the attack of the hill, following himself with the centre. The approach of Clinton was now discovered by the American left, which immediately endeavoured to regain the camp at Brooklyn. They were retiring from the woods by regiments, with their cannon, when they encountered the front of the British, consisting of the light infantry and light dragoons, who were soon supported by the guards. About the same time, the Hessians advanced from Flatbush, against that part of the detachment which occupied the direct road to Brooklyn.* Here General Sullivan commanded in person; but he found it difficult to make his troops sustain the first attack. The firing towards Bedford had disclosed to them the alarming fact, that the British had turned their left flank, and were getting into their rear. Perceiving, at once, their danger, they sought to escape, by regaining the camp with the utmost celerity. The sudden route of this party enabled De Heister to detach a part of his force against that engaged near Bedford. In that quarter, too, the Americans were broken and driven back into the woods, and the front of the column led by General Clinton, continuing to move forward, intercepted and engaged those who were retreating along the direct road from Flatbush. Thus attacked in front and rear, and alternately driven by the British on the Hessians, and by the Hessians on the British, a succession of skirmishes took place in the woods, in the course of which, some parts of corps forced their way through the enemy, and regained the lines of Brooklyn, and several individuals saved themselves under cover of the forest; but a greater proportion of the detachment was killed or taken. The fugitives were pursued to the American works, and such was the ardour of the British soldiery, that their cautious commander could scarce prevent an immediate assault.

The fire towards Brooklyn gave the first intimation to the American right, that the enemy had gained their rear. Lord Stirling perceived that he could escape only by instantly retreating across the creek, near the Yellow Mills, not far from the cove. Orders to this effect were immediately given, and the more effectually to secure the retreat of the main body of the detachment, he determined to attack, in person, a corps of the British, under Lord Cornwallis, stationed at a house somewhat above the place at which he proposed crossing the creek. About four hundred of Smallwood's regiment were drawn out for this purpose, and the assault was made with great spirit. This small corps was brought several times to the charge, and Lord Stirling was on the point of dislodging Lord Cornwallis, when the force in his front increasing, and General Grant also advancing on his rear, he could no longer oppose the superior numbers which assailed him, on every quarter; and the survivors of this brave party, with their general, became prisoners of war. This bold and well judged attempt, though unsuccessful, was not without its advantages; giving an opportunity to a large part of the detachment, to save themselves by crossing the creek.

The loss sustained by the American army on this occasion was considerable, but could not be accurately ascertained. Numbers were supposed to

* General Howe's Letter.

have been drowned in the creek, or suffocated in the marsh; and exact accounts from the militia could not be procured. General Washington did not admit it to exceed a thousand men, but in this estimate he could only have included the regular troops. General Howe states the prisoners to have amounted to one thousand and ninety-seven, among whom were Major-general Sullivan, and Brigadiers Lord Stirling, and Woodhull, by him named Udell. He computes the loss of the Americans at three thousand three hundred, but this computation is, probably, excessive. He supposes too, that the troops engaged on the heights, amounted to ten thousand; but it is impossible they could have much exceeded half that number. His own loss, he states at twenty-one officers, and three hundred and forty-six privates killed, wounded, and taken.

As the action became warm, General Washington passed over to the camp at Brooklyn, where he saw with inexpressible anguish, the destruction in which his best troops were involved, and from which it was impossible to extricate them. He could direct his efforts only to the preservation of those which remained.

Believing the Americans to be much stronger than they were in reality, and unwilling to commit any thing to hazard, General Howe made no immediate attempt to force their lines. He encamped in front, and on the twenty-eighth, at night, broke ground in form, within six hundred yards of a redoubt on the left.

VIII. Successful resistance to the victorious enemy being now hopeless, and the American troops, lying in the lines without shelter from the heavy rains, becoming daily more dispirited, the resolution was taken to withdraw the army from Long Island. This difficult movement was effected on the night of the 28th, with such silence and despatch, that all the troops and military stores, with a greater part of the provisions, and all the artillery except some heavy pieces, which, in the state of the roads, could not be drawn, were carried over in safety. Early the next morning, the British outposts perceived the rear-guard crossing the East river, out of reach of their fire. If the attempt to defend Long Island, so disastrous in its issue, impeach the judgment of the commander-in-chief, his masterly retreat, justly, added to his reputation among military men.

IX. But the effect of this defeat was most injurious to the American cause. It took from the troops the confidence which preceding events had created, and planted in its place, a dread of the enemy, to whom the perfection of military skill was now ascribed.

In a letter from General Washington to Congress, the state of the army, after this event, was thus feelingly described. "Our situation is truly distressing. The check our detachment sustained on the 27th ultimo, has dispirited too great a proportion of our troops, and filled their minds with apprehension and despair. The militia, instead of calling forth their utmost efforts to a brave and manly opposition, in order to repair our losses, are dismayed, intractable, and impatient to return. Great numbers of them have gone off, in some instances, almost by whole regiments, in many, by half ones, and by companies at a time. This circumstance of itself, independent of others, when fronted by a well appointed enemy, superior in number to our whole collected force, would be sufficiently disagreeable: but when it is added, that their example has infected another party of the army; that their want of discipline, and refusal of almost every kind of restraint and government, have rendered a like conduct but too common in the whole; and have produced an entire disregard of that order and subordination necessary for the well doing of an army, and which had been before inculcated as well as the nature of our military establishment would admit; our condition is still more alarming, and with the deepest concern I am obliged to confess my want of confidence in the generality of the troops.

"All these circumstances fully confirm the opinion I ever entertained, and which I, more than once, in my letters, took the liberty of mentioning to Congress; that no dependance could be put in a militia, or other troops than those enlisted and embodied for a longer period than our regulations have hitherto prescribed. I am persuaded, and am as fully convinced as of any one fact that has happened, that our liberties must, of necessity, be greatly hazarded, if not entirely lost, if their defence be left to any but a permanent army.

"Nor would the expense incident to the support of such a body of troops, as would be competent to every exigency, far exceed that which is incurred by calling in daily succours, and new enlistments, which when effected, are not attended with any good consequences. Men who have been free, and subject to no control, cannot be reduced to order in an instant; and the privileges and exemptions they claim, and will have, influence the conduct of others in such a manner, that the aid derived from them is nearly counterbalanced by the disorder, irregularity, and confusion they occasion."

The frequent remonstrances of the commander-in-chief, the opinions of all military men, and the severe correcting hand of experience, at length, produced their effect on the government of the union; and soon after the defeat on Long Island, it had been referred to the committee composing the board of war, to prepare a plan of operations for the next succeeding campaign. Their report, which was adopted, proposed a permanent army to be enlisted for the war, and to be composed of eighty-eight battalions, to be raised by the several states in proportion to their ability.* As inducements to enlist, a bounty of twenty dollars was allowed to each recruit, and small portions of vacant lands promised to every officer and soldier."†

X. Lord Howe, in his character of commissioner, sought, immediately, to avail himself of the impression, which he supposed the victory of the twenty-seventh might have made on Congress. For this purpose, General Sullivan was sent on parole, to Philadelphia, with a verbal message, purporting, that though his lordship could not, at present, treat with Congress as a political body, yet he was desirous to confer with some of its members, as private gentlemen, and to meet them at such place as they would appoint: That, with General Howe, he had full powers to compromise the dispute between Great Britain and America; the obtaining of which had delayed him near two months in England, and prevented his arrival at New York before the declaration of independence: That he wished a compact to be settled, at this time, when no decisive blow was struck, and neither party could feel compulsion to enter into an agreement: That, if Congress were disposed to treat, many things which they had not yet asked, might, and ought to be, granted; and that if, upon conference, there should be a probability of accommodation, the authority of Congress would be recognised, as indispensable to the completion of the compact.

This proposition was embarrassing. Absolute rejection might give colour to the opinion, that, if independence were waved, restoration of the ancient connexion, on principles, formerly deemed constitutional, was practicable;

* New Hampshire 3, Massachusetts 15, Rhode Island 2, Connecticut 8, New York 4, New Jersey 4, Pennsylvania 12, Delaware 1, Maryland 3, Virginia 15, North Carolina 9, South Carolina 6, Georgia 1.—88.

† To a colonel 500 acres, lieutenant-colonel 450, major 400, captain 300, lieutenant 200, ensign 150, and a non-commissioned officer or private 100 acres.

The resolution was afterwards changed so as to give the option to enlist for three years, or during the war. Those enlisting for three years not to be entitled to land.

whilst to enter upon negotiation under existing circumstances might impair confidence, in the determination of Congress, to maintain the independence they had declared. The difficulty was, in a measure, surmounted by the reply, "that Congress, being the representatives of the free and independent states of America, could not, with propriety, send any of its members to confer with his lordship in their private characters; but, that ever desirous of establishing peace upon reasonable terms, they would send a committee of their body, to know whether he had authority to treat with persons authorized by Congress for that purpose, on behalf of America; and what that authority is; and to hear such propositions as he shall think proper to make respecting the same." General Washington was, at the same time, instructed, that no proposition for peace ought to be regarded, unless made in writing, and addressed to the representatives of the United States in Congress, or to persons authorized by them; and that if application were made to him, on the subject, by any of the British commanders, he should inform them, that the United States having entered into the war, only, for the defence of their lives and liberties, would cheerfully agree to peace on reasonable terms, whenever it should be so proposed to them. These resolutions had the appearance of maintaining independence, without making it the condition of peace.

Dr. Franklin, John Adams, and Edward Rutledge, the committee of Congress, met Lord Howe on Staten Island. The conference was fruitless. The committee, in their report, gave a summary of its matter, saying, "It did not appear, that his lordship's commission contained any other authority than that expressed in the act of Parliament; namely, that of granting pardons, with such exceptions as the commissioners should think proper to make; and of declaring America, or any part of it, to be in the King's peace on submission: for as to the power of inquiring into the state of America, which his lordship mentioned to us, and of conferring and consulting with any persons the commissioners might think proper, and representing the result of conversation to the ministry, who, provided the colonists would subject themselves, might, after all, or might not, at their pleasure, make any alterations in the former instructions to governors, or propose, in Parliament, any amendment of the acts complained of; we apprehended any expectation from the effect of such a power, would have been too uncertain and precarious to be relied on by America, had she still continued in her state of dependence."

XI. A council of war, convoked by Washington, resolved to act on the defensive, and not to risk the army for the state of New York; but a middle line between abandonment and defence, was, for a short time, adopted. The public stores were removed to Dobb's Ferry, about twenty-six miles from New York. Twelve thousand men were ordered to the northern extremity of York Island, and four thousand five hundred returned for the defence of the city: the remainder occupied the intermediate space, with directions to support the city or the camp, at King's Bridge, as exigencies might require. As it was impossible to determine where the British would attempt to land, it was necessary, pursuant to the system of procrastination, and the determination to gain time to raise works for defence at various points. At length, (September 12th) another council of war directed the abandonment of the city. General Mercer, who commanded the flying camp on the Jersey shore, also, moved up the North river, to a post opposite Fort Washington.

On the fifteenth General Howe commenced to land his forces, under cover of some ships of war, on the East river, between Kipp's and Turtle Bays. The works, at this point, were capable of defence for some time; but the troops, stationed in them, terrified at the fire from the ships, abandoned them without waiting an attack, and fled with precipitation. When the cannonade had commenced, the brigades of Generals Parsons and Fellows were put in motion, and marched to the support of the lines, and General Washington, himself, rode towards the scene of action. The panic of the fugitives, from the works, was communicated to the advancing troops, and the commander-in-chief, had the extreme mortification to meet the whole retreating in the utmost disorder, despite the great efforts of their generals to check the disgraceful flight; and whilst he, himself, attempted to rally them, a small corps of the enemy coming in sight, they again broke and fled in the utmost confusion. The usually firm and equable mind of this admirable man, seems, on this occasion, to have been swayed by a gust of natural passion; and for the first, and perhaps, the only time, he despaired of the cause in which he had embarked his fortune, his life, and his fame. In the rear of his dastardly troops, with his face to the enemy, he appeared willing to bury the pangs of the present, and the dreaded infamy of the future, in an honourable grave. His aids and friends, who surrounded his person, by indirect violence, compelled him to retire, and preserved a life, perhaps, indispensable to the independence of his country.*

The only part remaining to be taken after this dereliction, was to withdraw the few remaining troops from New York, and to secure the posts on the heights. For the latter purpose, the lines were instantly manned, but no attempt was made on them. The retreat from New York was effected with an inconsiderable loss of men, in a skirmish at Bloomingdale; but all the heavy artillery, and a large portion of the baggage, provisions, and military stores, were unavoidably abandoned. No part of this loss was more severely felt, than that of the tents. In this shameful day, one colonel, one captain, three subalterns, and ten privates, were certainly killed; one lieutenant-colonel, one captain, and one hundred and fifty-seven privates were missing. The conduct of the troops on this occasion, calls for remarks which are alike applicable to the prior and subsequent armies of the United States. They had not the experience which teaches the veteran to do his duty, wherever he may be placed; in the assurance, that others will likewise do theirs; and to rely, that those who direct the whole will not expose him to useless hazard nor neglect those precautions which the safety of the whole may require.†

Unfortunately, there existed in many parts of the army, other causes beside the shortness of the terms of enlistment, and the inefficiency of the militia, which prevented the acquisition of these military sentiments. In New England, whence the war had been principally supported, the zeal excited by the revolution had taken such a direction, as in a great measure to abolish those distinctions between the platoon officers and the soldiers, which are indispensable to the formation of an efficient army. Many of these officers, here, as in other parts of the union, were elected by the men, and were, consequently, disposed to associate with them on the footing of equality. In some instances, those were chosen who had agreed to put their pay in common stock with that of the soldiers, and to divide equally with them. It is not cause of wonder, that among such officers, the most disgraceful and unmilitary practices should sometimes prevail; nor that privates should fail in respect, sub-

* Ramsay's American Revolution, vol. i. p. 392. Mr. Marshall does not notice, to affirm or deny, this statement of Mr. Ramsay. If the suppression have been made for the purpose of aggrandizing the hero of the biographer, it is reprehensible.—The office of apotheosis belongs to the poet or the slave. It is above or below the historian. And no human character can suffer less, from full disclosure, than that of General Washington. Such shades, as this, are but the foil of the brilliant, serving to perfect its lustre. Such instances of weakness, improve the exemplar which his life affords. Were it marked by unvarying wisdom, it would be rejected in despair, as unattainable.

† Marshall's Washington, vol. ii. 434.

ordination, and obedience. Orders of this period show, that several officers of inferior grade were not themselves exempt from the general spirit of pillage, which then disgraced the American troops.*

Having possessed himself of the city, (15th September, 1776,) the British general stationed a few troops in the town, and with the main body of the army encamped near the American lines. His right was at Horen's Hook, on the East river, and his left reached the North river, near Bloomingdale, so that his encampment extended quite across the island, here, about two miles wide, and his flanks were both covered by his ships. The strongest point of the American lines was at King's Bridge, preserving their communication with the continent. They also occupied in considerable force, M'Gowan's Pass, and Morris' Heights, which were fortified and rendered capable of defence against superior numbers. On the heights of Haerlem, still nearer the British lines, within a mile and a half of them, a strong detachment was posted in an intrenched camp.

The present position of the armies favoured the wishes of the American commander, to habituate his soldiers by a series of successful skirmishes, to meet the enemy in the field. Opportunities for this purpose were not long wanting. The day after the retreat from New York, the British appeared in considerable force in the plains between the camps. Washington ordered Colonel Knowlton of the volunteer corps of New England rangers, and Major Leitch with three companies of the third Virginia regiment, which had joined the army only the preceding day, to endeavour to get into their rear, whilst he amused them with demonstrations of an attack in front. The plan was successful; the British advanced eagerly to an advantageous position in front, and a firing commenced, but at too great a distance for execution. In the mean time, Colonel Knowlton, unacquainted with their new position, made his attack rather on their flank, than their rear. Very soon, Major Leitch, who had gallantly led the detachment, was brought off the ground mortally wounded, and not long afterwards, Colonel Knowlton also fell, bravely fighting at the head of his troops. Not discouraged by the loss of their field officers, the captains maintained their ground, and continued the action with great animation. The British were reinforced, and General Washington ordered on detachments from the adjacent regiments of New England and Maryland. The Americans, thus strengthened, charged the enemy, drove them from the woods into the plains, and were pressing them still further, when the general apprehending the approach of a large body of the foe, recalled his troops to their entrenchments. In this sharp conflict, many who had so disgracefully fled on the preceding day, now, with much inferior force, had engaged a battalion of light infantry, another of Highlanders, and three companies of Hessian riflemen, sustaining a loss in killed and wounded of not more than fifty men, whilst the British lost more than double that number. The effect of this first success of the campaign, was visible upon the spirits of the men, restoring them in some measure to their own esteem.

The armies did not long retain their position. General Howe, sensible of the strength of the American camp, had no inclination to force it. His plan was, to compel General Washington either to abandon it, or to fight in a position, where defeat would result in a total destruction of his army. With this view, after throwing up intrenchments on M'Gowan's Hill, for the protection of New York, he proposed to gain the rear of the American camp, and to possess himself of the North river, above King's Bridge. To ascertain the practicability of the latter, three frigates passed up, under the fire of

* Marshall's Life of Washington, vol. ii. 434.

Forts Washington and Lee, without injury from the batteries, or impediment from the *chevaux-de-frise*, which had been sunk in the channel, between those forts. This point being attained, the greater part of his army passed through Hellgate, into the Sound, and landed on Frog's Neck, in West Chester county, about nine miles from the camp, on the heights of Haerlem.* He continued here some days, quietly waiting for his artillery, military stores, and reinforcements, from Staten Island, which were detained by unfavourable winds.

XII. In the mean time, General Lee arrived,† from his late successful command, to the southward; and finding a disposition prevalent among the officers of the American army, to continue on York Island, he induced the call of a council of war, to consult on its propriety. He urged its entire relinquishment—dwelling upon the impracticability of stopping the ascent of the enemy's ships, upon the river, the possession of Frog's Neck, on the Sound, by the British, the absolute impossibility of preserving the communication with the country, and the imminent danger that the army must fight under disadvantages, or become prisoners of war. His views, so far as they regarded the army, were adopted; but unfortunately, the representations of General Greene prevailed, in relation to Fort Washington, the occupation of which, he contended, would divert a large portion of the enemy's force from the main body, and in conjunction with Fort Lee, would cover the transportation of supplies, up the river, for the service of the American troops. He further represented, that the garrison could be brought off, at any time, by boats from the Jersey shore.

XIII. On the 18th of October, General Howe moved forward his whole army, except four regiments destined for New York, towards New Rochelle. Some skirmishing took place, near East Chester, with part of Glover's brigade, in which the conduct of the Americans was courageous. As Howe took post at New Rochelle, Washington occupied the heights between it and the North river. The British general received here, the second division of Germans, under General Knyphausen, and an incomplete regiment of cavalry, from Ireland. Both armies now moved towards the White Plains, a strong piece of ground, where a large camp had been marked out, and occupied by a detachment of militia, sent to guard some magazines there collected. The main body of the Americans formed a long line of entrenched camps, extending from twelve to thirteen miles, on the heights from Valentine's Hill, near King's Bridge, to the White Plains; fronting the British line of march, and the Brunx, which lay between them, so as to collect in full force at any point, as circumstances might require. While the British army lay about New Rochelle, Major Rodgers, with his regiment (of tories), was advanced eastward towards Mamoraneck, on the Sound, where he was believed to be covered by the position of the other troops. An attempt was made to surprise him in the night; but it was not wholly successful. About sixty of his corps were killed or taken, with a loss to the Americans of two killed, and eight or ten wounded; among the latter, was Major Green, of Virginia, a brave officer, who led the advance, and who received a ball through his body. Not long after, a regiment of Pennsylvania riflemen, under Colonel Hand, fell in with and engaged an equal number of Hessian chasseurs, over whom they obtained some advantage.

The caution of the English general was increased by these evidences of enterprise in his adversary. His object seems to have been to avoid skirmishing, and to bring on a general action, if that could be effected under favourable circumstances; if not, he knew too well, the approaching dissolu-

* October 12th, 1776.

† October 14th.

tion of the American army, and calculated, not without reason, on deriving from that event nearly all the advantages of a victory. He proceeded therefore slowly. His marches were in close order, his encampments compact, and well guarded with artillery; and the utmost circumspection was used not to expose any part which might be vulnerable.*

As the sick and baggage reached a place of safety, General Washington gradually drew in his out-posts, and took possession of the heights on the east side of the Brunx fronting the head of the British columns. He was there joined by General Lee, who, after securing the sick and the baggage, had, with considerable address, brought up the rear division of the army.

General Washington was encamped on high, broken grounds, with his right flank covered by the Brunx, which also covered the front of his right wing, extending along the road on the east side of that river, towards New Rochelle, as far as the brow of the hill where his centre was posted. His left, forming almost a right angle with his centre, and nearly parallel to his right, extended along the hills northwardly, so as to keep possession of the commanding ground, and secure a retreat should it be necessary, from the present position, to one still more advantageous in his rear.

On the right of the army, and on the west side of the Brunx, about one mile from the camp, on the road leading from the North river, was a hill, of which General M'Dougal took possession, for the purpose of covering the right flank. His detachment consisted of about sixteen hundred men, principally militia; and his communication with the main army was perfectly open; that part of the river being every where passable, without difficulty. Hasty intrenchments were thrown up to strengthen every part of the lines, and to make them as defensible as possible.

On the 25th of October, General Howe, who had advanced from New Rochelle and Mamaroneck, prepared to attack General Washington in his camp. Early in the morning, the British approached in two columns, the right commanded by Sir Henry Clinton, and the left by General Knyphausen, accompanied by General Howe, in person. Their advanced parties having encountered, and driven in the patroles, their van appeared, about ten o'clock, in full view of the American lines; a cannonade commenced, without much execution, on either side. The British right formed behind a rising ground, about a mile in front of the American camp, and extended from the road leading from Mamaroneck, towards the Brunx; so that it was opposed to the centre of the American army.

On viewing General Washington's situation, Howe determined to possess himself of the hill occupied by M'Dougal. He directed Colonel Rawle, with his corps of Hessians, to cross the Brunx, and by a circuit, to gain a position from which he might annoy the right flank of M'Dougal, while Brigadier-general Leslie, with the second brigade of British troops, the Hessian grenadiers under Colonel Donop, and a Hessian battalion, should attack him in front. When Rawle had gained the designated position, the detachment under Leslie also crossed the Brunx, and commenced a vigorous attack on the Americans.† The militia immediately fled; but the regulars behaved with great gallantry. Colonel Smallwood's regiment of Maryland, and Colonel Reitzimar's of New York, advanced boldly towards the foot of the hill to meet Leslie; but after a sharp encounter, were overpowered by numbers, and compelled to retreat. Leslie then attacked the remaining part of M'Dougal's forces, consisting of his own brigade, the Delaware battalion, and a small regiment of Connecticut militia. They were soon driven from

* Annual Register.

† General Howe's letter.

the hill, but kept up, for some time, an irregular fire from the stone walls, and other enclosures about the scene of action. General Putnam, with Beal's brigade, was ordered to support them; but not arriving while they were in possession of the hill, he deemed it improper to attempt to regain it, and the troops retreated to the main army.

In this engagement, which, during its continuance, was very animated on both sides, the loss was supposed to have been about equal. That of the Americans was between three and four hundred in killed, wounded, and taken. Colonel Smallwood was among the wounded.

General Washington continued in his lines, expecting to be attacked. His sick and baggage were removed into his rear. But a considerable part of the day having been spent in gaining the hill, which had been occupied by M'Dougal, all attempts on his intrenchments were postponed until the next morning; and the whole British army lay on their arms the following night, in order of battle, and on the ground they had taken during the day.

This interval was employed by General Washington in strengthening his works, removing his sick and baggage, and preparing, by changing the arrangement of his troops, for the expected attack. His left maintained its position, but his right was drawn back to stronger ground. Perceiving this, and unwilling to leave any thing to hazard, Howe resolved to postpone further offensive operations, until Lord Percy should arrive with four battalions from New York, and two from the post at Mamaroneck. This reinforcement was received on the evening of the 30th, and preparations were then made to attack the American intrenchments the next morning. In the night and during the early part of the succeeding day, a violent rain fell, which induced a further postponement of the assault.* The provisions and heavy baggage being now removed, and apprehensions being entertained, that the British general, whose left wing extended along the height taken from M'Dougal, to his rear, might turn his camp, and occupy the post to which he designed to retreat, if an attempt on his lines should terminate unfortunately, General Washington changed his position in the night, and withdrew to the heights of North Castle, about five miles from White Plains. At the same time he detached Beal's brigade to take possession of the bridge on Croton river, a few miles in his rear, and over which is the road leading up the Hudson.

This position was so strong, that an attempt to force it was deemed imprudent. General Howe, therefore, gave a new direction to his efforts.†

XIV. The anxiety to preserve, if possible, the navigation of the Hudson, above King's Bridge, had induced the American general to maintain the posts of Forts Washington and Lee, on either side of that river. They essentially checked the movements of General Howe, who justly deemed the complete possession of York Island an object of too much importance to be longer neglected. He, therefore, directed General Knyphausen to cross the country from New Rochelle, and to take possession of King's Bridge, where a small party of Americans were stationed in Fort Independence. This was effected without opposition;—the Americans retiring to Fort Washington, and Knyphausen encamping between that place and King's Bridge.

In the mean time, Howe broke up his camp at White Plains, and marched to Dobbs' Ferry, whence he retired slowly down the North river, towards King's Bridge. The American general was immediately aware of the design against Fort Washington, and the Jerseys; but, apprehending that his adversary might return suddenly, and endeavour by a rapid movement, to execute the original plan of getting in his rear, he observed great caution,

* General Howe's letter.

† Ibid.

and maintained his position, until assured that the movement towards King's Bridge, was not a feint.

On the movement of the British army towards New York, General Washington perceived the neccessity of throwing a part of his troops into New Jersey, should Howe design to change the scene of action. A council of war, therefore, was immediately called, (November 6th,) which determined, unanimously, should Howe continue his march, that all the troops raised on the west side of the Hudson, should cross that river, to be afterwards followed, if necessary, by those raised on the eastern part of the continent; and that, for the preservation of the highlands, about the North river, three thousand men should be stationed at Peck's-kill, and in the passes of the mountains.

General Washington addressed a letter to Governor Livingston, advising him of the movement then making, and expressing a decided opinion that General Howe would not content himself with investing Fort Washington, but would invade the Jerseys. He urged the governor to put the militia in condition to reinforce the continental army, and to take the place of the new levies, a term designating a body of men between militia and regulars, raised to serve until the first of December, who could not be depended on to continue with the army one day longer than the time for which they were engaged. He also pressed, very earnestly, the removal of all the stock, and other provisions, of which the enemy might avail himself, from the sea-coast, and the neighbourhood of New York.

Immediate intelligence of this movement was likewise given to General Greene, who commanded in the Jerseys; and his attention was particularly pointed to Fort Washington. He was advised to increase his magazines about Princeton, and to diminish those near New York; as experience had demonstrated the difficulty of removing them on the advance of the enemy. Some apprehension was also entertained, that Howe would attempt to cross at Dobbs' Ferry, and envelop the troops about Fort Lee, as well as those in Fort Washington. Of this, too, General Greene was advised, and thereupon drew in his parties from about Amboy, and posted a body of troops on the heights to defend the passage at Dobbs' Ferry.

On the 13th of November, General Washington crossed the North river, with the selected portion of the army, leaving the eastern regiments under the command of General Lee, with orders, also, to cross the river, should General Howe effect it; but in the mean time, to assume the strong grounds, behind the Croton, at Pine Bridge.

Discretionary orders had been given to General Greene, to abandon Fort Washington, but which, for the reasons already stated, he delayed to execute. This fort was on a high piece of ground, near the North river, very difficult of ascent, especially, on the northern side. It was capable of containing about a thousand men; but the lines and out-works, chiefly on the southern side, were drawn quite across the island. The position was naturally strong, the approaches difficult, and the fortifications, though not sufficient to resist heavy artillery, were believed capable of sustaining any attempt at storm. The garrison containing some of the best troops of the American army, was commanded by Colonel Magaw, a brave and intelligent officer.

General Howe, who had retired slowly from the White Plains, encamped at a small distance from King's Bridge, on the heights of Fordham, with his right towards the North river, and his left on the Brunx. Detachments from his army having previously taken possession of the ground about West Chester, works were erected at Haerlem creek, to play on the opposite works of the Americans, and every preparation being made for an assault, the garrison was summoned (on the 15th of November,) to surrender on pain of being put to the sword. Colonel Magaw replied, that he should defend the place to the last extremity. The summons was immediately communicated to General Greene, at Fort Lee, and by him to the commander-in-chief, then at Hackensack. He immediately rode to Fort Lee, and though late in the night, was proceeding to Fort Washington, where he expected to find Generals Putnam and Greene, when, in crossing the river, he met those officers, returning from visiting that post. They reported that the garrison was in high spirits, and would make a good defence; on which, he returned with them to Fort Lee.

Early next morning, Colonel Magaw posted his troops partly in the outermost lines, partly between those lines, on the woody and rocky heights, fronting Haerlem river, where the ground being extremely difficult of ascent, the works were not closed; and partly on a commanding hill, lying north of the fort. Colonel Cadwalader, of Pennsylvania, commanded in the lines, Colonel Rawlings, of Maryland, on the hill towards King's Bridge, where his regiment of riflemen was posted among trees, and Colonel Magaw, himself, in the fort.

The strength of the place did not deter the British general from attempting to carry it by storm. A desire to save time, at this late season of the year, was the principal inducement to this determination. About ten o'clock, the assailants appeared before the works, and moved on to the assault in four quarters. Their first division, consisting of two columns of Hessians and Waldeckers, amounted to about five thousand men, under the command of General Knyphausen, advanced on the north side of the fort against the hill where Colonel Rawlings commanded, who received them with great gallantry. The second, on the east, consisting of the first and second battalions of British light infantry, and two battalions of guards, was led on by Brigadier-general Mathews, supported by Lord Cornwallis, at the head of the first and second battalions of grenadiers, and the thirty-third regiment. These troops crossed Haerlem river, in boats, under cover of the artillery planted in works which had been erected for the purpose, on the opposite side of the river, and landed within the third line of defence, which crossed the island. The third division was conducted by Lieutenant-colonel Stirling, who passed the river higher up; and the fourth, by Lord Percy, accompanied by General Howe, in person. This division was to attack the lines in front, on the south side.*

The attacks on the north, and south, by General Knyphausen, and Lord Percy, were made about the same instant on Colonels Rawlings and Cadwalader, who maintained their ground for a considerable time; but while Colonel Cadwalader was engaged in the first line against Lord Percy, on the south, the second and third divisions, which had crossed Haerlem river, made good their landing, and soon dispersed the troops fronting that river, as well as a detachment sent by Colonel Cadwalader, to support them. These being overpowered, he deemed it necessary to abandon the lines, and a retreat was commenced towards the fort, which, being conducted with confusion, a part of his men were intercepted by the division under Colonel Stirling, and made prisoners. The resistance on the north, was conducted with more courage, and was of longer duration. Rawlings maintained his ground with firmness, and his riflemen did vast execution. A three gun battery, north of the fort, also played on Knyphausen, with much effect. The Germans were repulsed several times with great loss; and, had every other part of the action been equally well maintained, the assailants, if ulti-

* General Howe's letter.

mately successful, would have had much reason to deplore their victory. At length, by dint of perseverance and numbers, the Hessian columns gained the summit of the hill; after which, Colonel Rawlings, perceiving the danger which threatened his rear, retreated under the guns of the fort.

Having carried the lines, and all the strong ground adjoining them, the British general again summoned Colonel Magaw to surrender. While the capitulation was progressing, General Washington sent him a billet, requesting him to hold out until the evening, when he would endeavour to bring off the garrison; but Magaw had already proceeded too far to retract; and it is probable the place could not have resisted an assault from so formidable a force as threatened it on every side. The most essential difficulties had been overcome: the fort was too small to contain all the men; and their ammunition was nearly exhausted. Under these circumstances, the garrison surrendered prisoners of war.

The loss on this occasion was the greatest the Americans had sustained. The garrison was stated by General Washington, at about two thousand men; yet, in a report published as from General Howe, the number of prisoners is stated at two thousand six hundred, exclusive of officers. Either General Howe must have included in his report, persons who were not soldiers, or General Washington, in his letter, must have comprised only the regulars. The last conjecture is most probably correct. The loss of the assailants is variously stated, at from eight to eleven hundred men. It fell heaviest on the Germans.

XV. The surrender of Fort Washington, induced a determination to evacuate Fort Lee; and a removal of the stores to the interior of Jersey, immediately, commenced. But on the 19th of November, before this could be completed, a detachment of the enemy, commanded by Lord Cornwallis, amounting to about six thousand men, crossed the North river, below Dobbs' Ferry, and endeavoured by a rapid march, to enclose the garrison between the Hudson and the Hackensack rivers. The safety of the garrison required its instant withdrawal from the narrow neck of land, which was with great difficulty effected, by a bridge over the latter river. With Fort Lee, all the heavy cannon, except two twelve pounders, together with a large quantity of provisions and military stores, fell into the hands of the enemy. The want of wagons rendered this loss inevitable.

After crossing the Hackensack, General Washington posted his troops along the western bank; but he could not defend it with an army of only three thousand effectives, exposed, without tents, to the inclement season which already prevailed, in a level country without an entrenching tool, and among people no wise zealous for the American cause; and being still enclosed by two rivers, the Hackensack and Passaic, his position was, thereby, rendered more dangerous. This gloomy condition was not cheered by the prospect of the future. No reliance could be placed on reinforcements from any quarter. The general made every exertion to collect an army, and in the mean time to impede, as much as possible, the progress of the enemy. General Carleton having retired from before Ticonderoga, he directed General Schuyler to hasten to his assistance, the troops of Pennsylvania and New Jersey. But the march was long, their term of service nearly expired, and they refused to re-enlist. General Lee was directed to cross the North river, and hold himself in readiness, if the enemy should continue the campaign, to join the commander-in-chief; but his army, too, from the same fatal cause, was melting away, and would soon be totally dissolved. General Mercer, who commanded part of the flying camp stationed about Bergen, was called in, but these troops had engaged to serve, only, until the first of December, and like other six months' men, had abandoned the army in great numbers. No hope existed of retaining the remnant, after they should possess a legal right to depart.

Under these circumstances, no serious design could be entertained of defending the Hackensack. A show of resistance was momentarily preserved, with a view of covering the few stores which could be removed. General Washington, with Beal's, Heard's, and part of Irvine's brigades, crossed at Acquackanonck Bridge, and took post at Newark, on the south side of the Passaic. Soon after he had marched, Major-general Vaughan, at the head of the British dragoons, grenadiers, and light infantry, appeared before the new bridge over Hackensack, and the American detachment in the rear being wholly unable to defend it, could only break it down, and retire before him over the Passaic.

General Washington having entered the open country, halted for a few days, to endeavour to collect such a force, as might preserve the semblance of an army. The better to effect this, he despatched General Mifflin to Pennsylvania, where he possessed great influence, and Colonel Joseph Reed, his adjutant-general, long known and highly valued in New Jersey, to Governor Livingston, to press upon him the absolute and immediate necessity of making further exertions to prevent the whole state from being overrun.

In this perilous state of things, he found it necessary to detach Colonel Forman of the New Jersey militia, to suppress an insurrection which threatened to break out in the county of Monmouth, where great numbers were well disposed to the royal cause. Nor was this the only place from which there was reason to expect the enemy might derive aid. Such an indisposition to further resistance began to be manifested throughout the state, as to excite serious fears respecting the conduct which might be observed when Lord Cornwallis should penetrate further into the country.*

Unable to make effective resistance, as the British crossed the Passaic, General Washington abandoned his position behind it; and on the 28th of November, as Lord Cornwallis entered Newark, he retreated thence to Brunswick. The time had now come, (December 1,) when the Maryland and Jersey levies in the flying camp, became entitled to their discharge, and he had the extreme mortification to behold his small army, still more enfeebled by the abandonment of these troops almost in sight of an advancing enemy. The Pennsylvania militia of the same class had engaged to serve until the first of January; but so many of them deserted, that it became necessary to place guards on the roads and ferries over the Delaware to apprehend the fugitives.

From New Brunswick, the commander-in-chief, again, urged upon Governor Livingston, that the intention of the enemy was, to pass through New Jersey to Philadelphia, and that some efficacious measures should be adopted to call out the strength of the state to his support, and its own defence. But it was not in the power of the governor to furnish the aid required. The Legislature, which had removed from Princeton to Trenton, and from Trenton to Burlington, had now adjourned, and the members had returned to their homes to protect their own more peculiar interests. The well affected part of the middle counties was overawed by the British army. The lower counties were haunted by tories, or paralyzed by their non-combatting Quaker population, and the militia of Morris and Sussex turned out slowly and reluctantly.† Washington, also, again urged General Lee to hasten to his assistance.

The troops were continued in motion for the purpose of concealing their weakness, and of retarding the advance of Cornwallis, by creating an opinion

* Marshall, Wash. Lett. † Ibid.

that the Americans meditated to attack him; but as the British van came in view, and approached the opposite side of the bridge, he was compelled to quit New Brunswick. Leaving Lord Stirling in Princeton with two brigades from Virginia and Delaware, amounting to twelve hundred men, to watch the enemy, he continued his march with the residue of the army to Trenton. Directions had already been given to collect and place under sufficient guard, all the boats on the Delaware, from Philadelphia upwards, for seventy miles, so that a hope might be reasonably entertained that the progress of the enemy would be stopped at this river; and that in the mean time, reinforcements might arrive, which would enable him to dispute its passage. Having, with great labour, transported the few remaining military stores and baggage over the Delaware, he determined to remain as long as possible with the small force which still adhered to him on the northern banks of that river.*

This retreat into, and through New Jersey, was attended with almost every circumstance that could embarrass and depress the spirits. It commenced immediately after the heavy loss at Fort Washington. In fourteen days after that event, the whole flying camp claimed its discharge, and other troops also, whose engagements terminated about the same time, daily departed. The two Jersey regiments which had been forwarded by General Gates, under General St. Clair, went off to a man, the moment they entered their own state. A few officers without a single private, were all of these regiments which St. Clair brought to the commander-in-chief. The troops who were with Washington, mostly of the garrison of Fort Lee, were without tents, blankets, shoes, and the necessary utensils to dress their provisions. In this situation, the general had the address to prolong a march of ninety miles, to the space of nineteen days. During his retreat, scarce an inhabitant joined him, whilst numbers daily flocked to the royal army, to make their peace, and beg protection. On the one side, was a well appointed full clad army, dazzling by its brilliance, and imposing by its success; on the other, a few poor fellows whose tattered raiment but too well justified the *soubriquet* of "ragamuffins," with which the sneering tories reproached them, fleeing for their safety. The British commissioners issued a proclamation commanding all persons assembled in arms against his Majesty's government, to disband and return to their homes; and all civil officers to desist from their treasonable practices, and to relinquish their usurped authority. A full pardon was offered to all, who within sixty days would appear before an officer of the crown, claim the benefit of the proclamation, and subscribe a declaration of his submission to the royal authority. Seduced by this proclamation, not only the ordinary people shrunk from the apparent fate of the country in this its murkiest hour, but the vapouring patriots who sought office and distinction at the hands of their countrymen, when danger in their service was distant, now crawled into the British lines, humbly craving the mercy of *their* conquerors; and whined out, as justification, that though they had united with others, in seeking a constitutional redress of grievances, they approved not the measures lately adopted, and were at all times opposed to independence.†

General Washington having secured his baggage and stores, and finding Cornwallis pause at Brunswick, he, on the 6th of December, detached twelve hundred men to Princeton, in hope, that by appearing to advance, he might not only delay the progress of the British, but in some degree, cover the country and re-animate the people of New Jersey.

XVI. The exertions of General Mifflin, though making little impression

* Marshall.

† Dr. Ramsay has given to political infamy, the names of Galloway and Allen, of Pennsylvania, he might have added those of Tucker, and others, of New Jersey.

on the state of Pennsylvania at large, were highly successful in Philadelphia. A large proportion of that city, capable of bearing arms, had associated for the defence of the country; and fifteen hundred now marched to Trenton. A German battalion was also ordered by Congress to the same place. On receiving this reinforcement, Washington commenced his march to Princeton; but before he could reach it, he received intelligence that Lord Cornwallis, also, strongly reinforced, was rapidly advancing from Brunswick by different routes to get into his rear. Thus a retreat even across the Delaware, became indispensable.

On the 8th of December, having secured the boats, and broken down the bridges on the roads leading along the Jersey shore, he posted his army on the western bank in such a manner, as to observe the fords by which the enemy must pass. As the American rear guard crossed the river, the British army came in sight. The main body halted at Trenton, whence detachments were thrown out above and below, so as to render uncertain where they might attempt to pass. Small parties, unimpeded by the people of the country, reconnoitred the river for a considerable distance. If the British general as reported, had brought boats with him, it would have been impossible for Washington, with his small force, to prevent the passage. From Bordentown, four miles below Trenton, the Delaware turns westward, and forms an acute angle with its upper course, so that Cornwallis might cross high up and be as near Philadelphia as the American army. For this reason, Washington advised, that lines of defence should be drawn from the Schuylkill about the heights of Springetsbury, eastward to the Delaware, and General Putnam was ordered to superintend them. General Mifflin, who had just returned to camp, was again despatched to the city to take charge of the numerous stores it contained.

Cornwallis made some unsuccessful attempts to seize a number of boats, guarded by Lord Stirling, about Coryell's Ferry; and having repaired the bridges below Trenton, advanced a strong detachment to Bordentown, demonstrating the design of crossing the river at points above and below Trenton, and to march in two columns, directly, to Philadelphia; or completely to envelope the American army.

To counteract this plan, some galleys were stationed, so as to communicate the earliest intelligence of movements below, and to afford aid in repelling an attempt to cross the river, whilst the commander-in-chief made other dispositions to prevent the passage above, which, he believed, the real object of the enemy. Four brigades under Generals Lord Stirling, Mercer, Stephens, and De Fermoy, were posted from Yardley's to Coryell's Ferry, in such manner as to guard every suspicious point of the river, and to assist each other in case of attack. General Irvine, with the Pennsylvania remnant of the flying camp, and some Jersey militia under General Dickenson, were posted from Yardley's down to the ferry opposite Bordentown. Colonel Cadwalader, brother of him taken at Fort Washington, with the Pennsylvania militia, occupied the ground on either side of the Neshaminy as far as Dunk's Ferry, where Colonel Nixon was posted with the third Philadelphia battalion. Precise orders were given to the commanding officer of each detachment for his conduct, directing his route in case he should be driven from his post, and the passes he should endeavour to defend, on his way to the high grounds of Germantown, where the army was to rendezvous if forced from the river.

In the mean time, General Washington continued his exertions to augment his army. Expresses were sent through the counties of Pennsylvania, and to the governments of Delaware and Maryland, urging them to forward their militia without delay. General Mifflin, whose popular eloquence had been most serviceable, was again directed to repair immediately to the neighbouring counties, and Congress declared it of the highest importance, that he should make a progress through the state of Pennsylvania, to rouse its freemen to the immediate defence of the city and country; naming a committee to assist him in the good and necessary work. General Armstrong of Pennsylvania, was, at the same time, despatched by General Washington, into that part of the state, where he possessed most influence. In the hope of thus obtaining adequate force, even for offensive operations, General Heath was called from Peck's-kill, and General Gates ordered on with regulars of the northern army.

XVII. Although General Lee had been frequently directed to join the commander-in-chief, he tardily obeyed, manifesting a strong disposition to retain his separate command, and rather to hang on, and threaten the rear of the British army, than to strengthen that in their front. With this view, in opposition to the judgment of Washington, he proposed to establish himself at Morristown. Again urged to march, still declaring his opinion in favour of his own proposition, he proceeded, reluctantly, towards the Delaware. Whilst passing through Morris county, near Baskingridge, at the distance of about twenty miles from the British encampment, he, very indiscreetly, quartered, under a slight guard, in a house about three miles from his troops. Information of this circumstance was given, by a countryman, to Colonel Harcourt, then, with a body of cavalry, watching his movements, who, immediately, formed and executed the design of seizing him. Early in the morning of the twelfth of December, by a rapid march, his corps reached Lee's quarters. The general, receiving no intimation of his approach, until the house was surrounded, became a prisoner, and was borne off in triumph to the British army; where, for some time, he was treated, not as a prisoner of war, but as a deserter from the British service.

This misfortune made a painful impression throughout America. The confidence, originally placed in General Lee, alike due to his experience and talents, had been increased by his success, whilst commanding the southern department, and by the conviction, that his advice, to which was ascribed the operations in New York, which defeated the plans of General Howe, would, if more closely followed, have prevented the losses at Fort Washington and Fort Lee. No officer, save the commmander-in-chief, had so large a share of the confidence of the army and country, and his capture was universally bewailed, as the greatest calamity which had befallen the American arms.

XVIII. General Sullivan, on whom the command devolved after the loss of Lee, promptly obeying the orders which had been given to that officer, joined Washington, by the way of Phillipsburg, on the twentieth of December. On the same day, General Gates arrived with some northern troops. By these and other reinforcements, the American army was augmented to about seven thousand effective men.

Having failed to obtain boats for crossing the Delaware, the British general determined to close the campaign, and retire into winter quarters. About four thousand men were cantoned, on the Delaware at Trenton and Bordentown, at the White Horse and Mount Holly; and the remainder of the army was distributed from that river to the Hackensack. Still, Washington believed, that an attempt to gain Philadelphia would be made, should the ice become sufficiently firm to bear the army. He supposed, also, that one of the objects of General Howe, in covering so large a portion of New Jersey, was to impede the recruiting service. To counteract this, three regiments marching from Peck's-kill, were halted at Morristown, and united with about eight hundred Jersey militia, who had collected at the same place, under Colonel Ford, the whole being placed under the command of General Maxwell of New Jersey. He had orders to watch the motions of the enemy, to harass their marches, give intelligence of their movements, especially, of such as might be made from Brunswick towards Princeton or Trenton, to keep up the spirits of the militia, and to prevent the inhabitants from going within the British lines, from making their submission, and taking protections.

Whilst these measures were in progress, the commander-in-chief laboured to impress upon Congress, the necessity of still further exertions to form a permanent army, particularly, to increase the cavalry, artillery, and engineers, and, also, to enlarge his own powers, which were incompetent to many cases that daily occurred. The moment was certainly one of fearful interest. The existing army, except a few regiments from Virginia, Pennsylvania, Maryland, and New York, affording an effective force of about fifteen hundred men, would dissolve in a few days. New Jersey had, in a great measure, submitted, and the militia of Pennsylvania had not displayed the alacrity which had been expected; and should the frost bridge the Delaware, it was to be dreaded, that General Howe would seize Philadelphia, and that its capture might induce the belief, that the contest had become desperate.

XIX. But even this deepest gloom had its ray of hope,—the first beam of a rising sun of unparalleled brightness. In the dispersed situation of the British army, General Washington perceived the opportunity of striking a blow which might retrieve the holy cause, in the public opinion, and recover the ground he had lost. He formed the daring plan of attacking, at the same instant, all the British posts on the Delaware. If successful in whole or in part, he would erase the impression made by his losses and retreat, would compel his adversary to compress himself so, as no longer to cover New Jersey, and would remove from Philadelphia the imminent danger which threatened it. The merit of having originally suggested this attack, may, according to Dr. Gordon, be claimed for General Joseph Reed.*

Washington proposed to cross the river, in the night, at M'Konky's Ferry, about nine miles above Trenton, with four thousand troops, under his own immediate command, assisted by Generals Sullivan and Greene, and Colonel Knox, of the artillery; to march down in two divisions, one by the river, and the other by the Pennington road, both leading to the town,—and that they might reach their destination by five o'clock of the next day, to pass them over the river by twelve o'clock. General Irvine was directed to cross at the Trenton Ferry, and to secure the bridge below the town, to prevent the escape of any part of the enemy by that road; and General Cadwalader to pass at Dunks' Ferry, and carry the post at Mount Holly. It had been designed to unite the troops engaged in fortifying the city of Philadelphia, with those of Bristol, and to place them under the command of General Putnam; but there were such indications, in that city, of an insurrection in favour of the royal cause, that it was deemed unsafe to withdraw them.

The weather, on the night of the twenty-fifth of December, was very severe; mingled snow, hail, and rain, fell in great quantities, and so much ice was made in the river, that, the division passing at M'Konky's Ferry could not be gotten over, before three o'clock, and it was near four, before the line of march could be taken up. As the distance by either road to Trenton was the same, it was supposed that each column would arrive there about the same time. Orders were, therefore, given to attack at the instant of arrival, and after driving in the out-guards, to press rapidly after them into the town, so as to prevent the main body from forming.

* Gordon's American Revolution, vol. ii. p. 391.

General Washington accompanied the upper column; and arrived at the out-post on that road precisely at eight o'clock. He immediately drove it in, and in three minutes heard the discharge from the column on the river road. The picket guard kept up a fire from behind houses as they retreated, but the Americans followed with such ardour and rapidity, that they could make no stand. Colonel Rawle,* a gallant officer who commanded in Trenton, paraded his men, in order to meet the assailants. In the commencement of the action he was mortally wounded; upon which his troops attempted to file off from the right, and gain the road to Princeton. Washington threw a detachment in their front, and at the same time advanced rapidly on them in person. Being surrounded, and their artillery already seized, they laid down their arms, and surrendered themselves prisoners of war.

Unfortunately, the quantity of ice rendered it impracticable for General Irvine to execute the part of the plan allotted to him. He was unable to cross the river; and of consequence the lower road towards Bordentown remained open. About five hundred men, among whom was a troop of cavalry, stationed at the lower end of Trenton, availed themselves of this circumstance, and crossing the bridge in the commencement of the action, escaped. The same cause prevented General Cadwalader from attacking the post at Mount Holly. With infinite difficulty, he got over a part of his infantry; but it being impracticable to transport the artillery, the infantry returned.†

Although in consequence of the extreme severity of the night, the plan failed in many of its parts, the success attending that assumed by General Washington in person was complete. One thousand of the enemy were made prisoners, and as many stands of arms, with six field pieces, were secured. About twenty of the enemy were killed, including officers. On the part of the Americans, two privates were killed, two frozen to death, and one officer, and three or four privates, were wounded.

Had the divisions of General Irvine and Cadwalader crossed the river, the British would, probably, have been swept from the banks of the Delaware,‡ and Washington would have taken a position in the Jerseys. But it was now deemed unadvisable to hazard the loss of the advantage already gained, and the general crossed the river with the prisoners and stores he had taken.

XX. The British commander was greatly astonished by this unexpected display of vigour on the part of the American General. Knowing the enfeebled condition of his army, and the expectation of its immediate dissolution, he had supposed the war almost at an end; and, probably, looked forward to a triumph at Philadelphia, so soon as the river Delaware should be rendered passable by frost, when this energetic apparition, as if from the dead, awakened him from a delightful dream. He determined, though in the depth of winter, to recommence active operations; and Lord Cornwallis, who had retired to New York, for the purpose of embarking for Europe, suspended his departure and returned, to the Jerseys, in great force, for the purpose of regaining the ground which had been lost.

Meanwhile, Count Donop; who commanded the troops posted below

* Quere? Rahl.

† Marshall. Wash. Lett.

‡ How practicable this would have been, appears from the following fact. Colonel Reed, who was with the division of Cadwalader, passed the ferry with the van of the infantry. He immediately despatched some trusty persons to examine the situation of the troops at Mount Holly. The report made by his messengers was, that they had looked into several houses in which the soldiers were quartered, and had found them, generally, fast asleep, under the influence, as was conceived, of the spirituous liquors they had drank the preceding day, which was Christmas. That there appeared to be no apprehension of danger, nor precautions against it.

Trenton, learning the disaster which had befallen Colonel Rawle, immediately commenced his retreat by the road leading to Amboy, and joined General Leslie at Princeton. The next day General Cadwalader took post on the Jersey shore, with orders to harass the enemy if he could do so safely, but to put nothing to hazard until he should be joined by the continental battalions. General Mifflin now joined General Irvine with a detachment of Pennsylvania militia, amounting to about fifteen hundred men, who were also ordered to cross the Delaware.

XXV. Once more at the head of a force with which he might attempt something, the general-in-chief resolved not to remain inactive. Inferior as he was to the enemy, he yet determined to employ the winter in endeavouring to recover the whole, or the greater part of Jersey.

With this view, he ordered General Heath, at Peck's-kill, on the North river, to leave a small detachment of troops at that place, and, with the main body of the New England militia, to move into Jersey, and approach the British cantonments. General Maxwell was directed to collect the militia, to harass their flank and rear, and to attack their out-posts. Having made these dispositions, Washington again crossed the Delaware, with his continental regiments, and took post at Trenton. Here he exerted all his influence to prevail on the troops from New England, whose terms of service expired on the last day of December, to continue during the present exigency, and, with infinite difficulty, and a bounty of ten dollars, many were induced to re-engage for six weeks.

The British were now (January, 1777) collected in force at Princeton, under Lord Cornwallis, where some works were thrown up; and, as they advanced a strong corps towards Trenton, and knew that the troops from New England were entitled to be discharged, it was justly expected they would attack the American army.

Generals Mifflin and Cadwalader, who lay at Bordentown and Crosswicks, with three thousand six hundred militia, on the night of the first of January, joined the commander-in-chief, whose whole effective force, with this addition, did not exceed five thousand men.

Lord Cornwallis advanced the next morning. About four o'clock in the afternoon, after some slight skirmishing with a small party detached to Maidenhead to harass and delay his march, his van reached Trenton, while the rear was at Maidenhead, about half way between Princeton and Trenton. On his approach, General Washington retired across the Assunpink, a creek which runs through the town, behind which he drew up his army. The British attempted to cross at several places, but the fords being guarded, they halted and kindled their fires. The American troops kindled their fires likewise, and a cannonade was kept up on both sides until dark.

The situation of General Wsshington was, now, again extremely critical. If he maintained his present position, it was certain that he would be attacked, next morning, by a force, in all respects, superior to his own; and the result would, most probably, be the destruction of his little army. If he attempted to retreat over the Delaware, now covered with ice, which, in consequence of a few mild and foggy days, was not firm enough to march upon, a considerable loss, perhaps a total defeat, would be sustained. In any event, the Jerseys would once more be entirely in possession of the enemy; the public mind would again be depressed, recruiting be discouraged by his apparent inferiority; and Philadelphia would a second time be in the grasp of General Howe. It was obvious, that the one event or the other would deduct greatly from the advantages promised by his late success; and, if it should not render the American cause, absolutely, desperate, would very essentially injure it.

XXII. In this state of things, he formed the bold and judicious design of abandoning the Delaware, and marching silently in the night by a circuitous route, along the left flank of the British army, into their rear at Princeton, where he knew they could not be very strong. After beating them there, he proposed to make a rapid movement to Brunswick, where their baggage and principal magazines lay, under a weak guard.

A council of war having approved this plan, preparations were immediately made for its execution. As soon as it was dark, the baggage was removed silently to Burlington; and about one o'clock in the morning of the third, after renewing their fires, and leaving their guards at the bridge and other passes over the creek, the army decamped with perfect secrecy, taking the Quaker road to Princeton. Here, three British regiments had encamped the preceding night, two of which commenced their march early in the morning to join the rear of their army at Maidenhead. About sunrise,* when they had proceeded about two miles, they saw the Americans advancing on the left, in a direction which would enter the road in their rear. They immediately faced about, and, repassing Stonybrook, moved under cover of a copse of woods towards the Americans, whose van was conducted by General Mercer. A sharp action ensued, which, however, was not of long duration. The militia, of which the advanced party was principally composed, soon gave way, and the few regulars attached to them were not strong enough to maintain their ground. While gallantly exerting himself to rally his broken troops, General Mercer was mortally wounded, and the van was entirely routed. But the fortune of the day was soon changed. The main body of the army, led by General Washington in person, followed close in the rear, and attacked the enemy with great spirit. Persuaded that defeat would irretrievably ruin the affairs of America, he advanced in the very front of the battle, and exposed himself to the hottest fire of the enemy. He was so well supported by the same troops who, a few days before, had served at Trenton, that the British, in turn, were compelled to give way. Their line was broken, and the two regiments separated from each other. Colonel Mawhood, who commanded that in front, and who, being, therefore, on the right, was nearest the rear division of the army under Lord Cornwallis, retired to the main road and continued his route to Maidenhead. The fifty-fifth regiment, which was on the British left, being hard pressed, fled, in confusion, across the fields and great road, into a back road leading between Hillsborough and Kingston towards Brunswick.† The vicinity of the British forces at Maidenhead, secured Colonel Mawhood from pursuit, and General Washington pressed forward to Princeton. The regiment remaining in that place took post in the college, and made some show of resistance; but the artillery being brought up, it was abandoned, and the greater part of them were made prisoners. A few saved themselves by a precipitate retreat to Brunswick.

In this action, upwards of one hundred of the British were killed, and near three hundred were taken prisoners. The loss of the Americans in killed was somewhat less, but in this number was included General Mercer,

* "The march of the army had been rendered much more expeditious, than it could otherwise have been, by a fortunate change of weather. On the evening of the second, it became excessively cold, and the roads which had become soft, were rendered as hard as pavement."

† "This account of the battle of Princeton varies, in some of its circumstances, especially in the manner of meeting the enemy, from that originally given. The papers in possession of the author do not state the relative situation of the armies when the action commenced. He is indebted for that information to a very intelligent friend, to whom he feels great obligation, which it gives him much gratification to acknowledge."—*Marshall.*

a very valuable officer from Virginia, who had served with the commander-in-chief in the war against the French and Indians, which terminated in 1763, and was greatly esteemed by him. Colonels Haslett and Potter, brave and excellent officers from Delaware and Pennsylvania; Captain Neal of the artillery, Captain Fleming, who on that day commanded the seventh Virginia regiment, and five other valuable officers, were also among the slain.

On the appearance of daylight,* Lord Cornwallis discovered that the American army had moved off in the night, and immediately conceived the plan of Washington. He was under extreme apprehension for Brunswick, where were magazines of great value, with the military chest containing about seventy thousand pounds. Breaking up his camp, he commenced a rapid march to that place, for the purpose of affording it protection; and was close in the rear of the American army before it could leave Princeton.

XXIII. General Washington was again in a very perilous situation. His small army was exhausted with extreme fatigue. His troops had been without sleep, all of them one night, and some of them two. They were without blankets; many of them barefooted, and otherwise thinly clad; and he was eighteen miles from his point of destination. He was closely pursued by an enemy, much superior in point of numbers, well clothed and fresh, and who must necessarily come up with him before he could accomplish his designs on Brunswick, if any opposition should there be made to him. He, therefore, wisely, determined to abandon the remaining part of his plan;† and breaking down the bridges over Millstone Creek, between Princeton and Brunswick, he took the road leading up the country to Pluckemin, where his troops were permitted to refresh themselves, and to take that rest which they so greatly required. Lord Cornwallis continued his march to Brunswick, which he reached in the course of that night. General Matthews, who commanded at that place, had been greatly alarmed; and while he took measures to defend himself, the utmost industry was used to remove the military stores to a place of greater safety.

The sufferings of the American army had been so great, from the severity of the season, and the active service in which they had been engaged;

* "The time when this movement of the American army was discovered by Lord Cornwallis, is taken from the British accounts. In the United States it was understood that the firing towards Princeton gave him the first intimation of the skilful manœuvre of the preceding night. It was also generally said at the time, that in the preceding evening, when the British army reached Trenton, Sir William Erskine urged an immediate attack, but Lord Cornwallis was disposed to defer it until the next morning, as his troops were fatigued by their day's march from Princeton, and the Americans were so hemmed in by the Delaware, filled with ice, on one side, and Crosswick's Creek, which is navigable for sloops, in their rear, that a retreat was impossible, and he could make sure work in the morning. To this observation, Sir William is said to have replied, "If Washington is the general I take him to be, his army will not be found on its present ground in the morning." The author has lately received this anecdote in a manner which induces him to think it worthy of more credit, than he had supposed it to be entitled to, while he received it merely as the report of the day."—*Marshall.*

"It is also an additional proof of the secrecy with which this manœuvre was executed, that some militia field officers who had retired into the rear, to get a good night's sleep, were, next morning, absolutely unable to say, what had become of the American army."—*Ibid.*

† "A council was held on horseback, and some gentlemen advised that he should file off to the southward. On crossing the Millstone river at Kingston, the guides were directed to take the road leading to the northward, through Hillsborough, but before they reached Somerset court-house, many of the infantry, worn out with fatigue, fasting and want of rest, lay down and fell asleep by the way. But the object of Lord Cornwallis being to save Brunswick, he did not turn aside to molest the American army."—*Ibid.*

their complaints, especially on the part of the militia, were so loud, their numbers were reducing so fast, by returning home, and by sickness, that General Washington found it impracticable, further to prosecute offensive operations. It was, therefore, deemed absolutely necessary to retire to Morristown, in order to put his men under cover, and to give them some repose.

The affairs of Trenton and Princeton were represented, and considered as great victories. They were believed, by the body of the people, to evidence the superiority of their army, and of their general. The opinion that they were engaged in a hopeless contest, yielded to a confidence that proper exertions on their part, would be crowned with ultimate success.

This change of opinion relative to the issue of the war, was accompanied with an essential change in conduct; and although the regiments required by Congress were not completed, they were made much stronger than, before this happy revolution in the aspect of public affairs, was believed to have been possible.

XXIV. The firmness manifested by Congress throughout the gloomy and trying period which intervened between the loss of Fort Washington, and the battle of Princeton, gives the members of that period a just claim to the admiration of the world, and to the gratitude of their fellow citizens. Unawed by the dangers which threatened them, and regardless of personal safety, they did not for an instant admit the idea, that the independence they had declared was to be surrendered, and peace to be purchased by returning to their ancient colonial situation. As the British army advanced through Jersey, and the consequent insecurity of Philadelphia rendered an adjournment of Congress from that place to one further removed from the seat of war, a necessary measure of precaution, their exertions seemed to increase with their difficulties. They sought to remove the despondence which was seizing and paralyzing the public mind, by an address to the states, in which every argument was suggested which could rouse them to vigorous action. They made the most strenuous efforts to animate the militia, and impel them to the field, by the agency of those whose popular eloquence best fitted them for such a service.

When reassembled at Baltimore, their resolutions exhibited no evidences of confusion or dismay; and the most judicious efforts were made, by collecting, as soon as possible, a respectable military force, to repair the mischief produced by past errors.

Declaring, that in the present situation of things, the very existence of civil liberty depended on the right execution of military powers, to a vigorous direction of which, distant, numerous, and deliberative bodies were entirely unequal, they authorized General Washington to raise sixteen additional regiments, and conferred upon him, for six months, powers for the conduct of the war, which were almost unlimited.*

XXV. And that no doubt might be entertained among foreign nations, and, particularly, in France, whose aid they were soliciting, Congress declared their determination, to listen to no terms founded on their resumption of the character of British subjects: but trusting the event to Providence, and risking all consequences, they resolved to adhere to the independence they had declared, and to the freedom of trade they had proposed to all nations. Copies of these resolutions were sent to the principal courts in Europe, and proper persons appointed to solicit their friendship to the new formed states. These despatches fell into the hands of the British, and by them were published; a circumstance, by no means, unacceptable to the Congress, who were persuaded, that an apprehension of an accommodation with Great

* Marshall.

Britain, was a principal objection to the interference of foreign courts, in what was represented to be no more than a domestic quarrel. A resolution, adopted in the worst fortune, that Congress would listen to no terms of re-union with the parent state, would, it was believed, convince those who wished for the dismemberment of the British empire, that it was sound policy to prevent the conquest of the United States.

XXVI. The favourable change in the affairs of the Americans, was in no place so sensibly felt as in New Jersey, where the people suffered all the horrors which could flow from a licentious and almost unrestrained soldiery. When the royal army entered Jersey, the inhabitants, pretty generally, remained in their houses, and many thousands received printed protections, signed by order of the British commander-in-chief. This event, in the language of Governor Livingston, "enabled the patriots more effectually to distinguish their friends from their enemies. It winnowed the chaff from the grain. It discriminated the temporizing politician, who, on the first appearance of danger, determined to secure his idol—property, at the hazard of the general weal, from the persevering patriot, who, having embarked his all in the common cause, chose rather, to risk, rather, to lose that *all* for the preservation of the more inestimable treasure *Liberty*, than to possess it upon the ignominious terms of tamely resigning his country and posterity to perpetual servitude." But it did more, "It opened the eyes of those who were made to believe that their impious merit in abetting the persecutors, would exempt them from being involved in the common calamity."* Neither the proclamation of the commissioners, nor protections, saved the people from plunder, or insult. Their property was taken and destroyed without distinction of persons. They exhibited their protections, but the Hessians could not read and would not understand them, and the British soldiers deemed it foul disgrace that the Hessians should be the only plunderers. Discontents and murmurs increased every hour with the ravages of both, which were almost sanctioned by general orders,† and which spared neither friend nor foe. Neither age nor sex protected from outrage. Infants, children, old men, and women, were left naked and exposed, without a blanket to cover them from the inclemency of winter. Furniture which could not be carried away, was wantonly destroyed; dwellings and out-houses burned, or rendered uninhabitable; churches, and other public buildings consumed; and the rape of women, and even very young girls filled the measure of woe. Such miseries are the usual fate of the conquered, nor were they inflicted with less reserve, that the patients were rebellious subjects. But even the worm will turn upon the oppressor. Had every citizen been secured in his rights, protected in his property, and paid for his supplies, the consequence might have been fatal to the cause of independence. What the earnest commendations of Congress, the zealous exertions of Governor Livingston, and the state authorities, and the ardent supplications of Washington could not effect, was produced by the rapine and devastations of the royal forces.

The whole country became instantly hostile to the invaders. Sufferers of all parties rose as one man, to revenge their personal injuries. Those who from age and infirmities were incapable of military service, kept a strict watch upon the movements of the royal army, and from time to time, com-

* Livingston's Address to the Assembly, 28th February, 1777.

† The orders of General Howe to Count Donop, directed that "all salted and meal provisions, which may be judged to exceed the quantity necessary for the subsistence of an ordinary family, shall be considered a magazine of the enemy, and seized for the King, and given to the troops as a saving for the public." Under such an order, the pickling tubs, and garners of every Jersey farmer became lawful prize; the captor being judge of the necessary quantity for the family subsistence.

municated information to their countrymen in arms. Those who lately declined all opposition though called on by the sacred tie of honour, pledged to each other in the declaration of independence, cheerfully embodied, when they found submission to be unavailing for the security of their estates. This is not to be attributed wholly to the victories of Trenton and Princeton. In the very moment of these actions, or before the results were known, individuals, ignorant of Washington's movements, concerted insurrections to revenge their peculiar injuries. The contest had its source in the unrighteous claim of the British statesmen, to appropriate the property of the colonists against their consent. It was reanimated by a new and direct application of the principle by the British army. Men who could not apprehend the consequences of British taxation, nor of American independence, could feel the injuries inflicted by insolent, and cruel, and brutal soldiers. The militia of New Jersey, who had hitherto behaved shamefully, from this time forward, generally, acquired high reputation; and throughout a long and tedious war, conducted themselves with spirit and discipline scarce surpassed by the regular troops.* In small parties they now scoured the country in every direction, seized on stragglers, in several slight skirmishes behaved unexceptionably well, and collected in such numbers as to threaten the weaker British posts, with the fate which those at Trenton and Princeton had already experienced. In a few days, indeed, the Americans had overrun the Jerseys. The enemy was forced from Woodbridge; General Maxwell surprised Elizabethtown, and took near one hundred prisoners with a quantity of baggage; Newark was abandoned, and the royal troops were confined to New Brunswick and Amboy, judiciously selected for the double purpose of again penetrating the country, and of keeping up a safe communication with New York. Within four days after the affair at Princeton, between forty and fifty Waldeckers were killed, wounded, or taken, at Springfield, by an equal number of the same Jersey militia, which but a month before, had abandoned all opposition. This enterprise was conducted by Colonel Spencer, whose gallantry was rewarded with the command of a regiment. On the 20th of January, General Dickenson, with about four hundred militia, and fifty of the Pennsylvania riflemen, defeated near Somerset court-house, on the Millstone river, a foraging party of the enemy of about equal number, and took forty wagons, upwards of one hundred horses, and many cattle and sheep, which they had collected. They retreated so precipitately, that he made but nine prisoners, but many dead and wounded were carried off in light wagons. The general received much praise for his courage and conduct; for though his troops were raw, he led them through the river middle deep, and charged with so much impetuosity, that the enemy, notwithstanding he had three field pieces, gave way and left the convoy. About a month after this affair, Colonel Neilson of New Brunswick, with a detachment of one hundred and fifty militia, surprised and captured Major Stockton, (one of the numerous family of that name, who, from his treachery, was called "double Dick,") at the head of fifty-nine privates, refugees, in British pay.

The three months which followed the battle of Trenton, passed away without any important military enterprise, other than we have described. Major-general Putnam took post at Princeton, in order to cover the country in the vicinity. He had only a few hundred troops, though he was no more than eighteen miles distant from the strong garrison of the British at Brunswick. At one period, he had fewer men for duty, than miles of frontier to guard. The situation of General Washington at Morristown, was not more eligible. His force was inconsiderable, compared with that of the British;

* Ramsay.

but the enemy and his own countrymen believed the contrary. Their deception was cherished and artfully continued by the specious parade of a numerous army. The officers, in positions difficult of access, by a constant communication with each other, secured themselves from insult and surprise.

XXVI. While the enemy was thus surrounded, and harassed by an almost imaginary army, whose parts disappeared at the approach of any considerable force, but instantly presented themselves when that force retreated, General Washington came to the hazardous, but judicious, resolution, of delivering himself and his future force from the dread of a calamity, which he could not elude, and which had been more fatal in his camp, than the sword of the enemy.

The small-pox, of all the agents of death, was the most painful and hideous. Inoculation had not yet in America, stripped it of its terrors; nor vaccination rendered it impotent. In despite of the utmost vigilance, it had penetrated to the northern and middle armies, and impaired the strength of both. In the northern, especially, its havoc had been so great, that the delay, requisite to obtain the command of Lake Champlain, alone, prevented the British army from reaching the Hudson. To neutralize the virulence of the pest, inoculation was now resorted to. With all possible secrecy, preparations were made to give the infection to the troops in camp, at Philadelphia, and other places; and thus an army was procured exempt from a calamity, the very fear of which endangered the most important operations.

XXVII. The hostile spirit which now displayed itself in the State of New Jersey, was encouraged by a politic and humane proclamation, issued by the commander-in-chief, about the last of January, directed to those who had submitted to, and taken protection from, the enemy; discharging the obligations created by their oaths of allegiance to the king, and requiring them to repair to head quarters, or to the quarters of the nearest general officer, and to swear allegiance to the United States, as the condition of a full pardon. An act of Assembly, conceived in the same spirit, was passed a few months after. The beneficial effects of these measures were soon visible. The people flocked in from every quarter, to take the oaths; but the Legislature could not, yet, be induced to pass an act, to bring the militia certainly into the field.

XXVIII. Amid these testimonies of reviving patriotism, it is painful to record the crimes which were committed by American soldiers, and which were but too much encouraged by the heterogeneous organization of the army; for the correction of which, General Washington found it necessary, by proclamation, to prohibit, "both in the militia and continental troops, in the most positive terms, the infamous practices of plundering the inhabitants, under the specious pretence of their being tories. It is our duty," continued the proclamation, "to give protection and support to the poor, distressed inhabitants, not to multiply their calamities. After this order, any officer found plundering the inhabitants, under the pretence of their being tories, may expect to be punished in the severest manner."

CHAPTER XIV.

I. Organization of the New Jersey State Government—II. First Address of the Governor—Other principal Officers.—III. Condition of the State at this period. IV. State of the Northern Department—Operations on the Lakes.—V. The British seize Rhode Island.—VI. Demonstration of General Heath, on Long Island. —Condition of the American Army, in New Jersey—Skirmishing.—VII. Early efforts of Sir William Howe, to destroy the American Magazines—Stores burned at Peck's-kill—at Danbury.—VIII. Successful enterprise of Colonel Meigs, against Sagg Harbour.—IX. Movements of General Washington, on opening the Campaign—Removal of the Army to Middlebrook—Disposition of the Troops. X. Operations of the Army under General Howe—Feint to cross the Delaware—Retreat from New Jersey—Returns, and attacks the American Army.—XI. Perplexity of Washington, caused by the Movements of the British Forces.—XII. Capture of Major-general Prescott, by Major Barton.—XIII. General Howe embarks for the southward—Measures of Washington thereon.—XIV. Attempt of General Sullivan, with Colonel Ogden, upon the Tories on Staten Island.—XV. Arrival of the British Army at Elk River—its Progress—Operations of the American Army—Battle of Brandywine.—XVI. Subsequent movement of the Armies.—XVII. Second encounter of the hostile Armies—they are separated by rain.—XVIII. Affairs of Paoli.—XIX. The British enter Philadelphia.—XX. Congress remove to Lancaster, thence to York.—XXI. Attack and defence of the Fortifications on the Delaware.—XXII. Battle of Germantown.—XXIII. Operations in New Jersey.—XXIV. Further proceedings on the Delaware.—XXV. Repulse of Count Donop, from Fort Mercer.—XXVI. General Greene despatched to New Jersey.—XXVII. Capture of Fort Mifflin, and abandonment of Fort Mercer.—XXVIII. Attempt of General Dickenson on Staten Island.—XXIX. American Army reinforced.—XXX. Attacked at White Marsh, by the British.—XXXI. The American Army retires into Winter Quarters.—XXXII. English plans for the Northern Campaign.—XXXIII. Condition of the American Northern Department.—XXXIV. Burgoyne captures the Forts on the Lakes, and disperses the American Army.—XXXV. Recuperative measures of General Schuyler.—XXXVI. Repulse of St. Leger, from Fort Schuyler.—XXXVII. Defeat of Colonel Baum, at Bennington.—XXXVIII. Beneficial result of these fortunate Events.—XXXIX. Battles on the Hudson, and Capture of Burgoyne.—XL. Movements of Sir Henry Clinton, in the Highlands.—XLI. Effect of the Capture of Burgoyne—at home and abroad.—XLII. Congress refuse to execute the Articles of Capitulation—their reasons.

I. The first Legislature of independent New Jersey, convened at Princeton, on the 27th of August, 1776. John Stephens was elected vice-president of the Council, and John Hart, speaker of the House of Representatives; and on the 31st of the month, William Livingston, Esq., was chosen in joint ballot, governor of the new State. This appointment removed him from a military command, at Elizabethtown, alike incompatible with his years, his habits, and his previous studies, to one, for which the employments of his life had admirably prepared him. On the first ballot, the votes were equally divided, between him and Richard Stockton; but on the second, on the succeeding day, he had a majority, of how many does not appear.* His rival,

* Dr. Gordon, (Hist. Revolution, vol. ii. p. 300,) says—"There was an equal number of votes for him and Mr. Stockton; but the latter having, just at the moment, refused to furnish his team of horses, for the service of the public, and the Legislature coming to the knowledge, the choice of Mr. Livingston took place immediately."—Mr. Sedgwick, in his life of Governor Livingston, very properly repudiates this reason, and observes—"I am told by a person formerly intimate with John Cleve Symmes, at this time a member of council, that he had often said between jest and earnest, 'that he had made Mr. Livingston governor.' Whether by this, is meant, that, on the

who, previous to the revolution, held a seat on the bench of the Supreme Court, was named chief-justice, but he refused the office. Governor Livingston continued to fulfil the duties of the executive, from this period until his death, a space of fourteen years, being annually re-elected, either, unanimously, or by large majorities.

II. His first address to the Assembly, displays that deep devotion to liberty, that religious confidence in final success, that inextinguishable hatred of British oppression, with that attention to affairs, which made him one of the most efficient agents of American deliverance. "Let us, gentlemen," so closes this earnest call for their warmest sympathy, and most vigorous exertions, in the American cause, "both by precept and practice, encourage a spirit of economy, industry and patriotism, and that public integrity and righteousness, which cannot fail to exalt a nation; setting our faces, at the same time, *like a flint*, against that dissoluteness of manners and political corruption, which will ever be the reproach of any people. May the foundation of our infant State, be laid in virtue and the fear of God—and the superstructure will rise glorious, and endure for ages. Then may we humbly expect the blessing of the Most High, who *divides* to the nations their inheritance, and *separates* the sons of Adam.* In fine, gentlemen, whilst we are applauded by the whole world, for demolishing the old fabric, rotten and ruinous as it is, let us unitedly strive to approve ourselves master builders, by giving beauty, strength and stability to the new."†

The other principal officers chosen for the organization of the government were, John De Hart, chief justice, Samuel Tucker, second, and Francis Hopkinson, third justices, and Jonathan D. Sergeant, clerk of the Supreme Court; Charles Petit secretary of state, and Richard Smith treasurer. Mr. De Hart refusing the office of chief justice, Mr. Robert Morris was appointed; the place of Mr. Tucker upon his declination, was given to Isaac Smith, and that of Mr. Hopkinson, on his acceptance of the admiralty in Philadelphia, was filled by John Cleves Symmes; Mr. Sergeant refusing to act as clerk, Bowes Reed was appointed.

III. The officers however, were continually changing, both military and civil; and for the services of the latter, there was at this period, but too little occasion. The campaign of 1776, was the most trying period of the war, and drew largely upon the ability and fortitude of the governor and other constituted authorities of the state. On the 15th September, the city of New York fell into the hands of the enemy. Two months were consumed by the hostile armies on the east bank of the Hudson. But when, on the 10th of November, the fall of Fort Washington was followed by the passage of the North river, by the British forces under Cornwallis, by the abandonment of Fort Lee, and the rapid retreat of the American army, the scene of action was immediately transferred to the heart of New Jersey.

Governor Livingston made the most strenuous exertions with the Assembly and with the people, to have the militia in the field to oppose the invading force. But it was not practicable to control the panic which had seized upon the mass of the population. The barefooted, and almost naked continental

final vote, Governor Livingston had only a bare majority, or that Mr. Symmes induced the adherents of Mr. Stockton to join those who were in favour of his rival, I doubt whether there are now any means of ascertaining."—p. 206. *n*.

* Deut. xxxii. 8.

† Votes of Assembly. From an expression in this paragraph, and his inflexible disposition, the governor was, for some time after this, known by the name of *Dr. Flint;* and an anecdote is told of Mr. Ames, who, in some momentary confusion of ideas, at a dinner in New York, where he met Governor Livingston, asked *Dr. Flint*, whether the town of Trenton was well or ill disposed to the new constitution.—*Sedgwick's Livingston*, 207.

army, retreating before the well appointed battalions of the enemy, impaired the confidence of the people, not less in the commander-in-chief, than in their own resources. The defenceless Legislature, with the governor at their head, removed from Princeton to Burlington, where they adjourned on the 2d of December, each man retiring to his home, to take charge of his peculiar interests. There scarcely remained a vestige of the lately constituted government, or any who owed it allegiance; and until the battle of Trenton, (25th December) New Jersey might have been considered a conquered country.*

IV. Although the Americans had been driven from Canada, and the hope of its conquest, was, for the present abandoned, the defence of the northern department of the United States was of the greatest importance. The possession of lakes Champlain and George, by the enemy, might induce that of Albany and all the upper parts of the Hudson, and opening a free communication between the northern British army, and that in New York, sever the eastern from the middle and southern states, and encourage the royalists of the middle and upper country, who were numerous, to show themselves in force. Under these impressions, such detachments were made from the army under Washington, on the opening of the campaign of 1776, as to expose him to the greatest hazards.

The northern department had been entrusted to General Schuyler, who, with high talents, possessed great influence in the country. General Gates had been named to the army in Canada, and though that army was now in the department of Schuyler, his senior officer, he still claimed the command. But Congress removed this difficulty by declaring, it was not their intention to place the former over the latter, and recommending them to co-operate harmoniously.

When expelled from Canada, the Americans had retired to the strong post of Crown Point, at the south end of Lake Champlain, whither General Carleton, for want of vessels, was unable immediately to follow them. But this obstacle was removed by the incredible exertions, with which a considerable fleet was built and equipped. General Schuyler, on his part, strenuously endeavoured to strengthen his little fleet, and to preserve the command of the lakes; but it was impracticable to obtain artillery, materials for ship building, or workmen, and his force was consequently much inferior to that of the enemy. Its command was given to the intrepid Arnold, from whom every thing was expected which courage could perform.

The small pox, which had made such ravages in the preceding campaign, still infected the army, and communicating itself to the reinforcements, rendered it necessary to stop many on their march: and mortality from this and other causes, induced the general officers in council, in the month of July, to resolve on evacuating Crown Point, and to concentrate their forces about Ticonderoga, a strong post, twelve miles from the former. This measure, apparently unavoidable, gave great chagrin to Congress, who entertained hopes of extending their operations to lakes Erie, and Ontario.

The British, by the first of October, had upon the lake, a fleet carrying more than an hundred guns, navigated by seven hundred prime sailors, and conducted by Captain Pringle; on board of which was General Carleton himself. On the 11th it proceeded to attack Arnold, then very advantageously

* The case of Samuel Tucker strongly illustrates the panic which prevailed among some of the whigs, on the invasion of the British. President of the convention which formed the constitution of the State—Chairman of the committee of safety, treasurer, aud subsequently, Judge of the Supreme Court, he took a protection of the British, and thus renounced allegiance to the state, and vacated his offices. Journal of Assembly, 17th December, 1777, and votes passim. *Sedgwick's Livingston*, 209, &c.

posted with a much inferior force, in the passage between the island of Valicour, and the western main. The wind favouring him, he was enabled to keep up the engagement for several hours, during which, his best schooner was burnt, and another vessel was sunk; but the enemy did not suffer less. Finding it impossible to renew the action with hopes of success, Arnold made his escape during the night, and was the next morning out of view of his pursuers, hastening to obtain shelter under the guns of the fort at Ticonderoga. But the enemy came up with him at noon, and he was compelled, after a spirited resistance of two hours, and the loss of another of his ships, with the second in command on board, to run the greater part of his vessels on shore, a few leagues from Crown Point, where he landed their crews in safety. A portion of his squadron passed Crown Point, and escaped to Ticonderoga. Those run on shore he burned, to prevent their capture by the conquerors.

Crown Point was seized by General Carleton, who advanced part of his fleet into Lake George, within view of Ticonderoga, and his army approached that place as if to lay siege to it. But after reconnoitering the works, and observing the steady countenance of the garrison, which consisted of between eight and nine thousand men, he concluded that it was too late in the season to invest the fortress, and returned to Canada, placing his troops in winter quarters, and making the Isle aux Noix his most advanced post. This retreat relieved the apprehensions of the Americans, and enabled General Gates, as we have seen, to march with a detachment of the northern army, to aid the commander-in-chief on the Delaware.

V. With the view of making his power more extensively felt, and of impeding the march of the troops about to be raised in New England, for the reinforcement of the army of General Washington, General Howe despatched an expedition consisting of a land force of three thousand men, under Sir Henry Clinton, and a fleet commanded by Sir Peter Parker, to take possession of Rhode Island, which was accomplished about the last of November, without material opposition. This diversion was effective in its main object; and the English derived permanent advantage, and the Americans sustained lasting inconvenience, from their possession of this post. The last were deprived of a harbour, admirably adapted to serve their maritime expeditions.

VI. With these concise notices of events in the northern and eastern sections of the country, we proceed to a more particular detail of those in New Jersey and the neighbouring states. Whilst Philadelphia was supposed to be in imminent danger, the militia of New England, in considerable numbers, had been ordered to the Delaware; and although many were detained by the invasion of Rhode Island, a few regiments reached the camp of General Heath, upon the North river, where they were arrested by the order of the commander-in-chief, for the purpose of making a diversion on the side of New York. The army in New Jersey, with the detachment to Rhode Island, it was supposed, had greatly reduced the British force in the city. About two thousand men were in the neighbourhood of King's Bridge, and all the other troops on the island were not estimated at a greater number. On Long Island, it was said, there was only Delancy's brigade of American loyalists, amounting to less than one thousand men. Under these circumstances, it was presumed, that the New York and New Jersey militia might form a respectable army, with which General Heath might alarm, and, perhaps, more than alarm that important post. He was directed to approach King's Bridge, to carry off the forage and provisions with which the enemy might be supplied, and if circumstances should justify, to attack the forts which guarded the entrance into the island. In such event, it was anticipated, that fears for New York would induce General Howe, either to abandon the Jerseys entirely, when his troops would suffer extremely through the winter, for fuel, forage and provisions, or so to weaken his posts at Brunswick and Amboy, as to permit General Washington to attack them with advantage. Should neither of these results be produced, some advantages might be gained on York or Long Island.

Pursuant to these views, General Heath marched* towards West Chester, and summoned Fort Independence; but the garrison refusing to surrender, he did not venture an assault with militia. Receiving intelligence that the British army had embarked from Rhode Island, and might, by entering the Sound, land in his rear, he was compelled to withdraw into the Highlands; not however, without the acquisition of considerable quantities of forage and cattle.

VII. In the mean time, repeated skirmishes on the lines increased the distress of the enemy, and the confidence of the Americans in themselves. The British found it totally unsafe to forage but with large covering parties, which were often attacked with advantage, and their horses frequently taken. Their miserable appearance evinced the scarcity which prevailed in the camp. In these skirmishes, prisoners were often made; and frequent small successes, the details of which filled the papers throughout America, served to animate the people at large, who even supposed that the British would be driven to their ships for protection, so soon as the season would permit the armies to take the field. Yet the real situation of General Washington, happily concealed, both from the enemy and from his own countrymen, was extremely critical. He was often abandoned by bodies of the militia, before their places were filled by others; and, thus, left in a state of dangerous weakness, with all his positions exposed to imminent hazard. This was not the only inconvenience resulting from this fluctuating army. The soldiers carried off arms and blankets which had been unavoidably delivered to them, to be used while in camp, and thus wasted in advance, the military stores collected for the ensuing campaign.†

While exposed to these embarrassing inconveniences, the general received intelligence, that reinforcements were arriving from Rhode Island, and that the movement of General Heath had not produced the effects he had expected. His fears for Philadelphia revived; and the New England troops, except so many as might be deemed necessary to guard the Highlands, were ordered immediately to join him. Heavy requisitions were also made on the neighbouring militia, especially of New Jersey.

The movement so much apprehended, was not made; and the war of skirmishes on the side of Jersey, continued throughout the winter. In the course of it, the British loss was supposed to be more considerable than they had sustained at Trenton and Princeton; and hopes were entertained that, from the scarcity of forage, neither their cavalry, nor draught horses would be in a condition to take the field, when the campaign should open.

This light war was far short of the hopes of the American General, who submitted, with infinite reluctance, to the inactivity his weakness imposed on him. He had flattered himself that the reviving courage of his countrymen would have placed at his disposal a force which would enable him to beat the enemy in detail, during the winter, and to repel the great exertions which would be made for the conquest of America in the ensuing summer.

All the intelligence from Europe concurred in demonstrating the fallacy of the hope, still cherished by many, that the war would be abandoned. Never had the administration been supported by greater majorities in Parliament; and the body of the nation appeared well disposed to employ all its means to reannex to the empire its revolted colonies. The importance of

* June, 1776.

† Marshall's Washington.

destroying, or maiming the present army before it could be reinforced was, consequently, felt in its full extent; and the commander-in-chief made the most strenuous endeavours to promote the recruiting service, and to collect the recruits in such numbers, as would enable him successfully to attack the British posts, either in Rhode Island, New York, or New Jersey. The state sovereignties, where the real energies of government resided, were, incessantly, urged to take effectual measures to fill their regiments, and to bring their respective quotas early into the field. They were pressed to march their recruits, so soon as they could be cleansed from the small-pox, by companies, and even by parts of companies, to the several stations assigned them; and those general officers, who were supposed to possess most influence, were detached to their respective states, for the purpose of promoting and superintending the recruiting service.

At the instance of the commander-in-chief, Congress passed such resolutions as were calculated to second his views. They authorized him to draw the eastern troops from Peck's-kill, who were to be replaced by New York militia; and required the executive of New Jersey, to order out the whole militia of that state, and the executive of Pennsylvania, such part of their militia as was contiguous to New Jersey, properly armed and equipped, to the aid of the general.

When the season for active operations approached, General Howe directed his first attention to the destruction of the scanty resources prepared by the Americans for the ensuing campaign. Magazines had been collected at Peck's-kill, in the Highlands, where mills had been erected, and the headquarters of the general commanding, had been established. On the recall of General Heath, to Boston, the command had devolved on General M'Dougal. The strength of this post, like others depending upon militia, was subject to great fluctuation; consisting, at times, of several thousand men, at others, reduced to as many hundred. The stores collected here, were at this time inconsiderable; but the British general supposing them of great value, and slightly defended, on the 23d of March, 1777, despatched Colonel Bird, against the post, with five hundred men, under convoy of a frigate, and some smaller armed vessels. General M'Dougal, whose force did not exceed two hundred and fifty men, exerted himself to remove the magazines into the strong country, in his rear; but before this could be effected, the enemy approached, and compelled him to retire, having first set fire to the store-houses and barracks. Colonel Bird completed the destruction, and returned to New York.

Danbury, on the western frontier of Connecticut, contained a valuable deposit of military stores, and though not more than twenty miles from the Sound, its safety was supposed to be assured by the nature of the country, the zeal of the militia, and by a portion of the Connecticut draughts, assembled there. But on the 25th of April, Governor Tryon, major-general of the provincials, in the British service, with Brigadiers Agnew, and Sir William Erskine, entered and fired the town, with all the stores it contained. Upon his retreat, he was assailed by about thirteen hundred militia, in several detachments, commanded by Generals Arnold, Silliman, and Wooster. In one of the several skirmishes, the last was killed. The enemy spent the night of the 27th at Ridgefield, and in the following morning resumed his retreat, and was again met by Arnold, with a force of one thousand, among whom were some continental artillery and infantry; but he attained his shipping, with a loss of one hundred and seventy men, killed, wounded and taken prisoners. The loss of the Americans was nearly the same, but it included several officers of rank, besides General Wooster. General M'Dougal had learned the intention of Tryon, and endeavoured to intercept his retreat by a rapid march, with twelve hundred men, to which number his forces had increased; but he could not arrive before the enemy had retired; and therefore hastily returned to his post at Peck's-kill.

VIII. This enterprise was soon after retaliated by an expedition, under Lieutenant-colonel Meigs, who, on the 23d of May, with two hundred and thirty men, carried and destroyed a large depot of provisions and forage, at Sagg Harbour, on Long Island; eluding the numerous cruizers of the enemy, and making near a hundred prisoners, without the loss of a single man. Such was the celerity of Colonel Meigs's movements, that he transported his men, between Guilford and Sagg Harbour, ninety miles, by land and water, in twenty-five hours.

IX. In the mean time, the American commander-in-chief, had formed his plan for the disposition of the army, when it should take the field. He was convinced, that while General Burgoyne, now in command of the British northern army, would either endeavour to take Ticonderoga, and penetrate to the Hudson, or join the grand army by sea, General Howe would endeavour, by moving up the North river, to possess himself of the forts and high grounds, at present occupied by the Americans, or would attempt Philadelphia. Yet uncertain as to which of those courses would be adopted, he determined to keep the high grounds of New Jersey, somewhat north of the road leading from Brunswick to Trenton. Encamped here, the army would cover New Jersey, and be at a convenient point to move, either for the protection of Philadelphia, on the west, or the Highlands, on the east. In the uncertainty with which the first movements of the enemy were enveloped, and the equal necessity of defending the three great points, Ticonderoga, the Highlands of New York and Philadelphia, against two powerful armies, superior to him, in arms, numbers and discipline, it was necessary so to arrange his force, as to enable the parts reciprocally to aid each other. To effect these purposes, the northern troops, including those of New York, were divided between Ticonderoga and Peck's-kill, while those from Jersey to the south, including North Carolina, were directed to assemble in New Jersey. If the army of Canada should join that of New York, by sea, the troops at Peck's-kill, and those in Jersey, could readily be united, either for defence of the Highlands, or of Philadelphia. If Burgoyne should attempt Ticonderoga, by way of the lakes, the force at Peck's-kill would afford aid to the army opposed to him.

Upon these arrangements being made, the camp at Morristown was broken up, and the army removed to Middlebrook, behind a ridge of strong and commanding heights, not far from the Raritan, about ten miles from Brunswick; where General Washington repaired, in person, on the 28th of May, 1777. The heights, in front of the camp, commanded the course of the Raritan, the road to Philadelphia, the hills about Brunswick, and a considerable part of the country between that place and Amboy; affording a full view of the most interesting movements of the enemy.

The force brought into the field by America, required all the aid of strong positions, and the most unremitting vigilance. On the 21st of May, the total of the army in Jersey, exclusive of the cavalry and artillery, amounted, only, to eight thousand three hundred and seventy-eight men, of whom, upwards of two thousand were sick. The effective rank and file were only five thousand seven hundred and thirty-eight. In this return, the troops of North Carolina were not included, as they had not then joined the army; and the militia of New Jersey, amounting to about five hundred men, were also omitted. Had this army been composed of the best disciplined troops, its inferiority in numbers must have limited its operations to defensive war; and have rendered it incompetent to protect any place, which could be defended only by battle in the open field. But more than half the troops* were unacquainted with military duty, and had never looked an enemy in the face.

A large proportion, especially from the middle states, were foreigners; many of them servants, on whose attachment to the American cause it was not safe to rely. To avail himself of this unfavourable circumstance, General Howe had offered a large reward to every soldier who would desert, and additional compensation to those who would bring their arms. The effect of these promises had been seriously felt; and their future operation, was greatly dreaded. To diminish this, and to allure, from the service of the enemy, those misguided Americans who had engaged with them, but might now wish to be again received into the bosom of their country, General Washington had urged on Congress the policy of allowing all the advantages of freemen to the servants who had enlisted; and of giving full pardon to all Americans, who would quit the British service. These recommendations, like almost every other proceeding from the same source, received the ready attention of Congress, and resolutions were passed in conformity with them.

As a movement of the enemy by land towards Philadelphia was probable, it was an important part of the plan of the campaign, to constitute on the western bank of the Delaware, an army of militia, strengthened by a few continental troops, under an experienced officer, to defend, in front, the passage of that river. To Arnold, then in Philadelphia, employed in the settlement of his accounts, this service was intrusted.

General Sullivan lay at Princeton with a body of continental troops, increasing in number by recruits from the southward, and some Jersey militia. He was directed to hold himself in perpetual expectation of attack, to send his baggage and provisions to places less exposed, and to be in readiness to move at any instant to a place of greater security, where his left could not be so readily turned, and whence he might harass the flanks of the enemy on a march, and preserve a communication with the army at Middlebrook—by no means to risk a general action, but to act entirely as a partisan corps; and on the first movement of the British army to place his main body in security, and to harass them with parties detached for that purpose. Measures were also taken to put the militia of Jersey in readiness to take the field so soon as offensive operations should commence. It was intended, not that they should remain embodied for the purpose of strengthening and acting with the continental army; but that, ranging the country in small parties, they should hang upon, and harass the flanks of the enemy.

X. The first and great object of the campaign, on the part of General Howe, was the acquisition of Philadelphia, which he originally designed to attain, by marching through New Jersey, and crossing the Delaware by a portable bridge, constructed during the winter. But the delay in the arrival of the tents and camp equipage, from Europe, and the early organization, and favourable position of the American army, caused him to devise another plan of operations, in case he could not draw the American general from his present advantageous position. This was to attempt Philadelphia by the Delaware or Chesapeake Bay. A demonstration was acordingly made, of proceeding to Philadelphia, by land. General Washington summoned to his assistance the continental troops, at Peck's-kill, with the exception of one thousand effectives, and in the mean time formed a select corps of riflemen,

* The extreme severity of the service, aided perhaps by the state of the hospitals, had carried to the grave, more than two-thirds of the soldiers, who had served the preceding campaign and been engaged for more than one year.

under Colonel Morgan, which was posted at Vanvechten's-bridge, on the Raritan, just above its confluence with the Millstone river, with orders to watch the left flank of the British army. On any movement of the enemy, he was instructed to seize every opportunity to fall on their flank, to gall them as much as possible, but to take especial care not to permit himself to be surrounded, or to have his retreat to the army cut off. General Sullivan was directed to change his position, and to occupy the high grounds of Rocky Hill, as a place of greater security.

With the view of inducing General Washington to quit his fortified camp, and to approach the Delaware, where he might bring on a general engagement, on ground more advantageous to himself, General Howe, leaving two thousand men at Brunswick, under the command of General Matthews, advanced, on the morning of the 14th of June, in two columns, towards that river. The front of the first, under Lord Cornwallis, reached Somerset Court House, by the break of day; and about the same time, the second, under General de Heister, arrived at Middlebush, between Brunswick and Somerville, on a road east of that taken by Cornwallis. The feint was unsuccessful. On the first intelligence that the enemy was approaching, Washington posted his whole army, with great advantage, in order of battle, on the heights in front of his camp. This position he maintained during the day, and at night the troops slept on the ground to be defended. In the mean time, the militia of New Jersey, with an alacrity, heretofore unexampled in the state, took the field in great numbers; principally joining General Sullivan, who had retired behind the Sourland hills, towards Flemington, where a considerable army was forming.

Finding that the American army could not be drawn from its position, and, probably, influenced in some degree, by the temper now manifested by the militia, General Howe determined to waste no more time in threatening Philadelphia by land, but to withdraw his army from Jersey; and, pursuing the principal object of the campaign, to embark them, for the Chesapeak or the Delaware. On the 19th, in the night, he returned to Brunswick, and on the 22d, to Amboy; where he threw over the channel which separates the continent from Staten Island, the bridge designed for the Delaware, and passed over the heavy baggage and a few of his troops to that island, whence the embarkation of his army was to be made. This retreat was conducted with some marks of precipitation, and many of the farm houses on the route are said to have been burned.

General Washington, expecting the movement from Brunswick, had made dispositions to derive some advantages from it. He detached General Greene, with three brigades, for the purpose of falling on, and annoying the British rear. General Sullivan was directed to move with his division, in order to co-operate with Greene, and Maxwell to fall on the flank of the enemy. In the mean time, the main army paraded on the heights of Middlebrook, ready to act as circumstances might require.

About sunrise, Colonel Morgan attacked and drove in a picquet guard; the enemy throwing themselves into some redoubts, which, on the approach of Wayne and Morgan they evacuated; immediately after, they commenced their march to Amboy. Some sharp skirmishing took place between them and Morgan's regiment, in which the latter acted to the entire satisfaction of their general; but the hope of gaining any important advantage was entirely disappointed. From his distance, and the late hour at which he received his orders, Sullivan was unable to come up in time; the express sent to General Maxwell either deserted to the enemy, or was taken; and the rear division of the British being stronger than was expected, the force on the lines could make no impression on it. From these causes, the retreat to Amboy was effected without any considerable loss.

In order to cover his light parties, which still hung on the British flank and rear, and to injure the enemy, General Washington advanced six or seven miles from his strong camp at Middlebrook, to Quibbletown, on the road to Amboy. Lord Stirling's division proceeded a few miles still nearer, to the neighbourhood of Matouchin meeting-house, in order to act with the parties which were on the lines, should an opportunity offer for attack.

In this state of things, it appeared practicable to General Howe to bring on an engagement. With this view, and probably in the hope of turning the left of the American army, and gaining the heights behind them, on the night of the 25th, he recalled the troops which had passed over to Staten Island; and early next morning, made a rapid movement in two columns towards Westfield. The right, under the command of Lord Cornwallis, took the route by Woodbridge to the Scotch Plains; and the left, accompanied by Sir William Howe in person, marched by Matouchin meeting-house, to fall into the rear of the right column. It was intended that the left should take a separate route, about two miles after their junction with the other column, in order to attack the left flank of the American army at Quibbletown; while Lord Cornwallis should gain the heights on the left of the camp at Middlebrook. Four battalions, with six pieces of cannon, were detached to take post at Bonhamtown.*

About Woodbridge, the right column of the British fell in with one of the light parties detached to watch their motions; and notice being thus received of this movement, General Washington immediately penetrated its object, and discerned his danger. The whole army was instantly put in motion. It regained with the utmost celerity the camp at Middlebrook, and took possession of the heights on the left, which it was supposed the enemy had designed to seize. Lord Cornwallis, on his route encountered Lord Stirling, and a smart skirmish ensued, in which the latter was driven from his ground with the loss of three field pieces and a few men. He retreated to the hills about the Scotch Plains, and was pursued as far as Westfield. Here Lord Cornwallis halted. Perceiving the passes in the mountains on the left of the American camp to be guarded, and, of consequence, that the object for which this skilful manœuvre had been made was unattainable, he returned through Rahway to Amboy; and, on the 30th of June, the whole army crossed over to Staten Island.

While retiring from Westfield, the British army was watched by the brigades of Scott and Conway; the former entered Amboy immediately after that place had been evacuated; but no opportunity was given, during the retreat, of attacking it to advantage.

XI. About this time, news was received of the advance of General Burgoyne, towards Ticonderoga, which, with the delay in the embarkation of Sir William Howe's forces, kept the American commander-in-chief in great uncertainty as to the designs of the enemy; and occasioned him to give orders for the return of two brigades to Peck's-kill, which had proceeded to Pompton Plains, to join him, and to despatch Parson's and Varnum's brigades to that post. Still he could not divest himself of the opinion, that the attempt to cross the Delaware would be renewed; and for some days he remained in his camp, at Middlebrook. A change of position from Prince's Bay, to the watering place, and a movement of the army to the latter, with the military stores and baggage from the coast opposite Amboy, at

* General Howe's letter.

length, relieved him from apprehensions of a sudden march on Philadelphia, and determined him to change his own position. He removed the main body of the army to Morristown, and advanced General Sullivan with his division, on the way to Peck's-kill, as far as Pompton Plains.

The preparations for embarkation of the British general, indicated the inception of a much longer voyage than that up the North river; and notice of these appearances were given to the eastern states; but the advance of Burgoyne, with a powerful army, against Ticonderoga, still induced the opinion, that the main object of Howe, must be to effect a junction with him, on the North river. Under this impression, Sullivan was ordered to Peck's-kill, and Washington, himself, proceeded to Pompton Plains, and on the 16th of July, to the Clove; where he determined to remain until the views of the enemy should be completely disclosed.

In this position, he, at first, commanded, that the North Carolina troops which had stopped at Philadelphia, should join him; but on receiving information that a great part of the British fleet had fallen down to the Hook, these forces were stopped at Trenton, and General Sullivan was directed not to cross the North river. General Putnam, who now commanded at Peck's-kill, was cautioned to guard against any sudden attack from New York; success in which, would be the more deeply felt, in consequence of the loss of Ticonderoga, and Mount Independence, which had fallen into the hands of Burgoyne. The information, that part of the fleet had dropped down to the Hook, was soon followed by intelligence, that the shipping were moving from the watering place to New York, and that several transports, convoyed by a ship of war, had proceeded as high as Dobbs' ferry. The passes in the Highlands were now supposed to be certainly their object, and Sullivan, who had been advanced as far as New Windsor, was ordered immediately to cross the Hudson, and to take post in the rear of Peck's-kill, on the east side of that river. Lord Stirling was also commanded to cross the river and join General Putnam.

XII. The perplexities of this moment were cheered by the intelligence of the capture of Major-general Prescott, the commander of the British troops on Rhode Island. Believing himself perfectly secure, guarded by his cruizers and at the head of an army greatly superior to any force collected in the eastern department, he indulged in convenient quarters, distant from camp, and with few guards about his person. Information of this negligence being communicated to the main, Colonel Barton, of the Rhode Island militia, planned with success, the capture of the general, in his quarters. On the night of the 10th of July, with a party of about forty persons, including captains Adams and Phillips, in four whale boats, he crossed the water, a distance of ten miles, deceived the vigilance of the guard boats, landed, marched a mile to the general's quarters, seized the sentinel at the door, and one of the aid-de-camps, took the general from his bed, and without allowing him time to dress, carried him with secrecy and despatch to a place of safety. This clever exploit was the more highly appreciated, as it gave the Americans an officer of equal rank to exchange for General Lee. Congress presented Colonel Barton with a sword, as a mark of their approbation.

XIII. At length, the British fleet put to sea; having on board General Howe, and thirty-six British and Hessian battalions, including light infantry and grenadiers, with a powerful artillery, a New York corps, called the Queen's Rangers, and a regiment of light horse. The residue of the army was divided between New York and Rhode Island. On the receipt of the intelligence, the American army commenced its march, (July, 1777,) for the Delaware, under the conviction, that the fleet was destined for Philadelphia. But whilst preparing to meet Sir William Howe on a new theatre, the commander-in-chief took measures, also, to check the progress of Burgoyne; who, having obtained possession, by a greatly superior force, of Ticonderoga, and the lakes, was advancing southward towards New York. Letters were addressed to the governments of the eastern states, urging them to reinforce with their militia, the retreating northern army. Major-generals Arnold and Lincoln, both influential with the eastern militia, were directed to join it; and three brigades of New England continental troops from Peck's-kill, Morgan's rifle regiment, and two regiments from New York, were ordered upon the same service.

On the 30th July, the enemy's fleet appeared off the capes of the Delaware, and orders were given by Washington for concentrating his forces at Philadelphia. They were scarce issued, when a new disposition was occasioned, by tidings, that the fleet had departed from the Delaware Bay, and was proceeding eastwardly. No further intelligence of it was received, until the 7th of August, when it was seen a few leagues southward of the Delaware capes; after which it disappeared, and was not again heard of, until late in that month. Meanwhile, the most perplexing uncertainty concerning its destination, was universal. On entering the capes of the Delaware, the general was deterred by the difficulties of that river from ascending it, and resolved to proceed to the Chesapeake; but was prevented by contrary winds, from reaching the mouth of the latter bay, until the 16th of August.

Washington employed this interval in examining the country about Philadelphia, and the works below the city; and he came to the conclusion, that the defence of the river should be confined to the fort on Mud Island, and to Red Bank, a piece of high ground on the Jersey shore, opposite to the island. This opinion he communicated to Congress, with his intention to march to Coryell's ferry, (New Hope,) sufficiently near Philadelphia, whence he might readily regain the North river, should it be necessary. Upon the protracted absence of the British fleet, he determined to march thither, but on the very day of this determination, learned the arrival of the whole fleet in the Chesapeake.

XIV. The different divisions of the army were immediately ordered to unite, with the utmost expedition, in the neighbourhood of Philadelphia, and the militia of Pennsylvania, Maryland, Delaware, and the northern counties of Virginia to take the field. These orders were received by General Sullivan, who had been encamped in Jersey about Hanover, just on his return from an expedition to Staten Island. The British force there amounted to between two and three thousand men; of whom nearly one thousand were provincials, stationed at different places on the coast opposite the Jersey shore. The European troops, amounting to sixteen hundred men, were in a fortified camp near the watering place. General Sullivan thought it practicable to surprise and bring off the provincials before they could be supported by the Europeans; and he was the more stimulated to the attempt, by their occasional incursions into Jersey. They had lately penetrated as far as Woodbridge, and had carried off twelve individuals, noted for their attachment to the American cause.* This expedition was undertaken by Sullivan with the select troops of his division, aided by a few Jersey militia, under Colonel Frelinghuysen. They had to march about twenty miles to the place of embarkation; where, only, six boats had been procured. Three of these were allotted to Colonel Ogden, who commanded one detach-

* Mr. Stockton, member of Congress, and Mr. Fell, member of council, had previously been made prisoners, and the person, nay, the life of Governor Livingston was daily threatened. Two thousand guineas are said to have been offered by the enemy for his capture.

ment intended to attack Colonel Lawrence, lying near the old Blazing Star ferry, and Colonels Dungan, and Allen, who lay about two miles from each other, towards Amboy. The other three were taken by General Deborre, accompanied by General Sullivan in person. He was to attack Colonel Barton near the new Blazing Star ferry, and, after securing that party, to assist Ogden. General Smallwood, with his brigade was to cross at Halsey point, and attack Buskirk's regiment near Decker's ferry. All the troops crossed before day, unperceived by the enemy. But, misconducted by his guides, Smallwood began his attack on a different point from that which was intended, in consequence of which, Buskirk's regiment made its escape; but Ogden and Deborre, were more successful. Lawrence and Barton were surprised, and, with several of their officers and men, were taken. The alarm being given, it became necessary for Sullivan precipitately to withdraw his forces from the island. It had been impracticable to obtain a sufficient number of boats to embark all the troops at the same time; and some confusion appears to have prevailed in this part of the business. General Campbell, with a considerable force advanced upon them; and the rear guard, after defending themselves for some time with great gallantry, were under the necessity of surrendering prisoners of war.

In his letters to the commander-in-chief, and to Congress, General Sullivan reported, that he had brought off eleven officers, and one hundred and thirty privates; and that a considerable number must have been killed in the different skirmishes. He stated his own loss to have been one major, one captain, one lieutenant, and ten privates killed, and fifteen wounded; and nine officers, among whom were Majors Stewart, Tillard, and Woodson, and one hundred and twenty-seven privates, prisoners.

In the account given by General Campbell, he claims to have made two hundred and fifty-nine prisoners, among whom were one lieutenant-colonel, three majors, two captains, and fifteen inferior officers.

XV. The British fleet ascended the Chesapeake Bay, and the Elk river; and on the 25th of August, landed the army at the ferry, without a show of opposition. Their whole force was computed at eighteen thousand men, in good health and spirits, trained to the service, abundantly supplied with the *materiel* of war, and led by a general of experience and military talent. If it were deficient in aught, it was in horses, which had suffered much during the preceding winter, and in the long voyage from New York to the Elk river.

Great effort was made to increase the American army. The militia responded to the call of their country in greater numbers than could be armed. The whole force was estimated at fifteen thousand, but the effectives, at not more than eleven thousand. Morgan's regiment of riflemen having been sent to the northern army, a light corps was formed by detachments from each brigade, and put under the command of General Maxwell; who, during the preceding winter, had acquired reputation as a partisan officer. This corps was thrown in advance of the American army, but was driven in by a column under Lord Cornwallis with considerable loss. The conduct of General Maxwell was much condemned by his officers, but he was acquitted of blame by a court-martial. Washington felt and deplored the absence of Morgan and his rifle corps. On the 3d of September, the British were encamped with their right about Pencader, with their left extending across Christiana creek, towards Newark. On the 5th, the whole American army, except the light infantry, took position behind Red Clay creek, having its left at Newport, on the Christiana, and on the road leading directly from the camp of Sir William Howe to Philadelphia. On the 8th, the main body of the enemy advanced by Newark upon the right of the American encampment, and took post within four miles of that place; whilst a strong column made a show of attacking in front, and after manœuvring for some time, halted at Milton, within two miles of the centre. General Washington perceived that the column in front was designed only to amuse, whilst the left should endeavour to turn his right, and, suddenly crossing the Brandywine, seize the heights on the north of that river, and cut off his communication with Philadelphia. To prevent this, he moved during the night over the Brandywine, and took post next morning behind the river, at Chad's Ford. The light corps under General Maxwell, was advanced in front, and the Pennsylvania militia under General Armstrong, were placed at a ford two miles below Chad's; the right extended some miles above that place, with a view to other passes deemed less practicable. In this position, the general awaited the movement of his adversary.

On the morning of the 11th, the whole British army advanced on the road leading over Chad's Ford, and the Americans prepared to defend the passage of the river. Some sharp skirmishing between the advanced column under Knyphausen, and the light corps of Maxwell, took place on either side, below the ford, with little damage to either party. About 11 o'clock, Washington, instructed that a division of the enemy had marched up the country, on the south of the Brandywine, formed the bold design of detaching Sullivan and Stirling to fall on its left, while he should cross the ford, and with the centre and left wing attack Knyphausen. At the critical moment, unhappily, erroneous intelligence was received that the movement of the British on the left, was a feint only; and about two o'clock, it was ascertained that a column, led by Cornwallis, having taken a circuit of seventeen miles, had passed the river above its forks, and was advancing in great force. The divisions of Sullivan, Stirling, and Stephens, marched to meet it; and that lately commanded by Lincoln, now by Wayne, remained at Chad's Ford, with Maxwell's corps, to check Knyphausen; whilst Green's division, and General Washington in person, formed a reserve and took a central position.

The divisions detached against Cornwallis, had scarcely formed on advantageous ground, above Birmingham meeting-house, when the attack commenced, at about half past four o'clock, and was for a season firmly sustained. The American right first gave way, exposing the flank of the remaining divisions to a galling fire; and in a short time, the whole line was routed. General Washington pressed forward to support this wing, but arrived only in time to check the pursuit. This service was efficiently rendered by a Pennsylvania regiment under Colonel Stewart, and a Virginia regiment under Colonel Stephens. Whilst the right was thus engaged, Knyphausen forced the ford. The whole American army retreated that night to Chester, and the next day to Philadelphia. Its loss was estimated at three hundred killed and six hundred wounded, and three or four hundred, principally of the wounded, made prisoners. That sustained by the enemy was reported at one hundred killed, and four hundred wounded. Among the wounded of the Americans, were Brigadier-general Woodford, and the Marquis de La Fayette.

XVI. The disposition to risk another battle was general, on the part of Congress, and the army. An opinion prevailed, which was carefully cherished, that the British had gained, only, the ground. Fifteen hundred continental troops were ordered from Peck's-kill, and directions given to the militia of New Jersey, Pennsylvania, and the remaining adjacent country, to march to the aid of the army, whilst due measures were taken to complete the defences of the Delaware river.

Sir William Howe, lay on the night of the 11th, on the field of battle. On the succeeding day, Major-general Grant, with two brigades, took post at Concord meeting-house. On the 13th, Lord Cornwallis having united with

Grant, marched towards Chester. Another detachment seized Wilmington, whither the wounded were escorted.

XVII. On the 15th, the American army was again collected, and intending to gain the left of the British, had reached the Warren tavern, on the Lancaster road, when intelligence was received of the approach of the enemy. Washington hastened to meet, and attack him in front. Both armies, eager for battle, had scarce engaged, when they were separated by a tremendous storm of rain, which rendered the retreat of the Americans indispensable. The wretched condition of their arms, produced, at all times, an inequality between them and the British; and, on this occasion, caused them the most imminent peril. Such was the effect of the rain upon the muskets and cartridge boxes, that of the former, scarce one in a regiment could be fired; and in the latter, of forty rounds per man, scarce one was fit for use. The retreat was continued all the day, and the greater part of the night, through a cold and most distressing rain, and very deep roads, to the Yellow Springs; and subsequently, to Warwick Furnace, on French Creek.

The weather, which compelled the flight of the American, arrested the progress of the British, army; and, until the 18th, it made no other movement, than to unite the columns. It then took post at Trydriffin, whence a party was detached to destroy a magazine of flour and other stores, at the Valley Forge. The American commander, as soon as circumstances would permit, ordered General Wayne to join General Smallwood, in the rear of the enemy; and, carefully concealing himself and his movements, to seize any occasion which might offer, to engage them with advantage. Meanwhile, he himself crossed the Schuylkill at Parker's ferry, and encamped on both sides of Perkiomen Creek; posting detachments at the several fords, by which it was presumed the enemy would attempt a passage.

XVIII. Wayne had taken a position near the Paoli tavern, about three miles in the rear of the left wing of the British. Notwithstanding his precautions he was betrayed by some of the disaffected inhabitants; and about eleven o'clock of the night of the twentieth, was surprised by a party of the enemy under Major-general Gray. His pickets were driven in, and gave the first intimation of Gray's approach. Wayne, instantly, formed his division; and whilst his right was fiercely assailed, directed a retreat by the left, under cover of a few regiments, who, for a short time, withstood the shock. The British, aided by the light of the American fires, put to death three hundred of his troops, by the free and exclusive use of the bayonet; sustaining a loss, themselves, of eight men, only. In consequence of animadversions on his conduct, Wayne demanded a court-martial, which unanimously acquitted him with honour.

XIX. Sir William Howe marched from his position, along the valley road to the Schuylkill, and encamped on the banks of the river, his line extending to French Creek, along the front of the American army. This arrangement seeming to threaten Reading, which contained a large depot of stores, Washington changed his position and marched towards Pottsgrove, with his left above, but near, the British right. This movement left the roads to Philadelphia open to the enemy, and the capture of the city could be prevented, only, by an engagement. Though urged to this, by public opinion, Washington prudently declined it. His forces were not concentrated. Wayne and Smallwood had not joined him, nor had he received the Jersey militia he expected under General Dickenson. Of the actual state of his army, it may be enough to say, that more than a thousand of his troops were barefooted, and had performed the late evolutions in that condition. The want of necessaries was such, that Colonel Hamilton, one of the general's aids, had been authorized and employed to take forcible possession of such linen, woollens, shoes, spirits, and other stores, as might be found in Philadelphia, giving certificates of quantity and value to the owners. "Your own prudence," said the general to him, "will point out the least exceptionable means to be pursued; but remember, delicacy and a strict adherence to the ordinary mode of application must give place to our necessities." But no effort could obtain a supply for the pressing and growing wants of the army. The duty of securing the public stores, was, also, assigned to Colonel Hamilton, which he executed by transporting them up the Delaware. On the twenty-sixth of September, Lord Cornwallis, at the head of the British and Hessian grenadiers, entered Philadelphia, and the main body of the British army encamped at Germantown.

XX. On the loss of the battle of the Brandywine, Congress resolved to remove to Lancaster. At this town they assembled on the twenty-seventh of the month, and soon after adjourned to Yorktown.

XXI. To the secure possession of the city and the comfort of his army, General Howe found the free navigation of the Delaware indispensable. But of this, he was wholly debarred by the fortifications, of Fort Mifflin, on Mud Island, at the confluence of the Schuylkill and the Delaware, and of Red Bank on the eastern shore; and by the *chevaux de frise* sunk in the channel, between these batteries, and at a point three miles below, opposite to Byllingsport, where some imperfect works had been erected for their protection. Whilst these defences were maintained, Howe could not communicate with his fleet; and the American vessels in the river, above the forts, would prevent him from foraging and obtaining provisions in New Jersey; whilst the army of Washington might cut off his supplies from Pennsylvania. The disadvantages resulting from the vessels, however, were soon diminished by the capture of the Delaware frigate, the largest of them.

Some British ships of war were already in the Delaware, and Captain Hammond, who commanded one of them, represented, that the possession of the fort at Byllingsport, which was feebly garrisoned, would enable him to raise the lower line of obstructions, and admit the fleet to Fort Mifflin. On the twenty-ninth of September, Colonel Stirling, with two regiments, captured it, without opposition; the garrison, on his approach, having spiked the artillery, and fired the barracks, withdrew without discharging a gun. This service performed, the detachment returned to Chester. On the third of October, another regiment was called from Germantown to Philadelphia, with orders to unite, on the next day, with Colonel Stirling.

Washington had now received all the reinforcements he expected; consisting of nine hundred continental troops from Peck's-kill, under General M'Dougal; about six hundred militia from Jersey, under Brigadier-general Forman, (General Dickenson having been detained by the apprehension of a second invasion from New York) and about eleven hundred from Maryland, under General Smallwood. His effective strength, rank and file, amounted to eight thousand continental troops and three thousand militia. With this force, he, on the thirtieth of September, took a position on the Skippack road, twelve miles from the enemy's camp, sixteen from Germantown, and twenty from Philadelphia. The line of encampment of the British army crossed Germantown at right angles with the main street, somewhat south of its centre, the left wing extending to the Schuylkill. Lord Cornwallis continued at Philadelphia.

Washington observing this division of the British force, formed the design of surprising the camp at Germantown, and thus giving a blow, which might decide the fate of the war. He proposed a simultaneous attack upon the wings, front and rear, which should be suddenly and vigorously made, and from which, the troops might expeditiously retreat, if it were unsuccessful.

Pursuant to his plan, the divisions of Sullivan and Wayne, flanked by Conway's brigade, were ordered to enter Germantown, by the way of Chesnut Hill, while General Armstrong, with the Pennsylvania militia, should fall down the Manatawny or Ridge road, and gain the British left, and by Vandeering's or Robinson's Mill, attack its rear: the divisions of Greene and Stephens, flanked by M'Dougal's brigade, to take a circuit by way of the Limekiln road, and entering the town at the market house, attack the right wing: the militia of Maryland and Jersey, under Generals Smallwood and Forman, to march by the Old York road, and turning the right, to fall on its rear: the division of Lord Stirling, and the brigades of Nash and Maxwell to form a corps de reserve: and parties of cavalry silently to scour the roads to prevent observation, and to keep up the communication between the heads of the columns.

XXII. With these dispositions the army moved on the third of October, about seven in the afternoon. About sunrise the next morning, the advance of the column led by Sullivan, encountered and drove in a picket placed at Mount Airy, or Mr. Allen's house.

The main body followed close, driving before it the fortieth regiment, commanded by Colonel Musgrave, until that officer threw himself, with six companies, into the large stone house of Mr. Chew, from which they galled the Americans, with a heavy and constant fire of musketry. Some attempts to storm this house, and an effort to bring a field piece to bear upon it, broke the line of the right wing, and with the darkness caused by an extraordinary fog, threw it into great confusion. The column led by Greene, arrived on its ground, and commenced an attack on the light infantry, in front of the British right wing. It was at first successful, and after driving in the pickets, forced the battalion of light infantry to give way.

The country through which the army was advancing, abounded with many small and strong enclosures, which broke the line, in every direction; the fog obscured surrounding objects, and the commander-in-chief, could neither observe nor correct the confusion that commenced. The causes which separated the regiments, prevented them from discerning the situation of the enemy, and from improving the first impression, and directing their after efforts to advantage. The attacks on the flanks and rear were not made. The Pennsylvania militia came in view of the chasseurs, who flanked the left of the British line, but did not engage them, closely. The Maryland and Jersey militia just showed themselves, on the right flank, about the time Greene's column was commencing a retreat.

These embarrassments gave the British time to recover from the consternation into which they had been thrown. Knyphausen, who commanded their left, detached one battalion to support the chasseurs; and part of the third and fourth brigades, under Generals Gray and Agnew, to attack the front of the column led by Sullivan, which had penetrated far into the village. Scott's and Muhlenberg's brigades were surrounded and made prisoners. The broken parts mistook each other for the enemy, and, whilst warmly engaged and sanguine of success, the main body of the army began to retreat. Washington was compelled to relinquish a victory he thought within his grasp, and to endeavour to secure his army. His retreat was, however, made without loss; the enemy being unable to pursue. In the battle, about two hundred were killed and six hundred wounded. The principal damage was sustained from Chew's house, and in Germantown. About four hundred were made prisoners. Among the killed was General Nash of North Carolina; and among the prisoners, Colonel Matthews of Virginia. The British loss, as stated by General Howe, was one hundred killed and four hundred wounded. Among the former were Brigadier-general Agnew and

Colonel Bird. The grenadiers in Philadelphia, under Cornwallis, hastened to the field of battle on the first alarm, running the whole distance, and reaching it, as the action terminated.

The American army retreated, the same day, about twenty miles, to the Perkiomen Creek; but soon after, resumed its former encampment on the Skippack.

XXIII. Immediately after the battle of Brandywine, New Jersey was required to furnish the army with reinforcements of militia, and General Putnam to detach fifteen hundred continental troops; and, at the same time, to cover the Jerseys with an equal number. The militia of Connecticut were relied upon to supply the vacuum in the posts on the North river, occasioned by these heavy draughts. These troops were, however, detained by the demonstrations made from New York. Sir Henry Clinton who commanded there, supposed, that, an alarm might serve both Howe and Burgoyne, by diverting, for a time, the aids which were designed for Washington and Gates. With this view, he entered East Jersey, at the head of three thousand men, by the way of Elizabethtown Point and Fort Lee; the columns uniting at the New Bridge, above Hackensack, on the twelfth of September. They encountered little opposition, and collected, on their way, large quantities of fresh provisions. About the fifteenth, observing that the continental troops under M'Dougal were approaching, and that, General Dickenson, with great exertion, was assembling the Jersey militia, he returned to New York and Staten Island, having lost in the excursion, only eight men killed and sixteen wounded. The supply of militia, for the continental army, collected very slowly, notwithstanding the efforts of Governor Livingston and General Dickenson. Accustomed to judge for themselves, they declared, that the danger of another invasion, rendered their services essential on the eastern frontier. Five or six hundred, however, crossed the Delaware at Philadelphia, about the time Sir William Howe passed the Schuylkill, and were employed in the removal of stores. As the enemy approached the city they retired from it, by the Frankford road; but the commanding officer having separated himself from his corps, was captured by a small party of the British light horse; on which the regiment dispersed and made its way, by different roads, to New Jersey. With much labour General Dickenson had collected two other corps, amounting to nine hundred men, with whom he was about to cross the Delaware, when he received intelligence of the arrival from Europe, of an additional force at New York. He returned, himself, with part of his levies, from Trenton toward Elizabethtown, whilst the remainder proceeded to Pennsylvania, under General Forman; but they, immediately after the battle of Germantown, were discharged.

XXIV. The attention of both commanders was, now, almost wholly given to the Delaware;—the one to remove, the other to sustain, the impediments to its navigation. Lord Howe had early brought round the ships of war and transports from the Chesapeake, and they were stretched along the Delaware shore from Reedy Island to Newcastle. But, although, with great difficulty, the *chevaux de frise* had been raised from the channel opposite to Byllingsport, so as to admit the passage of vessels of force, it was impracticable to proceed above the line from Fort Mifflin to Fort Mercer, or Red Bank. Every effort was consequently made for the destruction of these forts. Batteries were erected on the Pennsylvania shore, to play upon Mud Island, whilst a fierce attack was directed against the redoubts on the Jersey shore.

XXV. On the twenty-first of October, Colonel Count Donop, a distinguished German officer crossed the Delaware at Cooper's Ferry, at the head of a detachment of Hessians, amounting to about twelve hundred men, in order to proceed the next day to the attack of Red Bank.

It was part of the plan, that, so soon as the assault should commence, a heavy cannonade on Fort Mifflin should be made from the batteries on the Pennsylvania shore; and that the Vigilant ship of war, should pass through a narrow channel between Hog Island, next below Mud Island, and the Maine, so as to attack the fort in the rear. Meanwhile, to divert the attention of the garrison and marine force, from the Vigilant, and other serious attacks, the advanced frigates, with the Isis and Augusta, were to approach Fort Mifflin in front, by the main channel, as far as the impediments would admit, and to batter the works.

The fortifications at Red Bank consisted of extensive outer works, within which, was an intrenchment eight or nine feet high, boarded and fraized, on which Colonel Greene of Rhode Island, the commander, had bestowed great labour. Late in the evening of the 22d, Count Donop attacked it with great intrepidity; it was defended with equal resolution. The outer works being too extensive to be manned by the garrison, which did not exceed five hundred men, were only used to gall the assailants; and on their near approach, were abandoned by the Americans, who retired within the inner intrenchment, whence they poured upon the Hessians, pressing on with great gallantry, a most destructive fire. Colonel Donop, leading his troops, received a mortal wound, and Lieutenant-colonel Mingerode, second in command, fell about the same time. Lieutenant-colonel Linsing drew off the detachment; and being favoured by the darkness of the night, collected many of the wounded. He marched about five miles that night, and returned next day to Philadelphia. The loss of the assailants was estimated at four hundred men. The garrison, reinforced from Fort Mifflin, and aided by the gallies, which flanked the Hessians both advancing and retreating, fought under cover, and lost only thirty-two, killed and wounded. It would appear from the statement given by General Howe of this enterprise, that the inner works could not be carried without scaling ladders, which had not been furnished.

In performance of the part of the plan allotted to the navy, the Augusta, a sixty-four gun ship, the Merlin sloop of war, and four smaller vessels, strove to get within cannon shot of Fort Mifflin. But the two first got aground, and were, on the next day, set on fire and abandoned. The Augusta blew up. The repulse of the Hessians from Fort Mercer, and the able defence of Colonel Smith, at Fort Mifflin, inspired Congress with hopes, that these posts might be permanently maintained; and that body voted a sword to each of these officers, and one to Commodore Hazlewood, who commanded the gallies, as a testimony of the national gratitude.

XXVI. On the march of Donop to Jersey, Washington presumed, that his design was not to carry Fort Mercer by storm, but regularly to invest it. Immediate efforts were, therefore, made to get out the Jersey militia; but owing to the perpetual calls for service, on the eastern frontier, and there being, at the moment, no governor in the state, the gubernatorial term having expired before the re-election, a very inefficient force was gotten into the field; and had not General Dickenson ventured to give orders by his own authority, none would have been put in motion. Unable to obtain a sufficient aid from Jersey, Washington, on the twenty-ninth of October, sent over some Pennsylvania militia; and a few days after, General Varnum, with his brigade, were posted about Woodbury, having orders to relieve and reinforce both forts, as his strength would permit. General Forman, with such militia as could be brought into the field, was directed to join him.

XXVII. The operations of the enemy against Fort Mifflin, were uninterrupted. They had command of the Schuylkill, and of Province and Carpenter's islands, at its mouth. On both, batteries had been constructed, to play on the fort, from which they were separated by a narrow passage, between four and five hundred yards wide, in which were floating batteries. They had driven thence the American moveable water force, originally relied on, for security in that quarter. Its chief employment, now, was to defeat preparations making at Philadelphia against the fort, by descending the river. The garrison consisted of three hundred continental troops, only; a number insufficient to place a single line around the works.

On the 10th November, a new and large battery was opened from Province Island, which kept up an incessant fire throughout that day, and several successive days. The block-houses of the fort were reduced to a heap of ruins, the palisades were beaten down, and most of the guns dismounted, or otherwise disabled. The barracks were battered in every part, so that the troops could not continue in them. The night was spent in repairing the damages of the day, and guarding against storm, of which they were in perpetual apprehension. If in the day a few moments were allowed for repose, it was taken on the wet earth, rendered, by the heavy rains, a soft mud. The garrison was relieved by General Varnum every forty-eight hours, and one-half of his brigade was constantly on duty. Colonel Smith, with the concurrence of General Varnum, believed the garrison ought to be withdrawn. But the commander-in-chief cherished the hope that it might be maintained, until he, reinforced by the northern army, could make a successful effort for its protection; and therefore he directed that it should be defended to the last extremity. Never were orders better obeyed. On the 11th, Colonel Smith was wounded, and was obliged to yield the command, which was taken first by Colonel Russell, and afterwards by Major Thayer. On the 15th, the enemy brought up their ships so far as the obstructions would permit, and having discovered that the channel between Mud and Province Islands would admit of large vessels, introduced a frigate and sloop of war, within one hundred yards of the works. They not only kept up a most destructive cannonade, but threw hand grenades into them; and the musketry from the round-top of the frigate, killed every man that appeared on the platform. Orders were given to Commodore Hazlewood, to attempt the removal of these vessels, but he deemed it impracticable. The place was consequently no longer tenable, and at 11 o'clock of the night of the 16th, the garrison was withdrawn.

From the position of Fort Mercer, its safety depended, almost wholly, upon the possession of Fort Mifflin. Still it was resolved to defend it. On the 17th, Cornwallis marched against it by the way of Chester; and, notwithstanding General Washington was apprized of his intention, no effort which he could make could bring together, in season, a sufficient force to protect it, and the fort was evacuated. A few of the smaller American galleys escaped up the river, the rest were captured or burned. The passage of the Delaware was thus opened.

Lord Cornwallis, with a force of about five thousand men, availed himself of this incursion, to collect large quantities of fresh provisions for the relief of the British army, and had taken post on Gloucester Point, which was entirely under cover of the guns of the ships. General Greene commanded an almost equal body of troops in New Jersey, a part of which was militia, and awaited the arrival of Glover's brigade from the north, in order to take offensive measures against Cornwallis. But an attack upon the British, in their present advantageous position, would have been unwarrantable. Yet, a small, but brilliant affair was performed, by a detachment of about one hundred and fifty men from Morgan's rifle corps, under Lieutenant-colonel Butler, and a like number of militia, under the Marquis La Fayette, who served as a volunteer. They attacked a picket of the enemy, consisting of about three hundred men, and drove them, with the loss of twenty or thirty killed, and a great number wounded, quite into their camp; retiring themselves without pursuit. "I found the riflemen," said La Fayette, in a letter to Washington, "even above *their* reputation, and the militia above all expectation I could have formed of them." Cornwallis, soon after, returned to Philadelphia, and Greene joined the main army under the commander-in-chief.

XXVIII. During these transactions on the Delaware, General Dickenson, whose perfect knowledge of the country gave every hope of success, made another attempt to cut off Skinner's brigade of loyalists, stationed on Staten Island. He collected about two thousand men, and requested from General Putnam, commanding the continental troops, a diversion on the side of King's Bridge, in order to prevent a sudden reinforcement from New York. As his success depended upon secrecy, he concealed his object even from his field officers, until eight o'clock of the night on which it was to be executed; yet, by three next morning, Skinner was apprized of his intention, and saved his brigade by retiring into works too strong to be carried by assault. In the flight, a few prisoners were made and a few men killed. General Dickenson returned with the loss of three killed and ten slightly wounded.

XXIX. By the capture of Burgoyne and his army, part of the force of the northern department might be called to Philadelphia. But neither General Gates nor General Putnam were disposed to part, readily, with their troops. A considerable portion of them, however, after some delay, reached the camp under General Washington, whose army, thus reinforced, amounted to twelve thousand one hundred and sixty-one continental troops, and three thousand two hundred and forty-one militia. The force of the enemy, with some detachments lately received from New York, has been stated, variously, at from twelve to fourteen thousand men. This equality induced many persons to urge upon the commander-in-chief, an attack upon Howe in Philadelphia, notwithstanding that position was covered by the Delaware on the right, by the Schuylkill on the left, by the junction of these rivers on the rear, and by a line of fourteen redoubts on the front, extending from river to river, connected by abbatis and circular works. Happily, the prudence of the general, sustained by the advice of his superior officers, resisted the effort.

XXX. Master of the river Delaware, from Philadelphia to the sea, and of the country on both shores to the south, the British general was relieved of the apprehension of suffering from a scarcity of provisions, and was at leisure to turn his whole force upon the American army, circumscribing him on the north and west; which he proposed not only to force from its present position, but to drive beyond the mountains.

On the fourth of December, General Washington was apprized that an attempt would be immediately made upon his camp at White Marsh; and on the evening of the same day, Sir William Howe marched from the city with his whole force. About eleven at night, Captain Allen M'Lane, who had been detached with one hundred men, selected from several divisions, fell in with and attacked the British van, at the Three Mile Run, on the Germantown road, compelling their front division to change their line of march. At three next morning, the advancing army encamped on Chesnut Hill, in front of the American right, and distant from it three miles. Three days were spent in various manœuvres by the British forces, during which there were several skirmishes, with Morgan's riflemen and some militia under General

Irvine of Pennsylvania. The general was wounded, and with a small portion of his detachment, made prisoner. A general action was hourly expected, but Howe would not attack the American camp, admirably placed; nor would Washington engage in a position less advantageous. He desired to be attacked, and felt confident that Sir William Howe, strongly enforced, would not march out with his whole army, only, to march back again. But, on the morning of the nineteenth, he filed off from the right by several routes, in full march for Philadelpha. This movement prevented the execution of a daring design of the American general, (formed on observing the caution of Howe,) to surprise and seize Philadelphia.*

XXXI. The season had now become extremely severe, and it was impossible, without intense suffering, for an army so wretchedly furnished as was the American, longer to keep the field, in tents. That it might still continue to cover the country, it was resolved to take a strong position at the Valley Forge, and there to erect huts in the form of a regular encampment. Thither the army was removed on the 12th of December. Its course from White Marsh, might have been tracked by the blood which flowed from the bare feet of the soldiery. Though somewhat more comfortable in their huts, their winter was one of great privation and suffering, the details of which are foreign from our present purpose.

In order to have a full view of the campaign of 1777, it will be necessary that we, successively, narrate the progress of General Burgoyne, and the circumstances which produced the important event of his capture.

XXXII. When General Carleton had retired into winter quarters, General Burgoyne, who had served under him, returned to England, to communicate fully to the administration, the condition of affairs in the northern department, and to make arrangements for the ensuing campaign. With the cabinet, he digested a plan for penetrating to the Hudson, from Canada, by way of the lakes. A formidable army was to be put under his command, to proceed against Ticonderoga as soon as the season would permit; whilst a smaller force, under Col. St: Leger, composed of Canadians, American refugees, a few Europeans, and many Indians, should march from Oswego, by way of the Mohawk, and unite with the grand army on the North river.

* Mr. Marshall says, vol. iii. p. 289, Life of Washington, "Captain Allen M'Lane discovered, that an attempt was about to be made to surprise the camp at White Marsh," &c. Another version is given of this matter, by the American Quarterly Review, vol. i. p. 32, 1827. Possibly the officer to whom information was given was M'Lane instead of Craig. Both accounts, however, may be true. By the last it seems, that some British officers occasionally met for conference, at the house of William and Lydia Darrach, Quakers, resident in the city. On the second of December, they requested that the family would retire early in the evening, as they would be at their room, and remain late; and added, that, when about to depart, they would call the wife to let them out. Curiosity, the first tempter, induced Lydia to approach the door of the conference chamber, shod in felt, only, and to put her ear to the key hole, where she heard, in detail, the plan of attack for the fourth. Under pretence of procuring flour from Frankford, she obtained a pass from Sir William Howe. Leaving her bag at the mill, she hastened towards the American lines, and encountered on the way, the American Colonel Craig, of the light horse; to whom she communicated the important information. The necessary preparations were, of course, made. Lydia returned home with her flour; and anxiously awaited news of the event; but when the British returned, did not dare to ask a question. On the next evening, one of the officers who frequented the house, requested her to come to his room, that he might submit some questions to her. He inquired, earnestly, whether any of her family were up, the last night he was there. She told him, that all had retired at 8 o'clock. He observed, "I know *you* were asleep, for I knocked at your chamber door, three times, before you heard me. I am entirely at a loss, to imagine who gave General Washington information of our intended attack. When we arrived near White Marsh, we found all their cannon mounted, and the troops prepared to receive us, and we have marched back like a parcel of fools."

The invading force, immediately under the commander-in-chief, amounted to about 9000 men. He was supported by Major-general Phillips, of the artillery, Major-general Reidesel, and Brigadier-general Sprecht, of the German troops, together with the British Generals, Frazer, Powell, and Hamilton; all officers of distinguished merit. The detachment under St. Leger, consisted of about 1800 men; one-half of whom were Indians, and the greater proportion of the other half, American loyalists, under the command of Sir John Johnstone. A considerable force was left in Canada, under Sir Guy Carleton, whose military command was restricted to the province. This able and humane officer, though indignant at having been suspended, displayed the greatness of his mind, by his ready and effective assistance, in promoting the objects of the campaign.

XXXIII. The northern American army, which had been formed only for the year, dissolved with that term. So far from being in condition for offensive operations, scarce a show of defence could be preserved in the forts. The charge of this frontier was assigned to troops to be furnished by Massachusetts, New Hampshire, and the north-western parts of New York; but the recruiting proceeded so slowly, that it became necessary to call in the aid of the northern militia. General Gates, having joined General Washington, this department was solely under the command of General Schuyler, who failed in no effort to fulfil its duties. His plans for the ensuing campaign required 15,000 men; a very small portion of which could be supplied to him in season. The services of this officer had been more solid than brilliant, and were not, generally, nor duly, appreciated. Dissatisfied with their acceptation, his resignation was delayed, only, by patriotic motives. When the fear of a winter attack upon Ticonderoga had been removed, by the open state of Lake Champlain, he repaired to Congress to have his complicated accounts adjusted, his conduct inquired of, and his plans of future action approved and sustained. When his many and arduous services had, thus, became fully known, Congress deemed it essential to the public interests, to prevail on him to retain his commission. Repealing the resolution of the 6th March, 1776, which fixed his head-quarters at Albany, they directed him on 22d May, 1777, to assume the command of the whole northern department, consisting of Albany, Ticonderoga, Fort Stanwix, and their dependencies.

XXXIV. Sensible of the dangers which surrounded him, he made every exertion to meet them; visiting in person the several posts, and obtaining supplies of provisions. He was at Albany, for these services, and for hastening the march of reinforcements, when he received intelligence, from General St. Clair, commanding at Ticonderoga, that General Burgoyne had appeared before that fortress.*

The royal army approached by the unimpeded route of the lake; and advanced from Crown Point, with equal caution and order, on both sides of the strait, through which their naval force proceeded. In a few days they surrounded three-fourths of the American works at Ticonderoga and Mount Independence, and erected a battery on Sugar Hill, commanding both positions. The defence of the lines required ten thousand men; the actual force within them, was twenty-five hundred and forty-six continentals, and nine hundred militia, badly equipped, worse armed, and with provisions for twenty days, only. Had it been practicable to obtain an accurate knowledge of the strength of the besieging army, in due season, prudence would have required the abandonment of the post and removal of the stores, before its close approximation. Under existing circumstances, speedy retreat of the garrison was indispensable to the safety of the troops; and though General

* July 1st, 1777.

St. Clair knew, that the whole country relied, confidently, on the maintenance of the post, he wisely and heroically resolved, with the unanimous consent of his officers, to abandon it, and to preserve his army, if possible, for a future service. The execution of this resolution astounded and disgusted the nation; but its propriety became evident, so soon as circumstances permitted inquiry. A few days before the place was invested, General Schuyler, from the inspection of the muster rolls, and other reports alike erroneous, had stated the strength of the garrison at five thousand men, and its provisions abundant; and the invading force was, generally, supposed to be inferior. When, therefore, it was known, that the fortifications, on which much money and labour had been expended, and which were deemed the key of the whole western country, had been abandoned without an effort to sustain them—that an immense train of artillery, consisting of one hundred and twenty-eight pieces, and all the baggage, military stores, and provisions, had fallen into the hands of the enemy—that the army on its retreat, had been attacked, defeated and dispersed, astonishment pervaded all ranks of men, and the conduct of the officers was universally condemned. Congress directed a recall of all the generals of the department, and an inquiry into their conduct. Through New England, especially, the most malignant aspersions were cast on them; and General Schuyler, who, from some unknown cause, had never been viewed with favour in that part of the continent, was involved in the common charge of treason, to which this accumulation of unlooked for calamity was generally attributed, by the mass of the people. On the representation of Washington, the recall of the officers was suspended, until he should be of the opinion, that the state of things would admit such a measure. Gates, however, was directed to take the place of Schuyler. This substitution was warranted by policy; since it put at the head of the department, a general who enjoyed the public confidence, in the place of one who had lost it.

On abandoning the fort, St. Clair retreated rapidly to Castletown, thirty miles from Ticonderoga. In the pursuit, the enemy, with eight hundred and fifty men, under General Frazer, came up with his rear guard, under Colonel Warner, which, amounting to about one thousand men, had halted six miles short of that place. A sharp action ensued, terminating in the dispersion of the Americans, with great loss, by the aid of General Reidesel, who arrived with his division of Germans, during the heat of the contest. About the same time, Colonel Long was driven, with his detachment, from Skeenesborough, and the stores there collected, comprising nearly all that had been saved from the garrison, were destroyed. Long retired to Fort Anne, and soon afterwards to Fort Edward, the head-quarters of General Schuyler; whither St. Clair, after collecting the scattered remains of his army, also, retreated.

XXXV. Burgoyne remained some days at Skeenesborough, to collect and refresh his men; whilst Schuyler employed himself in removing the stores from Fort Edward, sweeping the country of every thing which could sustain an enemy, and throwing obstructions into the streams and roads, to check his course. Nor did he cease his endeavours to arouse the surrounding country to activity. Great exertion was also made by General Washington, to re-establish the northern army. Troops, artillery and ammunition, were despatched from Massachusetts and Peck's-kill. Generals Lincoln and Arnold, popular officers, especially, with their countrymen, and the not less popular Colonel Morgan, with his indefatigable rifle corps, were ordered to repair to it. In the very success of Burgoyne, this able and prudent man saw the source of his defeat, and foretold " that the confidence derived from success," would hurry him into measures that would effect his ruin.

In dispersing the American army, the British general had not completed half that was necessary, to enable him to reach the Hudson. The country through which he was to pass was in a great measure, in a primitive condition. Its roads bad, at the best, were obstructed by hundreds of trees, which had been felled across them. The bridges were broken down, and his provisions, batteaux, and artillery, were to be transported over this almost impassable route. Checked by these impediments, he did not reach that river, in the neighbourhood of Fort Edward, until the 30th of July. Schuyler, who had been daily gathering strength, but not yet strong enough to meet him, on his approach, retired over the Hudson to Saratoga, a few miles below that place, and soon after, to Stillwater, near the mouth of the Mohawk; where he fortified a camp, in hopes that he should soon be in condition to defend it.

But he did not confine himself wholly to defensive operations. The advance of Burgoyne left the posts in his rear uncovered, and General Lincoln was ordered, instead of immediately joining Schuyler, to attempt, with about two thousand men, to cut off the communication of the British with the lakes; whilst Arnold was despatched with three continental regiments to raise the siege of Fort Schuyler, which had been commenced by St. Leger, and to prevent the junction of the two portions of Burgoyne's army.

XXXVI. On the 3d of August, St. Leger invested Fort Schuyler, formerly Fort Stanwix. It was garrisoned by six hundred continental troops, commanded by Colonel Gansevoort. On his approach, General Herkimer assembled the militia of Tryon county, for the purpose of relieving the garrison. Gansevoort, apprized of this intention, resolved on a vigorous sortie, to second it. Unhappily, St. Leger had learned the movement of the former, and formed an ambuscade, into which Herkimer fell. His party was defeated with great slaughter; and the general and many officers were wounded. Its entire destruction was prevented by the timely sortie, under lieutenant-colonel Willet, who fell upon the feebly guarded camp of the besiegers, drove the soldiery into the woods, and brought off considerable plunder, several Indian weapons, and other articles much valued. His party killed several of the enemy, of whom were some Indian chiefs.

But a change was about to come over the fortune of Burgoyne. His star had reached its culminating point, and its decline was as rapid as its ascension. Fort Schuyler was well fortified, and held out. The Indians of St. Leger, always fickle, never persevering in continuous labour, became disgusted with the service, and impatient of the losses which they had sustained in the late skirmishes. At length, learning that Arnold was advancing, and a report prevailing, that Burgoyne had been routed, part of them slunk away, and the remainder threatened to follow. The siege was raised with great precipitation; the tents left standing, and the artillery, with great part of the baggage, ammunition, and provisions, fell into the hands of the Americans. The retreating army was pursued by a detachment from the garrison; and the Indians plundered the remaining baggage of the officers, and massacred such soldiers as could not keep up with the line of march. St. Leger returned to Montreal, whence he proceeded to Ticonderoga, with intention to join Burgoyne by that route.

XXXVII. To prevent relief to the garrison of Fort Schuyler, an attack on the American army was suggested by St. Leger; and Burgoyne was well disposed to an immediate and rapid movement down the Hudson, in hopes thereby, to drive his enemy before him, and free the whole of the upper country. But his supply of provisions was with great difficulty kept up, and such a movement would greatly increase that difficulty, as the communication with Fort George, already endangered by the body of militia assembling at White Creek, must be preserved by larger detachments from his army than he was in condition to make. In this dilemma, he resolved to attempt the large magazines of provisions at Bennington. Lieutenant-colonel Baum, with about five hundred men, was detached upon this service, to facilitate which, Burgoyne moved down the Hudson, and threw part of his army across it to Saratoga; and Lieutenant-colonel Brechman with his corps, was ordered to support Baum. Happily, General Stark, with the New Hampshire militia, was now at Bennington, on his way to camp, together with the remains of Colonel Warner's continental regiment; making in the whole, a force of two thousand men. Apprized of his danger, Baum entrenched himself four miles from the town, and despatched an express for a reinforcement. But before Brechman could arrive, Stark carried the works by assault, and the greater part of his detachment was killed or taken prisoners. Brechman came up in time to encounter the pursuing Americans, and he also, was compelled to retreat with the loss of many men, his artillery and baggage. Five hundred and sixty-four privates were taken prisoners, but the number of killed could not be ascertained; the most important acquisition, at the moment, of one thousand stand of arms, and nine hundred swords, was obtained.

XXXVIII. These fortunate affairs had the most important consequences. The whole Mohawk country was liberated from the foe—the Americans were at liberty to unite the whole of their forces in the northern department against Burgoyne—the militia and continental troops recovered confidence in themselves—the opinion prevailed, that the enemy was already beaten, and that the assembling of the great body of the militia, only, was necessary to compel him to yield his arms. The disaffected became timid, and the wavering were no longer disposed to join an army whose capture was doomed. But other causes, also, united to produce the great result. Vengeance for the barbarities of the savages, fired every breast, and overcame the terror they had created; the last reinforcements of continental troops had arrived—the harvest which had detained the militia was gathered, and General Gates had succeeded the unfortunate, unpopular, but meritorious Schuyler.*

XXXIX. Notwithstanding these disasters, Burgoyne adhered to his original purpose. By a slow and toilsome mode, having collected provisions from Fort George, sufficient for thirty days, he crossed the Hudson with his whole army on the 14th September, and encamped on the heights and plains of Saratoga, with the determination of deciding in a general engagement, the fate of the expedition.

Gates had removed his camp from the islands at the mouth of the Mohawk, to the neighbourhood of Stillwater. On the 17th, Burgoyne encamped within four miles of the American army; and, the interval being employed in the necessary repair of bridges between the two camps, on the 19th, a general engagement was fought, which terminated only with the day, and was in every respect favourable to the Americans. Beside the actual loss in battle, the Indians, Canadians, and provincialists, deserted in great numbers. The next day, intelligence was received from the north, which gave additional animation to the Americans. Detachments from General Lincoln's force had been sent against the forts on the lakes, and Colonel Brown had succeeded in capturing Mount Defiance, Mount Hope, the old French lines, the landing, and about two hundred batteaux at the north end of Lake George; and with the loss of only three killed, and five wounded, had liberated one hundred American prisoners, and taken two hundred and ninety-three British. This success was magnified into the reduction of Ticonderoga, and Mount Independence; but the attempt on these posts had been repulsed.

The armies retained their positions at Stillwater, until the 7th Oct.; Bur-

* August 21.

goyne, in hopes of relief, which had been promised him before the 12th, by Sir Henry Clinton, from New York; and Gates in gathering in the militia of the country. At length, the British general being obliged to diminish the rations of his men, resolved on another trial of strength with his adversary. This, like the preceding battle, was maintained until night, and the advantage was, again, decisively, with the Americans. Burgoyne was compelled to change his position, in order to avoid the renewal of the action, on the next day, with part of his works in possesion of the assailants. He subsequently retired to Saratoga, and endeavoured to open the road to Fort Edward. But being surrounded, and his provisions reduced to a three days' supply, even at short allowance, he was constrained by the most humiliating necessity, to open a negotiation with the American general, and finally to surrender himself and his army, prisoners of war, upon condition, that he should march out of his camp with the usual honours, with permission to return to England, but not to serve against the United States until exchanged.* At the time of the convention, the American force amounted to 9093 continental troops, and 4129 militia; but the sick exceeded 2500 men. The British force was 5752; having been reduced since it left Ticonderoga, 3248 men. In addition to this very great military force, the British lost, and the Americans acquired a fine train of artillery, seven thousand stand of excellent arms, clothing for seven thousand recruits, with tents, and other military stores, to a very considerable amount.

XL. During these important events, Sir Henry Clinton had endeavoured, not very judiciously, certainly, to assist Burgoyne, by his operations in the south. He succeeded in capturing the forts in the Highlands, and in removing the obstructions to the passage of the North river. But so much time was spent in burning the continental villages, and Esopus, and in devastating the country, that he was too late to save or serve his countryman. Upon the capture of Burgoyne, the troops employed in this odious service returned to New York, having inflicted much injury upon the Americans, and added new intensity to their hatred; but, having done no good, to their own cause.

About the same time, the British, who had been left in the rear of Burgoyne, destroying their stores, and abandoning their cannon, retreated to Canada, leaving the country, so late the seat of furious war, restored to perfect tranquillity.

XLI. The effect produced by the capture of this whole British army was of the highest importance, in three points of view. It established, incontestably, the ability of the United States to maintain their independence; and though the contest might be prolonged, its ultimate result was no longer doubtful. It created doubts in Great Britain of the success in the war—and it taught foreigners to confide in, and confiding, to aid, the exertions of the States.

XLII. The captured army was marched to the vicinity of Boston, where some difficulties in procuring proper quarters for the officers, induced a remonstrance from the General to Gates, in which he observed—"the public faith is broken." This expression led Congress to believe, that, if liberated, the troops would immediately join the British garrisons in America; and they passed a resolution suspending the embarkation, till a distinct and explicit ratification of the convention of Saratoga should be properly notified by the court of Great Britain. This event did not take place for many months, during which the troops continued prisoners.

* October 13.

CHAPTER XV.

Campaign of 1778.—I. Condition of the Army at the Valley Forge and at the commencement of the Campaign.—II. British foraging excursions in New Jersey.—III. Fortunate escape of an advance party under La Fayette.—IV. Effect of the American successes abroad—Efforts of American Agents.—V. Measures for Foreign Alliances—Duplicity of France—Treaties with her.—VI. War between Great Britain and France.—VII. Opinions in Great Britain—Ministerial measures.—VIII. Reception of those measures in America.—IX. Arrival of a French Minister Plenipotentiary.—X. The British Army evacuates Philadelphia—March through Jersey.—XI. Battle of Monmouth—British Army regains New York.—XII. Arrival of the French Fleet—proceeds to Rhode Island.—XIII. Attempt on Newport—Appearance of the English Fleet—French and English Fleets put to Sea—dispersed by Storm.—XIV. British Incursions in Connecticut.—XV. Disposition of the American Army.—XVI. British Incursions into New Jersey.—XVII. Movements of the adverse Fleets—Detachment against the Southern States.—XVIII. American Army retires to winter quarters—Its improved condition.—XIX. Indian devastations—Massacre at Wyoming.—XX. Operations against the Indians.—XXI. Discontent in the Jersey line.—XXII. March of General Sullivan to the Indian country—Events there,—XXIII. Expedition under Colonel Broadhead by the Allegheny River.—XXIV. Expedition against the Cherokees under General Pickens.—XXV. Unprovoked Slaughter of the Indians at Muskingum.

I. During the winter of 1777, 1778, the condition of the American army at the Valley Forge was one of great peril and suffering; requiring all the attractive powers of the cause and of the general in command, to preserve that army from dissolution. Every department was imperfectly organized. But the want of system and experience was no where more visible than in those of the quartermaster and the commissariat. Stores of the first necessity, invaluable from their scarcity, were carelessly abandoned, lost, or embezzled; and in a plentiful country, the troops were in danger of perishing for want of food. Tempting opportunities of annoying the enemy were frequently lost from the absolute impossibility of supplying the parties detailed with the indispensable provisions. Several times, during the winter, the soldiers were days without meat; and vegetables and other articles, indispensable to health, were almost unknown to them. The subsistence of an army, and the agents engaged in it, should be as dependent on, and responsible to, the commander-in-chief, as its military movements, and the officers who conduct them; and the negligence, fraud, or sluggishness of the commissary should be as promptly and severely punishable as the cowardice or treachery of the combatant. But this dependence was denied by that passion for engrossing power, and the jealousy which refuses it to others, inherent in popular assemblies. Congress would relinquish no powers which it could, itself, exercise. Early in the war, the office of commissary-general had been conferred upon Colonel Trumbull, of Connecticut, a gentleman well qualified for its duties, but who, notwithstanding, having to struggle through the difficulties of inexperience and original organization, could not fulfil them with universal satisfaction. The remedy resorted to by Congress increased the disease. They rendered his subordinates independent of the head, and made them accountable only to their body. Disgusted with a system, which subjected him to all the danger of responsibility, without the means of protection and indemnity, Mr. Trumbull threw up his commission. Consequently, the army was subjected to the dread, and, not unfrequently, to the pain, of famine. Relief was to be obtained only by compulsory military requisitions, and the whole country within seventy miles of head quarters was, by the resolutions of Congress, placed at the disposition of the commander-in-chief, whereon to levy whatever might be necessary for his army. That patriotism which rises and expends itself in sudden ebullition, is of ordinary growth—is a fever contagious in crowds—whilst that which endures under the deprivation of food and raiment, amid the severities of winter, and the perils of disease and battle, is as rare as it is estimable—but it is not so rare as that, which in the non-combatant, withstands the forcible, hourly, hopeless, unremunerated drain of the purse. Against the exactions, therefore, of the army, even the friendly farmer or dealer opposed the resources of his cunning; and though he did not furnish supplies to the enemy who tempted him with gold, he concealed them from his friends who could pay for them, at best, in almost worthless paper, and frequently, only, in naked promises. But many, very many, had not the negative merit of forbearing to supply the foe; in despite of the unceasing efforts of the American army, they carried large quantities of provisions to British quarters. General Washington could obtain relief, only, by the strenuous exertions of his best officers. General Greene, with a strong detachment, searched the surrounding country. Captain Lee and Captain M'Lane, excellent partisans, were despatched to Delaware and Maryland, and Colonel Tilghman into New Jersey—at the same time Washington urged upon the executives of the several states, to exert themselves for the army and the nation. But the appointment of General Greene to the office of commissary general, under the immediate direction of the commander-in-chief, in March, 1777, was the most efficient remedy.

The sufferings of the troops for want of proper clothing, was not less than from want of food. Their deplorable condition, in this respect, disabled them from keeping the field. The returns of the first of February, exhibit the astonishing number of three thousand nine hundred and eighty-nine men, in camp, unfit for duty, for want of clothes; of whom, scare one had shoes. Even among those returned, capable of duty, very many were so badly clad, that exposure to the colds of the season, must have destroyed them. Although the total of the army then exceeded seventeen thousand men, the effective rank and file, amounted, only, to five thousand and twelve. Nakedness amid frost, unhealthy food, and hunger, filled the hospitals with patients. In these miserable receptacles, death was most frequently found by those who sought for health. The provision made for them, at all times inadequate to their wants, was misapplied. They were crowded in small apartments, and a violent putrid fever raged among them, destroying more than all the other diseases of the camp. Had the British army, at this season, taken the field, it might, though with great suffering to itself, have compelled the American general, either to fight with inferior numbers, and to stake his army upon a battle, or to retreat further into the country; which could not have been effected without great loss, with his naked and barefooted soldiers.

Happily, the real condition of this army was not fully known to Sir William Howe. The present position had been assumed for the purpose of covering the country of Pennsylvania, protecting the magazines laid up in it, and cutting off the supplies of the British army. The plan extended no further than to guard, with the militia, the north of the Schuylkill, and the east of the Delaware, so as to restrain the people of the country from carrying in their provisions to market, to which they were irresistibly allured, by specie payments. These objects were, in a great measure, though not effectually, gained; nor, however, without occasionally inflicting personal chastisement upon delinquents.

II. In the species of war which this state of things produced, the advantage was with the British, who, being unassailable in their quarters, and possessing the command of the Delaware, might, at any time, ravage the coast of Jersey, before assistance could be rendered by the continental troops. The resistance of the militia was inconsiderable, and scarce expected. Yet the wants of such a number of persons and horses, required a greater supply of fresh provisions and forage than could be procured, by light parties or ordinary means. And as the spring opened, with the design to relieve their own army, and to distress that of the United States, about the middle of March, Colonel Mahwood and Major Simcoe were detached into Jersey, at the head of about twelve hundred men. They landed at Salem, and dispersed the small bodies of militia stationed in that part of the country, under Colonels Hand and Holme. The militia were posted at Quinton's Bridge, Alloways' Creek, over which it was supposed the British would endeavour to force a passage. Their numbers being unequal to an effectual resistance, it was only intended to keep the enemy in some check, until they should be reinforced. A judicious plan to surprise them, was skilfully executed by Major Simcoe, one of the best partisans in the British service, and their guard was cut to pieces. The loss of the militia, in several skirmishes, in killed and taken, was between fifty and sixty.

General Washington had received early intelligence of this expedition, which he communicated to Governor Livingston, with a request, that he would immediately order out the militia in force, to join Colonel Shreve, whose regiment was detached into Jersey to aid in protecting the country. The governor could not bring his militia with sufficient expedition into the field. The Legislature had neglected to make provision for paying them; and the repugnance to military duty which this circumstance could not fail to occasion, received no small addition from their unwillingness to expose themselves to its dangers, until a continental force should appear, as a point around which they might rally. On the arrival of Colonel Shreve at Haddonfield, he found, that the militia who had been assembled to aid him, and to intercept the communication with Philadelphia, amounted to less than one hundred men; and Colonel Ellis, their commanding officer, remarked, in a letter to the governor, that, "without some standing force, little was to be expected from the militia, who being, alone, not sufficient to prevent the incursions of the enemy, each one naturally consults his own safety, by not being found in arms."

Mahwood wrote to Colonel Hand, proposing to re-embark his troops, to refrain from further injury to the country, and to pay for the cattle and forage he had taken, in sterling money, on condition, that the militia would lay down their arms and depart to their homes; threatening, on refusal, to arm the tories, to attack all persons he found in arms, burn their dwellings, and reduce their families to the utmost distress. And that his threats might not be supposed in vain, he subjoined a list of the first objects of his intended vengeance.* Colonel Hand indignantly rejected the proposition, and Mahwood, but too faithfully, executed his threat; and, although his incursion continued six or seven days, he returned to Philadelphia unmolested. Not more than two hundred men could be collected to reinforce Colonel Shreve, who, unable to act with effect, did not even march to the lower parts of Jersey, which were plundered without restraint.

* These were, Edmund Keasby, Thomas Sinnickson, Samuel Dick, Whitten Crips, Ebenezer Howell, Edward Hall, John Bowen, Thomas Thompson, George Trenchard, Elisha Cattle, Andrew Sinnickson, Nicholas Keen, Jacob Hufty, Benjamin Holmes, William Schute, Anthony Sharpe, and Abner Penton.

Applications to General Washington for detachments of continental troops, sufficient to cover the country, were necessarily rejected, as the enemy could reinforce with more facility than he, and could, consequently, maintain his superiority until the whole war would be transferred to Jersey. He, however, permitted Colonel Shreve to remain on the east side of the Delaware, and reinforced him with an additional regiment; but would not consent to add to the strength of this detachment, or to depart from his design to keep on that side of the Delaware, only, such force as would break off the ordinary intercourse between the town and country. A larger one would only direct the attention of Sir William Howe towards it, and induce him to plan its destruction. Such an attempt on Colonel Shreve, was disappointed by a precipitate retreat, attended with some loss.

In addition to the vessels which had been engaged in defence of Fort Mifflin, others had been commenced above Philadelphia, but were not completed, when the British obtained possession of the river. To protect these from the enemy, Washington had directed them to be sunk in such a manner as to be weighed with difficulty. This order was disregarded. Against these vessels and some stores collected at Bordentown, an expedition was successfully sent. General Dickenson was in the neighbourhood, but his force was too small to interrupt the enterprise; and General Maxwell, who had been detached on the first intelligence, that the enemy was advancing up the Delaware, was retarded in his march by a heavy rain, which did not delay the movement of the British troops, on board of vessels in the river.

III. To cover the country effectually on the north of the Schuylkill, and to form an advance guard, which might annoy the rear of the enemy, should he evacuate the city, an event, deemed daily more probable, the Marquis de La Fayette was detached, with more than two thousand choice troops, and a few pieces of cannon, to take post on the lines, with orders to occupy no station, permanently, lest the enemy should successfully concert an attack upon him. Having taken a momentary position at Barren Hill, ten miles in front of the army, at the Valley Forge, notice thereof was given to General Howe; who, having reconnoitred his post, despatched General Grant, on the night of the nineteenth of May, against him. He succeeded in getting, undiscovered, into the rear of the Marquis, whilst General Gray, with a strong detachment, advanced by the south side of the Schuylkill, to a ford, two or three miles in front of his right flank, and the residue of the army encamped on Chesnut Hill. The Marquis discovered the perils which environed him, just in season, by a dexterous movement, to avoid them. He rapidly recrossed the Schuylkill by Matson's Ford, and took a post so favourable for defence, that although the enemy pursued him to the bank, he did not dare to wade the river to assail him. From the apparent imprudence, which might be inferred by his surprise, the Marquis is exonerated, by the fact, that the troops placed by him on his left flank, had, without his knowledge, changed their position.

IV. In the course of the winter, the effect, abroad, of the success of the American arms, began to develope itself. The government of France could not observe, without deep interest, the contest which was about to shake, to the foundation, the empire of her great enemy and rival. Though, labouring under financial embarrassments resulting from her late wars, she could not, hastily, involve herself in new expenses, yet the ministry and the nation, longed for an opportunity of retaliating the mortifications and defeat they had sustained. When the discontents of the colonies had broken into open hostilities, M. de Vergennes and other members of the French ministry, declared it to be the policy of France and Spain, to avoid aggression, for three causes; the two latter of which, were, doubtless, founded in truth, and are entirely comprehensible:—First, for moral reasons, which were conformable to the known opinions of the two monarchs: secondly, on account of the condition of the finances, the necessity of time for recovery of exhaustion, and the danger of perpetuating their weakness by premature exertion; and thirdly, that an offensive war, on the part of France and Spain, might reconcile the mother and her colonies; giving the minister a pretext for yielding, and the provinces a motive for acceding to his propositions, in order to obtain time to consolidate themselves, to ripen their plans, and to increase their means. They came to the conclusion, therefore, to watch events in Europe and America; avoiding every thing which might create an opinion that they had, in the latter, any authorized agent; to facilitate to the colonists, the means of procuring, by commerce, the articles, and even the money which they needed, but without a departure from neutrality; to refit and prepare for sea, the naval force; but to precipitate nothing, unless the conduct of England should afford real cause to believe, that she had determined to commence hostilities. Upon these principles, the conduct of the cabinet of Versailles was, for a time, regulated. A party, however, existed in that cabinet, at whose head was the Queen, which avowed a disposition to seize the present moment for revenge, by humbling Great Britain, and dismembering her empire.

The Americans had early sought the countenance of foreign powers, and, particularly, of France. The impossibility of obtaining a supply of arms and ammunition by ordinary means, had, in 1775, induced the appointment of agents to procure military stores abroad; who communed with a secret committee of Congress, empowered to correspond with their friends in Great Britain, Ireland, and other parts of the world. In the spring of 1776, Mr. Silas Deane appeared in Paris, as a political and commercial agent, with instructions to ascertain the disposition of the French king. That monarch, was still reluctant to do any act which might commit him with his enemies. The declaration of independence encouraged the court of Versailles to furnish, privately, means for continuing the war; but it was neither willing, nor prepared, to acknowledge the independence of the United States.

V. As soon as Congress had resolved on the declaration of independence, but before it was published, a project for treaties with foreign powers was prepared, and ministers appointed to negotiate them. Mr. Franklin, Mr. Deane, and Mr. Jefferson, were nominated; but the last named, declining the appointment, Mr. Arthur Lee, then in London, was substituted. They assembled in Paris, early in the winter, were favourably, but not publicly, received; and were assured, that the ports of France would remain open to their ships, and that free commercial relations should be cherished. So closely did the Count de Vergennes conform to his system of caution, that, though the fact was known to the American commissioners, that military stores had been exported from the king's magazines to America, he affected, in their presence, to be wholly ignorant of it. In this state of the negotiation, the utmost circumspection was observed in regard to Great Britain. Every step was taken publicly to gratify her. The remonstrances of her ambassador were scrupulously attended to; the departure of ships, having military stores was forbidden, although they were privately permitted to sail, or sailed without permission; officers having leave of absence, and about to join the Americans, were recalled; strict orders were given, that American prizes should not be sold in French ports; and in some cases, cruisers were compelled to give up the ships they had captured, and to enter into security to cruise no more in the European seas. At the same time, the American agents were privately informed, that in despite of these exactions of policy, they might confide in the good will of the government. Means were also taken to facilitate to them the negotiation of loans, and the owners of privateers were permitted, privately, to dispose of their prizes.

This perplexing and uncertain state, continued from December, 1776, to December, 1777. The success of the campaign of the latter year placed the Americans in a more favourable light, as possible instruments for the gratification of Gallic vengeance, and disposed the ministers to draw the relations with them more closely. The capture of Burgoyne determined them to acknowledge and support the independence of the United States. France frankly avowed, what folly alone could tempt her to conceal, that in this measure, she sought her own interest. Though war with Great Britain would probably be the consequence, there was a generosity displayed in abstaining from requiring any preference over other nations, and in treating with the new states as if they had been long established, and were in the fulness of strength and power.

Two treaties were formed. One, of friendship and commerce, recognised the independence of America. The other, of alliance, eventual and defensive, between the two nations, stipulated, that should a war arise between Great Britain and France during the existence of that with the United States, it should become a common cause, and that neither of the contracting parties should conclude either truce or peace with Great Britain, without the formal assent of the other. They mutually engaged not to lay down their arms, until the independence of the United States should be assured by treaty terminating the war. There were other provisions in this contract, which in their result did not affect the revolution.

VI. Soon after, the treaty of friendship and commerce was communicated by the representative of France to the British court; which, readily, conceiving, that France had not taken this step without a resolution to follow it through all its consequences, considered the notification a declaration of war; and immediately published a memorial for the justification of the hostilities she resolved to commence.

The French ministry received private intelligence, that the English cabinet contemplated to offer to the United States the acknowledgment of their independence, on condition of a separate peace. They communicated this to the American commissioners, urging them to lose no time in representing, that the war, though not declared in form, had actually commenced, and that they, deeming the treaty of alliance in full force, considered neither party at liberty to make a separate peace.

The despatches containing the treaties were received by the president of Congress, on Saturday, the second of May, after the House had adjourned. That body was immediately convened, and the joyful tidings communicated. The treaties were ratified, on Monday, with a resolution highly complimentary to the magnanimity and wisdom of the French monarch. But the intoxication of joy led this grave assembly into the error of publishing both, the avowed and concealed; or it served as an excuse for involving France, inextricably, in their cause, by confirming the indignation of Great Britain at her duplicity.

VII. The impression made upon the British nation, though different, was not less, than that upon the French, by the capture of Burgoyne; and produced even in the cabinet, resolutions in favour of pacific measures. In February, 1778, Lord North gave notice in the House of Commons, of his intention to propose a plan of conciliation. In conformity with which, he moved to bring in "a bill for removing all doubts and apprehensions concerning taxation by the Parliament of Great Britain, in any of the colonies and plantations of North America," and "a bill to enable his Majesty to appoint commissioners, with sufficient powers to treat, consult, and agree upon the means of quieting the disorders now subsisting in certain of the colonies of America.

The first declared that Parliament would impose no duty payable in America, except such as might be expedient for the purposes of commerce, the net produce of which, should be paid and applied for the use of the colony in which it should be levied, as other duties collected under the authority of the Legislature. The second, authorized the appointment of commissioners by the Crown, with power to treat, either with the constituted authorities, or with individuals in America,—the stipulations which might be entered into, to be subject to the approbation of Parliament. They were also empowered to proclaim a cessation of hostilities in any of the colonies; to suspend the operation of the non-intercourse law, and, during the continuance of the act, so much of all or any of the acts of Parliament, which had passed since the 10th of February, 1773, relating to the colonies; to grant pardon to any number or description of persons; and to appoint a governor in any colony, in which his Majesty had, theretofore, made such appointments. The duration of the last act was limited to the first of June, 1779. Both were sanctioned by Parliament with little opposition. Their great defect was, that they came too late. The spirit upon which they might have wrought was no more. It had been succeeded by one to which the demand of subjection, and the offer of pardon were irreparable insults.

Before these bills could be gotten through the customary forms, intelligence was received of the treaty with France. Copies were, therefore, hurried to America, to be laid before Congress, and the public, that they might counteract the effect of the treaty.

VIII. Washington was instructed of the nature of these bills, as well by letters, from Major-general Tryon, the British governor of New York, as from other sources. The communication from Tryon, containing the extraordinary and impertinent request, "that it should be published to the army," was immediately despatched to Congress. The committee to whom it was referred, reported, That the bills were designed to create division among the people, and to encourage desertion from the common cause, and were the sequel of the insidious plan, which, from the days of the stamp act, had involved the country in contention and blood; and though circumstances might, now, cause a recession from unjustifiable claims, they would not fail to be renewed upon the first favourable occasion:—That, as the union of the Americans, upon principles of common interest in defence of common rights, was cemented by common calamities and mutual good offices and affection, so the cause for which they contended, and in which all mankind were interested, must derive its success from the continuance of such union; and that, whoever should presume to make any separate or partial convention, with the commissioners under the crown, ought to be considered and treated as open and avowed enemies of the United States:—That, the United States could not, with propriety, hold conference with commissioners from Great Britain, unless as a preliminary, they should withdraw their fleets and armies, or in express terms acknowledge the independence of the States: And that, as it appeared to be the design of the enemies of the States, to lull them into fatal security, the States should be called upon to use the most strenuous exertions, to send their respective quotas of troops into the field, and to maintain their militia in readiness. Fearless of the effect of these measures upon the public mind, Congress ordered the report and resolutions to be published. The alliance with France, which had been long expected, was believed by every patriot to assure the national independence,—and this had become an object too dear to be easily abandoned.

Subsequently to the reception of the copies of the bills, letters were received by Congress, in the close of May, from Lord Howe and Sir Henry Clinton, enclosing the acts of Parliament, themselves. Congress replied—"Your lordship may be assured, that when the king of Great Britain shall be seriously disposed to put an end to the unprovoked and cruel war waged against these United States, Congress will readily attend to such terms of peace, as may consist with the honour of independent nations, the interest of their constituents, and the sacred regard they mean to pay to treaties."

The commissioners appointed to give effect to those conciliatory bills, consisted of Governor Johnstone, Lord Carlisle, and Mr. Eden, to whom Sir Henry Clinton was added. The three first arrived in Philadelphia, while the city was in possession of the British. On the 9th of June they requested, from General Washington, a passport for their secretary, Dr. Ferguson, with a letter from them to Congress; but this was refused. They, then, addressed a letter to Congress, in due form, communicating a copy of their commission, and of the acts of Parliament, and proposing among other things, to consent to a cessation of hostilities by sea and land; to restore free intercourse, to revive mutual affection, and renew the common benefits of naturalization, through the several parts of the empire: To extend every freedom to trade, that the respective interest of Britain and America could require: To agree that no military forces should be kept up in North America, without the consent of the general Congress, or particular Assemblies: To concur in measures "calculated to discharge the debts of America, and to raise the credit and value of the paper circulation:" To perpetuate the union, by a reciprocal deputation of agent or agents, who should have the privilege of a seat and voice in the Parliament of Great Britain, or if sent from Britain, in the Assemblies of the different colonies, to which they might be deputed, respectively. In short, to establish the power of the respective Legislatures in each particular colony, to settle its revenue in civil and military establishment, and to exercise a perfect freedom in legislation and internal government; so that the British colonies in North America, acting with Great Britain, in peace and in war, under one common sovereign, might have the irrevocable enjoyment of every privilege, short of a total separation of interests, or consistent with that union of force, on which the safety of their common religion and liberty depended."

The letter containing these propositions, also, contained some observations reflecting on the conduct of France, which gave so much offence in Congress, as to cause a suspension of the proceedings on the communication. But at length, an answer was agreed upon, signed by the president, and transmitted to the commissioners, rejecting their propositions, and assigning reasons therefor.

A reply from the commissioners followed the rejection of Congress, and the negotiation was thus, for a short period, continued, during which Mr. Johnstone caused certain propositions, in the nature of a bribe, to be made to Mr. Joseph Reed, which were not only indignantly rejected by that gentleman, but which induced Congress to refuse intercourse with the proposer. Mr. Johnstone, thereupon, retired from the commission, whilst his colleagues endeavoured to press their views upon the Congress and the nation. To the latter, both parties appealed through the press, but the British agents were, in every effort, unsuccessful.

IX. In the midst of these transactions, the Sieur Girard, who had negotiated the treaties between France and the United States, arrived at Philadelphia, in the character of minister plenipotentiary of his most Christian Majesty. This event produced unbounded joy among the people and Congress, by whom the minister was received with every demonstration of respect.

X. About the time the command of the army devolved on Sir Henry Clinton, orders were received for the evacuation of Philadelphia. The part which France was about to take in the war, with the naval force she had prepared, rendered this city a dangerous position, and determined the administration, entirely, to abandon the Delaware. Preparations to this end were actively pursued, but it was some time uncertain, to what point the army was destined. At length, the intention was apparent to reach New York through the Jerseys. Upon this presumption, General Washington conducted his operations.

General Maxwell, with the Jersey brigade, was ordered to take post about Mount Holly, and to unite with Major-general Dickenson, who was assembling the militia, for the purpose of breaking down the bridges, falling trees in the roads, and otherwise embarrassing the march of the British general. Instructions were given to these officers, to guard carefully against a *coup de main*, and to keep the militia, in small light parties, on his flanks.

When Washington learned, that the greater proportion of the British army had crossed the Delaware,* he convened a council of general officers, to determine on his course. The force of the armies was nearly equal, the numerical advantage being with the Americans; the British having ten, and the Americans between ten and eleven, thousand. Of seventeen general officers, Wayne and Cadwalader, alone, were decidedly in favour of attacking the enemy. Fayette inclined to that opinion without openly embracing it. Consequently, it was resolved, not to risk a battle.

Sir Henry Clinton moved with great deliberation; seeming to await the approach of his adversary. He proceeded through Haddonfield,† Mount Holly, Slabtown, and Crosswicks, to Allentown and Imlaytown, which he reached, on the twenty-fourth. Dickenson and Maxwell retired before him, unable to obstruct his march otherwise than by destroying the bridges. As his route, until he passed Crosswicks, lay directly up the Delaware, and at no great distance from it, General Washington found it necessary to make an extensive circuit, to pass the river at Coryell's Ferry. Pursuant to the settled plan of avoiding an engagement, he kept the high grounds, directing his course so as to cover the important passes of the Highlands. He crossed the river on the twenty-second, and remained the twenty-third at Hopewell, in the elevated country, adjacent to the river.

General Arnold, whose wounds yet unfitted him for service, was directed to possess himself of Philadelphia, and to detach four hundred continental troops, and such militia as could be collected, to harass the rear of the enemy. This service, by the order of the commander-in-chief, was confided to General Cadwalader, who could only add to his continental force, fifty volunteers and forty militia, commanded by General Lacy. From Hopewell, Morgan, with six hundred riflemen, was detached to annoy his right flank; Dickenson, with about one thousand Jersey militia, and Maxwell's brigade, hung on his left.

XI. In this position of the armies, General Washington, who had rather acquiesced in, than approved, the decision of the late council of war, and was disposed to seek battle, again submitted the proposal to the consideration of the general officers, by whom it was, again, negatived. By their advice a chosen body of fifteen hundred men, under Brigadier-general Scott, was added to the corps on the left flank of the enemy. But Washington being

* June 18th, 1777.

† The night that the British encamped at Haddonfield, Captain M'Lane, by orders from General Arnold, passed through their camp, and reported their situation to the general.

supported by the wishes of some officers whom he highly valued, determined, on his own responsibility, to bring on a general engagement. The enemy being on his march to Monmouth court-house, he resolved to strengthen the force on his lines, by despatching General Wayne with an additional corps of one thousand men. The continental troops, now, thrown in front of the army, amounted to four thousand men, a force sufficient to require the direction of a major-general. The tour of duty was General Lee's; but, he, having declared, strongly, against hazarding, even a partial engagement, and supposing that, in conformity with the advice signed by all the generals in camp, save one, nothing would be attempted beyond reconnoitring the enemy, and restraining the plundering parties, showed no disposition to assert his claim; but yielded the command to General La Fayette. All the continental parties on the lines were placed under his direction, with orders to take measures, in concert with General Dickenson, to impede the march of the British, and to occasion them the greatest loss. These measures demonstrated the wishes of the commander-in-chief, tending almost inevitably to a general battle. Wayne had earnestly advised it, and La Fayette inclined towards a partial engagement. Colonel Hamilton, who accompanied him, had the strongest desire to signalize the detachment, and to accomplish all the wishes of Washington. These dispositions having been made, the main army was moved to Cranberry, on the 26th, to support the advance. The intense heat of the weather, a heavy storm, and a temporary want of provisions, prevented it from proceeding further next day. The advanced corps had pressed forward and taken a position on the Monmouth road, about five miles in the rear of the enemy, with the intention of attacking him on the next morning. It was now, however, too remote, and too far on the right, to be supported in case of action; and pursuant to orders, the Marquis filed off by his left, towards Englishtown, early on the morning of the 27th.

General Lee had declined the command of the advance party, under the opinion, that it was not designed for effective service; but perceiving, soon after its march, that much importance was attached to it, and dreading lest his reputation might suffer, he earnestly solicited to be placed at its head. To relieve his feelings, without wounding those of La Fayette, Washington detached the former, with two other brigades, to support the Marquis. Lee would, of course, have the direction of the whole front division, amounting now to five thousand men; but he stipulated, that if any enterprise had been formed by La Fayette, it should be executed as if the commanding officer had not been changed.

Sir Henry Clinton had taken a strong position, on the high grounds about Monmouth court-house; having his right flank in the skirt of a small wood, his left secured by a thick one, and a morass towards his rear. His whole front was, also, covered by a wood, and, for a considerable distance towards his left, by a morass, and he was within twelve miles of the high grounds about Middletown; after reaching which, he would be perfectly secure.

Under these circumstances, General Washington determined to attack their rear, the moment they should move from their ground. This determination was communicated to Lee, with orders to make his dispositions, and to keep his troops constantly lying on their arms, that he might be in readiness to take advantage of the first movement. Corresponding orders were also given to the rear division.

About five in the morning of the twenty-eighth, intelligence was received from General Dickenson, that the front of the enemy was in motion. The troops were immediately under arms, and Lee was directed to move on, and attack the rear, "unless there should be powerful reasons to the contrary."

He was, at the same time, informed, that the main army would march to support him.

Sir Henry Clinton, perceiving that the Americans were in his neighbourhood, changed the order of his march. The baggage was placed under the care of General Knyphausen, while the flower of his army, unincumbered, formed the rear division commanded by Lord Cornwallis; who, to avoid pressing on Knyphausen, remained on his ground until about eight, and then descending from the heights of Freehold, into a plain of about three miles in extent, took up his line of march in rear of the front division.*

General Lee made the dispositions necessary for executing his orders; and, soon after the rear of the enemy was in motion, prepared to attack it. General Dickenson had been directed, to detach some of his best troops, to co-operate with him; and Morgan to act on the enemy's right flank, but with so much caution, as to be able readily to extricate himself, and to form a junction with the main body.

Lee appeared on the heights of Freehold, soon after the enemy had left them, and following the British into the plain, gave directions to General Wayne to attack their covering party, so as to halt them, but not to press them sufficiently to force them up to the main body, or to draw reinforcements from thence, to their aid. In the mean time, he proposed to gain their front by a shorter road on their left, and entirely intercepting their communication with the line, to bear them off before they could be assisted.

While in the execution of this design, a gentleman of General Washington's suite came up to gain intelligence, and to him, Lee communicated his present object.

Sir Henry Clinton, soon after the rear division was in full march, observed a column of the Americans on his left flank. This being militia, was soon dispersed. When his rear guard had descended from the hills, it was followed by a strong corps; soon after which, a cannonade upon it was commenced from some pieces commanded by Colonel Oswald, and, at the same time, he received intelligence, that a respectable force had shown itself on both his flanks. Believing a design to have been formed on his baggage, which in the defiles would be exposed, he determined, in order to secure it, to attack the troops in his rear, so vigorously, as to compel them to call off those on his flanks. This induced him to march back his whole rear division, which movement was making, as Lee advanced for the purpose of reconnoitring, to the front of the wood, adjoining the plain. He soon perceived himself to have mistaken the force which formed the rear of the British; but he yet proposed to engage on that ground, although his judgment, as was afterwards stated by himself, on an inquiry into his conduct, disapproved of it; there being a morass immediately in his rear, which could not be passed without difficulty, and which would necessarily impede the arrival of reinforcements to his aid, and embarrass his retreat should he be finally overpowered.

This was about ten o'clock. While both armies were preparing for action, General Scott (as stated by General Lee) mistook an oblique march of an American column for a retreat; and, in the apprehension of being abandoned, left his position, and repassed the ravine in his rear. Being himself of opinion, that the ground on which the army was drawn up, was by no means favourable to them, Lee did not correct the error Scott had committed, but directed the whole detachment to regain the heights they had passed. He was pressed by the enemy, and some slight skirmishing ensued, during this retrograde movement, in which not much loss was sustained on either side.

* Letter of Sir Henry Clinton.

When the first firing announced the commencement of the action, the rear division threw off their packs, and advanced rapidly to support the front. As they approached the scene of action, Washington, who had received no intelligence from Lee, notifying his retreat, rode forward; and about noon, after the army had marched five miles, to his utter astonishment and mortification, met the advanced corps retiring before the enemy, without having made a single effort to maintain their ground. Those whom he first fell in with, neither understood the motives which had governed General Lee, nor his present design; and could give no other information than that, by his orders, they had fled without fighting.

Washington rode to the rear of the division, which was closely pressed. There he met Lee, to whom he spoke in terms of some warmth, implying disapprobation of his conduct. He also gave immediate orders to the regiments commanded by Colonel Stewart and Lieutenant-colonel Ramsay, to form on a piece of ground which he deemed proper for the purpose of checking the enemy, who were advancing rapidly on them. General Lee was then directed to take proper measures, with the residue of his force, to stop the British column on that ground, and the commander-in-chief rode back, himself, to arrange the rear division of the army.

These orders were executed with firmness. A sharp conflict ensued, and when forced from the ground on which he had been placed, Lee brought off his troops in good order, and was, then, directed to form in the rear of Englishtown.

The check thus given the enemy, afforded time to draw up the left wing and second line of the American army, on an eminence, partly in a wood, and partly in an open field, covered by a morass in front. Lord Stirling, who commanded the wing, brought up a detachment of artillery, under Lieutenant-colonel Carrington, with some field pieces, which played with considerable effect on the enemy, who had passed the morass, and were pressing on to the charge. These pieces, with the aid of several parties of infantry, detached for the purpose, effectually put a stop to their advance. The American artillery were drawn up in the open field, and maintained their ground with admirable firmness, under a heavy and persevering fire from the British.

The right wing was, for the day, commanded by General Greene. To expedite the march, and to prevent the enemy from turning the right flank, he had been ordered to file off by the new church, two miles from Englishtown, and to fall into the Monmouth road, a small distance in the rear of the court-house, while the residue of the army proceeded directly to that place. He had advanced on this road considerably to the right of, and rather beyond, the ground on which the armies were now engaged, when he was informed of the retreat of Lee, and of the new disposition of the troops. He immediately changed his route, and took an advantageous position on the right.

Warmly opposed in front, the enemy attempted to turn the left flank of the American army, but were repulsed, and driven back by parties of infantry. They then attempted the right, with as little success. General Greene had advanced a body of troops, with artillery, to a commanding piece of ground in his front, which not only marred their design of turning the right, but severely enfiladed the party which yet remained in front of the left, wing. At this moment, General Wayne advanced with a body of infantry in front, who kept up so hot and well directed a fire of musketry, that the British soon gave way, and withdrew behind the ravine, to the ground on which the first halt had been made.

Here the British line was formed on very strong ground. Both flanks were secured by thick woods and morasses, while their front could be reached, only, through a narrow pass. The day had been intensely hot, and the troops were much fatigued. Still Washington resolved to renew the engagement. For this purpose, Brigadier-general Poor, with his own and the Carolina brigade, gained the enemy's right flank, while Woodford, with his brigade, turned their left, and the artillery advanced on them in front. But the impediments on the flanks of the enemy were so considerable, that before they could be overcome, and the troops approach near enough to commence the attack, it was nearly dark. Under these circumstances, further operations were deferred until morning. The brigades on the flanks kept their ground through the night, and the other troops lay on their arms in the field of battle, in order to be in perfect readiness to support them. General Washington, who had, through the day, been extremely active, passed the night, in his cloak in the midst of his soldiers.

In the mean time, the British were employed in removing their wounded. About midnight they marched away in such silence, that their retreat was without the knowledge of General Poor, who lay very near them.

As it was perfectly certain, that they would gain the high grounds about Middletown, before they could be overtaken, where they could not be attacked with advantage; as the face of the country afforded no prospect of opposing their embarkation; and as the battle, already, fought had terminated favourably to the reputation of the American arms; it was thought advisable to relinquish the pursuit. Leaving the Jersey brigade, Morgan's corps, and M'Lane's command * to hover about them, to countenance desertion, and protect the country from their depredations, it was resolved to move the main body of the army to the Hudson, and take a position which should effectually cover the important passes in the Highlands.

The loss of the Americans was eight officers and sixty-one privates killed, and about one hundred and sixty wounded. Among the slain were Lieutenant-colonel Bonner of Pennsylvania, and Major Dickenson of Virginia, both much regretted. One hundred and thirty were missing; of whom many afterwards rejoined their regiments.

Sir Henry Clinton stated his dead and missing at four officers, and one hundred and eighty-four privates; his wounded, at sixteen officers, and one hundred and fifty-four privates. This account, so far as respects the dead, cannot be correct, as four officers, and two hundred and forty-five privates were buried on the field, and some few were afterwards found and buried, so as to increase the number to nearly three hundred. The uncommon heat of the day was fatal to several on both sides.

As usual, when a battle has not been decisive, both parties claimed the victory. In the early part of the day, the advantage was certainly with the British; in the latter part, it may be pronounced, with equal certainty, to have been with the Americans. They maintained their ground, repulsed the enemy by whom they were attacked, were prevented only by the night, and the retreat of Sir Henry Clinton, from renewing the action, and suffered in killed and wounded less than their adversaries.

Independent of the loss sustained in the action, the British army was considerably weakened in its way from Philadelphia to New York. About one hundred prisoners were made, and near a thousand soldiers, principally foreigners, many of whom had married in Philadelphia, deserted the British standard during the march.

Whilst the armies were traversing the Jerseys, Gates, who commanded on the North river, by a well timed and judicious movement down the Hud-

* The militia had returned to their homes immediately after the action.

son, threatened New York, for the purpose of restraining the garrison of that place, from reinforcing Sir Henry Clinton, should such a measure be contemplated.

The conduct of Lee was generally disapproved. As, however, he had possessed a large share of the confidence of the commander-in-chief, it is probable, that explanations might have been made, which would have rescued him from the imputations cast on him, and have restored him to the esteem of the army, could his haughty temper have brooked the indignity he believed to have been offered him on the field of battle. General Washington had taken no measures in consequence of the events of that day, and, probably, would have come to no resolution concerning them, without an amicable explanation, had he not received from Lee a letter, in very unbecoming terms, in which he manifestly assumed the station of a superior, and required reparation for the injury sustained, from the very singular expressions, said to have been used, on the day of the action, by the commander-in-chief.

This letter was answered by an assurance, that so soon as circumstances would admit of an inquiry, he should have an opportunity of justifying himself to the army, to America, and to the world in general, or of convincing them that he had been guilty of disobedience of orders, and misbehaviour before the enemy. On the same day, on Lee's expressing a wish for a speedy investigation of his conduct, and for a court-martial, rather than a court of inquiry, he was arrested,

First. For disobedience of orders in not attacking the enemy on the 28th of June, agreeably to repeated instructions. Secondly. For misbehaviour before the enemy on the same day, in making an unnecessary, disorderly, and shameful retreat. Thirdly. For disrespect to the commander-in-chief in two letters. Before this correspondence had taken place, strong and specific charges of misconduct had been made against General Lee, by several officers of his detachment, and particularly, by Generals Wayne and Scott. In these the transactions of the day, not being well understood, were represented in colours much more unfavourable to Lee, than facts would justify. These representations, most probably, produced the strength of the expressions contained in the second article of the charge. A court-martial was soon called, over which Lord Stirling presided; and, after a full investigation, Lee was found guilty of all the charges exhibited against him, and sentenced to be suspended for one year. This sentence was afterwards, though with some hesitation, approved, almost unanimously, by Congress. The court softened, in some degree, the severity of the second charge, by finding him guilty, not in its very words, but of misbehaviour before the enemy, by making an unnecessary, and, in some few instances, a disorderly retreat.

Lee defended himself with his accustomed ability. He suggested a variety of reasons justifying his retreat, which, if they do not absolutely establish its propriety, give it so questionable a form, as to render it probable that a public examination never would have taken place, could his proud spirit have stooped to offer explanation, instead of outrage, to the commander-in-chief.

The attention of General Washington was now turned, principally, to the North river, towards which the march of his army was directed, with the intention of continuing some time about Haverstraw. And soon after he crossed the North river to the White Plains.

After remaining a few days on the high grounds of Middletown, Sir Henry Clinton proceeded to Sandy Hook; whence he passed his army over to New York. This transit was effected by means of the fleet under Lord Howe, which had arrived off the Hook on the 28th of June.

XII. Upon the day of battle, the French fleet, under Count d'Estaing, having on board a respectable body of land forces, made the coast, off Chincoteague inlet. Had it arrived a few days earlier, its superior force would have shut Lord Howe, and the British fleet, in the Delaware; and the capture of the army, under Sir Henry Clinton would, probably, have followed. The count proceeded to Sandy Hook, for the purpose of attacking the British fleet in port; and should this be found impracticable, to make an attempt on Rhode Island. The first was defeated by the shoalness of the bar, at the mouth of the harbour.

XIII. In the preceding winter, General Sullivan had been detached to command the troops in Rhode Island, and he was now directed to make such requisitions on the militia of New England, and to prepare such measures, as would enable him to attempt the town of Newport. General La Fayette joined him with two brigades; and soon after, General Greene assumed command of the whole force. On the 26th of July, the French fleet appeared off Newport, and cast anchor about five miles from that place, without Brenton's Ledge.

Sir Henry Clinton, apprehensive for the safety of his troops at Newport, had reinforced Major-general Pigot, who commanded on Rhode Island, and the garrison, now, amounted to six thousand effectives. Their main body lay at Newport; and the American army, under Sullivan, about the town of Providence. A plan for the reduction of Newport, was concerted between D'Estaing and Sullivan, in pursuance of which, the latter landed a force of near nine thousand men, on the island. But having, as the count supposed, improperly, taken preference of the French, he became offended, and some delay occurred in the co-operation of the French forces. In the mean time, a reinforcement to the British fleet arrived from Europe, under Admiral Byron, who came out to relieve Lord Howe. This circumstance determined the latter, though still superior in force, to attack the French fleet before Newport. Having approached that town, D'Estaing, with the weather gage, left the harbour to give battle. Howe deemed this an advantage in addition to numerical superiority, too great to encounter, and immediately put to sea, followed by the French. Two days were spent in fruitless manœuvres; and on the third, the fleets were separated and dispersed, by a storm. In a shattered condition, the English vessels sailed for New York, and the French for Rhode Island. D'Estaing, alleging his instructions to repair to Boston, should a superior British force reach America, refused to renew the attempt on the island, and left the American army there, to contend alone with the British in their entrenchments. Against this measure, all the general officers, except La Fayette, warmly protested. But thus deserted, the siege of Newport was broken up, on the night of the 28th of August; the army retiring, unobserved, to the northern end of the island. The British followed in two columns, and a smart action was fought, in which the American troops showed great firmness and courage. The battle ended with the day; both parties claiming the victory. Sullivan retreated from the island on the 30th, just in season to save his army; for on the next day, Sir Henry Clinton arrived with a force which would have rendered it impracticable. The conduct of the general was highly approved by Congress. But an unfortunate expression, in his general orders, seemingly, reflecting on the conduct of the French, gave the officers of their fleet and army some offence, which induced a representation from D'Estaing to the national council. The inhabitants of New England, generally, were so much discontented with the conduct of the fleet, that fears were entertained, lest the means of repairing the ships, could not be procured. These dangerous and irritating dissentions were appeased by the interference of Washington, Hancock, Greene, and other American patriots, who justly dreaded their effect on the fate of the country.

The English fleet had suffered less from the storm than the French; and Lord Howe, after refitting at New York, sailed for Boston, in hope of intercepting D'Estaing; but failing in this, and finding him safely moored in the harbour, he returned to New York, where receiving such additions to his force, as rendered him decidedly superior to his adversary, he resigned the command to Admiral Gambier, until the arrival of Admiral Byron, daily expected from Halifax.

XIV. On his way from Rhode Island to New York, Sir Henry Clinton prepared to make a descent on New London; but the winds proving adverse, he left the troops and transports, under Major-general Gray, to conduct an expedition to the eastward, as far as Buzzard's Bay. Gray destroyed a number of privateers, with their prizes, and some merchant vessels in Acushnet river, and reduced, on the 5th of September, great part of the towns of Bedford and Fairhaven, where a considerable quantity of provisions, military and naval stores, were reduced to ashes. At Martha's Vineyard, several vessels and salt works were destroyed, and a heavy contribution of live stock, levied on the inhabitants.

XV. Apprehensive that a combined attack of the land and naval force of the British, would be made on the French, fleet, General Gates was directed with three brigades to proceed as far as Danbury, in Connecticut, there to await orders. And with a view, both to the passes of the Highlands, and the eastern States, the camp at White Plains was broken up, and the main body of the army took a position further north, at Fredericksburg; while General Putnam was detached with two brigades, to the neighbourhood of West Point, and General M'Dougal with two others to Danbury, to join General Gates.

XVI. Soon after the return of Gray, a large British force from New York, in two columns, ascended the North river, by either bank. That on the west, of five thousand men, was commanded by Cornwallis, and that on the east, of three thousand, by Knyphausen. Their principal object was conjectured to be forage. The west corps surprised the cavalry regiment of Colonel Baylor, at Taupan, or Harrington. The British troops, on the 27th of September, rushed upon them in a barn where they slept, and refusing quarter, used the bayonet with savage cruelty. Of one hundred and four privates, sixty-seven were killed, wounded or taken—Colonel Baylor and Major Clough, both wounded, the former dangerously, the latter mortally, were among the prisoners. Some militia in the same neighbourhood, apprized of the approach of Colonel Campbell, who was sent against them, made their escape. The cruelty exercised on this occasion was, by the request of Congress, established by an inquisition instituted by Governor Livingston. This affair was in some degree balanced by one which occurred three days after. Colonel Richard Butler, assisted by Major Lee, with part of his cavalry, fell in with a party of fifteen chasseurs, and an hundred yagers, under Captain Donop, on whom they made so rapid a charge, that, without the loss of a man, they killed ten of the enemy on the spot, and took the officer commanding the chasseurs, and eighteen of the yagers, prisoners.

This movement had been, in part, designed to favour an expedition against Little Egg Harbour. Count Pulaski had been appointed general of the American cavalry, but the dissatisfaction of the officers induced him to resign his commission. He obtained permission to raise a legionary corps, consisting of three incomplete companies of horse, and the like number of foot, officered by foreigners, among whom was one Juliet, a deserter from the enemy. The Count had been ordered from Trenton to Little Egg Harbour, and was lying eight or ten miles from the coast, when his position was betrayed by Juliet. The plan to surprise him was successful, with respect to his infantry, who were put to the bayonet. The British account represents the whole corps to have been destroyed; but the Count admitted a loss of about forty only—and averred, that with his cavalry, he drove the enemy from the ground.

XVII. Admiral Byron assumed the command of the British fleet at New York, in September, and in October, appeared before Boston, for the purpose of blocking up D'Estaing, and availing himself of any circumstance which might favour an attack on the French fleet. But a furious storm driving him to sea, and essentially injuring him, he was compelled to put into Rhode Island, to refit. The French admiral, improving the favourable opportunity, sailed on the 3d of November, for the West Indies. Thus terminated, without material advantage, an expedition, of whose success the most sanguine expectations had been entertained.

Upon the same day, a detachment of five thousand men, from the British army, sailed from New York, under Major-general Grant, with the like destination; and towards the close of the month, another under Colonel Campbell, embarked, to act offensively, against the southern States.

XVIII. As there yet remained in New York a force sufficient for its defence, the American army retired, in December, into winter quarters. The main body was cantoned in Connecticut, on both sides of the North river, about West Point, and at Middlebrook. The troops again wintered in huts, to which they had become accustomed; and though far from being well clad, their condition was in this respect, so much ameliorated, by supplies from France, that they bore every inconvenience without repining.

The errors of the first years of the war had produced some useful reforms. The insufficiency of the provision for the support of the military officers, had caused the resignation of many, to the great injury of the service. From the convictions of justice and policy, and from respect to the earnest and disinterested recommendation of General Washington, Congress allowed half pay, for seven years after the expiration of service; which was subsequently extended to the end of their lives, but was finally commuted for full pay, for five years. Resignations were afterwards rare, and the States reaped the benefit of experienced officers, until the war was ended. A system of more regular discipline was introduced into the army, by Baron de Steuben, who had served under the King of Prussia. A very important amelioration was effected in the medical department, by appointing different officers to discharge the directing and purveying business of the military hospitals, which had been before united in the same hands. The merit of this change is due to Dr. Rush. And the ordinances limiting prices, being found utterly impracticable, were abolished.

XIX. Throughout all the borders of the land, a barbarous war was carried on by the savages, in which the usual restraints on the worst passions of our nature were abandoned. The American tories and refugees, who had fled to the wilds, under the disguise of Indians, indulged an unbounded lust for rapine. These tutored savages acted as guides to the war parties, leading them into the richest and undefended settlements, and enabling them frequently to escape with impunity. Any reverses they might occasionally suffer, were amply compensated by the British agents, whose inhuman policy had armed the murderers' hands, and daily urged them to action. Whilst the war was distant from the Indian country, the Indians experienced none of its evils. It produced only the pleasure of adventure, and of sudden and extraordinary acquisition. A particular detail of the devastations of property, of the distress of all sexes, ages and conditions, who were driven from their conflagrated homes, and wasted farms, to seek precarious shelter in the forest, and to subsist upon the spontaneous productions of the earth, and an account of the barbarous murders, would exceed our limits, and be but repetitions of disgusting scenes of horror. We will dwell only on the massacre at Wyoming, in Luzerne county, Pennsylvania, perpetrated under Colonel John Butler, a Connecticut tory, and an inhabitant of that charming valley, which in atrocity has never been surpassed. Early in July, 1778, a party of one thousand one hundred, of whom nine hundred were Indians, entered this new settlement. One of the forts, which had been constructed for the security of the inhabitants, being garrisoned by concealed tories, was surrendered, without opposition. Another was taken, part of the garrison having retired. The two principal forts, however, were Kingston and Wilkesbarre, near each other, on opposite sides of the Susquehanna river. The first contained Colonel Zebulon Butler, a cousin of the tory chieftain, with the greatest part of the armed force of the country, and a number of women and children. After rejecting a summons to surrender, he agreed to a parley at some distance from the fort, and marched to the appointed spot, with four hundred men. No person was, there, visible; but at a greater distance a flag was seen, which retired towards the mountain as he advanced, until it led him into an ambush, where, almost enveloped, he was suddenly attacked by the enemy. His troops, with great presence of mind and courage, instantly returned the fire, and were gaining the advantage in the combat, when some one, either coward or traitor, cried out, "the Colonel has ordered a retreat!" upon which immediate confusion was succeeded by a total rout. The troops endeavoured to cross the river to Wilkesbarre, but twenty only escaped from slaughter. Fort Kingston was immediately invested, and, to increase the terror of the garrison, the green and bleeding scalps of their wounded countrymen were sent in for their inspection. Colonel Zebulon Butler having withdrawn himself and family down the river, Colonel Dennison, the commanding officer, went out with a flag, to inquire what terms would be allowed the garrison. He received for answer, two words, uniting Spartan brevity with cannibal ferocity—"The hatchet." This condition, so merciless, he, unhappily, believed would not be inflicted, and surrendered at discretion. But the threat was in execution, more barbarous than in the letter. After selecting a few prisoners, the great body of the captives were enclosed in the houses, fire was applied to them, and they were consumed together.

Wilkesbarre surrendered without resistance, in the vain hope to mollify the fury of the invaders. The continental soldiers, amounting to about seventy, were hacked to pieces. The remaining men, with the women and children, shared the fate of the sufferers in Kingston; they perished in the flames. Although all show of resistance had terminated, the ruin was not yet complete. Near three thousand persons had escaped. Flying without money, clothes, or food, they sought safety in the interior country. To prevent their return, every thing remaining was destroyed. All the dwellings, and other improvements which the labour of years had provided, as well as every living animal which was discovered, was extirpated. The settlements of the tories, alone were preserved; an oasis amid the desert.* Some particular instances of barbarity occurred in this expedition, which stain only civil wars. Parents were murdered by their children, and brothers and sisters fell by the hands of brothers.

A repetition of these scenes, was attempted by a body of about five hundred men, composed of Indians, tories, and a few regulars, who broke into the Cherry Valley settlement, in the state of New York, where Colonel

* Marshall, Ramsay, Gordon.

Alden was posted with a continental regiment. A serjeant, with a small patrole, was cut off; in consequence of which, the colonel was completely surprised, and, while endeavouring to regain the fort, was killed, with ten of his soldiers; and the lieutenant-colonel, and two subaltern-officers, were made prisoners. The fort was assaulted, but a resolute defence being made, and the assailants having intelligence that relief was approaching the garrison, the enterprise was abandoned, and the party, after repeating the horrors practised in Wyoming, departed from the settlement.

XX. These injuries were in a small degree retaliated—by inroads into the Indian country from Schoharie, under Colonel William Butler; who penetrated as far as the towns of Unandilla, and Anaquaqua, the head-quarters of the celebrated Col. Brandt, an Indian of the half-breed, distinguished for his courage and his cruelty, which he destroyed, with a considerable quantity of corn, laid up for the winter's supply, without discovering an enemy:—By Colonel Hartley, who had been despatched with his regiment, and two companies of militia, to Wyoming—and by Colonel George Rogers Clarke, of Virginia, who, with a small force, and extraordinary exertions, averted the Indian war from his state, and captured the fort at St. Vincents, with its commander, Colonel Hamilton. This officer, with a few of his immediate agents and counsellors, who had been instrumental in the savage barbarities he had encouraged, were by the executive of Virginia, imprisoned in irons.

These expeditions, however beneficial, procured only partial relief. Congress, on being informed that the Indians were fortifying at Chemung, a large settlement about twelve miles from the mouth of Cayuga, a river emptying into the Susquehanna, where a large body of tories was collected, directed General Washington to take measures to disperse this encampment, and to repel the invasion of the savages on the frontiers of New York, New Jersey, and Pennsylvania. But the season of the year being unfit for such an enterprise, it was postponed.

Early in 1779, an extensive plan of operations was devised by General Washington, against the broad and fertile country, lying between the then westernmost settlements of Pennsylvania and New York, and the great lakes, occupied by the Six Nation Indians. These tribes had, from long intercourse with the whites, acquired many of the comforts of civilized life, with enlarged ideas of the advantages of private property. Their populous villages contained some good houses, their fertile fields yielded an abundant supply of corn, and their thrifty orchards, of fruit. A few of their towns were attached to the United States, but the greater portion was under the influence of the British. In the commencement of the war, they had engaged to be neutral; but were unable to resist the seduction of British presents, and their own longings for plunder and slaughter. Many of the loyalists driven from the United States, had taken refuge among them, increasing their strength, without diminishing their ferocity. Into the heart of these villages of mingled whites and Indians, it was now determined to lead a force, which, overpowering any numbers they could bring in the field, would inflict on them a merited punishment for their cruelties of the past year.

The country was to be entered in three divisions. The principal, consisting of three thousand men, marching by the Susquehanna, was to penetrate into the settlements of the Senecas; the second, of one thousand, to proceed by the Mohawk; and the third, of five hundred, by the Alleghany river. To prevent relief from Canada, demonstrations were made of a design to attack that province by the way of Lake Champlain.

XXI. As the army destined for the expedition, was about to move, alarming symptoms of discontent appeared in part of it. The Jersey brigade had been stationed through the winter at Elizabethtown, for the purpose of covering the adjacent country from the incursions of the British troops, on Staten Island. It was ordered, early in May, to march by regiments. To this order, General Maxwell replied, in a letter to the commander-in-chief, that the officers of the first regiment had delivered to their colonel, a remonstrance, addressed to the State Legislature, declaring, that, unless their complaints on the subjects of pay and subsistence obtained immediate attention, they were, at the expiration of three days, to be considered as having resigned; and requesting the Legislature in that event, to appoint other officers. General Maxwell added, "this is a step they are extremely unwilling to take; but is such, as I make no doubt, they will all take. Nothing but necessity, their not being able to support themselves in time to come, and being loaded with debts contracted in time past, would have induced them to resign at so critical a juncture." They declared, however, their readiness to make every necessary preparation for obeying the marching orders which had been given, and to continue their attention to the regiment, until a reasonable time for the appointment of their successors should elapse.

General Washington was much afflicted by this intelligence, and sought, in vain, by paternal remonstrance, to change their determination.

The condition of these officers seems to have been one of extreme privation. By a resolution of December, 1777, Congress had recommended to the several States to furnish the officers of their respective quotas, with certain clothing, at the prices current, when the army was established, in the year 1776, the surplus to be charged to the United States. This resolution seems to have been tardily and imperfectly obeyed, notwithstanding the repeated applications of the soldiery. Their pretensions were probably more strenuously urged in a memorial presented to the Assembly, on the 27th of April, 1779, respecting their pay, subsistence and clothing, and were supported by an energetic letter from General Maxwell; all of which were referred to a joint committee of both Houses. That committee reported, "That provision had been already agreed upon, as far as was consistent, previous to an application to Congress; and that if upon such application, no measures are by them adopted in that behalf, it will then be the duty of this State, to provide for its quota of troops, in the best manner they can devise." This resolution was duly approved; but another offered by the same committee, that the letter of General Maxwell contains indecent and undeserved reflections upon the representatives of the State; and that the same be transmitted to Congress, with a proper expression of the disapprobation and displeasure of the Legislature, was negatived.

Moved by the wretchedness of these officers, and the troops they commanded, Governor Livingston, John Cooper, Andrew Sinnickson, Joseph Holmes, Robert Morris, Peter Tallman, Abraham Vannest, Silas Condict, and William Churchill Houston, during the recess of the Legislature, on the fifteenth of January, requested the treasurer to pay into the hands of Enos Kelsey, commissioner for the purchase of clothing, the sum of seven thousand pounds, to be applied in procuring clothes for the officers, agreeably to the resolution of Congress, engaging to replace that sum in the treasury, provided the Legislature, at their next sitting, should not direct it to be credited in the accounts of the treasurer. On the 30th of April, this direction was given by the House, with orders to the commissioners to draw the further sum of twenty-five thousand pounds, for the purpose of furnishing to certain officers, clothing to the amount of two hundred pounds, as the prices then were, upon their paying the sum it would have cost, in the year 1776.

Still there were conditions annexed to these grants, which rendered them ineffective

On the 7th of May, the remonstrance of the officers was repeated, stating, that they were under marching orders, and in immediate want of a necessary supply. Upon which the House directed the commissioner to furnish them with clothing immediately, to the amount of two hundred pounds, and to pay to the soldiers of the brigade, the sum of forty dollars each. This disbursement removed the obstacle to the march of the brigade. The reason of the delay of the State, in supplying her forces, would seem to be a desire, that some uniform rule to this end, should be adopted by Congress, or that the confederacy should assume the whole duty to itself.

XXII. Before the grand expedition against the Indians, was put in motion, an enterprise of less extent, was successfully undertaken by Colonel Van Schaick, assisted by Lieutenant-colonel Willet, and Major Cochran, and between five and six hundred men, from Fort Schuyler, against the Onondago settlements. Most of the Indians escaped—but twelve were killed, and thirty-four made prisoners, including one white man. The houses and provisions were burned, the country devastated, and the horses and stock slain. The party returned without the loss of a man; and the colonel received thanks of Congress.

The largest division of the western army reached Wyoming, under General Sullivan, in the month of June. Its further progress was delayed for want of provisions and military stores, until the last of July. In the mean while, the enemy was not inactive. Brandt, at the head of some whites and Indians, fell upon the frontiers of New York, murdered many of the inhabitants, carried others into captivity, and burned and destroyed several houses. He was pursued by one hundred and fifty militia, whom he drew into an ambuscade and entirely defeated. A few days afterwards, Captain M'Donald, at the head of another small party, of whom a third were British, took a small fort on the west branch of the Susquehanna, making the garrison, of thirty men, prisoners of war; the women and children, contrary to the usages of the savages, were permitted to retire into the settled country.

Another body of troops designed to compose a part of the western army, had passed the winter on the Mohawk, and early in the season, under the command of General Clinton, marched to Lake Otsego, and thence descending the Susquehanna, united with the main division on the 22d of August. The whole army, amounting to five thousand men, proceeded, by the Cayuga, into the heart of the Indian country. The Indians, apprized of its approach, selected and fortified the ground on which to fight a general action, with no inconsiderable skill. About a mile in front of Newton, and some miles above Chemung, they collected their whole force, consisting, by the computation of Sullivan, of fifteen hundred, but by their own, of eight hundred men, only; with whom were united five companies of whites, comprising two hundred men. They were commanded by the two Butlers, Grey, Johnston, M'Donald, and Brandt. A breastwork had been constructed about half a mile in length, upon a piece of rising ground, having its flank and rear covered by the river, and in other respects, naturally strengthened.

About eleven in the morning of the 29th of August, this work was discovered by Major Par, of the advance rifle corps. General Hand formed his light infantry in a wood a few hundred yards from the enemy, and awaited the arrival of the main body; skirmishing with parties of Indians, who endeavoured to entice them to an incautious pursuit. Conjecturing that the hills on his right, were occupied by the enemy, Sullivan ordered General Poor, supported by General Clinton, to possess himself of them, to turn the left and gain the rear of the breastwork, while Hand and Maxwell should attack in front. This manœuvre was speedily decisive. The savages finding their flank uncovered, abandoned their works, and crossing the river, fled with the utmost precipitation. An unavailing pursuit was kept up for a few miles. Their ascertained loss was inconsiderable; but they were so intimidated, that they abandoned all idea of further resistance. The American loss did not exceed thirty. Sullivan penetrated into the heart of the country; which his parties scoured and laid waste in every direction. Every lake, river, and creek, was traced for villages, and no vestige of human industry was spared. Houses, cornfields, gardens, and fruit-trees, shared one common fate; the commanding general strictly executing the severe, but necessary orders he had received, to render the country completely uninhabitable, and thus to compel the Indians to remove to a greater distance. Eighteen villages, a number of detached buildings, one hundred and sixty thousand bushels of corn, and all those fruits and vegetables which conduce to the comfort and subsistence of man, were utterly destroyed. Five weeks were spent in this work of devastation. The want of provisions, alone, prevented Sullivan from endeavouring to render the campaign more decisive, by an attempt on the British post at Niagara.

XXIII. While Sullivan laid waste the country on the Susquehanna, another expedition, under Colonel Broadhead, ascended the Allegheny, against the Mingo, Muncey, and Seneca tribes. With more than six hundred men, he advanced two hundred miles up that stream, and destroyed the villages and cornfields on its head branches, with their wretched proprietors.

This chastisement of the savages was most savage, and is defensible, only, on the ground, that experience had taught, that nothing short of such severity could deter them from the yearly, perhaps, the more frequent, repetition of the scenes at Wyoming. Although the object of the campaign was not thoroughly obtained by terminating the Indian war, the Indians were intimidated; they became less terrible, their excursions less formidable, and less frequent.

XXIV. In the following year, (1780) the Cherokees, forgetting a severe chastisement given them in 1776, made an excursion into Ninety-Six district, South Carolina, massacred some families and burned several houses. General Pickens, with three hundred and sixty-four horsemen, penetrated the recesses of their country; killed forty of the enemy, took several prisoners, and burned thirteen towns and villages. Of his party, one only was killed and two were wounded. No expedition against the Indians was more rapid and decisive than this. The whites did not expend three rounds of ammunition; and yet, of the Indians who made themselves visible, three only escaped. A new and successful mode of fighting was introduced; the horsemen charging with reliance only upon their swords. The vanquished humbly sued for peace, which was granted, on condition, that they would deliver up all British emissaries, who should stimulate them to war.

XXV. These severe inflictions upon the Indian tribes, were the rigid exactions of duty; but we are required to record a massacre by the whites, that may be a pendant for that of Wyoming. An English poet* has, gracefully, sung the sufferings in the last, but no bard has described the horrors of the slaughter at Muskingum. At this place some Indian converts of the Moravians had settled. Under the care of pious missionaries, they had been formed into some degree of civil and religious order, and had adopted the faith, that "The Great Being did not make men to destroy men, but to love and assist each other." Upon this principle, they advised other tribes

* Campbell.

to desist from war: and from humanity, they premonished the whites, from time to time, of the dangers that threatened them. Provoked by this interference, the hostile Indians removed their pacific countrymen to the banks of the Sandusky. They obtained permission, however, in the fall of the year, to return and collect the crops they had planted. The whites, on the Monongahela, either through misconception or malice, reported, that their designs were inimical; and without due inquiry, one hundred and sixty crossed the Ohio, and slaughtered these inoffensive people, who fell martyrs to their principles of non-resistance. Not less than ninety were thus immolated.

Retribution, however, was not long delayed. Soon after this unprovoked butchery, a party of whites set out with the purpose of destroying the Indian towns on the Sandusky. But being encountered by the Delawares and Wyandots, they were repelled, with the loss of several prisoners, among whom, were Colonel Crawford and his son-in-law. All were offered up to the manes which haunted the Moravian towns of the Muskingum.

CHAPTER XVI.

Comprising a View of the War in the South.—I. Inert state of the Country in 1779. —II. The British Government adopts views of partial Conquest.—III. Georgia overrun--and Charleston threatened—Unsuccessful Siege of Savannah.—IV. Sir Henry Clinton subdues South Carolina.—V. His measures induce Revolt.—VI. General Gates assumes command of the Southern Army—Battle of Camden.—VII. Battle of King's Mountain.—VIII. Cornwallis reinforced.—IX. General Greene appointed to the Southern Department—Battle of the Cowpens—Retreat to Virginia.—X. Cornwallis retires, is pursued—Battle of Guilford Court House. —XI. Cornwallis marches for Petersburg—Greene for South Carolina—Expedition of Arnold against Virginia—Preparations against him—Defence of Virginia entrusted to La Fayette—Cornwallis takes command of the British Forces in Virginia.—XII. Progress of Greene in recovering the Southern States.—XIII. Sufferings of the Inhabitants.

I. The exertions made by the United States, though not beyond their strength, if put forth with system and discretion, were irregular and violent, and followed by that syncope which invariably attends undue efforts. A general langour had diffused itself through all the civil departments. The alliance with France was supposed to have secured independence, and a confidence that the enemy could not longer prosecute the war with success, prevented that activity which was painful to exert. The wretched policy of short enlistments had been pursued, until correction was impossible. The enthusiasm, which, at the commencement of the contest had overcome all personal considerations, had subsided, and was succeeded by views more particularly selfish, and more durable. From these considerations, it was not until the 23d January, 1779, that Congress authorized the re-enlistment of the army; nor until the 9th March, that requisition was made upon the States, for their respective quotas. The bounty offered, being insufficient to bring the men into the field, resort was again had to the special authority of the States. Thus, at a season when the recruits should have been in camp, they were yet to be obtained; and the public service was exposed to great hazard from the delay. At this period, too, several circumstances conspired to foment pernicious divisions and factions in Congress, which greater danger might have prevented or suppressed.

These dissentions, the removal of individuals of the highest influence, from the national councils to offices in the state governments; the depreciation of the paper currency; the destructive spirit of speculation caused by imaginary gain from this depreciation; a general laxity of principles, the inseparable concomitant of civil war and revolution; the indisposition to sacrifice personal convenience for the public weal; were rocks, on which the vessel of state might yet split, and which required the care of those whom influence and patriotism placed at the helm.*

The knowledge of these facts, deeply affected the mind of the commander-in-chief of the American armies, and gave him many apprehensions for the final result of the contest. They, also, had probably great effect upon the British commissioners; who inferred that the people, worn out by the complicated calamities of the struggle, desired an accommodation on the terms proposed by the ministry, and that the increasing difficulties necessarily resulting from the failure of public credit, would induce them to desert Con-

* Letter of Washington, Marshall, iv. p. 6.

gress, or compel that body to accede to those terms. These opinions, communicated to their government, undoubtedly continued to protract the contest.

II. The British government, confident of complete conquest, had prosecuted the war with a view to the recovery of the whole of its dominions in America. But the reverses they had sustained, the alliance with France, and the firmness with which the contest had been maintained, together with the rejection of the late pacific propositions, induced a change in the plan of operations. The islands about New York were retained, whilst their arms were principally directed against the southern States, which were less capable of resistance, and on which a considerable impression might certainly be made, and probably extended northward; but, however this might be, the possession of several States, at the negotiation for general peace, would afford plausible ground for claiming to retain them. Of the succeeding campaigns, therefore, the most active and interesting operations were in the southern country. But our limits and our purpose, forbid us to do more than shortly to advert to them.

III. Lieutenant-colonel Campbell, who sailed from New York, in December, 1777, arrived soon after at Savannah, and, in despite of the opposing efforts of General Howe, captured that place; and, aided by General Prevost, who advanced from Florida, reduced without difficulty, the whole state of Georgia; the inhabitants flocking in numbers to the royal standard. This rapid progress of the enemy calling for more efficient measures of resistance, General Lincoln was appointed to the southern command, in September, 1778. Previously, considerable reinforcements had been ordered from the northern army, particularly in the cavalry regiments of Bland, and Lieutenant-colonel Washington. Their march was, however, some time delayed, in consequence of the invasion of Virginia, in May, by Brigadier-general Matthews. His expedition, undertaken principally with the view of destroying the stores which had been laid up on the waters of that State, was but too successful; he having destroyed, in a few weeks, public and private property of immense value, at Norfolk, Portsmouth, Gosport, and the adjacent country.

The greatest force under Lincoln, assembled and armed with much difficulty, amounted to three thousand six hundred and thirty-nine, of whom two thousand four hundred and twenty eight, rank and file, were effectives; one-half, however, were militia; whilst Prevost commanded three thousand effective regulars, aided by many provincials. Lincoln proceeded from Purysburg, into Georgia; and, in the mean time, Provost marched on Charleston with two thousand four hundred regular troops, and a considerable body of Indians, driving before him General Moultrie, at the head of an inferior force. He summoned the town, on the 11th of May, 1779, but was compelled soon after, to raise the siege, by the approach of Lincoln, and to retire to the islands on the coast. On the 20th of June, a sharp but indecisive affair took place between twelve hundred Americans and seven hundred British, at Stono Ferry, in which the former lost one hundred and fifty men, with the much lamented Colonel Roberts. Prevost, retreating from island to island, soon after returned to Port Royal and Savannah, his troops enriched by the indiscriminate plunder they had made.

The Count D'Estaing, after a successful cruise to the West Indies, pursuant to the instructions of his court, and the solicitations of Lincoln and the authorities of South Carolina, arrived (September 1st,) on the coast of Georgia. He summoned Savannah, but suffered himself to be amused by Prevost for several days, until the latter had called in his troops, and was fully prepared for defence. Being joined by Lincoln, a formal siege was commenced; the ground being broken on the 23d of the month, and the advances made with every prospect of final success. The impatience of the French commander and his officers, excited by the dangers of the hurricane season, induced an assault on the 9th of October, with thirty-five hundred French, and six hundred continental troops; which, though bravely made, was bravely and successfully repelled. Count D'Estaing and Count Pulaski, were both wounded,—the former slightly, the latter mortally. The loss of the French was six hundred and thirty-seven, and of the Americans two hundred, men. The militia returned to their homes, and the French fleet and army to the West Indies. This visit of the fleet, however, disconcerted the British plans for the campaign, and occasioned the withdrawal of their army from Rhode Island; and their efforts in the south resulted in the possession of Savannah merely.

IV. Upon intelligence of these events, both parties sought to strengthen their respective forces, in the south. A large detachment, under Sir Henry Clinton, in person, sailed from New York, late in December, leaving the defence of that city to General Knyphausen; whilst Washington despatched southward, the troops of North Carolina, the new levies of Virginia, the rear division of Bland's and Baylor's cavalry, and afterwards, the Virginia line. In his passage, Sir Henry encountered a storm, which endamaged him so much as to require a reinforcement and supplies from New York. Charleston was his primary object, against which he proceeded from Savannah, on the 10th of February, 1780; approaching by way of the islands with great caution. On the first of April, he broke ground, within eight hundred yards of the American works, and on the 12th of May, the town capitulated. General Lincoln and his army, consisting of two thousand effectives, became prisoners. During the progress of the expedition, several sharp encounters took place, between small parties. The cavalry under General Huger, stationed about thirty miles above Charleston, was attacked and routed by Colonel Tarleton and Major Ferguson, on the morning of the 14th of April, and four hundred horses captured; and on the 7th of May, the remnant collected under Colonel White, of New Jersey, at Monk's Corner, was again charged and dispersed by the same active British officers.

Having possession of the capital, Sir Henry employed himself in reducing the country; despatching parties in various directions over it. The inhabitants vied with each other in devotion to the royal cause, and many, even of the citizens of Charleston, enlisted under the royal banners. In these operations, the only circumstance meriting special notice, was the surprise and defeat of Colonel Burford, by Colonel Tarleton. Burford commanded a regiment of new levies from Virginia, who arrived too late to aid Charleston. Upon the surrender of the city, he commenced his retreat, but was overtaken by a rapid march of one hundred and five miles in fifty-four hours. No quarter was given, and the carnage was horrible; one hundred and thirteen were killed on the spot; and one hundred and fifty so badly wounded, that they could not be removed. So confident was Sir Henry of having conquered the State, that he proclaimed the pacification, and released from their parole his militia prisoners, those taken in Charleston and Fort Moultrie excepted; and with the most sanguine hope of the recovery of all the southern States, he embarked for New York, on the 5th of June, leaving in South Carolina, about four thousand regulars, under Lord Cornwallis.

V. The parole of the American prisoners recognised their character of aliens to Great Britain; their release from it, avowedly, restored, without their assent, their relation of subjects; and its effect was to compel them to assume arms against their countrymen. Had they been suffered to enjoy the quiet of non-combatants, they might have remained unarmed; but they would not submit to the degradation of fighting the battles of the oppressor.

The proclamation sowed the teeth of the hydra, and armed men sprang up in every direction, to resist the British power.

The Delaware and Maryland lines, with the first regiment of artillery, were ordered to South Carolina, under General de Kalb; and exertions were made in Virginia to increase this force. The exiles from the north and west parts of the State, to the number of six hundred, collected under Colonel Sumpter, and were soon strengthened by a corps of militia, which had been collected by Cornwallis. The latter circumstance demonstrating the temper of the people, induced the British general to draw in his outposts, and arrange his troops in larger bodies.

VI. An army of two thousand men was thus formed, of which General Gates took the command, on the 25th of July. He, changing the dispositions of De Kalb, marched by the most direct route towards the enemy's post at Camden; and, unhappily, through a barren country, in which his troops suffered greatly from famine and unwholesome food. On his way he was joined by the North Carolina militia, under General Caswell, and some troops commanded by Lieutenant-colonel Peterfield. He arrived on the 13th of August, at Clermont, or Rugely's Mills, whence Lord Rawdon withdrew at his approach. And, here, the militia from Virginia, under General Stevens, also came to his aid. With a force, now, of about four thousand men, he marched rapidly, in the hope of surprising Camden. At the very hour of his departure from Clermont, Lord Cornwallis left Camden, with the design of striking him a sudden blow; and, to their mutual surprise, the hostile armies encountered in the woods, at about two o'clock of the morning of the 16th of August. The ground did not permit Gates to avail himself of his superiority in numbers, and Cornwallis restrained the ardour of his troops, that he might, with the light, better direct their disciplined valour. With the dawn the action commenced. The militia shamefully fled, carrying Gates with them, from the field of battle, in his endeavours to rally them. De Kalb, at the head of the continental troops, maintained the fight with some success, until overpowered by numbers, they were broken, and he fell under eleven mortal wounds. The Americans lost the greater part of their baggage, stores, and artillery; and by the estimate of the enemy, eight hundred men killed, and one thousand prisoners. Previous to the battle, a party was detached under Lieutenant-colonel Woolford, of Maryland, to unite with Sumpter, to intercept an escort of stores, for the garrison at Camden. This enterprise was successful; but the party was, afterwards, surprised by Tarleton, near the Catawba Ford, and was beaten and dispersed with the loss of between three and four hundred men, killed and wounded.

Notwithstanding the victory, Lord Cornwallis was unable to proceed against North Carolina, and to prosecute the career which he had proposed; his troops being enfeebled by sickness, and the hostile disposition of the citizens rendering it unsafe to remove any considerable portion of them from the State. The disasters, however, of the American arms, chilled the spirit of resistance; yet it was kept alive by the exertions of those able partisans, Sumpter and Marion, and was again reanimated, by the severity with which Cornwallis punished, as traitors, the militia who deserted his standard—producing but a fiercer resistance, and a capacity to brave and to bear the extremity of suffering. But the designs of the British commander were only suspended. He resumed them by despatching Major Ferguson into the western part of North Carolina, to rouse and organize the tory inhabitants; whilst he marched himself, late in September, to Charlotte, where he proposed to await the result of Ferguson's endeavours. That officer, attempting to intercept Colonel Clarke of Georgia, in his retreat from an unsuccessful attack upon Augusta, removed nearer to the mountains, where a short delay proved fatal to him. Several corps of hardy mountaineers, from the western parts of Virginia and North Carolina, under Colonels Campbell, Cleaveland, Shelby, and Servier, moved upon him with great celerity, whilst Colonels Williams, Tracy, and Brannan, from South Carolina, approached the same point. These forces, together three thousand strong, united at Gilbertstown. Sixteen hundred of the best mounted marksmen pursued Ferguson, who, apprized of their approach, pushed for Charlotte. He was overtaken, on the seventh of October, upon King's Mountain, attacked by three divisions, respectively, commanded by Shelby, Campbell, and Cleaveland, against each of whom, in the order of their arrival, he turned with considerable effect, the fearful bayonet; sustaining the conflict for more than an hour, and until he received a wound which caused his instant death. His second in command instantly demanded quarter. Of the enemy one hundred and fifty were killed, as many wounded, and eight hundred and ten were made prisoners; among the latter were one hundred English regulars. A valuable and timely prize was obtained in fifteen hundred stand of arms. The American loss was inconsiderable, but among the slain was Colonel Williams. Ten of the most active tories were selected and hung on the spot, in retaliation of the cruelties committed on the whigs at Camden. This misfortune compelled Cornwallis, who had crossed the Yadkin, to retrace his steps as far as Wynnesborough, where he awaited reinforcement. The militia were unable to follow up their successful blow for want of provisions.

VIII. Confident in the progress of Cornwallis, Sir Henry Clinton despatched from New York, on the 16th of October, three thousand men, under General Leslie, against Virginia, who, after some depredations, were ordered to Charleston, by sea, in consequence of the defeat of Ferguson. In the interim, Cornwallis was employed in suppressing the hostile efforts of the inhabitants, under Marion, Sumpter, Clarke, and Brannan. The most important of these affairs was that with Sumpter, on November 20th, at Blackstocks, near Tyger river, in which he repulsed Colonel Tarleton, with great loss.

IX. Gates slowly collected, at Hillsborough, the shattered remains of his army defeated at Camden. Being recalled, he delivered the command to his successor, General Greene, at Charlotte, on the 2d of December. His greatest efforts had not collected more than two thousand men, of whom a full third were militia, with which Greene took the field against a superior regular force, flushed with successive victories. But even this small army he soon divided; sending Morgan, with a considerable detachment to the western extremity of South Carolina, whilst he conducted the main body to Hicks's Creek, on the north side of the Pedee river, opposite the Cheraw Hills. Cornwallis, who was, again, preparing to proceed against North Carolina, but could not leave Morgan in his rear, sent Carleton against him, with orders to push him to the utmost. Morgan, with an inferior force, consisting, in a great measure, of militia, firmly awaited his approach, at the Cowpens, three miles from the line separating North and South Carolina. In the encounter which ensued, on the 17th of January, 1781, Tarleton was defeated with the loss of three hundred killed and wounded, and five hundred prisoners, eight hundred muskets, thirty-five baggage wagons, and one hundred dragoon horses. The impetuosity which had frequently served this energetic partisan, was, now, the cause of his defeat. Upon tidings of this victory, Greene hastened to join Morgan, directing his own corps to Guilford Court-house; and with great exertions, the prisoners and baggage were secured. In the pursuit, the British army sacrificed its baggage and every thing, not indispensable to action or the existence of the troops, and hung, almost constantly, on the American rear. Twice, at the Catawba and the Yadkin, the Americans were saved by the rising of the waters after their passage and before the arrival of the British. The two divisions of the American army united at Guilford Court-house; but too feeble for combat, the commander resolved to continue his retreat across the Dan to Virginia. The pursuit was so hotly followed, that as his rear crossed that river, the British van was in sight.* Thus baffled, Cornwallis retired to Hillsborough, with the view of rousing the tories; whilst Greene immediately recrossed the river to mar his labours,† in which he was eminently successful. General Pickens and Colonel Lee fell in with three hundred and fifty tories, under Colonel Pyle, on their way to the British army, whom they cut to pieces amid their shouts of "God save the King," and protestations of loyalty, which they uttered in the belief, that the assailants were royalists.

Cornwallis now retired, yet seeking a proper occasion for battle; sometimes turning upon the pursuer, and compelling him to retread his steps. At length, Greene having received all the reinforcements he had reason to expect, resolved to give battle, and marched, for that purpose, to Guilford Court-house. Cornwallis promptly accepted the offer. The American troops amounted to four thousand two hundred and sixty-two, of whom one thousand four hundred and ninety were regulars; the British did not exceed two thousand four hundred veterans. Greene selected his ground, and the issue was joined on the 15th of March. After a fierce combat, in which his troops, generally, behaved well, Greene was compelled to retreat; but the victory was dearly purchased, by the loss of five hundred and thirty-two killed and wounded, being much greater than that sustained by the Americans. Greene retired but a few miles, and awaited another attack; but Cornwallis, much enfeebled, left his wounded to the care of the loyalists in the neighbourhood, and pushed rapidly for Wilmington, where stores had been lodged and supplies might be obtained. Greene, also, leaving his hospital to the Quakers of the vicinage, whom he reminded of his former fraternization, as rapidly followed to Ramsay's Mills, on Deep River; where excessive fatigue, the want of food, and the release of his militia, compelled him to stop.

XI. After resting his troops, for about three weeks, at Wilmington, Cornwallis crossed the country to Petersburg. He pondered long before he adopted this northern course, when informed that Greene had taken the bold resolution to attempt the recovery of the southern country. He concluded, at length, that if Lord Rawdon, who commanded there, should have been defeated, he might dread his own safety; but if he had sustained himself, a return would be an useless abandonment of the ground he had gained. On the departure of Leslie from Virginia, the traitor, Arnold, entered that State, (on the 30th of December) and after committing many depredations, established himself at Portsmouth, on the 20th of January. Against him, Washington proposed to send, under La Fayette, twelve hundred men, of the New England and New Jersey lines, and, also, to employ the whole French fleet from Newport. Two frigates, however, only, sailed, which though inoperative in the original design, captured the Romulus, of fifty guns, passing from Charleston to the Chesapeake. Flattered by this success, the French admiral despatched a larger expedition to the same point; which encountering a British fleet, under Arbuthnot, near the Capes of Virginia, was so much endamaged as to return to Newport, leaving La Fayette at Annapolis, where he had repaired for convoy. That general returned to the head of Elk, whence he was directed to join the southern army. In the interim, General Phillips had embarked for the Chesapeake, with two thousand men, and arrived at Portsmouth on the 26th of March, 1781. This reinforcement, giving the British a decisive superiority in Virginia, changed the des-

* February 14th, 1781. † February 21st.

tination of La Fayette, to whom the defence of that State was now committed. For near two months, Phillips and Arnold prosecuted a predatory war, destroying immense quantities of tobacco and stores, and marking their course by terrible devastations; La Fayette and Steuben, endeavouring in vain to stay them, except in the protection of the magazines at Richmond. On the 20th May, Lord Cornwallis joined Arnold at Petersburg, a few days after the death of Phillips, and assumed the command of the whole British force in the State.

Against him, General La Fayette, aided by General Wayne, maintained a war of posts for the space of three months; until Cornwallis, impressed with the necessity of providing a strong place of arms in the Chesapeake, selected Yorktown, as a station for his army, and Gloucester Point, for his fleet, to which he retired with his whole force, increased to seven thousand men. From the Virginians, he had derived little aid. They either united with the continental army, or, more commonly, kept out of the way of the British. Few purchased safety by submission.

XII. Having thus followed Lord Cornwallis to an hour big with his own fate, and that of the war, we return to General Greene, who, with equal courage and ability, had turned his arms to the south. A line of posts had been constructed by the British from Charleston, by the way of Camden and Ninety-Six, to Augusta, in Georgia, the most important point of which was Camden. The forts, generally garrisoned by a few regular troops, united with the tory militia, were only slightly fortified to resist the sudden attack of the militia of the neighbouring country, no apprehensions being entertained of a more formidable enemy. Greene was fully aware of these unfavourable circumstances. "I shall take," said he, in a letter to General Washington, "every measure to avoid misfortune. But necessity obliges me to commit myself to chance, and if any accident should attend me, I trust my friends will do justice to my reputation." He detached Lee to unite with Marion, and Pickens, to assemble the western militia, and lay siege to Ninety-Six; and, marching himself on Camden, encamped before it on the 19th April. He manœuvred several days around the place, and, on the 25th, fought a severe battle with Lord Rawdon, at Hobkirk's Hill, with loss to either party, of about two hundred and fifty men. Although Greene retreated from the field, he did not abandon his views on Camden, until Rawdon was reinforced in the close of the month, by the corps of Colonel Watson, amounting to five hundred men. He then withdrew behind Sawney's Creek, and declined the battle, which Rawdon again offered. In the mean time, Forts Watson and Mottehouse, had surrendered to Marion and Lee, and Fort Orange, to Sumpter. Rawdon, abandoning the upper country, retired to Monk's Corner, to protect the district around Charleston. Compelled thus to comparative inactivity, he beheld the smaller posts reduced, and Seventy-Six in imminent danger from the attack of General Greene. From this mortifying state, he was relieved by the arrival of three regiments from Ireland, which again enabled him to overrun the state, and forced Greene to retreat before him, by the road to Charlotte. An eager race ensued, in which both parties divested themselves of whatever could stay their speed. But at the Ennoree, Lord Rawdon gave it over as hopeless. The retreat ceased with the pursuit, Greene halting on the north side of the Broad river; and, on the 13th July, he took post on the high hills of Santee.

Lord Rawdon, still holding his purpose of concentrating his forces in the lower country, withdrew his garrison; but soon after availed himself of permission to return to Europe. The command devolved on Colonel Stuart, who advanced to the post near the junction of the Congaree, and Wateree, where he was greatly annoyed by the corps of Marion and Washington. After a period of comparative repose, Greene recommenced active operations on the 22d of August, and, being strengthened by the militia and state troops of South Carolina, followed the British army to Eutaw, where it was reinforced by a detachment from Charleston. Greene was here joined by Marion, on the 7th September, and resolved to attack the British camp next day.

The battle of Eutaw Springs, was one of the most obstinate of the war. It was fought with about equal numbers, (2000) and ended in equal loss. The American killed, wounded, and missing, were estimated at five hundred and fifty-five; the British, at six hundred and ninety-three. But the American dead, owing to an obstinate contest on unfavourable ground, was most numerous. Among them, was Lieutenant-colonel Campbell, who fell whilst leading the Virginia brigade with trailed arms to a bold and decisive charge, which broke the British line. Colonel Washington was taken prisoner, having been unable to extricate himself from his horse, which, being killed, had fallen upon him. Both parties claimed the victory, but Stuart was compelled to withdraw to Monk's Corner, whilst Greene returned to the high hills of Santee, where his troops became too much enfeebled by disease, for active enterprise. The battle of Eutaw may be considered as closing the national war in South Carolina. A few excursions were afterwards made by the British, but with no more consequence than the loss of property and individual lives. On the 18th November, Greene moved down into the lower country, and the British retired with their whole force to the quarter-house within Charleston Neck, and the conquerors, who had carried their arms to the extent of the State, aimed at nothing more, than to secure themselves. After the capitulation at Yorktown, the British post at Wilmington, in North Carolina, was evacuated, and the troops in Georgia, were concentrated in Savannah.

The labours and exertions of the southern army were highly meritorious, but the successful activity of the legion under Lee, claims particular attention. It was, from its structure, peculiarly adapted to partisan war; and, being detached against the weaker posts of the enemy, had opportunities for displaying all its energies. In the extensive sweep from the Santee to Augusta, which employed, from the 15th April, to the 5th June, 1781, acting in junction, first with Marion, afterwards with Pickens, and sometimes alone, it constituted the principal force which carried five British posts, and made eleven hundred prisoners. At the commencement of the campaign of 1781, the British were in force all over the state; at its close, they durst scarce venture twenty miles from Charleston. At its commencement, the country had been completely conquered, and was defended by a regular army, estimated at four thousand men. The inhabitants were so divided, as to render it doubtful, to which side the majority was attached. At no time did the effectual continental force, which General Greene could bring into the field, amount to two thousand men; of whom a considerable portion were raw troops. Yet, by a course of judicious movement, bold action, and hardy enterprise, in which he displayed invincible constancy and courage, happily, tempered with prudence, he recovered the southern States; and, at the close of the year, civil government was fully established therein. A full portion of praise due to these achievements, belong to his troops. They bore every hardship and privation with patience and constancy. In his officers, the general was peculiarly happy. Unshackled by those, who, without military talent, had, through political influence, obtained high rank, his orders were executed by young men of equal spirit and intelligence, formed in the severe service of the north.

XIII. The sufferings occasioned by the ardent struggle for the southern States, were not confined to the armies. The inhabitants underwent the severest inflictions. Reciprocal injuries sharpened the resentment of contending parties, and armed neighbour against neighbour, in a war of extermination. As the parties, alternately, triumphed, opportunity was given to either for the exercise of vindictive passions, which derived new virulence from the example of the British commanders. When they had overrun Georgia, and South Carolina, they considered these States as reannexed to the British empire, and manifested a disposition to treat as rebels, all who, having submitted, resumed arms. One of their executions, that of Colonel Hayne, took place on the 3d of August, whilst Lord Rawdon was in Charleston, preparing to sail for Europe. The disposition to retaliate, to the full extent of their power, was equally strong in the opposite party. When Fort Granby surrendered, the militia attached to the legion, manifested so strong a desire to break the capitulation, and to kill the most obnoxious of the prisoners, who were tories, as to produce a solemn declaration from Greene, that he would put any man to death, who should commit an act so atrocious. Lieutenant-colonel Grierson, of the loyal militia, was shot by unknown marksmen; and, though a reward of one hundred guineas was offered for the perpetrator, he was never discovered. "The whole country," said the general, "is a continued scene of blood and carnage."*

* Ramsay, Gordon, Marshall.

CHAPTER XVII.

I. Condition of the Armies in the North.—II. British Expedition against the Forts on the North River.—III. Expedition under Tryon, against Connecticut.—IV. Capture of Stony Point, by Wayne.—V. Attack of the British Post, on Penobscot river.—VI. Major Lee assaults Paules Hook.—VII. Effects of the System of Paper Currency.—VIII. Spain declares War against England.—IX. Prospects of the Campaign of 1780.—X. The American Army retires into winter quarters.—XI. Marauding Parties of the Enemy in New Jersey.—XII. The Army at Morristown supplied by forced levies of Provisions.—XIII. Washington attempts the British Post at Staten Island—XIV. Difficulties arising from the want of political power in Congress.—XV. Discontents of the Army—Mutiny of the Connecticut troops.—XVI. Knyphausen invades New Jersey—Murder of Mrs. Caldwell, and of her Husband.—XVII. Battle of Springfield.—XVIII. La Fayette returns to the United States.—XIX. Renewed efforts for the Defence of the Country.—XX. Arrival of the French Fleet and Army—Plans consequent thereon.—XXI. Treason of Arnold.—XXII. American Army retires into winter quarters.—XXIII. European combinations against Great Britain.—XXIV. Revolt of the Pennsylvania line—of the Jersey line—Discontent of the Inhabitants of New Jersey.—XXV. Gloomy Prospect for the year 1781.—XXVI. Combined Operations of the French Fleet and Allied Armies, against Cornwallis—His Capture.—XXVII. New London taken and burned by Arnold.—XXVIII. Condition of the Country for the Campaign of 1782—Resolutions of the British Parliament in favour of Peace.—XXIX. Malignity of the Tories—Murder of Captain Huddy.—XXX. Cessation of Hostilities—Treaty of Peace.—XXXI. Disbanding of the Army.—XXXII. Public Entry of Washington to New York—takes leave of his Officers—Surrenders his Commission to Congress.

I. The apathy which we have noticed, as paralyzing the efforts of the people of the United States, at the commencement of the year 1779, was also visible in the operations of the British government. The ministry had lost the hope of reducing all the revolted colonies to obedience, and the desire of vengeance alone seems to have inspired the plan of the ensuing campaign, which was publicly announced to be that of rendering the colonies of as little avail as possible to their new connexions. With this view the operations in the northern States were conducted.

The force under Sir Henry Clinton, at New York, Rhode Island, and Virginia, was estimated at more than sixteen thousand men, whose efficiency was greatly increased by the co-operation of a powerful fleet, enabling the general to concentrate and direct it, at pleasure. The grand total of the American army, exclusive of the troops in the south and west, was also about sixteen thousand; of whom three thousand were with Gates, in New England—seven thousand with Washington, at Middlebrook, and the residue in the Highlands, under M'Dougals, and on the east side of the Hudson, under Putnam.

II. After the destruction of Forts Clinton and Montgomery, in 1777, the fortifications for defending the Hudson, were established at West Point, and at Stony and Verplank's Points, at King's Ferry, over which the great road between the middle and eastern States passed. Against these posts Sir Henry Clinton proposed to open the campaign by a brilliant *coup de main.* Washington, notwithstanding the financial embarrassments of the country, having always specie to reward spies, soon learned this intention, and made his dispositions to repel the attack. On the 30th of May, the forces selected for the expedition united with that from Virginia under Mathews, which arrived on that day, at New York, were conveyed to their destined point, by the fleet under Sir George Collier. The works at Stony Point being incomplete, were abandoned without resistance, and as they commanded those on the other bank, the latter were surrendered—Captain Armstrong and his garrison becoming prisoners. Both forts were completed by the enemy, and put into the best state of defence.

III. The contiguity of Connecticut to New York, its extent of coast, the supplies which it furnished to the continental army, and the many cruisers which plied in the Sound, rendered that State peculiarly obnoxious to the enemy, and provoked an enterprise against it, which was stimulated, also, by the hope, that Washington might thereby be drawn from his impregnable position on the North river. Governor Tryon, with a force of twenty-six hundred men, reached New Haven on the 5th of July, before the inhabitants had notice of his approach. The militia hastily assembled, but their opposition was feeble. The invaders having seized the town, and destroyed the naval and military stores, proceeded on the succeeding day, along the coast to the village of Fairfield. They experienced more resistance here, yet the spirited conduct of the people served but as a pretext for reducing the town to ashes, for the wanton destruction of private property, and for the maltreatment of the unarmed inhabitants of both sexes. From Fairfield, the British troops passed over the Sound to Huntingdon Bay, where they remained until the 11th, when they recrossed the water to the Cow Pasture, a peninsula on the east of Newark. At the same time a larger detachment from the main army approached Horse Neck, demonstrating a design of penetrating the country in that direction.

General Parsons, who had been despatched by Washington, to aid and direct the efforts of his countrymen, attacked the British with a considerable militia force, on the morning of the 12th, so soon as they were in motion, and kept up throughout the day an irregular and distant fire, but was unable to check their progress. After burning the town of Norwalk, Tryon returned to Huntingdon Bay, to await supplies and reinforcements; and was thence ordered to White Stone, where, in conference with Sir Henry Clinton, and Admiral Collier, it was determined to proceed, with increased force against New London. But this incursion was postponed by the assault of the American army, on the newly captured posts on the North river.

IV. By an original plan a simultaneous attack on both posts was intended; but it was, subsequently, resolved to proceed against Stony Point, as a distinct object. The enterprise was committed to General Wayne, with whom Major Lee was associated. He set out at the head of a strong detachment, at noon, and completed a march of about fourteen miles, by eight o'clock of the evening of the 15th of July; the hour of twelve being fixed for the assault. The garrison consisted of six hundred men, commanded by Lieutenant-colonel Johnston. The dispositions for the assault were made at Spring Steels, one and a-half mile from the fort. Instructions were given to attack the works on the right and left flank, at the same moment. The regiments of Febiger and Meiggs, with Major Hull's detachment, formed the right column, and Butler's regiment, with two companies under Major Murphrey, the left. One hundred and fifty volunteers, led by Lieutenant-colonel Fleury, and Major Posey, constituted the van of the right; and one hundred, under Major Stewart, that of the left. At half past eleven, the two columns moved on to the charge, the van of each, with unloaded muskets, and fixed bayonets; each preceded by a forlorn hope of twenty men, commanded, respectively, by Lieutenants Gibbon and Knox. The assailants reached the marsh, in front of the fort, undiscovered. Both columns rushed forward, under a tremendous fire of musketry and grape shot, and entered the works at the point of the bayonet, and without discharging a single piece, obtained possession of the post. The humanity of the conquerors was not less honourable than their courage. Not a single individual suffered after resistance had ceased.

All the troops distinguished themselves, whose situation enabled them so to do. Colonel Fleury was the first to enter the fort, and to strike the British standard. Major Posey mounted the works almost at the same instant, and gave the watch word, "*The fort is our own.*" Lieutenants Gibbon and Knox executed the service allotted to them, with intrepidity which could not be surpassed. Of the party of the former, seventeen were killed or wounded; and the whole loss was a hundred. Of the garrison, sixty-three were killed, and five hundred and forty-three made prisoners; and a large quantity of military stores was taken.

The attack on Fort Fayette, though postponed, to that on Stony Point, was not abandoned. Two brigades, under General M'Dougal, had been ordered to attempt the works at Verplank's, where Colonel Webster commanded, so soon as Wayne should obtain possession of Stony Point. The messenger, directed to apprize M'Dougal of Wayne's success, did not communicate with him on his way to camp; and this error, or negligence, was followed by others, which defeated subsequent efforts upon the place, until it was relieved by Sir Henry Clinton, who, to save it, relinquished his views upon Connecticut. The failure to obtain the fort on the east side of the river, diminished the advantages expected from that on the west; and the latter, requiring for its defence, a much larger force than could be spared for such a purpose, was abandoned. Sir Henry, immediately, resumed possession, repaired the fortifications, and regarrisoned it; and afterward retired to Philipsburg. General Washington maintained his post in the Highlands. While the armies watched each other, frequent rencounters took place, between small parties, which were of no other importance, than to evince the intrepidity, common to the junior officers, who had been formed during the war. At length, Sir Henry Clinton withdrew into York Island, and employed himself in strengthening its fortifications, that he might direct his principal efforts against the southern States, and compensate for the abstraction of the fleet, now sent to relieve Penobscot.

V. Early in June, Colonel M'Clean from Nova Scotia, with six hundred and fifty men, had taken possession of a defensible piece of ground on the Penobscot river, where he commenced such fortifications, as intimated a design to maintain the position. This measure threatened a serious diminution of the territory of the State of Massachusetts, and great exertions were, consequently, made to dislodge him. A considerable naval force, under Commodore Saltonstall, carried out, between three and four thousand men, commanded by General Lovell, which appeared before the new and unfinished work, on the 25th of June. Lovell effected a landing, with the loss of fifty men killed and wounded; erected a battery within seven hundred and fifty yards of the main work of the enemy, and kept up a warm cannonade for several days. Making little progress with his militia, he applied, through the governor of Massachusetts, to General Gates, commanding at Providence, for a reinforcement of four hundred continental troops; and Colonel Jackson and his regiment were immediately put in motion. But, on the 13th of August, Sir George Collier arrived in the river, with a superior naval force. Lovell immediately re-embarked his army, so silently as to be undiscovered by the garrison, who, in their lines, awaited an expected assault. His fleet offered a show of resistance, that the transports might escape up the river, and land the troops at a convenient point for further retreat. But the British admiral disregarded this stratagem; the Americans gave way, and a general chase and unresisted destruction ensued. The troops landed in a wild desert country, through which they had to explore their way without provision or other necessaries, for more than a hundred miles, before they could obtain supplies.

VI. The successful enterprise at Stony Point, was speedily followed by another, which equalled it in boldness of design. After Sir Henry Clinton had retired down the Hudson, Major Lee was employed on the west side of the river, to watch the proceedings of the British at Paules Hook, and the motions of their main army. The careless confidence of the garrison of the Hook, suggested to him the idea of surprising and carrying it off. The attempt was one of much danger, owing to the difficulty of access, and the greater difficulty of safe retreat, which, without boats to cross the Hackensack, must be made for many miles up that river, on the narrow neck between it and the Hudson, and could be secured, only, by its celerity. On the night of the 18th of August, a detachment from the division of Lord Stirling, including three hundred men designed for the expedition, was ordered down, as a foraging party. The American troops having frequently foraged in this vicinage, the movement excited no suspicion. Lord Stirling followed, with five hundred men, and posted himself at the New Bridge, over the Hackensack, so as to afford assistance, should it be necessary. The assailing party, under Major Lee, having passed the outworks, undiscovered, entered the main work at the Hook, at about three o'clock in the morning; and after a feeble resistance, with the loss of only two killed and three wounded, made one hundred and fifty-nine prisoners, including some officers. Very few of the British were killed. Major Sutherland, who commanded the garrison, threw himself, with forty or fifty Hessians, into a strong redoubt, which it was thought unadvisable to attack, lest the time employed, should endanger the retreat; the guns fired in New York and from the ships in the harbour, giving full evidence, that the alarm was complete. Wasting no time, therefore, in destroying works, which could easily be replaced, Lee, expeditiously, withdrew with his prisoners. To favour his retreat, boats had been placed at Dow's Ferry, on the Hackensack, near the Hook, with instructions to the officer in command, to await his arrival, which it was supposed would be before morning. Day appearing without the detachment, the officer supposed the attack had been postponed, and retired with his boats to Newark. The column, though greatly fatigued, was compelled to proceed to New Bridge, covered by the force of Lord Stirling. By mutual mistake, this party, and a party under the tory Colonel, Vanbuskirk, which crossed each other, avoided a battle, each supposing, that it was opposed by a superior force.

VII. Among the causes which now operated to paralyze the exertions of the Americans, was the depreciation of the paper currency. We have seen the extraordinary spectacle of thirteen colonies, and afterwards States, wholly independent of each other, carrying on, by themselves and their deputies, a burdensome war, against one of the most powerful nations of the earth; raising armies on the most expensive, as well as dangerous, establishment; carrying war into a neighbouring State, and equipping an efficient, though small navy;—without commerce and without revenue. These almost miraculous events were produced, in a great measure, by a paper currency, sustained by the ignorance, the confidence, and the patriotism of the people.

Paper money was a familiar agent throughout the continent; and south of New England, with the exception of South Carolina, its credit had been, generally, well preserved; the quantity being much below the demand of commercial exchange. Its extension, therefore, in the first stages of the revolution, was hailed by all classes as a real benefit—as a supply of vital fluid to the body politic, which renewed and increased its vigour. The commerce of

2 P

the colonies with England was a perpetual drain of their specie; and the business of the continent, always languished for want of a circulating medium. At the commencement of the revolution, too, the quantity of coin usually in the country, was greatly diminished. When the intercourse with Great Britain had ceased, and the credit of the colonists with their merchants was discontinued, part of the current gold and silver was absorbed in the payment of balances; part by the operations of the new authorities, particularly, in the expedition to Canada; and part by the hoarding of those, who foresaw the effects of the almost boundless extension of the paper system.

The necessity, therefore, of a circulating medium co-operated, admirably, with the patriotism of the people, to facilitate the use of the continental bills of credit; and, though, no specific funds were pledged for their redemption, and the government had none competent to that object, the occasion and the circumstances, gave such confidence in their value, that he was deemed a traitor to his country, who manifested a suspicion, that the public faith would not be religiously observed. So early as January, 1776, Congress passed a resolution on this delicate subject, denouncing against those who should discourage the circulation of the bills, the penalty of being deemed enemies to their country.* But this delusion could not be complete with thinking men, nor permanent with any class. As the quantity of bills daily increased, and soon exceeded all demands for commercial purposes, and could neither find their way into foreign countries nor be absorbed at home, their value became, necessarily, greatly impaired, and their redemption at par impracticable.

Aware that this truth must be betrayed, to all, by its effects, Congress laboured to procrastinate an event, pregnant with difficulties, they could not surmount. The emissions were small, as possible, and disbursements so parsimonious, as almost to produce the mischief dreaded, from that want of pecuniary resources which might result from the failure of public credit. The first emission was of two millions of dollars, in June, 1775, to which a further million was added, on the 25th of the following month, and on the 29th of November, an additional three millions. All these sums were to be redeemed by four annual payments, the first of which, on the last emission, to be made, on or before the last day of November, 1783; and the quota of each colony, was apportioned to the relative number of its inhabitants. These sums were supposed to be adequate to defray expenses to the 10th of June, 1776. But the march of events, soon required further issues, and by the 22d of July, 1776, they amounted to twenty millions, which, for some months, were, almost universally, received at par. Thus, whilst the ministry of England were perplexed to raise supplies, the American patriots, gave the power of gold to paper rags, by simple volition.

But it was not in the power of Congress to limit the issue of paper money; the right to emit it pertaining to every State, and being liberally exercised. To economise disbursements, to call in by taxes a part of the sums disbursed, thereby, diminishing the quantity, and increasing the demand, were the only possible means of preventing such an accumulation, as infallibly to continue its depreciation, until it should, entirely, cease to be a circulating medium. But the disbursements were made by too many hands to be economised, and the power of taxation was not in Congress. That body could, only, recommend the imposition of taxes, and their recommendations were, perhaps, the less attended to, because, whatever might be the public exigencies, the measure was, at all times, unpopular, and could, only, be effectual, by being universal. It was earnestly recommended, to the several colonies, and after-

* Marshall.

wards to the States, to adopt measures to redeem their quotas of the bills of credit emitted by Congress; but such was the danger apprehended from immediate taxation, that the payment of the first instalment of the first emission, was to be postponed until 1779, by which time it was certain the depreciation must be considerable.

Depreciation had made much progress, before the taxation commenced, and the remedy was so sparingly applied, as little to affect the disease. It is yet a problem unsolved, whether the revolution would have been aided by a more liberal resort to taxes. As it was dangerous to attempt the enforcement of taxation, palliatives were necessarily resorted to. A loan of five millions was proposed, at an interest of four per cent.; the principal to be repaid in three years, and for the greater accommodation of lenders, a loan office was to be established in each State. No certificate of loan to be less than three hundred dollars. A hope was entertained, that the loan would fill immediately, and would diminish the bills in circulation; and that the certificates being of large amount, would not be adapted to ordinary use. A lottery of four classes was also suggested, by which it was proposed to raise one million and five hundred thousand dollars; to draw in a large sum of continental money by the sale of the tickets; to retain, with the consent of the successful adventurers, the small prizes in each class, for tickets in the succeeding one, and the large prizes on loan. These means were wholly inadequate to the proposed object.

The faith of the people, however, supported the paper currency in undiminished reputation, until near the close of the campaign of 1776. Early in 1777, the depreciation became considerable; but, it was, generally, mistaken for the rise of prices; and in the ignorance of political economy which prevailed, it was supposed, that such effect might be violently restrained. To this end, Congress declared, that, whoever, in any purchase, sale, or barter, whatever, should rate gold or silver coin, higher than the continental bills of credit, ought to be deemed an enemy to the liberties of the United States, and to forfeit the value of the subject, in which such difference was made. And by most, perhaps, by all of the States, the paper bills were made a tender in payment of debts. But, a more effective and wise measure was, at the same time, devised. The States were urged, respectively, to support the credit of the Union, by a direct engagement to redeem these bills at the times fixed by Congress, and, immediately, to impose such taxes as the people were in condition to pay. They were assured, that, for all moneys thus raised, each State should receive a credit, with the United States, in its quota of the public debt, that had been apportioned to them. At the same time, a further loan of two millions was voted. The recommendations of Congress were complied with. The situation of the south, in these circumstances, required additional measures for relief. That portion of the country had been supplied by British merchants and British capital. The colonial traders had credit with such merchants; and large balances were annually owing, and in the hands of the planters, who, generally, preserved a credit to the value of their crops. To compel the American merchant to receive his debts, in paper, whilst he was bound to pay, in specie, would have been highly unjust; and he was, therefore, authorized to pay those due from him, into the public treasury, and was assured, that he should be, thereby, discharged from the claims of his creditor.

But neither loans nor taxes could be obtained in sufficient sums to prevent recourse to new issues of bills, and with every issue their value continued to decrease. Congress, in 1779, made a second effort to limit the flood of paper. They required of the States, on the first of January, to pay into the continental treasury, their respective quotas of fifteen millions for the service of that year, and of six millions, annually, from and after the year 1779, as a fund for reducing their early emissions and loans; and on the 21st of May, they further required, within the current year, forty-five millions of dollars. Large as these requisitions nominally were, they were wholly insufficient. The depreciation increased so rapidly as to defy all calculation. Towards the close of 1777, it was two or three for one—in 1778, five or six for one—in 1779, twenty-eight for one—in 1780, sixty for one, in the first half of the year; and near its close, it fell to one hundred and fifty for one. In some few places it continued in circulation for the first four or five months of 1781; but, in this last period, many would not take it at any rate, whilst others received it at a depreciation of several hundred for one.

To still the clamour which prevailed against these excessive issues, Congress resolved, in October, 1779, that no further sum should be issued, on any account, than would increase the circulation to two hundred millions, and no greater part of the sum, wanting to that amount, than was indispensable for the public exigencies, until adequate supplies could be otherwise obtained, for which reliance was placed upon the States. But Congress could not maintain its resolution; and soon completed the sum they had fixed as the maximum. At length, their paper became absolutely worthless; and they were almost wholly deprived of pecuniary means. Yet an effort was made to revive the credit of their bills, by a new issue under State guarantees—the old to be called in by taxes, and burned; and one dollar in new, to be emitted for every twenty of the old. Of the ten millions thus to be substituted, four were to be subject to the orders of Congress, and the remainder to that of the several States—the whole to be redeemable in specie, within six years; to bear an interest at the rate of five per cent., to be paid, also, in specie, at the redemption of the bills, or at the election of the owner, annually, in bills of exchange, on the American commissioners in Europe. This plan was soon found impracticable, and public credit being at the lowest ebb, the army was well nigh dissolved, and the country opened in every direction, to British excursions.

The crisis was a trying one, but it was happily past. New resources were discovered, and the war carried on with vigour. Much specie was about this time (1781) introduced into the United States, by trade with the French and Spanish West Indies, and by means of the French army in Rhode Island. The King of France gave the United States a subsidy of six millions of livres, and became their security for ten millions more, borrowed by them in the Netherlands. A regular system of finance was introduced by Mr. Robert Morris, who was placed at its head, and whose individual credit was liberally and advantageously used. The Bank of North America was established, and thus Congress and the country were extricated from the most imminent peril. By the scale of depreciation, the war was carried on for almost five years, for little more than a million sterling, and two hundred millions of paper dollars, were made redeemable by five silver ones.

New Jersey seems to have used her right of making money, with great moderation, and that dread of debt, which has peculiarly characterized her. By the act of June 8th, 1779, she called in all the bills of credit issued during her colonial state; and directed, that all not presented before the first of January, 1780, should be irredeemable. The provincial conventions, before the constitution of the State, authorized the issue of sixty thousand pounds, and provided for its extinction by taxation. This debt was adopted by the State. Under the requisition of Congress, March, 1780, the State authorized the issue of two hundred and twenty-five thousand pounds, payable with interest in yearly instalments, and the whole within six years.

But of this sum the whole was not emitted. On the 9th of January, 1781, a further emission of thirty thousand pounds was authorized, also, redeemable within six years. This sum was in small bills. And there were, probably, some other inconsiderable issues. But for the redemption of all, taxes were duly and timely laid. The State bills ceased to be a tender under the act of June 13th, 1781; and the continental bills, by an act of the 22d of the same month. The taxes were, during the depreciation, nominally enormous; and the amounts proposed to be raised at different times, strongly mark the course of depreciation. By a resolution of November, 1778, the Assembly proposed to raise one hundred thousand pounds, for the support of the government during the succeeding year; of which sum they proposed to pay to the governor one thousand pounds, and to Robert Morris, chief-justice, five hundred pounds, and the salaries of the other officers proportionately. And in November 20th, 1779, they resolved to raise *nine millions of dollars*, by the first of October following; and appropriated for the salary of the governor, seven thousand pounds, and for that of David Brearly, chief-justice, five thousand, and to the other officers proportionably.

During the war, there were large amounts of property belonging to the tories, confiscated; but they proved of little avail to the public treasury. The sales were generally made on credit, and by the progressive depreciation, what might have been dear at the time of purchase, became dog cheap at the time of payment.

The most extensive evils resulted from making the paper bills a tender in payment of debts contracted to be payable in gold and silver. They fell chiefly on those who lived upon fixed incomes, or possessed capitals, previously accumulated or invested. The annuitant, the widow, the heir, and the legatee, in receiving the nominal amount of their respective interests, did not, in many cases, receive a cent in the dollar. In a vast number of instances, the earnings of a long life of care and diligence, were wrested from their possessors. But the subject was not one of unmixed evil. It was generally useful to the poor; to those who hoarded not, but lived to-day upon the labour of yesterday or to-morrow. Whilst the paper money was current, none were idle from want of employment. Expending their money as fast as they received it, they always had its full value. No Agrarian law could have more effectually equalized the conditions of the State, than the tender of these depreciating bills. The poor became rich, the rich poor. All that the money lost in value was taken from the capitalists; but the active and industrious were safe, in conforming the price of their services to the state of the depreciation. The debtor who possessed property of any kind, could easily extinguish his debts. Every thing useful found a ready purchaser. The price of a bullock to-day would pay that of a slave purchased a few months before—that of a good horse, the value of an improved plantation.

The worst evil of the paper system was its demoralizing effect upon the community. The nature of obligations was so far changed, that the honest man, only, withheld the payment of his debts. A flood of speculation and fraud deluged the land, and found its way into its courts and its legislative halls, overwhelming truth, honour and justice.*

VIII. The summer of 1779 passed away, without furnishing, in America, any event which could have a material influence on the issue of the war. But it was otherwise in Europe, where a coalition, long looked for, and from which arose sanguine expectations, was effected. Spain resolved to unite with France, and to make, with her, common cause against Great Britain.

* Ramsay.

These two powers, it was believed, would be able to obtain complete ascendency at sea, and their fleets to maintain their superiority on the American coast, as well as in Europe. Yet, the United States were not acknowledged by Spain, as sovereign and independent; nor was their minister, Mr. Jay, who had been, some time before, sent to the Spanish court, accredited.

IX. As the campaign drew towards a close, without realizing the hope which had been cherished, that the war would terminate with it, General Washington laboured to induce the civil authorities to prepare in season for the ensuing campaign, exhibiting the alarming fact, that between October, 1779, and the last of June, of the coming year, the terms of service of near one-half of the soldiers of the army would expire. But it was impossible to remove the obstacles to prompt and united action. They were inherent in the system of confederation, in the novelty and untried circumstances of the States, and in that selfishness which had succeeded the first glow of patriotic indignation. Thus, the resolutions of Congress, relating to the military establishment, were not passed until the 9th of February, 1780; and did not require the troops to rendezvous before the first of April. The necessary acts of the State Legislatures, to give effect to these resolutions, were slow and irregular, uncertain and unseasonable; and the army could not possess that consistency and stability, which a better system would have given.

X. The season for active operations, in a northern climate, having ceased, the army retired into winter quarters. It was divided into two divisions—the northern under the command of Major-general Heath, had for its principal object, the security of West Point, and the posts on the North river, as low as King's Ferry; subordinate to which, was the protection of the country on the Sound, and the Hudson towards King's Bridge. The other and principal division, under Washington, originally proposed to encamp on the heights in the rear of the Scotch Plains, New Jersey; but Morristown was subsequently chosen, near which, the army was disposed in huts, late in December. From this post detachments were thrown out, towards the North river and Staten Island, for the purpose of covering the country from the depredations of the enemy.

XI. During the year 1779, the marauding parties of tories from New York and Staten Island, and occasionally, some of the enemy's regular troops, made devastating excursions into the State; the former for the purpose of plundering and capturing the unarmed inhabitants, and the latter, under the cover of legitimate war, to do the office of brigands. The enormities thus inflicted, were greatly increased, by associates sheltering themselves in the deep pine forests of Monmouth county, who, scarce regarding the distinctions of whig and tory, preyed on all within their power. Of these freebooters, Fagan, Bourke alias Emmons, Stephen West, Ezekiel Williams, and one Fenton, were most noted. Fagan was hunted and killed by a party of militia, under Captain Benjamin Dennis, who soon after, (January) by the agency of one Vankirk, entrapped Bourke, West, and Williams, whilst setting off from Rock Pond, for New York, with their booty. A small party, which lay concealed, shot them as they approached their boats. Their bodies, with that of Fagan, were hung in chains. Fenton was soon after killed by stratagem.

Bergen county was particularly exposed to hostile inroads, and the malice of the tories. On the 10th of May, about an hundred of the latter approached, by the way of New Dock, the settlements of Closter, and carried off Cornelius Tallman, Samuel Demarest, Jacob Cole, and George Buskirk; killed Cornelius Demarest, wounded Hendrick Demarest, Jeremiah Westervelt, Dow Tallman, and others; burned the dwellings of Peter Demarest, Matthias Bogart, Cornelius Kuyler, Samuel Demarest, together with many out-houses of other persons. They attempted to consume every dwelling they entered, but the fire was, in some, extinguished. They wantonly destroyed the furniture and stock, and abused the women. They were so closely pursued in their retreat, by the militia and a few continental troops, that they carried off no cattle, although that was a principal object of the incursion. This party belonged to the provincial corps of Colonel Vanbuskirk, an active and violent tory partisan, and consisted of former residents of Closter and Tappan, and some negroes.

On the 17th of May, a detachment of one thousand men, under that commander in person, swept over the county, marking their course with desolation and slaughter. Not a house within their reach, belonging to a whig inhabitant, escaped. Mr. Abraham Allen, and Mr. George Campbell, were barbarously murdered; Mr. Joost Zabriskie was stabbed in fifteen places, and two negro women were shot down, whilst endeavouring to drive off their master's cattle. The party avoided the vengeance of the militia by a speedy retreat with their plunder.

On the 9th of June, a party of more than fifty tories, from New York, landed in Monmouth county, and reached Tinton Falls undiscovered. They surprised and carried off Colonel Hendrickson, Lieutenant-colonel Wikoff, Captains Shadwick and Mr. Knight, with several privates of the militia, and drove away a few sheep and horned cattle. They were assailed by about thirty militia, whom they repelled, with the loss of two killed and ten wounded.

About the first of August, the house of Mr. Thomas Farr, near Crosswicks Baptist Church, was attacked by several of the forest ruffians. The family consisted of himself, wife and daughter. The assailants broke into the dwelling, mortally wounded Mr. Farr, and slew his wife outright. The daughter escaped to the house of a neighbour; and the alarmed villains fled without plunder.

On the 18th of October, a party of the enemy's light dragoons landed at Sandy Point, above Amboy, and proceeding to Bound Brook, burned some stores; thence by Van Veighton's Bridge, where they destroyed a number of boats, they marched to Somerset Court-house, which they fired. On their return, by the way of Brunswick, to South Amboy, they were annoyed by the militia. Their colonel and commandant, had his horse killed under him, and was himself made prisoner.

XII. Among the evils most dreaded, from the depreciation of the continental currency, was the difficulty which must necessarily arise in subsisting the army. This calamity was more hastened than deferred, by the parsimony with which Congress withheld, from the public agents, the money necessary for public purposes. Contracts could not be made co-extensive with the public wants, and many formed, were not fulfilled. A modification of the commissary department, in January, 1780, unfortunately, produced new embarrassments, and, at length, the credit of the purveying agents was wholly destroyed. Gaunt famine invaded the American camp at Morristown; and the procurement of supplies, by forced levies, became indispensable.

The commander-in-chief required, from each county in the State of New Jersey, a quantity of meat and flour proportioned to its resources, to be forwarded to the army within six days. To mitigate the odium of this measure, he addressed a circular letter to the magistrates, stating the urgency of the wants of the army, but with assurances, that if voluntary relief could not be obtained, a resort to force would be inevitable. To the honour of the State, notwithstanding its exhaustion, the required supplies were instantly furnished. Nor is less honour due to the soldiery, for the patient and unrepining fortitude with which they bore their sufferings. In the Highlands, similar wants were relieved by similar measures, which were more than once necessary to both camps. Soon after, the energies which the French displayed in the war, awakened a corresponding disposition in Congress, and in several States, which, in a new system of finance, gave adequate relief; but not until more serious evils, as will appear in the progress of the narrative, had developed themselves.

XIII. The isolated position of New York, had been much relied upon by the British commander for its defence. But the barrier which the waters afforded, was entirely removed by the severity of the frost in the winter of 1779, 1780. The ice becoming of such thickness, as to permit the army, with its wagons and artillery, to pass without danger, invited the enterprise of the commander-in-chief. His judgment and love of fame, alike, prompted him to attempt the city; but, the numerical inferiority of his force, still more the feebleness of his troops from the want of food and raiment, were insuperable obstacles. He eagerly engaged, however, in such enterprises to distress the enemy, as were in his power, without departure from the cautious system which had proven so beneficial to his country. The British troops, on Staten Island, were computed at twelve hundred men. The bridge of ice, over the waters, offered him, seemingly, a fair opportunity to surprise and bear off this corps, particularly, as the communication between Staten, and Long, and York islands, was supposed impracticable.

The enterprise was confided to General Lord Stirling, with a force of two thousand five hundred men, united to a detachment under General Irvine. On the night of the 14th of January, 1780, he moved from Dehart's Point; and detaching Lieutenant-colonel Willet to Decker's house, where Buskirk's regiment of two hundred men was stationed, proceeded, himself, to the watering place, where the main body was posted. But the enemy, apprehensive of attack, was abundantly vigilant; and, contrary to the intelligence previously received, the communication between the island and New York was still open. The object of the expedition, therefore, was unattainable, unless at an unjustifiable risk, as a reinforcement from New York might endanger the American detachment. Lord Stirling retreated on the morning of the 17th, sustaining an inconsiderable loss by a charge of cavalry on his rear. The excessive cold continuing, the rivers were soon afterwards completely blocked up. Even arms of the sea were passable on the ice, and the islands, about the mouth of the Hudson, presented to the view, and in effect, an unbroken continent.

XIV. The want of power in Congress, to raise funds, and to enforce its decrees of every character, almost deprived it of the semblance of a national council. The articles of confederation had been slowly approved, and were totally inefficient to protect the many general interests which it embraced. The establishment of the army, for the ensuing campaign, was fixed at thirty-five thousand two hundred and eleven men, and the measures for recruiting it, which preceded, a few days, those for its support, partook of the State system, which was entirely predominant. No means were used for raising men under the authority of Congress; and the several States were required by draught, or otherwise, to bring into the field, by the first day of April, the numbers necessary to their respective quotas. This course gave, unhappily, to the American confederacy, the semblance, nay, substantially, the character of an alliance of independent nations, whose embassadors assembled in general Congress, to recommend to their respective sovereigns, a plan of operations which each might pursue at pleasure. The measures productive of great uncertainty and delay, were reprobated by the commander-in-chief in vain, and he was doomed to struggle with embarrassments, of which he had never ceased to complain.

Famine was not the only great evil which beset the military service in 1780. Others, of a serious nature, presented themselves. The pay of an officer was reduced, by the depreciation of money, to a pittance wholly incompetent to his wants. That of a major-general would not compensate an express rider; nor that of the captain, furnish the shoes in which he marched. Generally, without fortune, the officers had expended the little they possessed, in the first equipments for their station; and were, now, compelled to rely on the States, to which they respectively belonged, for such clothing as they might furnish; which was so insufficient and unequal, as to produce extreme dissatisfaction, and great reluctance to remain in service.

XV. Among the privates there grew out of the very composition of the army, causes of disgust, which increased the dissatisfaction flowing from their multiplied wants. The first effort, towards the end of the campaign of 1776, to enlist troops for the war, had, in some degree, succeeded. In some States, especially in Pennsylvania, many recruits had, for small bounties, thus engaged. Whilst they served without pay, and almost without the necessaries of life, they had the mortification to behold their vacant ranks filled by men, who enlisted for a few months, only, and, for that short service, received high bounties, which, in depreciated money, seemed immense. In their chagrin, many were induced to contest their engagements, and others to desert. A representation of these circumstances, to Congress, produced a committee of inquiry, who reported, "that the army was unpaid for five months; that it seldom had more than six days' provisions in advance; and was, on several occasions, for sundry successive days, without meat; that it was destitute of forage; that the medical department had neither sugar, tea, chocolate, wine, or spirituous liquors of any kind; that every department was without money, and had not even the shadow of credit left; and that, the patience of the soldiers, borne down by the pressure of complicated sufferings, was on the point of being exhausted." In the mean time, Congress resolved, that they would make good to the line, and independent corps of the army, the depreciation of their pay, by which all the troops should be placed on an equal footing. But this benefit, dictated by simple justice, was limited to those in actual service, and to those who, after, came into it, engaging for three years, or the war.

These resolutions mitigated, but did not cure the prevailing griefs. A long course of suffering had produced some relaxation of discipline, and the discontents of the soldiery, at length, broke forth into actual mutiny.

On the 25th of May, two regiments from Connecticut, paraded under arms, with a declared resolution to return home, or to obtain subsistence at the point of the bayonet. The soldiers of other regiments, though not actually uniting with the mutineers, showed no disposition to suppress the mutiny. By great exertions of the officers, and the appearance of a neighbouring brigade of Pennsylvanians, then commanded by Colonel Stuart, the leaders were secured, and the troops brought back to their duty. But the temper of the soldiers, as apparent in their replies to the remonstrances of their officers, was of an alarming nature. They turned a deaf ear to the promises of Congress, and demanded some present, substantial, recompense for their services. A paper was found in the brigade, supposed from New York, stimulating the troops to abandon the cause of their country.

XVI. The discontents of the army, and the complaints of the people of New Jersey, on account of the repeated requisitions upon them, had been communicated, with such exaggerations, to the general, commanding in New York, as to induce the belief, that the American soldiers were ready to desert their standards, and the people of New Jersey to change their government. To avail himself of these dispositions, Knyphausen crossed over, on the sixth of

June, with about five thousand men, from Staten Island, and landed in the night at Elizabethtown Point. Early next morning he marched towards Springfield, by the way of Connecticut Farms, but soon perceived, that the temper of the country and army, had been misapprehended.

Washington had taken measures, in concert with the government of New Jersey, to call out the militia, so soon as occasion should require; and, on the appearance of the invading army, they assembled with great alacrity. On their march to Connecticut Farms, distant five or six miles from Elizabethtown, the British were harassed by small parties of continental troops, whose numbers were augmented, every instant, by the neighbouring militia. This resistance manifested, too clearly to be misunderstood, the resolution and temper to be encountered in the further progress of the expedition. A halt was made at the Connecticut Farms, where a spirit of revenge, more probably dwelling in the bosom of Governor Tryon, who was present, than in that of Knyphausen, who commanded, directed this village, with its church and parsonage, to be reduced to ashes. Another enormity was committed, at the same place, which aroused great indignation, not only in the vicinage, but every where throughout the Union. Mrs. Caldwell, the wife of the clergyman, had remained in her house, under the conviction, that her presence would protect it from pillage; and, that her person would not be endangered, as in the hope of preserving the Farms, Colonel Dayton, then commanding the militia, had determined not to halt in the settlement, but to take post, at a narrow pass, on the road leading to Springfield. Whilst sitting in the midst of her children, having a sucking infant in her arms, a soldier came to the window, and discharged his musket at her. She received the ball in her bosom and instantly expired. Ashamed of an act so universally execrated, the British contended, that the lady was the victim of a random shot from the militia. Circumstances, however, too strongly negatived this assertion, and a pathetic representation of the fact, published by the afflicted husband, received universal credit. The husband was distinguished for zeal to the American cause, and his fate was very like that of his wife. He was, some months after her decease, also shot to death, by a drunken tory, or British soldier, at Elizabethtown Point.

From the Farms, Knyphausen proceeded towards Springfield. The Jersey brigade, under General Maxwell, and the militia of the neighbourhood, who assembled in great force, took an advantageous position at that place, with the resolution to defend it. Knyphausen halted, and remained on the ground all night; but made no effort to dislodge the Americans. Washington having intelligence of this movement, marched his army early in the morning that Knyphausen left Elizabethtown Point, and advanced to the Short Hills, in the rear of Springfield. An impending battle was avoided by the German commander, who, hopeless of success, retired to the Point from which he had marched. He was followed by a detachment, which attacked his out-posts, supposing it had to contend with the rear of his army only; but on discovery, that the main body was still at the Point, the pursuers were recalled.

XVII. At this period, the numerical force of the American army, was fifty-five hundred and fifty-eight continental troops, of whom, only three thousand were effective. By return of Sir Henry Clinton, from his southern conquests, the British regular force, in New York, and its dependencies, was increased to full twelve thousand, which could be employed in the field, whilst four thousand militia and refugees performed garrison duty. With this disparity of numbers, the British commander might well hope to gather important fruits from again invading New Jersey, particularly, by penetrating to the American stores near Morristown. After masking his purpose, and dividing the small force of his adversary, by demonstrations against West

Point, he marched, on the morning of the 23d of June, from Elizabethtown, with five thousand infantry, a large body of cavalry, and from ten to twenty field pieces, towards Springfield.

In anticipation of this enterprise, General Greene had remained at Springfield, with two brigades of continental troops, and the Jersey militia: but in apprehension for the posts in the Highlands, the greater part of the army had been directed, slowly, towards Pompton. On observing the force which had entered the State, Washington halted and detached a brigade to hang on its right flank, whilst he prepared himself to support Greene, or otherwise to counteract the designs of the enemy.

At Springfield, Major Lee was advanced on the Vauxhall road, taken by the British right column; and Colonel Dayton, on the direct road, pursued by the left. As the enemy approached the town, a cannonade commenced, between their van and the American artillery, which had been posted to defend a bridge over the Rahway, guarded by Colonel Angel, with less than two hundred men. Colonel Shreve, with his regiment, occupied a second bridge, in order to cover the retreat of Angel. Major Lee, with his dragoons, and the piquets under Captain Walker, supported by Colonel Ogden, defended a bridge on the Vauxhall road. The residue of the continental troops, were drawn up on high ground, in the rear of the town, with the militia on the flanks.

The right column of the British, advanced on Lee, who resisted their passage until a body of the enemy had forded the river above him, when he withdrew his corps to avoid being surrounded. At this instant, their left attacked Angel, who maintained his ground with persevering gallantry, until compelled, after thirty minutes struggle, to yield to superior numbers; but he retired in perfect order, and brought off his wounded. Shreve, after covering Angel's retreat, rejoined his brigade. The English then took possession of the town and reduced it to ashes. The stern resistance he had encountered, the gallantry and discipline of the continental troops, their firm countenance displayed in continual skirmishing, and the strength of Greene's position, together with tidings, that a formidable fleet and army was daily expected from France, deterred Sir Henry from prosecuting his original design. He withdrew that afternoon from Elizabethtown; and in the same night passed over to Staten Island. In this battle the Jersey brigade and militia, bore a conspicuous and honourable part.

XVIII. There is, perhaps, no event connected with the American revolution, of more extraordinary character, than the devotion displayed towards it, by the Marquis de La Fayette. Of high aristocratic descent, rich, and with every prospect of flattering consideration, at the court of his king, he became enamoured of the principles of freedom and equality, in a distant and a foreign land; and against the remonstrances of his friends, and the disapprobation of his prince, devoted his life and fortune to their support. At the close of 1776, he communicated to the American commissioners, at Paris, his determination to repair to the United States. The encouragement which they gave to his wishes was retracted, when the reverses in New Jersey were known. But his enthusiasm was not to be thus extinguished; and he replied, that these circumstances rendered even inconsiderable aids more necessary; and that if they could not furnish him with a ship, he would freight one himself, to convey him and their despatches. This he did. At the age of nineteen years, newly wedded to a wife whom he loved, and tempted by the pleasures of a luxurious court, he voluntarily rejected the ready enjoyments of his condition, and sailed to America. He was received with such sentiments as his disinterestedness merited. But, instead of using this grateful disposition, to obtain extraordinary distinction, in the rendition of his services, as was generally the case with foreigners, who then sought employment in America, he, modestly and generously, declined a commission, and requested leave to serve as a volunteer. Nor were the virtues of this extraordinary man, thus displayed, the temporary fruits of momentary and youthful excitement. His love of freedom and political equality, and his disinterested pursuit of them, have rendered illustrious a long life; and it would seem, that with him, at least, the exercise of virtuous passions had the power to give increase of days. He became the friend of Washington. And if a nation's gratitude be the appropriate meed for national services, La Fayette has been rewarded, by his triumphal procession, of months, through the North American continent.

When war was declared between France and England, La Fayette deemed, that his duty required him to tender his services to his own sovereign. He obtained the permission of Congress, to return, preserving his rank of major-general, in the American army, and all his zeal for American interests. He was received at court with favour and distinction, and successfully employed his influence, in persuading the cabinet to grant efficient succours to the United States. There being no probability of active employment in Europe, he returned to America, in April, 1780; bearing the grateful intelligence, that France would immediately despatch a considerable land and naval armament, for the ensuing campaign.

XIX. These tidings gave, indeed, a new impulse to Congress, the State Legislatures, and the people. The first adopted vigorous resolutions for raising money and troops, which were transferred into the laws of the several States. But, unfortunately, the energy displayed in the enactment, did not extend to the execution of the laws; the troops being slowly raised, and in numbers far less than the service required. Several patriotic individuals contributed largely to the public funds. The citizens of Philadelphia established a bank, subscribing £315,000, Pennsylvania currency, payable in specie; principally, with a view to provide the army with provisions, and without contemplation of profit to the founders. The ladies of that city set a splendid example of patriotism, devoting large sums for the relief of suffering soldiers, which was, generally, followed throughout the country.* Yet, despite of all these exertions, the condition of the army continued deplorable.

XX. On the 10th of July, before Washington could fill his ranks, or had prepared any plan for the campaign, the first division of the French auxiliaries arrived at Newport, with more than five thousand troops, and intelligence, that a second division might be speedily expected. The instructions of General Rochambeau, placed him, entirely, under the command of Washington, and required his forces, as allies, to cede the post of honour to the Americans. In reliance on the French naval superiority, Washington proposed a joint attack on New York; fixing the 5th of August, for the reembarkation of the French troops, and the assembling of his army at Morrisania. But this design was procrastinated and finally defeated, by the successive arrival of British squadrons, which gave them the command of the sea, and confined the French to the harbour. In its prosecution, however, the commander-in-chief visited Hartford, that by personal conference with the French officers, he might concert measures for this and other objects.

During his absence from camp, the long meditated treason of General Arnold exploded, destroying, however, only, the most active auxiliary of his

* On the 4th of July, the ladies of Trenton appointed Mrs. Cox, Mrs. Dickenson, Mrs. Forman, and Miss Cadwalader, to open a subscription, and to correspond with the ladies in the different counties of the State, whom they named on committees.

guilt; whose merit caused him to be wept, even by his enemies. General Arnold possessed great courage, enterprise, patience, and fortitude, with other qualities essential to the able soldier. But without moral principle, or sound judgment, he estimated greatness to consist in ostentatious display, and the liberal indulgence of the senses. Previous to the revolution his poverty denied these enjoyments. His sudden elevation, whilst stimulating his appetites, gave him, justly or unjustly, the means for their gratification. A short period of success filled him with that disposition, which leads inevitably to ruin. He became prodigal of his own, and avaricious of the property of others. The wounds he received at Quebec and Saratoga, unfitted him for active service; and having large accounts to settle with Congress, he was, on the evacuation of Philadelphia in 1778, appointed to the command of that city. Here, yielding to his vain propensities, he incurred large expenses, for a sumptuous table and splendid equipage. To sustain these, with the spirit of the gambler, he embarked in perilous and unfortunate commercial speculations, and in unsuccessful privateer adventures. His accounts with the United States were intricate, and the enormous balances he claimed, were reduced, not only by a committee of Congress, but by the House, on the report of its committee. Charged with various acts of extortion upon the citizens, and peculation in the funds, detected and degraded, he reproached his country with ingratitude, and giving general offence, was arrested, tried, and sentenced by a court martial, and publicly reprimanded by the commander-in-chief.

From this hour, his haughty spirit is supposed to have devoted his country to the direst vengeance. Knowing well the importance of the post at West Point, he deliberately and successfully sought its command, with the view of betraying it to the enemy. To this end, a correspondence was for some time carried on, under mercantile disguise, in the names of Gustavus and Anderson, between him and Major John André, aid-de-camp of Sir Henry Clinton, and adjutant-general of the British army. To facilitate their communication, the Vulture, sloop of war, took a station on the North river; and the visit of General Washington, at Hartford, was improved, for adjusting their plans by a personal interview. André landed from the sloop, without the American lines, under a flag sent by Arnold. Their conference having been protracted, into the succeeding day, it became necessary that André should be concealed, until the night afforded him a safe opportunity to re-embark. He refused, peremptorily, to enter within the lines, but the respect promised to this objection, was not preserved. They continued together during the day, in which the Vulture shifted her position, in consequence of a gun having, without the knowledge of Arnold, been brought to bear upon her. The boatmen, on the following night, refusing to carry André on board, he attempted to reach New York, by land. Reluctantly yielding to the representations of Arnold, he exchanged his uniform, which he had hitherto worn beneath his surtout, for plain clothes, and set forth with a permit, authorizing him, under the name of John Anderson, to proceed on the public service to the White Plains, or lower, if he thought proper.

He had safely passed the posts, when he was arrested by one of three militiamen, on a scouting party. With a self-abandonment, extraordinary in one equally brave and intelligent, instead of producing his pass, he hastily asked the soldier, who had seized his bridle, "where he belonged to?" The reply, "to below," designating him to be from New York, André said, "And so am I;"—and declaring himself to be a British officer, on urgent business, begged that he might not be detained. The other militiamen coming up, he discovered his mistake too late to repair it. His most tempting offers for permission to escape, were rejected by his captors, who, on searching him, found concealed, in his boots, among other interesting papers, exact returns, in the hand-writing of Arnold, of the state of West Point, and its dependencies. Carried before Colonel Jameson, who commanded the scouts on the lines, he, anxious for the safety of Arnold, requested, that he should be informed, that Anderson was taken. An express was despatched with the communication. On receiving it, Arnold took refuge on board the Vulture, whence he proceeded to New York. Sufficient time being allowed for his escape, André no longer affected concealment, but avowed himself the adjutant-general of the British army.

This gallant and unfortunate man suffered the penalty which would have more justly fallen upon the fugitive traitor. He was condemned as a spy, by a court-martial, of which General Greene was president, and La Fayette, Steuben, and others, were members. And notwithstanding the earnest endeavours of Sir Henry Clinton, to save him, and the tears even of his judges, the sentence, sternly exacted by duty, was executed. Arnold became a brigadier in the British service, universally contemned as a vile and sordid traitor, who had been redeemed from the gallows, by the blood of one of the most accomplished officers of the British army.

The thanks of Congress were given, with a silver medal, bearing an inscription, expressive of their fidelity, to John Paulding, David Williams, and Isaac Vanvert; and subsequently, a pension of two hundred dollars per annum—a reward, better proportioned to the state of the treasury, than their services—was settled upon them, respectively.

XXII. Early in December, 1780, the American army retired to winter quarters. The Pennsylvania line was stationed near Morristown, the Jersey line about Pompton, on the confines of New York, and the troops of the New England States, at and near West Point, on both sides of the river. The line of New York remained at Albany, to which place it had been sent to aid in opposing a temporary invasion from Canada.

XXIII. In Europe, Great Britain, at war with France and Spain, was threatened by the northern powers, Russia, Sweden, and Norway, who, in the summer of 1780, entered into the celebrated compact known as "*The armed neutrality*." Holland showed a disposition not only to join this alliance, but to enter into a treaty with the United States of America. Both were offences which the English ministers were not disposed to overlook, and war was declared against that nation.

XXIV. The state of the American army was little improved during the year 1780. Discontent gained ground, and even the officers could not always restrain their repinings, in contrasting their condition with that of other classes in the country. These had, inevitably, an influence upon the disposition of the soldier. In addition to the general causes of dissatisfaction, the Pennsylvania line had one, almost, peculiar to itself. When Congress directed enlistments to be made for "*three years or during the war*," the recruiting officers of that line engaged many men on those ambiguous terms. As a consequence, the soldier claimed his discharge, at the expiration of three years; whilst the officer insisted, upon detaining him during the war. The imposition, as the soldier viewed it, was more impatiently borne, whilst he witnessed the large bounties given to the new recruits. The discontent which had been long fomenting, broke out on the night of the first of January, 1781, in open and almost universal revolt of this line.

Upon a signal given, all the regiments, except three, turned out under arms; avowing their determination to march to the seat of Congress, and obtain redress for their grievances, or to serve no longer. The officers endeavoured, in vain, to quell them. Several were wounded, and a Captain Billing killed, in the attempt. General Wayne presented his pistols, as if about to fire; but the bayonet was put to his breast, whilst, with expressions of respect and affection, he was told, "If you fire, you are a dead man. We are not going to the enemy; should he approach, we will fight him under your orders. But we will be no longer amused, and are resolved to obtain our just rights." In this temper, thirteen hundred men marched from Morristown to Princeton, with their arms and six pieces of cannon, in good order, with officers appointed from themselves, a sergeant-major, who had deserted from the British, being commander. They resisted attempts at accommodation, made, severally, by General Wayne and a committee of Congress. But, at length, at the instance of President Reed of Pennsylvania, they marched to Trenton, and submitted, on condition,—1. That those enlisted for "*three years or during the war*," should be discharged; such enlistment to be determined by commissioners mutually chosen, on the oath of the soldier, where the written contract could not be found; 2. That certificates for the depreciation of their pay should be immediately given, the arrearages to be paid as soon as circumstances would permit; 3. That certain specified articles of clothing, greatly needed, should be immediately furnished. In consequence of the irksomeness of this affair, the whole of the artillery, and of the five first regiments of infantry, were discharged before the contracts of enlistment could be brought from Morristown. On their production, it appeared, that the engagements of the remaining regiments did not entitle them to their discharge, and that, of those actually dismissed, the far greater number had enlisted for the war. The discharges, however, were not revoked, and those who were to remain in service, received furloughs for forty days, with orders to rendezvous at designated places in Pennsylvania.

Sir Henry Clinton, apprized of the revolt, on the third of January, sent his emissaries, with highly tempting offers, to the line, to engage them in his service. The offers were communicated to General Wayne, the agents seized and confined, and after the accommodation, they were tried and executed as spies.

General Washington, who, for prudential reasons, did not approach the mutineers, took measures to avail himself of the regular troops, and the militia of New York, for offence or defence. And, on the first notice of the mutiny, the militia of New Jersey, under General Dickenson, took the field, for the purpose of opposing any incursion which might be made in the State, and of co-operating with such of the regular troops as it might be necessary to employ.

The danger of yielding, even to the just demands of soldiers, with arms in their hands, was soon evident. The success of the Pennsylvania line stimulated part of that of Jersey, many of whom were foreigners, in the hope of like advantages, to a similar attempt. On the night of the 20th of January, part of the Jersey brigade, stationed at Pompton, rose in arms, and making the same claims which had been granted to the Pennsylvanians, marched to Chatham, where another portion of the brigade was posted, in expectation, that it would join in the revolt. But, the commander-in-chief, chagrined at the result of the late mutiny, and confident in the faith of the eastern troops, resolved on strong measures to stop the further progress of a spirit which threatened the total destruction of the army. A detachment, under General Howe, was immediately sent against the mutineers, with orders to bring them to unconditional submission, and to execute some of the most active of the leaders. Howe marched from Kingwood about midnight, and by the dawning of the next day, had so posted his force as to prevent the escape of the revolters. Colonel Barber, of the Jersey line, commanded them to parade without arms, and to march to designated ground. Upon their hesitation, Colonel Sprout advanced, giving them five minutes, only, for compliance. Intimidated, they instantly obeyed. The Jersey officers gave a list of the leaders of the revolt, from whom three of the most active were selected, who were executed upon the spot, by the other prominent mutineers. The vast disparity of numbers engaged in these mutinies, accounts for the difference in the results. The disaffected in the Jersey line did not exceed one hundred and sixty men.

Sir Henry Clinton offered to the Jersey mutineers the same terms as to the Pennsylvania line; and General Robertson, at the head of three thousand men, was detached to Staten Island, for the purpose of entering Jersey, and covering any movement which they might make towards New York. The emissary employed, proved to be in the American interest, and delivered his papers to Colonel Dayton, commanding at the first station to which he came. Other papers were dispersed among the mutineers, promising rewards to every soldier who should join the British troops when landed at Elizabethtown; but the mutiny was crushed so suddenly, as to allow no time for the operation of these proposals.

The vigorous steps now taken, were, happily, followed by such attention, on the part of the States, to the wants of the army, as checked the further progress of discontent. Although the army was reduced to almost insupportable distress, by the scantiness of supplies, the discontents of the people were daily multiplied, by enforced contributions, and the offensive manner in which they were levied. Every article for public use, was obtained by impressment, and the taxes, being chiefly specific, were either unpaid or collected by coercion. Strong representations were made against this system, and committees were, in some places, raised to express the public complaints. The dissatisfaction, therefore, which pervaded the mass of the community, was scarcely less dangerous, than that which had been manifested by the army.

XXV. The year 1781 commenced in gloom and despondency. The hopes founded on French aid had been disappointed; the sufferings of the army were unalleviated, and the prospect of its increase, discouraging. Of thirty-seven thousand troops, voted by Congress, to be in camp on the first of January, not more than fourteen thousand, two-thirds of whom, only, were effective, had been raised, in all the Union, in June, when the campaign opened. Food and raiment were still scantily supplied; the latter, contracted for in France, having been unaccountably delayed. In the mean time, the country was threatened from every quarter,—in the west, by new combinations of the Indians—in the north, from Canada, and the discontented residents of Vermont, whose contention for jurisdiction, with the State of New York, made them cold in the common cause—on the eastern border, by the increased force of Sir Henry Clinton—on the south, by Rawdon and Cornwallis. To supply the American army with food, would, perhaps, have been impossible, but for the efforts of the financier, Mr. Robert Morris; whose mercantile capital and credit were, judiciously, called to aid his official duties, without which, the decisive operations of the campaign, might have been defeated.

XXVI. Washington still cherished the design of attacking New York, and the French troops were ordered from Newport, late in June, for this purpose, The intention was abandoned, however, in August, in consequence of large reinforcements having been received, from Germany, by Clinton, the tardiness with which the American ranks were filled, and the prospect of striking a successful blow in the south. A large fleet, commanded by the Count de Grasse, was expected, daily, to arrive in the Chesapeake, affording, if conjoined in operation with the army, the most flattering hopes of the capture of Cornwallis.

The appearance of an attack on New York, was still kept up, whilst the allied army crossed the North river, and passed, by way of Philadelphia, to Yorktown. This march would, probably, have been interrupted, had not Sir Henry Clinton, relying, confidently, on some intercepted letters, developing the plan of the intended attempt on New York, believed the present movement to be a feint, until it was too far completed to be opposed. The order observed by the French troops, has, with great reason, called forth the plaudits of the historian. In a march of five hundred miles, through a country abounding in fruit, not a peach nor an apple was taken without leave. General Washington and Count Rochambeau, reached Williamsburg on the 14th of September; and visiting Count de Grasse, on board his ship, the ***Ville de Paris***, concerted the plan of future operations.

De Grasse arrived in the Chesapeake, from Cape Francoise, late in August, with twenty-eight sail of the line, and several frigates. At Cape Henry, an officer from La Fayette informed him of the situation of the armies in Virginia. Lord Cornwallis, who had received notice that a French fleet was to be expected on the coast, had collected his whole force at Yorktown and Gloucester Point; and the Marquis had taken a position on James River, for the purpose of opposing any attempt, which the British might make, to escape into South Carolina. Four ships of the line and several frigates, were detached for the purpose of blocking up the mouth of York River, and of conveying the French land forces, under the Marquis of St. Simon, up the James River, to form a junction with La Fayette. In the mean time, the fleet lay at anchor just within the capes. On the 25th of August, the Count de Barras sailed from Newport for the Chesapeake.

Admiral Rodney, who commanded in the West Indies, supposing that the greater part of the fleet of De Grasse, had proceeded to Europe, and that a part, only, of his own squadron, would suffice to maintain an equality of force in the American seas, detached Sir Samuel Hood to the continent, with fourteen sail of the line. That officer made land south of the capes of Virginia, a few days before De Grasse's arrival, and proceeded, thence, to Sandy Hook, which he reached on the 28th of August. Uniting with the force under Admiral Greaves, who, as senior officer, took the command, the whole fleet, amounting to nineteen sail of the line, set sail, immediately, in hopes of falling in with De Barras or De Grasse, wholly unsuspicious of the force of the latter. On the morning of the fifth of September, the fleet of De Grasse was discovered, consisting of twenty-four sail of the line, in the mouth of the Chesapeake. An engagement ensued, for several hours, in which neither party could claim the victory. Some days were spent in manœuvres, during which De Grasse, having the wind, might have brought on another battle; but it was declined, that the capture of the British army, now deemed almost certain, might not be put to hazard. In the mean time, De Barras arrived with his squadron, and fourteen transports laden with artillery and stores, proper to carry on the siege. The English fleet retired before this superior force, and returned to New York.

At length, the post of Lord Cornwallis was formally besieged, and the first parallel commenced, on the night of the sixth of October. The siege was prosecuted with great vigour, courage, and skill; the officers and soldiers of France and America, striving who should display most, these qualities. The defence was maintained, with equal spirit, against a vastly superior force, during thirteen days; until almost every gun on the fortifications was dismounted, and the batteries prostrated. On the nineteenth, Lord Cornwallis surrendered the posts of Yorktown and Gloucester Point, with their garrisons, and the shipping in the harbour with the seamen; the army and arms, military chest and stores, to Washington; the ships and seamen to the Count de Grasse. The total amount of prisoners, exclusive of seamen, exceeded seven thousand men. The allied army may be estimated at sixteen thousand; the French at seven thousand; the continental troops at five thousand five hundred, and the militia at three thousand five hundred. Sir Henry Clinton, fully apprized of the influence which the fate of the army, in Virginia, must have on the war, exerted himself, strenuously, for its preservation; and having embarked about seven thousand of his best troops, sailed for the Chesapeake, under convoy of twenty-five sail of the line. This armament left the Hook on the day the capitulation was signed at Yorktown, and appeared off the capes of Virginia, to learn the tidings of surrender, and to return to New York; no sufficient motive remaining for attacking the greatly superior force of De Grasse.

The exultation throughout the United States, at the capture of this formidable army, which had inflicted incalculable misery over an immense space of territory, was equal to the terror which it had inspired. The opinion became universal, that the great struggle was over, that the object of the contest had been fully gained, and every demonstration of gratitude was poured forth by Congress and the people, to heaven, and its agents in their deliverance.

XXVII. Whilst the allied armies were on march for Virginia, Sir Henry Clinton, probably, with the hope of recalling Washington, sent an expedition under Arnold, against New London, which landed in the port on the 6th of September. Fort Griswold, on one side of the harbour, made an obstinate resistance. It was garrisoned by Colonel Ledyard, and one hundred and sixty men. But being taken by storm, the captors disgraced their triumph, by the slaughter of the brave and unresisting defenders. Colonel Ledyard presented his sword to the commanding officer of the assailants, which the barbarian instantly plunged into his bosom, and the carnage was kept up, until the greater part of the garrison was killed or wounded. If such vengeance could be justified, there was, indeed, cause for it. Colonel Eyre, and Major Montgomery, the second in command, together with two hundred men, fell in the assault. The town of New London, and the stores which it contained, were consumed by fire.

XXVIII. The capture of Cornwallis was the conclusion of the war. A show of hostility was preserved for a few months, and some skirmishing was had, of no great interest, between the parties, near New York, and in the vicinity of Charleston. But no military event of importance, afterwards took place. Count de Grasse sailed for the West Indies, Wayne and Gest's brigades marched under General St. Clair, to the aid of Greene, in the south; the French troops remained in Virginia, and the eastern regiments returned to New Jersey and New York, under the immediate command of General Lincoln.

Stimulated by these successes, the preparations for another campaign were commenced, with much alacrity. The resolutions respecting the military establishment, were adopted by Congress, so early as the 10th of December; and those providing for the expenses of the war, substituting a vigorous system of taxation, for the demoralizing and unjust practice of extortion, and requiring eight millions of dollars, in specie, to be paid by the States, quarterly, were passed so early as the 10th of October. But the country was exhausted. The obstacles to raising revenue, were almost insuperable. At the commencement of the year 1782, not a dollar remained in the public treasury; and although the payment of two millions had been required by the first of April, on the twenty-third of that month, not a cent had been received. On the first of June, twenty thousand dollars, scarce more than sufficient for a single day's service, had been paid. In July, when a half years' tax was due, the minister of finance was informed by his agents, that in some States, nothing would be received before the month of December. The country was, therefore, indebted for indispensable supplies, to the funds and credit of the financier; but the public creditors were unpaid, and no one could look forward, without deep anxiety, to the perpetuation of the system of forced contribution.

Happily for the United States, the people of Great Britain had wearied of the contest, and constrained their King, and his ministers, to think of peace. Strong resolutions were adopted by Parliament late in February, which not being promptly acted upon by the ministry, were followed on the 4th of March, by a vote of the House of Commons, denouncing as enemies to his Majesty and the country, all who should advise or attempt, a further prosecution of offensive war on the continent of North America. A change of ministry succeeded these votes, with instructions to the commanding officers in America, which conformed to them.

XXIX. Although the spirit of animosity between the two nations, Great Britain and the United States of America, began to yield to policy and humanity, the ire which dwelt in the bosoms of the tories, seemed to wax stronger, as their hopes of restitution waned. In the depredations of Arnold, and in the border war of New Jersey, the injuries done by them, were the most malignant; and their vengeance was still poured out upon New Jersey. From many outrages, we select the following, as most prominent.

On the 2d of April, 1782, Captain Joshua Huddy was captured, with the block-house he defended, on Tom's river, by a party of refugees, after a gallant resistance. He was carried to New York, and detained in close confinement for some days, and then told, that he was to be hanged. Four days after (on the 12th,) he was carried by a party of tories to Middletown Heights, where he was deliberately executed, with the following label affixed to his breast.—"We, the refugees, having long, with grief, beheld the cruel murders of our brethren, and finding nothing but such measures daily carrying into execution;—we, therefore, determine not to suffer without taking vengeance for the numerous cruelties; and thus begin, having made use of Captain Huddy, as the first object to present to your view; and further determine, to hang man for man, while there is a refugee existing. Up goes Huddy, for Philip White."

The Philip White here named, was a tory, who had been taken by a party of Jersey militia, and killed, in attempting to escape. His death was, falsely, charged upon this victim. Huddy was a man of extraordinary bravery, and met his hard fate, with rare fortitude and composure of mind. He executed his will, under the gallows, upon the head of the barrel, from which he was immediately to make his exit—and in a hand-writing, fairer than usual. Greatly indignant at this wanton murder, Washington wrote to Sir Henry Clinton, threatening, that unless the murderers were surrendered, he would retaliate. The demand being refused, Captain Asgill was designated by lot, as the subject. In the mean time the British instituted a court-martial, for the trial of Captain Lippincott, the principal agent in the nefarious deed; when it appeared, that Governor Franklin, president of the board of associated loyalists, had given verbal orders to Lippincott, designating Huddy as a proper object for vengeance, as one who had persecuted the loyalists, and had been especially instrumental in hanging Stephen Edwards, a refugee. The court acquitted Lippincott, stating, that his conduct was dictated by the conviction, that duty required him to obey the orders of the board, as he did not doubt their authority. Sir Guy Carleton, who had succeeded to the chief command of the British army, notwithstanding the acquittal, reprobated the measure, gave assurance of further inquiry, and broke up the board of associated loyalists, to prevent the repetition of such excesses. Asgill was rescued from various reasons. The end of the war rapidly and visibly approached—the Count de Vergennes interceded for him, by letter, enclosing one from Mrs. Asgill, his mother, and Congress (November 7th,) directed the commander-in-chief, to his great satisfaction, to set the captain at liberty.

XXX. Sir Guy Carleton, with Admiral Digby, was commissioned to negotiate a separate peace with the Americans; but their efforts were futile, as such a course, being dishonourable to the States, was inadmissible. Nor was it apparent, that the powers of the commissioners were sufficiently full for the object. But the public votes we have stated, and, probably, the private instructions given to the British general, restrained him from offensive war; and the state of the American army, disabled Washington from any attempt on posts held by the enemy. These causes of inactivity in the north, extended also to the south.

After an intricate negotiation, in which the penetration, judgment, and firmness of the American commissioners* were eminently displayed, eventual and preliminary articles of peace were signed on the 30th of November. The treaty, however, did not take effect, until the general pacification, on the 20th of January, 1783. Tidings of the latter event were communicated by M. de La Fayette, by letter, received 24th of March. Early in April, came a copy of the treaty, from the American commissioners, and on the 19th of that month, the cessation of hostilities was proclaimed. On the 15th, the execution of the treaty was publicly celebrated, at Trenton.

XXXI. To the restoration of the blessings of peace, one important measure, the dissolution of the army, was indispensable. Military habits, and the spirit of segregation which they engender, are incompatible with the order and equality of civil life. The general and corporal are alike tenacious of command; and the soldier, reluctantly, lays aside the casque, the uniform and arms, the idleness and the license, which distinguish him from the citizen. The camp becomes his country—his fellows in arms, his only compatriots, and the articles of war, and the will of his officers, his only laws. His whole being is newly, but not beneficially, modified. His intellectual powers and employments are confined to narrow limits, whilst his physical force and sensual appetites, are generally increased, and often indulged, by irregular gratification. To dissolve an army which has no cause of complaint against the State, is often a difficult and dangerous duty—to disarm men, to whom the State, without the means of payment, is deeply indebted; who, poor and naked, look, confidently, on their return to civil life, only, to servile labour, beggary and oblivion, is indeed a perilous task; yet one, which among the miracles of the American revolution, was accomplished. A happiness, for which the country was as much indebted to the commander-in-chief, as for his military services. The traits of character displayed by him in attaining this object, are more valuable than any exhibited in his previous and after life, excellent as these, certainly, were. He had his equals, perhaps superiors, in his own country, in military talent and political science; but in magnanimity, self-control, and true appreciation of fame, he was unrivalled. Had he been animated by ordinary ambition, the passion common to an Alexander, a Cæsar, a Cromwell, and a Bonaparte, he might readily have availed himself of the discontents of the army to gratify it; he might have loosed upon his country, the most ferocious of animals, an irritated soldiery, and have compelled that country to fly to military despotism, as a refuge against the worse evils of anarchy. But, with the love of

* Messrs. John Adams, Benjamin Franklin, John Jay, and Henry Laurens.

peace, of order, of social feeling and political equality, which can never be too much praised, he said to the angry elements of discord, be still, and they obeyed his voice.

When the prospect of peace became certain, the officers of the army turned anxiously to their own condition, and asked, as an act of justice, payment of arrears, and compensation for losses sustained by a depreciated currency; and, as an act of gratitude, a reward, for services which were inestimable. To the immediate gratification of these demands, the obstacle was obvious, as irremediable, in an empty treasury. But there was a party in the national councils, who were indisposed to accept, without question, the high estimate of services made by the military—who believed that the life of the soldier, had, like other conditions, mingled good and evil, the one compensating the other; and who would not admit, that the distinction sought by thousands, despite of the labours and privations which it imposed, gave extraordinary and preferable claims upon the country. However sound, in general, might be this view of military merit, it was less just when applied to the continental army. There is no evil, it is true, which afflicted the American soldier, that had not been borne in pursuit of the very worst objects of human ambition, of absolute and unhallowed power, of the sordid love of gold. But the motive elevated the service; yet, only so long, as that motive was disinterestedly patriotic. Every effort to obtain pecuniary compensation, made *by the soldier*, stripped his pretensions of their gilding, and reduced him nearer to the grade of the ordinary mercenary. The country, but more, especially, posterity, owed to the men of the revolution, a deep debt of gratitude. But was that more due to the suffering soldier, than the suffering citizen—to him who met the enemy in arms, manfully returning blow for blow, than to him, who encountered the foe upon his hearth-stone, and unresistingly beheld his barns and his byres plundered, the wife of his bosom, and the children of his love, violated or slaughtered—to him, who, though, occasionally, scantily and precariously fed, had some assurance in the care of the nation, and in his own arms, that he should not starve, than to him, who was stripped of the loaf that he had garnered for his infants, that the soldier might not want—to him whom, depreciation of the currency, left as it found him, a pennyless man, than to him whom that depreciation despoiled of the hoards of his ancestors, and of the stores laid up during a long life of unremitting industry? Let the suffering of the soldier and the citizen, be duly compared; they will not be found more unequal than were the enjoyments for which they contended. An extraordinary gratitude continues even now, to repay the one, but no pension, no praise, has smoothed the thorny path of the other, to the grave.

With views such as we have glanced at, Congress lent a dull and unwilling ear, in the depth of pecuniary distress, to the vehement cries of the soldier; and in consonance with the experience of all times past, he demonstrated the disposition to redress his own grievances, and in his own way. An anonymous, but eloquent and inflammatory address, was circulated through the army,* exciting to this course; whilst another missive summoned the general and field-officers, to convene on the succeeding day. A crisis had thus approached, big with the fate of the nation. It was possible, for the commander-in-chief, by prompt, decisive and steady action, to avert the threatened evil; and he did not shrink from the service. He instantly noticed the seditious papers, in general orders, and called the general and field-officers, with one officer from each company, and a representation from the staff of the army, to assemble on the 15th, to consider the report of a com-

* March 10th, 1783.

mittee which had been deputed from the army to Congress. He employed the interval, successfully, in preparing the minds of all for moderate measures. At the convention, General Gates took the chair, and Washington addressed the officers, reprobating, in the strongest terms, the anonymous addresses, not only as to the mode of communication, but, also, as to the spirit which indicted them—dwelling on the character which the army had acquired for patriotism and order—expressing undiminished confidence in the justice and gratitude of the country, and conjuring them, as they valued their honour, as they respected the rights of humanity, and as they regarded their military and national character, to express their utmost detestation of the man who was attempting to open the floodgates of civil discord, and to deluge the rising empire with blood. So absolute was the power of virtue, on this occasion, that not a voice was raised to oppose its behests. Resolutions were, unanimously, adopted, echoing the sentiments of the commander-in-chief.

These events hastened the adoption of a resolution, which had been, some time, pending before Congress, giving to the officers who preferred a sum in gross to an annuity, five years full pay, in money, or in securities at six per cent., instead of the half-pay for life, which had previously been promised them; and measures were also taken, to obtain for the troops, three months' pay in hand. At the same time, a happy mean was pursued, of dispersing the dangerous mass. The commander-in-chief was instructed, to grant furloughs to the non-commissioned officers and privates, with an intention, which, of course, was persevered in, that they should not be required to rejoin their regiments. The officers remonstrated; but the general again appeased them, and gained their acquiescence. In the course of the summer, a great proportion of the troops, who had enlisted for three years, returned to their homes; and on the third of November, 1783, all who had engaged for the war, were discharged.

By these means, an unpaid army was disbanded and dispersed;—the privates betaking themselves to labour—the officers, who had been drawn from every condition of society, from the professions, from husbandry and from trade, and the mechanic arts, returned, generally, to their primary pursuits.

One, only, exception stands forth from this scene of honourable and patriotic devotion. About eighty of the new Pennsylvania levies, who were without pretensions of suffering and service, in despite of their officers, marched from Lancaster to Philadelphia,* to seek a redress of grievances. Joining with some troops, in the barracks of the city, their force was increased to three hundred, which proceeded with fixed bayonets and drums, to the state-house, where Congress, and the supreme executive council of Pennsylvania, held their sessions. They placed guards at every door, and sent to the council a written message, threatening to loose the soldiery upon them, if their demands were not granted within twenty minutes. Congress, though not the object of the soldiers resentment, deemed themselves grossly insulted, having been restrained of their liberty for several hours. Apprehensive of further ill consequence, from this insurrection, that body adjourned, to meet at Princeton, the next place of their assemblage. General Washington, informed of this outrage, despatched fifteen hundred men, under General Howe, to quell the mutiny, which, previously to their arrival, was suppressed, without bloodshed. Several of the mutineers were tried and condemned, two, to suffer death; and four, to receive corporal punishment; but all were afterwards pardoned.

XXXII. On the 25th of November, 1783, the British evacuated New

* June 20th, 1783.

York, and General Washington, attended by General Clinton, many civil and military officers, and a cavalcade of citizens, made a public entry into that city.

His military career was now on the point of terminating; but previously to divesting himself of his command, he proposed to bid adieu to his comrades in arms. The interview, for this purpose, took place on the fourth of December, at Francis' tavern. At noon, the principal officers had assembled, when he entered the room. His emotions were too strong to be concealed. Filling a glass with wine, he turned to them and said, "with a heart full of love and gratitude, I now take leave of you. I most devoutly wish, that your latter days may be as prosperous and happy as your former ones have been glorious and honourable." Having drank, he added, "I cannot come to each of you to take leave, but shall be obliged, if each will come and take me by the hand." General Knox being nearest, turned to him. Incapable of utterance, Washington grasped his hand, and embraced him. In the same affectionate manner, he took leave of all. Every eye was suffused with tears, and not a word broke the deep silence and tenderness of the scene. Leaving the room, he passed through the corps of light infantry, and walked to White Hall, where a barge waited to convey him to Paules Hook. The whole company followed in mute and solemn procession, testifying feelings of delicious melancholy, which no language can describe. Having entered the barge, he turned to his companions, and waving his hat, bade them a silent adieu. They returned the affectionate salute, and when the barge had left them, marched, in the same solemn manner, to the place where they had assembled.*

One other act remained, to render the fame of Washington, as imperishable as the globe on which he lived—to set an example of virtue and patriotism, which, through all time, shall inspire the good with the desire of imitation, and curb and defeat the demagogue, and the tyrant, who use political power for private ends. This was, the voluntary surrender of that almost dictatorial power, which had been granted by the sages of his country, and which he had used with unequalled prudence and conscientious reserve. This solemn and impressive duty, he performed at Annapolis, on the 23d of December, 1783, delivering his commission to the assembled council of the nation, from whom, eight years before, he had received it; and retiring to become, the first in peace, as he had been first in war, and first in the hearts of his countrymen.

* Marshall. Gordon.

CHAPTER XVIII.

I. Peculiar sufferings of the State of New Jersey from the War.—II. Laws in New Jersey relative to the Militia.—III. Council of Safety.—IV. Military efforts of New Jersey.—V. State Representatives in Congress.—VI. Establishment of the New Jersey Gazette.—VII. Unhappy Condition of the States after the return of Peace.—VIII. Inefficiency of the Articles of Confederation—Part of New Jersey in their Adoption.—IX. Measures proposed in Congress for maintaining Public Credit—Efforts of New Jersey upon this subject.—X. She resorts to Paper Currency and Loan Office for Relief.—XI. Difficulties with Great Britain relative to the Execution of the Treaty.—XII. Measures for regulating the Trade of the Union—Result in a Proposition for Revision of the Articles of Confederation.—XIII. Adoption of the New Constitution—Ratified by New Jersey.

I. In the rapid sketch we have given of the revolutionary war, we have endeavoured to place in full relief, those events, in which the State of New Jersey bore a distinguished part, or claimed a peculiar interest. We have, thus, noticed the battles and skirmishes which took place within and around her borders, and the injuries she sustained from the marauding parties of the enemy, and the requisitions of her friends. We have seen, that the American grand army, except for a period of nine months, between September, 1777, and June, 1778, when the British occupied Philadelphia, and for the two months of the autumn of 1781, employed against Cornwallis, in Virginia, was, during the whole war, within, or on the confines of, the State. Its presence necessarily drew upon her, the perpetual observation and frequent inroads of the enemy; so that her citizens were, at no time, relieved from the evils of war. Had the American army been regularly and fully paid, some, though inadequate compensation, might have been derived from the sale of her products to additional consumers. But, unhappily, those products were, too frequently, taken without payment, or were paid for in certificates, which, for the time, were worthless.

New Jersey, therefore, in the contest, to which she was as disinterested a party as any State in the Union, suffered more than her proportion, more than any other State, South Carolina excepted. Under these inflictions, the patriotism, patience, and fortitude of her people, were merits of the highest order. Her Legislature shrunk from no effort which the general interest required, and was, commonly, among the first to act upon the suggestions of Congress. After the victories of Trenton and Princeton, her militia, though continually harassed, by the cares of defending a long line of coast, turned out with promptness and energy, at the frequent calls of the commander-in-chief; and when actually invaded, in force, upon her eastern border, despatched considerable aid to her western sister State. The commander-in-chief, and his principal officers, bear abundant testimony to the activity, courage, and patriotism of her regular troops. Still, it remains, in order to display the part borne by the State, in the revolution, that we enter somewhat more fully into the peculiar measures she pursued.

II. The subject of militia service was then, as now, one of much difficulty, in all communities where the Quakers are numerous. The doctrine of non-resistance is more admirable in theory, than admissible in practice. Probably, it can exist, only, where the State possesses an adequate number of members, who are conscientiously scrupulous in defending their rights; and that a community of non-combatants, having wherewith to excite the cupidity of others, would be converted into soldiers or slaves. In

West Jersey, the Quakers were numerous, rich, and, as in Pennsylvania, many were not unfriendly to British pretensions. Their influence was sufficient to enervate the militia system. The ordinances of the Convention betrayed this; and the system became one of the first subjects of attention for the Legislature of the new State.

In a letter of the 24th of January, 1777, to Governor Livingston, General Washington complained of its inefficiency, and strenuously urged, that "every man capable of bearing arms, should be obliged to turn out, and not permitted to buy off his services for a trifling sum." The governor communicated and enforced this sentiment to the Legislature, whilst General Putnam, at this time, stationed at Princeton, irritated by the refusal of numbers to perform military duty, gave peremptory orders to apprehend delinquents, and to exact personal service, or to levy what he deemed proportionate fines. This arbitrary and illegal measure was properly reproved by the governor; but the general seems neither to have understood, nor relished the forbearance enjoined upon him, although sustained by orders of the commander-in-chief. In framing the new militia bill, the principle of pecuniary composition for service, was, tenaciously, retained. Again, Washington interfered, exclaiming, "How can an Assembly of gentlemen, eye witnesses to the distresses and inconveniences that have their principal source in the want of a well regulated militia, hesitate to adopt the only remedy that can remove them! And stranger still; think of a law, that must, necessarily, add to the accumulated load of confusion! For Heaven's sake, entreat them to lay aside their present opinions, and waving every other consideration, let the public good be singularly attended to! The ease they design their constituents, by composition, must be delusive. Every distinction between rich and poor, must be laid aside now."* Still the militia law, passed on the 15th of March, 1777, authorized the commutation of service, during the war.

III. More energy was infused into another act of the Legislature, enacted at this period, on the recommendation of the executive, constituting the governor, and twelve members of the Assembly, "a council of safety," with extraordinary and summary powers. The members had the authority of justices of the peace throughout the State,—they might fill vacancies in all offices during the recess of the Legislature—might correspond with Congress and other States, transact business with the officers of government, and prepare bills for the General Assembly—might apprehend disaffected persons, and imprison them, without bail or mainprize—might cause the laws to be faithfully executed, enforce the resolutions of the Assembly, and recommend to the speaker, to convene that body—and might call out such portions of the militia, as they should deem necessary, to execute the laws or protect themselves. The original act was limited to six months, but the powers given were continued and enlarged from time to time, until the middle of the year 1778. An attempt was unsuccessfully made, to revive this power in 1780. It was most usefully employed in detecting and punishing the tories.

IV. There is much difficulty in giving a minute and accurate account of the military efforts of the State. Those of the militia were, generally, desultory and momentary, whilst those of the regular troops are involved in the operations of the continental armies. All officers of the militia, above the grade of captain, were appointed by the council and Assembly, in joint meeting, who, also, nominated *all* the officers of the continental brigade, below the rank of brigadier. The militia officers, of all ranks, were frequently changed; but the changes in the brigade were little more than such as were occasioned by death and promotion.

* Sedgwick's Livingston—Vote of Assembly—State Laws.

The first brigadiers of militia were Philemon Dickenson, Isaac Williamson, and William Livingston. General Williamson resigned sixth of February, 1777. Mr. Livingston's commission was vacated by his election as governor. On the close of June, 1776, when the militia were ordered to meet the enemy operating against New York, Colonel Nathaniel Heard was promoted to the command of the detachment of three thousand three hundred volunteers, engaged to serve until December, which had been offered to Joseph Reed, who, about this time, entered the continental service. The colonels were Philip Van Cortland, Ephraim Martin, Stephen Hunt, Silas Newcomb; lieutenant-colonels, David Brearley, David Forman, John Munson, Philip Johnson, and Bowes Reed; brigade-major, Robert Hoopes. On the eighteenth of July, Congress having authorized the commander-in-chief to call to his assistance, two thousand men from the flying camp, the Convention of New Jersey supplied their place by a like number of militia. As the success of the enemy increased, and the danger to the State became imminent, still more strenuous measures were adopted. On the 11th of August, 1776, the Convention, by ordinance, divided the militia into two classes, ordering one-half into immediate service, to be relieved, monthly. The fine imposed on privates, refusing to serve, was three pounds, only. This forced effort was, necessarily, of short duration.

On the 15th of February, 1777, General Dickenson proposing to remove from the State, tendered to the Assembly his commission of brigadier, which was accepted with a vote of thanks, for his spirited and prudent conduct whilst in office. Joseph Ellis was named his successor, but declined the commission. On the twenty-first of February, David Potter and John Neilson, on the fourth of March, Colonel William Winds, on the fifth, David Forman, and on the fifteenth Silas Newcomb, were named brigadiers. Mr. Potter declined to serve. General Forman resigned on the 6th of November, and General Newcomb on the 4th of the following month. On the 6th of June, Mr. Dickenson, having abandoned his intention of leaving the State, was appointed major-general; he held this post during the war, was frequently, as we have seen, engaged in active service, giving high satisfaction to the commander-in-chief, the constituted authorities of the State, and the troops under his command.

To the continental army, New Jersey supplied two highly distinguished general officers, and a brigade, certainly, inferior to none in the service. Lord Sterling, remarkable for his zeal and energy as a whig, was, in October, 1775, a colonel in the militia of Somerset county. He was soon after appointed to the same rank, in the first continental regiment from the province, whilst William Maxwell received the colonelcy of the second. In December, of the same year, Lord Stirling was suspended by Governor Franklin, from his seat in Council. In January, 1776, he received the thanks of Congress, for the capture of the ship Blue Mountain Valley, which, with the aid of several gentlemen, volunteers from Elizabethtown, he surprised. In March following, he became brigadier, and in February, 1777, major-general, in the continental army. He died at Albany, 15th of January, 1783, whilst in chief command of the northern department. During the war, he rendered as much personal service as any officer of his rank; and to his military merit, General Washington has borne honourable testimony.*

* William Alexander, Earl of Stirling, was the only son of James Alexander, a distinguished lawyer, of New York, and at one time, Secretary of the Province of New Jersey. William commenced business as a merchant, in New York. In 1755, he was appointed one of the army contractors, by General Shirley; and, subsequently, private secretary to that commander. Being skilled in theoretic and practical

In February, 1776, a third battalion was raised in New Jersey, placed under the command of Colonel Maxwell, and marched for Canada. Under the resolutions of Congress, authorizing the raising of eighty-eight battalions, for the war, four were allowed to that State. In fitting them, recourse was had to the three battalions already in service, northward of Albany, and for the deficiency, to the five battalions, raised for one year, under the command of General Heard. Pursuant to the recommendation of Congress, of the 8th of October, 1779, the Assembly appointed a committee, consisting of Theophilus Elmer and Abraham Clark, to nominate the officers for the battalions, subject to the revision and confirmation of the Legislature. The first field-officers confirmed in joint meeting, were Colonels Elias Dayton, Ephraim Martin, Silas Newcomb, Isaac Shreve; Lieutenant-colonels David Brearley, Matthias Ogden, David Rhea, and Francis Barber; Majors William De Hart, Richard Howell, Joseph Bloomfield, and E. Howell. The company officers were appointed at the same time. Several changes in the field-officers, almost immediately took place.

Under the authority of Congress, in 1780, a new arrangement of the Jersey brigade was made, reducing the four battalions to three regiments, which was confirmed by the Assembly of the State, on the 26th of September, in the following manner, as to the field-officers. Of the first regiment, Matthias Ogden, colonel, David Brearley, lieutenant-colonel, Daniel Piatt, major; of the second regiment, Isaac Shreve, colonel, William De Hart, lieutenant-colonel, and Richard Howell, major; of the third, Elias Dayton, colonel, Francis Barber, lieutenant-colonel, and John Conway, major. The brigade, before and after it was thus constituted, was commanded by Brigadier-general Maxwell, and was employed, at times, in every part of the continent; wherever hard service was required, in the north, south, centre, and west.* Besides the distinguished military officers, we have above named, New Jersey gave to the continental army, Adjutant-general Joseph Reed, subsequently President of the Executive Council of Pennsylvania, and Elias Boudinot, the commissary-general of prisoners. This gentleman was, also, in 1783, President of Congress. In the civil department, she gave to the United States, a judge of admiralty, in Francis Hopkinson, and to Pennsylvania, an attorney-general, in Jonathan D. Sergeant.

V. In Congress, the State appears to have been uniformly and efficiently represented, and her delegates chosen, annually, by the Assembly, in joint ballot, to have borne an active part in all the important business of that body. We have heretofore given the names of her representatives, up to the adoption of the constitution of the State, and now append the names of those

mathematics, he was made surveyor-general of East Jersey. In September, 1756, he accompanied Shirley to England, and by his persuasions, was induced to claim the Scottish earldom of Stirling, of which he bore the family name, and which had been in abeyance, since 1739. He succeeded in establishing, in 1759, his direct descent from the titled family, before a jury of service, as required by the Scotch law, and, confident of final success, assumed the title, which was, at the same time, adopted by several other claimants. But the final decision depended on the House of Peers, which forbade all claimants of peerages to use the titles, until their rights were established. The decision was ultimately against him; but the title was given to him by courtesy, during the remainder of his life. Shortly after his return to America, he removed to Baskingridge, in the county of Somerset, New Jersey, where his father had owned extensive tracts of land; and being soon afterwards appointed a member of the King's Council, he remained at this place until the revolution. His letters to the Lords Bute and Shelburne, some of which remain, show an earnest desire to develope the resources of the colony. He made a map of the province, and endeavoured to foster its manufactures. In the year 1773, he exerted himself to discover the agents in the robbery of the treasurer, Stephen Skinner.—*Sedgwick's Life of Livingston.*

* General Maxwell resigned, 20th of July, 1780.

who served from that period, to the organization of the present federal government.*

VI. Among other measures, and certainly not the least efficient, adopted by the Legislature, in aid of the revolution, was the establishment of the public press, and the New Jersey Gazette; designed, among other good purposes, to counteract the influence of the Royal Gazette, published by Rivington, in New York. This matter was proposed to the Assembly on the 11th of October, 1777, and was undertaken by Mr. Isaac Collins, who had been printer to the province for some years; the Legislature engaging, for seven hundred subscribers, to establish a post from the printing office to the nearest continental post office, and to exempt the printer and four workmen from militia service. Mr. Collins was a Quaker, a whig, a man of enterprise, courage and discretion. The gazette was regularly published, until the 25th of November, 1786, when other presses having been established, it was discontinued, for want of patronage. It rendered essential service to the patriot cause, and was the vehicle for the lucubrations of Governor Livingston, and other writers, who animated and directed the efforts of their countrymen.

VII. The States had universally looked forward to the return of peace, with the establishment of their independence, as to a condition of unalloyed happiness. The unyielding firmness with which their trials had been borne, and the glorious termination of the contest, gave to the people much self-satisfaction, at home, and an honourable reputation, abroad, which served as powerful stimulus to pursue their high destinies with vigour. But many obstacles opposed the rapid progress which their hopes had predicted. In the course of the long war, the people had been greatly impoverished—their property had been seized for the support of both armies, and their labour had been much devoted to military service. The naval power of the enemy had almost annihilated their commerce; the price of imports was enhanced, whilst exports were reduced much below their ordinary value. On opening their ports, an immense quantity of foreign merchandise was poured into the country; and the citizens were, generally, tempted by the sudden cheapness of goods, and by their own wants, to purchase far beyond their means of payment. Into this indiscretion they were, in some measure, beguiled, by their own sanguine calculations, on the rise of the value of their products,

* The following named gentlemen were elected to Congress at the times respectively designated.—

1776, November 30th, Richard Stockton, Jonathan Dickenson Sergeant, Dr. John Witherspoon, Abraham Clark, and Jonathan Elmer. Mr. Stockton resigned, 10th of February, 1777.

1777, November 20th, Messrs. Witherspoon, Clark, and Elmer, Nathaniel Scudder, and Elias Boudinot.

1778, November 6th, Witherspoon, Scudder, Frederick Frelinghuysen, John Fell, and John Neilson.

1779, November 17th. The delegates were reduced to three, and were, John Fell, William Churchill Houston, and Thomas Henderson.

1780, November 23d, Witherspoon, Clark, Houston, William Patterson, and William Burnett.

1781, November 2d, Clark, Houston, Elmer, Boudinot, and Silas Condict.

1782, October 30th, Boudinot, Clark, Elmer, Condict, and Frelinghausen.

1783, November 6th, Elmer, Condict, John Stephens, sen., John Beatty, and Samuel Dick.

1784, October 29th, Houston, Beatty, Dick, Lambert Cadwallader, John Cleves Symmes, and Josiah Hornblower.

1785, October 28th, Cadwallader, Symmes, and Hornblower.

1786, November 7th, Cadwallader, Clark, and James Schureman.

1787, October 31st, Clark, Elmer, Patterson.

1788, Clark, Elmer, Jonathan Dayton.

and the evidences of the public debt, which were in the hands of most men. Extravagant estimates were made of the demand for lands, by the vast concourse of emigrants, which it was supposed equal liberty would bring from Europe; and adverting to the advantages gained by those who purchased on credit, during the prevalence of paper money, many individuals made extensive purchases at very high prices. The delusions, however, were soon dissipated, and a greater proportion of the inhabitants found themselves involved in debts they were unable to discharge. One of the consequences of this state of things, was a general discontent with the course of trade. From their superior skill and capital, and free admission to American ports, the British merchants had greater advantage in the American trade, than when the States were colonies; whilst the navigation of American ships to British ports, was prohibited, and American exports refused admission, or burdened with heavy duties. In the rich trade of the neighbouring colonies, the Americans were not permitted to participate, and in the ports of Europe they encountered embarrassing regulations. From the Mediterranean, they were excluded by the Barbary powers, whose hostility they could not subdue, and whose friendship they could not purchase.

The unpaid debt of the war was a source of great inconvenience to the country at home, whilst it caused ignominy and contempt abroad, from which there was no chance of escape, whilst the means of payment were derived from the State sovereignties. The debts of the union were computed to amount, on the first of January, 1783, to somewhat more than forty millions of dollars, which were due to three classes of highly meritorious creditors. To an *ally*, who, to the extensions of his arms, had added generous loans, and liberal donations;—to individuals in Holland, who, besides this precious token of confidence, were members of a republic, which was second in espousing our rank among nations—and to the soldiers of the war, whose patience and services, merited any other reward, than neglect and procrastination of payment; and to citizens who had originally loaned their funds, or had become purchasers of public securities.

This debt was due, part from the United States, and part from the individual States, who became immediately responsible to the creditors, retaining a claim against the general government, for the balance, which might appear on the settlement of accounts. The depreciation of the debts due from the Union, was consequent on its poverty, and inability to acquire funds; whilst the depreciation of the State debt, can be ascribed only to the want of confidence in governments controlled by no fixed principles.* In many of the States, public securities were sold at a discount of seventeen shillings in the pound. In private transactions, a great degree of distrust, also, prevailed. The bonds of debtors, of unquestioned solvency, were sold at fifty per cent. reduction; real estate was scarce vendible, and few articles could be sold for ready money, unless at a ruinous loss.

VIII. Much of the evils of this condition might have been readily removed, by an efficient general government, which could call forth and direct the wealth and energies of the people. But no such power could be derived from the loose articles of confederation, which had been, after much delay and reluctance, on the part of the States, finally adopted in 1781. These articles were laid before the Assembly of New Jersey, on the 4th of December, 1777. No action was had upon them during the then session, nor until the 15th of June, 1778, when the joint committee reported them, with sundry propositions of amendment:—1. That the delegates in Congress

* New Jersey provided for the payment of the interest, and for the final redemption of her domestic debt, by taxation.

should take an obligation to pursue the interests of the confederation, and, particularly, to assent to no measure which might violate it; 2. That the sole and exclusive power of regulating the trade of the United States with foreign nations, should be vested in Congress; and the revenue arising from the customs, should be appropriated to the establishment of a navy, and to other public and general purposes; 3. That no body of troops should be kept up by the United States in time of peace, except by the assent of nine States; 4. That the quotas of aids and supplies from the several States should be settled every five years; 5. That the boundaries of the several States should be fully and finally established, as soon as practicable within five years; 6. That the vacant crown lands should be deemed the spoils of the war, to be applied for the general benefit; and that whilst the jurisdiction of the several States was preserved with chartered or determined limits, the vacant lands should be vested in Congress, in trust for the United States; 7. That the requisitions on the several States for land forces, should be apportioned to the *whole* of the respective population, and not to the number of white inhabitants only; 8. That for equitably ascertaining the quota of troops of each State, a census of the inhabitants should be taken every five years; 9, and lastly, That the provision which required the assent of nine out of thirteen States, in certain cases, should be so modified, that the proportion should be preserved upon an increase of the number of States.

Although the inconvenience of amending the articles of confederation, may have prevented the incorporation of these propositions, it is obvious that the statesmen of New Jersey had foreseen and supplied the omission of many principles which were essential to the welfare, nay, the existence of the Union. At various times she enforced the propriety of the general regulation of trade, and of making the crown lands a common fund; and, finally, all her suggestions were adopted in the establishment of the Union. On the 14th of November, 1778, the Assembly, reasserting the propriety and expediency of their propositions, which they forebore to press, on account of the urgency of the case, and in the hope that the States would, in due time, remove the existing inequality, adopted the articles of confederation. And on the 20th, a law authorized their delegates in Congress, to subscribe them.

IX. The utter inefficiency of the articles of confederation, became apparent almost as soon as they were adopted, and was most conclusively exemplified, in the failure of the earnest endeavour to provide for the public debt, made in 1783. Two parties, as we have elsewhere observed, began to pervade the Union. One contemplated America as a nation, and laboured incessantly to invest the federal head with powers competent to the preservation of the Union. The other, attached to the State authorities, viewed all the powers of Congress with jealousy, and assented, reluctantly, to measures which tended to render them independent of the States. Sensible that the character of the government would be determined by the measures which should immediately follow the treaty of peace, gentlemen of distinguished political acquirements, among whom were some conspicuous officers of the late army, sought a place in the Congress of 1783. They procured the assent of the House, to a system, the best that circumstances would admit, to restore and support public credit, and to obtain from the States substantial means for the funding the whole debt of the nation. They proposed that adequate funds should be raised by duties on imports, and by internal taxes, for the immediate payment of the interest, and gradual extinction of the principal; and that the quotas of the several States, should be determined, not by the value of the located lands, but by the extent of its population. It was proposed, also, as an amendment to the 8th article of the confederation, that the taxes for the use of the continent, should be levied, separately, from other taxes, and paid directly into the national treasury, and that the collectors should be subject and responsible to Congress. To prevent the preference in payment, for part of the debts, which might result from a partial adoption of the system, it was declared, that no part of the revenue system should take effect, until the whole had been adopted by all the States; after which, the grant was to be irrevocable, except by the concurrence of the whole, or by a majority of the United States in Congress assembled. But to remove the jealousy which obstructed the grant of power, to collect an indefinite sum for an indefinite time, the proposition was modified, so that the grant was to be limited to twenty-five years, to be strictly appropriated to the debt contracted on account of the war, and collected by persons appointed by the respective States. These resolutions were adopted on the 18th of April, 1783; and a committee, consisting of Mr. Madison, Mr. Hamilton, and Mr. Ellsworth, was appointed to recommend them by an address to the people, and Washington, himself, joined in this object, by a circular addressed to the governors of the States, respectively.*

While the fate of these measures remained undecided, requisitions for the intermediate supply of the national demands, were annually repeated, but annually neglected. From the first of November, 1784, to the first of January, 1786, there had been paid to the public treasury, only 482,397 dollars. Happily, a loan had been negotiated in Holland, by Mr. Adams, after the termination of the war, out of which the interest of the foreign debt had been partly paid; but that fund was exhausted. Unable to pay the interest, the United States would, in the course of the succeeding year, be liable for the first instalment of the principal; and the humiliation of total failure, in the fulfilment of her engagements, would be accompanied with no hope of future ability. If the condition of the domestic creditors was not absolutely hopeless, their prospect of payment was so remote, that the evidences of their claim were transferred at a tenth of their nominal value. In a word, in 1786, a crisis had arrived, when the *people of the United States* were required to decide, whether, by the establishment of a secure and permanent revenue, and the maintenance of public faith, at home and abroad, they would sustain their rank as a *nation*.

In the course of the year 1786, the revenue system, proposed in April, 1783, had been adopted by every State in the Union, New York excepted. That State had passed an act upon the subject, but influenced by its jealousy of the Federal Government, had not vested in Congress the power of collecting the duties specified in their resolutions; but had reserved to itself the levying of the duties according to its own laws, made the collectors answerable only to the State, and the duties payable in State bills, which were liable to depreciation. As the assent of every State was indispensable to the success of the plan, it was thus, wholly defeated.

New Jersey, overshadowed by her overgrown neighbours, New York and Pennsylvania, whose capitals and whose ports, made them importers, not only for themselves, but for her, had a grievance peculiarly her own—paying the duties which those States, severally, levied upon the merchandise she consumed. She was, therefore, induced, by the strongest ties of interest, to support the federative system, by which such duties, instead of being levied by individual States for their special benefit, would be received and expended for the general weal of the nation; and was indignant, that the system had been rejected by New York. Certain resolutions, expressive of her sense, upon this and other momentous subjects, were reported to the Assembly, by Mr. Abraham Clarke, on the 20th of February, 1786, and

* Dated June 8th, 1783.

afterwards embodied in instructions to her delegates in Congress, to the following effect.

"When the revenue system of April 18th, 1783, was passed in Congress, we were then in hopes that our situation, between two commercial States, would no longer operate to our detriment; and that, those States, and others in their predicament, were, at length, convinced of the selfish and palpable injustice of subjecting others to their exactions, and then applying those exactions to the augmentation of their respective private revenues."

"The same contracted and destructive policy, that has long subsisted, still continues; and as we are convinced, that neither the public credit can be supported, the public debts paid, or the existence of the Union maintained, without the impost revenue, in some beneficial effective manner, it has become our duty to instruct you, to vote against each and every ordinance, resolution, or proceeding, whatever, which shall produce any expense to New Jersey, for the promotion or security of the commerce of these States, or any of them, from which neither the Union, in general, nor this State, in particular, derives any advantage, until all the States shall, effectually, and substantially, adopt and carry into execution, the impost above mentioned. You will see, by the representation of this State, June 25th, 1778, that the Legislature have, uniformly, held the same justice of sentiment, respecting the vacant or crown lands; relative to which, you are instructed—to vote against every proceeding, which shall tend to charge this State with any expense for acquiring, gaining possession of, or defending such territory, claimed by, or which is to accrue to, the exclusive benefit of any particular State or States, and not the Union at large."

"The Legislature has beheld, with much concern, gratuitous advances of money and partial payments, made by Congress, to importuning creditors and others, not regulated by any general and equal system, which not only impoverish the treasury, but produce discontents, and furnish bad precedents. You are, therefore, instructed not to assent to any such payments, or to the payment of any particular debts, other than foreign loans, in preference to others of a like nature, whereby a discrimination of creditors may take place. It were well if the public could pay all, promptly, but as that is impracticable, it is absolutely necessary, to act upon settled uniform plans, in paying as far as the revenue can extend."

The Assembly, also, resolved, for these reasons, "that they could not, consistently with the duty they owed to their constituents, comply with the requisition of Congress of the 27th of September, 1785, or any other of a similar nature, requiring specie contributions, until all the States in the Union should comply with the requisition of April, 1783, or at least, until the several States, having the advantage of commerce, which they now enjoy, solely from the joint exertions of the United States, shall forbear exacting duties upon merchandise, for the particular benefit of their respective States, thereby drawing revenues from other States, whose local situation and circumstances, would not admit their enjoying similar advantages from commerce."

This resolution proved so embarrassing to Congress, that a committee was appointed from that body, personally, to remonstrate with the Legislature of New Jersey, and to endeavour to procure its repeal. Whereupon, the House resolved, that "being willing to remove, as far as in their power, every embarrassment, from the councils of the Union, and that the failure of supplies from temporary demands, though clearly evinced from experience, may not be imputed to the State of New Jersey, only, the resolution of the twentieth of February, should be rescinded." Thus disappointed in procuring an equalization of the customs, the State, from the many petitions upon this subject, seems to have prepared itself for the establishment of a tariff of duties, upon all goods imported from the adjacent States. A measure which could have resulted only in awakening dangerous feuds with her neighbours, and in the greater oppression of her own citizens.

X. To relieve the pecuniary distress which weighed upon this State, in common with the rest of the Union, the Legislature resorted to the old expedient of issuing bills of credit, and lending them upon mortgage, through loan offices, established in the several counties. A bill for striking and making current, one hundred thousand pounds, was passed by the Assembly, in March, 1786, but was rejected in Council. The cries of the people, however, were too general and loud, to be thus disregarded; and a special session of the Legislature was holden on the 17th of May, following, when the bill passed both Houses.

XI. To increase the gloom which hung over the Union, difficulties had arisen relative to the execution of the treaty with Great Britain, which had been broken by both parties. The British had not delivered up, nor paid for, the slaves of the southern planters, nor surrendered the military posts upon the borders. Nor had the United States complied with the 4th, 5th, and 6th articles, containing agreements respecting the payment of private debts, due the British merchants, the confiscation of property, and the prosecution of individuals, for the part taken by them, during the war. Complaints were also, made, of British encroachments on the territory of the United States, from the eastern frontier. But the cause of the greatest disquiet, was the rigorous commercial system, pursued by Great Britain. To settle these vexatious questions, Mr. John Adams was, in February, 1785, appointed plenipotentiary of the United States to the British court. His efforts to give reciprocity and stability to the commercial relations, between the two countries, were unavailing; the cabinet of London declining negotiation with a government, which was unable to secure the observance of any general regulation, and to make the obligations of a treaty reciprocal.

XII. All these circumstances rendered a modification of the compact between the States, not only desirable, but inevitable, if their union was to be preserved. The immediate measures leading to a change, commenced in Virginia. On the 21st of January, 1786, a resolution was adopted in the Legislature of that State, appointing commissioners "to meet such as might be appointed by the other States in the Union, at a time and place to be agreed on, to take into consideration the trade of the United States; to examine the relative situation and trade of the said States; to consider how far a uniform system in their commercial relations may be necessary to their common interests, and their present harmony, and to report to the several States, such an act, relative to this great object, as when unanimously ratified by them, will enable the United States, in Congress assembled, effectually, to provide for the same." In the circular letter transmitting these resolutions to the respective States, Annapolis, in Maryland, was proposed as the place, and the ensuing September as the time, of meeting.

This resolution was submitted to the Legislature of New Jersey, on the 14th of March, 1786, and concurred in, a few days after. On the 21st, in joint meeting, Messrs. Abraham Clarke, William C. Houston, and James Schureman, were appointed delegates to the convention at Annapolis.

But five States,* only, were represented, on this important occasion. The delegates having appointed Mr. John Dickinson their chairman, proceeded to discuss the objects of their convention; when they soon perceived, that more ample powers were requisite to effect their contemplated purpose. They

* New York, New Jersey, Pennsylvania, Delaware, and Maryland.

rose, therefore, without coming to any resolution, save that of recommending, to the several States, the necessity of extending the revision of the federal system, to all its defects, and the appointment of deputies for that purpose, to meet in convention, in the city of Philadelphia, on the second day of the ensuing May.

This proposition was variously received, in accordance with the temper of the several parties in the Union. Those who sought the energetic government of monarchy, and those who earnestly desired to break up the old confederation, believed, that the public affairs had not yet reached their worst state—that state which would compel a change; and, therefore, they looked coldly upon it. Others deemed the mode of calling the convention, irregular; whilst others objected to it, because it gave no authority to the plan, which should be devised. But its most active opponents were the devotees of state sovereignty, who deprecated any considerable augmentation of federal power. The ultimate decision of the States, in favour of the proposition, is supposed to have been produced, by the commotions which at that time agitated all New England, and particularly Massachusetts. Congress was restrained from giving its sanction to the measure, by an apprehension, that their action upon it would impede, rather than promote, it. From this fear, they were relieved by the Legislature of New York, which, by a majority of one voice, only, instructed its delegation to move in Congress, a resolution, recommending to the several States, to appoint deputies to meet in convention, for the purpose of revising, and proposing amendments to, the federal constitution. On the 21st of February, 1787, the day succeeding the instructions given by New York, Congress resolved it "to be expedient, that on the second Monday in May next, a convention of delegates, who shall have been appointed by the several States, be held at Philadelphia, for the sole and express purpose of revising the articles of confederation, and reporting to Congress, and the several Legislatures, such alterations and provisions, therein, as shall, when agreed to, in Congress, and confirmed by the States, render the federal constitution adequate to the exigencies of government, and the preservation of the Union."

On the 24th of November, 1786, New Jersey had approved the measure, and nominated David Brearley, William C. Houston, William Patterson, and John Neilson, commissioners on her part; to whom she afterwards added, Governor Livingston, and Abraham Clark, on the 19th of May, 1787, (omitting the name of Mr. Nielson,) and Jonathan Dayton, on the 7th of June.

XIII. The representatives of twelve States convened at the time and place appointed; Rhode Island, alone, having refused to send deputies. Having, unanimously, chosen General Washington their president, they proceeded with closed doors, to discuss the interesting subject submitted to them. Upon the great principles of the system, not much contrariety of opinion is understood to have prevailed; but the various and intricate modifications of those principles, presented much difficulty. More than once, there was reason to fear, that the convention would rise without effecting the object for which it was formed. Happily, the advantages of the Union triumphed over local interests. And at length, on the 17th of September, the constitution of the United States of America, was given to the world.

Although earnestly devoted to the establishment of a strong and permanent government for the Union, New Jersey was anxious to preserve the original equality of the States, which had given to each, in Congress, before and after the adoption of the articles of confederation, a voice alike potential. The pretension was unjust, considering the United States as composed of one people, but had a colour of propriety when they were viewed as a confederation of independent States. The "New Jersey plan," as it was termed, was proposed by Mr. Patterson, and sustained by the delegates of New Jersey, Connecticut, Delaware, and in part of Maryland. To its introduction we, probably, owe that provision of the constitution of the United States, which gave from the several States, an equal representation in the Senate.*

The convention directed the result of their labours to be laid before Congress; and that it should afterwards be submitted to a convention of delegates, chosen in each State by the *people*, thereof, under the recommendation of its Legislature, for their assent and ratification; and that so soon as the conventions of nine States should have ratified it, it should be carried into operation by Congress, in a mode prescribed.

When submitted to the *people*, the merits of this constitution were fully and rigorously discussed, not only in the several conventions, but in the periodical papers of the day. The federal, and the State-right parties, which divided the country, maintained their views with equal zeal; but the first, after an arduous struggle, prevailed. In producing this result, Messrs. Madison, Jay, and Hamilton, were among the most efficient and distinguished agents, and their essays under the title of the ***Federalist***, form a valuable treatise on government, which must continue to be the text book for, at least, the statesmen of North America.

So balanced were the parties in some of the States, that even after the constitution had been long discussed, its fate could scarcely be conjectured; and so small in many instances, was the majority in its favour, as to afford ground to believe, that had the influence of character been removed, the merits of the instrument would not have secured its adoption. And in some of the adopting States, a majority of the people are supposed to have been opposed to it. The commissioners of New Jersey, reported to the Assembly the proceedings of the Convention, on the 25th of October, 1787. And Congress having unanimously resolved, that the constitution be transmitted to the several States, for consideration, the House, unanimously, on the 29th of October, recommended, such inhabitants of the State as were entitled to vote for representatives in the General Assembly, to elect on the fourth Tuesday of November, from each county, three delegates to a convention, to meet at Trenton, on the second Tuesday of December, to consider, and if approved, to ratify, the constitution.

The State Convention met on the 11th of December, 1787, and chose John Stephens, president, and Samuel Witham Stockton, secretary. After establishing rules for its government, it resolved, "that the federal constitu-

* The plan of Mr. Patterson contemplated the amendment of the articles of confederation—By vesting in Congress power—To raise a revenue by duties on imposts, stamps, and postage—To regulate trade and commerce with foreign nations, and between the States; all punishments, fines, forfeitures, and penalties, to be adjudged by the common law judiciary of the State, in which the offence should be committed, subject to an appeal to the judiciary of the United States—To make requisitions upon the several States, in proportion to the whole number of inhabitants, including those bound to servitude for a term of years, and three-fifths of slaves; and in case of non-compliance, to direct the collection of the same—To elect a Federal Executive to consist of several persons, paid by Congress, having power to appoint all Federal officers, &c.—To establish a Federal Judiciary, consisting of a supreme tribunal, appointed by the Executive, during good behaviour, to have original jurisdiction in case of impeachment, and appellate jurisdiction in cases relating to ambassadors, captures, piracy and felony on the sea—To impose an oath of fidelity, &c. on all officers—To make the Federal laws and treaties the supreme laws of the land, and to call forth the military powers of the confederated States, to enforce such laws—To provide for the admission of new States into the Union—To provide for deciding upon all disputes between the United States and an individual State, respecting territory—To make a uniform rule of naturalization, &c. &c.

tion be read, by sections, and that, as so read, every member make his observations thereon; that after debating such section, the question be taken, whether further debate be had thereon; and if determined in the negative, that the convention proceed in like manner to the next section, until the whole be gone through; upon which the general question shall be taken, Whether the Convention in the name, and on behalf of the people of this State, do ratify and confirm the said constitution?" And on Tuesday, the 18th of December, the constitution was, unanimously, adopted, without a single amendment. On the 19th, the members of the Convention went in solemn procession, to the Court House, where the ratification was publicly read to the people.*

The twelve articles of amendment, which were proposed and adopted, at the first session of the first Congress, were ratified by this State, by an act passed on the 20th of November, 1789. That the happiness of all the citizens of the United States has been promoted and secured, by the Federal Constitution, admits not of doubt. But, to New Jersey, especially, that instrument brought peace, protection and prosperity. Condemned, by circumstances, which she could not control, to abandon all prospect of foreign commerce, she would have been dependant upon New York on the east, and Pennsylvania on the west, for her supplies of foreign merchandise. For so valuable a customer, those States would, probably, have contended between themselves; and the inhabitants on the shores of the Delaware and its tributaries, would have made common interest with Philadelphia, whilst those on the banks of the Hudson and the sea coast, would have been controlled by the merchants of New York. Less causes have divided States, have given birth to civil wars, followed by the subjection of the country. New Jersey might have become the prize for which her great neighbours would have resorted to arms; and her greatest happiness might have been, to be conquered by the strongest.

From the dread of these evils, the Union has, happily, delivered her, and left her at perfect liberty to pursue, with unerring certainty, the welfare of her citizens. Debarred from foreign commerce, she has turned her providence to agriculture and manufactures. For the first, the diversity of her soils is admirably adapted. For the second, her mines and her streams have fitly prepared her. From both, she has continued to derive, abundantly, morals, wealth, and happiness. Since the adoption of the Federal Constitution, few subjects of historical interest have occurred,—public business has flowed in a silent and tranquil stream, and individual prosperity has been uninterrupted. The fondest wish of the patriot heart, must be, that the Union, the Federal Constitution, and the weal of the State, which are inseparable, may, also, be perpetual.

* New Jersey was the third State to ratify the constitution, being preceded only by Delaware, on the 7th, and Pennsylvania, on the 12th, of December.

APPENDIX.

NOTE A.—Page 6.

The Hudson and Delaware rivers have been known under various names, by the aborigines and the whites. Thus, the Hudson was called *Manahatta*, from an Indian nation near its mouth. *Mahakaneghtaç*, or *Mohican-nittuck*, and *Mohegan*, from the Mohicans; *Shattemuck*, perhaps a corruption of the preceding; and *Cohetaba*, by the Iroquois. The Dutch and English termed it the North, to distinguish it from the Delaware, or South river. The Dutch also called it Mauritius river, in honour of Prince Maurice. The Spaniards are supposed to have called it *Riviere de Montagnes*, from the Highlands through which it passes.

The Delaware, among the natives, was known as the *Poutaxat*, *Marisqueton*, *Makeriskitton*, and *Makerisk-kiskon*, and *Lenape-wihittuck*, stream of the Lenape. By the Dutch it was called Zuydt, or South, Nassau, Prince Kendrick's, or Charles' river; and by the English, the Delaware. The derivation of the last name is doubtful. Campanius says it was so named, from Mons. De la Warre, a captain under Chartier; and that it was discovered in 1600; whilst Stith informs us, that Thomas West, Lord Delaware, discovered and gave it his name, in 1610, and that he died opposite its mouth, on a second voyage to Virginia, in 1618. In Heylin's Cosmography, originally written in 1648, but continued by Edward Bohun to 1703, this river is called *Arasapha*.

NOTE B.—Page 18.

The description given by Plantagenet, was doubtless very enticing, and it would seem that the country had been pretty well explored, since he speaks familiarly of "iron stone, and by it, waters and falls, to drive iron-works, in an uninhabited desert." He speaks also, of lions, for which probably the panthers were taken. On religious subjects, the views of the projectors were liberal for the age, since there was to be "no persecution to any dissenting; and to all such, as to the Walloons, in Holland, free chapels; and to punish all as seditious, and for contempt, as bitter rail, and condemn others of the contrary."

NOTE C.—Page 34.

There is a singular pleasure in contrasting the order and moral beauty which has arisen from the chaotic materials of primitive Quakerism. To the philosophic mind, the dependence on the *divine light within*, as the guide of moral action, is little else than an abandonment of the understanding to every capricious impulse, and "wind of doctrine." Intense zeal has but two modes of expending itself—by action upon others, or upon ourselves. In the first case, its fruits are, commonly, active force and oppression, of which the history of every sect, is but too full of example; and in the second, it is passive resistance, whose reaction is equal to any power that can be brought to bear upon it. But this species of force requires the homogeneity and condensation of the parts of the suffering body. These were given by the establishment of the "discipline" of the Quakers, providing practical rules of action for life, and requiring the assent of a large portion of the society, to all public demonstrations of its faith and doctrines; whilst, at the same time, watchful guardians observed and regulated, by timely monition, the walking of the brethren. In these causes, of which the peculiarity of garb, the Quaker uniform, is but part, lay the strength of the society. The persecution it sustained, was an exterior force aiding its integrity and preservation, and without which, it is possible, the society cannot resist the centrifugal power of the *inward divine light*. For, when that ceased, a disintegration commenced, which has already produced a broad separation of the parts, and may ultimately resolve the whole body into primitive monads.

From the writings of modern historians, and apologists of Quakerism, we might suppose, that none of the Quakers, who were imprisoned by the magistrates, at this period, had been accused of aught but the profession of their peculiar doctrines, or attendance at their peculiar places of worship.. But very different causes of their imprisonment, have been transmitted to us, even by the sufferers themselves, and which leave it questionable whether the greatest wrong they sustained, was not the committal to the gaol, instead of the lunatic hospital. These sectarians, who have always professed and inculcated the maxims of inviolable peace, who not many years after their association, were accounted philosophical deists, seeking to pave the way to a scheme of natural religion, by allegorizing the distinguishing articles of the Christian faith, and who are, now, in general, remarkable for calm benevolence, and peculiar remoteness from active efforts to make proselytes, were, in their infancy, the most impetuous zealots, and inveterate disputers. In their eagerness to convict the world, and to bear witness from the fountain of oracular testimony, which they supposed to reside within them, against a regular ministry, which they called a priesthood of Baal, and against the sacraments, which they termed carnal and idolatrous observances, many committed the most revolting blasphemy, indecency, and disorderly outrage.

We refer our readers, on this subject, to *Sewal's History*, Howell's State Trials, vol. v. p. 801—vol. vi. p. 998; Hume's History of England, vol. vii. p. 336; Besse's "Collection of the Sufferings of the People called Quakers;" Fox's Journal, &c.

NOTE D.—Page 37.

The being a party to this agreement, constitution, or concessions, confers an honour upon a descendant, of which many inhabitants of New Jersey may now justly boast. The names of the signers, one hundred and fifty in number, may be found in the Appendix to Smith's History, page 538, and Leaming and Spicer's Collection, page 409.

NOTE E.—Page 38.

Thomas Hutchinson, of Beverley; Thomas Pierson, of Bonwicke, yeoman; Joseph Helmsly, of Great Kelke, yeoman; George Hutchinson, of Sheffield, distiller; and Mahlon Stacy, of Hansworth, tanner; all of the county of York, were principal creditors of E. Byllinge, to whom several of the other creditors made assignments of their debts, which together amounted to the sum of £2450 sterling, and who took in satisfaction, seven full, equal and undivided ninetieth parts of ninety equal and undivided hundred parts of West Jersey; and the same was conveyed to them, their heirs and assigns, by William Penn, Gawen Lawrie, Nicholas Lucas, and E. Byllinge, by deed, bearing date, *the first of the month called March*, 1676: And by another conveyance of the same date, from and to the same persons, in satisfaction for other debts, to the amount of £1050 sterling, three other full, equal and undivided ninetieth parts of the aforesaid ninety equal and undivided hundred parts of West Jersey, were also conveyed.—*Smith's Hist. New Jersey*, p. 92, *n.*

NOTE F.—Page 39.

Among these first settlers of Burlington, were Thomas Olive, Daniel Wills, William Peachy, William Clayton, John Crips, Thomas Eves, Thomas Harding, Thomas Nositer, Thomas Farnworth, Morgan Drewet, William Pennton, Henry Jennings, William Hibes, Samuel Lovett, John Woolston, William Woodmaney, Christopher Saunders, and Robert Powell. John Wilkinson and William Perkins were with their families, passengers, but dying on the voyage, the latter were duly protected, and aided by their fellow passengers. Perkins became a Quaker, early in life, and lived well in Leicestershire; but, in the fifty-second year of his age, was induced, by a favourable account of New Jersey, written by Richard Hartshorne, to embark with his wife, four children, and some servants. Among the last, was one Marshall, a carpenter, whose services were most useful in setting up the habitations of the new comers.

NOTE G.—Page 40.

In the *Willing Mind* came James Nevill, Henry Salter, George Deacon, and other families; in the *Martha*, Thomas Wright, William Goforth, John Lynam, Edward Season, William Black, Richard Dungworth, George Miles, William Wood, Thomas

Schooley, Richard Harrison, Thomas Hooten, Samuel Taylor, Marmaduke Horseman, William Oxley, William Lex, Nathaniel Luke, the families of Robert Stacy, and Samuel Odas, and Thomas Ellis, and John Barts, servants sent by George Hutchinson. Letters from the first emigrants, from John Cripps, Thomas Hooten, William Clark, and others, to their friends in England, descriptive of the richness and capabilities of the soil, abundance of game and fruits, temperature of the climate, excellence of the water, and kindness of the aborigines, induced many to emigrate. In *The Shield*, came William Emley, the second time, with his wife, two children, one born by the way, two men, and two women servants; Mahlon Stacy, his wife, children, and several servants, men and women; Thomas Lambert, his wife, children, and several men and women servants; John Lambert and servant; Thomas Revell, his wife, children, and servants; Godfrey Hancock, his wife, children, and servants; Thomas Potts, his wife, and children; John Wood and four children; Thomas Wood, wife, and children; Robert Murfin, his wife, and two children; Robert Schooley, his wife, and children; James Pharo, wife, and children; Susannah Farnsworth, her children, and two servants; Richard Tattersal, his wife, and children; Godfrey Newbold, John Dewsbury; Richard Green, Peter and John Fretwell; John Newbold; one Barns, a merchant from Hull, Francis Barwick, George Parks, George Hill, John Heyres, and several more.

In the ship from London, 1678, came John Denn, Thomas Kent, John Hollinshead, with their families; William Hewlings, Abraham Hewlings, Jonathan Eldridge, John Petty, Thomas Kirby, with others: the first of these settled about Salem, the rest at Burlington. About this time, and a few years afterwards, arrived at Burlington, the following settlers from England, viz. John Butcher, Henry Grubb, William Butcher, William Brightwin, Thomas Gardner, John Budd, John Bourten, Seth Smith, Walter Pumphrey, Thomas Ellis, James Satterthwaite, Richard Arnold, John Woolman, John Stacy, Thomas Eves, Benjamin Duffeld, John Payne, Samuel Cleft, William Cooper, John Shinn, William Biles, John Skein, John Warrel, Anthony Morris, Samuel Bunting, Charles Read, Francis Collins, Thomas Mathews, Christopher Wetherill, John Dewsbury, John Day, Richard Basnett, John Antrem, William Biddle, Samuel Furnace, John Ladd, Thomas Raper, Roger Huggins, and Thomas Wood.

About this time also, arrived John Kinsey. His father, one of the commissioners, dying on his arrival, the charge of the family fell upon him. He and his son became much distinguished in the province, holding many public stations. The latter died chief justice of Pennsylvania.

NOTE H.—Page 43.

The names of this Assembly and Council, and the forms of their engagements, may be seen in Leaming and Spicer's Collection of Grants, &c. p. 456.

NOTE I.—Page 46.

We purposed to reprint here, the act relating to the Confession of Faith; but our space does not permit it. It will be found in Leaming and Spicer's Collection, p. 548.

NOTE K.—Page 48.

The salary of the Governor was, generally, fifty pounds a year, paid in country produce, at prices fixed by law, and sometimes, four shillings a day besides, to defray the charges while a session was held: the wages of the Council and Assembly, during the sitting in legislation, was, to each member, three shillings a day: the rates for public charges, were levied at two shillings a head, for every male above fourteen years.

In 1668 the council consisted of six, viz. Nicholas Verlet, Robert Bond, Robert Vanquellin, Daniel Price, Samuel Edsall, and William Pardon; the Assembly of twelve, viz. Casper Steenmets, Baltazar Bayard for Bergen, John Ogden, senior, John Brackett for Elizabethtown, Robert Treat and Samuel Swame for Newark, John Bishop and Robert Dennis for Woodbridge, James Grover and John Bound for Middletown and Shrewsbury.

NOTE L.—Page 51.

It is not difficult to understand how a friendly intercourse originated between the leading persons among the Quakers, and Charles II. and his brother. The

Quakers desired to avail themselves of the authority of the King, for the establishment of a general toleration, and for their own especial defence against the enmity and dislike of their numerous adversaries. The King and his brother regarded, with great benevolence, the principles of non-resistance, professed by Friends, and found in them, the only class of Protestants, who could be rendered instrumental to their design of re-establishing Popery, by the preparatory measure of general toleration. But how the friendly relation thus created, between the royal brothers, and such men as Penn and Barclay, should have continued to exist, uninterrupted by all the tyranny and treachery which the reigns of these princes disclosed, is a difficulty which their contemporaries were unable to solve, otherwise than by considering the Quakers, as at bottom, the votaries of Popery and arbitrary power. The more modern and juster, as well as more charitable censure is, that they were dupes of kingly courtesy, craft, and dissimulation. They endeavoured to make an instrument of the King; while he permitted them to flatter themselves with this hope, that he might avail himself of their instrumentality, for the accomplishment of his own designs.—*Grahame's Col. Hist.*

NOTE M.—Page 51.

By recurring to the letters of Rudyard, first deputy-governor of East Jersey, Samuel Groome, surveyor, Lawrie, deputy-governor, John Barclay, and Arthur Forbes, to the proprietaries in London, the reader will perceive how strong and favourable were the impressions on the minds of the first settlers, in relation to the country. See Smith's Hist. New Jersey, from page 168 to 188.

NOTE N.—Page 55.

The counsellors named in the instructions were Edward Hunlake, Lewis Morris, Andrew Bowne, Samuel Jennings, Thomas Revel, Francis Davenport, William Pinhorne, Samuel Leonard, George Deacon, Samuel Walker, Daniel Leeds, William Sanford, and Robert Quarry. Quarry was said to be of the council of five governments at one time; viz. New York, New Jersey, Pennsylvania, Maryland, and Virginia. He died about the year 1712.—*Smith*, p. 231, *n*.

NOTE O.—Page 66.

A dispute was long pending between the general proprietors and the inhabitants of Newark, relating to lands included within the bounds of three Indian purchases, called the Mountain, the Horse Neck, and Van Gieson's. After several suits at law and equity, the contest was referred to arbitrators, mutually chosen by the parties, who awarded in favour of the general proprietors. Some of the defendants, dissatisfied with the award, endeavoured to excite the others to further contest, gave occasion for the letter of Mr. Ogden, who was council for the proprietors. His clear and satisfactory exposition of the case, most probably prevented a continuation of the controversy. We find the letter too long to be copied. It may be seen in a small pamphlet, in the Philadelphia Library, as noted, at page 66 of the text.

NOTE P.—Page 77.

The curious reader will find at the end of vol. iv. of the printed Minutes of the Assembly, in the State Library, at Trenton, a MSS. "table of the sittings of Assembly, from the surrender, in the year 1702, to the revolution, in 1776, with the names of the governors and speakers;" and also, "a list of the members of Assembly during the same period."

NOTE Q.—Page 81.

Names of the Legislative Council, in 1707, Richard Ingoldsby, lieutenant-governor, William Pinhorne, R. Mompesson, Thomas Revell, Daniel Leeds, Daniel Coxe, Richard Townly, Robert Quarry, and William Sandford.

NOTE R.—Page 82.

This illness of Jennings proved mortal, after a year's duration. He was a zealous minister among "Friends;" and upon all occasions took an active part in public affairs, in which he was alike distinguished by ability and integrity. His warm and sanguine temperament, was ordinarily controlled by a sound and experienced judgment; but it sometimes betrayed him into hasty and passionate conduct, of which his treatment to Keith, the apostate Quaker, whilst on trial before the court at Philadelphia, was a remarkable instance, and perhaps justified the charge made by the schismatic, that " he was too high and imperious, in worldly courts." He was an ardent lover of liberty, and firm and fearless in its defence. And though his manners were stern and severe, he was always sought by the people when important services were required. Twenty-eight years of his life were devoted to public employment; part of which, in Philadelphia. In private life, says Smith, " alive to the more generous emotions of a mind formed to benevolence, and acts of humanity, he was a friend to the widow, the fatherless, and the unhappy; tender, compassionate, disinterested, and with great opportunities, he left but a small estate; abhorring oppression in every shape, his whole conduct, a will to relieve and befriend mankind, far above the littleness of party and sinister views. He left three daughters, who intermarried with three brothers, by the name of Stevenson, whose posterity reside in New Jersey and Pennsylvania."

Thomas Gordon, his successor, was intimately connected with the proprietaries of East Jersey, before the surrender of the government in 1702. In 1697–8, he was deputy-secretary, and register of the province, and one of the council; and in 1702, on the removal of William Dockwra, he was appointed principal secretary. He was several years a representative in the Assembly, after the surrender; was treasurer for the eastern divison of the province, and distinguished in Perth Amboy as a pious member and liberal patron of the Episcopal church. He died on the 28th of April, 1722, aged seventy years. A tomb-stone in the grave-yard of St. Peter's church, at Amboy, with a long Latin inscription, commemorates his virtues.

NOTE S.—Page 83.

The Assembly of New York adopted resolutions, declaring, that the levying money on her Majesty's subjects of the colony, under any pretence, without the consent of the General Assembly, was a violation of the people's property; and that the freemen of the colony had an unquestionable, perfect and entire property in their goods and estate. We recognise here, the principles which subsequently led to the revolution. The Assembly, also, denounced the practice of Cornbury, in levying imposts on trade, and establishing fees without the sanction of law.

NOTE T.—Page 86.

The members of Council named in the instructions of Governor Hunter, were Lewis Morris, William Pinhorne, George Deacon, Richard Townley, Daniel Coxe, Roger Mompesson, Peter Sonmans, Hugh Huddy, William Hall, Thomas Gordon, Thomas Gardiner, Colonel Robert Quarry. The Queen, on the receipt of the remonstrance of the Assembly, appointed John Anderson, Elisha Parker, Thomas Byerly, John Hamilton, and John Reading; removing Pinhorne, Coxe, Sonmans, and Hall.

NOTE U.—Page 94.

We give the following abstract from the minutes of the Assembly, indicative of the spirit of the times, and exemplifying the matter which occasionally occupied the Legislature. On the 24th of January, 1719, the House appointed a committee to inquire into certain printed libels, and personal abuse against its members. One Benjamin Johnson, of Monmouth, had said to William Lawrence, a member from that county, "You Lawrence, are a pitiful pimping fellow, and have been false to your trust in the Assembly." On the complaint of Lawrence, Johnson was ordered into arrest by the House; but he avoided its displeasure by absconding. A passage in Titan Leeds' Almanac, for 1718, was voted libellous, and the author and printer were ordered into the custody of the sergeant-at-arms. Leeds was apprehended; but we do not know how punished. Two pamphlets, one entitled, "*A further discovery of the mystery of trade, proposed by A B,*" and the other, "*Proposals for traffic and commerce in New Jersey,*" were also declared to be libellous, the books condemned to be burned by the common hangman, and a reward offered for the apprehension of the authors. William Sandford and Thomas Buskirk, Esq. of Bergen county, were arrested on the speaker's warrant, for having reported, that Mr. Philip Schuyler, a member of the House, "*had drank a health to the damnation of the governor and the justices of the peace.*" Sandford admitted and justified the declaration; producing the affidavit of the coroner of the county, to the uttering of the words by Schuyler. Schuyler denied the words, but said, that he had quarrelled with the coroner, and had kicked him. Whereupon, the House gave the member permission to withdraw and go home, that he might procure evidence to disprove the charge thus brought against him. Sandford and Buskirk were discharged from custody. A copy of the affidavit was denied to Schuyler. Subsequently, the coroner was required to name the persons present, when the offensive words were alleged to have been uttered. These persons having no remembrance of the words, Schuyler was acquitted by a solemn vote, and permitted again to take his seat. But the proceedings against Sandford and Buskirk were not renewed.

NOTE V.—Page 97.

The members of council, named in the instructions of Governor Burnet, were Lewis Morris, Thomas Gordon, John Anderson, John Hamilton, Thomas Byerly, David Lyell, John Parker, John Wills, John Hugg, John Johnson, junior, John Reading, and Peter Bard.

NOTE W.—Page 105.

We refer the reader to Sparks' Life of Governeur Morris, for a full account of this family, which has been distinguished for so many years in New York and New Jersey.

NOTE Z.—Page 121.

"It was rumoured at an early period, that Braddock had been shot by his men. More recently, it has been stated, by one who could not be mistaken, that in the course of the battle, Braddock ordered the provincial troops to form a column. They, however, adhered to the Indian mode of firing, severally, from the shelter of the trees. Braddock, in his vexation, rode up to a young man by the name of Fawcett, and with his sword, rashly cut him down. Thomas Fawcett, a brother of the killed, soon learned his fate, and watching his opportunity, revenged his brother's blood, by shooting Braddock, mortally, through the body. Thomas Fawcett dwelt near Laurel Hill, Pennsylvania, until above ninety-seven years of age."—*Register of Pennsylvania, by S. Hazard, Jan. 28th*, 1828.

NOTE AA.—Page 140.

The following abstract from the address of Mr. Speaker Ogden to the House, exhibits, strongly, the state of the public feeling. "I am so unhappy as to find, that my conduct, which was the consequence of this opinion, formed on the most deliberate, impartial, and disinterested reasoning on the subject, has been put in an unfavourable light, and has made me the object of too general a resentment; I trust, that Providence will, in due time, make the rectitude of my heart, and my inviolable affection to my country, appear in a fair light to the world, and that my sole aim was the happiness of New Jersey. But, as at present, there appears a great dissatisfaction at my conduct, that has spread even among some of my constituents, whom I have served many years in General Assembly, to the utmost of my abilities, I beg leave of the House, to resign my seat in it, whereby my constituents may have an opportunity of sending another person in my room, who may act more agreeable to their present sentiments: though I am well assured, that no person can be found, who will study their welfare more sincerely, nor pursue it with more steadiness and integrity than I have done."—*Votes of Assembly*. Mr. Stephen Crane was elected in the place of Mr. Ogden.

NOTE BB.—Page 152.

The suit instituted, if any, against the treasurer, Stephen Skinner, was never brought to trial. He adhered to the British in the revolutionary war, and all his property in New Jersey, was confiscated and sold for the benefit of the State.

NOTE CC.—Page 164.

List of deputies in the provincial Congress, May, June, and August, 1775.

Bergen County, John Fell, John Demarest, Hendrick Kuyper, Abraham Van Buskirk, Edw. Merselius. *Essex*, Henry Garritse, Michael Vreeland, Robert Drummond, John Berry, William P. Smith, John Stiles, John Chetwood, Abraham Clark, Elias Boudinot, Isaac Ogden, Philip Van-Cortlandt, Bethuel Pierson, Caleb Camp. *Middlesex*, Nathaniel Heard, William Smith, John Dunn, John Lloyd, Azariah Dunham, John Schurman, John Wetherill, David Williamson, Jonathan Sergeant, Jonathan Baldwin, Jonathan Deare. *Morris*, William Winds, William De Hart, Peter Dickerson, Jacob Drake, Ellis Cooke, Silas Condict. *Somerset*, Hendrick Fisher, John Roy, Peter Schenk, Abraham Van Neste, Enos Kelsey, Jonathan D. Sergeant, Frederick Frelinghuysen, William Patterson, Archibald Stewart, Edward Dumont, William Maxwell, Ephraim Martin. *Monmouth*, Edward Taylor, Joseph Saltar, Robert Montgomery, John Holmes, John Covenhoven, Daniel Hendrickson, Nicholas Van Brunt. *Hunterdon*, Samuel Tucker, John Mehelm, John Hart, John Stout, Jasper Smith, Thomas Lowry, Charles Stewart, Daniel Hunt, Ralph Hart, Jacob Jennings, Richard Stevens, John Stevens, junior, Thomas Stout, Thomas Jones, John Bassett. *Burlington*, Joseph Borden, Isaac Pearson, Colin Campbell, Joseph Read, John Pope. *Gloucester*, John Cooper, Elijah Clark, John Sparks. *Cumberland*, Samuel Fithian, Jonathan Elmer, Thomas Ewing. *Salem*, Andrew Sinnickson, Robert Johnson, Samuel Dick, Jacob Scoggin, James James. *Cape May*, Jesse Hand.

NOTE DD.—Page 172.

List of the deputies of the provincial Congress, elected in September, 1775.

Bergen, John Demarest, Jacobus Post, Abraham Van Buskirk. *Essex*, Abraham Clark, Lewis Ogden, Samuel Potter, Caleb Camp, Robert Drummond. *Middlesex*, John Wetherill, John Dennis, Azariah Dunham. *Morris*, William Winds,* William De Hart,* Jacob Drake, Silas Condict, Ellis Cook. *Somerset*, Hendrick Fisher, Cornelius Van Muliner,* Ruloffe Van Dyke. *Sussex*, William Maxwell,* Ephraim Martin, Thomas Potts,* Abijah Brown, Mark Thompson. *Hunterdon*, Samuel Tucker, John Mehelm, John Hart, Charles Stewart, Augustine Stevenson.* *Monmouth*, Edward Taylor, John Covenhoven, Joseph Holmes. *Burlington*, Isaac Pierson, John Pope, Samuel How,* John Wood, Joseph Newbold. *Gloucester*, John Cooper,* Joseph Ellis, Thomas Clark,* Elijah Clark,* Richard Somers.* *Salem*, Grant Gibbon, Benjamin Holme, John Holme, Edward Keasby, John Carey. *Cumberland*, Theophilus Elmer, Jonathan Eyers. *Cape May*, Jesse Hand,* Elijah Hughes.

* The persons whose names are thus * marked did not attend this session of the Congress.

www.ingramcontent.com/pod-product-compliance
Lightning Source LLC
LaVergne TN
LVHW011245110826
845149LV00001B/53